Also from the Hound

VideoHound's® Golden Movie Retriever®

The

**VideoHound's War Movies:
Classic Conflict on Film**

VideoHound's Complete Guide to Cult Flicks and Trash Pics

**VideoHound's Horror Show:
999 Hair-Raising, Hellish, and Humorous Movies**

VideoHound's Vampires on Video

The St. James Film Directors Encyclopedia

**The St. James Women Filmmakers Encyclopedia:
Women on the Other Side of the Camera**

VideoHound's
INDEPENDENT FILM GUIDE

VideoHound's
INDEPE
FILM
GUIDE
Second Edition

NDENT

MONICA SULLIVAN

Foreword by
John Pierson

DETROIT • SAN FRANCISCO • LONDON • BOSTON • WOODBRIDGE, CT

VideoHound's® INDEPENDENT FILM GUIDE

Second Edition

Published by Visible Ink Press®, a division of the Gale Group.
27500 Drake Rd.
Farmington Hills, MI 48331-3535

Most Visible Ink books are available at special quantity discounts when purchased in bulk by corporations, organizations, or groups. Customized printings, special imprints, messages, and excerpts can be produced to meet your needs. For more information, contact Special Markets Manager, the Gale Group, 27500 Drake Rd., Farmington Hills, MI 48331-3535.

Art Direction Mary Claire Krzewinski and Pamela A. E. Galbreath

Photos The Kobal Collection

Cover/Back Cover Photos *Life Is Beautiful* (Miramax); *Affliction* (Lion's Gate); *High Art* (October Films); *Pecker* (Fine Line); *Gods and Monsters* (Lion's Gate); *Pi* (Harvest/Truth & Soul); and *The African Queen* (United Artists). All courtesy of the Kobal Collection.

Library of Congress Cataloging-in-Publication Data

Sullivan, Monica, 1950–
VideoHound's Independent Film Guide /
Monica Sullivan : foreword by John Pierson. — 2nd ed.
p. cm.
Includes bibliographical references and indexes.
ISBN 1-57859-090-6 (pbk.)
I. Motion pictures—Catalogs. 2. Video recordings—Catalogs
3. Low-budget motion pictures—Catalogs.
I. Title
PN1998.S84 1999
016.79143'75—dc21 99-26876
CIP

ISBN 1-57859-090-3 Printed in the United States of America

10 9 8 7 6 5 4 3 2 1

A Cunning Canine Production®

Contents

Foreword by John Pierson ix
Foreword to the First Edition by Mare Winningham xiii
Introduction xvii
Acknowledgments xix
Video Sources xxi
Instructions for Use xxii

THE REVIEWS
A to Z with Photos and Quotes 1

Indie Connections 557

Alternative Titles Index 561

Cast Index 567

Director Index 639

Category Index 649

Sidebars

Samuel Goldwyn . . . 4
Maggie Greenwald . . . 28
Tom DiCillo . . . 50
Errol Morris . . . 56
Joe Berlinger . . . 58
Ann Turner . . . 74
Wendell B. Harris Jr. . . . 76
Patricia Medina . . . 124
Robert Rodriguez . . . 132
Sam Raimi . . . 144
Mark Rappaport . . . 164
Jim McKay and Anna Grace . . . 174
Eames Demetrios . . . 176
Sandra Goldbacher . . . 184
Iain Softley . . . 192
Orson Welles . . . 204
Ang Lee . . . 228
Carol Lynley . . . 232
Wilson Cruz . . . 248
Peter Coyote . . . 256
John Carradine . . . 258
Elisha Cook . . . 260
Ralph Meeker . . . 264
Maya Deren . . . 314
Billy Connolly . . . 320
P.J. Hogan . . . 330
Samuel Fuller . . . 338
Linda Lawson . . . 346
Laura San Giacomo and Paul Rhys . . . 348
F.W. Murnau . . . 352
Jennie Livingston . . . 368
Michael Powell . . . 372
Andre de Toth . . . 380
Conrad Brooks . . . 382
Betty Garrett Parks . . . 386
Ida Lupino . . . 390
David Carradine . . . 396
Lawrence Tierney . . . 404
Sylvia Sidney . . . 416
Terry Moore . . . 428
Scott Hicks . . . 434
Buzz Hayes . . . 468
Richard Fleischer . . . 472
Lorraine Devon and Patricia Royce . . . 488
Karl Kozak . . . 490
Devon Gummersall . . . 496
D.A. Pennebaker and Chris Hegedus . . . 522
Nobu McCarthy . . . 524
Lillian Gish . . . 528
Stephen Fry . . . 540
Peter Adair . . . 552

Foreword

by John Pierson

Unsurprisingly, *The Phantom Menace* is not listed in this brand new edition of *VideoHound's Independent Film Guide.* At the moment, it's a moot point, since the video release date is still a few parsecs away. But will it be in the next edition?

A few years ago I created an off-Hollywood cable television show called *Split Screen.* At the beginning of the 1999 season, as a total goof, we started waiting in line for the new *Star Wars* three months early. The initial concept was just dripping with irony. What could possibly be less "indiefilm" than George Lucas' juggernaut? Yet, ironically, as we were queued up at New York City's deluxe Ziegfeld Theater with lots of time to kill, Lucas began to loom larger and larger as the most independent filmmaker in history. After all, he self-financed the film, created his own special effects in-house, sold his own merchandise, selected a releasing studio as if he were hiring a butler, installed his own sound systems in theatres, and even equipped four screens with the very latest technology—digital projection. Now that's autonomy, when you can preserve your vision *and* control its presentation.

About halfway through our first-in-line vigil, another paradoxical event occurred. *The Matrix* opened. And it was full of surprises. And it was visually inspired. And it was wildly original even as it lifted ideas left and right from other movies and books. And it was directed by a pair of palooka brothers from Chicago who had indie credibility for making a lesbian-action-feminist-neonoir genre film that was discovered at the Sundance Film Festival. That movie, *Bound,* was a total miss for me, a good example of a bad indie getting some unwarranted sympathy. If you're politically correct, you're supposed to frown on the Wachowski Brothers selling out to a studio. But they made one of the most astonishing leaps from first to second feature ever. I'm sorry, but I'm going to say it: *The Matrix* may be my favorite film of the year!

Do I require an intervention? Imagine a group of concerned friends whisking me off the *Star Wars* line to get a little indiefilm rehab at the 1999 Los Angeles Independent Film Festival. Maybe I'd be scared straight by seeing Phil Joanou's *Entropy* on opening night. Joanou was discovered by Steven Spielberg and has directed studio features like *Three o'Clock High* and *State of Grace.* Recently he went back to his roots for a cheap $3 million picture about being a filmmaker—the foremost topic of interest to indies. According to the *New York Times,* he's been carrying his own 35mm print around. While you're wondering whether this exercise is just as good as a trip to the gym, here's another question to ponder: What do Amy Irving, Tom Arnold, David McCallum, Mia Farrow, Ryan O'Neal, Tom Sizemore, Hal Holbrook, Christina Ricci, Robert Wagner, Bono, Burt Reynolds, Kelly McGillis, Jonathan Taylor Thomas, Daryl Hannah, and Jim Varney have in common? They're all featured in films at the L.A. *Independent* Film Festival, along with all the regulars, like Lili Taylor, James LeGros, Heather Matarazzo, and Kevin Corrigan. Only Eric Stoltz is missing. Many of these actors will probably decide they want to direct an independent film before the next Sundance rolls around. In the meantime, their names will look really good on the video box. There are still pure, original, no-name, from-nowhere indie films (maybe one or two a year) like *In the Company of Men* and *Pi.* But for every *Pi,* there are two films with Tori Spelling.

In a word, I think we're in the middle of a huge meltdown. None of the definitions work anymore. It's nothing but a gigantic distraction to worry about whether Barry Diller, Ted Turner, and Harvey "Weisnerstein" are destroying independent film. (Alright, I admit I'm a little on edge at the moment as the fate of my buddy Kevin Smith's *Dogma* hangs in the balance.) It's time to stop fretting about the death of independent film and start noticing the dearth of independent viewers. George Lucas may be acting like an indie, but his global audience is not.

The theatrical distribution gateway has always been a bottleneck, and marketing costs have increased exponentially throughout this decade. These oppressive conditions make home video and cable television (a few channels, at least) a veritable nirvana for all the free thinkers out there. While video obviously reduces the picture, it enlarges and levels the playing field. You can be the judge, the arbiter of quality, one on one. With any film, it's not the millions who watch and blank out who count. It's the one single solitary viewer who sees an unexpectedly influential movie one day and is permanently changed as a result.

I've had a wonderful opportunity during off-Hollywood's boom years to be a professional champion of numerous films that have deeply affected other people and, in a few cases, the bigger culture—films like *She's Gotta Have*

It, Clerks, The Thin Blue Line, Slacker, Roger & Me, and Chris Smith's *American Job.* But first I had to see them for myself and feel their impact as an individual. That's the exact spirit that Monica Sullivan brings to this guide.

I love the idea that Monica writes every word in these pages. You can feel it; she's not farming anything out to any associates or interns. Of course, I probably disagree with about half of her opinions, some of them pretty vehemently (for example, Monica gave *Bound*). But the theme that dominates the world of video is that you should make up your own damn mind. In fact, I wish *VideoHound's Independent Film Guide* had a blank facing page format to encourage readers to log their own reactions and opinions after having seen each movie.

Now if you'll excuse me, I have to get back to the front of the *Star Wars* line.

by Mare Winningham

I remember where I was and what I was doing when I heard they wanted me for a part in the minuscule-budgeted 1988 independent feature film *Miracle Mile.* This isn't always the case. Usually I feel circumspective, weighing in my mind the factors of the production (who's responsible for the dang thing), the location (where do I have to move my family), the money (how much will they give me), and the talent (hmmmm), before I can find my way to excitement. But every so often I get the news, hang up the phone, shriek, and begin my happiness dance, the hope and euphoria spreading in my chest.

It happened with *Miracle Mile.* Indie heartthrob Anthony Edwards, who was so good in *Gotcha* and *Heart Like a Wheel,* was already cast in the role of Harry, Everyman on the day the *big one* comes to downtown L.A. I was to play his new-found love, Julie, spending the majority of the movie in a shopping cart, drugged. The script had been profiled in a 1983 article by Stephen Rebello in *American Film* magazine about the ten best unproduced screenplays, calling it "a rude and flashy piece of comic business by Steve DeJarnatt. The premise: An itinerant trombone player mistakenly intercepts a predawn pay phone call in the L.A. Miracle Mile district. The news isn't good: in precisely 70 minutes, Soviet warheads will nuke the United States into Kingdom Come." Rebello's article followed the movie's beleaguered path from being commissioned by Warner Bros., to writer/director DeJarnatt's refusal to change the fatalistic ending to an it's-only-a-dream finale, to his eventual reclamation and ownership with the hopes of shooting it himself.

Securing a budget of less than $3 million, DeJarnatt had brought his baby near to its start date when I interviewed with him in his office, his cartoons-in-checkered-boxes story board behind him, hearing his plans for our film. Our film. That's how it was to be. I was going to be included in the process of creating this visually stunning love-at-the-end-of-the-world-on-Wilshire-Boulevard movie. The independent film world was a collaborative feat of promise amid impossible monetary and time constraints that would somehow benefit the movie, in the same way sewing your own clothes can achieve a creation no department store can supply. It inspired the underdog in me.

When I was invited to present an award at the Independent Feature Project West's Independent Spirit Awards, held in a tiny restaurant on La Cienega Blvd. in Los Angeles in 1987, I was by then a certified TV-movie queen. I had starred in over 25 television movies, and my hopes for enjoying the more complex roles offered to my acting peers in independent features were dwindling. The tables at the restaurant held the shining talent of that year's successes—David Lynch and his stellar cast of *Blue Velvet,* Oliver Stone and his winning film *Platoon*—and the emcee was Buck Henry, who introduced one performer/presenter as being the actor from *Deliverance* who was sodomized by a hillbilly. The whole event seemed rebellious and happily low-brow and anti-establishment. Compared to the Academy Awards, which would be televised shortly thereafter, this was the younger, wilder, out-of-control baby brother you always wanted at a party. I couldn't figure out why I'd been invited, but I felt lucky and hoped it meant I had some indie madness in my future.

In 1990, when Steve and I were nominated for *Miracle Mile,* the venue had changed to the retro Roosevelt Hotel. Martin Scorsese and Jodie Foster were honored, and that same rebel appeal seemed even more provocative, with nominees *sex, lies and videotape* and *Drugstore Cowboy.* I lost, and felt like I won. Everyone in the room had participated in a movie that had been conceived in the peril of penny pinching, and celebrated in the grinning pride of the miraculous. It feels so good to participate in a project budgeted at $3 million, when most studio films refer to their $15 million projects as "the little guys," and the most expensive film ever made cost $200 million, with number two behind it at $145 million. My dad always said frugality can make you happy.

I wouldn't attend another Independent Film Awards ceremony until 1996, when my personal indie ship came in with the release of *Georgia,* by far the best role I had ever been offered in film. Made for around $6 million, written by my friend Barbara Turner (who scripted three TV movies I had been in), directed by the great Ulu Grosbard (filmmaker of indie grandpa *Straight Time*), and starring Jennifer Jason Leigh, an indie-movie crown jewel of an actress (*Miami Blues, Last Exit to Brooklyn*), *Georgia* lifted my acting spirits in every way imaginable. By now the Spirit Award ceremonies were situated in Santa Monica, inside a huge tent on the beach, and televised on cable. Sam Jackson was master of ceremonies, and he managed

to instill the event with irreverence and intelligent celebration. The list of nominees completely overlapped with that year's Academy Award nominations: *Dead Man Walking, Leaving Las Vegas.* I was sad to see the TV cameras, but it figured. Independent films had taken center stage in the world movie market, and 1997, the year of *The English Patient, Sling Blade,* and *Shine,* was around the corner. I lost the Academy Award for best supporting actress to Mira Sorvino for *Mighty Aphrodite,* but I won the Independent Spirit Award. These days, I'm shocked when I have an audition for a studio film, and I'm happily trying to figure out how to support my household of seven on a combination of indie film SAG minimum salary and a cable TV supplement.

I met Monica Sullivan, who wrote the reviews in this guide, when I was publicizing *Wyatt Earp,* a big-budget studio flop that I hope did okay overseas because the director was a sweetie. Monica and I did our radio interview, said goodbye, and were thrown together once again for the publicity of *Georgia.* I believe, at the time, *Georgia* was just beginning its descent into video shelf life, and Monica said she thought it was the best movie of 1996. Her praise for every facet of the film made me leave the interview and head to the phone to call Barbara. Since then, Monica has attended every loud, smoky, dirty bar gig that my band and I have played in the San Francisco area. I sing when I'm not acting, and she writes books when she's not interviewing. I hope you appreciate her reviews (there's an original, raucous, thoughtful mind at work) as much as we both seem to treasure the possibilities of the independent film world.

Introduction

Sunday, March 21, 1999: For the first time in recent memory, practically *no one* got the top five Academy Award winners right—including me, naturally, but I rarely get them right. As always, I saw plenty of movies in 1998, but, again as always, few of the quirky oddball flicks I love with a passion beyond reason were among the nominees. Where was *The Opposite of Sex*? Or *The Suicide Kings*? Or *Love and Death on Long Island*? Not weighty enough? Too goofy? Screenwriter Bill Condon's award for *Gods and Monsters* was a delightful surprise, Judi Dench finally received the appreciation from America that she's enjoyed in England for many years (ever watch her in 1965's *Four in the Morning* or *A Study in Terror*?), and it was cool to see James Coburn with an Oscar in his hands for *Affliction.* (I never could understand why his hugely enjoyable star turns in *Dead Heat on a Merry-Go-Round, Our Man Flint,* and *The President's Analyst* weren't nominated for ANYTHING!) From this pair of eyeballs, many of the movies released in 1998 seemed like two or three hours in a detention hall. After all the trials and tribulations of life, I have to go to a movie to be miserable...a movie that's supposed to be worthwhile just because it's weighty and not goofy? There has to be a better way to spend however many movie-going hours are left in my life.

Independent films are the main reason why I still love going to the movies or picking up an unfamiliar title from a video shelf. I don't want a film to reinforce an opinion I already have. I want to see and hear the world from a perspective other than my own. I love it when a filmmaker shares a world that is wildly different from the one I've experienced up till now. Indies fill that need. The folks in Hollywood realize the significance of indies, which was why there was more grumbling than usual in the days after 1999's Oscar ceremonies. It was one thing to see the cute little puppies in the indie world sit at the awards banquet in 1997, but to have TWO movies made outside the system win the top prize in THREE years? "That's not what the founding fathers had in mind," sniffed one studio executive who declined to attach his name to the opinion he gave to the *L.A. Times.*

The founding fathers? Not Thomas Jefferson, Benjamin Franklin, John Adams, and the other guys who signed the Declaration of Independence in 1776. Nope! He was referring to Louis B. Mayer, his lawyers, and the Academy's other founding fathers, mostly producers, who tried to clean up the scandal-ridden motion picture industry and curb the rise of unions with a self-congratulatory awards ceremony on May 16, 1929. While they dined on squab and lobster, films made by Paramount, Fox, United Artists, and

MGM received the first Academy Awards in the Blossom Room at Hollywood's Roosevelt Hotel. In the early years of the Academy, block voting by studio employees ensured that there were few surprises, and certainly none from maverick outsiders, in the entire process.

The phenomenon began with a mere trickle, but the current renaissance of independent filmmakers is the healthiest trend in the relatively short history of the movies. Indies offer us a steady supply of fresh faces, bright talent, and vigorous treatment of themes rarely explored by major studios in such original and unvetted ways.

Yet all is still not quite perfect in this best of all cinematic times. Three days after the 1999 Oscar ceremonies, I was invited to speak to a college class in one of the many small towns I lived in as a kid. When I was growing up, the town had two theatres owned by one guy. NOW, there's a couple of multiplexes, owned by another guy, and he never books indies because his most faithful patrons are 11-year-old boys who see the same blockbusters over and over and over again. If you want to catch an indie on the big screen, you have to go to the nearest city, 20 minutes away. I spent the entire time I lived in that town wanting to run away, and as an adult I'm ecstatic that I don't have to live there anymore. I wish I could have kept that feeling under better wraps from the people who still have to live there, but I couldn't. As I talked about some of the indies in this book, I saw many of the class members writing down every single title, none of which would ever play in their town. If it hadn't won seven Academy Awards, *Shakespeare in Love* would be among them! Afterwards, one woman said she'd written down 300 titles to take to her favorite video outlet, which shows what a motor mouth I can be on this subject.

If you're an exhibitor or a video outlet buyer reading the previous paragraph, that's a sledgehammer hint! One of the hottest dates on a weekend night in San Francisco is at any Landmark theatre where nothing *but* indies ever play. Long lines of avid moviegoers wait patiently to get into any of the packed screening rooms, since their first, second, or even third choices may be sold out. Give the indies a chance to surprise you and entertain you and enrich your lives. It may not be what the Academy's venerable founding fathers had in mind, but so WHAT? Like the movies they made (and wouldn't make), they're *so* 70 years ago!

Monica Sullivan
Founding Producer,
Movie Magazine International
http://www.shoestring.org

Acknowledgments

Love to:

Steve Rubenstein, for making my days so much fun and for making me laugh in the middle of the night.

Jonesy and Kelly, for always knowing just what to do and say.

Tom Backos, forever ready, willing, and able for an adventure!

Raymond Formanek, forever wise, witty, and wonderful.

Alvah Bessie, who knew how to fight and how to love.

Estela, Marty, and Maya Goldsmith, for believing in me.

Carol Schwartz, editor *extraordinaire;* and Lauri Taylor, Julia Furtaw, Marilou Carlin, Chris Tomassini, Wayne Fong, Michelle Lonoconus, Christa Brelin, Brad Morgan, Judy Galens, Justin Karr, Jeff Hermann, Dean Dauphinais, and all the other dynamos at Visible Ink Press.

Mary Krzewinski and Pamela Galbreath, *artistes,* and Marco DiVita, master typesetter.

Randy Parker, web maestro of www.shoestring.org and nothing like yours truly, which is why we've stayed friends and colleagues for so long!

Mad Professor Mike Marano, especially when he rants and raves!

Adam Ling, who's way cool and way tough.

Andrea Chase, an altogether wonderful writer, and Brandon Chase, our most loyal listener.

Heather Clisby, because everyone who knows her says it's so much fun knowing her (and it is!).

Kate Ingram, the BEST program director in alternative radio.

Leo C. Lee, whose spirit inspires us all at Western Public Radio.

Sean Simplicio, Carol Pearson, Caroline Van Putten, and Lynn Chadwick, for helping to keep my radio dreams alive and well.

PLUS: Lee Amazonas, Rob Avila, Frank Buske, Larry Carlin, Anita Monga/Castro Theatre, Mark Chase, Carol Compton, Chuck & Zoya Csavossy, Martha Daetwyler, Paul Daugherty, Deb, Zoe Elton, Karl Fleischman, Michael Fox, Geoffrey Gallegos, Alanna, Emma, Tess & John Green-

ham, Mim Herzenstein, Russ Hickman, Curtis & Heidi Huber, Claude Jarman, Karen Larsen, Alex Lau, Nancy Madden, Kara Marette, Julie Long, Father Harry Mack, Paul Mapes, Peggy Martinez, McB., George McRae, Mary Mirabel, Auzzie & Laela Mirhashemi, MPI Home Video, Frank Munnich, Mike Neumann, Nobby, NPR Distribution, Rebecca Peters, Erik Petersen, Damien Pickering, John Pierson, Henry Trentman, Recorded Books, Inc., Gina Restani, Bill Banning & Elliott Lavine, Roxie Cinema, Chris Salak, Sue Braviak/Science Fiction Continuum, Jim Shepard, Susan Stanton, Michael Stressinger, Jerome, Stephanie & Dr. Moira Sullivan, Kathryn Evans/Turner Classic Movies, Craig Valenza, Marisa Vela, Blue Velvet, Clinton Vidal, Miss X, B.K. Wells, Mare Winningham and her wonderful band, George C. Wolfe, and all our wonderful listeners on KUSF, San Francisco, and the Public Radio Satellite System.

Video Sources

Some of the movies in this book are not currently in print, and some of them that are may be difficult to find using conventional devices such as the neighborhood video rental chain. Many independent and mail-order video outlets specialize in rare or hard-to-find movies. We have included a small list of such outlets to assist you in your search.

Thomas Video
122 S. Main St.
Clawson MI 48017
248-280-2833
fax: 248-280-4463
tomvid@mich.com
www.thomasvideo.com

Movies Unlimited
3015 Darnell Rd.
Philadelphia PA 19154
800-4-MOVIES

Video Oyster
145 W. 12th St.
New York NY 10011
fax: 212-989-3533
video@videooyster.com
www.videooyster.com

Facets Video
1517 W. Fullerton Ave.
Chicago IL 60614
800-331-6197

A Million and One World-Wide Videos
PO Box 349
Orchard Hill GA 30266
800-849-7309
fax: 770-227-0873
fax: 800-849-0873
Deals exclusively with rare and out-of-print titles.

Home Film Festival
PO Box 2032
Scranton PA 18501
800-258-3456

Video Library
7157 Germantown Ave.
Philadelphia PA 19119
800-669-7157
fax: 215-248-5627
rentals@vlibrary.com
www.vlibrary.com

Alphabetization

Titles are arranged on a word-by-word basis, including articles and prepositions. Leading articles (A, An, The) are ignored in English-language titles; the equivalent foreign articles are not ignored (because so many people—not you, of course—don't recognize them as articles); thus, *The Brothers McMullen* appears in the Bs, but *La Femme Nikita* appears in the Ls. Acronyms appear alphabetically as if regular words; for example, *D.O.A.* is alphabetized as "DOA." Common abbreviations in titles file as if they were spelled out, so *The Island of Dr. Moreau* will be alphabetized as "Island of Doctor Moreau" and *Mr. North* as "Mister North." Movie titles with numbers, such as *8½*, are alphabetized as if the number were spelled out—so this title would appear in the Es as if it were "Eight and a Half."

1 Clerks

2 *Clerks* is a promising first film by Kevin Smith about a clerk in a convenience store and a clerk in a video store. It's everything a first film should be: funny, fresh, and original. It was shot in black and white on a budget of $27,000, and its gritty, cinema-verite quality made it seem almost like a slice-of-life documentary rather than the scripted fiction film it really was. Reportedly, preview audiences were so caught up in the lives of the two central characters that they responded negatively when one of them was shown being killed on duty. So the ending was re-shot, a wise choice, because to have turned an 88-minute comedy into an 89-minute tragedy at the last minute wouldn't have worked without some premonitory sequences—which wouldn't have worked, either, because of the scrappy, upbeat tone overall. When Smith made *Mallrats* a year later, the same critics who lionized *Clerks* beyond recognition jumped down hard on the filmmaker's second effort. Smith's *Chasing Amy*, his third picture, is drawing rave rev 3 ***AKA:*** *Randal and D* 4

5 **1994** 6 **(R)** 7 **89m/** 8 **B** 9 *US* 10 Brian O'Halloran, Jeff Anderson, Marilyn Ghigliotti, Lisa Spoonhauer, Jason Mewes; **Cameos:** Kevin Smith; 11 ***D:*** Kevin Smith; 12 ***W:*** Kevin Smith; 13 ***C:*** David Klein; 14 ***M:*** Scott Angley 15 Sundance Film Festival '94: Filmmakers Trophy; Nominations: Independent Spirit Awards '95: Best First Feature, Debut Performance (Anderson), First Screenplay. 16 **VHS, LV, Closed Caption** 17 *VTR, CRC*

Sample Review

Each review contains up to 16 tidbits of information, as enumerated below. Please realize that we faked a bit of info in this review for demonstration purposes.

1. Title (see also #3 below, and the **Alternative Titles Index**)
2. Synopsis/review
3. Alternative title (we faked it here)
4. One- to four-bone rating (or **woof!**), four bones being the ultimate praise
5. Year released
6. MPAA rating
7. Length in minutes
8. Black and white (B) or Color (C)
9. Country of origin (if other than the U.S.); see next column
10. Cast, including cameos and voice-overs (V)
11. Director(s)
12. Writer(s)
13. Cinematographer(s)
14. Music composer(s)/lyricist(s)
15. Awards, including nominations
16. Format(s), including VHS, laser videodisc (LV), DVD, CD-I, letterboxed, and closed captioned

Country of Origin Codes

The country of origin codes indicate the country or countries in which a film was produced or financed. A listing of films by country may also be found in the **Category Index** under the appropriate term below.

AL Algerian
AR Argentinian
AT Austrian
AU Australian
BE Belgian
BR Brazilian
GB British
CA Canadian
CH Chinese
CL Colombian
CU Cuban
CZ Czech
DK Danish
NL Dutch
PH Filipino
FI Finnish
FR French
GE German
GR Greek
HK Hong Kong
HU Hungarian
IC Icelandic
IN Indian
IA Iranian
IR Irish
IS Israeli
IT Italian
JP Japanese
KO Korean
LI Lithuanian
MA Macedonian
MX Mexican
NZ New Zealand
NI Nicaraguan
NO Norwegian
PL Polish
PT Portuguese
RU Russian
SA South African
SP Spanish
SW Swedish
SI Swiss
TU Turkish
TW Taiwanese
VT Vietnamese
VZ Venezuelan
YU Yugoslavian

A-Ge-Man: Tales of a Golden Geisha

Admirers of Juzo Itami *(The Funeral, Tampopo, A Taxing Woman, A Taxing Woman's Return)* will want to see his 1991 film, *A-Ge-Man: Tales of a Golden Geisha,* featuring a nicely shaded performance by its star Nobuko Miyamoto as Nayoko the geisha. Watching the sympathetic Nayoko do everything in the world for some of the biggest jerks in Japan can be a bit taxing after 108 minutes. At one point, she raises a billion yen for her true love, who promptly starts chasing after a younger women and Nayoko doesn't even sock him! Itami paces the film like a music video and some of the sequences with Toshiyuki Honda's romantic jazz score look like they're headed straight for the Asian video market as is. Although *A-Ge-Man*'s satire is far from subtle, it was still an entertaining and at times quite funny selection at 1991's Mill Valley Film Festival. 𝅘𝅥𝅮𝅘𝅥𝅮𝅘𝅥𝅮

1991 108m/C *JP* Nobuko Miyamoto, Masahiko Tsugawa, Shogo Shimada, Hideji Otaki, Mitsuko; ***D:*** Juzo Itami; ***W:*** Juzo Itami; ***C:*** Zenko Yamazaki; ***M:*** Toshiyuki Honda.

Abandon Ship

I wanted to include *Nightmare Alley* in this book, but there's no way it qualifies as an indie. How 20th Century Fox allowed Tyrone Power to sacrifice his spectacular good looks to play a carnival geek and how Edmund Goulding managed to make a movie that uncompromising under the studio system is one of the great mysteries of Hollywood, circa 1947. So I'm including this Brit flick produced independently by Power a decade later, some 20 months before his sudden death in Madrid after a make-believe sword fight with George Sanders. Power, who came from a long line of actors, desperately wanted to be taken seriously, but legions of female audience members preferred to see him as a sexy swashbuckler. And Power WAS sexy and hypnotic, no question about it. For the role of Alec Holmes, Power had to look haggard and driven, even as a sultry lifeboat passenger, Edith Middleton (Moira Lister), leered at him for the entire length of the film. As an officer on a mined ocean liner, Holmes is acting captain of a lifeboat designed to hold 14, but crammed with 17 survivors, with an additional 11 people tied

"The story which you have just seen is a true one. In real life, Captain Alexander Holmes was brought to trial on a charge of murder. He was convicted and given the minimum sentence of six months because of the unusual circumstances surrounding the incident. If you had been a member of the jury, how would you have voted? Guilty or innocent?"

—The narrator introduces the controversy in *Abandon Ship.*

to the boat. Since many have sustained critical injuries, dying crew member Frank Kelly (Lloyd Nolan) tells Holmes to abandon those who are too weak to work or all will die. Holmes resists at first, but gradually comes to realize that Kelly is right and starts ordering gravely wounded men and women into the sea. With every trace of Hollywood glamour stripped from his face, Power played Holmes as if his life depended on it—and, in a way, it did, since his critical reputation was so important to him at that point. The supporting cast is outstanding, especially Nolan, Lister, and Mai Zetterling. Director Richard Sale's tight screenplay is inspired by the true story of the William Brown, an American freighter en route from Liverpool to Philadelphia in 1841, with 17 crew members and 65 Irish and Scottish passengers on board. After hitting an iceberg, the freighter split into two pieces. Because the William Brown was not a passenger ship, it carried just two lifeboats. For an excellent account of the Alexander Holmes trial that followed in 1842, you might want to check out a copy of Edward W. Knappman's indispensable *Great American Trials,* published by Visible Ink Press. ***AKA:*** Seven Waves Away. 🦴🦴🦴🦴

1957 97m/B *GB* Tyrone Power, Mai Zetterling, Lloyd Nolan, Stephen Boyd, Moira Lister, James Hayter, Marie Lohr, Gordon Jackson, Finlay Currie, John Stratton, Victor Maddern, Eddie Byrne, Noel Willman, Ralph Michael, David Langton, Ferdinand "Ferdy" Mayne, Austin Trevor, Moultrie Kelsall, Jill Melford; ***D:*** Richard Sale; ***W:*** Richard Sale; ***C:*** Wilkie Cooper; ***M:*** Arthur Bliss. **VHS**

Abel

Abel is a weird little Dutch film written and directed by its star, Alex Van Warmerdam, who plays a 31-year-old child still living at home with his parents. The film makes an effort to satirize male vanity and male voyeurism, but when it looks at women, it is content simply to ridicule them. Successful satire requires some level of understanding, an element which is missing in this nonetheless amusing 1987 entry in the Mill Valley Film Festival. 🦴🦴½

1987 100m/C *NL* Alex Van Warmerdam, Henri Garcin, Olga Zuiderhoek, Annet Malherbe; ***D:*** Alex Van Warmerdam; ***W:*** Alex Van Warmerdam.

Absolute Beginners

Julien Temple's underrated *Absolute Beginners* provides an unsettling portrait of London circa 1958. The film has been criticized for its lack of character development and for its last-minute attack on racism, and although these flaws are real, there is much worth seeing and hearing in this flashy study of the emergence of the British teen. Magnetic performances by David Bowie and Sade, amusing bits by Ray Davies and Mandy Rice-Davies, and interesting work by Patsy Kensit and Anita Morris contribute to the striking atmosphere. The impressive photography and great jazz don't hurt, either. I'd like to see this one along with the 1960 Val Guest film *Expresso Bongo,* starring Laurence Harvey and Cliff Richard, which examines the same world from a slightly different perspective. 🦴🦴🦴

1986 (PG) 107m/C *GB* David Bowie, Ray Davies, Mandy Rice-Davies, James Fox, Eddie O'Connell, Patsy Kensit, Anita Morris, Sade Adu, Sandie Shaw; ***D:*** Julien Temple; ***W:*** Richard Burridge, Don MacPherson; ***C:*** Oliver Stapleton. **VHS, LV**

Acting on Impulse

Reviews for *Acting on Impulse* were decidedly mixed, but it's a hoot! Linda Fiorentino IS angry scream queen Susan Gittes, who's had it with her Hollywood "career" and walks off the movie set. She checks into a hotel (as "Dee Dee Slaughter") where a convention for pharmaceutical sales representatives is being held (zzzzzz...), leaving behind her boyfriend (Adam Ant), her P.O.'d director (Paul Bartel), and her murdered producer (Patrick Bachau), whose body is discovered in her trailer. That makes her a suspect, doesn't it? Detective Stubbs (Isaac Hayes) investigates! "Dee Dee" meets Paul Stevens and Cathy Thomas (C. Thomas Howell and Nancy Allen) at the convention, comes on to Paul, gets stalked by a fan, and then there's that suspicion of being a murderer that clings to her like underwear. And, speaking of underwear, there's this side-splitting sight gag about the physical illusion we have of scream queens that Susan/Dee Dee tears away with a single defiant gesture. Fiorentino has the ability to make a truly unpleasant character funny, which makes me like her and want to root for her in spite of myself. No comment on Howell, who's out of his league here, but Allen has a good time with her change-of-pace role. And look at the rest of that cast! Cult film freaks will have a feast! Based on a story by Sol Weingarten. 🦴🦴🦴

1993 (R) 94m/C Linda Fiorentino, C. Thomas Howell, Nancy Allen, Adam Ant, Judith Hoag, Patrick Bauchau, Isaac Hayes, Paul Bartel, Donny Most, Miles O'Keeffe, Dick Sargent, Charles Lane, Mary Woronov, Zelda Rubinstein, Nicholas Sadler, Peter Lupus, Kim McGuire, Cassandra Peterson, Brinke Stevens, Michael Talbot, Robert Alan Golub, Cliff Dorfman, Craig Shoemaker, Scott Thompson Stevens; ***D:*** Sam Irvin; ***W:*** Mark Pittman, Alan Moskowitz; ***C:*** Dean Lent; ***M:*** Daniel Licht. **VHS**

Actors and Sin

Actors and Sin is HALF of a very good movie, produced independently by Ben Hecht (1893–1964), who adapted two of his short stories for the silver screen. Hecht shared directing chores with cameraman Lee Garmes (1898–1978) and cast Edward G. Robinson (temporarily on the Hollywood grey list) and blacklisted Marsha Hunt in "Actor's Blood." It may have been a supportive professional gesture, but no one remembers the first segment of *Actors and Sin* today. Robinson played Maurice, the distraught father of unhappy Marcia, who killed herself because she failed to make good as an actress. In Hecht's contrived script, Maurice tries to make it seem as if Marcia was murdered so she will achieve the fame she never received in her lifetime. Fast forward through this segment, unless you just want to watch these stars work together. "Woman of Sin" is also contrived, but it's a funny, clever satire. Eddie Albert is Orlando Higgens, a Hollywood agent who receives a hot new (sexy) script from hot new screenwriter Daisy Marcher. Who IS Miss Marcher? Only Jenny Hecht, the nine-year-old daughter of Ben, who's extremely well directed by her father here. Ben Hecht must have nursed a grudge against obnoxious, precocious Hollywood moppets for 25 years! "Woman of Sin" has bite and snap and a beautifully sustained quality of long-simmering resentment. Hecht's wise to every single trick of devil child Daisy, and daughter Jenny acquits herself admirably in the role. The supporting cast adds to the fun; for a change, we get to SEE, as well as hear, Alan Reed (Fred Flintstone)! 🦴🦴🦴

1952 82m/B Edward G. Robinson, Eddie Albert, Marsha Hunt, Alan Reed, Dan O'Herlihy, Tracey Roberts, Rudolph Anders, Paul Guilfoyle, Alice Key, Douglas Evans, Rick Roman, Jenny Hecht, Jody Gilbert, John Crawford; ***D:*** Lee Garmes, Ben Hecht; ***W:*** Ben Hecht; ***C:*** Lee Garmes; ***M:*** George Antheil. **VHS, LV**

The Addiction

Abel Ferrara's *The Addiction* is to *Ms. 45* what Francis Coppola's *The Cotton Club* was to *The Godfather:* a structural re-tread only worshippers at directors' shrines could love. Lili Taylor is excellent as always in the protagonist role, and it's fun to see perennial good girl Annabella Sciorra as a vampire, but Christopher Walken wraps it up as usual in one scene-stealing sequence that makes you wish the rest of the movie had been that good and that funny instead of the pretentious mess it is. It's shot in jokey black and white to minimize the gore. 🦴🦴

1995 (R) 82m/B Lili Taylor, Christopher Walken, Annabella Sciorra, Edie Falco, Paul Calderone, Fredro Starr, Kathryn Erbe, Michael Imperioli; ***D:*** Abel Ferrara; ***W:*** Nicholas St. John; ***C:*** Ken Kelsch; ***M:*** Joe Delia. Nominations: Independent Spirit Awards '96: Best Actress (Taylor), Best Film. **VHS**

Adoption

Adoption focuses on a pair of women, one 42, one 17, both of whom are entrapped and want to free themselves. In their struggle to make new beginnings, they lend each other support and friendship, and the script makes it clear that this is not the sort of encouragement men are capable of giving. Sensitively directed and

The Hound Salutes:
SAMUEL GOLDWYN
(1882–1974)

Samuel Goldwyn was a one-of-a-kind guy in a dime-a-dozen town. Between 1923 and 1959, he independently produced 80 films, including 50 released through United Artists between 1925 and 1940. Goldwyn, whose name still appears on every MGM release, lost control of Goldwyn Pictures in 1922. When the corporation merged with Metro and Mayer, Goldwyn played no role in the new studio. Every single one of Goldwyn's own films began with the credit "Samuel Goldwyn Presents." He paid for all 80 of his productions with his own money. Being accountable to no one, he made sure that his films were PERSONAL in every sense of the word. Who decided which movie to make? He did. Who decided which star to cast? He did. Who had the final word with the director? He did. Who was in charge of the ballyhoo? Samuel Goldwyn, that's who!

After his start in life as a Polish immigrant and a one-time glove peddler, many of Goldwyn's films showed individuals in conflict with the society that engulfed them. His first film for United Artists (which he re-made as a 1937 talkie and his son re-made in color as 1990's *Stella*) was *Stella Dallas.* Belle Bennett (1890–1932) played the part of a small-town girl who married a rich man (Ronald Colman, 1891–1958) and became the mother of his daughter, Laurel (Lois Moran, 1907–90). Being of a lower social order, Stella soon realizes that she and Stephen are ill-suited and their separation follows, with Stella keeping Laurel. Since Stella's sexual tastes run to low-class horse trainers like Ed Munn (Jean Hersholt, 1886–1956), her conscience kicks in about Laurel's environment. Learning that her husband wants to marry a

photographed, *Adoption* emerges as a story of strong hope, with realistic performances giving it tenderness and integrity. ***AKA:*** Orkobefogadas.

1975 89m/B *HU* Kati Berek, Laszlo Szabo, Gyongyver Vigh, Dr. Arpad Perlaky; ***D:*** Marta Meszaros; ***W:*** Marta Meszaros, Gyula Hernadi; ***C:*** Lajos Koltai; ***M:*** Gyorgy Kovacs. Berlin International Film Festival '75: Golden Berlin Bear. **VHS**

The Adventures of Milo & Otis

It isn't everyday that I receive pawtographed press releases from a dog and a cat, so I have to admit I was more than a little curious about *The Adventures of Milo & Otis,* a 1989 Japanese blockbuster with obvious international appeal. I think that grown-ups will enjoy the picture as much as their kids, although I did notice three exhausted fathers snoozing during a Saturday morning matinee. For those who stay awake, however, the film provides 76 minutes of pure fun as well as dazzling cinematography and non-stop anthropomorphism. The plot revolves around Milo, a mischievous orange cat, and his best friend Otis, a pug-ugly, thoroughly responsible watchdog. When Milo is swept down a river, Otis begins a lengthy rescue operation. Along the way, there are bears, a waterfall, a snake, a fox, a train, a pit, snow, and, worst of all in male-dominated Japan, females. Milo's true love is Joyce, who is soon eating for eight; Otis stumbles across Saundra, who presents him with Jean-Pierre, François, and Suzette. Family responsibilities, it

Real Lady like Helen Morrison (Alice Joyce, 1889–1955), Stella gallantly divorces him. She is then self-sacrificing—she kicks her daughter out of her life so Laurel, too, can be a Real Lady under Helen's guidance. The heart and soul of the movie, during which every mother in the audience is presumably sobbing her way through six tissue boxes, occurs when Stella, who did not receive a wedding invitation, cries her eyes out in the rain watching Laurel marry Richard Grosvenor (Douglas Fairbanks Jr.). Yes, the narrative thread is on the side of Society, but who did the audience care about and identify with through all 11 reels? Not Stephen, not Laurel, and certainly not Ed, Helen, or Richard: Nope, Stella tapped into every woman's fear that she's not good enough, not smart enough, and doggone it, NO ONE likes her!

Goldwyn instinctively knew that America was a generation of immigrants, most of whom felt like outsiders their entire lives. Wealth and success undiluted by misery and tragedy were not subjects that moviegoers would turn out in droves to experience second-hand. When Goldwyn DID focus on a rich, "happily" married couple, as in 1932's *Cynara,* the emphasis was on how, by taking his privileged life for granted, the husband (Colman again as barrister Jim Warlock) destroys a young girl's life. The girl (Phyllis Barry as Doris Lea) is one of millions eking out a living. The attentions of the powerful Warlock quite melt her heart and turn her head. Warlock's wife Clemency (Kay Francis, 1899–1968) is complicit in Doris' fate because she leaves town just before a wedding anniversary in order to comfort her lovelorn sister. When Doris cannot speak for herself, her roommate Milly Miles (Viva Tattersall) speaks for her, forcing Warlock to face how his casual actions have led to disaster. Again, Society remains intact, but the sharp social critique is obvious. In other entries throughout these pages (e.g., *Bulldog Drummond, Street Scene, Dead End*), the guide will show how Samuel Goldwyn, whose taste strictly reflected the movies he would pay to see, revealed American culture as he knew it, just as contemporary indie filmmakers reflect the world as they know it.

would seem, threaten the friendship between Milo and Otis even more than the dangers in the countryside. I wonder how the filmmakers were able to obtain some of the amazing footage. Although the producer claims that the animals received no "overt" direction or training, 18 animal trainers are listed in the credits. Thirty cats wound up playing Milo. There are no people in the cast, unless you count Dudley Moore, who narrates the story and plays all the voices, too. (Incidentally, with the possible exception of *Arthur, Milo & Otis* is the only movie of the 1980s which was worthy of Moore's considerable talent.) ***AKA:*** Koneko Monogatari; The Adventures of Chatran. 🦴🦴🦴

1989 (G) 76m/C *JP* Dudley Moore; ***D:*** Masanori Hata; ***W:*** Mark Saltzman; ***C:*** Hideo Fujii, Shinji Tomita; ***M:*** Michael Boddicker. **VHS, LV, Closed Caption**

The Adventures of Priscilla, Queen of the Desert

When 1992's *Strictly Ballroom* became an international hit, exhibitors were eager for MORE offbeat Australian movies that would do as well. *The Adventures of Priscilla, Queen of the Desert* fit the bill. Who would ever imagine Terence Stamp, the Oscar-nominated, impossibly gorgeous Billy Budd in Peter Ustinov's superb 1962 film of the same name, would EVER play a drag queen named Bernadette? And yet, Stamp, who initially resisted the idea, discovered that Bernadette was a role he was destined to play. The camera is not overly kind to Stamp at 55, but he invests the role of

"Nature, Mr. Allnut, is what we are put in this world to rise above."

—Rose Sayer (Katharine Hepburn) to Charlie Allnut (Humphrey Bogart) in *The African Queen*.

Bernadette with dignity, elegance, intrigue, and mystery, all the qualities of a great diva. Hugo Weaving and Guy Pearce, too, are terrific as fellow divas Mitzi AKA Tick and Felicia AKA Adam. The three of them hit the road in the title character, an outdated bus. Along the way, Bernadette discovers romance, Tick experiences fatherhood, and Adam learns how not to behave with a gang of red-necked rowdies. The soundtrack is a keeper, with songs galore by Alicia Bridges, Gloria Gaynor, Peaches and Herb, The Village People, Charlene, R. B. Greaves, Lena Horne, Paper Lace, Patti Page, CeCe Peniston, Trudy Richards, White Plains, Vanessa Williams, and Abba. Cast Note: Terence Stamp and Bill Hunter, who plays a charmer named Bob, had previously worked together in the 1985 Stephen Frears film *The Hit.*

1994 (R) 102m/C *AU* Terence Stamp, Hugo Weaving, Guy Pearce, Bill Hunter, Sarah Chadwick, Mark Holmes, Julia Cortez; ***D:*** Stephan Elliott; ***W:*** Stephan Elliott; ***C:*** Brian J. Breheny; ***M:*** Guy Gross. Academy Awards '94: Best Costume Design; Australian Film Institute '94: Best Costume Design; Nominations: Australian Film Institute '94: Best Actor (Stamp), Best Actor (Weaving), Best Cinematography, Best Director (Elliott), Best Film, Best Screenplay; Golden Globe Awards '95: Best Actor—Musical/Comedy (Stamp), Best Film—Musical/Comedy. **VHS, LV**

Aelita: Queen of Mars

Okay, so this is no Fritz Lang masterpiece, but for science-fiction buffs, it's a genuinely intriguing curiosity. Made the year that Lenin died and Stalin took over, it looks like the production team had fun with this one, especially the three art directors and the costume designer. Even then, was anyone taking the script all that seriously? For instance, who gets to go to Mars? One inventor (of course), one soldier (why?), and one police informer (that would be Igor Illinski and he is SUCH a ham!). So they get to Mars and guess what they find there? (See alternative title.) That's right, boys, it's Yet Another Revolution, dang it! (Gee, we thought we applied for this job to get away from all that.) Queen Aelita is something to see, alright. Some stills of the Martian sets and fashions must have slipped over to the U.S. of A. at some point, because our action-packed serials clearly received inspiration from somewhere for those pace-setting styles (I wonder if Ed Bernds and Zsa Zsa Gabor got a good look at Aelita before they made *Queen of Outer Space*). *Aelita* isn't camp yet, not really, but naive perhaps, and a little giddy. Based on Alexei Tolstoy's play. ***AKA:*** Aelita: The Revolt of the Robots.

1924 113m/B *RU* Yulia Solntseva, Nikolai Batalov, Igor Illinski, Nikolai Tseretelli, Vera Orlova, Pavel Poi, Konstantin Eggert, Yuri Zavadski, Valentina Kuindzi, N. Tretyakova; ***D:*** Yakov Protazanov; ***W:*** Fedor Ozep, Aleksey Fajko; ***C:*** Yuri Zhelyabuzhsky, Emil Schoenemann. **VHS, LV**

Affliction

If you were born into a violent alcoholic family, *Affliction* is the last movie you'd want to see on a dark and rainy Monday night. Even strong men who watch action flicks without flinching find *Affliction* a deeply painful film to watch. That said, the sight of Nick Nolte sitting very still on Oscar night, March 21, 1999, while many of his colleagues gave director (and friendly HUAC witness) Elia Kazan a standing ovation, quite melted my heart. If Nolte had the guts to communicate such a powerful statement without saying a word or creating a scene, I HAD to work up the nerve to see his movie, which I'd been avoiding for weeks. Yes, *Affliction* is a very difficult story for an audience to experience. It is told by Rolfe (Willem Dafoe), the son of Glen Whitehouse (uncompromisingly played by Oscar winner James Coburn), a violent alcoholic father. Rolfe learned to detach as a child and he has remained detached as an adult, but his brother Wade (Nick Nolte) never learned how. Wade, a small-town cop, has been married twice to the same woman (Mary Beth Hurt as Lillian), and as the story begins he is trying, unsuccessfully, to bond with his daughter Jill (Brigid Tierney). Jill wants to be with her Mom, and who can blame her? Wade leaves Jill at a party and goes outside to wisecrack with his pal Jack Hewitt (Jim True); when he returns, Jill's already called Mom to pick her up. Wade is hurt, but leaves her to smoke a joint with Jack and arrives back at the party just in time to meet Lillian. There's a short verbal wrangle before Jill leaves with her mom. Wade is thus suffering from the following: alcoholism, an agonizing toothache, a daughter he can only see on visits and who clearly doesn't want to see him, a girlfriend (Sissy Spacek as Maggie Fogg) who loves him but can't cope with his nightmare existence and many haunting memories of the beatings he received from his father as a child. Think those stakes are rough? They get rougher. His mother dies as a result of his drunken father's negligence (Glen's too mean to keep the house warm in a cold winter) and Wade grudgingly accepts the responsibility for taking care of Dad. Old patterns are re-established, with deadly variations. Wade hires a lawyer to dig up dirt on Lillian so he can get custody of Jill. Oh, and there's an accidental hunting death in the woods and Wade suspects it's murder AND that his pal Jack may be involved. When folks who don't drink see how messy the lives of alcoholic families are, they may believe that all those pressures drove them to drink. As Paul Schrader's hard-hitting screenplay and direction make exquisitely clear, it's the other way around. Maybe the only thing you can do is detach like Rolfe, but for 113 tortured minutes, Nolte compels us to see the world through Wade's eyes. Wade wants to be responsible and be a decent person, but like his father Glen before him and Glen's father before HIM and Glen's grandfather before HIM, he's too damaged to clear a path out of his smashed life.

1997 (R) 113m/C Nick Nolte, James Coburn, Sissy Spacek, Willem Dafoe, Mary Beth Hurt, Jim True, Marian Seldes, Brigid Tierney, Sean McCann, Wayne Robson, Homes Osborne; ***D:*** Paul Schrader; ***W:*** Paul Schrader; ***C:*** Paul Sarossy; ***M:*** Michael Brook. Academy Awards '98: Best Supporting Actor (Coburn); New York Film Critics Awards '98: Best Actor (Nolte); National Society of Film Critics Awards '98: Best Actor (Nolte); Nominations: Academy Awards '98: Best Actor (Nolte); Golden Globe Awards '99: Best Actor—Drama (Nolte); Independent Spirit Awards '99: Best Actor (Nolte), Best Cinematography, Best Director (Schrader), Best Film, Best Screenplay, Best Supporting Actor (Coburn); Screen Actors Guild Award '98: Best Actor (Nolte), Best Supporting Actor (Coburn). **VHS**

The African Queen

John Huston cooperatively made films under the studio system between the ages of 35 and 45: five for Warner Bros., one for Columbia, and two for MGM. After chafing at the bit for a full decade, he wanted to make movies his way and without interference. (Huston's *The Red Badge of Courage* ended the 27-year reign of MGM's Louis B. Mayer, who lost a production dispute with Dore Schary in 1951.) Huston couldn't get much further away from Hollywood than the Belgian Congo, where he traveled with stars Humphrey Bogart, Katharine Hepburn, and with Mrs. Bogart, Lauren Bacall. *The African Queen,* Huston's first film in Technicolor, set the standard for the hard-drinking, tough-living man's man who winds up opening his heart to an uptight missionary spinster. Their mutual goals and their gradually evolving love for each other transform them both. Robert Morley, Peter Bull, Theodore Bikel, and Walter Gotell also appear in small but key roles in this British-financed independent feature, the first of five in a row Huston made outside of Hollywood. There's no question that *The African Queen* would have been a much different movie (less real and less exciting) if it had been shot on a studio back lot. It gave Bogie his one and only Oscar, and created a whole new image for Hepburn, one that she maintained for over 45 years. Based on the novel by C.S. Forester.

1951 105m/C *GB* Humphrey Bogart, Katharine Hepburn, Robert Morley, Theodore Bikel, Peter Bull, Walter Gotell, Peter Swanwick, Richard Marner; ***D:*** John Huston; ***W:*** John Huston, James Agee; ***C:*** Jack Cardiff. Academy Awards '51: Best Actor (Bogart); Nominations: Academy Awards '51: Best Actress (Hepburn), Best Director (Huston), Best Screenplay. **VHS, LV**

After Dark, My Sweet

Jim Thompson's tightly written novels grab you by the throat and never let go until you finish reading them, usually about an hour later. I wish I could say the same thing about James Foley's movie version of *After*

Lucky (Nick Nolte) and Phyllis (Julie Christie) in *Afterglow.* Sony Pictures Classics; courtesy of the Kobal Collection

Dark, My Sweet. But alas no, and definitely no. This is a clear case of aficionados being so in love with the original source material that they attempt a meticulous (i.e. laborious) translation to the big screen. The results will please neither film noir buffs nor contemporary thriller fans. Foley's previous credits include two Madonna videos ("Live to Tell" and "Papa Don't Preach") and the excruciating feature *Who's That Girl?,* also starring Madonna. For a guy who cut his teeth on fast-paced videos, Foley seems determined to prove that he also has a forte for sluggish direction, and prove it he does for nearly two hours. Jason Patric portrays a character distractingly named Kevin Collins, for reasons best known to Foley. In Thompson's 1955 novel, the protagonist's name was Bill Collins, so why change the name to that of one of the most famous missing children in America, especially in a film about kidnapping? He meets up with a widow named Fay and her cohort named Uncle Bud, who soon draw him into a not-terribly-well-organized kidnapping scheme. Most of the film looks like a series of acting school exercises, none of which makes the slender plot any more compelling. Foley fails to build any appreciable momentum, even at points that ordinarily lend themselves to SOME tension. Jason Patric is far from fascinating as Collins, Rachel Ward is somewhat less than beguiling as Fay, and Bruce Dern is way over the top as Uncle Bud. The only interesting performance is delivered by Corey Carrier as Jack, a bratty kid mistakenly targeted as the kidnapping victim. Unfortunately, he's only onscreen for a minute or two. For those who care, there is one love scene: you see quite a lot of Patric's derriere, hardly anything at all of Ward. If you've ever seen Stanley Kubrick's *Paths of Glory* or *The Killing,* both with Jim Thompson screenplays, I doubt that you'll agree with Bruce Dern that "Thompson would have been proud of what we did with his material." For a better interpretation of Thompson material, rent Burt Kennedy's *The*

Killer Inside Me with Stacy Keach, instead of *After Dark, My Sweet*!

1990 (R) 114m/C Jason Patric, Rachel Ward, Bruce Dern, George Dickerson, James Cotton, Corey Carrier, Rocky Giordani; ***D:*** James Foley; ***W:*** Robert Redlin, James Foley; ***C:*** Mark Plummer; ***M:*** Maurice Jarre. **VHS, LV, Closed Caption**

After Hours

Actor Griffin Dunne reportedly abstained from sex while making *After Hours* because director Martin Scorsese wanted to maintain the tension of his character throughout a long Soho night filled with weird experiences and strange prowlers-who-only-come-out-when-it's-dark. Dunne plays a Manhattan computer guy with no money who's confronted first by Rosanna Arquette, Linda Fiorentino, and Teri Garr, then, in rapid succession by Verna Bloom, Cheech and Chong, John Heard, Dick Miller, Catherine O'Hara, Will Patton, Bronson Pinchot, Rockets Redglare, and Scorsese himself in a nightclub sequence (the list goes on and on). Dunne, who went on to direct his father Dominick as a restaurant critic putting a cockroach-infested fork in his mouth no less than 10 times in 1997's *Addicted to Love,* told *US* magazine's Amy Taubin that *Hours* and *Love* are first cousins. (Except that *Love* is, in his words, "corny and old-fashioned." Either that or what was the ultimate Catholic nightmare in 1985 has evolved into aw-shucks romanticism in 1997.) P.S. WHY did it take movie goers so many years (and over 15 flicks!) to appreciate Linda Fiorentino?

1985 (R) 97m/C Griffin Dunne, Rosanna Arquette, John Heard, Teri Garr, Catherine O'Hara, Verna Bloom, Linda Fiorentino, Dick Miller, Bronson Pinchot, Will Patton, Rockets Redglare; ***Cameos:*** Richard "Cheech" Marin, Thomas Chong, Martin Scorsese; ***D:*** Martin Scorsese; ***W:*** Joe Minion; ***C:*** Michael Ballhaus; ***M:*** Howard Shore. Cannes Film Festival '86: Best Director (Scorsese); Independent Spirit Awards '86: Best Director (Scorsese), Best Film. **VHS, LV, Letterbox, Closed Caption**

Afterglow

This featherweight variation on *Who's Afraid of Virginia Woolf?* is only partly redeemed by the fact that the always-good Nick Nolte and the ever-charismatic Julie Christie are in it. Lara Flynn Boyle's character is so vapid, it sounds as if she were modeled after a single blind date in Hell. As for Jonny Lee Miller, I can take him as a trainspotter, as a hacker, but not as some romance-starved fop worshipping at the altar of La Christie and limping around in a cast he got in a hokey suicide bid. *Afterglow* goes on for hours, and at the end, just when you're crossing every finger and toe that the soundtrack doesn't break into some sappy love song, Tom Waits starts to sing "Somewhere"—AAARGH!!

1997 (R) 113m/C Nick Nolte, Julie Christie, Lara Flynn Boyle, Jonny Lee Miller, Jay Underwood, Domini Blythe; ***D:*** Alan Rudolph; ***W:*** Alan Rudolph; ***C:*** Toyomichi Kurita; ***M:*** Mark Isham. Independent Spirit Awards '98: Best Actress (Christie); New York Film Critics Awards '97: Best Actress (Christie); National Society of Film Critics Awards '97: Best Actress (Christie); Nominations: Academy Awards '97: Best Actress (Christie). **VHS, Closed Caption**

Alambrista!

The best scripted film of 1978's San Francisco International Film Festival may well have been Robert M. Young's *Alambrista!,* a compassionate study of the Mexican immigrants who entered the U.S. illegally in the late 1970s in search of better employment. Focusing on one unmarried father named Roberto (touchingly played by Domingo Ambriz), Young reveals the frightening, nomadic, and altogether unfree lives the Mexican farmworkers must lead in order to send money home to their families. *Alambrista!* has a strong documentary quality: Young's training was in that filmmaking tradition. He shows how Roberto goes from farm to farm, harvesting fruits and vegetables, and how he lives briefly with a Stockton waitress (stunningly played by Linda Gillin, who also made a couple of chiller-thrillers). For the most part, Roberto's new life is horrible: lonely and exhausting, and filled with the terror of discovery by immigration authorities. *Alambrista!* evokes memories of *The Grapes of Wrath,* and the picture deserves much wider distribution than it received on the now-defunct *Visions* series via PBS. A must on video, not only for Young's superb storytelling, but also because it gives a chance to see

Alfie (Michael Caine) and Gilda (Julia Foster) in *Alfie.* Paramount; courtesy of the Kobal Collection

the early work of Oscar nominees Ned Beatty and Edward James Olmos, as well as the late Trinidad Silva *(Crackers, Colors, The Night Before).* ☙☙☙☙

1977 110m/C Domingo Ambriz, Trinidad Silva, Linda Gillin, Ned Beatty, Julius W. Harris, Paul Berrones, Edward James Olmos, Stephen Walker, Blake Ritson; ***D:*** Robert M. Young; ***W:*** Robert M. Young; ***C:*** Robert M. Young.

Alfie

In 1965's *The Ipcress File,* Michael Caine as Harry Palmer made ordinary blokes with glasses seem as sexy in their own way as Sean Connery did in the James Bond films. In 1966, he won an Academy Award nomination for best actor in the title role of *Alfie,* as a rake who outsmarts himself. Alfie fancies himself a man about town. He wants to be free and easy, but he's as trapped by the seduction game as any member of a chain gang. There's Ruby (Shelley Winters), a plump older woman who grows tired of him. There's Annie (Jane Asher), who loves him but cuts her losses when she sees him as he really is. There's Siddie, Gilda, Carla, and then there's Lily (Vivien Merchant), the most unassuming of them all. Lily doesn't understand Alfie's games but gets dragged into them anyway, partly because of her own sad life, but mostly because Alfie believes he doesn't care whether he hurts her or not. He simply doesn't consider the possibility that the consequences of his actions might be irreparably devastating. The truth shatters and changes them both forever. The unique thing about Michael Caine as Alfie is that he isn't strong (he spends time in the hospital) or drop-dead gorgeous, nor is his technique anything special. He simply does what he does because he doesn't think about it. We know that, because he speaks to the audience all through the film. We see and hear what he does and says, not with the self-knowledge that he will have after 114 minutes, but with the limited (and frankly, untested) insight that he has as he makes one mistake after another. Merchant, who also won an Oscar nomination, is immeasurably touching as the lonely wife of Alfie's fellow patient, and Denholm Elliot's career went into high gear after he played a sleazy doctor here; he would remain constantly employed until his death in 1992. Caine has the lion's share of screen time, after a full decade of slogging around the industry in small parts. Few deserve stardom as much, or sustain it as well as he does. Caine continues to grow as an actor with every role and I've yet to see him coast through a performance. It all started with this film. If he could reveal the aching humanity in *Alfie,* he could and would do the same for any character, however sterling or reprehensible. 🦴🦴🦴🦴

1966 (PG) 114m/C *GB* Michael Caine, Shelley Winters, Millicent Martin, Vivien Merchant, Julia Foster, Jane Asher, Shirley Anne Field, Eleanor Bron, Denholm Elliott, Alfie Bass, Graham Stark, Murray Melvin, Sydney Tafler, Peter Graves, Queenie Watts; ***D:*** Lewis Gilbert; ***W:*** Bill Naughton; ***C:*** Otto Heller; ***M:*** Burt Bacharach, Sonny Rollins. Cannes Film Festival '67: Grand Jury Prize; Golden Globe Awards '67: Best Foreign Film; National Board of Review Awards '66: Best Supporting Actress (Merchant); National Society of Film Critics Awards '66: Best Actor (Caine); Nominations: Academy Awards '66: Best Actor (Caine), Best Adapted Screenplay, Best Picture, Best Song ("Alfie"), Best Supporting Actress (Merchant). **VHS**

Alice

Alice has been identified by the folks at Roxie Releasing as "militant surrealism." It was one of the San Francisco International Film Festival's rare treats in the spring of 1988, and although it is certainly an unusual adaptation of the Lewis Carroll Wonderland classic, it is not as obsessive and scary as many grown-ups might have you believe. When I saw it one Palm Sunday with a crowd of Berkeley youngsters, they appeared to relish Alice's adventures as much as I did. None seemed overly disturbed by the imagery, but every child is unique, so do preview this one before you organize a kindergarten birthday party with *Alice* as the centerpiece. ***AKA:*** Neco Z Alenky. 🦴🦴🦴

1988 84m/C *CZ* Kristina Kohoutova; ***D:*** Jan Svankmajer; ***W:*** Jan Svankmajer; ***C:*** Svatopluk Maly. **VHS**

All Over Me

All Over Me opened to mostly favorable reviews because of its sympathetic treatment of gay themes, and its fine cast, even though it's much clunkier than producer Dolly Hall's 1995 breakthrough release, *The Incredibly True Adventures of Two Girls in Love.* (Hall also produced *High Art* in 1998, which drew the best notices of Ally Sheedy's career.) This one's about best friends Claude (*To Die For*'s Alison Folland) and Ellen (Tara Subkoff). They're no longer as close now that Ellen's going out with stoner Mark (Cole Hauser), and Claude turns to the gay Jesse (Wilson Cruz) for friendship. Claude dreams about being in a band with Ellen and gay musician Luke (Pat Briggs) and also pays her first trip to a lesbian bar and meets a singer named Lucy (Leisha Hailey). Oh, and Claude also works in a pizza parlor and doesn't get along with her mother (Ann Dowd). It plays no more gracefully than it reads and mortality is tossed into the mix because it was in the script, I guess. Alison Folland et al are very good indeed, which helps a lot. I'm still waiting for a real, live Wilson Cruz feature: Is anybody listening? 🦴🦴🦴½

1996 (R) 90m/C Alison Folland, Tara Subkoff, Cole Hauser, Wilson Cruz, Leisha Hailey, Pat Briggs, Ann Dowd; ***D:*** Alex Sichel; ***W:*** Sylvia Sichel; ***C:*** Joe DeSalvo; ***M:*** Miki Navazio. Nominations: Independent Spirit Awards '98: Best Actress (Folland). **VHS**

Allonsanfan

Allonsanfan stars the wonderful Marcello Mastroianni as a grudging revolutionary, circa 1816. This early Taviani film is somewhat uneven compared to their later efforts, but Mastroianni, as usual, makes it all worthwhile. The most meaningful moments occur when the Tavianis permit

Jesse (Wilson Cruz) and Luke (Pat Briggs) in *All Over Me.* Fine Line; courtesy of the Kobal Collection

some honest emotion to creep into the story. The brilliant cinematography is by Giuseppe Ruzzolini. ♪♪♪

1973 115m/C *IT* Marcello Mastroianni, Laura Betti, Renato de Carmine, Lea Massari, Mimsy Farmer, Claudio Cassinelli, Bruno Cirino; ***D:*** Paolo Taviani, Vittorio Taviani; ***W:*** Paolo Taviani, Vittorio Taviani; ***C:*** Giuseppe Ruzzolini; ***M:*** Ennio Morricone. **VHS**

The Amazing Mr. X

When film lovers conjure up memories of strong women in the 1940s, they may recall Joan Crawford with her thick lipstick and huge shoulder pads, but my favorite unsung actress of that era is Lynn Bari. Bari was a cool brunette with a deep hypnotic voice who glided through 70 films for 20th Century Fox between 1934–56. In the early days of her career, she would pass in and out of the plot so fast that her appearances would only register with her most meticulous admirers. By the time she hit her stride, her film career was nearly over. Fans who appreciated her fresh and easy banter as the mystery writer with Randolph Scott in *Home Sweet Homicide* or as a murder suspect with George Raft in *Nocturne* would not have many more Lynn Bari movies to enjoy before she moved on to television and the stage. *The Amazing Mr. X/The Spiritualist* was Bari's last important film as a central character. Carole Landis had originally been cast as a woman haunted by the "ghost" of her husband, but the beautiful Landis was haunted by a life beyond her control, and killed herself a few weeks before shooting was due to begin. Bari, benefiting enormously from the breathtaking camera work of the great John Alton, gave the role a depth and understanding that the essentially comic Landis would not have been able to supply. Whether drifting along a dark beach in flowing white evening gowns or registering a wry awareness of her fiance's romantic limitations, Bari gracefully sustained the delicate balance between world weariness and genuine vulnerability. Also in the cast were the ubiquitous Richard Carlson as her earnest but awkward love interest, the gently appealing Cathy O'Donnell, and Turhan Bey, delivering a surprisingly textured performance in the title role. Because *The Amazing Mr. X/The Spiritualist* lapsed into the public domain and is so often televised in murky prints that fail to do justice to Alton's cinematography, it has yet to acquire the reputation that it deserves. If actualized, rumors of a 35mm video may help to redress that injustice. Afterward, you can try to find a rental copy of *Nocturne,* then join the throng of Lynn Bari aficionados who are mystified by why such an intriguing presence continues to remain an unknown quantity today. ***AKA:*** The Spiritualist. 🦴🦴🦴

1948 79m/B Turhan Bey, Lynn Bari, Cathy O'Donnell, Richard Carlson, Donald Curtis, Virginia Gregg; ***D:*** Bernard Vorhaus; ***W:*** Muriel Roy Boulton, Ian McLellan Hunter; ***C:*** John Alton. **VHS**

The Ambulance

The presence of Eric Roberts in a movie like Larry Cohen's *The Ambulance* shows how his career has changed from the heady days when he was an Oscar contender. *The Ambulance* has all the trappings of an old-fashioned mystery: Roberts plays a cartoonist who falls for a mystery woman (Janine Turner) on the street. Before she passes out and is taken away in an ambulance, she slips him the vital clue that she's a diabetic. Yep, it turns out that mad doctor Eric Braeden is abducting all the diabetics he can and selling them for medical research. Larry Cohen clearly doesn't want you to think about that premise too long, and energetic Roberts won't LET you in any case. Still, *The Ambulance* has a great femme cop (Megan Gallagher), an even better nutty cop (James Earl Jones), and the Oscar-winning, scene-stealing Red Buttons as a wily old reporter who tries to help our poor driven hero. *Return of the Killer Tomatoes! The Lift, The Refrigerator,* and now *The Ambulance.* What's next? 🦴🦴🦴

1990 (R) 95m/C Eric Roberts, James Earl Jones, Megan Gallagher, Richard Bright, Janine Turner, Eric (Hans Gudegast) Braeden, Red Buttons, Laurene Landon, Jill Gatsby, Nicholas Chinlund; ***D:*** Larry Cohen; ***W:*** Larry Cohen; ***C:*** Jacques Haitkin. **VHS, LV, Closed Caption**

American Boyfriends

Canadian writer/director Sandy Wilson came up with this sequel to her 1985 hit, *My American Cousin.* Although Wilson tends to rely too heavily on 1965 media caca, there is no denying the considerable charm of Margaret Langrick as Sandy Wilcox and the immense charisma of John Wildman, seen all too briefly in a reprise of his role as Butch Walker. 🦴🦴🦴

1989 (PG-13) 90m/C *CA* Margaret Langrick, John Wildman, Jason Blicker, Lisa Repo Martell; ***D:*** Sandy Wilson; ***W:*** Sandy Wilson; ***C:*** Brenton Spencer. **VHS, LV**

American Heart

Take a good look at Jeff Bridges' performance as Jack in *American Heart* and then ask yourself what this three-time Oscar nominee has to DO to win an Academy Award. Bridges deservedly received recognition as Best Actor at the Independent Spirit Awards for his lived-in performance as an ex-convict, filled with despair and forced by circumstances to care for his adolescent son, Nick (superbly played by Edward Furlong). Nick has an aching need for his father's love and approval, but Jack has been so beaten by life that at first he can only grudgingly tolerate his son's presence. Directed by Martin *(Streetwise)* Bell, who thoroughly understands the difficult subject matter, *American Heart* resists sentimental short cuts and simplistic resolutions to dig all the way down to the core of this wrenching situation, and there's nary a false note in Peter Silverman's gritty, hard-hitting script. Bridges co-produced this little-seen American masterpiece, which represents an unequivocal high point in his long career. 🦴🦴🦴🦴

1992 (R) 114m/C Jeff Bridges, Edward Furlong, Lucinda Jenney, Tracey Kapisky, Don Harvey, Margaret Welsh; ***D:*** Martin Bell; ***W:*** Peter Silverman; ***C:*** James R. Bagdonas; ***M:*** James Newton Howard. In-

The world was created in six days. It was beautiful. But it was way over budget!

—Tagline from the movie *...And God Spoke.*

dependent Spirit Awards '94: Best Actor (Bridges); Nominations: Independent Spirit Awards '94: Best Cinematography, Best First Feature, Best Supporting Actor (Furlong), Best Supporting Actress (Jenney). **VHS, LV**

American Matchmaker

American Matchmaker is an archival treasure filmed in Yiddish by legendary cult director Edgar Ulmer in 1940. You may remember its star, Leo Fuchs (1911–94), as a character actor in 1990's *Avalon.* But 60 years ago, the Polish emigre cut a dashing figure in the title role of a confirmed-bachelor-turned-Manhattan-matchmaker. Ulmer's escapist comedy is lighter than air; you'd never know from the subject matter that this gentle satire was released the year after the Nazi invasion of Poland. ***AKA:*** Amerikaner Shadkhn. 🦴🦴🦴

1940 87m/B Leo Fuchs, Judith Abarbanel, Rosetta Bialis, Yudel Dubinsky, Abe Lax; ***D:*** Edgar G. Ulmer; ***W:*** S. Castle; ***C:*** Edgar G. Ulmer. **VHS**

American Strays

The big name cast may lure you, but you'll be chafing at the bit within the first few seconds of Michael Covert's *American Strays.* If Luke Perry wanted to terminate his status as a heartthrob, this lousy movie would do the trick, if any of his fan club members ever bother to rent *American Strays.* And what is Oscar nominee Jennifer Tilly doing here—slumming? With bad luck, this one might be played endlessly on cable television, dissolving the luster of each and every participant. Disjointed and dumb. **woof!**

1996 (R) 97m/C Carol Kane, Jennifer Tilly, Eric Roberts, John Savage, Luke Perry, Joe Viterelli, James Russo, Vonte Sweet, Sam Jones, Brion James, Toni Kalem, Melora Walters; ***D:*** Michael Covert; ***W:*** Michael Covert; ***C:*** Sead Mutarevic; ***M:*** John Graham. **VHS, DVD**

...And God Spoke

Soupy Sales as Moses, Eve Plumb as Mrs. Noah, Lou Ferrigno as Cain; yeah, those are the first actors you think about when casting a Biblical epic, right? *...And God Spoke* is a mockumentary on the making of the nonexistent movie of the same name. It focuses on the trials and tribulations of two independent producers (Clive Walton and Marvin Handleman, played by Michael Riley and Stephen Rappaport) as they attempt to film the best-selling book of all time. The team, best known for *Alpha Deatha De Kappa, Dial S for Sex,* and *Nude Ninjas,* now go after a target audience of four billion Bible readers. Clearly, Clive and Marvin are not among that group; they're unsure whether there were eight or ten disciples, and their vision of the loaves and fishes sequence (later scrapped for budgetary reasons) includes Pepperidge Farm goldfish crackers standing in for the fishes. Later, when they get into deeper financial scrapes, Marvin agrees that Moses will include a product placement pitch, delivering 20th century soft drinks as well as Commandments to the stock footage multitude from the 19th century. And of course, despite scathing reviews, *...And God Spoke* is a huge $42 million hit, attracting long lines of devoted groupies who wear Biblical gear to repeat screenings. As good-natured satire, *...And God Spoke* falls somewhere in between *The Making of Bikini School III* and *This Is Spinal Tap.* The performances are energetic and clever; it's fun to see Sales, Jan Brady, and the incredible Hulk again, and all in the same movie (and it's blessedly short). If the entire film had been in the same vein as the auditions for casting agent Charlie Rose, or the power clash between Marvin and the A.D. in a staff meeting, *...And God Spoke* would have been a non-stop side-splitter. As is, it's still a painless way to spend 82 minutes. 🦴🦴

1994 (R) 82m/C Michael Riley, Stephen Rappaport, Soupy Sales, Lou Ferrigno, Eve Plumb, Andy Dick, R.C. Bates, Fred Kaz, Daniel Tisman; ***D:*** Arthur Borman; ***W:*** Gregory S. Malins, Michael Curtis; ***C:*** Lee Daniel. **VHS**

And the Band Played On

In spite of all the hands that have clearly fiddled with *And the Band Played On,* it is still as good a film as we are likely to get anytime soon about the early years of the AIDS epidemic. And if millions decide to watch it only to see dozens of big stars acting their hearts out in cameos, they may still learn more about AIDS than they have from the guarded sound bites that represent their major source of information to date. What will the inhabitants of this planet in the 25th century think of how we handled these plague years after watching a movie like *And the Band Played On*? Historically, deadly plagues have always revealed the dark side of human nature as this one does; plague victims are either shunned or rushed to their graves by the ignorance of both their communities and their doctors. Throughout much of the 20th century, we've clung to the touching notion that science could solve our every problem, forgetting that the great influenza plague of 1918 claimed twice as many lives as World War I. Because the progress of that virus was so swift and so deadly, its victims left behind very little documentation. But the AIDS epidemic has been with us for the better part of two decades with no respite in sight yet. There is certainly no happy ending from the guy on the white horse, the former Center for Disease Control researcher Don Francis, earnestly played by Matthew Modine. Except for his dedication to his work, we know nothing about him. In fact, we learn nothing about the cipher-like doctors who fight the government bureaucracy as they struggle to identify and treat the virus; Glenne Headly and Lily Tomlin are among them. Ronald Reagan and Jerry Falwell play themselves courtesy of old video tapes, and Robert Gallo, another bad guy fixated on winning the Nobel Prize, is well played by Alan Alda. When the film does try to show the private life of someone like the late gay activist Bill Kraus, it gets it wrong, by dredging up the old movie bio cliche of the discontented lover who's jealous of all that political activism. In trying to reach middle America, the film is scrupulous about not depicting anyone who appears to be TOO gay. It reinforces the point that straight people and hemophiliacs could contract the virus or that babies might be born with AIDS and THAT'S when government leaders began to focus on the spread of the disease, by then out of control. But as the first widely distributed major film to deal with the politics of AIDS, it is successful in attracting our attention, concern, and hopefully, effective international demands for a timely cure. *And the Band Played On,* based on the book by the late journalist Randy Shilts, originally aired on the Home Box Office cable network and was also released theatrically in Europe.

1993 (PG-13) 140m/C Matthew Modine, Alan Alda, Ian McKellen, Lily Tomlin, Glenne Headly, Richard Masur, Saul Rubinek, Charles Martin Smith, Patrick Bauchau, Nathalie Baye, Christian Clemenson; ***Cameos:*** Richard Gere, David Clennon, Phil Collins, Alex Courtney, David Dukes, David Marshall Grant, Ronald Guttman, Anjelica Huston, Ken Jenkins, Richard Jenkins, Tcheky Karyo, Swoosie Kurtz, Jack Laufer, Steve Martin, Dakin Matthews, Peter McRobbie, Lawrence Monoson, B.D. Wong, Donal Logue, Jeffrey Nordling, Stephen Spinella; ***D:*** Roger Spottiswoode; ***W:*** Arnold Schulman; ***C:*** Paul Elliott; ***M:*** Carter Burwell. **VHS, LV, Closed Caption**

An Angel at My Table

Jane Campion's *An Angel at My Table* began life as a three-part series on New Zealand television, which (dare I say this?) is the best way to see this 157-minute movie. After all, it is based on three different autobiographical novels by Janet Frame, *To the Island, An Angel at My Table,* and *The Envoy from Mirror City.* Kerry Fox plays Frame, who was misdiagnosed as a schizophrenic and spent eight years in a mental institution receiving electroshock therapy before the error was corrected. Extremely well acted and directed, *An Angel at My Table* is nonetheless very heavy going all at once—especially first thing in the morning, which is when most reviewers see new movies. This explains (if not excuses) all the bad tempers and bad manners one is likely to observe at press screenings. *An Angel at My Table* won many awards all over the world, but then so did *Breaking the Waves* and any number of worthy candidates which are long, depressing, and make you feel like a heel for wanting to watch *Sullivan's Travels* instead.

1989 (R) 157m/C *NZ* Kerry Fox, Alexia Keogh, Karen Fergusson, Iris Churn, K.J. Wilson, Martyn Sanderson; ***D:*** Jane Campion; ***W:*** Laura Jones; ***C:*** Stuart Dryburgh. Independent Spirit Awards '92: Best Foreign Film. **VHS**

Angela

This strange movie about two little girls growing up with a depressed mother (who somewhat resembles Marilyn Monroe) was written and directed by Rebecca Miller, the daughter of Arthur Miller. It's a moderately interesting (but slooow and rather heavy going) examination of a childhood dominated by a fear of the Devil. Miranda Stuart Rhyne and Charlotte Blythe are good as the kids, Angela, ten, and Ellie, six, and Anna Thomson is eerily evocative as their mother. Cinematographer Ellen Kuras won a Filmmakers Trophy at 1995's Sundance Film Festival. 🦴🦴🦴

1994 105m/C Miranda Stuart Rhyne, Charlotte Blythe, Anna Thomson, John Ventimiglia, Vincent Gallo; ***D:*** Rebecca Miller; ***W:*** Rebecca Miller; ***C:*** Ellen Kuras; ***M:*** Michael Rohatyn. Sundance Film Festival '95: Best Cinematography, Filmmakers Trophy. **VHS**

Angels and Insects

We know that something's off from the very beginning of *Angels and Insects;* Paul Brown's surreal costumes are a dead giveaway. In spite of or, perhaps, because of them, William Adamson (Mark Rylance) determines to marry Eugenia (Patsy Kensit). Eugenia is lovely, but vague. There's something wrong with the marriage from the start, and William isn't even close to solving the riddle when one day he receives a message to return home early and realizes, in an empirical flash, exactly why Eugenia has distanced herself from him for so long. Then Kristin Scott Thomas (made up to look severe and efficient, but secretly lusting for William all this time) makes HER move. Writer/director Philip Haas and co-scripter Belinda Haas succeed in drawing us into a weird and disturbing climate. (I'm trying to come up with a picture that revolves around insects where the central characters were quite normal, but I'm drawing a blank here.) Based on A.S. Byatt's novella *Morpho Eugenia.* 🦴🦴🦴

1995 (R) 116m/C *GB* Mark Rylance, Patsy Kensit, Kristin Scott Thomas, Jeremy Kemp, Douglas Henshall, Chris Larkin, Annette Badland, Anna Massey, Saskia Wickham; ***D:*** Philip Haas; ***W:*** Belinda Haas, Philip Haas; ***C:*** Bernard Zitzermann; ***M:*** Alexander Balanescu. Nominations: Academy Awards '96: Best Costume Design. **VHS**

Anna

Anna is a showcase for Sally Kirkland, who tears into the role of a neglected Czechoslovakian actress with all the passion of a neglected American actress who has no time to waste reserving her energy. Kirkland gets down and dirty with this part, and she has the artistic courage to sacrifice her own good looks in order to create a more believable portrait of Anna, who has both good and bad days. Life does things to people, and Kirkland doesn't hesitate to show the extremes. In some close-ups, as when a beloved old teacher brings her to tears, she resembles a small child fearful of being swallowed by the world's promises and its lies. In others, as when Anna realizes that her protegée has borrowed her life story and claimed it as her own, her rage is limitless and we share the agony of the older woman who has no resources left on which to draw, not even memory. "Oscar nomination" is written all over Sally Kirkland's star performance, and yet she is a real ensemble player, too, for her sequences with model Paulina Porizkova and Robert Fields would be nowhere near as moving without a powerful interplay between the characters. Yurek Bogayevicz directs with a sensitive understanding of the realities of the acting profession, and Agnieszka Holland's screenplay offers a sharp perspective on the generational conflicts between women. The film has been compared to both *All About Eve* and *Sunset Boulevard,* but it differs from both in significant respects. The expatriate theme, as well as the intense examination of trust lost and trust found, contribute to make *Anna* a fresh entry in the catalogue of show business sagas. 🦴🦴🦴🦴

1987 (PG-13) 101m/C Sally Kirkland, Paulina Porizkova, Robert Fields, Stefan Schnabel, Larry

Eugenia (Patsy Kensit) in *Angels and Insects.* Samuel Goldwyn Company; courtesy of the Kobal Collection

"Mrs. Hammond told me that God made my hair red on purpose and I've never cared for Him since."

—Anne Shirley (Megan Follows) in *Anne of Green Gables.*

Pine, Ruth Maleczech; ***D:*** Yurek Bogayevicz; ***W:*** Yurek Bogayevicz, Agnieszka Holland; ***C:*** Bobby Bukowski; ***M:*** Greg Hawkes. Golden Globe Awards '88: Best Actress—Drama (Kirkland); Independent Spirit Awards '88: Best Actress (Kirkland); Los Angeles Film Critics Association Awards '87: Best Actress (Kirkland); Nominations: Academy Awards '87: Best Actress (Kirkland). **VHS, LV, Closed Caption**

Anne of Green Gables

There were two prior movies of Lucy Maud Montgomery's (1874–1942) classic novel, but Kevin Sullivan's version starring Megan Follows is far and away the best. In 1911, William Desmond Taylor (1877–1922) directed Mary Miles Minter (1902–84) in a Paramount film scripted by Frances Marion (1886–1973). Minter was beautiful, but not much of an actress, and her association with Taylor seems to have led directly to his murder in 1922 and to her speedy retirement in 1923. Moreover, beloved Prince Edward Island received short shrift both from Taylor and from George Nicholls Jr. who made the 1934 talking picture starring Dawn O'Day (1918–93), re-named Anne Shirley for the title character. Shirley was a delightful Anne, but for readers who wanted to see every single incident they had read about in the 1908 book, a 79-minute film couldn't provide the detail craved by Anne-atics. And so it took 77 years for Kevin Sullivan and Joe Weisenfeld to come up with the perfect adaptation, and the perfect Anne, Marilla (Colleen Dewhurst), and Matthew (Richard Farnsworth). 1985 audiences treasured this 197-minute labor of love, turning it into an instant classic. I don't care how jaded you think you are, this irresistible red-haired motor mouth from another time (that would be Anne) will melt your cold, cold heart. Exquisitely filmed on Prince Edward Island by Rene Ohashi. Followed by an equally fine 1987 sequel *(Anne of Avonlea)* and a long-running series in the '90s, *Avonlea* (an Emmy winner as outstanding children's program). ♦♦♦♦

1985 197m/C *CA* Megan Follows, Colleen Dewhurst, Richard Farnsworth, Patricia Hamilton, Schuyler Grant, Jonathan Crombie, Marilyn Lightstone, Charmion King, Rosemary Radcliffe, Jackie Burroughs, Robert Collins, Joachim Hansen, Cedric Smith, Paul Brown, Miranda de Pencier, Jennifer Inch, Wendy Lyon, Christiane Krueger, Trish Nettleton, Morgan Chapman; ***D:*** Kevin Sullivan; ***W:*** Kevin Sullivan, Joe Weisenfeld; ***C:*** Rene Ohashi; ***M:*** Hagood Hardy. **VHS, LV, Closed Caption**

Another Country

One of the saddest things about 1987's *Less Than Zero* (besides watching the way-too-believable performance of real-life substance abuser Robert Downey Jr.) is realizing that the director of that abysmal flick, Marek Kanievska, had helmed one of my favorite films of 1984. How could the man who made *Another Country,* one of the most sensitive films EVER about homosexuality, appear to give homophobia equal screen time just three years later? Rupert Everett plays Guy Bennett, who's meant to be real-life spy Guy Burgess (1911–63). Journalist Betsy Brantley comes to interview him at his flat in Russia and discovers that the aging traitor is somewhat of a broken-hearted Anglophile. What happened? Guy talks about his schooldays when he befriended a Marxist named Tommy Judd (newcomer Colin Firth at his most luscious) and kvetched about Mummy Imogen (Anna Massey), and fell in love with Harcourt (angelic Cary Elwes before he began to pump iron). Guy wants to be accepted by his schoolmates, but the homosexual activity they enjoy in private and condemn in public is intrinsic to his nature. As his infatuation with Harcourt deepens, Guy becomes increasingly vulnerable to the forces that lead to his break from Great Britain's social structure. Once the break occurs, he accepts his lot as a permanent outsider with resignation, no longer feeling any loyalty to the country of his birth, only a wistful yearning for its trappings. A good companion piece to *Another Country* is Alan Bennett's *An Englishman Abroad,* directed by John Schlesinger in 1983 and based on star Coral Browne's (1913–91) real-life encounter with Guy Burgess (Alan Bates). Reportedly, American audiences have a rough time making sense of the Burgess-Maclean-Philby triumvirate or comprehending subsequent revelations about the Queen's de-knighted art historian Anthony Blunt (1907–83). Everett's poignant portrayal really ought to speak for itself, but if not, John Costello's *The Mask of Treachery* (Collins, 1988) is crammed with over 760 pages worth of information on the subject. Extra Note: As a teenager, the ninth Earl Spencer appeared in several sequences here, one where he sings his sister Princess Diana's favorite hymn, "I Vow to Thee My Country," and another sequence where he bares his backside in a community shower.

1984 90m/C *GB* Rupert Everett, Colin Firth, Michael Jenn, Robert Addie, Anna Massey, Betsy Brantley, Rupert Wainwright, Cary Elwes, Arthur Howard, Tristan Oliver, Frederick Alexander, Adrian Ross-Magenty, Geoffrey Bateman, Philip Dupuy, Jeffrey Wickham, Gideon Boulting, Ivor Howard, Charles Spencer; ***D:*** Marek Kanievska; ***W:*** Julian Mitchell; ***C:*** Peter Biziou; ***M:*** Michael Storey. Nominations: Cannes Film Festival '84: Best Film. **VHS, LV**

Antonia's Line

This is the most accessible film by Marleen Gorris, whose previous efforts include 1983's *A Question of Silence* and 1985's *Broken Mirrors.* It's a family saga revolving around matriarch Antonia (Willeke Van Ammelrooy) and her large clan. The male characters are mainly utilitarian necessities here, but that's a step up from the murder victim/serial killer roles they've been assigned in other Gorris pictures. Gorris' 1995 Oscar winner blends humor with feminist insights and is beautifully photographed by Willy Stassen. (In Dutch with English subtitles.)

1995 (R) 102m/C *NL* Willeke Van Ammelrooy, Els Dottermans, Veerle Van Overloop, Thyrza Ravesteijn, Jan Decleir, Mil Seghers, Jan Steen, Marina De Graaf; ***D:*** Marleen Gorris; ***W:*** Marleen Gorris; ***C:*** Willy Stassen; ***M:*** Ilona Seckaz. Academy Awards '95: Best Foreign Film; Nominations: British Academy Awards '96: Best Foreign Film. **VHS**

Apartment Zero

What do movie buffs do in the daytime? Some people wonder, but not for very long. If you go to the same theatre night after night, you'll see the guy who wears the same shirt every night and switches his seat six times during the movie, the guy who routinely arrives an hour late (or 23 hours early), the guy who chain smokes in between features and never looks at or talks to anyone, the guy who always sits in the front row and can't wait to see every movie Dennis O'Keefe played in as an extra, the guy who arrives unannounced at the residences of 90-year-old actresses with an armful of 8" by 10" studio stills and a marking pen, the guy who sits next to you and invites himself on your unplanned 500-mile trip to a fan convention the day after tomorrow. Yeah, they're mostly guys. If you're not, they'll tolerate you if you know who Bob Steele and Verna Hillie are, but they only have eyes for starlets whose careers ended before they were born. Half of them hate each other on sight, like territorial tom cats, the other half aren't on speaking terms, unless someone wants to show off because he's seen Lloyd Bridges in 1935's *Dancing Feet* in a bit and he's the only one who HAS (in a dungeon-God-knows-where). Ah, the magic of the movies...Adrian Le Duc (Colin Firth) would fit right in with this crowd, if he can ever tear himself away from his Buenos Aires projection booth and *Apartment Zero.* For all his hard-earned cinematic knowledge, Adrian is intrinsically lonely and desperately in need of deep friendship. Adrian is picky, though. If someone doesn't know who Geraldine Page is—that's it, Adrian gave him his chance. When delectable Jack Carney (Hart Bochner) turns up applying to be his flat mate, Adrian gazes on him as if he's all 42 reels of 1924's *Greed* or the nitrate original of 1928's *The Divine Woman.* Jack doesn't know anything about movies, though. He doesn't even recognize the beautifully framed photograph of Montgomery Clift on Adrian's wall. But it doesn't matter; Adrian is hooked. So is everyone else in Adrian's building, who absolutely adore Jack, especially after he rescues a pussy cat. Adrian is jealous; he doesn't mix with the neighbors. Adrian's obsession with his flat mate grows as Jack puts up with his moods and pacifies him at every turn. Jack even suggests picking up girls together, but Adrian doesn't like girls, only women like the framed supernovas back at the flat.

> **"If that is a mask, please take it off now—or keep it on forever."**
>
> **—Adrian Le Duc (Colin Firth) in *Apartment Zero.***

Then Adrian discovers that Jack isn't what he thought he was and vice-a versa. Things get dark and creepy and furtive and don't forget that we're not in Kansas, Toto, we're in Argentina where people come and go so quickly, Dear. This smashingly acted, wonderfully satisfying chiller is chock full of film lore (including a great movie game you can play at home with your friends) and plenty of surprises. Colin Firth, a sexy matinee idol since 1984's *Another Country,* is still a sexy matinee idol after playing Darcy in 1995's *Pride and Prejudice.* Hart Bochner spent a lot of time making LONG miniseries on American television before directing 1994's very funny *P.C.U.* with Jeremy Piven, David Spade, and Jessica Walters, followed by 1996's *High School High.* 🦴🦴🦴🦴

1988 (R) 124m/C *GB* Hart Bochner, Colin Firth, Fabrizio Bentivoglio, Liz Smith, Dora Bryan, James Telfer, Mirella D'Angelo, Juan Vitale, Francesca D'Aloja, Miguel Ligero, Elvia Andreoli, Marikeva Monti; ***D:*** Martin Donovan; ***W:*** Martin Donovan, David Koepp; ***C:*** Miguel Rodriguez; ***M:*** Elia Cmiral. **VHS, LV**

The Apostle

I once knew a character who joined a monastery to atone for his sins. The notion of making peace with the people he had hurt didn't occur to him. I thought he was full of hooey and wasn't surprised when he left the monastery to start a "new" life with an entirely different cast of supporting players. Not long into the 134-minute running time of *The Apostle,* Texas Preacher Euliss Dewey (Robert Duvall) commits a vicious and inexcusable act. He vanishes from the scene of the crime and passes himself off as Apostle E.F. in Bayou Boutte, Louisiana. He works as a mechanic so that he can have free air time over the radio to start a new ministry and soon assembles enough followers for a new church, "The One Way Road to Heaven." While he's gaining the love and respect of the Louisiana congregation, he learns about the consequences of his behavior back home. E.F. stays put and preaches and preaches and preaches until the end of the movie, right into the credits. Society forces him to pay for what he did, and the press kit says that he has found redemption, but I didn't buy it. He hurt people and he hurt those who loved the people he hurt and all the evangelistic hot air in Louisiana isn't a self-inflicted penance for what he did in Texas, although it plays that way. As an actor, Robert Duvall has few peers. As a writer/director...well, this IS his film and it says what he wants it to say. I believed in the sincerity of E.F.'s followers, but I didn't believe in his redemption for as long as it takes to bat an eyelash. Farrah Fawcett and Miranda Richardson are outstanding as wife Jessie and lady friend, Toosie, and so is Duvall in the title role, although they're all here strictly to serve the plot, such as it is. *The Apostle* gets four bones for its performances but two and a half overall, at least for this viewer. 🦴🦴½

1997 (PG-13) 134m/C Robert Duvall, Miranda Richardson, Farrah Fawcett, John Beasley, Todd Allen, June Carter Cash, Billy Bob Thornton, Rick Dial, Walton Goggins, Billy Joe Shaver; ***D:*** Robert Duvall; ***W:*** Robert Duvall; ***C:*** Barry Markowitz; ***M:*** David Mansfield. Independent Spirit Awards '98: Best Actor (Duvall), Best Director (Duvall), Best Film; Los Angeles Film Critics Association Awards '97: Best Actor (Duvall); National Society of Film Critics Awards '97: Best Actor (Duvall); Nominations: Academy Awards '97: Best Actor (Duvall); Independent Spirit Awards '98: Best Screenplay, Best Supporting Actress (Fawcett, Richardson); Screen Actors Guild Award '97: Best Actor (Duvall). **VHS, Closed Caption, DVD**

The Applegates

The Applegates is the story of a colony of misguided Amazonian arthropods who believe that their only chance for survival depends on the extermination of the human race. They send a family of four bugs to Ohio. Their mission: to impersonate a nuclear family of humans named Dick, Jane, Sally, and Johnny, and then blow up a nuclear power plant. Ed Begley Jr., Stockard Channing, Camile Cooper, and Bobby Jacoby star as the statistically average Applegate family, with Dabney Coleman as the leader of their colony, Aunt Bea. Director Michael *(Heathers, The Truth about Cats and Dogs)* Lehmann's script never does explain how the bugs transform themselves into humans. His satire focuses on how the bugs are twisted by American society. Dick has an affair with his secretary, Jane becomes a chargeaholic, Sally gets preg-

nant, and Johnny gets hooked on drugs. Whenever any humans threaten to expose them, the bugs-in-disguise turn them into hostages. What makes the movie work is the twisted characterizations of the family. Ed Begley Jr. is just right as Dick. He may know the definition of "normal," but he has no idea how he's supposed to act under the circumstances. Future Oscar nominee Stockard Channing, one of America's most underappreciated actresses, is a delight as Jane, her growing mania for possessions dissolving her carefully maintained facade. The kids are good, too. Cami Cooper's role requires her to shift from innocence to evil and back again in the blink of eye and she conveys both with enormous skill. As her little brother, Bobby Jacoby is heartbreakingly innocent before some drug-dealing twins get their clutches on him. Lehmann's satire gets really broad as the family members start lying to each other right and left; *The Applegates* may not appeal to you if you demand good taste from a movie. Its humor can be brutal, but on some weird level, I prefer Lehmann's good-natured, what-the-hell attack on Middle America here to Tim Burton's mean-spirited vision of suburbia in *Edward Scissorhands.* ***AKA:*** Meet the Applegates. 🦴🦴🦴

1989 (R) 90m/C Ed Begley Jr., Stockard Channing, Dabney Coleman, Camille (Cami) Cooper, Bobby Jacoby, Glenn Shadix, Susan Barnes, Adam Biesk, Savannah Smith Boucher; ***D:*** Michael Lehmann; ***W:*** Michael Lehmann, Redbeard Simmons. **VHS, LV, Closed Caption**

Art for Teachers of Children

I've listened to DOZENS of after-the-fact stories from teenage girls seduced by adult males and from adult males who seduced teenage girls. The girls always seem to affect a cynical tone about experiences that clearly turned their lives upside down. The men are more flip; it was no big deal, she wanted it, she was screwed up anyway, yackety-yack. So Jennifer Montgomery's *Art for Teachers of Children,* documenting a sexual relationship between a 14-year-old student and her 28-year-old married school counselor, is a major button pusher from frame one. Montgomery's black-and-white feature film debut is atrociously acted (with a 22-year-old woman and 40-year-old guy in the leading roles) and stubbornly resists expressing ANY point of view. "There's nothing worse than boring men who make bad art," Montgomery's real-life mother (and no actress) intones on the soundtrack. See, Montgomery, then 33, wanted to make her fact-based movie about art, but why choose this particular topic if she didn't want to make some sort of comment about men who lust after children and the children who love them? It's haunting, though, in the same way those flat narratives about being a sexual plaything tug at your heart when they're recited by women who are old at 18. 🦴🦴

1995 82m/B Caitlin Grace McDonnell, Duncan Hannah, Coles Burroughs, Bryan Keane; ***D:*** Jennifer Montgomery; ***W:*** Jennifer Montgomery; ***C:*** Jennifer Montgomery. **VHS**

Ashes and Diamonds

If you want to watch Zbigniew Cybulski (1927–67) when he helped to put Polish films on the international movie map, don't miss *Ashes and Diamonds.* For marketing purposes, American publicists referred to Cybulski as the Polish James Dean, an overconvenient but apt comparison. Cybulski wore tinted prescription glasses throughout *Ashes and Diamonds* because of vision problems, but they also increased his mysterious allure. In the film, set on the last day of the war, his character must kill a man he doesn't want to kill and probably doesn't have to kill. He resists the job, but fate in the form of a poorly timed order is against him. *Ashes and Diamonds* says more about the post-war world of 1958 than it does of wartime life in 1945, especially when it contrasts Cybulski's destiny with his haphazard and rather naive pursuit of a young barmaid. In real life, Cybulski lived fast and died young while trying to board a train. His death increased his legendary status and several of his films (1954's *A Generation,* 1960's *Innocent Sorcerers,* 1965's *The Saragos-*

In a world of make believe, Stella is about to discover the difference between true love...and real life.

—Tagline from the movie *An Awfully Big Adventure.*

sa Manuscript) are still shown constantly in art houses all over the world. It is perhaps besides the point that, for all his tremendous presence and seemingly careless appeal, Cybulski often overacted like mad. As is evident here, he seldom approached his roles in a disciplined way or gave careful shadings to the characters he portrayed. But TRY tearing your eyes away from Andrzej Wajda's *Ashes and Diamonds* for a single second when Cybulski is onscreen. ***AKA:*** Popiol i Diament. 𝔄𝔄𝔄𝔄

1958 105m/B *PL* Zbigniew Cybulski, Eva Krzyzewska, Adam Pawlikowski, Bogumil Kobiela, Waclaw Zastrzezynski; ***D:*** Andrzej Wajda; ***W:*** Andrzej Wajda, Jerzy Andrzejewski; ***C:*** Jerzy Wojcik; ***M:*** Filip Nowak, Jan Krenz. **VHS, LV**

Attica

Cinda Firestone made this documentary with her folk's money (the Firestone Tire and Rubber Company). Her honest study of the Attica uprising benefits from outstanding research. Firestone produced, directed, and edited (with Tucker Ashworth) *Attica* herself, and her frank interviews with Attica's inmates are shrewdly spliced next to contrasting statements by Attica's officials. 𝔄𝔄𝔄

1974 80m/C ***D:*** Cinda Firestone; ***C:*** Roland Barnes, Jay Lamarch, Mary Lampson, Jesse Goodman, Carol Stein, Kevin Keating.

Aventurera

For a film buff, discovering a movie like *Aventurera* is better than finding buried treasure. Before I saw it, I'd never heard of its star, Ninon Sevilla, and now I can't wait to see some of her other movies (like 1949's *Senora Tentacion* and 1956's *Yambao*) even without subtitles and cut up with commercials on Spanish-language television channels. The pace of this 1949 Mexican film noir is breathtaking. In the first few minutes of the movie, we meet Sevilla as an innocent young girl named Elena whose mother runs off with another man. After her broken-hearted father commits suicide, Elena must find work, but every job she takes results in unwanted pawing. Finally, an old acquaintance named Lucio takes her to a nightclub, plies her with champagne, and promises to help her become a well-paid secretary. Instead, Elena finds herself working for the ruthless Rosaura, owner of a Juarez brothel. Elena not only has to sing and dance for the nightclub patrons, but share her bed with them as well! As the plot thickens, we learn that Rosaura is leading a double life in Guadalajara, that Elena is a fast learner of most of life's bitter truths, and that even a knife-wielding hunchbacked thug named El Rengo is not all that he seems to be. The eight production numbers are on the same level as those in a low-budget Columbia musical of the '40s, but Sevilla's over-the-top sensuality makes them sparkle. And when she isn't singing and dancing, her skill at projecting rage and resentment helps the 101-minute running time whiz by. Many of Sevilla's best scenes are with Andrea Palma, who plays Rosaura. Both women have a million reasons to hate each other, and Sevilla and Palma give their convoluted characters a surprising degree of dramatic realism in their highly charged sequences together. None of the male actors (except for Miguel Incian as El Rengo) are in the same league as Sevilla or Palma, but at least none of them looks or sounds like Glenn Ford, the bane of bargain-basement California noir. How many more gems like *Aventurera* are shelved in the vaults of other countries, waiting to be brought to life again on the movie screens of today? For starters, at least give us more Ninon Sevilla films, especially those with tantalizing titles like *Victims of Sin* and *Sensuality.* San Francisco's legendary Castro Movie Palace deserves credit for bringing *Aventurera* to contemporary audiences—I had no idea what a cinematic treat I'd been missing all these years. 𝔄𝔄𝔄𝔄

1949 101m/B *MX* Ninon Sevilla, Andrea Palma, Miguel Incian, Tito Junco, Ruben Rojo; ***D:*** Alberto Gout; ***W:*** Agustin Lara; ***C:*** Alex Phillips Jr.

An Average Little Man

An Average Little Man is two films in one, really: half wildly funny, the other half gra-

tuitously violent. Alberto Sordi, Shelley Winters, and Vincenzo Crocitti deliver superb performances as an excited family preparing for the son's (Crocitti) first examinations for employment. Their lives are normal enough until something goes hideously wrong, and the family crumbles for reasons that have nothing to do with them. The point here seems to be that life, as silly, dull, ordinary, petty, wonderful, or rewarding as it is, can be disrupted. And when it IS, the people who are left behind can never return to what they were before. When deep love and happiness end for Sordi's character, he replaces them with other feelings equally intense, that draw him into an entirely different life. Over 30 audience members missed this important point altogether when they walked out of a screening at 1977's San Francisco International Film Festival, perhaps feeling that writer/director Mario Monicelli illustrated his viewpoint with excessive bloodletting. Based on the book by Vincenzo Cerami. ***AKA:*** Un Borghese Piccolo Piccolo; Gran Bollito; A Very Little Man; An Average Man. 🦴🦴🦴

1977 120m/C *IT* Alberto Sordi, Shelley Winters, Vincenzo Crocitti, Romolo Valli, Renzo Carboni; ***D:*** Mario Monicelli; ***W:*** Mario Monicelli, Sergio Amidei; ***C:*** Mario Vulpiani; ***M:*** Giancarlo Chiaramello.

An Awfully Big Adventure

After *Four Weddings and a Funeral,* everyone wanted Hugh Grant to be exactly like Charles, the eligible luvvie he'd played in the film, for the rest of his natural life. That's quite a severe sentence, when you think about it. And then *An Awfully Big Adventure* came out and Grant suggested (undoubtedly with tongue firmly in cheek) that he was more like evil Meredith Potter than dear, sweet Charles. When Grant's *Awfully Big Adventure* in his real life made international headlines, all hell broke loose and everyone forgot about this movie. A shame really, because it's an interesting and rather different look at theatrical life. Many who did see *Adventure* seemed to criticize it from a moral perspective, as if sordid stories ought not to be told by a filmmaker who'd previously lured audiences into theatres with love stories like *Enchanted April* and *Four Weddings and a Funeral.* Mike Newell has made all sorts of films (1977's *The Man in the Iron Mask,* 1980's *The Awakening,* 1985's *Dance with a Stranger,* 1987's *The Good Father, Bad Blood,* and *Amazing Grace and Chuck,* 1992's *Into the West,* and 1996's *Donnie Brasco*), so where is it ground in stone that he has to be chained to feel-good flicks? Meredith Potter is no one's idea of a benevolent theatre manager. He's cruel to stage manager Bunny (Peter Firth), who adores him for masochistic reasons of his own; he has sex with one of the young men in the company; and he's altogether snide and insufferable, the ideal crush for 16-year-old assistant stage manager Stella (Georgina Cates). When established actor P.L. O'Hara (Alan Rickman) arrives on the scene, he immediately seduces Stella, who submits but informs him that she loves someone else. O'Hara's just as much of a rake as the theatre manager, but he still has a wisp of a conscience, which gives him an undeserved sense of moral superiority over Potter. Meanwhile, the older members of the troupe wisely distance themselves from all this subterranean nonsense and collect their paychecks in peace. This matter-of-fact look at backstage life is based on a Beryl Bainbridge novel. Express writer Bainbridge also wrote the acclaimed novel *Every Man for Himself* about the Titanic disaster; he is unlikely to see THAT book filmed anytime soon, not with all those worshipful Cameron admirers out there who would prefer to see another love story as a sequel. Before this film, Cates had received credits under another name, but she auditioned for Stella, knowing the filmmakers wanted a newcomer. Once she got the role, she played a newcomer on the set and onscreen, waiting until the film was in the can to tell the truth about her actual identity. She got away with it and why ever not? The shelf life of movie actresses is so ridiculously short, all really ought to be fair in love, war, and show business. 🦴🦴🦴

P.L. O'Hara (Alan Rickman) and Stella (Georgina Cates) in *An Awfully Big Adventure.* Fine Line; courtesy of the Kobal Collection

1994 (R) 113m/C *GB* Georgina Cates, Hugh Grant, Alan Rickman, Peter Firth, Alun Armstrong, Prunella Scales, Rita Tushingham, Alan Cox, Edward Petherbridge, Nicola Pagett, Carol Drinkwater, Clive Merrison, Gerard McSorley; ***D:*** Mike Newell; ***W:*** Charles Wood; ***C:*** Dick Pope; ***M:*** Richard Hartley. **VHS, LV, Closed Caption**

Back Street Jane

First-time feature director Ronnie Cramer may indeed have made "excellent" rock videos for his Denver band, Alarming Trends, but *Back Street Jane* is a real snoozer. The characters, all of whom are mired in the drug scene, are dull and dumb. Maybe you have to have 99 joints on the wall to get into this one. Cramer's camera work is somewhat better than his directing, which is only slightly better than his script. **woof!**

1989 m/B Monica McFarland, Marlene Shapiro, Sheila Ivy Traister; ***D:*** Ronnie Cramer; ***W:*** Ronnie Cramer; ***C:*** Ronnie Cramer. **VHS**

Backbeat

Backbeat begins with stylish titles that capture the pace and feel of the early '60s and then cuts to an absolutely perfect girl singer in a club, circa 1960: cute, dressed to the nines in a bright yellow dress and demure hair bow, and singing drekky music slightly off-key. One thing leads to another, and the two young male protagonists are fighting in an alley with a gang of thugs much bigger than they are. One of them sustains severe head injuries, and his ultimate fate is left in no doubt. And somehow, in spite of all that, there's still no sense of *Here Comes Beethoven* or the lavish costume ball before the Battle of Waterloo, a real tribute to *Backbeat*'s director Iain Softley. Even though we know how the story of the Beatles will end (indeed, books exist which account for nearly every day of the group's entire career), Softley wisely chooses NOT to be comprehensive. Instead, he tells a short and simple story of how the friendship between

Stuart Sutcliffe (Stephen Dorff) and John Lennon (Ian Hart) evolved as the group paid their dues in a string of grimy nightclubs in Hamburg and Liverpool. The other Beatles appear in recognizable sketch form: ambitious Paul McCartney (Gary Bakewell), dweeby George Harrison (Chris O'Neill), laconic Pete Best (Scot Williams), and even Ringo Starr, who didn't become a Beatle until 1962, is represented in a brief cameo. And then there's Astrid Kirchherr (Sheryl Lee), whose "je ne sais effin' quoi" bewitches Sutcliffe into making a decision he needed to make anyway. Never much of a musician, Sutcliffe left the band to devote more time to his art. His best friend grumbles and grumbles and grumbles about his departure (after all, with whom else can he share an evening with a couple of girls on adjoining bunk beds?) but eventually adjusts. And then, because of Act One, Scene One, the movie is over, except for the overfamiliar epilogue crawl. Still, Softley approaches potentially intimidating material in a fresh and vibrant way. Luckily for today's audiences, he is not a reverent worshipper at a well-tread shrine; he is a fine, evocative storyteller. With the help of charismatic performances from Dorff, Hart, and Lee, *Backbeat* succeeds in conveying the frantic fun that was crammed into the eight days a week of another time. 🦴🦴🦴

1994 (R) 100m/C *GB* Stephen Dorff, Sheryl Lee, Ian Hart, Gary Bakewell, Chris O'Neill, Scot Williams, Kai Wiesinger, Jennifer Ehle; ***D:*** Iain Softley; ***W:*** Michael Thomas, Stephen Ward, Iain Softley; ***C:*** Ian Wilson; ***M:*** Don Was. **VHS, LV, Letterbox, Closed Caption**

Bad Lieutenant

This is a guy movie with heavy doses of Catholic gobbledy-gook. Harvey Keitel is the Bad Lieutenant, and his award-winning performance will keep you watching despite the scumminess of his character. In one sequence, he stops a couple of young girls in a car and won't let them go unless they'll let him masturbate while he ogles them—yuchhh.... "What a lech!" one male viewer yelled as he laughed affectionately. Some guys worship every frame of this film and re-play the final sequence over and over again on video. Whatever turns 'em on, I guess, but for this viewer, once was way too much. The script was co-written by Abel Ferrara and 1981's *Ms. 45* herself, Zoe Tamerlaine, now Zoe Lund. 🦴🦴

1992 (NC-17) 98m/C Harvey Keitel, Brian McElroy, Frankie Acciario, Peggy Gormley, Stella Keitel, Victor Argo, Paul Calderone, Leonard Thomas, Frankie Thorn; ***D:*** Abel Ferrara; ***W:*** Zoe Tamerlaine Lund, Abel Ferrara; ***M:*** Joe Delia. Independent Spirit Awards '93: Best Actor (Keitel). **VHS, LV, Closed Caption, DVD**

Badlands

Just as *Bonnie and Clyde* gave a 1967 vision of 1930–34, *Badlands* examined 1957–59 through eyes that saw 1974 parallels in every frame. Although *Bonnie and Clyde* used real names and *Badlands* made up new ones, both films are essentially fiction. Each re-invents legendary criminals for later generations living in an entirely different world. Martin Sheen, then 34, and Sissy Spacek, 25, were long past high school, but persuasively played Kit Carruthers, 25, and Holly Sargis, 15, a couple of detached young outlaws based on Charlie Starkweather (1940–59) and his 14-year-old girlfriend, Caril Ann Fugate. Starkweather's body count was ten; Kit Carruthers kills around six people, and the entire spree is described in a flat, uninterpretive voiceover by Spacek as Holly Sargis. Many of the original critics who saw the film blasted what they perceived as its numbing, indifferent point of view. Kit is a textbook psycho, and Holly drifts after him in a cloud, sprinkling her description of their "adventures" with cliches she's picked up from late '50s pop culture. Warren Oates delivers his usual sterling performance as Holly's father, who's light years away from these two misfits. Much of Holly's chatter with Kit's future victims is dreary, dull small talk, which makes the inevitable bloodletting even more meaningless and incomprehensible. Their moments alone are far from romantic, although Kit does see himself in a romantic light. Inside the great mystery of mortality, there is no mystery, only an idiot racing towards the electric chair as if it were written in the

stars. Terrence Malick, the 31-year-old free spirit who wrote, directed, and produced *Badlands,* made his second film, the much-acclaimed *Days of Heaven,* in 1978. The same critics who dissected his first feature spent 20 years wondering about his abrupt departure from the movie business. In December 1998, Terrence Malick returned with *The Thin Red Line.* 𝔄𝔄𝔄𝔄

1974 (PG) 94m/C Martin Sheen, Sissy Spacek, Warren Oates, Ramon Bieri, Alan Vint, Gary Littlejohn, Charles Fitzpatrick, Howard Ragsdale, John Womack Jr., Dona Baldwin; ***Cameos:*** Terrence Malick; ***D:*** Terrence Malick; ***W:*** Terrence Malick; ***C:*** Tak Fujimoto, Stevan Larner, Brian Probyn; ***M:*** Erik Satie, Carl Orff. National Film Registry '93. **VHS, LV**

The Balance

The Balance focuses on a strong, compassionate wife and career woman in her early 30s, who puts marriage, work, and self on the line for reasons that are not entirely clear to her. Maja Komorowska's performance is magnetic and warm, completely involving us in her story. The score has all the force of any of the actors here, strengthening the impact of the simplest of sequences. ***AKA:*** The Quarterly Balance; Balans Kwartalny. 𝔄𝔄𝔄

1975 99m/C *PL* Maja Komorowska, Piotr Fronczewski, Marek Piwowski, Zofia Mrozowska, William Powers; ***D:*** Krzysztof Zanussi; ***W:*** Krzysztof Zanussi; ***C:*** Slawomir Idziak; ***M:*** Wojciech Kilar.

The Balcony

Joseph Strick's *The Balcony* gave Lee Grant a chance to sink her teeth into a meaty character role 12 years after her movie career was put on hold because of the Hollywood blacklist. Grant and the always over-the-top Shelley Winters portray 1963-style lesbians in Madame Irma's House of Illusion brothel. Jean Genet's plot is played out against a revolutionary backdrop and Peter Falk and Leonard Nimoy are two of Madame Irma's customers. Note: Nimoy also co-starred with Paul Mazursky and Michael Forest in Jean Genet's *Deathwatch,* the 1967 directing debut of the late Vic Morrow (1932–82). 𝔄𝔄𝔄

1963 87m/B Peter Falk, Shelley Winters, Lee Grant, Kent Smith, Peter Brocco, Ruby Dee, Jeff Corey, Leonard Nimoy, Joyce Jameson; ***D:*** Joseph Strick; ***W:*** Ben Maddow; ***C:*** George Folsey. Nominations: Academy Awards '63: Best Black and White Cinematography. **VHS, LV**

The Ballad of Little Jo

Suzy Amis delivers an outstanding performance as a woman passing as a man, based on a real-life character of the Old West. As unwed mother Josephine Monaghan, she is rejected by her rich family and heads west. She quickly discovers how difficult life is for a woman alone, and invents a new identity for herself as a male loner named Little Jo (who rather resembles Eric Stoltz). Ornery men quit hassling her and hopeful mothers in the nearby town think that Little Jo might make a great catch for their daughters, but Little Jo wisely tends to business and remains a loner. That is, until Little Jo becomes attracted to the hired hand (wonderfully played by David Chung), who quickly recognizes her true identity. Their subsequent relationship eases the underlying loneliness Little Jo would otherwise feel, but the endless masquerade does exact an enormous internal toll, which Amis reveals with subtle skill. Engrossing from start to finish, the film made me want to see writer/director Maggie Greenwald's other pictures, which include 1988's *Home Remedy* and the 1989 film noir, *The Kill Off.* As for Suzy Amis, her splendid work in a starring role here definitely made me wonder why her considerable talents were so squandered a year later in a nothing part in 1994's *Blown Away.* 𝔄𝔄𝔄

1993 (R) 110m/C Suzy Amis, Bo Hopkins, Ian McKellen, Carrie Snodgress, David Chung, Rene Auberjonois, Heather Graham, Anthony Heald, Sam Robards, Ruth Maleczech; ***D:*** Maggie Greenwald; ***W:*** Maggie Greenwald; ***C:*** Declan Quinn; ***M:*** David Mansfield. Nominations: Independent Spirit Awards '94: Best Actress (Amis). **VHS, Closed Caption**

The Ballad of the Sad Cafe

Quick: you're casting a movie set in a Depression-era mill town in the South and

Kit Carruthers (Martin Sheen) in *Badlands.* Warner Bros.; courtesy of the Kobal Collection

The Hound Salutes:
MAGGIE GREENWALD
Director/writer, *The Ballad of Little Jo*

I picked Jo Monaghan to make a film about for several reasons. She was the first woman that I had ever heard of who masqueraded as a man. Since then, I've learned that, in fact, Jo Monaghan was one of hundreds and hundreds of women throughout time who've done that. There are records going back to the Middle Ages of women who've cross-dressed to live lives of their own choosing that were outside what was considered acceptable behavior for a woman. Conditions for women in the middle of the 19th century were brutal. There were very few women in the West. Those who were there were, for the most part, prostitutes or wives. The options in our society were very limited for a single woman, particularly a fallen woman. One would think, really, that she didn't have to go out in the world and tell everyone she had an illegitimate child. The very fact that she was a young woman of breeding and that she was alone in the world would indicate to everyone around her that she was a fallen woman and she would be an easy prey and would have very, very few choices.

"Finding the right actress was an incredible challenge. In fact, I saw hundreds of women before Suzy Amis walked in the door. I was very quickly taken with her. She had all the qualities that I

you need someone to play Miss Amelia, a love-starved local recluse. Who's the first person on your short list? Outstanding actress that she is, Vanessa Redgrave does not spring immediately to mind. Did anyone try to contact, say, Sissy Spacek or Shelley Duvall? This screen adaptation of Carson McCullers' *The Ballad of the Sad Cafe* shows how three miscast Oscar winners can flounder under the guidance of an inexperienced, first-time director. British character actor Simon Callow has been seen to good effect in the Merchant Ivory films *A Room with a View* and *Maurice* as well as *The Good Father,* but he's out of his depth with such an ambitious first project. The first few minutes offer a good clue as to what will be wrong with the rest of the film. There are several vignettes of varying length that are supposed to show something about the characters in this town, only they don't. Unfortunately, none of the vignettes build on each other and there's nothing particularly riveting about any of the images that Callow selects. After nearly an hour, the story begins with the arrival of Miss Amelia's husband, portrayed by Keith Carradine, and the last half of the film sets us up for their final confrontation, a fist fight in which neither pulls a single punch. It's probably the least exciting fist fight we've ever seen on film, although Callow certainly tries hard to make it seem as if it OUGHT to be. There are, for example, countless close-ups of the spectators wringing their handkerchiefs. I've never seen a screen fight in which both fighters lead with their chins so much. Redgrave and Carradine successfully aim for each other's teeth throughout the entire fight, and fail to lose a single tooth. Stylistic decision or bad choreography? Redgrave and Carradine ignite no onscreen sparks alone

was looking for in someone to play Jo. She's a great beauty and very, very feminine, but very quickly you can get past that and I realized she had an androgynous quality and would be very believable as a young boy, a young man. Her emotional range is incredible; she's a great actress and she's physically very capable, and embraced the physical challenges of the role with enormous gusto. For about six weeks we had her working with a trainer to build her body up so she looked like someone who did manual labor. She worked with a movement coach to learn to move like a man. She went to sheepherding school, to shooting school, to riding school. We immersed her in a full regiment as well as regular rehearsals. She went right after that to play another role where she played a sexpot and it was like a total antidote.

"The reason I chose to make the character who becomes her lover [David Chung] a Chinese workman was that, again, the Chinese were marginalized, invisible people in our history, in our landscape. And it's a perfect character of a man who also has one identity that the world sees, which has nothing to do with who he really is. I immersed myself in photographs and in fact the American West is well documented in photography. And really, many details of life have been passed down to us in those old photographs as well as in the diaries of young women in particular. Very often frontier wives were educated; they knew how to write and led very lonely lives and kept diaries. I have always started out only willing to make the movies I wanted to make. That's sort of my path and it's never occurred to me to make any other kind of film."

MAGGIE GREENWALD also wrote and directed *The Kill-Off* and *Home Remedy.*

or together. At one point, Redgrave and Cork Hubbert go to see a movie in a neighboring town. The newsreels are crammed with FDR, but the unlikely feature attraction is a 1929 Hoover-era flop with Norma Talmadge and Gilbert Roland, *New York Nights*. Of all the cast, Hubbert fares the best with Callow's over-the-top direction, but everyone, even Redgrave and the extras, is somewhat guilty of overacting. The worst offender is Rod Steiger, in a small part as a preacher who invests his relatively brief screen time with enough subtext for 25 roles. It's hard to tell whether Callow was intimidated by his star-studded cast, the material, the period, or the locale, but nothing about *The Ballad of the Sad Cafe* seems real. It's more like a travelog you might be forced to sit through in Quaintness 101. Callow will be more fondly remembered for the lovable character who stuck his finger down his throat in a folk-style wedding service during 1994's *Four Weddings and a Funeral*. ♪♪

1991 (PG-13) 100m/C *GB* Vanessa Redgrave, Keith Carradine, Cork Hubbert, Rod Steiger, Austin Pendleton, Beth Dixon, Lanny Flaherty, Mert Hatfield, Earl Hindman, Anne Pitoniak; ***D:*** Simon Callow; ***W:*** Michael Hirst; ***C:*** Walter Lassally; ***M:*** Richard Robbins. **VHS, LV, Closed Caption**

Bang

The powerlessness in the life of The Girl (eloquently played by Darling Narita) is eating her up. She goes on an acting audition and the scurvy producer hits on her, then Officer Rattler (Michael Newland) threatens to bust her on some trumped-up charge unless she gives him a blow job. She manages to grab his gun, forces him to strip, and handcuffs him to a tree. Once she replaces her clothes with the outfit of a uniformed authority figure, she is treated with

Neutron (Patrick McGaw), Pedro (James Madio), Mickey (Mark Wahlberg), and Jim (Leonardo DiCaprio) in ***The Basketball Diaries.*** New Line; courtesy of the Kobal Collection

enormous respect by just about everyone: waitresses, cops, gang members, drug dealers.... But with Power comes The Truth and it doesn't set her free—it breaks her heart. In the film's most disarming sequence, she gets a lift with Juan and Jesus (Art Cruz and Luis Guizar), two sweet young gang members. She splits some beer and shares a joint with them and assumptions on both sides break down during their brief time together. Darling Narita is incredibly moving as the down-on-her-luck L.A. girl who goes through the full range of emotional highs and lows during one action-packed day. Despite the catchy title, *Bang* is much, much more than you might expect it to be, and on a $20,000 budget, besides. Does writer/director Ash walk on water? ***AKA:*** The Big Bang Theory. ⚲⚲⚲

1995 98m/C Darling Narita, Peter Greene, Michael Newland, David Allen Graff, Eric Schrody, Michael Arturo, James Sharpe, Luis Guizar, Art Cruz, Stanley Herman; ***D:*** Ash; ***W:*** Ash; ***C:*** Dave Gasperik. Nominations: Independent Spirit Awards '98: Debut Performance (Narita). **VHS**

Barcelona

It's good to see Christopher Eigeman (as Fred) in a movie again, four years after *Metropolitan.* Taylor Nichols is in it, too, as his cousin Ted. I once traveled to Paris with a couple of brothers from Spain and the rivalry between them crowded out any other social possibilities for the trip. Like them, Fred and Ted's rivalry never lets up for an instant, but since they're in a movie and they are Eigeman and Nichols, it's a treat to listen to them bicker about sex and politics, politics and sex. (I might not want to travel with them, though.) Fred is beautifully unaware what a jerk he is, while Ted does have a nagging awareness that he IS a twit. Fred's first words to Ted in a Barcelona hospital are priceless. All this, and Mira Sorvino, too! Another winner for writer/director Whit Stillman. ⚲⚲⚲

1994 (PG-13) 102m/C Taylor Nichols, Christopher Eigeman, Tushka Bergen, Mira Sorvino, Pep Munne, Francis Creighton, Thomas Gibson, Jack Gilpin, Nuria Badia, Hellena Schmied; ***D:*** Whit Stillman; ***W:***

Whit Stillman; ***C:*** John Thomas; ***M:*** Tom Judson, Mark Suozzo. Independent Spirit Awards '95: Best Cinematography. **VHS, LV**

Barefoot Gen

Animation often has the curious effect of lulling me into a false sense of security. I expect that the appealing images onscreen will amuse and entertain me, but not make me think too deeply or cry. The 1955 British version of George Orwell's *Animal Farm* changed my perception of what an animated film could be. 1983's *Barefoot Gen* offers a devastating contrast to live-action films like MGM's *Above and Beyond,* which idealized the bombers of Hiroshima by casting cinematic icon Robert Taylor as the pilot. Artist Keiji Nakazawa was six years old when his home was destroyed by the bombing of Hiroshima on August 6, 1945. Miraculously, he survived, and 28 years later he published *Barefoot Gen,* based on his own experiences on that fateful day. Nakazawa hoped one day to develop the cartoon into a feature-length film, and at 48 he finally achieved his dream. *Barefoot Gen* is the powerful result. The film starts out by giving us a bit of background on World War II, then shifts to the antics of two little boys. We know what an impact the war has made on their lives; they fight over a potato before reluctantly sharing it with their mother who is expecting another baby. Because of their enormous vitality, the irrepressible children take center stage and the war seems like a distant backdrop. The impact of the bombing, however, is enormous and immediate. Familiar characters are reduced to skeletons within seconds. The collapse of Gen's world is shown in a wrenching sequence when he must decide to save himself and his expectant mother rather than die with the rest of his family. Except for the sudden loss of his hair, Gen appears to have emerged unscathed from the bombing, but the tragic aftereffects of the Hiroshima bombing are everywhere. A soldier, not realizing what has happened to him, dies in a daze right in front of Gen. Gen's frail mother gives birth to an adorable little girl, but cannot feed her. Another woman who has lost her child tries to kill the infant, but then bursts into tears and offers to nurse the baby for her. Gen forages for food, finally stumbling on an unaffected cache of rice. An orphan appears on the scene, the exact double of Gen's doomed brother. He is instantly adopted into the family and the film's lighthearted vitality returns, but with a difference. To earn money to buy milk for the baby, the children accept a disagreeable job: taking care of a former artist whose family has rejected him now that he is disabled. Simply by being children, the little boys ignite his flagging spirits and his will to live and work, but there are no Pollyanna endings in *Barefoot Gen.* Gen's resilience is the theme of this deeply disturbing movie, and it is highly recommended for both adults and older children (over age 12). 🦴🦴🦴🦴

1983 90m/C *JP* ***D:*** Mamoru Shinzaki; ***W:*** Keiji Nakazawa; ***M:*** Kentaro Hada.

The Basketball Diaries

Leonardo DiCaprio's tremendous performance as Jim Carroll is the main reason to watch *The Basketball Diaries,* which otherwise is your standard drugalogue flick, no better and no worse than many others. Two significant elements that might have supplied meaningful context for THIS drugalogue (Carroll's Catholicism and the time period of his addiction) have been given short shrift here. As long as the story stays focused on DiCaprio, *The Basketball Diaries* remains compelling. When it wanders into the background that contributed to his drug abuse, my eyes start to glaze over. Carroll's faithful diary entries reveal what seems an effortless glide into addiction, with drugs on hand before and after basketball games. Lorraine Bracco is excellent as Carroll's tough-loving mom, packing more into the role than is in the dialogue. *The Basketball Diaries* was the first of three depressing overnight videos rented by a 13-year-old house guest. *Dead Poet's Society* and *Forrest Gump* followed, and I was one very cynical viewer by

"Time! Time! What is time? The Swiss manufacture it. The French hoard it. Italians want it. Americans say it is money. Hindus say it does not exist. Do you know what I say? I say time is a crook!"

—O'Hara (Peter Lorre) in *Beat the Devil.*

evening's end. I don't think that I could have watched *The Basketball Diaries* AFTER those other two. ☙☙☙

1994 (R) 102m/C Leonardo DiCaprio, Mark Wahlberg, Patrick McGaw, James Madio, Bruno Kirby, Ernie Hudson, Lorraine Bracco, Juliette Lewis, Josh Mostel, Michael Rapaport, Michael Imperioli; ***Cameos:*** Jim Carroll; ***D:*** Scott Kalvert; ***W:*** Bryan Goluboff; ***C:*** David Phillips; ***M:*** Graeme Revell. **VHS**

Basquiat

Jean Michel Basquiat is not exactly a household name today, although he has all the ingredients for legendary status: early fame, early death, umpteen mentions in Andy Warhol's diary, etc. He was an artist who slept on the streets, but believed he was fresh as a daisy (although Warhol's diaries say otherwise). At his scruffiest, he romances waitress Gina Cardinale (Claire Forlani); their moments together are the least interesting in the film. There are other rewards in Julian Schnabel's onscreen study of his fellow artist, though. David Bowie, who had the benefit of the most personal contact with Warhol, is the third actor to play him since 1991. (Crispin Glover and Jared Harris preceded him in *The Doors* and *I Shot Andy Warhol.*) Although the physical resemblance isn't particularly striking, Bowie is otherwise persuasive as Basquiat's patron and friend. The fickle cruelty of the New York art world is rendered with economic precision in a vivid restaurant sequence. Moreover, the evolution of Basquiat's longtime friendship with Benny Dalmau (colorfully played by Benicio Del Toro) reveals how Basquiat is changed as the opinion of his new acquaintances comes to mean more to him than he may care to admit. Familiar folks from other indie flicks (Dennis Hopper as a shrewd art buyer, Gary Oldman as artist Albert Milo, plus Willem Dafoe, Parker Posey, Elina Lowensohn, Paul Bartel, and Courtney Love) help to enhance *Basquiat*'s sense of time and place. Christopher Walken has his usual one sequence as a nut (an interviewer this time), and Tatum O'Neal, then 32, drifts in and out of focus in a bit as a stereotypical (mindless, rich) customer. At the core, Jeffrey Wright plays Basquiat as gifted, sweet, and hell-bent on accumulating an impressive resume before the ultimate fix. *Basquiat* boasts an excellent soundtrack. (Recommended for further research: Mary Woronov's terrific 1995 book, *Swimming Underground,* which spares no one in Andy Warhol's set, least of all herself.) ***AKA:*** Build a Fort, Set It on Fire. ☙☙☙

1996 (R) 108m/C Jeffrey Wright, David Bowie, Dennis Hopper, Gary Oldman, Christopher Walken, Michael Wincott, Benicio Del Toro, Parker Posey, Elina Lowensohn, Courtney Love, Claire Forlani, Willem Dafoe, Paul Bartel, Tatum O'Neal, Chuck Pfeiffer; ***D:*** Julian Schnabel; ***W:*** Julian Schnabel; ***C:*** Ron Fortunato; ***M:*** John Cale. Independent Spirit Awards '97: Best Supporting Actor (Del Toro); Nominations: Independent Spirit Awards '97: Debut Performance (Wright). **VHS, LV, Closed Caption**

Bastard out of Carolina

This exceptional first film by director Anjelica Huston was first intended for broadcast on Turner Network Television, which would have aired it with commercials. It was actually a blessing that it first aired on the Showtime Network without interruption 10 days before Christmas. (Showtime had originally planned to make the film until director Allison Anders resigned, then it wound up at TNT with Huston and the rest is history.) There is no tasteful way to show the horror of child abuse on film without running into the *Rashomon* syndrome: did that nice-looking stepfather actually rape his wife's daughter? Did the little girl provoke him? Seduce him? Lie? Then it becomes a mystery and takes the point of view away from the child. Twelve-year-old Jena Malone is remarkable as "Bone" Boatwright, whose performance was partly inspired by her conversations with a close friend who experienced child abuse. With her sad little face and frail physical presence, Malone would break anyone's heart, but her ability to communicate how she internalizes her wretched life is her greatest strength as an actress here. Top-billed Jennifer Jason Leigh is less satisfactory as her mother, Anney. Leigh tends to work from the outside in; sometimes it works spectacularly well, sometimes it doesn't. By playing Anney in a perpetual daze, she's outclassed here by fellow cast members Grace Zabriskie, Diana Scarwid, Christina Ricci, and best of all, Glenne Headley. Fortunately, Leigh's straight-line, untextured interpretation doesn't compromise the film, since the toughest acting assignment belongs to Ron Eldard as Glen Waddell. Eldard had previously done an expert job playing a loose cannon with surface appeal named Shep opposite Julianna Margulies' Carol Hathaway on *E.R.* His violent impulses come from a different place as the repellent Glen, and you can see why he would attract outsiders while carrying on his own private war of nerves with Bone. He's diseased, but frighteningly sane, and his eroticism is clearly detached from the target of his abuse. The sequences revealing Glen's abuse of Bone are so clear and so real that you'll want to jump into the narrative and tear her away from him, which may be the whole point of *Bastard out of Carolina.* It isn't exposure of child abuse that destroys families, but the abuse itself, a distinction that hasn't always been made entirely clear in previous movies that focus on this crime against children. Huston's directorial debut is a bold, brave film with no easy answers, but with plenty of haunting questions about the never-ending nightmares that represent childhood for far too many children on this planet. Based on the best-selling novel by Dorothy Allison. ☙☙☙☙

1996 (R) 97m/C Jennifer Jason Leigh, Jena Malone, Ron Eldard, Glenne Headly, Lyle Lovett, Dermot Mulroney, Christina Ricci, Michael Rooker, Diana Scarwid, Susan Traylor, Grace Zabriskie; ***D:*** Anjelica Huston; ***W:*** Anne Meredith; ***C:*** Anthony B. Richmond; ***M:*** Van Dyke Parks. Nominations: Independent Spirit Awards '97: Debut Performance (Malone). **VHS**

The Battle of the Sexes

The Catbird Seat is treasured by James Thurber fans for taking the sort of teeth-gnashing experience everyone dreads and discovering an ingenious way out of it. Mr. Martin (Peter Sellers) is a quiet Edinburgh accountant for Mr. Macpherson's (Robert Morley) textile company. He wishes to be left alone and he certainly leaves everyone else alone. That is, until Angela Barrows (Constance Cummings) arrives on the job. Mrs. Barrows (there's no polite way to say this) is an...American efficiency expert. She has the effect on shy Mr. Martin of a new piece of chalk S-C-R-E-E-C-H-I-N-G against a chalk board. She's loud. She has her own, very definite agenda. She lives in her own world. Regrettably, that world happens to be Mr. Martin's world, too, and he was here first! Mr. Martin is very unhappy. But then he realizes there is a solution in sight; he decides there's nothing for it but to murder Mrs. Barrows. What happens next is the stuff of which classic British comedies are made. Director Charles Crichton skillfully escalates the war of nerves between Mrs. Barrows and old Mr. Martin (Cummings was 49 and Sellers was 34, but he'd specialized in playing elderly characters for years). The character actors are first rate; Ernest Thesiger is Mr. Macpherson, Senior (right!) and Michael Goodliffe is charmingly dry as a detective. ☙☙☙

1960 88m/B *GB* Peter Sellers, Robert Morley, Constance Cummings, Jameson Clark, Ernest Thesiger, Donald Pleasence, Moultrie Kelsall, Alex Mackenzie, Roddy McMillan, Michael Goodliffe, Norman MacOwen, William Mervyn, Sam Wanamaker; ***D:*** Charles Crichton; ***W:*** Monja Danischewsky; ***C:*** Freddie Francis; ***M:*** Stanley Black. **VHS**

Beat the Devil

This was Bogie's and Huston's sixth and final film together. Huston and Capote intended it to be an Italian-style satire of *The Maltese Falcon,* but audiences of the '50s failed to appreciate it on that level. Television viewers and revival house devotees finally got the joke. It's a kick to watch and so different from the studio films Bogie and Huston made in the '40s. NO ONE receives a flattering gaze from cinematographer Oswald Morris, and Jennifer Jones is not treated like a delicate china doll or an unearthly creature as she is in most of her other pictures. Robert Morley (who was in *The African Queen* with Bogie) is Petersen, a part clearly designed for Sydney Greenstreet, and Peter Lorre, in his fifth and final movie with Bogie, ap-

"He is suffering. He is more cruel to himself than he is to humans."

—Beauty (Josette Day) to her father (Marcel Andre), speaking of the Beast (Jean Marais), in *Beauty and the Beast.*

pears as O'Hara! At one point, Bogie, Jones, Gina Lollobrigida, Morley, Lorre, Edward Underdown, and Ivor Barnard are hauled into the police station and only released when Bogie promises the officer that he will arrange for him to meet his idol, Rita Hayworth! Great fun. Based on the novel by James Helvick. 𝓭𝓭𝓭

1953 89m/C Humphrey Bogart, Gina Lollobrigida, Peter Lorre, Robert Morley, Jennifer Jones, Edward Underdown, Ivor Barnard, Bernard Lee, Marco Tulli; ***D:*** John Huston; ***W:*** John Huston, Truman Capote; ***C:*** Oswald Morris. **VHS, LV, Closed Caption**

Beauty and the Beast

For many people, Jean Cocteau's 1946 version of *Beauty and the Beast* is the loveliest film ever made, and one of the few that I wish I could go back in time to see again for the very first time. (The only American film of that era with even a fraction of its sense of imagination, wonder, and style is Val Lewton's 1944 classic *Curse of the Cat People,* most notably the sequences in the enchanted garden when Simone Simon as an ethereal ghost romps with Ann Carter as a lonely little girl.) *Beauty and the Beast* is a classic fairy tale about loneliness and love. Beauty (Josette Day) is a hard-working girl with simple tastes and very few dreams. She agrees to stay with the Beast mainly to save her father's life after he steals a rose from the Beast's garden to bring home to her. But the Beast (Jean Marais) is gentle and honest with her and she begins to care about him. The Academy of Motion Picture Arts and Sciences was napping in 1946 when Cocteau's exquisite *La Belle et la Bête* was released. *Beauty and the Beast* seldom fails to wrap its spell around those who still believe in fairy tales and Jean Cocteau believed in them with a passion all his life. Although he is faithful to a child's-eye view of fairy tales, his film is filled with surreal visions and sly humor for adult appreciation. ***AKA:*** La Belle et la Bête. 𝓭𝓭𝓭𝓭

1946 90m/B *FR* Jean Marais, Josette Day, Marcel Andre, Mila Parely, Nane Germon, Michel Auclair, Georges Auric; ***D:*** Jean Cocteau; ***W:*** Jean Cocteau; ***C:*** Henri Alekan. **VHS, LV, DVD**

Bedazzled

Nowadays, when we discuss the Seven Deadly Sins, we don't kid around, but in the Swinging '60s, Peter Cook and Dudley Moore got away with it in this side-splitting Faustian comedy, co-scripted by its stars. Cook (1937–95) is The Devil, George Spiggot; Moore, then 32, is Stanley Moon, Wimpy's short-order cook. Stanley is desperately in love with Wimpy's counter girl, Margaret Spencer (Eleanor Bron, then 33), and George offers him seven wishes in exchange for his soul. In his pursuit of Margaret, Stanley squanders them, but he does get a rather good understanding of the Devil and the chance to meet all Seven Deadly Sins. Raquel Welch, then 27, is Lillian Lust. (And yes, that IS Edna Everage's alter ego as Envy!) The pleasure of watching Cook and Moore work together was shared by Brits and Americans alike for the better part of two decades. Some of the funniest sight gags and most incisive dialogue in *Bedazzled* represent the best of their work in British television. Cook and Moore also won two Tonys and a Grammy together (plus two other Grammy nominations) for their bright, satirical work as a team. At 43, Moore emigrated to Hollywood and quickly established himself as an Oscar-nominated movie star. Except for a 16-month comedy series in the early '80s (that lasted eight times longer than TWO of Moore's comedy series in the '90s), Cook remained in England. He drank, put on weight (he once joked about playing Fat King Farouk), accepted cameo roles, and died too young of an intestinal hemorrhage. Until another bright, satirical team, Stephen Fry and Hugh Laurie, arrived on the scene, Peter Cook and Dudley Moore were regarded by many comedy buffs as two of Britain's wittiest treasures. (Other Cook-Moore films: *The Wrong Box* and *Those Daring Young Men in Their Jaunty Jalopies.* Skip Paul Morissey's *The Hound of the Baskervilles*!) 𝓭𝓭𝓭𝓭

1968 (PG) 107m/C *GB* Dudley Moore, Peter Cook, Eleanor Bron, Michael Bates, Raquel Welch,

Bernard Spear, Parnell McGarry, Howard Goorney, Daniele Noel, Barry Humphries, Robert Russell, Lockwood West, Robin Hawdon, Evelyn Moore, Charles Lloyd Pack; ***D:*** Stanley Donen; ***W:*** Dudley Moore, Peter Cook; ***C:*** Austin Dempster; ***M:*** Dudley Moore. **VHS, LV, Letterbox**

Before the Rain

Aleksandar (Rade Serbedzija) left Macedonia to live and work in London as a photographer many years ago. He returns to his former homeland as a war correspondent and is saddened by what his country has become. He is witness to an execution in Bosnia shortly before he goes back to see what has become of his old village. War is everywhere, ignited by racial hatred. Milcho Manchevski divides the narrative into three chapters: "Words," which shows how a monk named Kiril (Gregoire Colin of 1993's *Pas Tres Catholique*) is affected by Zamira (Labina Mitevska) when she seeks shelter in a monastery; "Faces," which focuses on Aleksandar's intimate relationship with Anne (Katrin Cartlidge), a photographic editor who is expecting a baby; and "Pictures," revealing a country under siege. ***AKA:*** Po Dezju. 🦴🦴🦴

1994 120m/C *GB FR MA* Rade Serbedzija, Katrin Cartlidge, Gregoire Colin, Labina Mitevska; ***D:*** Milcho Manchevski; ***W:*** Milcho Manchevski; ***C:*** Manuel Teran; ***M:*** Anastasia. Independent Spirit Awards '96: Best Foreign Film; Venice Film Festival '94: Golden Lion; Nominations: Academy Awards '94: Best Foreign Film. **VHS**

The Belles of St. Trinian's

If there's anything more inviting than the prospect of the great Alastair Sim in a comedy, it would be TWO Alastair Sims, one of them in drag as Miss Fitton, Headmistress of St. Trinian's School for Young Ladies, the other as her brother, Clarence. The story is inspired by the cartoons of Ronald Searle, first published in *Punch* magazine. The Belles, to put it mildly, are bloody terrors—frightening schoolmistresses, local merchants, and even the police. The plot is a born-again screwball comedy, with Joyce Grenfell, Hermione Baddeley, Beryl Reid, Guy Middleton, and Richard Wattis getting mixed up in some of the funniest situations. Sidney James and Joan Sims would later work together in the long-running series of *Carry On* comedies. There were four *St. Trinian's* comedies in all: 1957's *Blue Murder at St. Trinian's,* 1960's *The Pure Hell of St. Trinian's,* and 1966's *The Great St. Trinian's Train Robbery.* George Cole was in all of them as Flash Harry, but he (and we) would miss Sim, who bowed out after handing over the reins to Terry Thomas in *Blue Murder.* (Cecil Parker and Frankie Howard received top billing in the last two entries.) 🦴🦴🦴

1953 86m/B *GB* Alastair Sim, Joyce Grenfell, Hermione Baddeley, George Cole, Eric Pohlmann, Renee Houston, Beryl Reid, Balbina, Jill Braidwood, Annabelle Covey, Betty Ann Davies, Diana Day, Jack Doyle, Irene Handl, Arthur Howard, Sidney James, Lloyd Lamble, Jean Langston, Belinda Lee, Vivian Martin, Andree Melly, Mary Merrall, Guy Middleton, Joan Sims, Jerry Verno, Richard Wattis; ***D:*** Frank Launder; ***W:*** Frank Launder, Sidney Gilliat, Val Valentine; ***C:*** Stanley Pavey; ***M:*** Malcolm Arnold. **VHS**

Bellissima

Luchino Visconti's *Bellissima* focuses on a marginal fixture at Cinecitta studios: the ubiquitous stage mother. Anna Magnani wants stardom for her little girl and a better life for her small brood. In America, the stage mother is rarely shown as anything other than a selfish, conniving bitch who mercilessly exploits her offspring; the 1955 performance of Jo Van Fleet as Lillian Roth's mother in Daniel Mann's *I'll Cry Tomorrow* is a good example. But in Italy, with a director willing to examine the economic conditions that ignited stage mothers, stardom for children is shown as an escape from poverty for entire families. Magnani's deep emotional understanding of her character lets her get away with sequences which few other actresses could inject with sympathy. *Bellissima* is marred by a moralistic and unbelievable conclusion that Visconti reportedly fought hard to resist. Like all of Magnani's films, however, *Bellissima* demands compulsive attention because of the riveting presence of its star. 🦴🦴🦴

1951 130m/B *IT* Anna Magnani, Walter Chiari, Alessandro Blasetti, Tina Apicella, Gastone Renzelli; ***D:*** Luchino Visconti; ***W:*** Luchino Visconti, Cesare

"The bank took my farm, and Vietnam took my son."

—Shorty (John Mahoney) to Katie/Cathy (Debra Winger) in *Betrayed.*

Zavattini, Francesco Rosi, Suso Cecchi D'Amico; ***C:*** Piero Portalupi, Paul Ronald. **VHS**

Bellman and True

Bellman and True, a British thriller produced by George Harrison, is a bare-bones crime saga about computers, blood, and money, with a no-star cast and senseless characters. At one point, one crook tells another not to try to be Michael Caine, but in fact, Caine or Bob Hoskins or Peter O'-Toole might be just what the doctor ordered to punch up this movie. I say "might be," because a magnetic star would still have to contend with novelist Desmond Lowden's script, which he wrote with director Richard Loncraine. What's supposed to be unusual about this story is that its central character, invisibly played by Bernard Hill, presumably cares about his young stepson, Kieran O'Brien. However, he's constantly endangering the kid's life and exposing him to vicious gangsters. There's a woman in the plot, Frances Tomelty, but she makes even less sense than the men. (Footnote: Bernard Hill played John Lennon in the 1974 Willy Russell musical, *John, Paul, George, Ringo...and Bert* opposite Trevor Eve as Paul McCartney, Phillip Joseph as George Harrison, and Antony Sher as Ringo Starr.)

1988 (R) 112m/C *GB* Bernard Hill, Kieran O'Brien, Richard Hope, Frances Tomelty, Derek Newark, John Kavanagh, Ken Bones; ***D:*** Richard Loncraine; ***W:*** Richard Loncraine, Desmond Lowden; ***C:*** Ken Westbury; ***M:*** Colin Towns. **VHS**

The Belly of an Architect

Many of the press corps laughed hysterically at Peter Greenaway's *The Belly of an Architect,* starring Brian Dennehy and Chloe Webb. They laughed at things like Dennehy plunging headfirst onto the roof of a car at the same time as wife Webb's baby was being born. Obviously, Greenaway's work is fraught with humor that you have to be on the same wave length to appreciate. The title, by the way, is literal. You will see more extreme close-ups of Dennehy's bulging stomach than you can possibly imagine. As counterpoint, much of the two-hour film was shot with the principal action in extreme long shots, which makes this film a nightmare to watch on television or video. When Dennehy goes berserk at an outdoor restaurant, for example, Greenaway focuses on two female extras. When Dennehy is spying on Webb's fling with a rotter named Caspasian Speckler, we can barely see either one of them. The plot is your standard older-man-is-dying-while-his-pretty-young-wife-has-an-affair-with-an-Italian, but it kept several film critics in stitches, anyway. Confession 1: I missed every single in-joke. Question 1: Why are figs funny? Confession 2: I do not know who Etienne-Louis Boullee is. Question 2: What is so side-splitting about the name Stourley Kracklite? This movie and Fred Zinneman's similarly themed *Five Days One Summer,* plus Mary Lambert's one-of-a-kind *Siesta,* is yet another addition to my growing list of triple bills from hell. Trivia Note: France's Lambert Wilson plays just about the same part in both the Zinneman film and in *The Belly of an Architect.* **woof!**

1991 (R) 119m/C *GB IT* Brian Dennehy, Chloe Webb, Lambert Wilson, Sergio Fantoni, Geoffrey Copleston, Marino Mase; ***D:*** Peter Greenaway; ***W:*** Peter Greenaway; ***C:*** Sacha Vierny; ***M:*** Glenn Branca, Wim Mertens. **VHS, LV**

The Best Way

Claude Miller worked with François Truffaut on eight movies before he made the shift from assistant to director. Unlike Truffaut, Miller's view of life is harsh and blunt. Marc, the major character in *The Best Way,* is discovered romping alone in woman's clothing by Philippe, a fellow boys' camp director. The two begin a brutal, uneasy relationship, with Marc (Patrick Bouchitey) consistently cast as underdog. Philippe (Patrick Dewaere) taunts Marc, belittles him, tosses him in the water, even hits him, and still Marc comes back for more. At the end, an unusual resolution occurs between the two, and Miller stages it with tense excitement. By this time, he has drawn us into Marc's humiliation so completely that we are nearly as involved in his pain as he is. Sadly, both Dewaere and Christine Pascal ended their thriving careers by committing suicide, Dewaere at 35 in 1982 and Pascal at 42 in 1996. ***AKA:*** The Best Way to Walk; La Meilleure Façon de Marcher. 🦴🦴🦴

1976 85m/C *FR* Patrick Dewaere, Patrick Bouchitey, Christine Pascal, Claude Pieplu; ***D:*** Claude Miller; ***W:*** Luc Beraud, Claude Miller; ***C:*** Bruno Nuytten; ***M:*** Alain Jomy. **VHS**

Betrayed

The films of Constantin Costa-Gavras are often complicated, controversial, or disturbing. *Betrayed* is all three. When we see a man onscreen who appears to be a dutiful son, a kind father, and a considerate lover, we draw certain conclusions about his character. So, unfortunately, does federal agent Debra Winger, who is assigned to investigate the allegedly homicidal white supremacist character portrayed by Tom Berenger. The film's approach requires considerable courage to sustain, and its harsh observations about some aspects of this country put some of its original audiences on the defensive. It may remind others of Alfred Hitchcock's 1946 classic *Notorious,* in which Ingrid Bergman sleeps with Nazi Claude Rains and reports to her lover, American agent Cary Grant, who punishes her with his obvious resentment and disapproval of the sexual work he requires her to do. *Notorious* was fairly kinky for its era, but with *Betrayed,* Costa-Gavras is concerned with far more fundamental issues. The rootless, parentless Winger finds herself falling in love with Berenger and disconnecting from her agency contact John Heard. If she loves her target, he can't be a neo-Nazi, can he? He even hates the Nazi uniform and those who wear it. Her job becomes uglier to her, and more duplicitous. Winger perfectly captures the numbness of a human being who must deny her own feelings in order to survive. Berenger, too, gives his impossible role so much understanding that it's hard to imagine almost any other contemporary actor in the role. Their gritty scenes together are stripped of glamour, which lends their tortured love considerable credibility. Also outstanding are John Mahoney, one of the finest character actors alive today, as a decent man who rationalizes the evil he does, and a beautiful seven-year-old child named Maria Valdez as Berenger's ingratiating daughter. Screenwriter Joe Eszterhas succeeds in showing how complicated personal ethics become once you start caring about someone. People outside gnarled relationships might wonder how anyone could give a damn about a homophobic, racist murderer, particularly a sane one. Costa-Gavras suggests some uncomfortable answers; it's well worth checking out *Betrayed* to discover them. 🦴🦴🦴

1988 (R) 112m/C Tom Berenger, Debra Winger, John Mahoney, John Heard, Albert Hall, Jeffrey DeMunn; ***D:*** Constantin Costa-Gavras; ***W:*** Joe Eszterhas; ***C:*** Patrick Blossier. **VHS, LV, Closed Caption**

Beware of Pity

Stefan Zweig was an idealistic Austrian writer whose dreams of a united Europe were shattered by World War II. In 1942, he fled with his wife to Brazil where both committed suicide. Zweig left behind an impressive body of work, including several biographies, a novel called *Beware of Pity,* and many short stories, including "The Royal Game" and "Letter from an Unknown Woman," filmed by Max Ophuls for Universal in 1948. Maurice Elvey directed *Beware of Pity* in 1946 as a vehicle for two German expatriate stars, Lilli Palmer and the formally cool Albert Lieven, then 40. Although Palmer was then 35, her onscreen specialty between 1935 and 1986 was playing bewitching leading ladies and she is altogether compelling as the rich and youthful Baroness Edith. An extended ballroom sequence reveals her immediate infatuation with Lieven's aloof Lieutenant Anton Marek. Unfortunately, the large-eyed beauty has been crippled by an accident, rendering her an unsuitable dance partner, not to mention an ineligible bride, at least in HIS eyes. Her crush evolves into a lifelong obsession, and Marek's distaste for her is barely concealed by patronizing segues and ultra-polite humor. The more she reveals her love for him, the more he

Lt. Anton Marek (Albert Lieven) and Baroness Edith Kekefalva (Lilli Palmer) in *Beware of Pity.*
Two Cities; courtesy of the Kobal Collection

shuns her, until she is forced to recognize how far apart their feelings are. The best acting in the film is delivered by Gladys Cooper, then 58, who began her movie career at 25 and was something of a real-life pin-up girl during World War I. There's not a shred of self-pity in her immaculate performance as the blind wife of the Baroness' doctor, who tries hard to change destiny. I can never figure out whether *Beware of Pity* is some sort of a tribute to a self-contained careerist or if the conscience-ridden Zweig was trying to show the enormous damage emotional clods wreak on their love-starved victims. Either way, *Beware of Pity* is a beautifully filmed tale of romantic longing with expert playing by the two leads. It is also a wistful reminder of the irreplaceable pre-Sarajevo days that inevitably evoke fairy tales through their sheer visual loveliness. But the emotional rot has sunk in already; there's never-ending isolation and suffering for the victimized Baroness and a pointless series of military pursuits for the walled-off Lieutenant.

1946 129m/B Lilli Palmer, Albert Lieven, Cedric Hardwicke, Gladys Cooper, Ernest Thesiger, Freda Jackson, Linden Travers, Ralph Truman, Peter Cotes, Jenny Laird, Emrys Jones, Gerhard Kempinski, John Salew, Kenneth Warrington; ***D:*** Maurice Elvey; ***W:*** W.P. Lipscomb, Elizabeth Barron, Margaret Steen; ***C:*** Derick Williams. **VHS**

The Big Easy

Although purists might deny that today's color film noir efforts approach the excellence of the crisp black-and-white noir visions of another time, *The Big Easy* by Daniel Petrie Jr. certainly comes close. One of the best things about the film is its realistic depiction of sex between two people who don't know each other very well. Only in the movies are such pairings flawless, and *The Big Easy* shows some of the timing and pacing problems that are more true to real life. Then, the script keeps the mismatched couple at odds with each other for most of the film, and with gifted actors like Dennis Quaid and Ellen Barkin, the resulting undercurrents in emotion between the pair are more erotic than a dozen bedroom scenes would be. The New Orleans atmosphere and music add spice to this tale of a cop and a lawyer investigating police corruption in the New South, and the supporting cast members, with the exception of one wimp of a villain, are extremely well chosen. A bit by perennial film noir heavy Marc Lawrence adds to the fun.

1987 (R) 101m/C Dennis Quaid, Ellen Barkin, Ned Beatty, John Goodman, Ebbe Roe Smith, Charles Ludlam, Lisa Jane Persky, Tom O'Brien, Grace Zabriskie, Marc Lawrence; ***D:*** Jim McBride; ***W:*** Dan Petrie Jr.; ***C:*** Alfonso Beato; ***M:*** Brad Fiedel. Independent Spirit Awards '88: Best Actor (Quaid). **VHS, LV, Closed Caption**

The Big Lebowski

Large or lean, Jeff Bridges is loaded with charisma, even when he's The Dude, who wants nothing more from life than a little weed and a lot of bowling. He's the sort of nowhere man who gets caught up in This Huge Plot and spends the whole time yearning to return to his leisurely life of restricted activities because he is, after all, The Dude. The Dude's bowling buddies are Walter (John Goodman) and Donny (Steve Buscemi). Walter is a huge, bombastic veteran who's still obsessed with Vietnam, and Donny is a sweet little guy who hardly ever talks. The Dude's life is forever changed when Bad Guys vandalize his crummy dump of an apartment, beat him up, and worst of all, pee on His Rug! The Bad Guys are looking for a Jeff Lebowski, which is The Dude's actual name, but he knows he's not That Jeff Lebowski. He wants justice. He wants to find The Big Lebowski (David Huddleston). And most of all, he wants A New Rug! As if the opening narrative weren't goofy enough, it gets even goofier after that. Along the way, The Dude meets an assortment of oddballs, played to the hilt by a lustrous cast. Like The Dude himself, the plot doesn't really lead anywhere. The fun for fans of the Coen Brothers will be reveling in every twist and turn their vivid imaginations take them. Jeff Bridges is luminous as The Dude; if his character is lazy and unmotivated, he is not, and it is his multitextured performance that makes us care what happens to The Dude for every second of the 117-minute running time.

1997 (R) 117m/C Jeff Bridges, John Goodman, Steve Buscemi, Julianne Moore, Peter Stormare, David Huddleston, Philip Seymour Hoffman, Flea, Leon Russom, Sam Elliott, John Turturro, David Thewlis, Ben Gazzara, Tara Reid; ***D:*** Joel Coen; ***W:*** Joel Coen, Ethan Coen; ***C:*** Roger Deakins; ***M:*** Carter Burwell. **VHS, LV, Closed Caption**

Big Night

This excellent film is to struggling owners of small Italian restaurants what *Strictly Ballroom* is to Open Amateurs dancing on Federation steps at the Pan Pacific Grand Prix championships. *Big Night* takes a look at Primo and Secondo Pilaggi, two Italian brothers living and working in 1950s New Jersey: Primo (Tony Shalhoub), a genius chef who can't promote, and Secondo (Stanley Tucci), a genius promoter who can't begin to approach his brother's skill in the kitchen. Each needs the other and each resents the other. They continue to do what they do best, and decide to splurge on a Big Night in honor of Louis Prima (1911–78). Primo cooks the meal of a lifetime, and Secondo hustles the potential backers of a lifetime. The cards in the brothers' pricey gamble are stacked against them, and Secondo knows it. Ian Holm gives another vintage performance as a sleazy business competitor, and Campbell Scott (who also co-directed), Isabella Rossellini, and Minnie Driver are also seen to good advantage. This is the perfect dinner and a video movie, although you're going to wish you could eat some of Primo's creations. The last sequence in the film is deservedly memorable because it is simultaneously complex and simple

"I think a girl knows instinctively when she can trust a man."

—Alice White (Anny Ondra) is not correct in ***Blackmail.***

(like Primo's masterpieces) and, even more extraordinary, it was shot all in one take. *Big Night* is a triumph for writer/director Tucci, who clearly learned a great deal about the art of filmmaking during the seven years he played character parts in the Hollywood fluff machine. 🦴🦴🦴½

1995 (R) 109m/C Tony Shalhoub, Stanley Tucci, Ian Holm, Minnie Driver, Campbell Scott, Isabella Rossellini, Mark Anthony, Allison Janney; ***D:*** Stanley Tucci, Campbell Scott; ***W:*** Stanley Tucci, Joseph Tropiano; ***C:*** Ken Kelsch. National Society of Film Critics Awards '96: Best Supporting Actor (Shalhoub); Sundance Film Festival '96: Best Screenplay; Nominations: Independent Spirit Awards '97: Best First Feature, Best First Feature (Shalhoub, Tucci). **VHS, LV, Closed Caption, DVD**

Black Beauty

Filmmakers have tried many times, with variable results, to transfer Anna Sewell's classic children's book *Black Beauty* to the screen. First published in 1877, when many regarded horses as mere vehicles for their convenience, Sewell's novel was a shocking consciousness raiser. Written for the audience who would be most vulnerable to its grim message, *Black Beauty* was so effective that no child could ever forget it. It's hard to imagine any young reader who could grow up without caring about the welfare of the horses who played such a crucial role in late 19th and early 20th century transportation. Unsurprisingly, the sheer brutality of the subject matter frightened movie producers. Films made in 1946 and 1971 softened the harshness of Black Beauty's plight by padding storylines with romantic triangles and cute kids. Caroline Thompson's faithful adaptation may have finally got it right. Beautifully filmed, many portions of the book survive intact: Black Beauty's idyllic infancy and adolescence, his subsequent sale to aristocratic owners who abuse him in the name of fashion, his hard life working for a poor but kindly cab driver, his unbearable existence pulling a cart, and finally his fairy tale reunion with the grown-up stable boy who cares for him in his retirement. Along the way, we see man's inhumanity to animals in many ways: ignorance, indifference, neglect, and drunkenness, as well as a near-fatal stable fire and the systematic destruction of a spirited horse named Ginger. For very small children, all this may be too strong a dose of reality. (Several cried and had to leave the screening of *Black Beauty* that I attended.) Director Thompson still deserves high marks for her sincere effort to capture the sadness, cruelty, and small joys of life in another time. (Cast Note: Eleanor Bron and Peter Cook co-starred in *Bedazzled.* Bron went on to play mean Miss Minchin in 1995's *A Little Princess.* Sadly, this was Cook's swan song. Only 57, he died in 1995.) 🦴🦴🦴

1994 (G) 88m/C Andrew Knott, Sean Bean, David Thewlis, Jim Carter, Alun Armstrong, Eleanor Bron, Peter Cook, Peter Davison, John McEnery, Nicholas Jones; ***D:*** Caroline Thompson; ***W:*** Caroline Thompson; ***C:*** Alex Thomson. **VHS, LV, Closed Caption**

Black Joy

Black Joy focuses on life in Brixton, a Jamaican neighborhood in London. Funny, well acted, and poetically written, the film lives up to its title and offers an appealing glimpse at the life of Trevor Thomas as Benjamin Jones, a new arrival from Guyana. He promptly becomes involved with the girlfriend of a gangster; repercussions follow! This was the first dramatic feature made by black artists to be released in Great Britain, where it originally ran 109 minutes. Based on Jamal Ali's play *Dark Days and Light Nights.* Simmons later directed 1990's *Little Sweetheart.* 🦴🦴🦴

1977 97m/C *GB* Norman Beaten, Trevor Thomas, Dawn Hope, Floella Benjamin, Oscar James, Paul Medford, Shangò Baku, Azad Ali, Charles Pemberton, Vivian Stanshall, Kevin O'Shea; ***D:*** Anthony Simmons; ***W:*** Anthony Simmons, Jamal Ali; ***C:*** Phil Meheux; ***M:*** Lou Reizner.

Black Litter

Widely praised for its frighteningly accurate view of the fascist mentality, *Black Litter,* for this viewer, anyway, fell into the Operation-Was-a-Success-but-the-Patient-Died file. Its brutal conclusion draws too heavily on Woman-As-Symbol gimmickry, which takes the edge off the 80-something minutes worth of satire that leads up to it. Nothing short of controversial and extremely well acted, *Black Litter* won Manuel Gutierrez Aragon the Director's Prize at the Berlin Film Festival. ***AKA:*** Camada Negra. 🦴🦴🦴

1977 84m/C *SP* Jose Alonso, Angela Molina, Maria Luisa Ponte, Joaquin Hinojosa, Emilio Fornet; ***D:*** Manuel Gutierrez Aragon; ***W:*** Manuel Gutierrez Aragon, Jose Luis Borau; ***C:*** Magi Torruella; ***M:*** Jose Nieto.

Black Moon

Black Moon is pure mumble-jumble, with gorgeous cinematography by Sven Nykvist and pretty faces belonging to Rex Harrison's granddaughter Cathryn, Joe Dallesandro, and Alexandra Stewart, to charm us into thinking that what we're watching can't be all that bad. But it is. It starts in a rather interesting way, with scary and seductive imagery. But then the lushness folds up on itself as if to protect us from the insight that no one really knows what the heck they're doing here. Vaguely reminiscent of *Last Year at Marienbad, Black Moon* is a colorful grab bag of garbled, pretentious goofiness. (Louis Malle's previous hits were *Murmur of the Heart* and *Lacombe, Lucien.* He would next make *Pretty Baby* and *Atlantic City.*) **woof!**

1975 100m/C *FR* Cathryn Harrison, Joe Dallesandro, Alexandra Stewart, Therese Giehse; ***D:*** Louis Malle; ***W:*** Louis Malle, Joyce Bunuel, Ghislain Uhry; ***C:*** Sven Nykvist.

Black Narcissus

In 1960, director Michael Powell enraged British audiences with *Peeping Tom,* a sympathetic look at a psychotic killer and the kinky upbringing that contributed to his adult illness. The fact that Alfred Hitchcock's *Psycho* was wildly successful that same year didn't matter. Contemporary critics resented such an in-depth view of the dark side of human nature from a staid and genteel filmmaker like Powell. If they'd really looked at Powell's earlier films with Emeric Pressburger, they might not have been so shocked. For all its elegant beauty, 1947's *Black Narcissus* might be the most subversive movie ever made about nuns. Based on a Rumer Godden novel about five nursing sisters who are sent to the Himalayas to convert an abandoned palace into a school and hospital, the resulting film focuses on the personality changes of women in isolation. The catalyst for their change is provided by Mr. Dean, the dashingly virile estate agent portrayed by David Farrar. He reminds Deborah Kerr's Sister Clodagh of her sensual girlhood in Ireland, but he represents something far more intense for bitter Sister Ruth, played to the hilt by Kathleen Byron. In the safety of their own country surrounded by other nuns, the women might have been spared the unrelieved temptations provided by nostalgia, lust, and envy. Powell and Pressburger show how their inability to cope with those temptations is due more to their reluctance to face themselves than to any lack of religious conviction. Although they are sent to the Himalayas to help the people there, they find that the people distract them from their vocations. Moreover, Sisters Clodagh and Ruth wind up competing for the attention of the preoccupied Mr. Dean. The scene in which the lonely Sister Ruth finally descends into madness is accomplished with a bit of music, a tube of lipstick, and superb direction, yet the effect is as shocking as if she'd stripped to her knickers. *Black Narcissus,* like *Peeping Tom,* is available on home video and is well worth a reappraisal or fresh discovery. 🦴🦴🦴🦴

1947 101m/C *GB* Deborah Kerr, David Farrar, Sabu, Jean Simmons, Kathleen Byron, Flora Robson, Esmond Knight, Jenny Laird, Judith Furse, May Hallitt, Nancy Roberts; ***D:*** Michael Powell, Emeric Pressburger; ***W:*** Michael Powell, Emeric Pressburger; ***C:*** Jack Cardiff; ***M:*** Brian Easdale. Academy Awards '47: Best Art Direction/Set Decoration (Color), Best Color Cinematography; New York Film Critics Awards '47: Best Actress (Kerr). **VHS, LV**

Blackmail

An archival print of the silent version of *Blackmail* still exists and, as good as the early talkie is, the silent version is an altogether better film, with a fluid style and a minimum of intertitles. Joan Barry (later to star in *Rich and Strange* for Hitchcock) read Anny Ondra's dialogue just offscreen and Harvey Braban plays the talking in-

Joey (Billy Zane) and Mona (Jennifer Beals) in *Blood & Concrete: A Love Story.*
Columbia Tri-Star; courtesy of the Kobal Collection

spector. (Sam Livesey had played the silent inspector.) The talkie grafts dialogue sequences onto long stretches of silent footage. But if you compare *Blackmail* with *Atlantic,* another 1929 British talkie, Hitchcock's skill with the new technique is clearly in evidence. Look at the breakfast sequence where the repetition of the word "knife" not only grates on the conscience of a guilty young girl, but on our nerves as well. In *Atlantic,* however, Titanic could have sunk many times over in the pauses between the following words: "Sir... I... have... something... to... tell... you... something... I... feel... you... should... know.... The... ship... has... one... hour... to... live." Movies, even the ones that talk, MOVE, and Hitchcock knew that better than any British director during the transition to sound. Oh, and you can't miss Hitchcock's cameo here: he's reading a newspaper on a subway while being bothered by a little boy.

1929 86m/B *GB* Anny Ondra, John Longden, Sara Allgood, Charles Paton, Cyril Ritchard, Donald Calthrop, Charles Paton, Hannah Jones, Percy Parsons, Johnny Butt, Harvey Braban, Phyllis Monkman; ***Cameos:*** Alfred Hitchcock; ***D:*** Alfred Hitchcock; ***W:*** Alfred Hitchcock, Charles Bennett, Benn W. Levy, Garnett Weston; ***C:*** Jack Cox. **VHS, LV**

Blessing

It's an unhappy time down on the Wisconsin dairy farm in this tale of family life. Embittered patriarch Jack (Guy Griffis) can barely make a go of it, and takes his frustrations out by beating his cows and climbing to the top of the silo. Despairing wife Arlene (Carlin Glynn) enters newspaper lotteries and collects religious statues while daughter Randi (Melora Griffis) keeps delaying leaving the farm because of a nagging sense of responsibility. Claustrophobic atmosphere. Writer/director Paul Zehrer was nominated for 1995's Independent Spirit Award for his first screenplay.

1994 94m/C Guy Griffis, Carlin Glynn, Melora Griffis, Gareth Williams, Clovis Siemon; ***D:*** Paul Zehrer; ***W:*** Paul Zehrer; ***C:*** Stephen Kazmierski; ***M:*** Joseph S. DeBeasi. Nominations: Independent Spirit Awards '95: First Screenplay. **VHS**

Blithe Spirit

Condomine (Rex Harrison) lives in the country with second wife Ruth (Constance Cummings), but the spirit of his delectable first wife Elvira (Kay Hammond) turns up to make mischief. Madame Arcati (Margaret Rutherford) tries to return Elvira to the spirit world where she belongs, but Elvira has other ideas. As you might expect from director David Lean and that cast, this tale by Coward is deliciously well paced and played and the film even won an Oscar for special effects, which were state of the art by 1945 standards. If Rutherford had done nothing else in her career, she would reign in immortality as THE Madame Arcati. Instead, she's also THE Miss Letitia Prism, THE Duchess of Brighton, THE Miss Jane Marple, et cetera. (For the record, THIS Kay Hammond is NOT the Kay Hammond who played Mary Todd in D.W. Griffith's *Abraham Lincoln* 15 years earlier.

Why do you think so many actors have three names today? Film historians have been trying to unravel the filmographies of same-named actors, like the Misses Hammond, for far too long.)

1945 96m/C *GB* Rex Harrison, Constance Cummings, Kay Hammond, Margaret Rutherford, Hugh Wakefield, Joyce Carey, Jacqueline Clarke; ***D:*** David Lean; ***W:*** Noel Coward, Anthony Havelock-Allan; ***C:*** Ronald Neame; ***M:*** Richard Addinsell. Academy Awards '46: Best Special Effects. **VHS, DVD**

Blood & Concrete: A Love Story

Joey Turks (Billy Zane) is a cute but dumb bottle-blonde car thief. Just because he tries to steal a drug dealer's television set, Mort the owner (William Bastiani) stabs him! Joey's still bleeding when he meets a gloomy singer named Mona (Jennifer Beals), and she's just about to commit suicide by slashing her wrists! Their meeting saves them both, but then Mort's body is discovered in a blood-red swimming pool and Joey's under suspicion for murdering him and stealing Mort's drugs! Hank Dick (Carl Kolchak—I mean Darren McGavin) investigates! (As does fat Spunz, the homosexual gangster played by Nicholas Worth.) Needless to say, Joey and Mona try to avoid these two and get out of Hollywood. Mona does her best to get rid of her ex-boyfriend Lance (the hilarious James LeGros as the yuckiest rocker ever), but he's incapable of taking a hint. Mark Pellegrino and Harry Shearer are also in this, as hustler Bart and Sammy the drug dealer. If you don't mind spending 97 minutes with this crowd, *Blood & Concrete*'s pretty funny. If you do mind, there's always *Remains of the Day.* The beautiful Beals does all her own singing, too.

1990 (R) 97m/C Billy Zane, Jennifer Beals, Darren McGavin, James LeGros, Nicholas Worth, Mark Pellegrino, Harry Shearer, Billy Bastiani; ***D:*** Jeff Reiner; ***W:*** Jeff Reiner, Richard LaBrie; ***C:*** Declan Quinn; ***M:*** Vinnie Golia. **VHS, LV, Letterbox**

Blood Simple

Blood Simple put the Coen Brothers on the map and deservedly so. M. Emmet Walsh is the slimiest private investigator you can possibly imagine, or he wouldn't have accepted an assignment to murder the lover (John Getz) of Dan Hedaya's wife, newcomer Frances McDormand. When this flick first came out, movie buffs said it was the *Citizen Kane* of film noir, and it did re-invent much of what we'd expected to see and hear in film-noir. Terrific performances, dazzling camera work, a passionate understanding of the genre, and a gleeful propensity to knock its viewers right out of their seats made *Blood Simple* a revolutionary picture in many ways. Unlike the 1981 neo-noir *Body Heat, Blood Simple* is not an homage, but a fiercely original work in every way. Dead men may wear yellow, but real detectives don't!

1985 (R) 96m/C John Getz, M. Emmet Walsh, Dan Hedaya, Frances McDormand, Samm-Art Williams; ***D:*** Joel Coen; ***W:*** Joel Coen, Ethan Coen; ***C:*** Barry Sonnenfeld; ***M:*** Carter Burwell. Independent Spirit Awards '86: Best Actor (Walsh), Best Director (Coen); Sundance Film Festival '85: Grand Jury Prize. **VHS, LV, Closed Caption**

Blow-Up

Under no circumstances were kids who went to Holy Rosary Convent School supposed to see this movie! David Hemmings is shown carousing with two naked school girls, which was absolutely outrageous for a major 1966 release. When movies as great as *Blow-Up* were condemned from the pulpit, the Catholic Legion of Decency began to lose its clout. Also, Jane Birkin and Gillian Hills were clearly NOT little kids, which was perfectly obvious to any real kid. A slender David Hemmings was at his all-time sexiest here as a selfish photographer (he was mean to his girlfriend Sarah Miles, made homophobic remarks, et cetera). He photographs a beautiful park and is delighted with the results. But then he notices something. He blows up the images again and again and puts the pictures in sequence to tell a story. And what a story it is. (Not until John Cazale's

sound work in 1974's *The Conversation* would the nitty-gritty details of work ever seem as fascinating onscreen.) A desperate Vanessa Redgrave, who was in the park that day, comes to his flat to retrieve the negatives, even if she has to resort to seduction. *Blow-Up* is SO 1966: Veruschka, the Yardbirds, the mimes, the fashions, the soundtrack, and all the hollow trappings of that so-called swinging year are examined in detail by Michelangelo Antonioni with as much passion as the photographer played so vividly by Hemmings. The year 1966 may not have been quite like this movie, but Antonioni's vision of the era turned out to be how we would remember it. *Blow-Up* has tremendous repeat value, a gripping story, and so many wonderful details that you discover new ones each time you see it.

1966 111m/C *GB IT* David Hemmings, Vanessa Redgrave, Sarah Miles, Jane Birkin, Veruschka, Peter Bowles, John Castle, Gillian Hills, Julian Chagrin, Harry Hutchinson, The Yardbirds; ***D:*** Michelangelo Antonioni; ***W:*** Michelangelo Antonioni, Tonino Guerra; ***C:*** Carlo Di Palma; ***M:*** Herbie Hancock. Cannes Film Festival '67: Best Film; National Society of Film Critics Awards '66: Best Director (Antonioni), Best Film; Nominations: Academy Awards '66: Best Director (Antonioni), Best Story & Screenplay. **VHS, LV, Letterbox**

Blue Country

Jean-Charles Tacchella, who gifted the world with 1976's *Cousin, Cousine,* serves up a new treat with 1977's *Blue Country.* A sparkling cast, headed by Brigitte Fossey and Jacques Serres, enlivens this very funny romp in the French countryside, with Tacchella's artfully shaded screenplay lending a bit of poignance to their stories. ***AKA:*** Le Pays Bleu.

1977 (PG) 104m/C *FR* Brigitte Fossey, Jacques Serres, Ginette Garcin, Armand Meffre, Ginette Mathieu, Roger Crouzet; ***D:*** Jean-Charles Tacchella; ***W:*** Jean-Charles Tacchella; ***C:*** Edmond Sechan; ***M:*** Gerard Anfosso. **VHS**

The Blue Kite

This Chinese nominee for 1995's Independent Spirit Award's Best Foreign Language Film appeared to be unavailable for reappraisal at San Francisco video outlets, although it can be purchased through Kino on Video. Fifteen years of political and cultural upheaval in China is shown through the eyes of young troublemaker Tietou, who certainly earns his nickname of "Ironhead" after his 1954 birth. Soon his father is sent to a labor reform camp and his mother remarries—only to be faced with more struggles as the years go by. The kite is Tietou's cherished toy, and it keeps getting lost or destroyed but is always being rebuilt, offering one token of hope. In Chinese with English subtitles.

1993 138m/C *CH* Lu Liping, Zhang Wenyao, Pu Quanxin; ***D:*** Tian Zhuangzhuang; ***W:*** Xiao Mao; ***C:*** Yong Hou; ***M:*** Yoshihide Otomo. Nominations: Independent Spirit Awards '95: Best Foreign Film. **VHS**

Blue Velvet

I don't know who ever came up with the idea that the suburbs are a great place to raise kids; they're absolutely terrifying! I spent 15 of the worst years of my life in the Sacramento Valley (first Davis, then Woodland) before making my escape on a Greyhound bus on Friday, August 31, at 5:30 a.m. David Lynch understands the true horror of suburbia. It looks okay, but underneath, there's all sorts of weird stuff going on. Kyle MacLachlan (as Jeffrey Beaumont, who finds an ear), Isabella Rossellini (as Dorothy), Dean Stockwell, AND Dennis Hopper (as Frank Booth) all in the same movie! What more could any Grand Guignol devotee ask for? Laura Dern is Beaumont's sweet, innocent girlfriend. Hope Lange, Brad Dourif, Priscilla Pointer, and Lynch regular Jack *(Eraserhead)* Nance (who was murdered in real life after a fight in a doughnut shop in 1996) round out the cast. A deeply disturbing movie with superb cinematography by Frederick Elmes, and a great evocative score by Angelo Badalamenti, who went on to compose Lynch's *Wild at Heart* (also starring Dern) and the classic *Twin Peaks* theme. *Blue Velvet* revitalized the careers of Stockwell and Hopper (although not, alas, the underrated Lange), and if it encouraged pigeons NOT to move into suburban nightmares like Lumberton, so much the better, dang it!

Jane (Vanessa Redgrave) and Thomas (David Hemmings) in *Blow-Up.* MGM; courtesy of the Kobal Collection

Burt Reynolds as Jack Horner and William H. Macy as Little Bill in *Boogie Nights.* New Line; courtesy of the Kobal Collection

1986 (R) 121m/C Brad Dourif, Kyle MacLachlan, Isabella Rossellini, Dennis Hopper, Laura Dern, Hope Lange, Jack Nance, Dean Stockwell, George Dickerson, Priscilla Pointer; ***D:*** David Lynch; ***W:*** David Lynch; ***C:*** Frederick Elmes; ***M:*** Angelo Badalamenti. Independent Spirit Awards '87: Best Actress (Rossellini); Los Angeles Film Critics Association Awards '86: Best Director (Lynch), Best Supporting Actor (Hopper); Montreal World Film Festival '86: Best Supporting Actor (Hopper); National Society of Film Critics Awards '86: Best Cinematography, Best Director (Lynch), Best Film, Best Supporting Actor (Hopper); Nominations: Academy Awards '86: Best Director (Lynch). **VHS, LV, Letterbox, Closed Caption**

Bodies, Rest & Motion

...I used to live in a town where the main extracurricular activity was having, talking about, or cleaning up after sex; no wonder the leading cause of death was cracking up on the county road that led into town. My driving ambition between ages 10 and 18 was to leave town, but if I'd been 28 at the time, it would have taken me all of eight minutes to get out. Welcome to 94 minutes of *Bodies, Rest & Motion,* which began life as a play by Roger Hedden. I'm trying to imagine if I would have enjoyed it more watching actual people drift across a stage at 50-odd bucks a performance. I don't think so, although the occasional quirky line might have benefited more from the give-and-take that exists between performers and their audiences in a live setting. Here is the minimalist plot: Nick (Tim Roth) and Beth (Bridget Fonda) plan to move from Enfield to Butte, only Nick runs out on Beth so she has a one-night stand with Sid the house painter (Eric Stoltz) and then runs out on him. At movie's end, Nick is outraged that Beth ran out on him after he ran out on her and Sid is wandering along a highway, looking for Beth. Window dressing is provided by Phoebe Cates as Beth's best friend, Carol, who is also Nick's ex-lover. And that, action lovers, is it, except for a heavenly choir that accompanies this riveting narrative at far-from-heavenly moments. Michael Steinberg's film apparently is trying to wring extra mileage out of the 1991 success of *Slacker*—only Richard Linklater's satire was fresher and funnier and he didn't force us to stick with the same set of banal characters for the length of HIS movie. The guy behind me laughed most of the way through *Bodies, Rest & Motion;* I wonder what he does for kicks when he's alone.

1993 (R) 94m/C Phoebe Cates, Bridget Fonda, Tim Roth, Eric Stoltz, Scott Frederick, Scott Johnson, Alicia Witt, Rich Wheeler, Peter Fonda; ***D:*** Michael Steinberg; ***W:*** Roger Hedden; ***C:*** Bernd Heinl; ***M:*** Michael Convertino. **VHS, LV, Closed Caption**

Body Count

Alyssa Milano has paid her dues in a number of flicks you wouldn't go near if she weren't in them. As these quickly made entries go, *Body Count* isn't bad. For key stretches of the film, director Kurt Voss employs the radio drama technique of letting the sounds within a house build an effective atmosphere of horror. Even if everything unravels at the end, the production team deserves credit for trying something different. Susanne (Milano) is in love with Daniel (Justin Theroux), and he's finally bringing her home to meet his well-heeled folks. They include familiar faces from the small screen: Marta (*Lost in Space*) Kristen as Marilyn, Ron (*Planet of the Apes*) Harper as Jack, and Robert (*CHIPS*) Pine as Wilson. The first part of the movie is your standard edgy gathering of relatives, but it gets interesting when Susanne and Daniel are alone in the dark and hear truly terrible things happening to Aunt Estelle, Cousin Allen, Justin, and the rest of the clan. THEY MAY BE NEXT. Is there anything they can do to save themselves from a danger they can't even see? Ice-T is co-billed with Milano, who also serves as executive producer. Both are good here and this modestly made chiller may actually succeed in giving you a chill or two. Voss' previous credits include *Border Radio* (co-directed with Alison Anders), *Genuine Risk, The Horseplayer, Baja, Amnesia,* and *Poison Ivy 3: The New Seduction.* ***AKA:*** Below Utopia.

1997 (R) 88m/C Ice-T, Alyssa Milano, Justin Theroux, Tommy (Tiny) Lister, Jeannette O'Connor, Nicholas Walker, Eric Saiet, Marta Kristen, Ron Harper, Robert Pine, Richard Danielson; ***D:*** Kurt Voss; ***W:*** David Diamond; ***C:*** Denis Maloney; ***M:*** Joseph Williams. **VHS, Closed Caption**

Bongwater

When I lived in Solano Park (that's a student housing tract, not a youth hostel camp), I used to hear geniuses-in-residence at the Davis campus of the University of California say, "Why don't more filmmakers show what getting stoned is really like?" As *Bongwater* clearly shows, the answer to that burning question is, "Because drugs on film slow down time, slow down plots, slow down character development, slow down everything!" *Bongwater* picks up speed when a red-haired tornado named Serena (Alicia Witt) is onscreen. She's mean and tough and she's nuts, but she's an INTERESTING mean, tough nut. As for the guys in the film...well, it's like being introduced to half a dozen indistinguishable dudes at a party. WHO'S DAVID? (Luke Wilson) WHO'S DEVLIN? (Jack Black) WHO'S TONY? (Andy Dick) WHO'S ROBERT? (Jeremy Sisto) WHO'S TOMMY? (Jamie Kennedy) WHO'S BOBBY? (Scott Caan) The difference between David and Tommy is that David's a Portland artist who takes drugs with Tony and Robert, and Tommy's a heroin addict/musician en route to New York. A huge chunk of screen time involves David's acid trip in the woods of Oregon where the ghost of his Mom (Patricia Wettig) drops by for a chat, but it doesn't have much to do with the rest of the story. (Guy meets Psycho, Psycho leaves Guy, Guy misses Psycho.) Did I mention that Serena burns down David's house during the opening credits and there's still a whole movie to plow through after that? Based on the book by Michael Hornburg. *Bongwater* played at San Francisco's Indie Fest in January 1999.

1998 98m/C Luke Wilson, Alicia Witt, Amy Locane, Brittany Murphy, Jack Black, Andy Dick, Jeremy Sisto, Jamie Kennedy, Scott Caan, Patricia Wettig; ***D:*** Richard Sears; ***W:*** Nora Macoby, Eric Weiss; ***C:*** Richard Crudo; ***M:*** Mark Mothersbaugh, Josh Mancell.

Boogie Nights

Much of *Boogie Nights* makes the pornographic film industry look as wholesome as

The year is 2024...a future you'll probably live to see.

—Tagline from the movie *A Boy and His Dog.*

a Sunday school picnic. Burt Reynolds and his brood of sex stars are like family, only their home movies make money. Long but absorbing throughout its 155-minute running time, the plot follows sex stars Mark Wahlberg, Julianne Moore, Heather Graham et al from the '70s into the '80s. If the entire movie were just one big set-up for the punchline (when Wahlberg unzips to reveal a rubber snake the length of ANACONDA), it'd be relegated to the cult movie bin. Instead, writer/director Paul Thomas Anderson develops each and every member of his large cast in interesting and surprising ways. Unlike the filmmakers of *Showgirls,* Anderson doesn't judge anyone for his or her choice of profession. Reynolds won an Oscar nomination and revitalized his career as an idealized producer who exists only in fantasy land. 🦴🦴🦴

1997 (R) 155m/C Mark Wahlberg, Burt Reynolds, Julianne Moore, Don Cheadle, William H. Macy, Heather Graham, John C. Reilly, Luis Guzman, Philip Seymour Hoffman, Alfred Molina, Philip Baker Hall, Robert Ridgely, Joanna Gleason, Thomas Jane, Ricky Jay, Nicole Parker, Melora Walters, Michael Jace, Jack Wallace, John Doe; ***Cameos:*** Robert Downey, Michael Penn; ***D:*** Paul Thomas Anderson; ***W:*** Paul Thomas Anderson; ***C:*** Robert Elswit; ***M:*** Michael Penn. Golden Globe Awards '98: Best Supporting Actor (Reynolds); Los Angeles Film Critics Association Awards '97: Best Supporting Actor (Reynolds), Best Supporting Actress (Moore); MTV Movie Awards '98: Breakthrough Performance (Graham); New York Film Critics Awards '97: Best Supporting Actor (Reynolds); National Society of Film Critics Awards '97: Best Supporting Actor (Reynolds), Best Supporting Actress (Moore); Nominations: Academy Awards '97: Best Original Screenplay, Best Supporting Actor (Reynolds), Best Supporting Actress (Moore); British Academy Awards '97: Best Original Screenplay, Best Supporting Actor (Reynolds); Golden Globe Awards '98: Best Supporting Actor (Reynolds), Best Supporting Actress (Moore); MTV Movie Awards '98: Best Dance Sequence (Mark Wahlberg/cast); Screen Actors Guild Award '97: Best Supporting Actor (Reynolds), Best Supporting Actress (Moore), Cast; Writers Guild of America '97: Best Original Screenplay. **VHS, LV, Closed Caption, DVD**

Boss' Son

This early Bobby Roth film is an autobiographical account of why he isn't taking over his father's job as boss of a carpet mill. Despite the extremely personal primary source material, Roth manages to achieve just enough emotional distance, to the great advantage of his film. Working on a tiny budget of $500,000, Roth assembled an impressive cast of veterans, all of whom outshine Asher Brauner as the protagonist. As young Bobby, Brauner is too cold and detached for us to care about his inner conflicts regarding his own class and that of his co-workers. The balance problems aren't fatal, but they do weaken a potentially dynamite study of the American class system. Roth's compassionate script and direction, plus Henry G. Sanders' poignant performance, make this a memorable, if incompletely realized, effort. Roth's future movies include 1984's *Heartbreakers* and 1992's *Keeper of the City,* both starring Peter Coyote. 🦴🦴🦴

1978 97m/C Rita Moreno, James Darren, Asher Brauner, Rudy Solari, Henry Sanders, Richie Havens, Piper Laurie, Elena Verdugo; ***D:*** Bobby Roth; ***W:*** Bobby Roth; ***C:*** Alfonso Beato. **VHS**

Bound

This sizzling neo-noir was just as much fun for me to watch as many classic entries of the 1940s and the '50s. Jennifer Tilly is femme fatale Violet stuck with a schmuck named Caesar (Joe Pantoliano). When a butch ex-convict named Corky (Gina Gershon) enters her life, it's love and lust at first sight. Many bodies later, the Wachowski Brothers use all the best ingredients to bring their film to a satisfying conclusion. As Violet, Tilly has the half-finished look of the women in the Superman cartoons made by the Fleischer Bros. in the early 1940s, while Gershon's Corky evokes countless noir heroes who've almost given up on life until they meet the right woman and come up with the perfect heist plan that no one else can understand, much less carry out. That's all there is to the narrative structure, but it's well acted and well scripted with some fresh twists in the imagery department. 🦴🦴🦴🦴

1996 (R) 107m/C Gina Gershon, Jennifer Tilly, Joe Pantoliano, John P. Ryan, Barry Kivel, Christopher Meloni, Peter Spellos, Richard Sarafian, Mary Mara, Susie Bright, Ivan Kane, Kevin M. Richardson, Gene Borkan; ***D:*** Andy Wachowski, Larry Wachowski; ***W:*** Andy Wachowski, Larry Wachowski; ***C:*** Bill Pope; ***M:*** Don Davis. Nominations: Independent Spirit Awards '97: Best Cinematography; MTV Movie Awards '97:

Best Kiss (Jennifer Tilly/Gina Gershon). **VHS, LV, Closed Caption, DVD**

Box of Moonlight

Tom DiCillo's *Box of Moonlight* is a beautifully observed story of how a tightly coiled electrical engineer learns how to appreciate life after a chance meeting with a free spirit known only as The Kid. It's the sort of movie that would have been trampled by too many conflicting approaches at too many studio story conferences. You can almost envision the artistic compromises that would have been made with the script, the cast, even the title. Maybe those compromises would have made the project more *commercial,* but 1997's *Box of Moonlight,* DiCillo's superb follow-up to 1995's *Living in Oblivion,* is an enchanting, fully realized film on its own unique terms, and a quintessential indie. John Turturro is Al Fountain, strict with the men who work for him, strict with his young son Bobby (Alexander Goodwin), and strict with himself. A colleague feels sorry for Al and invites him to a card game with some of the other crew members. Just before leaving for the game, Al notices a strand of grey hair, his first. Then, courtesy of a door that has been left ajar, Al finds out how the men really feel about him and he beats a hasty retreat. He begins to see time run backward (water pouring from the glass into the pitcher, a bicyclist riding in reverse) and decides that he needs to abandon his timetable for a day or two and take a break. He returns to the site of many happy childhood memories and sees that it has been abandoned. A nice-looking older man inquires about the state of Al's spiritual health and Al wisely leaves the answer to his imagination. (We hear from that kindly gent again later.) So: Who better for a journey into self-discovery than a reckless Kid (Sam Rockwell) who lives by his wits and is always one or two jumps ahead of the law and/or a good hiding? At first glance, the uptight Al and this wild Kid seem to be the unlikeliest of companions, but Al finds more and more reasons to stay on the road and, whenever he calls the stressed-out Bobby at home, he loosens up a bit on those stern directives about homework and flash cards and stuff. Al and the Kid spend an idyllic summer's day and night with Floatie (Catherine Keener) and Purlene (Lisa Blount), two women they meet at a secluded swimming hole. Al learns what his visions mean and he learns what HE means in a way he never would without the detour. Turturro gives a tour-de-force performance as Al; I don't need to call the Psychic Friends Network to see this tremendously gifted actor giving an Oscar acceptance speech in the not-too-far-distant future. Like its wonderfully symbolic title, *Box of Moonlight* is a treasure to be savored again and again on repeat viewings. 🦴🦴🦴🦴

1996 (R) 111m/C John Turturro, Sam Rockwell, Catherine Keener, Lisa Blount, Annie Corley, Dermot Mulroney, Alexander Goodwin; ***D:*** Tom DiCillo; ***W:*** Tom DiCillo; ***C:*** Paul Ryan; ***M:*** Jim Farmer. Nominations: Independent Spirit Awards '98: Best Actor (Turturro). **VHS, LV, Closed Caption**

A Boy and His Dog

Harlan Ellison has been outraging people through most of his career as a professional writer. He admits frankly that much of this is hype. Contemporary writers have to be strong personalities to get booked on the chat shows that will promote their work. Ellison considers *A Boy and His Dog* to be one of the best science-fiction novellas he's ever written, and director L.Q. Jones' screen adaptation became an instant cult film when it was first released in 1975. I have yet to meet a woman who wasn't offended by it or a man who wasn't amused by it. Halfway through a 1975 press screening of *A Boy and His Dog,* I walked out, seriously intending not to return. A nice man in the lobby stopped me, reassured me that the last half of the movie was much better than the first, and told me that I'd feel a lot better if I went back. I did not feel a lot better. In fact, I felt simply horrible when director/screenwriter L.Q. Jones and actor/producer Alvy Moore appeared out of nowhere directly after the film, and proceeded to say how great they were and how awful many of the critics in attendance were for not liking their movie. *A Boy and His Dog* features

The Hound Salutes:
TOM DICILLO
Writer/director, *Box of Moonlight*

B*ox of Moonlight* was supposed to have been my second film. It was motivated by what happened to me on *Johnny Suede,* the way that film ended up. *Johnny Suede* was my first film. I am the first one to tell you that it suffers from a first-time director's inexperience. There are some things in it that I would want to do differently. I wrote *Box of Moonlight* to address those things. I wanted to do a film that was outside of New York, that had nothing to do with guys in goatees in leather jackets and drug addiction and *Rebel without a Cause.* I was very excited and I thought that this film was about not such a limited focus of people and that it was about more of my experience as a child growing up in different towns all over this country. That was the idea. I wanted to make an existentialist action-adventure comedy.

"*Box of Moonlight* is a film that asks you to pay attention. The first shot of the film is this aerial view that glides over the landscape, goes into some foliage in a wooded glade and we see what appears to be a deer, munching on some leaves, when, in fact, the deer is a plastic fake. It was a very conscious effort on my part to open the film that way, so that the audience would say, 'Uh-oh. Let's pay attention. Not everything is what it seems.' And the film is that way.

"John Turturro's character is a rigid, uptight guy, but he's not only that. He's got lots of other interesting things going on. Sam Rockwell plays 'the free spirit,' but on the other hand, he's got a lot of problems. Part of his being free appears to be that he's afraid, he cannot live in society, he

fine performances by Susanne Benton as A Girl and an even better one by Tiger the Dog, who previously starred in *The Brady Bunch.* It also offers incredible sex, violence at its most vicious, and a theme that is embarrassing in its treatment, if thoughtful in its content. Oh, yeah, the plot. It's set in the future. It shows how a telepathic Boy (Don Johnson, then 25) and his Dog survive despite all those people out there. It's also supposed to be funny. *A Boy and His Dog* is still igniting controversy on home video over two decades after its theatrical release. Cutting-edge satire or yet another cinematic cheap shot at women? It's your call. **woof!**

1975 (R) 87m/C Don Johnson, Susanne Benton, Jason Robards Jr., Charles McGraw, Alvy Moore; ***D:*** L.Q. Jones; ***W:*** L.Q. Jones; ***C:*** John Morrill; ***V:*** Tim McIntire. **VHS, LV, DVD**

The Boy from Mercury

Martin Duffy's *The Boy from Mercury* looks like it was shot in saturated Technicolor from the 1940s, but it's actually a '90s movie from Ireland, starring Rita Tushingham, Tom Courtenay, and a young charmer named James Hickey as Harry, a fatherless child who's convinced he's a creature from another planet. (All those weekly Flash Gordon serials fuel his imagination.) Tushingham and Courtenay are more animated here than they've been in

doesn't seem capable of dealing with the complexities of real life. The film is not easily defined in black and white and I like that. Even if you go back to *Johnny Suede,* I ask you to take a look at what you see and really think about it. I don't like movie stereotypes. *Johnny Suede* is an idiot, he's a fool, and it was my pleasure to show that here's a guy who thinks he's cool, but he's a total idiot. It still blows my mind that some people did not get that. If they didn't get that, I'm sorry, I guess I should have carved it on the film with a razor blade. How could you have a guy think he's cool with a hairdo like that? He's an idiot! On the other hand, just because Al Fountain is a little restricted does not mean that he cannot be responsible and respectable, and have vitality and masculinity. He doesn't have to be a wimp and a frightened little mouse.

"I knew that I needed an actor like John Turturro to make Al Fountain into a real icon. That's what I wanted him to be, almost like the Washington Monument of Fatherhood—and then tip over that monument. Then you've got a story. The Kid played by Sam Rockwell has several functions in this movie. He's designed to annoy the hell out of Al Fountain. What would annoy Al more than a guy driving drunk, a guy who engages in petty thievery for a living, a guy who doesn't pay taxes, a guy who has no responsibilities? As I worked on his character, The Kid became a giant pool for my thoughts about America, the way it is now, the way it used to be, the way it could be.

"The Kid is an absolute innocent. He takes everything at face value. He's absolutely trusting and absolutely helpless. That's good and bad. He's incapable of seeing a joyful moment and NOT going right for it. Because he lives in the moment, he really does embody freedom in a real way. For The Kid, life's about tolerance and enjoying things as they are."

In between *Johnny Suede* and *Box of Moonlight*, TOM DICILLO made the indie classic *Living in Oblivion*.

quite some time, and Hickey is altogether winning as the little would-be alien. ♪♪♪

1996 99m/C *IR* James Hickey, Rita Tushingham, Tom Courtenay, Hugh O'Conner; ***D:*** Martin Duffy; ***W:*** Martin Duffy; ***C:*** Seamus Deasy; ***M:*** Stephen McKeon.

Boy Next Door

The BBC has always been fascinated by pop iconography, and *Boy Next Door* might easily qualify to be a segment on A&E's *Biography* series. This portrait of Boy George is chockful of clips and wistful ruminations about what went wrong and when and why. Boy George's story ends on a bright note with a career upswing and an apparent recovery from drug addition. (As of 1997, he's a weekly columnist for the *Express,* a British tabloid.) ♪♪♪

1993 50m/C *GB* ***D:*** Mark Kidel.

The Boys of St. Vincent

The Boys of St. Vincent is a hard-hitting Canadian drama set in a Newfoundland orphanage for boys run by the Catholic Brothers. But Brother Lavin, the orphanage's well-respected director, has a secret life with the children under his care. He uses them as sexual outlets and, if they reject his advances or his authority, he beats them until they require medical attention. The three-hour-plus plot revolves around Kevin, one of Brother Lavin's spe-

Love is a mighty power.

—Tagline from the movie *Breaking the Waves.*

cial boys, who runs away rather than submit to him. What happens next is the subject of a 15-year cover-up. Were children at the orphanage actually abused by the Brothers? Should the police have intervened more forcefully? Why did the Catholic authorities simply transfer the guilty Brothers rather than make them face criminal charges? The long-term effects of sexual abuse are finally being faced by international courts after decades of ignoring children's complaints against so-called pillars of the community, a theme which is strongly reinforced in *The Boys of St. Vincent.* The kids have no rights. They are harassed and intimidated by their abusers. Well-meaning social workers, detectives, friends, and family members are ineffectual. The drama also deals with the cyclical nature of child abuse, that the abused grow up to abuse others as well. One of the more likable of Kevin's fellow victims grows up to be a drug addict and a street hustler, and during his court appearance it is revealed that as a teenager he abused little boys half his age. We watch his horrifying and tragic descent from freckle-faced charmer to a broken man of 25 who would rather die than face himself. The script suggests that Brother Lavin, too, was abused as a child, but since we only see him as a menacing adult, filled with rage and self-pity, he has no claim whatever on our sympathy. Henry Czerny made the most of his 1993 role as Brother Lavin, subsequently attracting the attention of more than one Hollywood producer. (Follow-up projects included the indies *Northern Extremes* and *When Night Is Falling,* plus blockbusters like *Clear and Present Danger* and *Mission: Impossible.*) The timing of 1995's limited theatrical release of *The Boys of St. Vincent* was ironic, since Newt Gingrich seemed to feel that more orphanages were just what we needed at that point in his career as Speaker of the House. Viewers of *The Boys of St. Vincent* can weigh the pros and cons on THAT issue for themselves! ꝏꝏ

1993 186m/C *CA* Henry Czerny, Johnny Morina, Sebastian Spence, Brian Dodd, David Hewlett, Jonathan Lewis, Jeremy Keefe, Phillip Dinn, Brian Dooley, Greg Thomey, Michael Wade, Lise Roy, Timothy Webber, Kristine Demers, Ashley Billard, Sam Grana; ***D:*** John N. Smith; ***W:*** Sam Grana, John N. Smith, Des Walsh; ***C:*** Pierre Letarte; ***M:*** Neil Smolar. Nominations: Independent Spirit Awards '95: Best Foreign Film. **VHS**

The Brandon Teena Story

Teena R. Brandon's short life spanned from December 12, 1973, to December 31, 1993. Her coffin is inscribed "Daughter, Sister, Friend." And so she was to the people who loved her. Teena was having a sexual identity crisis. Born a girl in Lincoln, Nebraska, she felt like a boy, and as Brandon Teena, she dated a number of young women, all of whom liked Brandon very much. They appreciated Brandon's gentleness and kisses and gestures of affection, including flowers. When Brandon moved to Falls City, she began to date Lana Tisdel and to hang out with Thomas Nissen, 21, and John Lotter, 22. They liked Brandon when they thought she was a man. Then Brandon was arrested for passing a forged check and charged under the name of Teena Brandon. Even worse, none of the girls in Falls City seemed the least bit concerned that Brandon had deceived them, and this infuriated Nissen and Lotter. Both had served time, both had trouble with women. The fact that former date Lana Tisdel preferred Brandon Teena OVER John Lotter and that even John's own sister Michelle Lotter was Brandon's friend fanned a stockpile of angry resentment that ignited into two hate crimes. First Nissen and Lotter beat and raped Brandon. Even though Brandon complained to police, Nissen and Lotter remained free to come and go. On New Year's Eve, Brandon and another friend, Philip Devine, 22, sought refuge with a friend in Humboldt, Lisa Lambert, 24, the mother of a nine-month-old baby boy, Tanner. Nissen and Lotter tracked down Brandon's temporary sanctuary, 30 miles from Falls City, and executed all three adults in Lambert's farmhouse, sparing only baby Tanner. Into this troubled community, documentarians Susan Muska and Greta Olafsdottir went straight to the primary sources to tell *The Brandon Teena Story.* They talked with Brandon's family and friends, with Lana Tisdel, with Lotter's family, with Lambert's family, with the police, and with out-of-towners who came to Nebraska specifically to observe the trial. We hear the brutal police questioning of Brandon after she was beaten and raped. The filmmakers question the convicted killers in prison. (Nissen received life without parole, Lotter faces the death penalty.) They are scary-looking thugs and their lack of remorse, or of any feeling except hatred for each other, is chilling. Meanwhile, Lana Tisdel sings a tribute song to the martyred Brandon. One surprising element of the documentary is its levity of tone. The effect is incongruous, but in no way disrespectful to the victims. The welcoming sign to Nebraska proclaims the good life. If one young person in the midst of a sexual identity crisis is such a threat, how good can that life be and, moreover, how safe can any of us be? Played at the Berlin Film Festival in 1998. ℒℒℒ

1998 89m/C ***D:*** Susan Muska, Greta Olafsdottir; ***W:*** Susan Muska, Greta Olafsdottir; ***C:*** Susan Muska.

Breakaway

Well, what did we expect? A mere 16 months after Nancy Kerrigan was temporarily sidelined while training for the 1994 Olympics, Tonya Harding's first movie was rushed to the Cannes Film Festival. When Sonja Henie, Vera Hruba Ralston, Belita, Carol Heiss, and Lynn-Holly Johnson were introduced to international film fans, they were groomed and protected and shown in the best light possible for beginning actresses. But Tonya Harding is in a unique position. She can't skate, she can't teach, she can't sing, no one's hired her to wrestle lately, and if she takes a regular job to pay the bills, the tabloid press is there to record the event in exhaustive detail. The story here is a piece of nothing, poorly acted by all involved, with the possible exception of Teri Thompson as Myra Styles, whose looks, poise, punchy delivery, and O.K. action sequences outclass those of all of her male colleagues, and certainly Tonya Harding, who is "introduced" as Gina. Gina can take care of herself, which means that if a guy with a gun runs into her, he will acquiescently allow her to beat him up, because it's in the script. Harding's ragged eyebrows could have used a trimming, her wardrobe is unironed Goodwill, and her line readings and gestures are excruciatingly awkward. But why go on? She needed direction, she didn't get it, end of story. If it's any consolation, Joe Estevez (Martin Sheen's sibling) is no Sir John Gielgud, either. For the truly curious only, and expect to be disappointed. **woof!**

1995 (R) 94m/C Teri Thompson, Joe Estevez, Chris De Rose, Tonya Harding, Tony Noakes, Rick Beatty, Michael Garganese; ***D:*** Sean Dash; ***W:*** Sean Dash, Eric Gardner; ***C:*** Carlos Montaner; ***M:*** Robert Wait. **VHS**

Breaking the Waves

This extremely long film (17 minutes longer than *Secrets and Lies,* which felt like forever) is not suitable for everyone on Planet Earth, like, for example, ME. I suspect that it impressed the Grand Jury at the Cannes Film Festival because of its power and its sincerity, and because of Emily Watson's tremendously hard work as Bess. Obviously I can't speak for The Deity, with whom Bess has so MANY conversations, but I suspect that God is a lot more forgiving of us (and, consequently, Bess) than we are of ourselves or each other. Bess' course of action is entirely clear to her, but her masochism is a mystery to me for the entire length of the narrative. Why should she punish herself by sleeping with other men because her husband is in an accident? To demonstrate that religious fervor is irrational? Or pointless? One senses the Victorian sensibility of an Emily Brontë *(Wuthering Heights)* or a William Somerset Maugham *(Christmas Holiday)* lurking about this sad story set in the 1970s. For someone who grew up listening skeptically to old nun's tales of little boys pocketing the Communion wafer, thereby drowning the whole Congregation in the Blood of Christ, Bess' self-torture clearly made a heckuva lot more sense to

"His greatest ambition is to become immortal... then die."

—Parvulesco (Jean-Pierre Melville) speaks of petty crook Michel/Laszlo (Jean-Paul Belmondo) in *Breathless.*

the filmmakers than it did to me. The ending made me feel like I'd just walked in front of a Mack truck. According to the May 7, 1997, *Express,* Helena Bonham Carter withdrew from the role of Bess, explaining that she "loved the part, but had an allergic reaction to the idea of this girl, whose husband is a paraplegic, who goes and prostitutes herself in the belief that it will make him better." If *Breaking the Waves* is your favorite movie—and it was for two viewers who recommended it to me without reservations—great, but I've lost my early tenacity for sitting through films-as-agony except by accident!!!

1995 (R) 152m/C *DK FR* Emily Watson, Stellan Skarsgard, Katrin Cartlidge, Adrian Rawlins, Jean-Marc Barr, Sandra Voe, Udo Kier, Mikkel Gaup; ***D:*** Lars von Trier; ***W:*** Lars von Trier; ***C:*** Robby Muller; ***M:*** Joachim Holbek. Cannes Film Festival '96: Grand Jury Prize; Cesar Awards '97: Best Foreign Film; New York Film Critics Awards '96: Best Actress (Watson), Best Cinematography, Best Director (von Trier); National Society of Film Critics Awards '96: Best Actress (Watson), Best Cinematography, Best Director (von Trier), Best Film; Nominations: Academy Awards '96: Best Actress (Watson); British Academy Awards '96: Best Actress (Watson); Golden Globe Awards '97: Best Actress—Drama (Watson), Best Film—Drama; Independent Spirit Awards '97: Best Foreign Film. **VHS, Letterbox, Closed Caption**

Breathless

Iowa-born Jean Seberg was only 17 years old when director Otto Preminger chose her to play the title role in *Saint Joan.* It was a spectacular way to launch a career and her subsequent failure in the film was equally spectacular; *Saint Joan* was chosen as the worst movie of the century by the Harvard Lampoon. Preminger gave her another chance with *Bonjour Tristesse,* but Deborah Kerr attracted most of the critical attention for that Françoise Sagan adaptation. Seberg's career could have ended right there had she not been cast in Jean-Luc Godard's *Breathless.* All the things about Seberg that had seemed so out of place in splashy American movies were just right in this fast-paced New Wave film from the year 1959. Suddenly, her skin-deep qualities seemed mysterious, part of a larger phenomenon, and the less emotional understanding she brought to her interpretation of an essentially thoughtless young waif, the better. Or so it seemed at the time when *Breathless* was first released. In fact, when Seberg stares blankly into the camera after her lover calls her a little bitch and says, "A little what? I don't understand," it is her very lack of expression that haunts me today. *Breathless* is perhaps the most enjoyable of Godard's films (it didn't hurt that François Truffaut collaborated on the script) and it turned Jean-Paul Belmondo, then 26, into an overnight star. Seberg's career received a much-needed boost and she made dozens of international films over the next 18 years. Seberg's naivete was genuine: she took her life in 1979 after being hounded by the F.B.I. for her involvement with the Black Panthers. She once admitted that she had neither the will nor the way to cope with Hollywood pressures and added, "I don't think any healthy, well-balanced person would want to become an actress." She projected youth, health, and a superficial version of happiness in *Breathless,* which may well leave today's audiences out of breath. ***AKA:*** À Bout de Souffle.

1959 90m/B *FR* Jean-Paul Belmondo, Jean Seberg, Daniel Boulanger, Jean-Pierre Melville, Liliane Robin; ***D:*** Jean-Luc Godard; ***W:*** Jean-Luc Godard; ***C:*** Raoul Coutard; ***M:*** Martial Solal. Berlin International Film Festival '60: Best Director (Godard). **VHS**

Bride of the Monster

The 1994 movie *Ed Wood* wasn't kidding: In order to secure financing from Donald E. McCoy, the owner of the Packing Service Corporation, Wood had to hire his son Tony as Lieutenant Dick Craig. A star was born, but only for this movie. Bela Lugosi has a bit more oomph than usual as Dr. Eric Vornoff; he's a great mad scientist and his sequence opposite a rubber octopus in Griffith Park is a highlight. Tor Johnson is also a welcome presence as Lobo. The rest of the cast is your standard Ed Wood stock company—under-rehearsed and overacting! While lacking the rock bottom aesthetics and existential wretchedness of *Plan 9 from Outer Space, Bride* is still pretty terrible in its own right and it's a must-see for all true Wood buffs. ***AKA:*** Bride of the Atom. 🦴🦴🦴

1955 68m/B Bela Lugosi, Tor Johnson, Loretta King, Tony McCoy, Harvey B. Dunn, George Becwar, Paul Marco, Billy Benedict, Dolores Fuller, Don Nagel, Bud Osborne, Conrad Brooks; ***D:*** Edward D. Wood Jr.; ***W:*** Edward D. Wood Jr., Alex Gordon, Alex Gordon; ***C:*** William C. Thompson; ***M:*** Frank Worth. **VHS**

Bride to Be

Bride to Be is quite unintentionally funny. It's yet another Son-Wants-His-Dad's-Girl yarn, only this time, the kid's going to be a priest. (What about his immortal soul?) Peter Day does an unmemorable acting job as the son. Sarah Miles is so quiet in the title role that at first it does seem that she can neither hear nor speak (nope, the screenwriter just didn't give her any words to say!) and Stanley Baker looks thoroughly embarrassed here as the father. ***AKA:*** Pepita Jiminez. 🦴

1975 115m/C *SP* Sarah Miles, Stanley Baker, Peter Day, Eduardo Bea, Vicente Soler, Jose Maria Caffarell, Maria Vico; ***D:*** Rafael Morena Alba; ***C:*** Jose Luis Alcaine; ***M:*** Stelvio Cipriano.

Brief Encounter

Early in his long career, David Lean made several small, beautifully observed films about love, about death, about how people survive, and about how things end. My favorite David Lean film is *Brief Encounter;* I can watch it over and over again and never grow tired of it. The story is deceptively simple and we discover it in bits and pieces. We see a woman and a man talking quietly in a railway tea shop. Another woman joins them, chattering animatedly until the man leaves ever so quietly. The first woman nearly faints, but is soon en route home with her chattering companion. As far as real time goes after that, the woman sits quietly at home with her well-meaning husband and her own memories until the end of the film. But her memories, as Lean makes abundantly clear, have shattered her life and it is only her enormous capacity for traditional routines that saves her from death and despair. We learn why that ordinary little incident in the railway tea shop was the most heartrending time of her life. Lean and screenwriter Noel Coward chose just what to show with great care and the only choice that appears out of place, ironically, inspired Billy Wilder to make *The Apartment* in 1960. Because his canvas was so small in *Brief Encounter,* Lean embellished it further with sound: a haunting narration, a sweeping Rachmaninoff-based score, plus a batch of typically British catch phrases. The crisp acting by the supporting cast, and especially by its stars Celia Johnson and Trevor Howard, rooted *Brief Encounter* in a definite time and place and rinsed away excessive sentiment. Yet despite its very Englishness, *Brief Encounter* does not date. It doesn't matter how the world has changed. These people in these circumstances made these choices, and even today, we might well imagine people making the very same choices all over again. 🦴🦴🦴🦴

1946 86m/B *GB* Celia Johnson, Trevor Howard, Stanley Holloway, Cyril Raymond, Joyce Carey, Everley Gregg, Margaret Barton, Dennis Harkin, Valentine Dyall, Marjorie Mars, Irene Handl; ***D:*** David Lean; ***W:*** Noel Coward; ***C:*** Robert Krasker. New York Film Critics Awards '46: Best Actress (Johnson); Nominations: Academy Awards '46: Best Actress (Johnson), Best Director (Lean), Best Screenplay. **VHS**

A Brief History of Time

Theoretical physicist Stephen Hawking was given two years to live when he contracted Lou Gehrig's disease in the early 1960s, but, over three decades later, he shows no indications OR inclinations of fulfilling that prophecy. As always, Errol Morris does a remarkable job of communicating an interesting subject on his own unique terms. Even if you barely squeaked by with a "C" in physics, *A Brief History of Time* supplies many lucid and compelling visualizations of Hawking's theories. One quibble is that Morris does not identify the many speakers in the film until the final credits. This wouldn't even work in a book, much less a movie! We figure out who Hawking's mother and sister are, but the comments of his many scientific colleagues have less of a context, since non-scientists don't know who they are (until

The Hound Salutes:

ERROL MORRIS

Director, *A Brief History of Time, The Thin Blue Line*

Stephen Hawking's mother quotes Samuel Johnson, 'Knowledge that you are to be hanged in the morning concentrates the mind.' And this is her own analysis of what happened to Stephen. Stephen was always very, very bright, but it was only after he was diagnosed with having a fatal illness—an illness that would kill him in a matter of years—that he began to work and produce these amazing results about the universe. I think that he has always had his writing style, but certainly the way in which he has to communicate has forced him to be concise, to be clear, to be brief. To me it became so much a part of him it's hard to know what part is Stephen and what part is a result of the illness or how he has to communicate. But Stephen, of course, is a great communicator. He's a great communicator of science, of scientific ideas, and he's a great communicator of his love of life and learning.

"Years ago, before I became a filmmaker, I spent a year interviewing murderers in Wisconsin on audiotape, and I conducted these interviews in a certain way. I tried to say as little as possible. I have interviews from that period where people talk for an hour or two and my voice is not on the tape. These are interviews that I am very, very proud of. And over the years I've developed this interviewing style [where I am not seen or heard]. It has occurred to me that in order to keep people talking at length, the important thing is not to listen to what they say. Often, when you listen to what

after it's over) or what any of them have done, ever, unless they look it up. Yes, the movie is about Hawking, but who the heck ARE all these guys who talk about him at length? The final shot is both poignant and eloquent: Hawking's wheelchair, labeled "STEPHEN," is shown against a starry sky. Left out of the film is the fact that Hawking was then in the process of divorcing his longtime wife Jane, unseen except in early candids, but much-discussed on camera. He married his longtime nurse Elaine Mason in September, 1994. Hawking, who has not been able to speak since 1985, said his wedding vows through a voice synthesizer created by his bride's ex-husband. 𝄐𝄐𝄐

1992 (G) 85m/C Stephen Hawking; ***D:*** Errol Morris; ***W:*** Stephen Hawking; ***C:*** John Bailey; ***M:*** Philip Glass. Sundance Film Festival '92: Filmmakers Trophy. **VHS, Closed Caption**

Brilliant Lies

Richard Franklin's *Brilliant Lies* is talky and stage-bound, feeling much longer than its 93-minute running time. Susy Conner (*Strictly Ballroom*'s Gia Carides) is a definite target of Gary Fitzgerald's (Anthony LaPaglia) sexual harassment, or is she? She asks sister Katie (Gia's real-life sister, Zoe) to back up her version of events, but Katie recalls that some of the events Susy describes actually happened to them both as children abused by their father, Brian (Ray Barrett). The script buys into most of the commonly accepted myths about harassment allegations: that mercenary women lie, that child molesters grow old

people say it can be distracting. You feel the need to react in some way and the person seeing your need to react often stops and feels the need to ask you a question, find out what you're thinking. What I decided was to devote all of my energies to looking like I was listening, because if I spent all my time looking like I was listening, I could devote my energies entirely to keeping someone talking at length without interruptions. There is always plenty of opportunity after the fact to listen to what was said in the editing room. You don't have to listen when you are doing the interview.

"It surprises me that many of the interests that I had even before I became a filmmaker have certainly translated into the films that I have made. I like to think that all of my films, in some way, concern the relationship between that real-world fact and the various fictions that we construct about it. Certainly, *The Thin Blue Line* was on one level the story of a real-life murder investigation in Texas. But I also like to think of it as an essay on self-deception, on how we view evidence, on how we perceive the world around us. *A Brief History of Time* is also a story about someone trying to understand what might be out there in the universe. Stephen Hawking's mother, at the very end of the movie, speaks very, very eloquently and very movingly about her son. It's not the case that Stephen Hawking is in possession of certain truth, that he knows all there is to know about the universe. In his mother's words, he's a searcher—he is a person involved in trying to understand more about the world, of trying to uncover truth. And in my own small way, I like to think that I'm involved in some similar enterprise."

ERROL MORRIS also directed *Gates of Heaven; Vernon, Florida; The Dark Wind;* and *Fast, Cheap & Out of Control.*

and can be let off the hook for the sake of family harmony, that no one is truly innocent so everyone is somewhat guilty, and a lot of other rubbish that a good cast can't redeem. (Cast Note: Gia Carides and Anthony LaPaglia are real-life husband and wife.)

1996 93m/C *AU* Gia Carides, Anthony LaPaglia, Zoe Carides, Ray Barrett, Michael Veitch, Neil Melville, Catherine Wilkin, Grant Tilly; ***D:*** Richard Franklin; ***W:*** Richard Franklin, Peter Fitzpatrick; ***C:*** Geoff Burton; ***M:*** Nevida Tyson-Chew. Nominations: Australian Film Institute '95: Best Actress (Carides), Best Supporting Actor (Barrett), Best Supporting Actress (Carides). **VHS**

Brother's Keeper

In both *Brother's Keeper* and *Paradise Lost: The Child Murders of Robin Hood Hills,* the filmmakers take a look at a murder case in which community members have pretty much made up their minds about the innocence or guilt of the accused. There is also a heavily charged side issue in each case to cloud the evidence: in *Keeper,* it's incest; in *Paradise,* it's Satanism. I've heard audience members for both films insist that it's SO obvious what REALLY happened. (To them, maybe, but not to me!) Joe Berlinger and Bruce Sinofsky succeed in building reasonable doubts, which is all any investigative reporters can hope to do. There is one gory bloodletting sequence that has nothing to do with the rest of the story, but it emphasizes the pervasive atmosphere that the people in *Brother's Keeper* belong in another time and place, not in the New York countryside of the early 1990s.

The Hound Salutes:

JOE BERLINGER

Documentarian, *Brother's Keeper* and *Paradise Lost: The Child Murders at Robin Hood Hills* (with Bruce Sinofsky)

Jessie Miskelly Jr. [serving a life sentence] had his appeal at the state level an February 19, 1996, and he was not given a new trial. The Arkansas State Supreme Court determined that his confession, which was what his appeal was based on, was valid, so he was denied a new trial and then he tried for an appeal at the federal level. Jason Baldwin [serving a life sentence] and Damian Wayne Echols [on Death Row] had their appeals at the state level on December 9, 1996, and our hope was that this film [*Paradise Lost*], which created quite a stir in Arkansas, would have some sort of an effect. [Their appeals were rejected on December 23, 1996.] People have been quite shocked by some of the things that the local press never reported, but that are included in our film. We felt it was very important to ground people in the horror of the crime. Unfortunately, in our society, we turn on the news and there are up to 15 horrible stories every night and we tend to tune them out. There's only 45 seconds of admittedly very graphic police footage, but we felt that by actually showing the bodies of the eight-year-old boys [Steven Branch, Christopher Byers, and Michael Moore], it was the only way to show just how horrible the crime was. We wanted people to realize that and pay attention. More importantly, our film is about a community's desire for revenge without rational thought. There were so many holes in the prosecution's case. To begin to understand how a community could have this venomous hatred and the need for revenge without considering all those holes in the case, we wanted to give viewers a clue as to how they could become that way. The

1992 104m/C *D:* Joe Berlinger, Bruce Sinofsky; ***C:*** Douglas Cooper. National Board of Review Awards '92: Best Feature Documentary; New York Film Critics Awards '92: Best Feature Documentary; Sundance Film Festival '92: Audience Award. **VHS, LV**

The Brothers McMullen

This overpraised indie about three Irish Catholic brothers in Long Island, New York, is a guaranteed button pusher for Irish Catholic women, which is why I originally disqualified myself from reviewing it. (Hey, is anyone out there laboring under the delusion that movie reviewers are objective ROBOTS? Dream on, baby!) Ed Burns' next movie, *She's the One,* was widely panned, but the fact is they're both practically the same AVERAGE movie. Shortly before the release of the very funny date movie, *The Truth About Cats and Dogs,* Janeane Garafalo did stand-up at San Francisco's Punch Line and UNrecommended this one as a date movie. It is mortally depressing to think of guys as adolescents from the obstetrics ward to the funeral parlor, but *The Brothers McMullen* reinforces this largely accepted (and often true) myth about Irish Catholic men. That's why Irish Catholic women (often) hesitate before marrying them. Jack is married to a perfectly nice woman and has an affair with an irresponsible hedonist (or so Burns'

crime was so shocking, so horrifying, that we can understand the community's need to want to find the killer at all costs even if it meant setting aside some of the obvious questions in the prosecution's case. We debated it; in the first cut of the film, the police footage ran for three minutes and ultimately we wound up with 45 seconds. It seems longer and it is horrifying, but the way we looked at it, there's 150 minutes in the film and about 150 seconds of that is graphic footage, but it does stay with you.

"Since Bruce Sinofsky and I were both expectant fathers at the time, we each paid a very high emotional price by making *Paradise Lost.* Our previous film, *Brother's Keeper,* was a fairy tale by comparison. Making this film was a nightmare. We'd spend mornings with the families of the victims—they'd be spewing out venom and hatred. Then we'd spend afternoons with the families of the accused—they couldn't understand why people were vilifying them and why they weren't looking more closely at the prosecution's case. At night, we'd go back to our hotel rooms, thinking about the images we'd seen and all we'd heard and we'd just want to cry. The fact that our wives were pregnant while we were making this film—and that while editing this film, we each had a child—at times meant that the contrast between our nice comfortable homes with beautiful children and the images on our editing machines was simply too much to take. *Paradise Lost* is an important film with an important message: Sometimes there are people in prison for crimes they didn't commit. It's true that Damian Wayne Echols is a weird, strange character and a little frightening, but in this country, there's got to be more than weirdness to land you on Death Row. There are definitely some personality traits that we found alarming while making this film, but the bottom line is that the State of Arkansas had no case against these three kids and just because somebody's weird and strange, it doesn't mean that he's a baby killer."

Other Berlinger/Sinofsky projects include *Where It's At: The Rolling Stone State of the Union* (ABC, 1998) and *Paradise Lost: Revisited* (HBO, 1999).

script suggests) who IS responsible for two things: Jack's lapse from (1) his religious faith, and (2) his marital vows. Barry wants to be a writer and his perfectly nice girlfriend will interfere with that (or so Burns' script suggests), so quite a lot of screen time is devoted to that. Patrick is engaged to marry a Jewish-American princess, whose father would set him up for life, but he's seriously interested in a (lapsed Catholic) woman who wants to hit the road with him if he'll pay for half of the new car. Oh, and did you know that it's easy to be a Good Catholic if you marry your one True Love? Got an extra 98 minutes for burning issues like these? How about 193 minutes for a mediocre double feature that also includes *She's the One?* (Newcomer Maxine Bahns is charming in each flick.) 🦴🦴

1994 (R) 98m/C Edward Burns, Jack Mulcahy, Mike McGlone, Connie Britton, Shari Albert, Elizabeth P. McKay, Maxine Bahns, Jennifer Jostyn, Catharine Bolt, Peter Johansen; ***D:*** Edward Burns; ***W:*** Edward Burns; ***C:*** Dick Fisher; ***M:*** Seamus Egan. Independent Spirit Awards '96: Best First Feature; Sundance Film Festival '95: Grand Jury Prize. **VHS, Closed Caption**

Bulldog Drummond

It's hard to sit through early talkies made in 1929, even if they've been archivally restored until they're as glistening as the day they were released. There are, of

Erma Peterson (Lilyan Tashman) and "Bulldog" Drummond (Ronald Colman) in *Bulldog Drummond.* United Artists; courtesy of the Kobal Collection

course, exceptions: Alfred Hitchcock's *Blackmail,* F. Richard Jones' *Bulldog Drummond,* ahm....ahm...ahm...and I'm thinking it over! Well, definitely *Blackmail* and *Bulldog Drummond,* anyway. *Blackmail* also exists as a breezy silent film, but the charm of *Bulldog Drummond* is to hear, for the very first time, the beautiful voice of Ronald Colman, then 38, in the title role. Independent producer Samuel Goldwyn may not have been the first to crack the new market, but he was far and away the classiest. Captain Hugh Drummond is bored out of his skull, so he takes out a *London Times* advertisement announcing that he's ready for adventure. Phyllis Benton (Joan Bennett, then 19) asks him to rescue her uncle (Charles Sellon as Hiram J. Travers) from the clutches of the villainous Dr. Lakington (Lawrence Grant). Drummond and his loyal buddy Algy Longworth (Claud Allister) are on the job! Unlike many creaky vehicles of this transitional era, *Bulldog Drummond* moves at a breathless clip and there's even time for a 70-year-old gag about halitosis, drolly communicated to one of the bad guys by Bulldog: "Even your best friends won't tell you." It's also a treat to see Lilyan Tashman as the nasty femme fatale Erma. (Tashman was one of Hollywood's best-dressed blondes until her early death in 1934.) Everything about the production is fresh and funny and audiences clamored to pay the $2 (pre-Depression) admission fee. Colman worked 18-hour days to earn his first Oscar nomination for this one, although he finally demanded a less exhausting schedule. He made 26 more films over the next 28 years and finally won an Oscar on his third try for 1947's *A Double Life.* And Bennett, less alluring as a blonde than as the bottle brunette she would become in 1938, still had a sense of her own worth by refusing to make a screen test. (She was still working 75 films later, well into her 70s.) Based on the novel by Herman Cyril "Sapper" McNeile and the play by McNeile and Gerald DuMaurier.

1929 **85m/B** Ronald Colman, Joan Bennett, Montagu Love, Lilyan Tashman, Lawrence Grant, Wilson Benge, Claud Allister, Adolph Milar, Charles Sellon, Tetsu Komai, Donald Novis; ***D:*** F. Richard Jones; ***W:*** Sidney Howard, Wallace Smith; ***C:*** George Barnes, Gregg Toland. Nominations: Academy Awards '30: Best Actor (Colman), Best Interior Decoration, Best Interior Decoration. **VHS, LV**

Bullets over Broadway

This valentine to Broadway is a full notch above Tay Garnett's *Main Street to Broadway,* a star-studded fest that crammed the best theatrical troupers of that era (including wonderful Tallulah Bankhead) into a slight story about a first-time playwright (newcomer Tom Morton, whom no one got a chance to remember before he was forgotten). *Bullets'* story line involving fledgling writer David Shayne (John Cusack) basically functions as an immobile jungle gym around which colorful characters do cartwheels with intriguing subplots. Best of all are gangster Chazz Palminteri and his boss' no-talent girlfriend Jennifer Tilly, who both want to break into show business in the worst way. (Now why couldn't they have been cast in 1993's *Born Yesterday?*) The atmosphere and period details are simultaneously faithful and satirical. Every stock company has an idol whom the other members tolerate, but the audiences worship (that would be chain-eating Jim Broadbent here). Dianne Wiest, if not in Bankhead's league, won an Oscar as the stage diva who's on 24 hours a day, and Rob Reiner, Mary-Louise Parker, and Joe Viterelli add to the background flavor. You won't mind a bit that Cusack, at the center of this infectious whirlwind of energy, fades into the wallpaper most of the time.

1994 (R) 106m/C Dianne Wiest, John Cusack, Jennifer Tilly, Rob Reiner, Chazz Palminteri, Tracey Ullman, Mary-Louise Parker, Joe Viterelli, Jack Warden, Jim Broadbent, Harvey Fierstein, Annie-Joe Edwards; ***D:*** Woody Allen; ***W:*** Woody Allen, Douglas McGrath; ***C:*** Carlo Di Palma. Academy Awards '94: Best Supporting Actress (Wiest); Golden Globe Awards '95: Best Supporting Actress (Wiest); Independent Spirit Awards '95: Best Supporting Actor (Palminteri), Best Supporting Actress (Wiest); Los Angeles Film Critics Association Awards '94: Best Supporting Actress (Wiest); New York Film Critics Awards '94: Best Supporting Actress (Wiest); National Society of Film Critics Awards '94: Best Supporting Actress (Wiest); Screen Actors Guild Award '94: Best Supporting Actress (Wiest); Nominations: Academy Awards '94: Best Art Direction/Set Decoration, Best Costume Design, Best Director (Allen), Best Original Screenplay, Best Supporting Actor (Palminteri), Best Supporting Actress (Tilly); British Academy Awards '95: Best Original Screenplay; Independent Spirit Awards '95: Best Film, Best Screenplay. **VHS, LV, Closed Caption**

Burnt by the Sun

Burnt by the Sun deservedly won an Oscar for Best Foreign Language Film of 1994. It captures a heartbreakingly lovely summer day in the country. Bolshevik hero Serguei Kotov is madly in love with his wife and small daughter and their life together is joyful and serene. The arrival of his wife's former lover Dimitri appears to be no more than a catch-up-on-the-past visit at first. But gradually, Serguei realizes that he is about to give his family the ultimate gift: a treasured memory and the secure knowledge of his love for them. Director Nikita Mikhalkov skillfully weaves the light-hearted ambiance of a happy family with vaguely disturbing sexual games, far more disquieting political undercurrents, and finally, sheer horror. The unclouded sweetness of the relationship between Serguei and his little girl is beautifully conveyed by Mikhalkov and his real-life daughter Nadia. ***AKA:*** Outomlionnye Solntsem.

1994 (R) 134m/C *RU FR* Nikita Mikhalkov, Ingeborga Dapkounaite, Oleg Menshikov, Nadia Mikhalkov, Andre Oumansky, Viatcheslav Tikhonov, Svetlana Krioutchkova, Vladimir Ilyine; ***D:*** Nikita Mikhalkov; ***W:*** Nikita Mikhalkov, Rustam Ibragimbekov; ***C:*** Vilen Kalyuta; ***M:*** Eduard Artemyev. Academy Awards '94: Best Foreign Film; Cannes Film Festival '94: Grand Jury Prize; Nominations: Australian Film Institute '96: Best Foreign Film; British Academy Awards '95: Best Foreign Film. **VHS, LV**

Bury Me Dead

A movie as good as *The Amazing Mr. X* made me wonder if director Bernard Vorhaus and cinematographer John Alton worked together on anything else. They did, but the results were very different. *Bury Me Dead* originated as a radio drama by Irene Winston and was adapted for the

For those who were burnt by the sun of the revolution.

—Tagline from the movie *Burnt by the Sun.*

screen by Dwight V. Babcock and Karen De Wolf. Someone, somewhere, thought that he just might be able to make another *Laura* on the cheap. June Lockhart is Barbara Carlin, who attends her own funeral and then surprises her husband's lawyer, Michael Dunn (Hugh Beaumont) by hopping into his car afterwards. One by one, she further surprises the people who thought she was dead: her husband Rod (Mark Daniels), her troubled sister Rusty (Cathy O'Donnell), a flirtatious boxer (Greg McClure), the ghoulish butler (Milton Parsons), and so on. It must be noted that the costumes and sets here are ghastly, even for a grade-Z entry like this. Furthermore, the script is crammed with gallows humor—up to six funereal jokes in a row in one sequence. And as a special treat, neither Daniels nor McClure can act his way out of a paper bag and both left acting early to pursue other interests (television direction for Daniels, a singles bar for McClure), much to the relief of grade-Z film buffs everywhere. June Lockhart, however, is cute; her assurance at age 22 reminds you why she was able to sustain a 60-year career, from *A Christmas Carol* through *Beverly Hills 90210.* Cathy O'Donnell, no longer under the direction of her brother-in-law William *(Best Years of Our Lives)* Wyler, is less successful here as a vixen. She's SO sweet and soulful-looking; who'd ever believe HER as a bad girl? Also suffering from the loss of an A-list director (in her case, *The Big Sleep*'s Howard Hawks) is Sonia Darrin as temptress Helen Lawrence, wearing the worst clothes in the film. She evolves from bathing beauty to Amazon to a vamp so scrawny that her hip bones nearly pop out of her dress. Charles Lane plays a verbose police investigator who barely gives a suspect a chance to say one syllable! The guy next to me solved the mystery 40 minutes after the opening credits. You might get the impression from all of the above that *Bury Me Dead* is better buried. It is, in fact, a real hoot, and I wish it WERE on video or even late night television SOMEWHERE. ♪♪♪

1947 68m/B June Lockhart, Hugh Beaumont, Cathy O'Donnell, Mark Daniels, Sonia Darrin, Greg McClure, Virginia Farmer, Milton Parsons, Peggy Castle, Cliff Clark, John Dehner, Ned Glass, Charles Lane; ***D:*** Bernard Vorhaus; ***W:*** Dwight V. Babcock, Karen De Wolf; ***C:*** John Alton; ***M:*** Emil Cadkin.

Business As Usual

Economic sanctions may be the only thing that sexual bullies understand. This is the point that a gutsy young working-class filmmaker, Lezli-Ann Barrett, makes with her first movie, *Business As Usual.* Glenda Jackson plays the "manageress" of a Liverpool boutique to whom model Cathy Tyson appeals for help against the unwelcome advances of Mr. Barry, the area manager. None too thrilled to be caught in the middle, Jackson's character nonetheless complains to Barry, who promptly fires her without written notice. When she later asks for the reason for her dismissal in writing, Barry, who has already hired her replacement, has her removed from the store by the police. Her husband, a former embattled union leader, has lost his spirit and fears that she will lose hers by fighting back. However, her father and son, both labor organizers, are full of fight and urge her to enlist the help of her union. One of the interesting elements in *Business As Usual* is that the film shows how union leaders are sometimes willing to make harsh compromises with management in order to relieve tense labor struggles. By showing Jackson's husband (wonderfully played by John Thaw) as a defeated, weary, intensely proud man whose finest combats are behind him, Barrett's script also shows what an exhausting thing it is to fight on behalf of other workers. And the film certainly does not glamorize the long hours of picketing, the police harassment, and the media trivialization of sexual harassment issues. Barrett's screenplay is also interesting for her sensitive depiction of Tyson's boyfriend, well played by poet Craig Charles, Tyson's real-life husband. In the movies, targets of harassment are often aligned with some drippy character who first blames the victim and then withdraws emotional support. Tyson perfectly captures the pain and confusion of the harassment target and her scenes alone with

Charles are tender and believable. The source of all this agony, Mr. Barry, is hardly a villain, just an average, run-of-the-mill jerk, who thinks that downgrading women is funny. As portrayed by Eamon Boland, he is not particularly bright and rather frightened of both men and women. All that is beside the point, of course, when he tries to halt a woman's career simply because she sees through his games. Production values on *Business As Usual* are deliberately gritty, a far cry from the glossy films in which Jackson usually stars. When Barrett got nowhere trying to submit her scripts to Jackson through an agent, she went to see her in a play and personally asked her to read the script. Even with Jackson's acceptance, it took years for Barrett to raise the money and attract the connections that, luckily for viewers, made *Business As Usual* possible. Note: In real life, Jackson won a Labor seat in Parliament in 1992. 𝒱𝒱𝒱

1988 (PG) 89m/C Glenda Jackson, Cathy Tyson, John Thaw, Craig Charles, Eamon Boland; ***D:*** Lezli-Ann Barrett; ***W:*** Lezli-Ann Barrett; ***C:*** Ernest Vincze. **VHS, Closed Caption**

Butley

It's hard to imagine a story in which a man loses both his wife and his best friend in the same day could possibly be slow-paced. But it IS, and only Alan Bates' powerhouse performance in the title role keeps Simon Gray's attenuated structure from falling apart. If Jimmy Porter, the angry young man of the late John Osborne's *Look Back in Anger* had made it past the 1950s and gone on to be a university professor, he might have become just such a man as Butley. True, Butley does not have Jimmy Porter's savagery; he has replaced that with a humorous attitude that is both appealing and aggravating. He has become A Difficult Bloke to Understand. He's too pathetic to be truly comic, and too lacking in irony to be truly tragic. Nor does he have the richness of character that might at least make him a tragicomic figure. He stumbles through life, anyway, annoying the hell out of everyone in such a charming way that it is hard for anyone to leave him. But leave him they do, and this is what *Butley* is all about. There's not much else here: one dull office setting, people walking in and out. We meet these people only briefly, and we see them chiefly through Butley's eyes. We also hear far too many discussions of characters we only catch a glimpse of, or worse, never meet at all. Through it all, Bates injects passion into every one of his lines. Butley may be sloppy, lazy, and frustrated, but he is also filled with an intellectual vitality, and Bates makes the struggles of this man, lugging around both a liquor bottle and his long-unfinished book about T.S. Eliot in his briefcase, wholly worth two hours of our concern and attention. The late Jessica Tandy (1909–94) plays Edna Shaft, the only other role of any length. (*Butley* won the Evening Standard award as Best Play and was a 1973 Tony nominee for Best Play. Bates won the Tony for Best Dramatic Actor. *Butley* was released theatrically overseas in 1976.) An American Film Theatre production. 𝒱𝒱𝒱

1974 127m/C *GB CA* Alan Bates, Jessica Tandy, Richard O'Callaghan, Susan Engel, Michael Byrne, Georgina Hale, Simon Rouse, John Savident, Oliver Maguire, Susan Wooldridge; ***D:*** Harold Pinter; ***W:*** Simon Gray; ***C:*** Gerry Fisher. **VHS**

Butterfly Kiss

The May 1996 issue of *Films in Review* arrived three months late, as usual. It featured pages and pages about the so-called Golden Age of Hollywood, attenuated reviews of movies that have been out for ages, and a color cover shot of Dian Hanson. (Who?) But this quaint little publication also seemed to contain a few words of warning for folks like, well, me. It appears that contributor Rocco Simonelli is steamed about audience members with the NOIVE not to like Michael Winterbottom's *Butterfly Kiss,* starring Amanda Plummer and Saskia Reeves. Says Rocco: "It's viewers such as yourselves who are the true cause of Hollywood's decline in recent years, its pervasive unwillingness to take chances. The next time you're bitching about the tedium and lack of

"Killing people is nothing. I've done much worse than kill people."

—Eunice (Amanda Plummer) in *Butterfly Kiss.*

imagination embodied by most Hollywood fare, remember it was YOU who wielded the knife." Gee, Rocco, we thought that was Amanda Plummer! As far as we can recall, we sent all our knives to the cleaners before we saw *Butterfly Kiss.* Even if it didn't have Michael Winterbottom's mitts all over it, you wouldn't have to tell us it was a guy who came up with yet another psycho lesbian movie. What is so daring and innovative about *Basic Instinct* or *Single White Female*? Lesbian looney-tunes have been around at least as long as the early days of the silent flickers. Loving women equals killing people, especially men, and usually after sex. It goes with this particular stretch of cinematic territory. Casting Amanda Plummer as the homicidal Eunice is rather stacking the deck, because she can be every bit as much of a ham as her dad Christopher. The only surprise here is Saskia Reeves as Eunice's submissive lover Miriam. Reeves photographs entirely differently in color than she does in black and white. Through most of the film, Miriam drags herself through life like a wimpy Sigourney Weaver, but in black and white, she reveals flashes of wit, humor, and irony in the best tradition of Maggie Smith. This despite Winterbottom's edict for Reeves to make Miriam flat and boring. And what do lesbians do in the daytime besides get rid of the bodies they carved up the night before? After a 1996 screening at San Francisco's Lesbian and Gay Film Festival, *Butterfly Kiss* had a brief commercial run at nationwide Landmark Theatres, then made a fast flight to video. **woof!**

1994 85m/C *GB* Amanda Plummer, Saskia Reeves, Paul Brown, Des McAleer, Ricky Tomlinson; ***D:*** Michael Winterbottom; ***W:*** Frank Cottrell Boyce; ***C:*** Seamus McGarvey; ***M:*** John Harle. **VHS**

Cabeza de Vaca

I'm always leery of movies with the proviso "Patient viewers will be rewarded." That usually means that I will feel bored and guilty for 90 to 120 minutes, wondering what in the world is happening onscreen that is so blazingly wonderful. *Cabeza de Vaca* has received some nice notices from *Daily Variety,* the *Village Voice,* the *L.A. Times,* and *Time* magazine, but I felt like I wandered into Ethnography 101 by mistake. There is no character you can care about one way or the other with the exception of a short guy with no arms who yells a lot. The action takes place in the early 16th century and revolves around a Spanish explorer who lives among the Indians for eight years. There is more blood than dialogue in the movie, a bit of magic here and there, and the obligatory bare chest whenever a rare female drifts into focus. Thinking that the film might appeal more to men than to women, I asked for another opinion from a male viewer, but *Cabeza de Vaca* left him equally cold. The film on video may very well succeed in attracting a receptive audience who will appreciate this epic, which has been described as a Mexican *Dances with Wolves.* ✂✂

1990 (R) 111m/C *MX SP* Juan Diego, Daniel Gimenez Cacho, Roberto Sosa, Carlos Castanon, Gerardo Villarreal, Roberto Cobo, Jose Flores, Ramon Barragan; ***D:*** Nicolas Echevarria; ***W:*** Guillermo Sheridan, Nicolas Echevarria; ***C:*** Guillermo Navarro; ***M:*** Mario Lavista. **VHS**

Caddie

Based on the true story of an anonymous woman who raised her two children alone after her husband ran off with her best friend, *Caddie* makes a hopeful statement for strong, resilient women who don't spend their lives waiting for a romantic prince to sweep them off their feet, but make the best of circumstances, even when they're dreary. Unable to find any other job but as a bar maid, Caddie works energetically for her kids and herself. Director Donald Crombie suggests that the world is filled with Caddies, worthy of more dignity and respect than they've ever received. At one point, Peter, Caddie's true love from Greece (ably played by Takis Emmanuel), tells her that she isn't like all the other women who work in bars. Her snappy retort is filled with rage at the stereotype. Helen Morse is wonderful as Caddie, persuasively revealing the woman who can tackle everything, even the Great Depression, on her own terms. A guy at the screening I attended mentioned that

Caddie's poverty seemed too beautiful to be real, but I beg to differ. Early in the film, it is revealed that Caddie would transform the most sordid surroundings into a decent place for herself and her family. There ARE women like Caddie in the world and, luckily for us, screenwriter Joan Long wrote about one of them for all the world to see. 𝄢𝄢𝄢

1976 107m/C *AU* Helen Morse, Jack Thompson, Takis Emmanuel, Jacki Weaver; ***D:*** Donald Crombie; ***W:*** Joan Long; ***C:*** Peter James; ***M:*** Patrick Flynn. **VHS**

Cafe Nica: Portraits from Nicaragua

John Knoop's 45-minute documentary *Cafe Nica* is too short to do justice to its subjects, the Nicaraguan people affected by war. The film lacks a strong point of view as well as the depth that would lend meaning to all those fleeting talking heads. 𝄢𝄢

1987 45m/C Rene Auberjonois; ***D:*** John Knoop; ***C:*** John Knoop. **VHS**

Caged

Regardless of the budgetary constraints of *Caged,* which were clearly considerable, the stakes in this San Francisco indie by first-time director Rand Alexander are way too low for a feature. Charlie Caine (Michael Todd) has visions of being a director of commercials rather than the legal depositions his job requires him to record on video. But Charlie's life is as clueless as his ambitions. He goes to a bar to flirt with a girl friend where he knows that another girl friend is a waitress, then complains because the waitress isn't getting the message he's failed to deliver, that He's Moved On. Things get a little violent and the waitress gets hurt, although its obvious she still cares about Charlie. Worst of all, Charlie puts a kettle on the stove and leaves his apartment; the front door swings shut, trapping him between the locked front door and the locked security gate for DAYS. By this point, I'm thinking this guy is too stupid to live or for me to care about. There are funny lines and ideas in *Caged,* but the narrative, which sets up situations and then abandons them, hops all over the place. It's all supposed to be set against the backdrop of San Francisco's swing scene, but the soundtrack is basically wallpapered with old radio transcriptions of big band broadcasts from the 1940s. Videotapes are available through randFilms LTD., 1333 26th Avenue, San Francisco, California 94122. Played at San Francisco's Indie Fest in January 1999. 𝄢

1997 90m/C Denis Liliegren, Samantha Sams, Barry Smith, Pete Marvel, Michael Todd, Rand Alexander, Brent Deal; ***D:*** Rand Alexander; ***W:*** Rand Alexander; ***C:*** Brent Deal.

Camille Claudel

The life of Camille Claudel offers several good answers to the age-old question (probably asked by a man!): "Why are there no great woman artists?" For one thing, many make the mistake of sleeping with great male artists! For another, artistic cliques, standards, and histories are dominated by men. When I first tried to look up Camille Claudel, only recognized as a major sculptor since 1984, her name, predictably, was missing from the encyclopedia, although her brother Paul and her lover Auguste Rodin both received extensive entries. Luckily, her biography by Reine-Marie Paris is available in paperback, extensively illustrated with photographs of Camille's finest sculptures. Camille Claudel is also the focus of the fine French film starring Isabelle Adjani in the title role and Gerard Depardieu as Auguste Rodin. Marilyn Goldin's eloquent screenplay shows how difficult it was for Camille to establish herself as an artist in the late 19th and early 20th century. Like a benevolent despot, Rodin offered Camille a position in his studio, but he sealed himself off to her once their affair was over and he could no longer accept her unique, deeply threatening visions as an artist. According to her biographer, there is some evidence in the Rodin Museum to support Camille's belief that her consignment to artistic obscurity was the work of Rodin. In any event, Camille

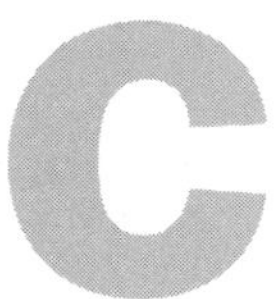

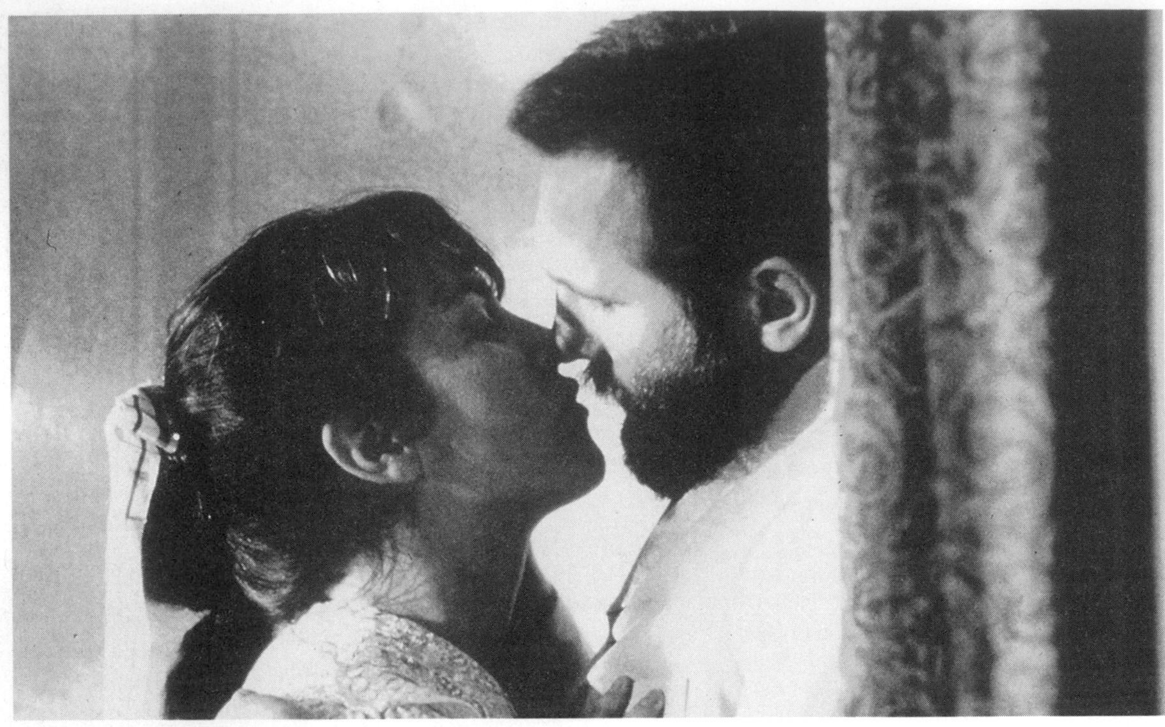

Isabelle Adjani and Gerard Depardieu as Camille Claudel and Auguste Rodin in *Camille Claudel.*
Canon/Fechner/Lilith/Gaumont/A2/DD; courtesy of the Kobal Collection

never recovered from Rodin's rejection; by 1913, her family committed her to an asylum, where she spent the last 30 years of her life before her death at the age of 78. She never sculpted again, although she wrote many lucid letters to her much-loved brother Paul, who was responsible for her confinement. Isabelle Adjani plays Camille to the hilt, perfectly capturing her clashing needs for love and work. Depardieu's Rodin is more of an enigma, but then so are most men who profess to love two women in different ways. Laurent Grevill plays Paul Claudel as a self-righteous drip, but Alain Cuny steals every scene he's in as Camille's father, the only man who seems to love and understand her exactly as she is. Note: A photograph of the real Camille Claudel at age 20 reveals intelligence, pride, strength, and beauty. All are assets for a woman and an artist but, as Bruno Nuytten's disturbing film shows, they are sometimes fatal for a student and a mistress. (In French with English subtitles.) 🦴🦴🦴🦴

1989 (R) 149m/C *FR* Isabelle Adjani, Gerard Depardieu, Laurent Grevill, Alain Cuny, Madeleine Robinson, Katrine Boorman; ***D:*** Bruno Nuytten; ***W:*** Bruno Nuytten, Marilyn Goldin; ***C:*** Pierre Lhomme; ***M:*** Gabriel Yared. Cesar Awards '89: Best Actress (Adjani), Best Art Direction/Set Decoration, Best Cinematography, Best Costume Design, Best Film; Nominations: Academy Awards '89: Best Actress (Adjani), Best Foreign Film. **VHS, LV**

Campfire Tales

Dead of Night initiated a long line of horror movies in which a framing device of people telling stories to each other turned out to be even scarier than the stories. *Campfire Tales* continues that esteemed tradition over half a century later and while not in the same league as its classic inspiration, it's still pretty scary. "The Hook" is a black-and-white nod to drive-in fodder of the '50s, and although it opens and closes the film, it doesn't have anything to do with the rest of the picture. Jay R. Ferguson, Christine Taylor, Kim Murphy, and Christopher Masterson play Cliff, Lauren, Alex, and Eric, four kids out on a joyride who go off the road one night. They tell each other eerie tales about the worst things that can happen on a honeymoon, over the Internet, and in a house that replays its grimmest tragedy over and over again. Then we go back to the kids' story and familiar faces from each tale intersect with their own, but as different characters. The Internet tale is the most disturbing as it shows a pre-teen girl from the perspective of her male stalker on the Internet, who pretends to be another young girl in a chat room, thus gaining access to all sorts of confidential information. Among the joyriders, Christine Taylor registers most strongly as Lauren and Jennifer MacDonald is also quite good as Valerie, a newlywed bride on a honeymoon in hell.

1998 (R) 103m/C James Marsden, Kim Murphy, Christine Taylor, Jay R. Ferguson, Christopher K. Masterson, Ron Livingston, Jennifer MacDonald, Hawthorne James, Alex McKenna, Glenn Quinn, Erick Fleeks, Amy Smart, Rick Lawrence, Suzanne Goddard; ***D:*** David Semel, Martin Kunert, Matt Cooper; ***W:*** Martin Kunert, Matt Cooper, Eric Manes; ***C:*** John Peters; ***M:*** Andrew Rose. **VHS, LV, Closed Caption**

Cannibal Women in the Avocado Jungle of Death

Cannibal Women in the Avocado Jungle of Death was my favorite of all the movies I rented in the month of March, 1990. It features a change of pace role for Shannon Tweed, who was then featured on the Playboy Channel in *Barbi, Shannon and Candy,* a tribute to three former Playmates. In *Cannibal Women,* she plays a feminist anthropology professor. My favorite character in the movie is Bunny, her worst student, who thinks that she's the best one in the class. Bunny, played by Karen *(Return of the Killer Tomatoes)* Mistal, is always talking about her sexual fantasies. The two of them have to go into the jungles of San Bernadino to find another feminist professor, Adrienne Barbeau. They enlist the aid of a fairly useless male guide (played by Bill Maher) with whom Bunny promptly falls in love. You see, Bunny would like to be a feminist, but she never CAN remember which side she's on. Also, she can't quite abandon her sexual fantasies of being wrapped up in red licorice and...love it! Great fun at a video party with plenty of free-spirited friends.

1989 (PG-13) 90m/C Shannon Tweed, Adrienne Barbeau, Karen Mistal, Barry Primus, Bill Maher; ***D:*** J.F. Lawton; ***W:*** J.F. Lawton. **VHS, LV, Closed Caption, DVD**

Careful

Careful is receiving the sort of ecstatic (and strategically placed) reviews that assure it a place in cult movie circles for many years to come. On the basis of its unique visual style alone, it is well worth a look, but whether *Careful* succeeds in luring you into its spell may depend on your ability to accept the artistic choices of its director, Guy Maddin. *Careful* is a movie I found easy to admire but hard to love, and I tried. Its striking use of colors; its playful nod to scratchy soundtracks, intertitles, and other outdated film conventions; its sincere attempt to reveal how repression ignites overwhelming passion—all provide clear evidence of the quirky and original talent of its director. But ultimately, Guy Maddin's limited abilities as a storyteller are not equal to his ambitious visions. His characters are more like puppets than flesh-and-blood people. If they make a sound when they are sexually aroused, they may be buried by an avalanche, a theoretically intriguing dilemma, but less than riveting to observe even when accompanied by a bag of visual tricks. None of the folks in this movie affect us quite as deeply as when they are in repose and no emotion or language gets in the way. Maddin's use of formal speech patterns is deliberate. The script was translated from English into Icelandic and then back again. Intellectuals may worship this approach, but I found it as draining as all the overproduced set pieces in Sergei Eisenstein's *Ivan the Terrible,* another so-called classic that's difficult to be moved by, however great it is to watch. Recommended for viewing after *Careful:* the great Gosia Do-

Rosealee and Joseph (Amy Irving and Dennis Hopper) in *Carried Away.*
Fine Line; courtesy of the Kobal Collection

browolska, rather underused here, in John Dingwall's Australian classic *Phobia,* which wrings more emotion out of two characters on a single set than Maddin does in this kaleidoscopic romp in a Canadian grain elevator. 𝄞𝄞

1992 100m/C Kyle McCulloch, Gosia Dobrowolska, Jackie Burroughs, Sarah Neville, Brent Neale, Paul Cox, Victor Cowie, Michael O'Sullivan, Vince Rimmer, Katya Gardner; ***D:*** Guy Maddin; ***W:*** Guy Maddin, George Toles; ***C:*** Guy Maddin; ***M:*** John McCulloch. **VHS**

Carmen Miranda: Bananas Is My Business

Carmen Miranda. The name alone conjures up memories of Technicolor Fox musicals of the '40s at their zenith. Carmen Miranda was a bundle of energy and mischief, and the first Brazilian entertainer to become an international superstar. She was also to solidify the Latina standard for the silver screen. As Rita Moreno, who won an Academy Award six years after Miranda's death, observed wryly, "We had to be peppy. But I wanted to be an actress." After *West Side Story,* the versatile Moreno made no movies for years. But if Carmen Miranda ever chafed at being a high-priced specialty act, she never seemed to show it, at least not onscreen. *Carmen Miranda: Bananas Is My Business,* Helena Solberg's documentary of her legendary career, is mainly valuable for its rare film clips, dating back to the '30s. But the subtext, that Miranda was "Our Carmen," namely Brazil's own, tends to grate after awhile. Once Miranda left Brazil for first Broadway and then Hollywood, she returned just three times in 16 years, once to be treated with indifference by upper-crust Brazilian audiences, once to recover from exhaustion, and finally for her funeral. It was because little Helena's parents wouldn't let her join the million people lining the streets for the services

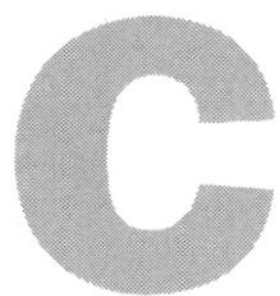

that she became obsessed with Carmen Miranda's complicated relationship with her homeland. But the evidence she chooses to illustrate her theories is largely supplied by subjective voiceovers and a few interviews with wistful friends, family, colleagues, and employees. Nowhere is it made clear that Miranda wanted any other life than the one she had. True, she died young, on the very night that a television performance left her breathless. (The actual clip is shown in slow motion.) But dying young doesn't necessarily mean living unhappily, and the unsupported gossip that Solberg includes only reveal her own iconographic obsession, not the real Carmen Miranda. If you want to know the real Carmen Miranda, rent one of her many festive movies on video: *Down Argentine Way, Weekend in Havana,* and *Springtime in the Rockies* are three of her best Fox vehicles; *A Date with Judy* and *Nancy Goes to Rio* are two examples of her years at MGM; *Doll Face* and *Lucky Stiff,* which are minor showcases of her work, are fun to watch today; *Copacabana* co-starring Groucho Marx has been colorized recently to fairly good advantage; and, best of all, *The Gang's All Here* is a constant cable attraction. (That's the Busby Berkeley confection in which Carmen Miranda immortalized "The Lady with the Tutti Frutti Hat" for posterity.) It's sad that Carmen Miranda probably loved Brazil far more than Brazil ever loved her back. Her legacy of 14 musicals ensures that she will be remembered far longer than the native audiences who scorned her for her success. ♪♪♪

1995 92m/C Helena Solberg, Alice Faye, Rita Moreno, Cesar Romero; ***D:*** Helena Solberg; ***W:*** Helena Solberg; ***C:*** Tomasz Magierski. **VHS**

Carnival of Souls

For many years, *Carnival of Souls* was my idea of a genuinely scary movie, far more frightening than *Frankenstein* or *Dracula.* In fact, if I watched *Carnival of Souls* while babysitting, I wanted to wake up all the kids so they could protect me from its terrors. *Carnival of Souls* was the only feature ever made by Herk Harvey, who was stiffed by distributors in 1962 and never made a dime on the film's original release. The film became a late-night television staple and gradually acquired a loyal audience. Harvey eventually bought back the movie rights and 1989 audiences were finally able to see his original uncut version in a 35mm print. Paradoxically, Harvey's film succeeds because and in spite of its tiny budget. The amateur performances and script banalities demand considerable viewer patience. With more generous funding, though, the film might have strayed from the once-in-a-lifetime cast and claustrophobic settings which make it so distinctive. We know we're not in Hollywood anymore from the very beginning. The flat Kansas landscapes and untrained faces have little connection with the cultural symbols that saturate most of the big studio films of 1962. We're light years away from the Warner Bros. and Paramount studios that are processing *The Music Man* and Elvis Presley musicals. A pretty girl appears to be the victim of a drowning accident, only she picks herself up and travels to another town where she is hired as a church organist and moves into a boarding house. As portrayed by Candace Hilligoss, the girl is extremely sensitive to her surroundings yet somehow disconnected from them. A slimy fellow boarder tries to pick her up. She vacillates between fending him off and encouraging his attention. She shops for clothes in a local department store until she realizes that no one can see her or hear her. She practices on the church organ until she discovers that she has no control over what she plays. She tries to get out of town only to be confronted with one obstacle after another. A psychiatrist and a priest offer empty reassurances. A Carnival of Souls beckons her to accept her true fate. *Frankenstein* and *Dracula* provide us with plenty of cheap thrills, but we are unlikely to bump into either of them in real life. All of us WILL come face to face with our own mortality, and *Carnival of Souls* reminds us that, no matter how much we resist, the outcome is inevitable. ♪♪♪

"It was as though for a time I didn't exist, as though I had no place in the world...I've no desire for the close contact of other people. I don't seem capable of being close to people."

—Mary Henry (Candace Hilligoss) explores her feelings with her doctor in *Carnival of Souls.*

1962 80m/B Candace Hilligoss, Sidney Berger, Frances Feist, Stan Levitt, Art Ellison, Harold (Herk) Harvey; ***D:*** Harold (Herk) Harvey; ***W:*** John Clifford; ***C:*** Maurice Prather. **VHS, LV**

Carried Away

Watching movies can be DANGEROUS! No, really. I read a decent review of this movie and went dashing out to see it before it closed. The first thing that happens, there's this jagged metal THING in the seat in front of me that gashes my knee and I'm bleeding all over a sticky theatre floor littered with dried-up popcorn and trampled-on bubble gum. Drat, and I left my hydrogen peroxide at home in the medicine cabinet. Like any dedicated movie buff, I let my knee heal itself for 107 minutes *sans* disinfectant. Was it worth it in this case? Uh...no. First off, Dennis Hopper is 60 here, and what's more, he looks older, as in WAY older. It looks like Amy Irving is meant to be his contemporary here, although she's actually 17 years younger. Even glammed down, she still looks WAY younger. Then there's seductress Amy Locane, who's really 25, but is meant to be 17. ("That," says a 16-year-old of my acquaintance, "is what grown-ups think teenagers look like. Any teenager knows what a teenager looks like.") But if they're all good actors, who cares? Now, if a 60-year-old *actress* is going with a 43-year-old *actor* who's supposed to be the same age and the *actress* is also having sex with a 25-year-old *actor* who's supposed to be 17, you'd hear "Get out of town!" way faster than you can say, "But they're all good actors!" Anyway, Hopper is Joseph Svendon, a teacher and a farmer with a limp who takes care of his frail mother (Julie Harris). He's keeping company with Irving as Rosealee Henson until Locane as Catherine Wheeler swings into his life. Catherine knows just how to vamp Joseph by expanding her chest while she's wearing a tight shirt, so they have sex right away and lots of it. Rosealee senses it and old Dr. Evan (Hal Holbrook) warns him about it, but what's an old guy like Joseph to do? Catherine *asked* for it. An extremely fit-looking Gary Busey, 52, is Major Nathan Wheeler, Catherine's father. From his very first appearance, I kept thinking how much better *Carried Away* would have been if Busey and Hopper had swapped roles from the start. Anyway, the situation goes on and on and there's full frontal nudity of Hopper and Irving, yet the picture as a whole is cool, clinical, and not very erotic. Even without a knee gash, I wasn't carried away by *Carried Away.* Its one asset for me is Busey, otherwise I'd give it a WOOF! Based on the Jim Thompson novel *Farmer.* ***AKA:*** Acts of Love.

1995 (R) 107m/C Dennis Hopper, Amy Irving, Amy Locane, Gary Busey, Julie Harris, Hal Holbrook, Christopher Pettiet, Priscilla Pointer, Gail Cronauer; ***D:*** Bruno Barreto; ***W:*** Ed Jones; ***C:*** Declan Quinn; ***M:*** Bruce Broughton. **VHS, LV, Closed Caption**

Carrington

People who say that a woman is ahead of her time are usually men. Since so little is expected of them, women often follow paths that make more sense to them as individuals than to anyone else, including many of their male biographers. Dora Carrington was an early 20th century eccentric and a wonderful painter. She fell in love with the witty, sickly, and broke gay writer Lytton Strachey. Although she didn't fully realize it until he was on his deathbed, Strachey fell in love with her, too. They lived together for many years, meeting their sexual needs with other partners, but arranging their entire lives so they could be together. Writer/director Christopher Hampton goes into considerable detail about the financial arrangements the two have to make to live together, and I'm afraid I lost track of the count and the amount during one of Carrington's many affairs. But Jonathan Pryce and Emma Thompson are just dear as the unlikely couple who wrote their own rules in the idyllic English countryside. What do they see in each other? It's only obvious. He is honest, charming, and fun; she is loyal, loving, and unique. Except for Strachey, Carrington is accountable to no one but herself, certainly not to a spouse or her many lovers. But she's as strung on Strachey as a woman can be. Strachey's light, dry, satirical books are still in print, including his biography of Queen Victoria, which is considered to be his masterpiece. For his time, Strachey's biographical approach was revolutionary; no previous writer had succeeded in revealing an icon like Victoria in such deeply human terms. Jonathan Pryce does a beautiful job showing just why Lytton Strachey captivated his generation, and Emma Thompson is an ideal foil as his much-loved companion who is quirky to everyone but herself. Art critics (who rarely ever wrote about her before this movie) complain that we don't get to see enough of Carrington's work in the film, but we don't get to read any of Strachey's work here either. This is above all a sensitively rendered love story, and Hampton and cast deserve high marks for making *Carrington* so vital and real to contemporary audiences.

1995 (R) 120m/C *FR GB* Emma Thompson, Jonathan Pryce, Steven Waddington, Samuel West, Rufus Sewell, Penelope Wilton, Jeremy Northam, Peter Blythe, Janet McTeer, Alex Kingston, Sebastian Harcombe, Richard Clifford; ***D:*** Christopher Hampton; ***W:*** Christopher Hampton; ***C:*** Denis Lenoir; ***M:*** Michael Nyman. Cannes Film Festival '95: Special Jury Prize, Best Actor (Pryce); National Board of Review Awards '95: Best Actress (Thompson); Nominations: British Academy Awards '95: Best Actor (Pryce), Best Film. **VHS, LV**

Castaway

The advertisements for *Castaway* promised romance on an idyllic island. This sort of promotion may be a publicist's dream, but audiences expecting a Harlequin-style fantasy won't find one in this 1987 Nicolas Roeg film starring Oliver Reed and newcomer Amanda Donohoe. Instead, the film asks author Lucy Irvine's question, "Why do I have to be stuck on an island with him of all people, in such a potentially wonderful situation?" At 25, Lucy, a former clerk, monkey keeper, and waitress, was looking for adventure when she responded to Gerald Kingsland's magazine ad: "Writer seeks 'wife' for year on tropical island." It was 1981, and London was preparing for the first installment in the 16-year media saga of Prince Charles and Lady Diana. Despite her reservations, Lucy agreed to marry Gerald in order to satisfy Australian immigration restrictions. She also learned that she would have to finance the trip as Gerald was broke. The less-than-happy couple wound up on Tuin, between New Guinea and Australia. Thirteen months later, Lucy returned to England alone, and her vividly written best-selling book on her experiences was dedicated to Gerald and published in 1984, six months before Gerald Kingsland's *The Islander* saw print. There is plenty of nudity in *Castaway* but not much sex. In Roeg's film, sex becomes a metaphor for power. Although Gerald, on his third island trip, is supposed to be the more experienced of the pair in matters of survival, Lucy actually thrives better on the island than he does. Sexual dependency on the frightened, complaining Gerald, who, as Lucy correctly observes, "copes with pain by sheathing himself in indifference," seems as unappealing to us as it does to Lucy. Gerald perks up a bit towards the end of the year, when he does mechanical repair work for nearby islanders. Losing her hold on Gerald, Lucy acts her way through sex with him, a power play that works. Oliver Reed, nearing 50, gives a heart-wrenching performance as a man who knows every trick in the book except how to hide from himself and from Lucy. In her second film, Amanda (*Foreign Body*) Donohoe portrays the resourceful, intelligent Lucy with a serene self-confidence any screen veteran would envy. Nicolas Roeg's vision of Tuin includes dazzling shots of clouds washing over the moon, as well as the pitiless depiction of this mismatched pair who learn to depend on each other in spite of themselves. Roeg and Reed took an admirable risk revealing the interior toll of false machismo, and for that reason I have a hunch men will be more uncomfortable with the sexual politics of this film than women.

1987 (R) 118m/C *GB* Oliver Reed, Amanda Donohoe, Tony Rickards, Georgina Hale, Frances Barber, Todd Rippon; ***D:*** Nicolas Roeg; ***W:*** Allan Scott; ***C:*** Harvey Harrison; ***M:*** Stanley Myers. **VHS, Closed Caption**

Cat and Mouse

Cat and Mouse is a straightforward murder mystery, graced by the presence of gorgeous Michele Morgan. The wry performance by Serge Reggiani as a single-mind-

“I’d give my life to be dead.”

—Francesco Dellamorte (Rupert Everett) in *Cemetery Man.*

ed detective is perfection itself. Claude Lelouch can't resist adding an obligatory (if excellent) car chase sequence. Great fun! ***AKA:*** Le Chat et la Souris.

1978 (PG) 107m/C *FR* Michele Morgan, Serge Reggiani, Jean-Pierre Aumont, Philippe Labro, Philippe Leotard, Valerie Lagrange, Michel Perelon, Christine Laurent; ***D:*** Claude Lelouch; ***W:*** Claude Lelouch; ***C:*** Andre Perlstein; ***M:*** Francis Lai. **VHS**

The Cater Street Hangman

Admirers of Inspector Thomas Pitt had to wait nearly 20 years to see him on film, and red-haired Eoin McCarthy fills the detective's shoes as if he'd been born to solve unspeakable crimes. One of the best things about *The Cater Street Hangman* is that the first credit reads *The Inspector Pitt Mysteries,* which means that we can expect *Callendar Square, Paragon Walk, Resurrection Row, Rutland Place, Bluegate Fields, Death in Devil's Acre, Cardington Crescent, Silence in Hanover Close, Bethlehem Road, Face of a Stranger, Dangerous Mourning, Defend and Betray,* et cetera, in due course. Not since the Sergeant Cribb mysteries of 1980–83 starring Alan Dobie has there been such a meticulously researched character, deeply entrenched in his own time and place. As Pitt explains in *The Cater Street Hangman,* he spent years trying and failing to save the good name of his father. Rather careless in appearance, he has an intimate appreciation of the working class into which he was born and his crime-solving approach tends to be empirical and visceral rather than cerebral and contemplative. Challenged by suspects, he continues his questioning without the slightest trace of irritation. The Pitt mysteries are further enriched by the deductive skills of Charlotte Ellison (beautifully played by Keeley Hawes), a misfit in her own well-born family. When a series of pious women become the victims of murder, Charlotte takes a special interest in the case and her prickly relationship with Thomas gradually takes on the nature of a true investigative team. The suspicious-looking suspects are well cast, from Peter Egan as Edward, Charlotte's stern papa, and John Castle as her nemesis, Reverend Prebble; to Richard Linton as brother-in-law Dominic Corde and Janet Maze as Martha Prebble. Also in the cast are David Roper as Maddock, Robert Reynolds as Dr. Hope, Jack Turlton as Sgt. Webster, Judy Campbell as Grandmama, and Sheila Ruskin, Sarah Woodward, and Katie Ryder Richardson as Caroline, Sarah, and Emily Ellison. Small touches like a street sprite singing for her supper, corsets that only allow one to breathe if released a notch, and satirical jabs at the Anglican Church all add to the unique flavor of what I hope will be the first entry in a looong series. Although June Wyndham Davies produced on a small budget of two million pounds ($3.5 million?), *The Cater Street Hangman* looks and feels far more expensive. Based on the 1979 novel by Anne Perry (see review for *Heavenly Creatures*). Cast Note: If Egan and Castle seem familiar, they play Oscar Wilde and Prince Louis Battenberg in 1978's *Lillie.* Egan also stars in *A Perfect Spy* and Castle appears in *The Bretts.*

1998 100m/C *GB* Eoin McCarthy, Keeley Hawes, Peter Egan, John Castle, Richard Linton, David Roper, Robert Reynolds, Judy Campbell, Sheila Ruskin, Sarah Woodward, Katie Ryder Richardson, Jack Turlton, Janet Maze; ***D:*** Sarah Hellings; ***W:*** T.R. Bowen; ***C:*** Doug Hallows; ***M:*** Christopher Gunning.

Caught

Caught is about Nick (Arie Verveen), a youthful drifter who gets caught up in the lives of a middle-aged couple, Betty and Joe (Maria Conchita Alonso and Edward James Olmos), who own a Mom-and-Pop fish store in Jersey City. When Betty and Joe's adult son Danny (Steve Schub), now a married parent, comes home, he is angered by the fact that his place in his parent's lives seems to have been usurped by Nick. Alonso and Robert Young–regular Olmos attracted good notices for their performances as Betty and Joe, and *Caught* also received attention for the “sexual steaminess” of some erotic sequences between Betty and Nick. Based on the novel *Into It* by screenwriter Edward Pomerantz.

1996 (R) 109m/C Edward James Olmos, Maria Conchita Alonso, Arie Verveen, Steven Schub, Bitty Schram, Shawn Elliot; ***D:*** Robert M. Young; ***W:*** Edward Pomerantz; ***C:*** Michael Barrow; ***M:*** Chris Botti. Nominations: Independent Spirit Awards '97: Best Actress (Alonso), Best Director (Young), Debut Performance (Verveen). **VHS, LV, Closed Caption**

Celia: Child of Terror

Australian writer/director Ann Turner offers one of the few honest depictions of the dark side of childhood, as seen by a nine-year-old girl growing up in the 1950s. Rebecca Smart is remarkable as the little girl who turns to voodoo magic in an effort to cope with unfair grown-ups, unyielding politicians, and cruel playmates. The character of Celia has been compared by some critics to Rhoda Penmark in *The Bad Seed,* but the comparison isn't especially apt. Under less stressful conditions, Celia might have resorted to less drastic remedies to solve her very real problems. But, as the film makes clear, friends and grown-ups who might have provided solid sympathetic support are torn away from her for reasons her family fails to make clear to her. The only things that really belong to her are her rabbit Murgatroyd and her violent fantasies, and both serve as catalytic agents for her ultimate corruption. (It isn't giving away too much if I advise you not to get too attached to Murgatroyd.) *Celia* may be an exaggeration of reality, but not by much, and *Celia* was by far the best of 1990's Women in Film festival entries. 🦴🦴🦴

1990 110m/C *AU* Rebecca Smart, Nicholas Eadie, Victoria Longley, Mary-Anne Fahey; ***D:*** Ann Turner; ***W:*** Ann Turner; ***C:*** Geoffrey Simpson. **VHS**

Cemetery Man

Michele Soavi's *Cemetery Man* played at selected Landmark Theatres in the spring of 1996 to generally grumpy reviews, but for goofball entertainment, I thought it was a kick to watch. It was certainly a helluva lot more fun than Paul Schrader's *My Dinner with Androids,* I mean, *The Comfort of Strangers,* which came and went in 1991. Rupert Everett stars again as a bit of an idiot, but at least he isn't bored in this one. He's Francesco Dellamorte, a grave keeper with a problem: the dead keep returning to life and he has to shoot them in the head to get rid of them once and for all. One day, an old geezer kicks off and his beautiful widow arrives on the scene to pay her respects. As soon as she says, "I love my husband," she and Dellamorte are frolicking on his gravestone. The husband returns as a zombie and proceeds to bite her to death. Or at least that's Dellamorte's first impression. Too late, he finds out that she was only frightened and, because of his usual approach with zombies, he's lost her forever, or at least until she returns as another character, and another. (Anna Falchi is the well-endowed object of his desire.) The plot takes increasingly strange turns as motorcyclists collide with Boy Scouts in a school bus and Dellamorte starts shooting the living as well as the dead. There's a rich, haunting look to the film that may remind you of the Mario Bava horror classics of the 1960s, or of the 1980s films of Dario Argento. It's no accident; Argento is Soavi's cinematic mentor. Three of the big gripes about this film are: (1) It seems to go around in circles; (2) It steals sequences from other movies; and (3) The frequent bloodletting is comedic to the point of absurdity. True enough, and that may be why *Cemetery Man* collected dust in an Italian studio vault for two years. But Rupert Everett is always an arresting presence, and if you're in the mood for this sort of senseless foolishness (as I obviously was), you may giggle your way into insensibility. Attention die-hard movie buffs: if character actor Mickey Knox looks familiar to you, he should! Once upon a time, he worked with Bogart, Cagney, and Lancaster in such film noir treats of 1949 as *Knock on Any Door, White Heat,* and *I Walk Alone.* ***AKA:*** Dellamorte Delamore; Of Death, Of Love. 🦴🦴🦴

1995 (R) 100m/C *IT* Rupert Everett, Anna Falchi, Francois Hadji-Lazaro, Mickey Knox, Fabiana Formica, Clive Riche; ***D:*** Michele (Michael) Soavi; ***W:*** Gianni Romoli; ***C:*** Mauro Marchetti; ***M:*** Manuel De Sica. **VHS, Closed Caption**

The Hound Salutes:
ANN TURNER
Director/writer, *Celia: Child of Terror*

The Australian rabbit massacre occurred in the late 1950s, when farmers had a real rabbit problem in the country where the rabbits were just stripping the pastures bare. The very conservative government at the time tried to appease them by rounding up children's pet rabbits in the cities. People just had to destroy their rabbits or take them to the zoos. I read that first in Victoria in the early 1980s in an article about rabbits finally being legalized; and what I loved was the fact that the government had to reverse its decision and people had to go and collect their pets, and chaos ensued when there were thousands of rabbits and hundreds of parents and children and all the rabbits looked the same. It just struck me as a wonderful metaphor for the way governments behave.

"The rabbit newsreels I show in the film are from archival footage with a new voiceover commentary, the Mike Mayfield detective serials are completely re-created, and the voodoo movie is a genuine old feature. Basically, all the voodoo games the kids play in the film come from my own childhood. We used to play voodoo games like that as kids. I thought back and reinterpreted the games. The more I thought about them, the more I realized how dangerous and how violent a lot of the games we played really were. At the time, we just thought they were funny. For instance, I remember as kids we used to dig holes in a beach and wait and listen at night in our beach house for people to fall down in the holes. We thought that was hysterically funny. I looked at the power games that we played as children. Something that's always fascinated me is how people acquire power and acquire the trappings of the adult world through their ritualized games as children.

Center Stage

In spite of the fact that portions of *Center Stage* were shown out of sequence at the Berlin Film Festival, Maggie Cheung still won a much-deserved Best Actress Award for her breathtaking performance as Ruan Ling-Yu. *Variety*'s review was just a tad chilly, although its critic neglected to mention the mixed-up reels at the screening in his report, tsk-tsk. He did describe the "inadequate" translation, which is exactly what occurred when I first saw it. Imagine, if you will, two Ruan Ling-Yu fans shaking a fellow viewer who could only read the Cantonese subtitles when many sequences (including the climax!) of an edited copy of the film were entirely in Mandarin. Luckily, Tai Seng Video has come up with the full (154 minute) version with English subtitles so Western audiences can savor Maggie Cheung's exquisite work here to full advantage. Ruan Ling-Yu was China's leading actress in 1935 when she committed suicide, leaving behind a note: "Gossip is a dreadful thing." Her offscreen life was difficult and complex, but on film Ruan Ling-Yu was wonderfully perceptive and deeply lucid. Cheung, with her own unique style and presence, succeeds in unlayering the mystery behind this legendary star. In one heartbreaking sequence, Cheung as Ling-Yu has already made her decision to die, but

"Celia is a very sensitive child, but I think she starts out as someone who's being very honest and really dedicated to her own way of seeing things. She's got a very vivid imagination, so she dips into the fantasy world and then the reality of life is parallel when she's going between the two. As the film progresses and Celia experiences severe losses in her life, she tips into a very unstable frame of mind, and she isn't helped by the society around her—the society that's forcing these losses upon her to some extent and isn't actually aware of the damage it's doing. We're actually looking at a child who's very much affected by everything around her, but her parents just aren't seeing what's going on in Celia's mind until far too late.

"I wanted to show Celia's mother through her child's eyes. Celia takes her mother absolutely for granted and she has very little in common with her. Celia's mother is quite remote from her at the start; at the same time, Celia is very close to her grandmother. As the film progresses, Celia's mother learns a lot from her next-door neighbor, Alice. And, as she grows up a bit, Celia learns to identify much more with her mother, who, in turn, stands up for Celia in a way that she wouldn't be capable of before her friendship with her neighbor Alice. I wanted to show the growth of a woman through a friendship.

"Working with Rebecca Smart (who was 11 at the time) and the other children in *Celia* was a fantastic experience. I was frightened about directing kids because I'd never done it before, and they were marvelous. We spent a lot of time casting and so the children I chose were people I really believed in. They were straightforward, they were honest, they were energetic, they were well behaved when they were required to be, and then they'd play like rowdy kids in between takes. They were simply incredible to work with and wonderful fun. The poor adults got less attention than they would normally if there hadn't been children in the cast, but we all worked very well together. Rebecca Smart is quite an experienced actress, so as the director, I was in the position of having the leading actress being much more experienced than I was, which really kept me humble."

she moves with elegant grace among the members of her profession, responding with warm affection to the well wishers who are already celebrating her introduction to talking pictures (Chinese films were silent until 1935). Director Stanley Kwan re-creates the look and feel of the '30s and includes footage of the real Ruan Ling-Yu in *The Peach Blossom Weeps Tears of Blood, The Goddess,* and *New Women.* Black-and-white interviews with aging contemporaries of the late actress are also included, as well as discussions with Cheung about her own approach to the material. Even die-hard movie buffs may never have heard of Ruan Ling-Yu; *Center Stage* is an excellent introduction to her life and work, and Cheung's riveting star turn is not to be missed! ***AKA:*** The Actress; Ruan Ling-Yu; The New China Woman. 🦴🦴🦴

1991 154m/C *HK* Maggie Cheung, Tony Leung Chiu-Wai, Shin Hong, Carina Lau, Lawrence Ng, Waise Lee, Cheung Chung, Siu Sheung, Yip Sang; ***D:*** Stanley Kwan; ***W:*** Yau Tai On-Ping; ***C:*** Poon Hang-Seng. **VHS**

Century

Century is everything *The Age of Innocence* wanted to be and wasn't: an atmospheric re-creation of the mood and feeling of a vanished time. Martin Scorsese tried to accomplish this with an extravagant budget and extended close-ups of lavish meals.

The Hound Salutes:
WENDELL B. HARRIS JR.
Director/writer/actor, *Chameleon Street*

Douglas Street performed 36 operations: hysterectomies, appendectomies, mastectomies... and whatever Doug does, he does very well. It's interesting. When he first performed a hysterectomy, he told me he made the incision twice as long as it would normally be so that he could get inside and search around for the uterus because he wasn't sure was where it was located. I think that our story *Chameleon Street* would be a lot different if Doug Street were going from episode to episode, from escapade to escapade, and screwing up. But the fact is, whatever Doug tries his hand at, he succeeds at. I mean he could walk in here and be an interviewer right now and interview me, because he knows what buttons to push. We met him back in June 1984. We interviewed him, but of course we first told him about our desire to make a film on his life, and at the time I think Doug was somewhat despondent, so he latched on right away. He was very interested in having a film and in fact he wanted to play himself, but unfortunately he was incarcerated.

"The moment that I first read an article in the *Detroit Free Press* about Doug, I wanted to play him. That was the first time I'd heard about Doug and the moment I read it, I realized that it was somewhat of a dream role for an actor, and since acting is everything to me, I embarked with my family and our company, Prismatic Images, on a seven-year odyssey which has led me to this moment. We spent four years raising the $2 million budget, based on a limited partnership of $25,000 a share, and during that four-year period, I continued to revise and rewrite the script through 28 revisions, and after that four-year period we began production. I wasn't initially supposed to direct, write, *and* act, but we approached several directors, among them Melvin Van Peebles, and Michael Apted, who directed *Coal Miner's Daughter.* Unfortunately, we could not afford those directors. And that's kind of a metaphor for the independent film experience. You end up being told by the money you have what you're going to do and what you're not going to do. So I was the cheapest director around."

But money and food, however useful in real life, shouldn't have the burden of stealing scenes from the actors. With a much smaller budget, writer/director Stephen Poliakoff has kept the focus where it belongs in *Century,* on the superb cast who interpret his excellent screenplay. As we approach the 21st century, we find ourselves evaluating the last few years of the 20th. Which of our customs and traditions will survive and endure, which will be hermetically sealed in this era and rendered obsolete by the year 2001? The progressive doctor, played with languid charm by Charles Dance, is a man who appears far ahead of the late 19th century, but, in fact, his influence is forever trapped within it because of a fatal flaw. The young medical student earnestly played by Clive Owen is inspired by Dance's character, but ultimately disillusioned by him. His immigrant father, wonderfully played by the late Robert Stephens (1931–95), wants to give a spectacular welcome to the new age in his adopted country, even though his neighbors in the British countryside avoid and distrust him because of his Eastern European background. And the shimmering Miranda Richardson, as one of the women employed in Dance's medical institute, is determined to make a free-spirited life for herself, regardless of the obstacles. The conflict between Dance and Owen is at the heart of the film: Dance hires women (and one black man) to work at his institute and treats them with respect. He gives his students valuable training and the chance to learn on the job. He even encourages Owen's independent medical research, as long as he and everyone else recognizes who's in charge. But Dance has his own murky agenda, carefully concealed from the wealthy benefactress who backs the institute (the great Joan Hickson, seen all too briefly in two marvelous sequences with Owen). After the frustrated Owen discovers what Dance is really up to, he enlists Richardson's help and graduates from devoted admirer to fierce adversary. The battle is only partly successful; the fledgling medical pioneer loses valuable research opportunities by taking on the system that once nurtured him. And that, in a way, is the point of *Century;* however much we rage against the inequities in our own time, it will always have the edge on us. Poliakoff and cast drive this concept home with fresh and startling meaning. 🦴🦴🦴🦴

1994 (R) 112m/C *GB* Clive Owen, Charles Dance, Miranda Richardson, Robert Stephens, Joan Hickson, Lena Headey, Neil Stuke; ***D:*** Stephen Poliakoff; ***W:*** Stephen Poliakoff; ***C:*** Witold Stok; ***M:*** Michael Gibbs. **VHS**

Chain of Desire

Remember Max Ophuls' classic 1950 film *La Ronde,* based on Arthur Schnitzler's play? The one in which just about everyone in an all-star cast (Anton Walbrook, Serge Reggiani, Simone Simon, Simone Signoret, Daniel Gelin, Danielle Darrieux, Fernand Gravet, Odette Joyeux, Jean-Louis Barrault, Isa Miranda, Gerard Philipe) had affairs with each other? So did Roger Vadim, who remade it, not very well, in 1964. So did Temistocles Lopez, who remade it in 1993. The "advantage" this time is that the Production Code of 1934–69 need be considered no longer when making a movie about pointless sex. Alma D'Angeli (Linda Fiorentino) and Jesus (Elias Koteas) are the first sexual adventurers. There are 14 lust-driven Manhattanites in this movie. In place of the sophisticated, dry humor of Ophuls, we get Lopez' message for the '90s, delivered in an understated way—but if you have a pulse, it will still hit you with a thud. 🦴🦴

1993 107m/C Linda Fiorentino, Elias Koteas, Malcolm McDowell, Grace Zabriskie, Tim Guinee, Assumpta Serna, Patrick Bauchau, Seymour Cassel, Kevin Conroy, Angel Aviles, Holly Marie Combs, Jamie Harold, Dewey Weber, Suzanne Douglas; ***D:*** Temistocles Lopez; ***W:*** Temistocles Lopez; ***C:*** Nancy Schreiber; ***M:*** Nathan Birnbaum. Nominations: Independent Spirit Awards '94: Best Cinematography. **VHS, LV**

Chameleon Street

I wonder if the real William Douglas Street ever saw 1960's *The Great Impostor,* in which Tony Curtis as Ferdinand Waldo Demara Jr. teaches school without a credential, impersonates a novice in a Trappist monastery, works as a prison warden's deputy, and performs a successful operation as a Canadian naval lieutenant without a medical degree. At any rate, Street (Wendell B. Harris) wanted a more interesting way of life than to work for a burglar alarm company in Detroit. Street, too, performs surgery AND impersonates a *Time* reporter AND pretends to be an exchange student from Africa AND speaks French AND practices law. *Chameleon Street* isn't particularly well acted or well directed, but it is fun and there's a great costume ball sequence. 🦴🦴🦴

1989 (R) 95m/C Wendell B. Harris Jr., Angela Leslie, Amina Fakir, Paula McGee, Mano Breckenridge, David Kiley, Anthony Ennis; ***Cameos:*** Coleman A. Young; ***D:*** Wendell B. Harris Jr.; ***W:*** Wendell B. Harris Jr.; ***C:*** Daniel S. Noga; ***M:*** Peter S. Moore. Sundance Film Festival '90: Grand Jury Prize. **VHS, LV**

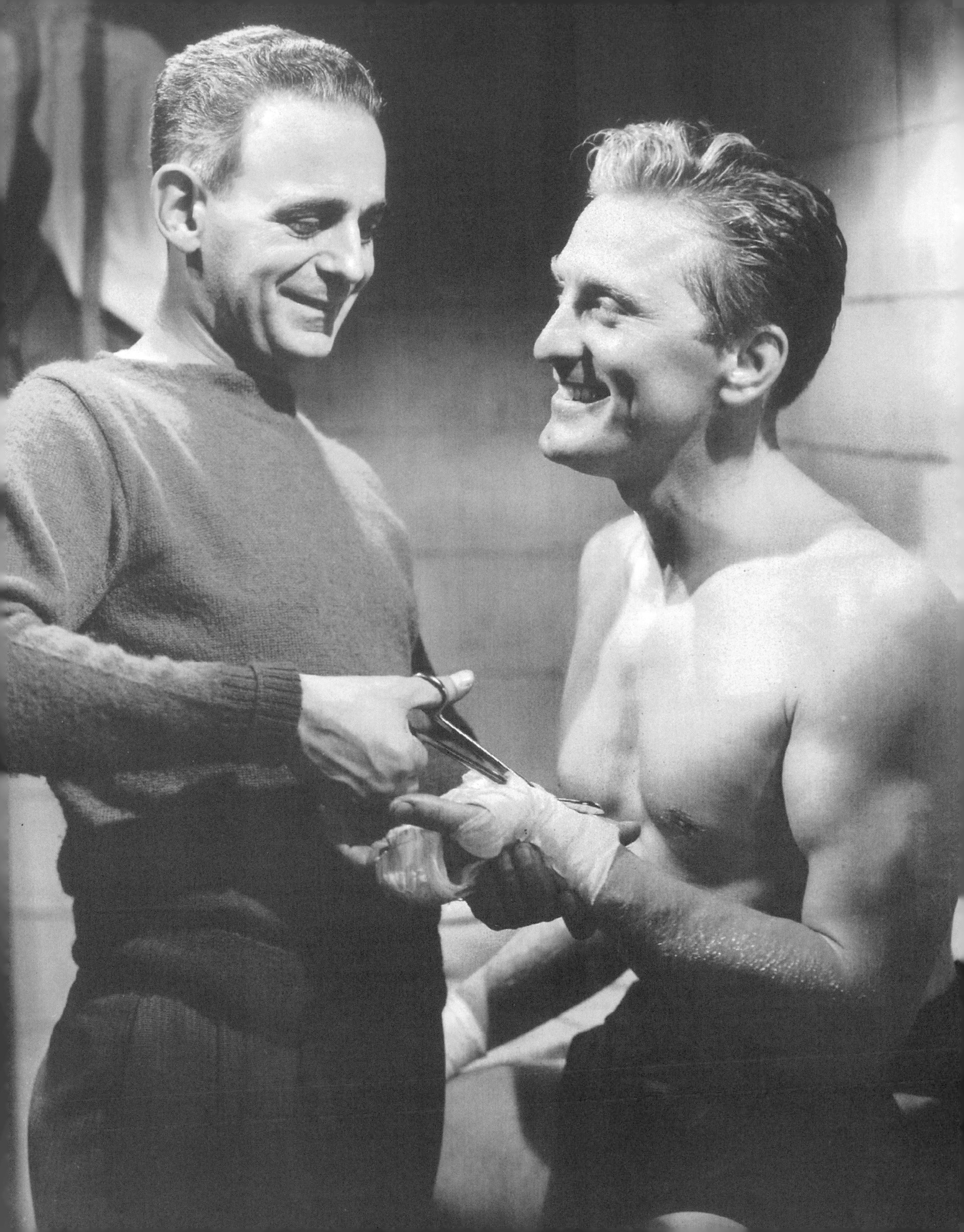

Champion

Ring Lardner's bitter short story about the lionization of a loser who bullied his way to the top of the fight game was transformed into a larger-than-life portrait of an anti-hero by the soon-to-be-blacklisted screenwriter Carl Foreman. Many of the illustrations that made the original yarn so cynical are included in the film, but the approach changed completely. Midge Kelly is a jerk because he is a jerk, according to Lardner. As portrayed by the likable Kirk Douglas, Midge Kelly is an ambitious young hustler who is jerked around by the circumstances of his limited life and who makes errors in judgment that propel him straight through his spectacular rise and inevitable fall. Therefore, even though Midge Kelly is shown beating up his crippled brother and abandoning his wife on their wedding day, neglecting his mother, pursuing and dumping a married woman, and using yet a third woman for his own gain, Kirk Douglas invests his pathetic character with such an unconscious, driven quality that we cannot help identifying with his struggle. He manipulates everyone in sight, yet when he says "I'm not going to be a 'hey, you' all my life. I'm going to make something of myself," it is not hard to sympathize with his desire to improve his wretched existence. Midge Kelly's going to be champion even if it kills him. When we watch his agonized scrambling for recognition and see his broken body and battered face, we understand his brother's refusal to condemn him and not for the hard-boiled reasons supplied by Lardner. This is what winning at any cost does to some people, says Foreman. Midge Kelly's victims, who learned to swallow their losses, are in far better shape than he is. He may be achieving immortality, but they are learning how to live.

1949 99m/B Kirk Douglas, Arthur Kennedy, Marilyn Maxwell, Ruth Roman, Lola Albright, Paul Stewart; ***D:*** Mark Robson; ***W:*** Carl Foreman; ***C:*** Franz Planer; ***M:*** Dimitri Tiomkin. Academy Awards '49: Best Film Editing (Harry Gerstad); Nominations: Academy Awards '49: Best Actor (Douglas), Best Black and White Cinematography (Planer), Best Screenplay (Foreman), Best Supporting Actor (Kennedy), Best Original Score (Tiomkin). **VHS, Closed Caption**

Chan Is Missing

Chan Is Missing is the first movie I saw in a theatre that I remember trying to press the pause button so I could rewind the film to see a favorite sequence twice (I got my first VCR in May, 1982). Obviously, I couldn't do it, but the impulse was there. It's about a couple of taxi drivers in San Francisco who hunt for Chan after he vanishes with their five grand meant to pay for a taxi license. The great black-and-white footage of Chinatown captures the look, pace, and feel of the neighborhood in the early '80s, and Wayne Wang gets performances out of his then-unknown cast. *Chan Is Missing* launched Wayne Wang's successful career as a director and also gave us a chance to see future director Peter Wang *(A Great Wall, Laserman)* as Henry the Cook. Laureen Chew (Amy) was in *Dim Sum,* Wayne Wang's next picture, and Marc Hayashi (Steve) co-starred with Peter Wang in *Laserman.*

1982 80m/B Wood Moy, Marc Hayashi, Laureen Chew, Judy Mihei, Peter Wang, Presco Tabios, Frankie Allarcon, Virginia Cerenio, Roy Chan, George Woo, Emily Yamasaki, Ellen Yeung; ***D:*** Wayne Wang; ***W:*** Wayne Wang, Terrel Seltzer, Isaac Cronin; ***C:*** Michael G. Chin; ***M:*** Robert Kikuchi-Yngojo. **VHS**

Chaplin

With Richard Attenborough at the helm, *Chaplin* promised to be yet another overblown movie biography, and that it certainly is. However, it is largely redeemed by the truth that its gifted cast succeeds in conveying onscreen. The centerpiece of the movie is Robert Downey Jr., who is nothing short of superb in the title role. Moira Kelly also delivers absolutely beguiling performances as Chaplin's first and last loves, Hetty Kelly and Oona O'Neill. There is a lovely early sequence with Downey and Kelly that effectively captures Chaplin's romantic spirit struggling to express itself against the backdrop of a frosty London night. Many of *Chaplin*'s finest moments deal with unfamiliar material like this encounter, and Chaplin's studio days are lovingly re-created with some

Tom Haley (Paul Stewart) and Midge Kelly (Kirk Douglas) in *Champion.* United Artists; courtesy of the Kobal Collection

Everyone has a wild side. Even a legend.

—Tagline from the movie *Chaplin*.

nice color work that takes on the patina of hand-painted tintypes. Attenborough and screenwriters William Boyd, Bryan Forbes, and William Goldman seem to fight their own film by establishing, but ineffectively reinforcing, a through-line from a not particularly memorable meeting between Chaplin and a young J. Edgar Hoover, to Chaplin's permanent exile from America over 30 years later. Kevin Dunn's portrayal of Hoover, of course, is your standard vindictive voyeur that's been floating around on movie screens since 1972. Moreover, Chaplin's legendary contemporaries like Mabel Normand and Mary Pickford are dismissed as overrated bitches, when they were every bit as wonderful in their own way as Chaplin was. You'd also think, to look at Paul Rhys' sincere interpretation of Syd Chaplin, that he functioned strictly as his brother's agent. In fact, he was a wonderfully talented comedian in his own right, and his 1925 production of *Charley's Aunt* is the best and funniest of all the movie versions of the Brandon Thomas classic. Admittedly, you'd expect a movie about Chaplin, based on his autobiography, to focus mainly on the title character. But when you see stars like Kevin Kline in a particularly sensitive turn as Douglas Fairbanks and Dan Aykroyd as Mack Sennett (God, where is his ego, to show his ENTIRE naked stomach in one shot?), and the enchanting Penelope Ann Miller as Edna Purviance and Diane Lane capturing a great deal of Paulette Goddard's vivacity, you can't help thinking that it was THIS crowd that represented Chaplin's world. Why couldn't we have seen more of them, instead of sporadic set pieces illustrating J. Edgar Hoover's detached paranoia? That the filmmakers attempted more than they could fully explore may have been somewhat of an error in judgment, but with all *Chaplin*'s flaws, there is still so much of value in this movie that it is definitely worth careful appraisal on video.

1992 (PG-13) 135m/C *GB* Robert Downey Jr., Dan Aykroyd, Geraldine Chaplin, Kevin Dunn, Anthony Hopkins, Milla Jovovich, Moira Kelly, Kevin Kline, Diane Lane, Penelope Ann Miller, Paul Rhys, John Thaw, Marisa Tomei, Nancy Travis, James Woods, David Duchovny, Deborah Maria Moore, Bill Paterson, John Standing, Robert Stephens, Peter Crook; ***D:*** Richard Attenborough; ***W:*** Bryan Forbes, William Boyd, William Goldman; ***C:*** Sven Nykvist; ***M:*** John Barry. British Academy Awards '92: Best Actor (Downey); Nominations: Academy Awards '92: Best Actor (Downey), Best Art Direction/Set Decoration, Best Original Score. **VHS, LV, Letterbox, Closed Caption**

Charley's Aunt

Sydney Chaplin (1885–1965) is the whole show in this delightful silent comedy. Charlie's handsome older brother is a charmer as Babbs (AKA Lord Fancourt Babberly), and he's even better as the sweet little old lady who's supposed to be "Charley's Aunt from Brazil, where the nuts came from." The REAL Donna Lucia D'Alvabarez is fetching Eulalie Jensen (1885–1952). Babbs is in love with Ela (Ethel Shannon, 1898–1951); Jack Chesney's (David James) in love with Kitty Verdun (Priscilla Bonner, 1899–1996); and Charley Whykeham's (Jimmy Harrison, 1908–77) in love with Amy (Mary Akin), but he's having a bit of a problem with her grumpy Uncle Stephen. When Babbs turns up at St. Olde's College in Oxford University as Donna Lucia, Uncle Stephen (James E. Page, 1870–1930) and Jack's father Sir Francis (Phillips Smalley, 1865–1939), compete for "her" attention. Meanwhile, Brassett the butler (Lucien Littlefield, 1895–1960) does his best to look befuddled. Littlefield lost his hair while still quite young, so he spent most of his long career playing much older men. I used to wonder about the enormous eyes of silent movie stars; was it just makeup or was it some sort of lighting effect? Then I saw Priscilla Bonner up close in San Francisco's Sheraton Palace Hotel in 1984. She looked very much like Kitty Verdun and her lovely large eyes were absolutely real. An early talkie version of *Charley's Aunt* was made in 1930 and it creaks in comparison with this lively farce. Based on Brandon Thomas' 1892 play, which is so fresh and so funny that it will probably make people laugh in the 21st century.

1925 75m/B Sydney Chaplin, Ethel Shannon, Lucien Littlefield, Alec B. Francis, Mary Akin, Priscilla Bonner, Jimmy Harrison, David James, Eulalie

Jensen, James E. Page, Phillips Smalley; ***D:*** Scott Sidney; ***W:*** F. McGrew Willis, Joe Farnham; ***C:*** Gus Peterson, Paul Garnett. **VHS**

Chasing Amy

After the award-winning *Clerks* and the critically panned *Mallrats,* writer/director Kevin Smith worked hard on his third film. The result, *Chasing Amy,* is his best effort to date. It certainly contains a beautifully written, star-making role for Joey Lauren Adams as its central character Alyssa, and two carefully observed male characters (Holden and Banky, played by Ben Affleck and Jason Lee) with more than enough shadings and textures to fill several features. Childhood friends Holden and Banky collaborate on a cult comic. Alyssa arrives on the scene, and Holden falls head over heels in love with her. There are only three problems: first, Alyssa is looking for a best friend, not a lover. Second, watch the movie! Third, watch the movie!! Smith's script is charged with honest intensity, and the performances by Adams, Affleck, and Lee are excellent. In the end credits, Smith apologizes to the critics who hated *Mallrats.* He won't have to apologize to anyone for *Chasing Amy* except to those who want to know what will happen to Alyssa, Holden, and Banky after the final reel. We sort of know, anyway, in the same bittersweet way we know about all the different scrawls on all the different candids in long-unopened high school yearbooks. 🦴🦴🦴

1997 (R) 105m/C Ben Affleck, Joey Lauren Adams, Jason Lee, Dwight Ewell, Jason Mewes, Kevin Smith; ***D:*** Kevin Smith; ***W:*** Kevin Smith; ***C:*** David Klein; ***M:*** David Pirner. **VHS, LV, Closed Caption**

Chicken Hawk

When you're looking for a third film to round out a triple feature for an upcoming N.A.M.B.L.A. meeting (the other movies being *For a Lost Soldier* and *Happiness,* naturally), *Chicken Hawk* is sure to fit the bill. Its filmmakers offer a platform to male lovers of boys, so you're mostly stuck with their rationales. The most extreme is a spacey older gent who's convinced that a mere exchange of smiles with a child represents "flirting" and/or mutual consent for sexual activity. (The identities of the kids in the film are disguised.) All the advocates of man-boy love claim to be "celibate" and some offer the argument that sex between adults and children has been permissible in societies outside of Western culture. Opposing views, mostly expressed by concerned parents, receive token attention. A fundamental ethical issue, the vast discrepancy between an adult's power to choose and a child's basic powerlessness to make an informed choice, is not really addressed in this scrupulously non-judgmental film. ***AKA:*** Chicken Hawk: Men Who Love Boys. 🦴

1994 58m/C Barbara Adler, Mimi Turner; ***D:*** Adi Sideman; ***C:*** Nadev Harel.

Children of Paradise

Children of Paradise/Les Enfants du Paradis was made in France over a two-year period between 1943 and 1945 during a time when the Nazis had overtaken the country. The Nazis demanded severe restrictions not only on the content of French films, but also on their length. Director Marcel Carne and screenwriter Jacques Prevert envisioned a lavish historical epic that was twice the length of an average feature, but told the Nazis that they were actually making two movies, secretly hoping, of course, that the war would be over long before their masterpiece was released. Moreover, Jewish composer Joseph Kosma and Jewish designer Alexandre Trauner were in danger at all times of being captured by the Nazis. Because she fell in love with a German officer, Arletty (1898–1992), the beautiful actress who played the leading role of Garance, was at one point imprisoned and sentenced to death. (She received a stay of execution and survived.) None of the incredible tensions that the cast and crew must have endured can be seen in the resulting three-plus hour film, released after the Allied liberation. Despite its length, this lyrical saga of love and longing moves like lightning. Because *Children of Paradise* showed the vanished world of the mid-19th century

"I'm free."

—Garance (Arletty) triumphs in *Children of Paradise.*

(magnificently photographed by Roger Hubert) and focused largely on a central female character, it has been favorably compared with *Gone with the Wind.* But for all its boisterous theatrical backdrops and passionate emotional undercurrents, *Paradise* is a far more subtle film. Jean-Louis Barrault (1910–94) plays Baptiste, a famous mime, who yearns for the elusive Garance as she moves from one man to another. She agrees to spend the night with this hopeless romantic with the words, "Love is so very simple." Baptiste turns her down and by the time the two get a second chance, love has become irretrievably complicated for them both. Arletty and Barrault have never been better, and the supporting cast (which includes Pierre Brasseur, Maria Casares, Albert Remy, Leon Larive, Marcel Herrand, Pierre Renoir, Jeanne Marken, and Gaston Modot) deliver vivid performances in carefully chosen roles. (Arletty and Barrault later made appearances in 1962's *The Longest Day.*) ***AKA:*** Les Enfants du Paradis.

1945 188m/B *FR* Jean-Louis Barrault, Arletty, Pierre Brasseur, Maria Casares, Albert Remy, Leon Larive, Marcel Herrand, Pierre Renoir, Gaston Modot, Jane Marken; ***D:*** Marcel Carne; ***W:*** Jacques Prevert; ***C:*** Roger Hubert; ***M:*** Maurice Thiriet, Joseph Kosma. **VHS, LV**

Children of the Damned

In the fall of 1963, Anton Leader tried to duplicate the success of the original *Village of the Damned* with *Children of the Damned.* Ian Hendry and Alan Badel (both wearing obvious rugs) run around town trying to figure out what an international batch of alien-spawned children have in mind. Barbara Ferris is on hand to translate because NONE of those whiz kiddies can act. To make a story like this work, you really have to go for the audience's visceral connection with the material. Long military strategy sequences and endless philosophizing just don't cut it. The lack of a deeply impassioned protagonist (which, yeah, even snide George Sanders could be when he halfway tried, as he did in *Village*) ultimately scuttled whatever dreams the producers may have had for 10 more damned children sequels.

1963 90m/B *GB* Ian Hendry, Alan Badel, Barbara Ferris, Alfred Burke, Sheila Allen, Clive Powell, Frank Summerscales, Mahdu Mathen, Gerald Delsol, Roberta Rex, Franchesca Lee, Harold Goldblatt, Ralph Michael, Martin Miller, Lee Yoke-Moon; ***D:*** Anton Leader; ***W:*** John Briley; ***C:*** David Boulton. **VHS, LV**

The Children of Theatre Street

The Children of Theatre Street marked Grace Kelly's (1928–82) return to the big screen after a two-decade absence. She narrated this circumspect examination of the Leningrad Academy, a Russian ballet school. The Soviet Union withdrew its endorsement of the film after its release because the names of three dancers who defected (including Rudolf Nureyev, 1938–93) were mentioned. Unfortunately, director Robert Dornhelm showed all the tedium of the ballet dancers in training, with very little of the excitement.

1977 92m/C *RU* Grace Kelly, Angelina Armeiskaya, Alec Timoushin, Lena Voronzova, Michaela Cerna, Galina Messenzeva, Konstantin Zaklinsky; ***D:*** Robert Dornhelm; ***W:*** Beth Gutcheon; ***C:*** Karl Kofler. Nominations: Academy Awards '77: Best Feature Documentary. **VHS**

The Chocolate War

The Chocolate War gets off to an irritating start. Writer/director Keith Gordon crams its first few minutes with stylistic flourishes that serve to confuse rather than intrigue, especially since this flashy approach is soon abandoned in favor of a straightforward narrative. Then it wrings more dramatic mileage out of the annual school candy sale than you would ever have thought possible. We are introduced to Brother Leon, a nutcase if ever there was one, who has his eyes on the headmastership of St. Trinity School for Boys. We also meet the conscienceless Archie, who leads the school's secret society, the Vigils. And then there is Jerry, who initially seeks their acceptance but winds up disillusioned and dispirited by what he learns about both. Former actor

Keith Gordon has assembled rather an off-beat cast: the great John Glover is over the top as always as weird Brother Leon, Ilan Mitchell-Smith seems a bit vague as Jerry, but Wally Ward is right on target as the sociopathic Archie. Adam Baldwin is still in high school eight years after *My Bodyguard,* and the film's only comic relief is furnished by the reliable Bud Cort as Brother Jacques. Based on Robert Cormier's novel, *The Chocolate War* has nothing good to say about self-serving systems or about those who protect them; the film deserves credit for exploring some universal truths in the worthiest of settings, an all-male Catholic school. 🦴🦴🦴

1988 (R) 95m/C John Glover, Jenny Wright, Wally Ward, Bud Cort, Ilan Mitchell-Smith, Adam Baldwin; ***D:*** Keith Gordon; ***W:*** Keith Gordon. **VHS, LV, Closed Caption**

A Chorus of Disapproval

If you enjoyed Jeremy Irons' performance in Barbet Schroeder's vastly overrated *Reversal of Fortune,* or even if you didn't, you might enjoy seeing him in *A Chorus of Disapproval,* directed by Michael Winner. Winner began his career in 1957 by directing *This Is Belgium.* Strapped for funds, he shot much of the travelogue in the British suburban town of East Grinstead. He achieved fame and fortune with the American-made *Death Wish* movies, but his early work on films like *The Jokers* and *I'll Never Forget What's 'is Name* reveal a remarkable feeling for sharp satire that he seldom exploits. Winner was a good choice to direct Alan Ayckbourn's *A Chorus of Disapproval,* a charming satire about the antics of an amateur suburban theatrical troupe. Like many other Ayckbourn works, including *The Norman Conquests,* the satire is in-house. The characters may not behave in irreproachable ways, but they are not condemned for their shortcomings; they are simply shown as the intensely human lot they are. Jeremy Irons is ideally cast as a widowed twit who auditions for the company led by Anthony Hopkins. Hopkins is an insensitive boor, but he is completely devoted to the company and takes the newcomer under his wing. Faster than you can say, "What is there to do in this little town?," we learn that the chief indoor sport is extramarital affairs. There is a swinging couple played by the seductive Jenny Seagrove and a rather puffy Gareth Hunt, who invite Irons and a friend over for fun and games, but Irons is so dense that he brings a sweet little dowager who spends the evening sleeping through a television documentary. There is Hopkins' wife (Prunella Scales), who falls head over heels for the shy young stranger. Meanwhile, Alexandra Pigg and Patsy Kensit fight for the reluctant approval of a grungy kid in the troupe. For one of Britain's most prolific playwrights, Ayckbourn leads a somewhat insulated life. At one point in his career, he maintained that he wrote everything for a suburban repertory theatre, not for West End showcases, television, or the movies, and his work still remains untouched by urban sophistication. As a writer, his chief fascination remains suburbia, a world he observes with affection and wit. Along the way, we see pettiness and treachery, but we also see continuity and strength. Some of Britain's finest actors are in the cast of *A Chorus of Disapproval* (Sylvia Syms, Lionel Jeffries, Barbara Ferris, Richard Briers) and Winner's surprisingly low-key approach here is ideal for this sort of delicate material. 🦴🦴🦴

1989 (PG) 105m/C *GB* Jeremy Irons, Anthony Hopkins, Jenny Seagrove, Lionel Jeffries, Patsy Kensit, Gareth Hunt, Prunella Scales, Sylvia Syms, Richard Briers, Barbara Ferris, Alexandra Pigg; ***D:*** Michael Winner; ***W:*** Michael Winner, Alan Ayckbourn; ***M:*** John Du Prez. **VHS**

Christabel

Elizabeth Hurley is famous today for her boyfriend, her cleavage, her clothes, her commercials, and her delightful comedy performance in *Austin Powers: International Man of Mystery.* She also made quite a splash in England as the title character in *Christabel,* based on a true life story set in World War II. When I was looking for something else on the British Drama shelf at Le Video, I discovered *Christabel,* brought it home, and despite its length,

If my memory of her has an expiration date, let it be 10,000 years.

—Tagline from the movie *Chungking Express*.

couldn't stop watching. Adapted by Dennis Potter from *The Past Is Myself,* Christabel Bielenberg's memoir, the story opens in the early 1930s when the very English Christabel becomes the bride of Peter (Stephen Dillane), a German attorney. After war breaks out, Christabel retreats to the mountains with her little boys. She learns that Peter is in prison for taking part in an assassination plot against Hitler and she's determined to free him. Two sequences in particular require considerable skill from Hurley. In one, she must relay information via code in a story she tells to her imprisoned husband. She mouths the words "There's a microphone" and communicates the entire sad tale in code between sobs. In another, she must secure her husband's release from captivity by playing the role of a rich and influential friend of Winston Churchill in order to intimidate his captors. One false emotion or faulty line delivery in either sequence would have destroyed the point of the film, but newcomer Hurley does a remarkable job for any actress, much less a beginner. The lovely Ruth Etting standard from the year 1927, "Wherever You Go, Whatever You Do, I'm Following You," is used to haunting effect.

1989 148m/C *GB* Elizabeth Hurley, Stephen Dillane, Nigel le Vaillant, Geoffrey Palmer, Ann Bell, Ralph Brown, John Burgess, Suzan Crowley, Eileen Maciejewska, Hugh Simon, Nicola Wright; ***D:*** Adrian Shergold; ***W:*** Dennis Potter; ***C:*** Remi Adefarasin; ***M:*** Stanley Myers. **VHS, Closed Caption**

Chungking Express

The girlfriend of Cop 223 (Takeshi Kaneshiro) has just left him, and while he drowns his sorrows in a pineapple binge, he tries to see if any of his old girlfriends will go out with him. Then he meets a tough blonde drug dealer (superstar Bridget Lin)! The girlfriend (Valerie Chow) of Cop 663 (Superstar Tony Leung) has just left him, and while he's at a fast-food restaurant called the Midnight Express, counter girl Faye Wang makes it very clear that she wants him. So clear, in fact, that she completely obsesses on him, rather like the hero-worshipping kids in 1964's *The World of Henry Orient.* How many times can you listen to "California Dreamin'" withtout screamin'? (Wang's character plays the 1966 hit every chance she gets.) Terrific acting and direction plus stylish cinematography and editing made *Chungking Express* the premiere Rolling Thunder selection from Wong Kar-Wei aficionado Quentin Tarantino.

1995 (PG-13) 102m/C *HK* Bridget Lin, Takeshi Kaneshiro, Tony Leung Chiu-Wai, Faye Wang, Valerie Chow, Piggy Chan; ***D:*** Wong Kar-Wai; ***W:*** Wong Kar-Wai; ***C:*** Christopher Doyle, Lau Wai-Keung; ***M:*** Frankie Chan, Roel A. Garcia. Nominations: Independent Spirit Awards '97: Best Foreign Film. **VHS, LV, Closed Caption**

Cinema Europe

If you ever saw the 1979 Thames television series *Hollywood: The Pioneers,* you already know what meticulous documentarians Kevin Brownlow and David Gill are. Still available on home video, the series revealed the silent movie era, not as creaky, dusty subject matter suitable mainly for museum browsing, but as the vital, hypnotic period for art and entertainment that it really was. Well, Brownlow and Gill have produced a new BBC series that only the lucky subscribers to Turner Classic Movies were able to see in early July of 1996. Their *Cinema Europe* series is a sure bet for home video, so keep your eyes open for it at your favorite neighborhood outlet. *Cinema Europe* bypasses American movies entirely and focuses only on films that were made in Europe. We first discover where it all began and learn that European filmmaking techniques predated cinematic innovations long assumed to originate in America. Subsequent entries, such as *Art's Promised Land, The Unchained Cinema,* and *The Music of Light* show how lovely and lyrical silent films could be at their best: in Sweden, in Russia, in Germany, in France. The toning and tinting of silent pictures created and sustained moods and atmospheres we still can't take for granted in 1997 when we see them at their pristine best. There were even sound experiments as long ago as 1906, but the movies stayed silent through the late 1920s. For most of this study of European cinema, Brownlow and Gill seem

affectionate and awestruck by the artistic and technical wizardry of the early masters. And then they take a sharply critical look at the British film industry in a segment titled *Opportunity Lost.* Why couldn't England make films and develop stars as well as their European neighbors did? We see a 1913 version of *Hamlet* and note that the cameraman can't even keep up with the star! Actress/screenwriter Joan Morgan is unknown here, but her acting career began in 1914 at age nine and continued through 1938 in 37 films, as she explains in a lively series of anecdotes brimming with memories. British cinema didn't really come alive until Alfred Hitchcock, and he, as Kenneth Branagh's narration firmly reminds us, was far more influenced by German expressionism than by any homegrown celluloid endeavors. By the time we arrive, all too soon, at *End of an Era,* we're convinced: in leaving the silent era, we lost something precious, magical, and, all too often, irretrievable. You can still rent a few remaining silent treasures on video, but you may have to hunt for them or try one of the mail-order houses that still stocks them. In the meanwhile, *Cinema Europe* is a must for any true buff of the silent era.

1996 360m/C Kenneth Branagh; ***D:*** David Gill, Kevin Brownlow; ***W:*** David Gill, Kevin Brownlow; ***C:*** David Gill, Kevin Brownlow; ***M:*** Carl Davis, Philip Appleby.

Cinema Paradiso

Cinema Paradiso, Italy's winner in the 1989 Oscar competition, is half of a great movie. Its simple premise is that motion pictures have a profound effect on all our lives. For the first hour, this theme is charmingly illustrated by the evolving friendship between Alfredo, the movie projectionist in a small village, and Toto, a little boy who adores him. Toto also adores flammable nitrate film, the projection booth, and everything in sight in the "Cinema Paradiso." Seen through Toto's eyes, a movie theatre is an enchanted palace and we do not wonder why he idolizes Alfredo, despite the older man's insistence that only an imbecile would be a projectionist. (The film gets much of its strength from Philippe Noiret and Salvatore Cascio's beautiful performances as Alfredo and Toto.) The second hour looks and feels like a different movie: Toto saves Alfredo's life when the theatre is destroyed by fire and later takes over his job as projectionist. Every male fantasy appears to be carved in stone in the second half: the elusive girl who is seduced by relentless pursuit and then lost by circumstances, the young man who is forbidden to look fondly on his humble beginnings lest he be sidetracked from success by nostalgia, even the peculiar conviction that shunning loved ones is a necessary part of adult life. Just when it looks as if writer/director Giuseppe Tornatore has forgotten why he made the film, he floods the screen with fragments from Toto's magical childhood at the "Cinema Paradiso," all the love scenes that were censored by the village priest. It's pure mush, but it's irresistible mush. Most audiences will leave remembering the winning truths of Part One and forgetting the laborious falseness of Part Two. The last sequence succeeds in making *Cinema Paradiso* seem to be a much better film than it really is. ***AKA:*** Nuovo Cinema Paradiso.

1988 123m/C *IT* Philippe Noiret, Jacques Perrin, Salvatore Cascio, Marco Leonardi, Agnes Nano, Leopoldo Trieste; ***D:*** Giuseppe Tornatore; ***W:*** Giuseppe Tornatore; ***C:*** Basco Giurato; ***M:*** Ennio Morricone. Academy Awards '89: Best Foreign Film; British Academy Awards '90: Best Actor (Noiret), Best Foreign Film, Best Original Screenplay, Best Supporting Actor (Cascio); Cannes Film Festival '89: Grand Jury Prize; Golden Globe Awards '90: Best Foreign Film. **VHS, LV, 8mm**

Citizen Ruth

This superb satire takes no prisoners in a razor-sharp examination of both sides of the abortion issue. Laura Dern is terrific as Ruth, a glue-sniffing, pregnant, unfit mother of four who is busted for fetus endangerment, and then learns that the judge will go easy on her if there's no fetus to endanger. Faster than you can count up to 400 bucks, Kurtwood Smith and Mary Kay Place as Norm and Gail Stoney are paying Ruth's bail, and taking her home to stay in their immaculate Christian home. What's

Ruth (Laura Dern) and one of her mentors, Gail Stoney (Mary Kay Place) in *Citizen Ruth.* Miramax; courtesy of the Kobal Collection

the catch? Ruth has to HAVE Baby Tanya, of course, because it will send a powerful message to America from all those nice right-to-life folks. Ruth hears the word "message," panics, and hunts for the nearest tube of glue. Her next trial and tribulation is with the nice folks who believe in a woman's-right-to-her-own-body. They take Ruth home to stay with them, too. What's the catch? Ruth has to exercise her freedom to choose an abortion, of course, because it will send a powerful message to America from all those nice folks who believe in THAT freedom, of course. Ruth hears the word "message," panics again, and indulges in more substances! But there IS one non-partisan message in which Ruth has faith, and it is this delicious concept that wipes out every argument either side can contrive. The well-chosen supporting cast (Swoosie Kurtz, Kelly Preston, M.C. Gainey, Kenneth Mars, Alicia Witt, Tippi Hedren as Super Feminist Jessica Weiss, and even Diane Ladd as Ruth's mom) adds to the surreal quality of Ruth's dilemma and her wildly skewed alternatives. And check out the adolescent boy who's the constant attendant of Blaine Gibbons, the right-to-life spokesman played by Burt Reynolds. He's a subtle symbol of hypocrisy at the top of the power chain, reinforced by Norm Stoney's lustful leering at Ruth while playing the good Christian husband and father to the hilt. If even one whiff of politically correct banana oil makes you RETCH, *Citizen Ruth* is YOUR movie! ***AKA:*** Precious; Meet Ruth Stoops. ℒℒℒℒ

1996 (R) 104m/C Laura Dern, Swoosie Kurtz, Mary Kay Place, Kurtwood Smith, Kelly Preston, Burt Reynolds, M.C. Gainey, Kenneth Mars, Kathleen Noone, David Graf, Tippi Hedren, Alicia Witt, Diane Ladd; ***D:*** Alexander Payne; ***W:*** Alexander Payne, Jim Taylor; ***C:*** James Glennon; ***M:*** Rolfe Kent. Montreal World Film Festival '95: Best Actress (Dern). **VHS, LV, Closed Caption**

Citizen X

The story of Russian murderer Andrei Chikatilo and the 52 people he killed may have been too horrifying for the big screen, too horrifying and too difficult to access. No one except criminologists and scientific researchers wants to get inside the mind of such a man, and Soviet Russia denied he even existed between 1982 and 1990. The investigator assigned to the case is Dr. Viktor Burakov (Stephen Rea), whose dedication to stopping Chikatilo's deadly spree more than makes up for the fact that there is no genius lurking beneath his untidy exterior. Dr. Burakov's greatest ally is Colonel Fetisov (Donald Sutherland), a bureaucrat who IS a genius, especially when it comes to working within a flawed system that's staggering under the weight of a myriad of excuses and denials. Colonel Fetisov knows what Dr. Burakov does not, that the search for Chikatilo will be delayed and hampered at every turn by officious bureaucrats trying to protect themselves and bolster their reputations, at the expense of dozens of innocent lives. One such bureaucrat is Soviet official Bonarchuk (Joss Ackland) who states categorically that only Western societies are plagued by serial killers. He orders a policeman (John Wood) after his own heart to look for *Citizen X* among identifiable homosexuals and perverted criminals. Burakov and Fetisov are convinced that the killer is a more nondescript type since his youthful victims trusted him well enough to follow him into the woods where most of the bodies are discovered. Jeffrey DeMunn plays Chikatilo as the sort of man you might not notice in a group of three, a wimp who'd never pick on someone his own size; he only has the power to hurt the extremely young and vulnerable. After eight long years and the collapse of Soviet Russia, Chikatilo is finally placed in custody. In one long sequence with the skillful Russian psychiatrist played by Max von Sydow, the agonized Chikatilo finally confesses all. It is no comfort to the families or to the audiences who watch *Citizen X,* but the investigation clearly forced the Russian people (and international viewers) to see Death with a human face. Performances throughout are immaculate, particularly Sutherland's brilliant work as Colonel Fetisov. Chris Gerolmo's incisive script and careful direction make it possible for us to watch this horrifying nightmare without turning away. And Gerolmo's understated lucidity may help more than one viewer look twice before s/he follows a kind stranger ANYWHERE. 🦴🦴🦴

1995 (R) 100m/C Stephen Rea, Donald Sutherland, Jeffrey DeMunn, John Wood, Joss Ackland, Max von Sydow, Ralph Nossek, Imelda Staunton, Radu Amzulrescu, Czeskaw Grocholski, Ion Caramitru, Andras Balint, Tusse Silberg; ***D:*** Chris Gerolmo; ***W:*** Chris Gerolmo; ***C:*** Robert Fraisse; ***M:*** Randy Edelman. **VHS**

City of Hope

Again, no one asked me, but *City of Hope* was a much worthier contender for Picture of the Year than *Silence of the Lambs.* John Sayles' rich portrait of the complexity of urban life offers sharp, revealing performances from Vincent Spano as Nick, Joe Morton as Councilman Wynn, and Tony LoBianco as Nick's father Joe. Sayles exposes the "any means necessary" approach to deal-making in the city, even when it leads to tragedy. He also shows the inevitable malaise and despair that accompany such cold ruthlessness. Nick doesn't care and wants out; Wynn does care, but his reform efforts are blocked at every turn; and Joe loves his son, but establishes an impossible blueprint for his life. All the actors in the large cast are outstanding, including Sayles as a sleazebag named Carl. *City of Hope,* a far more cohesive film than *Lone Star,* is long overdue for a major reassessment. 🦴🦴🦴🦴

1991 (R) 132m/C Vincent Spano, Tony LoBianco, Joe Morton, Todd Graff, David Strathairn, Anthony John Denison, Barbara Williams, Angela Bassett, Gloria Foster, Lawrence Tierney, John Sayles, Maggie Renzi, Kevin Tighe, Chris Cooper, Jace Alexander, Frankie Faison, Michael Mantell, Josh Mostel, Joe Grifasi, Louis Zorich, Gina Gershon, Rose Gregorio, Bill Raymond, Maeve Kinkead, Ray Aranha; ***D:*** John Sayles; ***W:*** John Sayles; ***C:*** Robert Richardson; ***M:*** Mason Daring. Independent Spirit Awards '92: Best Supporting Actor (Strathairn). **VHS, LV, 8mm, Closed Caption**

The City of Lost Children

I'm one of the viewers who said, "Huh?" after watching this movie. Then I heard a

Clay (Joaquin Phoenix) and Amanda (Georgina Cates) in *Clay Pigeons.* Gramercy; courtesy of the Kobal Collection

much-televised promotion in which a critic described it as "eye candy." It isn't for children, but it focuses on them, so I guess it's for grown-ups who are on the edge of their seats at the notion of an inventor stealing kid's dreams because he can't have any. Best for those who like this sort of thing. ***AKA:*** La Cité des Enfants Perdus.

1995 (R) 114m/C *FR* Ron Perlman, Daniel Emilfork, Joseph Lucien, Judith Vittet, Dominique Pinon, Jean Claude Dreyfus, Odile Mallet, Genevieve Brunet, Mireille Mosse; ***D:*** Jean-Pierre Jeunet, Marc Caro; ***W:*** Jean-Pierre Jeunet, Marc Caro, Gilles Adrien; ***C:*** Darius Khondji; ***M:*** Angelo Badalamenti; ***V:*** Jean-Louis Trintignant. Cesar Awards '96: Best Art Direction/Set Decoration; Nominations: Cesar Awards '96: Best Cinematography, Best Costume Design, Best Score; Independent Spirit Awards '96: Best Foreign Film. **VHS, LV, Closed Caption**

Clay Pigeons

Vince Vaughn wants to play Lonesome Rhodes in a reprise of the role immortalized by Andy Griffith in 1957's *A Face in the Crowd.* Just thinking about the gifted Vaughn as a sleazy, media-driven character is a mouth-watering prospect, since Vaughn IS Lester Long in *Clay Pigeons,* the first film for screenwriter Matthew Healy and for director David Dobkin. Both Healy and Dobkin dive into the film noir genre like Philip Marlowe plunged into that bottomless black pool in *Murder, My Sweet.* But this is neo-noir, circa 1998, with its own weird twists and turns. The world of *Clay Pigeons* is savagely funny, with vast, bright Canadian landscapes supplying the background for all sorts of violent surprises. Clay Bidwell (Joaquin Phoenix) is best friends with Earl (Gregory Sporleder), who believes that his wife Amanda (Georgina Cates) was a virgin when he married her. After learning that Clay and Amanda are carrying on, and knowing that his good buddy Clay would never, ever shoot anyone, Earl comes up with a surefire scheme of vengeance. What's a peace-loving small town guy like Clay to do? Then, Earl's "virginal" bride Amanda proves to be pretty faithless, and she continues to practice her seductive tricks on poor Clay, who, it must be said, is not terribly bright. In frustration, he takes cute waitress Gloria (Nikki Arlyn) home to his water bed, a situation not missed by the also-frustrated Amanda. Nope, Clay and Amanda just can't seem to get along, a situation not missed by good old boy Lester Long. Ah, Lester, what can you say about him other than he's good-natured and clean-shaven and wears a big cowboy hat and has a silly laugh that you'd never miss in a crowded bar? How Clay and Gloria and Amanda and Lester and Monica Moench's Kimberly (Clay used to babysit her before SHE was a waitress) help each other fulfill their destinies is the tale that *Clay Pigeons* has to tell. That Healy and Dobkin make you laugh and shiver and look forward to every new sequence with breathless anticipation is a tribute to their fresh and vivid originality. Phoenix and Vaughn bring out the best in each other as actors (if not as characters) and every part down to the tiniest bit is splendidly cast. Once again, Janeane Garofalo is a delight as FBI agent Dale Shelby, and who should be her granite-jawed partner but Phil Morris (son of Greg, from *Mission Impossible*)? Scott *(In Cold Blood)* Wilson plays decent Sheriff Mooney with every bit as much intensity as he once played Dick Hickock, and if you remember Cates from her work in the Brit flicks *An Awfully Big Adventure* and *Frankie Starlight,* you'll be stunned at her unrecognizable transformation here as the trashy Amanda. 🦴🦴🦴🦴

1998 (R) 104m/C Vince Vaughn, Joaquin Rafael (Leaf) Phoenix, Janeane Garofalo, Scott Wilson, Georgina Cates, Phil Morris, Vince Vieluf, Nikki Arlyn, Monica Moench, Joseph D. Reitman, Gregory Sporleder; ***D:*** David Dobkin; ***W:*** Matthew Healy; ***C:*** Eric Alan Edwards; ***M:*** John Lurie. **VHS, LV, Closed Caption, DVD**

Clean, Shaven

Schizophrenic Peter Winter (Peter Greene in a stunning performance) is searching bleak Miscou Island, off the New Brunswick coast, for his young daughter, whom his mother put up for adoption after Peter was institutionalized and his wife died. Peter's being tailed by Detective McNally (Robert Albert), who suspects him of a child's murder, and his tenuous hold on reality slowly disintegrates into torment and self-mutilation. Debut for director/writer Lodge Kerrigan. Greene can also be seen in *Laws of Gravity, Judgment Night,* and *The Mask.* Jennifer MacDonald is in *Headless Body in Topless Bar.* 🦴🦴

1993 80m/C Peter Greene, Robert Albert, Jennifer MacDonald, Megan Owen, Molly Castelloe; ***D:*** Lodge Kerrigan; ***W:*** Lodge Kerrigan; ***C:*** Teodoro Maniaci; ***M:*** Hahn Rowe. Nominations: Independent Spirit Awards '95: Best First Feature. **VHS**

Clerks

Clerks is a promising first film by Kevin Smith about a clerk in a convenience store and a clerk in a video store. It's everything a first film should be: funny, fresh, and original. It was shot in black and white on a budget of $27,000, and its gritty, cinema-verite quality made it seem almost like a slice-of-life documentary rather than the scripted fiction film it really was. Reportedly, preview audiences were so caught up in the lives of the two central characters that they responded negatively when one of them was shown being killed on duty. So the ending was re-shot, a wise choice, because to have turned an 88-minute comedy into an 89-minute tragedy at the last minute wouldn't have worked without some premonitory sequences—which wouldn't have worked, either, because of the scrappy, upbeat tone overall. When Smith made *Mallrats* a year later, the same critics who lionized *Clerks* beyond recognition jumped down hard on the filmmaker's second effort. Smith's *Chasing Amy,* his third picture, drew rave reviews. 🦴🦴🦴

1994 (R) 89m/B Brian O'Halloran, Jeff Anderson, Marilyn Ghigliotti, Lisa Spoonhauer, Jason Mewes; ***Cameos:*** Kevin Smith; ***D:*** Kevin Smith; ***W:*** Kevin Smith; ***C:*** David Klein; ***M:*** Scott Angley. Sundance Film Festival '94: Filmmakers Trophy; Nominations:

"You can do anything with a child, as long as you play with him."

—Interrogator Alan Rickman's response to prisoner Madeleine Stowe's defense that she is only a writer of children's books, in *Closet Land*.

Independent Spirit Awards '95: Best First Feature, Debut Performance (Anderson), First Screenplay. **VHS, LV, Closed Caption**

Closet Land

Four audience members walked out of the advance screening of *Closet Land,* a heavy-handed and overly stylized film about the psychological torture of a female political prisoner. *Closet Land* is a "safe" propaganda film produced by Ron Howard with the blessing of Amnesty International. Who is going to be FOR the torture of a pretty young woman in a flowing white dress? Both actress Madeleine Stowe and the dress go through the entire 90-minute film looking absolutely terrific. Stowe is the captive of the plumby-voiced Alan Rickman, who wears a suit and tie most of the time and has just a hint of five o'clock shadow by film's end. So much for harsh realism. And where will we be watching this movie? In comfortable living rooms a few steps away from gleaming kitchens and light years away from the unnamed countries where torture occurs. Since few of us are likely to voluntarily place ourselves in danger in abusive faraway countries, the most we can do is give a few bucks to Amnesty International. But you can do that after watching television's short public service announcements from Glenn Close and Robin Willlams. So let's look at *Closet Land* as a film. The images reinforce the helplessness of women. The soundtrack reinforces the eroticism traditionally associated with the helplessness of women. And the rhetoric is foolhardy. It is the duty of a political prisoner to escape, not to engage in the lost cause of educating one's captors. This prisoner uses precisely the same techniques for escape that she did as a child, reinforcing the false notion that women learn nothing about self-protection between infancy and adulthood. There is even a moment when *Closet Land* appears to be veering in the kinky direction of Liliana Cavani's *The Night Porter,* but then Stowe makes a sacrificial speech. A much better, more realistic movie about this subject is Poland's long-banned *Interrogation,* also available on home video. But 1982's *Interrogation* is a film about survival, not martyrdom, and Krystyna Janda is not a pretty pin-up like Madeline Stowe. Janda's prison is a gritty, grimy place, not a polished, stage-bound chamber, and no one in *Interrogation* has cinematic credentials on the order of *Stakeout* or *Die Hard.* First-time writer/director Radha Bharadwaj is a talented, well-meaning artist who convinces only the faithful and the safe. Ultimately, her *Closet Land* is the politically correct equivalent of *Triumph of the Will.* **woof!**

1990 (R) 90m/C Madeleine Stowe, Alan Rickman; ***D:*** Radha Bharadwaj; ***W:*** Radha Bharadwaj; ***C:*** Bill Pope; ***M:*** Richard Einhorn. **VHS, LV, Closed Caption**

Closing Numbers

Strong performances and mature story lines distinguished many of 1994's entries at the 18th Annual International Lesbian and Gay Film Festival. The highlight of Stephen Whittaker's *Closing Numbers* is a bravura performance by the much underrated Jane Asher, who hasn't had this meaty a role since she made *Deep End* with Jerzy Skolimowski in 1970. Asher plays a happily married wife and mother without a clue that her husband is bisexual until she confronts the man with whom he's been having an affair. THEY'VE been having safe sex, the lover tells her, but SHE is at risk because of unprotected one-night stands in her husband's past. She reacts with rage at first, then numbly continues with the routine of her life, with a few differences. She has an HIV test and is introduced by the lover to working with one of his AIDS patients. All the while, her husband remains in deep denial, and their son is extremely hostile to his parent's much-changed relationship. Asher's beautifully drawn study of a woman in limbo is unforgettable.

1993 95m/C *GB* Jane Asher, Tim Woodward, Patrick Pearson, Nigel Charnock; ***D:*** Stephen Whittaker; ***W:*** David Cook; ***C:*** Nicholas D. Knowland.

Clouds over Europe

Tim Whelan's *Clouds over Europe/Q Planes,* released less than six months before World War II, shows how much Great Britain had changed in the 18 months since 1937's *Non-Stop New York.* There is a not-so-subtle grim edge to this playful treatment of pre-war espionage. *Clouds over Europe* made a great impression on 16-year-old movie fan Patrick MacNee, who stored away his impressions of Ralph Richardson's wry secret service agent for future reference. (MacNee's memory was to prove handy when he played John Steed in *The Avengers* television series.) Valerie Hobson, icily portrayed in 1989's *Scandal,* was a warm and lively presence in British films for over 20 years and she does a fine job here as a persistent journalist. Laurence Olivier costars as a dashing test pilot. ***AKA:*** Q Planes.

1939 82m/B Laurence Olivier, Valerie Hobson, Ralph Richardson, George Curzon, George Merritt, Gus McNaughton, David Tree, Sandra Storme, Hay Petrie, Frank Fox, Gordon McLeod, John Longden, Reginald Purdell, John Laurie, Pat Aherne; ***D:*** Tim Whelan; ***W:*** Ian Dalyrymple; ***C:*** Harry Stradling. **VHS, LV**

Coffee with Lemon

Award-winning actress Tatyana Vasilyeva stars in Leonid Gorovets' *Coffee with Lemon.* Great Russian actor Valery Ostrovsy (Alexander Abdulov) goes to Israel with his wife (Vasilyeva) and son, hoping for a better life. He winds up out of work because he can't speak Hebrew. Then he finds out he's won an award for his performance in a film he made before leaving Russia. This Israeli entry suggests that talent only appears to transcend the perennial challenge of a Jewish identity, and its downbeat conclusions indicate that, drawn to its most illogical extremes, belief in such an apparition leads to tragic consequences. By some startling coincidence, Alexander Proshkin's *To See Paris and Die,* made in Russia in 1993 and also starring Vasilyeva, had pretty much the same theme.

1994 94m/C *IS* Alexander Abdulov, Tatyana Vasilyeva, Bruria Albek; ***D:*** Leonid Gorovets; ***W:*** Semyon Vinokur; ***C:*** Valentin Belanogov.

Cold Feet

Someone must have had cold feet about making *Cold Feet* because Thomas McGuane's screenplay sat on the shelf for nearly 13 years. This starring vehicle for Oscar-nominee Sally Kirkland is supposed to be a comedy. The press kit even let reviewers know what the funny parts are and why; if you don't laugh, well, heck, maybe you just don't have a sense of humor. The film is 94 minutes long and Kirkland has a different costume change for every scene. She dives into the part with such enthusiasm that it almost doesn't matter that her role makes no sense at all. Her co-stars Keith Carradine and Tom Waits are supposed to be endearing in a peculiar sort of way. Carradine's irresponsible cowboy ditches fiancee Kirkland with Waits, a psychotic killer who's even played as a folk hero. (Waits shoots a doctor in cold blood and then overacts for the rest of the movie while Kirkland nibbles on Cheez Whiz and crackers.) Small details are ignored: if you cut a horse open to stuff him with emeralds, you always have to sew him back up again if you want him to live, except in this movie. Also, even though Waits slices Carradine's ear and Carradine did, after all, watch him shoot that doctor, Carradine still lets his much-loved nine-year-old daughter play with Waits without supervision. I thought that was really strange. I only laughed at one thing: a movie marquee features *Chicks with Zip Guns* as the main attraction and *Rancho Deluxe* as the second feature. It's an in-joke but at least I got this one. Thomas McGuane wrote *Rancho Deluxe* back in 1975 and its star Jeff Bridges has an unbilled bit in *Cold Feet* as a bartender. Another in-joke is the presence of Kirkland's real-life old flame Rip Torn as an all-purpose sheriff and minister at her onscreen wedding. If you agree with McGuane that Montana in and of itself is hilarious, then *Cold Feet* just may be your movie.

1989 (R) 94m/C Keith Carradine, Tom Waits, Sally Kirkland, Rip Torn, Kathleen York, Bill Pullman, Vincent Schiavelli, Jeff Bridges; ***D:*** Robert Dornhelm; ***W:*** Thomas McGuane, Jim Harrison; ***C:*** Bryan Duggan; ***M:*** Tom Bahler. **VHS, LV**

A Cold Wind in August

Lola Albright is a meltingly lovely blonde from Akron, Ohio, who will probably best be remembered for her role as a nightclub singer in television's *Peter Gunn* series. Although she created a vivid impression in 36 movies between 1948 and 1977, Albright received just one starring role onscreen, in 1961's *A Cold Wind in August,* based on the Burton Wohl novel. Albright plays a 40-week-a-year stripper who cherishes the 12 weeks she can try to lead a more conventional life in a New York apartment building. Among her own age group (36), she is hard and brittle, determined to distance herself from the fantasies of men who want her to fill their needs, not her own. On a sultry summer day, the 17-year-old son of the building supervisor arrives at her doorstep, ready to fix her air conditioner. Around this awkward, intimidated kid, her tough shell dissolves, and she finally allows herself to feel something. The kid is nicely played by Scott Marlowe, who had been playing troubled teens for over five years by this point, so the extreme difference in their ages had to be spelled out in the acting and by Alexander Singer's skillful direction, rather than the script. In fact, there is one sequence in a park where this supposedly mismatched couple draw stares that don't make sense since Albright looks so young and Marlowe is so obviously not a teenager. The moments when the film really works are when Albright brilliantly reveals her loss of self over a love that means everything in the world to her, yet is clearly, by its very nature, ephemeral. The rare quality of this film lies in its sympathetic understanding of the acting women have to do to survive, and in its depiction of the strong disapproval men feel when women stop acting. Strong supporting performances are delivered by two great character actors: Joe De Santis, as the kid's compassionate father, and another *Peter Gunn* alumnus, Herschel Bernardi, as a friend who stoically endures a friendship with Albright's character, suffering all the while from his unrequited love for her. *A Cold Wind in August* is a hard film to find today, not yet released on home video, and surfacing only very occasionally on television late at night. But when you consider the example of *Butterfield 8,* a slick and phony piece of splashy Metro drek that won Elizabeth Taylor the 1960 Oscar, the virtues of a small, independent gem like *A Cold Wind in August* sparkle in comparison. (Condemned by the Legion of Decency during its original release.) ℛℛℛℛ

1961 80m/B Lola Albright, Scott Marlowe, Herschel Bernardi, Joe De Santis; ***D:*** Alexander Singer; ***W:*** Burton Wohl; ***C:*** Floyd Crosby.

Coldblooded

The way that critics pounced on *Coldblooded,* I thought its filmmakers were trying to produce a snuff film or plagiarize *Pulp Fiction* or both. That's until I actually sat down and watched this low-key satire. Clearly, its original audiences didn't appreciate first-time director M. Wallace Wolodarsky's sense of humor at all, but I did. Jason Priestley is Cosmo Reif, the bookie of a mobster named Gordon (played by Robert Loggia). When Gordon needs a new hit man, he thinks first of Cosmo, even though he doesn't have any experience. That's all right; Steve, the other hit man, will train him. Peter Riegert, one of the great character actors of his generation, is so memorable as Steve that he steals every scene he's in, even when Wolodarsky didn't write them to favor him. Steve hates his job; he drinks alone and cries alone, then wakes up with a hangover and goes to work. Cosmo doesn't much like the job, either, but finds that he's surprisingly good at it. Instead of crying and drinking, he joins a health club and falls for Jasmine, the lovely yoga teacher, played by the lovely ingenue Kimberly Williams. Up to this point, Cosmo has only been able to retain the attention of Honey the Hooker (Janeane Garofalo). But now he has visions of a better life with Jasmine, but without Gordon, his henchman John, or even Steve. Only one hitch: Jasmine doesn't like the idea of living with a hit man; but then, neither does Cosmo. *Coldblooded* is played so broadly, it's hard to imagine that anyone thought it was a documentary or a justification of the need for hit men anymore than Jonathan Swift's modest proposal of the 18th century actually called for the children of the poor to be eaten by the rich. Who could believe that anyone who looked like Jason Priestley would lead such a dull, drab life? Or that a charmer like Peter Riegert couldn't talk his way out of any assignment? Or that Kimberly Williams would consider a hit man to be her nicest boyfriend? Hey, it's only a movie, but it made ME laugh! 🦴🦴🦴

1994 (R) 92m/C Jason Priestley, Peter Riegert, Kimberly Williams, Robert Loggia, Janeane Garofalo, Josh Charles, David Anthony Higgens, Doris Grau; ***Cameos:*** Talia Balsam, Michael J. Fox; ***D:*** M. Wallace Wolodarsky; ***W:*** M. Wallace Wolodarsky; ***C:*** Robert Yeoman; ***M:*** Steve Bartek. **VHS**

Color Adjustment

When we look at early images of television, an atmosphere of false innocence saturates everything we see. We don't think of the real-life Donna Reed, infuriated by relentless male visions of what the perfect wife and mother should be, we don't think of the real-life Robert Young and his offscreen struggles with alcoholism, we don't think of the real-life Nelson family, nearly torn apart by custody battles; we prefer to think of serene communities like Mayfield where Wally and the Beaver are always twelve and nine years old and Ward and June Cleaver are always there for their little boys. But as false as white images on television are, at least they exist. In the early 1950s, as *Color Adjustment,* Marlon Riggs' absorbing 1991 film shows, you could stop counting shows about black Americans after *Beulah* and *Amos 'n' Andy.* Both series were originally created and played by middle-aged white guys for radio. (Yes, Beulah, too. Marlin Hurt and Bob Corley were the voices of *Beulah* the maid long before Ethel Waters and Louise Beavers took over the role on television.) The N.A.A.C.P. fought hard to get the racial stereotypes of *Amos 'n' Andy* off the air and finally succeeded in 1953, although the show persisted in reruns through 1966. After that, there were only sporadic efforts to acknowledge black artists on television. Nat "King" Cole was given a shot at his own weekly variety show, but the series failed to attract a sponsor after its first season. Bill Cosby's role as Alexander Scott on *I Spy* provided a breakthrough of sorts, but the doors opened very slowly and only for the most non-threatening images of black Americans, like the nurse *Julia,* interpreted by Diahann Carroll. (*Room 222,* clearly inspired by the huge international success of *To Sir with Love,* gave slightly more realistic roles as teachers to the late Lloyd Haynes and to Denise Nicholas.) But it was Norman Lear's *All in the Family,* with two of its enormously popular spin-offs, *Good Times* and *The Jeffersons,* that finally convinced network executives that shows about black Americans could be ratings leaders. Even so, black images popularized by television in the 1990s are often just as unrealistic as their 1950s predecessors were. Television projects with a conscience like *East Side, West Side, Roots, Frank's Place,* and *The Cosby Show* are examined in the context of what is actually happening in the lives of television viewers and contrasted with thoughtful observations by the late James Baldwin, Diahann Carroll, Esther Rolle, Tim Reid, and others. As always, the late Marlon Riggs offers welcome counterpoint at a time when we are all challenging what we see and hear in the media. If you can find it, you won't want to miss *Color Adjustment.* 🦴🦴🦴🦴

1991 88m/C Ruby Dee; ***D:*** Marlon Riggs; ***W:*** Marlon Riggs; ***C:*** Rick Butler; ***M:*** Mary Watkins. **VHS**

Color of a Brisk and Leaping Day

While living in L.A. at the end of WWII, Chinese-American John Lee (Peter Alexander) learns that the Yosemite Valley Railroad is being scrapped and becomes determined to save it, in part as an homage to his grandfather, who emigrated to work as a railroad laborer. A romantic train fanatic himself, Lee arranges financing from

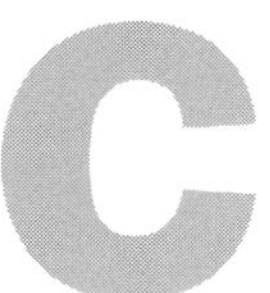

"My father was a very big man. And he wore a black mustache. When he grew older and it grew gray, he colored it with a pencil. The kind women use. Mascara."

—Robert (Christopher Walken) in *The Comfort of Strangers.*

wealthy businessman Pinchot (John Diehl) but must make the railroad pay within a year—unlikely, as the automobile rapidly takes over as preferred transportation. Well captures a 1940s atmosphere, but pacing and dialogue are uneven. Director/writer Christopher Munch is best known for *The Hours and Times.* ⅋⅋

1995 87m/B Peter Alexander, Jeri Arredondo, Henry Gibson, Michael Stipe, John Diehl, David Chung, Diana Larkin, Bok Yun Chon; ***D:*** Christopher Munch; ***W:*** Christopher Munch; ***C:*** Rob Sweeney. Sundance Film Festival '96: Best Cinematography; Nominations: Independent Spirit Awards '97: Best Cinematography. **VHS**

Combination Platter

Combination Platter was made by Tony Chan when he was only 23 years old. It gives us a light-hearted, sharply observed look at the immigration experience, as seen from the perspective of Robert (Jeff Lau), who comes to New York from Hong Kong without a green card. Robert's helpful friend Andy (Kenneth Lu) introduces him to women, even though Robert is shocked by the idea that he can become a citizen by marrying an American. His first job is as a waiter in a Chinese restaurant and this is where he learns about life in America. Chan and Edwin Baker won a much-deserved award for Best Screenplay at 1993's Sundance Film Festival. ⅋⅋⅋

1993 84m/C Jeff Lau, Colleen O'Brien, Lester Chan, Thomas S. Hsiung, David Chung, Colin Mitchell, Kenneth Lu, Eleonara Khilberg, James DuMont; ***D:*** Tony Chan; ***W:*** Tony Chan, Edwin Baker; ***C:*** Yoshifumi Hosoya; ***M:*** Brian Tibbs. Sundance Film Festival '93: Best Screenplay; Nominations: Independent Spirit Awards '94: Best First Feature, Best Screenplay, Best Supporting Actor (Chung). **VHS**

The Comfort of Strangers

1961's *Last Year at Marienbad* has gone begging for the perfect film to round out a double bill suitable for residents of Limbo and/or Purgatory. Now at last there IS one! *The Comfort of Strangers,* the latest from everybody's favorite divinity school dropout: Grand Rapids, Michigan's own Paul Schrader. Let's hear it! Or to be more precise, let's hear whaaat? How about some hot dialogue from the one and only Harold Pinter, Schrader's accomplice in this cinematic minefield. HE: "Why is there no other word for thigh?" SHE: "It's a perfectly good word, what's wrong with it?" HE: "Yes, but...." Then HE goes on to list a dreary and depressing series of anatomical euphemisms and bemoans the fate of the humble word "thigh." This riveting sequence says a lot about the rest of the film. Natasha Richardson plays a young British mother of two who leaves them at home to travel to Venice with her even-more British lover Rupert Everett. The match is not made in heaven, and it's clear that they are beginning to bore each other. There are only a zillion restaurants in Venice, but one night they can't find one and who should crawl out of the nearest dark alley but a slimy stranger in a white suit? (Christopher Walken, of course, typecast this time with an all-purpose Italian-Bavarian accent!) They follow the stranger down some dark alleys to a crummy bar he assures them is really good, but turns out to be HIS bar, where no food is available. They chew on breadsticks, swallow wine, and listen to stories from this character, who amazingly, is even more boring than they are. The next morning, the couple wakes up in the street where SHE gets sick. The next day, they try to avoid the stranger, but he drags them to his house, anyway. His "Canadian" wife is Helen Mirren, who watches them while they sleep and then tells them about it. Before they all have dinner that night, Walken punches Everett in the stomach for no good reason. The couple resumes their stupefyingly dull holiday until they see Mirren waving to them from her window. Not wishing to be rude, they pop in to say hello. Walken invites Everett to follow him down more dark alleys, Mirren prepares a drink for Natasha Richardson, and two people walk out of the movie theatre, one of them hissing, "Oh, the English!" Three guys in front of me are in stitches, I am in stitches, and at least one stuffed shirt is disgusted with all of us for not accepting this beautiful work of art with appropriate reverence. Our reaction probably counts as two venial sins, at least. I went home and enjoyed watching *Goldfinger* AND *Arsenic and Old Lace,* which just may count as FOUR mortal sins, oh dear. *My Dinner with Androids,* whoops, sooo sorry, we did mean *The Comfort of Strangers,* is available for your consideration on home video. **woof!**

1991 (R) 102m/C Christopher Walken, Natasha Richardson, Rupert Everett, Helen Mirren; ***D:*** Paul Schrader; ***W:*** Harold Pinter; ***C:*** Dante Spinotti; ***M:*** Angelo Badalamenti. **VHS, Closed Caption**

Confessions of a Window Cleaner

Robin Askwith looks as though someone once gave his face a severe punching. He stars as the "romantic" hero of four London-based comedies, in which he discovers new professions and different sets of women on the job. It's difficult to believe that Askwith could attract such frenzy from his female patrons, but he does have a certain awkward appeal. In spite of the relentless schoolboy-level humor, the film manages to garner some honest laughter, particularly in the family sequences co-starring Anthony Booth and Sheila White as Sidney and Rosie Noggett, and Bill Maynard and Dandy Nichols as Mr. and Mrs. Lea. Followed by *Confessions of a Pop Performer* (1975), *Confessions of a Driving Instructor,* and *Confessions from a Holiday Camp* (1977), all starring Robin Askwith as Timothy Lea and based on Lea's novels.

1974 m/C *GB* Robin Askwith, Anthony Booth, Sheila White, Bill Maynard, Dandy Nichols; ***D:*** Val Guest; ***W:*** Val Guest, Georges Lendi; ***C:*** Norman Warwick.

The Conformist

A chill sets in every time I see the gutless "Conformist" in Bernardo Bertolucci's classic adaptation of Alberto Moravia's 1951 novel. And then, a few years go by, and I'm swept up in the film's spell all over again as if I were watching it for the first time. I suspect that the film would have been unbearable to watch if any other artist than Bertolucci had been at the helm or any actor other than Jean-Louis Trintignant had been cast in the title role. Trintignant is the thinking man's wimp; as he is swept along by events and circumstances in Fascist Italy, his face maps out all the untaken roads and unmade choices. But if there is a heart and soul to the film, it is possessed by the cool lesbian played by Dominique Sanda. *The Conformist,* the film that launched Bertolucci's international career, cost just 3/4 of a million dollars to make, but Sanda's mere presence makes the film look and feel far more expensive. From her seduction on a polished table to her doomed flight from assassins, Sanda is the perfect sacrificial symbol of that era, a fact not lost on Vittorio De Sica, who went on to cast her in the Oscar-winning *Garden of the Finzi Continis.* Although Trintignant's internal angst and his aimless domestic life with Stefania Sandrelli (whom Sanda's character tries to lure both on and off the dance floor) receive most of the screen time, it is Sanda's haunting presence that lingers in the memory. Note: A new restored print of *The Conformist* surfaced in 1994, including the five-minute "Dance of the Blind" sequence shorn by Paramount from the original 1971 release. ***AKA:*** Il Conformist.

1971 (R) 108m/C *IT FR GE* Jean-Louis Trintignant, Stefania Sandrelli, Dominique Sanda, Pierre Clementi, Gastone Moschin, Pasquale Fortunato; ***D:*** Bernardo Bertolucci; ***W:*** Bernardo Bertolucci; ***C:*** Vittorio Storaro; ***M:*** Georges Delerue. National Society of Film Critics Awards '71: Best Cinematography (Storaro), Best Director (Bertolucci); Nominations: Academy Awards '71: Best Adapted Screenplay. **VHS, LV**

Cop Land

Sylvester Stallone gives the performance of his life in *Cop Land,* James Mangold's outstanding film noir about a rarefied community of policemen who take care of their own by any means necessary. The story opens with a high-speed police chase on the George Washington Bridge. Young cop Murray Babitch (Michael Rapaport) thinks he sees something in the car of two black kids out for a lark that night,

Tilden (Robert De Niro) and Heflin (Sylvester Stallone) in *Cop Land.* Miramax; courtesy of the Kobal Collection

but in his trigger-happy confusion, he's mistaken. His error in judgment sets the plot in motion and, like all great film noir, nothing is what it appears to be. Across the river from Manhattan is Garrison, New Jersey, a bedroom community for off-duty policemen and their families, population: 1,280. There is no crime in Garrison; Stallone as paunchy Sheriff Freddy Heflin spends his days as an all-purpose Mr. Fix It. When little boys fight, when next door neighbors are passive aggressive with each other, when a small child loses a stuffed toy, Freddy Heflin is on the job. Freddy wanted to be a real cop, but as a kid, he rescued a teenaged girl from drowning and lost his hearing in one ear. The girl grew up to be Liz Randone (Annabella Sciorra), unhappily married to Officer Joey Randone (Peter Berg). Freddy remains helpful to Liz, and she is kind to him, if more than a little resentful of the way life turned out for her. It is in Garrison that senior Officer Ray Donlan (Harvey Keitel) plans to solve the problem of his nephew Murray's error in judgment, and it is Ray's plan that unlayers the corrupt cesspool Garrison has become over the years. Internal Affairs investigator Moe Tilden (Robert De Niro) tries to solicit Freddy's help to get to the bottom of the cesspool, but Freddy doesn't want to see, hear, or know about the extent of the corruption. Ray Liotta is electrifying as Gary Figgis, an unhappy, angry cop who needles Freddy about his doughnut consumption and urges him to Do Something. When Freddy finally moves into action, it is nearly too late and the consequences are devastating. I could not stop crying over the sheer brilliance of Stallone's less-is-more performance as Freddy and

over Mangold's power as a writer/director in exquisite control of his material. The Blue-Ribbon ensemble cast, filled with acting gods all working for a fraction of their regular salaries in a character-driven indie, gives noir buffs and discriminating audiences the cinematic equivalent of nirvana. I was still crying a day later.

1997 (R) 105m/C Sylvester Stallone, Robert De Niro, Annabella Sciorra, Harvey Keitel, Peter Berg, Janeane Garofalo, Michael Rapaport, Ray Liotta, Cathy Moriarty, Robert Patrick, Noah Emmerich, John Spencer, Malik Yoba, Frank Vincent, Arthur J. Nascarelli, Edie Falco, Deborah Harry; ***D:*** James Mangold; ***W:*** James Mangold; ***C:*** Eric Alan Edwards; ***M:*** Howard Shore. **VHS, LV, Closed Caption**

Cosi

Cosi received a single press screening in San Francisco sometime in 1997, then the theatrical engagement was canceled and I heard no more about it until I saw it on a video shelf. It created quite a splash in Australia in the spring of 1996, so its last-minute yanking is something of a mystery. P.C. jitters, maybe? Who knows? It's about the determination of the residents of a mental hospital to stage Mozart's opera *Cosi Fan Tutte,* no matter WHAT obstacles get in their way. Lewis (Ben Mendelsohn) is the drifter/therapist who helps them turn their dream into a reality. The patients do a terrific job and the cast, including actors who appeared in Louis Nowra's original stage production, is a delight. Barry Otto, a scene stealer as Doug Hastings in 1992's *Strictly Ballroom,* is wonderful here as Roy, who insists that Lewis get the ball rolling despite the minor detail that no one knows a single word of Italian. An in-joke here is that the graceful Paul Mercurio (who co-starred as Scott Hastings with Otto) plays a clumsy auditioner who fails to receive a callback! (Ditto Greta Scacchi!) Toni (*Muriel's Wedding*) Colette is charming as Julie, whose big number in the show occurs when she sings "Stand by Me" during a production glitch. When theatrical folks talk about their fellow cast members being like "family," in the best sense of that word, they must mean something like the magic that binds the ragtag *Cosi* company together. This one's a winner! ***AKA:*** Caught in the Act.

1995 (R) 100m/C *AU* Ben Mendelsohn, Barry Otto, Aden Young, Toni Collette, Rachel Griffiths, Colin Friels, Paul Chubb, Pamela Rabe, Jacki Weaver, David Wenham, Colin Hay, Tony Llewellyn-Jones, Kerry Walker; ***Cameos:*** Greta Scacchi, Paul Mercurio; ***D:*** Mark Joffe; ***W:*** Louis Nowra; ***C:*** Ellery Ryan; ***M:*** Stephen Endelman. Australian Film Institute '96: Best Adapted Screenplay, Best Supporting Actress (Collette); Nominations: Australian Film Institute '96: Best Supporting Actor (Otto). **VHS, LV, Closed Caption**

Coup de Torchon

Jim Thompson was an Oklahoma-born paperback writer who wrote riveting tales about superficially boring people with humdrum routines and hellish interior lives. Thompson wrote two screenplays for Stanley Kubrick, and four of his novels have inspired both American and French filmmakers. In 1982, Bertrand Tavernier made *Coup de Torchon/Clean Slate,* switching Thompson's *Pop.1280* locale to Equatorial Africa, circa 1938. The film won an Oscar nomination, but to me, it was as jarring as watching Agatha Christie's Saint Mary Mead transformed into Beverly Hills with story line intact. Philippe Noiret is a lumbering, cuddly teddy bear of a man, totally incapable of projecting the dark side of his homicidal character. I knew the film was losing me when I asked myself, "Why does he kill?" and my only answer was, "Well, it's in the script." Stephane Audran and Isabelle Huppert contribute to the unreal proceedings and the whole thing is splashed with an overpowering jazz score by Philippe Sarde. The bizarre film has its aficionados, but the fact that the gruesome plot is played for laughs may strike some as obscene. Decide for yourself! ***AKA:*** Clean Slate.

1981 128m/C *FR* Philippe Noiret, Isabelle Huppert, Guy Marchand, Stephane Audran, Eddy Mitchell, Jean-Pierre Marielle, Irene Skobline; ***D:*** Bertrand Tavernier; ***W:*** Bertrand Tavernier; ***C:*** Pierre William Glenn; ***M:*** Philippe Sarde. Nominations: Academy Awards '81: Best Foreign Film. **VHS**

Bette (Jessica Lange) and Jenny (Elisabeth Shue) in *Cousin Bette.* Fox Searchlight; courtesy of the Kobal Collection

Cousin Bette

From *King Kong* to *Tootsie* to *Blue Sky* to *Cousin Bette,* Jessica Lange has worked hard on her unusual career. The large range of unconventional roles she has played would never have been offered to any one actress in the so-called Golden Age of Hollywood. *Cousin Bette* IS a part any full-blooded actress would sacrifice her beauty to portray and Lange is wise to take on character star turns at this stage in her 22 years as a movie star. Bette has lived a second-class life as the poor and plain relation of Baroness Adeline Hulot (Geraldine Chaplin), whom we see dying during the opening credits. Bette hopes to marry the widowed Baron Hulot (Hugh Laurie), but he, alas, only has eyes for the voluptuous dancer Jenny Cadine (Elisabeth Shue, stunningly costumed by Gabriella Pescucci) and therefore magnanimously offers to keep Cousin Bette on as the live-in housekeeper. She, needless to say, is filled with cold fury and dreams of revenge, but accepts the Baron's offer while refusing to live under the same roof. In her hovel, she plays patroness of the arts to an impoverished count and suicidal artist, Wenceslas Steinbach (gorgeous Aden Young). Meanwhile, Baron Hulot's daughter Hortense (Kelly Macdonald) is courted by a series of elderly suitors, including Bob Hoskins as Cesar Crevel, who says he will pay two hundred thousand francs to see her naked. She inhales as if she's sniffing men's drawers that have never been laundered and declines. All the ingredients are in place for Honore de Balzac's in-depth examination of a variety of truly sleazy characters in Paris, circa 1847–48. Lange's interpretation of Cousin Bette is subtle yet passionate, oozing with curdled sweetness on the surface and flashing sparks of the deep pain she's experiencing underneath. Elisabeth Shue is no less splendid as the treacherous Jenny. She's never been more beautiful, yet there is an underlying sense of exhaustion at the reality of being a plaything for an endless line of rich and powerful men. Shue does all her own singing; director Des McAnuff emphasizes the comedy in this tale of fairly brutal sex and money games; and you can expect to see stills from Aden Young's chocolate sauce romp with Shue in a future issue of *Celebrity Sleuth.* What more can you can ask for from a story that predates the mid-19th century? 🦴🦴🦴

1997 (R) 112m/C Jessica Lange, Elisabeth Shue, Aden Young, Bob Hoskins, Kelly Macdonald, Hugh Laurie, Geraldine Chaplin, Toby Stephens, John Sessions; ***D:*** Des McAnuff; ***W:*** Lynn Siefert, Susan Tarr; ***C:*** Andrzej Sekula; ***M:*** Simon Boswell. **VHS, Closed Caption**

Cousin, Cousine

One of the most delicious releases of 1976 was Jean-Charles Tacchella's *Cousin, Cousine.* This tender French offering is a gentle, lyrical story about two distant cousins who meet at various family gatherings and how they gradually fall in love. Marie-Christine Barrault and Victor Lanoux play the lovers with delightful subtlety. They are wonderfully supported by a cast that includes Guy Marchand and Marie-France Pisier as their spouses. There is also a rambunctiously real group of child actors. Director/screenwriter Tacchella suggests that it is the people who invest themselves fully in life who have the privilege of savoring love at its most profound. *Cousin, Cousine* is that rare film that gets remarkable mileage out of harmony. 🦴🦴🦴🦴

1976 (R) 95m/C *FR* Marie-Christine Barrault, Marie-France Pisier, Victor Lanoux, Guy Marchand, Ginette Garcin, Sybil Maas; ***D:*** Jean-Charles Tacchella; ***W:*** Jean-Charles Tacchella; ***C:*** Georges Lendi; ***M:*** Gerard Anfosso. Cesar Awards '76: Best Supporting Actress (Pisier); Nominations: Academy Awards '76: Best Actress (Barrault), Best Foreign Film, Best Original Screenplay. **VHS, LV**

Crash

No question about it, *Crash* is one strange flick. Only in the movies do we ever see couples with the same sexual intentions glance at each other for less than ONE second and find themselves in lustful embrace the very NEXT microsecond. In *Crash,* no one asks anyone, "Voulez-vous couchez avec moi ce soir?" or "Why don't we do it in the City Dump?" Everyone just KNOWS. It's a mystery, originally spun by J. G. Ballard in his 1973 novel. James Spader, who's played the full spectrum of sexual nuts onscreen, is married to Catherine (Deborah Unger). He gets in an accident with Helen (Holly Hunter) and her husband. The husband dies, James and Helen are injured, and both are soon "exploring their sexuality" at re-enactments of James Dean's and Jayne Mansfield's fatal crashes, at a greatest-hits video screening of car crashes, and best of all, in actual cars where actual people have died. My late friend Alvah might have said that a flick like *Crash* is symbolic of a disintegrating society. Well, we all bring our own baggage to a movie like this, so I asked my friend Raymond, "How and why are they getting off on all this stuff? Are they really as happy as they look?" Raymond said that they were experiencing pleasure, but not fulfillment, which is rather a difficult concept for a former convent school girl to unravel. *Crash* does take us into its own world in a way that David Lynch's *Lost Highway* (because of the intermittent boredom factor) does not. Unger (who appeared in 1993's *Hotel Room* along with Mariska Hargitay, a survivor of the Mansfield crash) has an intriguing aura and Rosanna Arquette, complete with leg brace, really looks as if she was BORN to be in *Crash.* This is the sort of movie that works for its NC-17 rating. No one but Cronenberg would touch a project like *Crash;* fortunately, he did. *Crash* may be weird, twisted, and sick, but it's always dispassionate, thoughtful, and riveting. 🦴🦴🦴

1995 (NC-17) 98m/C *CA* James Spader, Holly Hunter, Elias Koteas, Deborah Kara Unger, Rosanna Arquette, Peter MacNeill; ***D:*** David Cronenberg; ***W:*** David Cronenberg; ***C:*** Peter Suschitzsky; ***M:*** Howard Shore. Cannes Film Festival '96: Special Jury Prize; Genie Awards '96: Best Adapted Screenplay, Best Cinematography, Best Director (Cronenberg), Best Film Editing; Nominations: Genie Awards '96: Best Film, Best Sound. **VHS, LV, Closed Caption**

Crashout

If you want to make sure your script gets made right, produce it yourself: Hal E.

Alice Mosher (Beverly Michaels), Van Duff (William Bendix), and Swaner Remsen (William Talman) in *Crashout*. Courtesy of the Kobal Collection

Chester's tough, uncompromising drama of six convicts attempting a prison *Crashout* is dominated by the no-holds-barred performance of William Bendix as Van Duff, a badly wounded con. Duff has wild dreams of buried wealth, which he says he'll split with the other five if they'll do something about his wound and help him get to his stash. It's a dream ignited by feverish desperation and shared by Joe Quinn (Arthur Kennedy), Pete Mendoza (Luther Adler), Monk Collins (Gene Evans), Billy Lang (Marshall Thompson), and a religious fanatic named Swaner Remsen (William Talman). If you only know Talman from his work as Hamilton Burger on *Perry Mason,* you'll be mesmerized by his superb change-of-pace performance here. Quinn, the sanest of the bunch, seeks help from Alice Mosher (Beverly Michaels). For a few tense moments, the illusion of another life seems possible, but the psychodrama of Quinn's fellow inmates dominates the running time, as it must. The stark plight of the six men gives a timeless, existential quality to *Crashout.* If the big wigs ever decide to remake it with huge stars, they'll wreck it. Duff, Quinn, Mendoza, Remsen, Collins, and Lang could be anyone. The fact that these guys are among society's wretched and that they bring out the worst in each other is rendered more effective by the small, realistic details of the production. Twenty-one-year-old Melinda Markey, daughter of Joan Bennett and Gene Markey, plays a girl in the bar, Gloria Talbot plays a girl on a train, Morris Ankrum is the head guard, and wonderful little Percy Helton is Doctor Barnes. 🦴🦴🦴🦴

1955 88m/B William Bendix, Gene Evans, Arthur Kennedy, Luther Adler, William Talman, Marshall

Thompson, Beverly Michaels, Gloria Talbot, Adam Williams, Percy Helton, Melinda Markey, Morris Ankrum; ***D:*** Lewis R. Foster; ***W:*** Hal E. Chester; ***C:*** Russell Metty; ***M:*** Leith Stevens. **VHS**

Creepers

One of the best Dario Argento titles available on home video (if you're lucky enough to run across the uncut 109-minute original INSTEAD of the chopped-up 82-minute version) is the 1985 horror classic *Creepers.* It stars Jennifer Connelly, then 15, whose youthful beauty was strikingly comparable with that of the young Elizabeth Taylor, and who was certainly a much better actress than Taylor at the same age. As in many early Taylor films, Connelly's character gets along better with animals (particularly insects) than with people. Connelly is stuck in a crummy girls' school where she is susceptible to sleepwalking, especially when she hears about all the terrible things that are happening to the young girls in the area. The grisly violence in this film is SO overstated that it's doubtful that even the most squeamish viewer could take it TOO seriously. The over-the-top performances by Daria Nicolodi and the great Donald Pleasence emphasize the fact that IT'S ONLY A MOVIE, folks. Anyway, we KNOW that Dario Argento couldn't be such a churl as to let anything happen to Jennifer Connelly, who looks cool and elegant even when she's sticking her finger down her throat. He must be a nice man to provide such excellent acting opportunities for all those bees and maggots, not to mention one scene-stealing monkey! If you can't find Dario Argento movies at the local Bijou, the following titles are well worth the search: 1970's *The Bird with the Crystal Plumage* starring Tony Musante, 1971's *Cat o' Nine Tails* with the late James Franciscus and a great Ennio Morricone score, 1975's *Deep Red* starring David Hemmings, 1988's *Terror at the Opera* with the late Ian Charleson, 1982's *Unsane* starring Tony Franciosa, 1990's *Two Evil Eyes* with Harvey Keitel in an adaptation of Poe's *The Black Cat* and, of course, *Creepers,* the perfect movie to watch when you're all alone without a telephone on a dark and spooky night. ***AKA:*** Phenomena.

1985 (R) 82m/C *IT* Jennifer Connelly, Donald Pleasence, Daria Nicolodi, Elenora Giorgi, Dalia di Lazzaro, Patrick Bauchau, Fiore Argento, Federica Mastroianni, Michele (Michael) Soavi, Gavin Friday; ***D:*** Dario Argento; ***W:*** Dario Argento, Franco Ferrini; ***C:*** Romano Albani; ***M:*** Simon Boswell. **VHS**

Crime of Passion

Ah, the joys of 1957, when men were men and women twiddled their thumbs. Kathy Ferguson (Barbara Stanwyck) begins this movie with an exciting job as a columnist for a San Francisco newspaper. She even plays a key role in clearing up a murder case. She's en route to Manhattan on a fast-paced career track, when she makes a quick stop in Los Angeles to meet Detective Lieutenant Bill Doyle of the L.A.P.D. (Sterling Hayden) for dinner. One thing leads to another, and before you can say, "Darn my socks for me, Darling," she is MRS. Bill Doyle, trapped in a suburb, with no outlet for her tremendous energy. She's bored with her life and she hates Bill's friends on the force AND their wives, so she takes up a new hobby: promoting Bill's career. This means sleeping with his boss, Inspector Tony Pope (Raymond Burr), and alienating him from other detectives who might get the job she wants Bill to have. (See what happens when a gal leaves a great job to do nothing?) Even though Kathy Ferguson Doyle is basically a screw up, Stanwyck invests the role with eloquence and angst. The dull life that her character rails about IS everything that she says it is. The obvious choice over 40 years later isn't even mentioned as an option: go back to the work you love and if Bill doesn't like it, TOUGH! This seems eminently more sensible than: sleep with Bill's boss, but don't tell Bill, and make sure you do something to get caught, so Bill will feel like a sap, anyway. Yeah, there's a lot of rage against women in *Crime of Passion,* but you can't stop watching it because of Stanwyck and Burr. (Hayden's thankless part must have grated on him after starring in *The Asphalt*

Mylene Demongeot as Abigail Williams and Yves Montand as John Proctor in *The Crucible.* Courtesy of the Kobal Collection

Jungle for John Huston and *The Killing* for Stanley Kubrick.) And yes, that IS Stuart Whitman in a bit as a lab technician, four years away from his 1961 Academy Award nomination for *The Mark.* ☠☠☠

1957 85m/B Barbara Stanwyck, Sterling Hayden, Raymond Burr, Fay Wray, Royal Dano, Virginia Grey, Dennis Cross, Robert Griffin, Jay Adler, Malcolm Atterbury, S. John Launer, Brad Trumbull, Skipper McNally, Jean Howell, Peg La Centra, Nancy Reynolds, Marjorie Owens, Robert Quarry, Joe Conley, Stuart Whitman; ***D:*** Gerd Oswald; ***W:*** Jo Eisinger; ***C:*** Joseph LaShelle; ***M:*** Paul Dunlap. **VHS, Closed Caption**

Criminal Law

Criminal Law opens with a sequence in which attorney Gary Oldman is shown defending a wholesome-looking killer portrayed by Kevin Bacon. Oldman destroys an eyewitness account because she was wrong about when she last purchased diapers. If she was wrong about the diapers, Oldman contends, why couldn't she wrong about identifying the murderer? Sure, says the jury, and Bacon is a free man. At this point, the film could have gone anywhere, and that's the main problem with *Criminal Law.* It goes EVERYWHERE. At first, Mark Kasden's script appears to be commenting on a legal system that frees Bacon to kill again and again, with Oldman as his reluctant collaborator. But then, perhaps encouraged by the ongoing Wade vs. Roe controversy, Kasdan tries to show how having an abortionist for a mother unhinges Bacon. The images of the smoking and flaming victims are too grisly for us to feel sorry for this demented killer. So the script introduces a strong female character (Karen Young) who goes to bed with Oldman for reasons best known to Kasdan. Then she beats up Bacon before she vanishes from the plot. A dying professor is dragged in to make Oldman cry at the astonishing news that law and justice are different. When all else fails, Officer Joe Don Baker patiently explains that "Crazy killers are crazy," resulting in unintentional audience laughter and a bullet in the stomach. Bacon and Oldman beat each other up, sort of, in an empty courtroom. Bacon cries some more. It's a stretch for him as an actor. Oldman, too. And Martin Campbell's direction of this suspenseless thriller is "stylish." The producers say so. They aren't concerned about the reviews. *Criminal Law* was originally hyped by manipulative commercials in which nameless people were shown walking out of a theatre and saying how great the film and the actors are. Who were these people and why were they there? Why should anyone trust them? Most of THEM probably couldn't remember the last time THEY bought diapers!

1989 (R) 113m/C Kevin Bacon, Gary Oldman, Karen Young, Joe Don Baker, Tess Harper; ***D:*** Martin Campbell; ***W:*** Mark Kasden; ***C:*** Phil Meheux; ***M:*** Jerry Goldsmith. **VHS, LV**

Critical Care

Heck, even half the cast of *Critical Care* would drag me into a theatre. But the half-baked script by Steven S. Schwartz is crammed with meet cute/evolve cute/resolve cute situations, and in one unbearable sequence, a dry-eyed James Spader as Dr. Werner Ernst actually quivers his lip in the lackluster tradition of Douglass Montgomery. Who? My point, exactly. Let me outta here! The nadir of this excruciating hospital drama occurs in the consultations between Dr. Ernst and Dr. Butz. Why? Because Dr. Butz is Albert Brooks, wearing "old guy" makeup, best suited for a boardwalk fun house. And we're supposed to be moved by the rest of this movie? The Ethical Quandary here is whether or not Dr. Ernst should keep a rich old man alive to the tune of $112,800 monthly when he's in a "persistent vegetative state." One rich daughter says NO! One rich daughter says YES! Werner Ernst, who presumably passed an I.Q. test before he entered medical school, sleeps with one sister, is recorded on videotape (It Seems to Me I've Heard This Song Before), and faces Real Trouble, in addition to the aforementioned Ethical Quandary. Even if you must kill 105 minutes, you can do better than this absolutely ghastly entry which premiered at the Chicago Film Festival. **woof!**

1997 (R) 105m/C James Spader, Albert Brooks, Kyra Sedgwick, Helen Mirren, Margo Martindale, Jeffrey Wright, Wallace Shawn, Anne Bancroft, Philip Bosco, Edward Herrmann, Colm Feore, James Lally, Al Waxman, Harvey Atkin; ***D:*** Sidney Lumet; ***W:*** Steven S. Schwartz; ***C:*** David Watkin; ***M:*** Michael Convertino. **VHS, LV, DVD**

The Crossing Guard

Sean Penn comes of age as a mature screenwriter and director with this beautifully rendered study of forgiveness. Jack Nicholson and Anjelica Huston play the divorced parents of a little girl killed by hit-and-run drunk driver David Morse, who has just completed his term in prison for manslaughter. Huston is re-married to a patient, decent guy and has come to terms with her grief over her lost child, but the embittered Nicholson has not and cannot. All he can think of when Morse is released is that now he can finally kill him. He pays a visit to him, gun in hand, but it doesn't go off, and Morse asks him to reconsider his decision for a few days. Morse is genuinely regretful for his crime, and still feels enormous guilt as he remembers his victim's last words. Nicholson continues to stew in his own anguish and self-imposed isolation until his long-numbed conscience awakens him from a nightmare. In his terror, he calls his ex-wife for help, and then Huston and Nicholson share a sequence charged with gut-grinding emotional honesty. What follows for Nicholson is uglier than any nightmare, as he is finally forced to confront the potential killer within himself. Nicholson, Huston, and Morse are all outstanding. An interesting touch for film noir buffs is that classy chanteuse Hadda Brooks, who appeared in Nicholas Ray's *In a Lonely Place* in 1950 (in which Humphrey Bogart bat-

“Didja ever pick your teeth up with broken fingers?”

—Fergus/Jimmy (Stephen Rea) to his boss in *The Crying Game.*

tled with HIS private demons), is also in *The Crossing Guard,* looking as elegant as ever. ☙☙☙☙

1994 (R) 111m/C Jack Nicholson, Anjelica Huston, David Morse, Robin Wright Penn, Robbie Robertson, Piper Laurie, Richard Bradford, John Savage, Priscilla Barnes, Kari Wuhrer, Jennifer Leigh Warren, Richard Sarafian, Jeff Morris, Joe Viterelli, Eileen Ryan, Ryo Ishibashi, Michael Ryan, Nicky Blair, Gene Kirkwood, Jason Kristofer, Hadda Brooks; ***D:*** Sean Penn; ***W:*** Sean Penn; ***C:*** Vilmos Zsigmond; ***M:*** Jack Nitzsche. Nominations: Golden Globe Awards '96: Best Supporting Actress (Huston); Independent Spirit Awards '96: Best Supporting Actor (Morse); Screen Actors Guild Award '95: Best Supporting Actress (Huston). **VHS, LV, Closed Caption**

The Crucible

An American film of Arthur Miller's *The Crucible* would have to wait until 1996, but the landmark play WAS filmed in 1957 by a French production company in East Germany, which meant that only art house patrons got to see it in America. It starred Simone Signoret (1921–85), Yves Montand (1921–91), and Mylene Demongeot, then 20, and the screenplay was by none other than Jean-Paul Sartre (1905–80). In the bleak landscape of East Germany's countryside (which looks nothing at all like Salem, Massachusetts, in 1692), Elizabeth and John Proctor play out their troubled marriage with no help at all from that 17th century vixen, Abigail Williams. John is at odds with the community powers that be, Elizabeth is resigned to Abigail's mischief, and Abigail is made jealous by every moment that John spends away from her. The witch hunt is fueled by uncontrollable sexual tension, but the political nightmare that follows takes on a life of its own from which no one can escape. Reviews at the time of release were just fair, but the film holds up very well today. Montand's John Proctor may have deep political convictions, but he isn't terribly bright. Basically, he sets himself up with his own sexual brutality. Signoret has the challenge of repressing her natural sensuality and keen intelligence to play a good and simple woman whose chronic illness supplies her faithless husband with an excuse to have sex with the much younger Abigail. The sexy Demongeot (bearing a close resemblance to Jennie Garth) became an international star but rarely played a role with as much meat or range as Abigail. Director Raymond Rouleau also played the Governor. The interior sequences still sizzle today, but every single exterior sequence shoves us right into 1957. Couldn't the budget have been stretched to include a few trees or a better location scout? (*The Crucible* turned up on the small screen in America on CBS in 1967 with Colleen Dewhurst (1924–91), George C. Scott, and Tuesday Weld as Elizabeth, John, and Abigail.) ***AKA:*** The Witches of Salem; Les Sorcières de Salem. ☙☙☙

1957 135m/B *FR* Simone Signoret, Yves Montand, Mylene Demongeot, Jean Debucourt, Raymond Rouleau, Jean Gaven, Jeanne Fusier-Gir; ***D:*** Raymond Rouleau; ***W:*** Jean-Paul Sartre; ***C:*** Claude Renoir; ***M:*** Georges Auric. **VHS**

Crumb

Watching *Crumb* made me think about *Grey Gardens,* the 1975 documentary the Maysles brothers filmed about the odd mother and daughter who were related to Jacqueline Bouvier Kennedy. There are so many odd mothers and daughters on the planet; were those two chosen only because they were so closely related to the First Lady? Watching *Crumb* also made me think about *Gates of Heaven,* the 1978 documentary Errol Morris did about a pet cemetery and the two brothers who maintained it. As the camera focused on these cooperative subjects, it made them look rather foolish and rather odd. The Crumb family is also rather odd, but would we be so interested in these previously anonymous people if underground comic artist Robert Crumb weren't related to them? It's one thing to watch a movie about troubled make-believe people and feel relieved that we don't have to live their lives, but to watch *Crumb* and feel relieved that we aren't Max and Charles Crumb makes me wonder: how many families could be so closely scrutinized and emerge with any dignity whatsoever? Unfortunately, fame is the bench mark of success in America. If you don't achieve it (or don't want it), why does that invalidate your life when a documentary filmmaker comes to pay a call about a legendary sibling? (Two Crumb sisters refused to be a part of this film.) Every life has its patches of depression, imperfection, and inactivity. Many lives are conducted in seclusion. Many fathers are "sadistic bull(ies)." And it's unimaginable that there's a teenage boy alive who DOESN'T indulge in sexual fantasies. As a documentary, *Crumb* won wide acclaim for its director, Terry Zwigoff, who worked six years on the project. I wouldn't LET anyone into my life for six years who only wanted to examine it, good and bad, with a camera and then distribute the edited results all over the world. Would you? Are Robert Crumb and his family still speaking to Terry Zwigoff? If not, is that still okay because strangers enjoyed this film so much in neighborhood theatres? Were so-called primitive tribes that far off when they believed that a camera would steal their souls? I give it four bones for the cognoscenti, but for myself, no comment.

1994 (R) 119m/C ***D:*** Terry Zwigoff; ***C:*** Maryse Alberti. National Society of Film Critics Awards '95: Best Feature Documentary; Sundance Film Festival '95: Best Cinematography, Grand Jury Prize. **VHS, LV, Closed Caption, DVD**

Crush

There's something deeply satisfying about seeing a real menace onscreen. No explanations, no excuses—she's bad because she's bad and that's that! Marcia Gay Harden, who played sultry Ava Gardner in *Sinatra* and soft-hearted Shelby Goddard in *The Spitfire Grill,* IS Lane, a genuine Wicked Woman of the Silver Screen. Don't be her friend, don't go to bed with her, and don't, whatever you do, get in a car with her if she's behind the wheel. That's what Christina (Donough Rees) the literary critic does (it figures), and she's left for dead (uh-oh) when Lane crashes the car. Lane goes to the home of novelist Colin (William Zappa) and immediately seduces him, then goes to work on daughter Angela (Caitlin Bossley), who's still a teenager. No, this isn't a Shannon Tweed movie, although it does sound like one, doesn't it? The difference lies in Harden's brilliant, what-the-hell interpretation as Lane. I don't how she worked out her character but she's so damn funny, I was cracking up through most of the movie. Writer/director Alison Maclean has an eye and ear for this sort of satire, and she chose the right actors for the right jobs. 🦴🦴🦴

1993 97m/C *NZ* Marcia Gay Harden, Donough Rees, William Zappa, Caitlin Bossley; ***D:*** Alison Maclean; ***W:*** Alison Maclean, Anne Kennedy; ***C:*** Dion Beebe. **VHS**

The Crying Game

Amaze your friends! Ask them who was the first singer to make "The Crying Game" a number-five Brit Hit for 12 weeks. They will say, "Boy George, of course," and you will say, "No, Dave Berry, on August 6, 1964," and since the entire U.S. of A. was pre-occupied with The Beatles' first national tour in August, 1964, they will say, "Who?" Since, on college campuses, a generation seems to last about four years or so, it's possible that someone born in the '80s might not know the secret of *The Crying Game.* If you've already seen 1994's *Naked Gun 33 1/3: The Final Insult,* fergeddit, it's too late, but if you really have just arrived on Planet Earth from Planet Mars, *The Crying Game* is Neil Jordan's Oscar-winning story of Fergus (Stephen Rea), a member of the I.R.A., who becomes friends with Jody, a captive British soldier (Forest Whitaker), and who later looks up Jody's lover, Dil (Jaye Davidson). That's as far as I'm going with this, in case you WERE born in the '80s OR emigrated from Mars and didn't have to watch that *Naked Gun* movie on the flight to Earth. Acting by everyone (including Miranda Richardson as Jude, another I.R.A. member) is first rate. Like many classic movies, *The Crying Game* is so well made and so much a part of film lore that it's hard to remember that it really has only been part of our cinematic consciousness since 1992. 🦴🦴🦴🦴

1992 (R) 112m/C *IR* Stephen Rea, Jaye Davidson, Miranda Richardson, Forest Whitaker, Adrian Dun-

Cutter does everything his way. Fighting. Loving. Working. Tracking down a killer.

—Tagline from the movie *Cutter's Way.*

bar, Jim Broadbent, Ralph Brown, Breffini McKenna, Joe Savino, Birdie Sweeney, Andre Bernard; ***D:*** Neil Jordan; ***W:*** Neil Jordan; ***C:*** Ian Wilson; ***M:*** Anne Dudley. Academy Awards '92: Best Original Screenplay; Australian Film Institute '93: Best Foreign Film; Independent Spirit Awards '93: Best Foreign Film; Los Angeles Film Critics Association Awards '92: Best Foreign Film; New York Film Critics Awards '92: Best Screenplay, Best Supporting Actress (Richardson); National Society of Film Critics Awards '92: Best Actor (Rea); Writers Guild of America '92: Best Original Screenplay; Nominations: Academy Awards '92: Best Actor (Rea), Best Director (Jordan), Best Film Editing, Best Picture, Best Supporting Actor (Davidson). **VHS, LV, Letterbox, Closed Caption, DVD**

Curse of the Starving Class

Subtlety is in short supply in Sam Shepard's *Curse of the Starving Class,* a first effort by director J. Michael McClary. James Woods overacts like he never heard the expression "less is more," and his co-stars Kathy Bates, Randy Quaid, Louis Gossett Jr., and a maggot-ridden lamb all seem to follow his lead. I can imagine few movie experiences more painful than to watch this movie on a double bill with *Silent Tongue,* another Sam Shepard turkey. Would it have been any better if Bruce Beresford had directed as well as adapted the script? Maybe, but we'd still be stuck with the brother taking a leak on his sister's 4-H project, for reasons best known to Shepard. **woof!**

1994 (R) 102m/C James Woods, Kathy Bates, Henry Thomas, Kristin Fiorella, Randy Quaid, Louis Gossett Jr.; ***D:*** Michael McClary; ***W:*** Bruce Beresford; ***C:*** Dick Quinlan. **VHS, LV, Closed Caption**

Cutter's Way

Cutter's Way, by Ivan Passer, was quickly identified as new-age film noir by the few people who actually saw it during its original 1981 run. It is not, however, the comfortable sort of film noir which makes it easy for you to go willingly wherever the hero wants to take you. *Cutter's Way* is an intensely uncomfortable film to watch and there are no heroes anywhere in sight, just three ragged people who stumble on a brutal murder. In 1981, John Heard had the talent and drive to become one of the major actors of his generation. He didn't quite make it, but at least he got the chance to sink his teeth into the meaty role of Cutter, a crippled vet who hates the world for many good reasons. The perennially underrated Jeff Bridges slid into the role of Cutter's best friend Bone with his usual skill, and Lisa Eichhorn portrayed Cutter's bitter wife (and Bone's occasional bed partner). Their amateur murder investigation is conducted with rage and with plenty of mistakes made along the way. *Cutter's Way* was a pioneering noir effort of the '80s, not as atmospheric as the enormously successful *Body Heat,* also released in 1981, nor as likable as 1987's *The Big Heat.* Passer's film was an interesting study of three seedy low lifes mustering the conviction to clash with a corrupt and powerful killer in sunny Santa Barbara. ***AKA:*** Cutter and Bone.

1981 (R) 105m/C Jeff Bridges, John Heard, Lisa Eichhorn, Ann Dusenberry, Stephen Elliott, Nina Van Pallandt, George Dickerson; ***D:*** Ivan Passer; ***W:*** Jeffrey Alladin Fiskin; ***C:*** Jordan Cronenweth; ***M:*** Jack Nitzsche. **VHS, LV**

Daddy Nostalgia

Dirk Bogarde and Jane Birkin in a film by Bertrand Tavernier? Sounds pretty good, doesn't it? Regretfully, *Daddy Nostalgia,* which sounds terrific on paper, is slow as molasses to watch. Tavernier's own father was dying as the film was being made, but the director chose to approach the subject of mortality at an oblique angle and the results are false and boring. Birkin's character is filled with adolescent concerns and behavior, a bit weird to watch in a woman of 45. And sorry, I just can't accept a screen personality as strong as Bogarde as he mopes around a French villa, waiting to die. He may have been able to pull it off in *Death in Venice,* but Tavernier isn't Visconti and screenwriter Colo Tavernier O'Hagan isn't Thomas Mann. The threadbare premise of the film is that Birkin's character was neglected as a child and she still yearns for Daddy's approval 40 years later. Bogarde is an insensitive, unappealing lout who can't talk with either his French wife (Odette Laure) or his very

British daughter. Birkin has agreed to visit for a pre-determined amount of time, and when the time is up, she leaves. The last act occurs off camera, so nothing much happens for 105 minutes except that you get a chance to see how Bogarde looks and sounds these days (great, on both counts). Too bad his first theatrical feature since 1978 is such a sluggish vehicle. Bogarde deserves a much better swan song than *Daddy Nostalgia.* ***AKA:*** These Foolish Things; Daddy Nostalgie. 🦴🦴

1990 105m/C *FR* Dirk Bogarde, Jane Birkin, Odette Laure; ***D:*** Bertrand Tavernier; ***W:*** Colo Tavernier O'Hagan; ***C:*** Denis Lenoir; ***M:*** Antoine Duhamel. **VHS**

Dance with a Stranger

Dance with a Stranger made Miranda Richardson a star and ignited the career of director Mike Newell. Released midway through the Thatcher years (1979–91), the film was typical of its era in that it cast a harsh gaze on the early 1950s, while clearly reveling in their ambiance. Ruth Ellis (Richardson) is the tough-as-nails (translation: walking wounded) manageress of a bar. From the instant that race car driver David Blakely (kinky Rupert Everett) orders a gin and tonic, Ellis is hooked, although she does her best to feign indifference. In fact, at many points during their two-year (1953–55) affair, either Ellis or Blakely was heartily fed up with the other, although never at the same time. Ellis recognizes that they are out of each other's league and although Blakely denies it, he knows it, too. Complicating the situation is Ruth's sad-eyed little boy Andy (Matthew Carroll, in a heart-wringing performance), and Desmond Cussen (Ian Holm, in an on-target piece of work), who's obsessed with Ellis all the time, not just sporadically like Blakely. That cast of characters is just about all that anyone could ask for in a mad love story—only this story is true, brilliantly adapted by Shelagh *(A Taste of Honey)* Delaney, who was all of 16 when Cussen drove the love-crazed Ellis to the scene of the crime where she gunned down Blakely on Easter Sunday, 1955. Joanne Whalley is a bar girl named Christine. Historical Note: What *Dance with a Stranger* doesn't tell us is that Ellis (1926–55, and the last woman hanged in Great Britain) killed Blakely (1929–55) just before a newspaper strike. If the presses had been rolling at full speed, would Ellis' life have been spared? In France, the killing was widely regarded as a crime of passion, and hardly a candidate for the death penalty. Although 50,000 signatures were finally collected on one petition protesting her execution, Ellis was hanged with unseemly haste, less than 95 days after Blakely's death, and nowhere near enough time to launch an effective campaign to save her life, especially during the most crucial early days of the newspaper strike. 🦴🦴🦴🦴

1985 (R) 101m/C *GB* Miranda Richardson, Rupert Everett, Ian Holm, Joanne Whalley, Matthew Carroll, Tom Chadbon, Jane Bertish, David Trughton, Paul Mooney, Stratford Johns, Susan Kyd, Leslie Manville, Sallie-Anne Field, Martin Murphy, Michael Jenn, Daniel Massey; ***D:*** Mike Newell; ***W:*** Shelagh Delaney; ***C:*** Peter Hannan; ***M:*** Richard Hartley. Cannes Film Festival '85: Best Film. **VHS, LV, Closed Caption**

Dangerous Liaisons

Underwhelmed by 1988's *Dangerous Liaisons* with Glenn Close and John Malkovich? Then check out Roger Vadim's 1960 version of the 1782 novel by Choderlos de Laclos. Jeanne Moreau and the late Gerard Philipe star in this sexual tug of war between a ruthless husband and wife who get a bang out of tormenting their respective victims. Her target is an unsophisticated young man played by Jean-Louis Trintignant, his victim is a happily married (right!) bride portrayed by the director's wife, Annette Stroyberg. Moreau and Philipe are such cool customers that their roles make much more sense than they did with Close and Malkovich. The evil, beat atmosphere is enhanced by Thelonius Monk's timeless jazz score. ***AKA:*** Les Liaisons Dangereuses; Dangerous Love Affairs. 🦴🦴🦴

1960 111m/B *FR IT* Gerard Philipe, Jeanne Moreau, Jeanne Valeri, Annette Vadim, Simone Renant, Jean-Louis Trintignant, Nikolas Vogel; ***D:*** Roger

When the hunters become the hunted.

—Tagline from the movie *Das Boot.*

Vadim; ***W:*** Roger Vadim; ***C:*** Marcel Grignon; ***M:*** Thelonious Monk. **VHS, LV**

Dark Habits

Director Pedro Almodovar simmered in Madrid for a full decade while doing extra film jobs, making Super 8 movies and working for the telephone company. He made eleven movies between 1980 and 1995, of which 1986's *Matador* is the fifth and 1984's *Dark Habits* is the third. *Dark Habits* is the work of a still maturing artist. Sexual obsession is one thing, but Catholicism is a far more primal target for satire. The film gets free mileage out of nuns on acid, nuns shooting up, and nuns sniffing cocaine, plus the lesbian mother superior who must finance all these activities, not to mention their pet tiger's food expenses. Underneath all these absurdities, the story line is straightforward, as are most of Almodovar's plots. *Dark Habits* is one long joke, not too far removed from the playground fantasies of parochial schoolchildren, but it is basically a warm-up for the far more ambitious projects Almodovar was yet to make. His fourth and sixth films, 1985's *What Have I Done to Deserve This?* and 1986's *Law of Desire,* both starred the legendary Carmen Maura. ***AKA:*** Entre Tinieblas. 🦴🦴🦴

1984 116m/C *SP* Carmen Maura, Christina Pascual, Julieta Serrano, Marisa Paredes; ***D:*** Pedro Almodovar; ***W:*** Pedro Almodovar; ***C:*** Angel Luis Fernandez. **VHS, LV, Letterbox**

Das Boot

A two-and-a-half hour war movie set in a German submarine? Eh! So I passed on *Das Boot* in 1981. Then I read that it was being re-released in 1997 in a three-and-a-half hour version, and I even heard GUYS grumbling about it at that length. But the restored *Das Boot* was playing half a block away from my flat for what seemed like forever, so I went to the Bridge Theatre in the spring of 1997, determined to plow through it. I braced myself for the worst, namely, the same thing that happened when I went to see *Platoon* in 1986 or *Secrets and Lies* in 1997: Film As Agony. But *Das Boot* had me in its spell for every second of its 210-minute running time. Wolfgang Petersen, who definitely knows how to helm a thriller *(In the Line of Fire, Outbreak),* makes the day-to-day tasks aboard the submarine seem significant and vital. Because of the way it was shot, you almost feel as if you're a part of the crew, which must have been a much more shocking realization to American audiences in 1981. The men aboard the sub are doing a job; no one spouts Nazi propaganda. In fact, during one surreal sequence off the sub, when they are honored at a way-too-lavish buffet by beautifully dressed National Socialists, the captain (Juergen Prochnow) doesn't even respond when he's on the receiving end of the "Heil Hitler" salute. The German crew members are not cartoons, which is all I ever saw before *Das Boot.* And yet, even though I wince every time I hear a depth charge or watch the crew repair a potentially fatal leak, the film makes no attempt to whitewash or glorify the German military effort. In the final sequence, Peterson shows the futility of war as graphically as Lewis Milestone did over half a century earlier in *All Quiet on the Western Front.* If the longer version of *Das Boot* winds up in video stores, try breaking it up with an intermission. It's an excruciatingly intense experience. ***AKA:*** The Boat. 🦴🦴🦴🦴

1981 (R) 210m/C *GE* Juergen Prochnow, Herbert Gronemeyer, Klaus Wennemann, Hubertus Bengsch, Martin Semmelrogge, Bernd Tauber, Erwin Leder, Martin May, Heinz Honig, U. A. Ochsen, Claude-Oliver Rudolph, Jan Fedder, Ralph Richer, Joachim Bernhard, Oliver Stritzel, Konrad Becker, Lutz Schnell, Martin Hemme; ***D:*** Wolfgang Petersen; ***W:*** Wolfgang Petersen; ***C:*** Jost Vacano; ***M:*** Klaus Doldinger. Nominations: Academy Awards '82: Best Adapted Screenplay, Best Cinematography, Best Director (Petersen), Best Film Editing, Best Sound. **VHS, LV**

Daughters, Daughters

Sexist horsefeathers this, but I had yet another argument (with a guy) who went ballistic when I said so. When will I ever learn? HIS P.O.V.: "It's okay to zero in on a man's obsessive struggle to father a son after eight daughters, because it's a comedy from Israel." MY P.O.V.: "Director Moshe Mizrahi is condescending toward ALL his characters, male and female. Shai K. Ophir, who plays the father, is a competent actor, but the screenplay he writes with Mizrahi debases everyone. No one laughs WITH the characters because they're too crudely drawn and no one laughs AT them because they're not funny enough to carry the contrived premise." So there. 🦴

1974 88m/C *IS* Shai K. Ophir, Zaharira Harifai, Joseph Shiloah, Michal Bat-Adam; ***D:*** Moshe Mizrahi; ***W:*** Moshe Mizrahi, Shai K. Ophir; ***C:*** Adam Greenberg; ***M:*** Alex Cagan.

Daughters of the Country

Daughters of the Country is an intriguing series of four films beautifully produced by Norma Bailey for the National Film Board of Canada. The series spans the years 1770 through 1985, and each episode focuses on how a strong female character learns to deal with the clash between Native American and outside cultures. In the first episode, the title character, "Ikwe," leaves her Ojibwa village to begin a new life with a young Scottish trader, an alliance that seems promising at first, but disintegrates over time. (*Forever Knight* devotees note that Geraint ["Nick"] Wyn Davies stars as Angus.) "Mistress Madeleine" is a Metis woman of the 1850s caught in the middle of a clash between the Hudson Bay company monopoly and Native American freetraders. The conflict is intensified by the reality that her common-law husband is a company clerk and her own brother is among the freetraders. In "Places Not Our Own," set in 1929, a marvelous young actress named Diane Debassige plays Flora, whose dreams of attending school are shattered by the indifference of the white community. The small kindnesses she receives from individual townspeople do not compensate for the fact that Flora and her Metis family are not really considered part of the town. Diane Debassige also appears in "The Wake," a contemporary story in which the Metis and the white community in Alberta are still at odds, with heart-breaking consequences for four Native American kids. Throughout this outstanding series, the sheer inadequacy of well-meant white liberalism is under attack, but never more so than in "The Wake." A Native American woman and a white police officer fall in love amidst the racial tensions of the town, and again and again, in spite of his underlying intentions, it is easier on the officer's conscience that he take care of his own skin than face the very real danger his acquiescence represents to the people who are presumably under his care and protection. The overall effect of *Daughters of the Country* is "la plus ça change, la plus ça meme," but producer/director Bailey and the women who wrote the ambitious series deserve high marks for tackling their central premise with strong narrative skills and loving attention to details often overlooked in other studies of Native American life. Highly recommended for viewers of all ages. 🦴🦴🦴🦴

1986 228m/C *CA* William Ballantyne, Patrick Bruyere, Jamie Hardesty, Hazel King, Geraint Wyn Davies, Ken Charlette, Victor Cowie, Harry Daniels, Mireille Deyglun, Makka Kleist, William Ballantyne, Kate Berry, Diane DeBassige, Michael Fletcher, Damon Fontaine, Frank Adamson, Bill Alcorn, Cynthia Alcorn, Ken Charlette; ***D:*** Norma Bailey, Aaron Kim Johnston, Derek Mazur; ***W:*** Wendy Lill, Aaron Kim Johnston, Anne Cameron, Sandra Birdsell, Sharon Riis; ***C:*** Ian Elkin; ***M:*** John McCulloch, Pierre Guerin, Randolph Peters, Ron Halldorson. **VHS**

Daughters of the Dust

At 113 minutes, *Daughters of the Dust* deserved a context for its narrative. Instead, we get beautiful cinematography, and a very leisurely paced look at the lives of five women before they leave their island to emigrate to the Georgia coast. They can act, but Julie Dash's storytelling skills are decidedly embryonic. Set in 1902. 🦴🦴🦴

1991 113m/C Cora Lee Day, Barbara O, Alva Rogers, Kaycee Moore, Cheryl Lynn Bruce, Adisa Anderson, Eartha D. Robinson, Bahni Turpin,

Slater (Rory Cochrane) and Wooderson (Matthew McConaughey) are *Dazed and Confused.*
Gramercy; courtesy of the Kobal Collection

Tommy Redmond Hicks, Malik Farrakhan, Cornell (Kofi) Royal, Vertamae Crosvenor, Umar Abdurrahman, Sherry Jackson, Rev. Ervin Green; ***D:*** Julie Dash; ***W:*** Julie Dash; ***C:*** A. Jafa Fielder; ***M:*** John Barnes. Sundance Film Festival '91: Best Cinematography. **VHS**

Day for My Love

Day for My Love features the most adorable four-year-old child (Sylva Kamenicka). She dies very early in the story, but her laughing presence infects the entire movie. Marta Vancurova and Vlastimil Harapes star as the young couple who must cope with the loss of their young child, and build a new life for themselves while making peace with their past. Very well scripted by Marketa Zinnerova and a bit too artily shot by Jiri Machane, *Day for My Love* is enhanced by Juraj Herz's strong direction, as well as the excellent acting throughout.

1977 91m/C *CZ* Marta Vancurova, Vlastimil Harapes, Sylva Kamenicka, Dana Medricka, Jirinaova Sejbalova; ***D:*** Juraj Herz; ***W:*** Marketa Zinnerova; ***C:*** Jiri Machane; ***M:*** Petr Hapka.

The Daytrippers

Produced by Steven Soderbergh, Greg Mottola's *The Daytrippers* follows a family as they try to patch up the ailing marriage of the older daughter, Eliza (Hope Davis). Is husband Louis (Stanley Tucci) having an affair or what? *The Daytrippers* is more concerned with the "or what" than the affair. What adult daughter would let herself be dragged around by Mom and Dad (Anne Meara and Pat McNamara), sister Jo (Parker Posey), and would-be brother-in-law Carl (Liev Schreiber)? Somehow, Mottola makes the characters and situations seem funny and real and it doesn't hurt one bit that Marcia Gay Harden and co-producer Campbell Scott are also in the cast.

1996 m/C Hope Davis, Stanley Tucci, Parker Posey, Liev Schreiber, Pat McNamara, Anne Meara, Campbell Scott, Marcia Gay Harden, Andy Brown; ***D:*** Greg Mottola; ***W:*** Greg Mottola; ***C:*** John Inwood. **VHS, Closed Caption**

Dazed and Confused

No matter what your high school graduating class, most last-day-of-school movies have a universal appeal. We are all familiar with the rituals and the pain that follows them. In my case, I hung out with a guy whose parachute didn't open, danced with a guy who died too young of cancer, went to a rock concert with a neighbor who died at 22 of complications from a hole in her heart, and took walks in the country with a crash victim who took eight whole years to die, at age 20. Our shared experiences were often just as goofy as the ones in this film, which is why I thought *Dazed and Confused* was evocative and a more recent graduate thought they were pucrile. Well, he would, wouldn't he, being so close to the experience and so eager to escape it? Jason London is a football player with attitude named Randall "Pink" Floyd, who has a girlfriend we don't see and a gentle way with just about everyone that we do see. Wiley Wiggins is Mitch Kramer, a much younger, smaller boy who experiences some harsh rites of passage and gains considerable respect from everyone as a result. Ron Slater (Rory Cochrane) sees everything, even the history of George and Martha Washington, through a haze of marijuana. Ben Affleck, yes, THE Ben Affleck who went on to receive an Oscar for *Good Will Hunting,* is a nearly unrecognizable Big Bully named Fred O'Bannion. And a definitely unrecognizable Matthew McConaughey is David Wooderson, a graduate of uncertain vintage, who hangs out where high school girls hang out because "I get older, they stay the same age." But wait, there's more! Parker Posey as the bitchy Dana Marks, the very funny Adam Goldberg as Mike Newhouse, Anthony Rapp and Kristin Hinojosa as Tony Olson and Sabrina Davis, a really sweet couple, and Joey Lauren Adams as Simone Kerr! Not to mention all those smash hits of 1976 and gr-r-r-eat fashions. Richard Linklater was still wrapping up the song rights and had yet to reach a distribution agreement (with Universal) when *Dazed and Confused* premiered at the Seattle Film Festival. Within five years, many of its players became Movers and Shakers within the movie business. I kept renting this movie and renting this movie and renting this movie until I imagined it cut up on pay cable like *Fast Times at Ridgemont High* and I finally bought it. I still watch it and I still laugh. It's a keeper! 🦴🦴🦴

1993 (R) 97m/C Jason London, Rory Cochrane, Sasha Jensen, Wiley Wiggins, Michelle Burke, Adam Goldberg, Anthony Rapp, Marissa Ribisi, Parker Posey, Joey Lauren Adams, Ben Affleck, Milla Jovovich, Cole Hauser, Matthew McConaughey, Kristin Hinojosa; ***D:*** Richard Linklater; ***W:*** Richard Linklater; ***C:*** Lee Daniel. **VHS, LV, Letterbox, Closed Caption, DVD**

The Dead

Nothing would have kept me away from John Huston's swan song, *The Dead,* but I suspect that the overall sentimental response to the film is based more on a lifelong admiration for Huston's work than to the film itself. I have a hunch that some audience members find all these Irish bores quaint or precious, but I did NOT. James Joyce's 1914 story is a pleasure to read for the loveliness of its language, but *The Dead* was harder for me to sit through in a theatre. I would cheerfully pay to avoid the dull family get-together shown on film, or to listen to an elderly woman sing off-key, and she does over and over again. Maybe I would have to be 81 years old to find the experience, as Huston did, "funny and dear and terribly sad," or to find the film itself "a soul-shaking experience," but I tend to doubt it. Huston includes one beautiful exterior shot at night that evokes the frailty of time in a way that the rest of the film does not. 🦴🦴

1987 (PG) 82m/C *GB* Anjelica Huston, Donal McCann, Marie Kean, Donal Donnelly, Dan O'Herlihy, Helen Carroll, Frank Patterson; ***D:*** John Huston; ***W:*** Tony Huston; ***C:*** Fred Murphy; ***M:*** Alex North. Independent Spirit Awards '88: Best Director (Huston), Best Supporting Actress (Huston); National Society of Film Critics Awards '87: Best Film; Nominations: Academy Awards '87: Best Adapted Screenplay, Best Costume Design. **VHS, LV, Closed Caption**

Dave Connell (Joel McCrea) and Baby Face Martin (Humphrey Bogart) in *Dead End.* Goldwyn/United Artists; courtesy of the Kobal Collection

Dead Calm

Nicole Kidman and Sam Neill are a cute couple, but I wouldn't get in a car with her or on a boat with either one of them. Five minutes into *Dead Calm,* her baby is hurled through a windshield. There is actually no reason for this sequence except to establish why Kidman and Neill go on a sea cruise alone to recover. It also prepares you for the violence this accident-prone couple will experience throughout the rest of the film. When a psycho (screechingly overacted by Billy Zane) rows over to their boat from his own doomed vessel, Neill doesn't believe their visitor's tall tale of botulism and death from contaminated salmon. Neill rows to the vessel to investigate, leaving Kidman and their pet dog alone with the psycho. (Warning: don't get too attached to that mutt.) You see, Neill has 25 years experience at sea, but you'll have to take his word for it. For a small craft skipper, he is constantly endangering his boat, his crew, and himself. He spends what seems like half the movie trying to save himself from drowning by breaking down a vessel door he had no reason to go through at all. Meanwhile, Kidman and that psycho just never can seem to get along. He beats her up, rapes her, kicks down doors, and destroys her radio. She drugs his lemonade, shoots him with an arrow, ties him up, and tries to throw him overboard. Australian director Phillip Noyce, also responsible for the 1986 dud *Echoes of Paradise,* telegraphs each move by all three well in advance. Try to imagine the dumbest thing any of them can do and sure enough, there it is, right onscreen. Was the Charles Williams novel this much of a mess? Tantalizing Back

Story: one of Orson Welles' many unfinished films was an earlier version of *Dead Calm* entitled *Dead Reckoning,* starring Jeanne Moreau and himself in the Kidman/Neill roles and Laurence Harvey as the psycho. Financing and/or Harvey's early death scuttled the project, although footage from this incomplete work survives. 🦴🦴🦴

1989 (R) 97m/C *AU* Sam Neill, Billy Zane, Nicole Kidman, Rod Mullinar; ***D:*** Phillip Noyce; ***W:*** Terry Hayes; ***C:*** Dean Semler; ***M:*** Graeme Revell. **VHS, LV, 8mm, Letterbox, Closed Caption, DVD**

Dead End

It was the summer of 1937 and happy days weren't here again. It would take a second world war to end the international depression. Sidney Kingsley (*Men in White, The Patriots, Detective Story*) had won a Pulitzer Prize for the original play *Dead End* in 1935, when he was only 29. Lillian Hellman (1905–84) was on Samuel Goldwyn's payroll, so she wrote the screenplay. Director William Wyler wanted to film the picture on the sidewalks of New York, but Goldwyn, like so many Hollywood producers, insisted that his Oscar-winning art director (Richard Day, 1896–1972) could transform the back lot into an East Side neighborhood. Well, you never forget it's a set, but what a set (!), filled with nooks and crannies and back alleys and dark stairs and a sharp contrast between the poverty line and the exterior of a luxury apartment building. *Dead End* wasn't a bromide for those 20th century blues, it was a hard-hitting look at how the Depression affected everyone. Drina Gordon (Sylvia Sidney) is the sole source of support for her teenage brother Tommy (Billy Halop), but she's currently picketing her place of work. (Check out other films of the '30s to see how often members of picket lines are shown in such a compassionate light, if at all.) Drina's in love with architect Dave Connell (Joel McCrea), but he's between jobs and lusting after gangland moll Kay Burton (Wendy Barrie, who had a reputation for socializing with gangsters in real life). Tommy and the other Dead End Kids—Dippy, Angel, T.B., Spit, and Milty—worship their gangland ideal, Baby Face Martin (Humphrey Bogart): He got out. But Martin is back (with Allen Jenkins as a thug named Hunk) to pay a call on his girlfriend, Francey (Claire Trevor) and to see his mother (Marjorie Main). Despite Goldwyn's clout as an independent producer and Wyler's sensitivity as a director, this stage-to-screen transfer had to get past the Hays Office, and that meant that Kay Burton's status and Francey's syphilis could be suggested obliquely, but not mentioned out loud. But all the other theatrical elements remain intact, including the corrosive effect of slum life on children, as well as adults. The Dead End Kids evolved into the Bowery Boys, giving several of the kids here a regular paycheck well into middle age. They became a comic distortion of their desperate *Dead End* characters, all of whom seemed destined to wisecrack their way into early graves. ***AKA:*** Cradle of Crime. 🦴🦴🦴🦴

1937 92m/B Sylvia Sidney, Joel McCrea, Humphrey Bogart, Wendy Barrie, Claire Trevor, Allen Jenkins, Marjorie Main, Billy Halop, Huntz Hall, Bobby Jordan, Gabriel Dell, Leo Gorcey, Charles Halton, Bernard Punsley, Minor Watson, James Burke; ***D:*** William Wyler; ***W:*** Lillian Hellman; ***C:*** Gregg Toland; ***M:*** Alfred Newman. Nominations: Academy Awards '37: Best Cinematography, Best Interior Decoration, Best Picture, Best Supporting Actress (Trevor). **VHS, LV**

Dead Man

I fidgeted all the way through Jim Jarmusch's *Dead Man.* This is one of those long-winded black-and-white Westerns that makes you want to bag the screening and spend the time necking instead. Johnny Depp plays the title role with excruciating fidelity, and Robert Mitchum plays a cameo role, but that's about it. There's a line at the beginning that pretty much says it all, unless you need empirical evidence of just how soporific Depp can be. 🦴🦴

1995 (R) 121m/B Johnny Depp, Gary Farmer, Lance Henriksen, Michael Wincott, Mili Avital, Crispin Glover, Gabriel Byrne, Iggy Pop, Billy Bob Thornton, Jared Harris, Jimmie Ray Weeks, Mark Bringleson, John Hurt, Alfred Molina, Robert Mitchum; ***D:*** Jim Jarmusch; ***W:*** Jim Jarmusch; ***C:*** Robby Muller; ***M:*** Neil Young. New York Film Critics Awards '96: Best Cinematography; National Society of Film Critics Awards '96: Best Cinematography; Nominations: Independent Spirit Awards '97: Best Cinematography, Best Film, Best Screenplay, Best Supporting Actor (Farmer). **VHS, LV, Closed Caption**

"I want the last face you see in this world to be the face of love, so you look at me when they do this thing. I'll be the face of love for you."

—Sister Helen Prejean (Susan Sarandon) in *Dead Man Walking.*

Dead Man Walking

Susan Sarandon is Sister Helen Prejean, death row inmate Matthew Poncelet's (Sean Penn) last chance at spiritual salvation. Poncelet murdered two young people in cold blood and is numb to the horror of his crime. Seeing Sister Helen is better than nothing, so he asks her to keep visiting him at Angola prison in New Orleans where he waits to die. On an early visit, he tries to hit on her, but she slaps him down with a sarcastic verbal retort and continues with the serious work of saving his soul. Although Sister Helen is opposed to the death penalty, Oscar nominee Tim Robbins' superb film shows both sides with careful, non-judgmental attention. The victims' parents are in agony, Poncelet has a shattering change of heart due to Sister Helen's steady influence, and there is a vivid sequence showing his emotion-charged encounter with his family at the prison. Penn won an Oscar nomination as Matthew Poncelet and, after a career filled with outstanding performances, Sarandon won her first Academy Award for her unforgettable portrait of Sister Helen Prejean. Scott Wilson (Chaplain Farley) starred as Dick Hickock in 1967's *In Cold Blood.* 🦴🦴🦴🦴

1995 (R) 122m/C Susan Sarandon, Sean Penn, Robert Prosky, Raymond J. Barry, R. Lee Ermey, Celia Weston, Lois Smith, Scott Wilson, Roberta Maxwell, Margo Martindale, Barton Heyman, Larry Pine; ***D:*** Tim Robbins; ***W:*** Tim Robbins; ***C:*** Roger Deakins; ***M:*** David Robbins. Academy Awards '95: Best Actress (Sarandon); Independent Spirit Awards '96: Best Actor (Penn); Screen Actors Guild Award '95: Best Actress (Sarandon); Nominations: Academy Awards '95: Best Actor (Penn), Best Director (Robbins), Best Song ("Dead Man Walking"); Australian Film Institute '96: Best Foreign Film; Golden Globe Awards '96: Best Actor—Drama (Penn), Best Actress—Drama (Sarandon), Best Screenplay; Independent Spirit Awards '96: Best Supporting Actress (Weston); MTV Movie Awards '96: Best Female Performance (Sarandon); Screen Actors Guild Award '95: Best Actor (Penn). **VHS, LV, DVD**

Dead of Night

For those who believe that Hell may mean repeating your earthly mistakes over and over again with one agonizing moment of realization every time that THIS is to be your fate for the rest of eternity, *Dead of Night* is one very scary flick, best seen with lots of friends who won't leave you alone afterward. Mervyn Johns plays an architect who wakes up after a nightmare and then goes to a farmhouse where he has an appointment. He thinks he's seen it before! The guests then tell scary stories to each other. A race car driver tells the story of his dream about a hearse driver who has room for one more. When he later hears a bus driver say the same thing, he refuses to get on and watches in horror as the bus crashes right afterward. Then a young girl (Sally Ann Howes) tells about a Christmas party where she runs into a little boy named Francis, the brother of Constance Kent, who was accused of his murder in 1860. This Alberto Cavalcanti entry is followed by John Baines' "The Haunted Mirror" (directed by Robert Hamer), in which a young wife watches as her new husband is nearly driven mad by an antique mirror that takes over his personality. Basil Radford and Naunton Wayne then provide comedy relief in H.G. Wells' "The Inexperienced Ghost" (directed by Charles Crichton), about two golfers who both want the same girl. It's a trifle, but a welcome one. The tension would have been nearly unbearable if we'd gone straight from the "The Haunted Mirror" into Cavalcanti's justly famous "Ventriloquist's Dummy" (starring Michael Redgrave) and then back to the chilling story of the nightmare-ridden architect. *Dead of Night* has a cumulative effect. It lulls us with sly humor, then makes the hair stand up on the back of our necks with sheer terror. The linking story and the hearse driver dream are based on the E.F. Benson stories "Room in the Tower" and "The Bus Conductor" and are both directed by Basil Dearden. Ealing forever, and not only for comedies! 🦴🦴🦴🦴

1945 102m/B *GB* Michael Redgrave, Sally Ann Howes, Basil Radford, Naunton Wayne, Mervyn Johns, Roland Culver, Googie Withers, Frederick Valk, Antony Baird, Judy Kelly, Miles Malleson, Ralph Michael, Mary Merrall, Renee Gadd, Michael Allan, Robert Wyndham, Esme Percy, Peggy Bryan, Hartley Power, Elizabeth Welch, Magda Kun, Carry Marsh; ***D:*** Alberto Cavalcanti, Charles Crichton, Basil Dearden, Robert Hamer; ***W:*** T.E.B. Clarke,

John Baines, Angus MacPhail; ***C:*** Jack Parker, H. Julius; ***M:*** Georges Auric. **VHS**

Dealers

If you like to watch Rebecca DeMornay and Paul McGann work, you can see them in *Dealers,* an incomprehensible drama about London high finance. For much of the film's running time, I had no idea what was going on or why. DeMornay and McGann work themselves into a frenzy to achieve a goal that neither seems to care about. After reading the press kit, which clarifies stuff that screenwriter Andrew Maclear should have explained onscreen, I didn't care, either. That's a fatal flaw for a 92-minute movie. Colin Bucksey's crisp direction and the attractive leads would be more effective in a better film. Also worth noting is Derrick O'Connor, who does wonders with a sparsely written character role. **woof!**

1989 (R) 92m/C *GB* Rebecca DeMornay, Paul McGann, Derrick O'Connor; ***D:*** Colin Bucksey; ***W:*** Andrew Maclear; ***C:*** Peter Sinclair. **VHS, LV**

Dear Michael

The excellent Italian picture *Dear Michael* explores the wanderings of Mara, a gypsyish mother (Mariangela Melato) and her baby. Mara has an idea who the father is, and spends her time moving in and out of the homes of his friends and relatives. Melato, so effective in the Lina Wertmuller films *Seduction of Mimi, Love and Anarchy, Swept Away,* and *Summer Night...,* wrings enormous sympathy out of her role here. Her ability to add new dimensions to her sometimes unbearable characters are truly imaginative. Whether she's breaking up with a lover who cannot stand her, scolding an impatient cab driver, or enduring a boring social evening with a group of "intellectuals," Melato provides *Dear Michael* with its funniest and most human moments. Director Mario Monicelli and screenwriters Suso Cecchi D'Amico and Tonino Guerra skillfully blend Mara's story into that of her former lover's family. With the addition of superb, understated performances by the late Delphine Seyrig, Aurore Clement, and particularly Fabio Carpi as one of Mara's befuddled lovers, *Dear Michael* is among the most memorable films of 1976. Melato's other films on video include: *By the Blood of Others, To Forget Venice, So Fine,* and *Dancers.* ***AKA:*** Caro Michele.

1976 108m/C *IT* Mariangela Melato, Delphine Seyrig, Aurore Clement, Lou Castel, Marcella Michelangeli, Fabio Carpi; ***D:*** Mario Monicelli; ***W:*** Suso Cecchi D'Amico, Tonino Guerra; ***C:*** Tonino Delli Colli; ***M:*** Nino Rota.

Dear Victor

At first, *Dear Victor* gives every indication that it's going to be a comedy, then a savage plot twist occurs: Film Festivalitis? Yes, that strange and sometimes frightening condition that afflicts directors who don't want to make a choice about the direction of their narratives, so the choice is made FOR them by tuned-out audiences! The compensatory surprise here is Alida Valli, who's simply wonderful and very funny as a singer who COULD have been an opera star. ***AKA:*** Ce Cher Victor.

1975 102m/C *FR* Bernard Blier, Jacques Dufilho, Alida Valli, Alice Reichen, Jacqueline Doyen, Philippe Castelli, Jacques Rispal; ***D:*** Robin Davis; ***W:*** Robin Davis, Robin Laurent; ***C:*** Yves Lafaye; ***M:*** Bernard Gerard.

Death and the Maiden

Roman Polanski sets up a gripping dilemma here and then dribbles it. Why do we have to forgive the unforgivable? Why do we have to live and let live when we've been victimized by a person who clearly didn't care whether or not we lived or died? Three fine actors (Ben Kingsley, Sigourney Weaver, Stuart Wilson) grapple with this situation for 103 minutes until the credits roll. In a number of ways, it rather reminds me of 1986's *Extremities,* where we are reminded over and over again that a reprehensible character deserves for the woman he raped to treat him like a human being. Can't someone, ANYONE else do that little thing? Polanski succeeds in making us feel as trapped as his characters, but the muddled, well-intentioned narrative thread tends to be unplayable at times, especially by Weaver,

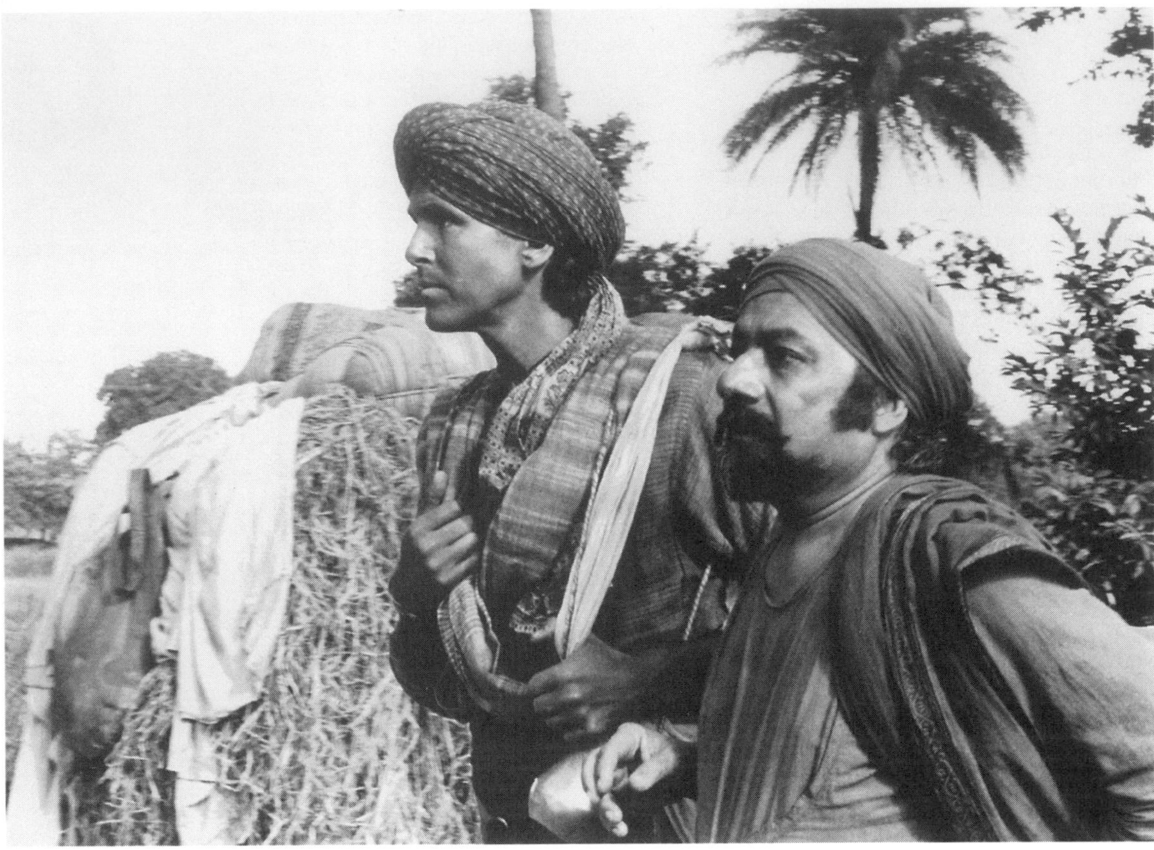

Pierce Brosnan and Saeed Jaffrey in *The Deceivers.*
Cinecom-Film Four; courtesy of the Kobal Collection

who has the hardest job here. Based on the play by Ariel Dorfman. ***AKA:*** La Jeune Fille et la Mort. ☙☙☙

1994 (R) 103m/C Sigourney Weaver, Ben Kingsley, Stuart Wilson; ***D:*** Roman Polanski; ***W:*** Rafael Yglesias, Ariel Dorfman; ***C:*** Tonino Delli Colli; ***M:*** Wojciech Kilar. Nominations: Independent Spirit Awards '95: Best Director (Polanski). **VHS, LV, Closed Caption**

Death of a Schoolboy

I once saw a movie about Bismarck made during the Third Reich that didn't have a single battle sequence, for who knows what reason. It played out rather like a chess game. It reminded me of THIS movie, about the 16-year-old kid who started World War I (and, consequently, II) by shooting Archduke Franz Ferdinand and his wife during a holiday parade in Sarajevo on June 28, 1914. *Death of a Schoolboy* is all about Gavre Princip without showing what he did or what it meant. You see him before and after the parade, you see what he's like and how he evolved from schoolboy to assassin and...that's the movie. Even if Peter Patzak was broke, even if he couldn't afford the extras or the props to recreate the parade, there is an abundance of stock footage and stills collecting dust on the shelves of archives and libraries, so why not show them? To take the emphasis off the single act that placed Princip in the encyclopedia and not to show that act is simply inexplicable. The story begins in Bosnia-Herzegovina when Princip (Reuben Pillsbury) is a baby-faced, 17-year-old idealist who hates the monarchy. He considers Franz Ferdinand's visit on a Serbian national holiday to be an insult and prepares to do away with him. (In the film, he expresses regret to Phillipe Leotard's Dr. Levin about killing the Archduke's morganatic wife as well and it's clear that he hasn't a clue about how and why the Great War started.) He considers the assassination, makes his plans carefully...and then we see him as a reflective inmate in the prison where he died of tuberculosis in 1918, a Serbian "hero" and no longer a schoolboy. This could have been a fascinating picture instead of the rambling assembly of unfinished ideas that it is. ***AKA:*** Gavre Princip Himmel Unter Steinen. 𝄞𝄞

1991 93m/C Reuben Pillsbury, Christopher Chaplin, Robert Munic, Sinolicka Trpkova, Michele Melega, Alan Cox, Hans-Michael Rehberg, Philippe Leotard, Alexis Arquette; ***D:*** Peter Patzak; ***W:*** David Anton, Hans Konig; ***C:*** Igor Luther; ***M:*** Peter Ponger.

The Deceivers

The Deceivers appears to have everything going for it: a handsome hero (Pierce Brosnan), fine support from excellent character actors Shashi Kapoor and Saeed Jaffrey, fascinating Indian locations, and a plot that promises mystery, suspense, and danger. It bogs down in murky character development, a fatal lack of conviction about who the villains are, and an obvious series of false discussions that drag the plot down at every turn. ("I can't do it." "Yes, you can." "No, I can't." "You must." and so forth until we cut to the next scene with Brosnan doing what he couldn't with no effort at all.) Based on a true story, *The Deceivers* are also known as Thugees, a weird, murderous cult that thrived in India, circa 1825. I tend to be suspicious of internal problems that can only be sorted out by British outsiders or by Shirley Temple; after all, Great Britain had and has its share of weird murderers and nobody ever suggests that Rajahs be imported to clear up those problems. That said, the film is further burdened by Brosnan's bewildered performance. When the Irish actor appeared in *The Long Good Friday* with Bob Hoskins, he delivered a crisp, menacing performance, quite free of any tendency to sweeten his character. After four years of playing a heroic television detective, Brosnan seems more interested in stardom (with substance, of course!) than in acting. It's hard to figure out what he's trying to do with his character, a problem we don't have with co-stars Kapoor and Jaffrey. Also in the cast are David Robb, who specializes in playing husbands of icons of the '60s (Hayley Mills) and the '80s (Diana, Princess of Wales). Keith Michell, considerably puffier than in his lean days onstage in the '70s when he played Peter Abelard in the nude, is virtually unrecognizable here. *The Deceivers* is produced by Ismail Merchant, taking a busman's holiday from his meticulous production team of Ruth Prawer Jhabvala and James Ivory. With a script straight out of Screenwriting I by Michael Hirst (from John Masters' novel) and clumsy schoolboy direction by Nicholas Meyer, Merchant seems to be taking a crash course in the *Classics Illustrated* school of filmmaking. 𝄞𝄞

1988 (PG-13) 112m/C *IN GB* Pierce Brosnan, Saeed Jaffrey, Shashi Kapoor, Keith Michell, David Robb; ***D:*** Nicholas Meyer; ***W:*** Michael Hirst; ***C:*** Walter Lassally. **VHS, LV, Closed Caption**

Deep End

Jane Asher is a fine actress whose well-publicized social life offscreen has eclipsed virtually everything she's ever done onscreen. In the case of the rarely shown *Deep End,* it's a shame, because her performance here is outstanding. John Moulder-Brown is 15-year-old Michael, who gets a job as a Men's Attendant at London's Newford public bathhouse. He falls hard for Women's Attendant Susan (Asher), who's about eight years older. She's having a not particularly satisfying relationship with an older man and is touched, at least at first, by Michael's crush on her. But as time wears on, she can no longer juggle all the disparate elements of her life, and Michael is devastated by her growing disinterest in his devotion to her. Inevitably, something has to give, and it does in a way that startles this mismatched pair as much as it does us. *Deep End* is a shockingly overlooked study of adolescent obsession at its most extreme, meticulously scripted and directed

Katharine Hepburn and Paul Scofield in *A Delicate Balance.* American Film Theatre; courtesy of the Kobal Collection

and remarkably acted by the two leads. Don't miss it! 🦴🦴🦴🦴

1970 88m/C *GB GE* Jane Asher, John Moulder-Brown, Diana Dors, Karl Michael Vogler, Christopher Sandord; ***D:*** Jerzy Skolimowski; ***W:*** Jerzy Skolimowski, Jerry Gruza, Bloeslav Sulik; ***C:*** Charly Steinberger; ***M:*** Cat Stevens. **VHS**

Def by Temptation

Ah, those demon temptresses, preying on innocent divinity students. James Bond III wrote, directed, and starred as Joel in *Def by Temptation,* which horror devotees consider to be the *pièce de résistance* of Troma Films' oeuvre. The rest of the cast received high praise, too, especially seductive Cynthia Bond, and the soundtrack became a collectors' item. Cinematographer Ernest Dickerson, who also shot *She's Gotta Have It* (with John Canada Terrell), went on to direct *Juice* (with Samuel L. Jackson) and *Blind Faith* (with Kadeem Hardison). 🦴🦴🦴

1990 (R) 95m/C James Bond III, Kadeem Hardison, Bill Nunn, Samuel L. Jackson, Minnie Gentry, Rony Clanton, Cynthia Bond, John Canada Terrell; ***D:*** James Bond III; ***W:*** James Bond III; ***C:*** Ernest R. Dickerson; ***M:*** Paul Lawrence. **VHS, LV, DVD**

A Delicate Balance

The credits for *A Delicate Balance* sound so tantalizing, it's sad that the film itself is such a drag to watch. Six years earlier on Broadway, the original play by Edward Albee had won the Pulitzer Prize, and actress Marian Seldes won a Tony for her performance. (Co-stars Hume Cronyn and Rosemary Murphy were also nominated, and the venerable Jessica Tandy was in it, too.) Maybe it was one of those unfilmable plays, or maybe its stars were too high profile to be persuasive in roles they weren't exactly born to play, or maybe it simply wasn't Tony Richardson's cup of tea. Luis Buñel's, maybe? Edward Albee and Eugene O'Neill were the only American playwrights represented in 13 American Film Theatre productions of the early 1970s. *A Delicate Balance* was released theatrically overseas in 1976. The only noteworthy thing about this movie was meeting Celeste Holm at a San Francisco matinee screening in the theatre lobby. She asked me if I accepted the premise of the film (No!) and if I wanted an autograph, would I give her a quarter for UNICEF? (Yes!) 🦴🦴

1973 134m/C *GB CA* Katharine Hepburn, Paul Scofield, Lee Remick, Kate Reid, Joseph Cotten, Betsy Blair; ***D:*** Tony Richardson; ***W:*** Edward Albee; ***C:*** David Watkin. **VHS**

Delusion

Delusion is an accurate title for a movie that is deliberately reminiscent of many other noir films. Those films, which include Edgar Ulmer's *Detour* and Alfred Hitchcock's *Vertigo,* deliver a lot more than *Delusion* ever does. It starts out well: a schnook named George (Jim Metzler) steals nearly $250,000 to save his ailing company, then drives his Volvo into the desert with the loot. Faster than you can say *Psycho,* George runs into a fruitcake named Chevy (Kyle Secour) with a weak stomach and a girlfriend named Patti. Patti is sporadically crafty, especially when craftiness will advance the plot. But George is always a schnook and Chevy is always a fruitcake and 100 minutes of these two tend to make Patti's cipher-like personality seem more complex than it really is. Jerry Orbach is seen in a brief appearance. So is Jennifer Rubin's bare chest. And so is a moderately intriguing plot twist that Patti and the audience know about, but not George or Chevy. Don't be misled, though: writer/director Carl Colpaert takes that title very seriously. Everything in his picture is a tease, from the spectacular golden landscapes, to the deceptively provocative emotional subtext, to the emptiness of the treasure that lies within everyone's reach and no one's grasp. *Delusion* is a film about hard-core losers living by rules that don't work. There is not even a minimal effort to supply the characters with depth; you already know much more about them than you'll ever want to know. *Delusion*'s very emptiness may guarantee it an audience. But for anyone who really loves film noir, Colpaert's decision to tie up the plot with Lee Hazelwood's *These Boots Are Made for Walking* reveals *Delusion*'s threadbare ingredients: something old, nothing new, something borrowed, nothing blue. 🦴🦴

1991 (R) 100m/C Jim Metzler, Jennifer Rubin, Kyle Secor, Robert Costanzo, Tracey Walter, Jerry Orbach; ***D:*** Carl Colpaert; ***W:*** Carl Colpaert, Kurt Voss; ***C:*** Geza Sinkovics; ***M:*** Barry Adamson. **VHS, LV, Letterbox**

Destiny Turns on the Radio

Quentin Tarantino as Johnny Destiny. Right. And the Emperor was really wearing clothes. But Mr. T is an Oscar winner. He's the 1990s' Big Thing. Why not be a movie star and an influential screenwriter and a hot director, too? Tarantino was promoted more in the television spots than the so-called stars, Dylan McDermott, Nancy Travis, James LeGros, and James Belushi, as if his Midas touch could rub off on first-time screenwriters Robert Ramsey and Matthew Stone and on fledgling director Jack Baran. It can't, of course. The script is the stuff of formulaic hacks, and Baran's idea of great direction is to tell McDermott he's in an action flick, THEN tell Travis she's in a romantic comedy, THEN tell LeGros his character is brain dead, and THEN tell Belushi and his henchmen that their characters require constant reassurances about their virility; they even scratch their crotches in synch. All of this was developed at The Sundance Institute, so some critics have been charitable about this maiden effort. But it's a mess. Travis is a nightclub singer whose voice is dubbed by a singer who's ever so slightly off-key, so the Hoagy Carmichael classic "Baltimore Oriole" is ruined, ditto "That Old Black Magic." (You can hear Louis Prima and Keely Smith sing it right on the soundtrack.) A restrained Bobcat Goldthwaite plays an undercover cop who

"I keep trying to forget what happened and wonder what my life would have been like if that car of Haskell's hadn't stopped. But one thing I don't have to wonder about—I know. Some day a car will stop to pick me up that I never thumbed. Yes, fate—or some mysterious force—can put the finger on you, for no good reason at all.... No matter what you do, no matter where you turn, fate sticks out its foot to trip you."

—Al Roberts (Tom Neal) in *Detour.*

spends most of the movie tied to a vibrating bed with an apple taped in his mouth. A real knee slapper, no? Tarantino has set the world on fire as a screenwriter and director, but he is not of strong enough presence to dazzle anyone as Johnny Destiny. And for critics to be kind to *Destiny Turns on the Radio* sets Baran, Ramsay, and Stone up for their second effort to be (surprise) received far worse than their dreadful debut, since it lacks the je ne sais quoi of *Destiny.* It's a curiosity piece all right, but it's lucky that night prowling movie cats usually have eight or nine lives to spare. **woof!**

1995 (R) 101m/C Dylan McDermott, Nancy Travis, James LeGros, Quentin Tarantino, Allen (Goorwitz) Garfield, James Belushi, Tracey Walter, Bob(cat) Goldthwait; ***D:*** Jack Baran; ***W:*** Robert Ramsey, Matthew Stone; ***C:*** James L. Carter; ***M:*** Steven Soles. **VHS, Closed Caption**

Detour

Detour is THE grunge classic of all time. In most cases, when you watch a poverty row film, you find yourself wishing that they had just a bit more time or money to do things properly: if only the wallpaper in the hero's apartment and the police station weren't identical; if only the same three extras weren't in the background in every single sequence. But *Detour,* shot on a next-to-nothing budget in less than a week, is perfect just the way it is. The main reason, of course, is that Edgar G. Ulmer, a brilliant director who rarely got a chance at an "A" movie, was at the helm. No one could wring more from a poverty row effort than Ulmer, as he demonstrated in his superior work on films like *Bluebeard* and *Strange Illusion.* Superstar John Garfield might have seemed like an ideal choice for the role of the protagonist in *Detour,* but in fact, Tom Neal WAS Al Roberts. Neal kicked around Hollywood from the late '30s through the early '50s, launching his career at the prestigious MGM studios, but he descended swiftly to grade-Z programmers, in part because of his unsavory offscreen behavior. (He later wound up in prison for killing one of his wives.) If ever a camera recorded the face of a loser, Tom Neal was the quintessential loser. He was 31 in 1945, the year *Detour* was shot, and while superficially attractive, he seemed drenched in world-weariness and defeatism. Ann Savage, then a 24-year-old starlet, sacrificed her good looks to play the role of Vera, a femme fatale with a vengeance. No other young actress of her era ever made herself so unlovely for the sake of a role: no make-up, ragged hair, a wardrobe from Hell. If you catch a dolled-up version of Savage in any of her glossy Columbia films, you'll find it hard to believe you're looking at the same person. In the course of little over an hour, Al and Vera meet, join forces, and destroy each other on the road, spitting dialogue at each other that you're unlikely to hear in any other '40s movie. Among the lighter-than-air films of that time, *Detour* stands alone as a grim chunk of realism and it's still every bit as hard-hitting in the '90s.

1946 67m/B Tom Neal, Ann Savage, Claudia Drake, Edmund MacDonald, Tim Ryan, Esther Howard; ***D:*** Edgar G. Ulmer; ***W:*** Martin Goldsmith; ***C:*** Benjamin Kline; ***M:*** Erdody. **VHS, LV**

The Devil Is a Woman

Maybe it was movies like *The Devil Is a Woman* that eventually lured Glenda Jackson off the sound stages and into Parliament. She dons spiked belts here in her role as a weird mother superior who keeps the residents of her convent under her thumb. The script is your basic, silly, half-baked attack on the Catholic hierarchy—not a bad target, perhaps, but if you're going to satirize an institution, at least deal with it on its own terms. Unconvincing and ridiculous beyond belief, *Devil* doesn't even come close. ***AKA:*** Il Sorriso del Grande Tentatore. **woof!**

1975 185m/C *GB IT* Glenda Jackson, Claudio Cassinelli, Lisa Harrow, Adolfo Celi, Arnoldo Foa, Rolf Tasna, Dulio Del Prete, Gabriele Lavia, Francesco Rabal; ***D:*** Damiano Damiani; ***W:*** Damiano Damiani, Fabrizio Onofri, Audrey Nohra; ***C:*** Mario Vulpiani; ***M:*** Ennio Morricone.

Diamonds in the Snow

In the city of Bendzin, Poland, three small children among thousands were being torn away from their families during the Nazi occupation. The little girls grew up to participate in the making of *Diamonds in the Snow.* The award-winning documentary is directed by Mira Reym Binford, who recalls her own experiences and interviews two others among the 12 surviving children of the town, Ada Raviv and Shulamit Levin. In Dr. Binford's case, her life was protected by another refugee who nonetheless beat her up. As an adult, she searches for his own children and learns that after the war they were treated no better than she was, a discovery that helps to heal much of her early pain and confusion. 🦴🦴🦴

1994 59m/C *D:* Mira Reym Binford. **VHS**

Diary of a Hitman

Sherilyn Fenn may not have the marquee value of Kim Basinger—yet—but just wait. The smashingly talented alumnus of *Twin Peaks* can act rings around most other actresses of her generation as she demonstrates in Roy London's 1992 film noir sleeper, *Diary of a Hitman,* starring Forest Whitaker. Whitaker plays a hired gun who is paid by Lewis Smith to execute his wife (Fenn) and their baby. Whitaker's character has already begun to agonize over his profession, but he is unprepared for Fenn's sheer vivacity. He hesitates, and that hesitation forms the basis for Kenneth Pressman's narrative (based on his play, *Insider's Price*). Fenn gives extraordinary dimension to the role of the would-be victim. First, she can't wait for her husband to come home; then, as she realizes that Whitaker has come to kill her baby and herself on her husband's orders, she fights like a tiger to survive. One by one, she tries every resource at her disposal, always tapping into her internal strengths as an actress, never employing the easy external tricks that might have created a flashy, but far less real, character. Whitaker, too, is quite moving as the conscience-stricken assassin. With a brilliant series of emotional mood swings, he captures both the extreme danger and the capacity for deep feeling that are central to the life-and-death conflict in *Diary of a Hitman.* Michel Columbier's fine jazz score enhances Roy London's striking visual style, and the supporting cast members (James Belushi, Seymour Cassel, Lois Chiles, and a nearly unrecognizable Sharon Stone) are exceptionally good; they are usually the stars in other films. The killer with a heart of gold is the stuff of pure theatre, nearly a cliche. Thanks to the expert work of Forest Whitaker and Sherilyn Fenn, the complex relationship between killer and victim also serves to reveal the existential angst lurking beneath all our meaningless rituals. 🦴🦴🦴

1991 (R) 90m/C Forest Whitaker, James Belushi, Sherilyn Fenn, Sharon Stone, Seymour Cassel, Lewis Smith, Lois Chiles, John Bedford-Lloyd; ***D:*** Roy London; ***W:*** Kenneth Pressman; ***M:*** Michel Colombier. **VHS, LV, Closed Caption**

Different for Girls

Richard Spence's *Different for Girls* is a love story with a twist. It's the tale of Kim Foyle and Paul Prentice (well played by Steven Mackintosh and Rupert Graves), who develop a romance under unusual circumstances. It seems that once upon a time Prentice was friends with a classmate named Karl at a Catholic school for boys. The boy Karl evolved into the girl Kim after a sex change operation and the mutual attraction between Kim and Prentice needs some sort of reassuring context since they both consider themselves to be straight. Got that? The film is nothing earth-shattering, but it is well made, pleasant, and straightforward. 🦴🦴½

1996 (R) 92m/C *GB* Rupert Graves, Steven Mackintosh, Miriam Margolyes, Saskia Reeves, Neil Dudgeon, Charlotte Coleman; ***D:*** Richard Spence; ***W:*** Tony Merchant; ***C:*** Sean Van Hales; ***M:*** Stephen Warbeck. Montreal World Film Festival '95: Best Film. **VHS**

"You're just like any other man only a little more so. You have a feeling of being trapped, hemmed in, and you don't know whether or not you like it."

—Paula Gibson (Pamela Britton) on fiancé Frank Bigelow (Edmond O'Brien) in *D.O.A.*

Dinner for Adele

This charming film from Czechoslovakia, a surprise hit at international film festivals, is inspired by the Nick Carter detective stories that enjoyed a vogue at the turn of the 20th century. *Dinner for Adele/Adele Hasn't Had Her Supper Yet* is about a man-eating plant, some early flying machines, a mad scientist, a sane scientist, a delightful strudel of a girl who makes terrific strawberry dumplings, a fat detective and, last but not least, the famous slender detective Nick Carter whose motto is "Always prepared!" How do they all fit together? Hopefully, a shrewd American distributor will acquire the video rights, so more viewers will have the fun of discovering Adele all over again. (Adele is the animated plant. The wonderfully capable Czech actor Michal Docolomansky plays Nick Carter.) ***AKA:*** Adele Hasn't Had Her Supper Yet; Nick Carter in Prague. 🦴🦴🦴🦴

1978 100m/C *CZ* Michal Docolomansky, Rudolf Hrusinsky, Milos Kopecky, Nada Konvalinkova, Ladislav Pesek; ***D:*** Oldrich Lipsky; ***W:*** Jiri Brdecka; ***C:*** Jaroslav Kucera.

Dirty Dancing

I used to love Jennifer Grey when she had her own nose on her face in the 1980s; it was cute, it gave her character, and it suited her. Now, I don't always recognize her face on the video boxes and she's indistinguishable from so many other ingenues of the 1990s. For the long summer of 1987, Grey and co-star Patrick Swayze epitomized romance as they danced together all night long. It's set in another place (the Catskills) and time (1963), when teenagers still spent summers with their parents at resort hotels in the country. More accurately, *Dirty Dancing* is 1963 grafted onto 1987, because the music and the dance styles are from the later era. But female audiences identified with Grey's character, and empathized with her discovery of the universal truths about that age in that rarefied atmosphere. *Dirty Dancing* isn't a perfect movie, but it's a very pleasant way to spend 97 minutes. Emile Ardolino also directed 1992's *Sister Act.* 🦴🦴🦴

1987 (PG-13) 97m/C Patrick Swayze, Jennifer Grey, Cynthia Rhodes, Jerry Orbach, Jack Weston, Jane Brucker, Kelly Bishop, Lonny Price, Charles "Honi" Coles, Bruce Morrow; ***D:*** Emile Ardolino; ***W:*** Eleanor Bergstein; ***C:*** Jeffrey Jur; ***M:*** John Morris. Academy Awards '87: Best Song ("(I've Had) the Time of My Life"); Golden Globe Awards '88: Best Song ("(I've Had) the Time of My Life"); Independent Spirit Awards '88: Best First Feature. **VHS, LV, Closed Caption, DVD**

Dites-Lui Que Je L'Aime

Dites-Lui Que Je L'Aime is a disappointing second film by Claude Miller, who made such a promising debut with 1976's *The Best Way. Dites-Lui...* seems to have been crafted by a self-indulgent film student. Based on a Patricia Highsmith novel, the plot revolves around a completely unsympathetic accountant (listlessly played by Gerard Depardieu), who pursues former girlfriend Dominique Laffin, now a married mother. Meanwhile, gorgeous masochist Miou-Miou pursues Depardieu, and a married drip subsequently pursues Miou-Miou. For 107 minutes, all the characters throw each other around and yell a lot. The best moment occurs when Gerard Depardieu kicks in a television set while Paul Anka is singing, which gives you some idea how droll the rest of this flick is. ***AKA:*** This Sweet Sickness; Tell Her I Love Her. 🦴🦴

1977 107m/C *FR* Gerard Depardieu, Miou-Miou, Dominique Laffin, Claude Pieplu, Christian Clavier, Jacques Denis, Josiane Balasko, Veronique Silver, Jacqueline Jeanne, Michel Such; ***D:*** Claude Miller; ***W:*** Claude Miller, Luc Beraud; ***C:*** Pierre Lhomme. **VHS**

D.O.A.

Independent producer Harry M. Popkin made several interesting films in the late 1940s and early 1950s, most with an emphasis on location shooting. *D.O.A.* is extremely effective in this respect because when Edmond O'Brien as Frank Bigelow runs through the streets of San Francisco and Los Angeles, the actual neighborhoods give his story a realistic touch that no lighting tricks or rear screen projections could match. Bigelow is a C.P.A. in the small town of Banning. He wants to have fun in San Francisco, alone, without Pamela Britton along as his girlfriend Paula Gibson. Oddly, his first few hours in the city have a comedic feel, which makes his subsequent predicament all the more terrifying. He goes to a jazz bar at Fisherman's Wharf, meets a cute girl named Jeanie (Virginia Lee), takes one small sip of the wrong drink and his fate is sealed, permanently, although he doesn't know it yet. By the time he gets around to seeking medical attention, it's too late—he's already dying of radiation poisoning. The rest of the movie follows Bigelow as he tries to trace who did this to him and why. I don't know of any other film noir where the victim is able to investigate his own murder in advance (except for the re-makes of this one), although Ephraim Katz's *Film Encyclopedia* lists a 1931 German movie by Robert Siodmak, *Looking for His Murderer/Der Mann der Seinen Morder Sucht.* (Anyone know if that movie still survives?) The application of radioactive poison as an instrument of death was an example of the postwar paranoia that would reach its zenith in Robert Aldrich's 1955 indie, *Kiss Me Deadly.* Future Oscar winner O'Brien is excellent, and *D.O.A.* is undoubtedly director Rudolph Mate's finest work. This was the debut film for Beverly Garland as Miss Campbell and also for Neville Brand as Chester. Brand had the interesting talent of projecting charisma AND ugliness in the same shot. A great screen villain was born! WARNING: Oscar-winning cameraman Ernest Laszlo (1905–84) did NOT work his fingers to the bone on this film noir to have someone colorize his efforts! Please buy/rent *D.O.A.* in black and white! 🦴🦴🦴

1949 83m/B Edmond O'Brien, Pamela Britton, Luther Adler, Neville Brand, Beverly Garland, Lynne Baggett, William Ching, Henry Hart, Laurette Luez, Virginia Lee, Jess Kirkland, Cay Forrester, Michael Ross; ***D:*** Rudolph Mate; ***W:*** Russel Rouse, Clarence Green; ***C:*** Ernest Laszlo; ***M:*** Dimitri Tiomkin. **VHS, DVD**

The Dog Who Loved Trains

This early film by Goran *(Someone Else's America)* Paskalyevic tells the story of Mika, an escaped prisoner (Svetlana Bojakvic), and the two men who "help" her. One is a cowboy stuntman who once doubled for Kirk Douglas (Bata Zivojinovic). The other is a slightly mentally disabled young man (beautifully played by Irfan Mensur) who is searching for his childhood dog. For Mika, there seems to be no escape, only a never-ending series of geographical transitions. The gripping direction throughout retains our interest in Mika's flight. 🦴🦴½

1978 ?m/C *YU* Svetlana Bojakvic, Bata Zivojinovic, Irfan Mensur; ***D:*** Goran Paskalyevic.

Don's Party

All director Bruce Beresford does with David Williamson's stage play *Don's Party* is show that when people drink too much they become obnoxious. They tell each other What They Really Think and flirt with each other's spouses. In the morning, of course, all their sharp insights dissolve into hangovers. Harmless, but silly. Beresford went on to a distinguished career as an international director. Williamson worked again with Beresford and wrote screenplays for Peter Weir and other directors. 🦴🦴

1976 90m/C *AU* Pat Bishop, Graham Kennedy, Candy Raymond, Veronica Lang, John Hargreaves, Ray Barrett, Claire Binney, Graeme Blundell, Jeanie Drynan; ***D:*** Bruce Beresford; ***W:*** David Williamson; ***C:*** Donald McAlpine. Australian Film Institute '77: Best Actress (Bishop). **VHS**

Don't Take It to Heart

Don't Take It to Heart has no reputation whatsoever, but is a lovely surprise for those who stumble on it by accident. Its stars are dashing Richard *(Robin Hood)* Greene and beautiful Patricia Medina, his wife at the time. He's Peter Hayward, a helpful solicitor with a secret; she's Lady Mary, the socialist daughter of the Earl of

The Hound Salutes: PATRICIA MEDINA

Don't Take It to Heart

I started to write my book *Laid Back in Hollywood* after I lost my husband, Joseph Cotten. I was grieving for him and I thought a catharsis would help. I'm not the only person who's lost someone she loved dearly. Anyone who's going through it or who's been through it, please don't go into the deep, dark pit of depression as I did. It held me up for years; it didn't help at all and it didn't bring anyone back. You have to grieve and put the loved one in his natural place in your heart and then be a part of the world. That's what I recommend and that's what I'm trying to do now.

"At first, *Laid Back in Hollywood* was mainly all about my husband and then I realized I was so much a part of him that I'd better start with myself and my life and how it evolved, how I made pictures and all these things and how finally I found the perfect love. I made the 1944 film *Don't Take It to Heart* with my first husband, Richard Greene, and the director, Jeffrey Dell, came to me after we made the test and he said, 'We have a problem.' And I thought, 'Oh, dear God, what is this?' So I said, 'A problem? What is it?' He said, 'Patricia, you have to look down all the way through the picture.' I said, 'That's going to be a little awkward. After all, Richard's considerably taller than I am.' And he said, 'Yes, but I ran the test for some fellows in the screening room and whenever you looked up, they all whistled and we can't have that!' I said, 'Perhaps you can have Richard sitting down? He's going to look so ill-mannered when he's sitting down and I'm looking down at him.' I don't know what happened, but I believe it was quite a delightful movie and I think I sort of looked in between faces all the way through the picture. Then I came out to Hollywood and the directors

Chanduyt (the wonderful Irish character actor Brefni O'Rorke). The village of Chanduyt becomes notorious when a ghost turns up in the Earl's castle. This British screwball comedy is filled with all the top character actors of the period (including Ernest Thesiger and Joan Hickson), and Jeffrey Dell's clever direction and screenplay has a bright, irreverent attitude towards the rigid British class structure. If you wonder why Medina is always looking down in every sequence, it's because test screenings revealed that loud and distracting wolf whistles followed whenever her gorgeous brown eyes were seen in full-face close-ups! 🦴🦴🦴

1944 91m/B *GB* Richard Greene, Patricia Medina, Brefni O'Rorke, Alfred Drayton, Joan Hickson, Richard Bird, Joyce Barbour, Moore Marriott, Edward Rigby, Wylie Watson, Ernest Thesiger; ***D:*** Jeffrey Dell; ***W:*** Jeffrey Dell.

The Doom Generation

"A Heterosexual Movie by Gregg Araki"? How about a re-tread of 1987's *Three Bewildered People in the Night,* also by Araki? Rose McGowan gives a vivid performance as Amy Blue, but the theme here, that figurative and literal lost puppies deserve whatever they get, is illustrated in nauseating detail, rather like a low-budget homage to *Natural Born Killers,* released the previous year. One particularly gory sequence also recalls

here said, 'Oh my God, use your eyes!' I said, 'I'm using them! I can see!' It was the opposite, in other words, 'Look up, please': American directors liked the whistles.

"Orson Welles was (and is!) the best director in the world and one of my all-time favorites. He was absolutely unique. Working with him was sheer joy. You could learn so much with him every step of the way. I loved every minute of it. I think he was treated very badly in Hollywood, though, I really do. They said that he wasted money, and when you think of the millions and millions they're spending today—and that Orson brought in *Citizen Kane* for under a million. He was a fine actor and no one could touch him as a director.

"There were problems when he was making *Mr. Arkadin.* They called me up and they wanted to put more of me in it. I said, 'That would be very nice. I'd better get together with Orson.' They said, 'We're not going to have Orson do it.' And I said, 'Then you don't get me, because it's Orson's picture and if you're going to tamper with it, that isn't fair at all.' I think *Mr. Arkadin* came out more or less the way Orson wanted it. My swashbuckling pictures were merely a means to an end; I was quite happy making them and I suppose I looked alright in costume. I always wanted to be a comedienne and when *The Killing of Sister George* came around, there was a marvelous comedy sequence near the end. I think the character of Sister George had died and I was getting telephone calls from all the men in the world and flowers were coming in; it was really funny, but they cut it out for the X-rated love scene with Coral Browne and Susannah York. I thought it ruined the picture. I know I have a chip on my shoulder because I lost my comedy sequence, but I do believe if it hadn't been for that love scene, Beryl Reid would have been put up for an Academy Award. She gave a marvelously humorous, tender, touching, excellent performance."

Other PATRICIA MEDINA titles on video include: *Spitfire, The Day Will Dawn, Hotel Reserve, The Three Musketeers, Francis the Talking Mule, The Jackpot, Abbott and Costello in the Foreign Legion, Botany Bay, Snow White and the Three Stooges,* and *The Big Push.*

1995's *Dead Presidents,* although the brutal imagery made more sense in the context of the Hughes brothers film. How many ways can you show a menage a trois in which the object of the film is to get the guys alone together? Ditch the impediment? (Although in this case you'd be losing the best actor in the film.) Araki's first flick was lionized beyond recognition at 1988's Lesbian and Gay Film Festival. By the time 1989's fest rolled around, the critics were back to normal with mixed reactions to *The Long Weekend (o' despair). The Living End, Totally F***ed Up, The Doom Generation,* and *Nowhere* followed. Look for *The Love Boat*'s Lauren ("Cruise Director Julie McCoy") Tewes and *The Brady Bunch*'s Christopher ("Peter") Knight as television news anchors.

1995 (R) 84m/C Rose McGowan, James Duval, Johnathon Schaech; ***Cameos:*** Parker Posey, Lauren Tewes, Christopher Knight, Margaret Cho, Skinny Puppy; ***D:*** Gregg Araki; ***W:*** Gregg Araki; ***C:*** Jim Fealy. Nominations: Independent Spirit Awards '96: Debut Performance (McGowan). **VHS, DVD**

Down & Dirty

In *A Special Day,* Ettore Scola already demonstrated his unique gift for tackling a difficult subject with sensitivity, and then shaping a lovely and graceful film. The hilarious *Down & Dirty* is about a large Italian family who live in a hovel and who spend most of their time trying to kill each other. The humor here isn't the least bit

polite, with Scola (who collaborated on the script with his *Special Day* co-writer, Ruggero Maccari) aiming for the broadest possible laughter. The impact of *Down & Dirty* is even more amazing because its entire cast looks, acts, and IS non-professional, with the exception of Nino Manfredi, the leader of this lavishly gross clan. ***AKA:*** Dirty, Mean and Nasty; Brutti, Sporchi e Cattivi; Ugly, Dirty and Bad. 🦴🦴🦴

1976 115m/C *IT* Nino Manfredi, Francesco Anniballi, Maria Bosco; ***D:*** Ettore Scola; ***W:*** Ettore Scola, Ruggero Maccari; ***C:*** Dario Di Palma; ***M:*** Armando Trovajoli. Cannes Film Festival '76: Best Director (Scola). **VHS, Closed Caption**

A Dream of Passion

Jules Dassin's contemporary vision of the Medea myth was dissolved by critics, who thought that Melina Mercouri overacted and the update itself was just plain silly. It isn't great, but it isn't the wretched mess they insisted it was upon release. *A Dream of Passion* actually serves up some pretty good acting by Mercouri, Ellen Burstyn, and Andreas Voutsinas (best known for being Christopher Hewett's partner in 1968's *The Producers*). Mercouri plays an actress playing Medea, Burstyn plays a tormented religious fanatic whose real-life actions parallel that of the tragic Medea. They share some nerve-shattering sequences and there are also some mesmerizing moments when Mercouri's character speaks directly to the camera. Eighteen years after taking the world by storm with her Oscar-nominated performance in Dassin's *Never on Sunday, A Dream of Passion* was very nearly the end of the line for Mercouri (1923–94), at least onscreen. By 1978, she was a major player in Greek politics. Burstyn, of course, went on to make many more films as one of America's leading actresses. 🦴🦴½

1978 (R) 105m/C *GR SI* Ellen Burstyn, Melina Mercouri, Andreas Voutsinas; ***D:*** Jules Dassin; ***W:*** Jules Dassin; ***C:*** Yorgos Arvanitis. **VHS**

Dreamchild

When Gavin Millar's *Dreamchild* was released in 1985, its star Coral Browne (1913–91) seemed a sure bet for an Oscar nomination. The film won favorable attention on the art house circuit for its unusual approach to the true-life story of Alice Hargreaves, who inspired Charles Dodgson to write *Alice in Wonderland.* As written by Dennis Potter, *Dreamchild* is a film of great imagination and style, enhanced by Ian Holm's touching performance as Charles Dodgson and by Coral Browne's commanding presence as 80-year-old Alice. 🦴🦴🦴

1985 (PG) 94m/C *GB* Coral Browne, Ian Holm, Peter Gallagher, Jane Asher, Nicola Cowper, Amelia Shankley, Caris Corfman, Shane Rimmer, James Wilby; ***D:*** Gavin Millar; ***W:*** Dennis Potter; ***C:*** Billy Williams; ***M:*** Max Harris, Stanley Myers. **VHS**

Drugstore Cowboy

Before there was *Trainspotting* and Ewan McGregor, there was *Drugstore Cowboy* and Matt Dillon. He's excellent here as a junkie trying to escape the drug scene, circa 1971. Delicately lovely teenager Heather Graham (the real-life daughter of an FBI agent, she later starred as Annie Blackburne on *Twin Peaks*) is the sacrificial lamb of the group, and the impetus for Matt's driving ambition to turn his life around. His girlfriend, well played by Kelly Lynch, finds it harder to leave the scene. Max Perlich played a similar role in 1991's *Rush.* William S. Burroughs, then 75, also makes an appearance. This scrupulously detailed study of drugstore thieves and junkies seems to deglamorize their lives without any intrusive commentary, but I've heard more than one former drug abuser say that this movie makes them homesick for the good old days, B.C. (Before Crack!). 🦴🦴🦴½

1989 (R) 100m/C Matt Dillon, Kelly Lynch, James Remar, James LeGros, Heather Graham, William S. Burroughs, Beah Richards, Grace Zabriskie, Max Perlich; ***D:*** Gus Van Sant; ***W:*** Gus Van Sant, Daniel Yost; ***C:*** Robert Yeoman; ***M:*** Elliot Goldenthal. Independent Spirit Awards '90: Best Actor (Dillon), Best Cinematography, Best Screenplay, Best Supporting Actor (Perlich); Los Angeles Film Critics Association Awards '89: Best Screenplay; New York Film Critics Awards '89: Best Screenplay; National Society of Film Critics Awards '89: Best Director (Van Sant), Best Film, Best Screenplay. **VHS, LV**

Jordan (James Duval), Amy (Rose McGowan), and Xavier (Johnathon Schaech) in *The Doom Generation.* Samuel Goldwyn Company; courtesy of the Kobal Collection

Paul and Mary Bland (Paul Bartel and Mary Woronov) in *Eating Raoul.*
20th Century Fox; courtesy of the Kobal Collection

East and West

East and West is an Austrian re-discovery from the year 1924 starring Molly Picon. Picon, then 26, was something of a Yiddish "It" girl, just as rambunctious as Clara Bow, although far more wholesome, of course. Still, she does eat up a storm on the Day of Atonement and clearly loves to dance with the boys. Unlike the fragile Miss Bow, Molly Picon was built to last; she was still making movies until eight years before her death in 1992 at the age of 94. *East and West* is a fine showcase for Picon's boundless energy and charm. ***AKA:*** Ost und West. 🦴🦴🦴

1924 85m/B *AT* Molly Picon, Jacob Kalish, Sidney Goldin; ***D:*** Ivan Abramson, Sidney Goldin. **VHS**

Easy Rider

In his 1995 autobiography *Endless Highway,* David Carradine writes that *Easy Rider* was financed by Peter Fonda's Diner's Club card. Eventually, of course, it was picked up by Columbia, made everyone a fortune and gave Jack Nicholson the first of his many Oscar nominations. The turning point was the Cannes Film Festival, where this $375,000 road movie, partly shot in 16mm, won the First Film prize for director Dennis Hopper. (Although, as Vincent Canby sniffed in opposite full-page ads in the *New York Times,* "there was only one other picture competing in that category." Let HIM try making an indie someday!) Then other honors began flooding in: Hopper received a special award from the National Society of Film Critics, which also named Jack Nicholson best supporting actor. The New York Film Critics Circle gave supporting actor recognition to Nicholson. Columbia poured money into *Easy Rider*'s advertising campaign and the film became a blockbuster, winding up among the studio's top four moneymakers of the decade. But if Columbia executives had monkeyed around with *Easy Rider* from its inception, it would have emerged as a very different film. As a first-time viewer, I found the Oscar-nominated screenplay to be extremely uneven, but every guy I ever saw it with thought it was perfect. The mood of the film is bleak and depressing. (There are few things youthful international audiences appreciate more than a sharply critical view of the Land of Opportunity.) Lost in their drug haze, Wyatt (Fonda) and Billy (Hopper) are a deeply boring team, but most of the guys I knew in 1969 worshipped the both of them. The movie didn't kick into gear for me until Nicholson, as George Hanson, arrives on the scene. He is such a free spirit, far freer than either Wyatt or Billy, and his sheer pleasure at the prospect of a free life is a joy to see. I wouldn't follow Wyatt or Billy anywhere, but George is such a bright, sweet clueless soul that you can't help falling in love with him. You WANT his life to have a happy ending and when he isn't around, the bleakness and depression engulf the screen once more. *Easy Rider* also paints an unbelievably ugly portrait of the South. Even New Orleans, as seen by the perpetually stoned Wyatt and Billy, looks creepy and sinister. Many of the younger audiences in the San Francisco Bay Area thought that *Easy Rider*'s depiction of the South was as accurate as a documentary (it isn't) and were afraid to travel there, just because of this movie (THEIR loss)! The rock soundtrack is a great time capsule of its era. 🦴🦴🦴

1969 (R) 94m/C Peter Fonda, Dennis Hopper, Jack Nicholson, Karen Black, Toni Basil, Robert Walker Jr., Luana Anders, Luke Askew, Toni Basil, Warren Finnerty, Mac Mashorian, Antonio Mendoza, Sabrina Scharf, Phil Spector; ***D:*** Dennis Hopper; ***W:*** Terry Southern, Peter Fonda, Dennis Hopper; ***C:*** Laszlo Kovacs. Cannes Film Festival '69: Best First Feature (Hopper); New York Film Critics Awards '69: Best Supporting Actor (Nicholson); National Society of Film Critics Awards '69: Best Supporting Actor (Nicholson); Nominations: Academy Awards '69: Best Story & Screenplay, Best Supporting Actor (Nicholson); Cannes Film Festival '69: Best Film. **VHS, LV, 8mm**

Eat a Bowl of Tea

After the 1987 bomb *Slamdance,* director Wayne Wang returns to the low-key, personal style of filmmaking that won critical praise for his earlier movies, *Chan Is Missing* and *Dim Sum. Eat a Bowl of Tea* focuses on the family pressures that nearly destroy the marriage of a young Chinese couple, circa 1949. I first thought that the husband was suffering from a problem that was far more easily correctable than impotence, but it's so rare for any film to focus serious attention on the sexual difficulties within marriage, that Wang's sensitive entry deserves high marks for making the effort. *Eat a Bowl of Tea* is beautifully atmospheric, with lush period detail and sympathetic performances by Cora Miao and Russell Wong as the confused partners. 🦴🦴🦴

1989 (PG-13) 102m/C Cora Miao, Russell Wong, Lau Siu Ming, Eric Tsiang Chi Wai, Victor Wong, Jessica Harper, Lee Sau Kee; ***D:*** Wayne Wang; ***W:*** Judith Rascoe; ***C:*** Amir M. Mokri; ***M:*** Mark Adler. **VHS, LV, Closed Caption**

Eat Drink Man Woman

This mouth-watering film by Ang Lee shows a great chef (Sihung Lung as Chu) at work making superb meals every Sunday for his three daughters (a teacher, an executive, and a clerk at Wendy's). Since he IS their father, he is filled with opinions about what his grown children (who still live with him) should do with their lives. Lung, Ah-Leh Gua, and Winston Chao also starred in Ang Lee's *The Wedding Banquet* the previous year. An absolutely scrumptious date movie, but eat FIRST! 🦴🦴🦴🦴

1994 (R) 123m/C *TW* Sihung Lung, Kuei-Mei Yang, Yu-Wen Wang, Chien-Lien Wu, Sylvia Chang, Winston Chao, Ah-Leh Gua, Lester Chen; ***D:*** Ang Lee; ***W:*** Ang Lee, James Schamus, Hui-Ling Wang; ***C:*** Jong Lin; ***M:*** Mader. National Board of Review Awards '94: Best Foreign Film; Nominations: Academy Awards '94: Best Foreign Film; Golden Globe Awards '95: Best Foreign Film; Independent Spirit Awards '95:

"Paul, do you think you could buy another frying pan? I'm just a little squeamish about cooking in the one we use to kill people."

—Mary Bland (Mary Woronov) voices one of the drawbacks of killing for a living in *Eating Raoul.*

Best Actor (Lung), Best Actress (Wu), Best Cinematography, Best Director (Lee), Best Film, Best Screenplay. **VHS, LV**

Eat the Rich

Eat the Rich, a British comedy featuring cameo appearances by Paul and Linda McCartney, is about restaurants, blood, and money. It stars Lanah Pellay, a whining London drag queen whose number-one hit, *Pistol in My Pocket,* can be heard on the movie's soundtrack. When Lanah, as Alex the waiter, is fired from a posh eatery, s/he forms a gang and vows revenge. So, yes, you can take that title literally. In addition to the McCartneys, Angie Bowie, Sandie Shaw, Koo Stark, and Miranda Richardson pop up in small parts. Peter Richardson (any relation?) wrote and directed *Eat the Rich,* which I had the bad luck to see before breakfast. *Eat the Rich* is no great shakes, but may attract what is tactfully known as a cult audience. **woof!**

1987 (R) 89m/C *GB* Nosher Powell, Lanah Pellay, Fiona Richmond, Ronald Allen, Sandra Dorne, Angie Bowie, Sandie Shaw; ***Cameos:*** Paul McCartney, Linda McCartney, Bill Wyman, Koo Stark, Miranda Richardson; ***D:*** Peter Richardson; ***W:*** Peter Richardson; ***C:*** Witold Stok. **VHS**

Eating Raoul

I really love Paul and Mary Bland. I don't know that I'd want to live next door to them, but they're so nice and so much in love and so happy, sort of like Gomez and Morticia Addams. Their dream is to open a restaurant, and, as luck would have it, this real creep tries to attack Mary and when Paul kills him by mistake, they realize that the creep has money and it's THEIRS, THEIRS, THEIRS!!! But they can't just leave the creep lying there dead like that, it's unhygenic or something. Paul and Mary figure it out, along with a sure-fire scheme to make even more MONEY! MONEY! MONEY! Is this a great country or what? Paul Bartel and Mary Woronov, who co-directed, have terrific chemistry together, and take a look at that supporting cast! Endless repeat value on this one. (Robert Beltran went on to play First Officer Chakotay on *Star Trek: Voyager.*) ♫♫♫♫

1982 (R) 83m/C Mary Woronov, Paul Bartel, Robert Beltran, Buck Henry, Ed Begley Jr., Edie McClurg, John Paragon, Richard Blackburn, Hamilton Camp, Bill Curtis, Susan Saiger; ***D:*** Mary Woronov, Paul Bartel; ***W:*** Paul Bartel, Richard Blackburn; ***C:*** Gary Thieltges. **VHS**

Echoes of Paradise

Philip Noyce's *Echoes of Paradise/Shadows of the Peacock* treats the age-old theme of the married woman with young children who has a fling with a promiscuous young man who is totally wrong for her, who realizes it 90 long minutes later, and who returns to her family with an experience she appears to have placed well behind her. It fails to answer the question of the '80s (and '90s): if yesterday's filmmakers could treat international crises like two World Wars and the Great Depression within months of their respective beginnings, why don't many of today's filmmakers wake up to the fact that the '80s (and the '90s) are the Plague Years? A woman who hops into bed with an obvious gigolo or male prostitute isn't looking for mere adventure or heightened identity anymore. She's risking a long, painful death for herself and agony for her family who watch her die. If condoms are too threatening to deal with on film, then filmmakers can always set the film in another period when casual sex was less deadly. Even if Noyce HAD done that, though, this movie would still be an uninvolving snoozer, with little but the scenery to recommend it. ***AKA:*** Shadows of the Peacock. **woof!**

1986 (R) 90m/C *AU* Wendy Hughes, John Lone, Rod Mullinar, Peta Toppano, Steve Jacobs, Gillian Jones; ***D:*** Phillip Noyce; ***C:*** Peter James. **VHS, LV**

Eddie and the Cruisers

The coming attractions trailer for *Eddie and the Cruisers* was so awful that I almost didn't see it theatrically. Apparently, there were quite a few other people who felt the same way because *Eddie and the Cruisers* didn't attract much attention until it hit the video stores. Then it became so famous that the soundtrack became a hot item, and a 1989 sequel was filmed in Canada with Michael Pare and Matthew Laurance (but none of the other original participants). Anyway, you either like this movie or you don't. Ellen Barkin (as reporter Maggie Foley) doesn't. She is quoted as saying, "(It's) the only movie I've made that really upsets me. I hate it. And now it's out on video, so it never dies. People come up to me and say, 'You were great in (it).' And I say, 'Sorry, that wasn't me.'" She says all those mean things about THIS movie and not one squawk about Mary Lambert's *Siesta*??? Aaargh.... I enjoy *Eddie and the Cruisers.* Barkin IS great in it. Pare was then at a fairly confident point in his career when you could actually see how Eddie Wilson could become the focal point of a cult. Tom Berenger as outsider Frank Ridgeway gives the viewers someone with whom to identify during Eddie and the Cruisers' many in-house fights. And Joe Pantoliano is especially good as Doc, the group-manager-turned-dee-jay. Another probable factor in the film's popularity is the fact that, a dozen years after Jim Morrison's death, there were many fans who wished he were still around to create music; the script here plays around with that wish fulfillment fantasy quite a bit. You could do a lot worse on a rainy night than to rent this well-acted little film from 1983.

1983 (PG) 90m/C Tom Berenger, Michael Pare, Ellen Barkin, Joe Pantoliano, Matthew Laurance, Helen Schneider, David Wilson, Michael "Tunes" Antunes, Joe Cates, John Stockwell, Barry Sand, Howard Johnson, Robin Karfo, Rufus Harley, Bruce Brown, Louis D'Esposito, Michael Toland, Bob Garrett, Joanne Collins; ***D:*** Martin Davidson; ***W:*** Martin Davidson, Arlene Davidson; ***C:*** Fred Murphy; ***M:*** John Cafferty. **VHS, LV, 8mm, Closed Caption**

Eddie and the Cruisers 2: Eddie Lives!

Eddie and the Cruisers was far from a masterpiece, but it boasted an intriguing mystery, a satisfying structure, and a fine cast which included Tom Berenger, Ellen Barkin, Joe Pantoliano, and Helen Schneider, none of whom returned for *Eddie Lives!* The ineptly promoted 1983 film also earned the reputation of being better than it was because it attracted a huge audience when it was released on video. Some of the excruciating dialogue wasn't quite so painful on the small screen, and the excellent soundtrack performed by John Cafferty and the Beaver Brown Band sold in the millions. The sequel reveals that Eddie Wilson as portrayed by Michael Pare was to the first film what Tweety Bird was to the Sylvester the Cat cartoons. (Try imagining Tweety without Sylvester and you realize how dependent this non-character is on the much more interesting personality whose life revolves around him.) For those who care, Michael Pare is back as Eddie and a Canadian Geena Davis lookalike named Marina Orsini's got him. Eddie, also known as Joe West, is just as obnoxious as ever, but he meets an equally obnoxious young rocker who tries to lure him back into show business. Eddie drags his heels at first (they have to pad the running time somehow), but he is soon back to his old self, ordering everyone around just like in the old days. Meanwhile, greedy promoters (is that redundant?) are trying to cash in on Eddie's old records and tapes, encouraging Eddie sightings and lookalike contests. The only mystery in *Eddie Lives!* is whether transferring it to video will shrink its enormous flaws. Jean-Claude Lord's direction varies between mediocre and so-bad-I-can't-believe-I'm-watching-this, the acting is mostly wretched (three of the members of Eddie's new band cannot act at all so they just sit there when they're not playing, how exciting), and the script is strictly from hunger. The better cast members include Bernie Coulson and Anthony Sherwood plus Matthew Laurance from the original cast, who's already talking about *Eddie 3.* Larry King, Bo Diddley, Martha Quinn, and Merrill Shindler play themselves. You could probably pick up the album somewhere for the price of a movie ticket and spare yourself 106 minutes of squirming through the resuscitation of a jerk who still looks 29 long after he took that dive off the pier in 1964. **woof!**

The Hound Salutes:
ROBERT RODRIGUEZ
Director/writer/cinematographer, *El Mariachi*

A couple of years ago, one short film that I made—my first film that I shot on film and edited on video—went on to win many film festivals. I started thinking that maybe some day someone who'll see this might ask me to make a feature film for them, and I never made a feature film before. I'd only been making short stories and I saw how each short story I did got a little better. I would get better by practicing. The movies, the storytelling, got better. So I decided what I needed to do was get practice making a feature film—like I'd gotten practice by making a short film—before going to Hollywood and trying to get real work, because I didn't want to fall on my face if someone gave me a feature project. And you've heard of filmmakers who make it big and then they disappear because they're so scrutinized on their second film and never really had a chance to develop a style or to experiment. So my plan was to make my first, second, and third movie in a way that no one would ever see it if they weren't any good and in a way that I could experiment freely without having anyone watch me.

"$7,000 is a lot of money to a young filmmaker. Everyone in Hollywood says, 'That's nothing, that's nothing.' But when you don't have any money and you're from a family of 10 like me or just a college student working two jobs to pay yourself through school, you don't have any money to go and make a film, even like this. So it was a big risk at the time. The guy who played the Mariachi [Carlos Gallardo], he sold some land his father had left him. And I'd sold my body to science. I'd done that before for my short film. They have these medical research centers; they're usually in college towns. They're all over the country. So summer came, I checked into this place. I wrote my script in there. I

1989 (PG-13) 106m/C *CA* Michael Pare, Marina Orsini, Matthew Laurance, Bernie Coulson, Anthony Sherwood; ***Cameos:*** Larry King, Bo Diddley, Martha Quinn, Merrill Shindler; ***D:*** Jean-Claude Lord; ***W:*** Charles Zev Cohen; ***C:*** Rene Verzier; ***M:*** Leon Aronson. **VHS, LV**

8½

Federico Fellini's *8½* was one of the loveliest films of 1963 and it's every bit as exquisite today. The dream cast is headlined by Marcello Mastroianni, Claudia Cardinale, Anouk Aimee, and Barbara Steele. All this plus Nino Rota's haunting score and the brilliant cinematography of Gianni Di Venanzo combined to make *8½* one of the most widely admired and relentlessly imitated movies of its era. Many tried, but none quite captured the overwhelming sense of love and longing the great Fellini gave to this unsparingly honest examination of a successful director on the verge of a nervous breakdown. Cast Notes: Madeleine LeBeau played Yvonne in *Casablanca* 20 years earlier; Mark Herron was Judy Garland's fourth husband from 1965 to 1967. ***AKA:*** Otto E Mezzo; Federico Fellini's *8½*.

1963 135m/B *IT* Marcello Mastroianni, Claudia Cardinale, Anouk Aimee, Sandra Milo, Barbara Steele, Rossella Falk, Eddra Gale, Mark Herron, Madeleine LeBeau, Caterina Boratto; ***D:*** Federico

was in there a whole month. You can't leave—that's part of the testing. They test some drug on you; this one was supposed to lower your cholesterol. While I was in there I finished the script. I met one of my actors, who was in the bunk next to me. He's the guy who played the Man in White. I earned $3000 in one month.

"We took our finished tape to Los Angeles to sell it to the Spanish home video market. So, while I was waiting, I dropped a demo tape off at ICM [International Creative Management]. They represent Arnold Schwarzenegger and other biggies. They wouldn't sign someone off the streets. I knew that; I just called them up and said, 'I'm in town. I know you guys don't sign people off the streets. That's not what I want. Here's a compilation of my work: a two-minute trailer from the movie and my short movie. Ten minutes total. All I want you to do is watch it because I'm going to go off and make two more movies in Spanish—action movies in Mexico, to get more experience. And maybe in a year or so I can show you that stuff and see if you like that and can give me some guidance down the line. I just want you to know who I am now and give me your honest opinion of what my work is at this stage and what you think I need.' And they watched it that night. They called me the next day and said, 'We want to work with you.' Unbelievable. It was the first door I knocked on. They started sending copies of *El Mariachi* all over Hollywood with their endorsement—to the studios, to other independent producers all over. Telling people to watch it. Saying, 'This kid, we think he's the next hot thing; he just did this movie for very low money and no crew.' I started getting calls right away. With their endorsement, everyone watched the movie that weekend. I started getting calls from Tristar, from Paramount, from Disney, and from Columbia. Not interested, really, in *El Mariachi,* but in the body of work they had seen and they wanted to talk about future projects. So I started talking to those people, giving them all my ideas, and Columbia signed me to a two-year writing and directing contract."

ROBERT RODRIGUEZ on video: *Desperado, From Dusk to Dawn, Four Rooms,* and *Roadracers.*

Fellini; ***W:*** Tullio Pinelli, Ennio Flaiano, Brunello Rondi, Federico Fellini; ***C:*** Gianni Di Venanzo; ***M:*** Nino Rota. Academy Awards '63: Best Costume Design (B & W); New York Film Critics Awards '63: Best Foreign Film; Nominations: Academy Awards '63: Best Art Direction/Set Decoration (B & W), Best Director (Fellini), Best Story & Screenplay. **VHS, LV, Letterbox**

Eight Men Out

If there is any financial protection at all for ballplayers today, it is probably because, over 75 years later, we are still haunted by the 1919 World Series scandal that inspired John Sayles to write and direct *Eight Men Out.* The film reveals how vulnerable the underpaid Chicago White Sox were to self-serving operators like Arnold Rothstein, Bill Burns, and Abe Attell. The team's grievances against club owner Charles Comiskey were real, but their decision to profit by throwing the series was a sickening one. The games in which the players listlessly go through the motions are as painful to watch as they must have been for the original players to experience. Sayles also shows, on at least one occasion, the threat of physical violence, when a thug threatens to kill a team player's wife if he doesn't comply with the fix. *Eight Men Out* succeeds in making its point that good people can and do go wrong under

"Destroy all values, conformity, and morals. Throw away the pleasure of love, and realize the dream of eroticism."

—Mario (Alain Cuny) instructs Emmanuelle (Sylvia Kristel) in *Emmanuelle.*

certain circumstances and it also fills today's audiences with sadness that eight gifted players lost their careers and their reputations when they allowed themselves to be manipulated by opportunistic gamblers. For a movie with so many stellar names in the cast, there is a real ensemble feel to the production, which greatly enhances its message. John Cusack, Charlie Sheen, and D.B. Sweeney deliver three of the eight extremely effective performances by the team, and John Mahoney does another solid character turn as their coach. Michael Lerner and Christopher Lloyd are appropriately slimy as Rothstein and Burns, and the late John Anderson (1922–92) steals a magnificent scene as the new baseball commissioner. Robert Richardson's cinematography helps to capture the atmosphere of the era, particularly in the film's striking conclusion. With Sayles at the helm (and in a cameo as Ring Lardner), *Eight Men Out* is highly recommended even if you don't particularly care for baseball. 𝒥𝒥𝒥

1988 (PG) 121m/C John Cusack, D.B. Sweeney, Perry Lang, Jace Alexander, Bill Irwin, Clifton James, Michael Rooker, Michael Lerner, Christopher Lloyd, Studs Terkel, David Strathairn, Charlie Sheen, Kevin Tighe, John Mahoney, John Sayles, Gordon Clapp, Richard Edson, James Reed, Don Harvey, John Anderson, Maggie Renzi; ***Cameos:*** John Sayles; ***D:*** John Sayles; ***W:*** John Sayles; ***C:*** Robert Richardson; ***M:*** Mason Daring. **VHS, LV, Closed Caption**

El Mariachi

Robert Rodriguez kept it simple for his first film and, as a result, plunged head first into the movie business with a splash at age 24. All El Mariachi (Carlos Gallardo) wants is a chance to sing. All drug dealer Azul (Reinol Martinez) wants is a chance to avenge himself on Moco (Peter Marquardt), his former partner. Unhappily, El Mariachi and Azul are identically dressed in black and each carry a guitar case, but Azul's case...does NOT carry a guitar! Consuelo Gomez is sexy Domino, who thinks El Mariachi is cute, but the bloodthirsty Moco thinks Domino is cute, so that's a problem. In 1995, Rodriguez directed *Desperado,* his own expensive 106-minute remake of this violent, funny little film, but it's the $7,000 81-minute original version that everyone will remember. Filmed in Acuna, Mexico. 𝒥𝒥𝒥

1993 (R) 81m/C *MX* Carlos Gallardo, Consuelo Gomez, Peter Marquardt, Jaime de Hoyos, Reinol Martinez, Ramiro Gomez; ***D:*** Robert Rodriguez; ***W:*** Robert Rodriguez, Carlos Gallardo; ***C:*** Robert Rodriguez. Independent Spirit Awards '94: Best First Feature; Sundance Film Festival '93: Audience Award; Nominations: Independent Spirit Awards '94: Best Director (Rodriguez). **VHS, LV, 8mm, DVD**

Emmanuelle

In 1975, *Emmanuelle* was the most popular movie in France. It was called "a sexual Vogue" by someone or other and also an "'X' you can take your wife to." If adult audiences required THAT much assurance, they needed more help than mere publicity hacks could provide! The ultimate comment on the film? *Emmanuelle* stinks, then and now. It is the story of an innocent young girl (Sylvia Kristel) who joins her husband (Daniel Sarky) in Bangkok. Just how innocent any girl can be who seduces two men on the flight to Bangkok is left to our imaginations. But no matter. All the wives in Bangkok are bored; there is nothing for them to do. This is the stuff that old X-rated films are made of. Emmanuelle befriends a young archaeologist (Marika Green, who'd once worked with Bresson). The tension mounts; maybe Emmanuelle will get a job, too? Maybe then she won't be so bored! But no. She has a disillusioning fling with the archaeologist, and then searches for "fulfillment" with a 67-year-old "expert" named Mario (played by Alain Cuny, a Shakespearean actor who'd worked with Carne, Malle, Fellini, Buñuel, and Rosi and now with JUST JAECKIN on THIS?!). The film gets very cerebral after that. "What's eroticism to you?" Mario asks Emmanuelle. Well, Emmanuelle is not sure. She thinks maybe it's the "cult of sensual joy," or something like that. Wrong, says Mario. It's really the "rejection of the subterfuge to lucidity." Well, I'm certainly glad Mario cleared THAT up, or I'd never have known. Mario also tells her that "to arrive at the unknown, you must leave reason behind." (Translate that:

rape can set you free.) Then, director Jaeckin decides that what his X-rated French masterpiece really needs is symbolism. See, there's this chicken at the beginning of the film that gets his head cut off. Are you following? Later on, Emmanuelle smears on enough mascara to initiate a worldwide Maybelline shortage, and—SURPRISE!—dons feathers. She hates uptight people now. She's ready to compete with Ziggy Stardust anytime. The film is only 92 minutes long, but you could have fooled me. If it weren't for Richard Suzuki's impressive cinematography, I wouldn't have one good thing to say about this movie. If you're looking for a film that puts women in their place and that gives new meaning to words like dull and annoying, by all means, indulge in *Emmanuelle*'s endless psychological inanities. **woof!**

1974 92m/C *FR* Sylvia Kristel, Alain Cuny, Marika Green, Daniel Sarky; ***D:*** Just Jaeckin; ***W:*** Jean-Louis Richard; ***C:*** Richard Suzuki; ***M:*** Pierre Bachelet. **VHS, DVD**

Emma's Shadow

"The Poor Little Rich Girl" is among the most familiar images on the silver screen. Mary Pickford first played her in a strange little film from 1917. Her only escape from her emotionally deprived life is through an accidental drug overdose! In 1936, Shirley Temple preferred the company of radio troupers Alice Faye and Jack Haley to benign neglect from Michael Whalen, her tycoon father. (The Depression twist in this one was the threatening presence of a sex maniac down the hall.) In 1982, Bridgette Anderson orchestrated her own kidnapping in *Savannah Smiles.* The 1988 Danish film *Emma's Shadow* explores many of these tried and true situations, but with a fresh, strong approach that helped it to become a prize winner at the Cannes Film Festival. Emma, beautifully played by Line Kruse, is the 11-year-old child of a wealthy couple who barely notice she's alive. She runs away and literally bumps into a sewer worker whom she adopts as her best friend on sight. Although he is an ex-convict and far from the brightest man in the world, Emma nonetheless adores him and starts cooking up a successful scheme to wring money out of her folks. She spends the money on an elaborate meal at a deluxe hotel, to be shared by her new friend and two little boys in the neighborhood. The boys pile into a bubble bath and Emma gazes worshipfully at her friend as he drinks himself silly. The in-joke here is that Emma's friend is played by Borje Ahlstedt, so good in *Fanny and Alexander,* who launched his career 25 years ago in the *I Am Curious, Yellow and Blue* films. Writer/director Soeren Kragh-Jacobsen treads a very fine line here, so that you're always aware of the underlying sensuality, but are relieved that it STAYS underlying. As in most films of this type, the child is the focal point throughout and Line Kruse delivers a wonderfully shaded performance as Emma. She is fiercely protective of Ahlstedt's character, seeing through his rough, bumbling exterior into the kind, decent, and considerate soul who is able to give her far more than her high-rolling but uncomprehending parents. Despite its award-winning status and excellent reviews, *Emma's Shadow* has yet to acquire the reputation it deserves in this country, but it's been given a new life on video. See it before a Hollywood studio turns it into a yucky American transplant. ***AKA:*** Skyggen Af Emma. 🦴🦴🦴🦴

1988 93m/C *DK* Borje Ahlstedt, Line Kruse; ***D:*** Soeren Kragh-Jacobsen; ***W:*** Soeren Kragh-Jacobsen; ***C:*** Dan Laustsen. **VHS**

Enchanted April

In the 1980s, Mike Newell was best known for his work on tough, gritty projects like *Blood Feud, Dance with a Stranger,* and *The Good Father. Enchanted April,* a delicate comedy of manners and wishful thinking at best, seemed an odd choice for this hard-hitting director. Based on a novel by Elizabeth von Arnim (who was the Countess Russell in real life), *Enchanted April* was a resounding flop when Harry Beaumont first filmed it for RKO studios in 1935. Ann Harding portrayed a middle-aged Shirley Temple who brought joy into every life she touched, with the notable exception of the audience.

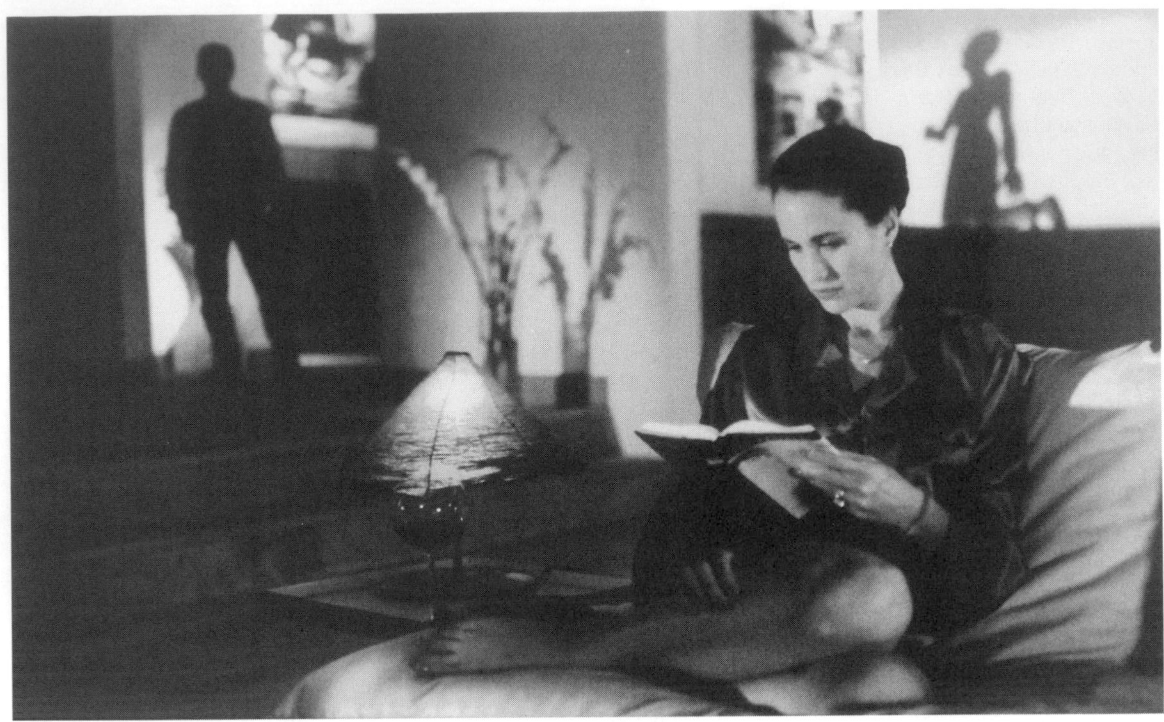

Andie MacDowell as Paige Stockard in *The End of Violence.* MGM; courtesy of the Kobal Collection

In 66 interminable minutes, Harding was able to lure back her straying husband, Frank Morgan, bring two young lovers together, patch up the marriage of Kay Alexander and Reginald Owen, AND warm the heart of a gruff old lady played by Jessie Ralph. Unsurprisingly, Ralph and Owen stole every sequence they were in, and, equally unsurprisingly, *Enchanted April* brought Ann Harding's reign as grande dame of the RKO lot to a grinding halt. The new version of *Enchanted April* is a VAST improvement over the original, which is not to say that it will succeed in bringing joy into every life it touches. The Ann Harding role this time around is played by comedienne Josie Lawrence, who at least is able to bring a down-to-earth foundation to the endless whimsicality of her character. Miranda Richardson seems more uncomfortable in a repressed role, although she does her best with it. In the role of the aristocratic beauty who was originally played by the serenely lovely Jane Baxter, Polly Walker tries hard as Lady Caroline Dester, but she looks and sounds like a contemporary punk, nothing at all like a 1922 deb chafing at the bit. The male parts are much less crucial, but Michael Kitchen comes off best as Mr. Briggs, a shell-shocked vet turned landlord, who can barely distinguish between one discontented tenant and another. Briggs is interesting as a representative of the dwindling romantic choices open to British women of the early 1920s. Many of their generation's most dazzling charmers had been blown to bits in World War I and the men who were left, like Briggs, were irreversibly changed. *Enchanted April* may mean less to California audiences than to British viewers, used to the cold rain and a relentless parade of twits. For four women (including the scene-stealing Joan Plowright) to flower in the very villa where von Arnim wrote her novel clearly might have meant something to 1922 readers, but it meant nothing at all to 1935 moviegoers and will probably be regarded as a mere historical curiosity today. One can only hope that the works of von Arnim will not be run into the ground by filmmakers like every syllable of E. M. Forster has been over the last decade. P.S. If you're truly enthralled by von Arnim, 1944's *Mr. Skeffington* with Bette Davis and Claude Rains (all 146 minutes of it!) is also available on video.

1992 (PG) 93m/C *GB* Miranda Richardson, Joan Plowright, Josie Lawrence, Polly Walker, Alfred Molina, Jim Broadbent, Michael Kitchen, Adriana Fachetti; ***D:*** Mike Newell; ***W:*** Peter Barnes; ***C:*** Richard Maidment; ***M:*** Richard Rodney Bennett. Golden Globe Awards '93: Best Actress—Musical/Comedy (Richardson), Best Supporting Actress (Plowright); Nominations: Academy Awards '92: Best Adapted Screenplay, Best Costume Design, Best Supporting Actress (Plowright). **VHS, LV, Closed Caption**

The End of Violence

The End of Violence disappointed Wim Wenders fans who wanted it to be another *Paris, Texas* or *Wings of Desire,* but *Wings of Desire* did nothing for me, unlike *The End of Violence.* It's an absorbing story with an extremely interesting cast. Bill Pullman is Mike Max, a director who gets kidnapped at gunpoint by two idiots who wind up with their heads blown off and not by Mike Max. He escapes into a low-key life with a family headed by Juan Emilio (Henry Silva, who hasn't aged much since 1962's *The Manchurian Candidate*). Paige Stockard (Andie MacDowell) is Mad Mike's wife, who was planning to leave him before the kidnapping. She takes over his business interests and finds a new guy. The surprise of the film is Traci Lind as Cat, an injured stuntwoman who becomes an actress after Mike Max takes an interest in her career. Lind steals every scene she's in, no mean feat when Udo Keir as her director Zoltan Koyacs is talking dirty to her. (I guess it's a step up from his smallish roles in *Breaking the Waves* and *Barb Wire.*) Daniel Benzali is typecast as a creepy-looking shadowy figure in a suit named Brice Phelps. Samuel Fuller plays Louis Bering, Gabriel Byrne's father! Now THAT's a stretch. Byrne is Ray, who knows more than he ever tells about the kidnapping of Mike Max. Loren Dean as Doc Block (he looks like a young Chris Isaak) investigates AND gets to meet Cat! Yeah, it is pretty complicated and you do have to pay attention, but the dots eventually connect. Wenders makes the 122-minute running time worth your while and gets terrific performances out of every actor, down to the tiniest bit part. And Ry Cooder (who also composed the *Paris, Texas* soundtrack) comes up with another effective score. All this and Pascal Rabaud's stunning camera work, too? Who needs an Angel in the Pizza Parlor?

1997 (R) 122m/C *FR* Bill Pullman, Gabriel Byrne, Andie MacDowell, Daniel Benzali, Traci Lind, Rosalind Chao, Loren Dean, Nicole Parker, Enrique Castillo, K. Todd Freeman, John Diehl, Pruitt Taylor Vince, Peter Horton, Udo Kier, Marshall Bell, Frederic Forrest, Henry Silva, Samuel Fuller; ***D:*** Wim Wenders; ***W:*** Nicholas Klein; ***C:*** Pascal Rabaud; ***M:*** Ry Cooder. Nominations: Independent Spirit Awards '98: Best Director (Wenders). **VHS, Closed Caption, DVD**

The English Patient

Once, a long time ago, I was a member of the National Academy of Television Arts and Sciences. After a few bewildering industry functions, I let my membership lapse. So I'm not even marginally qualified to vote with the members of the Academy for Best Picture of the Year. But if I could have voted in 1996, I would have, for *Fargo*! More than enough people are worshipping *The English Patient* that I don't need to join them. It's the sort of big, circuitous movie that always wins Best Picture. Okay, so it's an indie, but it's an indie that looks, sounds, and feels like *Gandhi,* except for Juliette Binoche and Naveen Andrews as Hana and Kip. This is not to knock Ralph Fiennes and Kristin Scott Thomas, who are very good, just the picture's naggingly pompous undertones AND overtones. Fiennes' character (Hungary's own Count Almasy) falls hard for Katherine, AKA Mrs. Geoffrey Clifton (Scott Thomas). Since boring old Geoffrey is played by Colin Firth, he's practically asking for his wife to be whisked away by a handsome count. The climax of this film may be terribly romantic in a gloppy sort of way, but it's all so avoidable that you can't blame destiny for this one. Oh well, people in love WILL do anything, won't they? Like lose their minds. And their wits. And their humility.

Mr. Sloane (Peter McEnery), flanked by Ed (Harry Andrews) and Kath (Beryl Reid) in *Entertaining Mr. Sloane.* Warner Bros.; courtesy of the Kobal Collection

And their sense of logic...and proportion. There was this skirmish going on at the time, World War II, I believe it was called? Am I supposed to quiver with anticipation every time Katherine and the Count exchange a guilty glance? Because I don't. Best Pictures of the Year don't really do it for me, anyway (I've concurred with precisely five choices in the entire history of the Academy). I can (almost) stand the very best ones every 10 or 20 years. As for the rest, once is enough, thanks. In order for a movie to be acceptable to the Academy membership, it can't be quirky or cutting edge, it has to say something positive about the human spirit, which must be Binoche's and Andrews' function here. To be honest, Hana and Kip are worth a heckuva lot more attention than the central characters, mainly because they ARE played by Binoche and Andrews. Oh, and the costumes here are nearly as ghastly as the ones in *Secrets and Lies.* 🦴🦴

1996 (R) 162m/C Ralph Fiennes, Kristin Scott Thomas, Juliette Binoche, Willem Dafoe, Naveen Andrews, Colin Firth, Julian Wadham, Juergen Prochnow, Kevin Whately, Clive Merrison, Nino Castelnuovo; ***D:*** Anthony Minghella; ***W:*** Anthony Minghella; ***C:*** John Seale; ***M:*** Gabriel Yared. Academy Awards '96: Best Art Direction/Set Decoration, Best Cinematography, Best Costume Design, Best Director (Minghella), Best Film Editing, Best Picture, Best Sound, Best Supporting Actress (Binoche), Best Original Dramatic Score; Directors Guild of America Awards '96: Best Director (Minghella); Golden Globe Awards '97: Best Film—Drama, Best Original Score; Los Angeles Film Critics Association Awards '96: Best Cinematography; National Board of Review Awards '96: Best Supporting Actress (Binoche), Best Supporting Actress (Scott Thomas); Broadcast Film Critics Association Awards '96: Best Director (Minghella), Best Screenplay; Nominations: Academy Awards '96: Best Actor (Fiennes), Best Actress (Scott Thomas), Best Adapted Screenplay, Best Sound Effects Editing; British Academy Awards '96: Best Actor (Fiennes), Best Actress (Scott Thomas), Best Adapted Screenplay, Best Director

(Minghella), Best Film, Best Supporting Actress (Binoche); Golden Globe Awards '97: Best Actor—Drama (Fiennes), Best Actress—Drama (Scott Thomas), Best Director (Minghella), Best Screenplay, Best Supporting Actress (Binoche); Screen Actors Guild Award '96: Best Actor (Fiennes), Best Actress (Scott Thomas), Best Supporting Actress (Binoche), Cast; Writers Guild of America '96: Best Adapted Screenplay. **VHS, LV, Closed Caption, DVD**

The Englishman Who Went up a Hill But Came down a Mountain

The Englishman Who Went Up a Hill But Came Down a Mountain is a direct descendant of the classic Ealing comedies circa 1949. A quaint, decidedly regional British situation is gently but persistently satirized for the entire film. In this case, we are looking at a small village in Wales, where a visual quote about the chief recreational activity (i.e. making babies) is affectionately reminiscent of the opening shot of *Whisky Galore.* The point of the story—that World War I has so devastated the young male population of Ffynnon Garw that the village needs a symbol like the first mountain in Wales to bolster its identity—is lighter than air. (For that matter, so was the premise of *Whisky Galore.*) Writer/director Christopher Monger embroiders this delicate tale, derived from his grandfather's bedtime stories, with loving detail. Hugh Grant is Reginald, the English twit who comes to survey Ffynnon Garw's so-called mountain and winds up falling in love with the place. As usual, the devilishly attractive Grant, stutters and mumbles his way through the plot as if he'd never been out on a date. But this time at least, there's a plausible reason for his social jitters. Tara Fitzgerald, Grant's restless bride in *Sirens,* is bewitching here as Betty of Cardiff, who persuades Reginald and his drunk surveying partner George Garrad (ever so drily played by Ian McNeice) to stick around the village a bit longer. The lynchpin of the community is Colm Meaney as bartender Morgan the Goat, who's responsible for so many ginger-haired babies born during the war years. And then there is Ian Hart as a shell-shocked war veteran named Johnny (not Lennon for a change), and Kenneth Griffith, then 74, who began his career playing small roles in Will Hay comedies at Ealing while barely out of his teens. In recent years, he's often cast as venerable clerics (he had previously worked with Grant in *Four Weddings and a Funeral*) and he makes a nice foil here as Morgan's fire and brimstone nemesis. *The Englishman Who Went Up a Hill But Came Down a Mountain* hasn't a smidgin of breathtaking suspense, but it's lovely to look at and its gentle humor wins this delightful entry the status of one of 1995's most charming sleepers. 🦴🦴🦴

1995 (PG) 96m/C *GB* Hugh Grant, Tara Fitzgerald, Colm Meaney, Ian McNeice, Ian Hart, Kenneth Griffith; ***D:*** Christopher Monger; ***W:*** Christopher Monger; ***C:*** Vernon Layton; ***M:*** Stephen Endelman. **VHS, LV, Closed Caption**

Enid Is Sleeping

When I first saw *About Last Night* in 1986, I was enormously impressed by the quirky talent of a young actress named Elizabeth Perkins. In 1988, she made *Big* and *Sweet Hearts Dance,* both so saturated by cutesy concepts that she tended to get lost in the proceedings. Then there was 1986's *From the Hip,* 1993's *Indian Summer,* and 1995's *Moonlight and Valentino* in which she was even MORE lost, PLUS 1991's *He Said, She Said,* more cutesy conceptual crap. Just when it seemed like Perkins was stuck in a conventional leading lady rut, she made a little-heralded black comedy with Judge Reinhold, 1990's *Enid Is Sleeping.* Since it came along not long after 1989's *Weekend at Bernie's* and may have seemed to share the same concept, *Enid* might easily have died an unfair death, except for one thing. Perkins and director Maurice Phillips rescued the badly edited film from the ailing studio that ordered the cuts and assembled the film as THEY wanted it to be shown. The delightful results have been retitled *Over Her Dead Body.* Maureen Mueller IS Enid, the

Jack Nance is *Eraserhead.*
Courtesy of the Kobal Collection

sister from Hell. June (Perkins) is her little sister who has been having an affair with Enid's husband (Reinhold), a cop in a sleepy Southwestern town. Enid surprises them in bed, one thing leads to another, and the rest of the movie shows how June tries to get rid of Enid. The hilarious script gets astonishing mileage out of the dumbest cast of characters you can possibly imagine. Reinhold's character continues his daily routine with his partner Jeffrey Jones, who watches too many movies along the lines of *Beverly Hills Cop.* When he's actually confronted with violence, he's filled with panic and nausea. Rhea Perlman is their ditzy dispatcher. Meanwhile, Perkins brilliantly runs the full gamut of emotional distress as she tries to deal with Enid and every lowlife in the Southwest, including Michael J. Pollard. I've seldom laughed at a video as much as I did with *Over Her Dead Body,* and although most outlets won't have 128 copies of this sleeper, it's well worth searching for, anyway. Perkins went on to break hearts in 1991's *The Doctor* and to pick up (hopefully) fat paychecks for *The Flintstones* and *Miracle on 34th Street* in 1994. What, and give up show business? Make your own movie, Elizabeth! If you can work wonders rescuing *Enid,* you can work miracles with an indie that's yours from opening to closing credits! ***AKA:*** Over Her Dead Body. 🦴🦴🦴🦴

1990 (R) 105m/C Elizabeth Perkins, Judge Reinhold, Rhea Perlman, Maureen Mueller, Jeffrey Jones, Michael J. Pollard; ***D:*** Maurice Phillips; ***W:*** Maurice Phillips; ***C:*** Alfonso Beato. **VHS**

The Entertainer

The Entertainer is the 1960 film in which Laurence Olivier, then 53, bid farewell to the romantic roles of his youth. Olivier surrounded himself with the angry young men of that era: director Tony Richardson, writer John Osborne, and unknown actors Albert Finney and Alan Bates. The bitter film represents a complete departure from his previous work. It also ended his 20-year marriage to actress Vivien Leigh; Joan Plowright, the young actress who played his daughter, would become Lady Olivier within the year. *The Entertainer* is saturated with yearnings for a life which only seems desirable to outsiders. Olivier plays a seedy music hall artiste who lusts after beauty contest winner Shirley Anne Field. Meanwhile, he pretends not to know his own family, refusing to face his reflection in their eyes. It is a harsh portrait, unclouded by the sentiment which flaws his work in the 1952 film *Carrie.* Olivier won an Oscar nomination for *The Entertainer,* revitalizing his career as a strong character actor. 🦴🦴🦴½

1960 97m/B *GB* Laurence Olivier, Brenda de Banzie, Roger Livesey, Joan Plowright, Daniel Massey, Alan Bates, Shirley Anne Field, Albert Finney, Thora Hird; ***D:*** Tony Richardson; ***W:*** Nigel Kneale, John Osborne; ***C:*** Oswald Morris; ***M:*** John Addison. Nominations: Academy Awards '60: Best Actor (Olivier). **VHS**

Entertaining Mr. Sloane

Let me say something about the FASHIONS in *Entertaining Mr. Sloane.* Beryl Reid, a full-figured 52, must be among the least vain actresses of all time to wear the skimpy outfits designed for her by Emma Porteus. Well, Kath WOULD wear outfits like that to entice the new tenant, Mr. Sloane (Peter McEnery, then 30). HE, meanwhile, is wearing the tightest leather suit imaginable, which makes him just as desirable to Brother Ed (Harry Andrews, 59) as to Sister Kath. Upstairs, Dadda Kemp (Alan Webb, 64) is drooling his life away. Ed and Kath would do anything to make Mr. Sloane happy—yes, ANYTHING—and with that in mind, Mr. Sloane licks his chops and bides his time. This successful adaptation of the very funny black comedy from the savagely original mind of Joe Orton is filled with grotesque situations, violent undercurrents, and sly wit. Everyone plays this droll farce with tongues firmly in cheek: "And we sweat and we strain entertaining Mr. Sloane...." Well, it may not have made the Billboard charts like "Yeh Yeh" or "The Ballad of Bonnie and Clyde," but 26-year-old pop singer Georgie Fame undoubtedly earned a decent paycheck for writing the title song of this movie, which received a "X" rating in Great Britain. 🦴🦴🦴

1970 90m/C *GB* Beryl Reid, Harry Andrews, Peter McEnery, Alan Webb; ***D:*** Douglas Hickox; ***W:*** Clive Exton, Joe Orton; ***C:*** Wolfgang Suschitzky. **VHS**

Equinox

Someday, some Alan Rudolph devotee will come up with a book about why he or she IS one, and I have a hunch I will be no more enlightened than I am now. *Equinox* is well acted but sluggish hooey about twins Henry and Freddie (Matthew Modine in a dual role) who both inherit a fortune. An even more frustrating movie to watch than *Trouble in Mind,* if that's possible. 🦴🦴

1993 (R) 110m/C Matthew Modine, Lara Flynn Boyle, Lori Singer, Marisa Tomei, Fred Ward, M. Emmet Walsh, Tyra Ferrell, Tate Donovan, Kevin J. O'Connor, Gailard Sartain; ***D:*** Alan Rudolph; ***W:*** Alan Rudolph; ***C:*** Elliot Davis. Nominations: Independent Spirit Awards '94: Best Actor (Modine), Best Cinematography, Best Film, Best Supporting Actress (Boyle). **VHS, LV, Letterbox, Closed Caption**

Eraserhead

When David Lynch paid a visit to Berkeley in the '80s, an eager crowd begged for the secret of Baby Henry. Who or what had played the premature child of Henry Spencer, played by Jack Nance? Lynch wasn't talking, and no amount of groveling could persuade him to divulge this particular bit of casting for the benefit of posterity. And now Jack Nance (1943–96) is gone, so we're stuck with the crushingly confident speculations of film buffs. (My guess: An electrically charged lamb fetus.) As in the David Lynch films that followed this one, the currents of morality run strong and deep. Henry Spencer tries very hard to be a responsible father to Baby Henry, but his world is weird and strange and it's getting weirder and stranger by the second. Lynch received AFI funding to make *Eraserhead,* and for his very next feature, he received two Academy Award nominations for writing and directing *The Elephant Man* for Paramount! So make your first indie as bizarre and personal as you like; that way, everyone will get to know (and hire) the real you as you really are. You can't watch *Eraserhead* too often in a revival theatre, though. You might walk out of the lobby and find yourself trapped in Henry Spencer's world forever! Cast Note: Jennifer Lynch grew up to write *The Secret Diary of Laura Palmer* and to direct *Boxing Helena.* PLUS: In an episode of TV's *My So-Called Life,* Jack Nance plays a scrupulously conventional innkeeper who tries to keep order when Patty Chase (Bess Armstrong) has too much to drink and nearly strips in the dining room, yelling, "I am a grown-up." "That is a judgment call," Nance snaps back. 🦴🦴🦴

1978 90m/B Jack Nance, Charlotte Stewart, Allen Joseph, Jeanne Bates, Judith Anna Roberts, Laurel Near, V. Phipps-Willson, Jack Fisk, Jean Lange, Jennifer Lynch; ***D:*** David Lynch; ***W:*** David Lynch; ***C:*** Frederick Elmes, Herbert Cardwell; ***M:*** David Lynch, Fats Waller, Peter Ivers. **VHS, LV**

Evergreen

Once upon a time, going to talking pictures in America meant that we only saw American movies; 1933's *The Private Life of Henry VIII* changed all that. Not only did this very British film win its star, Charles Laughton, the Academy Award for best actor, but it also proved that audiences were receptive to pictures made outside of Hollywood. Unfortunately, musical comedies don't always travel well across the Atlantic, so, with one exception, British musicals didn't make a real splash in America until the Beatles made *A Hard Day's Night* in 1964. The one exception was the work of Jessie Matthews, and her greatest triumph was 1934's *Evergreen. Evergreen* co-stars Jessie Matthews' husband at the time, Sonnie Hale (1902–59) in a comic role, and they made several films together as a team throughout the decade. Barry MacKay, best remembered as Scrooge's nephew in MGM's *A Christmas Carol,* also plays opposite Matthews. Betty Balfour (1903–79), a big star in British silent comedies, plays the second lead, and the caddish blackmailer is played by an American-born character actor named Hartley Power (1894–1966). Everyone in the production is young, between 27 and 40, and they all breathe life into what is basically a pretty implausible tale. That may be why *Evergreen,* along with its many English cultural references, never made it to Broadway. Jessie Matthews always looks so cheerful onscreen that it's hard to believe that she was a woman on the verge of a nervous breakdown all through *Evergreen.* Only the careful handling of director Victor Saville (1897–1979) kept the production rolling along at a rapid clip. (Saville had a long career in both countries, eventually producing 1955's *Kiss Me Deadly.*) Matthews' personal problems and wrenching memories about the making of *Evergreen* did lead to a breakdown when it was shown at a retrospective in her honor many years later. None of her private unhappiness shows up on film, however. Matthews' graceful dancing and bright personality plus a lovely Rodgers and Hart score made *Evergreen* a smash hit. In her later years, Jessie Matthews wrote her autobiography, *Over My Shoulder,* and played a supporting role in *Edward and Mrs. Simpson* as Wallis' aunt. She was still working the year of her death at age 74 in 1981.

1934 91m/B *GB* Jessie Matthews, Sonnie Hale, Betty Balfour, Barry Mackay, Ivor McLaren, Hartley Power, Patrick Ludlow, Marjorie Gaffney; ***D:*** Victor Saville; ***W:*** Emlyn Williams; ***C:*** Glen MacWilliams; ***M:*** Richard Rodgers, Harry Woods, Lorenz Hart, Harry Woods. **VHS, LV**

Every Man for Himself & God against All

In 1828, a most unusual young man turned up in Nuremberg. For the next five years, he was a source of wonder and, perhaps, fear to the intelligentsia. Who was he? Where had he come from? Why had he been deprived of a normal existence his entire life? Was he descended from royalty? His murder in 1833 only intensified the riddle. Artists and scholars continue to study Kaspar Hauser to the present day. Possibly the most heartfelt view of the subject was provided by Werner Herzog's 1975 masterpiece, *Every Man for Himself & God Against All/The Mystery of Kaspar Hauser.* Under Herzog's brilliant direction, Bruno S attempts and succeeds at the impossible: stripping his entire personality of each and every trace of socialization. His Kaspar is like a baby who grows from infancy to adulthood without learning a thing. His social vulnerability is the quality that attracts small children who laboriously teach him how to speak, one word at a time; nursery rhymes, as one boy explains patiently to a little girl, are too difficult for him to learn. Kaspar is later exploited as a freak attraction, but he escapes and goes on to lead a life of what appears to be non-stop education in sheltered circumstances. His questions are strong, clear, and childlike, but because he is a man, they are interpreted as a threat. Or so Herzog suggests. The tenderness and compassion with which Kaspar is initially received evolves into suspicion and violence. Just when the whole world appears to be opening up for Kaspar, he is the object of

Dr. Louis Batiste (Samuel L. Jackson) and his wife, Roz (Lynn Whitfield), in *Eve's Bayou.* Trimark Pictures; courtesy of the Kobal Collection

The Hound Salutes:
SAM RAIMI
Director/writer, *Evil Dead*

I'd always hoped to make a movie professionally when I was a kid, but I never really thought that I'd get the chance to do it. I had no idea of even how to approach it. When I started out, I didn't come to Hollywood. I rounded up private investors with my two partners in the city of Detroit and, one by one, we raised investments for our first feature film ($5,000, $10,000) until we finally had enough money to go out and shoot a 16mm horror movie, eventually entitled *Evil Dead.*

"The Three Stooges are great comedians and great masters of slapstick. I also love Jerry Lewis and a lot of other comedians, but actually, for *The Quick and the Dead,* the influences were very different. This western was more about updating what the great Italian filmmaker Sergio Leone [1921–89] had done in the 1960s with his series of westerns with Clint Eastwood. Because the western has enjoyed a resurgence in Hollywood in the 1990s, the studios are willing to back that genre, but I was always interested in the spaghetti westerns of the '60s. What we've tried to do is take the role traditionally played by a male in those westerns and give it to a female, because we felt it was the right time

two murderous attacks, the second eventually proving fatal. His efforts at socialization end and he reverts to the infant's heartrending gestures for someone, anyone, to stop the pain. When Bruno S is onscreen, it's impossible to tear your eyes away from his one-of-a-kind performance, but Herzog wisely gives a spare but eloquent context for *Every Man for Himself & God Against All/The Mystery of Kaspar Hauser.* An anatomical dissection of Kaspar Hauser is quickly carried out, revealing nothing but our eagerness to search for answers, even when they're wrong. In contrast, Herzog shows us the landscapes that surround his story, recreating the lush color experiments of photographers of the mid-19th century. Herzog's anachronistic images and Bruno S' newly reborn eyes make more sense of the mystery than all the state-of-the-art scientific bumbling of 1833 or 1998. ***AKA:*** The Mystery of Kaspar Hauser; Jeder fur Sich und Gott gegen Alle; The Enigma of Kaspar Hauser. 🦴🦴🦴🦴

1975 110m/C *GE* Bruno S, Brigitte Mira, Walter Laderigast, Hans Musaus, Willy Semmelrogge, Michael Kroecher, Henry van Lyck; ***D:*** Werner Herzog; ***W:*** Werner Herzog; ***C:*** Jorge Schmidt-Reitwein; ***M:*** Albinoni Pachelbel, Orlando Di Lasso. Nominations: Cannes Film Festival '75: Best Film. **VHS**

Everything Ready, Nothing Works

This early Lina Wertmuller film is a fast, occasionally funny yarn about how some young Sicilian men and women make a start in Northern Italy (Milan, to be specific), even though they have no money and are constantly being victimized. There is one semi-rape sequence. The victim loves it. Wertmuller shows the moment, then lets it go without comment. She would explore sexual politics in much greater depth in 1975's *Swept Away....* 🦴🦴

1974 107m/C *IT* Luigi Diberti, Lina Polito, Nine Bignamini, Sara Rapisarda, Guiliana Calandra, Isa Danieli; ***D:*** Lina Wertmuller; ***W:*** Lina Wertmuller; ***C:*** Giuseppe Rotunno; ***M:*** Piero Piccioni.

for the audience to be able to accept a female protagonist, someone who doesn't sprain her ankle and say, 'I can't run anymore!', but rather someone like Sharon Stone who can slap leather with the best of them and come out with twin six-guns barking flame, leave the bodies smoldering in the dust, and ride on.

"I wanted to put my 1973 Oldsmobile in *The Quick and the Dead,* but I couldn't find a place for it and it's been in every movie I've ever made. It's had kisses filmed in its front and back seats, it's run over dummies, it's been in car chases and car battles, it's gone off the Belle Isle Bridge and plunged into the Detroit River, it's had its guts removed and was put in front of a front screen stage to film a front screen battle atop the automobiles, it's been transported back in time in motion pictures and landed in the Middle Ages, it's had its engine hauled out and replaced with a steam engine to form the Death Coaster, and it's been sent into the future in its 1992 incarnation at the end of *Army of Darkness,* but I just couldn't figure out a way to put it into the Old West without ruining the movie. The studio doesn't even know about it. I got it in a storage yard. I'm just waiting for a chance to use it again in the next picture."

SAM RAIMI directed *Evil Dead, Crimewave, Evil Dead 2: Dead by Dawn, Darkman, Army of Darkness, The Quick and the Dead,* and *A Simple Plan,* among other producing, writing, and acting credits.

Eve's Bayou

There are few tasks tougher on a writer than to reveal an unpleasant character, warts and all, through the eyes of a child who loves him with all her heart. First-time writer/director Kasi Lemmons has accomplished this stunning feat with an effortless skill and mature compassion that many grizzled veterans would envy. The story begins with the adult reflections of Eve Batiste, narrated by Tamara Tunie: "The summer I killed my father, I was 10 years old." Even though we know that at the outset, Lemmons' gripping tale is filled with 109 minutes of surprises. Jurnee Smollett is little Eve, the less-favored daughter of the much-admired Dr. Louis Batiste (Samuel L. Jackson) and his beautiful wife Roz (Lynn Whitfield). Eve's longing for her father's approval is revealed in a 1962 party sequence where he dances with her older sister Cisely (Meagan Good). Why, Eve wonders, doesn't Daddy ask her to dance FIRST? In the course of the party, Eve wanders out to the barn where she finds Daddy in flagrante delicto with Mrs. Matty Meraux (Lisa Nicole Carson). Daddy denies Eve's perception of the incident and, later that night, when Eve tells Cisely what happened in the barn, Cisely denies it, too, and deconstructs the episode to show Eve what might have happened instead. Nevertheless, Eve's idealization of Daddy ends that night, and so does her perception of her entire family. Home is no longer a safe harbor for the little girl anymore. Much of the running time is preoccupied with secret sex and voodoo magic. Do the sex and magic contribute to the outcome, or are they merely catalysts for everyone's inevitable destiny? The life of Aunt Mozelle Batiste Delacroix (Debbi Morgan) is dominated more by voodoo than by her much more reliable common sense. It is only the love of a good man (Vondie Curtis-Hall as Julian Greyraven) that convinces Mozelle to buck fate and follow her heart. Diahann Carroll has a flamboyant

Sam Raimi's *Evil Dead.* Courtesy of the Kobal Collection

star turn as voodoo queen Elzora, to whom little Eve turns for help when she can see no way out of her family's nightmare existence. *Eve's Bayou* is filled with beautiful performances and a shattering view of how a smart, charming womanizer can destroy the lives of everyone he touches, including his own.

1997 (R) 109m/C Samuel L. Jackson, Lynn Whitfield, Debbi Morgan, Diahann Carroll, Jurnee Smollett, Meagan Good, Vondie Curtis-Hall, Lisa Nicole Carson, Jake Smollett, Ethel Ayler; ***D:*** Kasi Lemmons; ***W:*** Kasi Lemmons; ***C:*** Amy Vincent; ***M:*** Terence Blanchard; ***V:*** Tamara Tunie. Independent Spirit Awards '98: Best First Feature, Best Supporting Actress (Morgan). **VHS**

Evil Dead

If you're ever trapped in a cabin with your friends and find the *Sumerian Book of the Dead,* do not open it, skim its incantations, or say even one of them out loud. If you do, you will wind up in pieces. That's what happens to the cast of 1983's *The Evil Dead.* Guys love this blood-and-guts fest, and even think it's funny. But the violence never (ever!) let's up, and we know next to nothing about any of the characters being sliced and diced ad nauseum. Director Sam Raimi's beloved 1973 Oldsmobile makes its movie debut here. *The Evil Dead,* filmed entirely in Michigan and Tennessee, was followed up by a 1987 sequel, *The Evil Dead 2: Dead by Dawn,* as well as a jump to the Middle Ages, with *Army of Darkness.* Three bones for fans, but for me, just

1983 (NC-17) 85m/C Bruce Campbell, Ellen Sandweiss, Betsy Baker, Hal Delrich, Sarah York, Theodore (Ted) Raimi; ***D:*** Sam Raimi; ***W:*** Sam Raimi; ***C:*** Tim Philo; ***M:*** Joseph LoDuca. **VHS, LV, DVD**

Exotica

Before he was *Nowhere Man,* Bruce Greenwood was Francis the tax inspector in Atom Egoyan's *Exotica.* Francis is a nightly customer at the Exotica strip club, mainly because Christina (Mia Kirschner) works there. Francis' interest in Christina disturbs Eric (Elias Koteas), the club dee jay who used to go with her. But obsession always finds a way to feed itself. There are many subterranean currents in *Exotica* and Egoyan gives us tantalizing glimpses of all of them. The club, a world in itself, taps into the fantasies of all who drift into it, yet there's a ubiquitous sense of unease that all is not well in that world. A fine cast, a hypnotic script, and lush art direction contribute to make *Exotica* an eerie experience with plenty of repeat value. ☙☙☙

1994 (R) 104m/C *CA* Mia Kirshner, Elias Koteas, Bruce Greenwood, Don McKellar, Victor Garber, Arsinee Khanjian, Sarah Polley, Calvin Green, David Hemblen; ***D:*** Atom Egoyan; ***W:*** Atom Egoyan; ***C:*** Paul Sarossy; ***M:*** Mychael Danna. Genie Awards '94: Best Art Direction/Set Decoration, Best Cinematography, Best Costume Design, Best Director (Egoyan), Best Film, Best Screenplay, Best Supporting Actor (McKellar), Best Original Score; Toronto-City Award '94: Best Canadian Feature Film; Nominations: Genie Awards '94: Best Actor (Greenwood), Best Actor (Koteas); Independent Spirit Awards '96: Best Foreign Film. **VHS, LV, Closed Caption**

Eye of the Needle

It's an old story: an attractive woman is married to a man who hasn't touched her in years. She preserves the conventions of the relationship, anyway, at least until the first devil-may-care stranger arrives on the scene. Well, okay, so far it's an old story. But in 1981's *Eye of the Needle,* based on the Ken Follett WWII suspense thriller, we see a rare example of a strong screen heroine whose power isn't drained by her libido. Kate Nelligan lives fitfully on an island with her husband (who's crippled emotionally as well as physically). When sad-eyed Donald Sutherland turns up, they're in bed together the first night they meet. Sutherland's well-drawn character has a dark secret: he's a vicious killer and Nazi spy determined to snafu the D-Day invasion. By the time he winds up on Nelligan's island, he's single-handedly racked up a distressingly high body count and her husband is next on the list. The violence is complemented by a lavish Miklos Rozsa score, as are the romantic sequences, so his transformation from conscienceless assassin to love-struck interloper is surreal. We're used to seeing the GOOD guy be accompanied by such a passionate soundtrack. The moment when Nelligan's character, who has had long years of practice concealing her emotions, realizes who Sutherland is, is subtle but extremely intense. Without a wasted word or gesture, she launches a strategy of attack. It has nothing to do with anything she has ever been before—she simply operates on pure emotions and sheer nerve to defend herself and her small child. It's unusual to watch a woman steel herself to be as ruthless as her male adversary, disregarding the deep pain she clearly feels in the process. Director Richard Marquand effectively captures the timeless existential conflict between Nelligan's and Sutherland's characters while still sustaining the mood and pace of a wartime thriller. ☙☙☙

1981 (R) 112m/C Donald Sutherland, Kate Nelligan, Ian Bannen, Christopher Cazenove, Philip Brown, Stephen MacKenna, Faith Brook, Colin Rix, Alex McCrindle, John Bennett, Sam Kydd, Rik Mayall, Bill Fraser; ***D:*** Richard Marquand; ***W:*** Stanley Mann; ***C:*** Alan Hume; ***M:*** Miklos Rozsa. **VHS**

The Fable of the Beautiful Pigeon Fancier

Ruy Guerra's attractive trifle about a vain and selfish dandy focuses on his obsession for a lovely young matron. It's hard to care much about the dandy since his obsession is so detached and it's harder still to care about the matron since she functions more as a symbol than as a real character. Based on the Gabriel Garcia Marquez novel, *Love in the Time of Cholera.* Garcia Marquez's *Letters from the Park* (also made in 1988) is much better. In Spanish

Elsie Wright (Florence Hoath) and a fairy in *FairyTale: A True Story.* Paramount; courtesy of the Kobal Collection

with English subtitles. ***AKA:*** Fabula de la Bella Palomera.

1988 73m/C *SP* Ney Latorraca, Claudia Ohana, Tonia Carrero, Dina Stat, Chico Diaz; ***D:*** Ruy Guerra; ***W:*** Ruy Guerra, Gabriel Garcia Marquez; ***C:*** Edgar Moura. **VHS, LV**

Face to Face

Face to Face is an unrelieved downer, but a brilliant one. Liv Ullman plays Jenny, a psychiatrist with a dull, mean family, who tries to kill herself. She is saved by a fellow doctor (Erland Josephson) with problems of his own: his young male lover just left him for a wealthy female patron. Jenny's world is SO unpleasant: her grandmother leaves her alone when she is ill, her husband flies back from America for ONE day after her suicide attempt, her daughter reproaches her with the information that her mother never really liked her anyway, Josephson leaves for Jamaica the day after her life-and-death crisis, Jenny is robbed and nearly raped when she tries to help a young patient...surprisingly, her suicide attempt has nothing to do with any of these situations. She is seeking, rather, the rare ability to FEEL things, truly and deeply. Her voyage through a terrible crisis forces her to test and tap this ability in a way she's never done before. Ingmar Bergman is at his most personal and self revealing here, and Sven Nykvist draws us into Jenny's electrifying world with harsh-tender close-ups. The picture ends on a sad, but hopeful note; its final image of two elderly people caressing one another was quite complete without Jenny's commentary: "Love embraces everything, even death." ***AKA:*** Ansikte mot Ansikte.

1976 136m/C *SW* Liv Ullmann, Erland Josephson, Gunnar Bjornstrand, Aino Taube-Henrikson, Sven Lindberg, Kary Sylway, Sif Ruud; ***D:*** Ingmar Bergman; ***W:*** Ingmar Bergman; ***C:*** Sven Nykvist. Golden Globe Awards '77: Best Foreign Film; Los Angeles Film Critics Association Awards '76: Best Actress (Ullmann), Best Foreign Film; National Board of Review Awards '76: Best Actress (Ullmann); New York Film Critics Awards '76: Best Actress (Ullmann); Nominations: Academy Awards '76: Best Actress (Ullmann), Best Director (Bergman). **VHS**

FairyTale: A True Story

It's hard to imagine that there are two more adorable little actresses than Florence Hoath and Elizabeth Earl as Elsie Wright and Frances Griffiths, two delightful amateur photographers who may or may not have captured real fairies on film. The filmmakers of *FairyTale: A True Story* more or less take the account at face value, showing contradictory evidence but preserving the pure enchantment of childhood when, for many kids, believing in fairies is absolutely essential! *FairyTale* takes place in 1917 when a generation of young men faced death everyday during what was then known as The Great War. Sir Arthur Conan Doyle, then 58 and the grieving father of a lost son, launched an investigation into psychic phenomena in order to comfort himself. After he learned of the fairies of Elsie and Frances, he wrote about them in *The Coming of the Fairies.* Although Doyle tried to conceal their identities, the investigative reporters of the day were just as diligent then as they are now, and the subsequent press attention brought the two girls much unwanted notoriety. *FairyTale* is charming and true when it focuses on Elsie and Frances and the beautiful surroundings in which they live. The introduction of computer animation for several of the fairy sequences is, unhappily, an imperfect artistic solution. Fairies are only magic when they're real and computer animation is too precise to look real. Shadows, soft focus, any elegant subterfuge would have eliminated the clash of 1997 technical wizardry grafted on an 80-year-old tale. Peter O'Toole at 65 doesn't much resemble the well-fed Doyle, and his eyes look like they're trying to escape from a face and frame that reveal every second of a wild Irish life. Harvey Keitel, 58, is 15 years older than his Harry Houdini character was at that point in that career. But, as anyone who has fidgeted through 1922's *The Man from Beyond* knows, Houdini had zero cinematic charisma and Keitel has plenty to spare. For the most part, *FairyTale: A True Story* has the look and feel of another era, but Misses Hoath and Earl breathe fresh life into that era and give it a very special meaning for contemporary audiences. ***AKA:*** Illumination. 🦴🦴🦴

1997 (PG) 99m/C Harvey Keitel, Peter O'Toole, Florence Hoath, Elizabeth Earl, Paul McGann, Phoebe Nicholls, Bill Nighy, Bob Peck, Tim McInnery; ***Cameos:*** Mel Gibson; ***D:*** Charles Sturridge; ***W:*** Ernie Contreras; ***C:*** Michael Coulter; ***M:*** Zbigniew Preisner. **VHS, Closed Caption**

The Fallen Idol

Baines and Julie (Ralph Richardson and Michele Morgan) are having an affair, and mean Mrs. Baines (Sonia Dresdel) doesn't like it. Meanwhile, Phillipe (Bobby Henrey, then 9) is bored and lonely (no parents in sight), so he hangs out with his hero Baines and with Julie, and steers clear of Mrs. Baines. Then Phillipe believes that he's witnessed the murder of Mrs. Baines by none other than Baines! This interesting study of adult behavior through a child's eyes is based on Graham Greene's *The Basement Room;* Greene also collaborated on the screenplay. The camera sticks with Phillipe. We see what he sees and even when he's wrong, we still root for things to go well for him. Henrey made just one other movie, 1951's *The Wonder Kid* with Oskar Werner and Sebastian Cabot. ***AKA:*** The Lost Illusion. 🦴🦴🦴🦴

1949 92m/B *GB* Ralph Richardson, Bobby Henrey, Michele Morgan, Sonia Dresdel, Jack Hawkins, Bernard Lee, Denis O'Dea, Dora Bryan, Walter Fitzgerald, Karel Stepanek, Geoffrey Keen, James Hayter, Dandy Nichols, George Woodbridge, John Ruddock, Joan Young, Gerard Heinz; ***D:*** Carol Reed; ***W:*** Graham Greene, Lesley Storm, William Templeton; ***C:*** Georges Perinal. British Academy Awards '48: Best Film; National Board of Review Awards '49: Best Actor (Richardson); New York Film Critics Awards '49: Best Director (Reed); Nominations: Academy Awards '49: Best Director (Reed), Best Screenplay. **VHS, LV**

False Weights

False Weights lumbers along for 145 minutes. We are stuck with an unsympathetic village official most of the time, with occasional relief supplied by subplots mashed into the major narrative. Jerzy Lipmann's cinematography is stunning, but this vague film doesn't work as a character study, so

"Say Lou, didya hear the one about the guy who couldn't afford personalized plates so he went and changed his name to J3L2404?"

—Marge Gunderson (Frances McDormand) in *Fargo.*

it certainly doesn't succeed as a social statement. Bernhard Wicki's previous efforts, 1959's *The Bridge* and 1965's *Morituri,* were better received in the U.S., winning a total of three Oscar nominations between them (he also wrote the screenplay for 1962's *The Longest Day*). 🦴

1974 145m/C *GE* Helmut Qualtinger, Agnes Fink, Bata Zivojinovic, Evelyne Opela, Kurt Sowinetz, Istvan Iglody; ***D:*** Bernhard Wicki; ***W:*** Fritz Hochwalder; ***C:*** Jerzy Lipmann; ***M:*** George Grutz.

Fargo

Fargo was 1996's sentimental favorite, according to longtime admirers of the Coen brothers' amazing body of work. From 1985's *Blood Simple* to 1987's *Raising Arizona,* from 1990's *Miller's Crossing* to 1991's *Barton Fink,* the Coen brothers have thrust their black comedies into the American consciousness in bold and inventive ways. The good-hearted police chief Marge Gunderson (Frances McDormand) is exactly what we NEVER see in a crime saga. She's pregnant, she has morning sickness, she's hasn't a duplicitous bone in her body, and yet she matter-of-factly gets to work SOLVING things, and then goes home to cuddle with her husband. The kidnap scheme dreamed up by Jerry Lundegaard (William H. Macy) is as screwed-up in the blueprint stage as it is in reality. The greedy kidnappers he hires are deadly serious, but bloody inept. Everything is played out against the snowy landscape of Minnesota, and even Harve Presnell (star of the '60s musicals *The Unsinkable Molly Brown* and *Paint Your Wagon*) puts in an appearance as the kidnap victim's father. Of all the top domestic indie releases of 1996, only Billy Bob Thornton's creation of Karl Childers in *Sling Blade* came anywhere near triggering the widespread adoption of catch phrases that *Fargo*'s Police Chief Marge Gunderson did. *Fargo* may be based an actual events from 1987, but the Coen brothers have clearly taken the inspiration for their screenplay from bits and pieces of several crimes of the Midwest. You may want to see this one twice. 🦴🦴🦴🦴

1996 (R) 97m/C William H. Macy, Frances McDormand, Steve Buscemi, Peter Stormare, Harve Presnell, Steve Reevis, John Carroll Lynch, Kristin Rudrud, Steve Park; ***Cameos:*** Jose Feliciano; ***D:*** Joel Coen; ***W:*** Ethan Coen, Joel Coen; ***C:*** Roger Deakins; ***M:*** Carter Burwell. Academy Awards '96: Best Actress (McDormand), Best Original Screenplay; Australian Film Institute '95: Best Foreign Film; Cannes Film Festival '96: Best Director (Coen); Independent Spirit Awards '97: Best Actor (Macy), Best Actress (McDormand), Best Cinematography, Best Director (Coen), Best Film, Best Screenplay; National Board of Review Awards '96: Best Actress (McDormand), Best Director (Coen); New York Film Critics Awards '96: Best Film; Screen Actors Guild Award '96: Best Actress (McDormand); Writers Guild of America '96: Best Original Screenplay; Broadcast Film Critics Association Awards '96: Best Actress (McDormand), Best Film; Nominations: Academy Awards '96: Best Cinematography, Best Director (Coen), Best Film Editing, Best Picture, Best Supporting Actor (Macy); British Academy Awards '96: Best Actress (McDormand), Best Director (Coen), Best Film, Best Original Screenplay; Cesar Awards '97: Best Foreign Film; Directors Guild of America Awards '96: Best Director (Coen); Golden Globe Awards '97: Best Actress—Musical/Comedy (McDormand), Best Director (Coen), Best Film—Musical/Comedy, Best Screenplay; MTV Movie Awards '97: Best On-Screen Duo (Peter Stormare/Steve Buscemi); Screen Actors Guild Award '96: Best Supporting Actor (Macy). **VHS, LV, Closed Caption, DVD**

Faster, Pussycat! Kill! Kill!

To see three voluptuous evil pussycats do bad things onscreen was an experience not to be missed in 1965! In fact, *Faster, Pussycat! Kill! Kill!* continues to play to packed art houses and commercial theatres to this day. It's a guaranteed rent payer! Tura Satana (*The Astro Zombies, The Doll Squad*) IS Varla, Haji (*Motor Psycho*) IS Rosie, Lori Williams IS Billie, Playboy pin-up Susan Bernard (*Teenager*) IS Linda, Ray Barlow IS Tommie, Paul Trinka IS Kirk, Stuart Lancaster (*Mantis in Lace, Mistress of the Apes, Beneath the Valley of the Ultra-Vixens*) IS The Old Man, Mickey Foxx IS the Service Station Attendant, and Dennis Busch IS The Vegetable! Satana is not only physically impressive, she also knows karate, so when Varla goes into action, she isn't kidding around! The body count in this flick is astonishingly high and so is the level of Jack Moran's fast-paced screenplay. Movie buffs will forever keep a special place in their hearts for director Russ Meyer. He was a sharp, shrewd operator who knew how to tell (and edit) a story, who kept the plots moving, and who had a particular genius for casting actors and actresses with spectacular physical dimensions. His ability to stretch bucks on a budget and his boxoffice receipts were so overwhelming that ailing 20th Century Fox studios invited him to direct *Beyond the Valley of the Dolls* when they urgently needed a hit in 1970. Anyone remember a few of Fox's other releases that year, like *Cover Me Babe, Hello-Goodbye, Move,* and *Myra Breckinridge*? Yeah, yeah, I know, *Patton, MASH,* and *Tora! Tora! Tora!,* war movies all. Meyer made love, not war, and even the violence is straight out of a comic book. And, according to *Valley* Girl Cynthia Myers, Russ Meyer was the most gentlemanly of directors; how many "respectable" male directors can make that claim without crossing their fingers behind their backs? P.S. The Spice Girls co-opted this movie for their *Say You'll Be There* video.

1965 83m/B Tura Satana, Haji, Lori Williams, Susan Bernard, Stuart Lancaster, Paul Trinka, Dennis Busch, Ray Barlow, Mickey Foxx; ***D:*** Russ Meyer; ***W:*** Jack Moran, Russ Meyer; ***C:*** Walter Schenk; ***M:*** Paul Sawtell, Bert Shefter, The Bostweeds. **VHS**

The Favor, the Watch, and the Very Big Fish

The Favor, the Watch, and the Very Big Fish might have been a screwball comedy for the early 1990s, if anyone had drifted into movie theatres to see it. It stars three endearing actors, Bob Hoskins, Jeff Goldblum, and Natasha Richardson, as three strangers who drift into an intriguing romantic triangle. Along the way, writer/director Ben Lewin (who based his film on the Marcel Ayme short story, "Rue Saint-Sulpice") pokes gentle fun at voiceover artists for pornographic films, the folks who manufacture religious art objects, and star-crossed lovers. Hoskins plays Louis Aubinard, an innocent (and virginal) French photographer who is looking for the ideal Jesus to pose for a series of devotional illustrations. After an idyllic chance meeting with a voiceover artist named Sybil (Richardson), he manages to connect with a former piano player played by Goldblum, who is still suffering after the death of his long-dead mother and also from the loss of the idyllic love of his life, a one-time waitress named Sybil. Yes, it's the same Sybil. For the rest of the movie, Sybil searches for each man so she can explain why she appears to have jilted him, the piano player suffers agonies because he suspects that his photographer friend Louis loves Sybil, and Louis stolidly remains a loyal friend to his new model while hoping against hope that he will one day be reunited with Sybil. The fun is watching the three leads at work. At one point, Hoskins exclaims with a perfectly straight face, "I'm not a great actor!," a line ONLY a great actor could safely deliver. As in his previous British films, *The Tall Guy* and *Mister Frost,* Goldblum chews the scenery in another bizarre role that only he could render plausible. The much-underrated Natasha Richardson is delightful as Sybil and a great supporting cast (Angela Pleasence, Jean-Pierre Cassel, and Michel Blanc as Louis' martinet employer) make *The Favor, the Watch, and the Very Big Fish* a pleasure to watch. (If you're easily offended by borderline satire, you can always watch Bing Crosby on video as Father O'Malley!)

1992 (R) 89m/C *GB FR* Bob Hoskins, Jeff Goldblum, Natasha Richardson, Michel Blanc, Jacques Villeret, Angela Pleasence, Jean-Pierre Cassel, Bruce Altman; ***D:*** Ben Lewin; ***W:*** Ben Lewin; ***C:*** Bernard Zitzermann; ***M:*** Vladimir Cosma. **VHS, LV, Closed Caption**

Fear

Fear begins promisingly and even features a low-budget earthquake sequence. Tomislav Pinter's cinematography is immaculate, the acting is impressive throughout, and the sets and costumes certainly convey the decadent atmosphere Matjaz Klopcic tries to explore here. The main problems with this attractive film are Klopcic's uncompelling screenplay and listless direc-

A high point in low taste.

—Tagline from the movie *Female Trouble*.

tion. Unfortunately, when film festival novices see a boring mess like this one, they often think it's THEIR fault, and that if they went to more movies or even flew to Yugoslavia, they would GET it. FERgeddit! If you think it's a thumping bore, it probably is. ***AKA:*** Strah. 🦴🦴

1975 105m/C *YU* Ljuba Tadic, Milena Zupancic, Anton Petje, Milena Dravic; ***D:*** Matjaz Klopcic; ***W:*** Matjaz Klopcic; ***C:*** Tomislav Pinter.

A Feast at Midnight

The posters for *A Feast at Midnight* are evocative of the heady days when Christopher Lee reigned supreme at Hammer Studios: "A 500-year-old school. A prehistoric form master...And a 10-year-old chef." The 10-year-old chef is Freddie Findlay, who is introduced as Magnus with this film. Lee is Major Longfellow (AKA Raptor), his mean Latin professor. And the 500-year-old school? The production company paid a visit to a boarding school in England, inquiring if they could use the school as an elaborate set for a five-week shooting schedule during the spring holidays. The producers then cast the students in the picture, and *A Feast at Midnight* was ready for the front burner. The premise is that Magnus is miserable at boarding school; he's no good at sports and the other boys bully him. Magnus IS good at one thing: creating elaborate desserts in the kitchen for a secret eating club called the Scoffers. The lighter-than-air story is enacted with great sweetness by the kids, and yes, this one WILL make you hungry. It's a charmer. (And it's a treat to see Christopher Lee in a movie, even if he isn't playing a vampire!) 🦴🦴🦴

1995 185m/C *AU* Christopher Lee, Robert Hardy, Edward Fox, Freddie Findlay, Lisa Faulkner, Samuel West; ***D:*** Justin Hardy; ***W:*** Justin Hardy, Yoshi Nishio; ***C:*** Tim Maurice-Jones; ***M:*** David A. Hughes, John Murphy.

Federal Hill

Ralph (Nicholas Turturro), Nicky (Anthony DeSando), Frank (Michael Raynor), Bobby (Jason Andrews), and Joey (Robert Turano) are longtime Italian buddies in Providence, Rhode Island, and they still meet at Joey's every week to play cards. Ralph (a thief) and Nicky (a drug dealer) are best friends. When Nicky sells some coke to Wendy (Libby Langdon) for a party, he shows up for it with Ralph. Ralph gets nowhere at the party, but Nicky winds up in a thing with Wendy and he decides to leave his pals for her. Ralph says that Wendy's just using Nicky for a fling, then loser Bobby gets in trouble and Ralph gets in trouble for helping Bobby. It all gets tied up in melodramatic fashion, but while it lasts, it's never dull, it's sometimes funny and it's always well acted in great black and white. Which makes more sense/cents? To light a film for black and white, but shoot it in color, finish it, then release it theatrically in black and white for film noir purists and in both versions for the home video market, OR to spend a small fortune colorizing a 1994 film? Michael Corrente colorized *Federal Hill*. I know why there are two versions: there are actually people (including my one-time upstairs neighbor) who refuse to look at any movie that's not in color. But to *colorize* your brand new movie? The mind boggles. 🦴🦴🦴½

1994 (R) 100m/B Anthony De Sando, Nicholas Turturro, Libby Langdon, Michael Raynor, Jason Andrews, Frank Vincent, Robert Turano, Michael Corrente; ***D:*** Michael Corrente; ***W:*** Michael Corrente; ***C:*** Richard Crudo; ***M:*** Bob Held, David Bravo. Nominations: Independent Spirit Awards '95: Best Supporting Actor (Turturro). **VHS, LV, Closed Caption**

Feed

With 27 days to go in the 1992 presidential campaign, Kevin Rafferty and James Ridgeway's *Feed* could not have been released at a better time. Here are the candidates as they would rather you had NEVER seen them, getting ready to go on television and trying to create a Presidential impression. Only Jerry Brown just can't seem to cover that dang bald spot of his, no matter how much he combs forward what's left of his hair. He wanted his campaign to seem effortlessly low-key, but he whines, whines, whines when a female aide can't straighten his tie just right. And HE can't do it, either. Bob Kerrey, sucking soda through a straw, just can't seem to erase the image of a choir boy, as a television moderator observes, supposedly off the record, but preserved forever on film. The late Paul Tsongas made the mistake of being photographed in swimming trunks, not even trying to suck in his stomach, and he also made a wild guess at the 1992 cost of a gallon of milk: $1.79! Ross Perot tells interminable dull jokes, always looking as if he's ready for an alien from outer space to give him advice. Bill Clinton doesn't seem to have any off-guard moments. He can always think of something to say, no matter how many times he's drilled about Gennifer Flowers. (Flowers makes an appearance, too, enthusing about Clinton's soft lips.) And George Bush can, does, and will sit in front of a television camera for long, long moments on end, rarely saying a word to break the ice. People click off to candidates for the most inconsequential of reasons: one voter rejected Tsongas because he wore a pocket protector. A Democratic candidate makes the mistake of trying to shake the hands of two Republican voters and is sternly admonished by one woman: "A lady always presents her hand first." All the footage comes from the 1992 New Hampshire primary when the candidates apparently felt that most of what they said and did would be unseen by the rest of the country. Seeing the candidates like this, unvarnished and totally dependent on the folks from the media who surround them is far more absorbing than watching them blather prepared speeches for hours on end. Even if it IS dated, *Feed* is fascinating and well worth a video search. 🦴🦴🦴

1992 76m/C *D:* Kevin Rafferty, James Ridgeway; ***C:*** Jenny Darrow. **VHS**

The Feldmann Case

The Feldmann Case represents the outstanding debut of director Bente Erichsen, who wrote her screenplay after reading the novel *Echo from Scream Pond,* based on a true World War II story about the Norwegian underground. There is a striking contrast between the official findings of the case and the director's own ethical viewpoint. The interpretative clash adds to the suspense: we know what happened to the rich Jewish couple who tried to escape the Nazis, what we don't know is why, and this is Erichsen's main concern. A well-acted, extremely gutsy film, *The Feldmann Case* is not yet available on video, although it should be! ***AKA:*** Feldmann Saken. 🦴🦴🦴🦴

1987 89m/C *NO* Finn Kvalen, Sverre Anker Ousdal, Bjorn Sundquist, Ingerid Vardung; ***D:*** Bente Erichson; ***W:*** Bente Erichson; ***C:*** Rolv Haan.

Female Trouble

Female Trouble is John Waters' favorite movie. It's all about the fictitious adventures of Dawn Davenport from her life as a suburban brat to her electrifying destiny. Divine gives another superstar performance in this underground classic, made for $25,000 in 1974. 🦴🦴

1974 (R) 95m/C Divine, David Lochary, Mary Vivian Pearce, Mink Stole, Edith Massey, Danny Mills, Cookie Mueller, Susan Walsh, Elizabeth Coffey, Channing Wilroy; ***D:*** John Waters; ***W:*** John Waters. **VHS**

Fire Maidens from Outer Space

I got yelled at for enjoying this movie and grilled afterward: "Wouldn't you rather watch a GOOD movie than a BAD one?" Not necessarily! *Fire Maidens from Outer Space,* which looks like it was shot in someone's backyard, revolves around the efforts of five astronauts to save the Fire Maidens of Jupiter's 13th moon from this whatchamacallit in wrinkled long underwear! Anthony Dexter, whose career hit the automatic skids after starring in 1951's *Valentino,* is Astronaut Luther Blair. Susan Shaw, one of Britain's most promising starlets of the late 1940s and early 1950s, is Hestia. Paul Carpenter, Harry Fowler, and Sydney Tafler are Astronauts Larson, Sydney Stanhope, and Dr. Higgins. Some of these actors deleted this movie from their resumes. I don't know a thing about any of the other actors. I stopped watching movies with the person who yelled at me, but I haven't stopped watch-

George Baker and Denzel Washington in *For Queen and Country.*
Paramount; courtesy of the Kobal Collection

ing this movie. There really IS something exhilarating about (a) stupefying cheapness, (b) technical incompetence, (c) artistic nadirs, (d) all of the above. **woof!**

1956 80m/B *GB* Anthony Dexter, Susan Shaw, Paul Carpenter, Harry Fowler, Jacqueline Curtiss, Sydney Tafler, Maya Koumani, Jan Holden, Kim Parker, Rodney Diak, Owen Berry; ***D:*** Cy Roth; ***W:*** Cy Roth; ***C:*** Ian Struthers. **VHS**

First Communion

Rene Feret's *First Communion* is a portrait of a family over a 100-year span; it has much the same effect as the spinning pages of a huge scrapbook filled with the faces of people who may mean a great deal to each other, but not to a stranger who casually picks up the scrapbook. Since Feret tells us that it isn't important who married whom over the years or who died, it's exactly like watching a bunch of someone else's home movies. The ballad that's supposed to hold everything together is insipid, but Jean-François Robin's cinematography is exquisite, and the main redeeming virtue of this immature first film. ***AKA:*** La Communion Solonnelle. 🦴🦴

1977 185m/C *FR* Claude-Emile Rosen, Claude Bouchery, Vincent Pinel, Yveline Ailhaud, Patrick Fierry, Jany Gastaldi, Marcel Dalio, Philippe Leotard, Rene Feret; ***D:*** Rene Feret; ***W:*** Rene Feret; ***C:*** Jean-Francois Robin; ***M:*** Sergio Ortego.

Five Corners

If you're looking for a pattern in the career of Oscar-winning screenwriter John Patrick Shanley, try to figure out what *Moonstruck, Five Corners, The January Man, Joe Versus the Volcano* (which he also directed), *Alive, We're Back! A Dinosaur's Story,* and *Congo* have in common. That isn't a trick question, because heck if I know, either. Shanley is capable of writing sequences of both heartfelt realism and mind-boggling mediocrity (contrast the first and second halves of *Joe*). Most of the story line of *Five Corners,* which played at the Mill Valley Film Festival in the fall of 1987, is strong and clear. At one point in this story about teens in 1964, though, violence occurs without warning, and the sequence is like "a stun gun to your brain," as Angela Chase, a teen from a later era, might say. Are these completely gratuitous moments really necessary? What do they give the narrative that it doesn't already have? Don't they, in fact, take away from the other 90 minutes that have already established the psychosis behind the violence? It is this lack of balance that would topple other Shanley screenplays. On the plus side, the acting by Jodie Foster (who won an Independent Spirit Award), Tim Robbins, and John Turturro is excellent, and so is James Newton Howard's score.

1988 (R) 92m/C Jodie Foster, John Turturro, Todd Graff, Tim Robbins, Elizabeth Berridge, Rose Gregorio, Gregory Rozakis, Rodney Harvey, John Seitz; ***D:*** Tony Bill; ***W:*** John Patrick Shanley; ***C:*** Fred Murphy; ***M:*** James Newton Howard. Independent Spirit Awards '89: Best Actress (Foster). **VHS**

Flirting with Disaster

There's something about Ben Stiller in a movie that just makes me go AAARGH. He shows up in *Reality Bites:* AARGH. He shows up in this one: AARGH. He may be a terrific guy offscreen, but onscreen he reeks of Yuppieville. Maybe he should grow a beard. Get a growl in his voice. Anything to give him an edge. David O. Russell's movie has so many edges, you might think that one of them would rub off on Ben Stiller. But noooooo.... Luckily, *Flirting with Disaster* has a large cast. There's Patricia Arquette, who looks as young here as she looked old in *Lost Highway.* Josh Brolin (NOT Ben Stiller) licks her armpit. Amazing. There's Tea Leoni as a shrink. Sure. There's Alan Alda and Lily Tomlin as a hippie dippie couple; now, there's a concept. There's George Segal and Mary Tyler Moore, who are SO uptight you could market the both of them as slingshots. Russell talked Moore into a few underwear sequences. No comment. In spite of the overall weirdness, everyone acts as if everything is normal; Moore flosses her teeth and asks Segal, "Where's your sense of romance?" It's funny!

1995 (R) 92m/C Ben Stiller, Patricia Arquette, Tea Leoni, Alan Alda, Mary Tyler Moore, George Segal, Lily Tomlin, Josh Brolin, Richard Jenkins, Celia Weston, Glenn Fitzgerald, Beth Ostrosky, Cynthia Lamontagne, David Patrick Kelly, John Ford Noonan, Charles Oberly; ***D:*** David O. Russell; ***W:*** David O. Russell; ***C:*** Eric Alan Edwards; ***M:*** Stephen Endelman. Nominations: Independent Spirit Awards '97: Best Director (Russell), Best Screenplay, Best Supporting Actor (Jenkins), Best Supporting Actress (Tomlin). **VHS, LV, Closed Caption**

Fly by Night

Slapdash, skin-deep look at a couple of rappers who team up with a third (authentic rapper Darryl Mitchell as Rich's cousin Kayam) to achieve fame. When they do, they hate it. Do Steve Gomer and Todd Graff know what makes their characters (Jeffrey Sams as Rich, Ron Brice as I) tick? If they do, it isn't onscreen. There's an exciting score, though.

1993 (PG-13) 93m/C Jeffrey D. Sams, Ron Brice, Darryl (Chill) Mitchell, Todd Graff, Leo Burmester, Soulfood Jed, Lawrence Gilliard, Omar Carter, Maura Tierney, Yul Vazquez, M.C. Lyte, Christopher-Michael Gerrard, Ebony Jo-Ann; ***D:*** Steve Gomer; ***W:*** Todd Graff; ***C:*** Larry Banks; ***M:*** Kris Parker, Sidney Mills, Dwayne Sumal. Sundance Film Festival '93: Filmmakers Trophy. **VHS, Closed Caption**

For a Lost Soldier

For a Lost Soldier was San Jose's opening night selection at the Gay and Lesbian Film Festival in 1993. It arrived with an impressive award from a festival in Turin. A grown-up choreographer (Jeroen Krabbe) reminisces about those good old World War II days when he was a boy of 12 or so and had a fling with a grown-up soldier. Their fairly explicit romps in bed are shown as warm and cozy, and we never see what happens to the child between the end of their affair and his well-established adult life. (It may have been in the original Dutch book, but it isn't onscreen.) Other short films at the festival that year were much more honest; several focused on how their protagonists are completely bewildered by conflicting emotions about sex and tormented by a fear of being abandoned as a

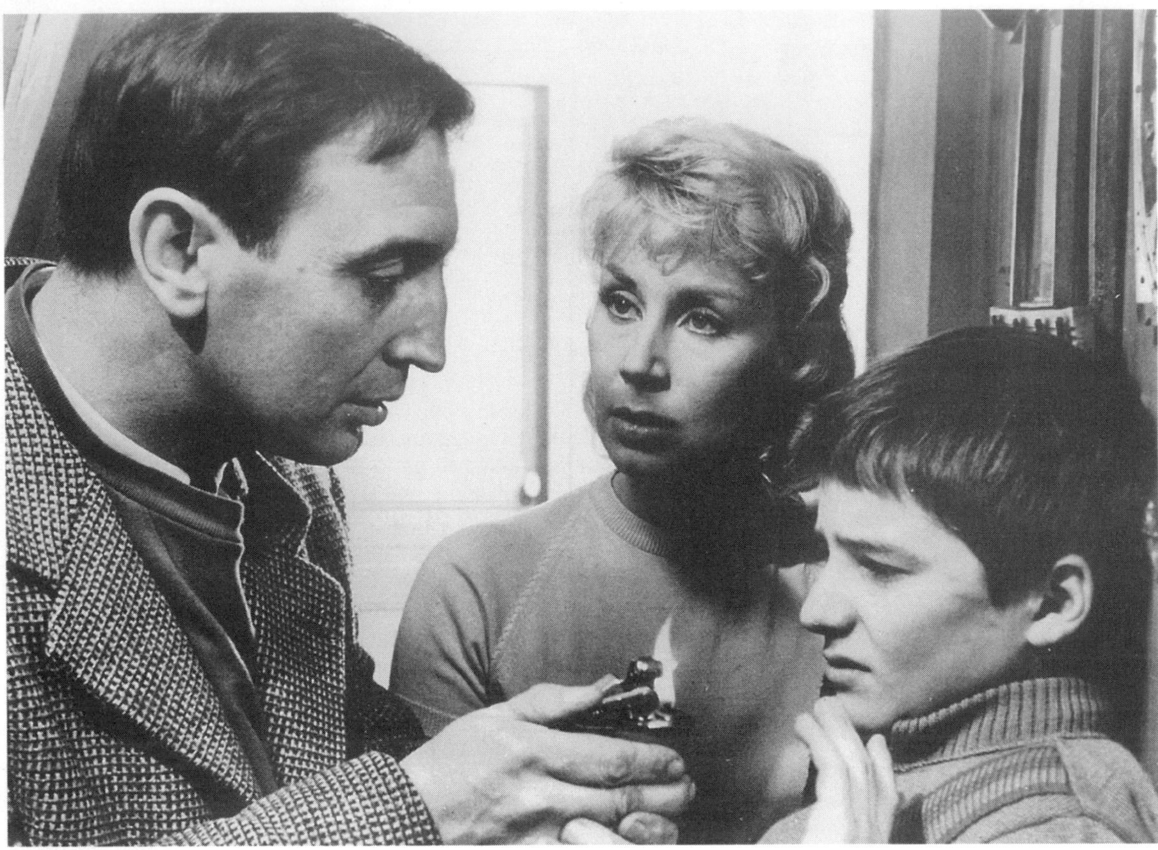

Albert Remy, Claire Maurier, and Jean-Pierre Leaud as the dysfunctional family in *The 400 Blows.*
Carosse; courtesy of the Kobal Collection

result of the choices they make. For grown-ups to convince themselves that very young children recover quickly from intense emotional experiences may be convenient for them, but the reality for the kids is much different. The unreal romantic lushness of *For a Lost Soldier,* therefore, makes it an ideal advert and/or propaganda for the North American Man/Boy Love Association. ***AKA:*** Voor een Verloren Soldaat. 🦴

1993 92m/C *NL* Marten Smit, Andrew Kelley, Jeroen Krabbe, Feark Smink, Elsje de Wijn, Derk-Jan Kroon; ***D:*** Roeland Kerbosch; ***W:*** Roeland Kerbosch; ***C:*** Nils Post; ***M:*** Joop Stokkermans. **VHS**

For Queen and Country

For Queen and Country is bogged down with good intentions and by characters who function as symbols rather than as people. The thrust of the film is that Great Britain does not care about the lower classes, and if the country makes use of a poor man in wartime, he can expect a life of hopelessness when he returns home. Denzel Washington is so good in the central character of Reuben that he grabs our attention and sympathy in spite of the rigid symbolism of his role. Also good are Dorian Healy as Fish, a friend crippled by his tour of duty, and Amanda Redman as Stacey, a woman who is interested in Reuben until she recognizes his evolving need for violent solutions. The rest of the cast, including veteran character actor George Baker, are given no chance to do much more than advance the plot. I have the same reservations about director Martin Stellman's turgid screenplay for 1987's *Defense of the Realm.* By wanting to make a predetermined point with as few words as possible, he reduces most of the characters to delivery people. In *For Queen and Country,* nearly all of the first 90 minutes of the plot are absorbed with establishing the unjust poverty suffered by Reuben and Fish, something a writer without such a rigid agenda could have shown in a fraction of the time. In fact, a single moment reveals that if the British bureaucracy had been a bit less unyielding, Reuben and Stacey might have been able to make a go of it. But Stellman chooses to show the moment as anticlimactic, then wraps it all up with violence and deja vu and says what? That because the British government is unfair to disconnected veterans that they might as well pack it in the day they get their discharge papers? That's what Stellman's persistent images indicate. There are suggestions of other resolutions, but that would have disturbed the conclusion's contrived symmetry. There are quite a few things wrong with *For Queen and Country* but Denzel Washington isn't one of them, and the film is worth seeing for his commanding performance alone. 🦴🦴🦴

1988 (R) 105m/C *GB* Denzel Washington, Dorian Healy, Amanda Redman, Sean Chapman, Bruce Payne, Geff Francis, George Baker; ***D:*** Martin Stellman; ***W:*** Trix Worrell, Martin Stellman; ***C:*** Richard Greatrex; ***M:*** Michael Kamen. **VHS**

Forbidden Choices

Yeah, if I made a fictional indie with a moniker like *The Beans of Egypt, Maine,* I'd consider giving it a catchier title, too. It sounds like a National Geographic documentary instead of the soap opera that it is. Actually, that IS the title of Carolyn Chute's novel and it IS about the Bean family who live in Egypt, Maine. The head of the Bean family of nine is Reuben (Rutger Hauer?!$#%), but he's in jail, so Roberta (Kelly Lynch) is raising them on her own. Earlene Pomerleau (Martha Plimpton, the film's chief virtue) thinks the Beans are neat, especially Beal (Patrick McGaw). Well, what else does she have in her life but a tyrannical, Bible-thumping Daddy (Richard Sanders)? Anyway, that new title refers to Beal and zzzzzz.... ***AKA:*** The Beans of Egypt, Maine. 🦴🦴

1994 (R) 109m/C Martha Plimpton, Kelly Lynch, Rutger Hauer, Patrick McGaw, Richard Sanders; ***D:*** Jennifer Warren; ***W:*** Bill Phillips; ***C:*** Stevan Larner; ***M:*** Peter Manning Rob. Nominations: Independent Spirit Awards '95: Best Cinematography, Best Supporting Actress (Lynch). **VHS, LV, Closed Caption**

Forbidden Games

François Boyer wrote the screenplay for *Les Jeux Interdits* in 1946, but World War II was over and no one wanted to see another war movie. So he turned it into a novel and producer Robert Dorfman WAS interested in making a movie of a successful book. An entirely new screenplay was drafted by Jean Aurenche and Pierre Bost with director Rene Clement (1913–96), who decided to film the story on a farm that was actually poor, as indicated in the script. He began a search for the two children who were to star in the picture. Brigitte Fossey, who was heartrending as the orphaned Paulette, was only five years old. Georges Poujouly, who would play Michel, was just eleven. The narrative sticks with the kids to show the horrors of war. Michel protects Paulette from the sadness and loneliness of her situation by coming up with a game to bury dead animals they find in the countryside and placing crosses (stolen from the church cemetery) on top of their homemade graves. The game comforts them both, although the adults are none too pleased by the sacrilegious aspect of the rituals. Under pressure, Michel says he will give up the crosses if the grown-ups promise they won't take Paulette away. They agree, and Michel learns, much too young, about the ugliness of betrayal. Paulette's fate, to wander among a crowd of other refugees, is devastating. She cries for "Michel!" over and over again. The "Forbidden Games," along with the kind little boy who nurtured her, are lost to her. Forever? We don't know about Paulette and Michel, but in real life, Fossey went on to a successful acting career when she grew up. In one of her most intriguing pictures, 1984's *The Future of Emily* (co-starring Ivan

A Terrifying Tale of Sluts and Bolts!

—Tagline from the movie *Frankenhooker.*

Desny and Hildegarde Knef), she played an actress reflecting on her career since childhood. At one point, she discusses a role she played at five, sighing, "it was my best performance." (Fossey's other films include *The Wanderer, Honor Among Thieves, Going Places, Blue Country, The Man Who Loved Women, Quintet, Chanel Solitaire, La Boum, Enigma,* and *The Last Butterfly.*) Poujouly also found work—as a supporting actor in other French films, including 1958's *Frantic.* And Jacques Marin, who plays Georges, continued to appear as a character actor in international films for many years. The initial reaction to Clement's film was mixed. Although *Forbidden Games* won many awards in Italy, Britain, and America, including an Oscar, the French were horrified by the way their post-war society appeared to the rest of the world. But *Forbidden Games* remains the best known and most treasured French film of its time. (Clement's other films include *The Walls of Malapaga, Gervaise, The Day and the Hour, Joy House, Is Paris Burning?, Rider on the Rain,* and *And Hope to Die*). ***AKA:*** Les Jeux Interdits. 🦴🦴🦴🦴

1952 90m/B *FR* Brigitte Fossey, Georges Poujouly, Amedee, Louis Herbert, Suzanne Courtal, Jacques Marin, Laurence Badie, Andre Wasley, Louis Sainteve; ***D:*** Rene Clement; ***W:*** Rene Clement, Jean Aurenche, Pierre Bost, Francois Boyer; ***C:*** Robert Juillard; ***M:*** Narciso Yepes. British Academy Awards '53: Best Film; New York Film Critics Awards '52: Best Foreign Film; Venice Film Festival '52: Best Film; Nominations: Academy Awards '54: Best Story. **VHS, LV**

Forgotten Silver

Peter Jackson's *Forgotten Silver* may be an eyelash too clever for its own good. It looks like a documentary of a forgotten New Zealand filmmaking pioneer named Colin McKenzie, but it's essentially a reconstruction of silent movie history if an obscure bloke, rather than D.W. Griffith, had been responsible for early cinematic innovations. (If you've ever seen *The Missing Reel,* a film by Christopher Rawlence about an authentic forgotten filmmaking pioneer, you're aware that stranger things have been known to happen.) Still, *Forgotten Silver* is obviously an affectionate look at a vanished era, and Jackson, Sam Neill, Leonard Maltin, et al obviously had a ball making it. 🦴🦴🦴

1996 53m/C *NZ* Sam Neill, Leonard Maltin, Harvey Weinstein, John O'Shea, Hannah McKenzie, Lindsay Shelton, Johnny Morris, Marguerite Hurst, Costa Botes, Jeffrey Thomas; ***D:*** Peter Jackson, Robert Sarkies, Costa Botes; ***W:*** Peter Jackson, Costa Botes; ***C:*** Alun Bollinger. **VHS**

The 400 Blows

Antoine Doinel (Jean-Pierre Leaud) is one troubled 12-year-old kid. His mother (Claire Maurier) wanted to have an abortion when she learned she was expecting him and Antoine knows it. She is unfaithful to his father (Albert Remy) and both are indifferent to Antoine. He skips school, steals, and lies about the cause of his behavior by saying that his mother is dead. He is sent to an institution but escapes, and the shot of Antoine on the beach is one of the most indelible images of childhood ever. Jean-Pierre Leaud seems so real as Antoine, it's hard to believe he's acting. But he is, and Truffaut took infinite care to see that his young discovery hit just the right notes in his first movie. Partly based on Truffaut's own life, *The 400 Blows* gave us a view of childhood that we'd never before seen in such realistic detail. A groundbreaking picture in every way, it was and still is an enormously influential film on more than two generation of filmmakers. ***AKA:*** Les Quartre Cents Coups. 🦴🦴🦴🦴

1959 97m/B *FR* Francois Truffaut, Jean-Pierre Leaud, Claire Maurier, Albert Remy, Guy Decomble, Georges Flament, Patrick Auffay, Jeanne Moreau, Jean-Claude Brialy, Jacques Demy, Robert Beauvais; ***D:*** Francois Truffaut; ***W:*** Francois Truffaut, Marcel Moussey; ***C:*** Henri Decae; ***M:*** Jean Constantin. Cannes Film Festival '59: Best Director (Truffaut); New York Film Critics Awards '59: Best Foreign Film; Nominations: Academy Awards '59: Best Story & Screenplay. **VHS, LV, Letterbox, DVD**

Four Weddings and a Funeral

Like 1992's *Strictly Ballroom, Four Weddings and a Funeral* is the sort of delicious confection that actually improves with repeat viewings. It's the story of a dashing bachelor named Charles (Hugh Grant) who goes to wedding after wedding, screwing up left and right (he loses vital wedding paraphernalia LIKE THE RING, has a severe case of foot-in-mouth disease, is forever at the wrong place at the wrong time, et cetera), until he finally comes to terms with how he can slip into the whole system with the least pain and effort. *Four Weddings* was a hit in England and an even bigger hit in America. The reasons for this transatlantic phenomenon are obvious: there are many flattering references to American cultural symbols; American songs galore on the soundtrack; and, of course, Gaffney, South Carolina's own Andie MacDowell as Carrie, the object of Charles' desire. This satire of love and death, moreover, is warm and affectionate. Lovely touches abound, like Simon Callow sticking his finger down his throat at a gloppy folk song during one ceremony, the picture-perfect casting-against-type of politically radical Corin Redgrave as an aristocrat, the bride who kisses total strangers and tells them how much she loves them to the accompaniment of the groom's assessment of her alcoholic intake, bridesmaid Lydia (Sophie Thompson) who doesn't want to scrape the bottom of the barrel with Bernard but engages in some lusty wedding-bound necking with him anyway, Charles' endearing roommate Scarlett (Charlotte Coleman) who dreams of meeting Rhett at one of these functions, and Charles' sharply observed friend (Kristin Scott Thomas), who calls his ex-girlfriend Duckface and who is, of course, madly in love with Charles. And these represent a very small fraction of my favorite sequences. (Two words more: Rowan Atkinson!) *Four Weddings and a Funeral* is a keeper, to savor during those hours when the world seems dreary and depressing and you really need a movie filled with laughter and wit. 🦴🦴🦴🦴

1994 (R) 118m/C *GB* Hugh Grant, Andie MacDowell, Simon Callow, Kristin Scott Thomas, James Fleet, John Hannah, Charlotte Coleman, David Bower, Corin Redgrave, Rowan Atkinson, Rosalie Crutchley, Kenneth Griffith, Jeremy Kemp, Sophie Thompson; ***D:*** Mike Newell; ***W:*** Richard Curtis; ***C:*** Michael Coulter; ***M:*** Richard Rodney Bennett. Australian Film Institute '94: Best Foreign Film; British Academy Awards '94: Best Actor (Grant), Best Director (Newell), Best Film, Best Supporting Actress (Scott Thomas); Golden Globe Awards '95: Best Actor—Musical/Comedy (Grant); Writers Guild of America '94: Best Original Screenplay; Nominations: Academy Awards '94: Best Original Screenplay, Best Picture; Directors Guild of America Awards '94: Best Director (Newell); Golden Globe Awards '95: Best Actress—Musical/Comedy (MacDowell), Best Film—Musical/Comedy, Best Screenplay; MTV Movie Awards '95: Breakthrough Performance (Grant). **VHS, LV, Letterbox, DVD**

France, Incorporated

Alain Corneau's *France, Incorporated* offers a shattering sci-fi speculation on what life would be like in the year 2222 if hard drugs were legalized. The versatile Canadian actress Allyn Ann McLerie *(Words and Music, Phantom of the Rue Morgue, The Reivers, They Shoot Horses, Don't They?, Cinderella Liberty, All the President's Men)* is well cast as a tough-minded businesswoman who attempts to commercialize heroin as aggressively as cigarettes were marketed in the 1950s. There is nothing pretty about the sex and violence in this X-rated fantasy. The interesting premise occasionally lapses into facile slickness, though. 🦴🦴🦴

1974 100m/C *FR* Michel Bouquet, Allyn Ann McLerie, Roland Dubillard, Joel Barcellos, Michel Vitold, Ann Zacarias, Francis Blanche, Daniel Ceccaldi, Gerard Desarthe; ***D:*** Alain Corneau; ***W:*** Alain Corneau, Jean-Claude Carriere; ***C:*** Pierre William Glenn; ***M:*** Clifton Chenier.

Frankenhooker

At the beginning of *Frankenhooker,* we see the extremely pretty Elizabeth, whom boyfriend Jeffrey Franken thinks is too fat. On the other hand, Jeffrey looks and is just plain weird. He wants Elizabeth to be perfect and when she meets her demise in a freak garden accident, he makes careful plans to reassemble her. And so yet another *Frankenstein* variation is born. This one is pretty good, probably because it doesn't pretend to be anything other than what it is, a low-budget black comedy for the midnight matinee crowd. James Lorinz and Patty Mullen have a good time in the leading roles, and cult favorites Shirley

"This is a crucial question, Bob. Do you believe in the lord Jesus Christ and take him for your personal savior?"

—Vanessa (Reese Witherspoon) has a gun to Bob's (Kiefer Sutherland) head in *Freeway.*

Stoler and Louise Lasser pop up in supporting roles. There are plenty of body parts in the picture, but they're so obviously clunky and fake that I can't imagine anyone being seriously frightened by them. *Frankenhooker* is the first movie I've seen that makes jokes about crack; a good companion piece would be the equally bizarre *Mystery of the Leaping Fish* made in 1916 by D.W. Griffith and Tod Browning with Douglas Fairbanks as Coke Ennyday. At the sold-out premiere screening I attended at San Francisco's Roxie Cinema, the audience was already having conversations with the characters onscreen, a sure sign that *Frankenhooker* will be around for some time to come. ☆☆☆

1990 (R) 90m/C James Lorinz, Patty Mullen, Charlotte J. Helmkamp, Louise Lasser, Shirley Stoler; ***D:*** Frank Henenlotter; ***W:*** Frank Henenlotter, Robert Martin; ***C:*** Robert M. Baldwin Jr. **VHS, LV, Closed Caption, DVD**

Frankenstein Unbound

There have been close to 100 movies made about Dr. Frankenstein and his monster, so why not yet another variation on the legend from the one and only Roger Corman, directing his first film in decades? This is the third film in four years to make use of the Byron-Godwin-Shelley triangle (*Gothic* and *Haunted Summer* were the others) but they're mainly in this picture as atmospheric window dressing. John Hurt plays who else but an American scientist from the future who has created a machine that is raising havoc with time and space. He is not as conscience-stricken as he could be, and when he winds up in early 19th century Switzerland, he heads straight for the nearest tavern. He asks if he can share a table with who else but Raul Julia's Dr. Frankenstein? (Do you ever wonder why time travelers never seem to run into ordinary blokes?) Hurt is staggered by the quick realization that Dr. Frankenstein is not a very nice man and resolves to Do Something About It. He meets Mary Godwin (Bridget Fonda) at a witchcraft trial for a little girl accused of a murder committed by Dr. Frankenstein's monster. When Mary expresses sympathy for the child, he follows his literary idol to the Swiss retreat she shares with Byron and Shelley. "You're not English, are you?" a prissy Byron (Jason Patric) inquires after hearing John Hurt's thick British accent. "No," Hurt answers heartily. "I'm Dr. Joe from America!" Bridget Fonda, fetchingly costumed as Mary Godwin, is unable to help save the world from Frankenstein, because she hasn't even written the book yet! Her presence in the film is explained when Dr. Joe goes to bed with her. And that's all we ever see of Mary Godwin. Dr. Frankenstein continues to be not very nice and we finally see his monster. His makeup is overdone, his dialogue is overwritten, and Roger Corman gets to stage all sorts of violence he could never get away with at American International Pictures. He still cuts corners in inimitable Roger Corman fashion, though. *Frankenstein Unbound* was backed by investors from Italy where the movie was shot on location. But Swiss and Italian vegetation are quite different: to the best of our knowledge, there aren't any palm trees in the Swiss Alps, are there? The conclusion looks like it was shot in the property department for every science-fiction movie made in Italy since 1979. There are some nice touches: my favorite character was Dr. Joe's talking car, which has the capacity to run off copies of entire books. The look of the film is extremely lush, but the editing is sloppy, as if Corman started out to make a pretty good movie and then someone from outside the project slapped it together. *Frankenstein Unbound* was basically dumped by its eventual distributor, 20th Century Fox, but in spite of this cavalier treatment, it may attract a cult viewing audience. ***AKA:*** Roger Corman's Frankenstein Unbound. ☆☆½

1990 (R) 86m/C John Hurt, Raul Julia, Bridget Fonda, Jason Patric, Michael Hutchence, Catherine Rabett, Nick Brimble, Catherine Corman, Mickey Knox; ***D:*** Roger Corman; ***W:*** F.X. Feeney, Roger Corman; ***C:*** Melissa Torpy, Armando Nannuzzi; ***M:*** Carl Davis; ***V:*** Terri Treas. **VHS, LV, Closed Caption**

Frankie Starlight

Frankie Starlight was among my favorites at 1995's crop of films at the San Francisco International Film Festival. The stars on the record are Anne Parrillaud, Matt Dillon, and Gabriel Byrne, but the real stars are Alan Pentony and Corban Walker, who play the title character as a child and as an adult. The film shows what led up to Walker writing a novel about his tragic mother (Parrillaud) and her lovers (Byrne and Dillon), as well as the repercussions after his book is published. Also in the cast is young Georgina Cates, who created such a vivid impression in Mike Newell's *An Awfully Big Adventure* earlier in 1995. Michael Lindsay-Hogg directs this beautifully filmed tale by Chet Raymo and Ronan O'Leary. 🦴🦴🦴

1995 (R) 100m/C *IR* Corban Walker, Alan Pentony, Gabriel Byrne, Anne Parillaud, Matt Dillon, Georgina Cates, Darbnia Molloy, Niall Toibin, Rudi Davies; ***D:*** Michael Lindsay-Hogg; ***W:*** Chet Raymo, Ronan O'Leary; ***C:*** Paul Laufer; ***M:*** Elmer Bernstein. **VHS, LV, Closed Caption**

Free Tibet

The Free Tibet movie is a lot like the Free Tibet concert of June 1996: One Big Blur. To truly enjoy the two-day event at the Polo Fields in San Francisco's Golden Gate Park, you didn't have to be 14 years old, but it helped. You didn't have to be bombed (I wasn't), but it helped. You didn't have to be an amnesiac about better concerts of the '90s, but it helped. *Free Tibet* was a concept no one seemed to get but the organizers, and they tried to drill it into everyone's head with lectures, eyewitnesses, and literature, none of which the audience members would have paid 50 bucks to experience. The audience came for the bands: Beastie Boys, Biz Markie, Cibo Matto, Foo Fighters, Richie Havens, John Lee Hooker, Hugh Masekela, Pavement, Smashing Pumpkins, and A Tribe Called Quest on Saturday; Beck, Biork, Fugees, Buddy Guy, Ima, Yoko and Sean Lennon, Rage Against the Machine, Red Hot Chili Peppers, Skatalites, and Sonic Youth on Sunday. Most of the bands were whisked on and off stage within 30 minutes, so at the exact moment you were beginning to get into a set, it was over. It's even less satisfying in the film, because between the backstage blather bits and the stock footage of Tibet, you get a few seconds of this and that without knowing why (or if) they're important. With the best intentions in the world, Free Tibet was a shapeless concert and Sarah Pirozek's film reflects that shapelessness without adding anything new and/or illuminating. Some 14-year-old runaways in my vicinity were so excited that they were actually seeing and hearing what they thought was the 1996 equivalent of Woodstock. I hope they're not disillusioned by this film. There's time enough for shattered illusions when they're 17 and beyond. 🦴🦴

1998 90m/C ***D:*** Sarah Pirozek; ***C:*** Evan Bernard, Roman Coppola, Spike Jonze.

Freeway

To me, THIS is the golden age of the movies. To be sure, Hollywood studios are still the same cumbersome, second-guessing, bandwagon-climbing monstrosities they've always been. But in the bad old days, actors who wanted to try something different in the low-budget independent arena found themselves in professional coventry for the duration. Some of their careers never recovered from the industry impression that they were on the skids. Today, careers get jump starts, actors receive Academy recognition, and hot new directors generally do their best work away from the meddling mitts of major studio flunkies. Reese Witherspoon, for example, has played peaches-and-cream roles for the last five years: for MGM in *Man in the Moon,* for Disney in *A Far Off Place,* for Polygram in *S.F.W.* Who better to cast as the ultimate Little Red Riding Hood in Matthew Bright's abrasively funny and ferociously smart *Freeway.* As Vanessa Lutz, Witherspoon digs into the DNA of every disadvantaged kid who ever got shafted by society and comes up with a scary portrait of exactly what makes her tick...AND explode. Vanessa's history includes shoplifting, prostitution, arson, and violence, but she remains unjaded and achingly vulnerable. She is, in fact, the ideal target for the Big Bad Wolf (Kiefer Sutherland as Bob Wolverton), a misleadingly sympathetic pillar of society who works with kids and lives in a nice house with his pretty wife,

Bob (Barry Foster) and Brenda (Barbara Leigh-Hunt) in *Frenzy.* Universal; courtesy of the Kobal Collection

Brooke Shields (giving her career a much-needed jump start after three years of cinematic inactivity). Shields doesn't know about her hubby's secret stash of porno magazines or the fact that HE is the I-5 serial killer, preying on defenseless hookers. Vanessa has any number of remarkable dimensions to her character, but "defenseless" is not among them. On her way to Granny's trailer, she accepts a Spanish gun from a doomed boyfriend, so when Bob moves in for the kill, Vanessa is ready. But the movie doesn't end there, Big Bad Bob Wolverton being one of those invincible types who just doesn't know how to lie down dead after being riddled in the head and back with bullets. Bright still has a great deal to say about how society has a firm grip on deceptively obvious formulas that are far more easily assimilated than the truth. Sutherland has a blast-and-a-half as the Wolf, but if they gave Oscars for the most outstanding hitchhiker since Ann Savage snagged Tom Neal in 1945's *Detour,* Witherspoon would win for *Freeway* with NO serious competition. Don't miss this once-in-a-lifetime performance! 🦴🦴🦴🦴

1995 (R) 102m/C Reese Witherspoon, Kiefer Sutherland, Brooke Shields, Wolfgang Bodison, Dan Hedaya, Amanda Plummer, Bokeem Woodbine, Brittany Murphy; ***D:*** Matthew Bright; ***W:*** Matthew Bright; ***C:*** John Thomas; ***M:*** Danny Elfman. **VHS, Closed Caption**

French Provincial

A BORING movie starring Jeanne Moreau and Marie-France Pisier? Sad, but true. Moreau starts out as a laundress and winds up as the president of a factory. Marrying well helped, but very little else is

explained in this deliberately enigmatic film spanning the years 1900–75. After this far-from-gripping start, Andre Techine went on to a career as a world-class filmmaker, directing *The Brontë Sisters, Rendezvous, Scene of the Crime,* and *Wild Reeds.* **AKA:** Souvenirs d'en France. 🦴

1975 95m/C *FR* Jeanne Moreau, Michel Auclair, Marie-France Pisier, Orane Demazis, Claude Mann, Julien Guiomar, Michele Moretti, Aram Stephane; ***D:*** Andre Techine; ***W:*** Andre Techine, Marilyn Goldin; ***C:*** Bruno Nuytten; ***M:*** Philippe Sarde.

Frenzy

After *Psycho,* Alfred Hitchcock made *The Birds* and *Marnie* with Tippi Hedren, a beautiful former model with serious limitations as an actress, then *Torn Curtain,* with the miscast and mismatched Paul Newman and Julie Andrews, then *Topaz,* which is so boring that it hardly seems like a Hitchcock movie at all. When *Frenzy,* his first British film since 1950's *Stage Fright,* was released in June 1972, the advance word was that it was vintage Hitchcock. That it was, and then some. *Frenzy* is murder most explicit AND murder most subtle. Jon Finch, not a star and therefore not someone in whom the audience has any emotional investment, is bartender Richard Blaney. After he gets fired from his job, only fruit stand owner Bob Rusk (Barry Foster) and cocktail waitress Babs Milligan (Anna Massey) seem to like him, so when his former wife Brenda (Barbara Leigh-Hunt) is strangled, he's the prime suspect. We know he didn't do it, because we saw the whole thing—but the police aren't grilling us. Babs tries to help him and Bob tries to help him. Another murder occurs in broad daylight. We don't see this one, but even before we see the body, we can imagine every grisly detail as the camera retreats from both killer and victim back down the stairs and out onto the bustling street. Alec McCowen and Vivien Merchant are wonderful as Inspector and Mrs. Oxford. They discuss every graphic aspect of the case as she tries to force inedible "gourmet" food down his throat and he tries to toss and/or spit it out behind her back. For some reason, Mrs. Oxford believes in Mr. Blaney, and while her husband dreams of humble cups of tea and coffee in truck stop diners, she lists the points of evidence that show how Richard Blaney couldn't possibly have committed ANY murders, let alone two. Although we never feel the same as Mrs. Oxford does about Blaney, that's hardly the point. A character doesn't have to be likeable to be innocent of murder. The reverse is true, too, of course. The most charming and appealing people can also be murderers. *Frenzy,* a striking and disturbing film, may be the most personal of all Hitchcock's pictures. No one shoved a star down his throat this time, so there are none in sight, and thus no narrative compromises. The humor has never been darker, the sexual undercurrents have never been as obvious. Hitchcock doesn't show us what we expect to see—he shows us what we don't want to see. Except with the Oxfords, we are always off balance and uneasy. We don't feel relief when the credits roll because Blaney's deliverance means nothing to us; two people we liked are dead and now we know what happens behind closed doors, even in the daytime. Based on the Arthur La Bern novel *Goodbye Piccadilly, Farewell Leicester Square.* 🦴🦴🦴🦴

1972 (R) 116m/C *GB* Jon Finch, Barry Foster, Barbara Leigh-Hunt, Anna Massey, Alec McCowen, Vivien Merchant, Billie Whitelaw, Jean Marsh, Bernard Cribbins, Michael Bates, Rita Webb, Jimmy Gardner, Clive Swift, Madge Ryan, George Tovey, Noel Johnson; ***D:*** Alfred Hitchcock; ***W:*** Anthony Shaffer; ***C:*** Gilbert Taylor; ***M:*** Ron Goodwin. **VHS, LV**

Fresh

Twelve-year-old "Fresh" (Sean Nelson) is a New York drug runner, working for heroin dealer Esteban (Giancarlo Esposito) while living with his Aunt Frances (Cheryl Freeman) and his many female cousins. He isn't supposed to see his down-and-out dad Sam (Samuel L. Jackson), but does so anyway, and learns how to play speed chess with him. Chess, the ultimate war game, gives Fresh a strategy for survival when he becomes an eyewitness to two murders committed by a terrifying crack dealer named Jake (Jean LaMarre). Boaz Yakin gives us a bleak view of childhood and brings out outstanding performances

The Hound Salutes:
MARK RAPPAPORT
Director/writer, *From the Journals of Jean Seberg, Rock Hudson's Home Movies*

How do you make a filmed biography true? Ultimately, biography is more reflective of the person who wrote it than of the person it's about, and autobiography is a total tissue of lies. It depends on what you remember, what you're willing to tell. It's like that song in *Gigi*: "Ah, Yes, I Remember It Well." That whole notion of objectivity and truth really has to be questioned. I don't think I'm lying or telling the wrong thing. In fact, I use the films of Jean Seberg as my main text and those are not lies. You're seeing exactly what was shot, the way it was written, lit, directed, and edited. That's the original source material and the facts of her life are almost incidental. I'm not an investigative reporter—I don't go and interview people who have the true dope. In fact, when the film first opened in New York, Mike Wallace came to the screening! And, in the Q and A, this stentorian voice booms out, filling the whole theatre, 'Well, I knew Jean Seberg and you didn't (of course); how can you make these connections between her and Jane Fonda and Vanessa Redgrave?' I think it was interesting that he came to the film and, furthermore, stayed for the Q and A. Obviously, the film got to him on some level.

"Seberg's most important work, of course, is Godard's *Breathless,* and if you haven't see that, you must see it immediately. It's an astonishing movie and it's as fresh now as when it was first made in 1959. Working on this film, I would say that I've seen parts of it hundreds of times and it's still a kick in the head. It's a great movie and an amazing tonic and she's incomparably wonderful in it. It's hard to imagine what *Breathless* could or would have been without Jean Seberg."

Other JEAN SEBERG titles on video include: *Saint Joan, Bonjour Tristesse, The Mouse That Roared, Playtime, The Five Day Lover, Lilith, A Fine Madness, Pendulum, Paint Your Wagon, Macho Callahan,* and *Airport.*

from veterans Esposito and Jackson, and also from young Nelson and LaMarre. And the well-developed chess angle provides *Fresh* with a fascinating, if cynical resolution. ☙☙☙

1994 (R) 114m/C *FR* Samuel L. Jackson, Giancarlo Esposito, Sean Nelson, N'Bushe Wright, Ron Brice, Jean LaMarre, Luis Lantigua, Yul Vazquez, Cheryl Freeman; ***D:*** Boaz Yakin; ***W:*** Boaz Yakin; ***C:*** Adam Holender. Independent Spirit Awards '95: Debut Performance (Nelson); Sundance Film Festival '94: Special Jury Prize, Filmmakers Trophy; Nominations: Independent Spirit Awards '95: Best Supporting Actor (Esposito). **VHS, LV, Closed Caption**

Fright

This is THE babysitter movie to watch when you're alone with a baby whose parents have gone out for dinner and your boyfriend wants to keep you company and you suspect that the baby's mother might have a homicidal ex-husband lurking about the house. This is Amanda's (Susan George) dilemma, and what she faces when nice Dr. and Mrs. Helen Cordell (John Gregson and Honor Blackman) leave her to mind baby Tara for the evening wouldn't even BEGIN to happen to any member of the Baby-Sitters Club. Saturated with blood and violence, *Fright* offers George a strong part as the resourceful Amanda, and also gives Ian Bannen plenty of chances to chew up the scenery. Baby Tara (the director's child) is cute. ***AKA:*** Night Legs.

1971 (PG) 84m/C *GB* Susan George, Honor Blackman, Ian Bannen, John Gregson, George Cole, Dennis Waterman, Tara Collinson, Maurice Kaufman, Michael Brennan, Roger Lloyd Pack; ***D:*** Peter Collinson; ***W:*** Tudor Gates; ***C:*** Ian Wilson; ***M:*** Harry Robinson. **VHS**

The Frightened City

The Frightened City has oodles of repeat value because the plot will zoom out of your head five minutes after you see it. Herbert Lom and John Gregson star as Waldo Zhernikov and Detective Inspector Sayers, and Sean Connery is billed third as Paddy Damion. His hairline is quite high here, so I suspect that IS a rug he's wearing in 1962's *Dr. No* and all the subsequent Bond films. All the pretty girls wear tight, low-cut dresses, and director John Lemont never misses a chance to emphasize their best assets—including their navels during one dance sequence in a nightclub. He's wise to do that because all the musical numbers here are ghastly. We see Connery doing manly things from the start, like judo, and then we watch him take a shower and change into an undershirt, slacks, and tight pullover shirt with no tie. There's plenty of American-style thugs in this one, with names like Tanky Thomas, Nero, Sanchetti, Salty Brewer, Lippy Green, and Basher Prebble (you get the idea), and many, many fights, which are a relief after all that singing and dancing. Composer Norrie Paramor, who appears here as the Taboo Club's pianist, wrote the film's featured songs, "Marvelous Lie" and "I Laughed at Love" with lyricist Bunny Lewis. Produced by Lemont and screenwriter Leigh Vance.

1961 91m/B *GB* Herbert Lom, John Gregson, Sean Connery, Alfred Marks, Yvonne Romain, Kenneth Griffith, Olive McFarland, Frederick Piper, John Stone, David Davies, Tom Bowman, Robert Cawdron, Norrie Paramor; ***D:*** John Lemont; ***W:*** Leigh Vance; ***C:*** Desmond Dickinson; ***M:*** Norrie Paramor. **VHS, Closed Caption**

From Hollywood to Deadwood

An interesting blend of humor and the private eye genre can be found in Rex Pickett's *From Hollywood to Deadwood.* Pickett's clever script helped to bolster the wonderful rapport between the two leads, played by San Francisco Bay Area actors Scott Paulin and Jim Haynie. They play two private eyes in search of Lana Dark, a mysterious actress who fled in the middle of her latest movie. Haynie and Paulin bring a likeable, self-effacing quality to their scuzzy roles, but Barbara Schock can't act worth beans in the film's pivotal role. Still, this is a pretty good little film.

1989 (R) 90m/C Scott Paulin, Jim Haynie, Barbara Schock; ***D:*** Rex Pickett; ***W:*** Rex Pickett; ***C:*** Peter Deming. **VHS, LV, Closed Caption**

From the Journals of Jean Seberg

Jean Seberg was a pretty blonde from Iowa who was voted "most likely to succeed" when she graduated from high school in 1956. The following year, she was the first teenager to play *Saint Joan* onscreen. She received enormous publicity prior to the film's release, but both Seberg and director Otto Preminger were raked over the coals by critics and audiences alike. (The Harvard Lampoon cited *Saint Joan* as the worst film of the century 1857–1957 and complained that Seberg was "soporific as a saint and insipid as a sinner.") After a start like that, there was nowhere to go but up, or back to Iowa. Seberg chose to make another film with Pre-

Gerald (Tom Wilkinson), Nathan (William Snape), Gaz (Robert Carlyle), Lomper (Steve Huison), Guy (Hugo Speer), Horse (Paul Barber), and Dave (Mark Addy) in *The Full Monty.* Fox Searchlight; courtesy of the Kobal Collection

minger, *Bonjour Tristesse.* If that movie had been her first, the career of Jean Seberg might have been quite different. As it was, her good work in her second movie still supplied her with a shot at international stardom in the heady early days of the French New Wave. Jean-Luc Godard's *Breathless,* written by François Truffaut and co-starring Jean-Paul Belmondo, gave Seberg her most fondly remembered role. As an American teen selling the N.Y. *Herald Tribune* on the streets of Paris, she was vivid and affecting, and her ultra-short haircut and off-the-rack wardrobe launched a new look for young girls of the late '50s to emulate. Jean Seberg appeared to be here to stay, but like her sophisticated facade, the public illusion was more persuasive than her private reality. Despite fine performances in dozens of underrated domestic and French movies, Seberg's life and career may well have been doomed from the moment she left her Midwestern home in Marshalltown. In *From the Journals of Jean Seberg,* Mark Rappaport's fictitious approach to her life, a former babysitting charge who grew up around the corner from Seberg tells the story of a sensitive small-town girl driven to professional and personal despair. Mary Beth Hurt, then 47, plays the Jean Seberg who might have been, had she overcome the tragedy of her life with Rappaport's blessed sense of irony. The film traces the work of such contemporaries as Jane Fonda and Vanessa Redgrave, who achieved greater fame and recognition than Seberg and were better protected emotionally during their days of political activism. The fragile Seberg tried to kill herself annually on the anniversary of her baby daughter's death, after being hounded by the FBI who leaked false rumors that the premature infant had been fathered by a Black Panther. In *From the Journals of Jean Seberg,* Rappaport (who also assembled 1992's *Rock Hudson's Home Movies*) tells an immensely sad story with effective detail and compassionate honesty.

1995 97m/C *D:* Mark Rappaport; *W:* Mark Rappaport; *C:* Mark Daniels. **VHS, DVD**

From the Pole to the Equator

Even if avant-garde film isn't your favorite type of movie, I highly recommend what Yervant Gianikian and Angela Ricci Lucchi have done with *From the Pole to the Equator.* These two filmmakers from Milan assembled their film from 35mm nitrate originals shot in 1910 by early Italian cinematographer Luca Comerio. Comerio traveled with an adventuring baron named Franchetti and captured some extraordinary footage of faraway lands, as well as early films of land and air vehicles. The old movies are in variable condition and are reprinted and hand-tinted by Gianikian and Ricci Lucchi, who add an effective score by California musicians Keith Ullrich and Charles Anderson. I couldn't take my eyes off the screen for the full 96 minutes when I saw it in 1987 at the Pacific Film Archive, and I predict that *From the Pole to the Equator* may have the same effect on those who discover it on a video shelf. 🦴🦴🦴

1987 96m/C *IT GB* ***D:*** Yervant Gianikian, Angela Ricci Lucchi; ***M:*** Keith Ullrich, Charles Anderson.

The Full Monty

There were a number of feel-good date movies in 1997: *The Full Monty* and *Good Will Hunting* were among them. They were both mainly about guys, but gals didn't mind going to see them because the male stars were so cute, did cute things, et cetera. In *The Full Monty,* they had cute butts. The word I heard over and over again from delirious fans about this Brit indie is "original." I'm reminded of a college dee jay who was offered five bucks an hour to do drive-time radio in a small town because the departing dee jay wanted to work full time at Safeway and when she asked about the local social life, she received a three-word reply before she turned down the job: "Unemployed married men." That's Gaz (Robert Carlyle), Dave (Mark Addy), and Gerald (Tom Wilkinson) in Sheffield for you. Along with Guy (Hugo Speer), Horse (Paul Barber), and Lomper (Steve Huison), they pick up some extra change by doing "The Full Monty": stripping in a nightclub. And that's the whole movie. Labor leaders lauded this film for its sympathetic portrayal of jobless workers, male and female audiences thought it was side-splitting, and I just thought, if you wouldn't want to go near Gaz-Dave-Gerald-Guy-Horse-Lomper in a town like Sheffield, why would you want to spend a whole movie with them just so you could see them without their skivvies? 🦴🦴🦴

1996 (R) 90m/C *GB* Robert Carlyle, Tom Wilkinson, Mark Addy, Steve Huison, William Snape, Paul Barber, Hugo Speer; ***D:*** Peter Cattaneo; ***W:*** Simon Beaufoy; ***C:*** John de Borman; ***M:*** Anne Dudley. Academy Awards '97: Best Original Musical/Comedy Score; British Academy Awards '97: Best Actor (Carlyle), Best Film, Best Supporting Actor (Wilkinson); Screen Actors Guild Award '97: Cast; Nominations: Academy Awards '97: Best Director (Cattaneo), Best Original Screenplay, Best Picture; Australian Film Institute '98: Best Foreign Film; British Academy Awards '97: Best Director (Cattaneo), Best Film Editing, Best Original Screenplay, Best Sound, Best Supporting Actor (Addy), Best Supporting Actress (Sharp), Best Score; Golden Globe Awards '98: Best Film—Musical/Comedy; MTV Movie Awards '98: Best Dance Sequence (Cast); Writers Guild of America '97: Best Original Screenplay. **VHS**

Fun

The past and the future are in color in *Fun,* the present is in grim black and white. The protagonists are two very young girls who share confidences and cuddle after spending the most fun day they'll ever have together. What's their idea of fun? Going to malls, hanging out, playing games, ringing doorbells, and yelling at the occupants. Oh, and brutally stabbing to death a sweet little old lady who is kind to them. Why? Counselor Leslie Hope and journalist William R. Moses attempt to find out during the course of this very disturbing character study, based on James Bosley's play. Renee Humphrey and Alicia Witt are remarkable as two troubled teens who manipulate their adult interrogators and resist every effort from those who want to help them understand their crime. Plenty of nightmares here! 🦴🦴🦴

1994 95m/C Alicia Witt, Renee Humphrey, Leslie Hope, William R. Moses, Ania Suli; ***D:*** Rafal

When Shade's good, she's very good. But when Trudi's bad, she's better.

—Tagline from the movie *Gas Food Lodging.*

Zielinksi; ***W:*** James Bosley; ***C:*** Jens Sturup; ***M:*** Marc Tschantz. Nominations: Independent Spirit Awards '95: Debut Performance (Witt), First Screenplay. **VHS**

The Funeral

Johnny Tempio (Vincent Gallo) has been murdered, and as Ray (Christopher Walken) and Chez (Christopher Penn) recall their brother's short life at his funeral, they are obsessed with avenging his death. Whodunit? Gangster Gaspare Spoglia (Benicio Del Toro)? Ray's and Chez's wives (Annabella Sciorra and Isabella Rossellini) don't care. They are in love with their husbands and don't want them to die. "When I'm dead, I'm gonna roast in Hell. I believe that," Walken as Ray says as only he can, then he adds fatalistically, "The trick is to get used to it." What the Tempio brothers choose to get used to may not be what viewers want to get used to, but *The Funeral,* set in the '30s and scripted by Nicholas *(King of New York)* St. John (instead of Abel Ferrara himself) is at least a full notch above the mindless symbolic whack-off of *Bad Lieutenant,* with sterling performances by all. ♪♪♪

1996 (R) 96m/C Christopher Walken, Benicio Del Toro, Vincent Gallo, Christopher Penn, Isabella Rossellini, Annabella Sciorra, John Ventimiglia, Paul Hipp, Gretchen Mol; ***D:*** Abel Ferrara; ***W:*** Nicholas St. John; ***C:*** Ken Kelsch; ***M:*** Joe Delia. Nominations: Independent Spirit Awards '97: Best Actor (Penn), Best Cinematography, Best Director (Ferrara), Best Film, Best Screenplay. **VHS**

Funny Bones

For me, the jewel of 1995's San Francisco International Film Festival was Peter Chelsom's *Funny Bones,* about which the less said the better. *Funny Bones* really must be seen to be believed and appreciated. This very black comedy stars young American character actor Oliver Platt and young Britcom newcomer Lee Evans. The film's extremely dark undercurrents aren't just plot driven—they give *Funny Bones* its emotional core. Shot at the legendary comedy factory of Ealing Studios, on location in Las Vegas, and in Blackpool, *Funny Bones* is the ideal blend of Golden Age tradition and Chelsom's cutting edge humor. What are Jerry Lewis, Ruta Lee, Oliver Reed, Leslie Caron, and Harold Nicholas all doing in the same movie? The enormous risks taken in *Funny Bones* wouldn't be nearly as breathtaking without their combined 231 years of razor-sharp timing and onscreen charisma. ♪♪♪

1994 (R) 128m/C Oliver Platt, Lee Evans, Leslie Caron, Jerry Lewis, Oliver Reed, Ian McNeice, Ruta Lee, Richard Griffith, George Carl, Freddie Davies; ***D:*** Peter Chelsom; ***W:*** Peter Chelsom, Peter Flannery; ***C:*** Eduardo Berra; ***M:*** John Altman. **VHS, LV, Closed Caption**

Gal Young 'Un

Winner of the Grand Jury Prize at the Sundance Film Festival in 1981, *Gal Young 'Un* is set during the Prohibition era, in which a rich, middle-aged woman living on her property in the Florida backwoods finds herself courted by a much younger man. She discovers she is being used to help him set up a moonshining business. Unsentimental story of a strong woman, based on a Marjorie Kinnan Rawlings story. Director Victor Nunez won his second Grand Jury Prize at the Sundance Film Festival in 1993 for *Ruby in Paradise,* starring 1994's Independent Spirit Award winning actress Ashley Judd. ♪♪♪

1979 105m/C Dana Preu, David Peck, J. Smith, Timothy McCormack, Gene Densmore, Jenny Stringfellow; ***D:*** Victor Nunez; ***W:*** Victor Nunez; ***C:*** Victor Nunez. Sundance Film Festival '81: Grand Jury Prize. **VHS**

Galileo

A fine supporting cast somewhat compensates for the casting of over-the-top Topol as Galileo. Otherwise, another American Film Theatre production with nothing special to recommend it. (*Galileo* was released theatrically overseas in 1976.) ♪♪½

1973 145m/C *GB CA* Chaim Topol, Edward Fox, Michael (Michel) Lonsdale, Richard O'Callaghan, Tom Conti, Mary Larkin, Judy Parfitt, John McEnery, Patrick Magee, Michael Gough, Colin Blakely, Clive Revill, Georgia Brown, Tim Woodward, John Gielgud, Margaret Leighton, Henry Woolf, Ronald Radd, Madeleine Smith; ***D:*** Joseph Losey; ***W:*** Joseph Losey, Bertolt Brecht, Barbara Bray; ***C:*** Michael Reed; ***M:*** Hanns Eisler. **VHS**

The Garden

This is the Melanie Griffith movie very few American audiences have ever seen. At a 1977 press conference during the San Francisco International Film Festival, several catty reviewers asked why SHE had been cast. One of its creators later told me, "Everyone seems to be making fun of us for casting Melanie Griffith in the movie. But she was the best American actress who would take her clothes off that we could get!" Well, the future Oscar nominee IS pretty awful as an ersatz angel. But the real star of the film is Jerusalem, which has never been lovelier, especially with Valery Galperin behind the camera. Victor Nord's interpretation of Yoseff Avissar's whimsical script is deft and there are some good performances here, most notably by Shai K. Ophir and Tuvio Tavi. 🦴🦴

1977 93m/C *IS* Shai K. Ophir, Melanie Griffith, Tuvio Tavi, Tsachi Noi, Shoshanah Duer, Seadia Damar; ***D:*** Victor Nord; ***W:*** Yosef Avissar; ***C:*** Valery Galperin; ***M:*** Noah Shariff.

Gas Food Lodging

This Allison Anders film takes its time showing the lives of waitress Nora (Brooke Adams) and her daughters Trudi (Ione Skye) and Shade (Fairuza Balk). The best thing about the movie is Balk's award-winning performance as a teenager confused by the haphazard life she shares with her mother and sister. James Brolin makes a classy, lived-in appearance as Shade's dad, John. Aside from that, things seem to lumber along almost as slowly in this one as they would in 1993's *Ruby in Paradise* by Victor Nunez (except *Ruby* is 15 minutes longer). Skye and Donovan Leitch are real-life siblings. Shot on location in Deming, New Mexico. 🦴🦴

1992 (R) 100m/C Brooke Adams, Ione Skye, Fairuza Balk, James Brolin, Rob Knepper, Donovan Leitch, David Lansbury, Jacob Vargas, Chris Mulkey, Tiffany Anders; ***D:*** Allison Anders; ***W:*** Allison Anders; ***C:*** Dean Lent; ***M:*** J. Mascis, Barry Adamson. Independent Spirit Awards '93: Best Actress (Balk). **VHS, LV, Letterbox, Closed Caption**

Gaslight

People who pine for the good old days when Hollywood studios had a stranglehold on the worldwide film industry might appreciate how good old MGM made an international hit out of 1944's *Gaslight. Gaslight* was originally made in England four years earlier with Diana Wynyard and Anton Walbrook. Since neither Wynyard nor Walbrook were MGM stars, what's a rich powerful studio to do? Bingo! Buy up all the prints, suppress them, and make a big, expensive movie with REAL stars, like Ingrid Bergman and Charles Boyer. I'm not knocking Bergman and Boyer. Two of Bergman's Swedish hits had already been re-made in Hollywood: *Intermezzo* with Bergman herself and *A Woman's Face* with Joan Crawford. But this original version, with far more subtle direction and performances, is actually far more terrifying than the best that Hollywood could buy! Only menacing teenager Angela Lansbury, as Hollywood's Nancy, is WAY superior to the original Nancy, Cathleen Cordell. Interestingly, Lansbury's mother, Moyna MacGill, has a small role in the first movie. You can still dig the re-make and deplore MGM's strategy in (nearly) destroying every trace of the existence of this film. ***AKA:*** Angel Street. 🦴🦴🦴🦴

1940 88m/C *GB* Anton Walbrook, Diana Wynyard, Frank Pettingell, Cathleen Cordell, Robert Newton, Jimmy Hanley, Minnie Rayner, Mary Hinton, Marie Wright, Jack Barty, Moyna MacGill, Darmora Ballet; ***D:*** Thorold Dickinson; ***W:*** A.H. Rawlinson, Bridget Boland; ***C:*** Bernard Knowles; ***M:*** Richard Addinsell. **VHS**

Genevieve

Genevieve is the perfect movie to watch when you're in the world's worst mood; it will cheer you up in no time. John Gregson and Kenneth More are two antique car buffs obsessed with winning the annual Brighten-to-London run. Dinah Sheridan and Kay Kendall are along for the ride. That's all there is to it, but with that cast and the gifted Henry Cornelius at the helm, *Genevieve* is fondly remembered as the brightest British comedy of the year. Not too many people remember Kay

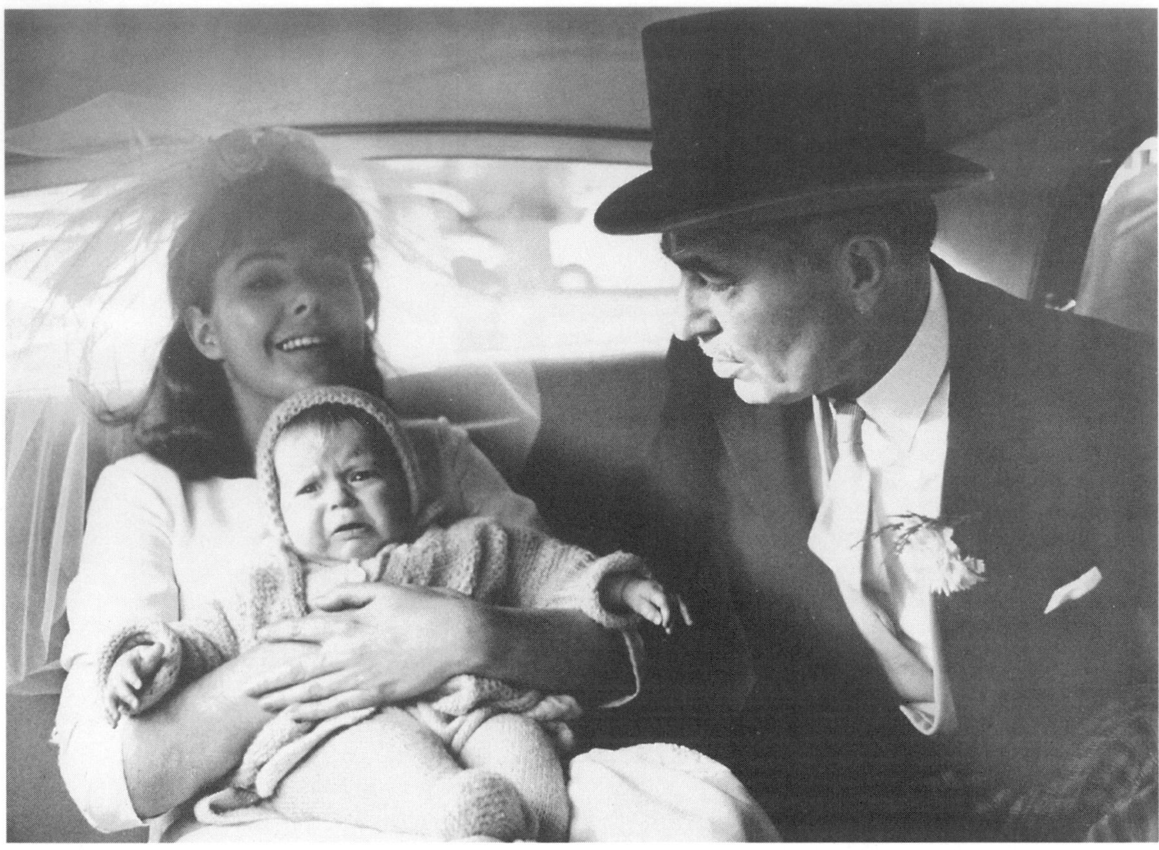

Georgy (Lynn Redgrave) and James (James Mason) in *Georgy Girl.*
Columbia; courtesy of the Kobal Collection

Kendall today, but with her breakthrough film *Genevieve,* she emerged as the funniest comedienne to hit the silver screen since Carole Lombard. Kendall played a trumpet-playing model with a huge dog named Suzy who's stuck for the weekend with the canine-loathing More. All four leads were charming in the film, but the extremely droll Kendall was the real surprise. William Rose's screenplay and Larry Adler's harmonica score (both Oscar nominees) added to the infectious fun, and the well-chosen supporting cast included one-time Sherlock Holmes star Arthur Wontner (1875–1960) and the delightful Joyce Grenfell. Not to mention that splendid title character in three-strip Technicolor! 🦴🦴🦴🦴

1953 86m/C *GB* John Gregson, Dinah Sheridan, Kenneth More, Kay Kendall, Geoffrey Keen, Reginald Beckwith, Arthur Wontner, Joyce Grenfell, Leslie Mitchell, Michael Medwin, Michael Balfour, Edie Martin, Harold Siddons; ***D:*** Henry Cornelius; ***W:*** William Rose; ***C:*** Christopher Challis; ***M:*** Larry Adler. British Academy Awards '53: Best Film; Golden Globe Awards '55: Best Foreign Film; Nominations: Academy Awards '54: Best Story & Screenplay, Best Original Score. **VHS**

Georgia

Addison DeWitt is alive and well and residing in the offices of *Time* magazine. His name these days is Richard Corliss, but his critical approach is the same, and one of his 1995 critiques is even semi-cobbled from *All About Eve.* Luckily, Richard Corliss was ineligible for 1995's Academy Awards. Unluckily he seemed to believe that he was on some sort of a mission from God to keep Jennifer Jason Leigh from winning an Oscar for her remarkable performance in *Georgia.* Leigh, claimed Corliss, is too "small" to deserve the critical raves she's received ever since *Georgia* was screened at Cannes in the spring of 1995. Such praise was like a "migraine" to Corliss and he insisted that "this racket must cease." Because he said so, of course. Because Leigh is good enough for cable but not for Oscar. Because she's so "very, very bad." Any poor dear who thinks otherwise must be delusional or at least "mistaken" about what constitutes good acting. *Georgia,* an outstanding independent release, was not made for the Addison DeWitts of this planet. Jennifer Jason Leigh is nothing short of electrifying as Sadie Flood, a down-and-out, not particularly talented singer who drinks and drugs up a storm while draining everyone who comes near her. Her far more gifted sister Georgia (beautifully played by Oscar-nominee Mare Winningham) wisely protects herself from Sadie's whirlwind existence, but at a price. Georgia is so self-contained that her life is blessed with every trapping of success but joy. When the sisters are together, their collective loneliness fills up the screen. Films that have attempted to show the lives of musicians at their grittiest always seem to miss several beats when it comes to conveying emotional honesty. Other writers and directors have tried to capture the Sadies and Georgias of the world, but never with such depth and passion. That's why Barbara Turner's skillfully constructed screenplay and Ulu Grosbard's scrupulous direction give the two stars such crucial support. Each and every character in *Georgia* brings a unique voice that supplies strong counterpoint to the hermetically sealed alliance between the sisters. Particularly fine performances are contributed here by Ted Levine and Max Perlich as the men in their lives. And Leigh and Winningham will tear the heart out of any innocent audience member who still has a pulse. Whichever way you look at it (unless you happen to be a latter-day Addison De HALF Witt!), *Georgia* is a tremendous achievement. I've already seen it six times (and counting!). 🎞🎞🎞🎞

1995 (R) 117m/C Jennifer Jason Leigh, Mare Winningham, Ted Levine, Max Perlich, John Doe, John C. Reilly, Jimmy Witherspoon; ***D:*** Ulu Grosbard; ***W:*** Barbara Turner; ***C:*** Jan Kiesser. Independent Spirit Awards '96: Best Supporting Actress (Winningham); Montreal World Film Festival '95: Best Actress (Leigh), Best Film; New York Film Critics Awards '95: Best Actress (Leigh); Nominations: Academy Awards '95: Best Supporting Actress (Winningham); Independent Spirit Awards '96: Best Actress (Leigh), Best Director (Grosbard), Best Supporting Actor (Perlich); Screen Actors Guild Award '95: Best Supporting Actress (Winningham). **VHS, LV, Closed Caption**

Georgy Girl

1966 was a heady year for the Redgrave sisters: both Lynn and Vanessa received Academy Award nominations for Best Actress. Elizabeth Taylor won that year, but Lynn and Vanessa established secure places for themselves on the international movie map. From then on, Michael Redgrave was more likely to be referred to as their father than they were to be mentioned in footnotes as simply his daughters. In many ways, *Georgy Girl* was a brave gamble for 23-year-old Lynn. Although she gained weight for the role, many audiences thought that Lynn WAS the hefty Georgy, and she seldom played willowy heroines in her subsequent career. But the whole point of the movie was that a girl didn't have to be a dolly bird (like Georgy's drop-dead-gorgeous roommate Meredith) to attract men and lead a fulfilling life. When we see Georgy dancing with a group of children, we can see that she's as free as the air when she isn't worried about peer judgments. And then there's James Leamington (deftly played by James Mason, then 57) who loves Georgy exactly as she is. As the movie begins, he's too old and serious for her, but as Georgy's life takes its course, what she needs takes precedence over what she thinks she wants. Meredith (played to the hilt by 21-year-old Charlotte Rampling) is a bored, conscienceless vamp who doesn't care about Georgy or her many boyfriends and who definitely doesn't give a damn about the prospect of motherhood. When she decides not to abort her latest baby, Georgy is in heaven. Glowing with joy about the prospect of a vicarious pregnancy, she rushes around getting ready for the new arrival. In the process, she becomes desirable to Mered-

> "You don't know what it means to us to see something that's not new."
>
> **—Peggy Martin (Jean Parker) tries to express her appreciation for antiques in *The Ghost Goes West.***

ith's boyfriend (played by the impossibly young and sexy Alan Bates, then 32) and he falls head over heels in love with her. By that point, so has everyone in the audience, and this is what made *Georgy Girl* so refreshing in 1966. Georgy is beautiful for who she is, not how she looks. In contrast, the selfish Meredith seems like a flavor of the month gone sour. This simple statement, filmed in a fast-paced, irresistible style by Silvio Narizzano, gave *Georgy Girl* plenty of repeat value in the decades to come. Lynn Redgrave's unforgettable portrait of Georgy with her uninhibited zest for life plus the droll dirty old man captured to perfection by James Mason will still be a pleasure to watch in 2016. ♪♪♪♪

1966 100m/B *GB* Lynn Redgrave, James Mason, Charlotte Rampling, Alan Bates, Bill Owen, Claire Kelly, Rachel Kempson, Denise Coffey, Dorothy Alison, Peggy Thorpe-Bates, Dandy Nichols; ***D:*** Silvio Narizzano; ***W:*** Margaret Forster, Peter Nichols; ***C:*** Ken Higgins. Golden Globe Awards '67: Best Actress—Musical/Comedy (Redgrave); New York Film Critics Awards '66: Best Actress (Redgrave); Nominations: Academy Awards '66: Best Actress (Redgrave), Best Black and White Cinematography, Best Song ("Georgy Girl"), Best Supporting Actor (Mason). **VHS, LV**

The Ghost Goes West

Robert Donat plays a dual role here as Murdoch and Donald Ghourie. Eugene Pallette is Joe Martin, who wants to buy a Scottish castle and take it home with him to Florida. Jean Parker is Joe's pretty daughter, Peggy. The only thing is the ghost has to stay with the castle, so when Joe and Peggy leave with their new purchase, the ghost goes with them. With Robert Sherwood and Geoffrey Kerr as screenwriters and the great Rene Clair at the helm, *The Ghost Goes West* promised to be very special, and it was. The fine supporting cast adds to the fun and you haven't lived 'til you've seen Eugene Pallette in a kilt! ♪♪♪

1936 90m/B *GB* Robert Donat, Jean Parker, Eugene Pallette, Elsa Lanchester, Ralph Bunker, Patricia Hilliard, Everley Gregg, Mortan Selten, Chili Bouchier, Mark Daly, Herbert Lomas, Elliot Mason, Jack Lambert, Hay Petrie; ***D:*** Rene Clair; ***W:*** Robert Sherwood, Geoffrey Kerr; ***C:*** Harold Rosson. **VHS**

Gimme Shelter

I was invited to the Altamont concert on Saturday, December 6, 1969, but the prospect of a free Rolling Stones concert was pretty terrifying for anyone with even a mild strain of agoraphobia so I declined. When I saw the Maysles Brothers magnificent film of the concert nearly 30 years later, I was stunned that they'd somehow managed to include one of the people who invited me: I'll never be able to get the image of that kid (staggering through the crowd while stoned to the gills) out of my head. Whatever happened to that kid and all the other kids that dozens of camera people—including George Lucas, Stephen Lighthill, and the late Peter (*Word Is Out*) Adair—recorded for all time? It was like watching some of the very first flickering images of the 1890s: Who were these people? What were they thinking about? Where were they going? Were they happy? Were their lives long or short? We know the fate of at least four of the audience members: three died in accidents and one, Meredith Hunter, was stabbed to death while the cameras were rolling. We know that Mick Jagger, Keith Richard, and Charlie Watts are still touring with the Stones, and that Bill Wyman and Mick Taylor are not. We know that Ike and Tina Turner broke up and that Tina is still a major force in the musical industry. We know that Jerry Garcia died at 53 in 1995 and the Grateful Dead disbanded shortly thereafter, although the members continue to play together and with other groups. The Jefferson Airplane and Crosby, Stills, and Nash are covered exhaustively on Video Hits One Profiles. Producer Bill Graham died at 60 in a helicopter crash after a concert on a dark and stormy night in 1991 and Melvin Belli, the Stones temporary lawyer, outlived him by five years, dying at 88 in 1996. But what the Maysles Brothers did in the year it took to edit and assemble *Gimme Shelter* was show a day in history that marked the end of one way of looking at the rock world and the beginning of another, much darker perspective. All through the '60s, rock 'n' roll music had been good clean fun, because good clean fun made money. *Woodstock,* which took forever to organize, looks happy and peaceful, because no one's going to make a movie about someone who's trapped in a car due to traffic gridlock and thus never makes it to the concert. The Altamont concert took less than a day to organize and it's obvious. A pharmaceuticals vendor peddles "Hashish, LSD, Psilocybin" as if they were popcorn, hot dogs, and cotton candy. Long before the concert started, people were experiencing psychotic reactions to the drugs and it is painful to watch. Tina Turner is great as always, an oasis before the Hells Angels, drunk on all the free beer they could stand, began to clash not only with kids on impure drug cocktails, but with the musicians themselves. Marty Balin of the Jefferson Airplane was knocked out by a Hell's Angel and an unrepentant Angel simply roared back when band mate Paul Kantner publicly complained. Grace Slick momentarily succeeded in neutralizing the situation, but the Angels were enraged when anyone went near their motorcycles or challenged their authority. They acted as if treating the Angels with respect, NOT listening to the music, was the whole point of the concert. When Mick Jagger (with a cultivated Cockney accent) is onstage, he talks to the crowd like a substitute teacher and is just as ineffective. The final moments of the concert are so violent, hellish, and out of control, it's no wonder that Jagger, who is filmed muttering, "Horrible..." while watching the concert footage later, looks like a threatened animal caught in the headlights of a car. The ghosts of Altamont haunted concert organizers for years as they planned every detail of every show WAY in advance. And of course the law took a firmer position on the safety measures established for guiding and controlling crowds. Would the December 1969 concert have been as ill-fated if it had been held in Golden Gate Park, the Stones' first choice of venue? Well, it wasn't held in Golden Gate Park because of fears about substance abuse and, as the Maysles Brothers make crystal clear in *Gimme Shelter,* substance abuse (and lousy planning) led straight to the Altamont disaster. But time passes and, 25 years later, a Rolling Stones concert was no more than a backdrop for a *Beverly Hills 90210* episode about Donna Martin, Ray Pruitt, Kelly Taylor, Steve Sanders, Claire Arnold, David Silver, Andrea Zuckerman, and Brandon Walsh. ♪♪♪♪

1970 91m/C Mick Jagger, Keith Richards, Charlie Watts, Bill Wyman, Mick Taylor, Marty Balin, Grace Slick, Paul Kantner, The Jefferson Airplane, Jerry Garcia, The Grateful Dead, David Crosby, Stephen Stills, Graham Nash, Tina Turner, Ike Turner, Melvin Belli, Bill Graham; ***D:*** David Maysles, Al Maysles, Charlotte Zwerlin; ***C:*** Haskell Wexler; ***M:*** Rolling Stones. **VHS, LV**

Girl Gang

This stunning film, which appears to violate every single item in the then-current production code, was considered lost for over 40 years. Joanne Arnold is a tall, voluptuous brunette who'll do anything for a fix, and Timothy *(Glen or Glenda?)* Farrell is the sleaziest dope dealer you'll ever see. *Girl Gang* reveals, in graphic detail, exactly how to shoot heroin PLUS how to remove a bullet from a college girl on a kitchen table (she doesn't make it). To join the local dope club, girls must have sex with five guys whether the girls (OR the guys) want to or not; it's a RULE! The acting and everything else about this shocking expose/searing indictment/lousy movie (take your pick) is dreadful, but you may not be able to keep from staring at it, like bugs under a rock. Expected to be available on video soon for Farrell's many loyal fans. **woof!**

1954 60m/B Joanne Arnold, Timothy Farrell; ***D:*** Robert Derteno.

Girlfriends

Nobody asked me, but I always thought that Melanie Mayron was among the most appealing actresses of her generation in the days when she created delightful characters like Ginger, Marsha, and Susan in enjoyable flicks like *Harry and Tonto, Car Wash,* and *Girlfriends.* She was healthy, self-possessed, and reassuring, with no actressy mannerisms or ticks. Even though Mayron, then 26, was cast as a young photographer opposite some formidable actors in *Girlfriends* (Bob Balaban, Christopher Guest,

The Hound Salutes:

JIM MCKAY AND ANNA GRACE

Girls Town

Jim McKay: "We sent the Sundance Film Festival a rough cut of *Girls Town* while it was still on video and called back a few times to see how it was doing. Thankfully, the people who saw it liked it and trusted that we could finish it in time to have it shown at the festival itself. I hadn't done any prior narrative projects. This was my first film. I had worked on short pieces on documentaries and music videos. I studied acting for nine months before we did the workshop for *Girls Town,* but I felt like coming out of my experience in a non-narrative world and not having worked with actors before, I needed to get with that, so that I knew what I was doing and could really understand and work with actors. For me, this process was how I wanted to develop a project because stylistically, I was looking for something that was very realistic and true to life and the language was right and the characters were right. Not having had the experience of being a teenage girl, I felt like it made sense to open up that thing and work with other people on it. We definitely made the film primarily for teenage girls. It turns out that everyone's relating to it and everyone's enjoying it, but if there's an audience that we would love to see it, it's teenage girls. I think it's one of the few films that gives

Kathryn Walker, Eli Wallach, Amy Wright, Kristopher Tabori, and the late Viveca Lindfors, Mike Kellin, and Kenneth McMillan), she walked off with the movie. But Warner Bros. in 1978 wasn't Warner Bros. in 1938. There were no Melanie Mayron projects in the works. Instead, there were a long series of prestigious character roles. By 1987, a lean, re-sculpted Mayron emerged as Melissa Steadman on *thirtysomething* (ABC, 1987–91). She was playing a photographer again, and she won her first Emmy, but she looked sad-eyed and high-strung, perfect for the series, but rather less so for those who remember her natural *joie de vivre* as Susan Weinblatt. (A hint of that playful quality could be seen when she played a cop named Crystal in 1990's *My Blue Heaven.*) *Girlfriends* was made in the very early days of the A.F.I. grant program, designed to encourage women to make their own films. The $10,000 seed money got the project off and rolling, but did not lead to a directing career for Claudia Weill. (Her two follow-up films included 1980's sprightly but little seen *It's My Turn* and 1988's *Once a Hero.*) Screenwriter Vicki Polon re-surfaced as a co-scripter on 1993's *Mr. Wonderful.* 🦴🦴🦴

1978 (PG) 87m/C Melanie Mayron, Anita Skinner, Eli Wallach, Christopher Guest, Amy Wright, Viveca Lindfors, Bob Balaban, Kathryn Walker, Kristopher Tabori, Mike Kellin, Kenneth McMillan; ***D:*** Claudia Weill; ***W:*** Vicki Polon; ***C:*** Fred Murphy. Sundance Film Festival '78: Grand Jury Prize. **VHS**

Girls in Chains

Hey, everybody, it's guilty pleasure time, and for tonight's snack, we are not featuring that bizarre (male) hot dog that leaps into a (female?) bun, but ta-dah!: *Fashion Victims of 1943,* also known as *Girls in Chains.* Talk about having to see a movie to believe how cheap it can really be. Director Edgar G. Ulmer must have been out to set some sort of a record with this one. Arline Judge, real-life veteran of seven

credit to young people and doesn't let adults in the film become the center of the story or let boys in the film become the center of the scene.

"I would definitely work under the same circumstances as our small-budget, 12-day shoot for *Girls Town.* I don't necessarily want any producer with a lot of money to know that, but I would really have no problem doing a film where I had the same amount of control that I had on this film if that was the only way to make it. As hard as it was, it was equally joyous and every moment in the editing room was a pleasure because we were working on OUR film. No one was telling us who to put in it or what to cut or what to change. Construction workers sit out on the sidewalk and eat their lunch everyday, they don't have catering. I don't know why films have to be that different. It was such a unique thing that we didn't have trailers for the actors."

Anna Grace: "After working on *Girls Town,* I starting writing another screenplay. I had done some improvisational workshops before I did this project. *Girls Town* was my first film, but not my first improvisational process, so it was a pretty good transition for me to go from improvisational theatre to an improvisational workshop for a film. I would also work under the same conditions that I did in *Girls Town.* We did what we really needed to do as actors. In a big production under studio constraints, I don't know whether actors would be given as much leeway. We could do what we wanted in order to tell the story truthfully and that way, making *Girls Town* was really a total joy."

well-publicized divorces, stars as MISS Helen Martin, who is trying to overhaul the women's prison system. She is handicapped in her sincere reformation efforts by the fact that her brother-in-law is none other than the notorious gangster, Johnny Moon. (In case we have trouble remembering his name, composer Erdody helpfully grafts Louis Lambert's "When Johnny Comes Marching Home" onto his "original" score, again and AGAIN.) And, then of course, there are life-and-death decisions to be made about what hat Helen should wear while breaking into an office to lift incriminating files. Helen chooses a creation with a far-reaching white net accentuated by what look like circles of white felt. Although her choice does not seem to have set off any hat purchase shock waves among other fashion victims of 1943, Helen likes it enough to wear it in ANOTHER sequence. (And yes, the shifty night watchman does notice her wearing that thing.) When Helen goes to nightclubs (with chandeliers, a juke box, armchairs, and a bartender who is always wiping the same glass), she likes to wear pace-setting print dresses with airplanes on them and styles her hair as if a lawnmower ran through the middle of it. The reason she goes to nightclubs is to be interrupted by an incoherent old drunk who leaks vital, but unintelligible, information. The bad guys decide that this blabbermouth needs to be taught a lesson, so they pick him up at midnight and toss him into some stock footage of Hoover Dam at high noon. He does not die or even stop talking, only winds up in traction at a hospital. The good guys corner the bad guys in a hallway cluttered with 19 or 20 chairs and then there's a nice expressionistic climax on a moonlit rooftop. By the way, the title characters, led by Barbara Pepper, do not wear chains, but most have higher heels than usual for prisoners in Cell Block Z. Accord-

The Hound Salutes: EAMES DEMETRIOS

Director/writer, *The Giving*

When we made *The Giving,* we made an effort to audition street poets and homeless people on the streets of Los Angeles. A dozen of the 22 cast members are either homeless, formerly homeless, or mentally ill, without compromising the quality of the performances. We just expanded the universe we were considering. I thought about what would happen if you allowed the despair that's on the streets to enter your heart, and how people who work in refugee camps or soup kitchens give themselves 100% rations when they can only afford to give 50% rations to refugees and the homeless. What's the emotional equation they're making in their heads? I also had an image in my mind about what would happen if I opened all the windows in my apartment for 20 years and let the wilderness take over. It took me about three years from the time I wrote the script to the time we started shooting *The Giving* and during that time seeds were planted. When I hooked up with my partner Tim, the co-producer, we created a limited partnership and started holding fundraisers and reaching out to people. We basically raised the money that way. I'd made some 16mm films and documentaries, but this was my first 35mm feature in black and white.

"When I first wrote the screenplay, my impulse was to make it right away, but the three years that passed gave me a richer background and richer experience, especially in regard to the issue of homelessness itself, because one of the documentaries I did was an interview project with a wide spectrum of 25 people, three of whom were homeless. Since I was interviewing these people every

ing to Edger G. Ulmer, this movie made a FORTUNE, which just goes to prove that I do not know how to recognize the unappreciated genius and stylish symbolism that were poured into *Girls in Chains.* 🦴🦴🦴

1943 72m/B Arline Judge, Roger Clark, Robin Raymond, Barbara Pepper, Dorothy Burgess, Clancy Cooper, Sid Melton, Betty Blythe, Peggy Stewart, Francis Ford; ***D:*** Edgar G. Ulmer; ***W:*** Albert Beich; ***C:*** Ira Morgan; ***M:*** Erdody. **VHS**

Girls Town

Nikki (Aunjanue Ellis), one of a group of four friends, kills herself after being raped. Patti (Lili Taylor), Emma (Anna Grace), and Angela (Bruklin Harris) try to come to terms with their loss and mostly wind up acting out (vandalizing the rapist's car, snapping at each other, et cetera). Although the actors have given themselves sharp dialogue to say, the sequences don't build on each other to increase the narrative's impact. Intriguing directions for character development are suggested and then abandoned. Good acting helps. 🦴🦴

1995 (R) 90m/C Lili Taylor, Anna Grace, Bruklin Harris, Aunjanue Ellis, Guillermo Diaz, John Ventimiglia; ***D:*** Jim McKay; ***W:*** Denise Casano, Jim McKay, Lili Taylor, Anna Grace, Bruklin Harris, Aunjanue Ellis; ***C:*** Russell Fine. Sundance Film Festival '96: Filmmakers Trophy; Nominations: Independent Spirit Awards '97: Best Supporting Actress (Taylor). **VHS**

three weeks, I really got to know them as I spent time on the streets and learned a little bit more about the vibe one needs to present on the streets. I also found out about some of the street poets and mental health groups I wanted to tap into for the performers. I feel like that is almost like the background I got after I wrote the script that enriched it. The cast really brought the characters to life. People often ask me if there was a lot of improvisation and I take that as a compliment, because actually there wasn't. If they hadn't enlivened those characters with their own experiences, there wouldn't be a movie there.

"The dual-duet relationship between Jeremiah, the non-homeless leading character, and Gregor, the leading homeless person, is really the core of the film. Jeremiah lets Gregor down at a critical moment and. the point is not that Jeremiah feels misunderstood, but something far more terrifying—he feels understood by Gregor. Jeremiah feels that Gregor understands all the doubts and the confused motives that go on inside his head while he's committing his acts of charity for the homeless community.

"For Jeremiah [Kevin Kildow], I really wanted the Byzantine look of medieval portraits of pure saints with haunted eyes and then to play off that look. Jeremiah is not a pure saint, at least as we conceive or imagine them to be. His motives are confused—sometimes you hate him, sometimes you like him, and sometimes you feel sorry for him, but I wanted him to appear like a tortured soul onto whom we've projected all our feelings. Gregor [Lee Hampton] has very complex feelings towards Jeremiah and society in general. He imagines that cities were created in 1819, almost by geological force, and that they've been decaying ever since and they're now just this frontier wilderness out of which one might homestead and carve a new living like the pioneers. Obviously, that isn't true—and to Lee Hampton's credit as an actor, Gregor understands the ways that is and is not true. At the beginning, Kevin Kildow's Jeremiah only understands the ways that it is not true. That strange understanding of the city is really a hard thing for an actor to pull off and both actors pull it off really well."

The Giving

Jeremiah Pollock (Kevin Kildow) is a Los Angeles bank executive riddled with guilt over the people on Skid Row. On an impulse, he decides to give $10,000 to the homeless. Perhaps unsurprisingly, Jeremiah's generosity is regarded with suspicion by a homeless spokesperson named Gregor (Lee Hampton). Jeremiah's intentions are serious, though. Already rail thin, he starves himself, sleeps on the streets, and shows homeless people how to get money out of automatic teller machines. Except for his occupation, Jeremiah is a man of mystery, as is the source of his very real guilt. Eames Demetrios appears to be more concerned with the look of this black-and-white entry than with a carefully crafted narrative in which all questions are asked (and answered); *The Giving* succeeds in working a dream-like spell over careful viewers and it does tend to linger in the mind afterwards. 🦴🦴🦴

1991 100m/B Kevin Kildow, Lee Hampton, Satya Cyprian, Kellie A. McKuen, Gail Green, Stephen Hornyak, Oliver Patterson, Paul Boesing, Russell Smith; ***D:*** Eames Demetrios; ***W:*** Eames Demetrios; ***C:*** Antonio Soriano; ***M:*** Stephen James Taylor.

Glen or Glenda?

The canon of Edward D. Wood Jr. holds a special place in the hearts of his many

Dr. Van Ness (Herbert Marshall), David Sheppard (Richard Egan), and Joanna Merritt (Constance Dowling) battle *Gog.* United Artists; courtesy of the Kobal Collection

fans because Wood really had faith in his subject matter; there isn't a trace element of condescension in any of his films. When Wood made *Glen or Glenda?* for producer George Weiss (who also appeared in the film), he thought enough of the material to retain the services of a medical adviser, Dr. Nathan Bailey. *Glen or Glenda?* is a sympathetic account of how Glen (played by Wood himself) is attracted to wearing the angora sweaters of his girlfriend Barbara (Dolores Fuller, then involved with Wood). To beef up the theme of the study, composite case studies are included of successful sex changes and of the sad ends of those who fail to realize their cross-dressing destinies for one reason or another. Bela Lugosi watches over mankind while intoning, "Pull the strings! Pull the strings!" Of course it's camp, but it's fun to watch; I will probably see *Glen or Glenda?* more times in my lifetime than *Gandhi.* (Once was enough, thanks.) Wood's colossal enthusiasm for creating a meaningful and socially important film along with his sheer genius for hokiness makes *Glen or Glenda?* a unique viewing experience. WARNING: Do not watch this movie with anyone who uses the "J" word ("juxtaposition") in every other sentence. S/he will just cramp your viewing style and you will not have fun. I'm serious! ***AKA:*** He or She; I Changed My Sex; I Led Two Lives; The Transvestite; Glen or Glenda: The Confessions of Ed Wood. ♪♪♪

1953 67m/B Edward D. Wood Jr., Bela Lugosi, Lyle Talbot, Timothy Farrell, Dolores Fuller, Charles Crafts, Tommy Haynes, Captain DeZita, Evelyn Wood, Shirley Speril, Conrad Brooks, Henry Bederski, William C. Thompson, Mr. Walter, Harry Thomas, George Weiss; ***D:*** Edward D. Wood Jr.; ***W:*** Edward D. Wood Jr.; ***C:*** William C. Thompson. **VHS**

Go Fish

Go Fish is a bit too self-consciously arty for its own good. I hope that the rules and regulations for P.C. lesbians are meant as satire, not as a code of conduct. It looks as though *Go Fish* were a fun movie to make, but it is less fun to listen to the copious self-analysis that accompanies each move that Max (Guinevere Turner) makes toward Ely (V.S. Brodie). *Maedchen in Uniform* and *These Three* are better acted, *Fried Green Tomatoes* and *The Incredibly True Adventure of Two Girls in Love* are livelier, *Nadja* and *French Twist* are funnier, *Daughters of Darkness* and *Bound* have better stories AND.... Okay, I confess, it was those damn toenails! Watching someone you barely know do any of the following on Date One (paring toenails, belching after chug-a-lugging beer, or asking you to slide egg albumen down each other's throats a la *Tampopo*) is not my idea of Nirvana. So happy that Max and Ely found each other!

1994 (R) 87m/B Guinevere Turner, V.S. Brodie, T. Wendy McMillan, Anastasia Sharp, Migdalia Melendez; ***D:*** Rose Troche; ***W:*** Guinevere Turner, Rose Troche; ***C:*** Ann T. Rossetti; ***M:*** Brendan Dolan, Jennifer Sharpe. Nominations: Independent Spirit Awards '95: Best Supporting Actress (Brodie). **VHS**

Gods and Monsters

Hollywood is the wrong place to be a Nobody, even if you previously were a Somebody of the Highest Wattage. *Gods and Monsters* is a speculation on the sad last days of the legendary director James Whale, who brought us *Frankenstein* just in time for Christmas 1931, plus *The Old Dark House* (1932's Halloween release), 1933's *The Invisible Man* and, just in time for Easter 1935, *Bride of Frankenstein.* As the story opens, we see the great Ian McKellen as Whale in the spring of 1957, very frail in his 60s, drifting in and out of full consciousness. His constant attendant is Hanna the housekeeper (a nearly unrecognizable Lynn Redgrave at 55), who is devoted to him, despite her deep disapproval of his homosexuality. A very young and gushy journalist (Jack Plotnick as Edmond Kay) comes to pay a call on his idol, but he only wants to talk about monsters and Whale wants to talk about anything else. To liven things up, he agrees to give a complete answer to every question but only if Kay removes an article of clothing per question. The game doesn't last long, as Whale is in very delicate health indeed. McKellen's shrewd understanding of the sharp intelligence trapped inside a failing body is the key to his performance, and he gets the balance just right in this Oscar-worthy interpretation. Whale can't stop staring at his beautiful young gardener (splendidly played by a very buff Brendan Fraser as Clayton Boone), and he invites him to swim in his pool, drink his iced tea, and even pose for his portrait. The relationship is primal for Whale, but is initially no more than a source of curiosity for Clay. Warned by his friends about Whale's homosexuality, the straight Clay continues the association anyway. He likes the stories—well, some of them, and he develops sympathy for his employer as he learns more about his lonely life from Hanna. Whale invites Clay to a garden party for Princess Margaret (who did not visit Hollywood until 1965) at the home of director George Cukor. H.R.H. mistakes Whale for Cecil Beaton (unlikely since she'd known Beaton from childhood) and greets Clay (dressed down in a T-shirt) graciously, although Cukor is clearly annoyed. The conceit of the garden party is intriguing because it strikes true and false notes throughout the sequence. The notes that ring true are Whale's increasing isolation in a society that has no further use for him, and the fear he ignites by being himself when every other gay man at the party is required to play the game. Rosalind Ayres is wonderful as Elsa Lanchester, and so much like the delightful character actress that it's a shock to realize you're not watching the genuine article. (Jack Betts, too, is eerily like Boris Karloff at age 70.) But the actors playing Cukor and the Princess only look right—they feel quite wrong, especially when sharing a moment with McKellen who's so real and so right as Whale. Bill Condon's *Gods and Monsters,* based on Christopher Brain's novel *Father of Frankenstein,* shows the dwindling light of a former

Some loves are impossible. But they are loves just the same.

—Tagline from the movie *Golden Gate.*

supernova in a frank and compassionate way. By showing an old man's agonizing desire for nostalgia, it owes more to *Death in Venice* than to *Sunset Boulevard.* And it's a rich and detailed portrait of one life's ultimate collision with destiny, as only Ian McKellen can etch it on our hearts and minds. (Clive Barker is among the executive producers on this one.)

1998 105m/C Ian McKellen, Brendan Fraser, Lynn Redgrave, Lolita Davidovich, David Dukes, Kevin J. O'Connor, Brandon Kleyla, Pamela Salem, Michael O'Hagan, Jack Plotnick, Sarah Ann Morris, Rosalind Ayers, Jack Betts; ***D:*** Bill Condon; ***W:*** Bill Condon; ***C:*** Stephen M. Katz; ***M:*** Carter Burwell. Academy Awards '98: Best Adapted Screenplay; Golden Globe Awards '99: Best Supporting Actress (Redgrave); Independent Spirit Awards '99: Best Actor (McKellen), Best Film, Best Supporting Actress (Redgrave); Los Angeles Film Critics Association Awards '98: Best Actor (McKellen); National Board of Review Awards '98: Best Actor (McKellen), Best Film; Broadcast Film Critics Association Awards '98: Best Actor (McKellen); Nominations: Academy Awards '98: Best Actor (McKellen), Best Supporting Actress (Redgrave); British Academy Awards '98: Best Supporting Actress; Golden Globe Awards '98: Best Actor—Drama (McKellen); Golden Globe Awards '99: Best Film—Drama; Independent Spirit Awards '99: Best Screenplay; Screen Actors Guild Award '98: Best Actor (McKellen), Best Supporting Actress (Redgrave); Writers Guild of America '98: Best Adapted Screenplay. **VHS**

Gog

Sure, *Gog* doesn't have the cachet of *Godzilla* or *Rodin,* but it did terrorize my friend Clinton Vidal as an *enfant terrible*, and he's one of the roughest, toughest guys I know, ROWR! So there. Richard Egan is David Sheppard, Security Agent for something called the Office of Scientific Investigation. At this point, I should mention the number of women in the cast, which is above average for a science-fiction flick of this era. This is probably because the movie was made in 3-D AND Cinecolor, but it does pare down the number of "How can you possibly concentrate on science when you're wearing a bra?" questions which are DE RIGUEUR when there's only one (1) female on the project. However, a significant amount of screen time is devoted to LONG scientific explanations, time that might be better spent on more Sabre Jet action sequences, more close-ups of Novac (Nuclear Operative Variable Automatic Confuser, a poor misunderstood computer), more fights with *Gog* and his fellow robots, et cetera. *Gog* is still enjoyable, anyhow. The title alone has resonance, ditto Herbert Marshall as Dr. Van Ness and William Schallert as Engle. They don't entirely compensate for Constance Dowling's unflattering hairstyle as Joanna Merritt (eight years earlier, she was the nasty, cat-like Mavis Marlowe in *Black Angel* with GREAT hairstyling by Carmen Dirigo!). But Ivan Tors is at the helm here, not Roy William Neill. Having saved the world in 1955, the busy Richard Egan dashed off to Afghanistan in the 1890s to wrangle with Raymond Burr and woo Dawn Addams in *Khyber Patrol.*

1954 82m/C Richard Egan, Constance Dowling, Herbert Marshall, John Wengraf, Philip Van Zandt, Steve Roberts, Valerie Vernon, Michael Fox, William Schallert, Byron Kane; ***D:*** Herbert L. Strock; ***W:*** Ivan Tors, Tom Taggart, Richard G. Taylor; ***C:*** Lothrop Worth; ***M:*** Harry Sukman.

Golden Gate

Okay, everybody, let's play movie producer! Here's the story: first, we need Matt Dillon in the lead, because at the age of 30, he can convincingly age from 22 to 38 without ever changing his suit or hair. Dillon starts out as eager beaver FBI agent Kevin Walker, who just wants to get laid and make a name for himself in the Bureau. So he tells this girl he wants to lay (Teri Polo as Cynthia) that justice means more to him than the law, and he deliberately frames a Chinese laundry worker for being part of a Communist conspiracy. Cynthia walks out on fledgling agent Walker. The Chinese laundry worker spends the years 1952 through 1962 in prison, during which time his motherless little girl grows up to be Joan Chen, 33, as Marilyn Song. Ordered by the FBI to continue surveillance on her newly released father, Walker stalks him into an early grave, courtesy of a suicide leap from the Golden Gate Bridge. Then, because Walker wants to lay Song, he tells her nice things about her father that he claims he learned as a public defender. They make out next to the Golden Gate Bridge where the proud agent can't help bragging about the original news coverage of her father's conviction.

Sure enough, Song finds the original front page picture of Walker framing her father and splits. Six years later, Agent Walker is ordered by the FBI to begin surveillance on Song, now an instructor at the University of California at Berkeley. Since Walker framed her father for being part of a Communist conspiracy, why not frame Song too, complete with the help of a University official? But this creep we've been stuck with for 95 minutes, who's never shown even a sliver of a conscience, suddenly has a change of heart in the final reel. So, there will be a karmic finale for FBI Agent Kevin Walker at the Golden Gate Bridge and a happy ending for Marilyn Song, so she can narrate the movie. PLUS: They can even say these lines to each other, to be excerpted in the coming attractions trailer and ALL the posters: "Some loves are impossible." "But they are loves just the same." What do you think? Great, huh? And producer Michael Brandman did think that David Henry Hwang's idea was great, just great: "When a playwright as uniquely talented as David has an idea he wants to pursue, I am smart enough simply to say yes." So now you know. The spirit of self-styled movie mogul Howard Hughes, who ran RKO into the ground with Red Menace flicks like *I Married a Communist,* is alive and well in 1994. We can't all be movie producers, but at least we can say some movies are stinkers. But they are made just the same. **woof!**

1993 (R) 95m/C Matt Dillon, Joan Chen, Bruno Kirby, Teri Polo, Tzi Ma, Stan Egi, Peter Murnik, Jack Shearer, George Giudall; ***D:*** John Madden; ***W:*** David Henry Hwang; ***C:*** Bobby Bukowski; ***M:*** Elliot Goldenthal. **VHS, LV, Closed Caption**

A Good Man in Africa

A Good Man in Africa is an odd hybrid of a film. For much of its running time, you may find yourself giggling at the sheer silliness of the situations its protagonist gets himself into, but the heart of the film seems to have been given short shrift. What's more, the whole thing ends on a flat, abrupt, and entirely unsatisfying note. The cast is as uneven as William Boyd's script. Colin Friels at 40 is a bit long in the tooth to be playing junior diplomat Morgan Leafy, a character whose approach to life is essentially adolescent; any 15-year-old kid of your acquaintance is likely to be more street savvy. (Friels' natural comedic gifts help somewhat.) John Lithgow, only nine years older than Friels, rather overdoes the aging British diplomat yearning for a knighthood and a cushy berth. By trying to get every detail just right, Lithgow loses the essence of his character. (Watch the fine actress playing the small role of a visiting Duchess to see how an understated Brit ought to be played.) Sadder still is Diana Rigg as Lithgow's frustrated wife, badly photographed, unflatteringly garbed, with god-awful dialogue to deliver. At one point, her character dashes into the night with Leafy, dodging bullets, racing through fields, ducking under fences. The brief interlude is evocative of the heady days when Mrs. Emma Peel was the classiest female sleuth on the planet, but it all ends with a thud when Rigg is given more wretched lines to say and then dismissed with Leafy's voiceover. Louis Gossett Jr. and Joanne Whalley are two halves of a match made in heaven: he's a crooked political leader, she supplies sexual favors in exchange for favors in the real world. And then there is the incorruptible title character, Dr. Alex Murray, played to cool perfection by Sean Connery. Like Rigg, Connery is given a chance to re-create a moment from another time: playing a golf game that isn't really a golf game. His opponent may not be in the same league as Auric Goldfinger, but in his own blundering way, Leafy is more of a threat. The two meet again and again, with Connery savoring all of the film's best lines and stealing every scene. Check out his last moment in the film; only Barbara Stanwyck has ever managed to achieve anything like it with such riveting subtlety. It's such a great moment, in fact, that you wonder why anyone would dare to tack on the inadequate sequence that follows it. Reportedly, *A Good Man in Africa* was re-edited after an earlier version mystified audiences, so we can expect Bruce Beresford to come up with the inevitable "director's cut." 🦴🦴

1994 (R) 95m/C Colin Friels, Sean Connery, Louis Gossett Jr., John Lithgow, Joanne Whalley, Diana

Chuckie (Ben Affleck) and Will (Matt Damon) in *Good Will Hunting.* Miramax; courtesy of the Kobal Collection

Rigg; ***D:*** Bruce Beresford; ***W:*** William Boyd; ***C:*** Andrzej Bartkowiak. **VHS**

The Good Soldier

Since this is the only filmed version of Ford Madox Ford's classic novel, it deserves a video release. Originally made for Granada television, it was nominated for an international Emmy and featured on-target performances by the late Jeremy Brett in the title role, the late Susan Fleetwood as his long-suffering wife Leonora Ashburnham, and Robin Ellis and Vickery Turner as dense John and despicable Florence Dowell. The novel was light years ahead of its time in tone and structure, and director Kevin Billington took extraordinary pains to preserve both its dark humor and its bitter irony. Acting throughout is first rate, and Elizabeth Garvie is especially affecting as Nancy Rufford. John Ratzenberger, then a British resident, makes a surprise cameo appearance, not long before his tenure on *Cheers.* Lushly filmed on location at Bad Nauheim, Marburg, and Wiesbaden, as well as Holker Hall, Cambria; Croxteth Hall, Liverpool; Stanway House, Gloucestershire; and Chetham's Library, Manchester. ☙☙☙

1981 113m/C *GB* Robin Ellis, Vickery Turner, Jeremy Brett, Susan Fleetwood, Elizabeth Garvie, Pauline Moran, John Ratzenberger, Geoffrey Chater, Roger Hammond, John Grillo, Alan Downer, Waldemar Ruhl, Kenneth Midwood, William Merrow; ***D:*** Kevin Billington.

The Good Wife

Once upon a time, there was a type of movie called a woman's picture, AKA a four-handkerchief weeper. These films were invariably written and directed by men, the plots usually involved the heroine having to choose between security and sex, and there were always strong undercurrents of moral disapproval, even when they were charged with considerable sympathy. Today the woman's picture has been inherited by a new breed of director, no longer restrained by an obsolete production code. In 1986, Ken Cameron made *The Good Wife* with Rachel Ward, Bryan Brown, and Sam Neill, working from an original screenplay by Peter Kenna. If the film is remembered at all today, it is largely because of the excellent performances by the three leading players, but it is also of interest for its mid-1980s perspective on the downward spiral of sexual addiction. Ward is the title character, living in rural Australia with her husband and his younger brother. The kindest way to describe the bedside manner of the two men is erotically challenged. Their brawls with each other last far longer than their encounters with Ward's character. Although she gets nothing that could remotely be described as a kick from either brother, she remains a dutiful companion to them both until the dapper stranger played by Neill arrives on the scene. When he makes a humiliating and perfunctory pass at her, she rebuffs him instinctively, even though it is clear that she is interested in him. He starts his new job at a local bar and she returns to her familiar work routines, but with a difference. When it is clear that the stylish bartender is an unabashed philanderer, she begins to stalk him. He has moved on to fresh prey, but her obsession has become impersonal and all-encompassing; she applies lipstick, buys a new dress, and hangs out at the bar, drinking brandy after brandy just so she can stare at him and give him endless opportunities to reject her in front of the entire town. She leaves her home and moves into a room across the street so she can watch him seduce another man's wife, hoping for some signal that will make sense of her self-inflicted torture. Screenwriter Kenna has a good grasp of the psychological makeup of his characters and their eloquent self-awareness is well accompanied by Cameron Allan's persistent neurotic score. Ward and the men eventually work themselves into the sort of frenzy for which there can be no satisfactory conclusion. For most of *The Good Wife*'s running time of 97 minutes, however, director Cameron does manage to reveal a bit of the mystery behind his title character's longing to feel something, anything, in her own lifetime, even if it's unrelieved despair from a cold-blooded stranger. ***AKA:*** The Umbrella Woman. 🦴🦴🦴

1986 (R) 97m/C *AU* Rachel Ward, Bryan Brown, Sam Neill, Steven Vidler, Bruce Barry, Jennifer Claire; ***D:*** Ken Cameron; ***C:*** James Bartle; ***M:*** Cameron Allan. **VHS, LV**

Good Will Hunting

Everyone raved about this feel-good date movie in 1997. If you couldn't get into *Titanic,* you saw *Good Will Hunting* instead. Matt (Will Hunting) Damon and Ben (Chuckie) Affleck got their very own magazines (just like Leonardo DiCaprio!) with HUNDREDS of color photographs and hardly any words to read. They won an Oscar for best original screenplay, Robin (Sean McGuire) Williams won an Oscar as best supporting actor, and nominee Minnie (Skylar) Driver, Damon's former girlfriend, showed up at the Academy Awards ceremony dressed to the nines and ALONE. *Good Will Hunting* shows how the adorable, messed-up title character learns to accept his great genius with the help of his messed-up therapist. Chuckie is Will's best friend and Skylar would like to be his girlfriend. After 126 minutes, all burning questions and issues are answered and resolved, all the couples in all the movie theatres on the planet depart happily and proceed to affirm life in their own respective ways and magazine publishers scramble to find more pictures of Damon and Affleck for their next iconographic issue. (NO ONE put Ben Affleck in the fan rags after he played Bully O'Bannion in 1993's *Dazed and Confused.*) Clearly, yours truly resisted *Good Will Hunting,* but it deserves at least 2 1/2 bones for being well acted, well directed, and well produced. 🦴🦴½

1997 (R) 126m/C Matt Damon, Robin Williams, Ben Affleck, Stellan Skarsgard, Minnie Driver, Casey Affleck, Cole Hauser; ***D:*** Gus Van Sant; ***W:*** Matt Damon, Ben Affleck; ***C:*** Jean-Yves Escoffier; ***M:*** Danny Elfman. Academy Awards '97: Best Original Screenplay, Best Supporting Actor (Williams); Golden Globe Awards '98: Best Screenplay; Screen Actors Guild Award '97: Best Supporting Actor (Williams); Broadcast Film Critics Association Awards '97: Breakthrough Performance (Damon), Best Original Screenplay; Nominations: Academy Awards '97: Best Actor (Damon), Best Director

The Hound Salutes:

SANDRA GOLDBACHER

Writer/director, *The Governess*

I was incredibly lucky. I sent the first draft of the screenplay to Minnie Driver, whom I'd always hoped that I could have for the part of Rosina Da Silva. I always had her in my head when I was writing the screenplay. She sent me a fax back to say that she loved it, so it was a dream come true, really. I'd grown up with the novels of the Brontë sisters and I'd always loved the wonderful, passionate 19th century heroines in those novels. But in those novels, the heroines always had to come to some terrible end. They'd either die of consumption or they'd just get married and you wouldn't know what happened, so it was interesting for me to bring a modern sensibility to one of those passionate stories.

"I set the story in 1840, because I wanted it to be JUST before the photographic process of salt fixation was discovered, which was a way of fixing photographic images permanently on the paper. There were a lot of people who worked trying to find this process, particularly in Scotland and Paris. They could make these beautiful images, but they'd disappear within a couple of days. That always fascinated me, that idea of trying to capture an image permanently.

"I started writing the screenplay as Rosina's diary, so that it would have a personal, subjective feel. My father is a Sephardic Jew from Italy near Venice and my mother's family are Protestant from the Isle of Skye in Scotland, so the idea of bringing together two people from different cultures

(Van Sant), Best Film Editing, Best Picture, Best Song ("Miss Misery"), Best Supporting Actress (Driver), Best Original Score; Directors Guild of America Awards '97: Best Director (Van Sant); Golden Globe Awards '98: Best Actor—Drama (Damon), Best Film—Drama, Best Supporting Actor (Williams); MTV Movie Awards '98: Best Film, Best Male Performance (Damon), Best On-Screen Duo (Matt Damon/Ben Affleck), Best Kiss (Matt Damon/Minnie Driver); Screen Actors Guild Award '97: Best Actor (Damon), Best Supporting Actress (Driver), Cast; Writers Guild of America '97: Best Original Screenplay. **VHS, LV, Closed Caption, DVD**

The Governess

Rosina Da Silva is a fiercely independent young Sephardic Jewish woman, who has spent all her life with her loving family in London, circa 1840. When tragedy strikes, Rosina must earn money to support them. She has always wanted to be a great actress, but impersonating a gentile governess named Mary Blackchurch wasn't quite the role she had in mind. Harsh times call for harsh measures and Rosina/Mary resolutely leaves her much-loved home for the Isle of Skye to play governess to little Clementina Cavendish (*FairyTale*'s delightful Florence Hoath). This is the premise of Sandra Goldbacher's *The Governess,* starring the vibrant Minnie Driver in the title role. Gothic conventions are strictly observed; Clementina must be a irrepressible imp determined to torture Miss Blackchurch until she recognizes who's boss. There must also be a delicate, fluttery Mrs. Cavendish (the wonderful Harriet Walter) who clearly hasn't slept with her husband in a while. And Mr.

was one I grew up with, literally. I shot the film on the Isle of Arran, which is next to the isle of Skye, because it had a wonderful castle we could use.

"Minnie Driver's dresses are made of Holland linen, but they have a shiny surface to them. She does wear a leather coat, though. What's fun about her clothes is that, because she came from a very different background from the sort of prim and proper governess she's pretending to be as Mary Blackchurch, her clothes are much too opulent and inappropriate—they're sort of Jewish princessy. She stands out.

"Rosina comes from a very loving, seemingly secure background, which is then torn apart. She's this mixture of the very strong, the very passionate, the very confused, and the very vulnerable, which I find interesting. Rosina is a one-off; she wants to be an actress, she loves the idea of play acting, and she embraces the theatrical, so she is an original, I think.

"I worked with a photographic artist on the film and he uses a lot of old processes in his work. He uses a lot of experimental processes on the photographs in the film. He didn't actually fix them with salt, because that's a hit-or-miss affair, although that was how the first prints were fixed. We based the look of the photographs on the work of Julia Margaret Cameron (1815–79). He uses a mixture of ad hoc things he's made himself, some old things and new processes, as well.

"The photographer Charles Cavendish (Tom Wilkinson) has a profound problem with love, but he comes to life when Rosina comes into his world and then it's too much for him and he shuts down again. I think that's the key to his character, really.

"The food on the Cavendish dinner table was all sorts of things: stuffed larks and a lot of semolina, the sort of sloppy white food you're forced to eat at boarding school. I think you call it 'cream of wheat' in America."

Charles Cavendish (Tom Wilkinson) must be a brooding, mysterious man of few words with a certain scruffy erotic appeal. There doesn't always have to be an odd son lusting after the governess, but this movie has one, with all the trimmings (Jonathan Rhys Meyers as Henry Cavendish). If you've seen *Jane Eyre,* you know what happens next—the variation on a theme here is that Charles is a pioneer in the infant art of photography. His work is the most interesting thing happening on the desolate isle, and Rosina soon shares his obsession, which leads to all sorts of shenanigans, of course. The charm of *The Governess* resides in the capable hands of Minnie Driver. Like the young Bette Davis, she dominates every frame in which she appears and that's practically the entire 114-minute running time. Whether she's conveying her aching loneliness for her own family, her unflappability in her sequences with the mischievous Clementina, or her growing attachment to her mentor Charles, Driver is an actress of enormous skill, sensuality, and power. Director Goldbacher makes an impressive debut: her vision of the early Victorian era is strikingly free of the most obvious cliches and costume designer Caroline Harris clearly had fun finding a way for Minnie Driver to wear black leather.

1998 (R) 114m/C Minnie Driver, Tom Wilkinson, Harriet Walter, Florence Hoath, Jonathan Rhys Myers, Arlene Cockburn, Emma Bird, Adam Levy, Bruce Meyers; ***D:*** Sandra Goldbacher; ***W:*** Sandra Goldbacher; ***C:*** Ashley Rowe; ***M:*** Ed Shearmur. **VHS, Closed Caption, DVD**

Benjamin (Dustin Hoffman) contemplates Mrs. Robinson (Anne Bancroft) in *The Graduate.*
Embassy Pictures; courtesy of the Kobal Collection

Grace of My Heart

I spent a dozen hours of my life in 1996 watching *The Beatles Anthology.* I don't know how much more thorough an in-house project could have been. It had every scrap of footage, with massive commentary by the group, their producer, their press officer, and their tour manager. Yet I found myself recalling, with increasing fondness, the devastating and very funny 70-minute satire *All You Need Is Cash,* made by Eric Idle and Neil Innes in 1978. Irreverent fiction sometimes does it better than the most scrupulously produced documentary. Allison Anders' *Grace of My Heart* pays tribute to the female songwriters of the '60s who slogged their youth away in tiny offices creating words and music for big stars to turn into hits. The two factors I most enjoyed about the film just as easily turn others off. Illeana Douglas, to me, is one of the great undiscovered treasures in movies today. In films like *Cape Fear, Grief, Search and Destroy,* and *To Die For,* Douglas has consistently turned in performances evocative of 1940s "B" queens, but with a daffy, vulnerable twist all her own. Illeana Douglas aficionados won't be able to get enough of her in *Grace of My Heart,* but if she ain't your type, this movie won't be either, since she's in virtually every sequence. And if you're sick to death of the 1960s, see something else! Unfortunately, I attended a screening with a group of bickering critics who had trouble with the star, the subject, or both, AND they were disappointed by the songwriter's romantic choices. They also complained because the soundtrack was dubbed by vocalists. Hey, we're talking Allison Anders here, not some megabuck studio with a demographic survey team. Anders' script and direction are terrific, filled with realistic observations and deft touches missing in male-oriented rock films like the otherwise excellent *Stardust.* John Turturro is exceptional as the no-nonsense producer, Bridget Fonda contributes a nice bit as a gay teen idol (her dad Peter was cut out of the film as Guru Dave, although his voice remains on the soundtrack), and Matt Dillon as a destructive genius sounds eerily like Dennis Hopper. *Grace of My Heart* is a charmingly gritty look at a grittily charming character. Regardless of what you may read about this one in print, give *Grace of My Heart* a chance. Recommended for further research on video: *Girl Groups,* crammed with colorful if not always accurate recollections as well as vintage clips of some terrific performances of that era.

1996 (R) 116m/C Illeana Douglas, John Turturro, Matt Dillon, Eric Stoltz, Bruce Davison, Patsy Kensit, Bridget Fonda, Jennifer Leigh Warren, Chris Isaak; ***D:*** Allison Anders; ***W:*** Allison Anders; ***C:*** Jean-Yves Escoffier; ***M:*** Larry Klein; ***V:*** Peter Fonda. **VHS, LV, Letterbox, Closed Caption**

The Graduate

The Graduate was the most successful independent film from 1967 through 1990, until the release of *Teenage Mutant Ninja Turtles*; indies that attract over $100 million in boxoffice receipts are on a very short list. Admittedly, *The Graduate*'s credentials were so impeccable that its first audiences may not have realized that they were watching a groundbreaking film in so many ways. Director Mike Nichols, screenwriters Buck Henry and Calder Willingham, cinematographer Robert L. Surtees, and composer Dave Grusin were all sizzling hot at that stage of their careers and everyone wanted to work with them. Everyone, that is, except Doris Day, who turned down the role of Mrs. Robinson. Would Simon and Garfunkel's "Mrs. Robinson" have given "Que Sera, Sera" a run for its money if we'd envisioned Day as Benjamin Braddock's seductress, instead of Anne Bancroft? Nah, I don't think so. Day, as the golden girl of 1948–73, would have been as miscast as Mrs. R. as Lucille Ball was as Mame or Tom Cruise was as Lestat or Ralph Fiennes was as John Steed! Anne Bancroft, however, was (and is) surprising me all the time with her range as an actress; who could have brought such razor sharp timing to the sequence where she kisses Benjamin BEFORE exhaling her cigarette? Dustin Hoffman, then 30 and just six years younger than Bancroft, was an unknown quantity at the time, unless you're among his relatives and caught his first flick, *Madigan's Millions.* Nichols had seen him in a play and insisted Hoffman would be perfect in the title role, despite his age. Katharine Ross became an overnight icon as Elaine, but Hollywood of the late '60s was no longer capable of sustaining or protecting its stars. Her career continued, but, except for *Butch Cassidy and the Sundance Kid,* not at the level of this star-making role. The week *The Graduate* opened in Woodland, California, students and teachers alike were sharing inside jokes, quoting lines, and acting out situations from the movie. The word "plastics" was like a password into *Graduate*-speak, ditto "ELAINE! ELAINE! ELAINE!" Graduates weren't QUITE like this in 1967; Benjamin looks more at home in 1962, but the way he fights for his happiness, despite all his flaws, struck a nerve with audiences of its era and, unsurprisingly, still does so today. As a San Franciscan, though, there's just one thing about *The Graduate* that will bug me to the end of time. Why didn't anyone notice that Benjamin was driving to SAN FRANCISCO on the Bay Bridge, not to BERKELEY? He couldn't get anywhere NEAR Elaine with that sense of direction!

1967 (PG) 106m/C Dustin Hoffman, Anne Bancroft, Katharine Ross, Murray Hamilton, Brian Avery, Marion Lorne, Alice Ghostley, William Daniels, Elizabeth Wilson, Norman Fell, Buck Henry, Richard Dreyfuss, Mike Farrell; ***D:*** Mike Nichols; ***W:*** Buck Henry, Calder Willingham; ***C:*** Robert L. Surtees; ***M:*** Paul Simon, Art Garfunkel, Dave Grusin. Academy Awards '67: Best Director (Nichols); American Film Institute (AFI) '98: Top 100; British Academy Awards '68: Best Director (Nichols), Best Film, Best Screenplay; Directors Guild of America Awards '67: Best Director (Nichols); Golden Globe Awards '68: Best Actress—Musical/Comedy (Bancroft), Best Director (Nichols), Best Film—Musical/Comedy, National Film Registry '96;; New York Film Critics Awards '67:

"I realized that in becoming a gentleman, I had only succeeded in becoming a snob."

—Pip (John Mills) in *Great Expectations.*

Best Director (Nichols); Nominations: Academy Awards '67: Best Actor (Hoffman), Best Actress (Bancroft), Best Adapted Screenplay, Best Cinematography, Best Picture, Best Supporting Actress (Ross). **VHS, LV, 8mm, Letterbox, Closed Caption**

Grand Isle

The opening night selection for 1991's On Screen: A Celebration of Women in Film Festival was *Grand Isle,* based on Kate Chopin's 1899 novel *The Awakening.* It's the story of a young mother married to a jerk who pines for another jerk who teaches her how to swim but who actually sleeps with a third jerk. She attempts art work in the nude, burns all her paintings, and drowns herself after her swimming teacher walks out on her twice. *The Awakening,* along with *Mill on the Floss* and *Wuthering Heights,* is required reading in feminist literature classes, especially if you subscribe to the theory that a woman's entire range of choices at the turn of the century consisted of three jerks or death. But heck, even Queen Victoria's granddaughter (Princess Marie Louise, 1872–1956) obtained a divorce in 1900, with grandma's blessing and consent and if she didn't walk into the sea afterward, the times couldn't have been all that repressive! The ideal director for this sort of delicate material would have been someone like Joan Micklin Silver, who has enormous skill at capturing the look, feel, and sensibility of other eras *(Hester Street, Bernice Bobs Her Hair)* without ever caricaturizing them. But instead, actress/producer Kelly McGillis chose Mary *(Siesta, Pet Semetary 1–2)* Lambert whose visions are invariably hermetically sealed and pretentious. If you can accept the fact that any of the shadowy guys in this story are capable of repressing a strapping creature like McGillis, you may like *Grand Isle,* which wound up on TNT a year after its premiere. (Actually, the underused Glenne Headly, who also appears in the film, would have been a far better casting choice in the lead.)

1991 94m/C Kelly McGillis, Adrian Pasdar, Julian Sands, Jon DeVries, Glenne Headly, Anthony De Sando, Ellen Burstyn; ***D:*** Mary Lambert; ***W:*** Hesper Anderson; ***C:*** Jonathan Tucker. **VHS, LV, Closed Caption**

Great Expectations

For David Lean's 1946 film of Charles Dickens' *Great Expectations,* John Mills and Valerie Hobson were cast as Pip and Estella, and a one-time advertising copywriter named Alec Guinness, then 32, was cast in the pivotal role of Herbert Pocket. It was the first of seven films Guinness would make with Lean over the next 38 years. *Great Expectations* and Lean received Best Picture and Best Director Oscar nominations, and the film won two Academy Awards for Guy Green's cinematography and Wilfred Shingleton's art direction. It is perhaps the best of the Dickensian movies, and it certainly etched some indelible impressions on its audiences: Martita Hunt's Miss Havisham chained to her memories and her dreams of revenge, Jean Simmons' haughty young Estella at the start of a gradual slide into near-madness, and the eerie opening graveyard scene between the boy Pip (Anthony Wager) and the convict Magwitch (Finlay Currie). The mid-Victorian era is captured with precision, as well as the brooding sadness that flavors much of the original novel.

1946 118m/B *GB* John Mills, Valerie Hobson, Anthony Wager, Alec Guinness, Finlay Currie, Jean Simmons, Bernard Miles, Francis L. Sullivan, Martita Hunt, Freda Jackson, Torin Thatcher, Hay Petrie, Eileen Erskine, George "Gabby" Hayes, Everley Gregg, O.B. Clarence; ***D:*** David Lean; ***W:*** David Lean, Ronald Neame; ***C:*** Guy Green. Academy Awards '47: Best Art Direction/Set Decoration (B & W), Best Black and White Cinematography; Nominations: Academy Awards '47: Best Director (Lean), Best Picture, Best Screenplay. **VHS, LV, DVD**

Grief

Mark (Craig Chester) is a writer on the syndicated daytime TV show *The Love Judge.* Still numb from his lover's death from AIDS the previous year, Mark begins to take an interest in fellow writer Bill (Alexis Arquette), while writer Paula (Lucy Gutteridge) desires to become the show's new producer and secretary Leslie (Illeana Douglas) wants to take her place as the new writer. Present producer Jo (Jackie Beat) tries to keep her office family in line while sorting out her personal life. Writer/director Richard Glatzer wrote *Divorce Court* scripts for five years, so you might think that his own screenplay would have a bit more bite. It does, but only during Illeana Douglas' sequences. 🦴🦴

1994 86m/C Craig Chester, Alexis Arquette, Lucy Gutteridge, Illeana Douglas, Jackie Beat, Carlton Wilborn, Paul Bartel, Mary Woronov; ***D:*** Richard Glatzer; ***W:*** Richard Glatzer; ***C:*** David Dechant. **VHS**

The Grifters

Jim Thompson's tightly written novels grab you by the throat and never let go until you finish reading them. *The Grifters* supplies movie audiences with an equivalent cinematic wallop. Ironically, it took a British director, Stephen Frears, to do full justice to Thompson, and *The Grifters* is arguably the finest film noir to emerge in recent years. *The Grifters* examines con artists in extreme close-up. For most of the narrative, Frears uses a straightforward matter-of-fact approach to tell a fairly bizarre, always chilling tale. In *The Grifters,* Anjelica Huston plays the sort of mother seldom seen on screen. As Lilly, her life has been one con after another, with no respite in sight. She is not devoid of feelings, she has simply learned that feelings are easily expendable in her line of work. Throughout the film, we see how other con artists retire after brutal experiences, which merely sideline Lilly for a moment or two. In contrast, her son Roy (John Cusack) doesn't have the stomach to be a con artist. His timing is off. His recovery time is slow. Worst of all, Roy lacks Lilly's sharp knack for reading people, especially a fellow grifter named Myra (Annette Bening). Cusack does his best job to date here and the usually elegant Bening is so grimy as Myra that she is able to achieve the effects of aromarama without the help of scratch-and-sniff cards. Veteran character actors Pat Hingle and Henry Jones also contribute to the film's pungent atmosphere. But it is Anjelica Huston's film all the way. Remember the final sequence in *Double Indemnity* when Barbara Stanwyck lies to Fred MacMurray for the umpteenth time and nearly gets away with it? Screen moments like this defy dissection and analysis, and Anjelica Huston has so many of them in *The Grifters:* the way she can take in stride a cigarette being ground onto her palm; the way she can work scams on everyone, even her own kid, without batting an eye. There was one point in the film when I thought she was going to bite the dust for sure and all I could think was, "I don't care what sort of a monster she is. If she dies, this movie is over!" And then there is the film's startling conclusion, which will knock you for a loop even if you've read the book. In 1969 at age 17, Anjelica was regarded as one of the world's worst actresses when she made her movie debut in *A Walk with Love and Death,* directed by father John. Over the years, she has emerged as a wise and charismatic presence onscreen, and her delicious portrayal in *Prizzi's Honor* was clearly just a warm-up for the work we will hopefully see her do in the future. In the meanwhile, Anjelica Huston's work in *The Grifters* simply has to rank among the all-time great noir performances ever. 🦴🦴🦴🦴

1990 (R) 114m/C Anjelica Huston, John Cusack, Annette Bening, Pat Hingle, J.T. Walsh, Charles Napier, Henry Jones, Gailard Sartain; ***D:*** Stephen Frears; ***W:*** Donald E. Westlake; ***C:*** Oliver Stapleton; ***M:*** Elmer Bernstein. Independent Spirit Awards '91: Best Actress (Huston), Best Film; Los Angeles Film Critics Association Awards '90: Best Actress (Huston); National Society of Film Critics Awards '90: Best Actress (Huston), Best Supporting Actress (Bening); Nominations: Academy Awards '90: Best Actress (Huston), Best Adapted Screenplay, Best Director (Frears), Best Supporting Actress (Bening). **VHS, LV, Closed Caption, DVD**

Grim Prairie Tales

Grim Prairie Tales is director/screenwriter Wayne Coe's first movie and his heart, if not his maturity as an artist, is definitely in the right place. Brad Dourif plays the sort of innocent who would have provided fodder for a monster in a different sort of movie. As it is, James Earl Jones comes barreling into his camp with a dead body in tow. Although Jones is armed with a full arsenal of death-dealing weapons, he proposes instead that he and Brad tell each other stories next to the campfire all night

Ann Proctor (Ruth Warrick) and Evelyn Heath (Anne Baxter) in *Guest in the House.*
United Artists; courtesy of the Kobal Collection

long. Only in the movies! The stories have the raw and unfinished feel of promising first drafts, but who knows what tales emerged from 19th century travelers when they didn't have pesky movie reviewers to evaluate their yarns? Coe's artistic, political, and sexual sensibilities belong strictly in the 20th century, however. For one sequence, he even thought it would be neat if the character had an animated nightmare. Not only is the animation poor, but the context is all wrong. Occasionally, Coe stumbles onto chilling home truths. His tale of a good family man who also happens to be a lyncher is well told from the perspective of the man's horrified daughter and deeply troubled wife. I also liked the dark little story about a misplaced act of chivalry resulting in an unexplained but definitely weird sexual encounter. Except for Dourif and Jones and the little girl who plays the lyncher's daughter, the casting could have been better, although Marc McClure, William Atherton, and Lisa Eichhorn fare the best.

1989 (R) 90m/C Brad Dourif, James Earl Jones, Marc McClure, William Atherton, Scott Paulin, Lisa Eichhorn; ***D:*** Wayne Coe; ***W:*** Wayne Coe; ***C:*** Janusz Kaminski. **VHS, LV**

Guest in the House

The interesting thing about *Guest in the House* is what it had to say about a frail 22-year-old girl whose manipulative behavior is plenty clear to the viewer, but not to any of the characters in the movie. Or is her behavior so strikingly clear because we know that the roles of Eve Harrington and Nefretiri are lurking in Anne Baxter's future? The part of Evelyn Heath is a preview of the many insincere vixens Baxter would play, but Douglas Proctor is unfamiliar erotic terrain for Ralph Bellamy. No less than three attractive women (including Ruth Warrick as wife Ann and Marie McDonald as Miriam, a voluptuous model) gaze at him like he's Mr. Sex whenever they're in his vicinity. Well, when the only other males around are Scott McKay, Jerome Cowan, and Percy Kilbride, it makes sense, sort of. Director John Brahm does a perceptive job exploring the film's many neurotic characters. (The conceit here is that you catch a neurosis as easily as a cold.) The sanest women in the joint are Margaret Hamilton and especially Aline MacMahon, who delivers her usual immaculate performance as shrewd Aunt Martha. The bonus is that *Guest in the House* is fraught with sexual tensions and all of them are explored as exhaustively as an independent production could get away with in 1944. 🦴🦴🦴

1944 121m/B Anne Baxter, Ralph Bellamy, Ruth Warrick, Marie McDonald, Margaret Hamilton, Aline MacMahon, Scott McKay, Jerome Cowan, Percy Kilbride, Connie Laird; ***D:*** John Brahm; ***W:*** Ketti Frings; ***C:*** Lee Garmes; ***M:*** Werner Janssen. Nominations: Academy Awards '45: Best Original Dramatic Score. **VHS**

Gun Crazy

Peggy Cummins IS Annie Laurie Starr in this film noir classic! Three years after her ignominious firing from Otto Preminger's *Forever Amber* (reportedly because she looked like a little girl playing dress-up in period costumes), Cummins showed that she could be every bit as sexy as her replacement, Linda Darnell, in a blonde wig. In this beautifully directed saga by Joseph H. Lewis, Starr is a sideshow attraction in a carnival, sleeping with her yucky boss Packett (Berry Kroeger), and impressing small town crowds with her shooting expertise. Then Bart Tare (John Dall) walks by with a couple of his friends. Bart's had an interesting history with guns. As a child (Russ Tamblyn), he was obsessed with them—not with killing, just with guns, and was sent to reform school by Judge Willougby (Morris Carnovsky). Bart quickly impresses Annie with HIS shooting expertise, and they fall into instant lust, sort of a menage a trois, really—Annie, Bart, and guns. Packett hires Bart for the act and he tours with the carnival, until he and Annie get married. Then a jealous Packett fires them both, and they lose their legitimate arena for expressing their passion with guns. It isn't really poverty that leads them to the next step, but Annie's desire to use a gun again. Bart resists her suggestion that they become bank robbers and tries to leave, but the bond between them is too strong and their fate is sealed. There is a wonderful sequence as they approach the bank, shot from the back seat of the car, with all-natural lighting. It just looks so real, and the acting by Cummins and Dall is so artless that for a moment we forget we're watching a movie with actors—it's like we intruded on an actual hold-up. If *Gun Crazy* were re-released today, it would bat most neo-noir entries out of the ball park. Independently produced by the King brothers, Frank and Maurice, who also made 1945's *Dillinger. Gun Crazy* is based on the *Saturday Evening Post* story by MacKinlay Kantor. Millard Kaufman fronted for blacklisted screenwriter Dalton Trumbo, who was the most prolific of the Hollywood Ten: he won Oscars for *Roman Holiday* (using a front) and *The Brave One* (with a pseudonym) while still on the blacklist. Lewis' other excellent noir films include *My Name Is Julia Ross, So Dark the Night, Undercover Man, A Lady Without Passport,* and *The Big Combo.* ***AKA:*** Deadly Is the Female. 🦴🦴🦴🦴

1949 87m/B Peggy Cummins, John Dall, Berry Kroeger, Morris Carnovsky, Anabel Shaw, Nedrick Young, Trevor Bardette, Russ Tamblyn, Harry Lewis, Mickey Little, Paul Frison, Dave Bair, Stanley Prager, Virginia Farmer, Anne O'Neal, Frances Irwin, Don Beddoe, Robert Osterloh, Shimen Ruskin, Harry Hayden; ***D:*** Joseph H. Lewis; ***W:*** Dalton Trumbo; ***C:*** Russell Harlan; ***M:*** Victor Young. **VHS**

Guncrazy

Drew Barrymore and James LeGros star in *Guncrazy,* a film that both exploits Barrymore's checkered offscreen image and protects her status as a 17-year-old minor. The result is a weak, if violent, story that backs away from every sexual issue it raises. Barrymore doesn't really have sufficient depth as an actress yet to play a junior league Bonnie Parker, although Ione Skye, another badly neglected member of the cast, could have tackled the leading role with ease and honors. Skip this one and rent Joseph H. Lewis' classic 1949 film noir *Gun Crazy* instead. 🦴

The Hound Salutes: IAIN SOFTLEY
Director, *Hackers*

I think that it was such a logical progression for me to go from *Backbeat* to *Hackers,* although I wasn't seeking out a stylistic consistency. I was just looking for something that caught my eye, made me laugh and got my pulse racing. After *Backbeat,* a lot of the scripts I was sent were very well written—technically brilliant, with snappy dialogue, but formulaic, with no originality or new perspective. I got to feeling, 'What else do I know about the world?' What really struck me about first-time writer Rafael Moreu's *Hackers* script was its freshness, its energy, and its sense of fun. More importantly, though, it was about a new world (the computer subculture or cyberculture), that I hadn't seen anyone try to reflect onscreen.

"It was a movie that I hadn't seen before, like *Blow-Up* reflected London's art, fashion, and music world in 1966 or *Easy Rider* reflected America's rock culture in 1969. That was a real plus for me. In addition, *Hackers* confounded my expectations. I expected a script about computer hackers would consist of white, middle-class, nerdy kids in suburban bedrooms. What we had in Rafael Moreu's script was a group of multi-ethnic, multi-racial, vibrant guys and girls on the streets of Manhattan (which itself is a technological crossroads and cultural melting pot). There was something very sexy and tribal about that. I liked the idea of these kids almost inhabiting the streets of Manhattan as a modern-day cyberpunk tribe. Obviously, that had great potential for visual interpretation, which isn't, to my mind, just flashiness for its own sake, but is actually an intrinsic part of the narrative storytelling—to try to create a world that gives people a sense of what the movie's trying to do.

1992 (R) 97m/C Drew Barrymore, James LeGros, Billy Drago, Rodney Harvey, Ione Skye, Joe Dallesandro, Michael Ironside; ***D:*** Tamra Davis; ***W:*** Matthew Bright; ***C:*** Lisa Rinzler. **VHS, LV, Closed Caption**

Habit

Vampires on a budget (!), only this time they're in color (unlike *The Addiction*) and glorious Pixelvision is nowhere in sight (unlike *Nadja*). Sam (Larry Fessenden) is an alcoholic, who isn't sure whether Anna (Meredith Snaider) is a vampire or not and is having too good a time with her in bed to give a hoot, one way or another. Ultra-cheap, but the cast is good and director Fessenden does what he can with his rock-bottom budget. 🦴🦴

1997 112m/C Larry Fessenden, Meredith Snaider, Aaron Beall, Heather Woodbury, Patricia Coleman; ***D:*** Larry Fessenden; ***W:*** Larry Fessenden; ***C:*** Frank DeMarco; ***M:*** Geoffrey Kidde. Nominations: Independent Spirit Awards '98: Best Cinematography, Best Director (Fessenden). **VHS**

Hackers

In the beginning, hackers were, well, sort of geeky. They could be supporting characters in the movies, the experts that the cool heroes went to see when they needed help. But they rarely left their computer terminals. Iain *(Backbeat)* Softley's movie, *Hackers,* is the latest cinematic effort to lionize hackers and turn them into the cool heroes. The protagonist hacker is state-of-the-art cute. His female nemesis (and

In order to tell the story, it was also very important to interpret the computer sequences and the battle in cyberspace at the end of the movie between all the hackers and the villain. It was necessary to find an absorbing, arresting, and involving way of depicting what is actually a two-dimensional screen. I wanted to show why hackers get so hooked on cyberspace, which in reality is a theoretical place. What is it that obsesses them? I got interested in the idea that it was a parallel reality that they surfed through with their minds, and where they existed in these labyrinths that connect computers together. I wanted to present this fantasy world as a physical reality to the cinema audience. I came up with a database that was a three-dimensional city of text, much like a mirror image of the city of Manhattan itself. There are many references to Manhattan being a technological fantasy island where the hackers feel at home and have a lot of fun.

"The styles and techniques of the stars [Jonny Lee Miller, Angelina Jolie, Fisher Stevens, Lorraine Bracco, Alberta Watson, Matthew Lillard, Penn Jillette] were very different. It was a bit like the movie; cyberculture is like a collage. You only need to flip through *Wired* or *Mondo 2000* to see that they use images like a photo montage. The *Hackers* script reflects that in a way. The hackers move around in very different worlds: the streets, their schools, their departments, their clubs, the Secret Service world, the oil company world, and all those worlds, with their different textures and feelings, are reflected in the acting styles. I had to stay on my toes to work out what was the best way for each actor. Some actors wanted to be told quite specifically what they were to do, other actors wanted a lot of freedom to improvise; some people's early takes turned out to be the best, other people's later takes were best. Sometimes, I'd just have to choose from the middle takes to get the best results from each actor. But it was a terrific experience and I think that everyone wound up bringing a helluva lot to the movie."

IAIN SOFTLEY also directed the indie films *Backbeat* and *The Wings of the Dove.*

eventual girlfriend) wears brown eyeshadow and black lipstick. Virtually all of their fellow hackers are whizzes on skateboards, a phenomenon that rarely occurs in real life. And as for the computer graphics, there's no such thing as a dull or undecorated screen. None of that "Do you really want to do this?" crap, just bold, colorful images, seamlessly edited into the dazzling, fast-paced lives that hackers lead. (And if you swallow the premise, I can make you a sensational deal on the Golden Gate Bridge.) The bad guys are Fisher Stevens (overacting as usual) and Lorraine Bracco (totally wasted). The main hacker's mother is Alberta Watson, who also played the incestuous mom in *Spanking the Monkey.* (In some sequences, she appears to be wearing the same bathrobe...an inside joke?) All the hackers seem to have "hot new star" stamped on their foreheads. They talk about megabytes and RAM as if they were discussing their favorite sexual positions. (True to hacker mythology, though, there isn't any real sex, only fantasies.) Everyone's an eyelash too old to be a pin-up in teen magazines Like *All Stars* or *Tiger Beat.* And the "hackers of the world unite" anthem is just dumb. The producers hope that the pulsing soundtrack, the fashions, and the erotically charged atmosphere will lure kiddies into theatres/video outlets in droves. (Jonny Lee Miller made a better career move by playing third lead in *Trainspotting* than by starring in this one.)

Laurie Strode AKA Keri Tate (Jamie Lee Curtis) engages in some violent sibling rivalry in *Halloween: H20.*
Dimension Films; courtesy of the Kobal Collection

1995 (PG-13) 105m/C Jonny Lee Miller, Angelina Jolie, Fisher Stevens, Lorraine Bracco, Jesse Bradford, Wendell Pierce, Alberta Watson, Laurence Mason, Renoly Santiago, Matthew Lillard, Penn Jillette; ***D:*** Iain Softley; ***W:*** Rafael Moreu; ***C:*** Andrzej Sekula; ***M:*** Simon Boswell. **VHS, LV, Closed Caption**

Halloween

Halloween, made on a budget of $300,000, brought in over $47 million in boxoffice receipts, which stunned the motion picture industry. It made John Carpenter and Jamie Lee Curtis famous and it became a model for countless other horror directors, not all of whom actually understood why *Halloween* quickened viewer's pulses. Carpenter recognized what Alfred Hitchcock, another great director in the horror genre, learned over 50 years before. When you force an audience to pay attention to a myriad of details in a suspenseful narrative where they know something terrible WILL occur, the violence actually RELIEVES their built-up tensions. Carpenter, who also wrote the effective, monotonous score, showed a fairly dull town on a fairly dull day. But we know from the prologue that an evil killer will return on Halloween night. He will kill because that's what he does; there's no sociological sympathy wasted on HIM—that's reserved for resourceful babysitter Laurie Strode, played by Curtis. My first impression of this second-generation actress, then 19, is that she has great presence and confidence, plus a low, forceful voice, PLUS a don't-mess-with-me veneer that makes her far more intriguing than the traditional squishy monster bait. The casting of Donald Pleasence as Dr. Samuel Loomis adds the resonance of countless prior horror classics to this groundbreaking 1978 entry in the genre. Moreover, the psychological landscape of *Halloween* is dominated by the indomitability of the killer. Later villains would become invincible to a ridiculous degree: five bullets and a burial service and their tickers are STILL ticking through multiple sequels. But *Halloween* plays it fair and square all the way through. It scares us because John Carpenter is a genius at what he does—scrambling our emotions for 93 minutes and always making us want to come back for more. Babysitter Advisory: Don't watch this one alone!

1978 (R) 93m/C Jamie Lee Curtis, Donald Pleasence, Nancy Loomis, P.J. Soles, Charles Cyphers, Kyle Richards, Brian Andrews, John Michael Graham, Nancy Stephens, Arthur Malet, Mickey Yablans, Brent Le Page, Adam Hollander, Robert Phalen, Sandy Johnson, David Kyle, Nick Castle; ***D:*** John Carpenter; ***W:*** John Carpenter, Debra Hill; ***C:*** Dean Cundey; ***M:*** John Carpenter. **VHS, LV**

Halloween: H20

In entertainment value, *Halloween: H20 (Twenty Years Later)* delivers four bones worth of fun; I was laughing for the last 35 minutes. Is this what Steve Miner et al had in mind? It raked in $55 million at the boxoffice within four months of its release, so maybe it is. Anyway, we're back with

Laurie Strode at age 37 (inimitably played by Jamie Lee Curtis, 39). She's a wreck, especially when October 31st rolls around every year. She's faked her own death, she's changed her name to Keri Tate, she drinks, she takes pills, and she imagines she sees Michael Myers everywhere. She's going with Will, sort of a loser shrink (Adam Arkin), who tries to talk her out of her justifiable paranoia. Scratch one bone! Laurie/Keri also has a 17-year-old kid named John (Josh Hartnett) who has NO idea what she's been through and is therefore chomping at the bit for some independence. He's supposed to be camping at Yosemite with his class, but decides to stay at school with girlfriend Molly (Michelle Williams) and pals Charlie (Adam Hann-Byrd) and Sarah (Jodi Lynn O'Keefe). I'll say one thing for Michael Myers' victims—they all put up one helluva fight. But you can't win against a guy who gets stabbed umpteen times, leaps off tall buildings with a sickening thud, crashes through windshields before getting run over by a car and falling off a cliff. And is he...? Yes, he is! Michael Myers is still ticking! It's got to be a fight to the bitter end for Laurie (what a woman) and Michael (Chris Durand). Scratch that! How about the next sequel? How can there be a sequel? Love and homicidal maniacs always find a way! Turn off the lights, lock the doors, look close for Janet Leigh's cameo as Norma, and check out Ronny, the invincible security guard played by L.L. Cool J. (what a man). Based on characters created by Debra Hill and John Carpenter. ***AKA:*** Halloween: H20 (Twenty Years Later); Halloween 7. 🦴🦴🦴

1998 (R) 86m/C Jamie Lee Curtis, Adam Arkin, Josh Hartnett, Michelle Williams, Adam Hann-Byrd, Jodi Lynn O'Keefe, Janet Leigh, L.L. Cool J., Joseph Gordon Levitt, Nancy Stephens, Branden Williams, Chris Durand; ***D:*** Steve Miner; ***W:*** Matt Greenberg, Robert Zappia; ***C:*** Daryn Okada; ***M:*** John Ottman, John Carpenter. **VHS, LV, Closed Caption**

Hand in Hand

This touching story of the friendship between a Roman Catholic boy (Philip Needs as Michael O'Malley) and a Jewish girl (Loretta Parry as Rachel Mathias) could easily have been heavy handed with the wrong director. Philip Leacock, who guided the very young Vincent Winter and Jon Whiteley to Academy Awards in 1953's *The Little Kidnappers,* was clearly the right guy for the job. Michael and Rachel get along just fine until he is teased about the friendship by his schoolmates, who tell him that Jesus Christ was killed by the Jewish people. Rachel is happily preparing an after school feast for him when he repeats what his friends told him. "We never killed anyone!" she cries and runs off. But the kids miss each other, and eventually run away together to speak to the Queen. They don't get to meet her, but they do have a chat with Lady Caroline (Sybil Thorndike) at one of the Queen's homes, and eventually, their respective parents enlist Father Timothy and a Cantor to help the kids with their dilemma. The best thing about *Hand in Hand* is the wonderful rapport between Needs and Parry. Their friendship is understated and most believable. (Parry was later signed by Walt Disney to appear in 1963's *The Horse Without a Head,* co-starring Vincent Winter.) 🦴🦴🦴

1960 78m/B *GB* John Gregson, Sybil Thorndike, Finlay Currie, Loretta Parry, Philip Needs, Miriam Karlin, Derek Sydney, Kathleen Byron; ***D:*** Philip Leacock; ***W:*** Leopold Atlas, Diana Morgan, Sidney Harmon; ***C:*** Frederick A. (Freddie) Young.

A Handful of Dust

Many feel the reason for the transatlantic success of *Dynasty* and *Brideshead Revisited* is that nothing delights Britishers and Americans more than watching their overseas cousins commit upper-class suicide. It makes sense, especially when you realize that hours and hours devoted to poverty-stricken characters in unphotogenic surroundings seldom pack the same visual wallop. Nope, if we're going to watch people run themselves into the ground, let's also have the startling insight that all those palaces and spectacular estates can't possibly save them from them-

“Well, this one has. You know, it’s stuck on good and proper now.”

—Ringo Starr’s response to a reporter’s question: “Do you think these haircuts have come to stay?” in *A Hard Day’s Night.*

selves. As *Brideshead Revisited* showed, Evelyn Waugh was passionately in love with the exclusive aristocratic world he satirized in so many of his books. *A Handful of Dust,* based on Waugh’s 1934 novel, provides more of the same rich and foolish twits, gorgeous and amoral wives, foolish pastimes that destroy the family heir, and the usual obligatory splendor as a backdrop. James Wilby, then 30, plays Lord Tony Last whose bride, Lady Brenda (Kristin Scott Thomas, then 28), develops a sudden craving to take an economics class, and we all know what THAT means. Faster than you can say “satin sheets,” Brenda is shown rolling in bed with a brainless, disloyal rotter named (of course) Beaver. The affair (of course) rocks the very foundations of what a proper upper-class marriage should be, but Brenda doesn’t have to pay too high a price for her bad manners. For reasons that make very little sense, though, poor Tony winds up stuck in a Brazilian jungle, forced to read Dickens novels to a loonie played by Alec Guinness. It takes about two hours to plow through this well-acted London Weekend Television production, directed by Charles Sturridge, who also helmed *Brideshead Revisited.* There’s one funny sequence when Lord Tony, eager to give the undeserving Lady Brenda grounds for divorce, dutifully trots off to a seaside hotel to stage his adultery with a woman who can’t find anyone to take care of her little girl. Private detective John Junkin, irritated when all he sees is Lord Tony babysitting the kid on the pier and in the hotel dining room, patiently explains that, no, this isn’t the way the game is played. The rest of the story is supposed to be hilarious too, and for those who believe that the rich are inherently cursed, it probably is—so if you enjoy this sort of fare, *A Handful of Dust* just may be your movie! 𝅘𝅥𝅘𝅥𝅘𝅥

1988 (PG) 114m/C *GB* James Wilby, Kristin Scott Thomas, Rupert Graves, Alec Guinness, Anjelica Huston, Judi Dench, Cathryn Harrison, Pip Torrens, John Junkin; ***D:*** Charles Sturridge; ***W:*** Charles Sturridge, Tim Sullivan, Derek Granger; ***C:*** Peter Hannan; ***M:*** George Fenton. British Academy Awards ’88: Best Supporting Actress (Dench); Nominations: Academy Awards ’88: Best Costume Design. **VHS**

The Hands of Orlac

When *The Hands of Orlac* was first shown in Vienna, grown women fainted and their male companions complained to the theatre manager. The manager asked Conrad Veidt if he would say something to the crowd to circumvent a riot. Reportedly, Veidt so moved the audience that, not only did he receive an ovation, but the movie went on to enjoy spectacular success (and with good reason). Is this silent movie better than 1935’s *Mad Love* starring Peter Lorre and 1960’s *The Hands of Orlac* with Mel Ferrer? Unquestionably! Veidt (1893–1943) was one of the most expressive actors of the silent screen. Moviegoers who know him only as *Caligari*’s Cesare the somnambulist or as Jaffar in *The Thief of Bagdad* or as *Casablanca*’s Major Strasser don’t really know Conrad Veidt. As pianist Paul Orlac, he believes that his hands (crushed in an accident) have been replaced with those of a murderer. He believes the murderer to be the sinister-looking gent played by Fritz Kortner (1892–1970), and so do we. Orlac feels that he can no longer touch his wife (Alexandra Sorina) or play ever again. Actually, screenwriter Ludwig Nerz and director Robert Wiene (1881–1938) are playing fast AND clever with us, but as long as the illusion lasts, we are nearly as caught up in Orlac’s torture as he is (and I’m not talking about a dream sequence here). In the best of all possible worlds, *The Hands of Orlac* would be released on video with the Clubfoot Orchestra’s outstanding score, first performed at San Francisco’s Castro Theatre in early 1997. (Based on the novel by Maurice Renard.) ***AKA:*** Orlacs Hände. 𝅘𝅥𝅘𝅥𝅘𝅥𝅘𝅥

1925 92m/B *AT* Conrad Veidt, Fritz Kortner, Carmen Cartellieri, Paul Askonas, Alexandra Sorina, Fritz Strassny; ***D:*** Robert Wiene; ***W:*** Ludwig Nerz; ***C:*** Gunther Krampf, Hans Androschin. **VHS**

Hangin’ with the Homeboys

Because *Hangin’ with the Home Boys* starred a cast of talented unknowns and New Line Cinema did not heavily promote it, the film needed (and deserved) favorable word-of-mouth reviews to do well at the boxoffice. It's exactly the TYPE of movie I ordinarily detest: four guys hang out together one night every week, preferring their own company to anyone else's, and of course ragging on every female that crosses their path. That said, *Hangin' with the Home Boys* is a delight to watch mainly because of writer/director Joseph B. Vasquez's superb understanding of what makes his characters tick. Moreover, the women in the story, although they are seen one-dimensionally by the four guys, are drawn with considerable depth. Willie (Doug E. Doug) is so convinced that his poverty is rooted in the fact he is black that he spends the entire evening sponging off his buddies. Tom (Mario Joyner) wants to be a great actor like William Shatner, even hustling agents as he peddles magazines over the telephone to survive. Johnny (John Leguizamo) works for a supermarket, has fantasies about women, and is terrified to apply for a scholarship that will free him from his safe, spare existence. The most obnoxious of the four is Fernando (Nestor Serrano), who lives off women and wants to be known as Vinny so people will think he's Italian instead of Puerto Rican. Kimberly Russell, Mary B. Ward, Christine Claravall, and Rosemarie Jackson are seen briefly but vividly as the women in their lives, and Reggie Montgomery has a sparkling cameo as a street person named Pasta. Because its executive producer Janet Grillo insisted that film companies take on the project or leave it exactly as is, Vasquez's film is strikingly free of all the telltale evidence that accompanies development process tampering. When 19 or 20 executives start monkeying around with someone's baby, the results are inevitably slick and riddled with cliches. (The difference between the very real confusion young men feel around women and Hollywood's exploitation of that confusion to justify onscreen female bashing is overwhelming.) Although Vaquez clearly likes Willie, Tom, Vinny, and Johnny, their rough edges have not been smoothed away to make them more conventionally appealing. *Hangin' with the Home Boys* is highly recommended as a compassionate, extremely funny film about an authentic time in the past of its creator. (Vasquez's other films include *The Bronx War* and *Street Hitz.*) 🎞🎞🎞

1991 (R) 89m/C Mario Joyner, Doug E. Doug, John Leguizamo, Nestor Serrano, Kimberly Russell, Mary B. Ward, Christine Claravall, Rosemark Jackson, Reggie Montgomery; ***D:*** Joseph B. Vasquez; ***W:*** Joseph B. Vasquez; ***C:*** Anghel Decca. Sundance Film Festival '91: Best Screenplay. **VHS, LV, Closed Caption**

Happiness

After watching 90 minutes of *Happiness* on a screening room floor, our esteemed colleague Andrea Chase sensibly announced that she'd had it and left. I stuck it out for the remaining 49 minutes and staggered out into the sunshine, desperate for fresh air and for *Buffy, the Vampire Slayer.* It is reassuring for me to think about Andrea Chase instead of Todd Solondz's *Happiness,* because she is real and his latest critical triumph is a sham. It is comforting for me to consider the virtues of Buffy because she represents goodness and strength in a murky, wimpy world. Apparently it is a source of ecstasy for most international critics to look down on New Jersey as the cesspool of the universe. I suspect that most have never been there. They are not like and do not know anyone like the people in *Happiness,* therefore all is well and good on our planet. *Happiness* is about pedophiliac psychiatrist Dr. Bill Maplewood (Dylan Baker), who arouses himself with teen beefcake magazines, drugs and sodomizes his 11-year-old son's classmate, Johnny Grasso (Evan Silverberg), and then sodomizes yet another classmate before law enforcement authorities finally catch on. It's about a large woman who cuts her doorman into little pieces and freezes them after he rapes her. Its about a sexual stalker who makes calls to fantasy objects who then lose their allure for him when he actually approaches them. It's about Joy Jordan (Jane Adams), a lonely and very bad songwriter wracked with guilt after she dumps loser Andy Kornbluth (Jon Lovitz), who only succeeds at killing himself and blaming her. After that, Vlad the Russian thief (Jared Harris) looks like an ever-so-tempting alter-

elest father-son dialogues ever filmed, including a harsh nine-word exchange I hope I can forget someday. Don't feel guilty if you skip *Happiness:* I wish I had! It's a real "Triumph of the Will" for N.A.M.B.L.A. members (North American Man-Boy Love Association). 🦴

1998 139m/C Jane Adams, Dylan Baker, Lara Flynn Boyle, Ben Gazzara, Jared Harris, Philip Seymour Hoffman, Jon Lovitz, Cynthia Stevenson, Elizabeth Ashley, Louise Lasser, Camryn Manheim, Anne Bobby, Evan Silverberg; ***D:*** Todd Solondz; ***W:*** Todd Solondz; ***C:*** Maryse Alberti; ***M:*** Robbie Kondor. **VHS**

Clementine (Gwyneth Paltrow) in *Hard Eight.* Goldwyn; courtesy of the Kobal Collection

native. There was a core of sweetness to *Welcome to the Dollhouse.* Solondz genuinely liked some, if not all, of the characters in *Dollhouse* (his second feature; 1989's *Fear, Anxiety and Depression* was the first) and there was a moral compass lurking on the margins of the story. However bizarre the worlds of, say, David Lynch and John Waters, their films are not long sociopathic rants. There is good and evil in the world and we never forget the difference. Solondz was quoted in *Newsweek* as saying, "If the audience looks at *Happiness* and says they're freaks, I've failed." There is nothing but horror in *Happiness* and eventually, if you don't tune out, you immunize yourself to 139 minutes of ugly despair. For expatriates who detest American culture, *Happiness* may be a comedy, but for me, the screening room became a virtual torture chamber, with some of the cru-

Happy Together

Happy Together looks great and Wang Kar-Wai aficionados will appreciate this movie that's about everything BUT the story of a relationship. For me, it was like flipping through the travelogues of strangers. It shows Hong Kong stars Leslie Cheung and Tony Leung Chiu-Wai as gay lovers in Buenos Aires, Argentina, who are together, then apart, then sort of but not really together again. Instead of listening to "California Dreaming" over and over again as we did in *Chung King Express,* we get to hear (what else?) "Happy Together." Christopher Doyle's cinematography is so spectacular, I wanted to be absorbed by this style-driven movie, but the 92-minute script says nothing about the characters that I couldn't get from a promotional poster. ***AKA:*** Cheun Gwong Tsa Sit; Spring Brilliance Suddenly Pours Out. 🦴🦴

1996 92m/C *HK* Leslie Cheung, Tony Leung Chiu-Wai, Chang Chen; ***D:*** Wong Kar-Wai; ***W:*** Wong Kar-Wai, Kar-Wei Wong; ***C:*** Christopher Doyle; ***M:*** Danny Chung. Cannes Film Festival '97: Best Director (Kar-Wai); Nominations: Independent Spirit Awards '98: Best Foreign Film. **VHS**

A Hard Day's Night

Yes, *A Hard Day's Night* was a Brit indie, made quickly to cash in on the Beatle's surge in popularity after their February 1964 appearance on *The Ed Sullivan Show.* Producer Walter Shenson hoped that Beatlemania would last at least through June, when the movie was due to hit theatres. The selection of Richard Lester as director was by no means a guarantee that the movie would be a blockbuster. He had, after all, helmed *It's Trad, Dad,* a little-known 1962 Helen Shapiro musical, remembered today only by die-hard film buffs. Also known as *Ring-A-Ding Rhythm,* this 73-minute film was packed with then-household names like Chubby Checker, John Leyton, Gary (U.S.) Bonds, and the late Gene Vincent and Del Shannon. It was also filled with Lester's then-innovative cinematic techniques, but it went nowhere fast, as did many Brit flicks of that era, like 1963's *Summer Holiday* and *It's All Happening* with, respectively, Cliff Richard and Tommy Steele. All right, the Beatles could sing, but could they act? Alun Owen prepared his Oscar-nominated screenplay with the assumption that they could not, and then, when the rushes revealed that at least three of the Beatles were surprisingly relaxed on camera (the dashing Paul McCartney was not among them), Owen quickly came up with more dialogue for them. An American tour that coincided with the film's U.S. release helped to make it one of 1964's most profitable releases. The international audiences of 1964 were clearly hungry for a lightning-paced, tongue-in-cheek glimpse of life in the fast lane, and *A Hard Day's Night* supplied it. We wanted to believe that being a Beatle was fun and zany, just like in this movie; it was a shock to discover in *Let It Be,* a mere six years later, how far the sparkling Beatle image was removed from a much-grittier reality. As fiction, *A Hard Day's Night* holds up. This is how we would like for the life of the Beatles to be, so this is what we want to remember. (Self-effacing Ringo Starr, the last to join the group, was, by virtue of being the best actor in the bunch, the quintessential Beatle; he went on to make the most films as an actor, and is, with shifting members of his All-Starr band, the only former Beatle to tour with any regularity into the 1990s.) ♨♨♨♨

1964 90m/B *GB* John Lennon, Paul McCartney, George Harrison, Ringo Starr, Wilfrid Brambell, Norman Rossington, John Junkin, Victor Spinetti, Anna Quayle, Deryck Guyler, Richard Vernon, Lionel Blair, Eddie Malin, Robin Ray, Alison Seebohm, David Saxon; ***D:*** Richard Lester; ***W:*** Alun Owen; ***C:*** Gilbert Taylor. Nominations: Academy Awards '64: Best Story & Screenplay (Owen), Best Original Score. **VHS, LV, CD-I, DVD**

Hard Eight

Sydney (Philip Baker Hall) is a man of mystery from the moment we first lay eyes on him. He's about 64 and he looks it. He's led a tough life which he doesn't discuss. He knows the rules of every game, but doesn't say how he learned them. He meets John (John C. Reilly) sitting outside a coffee shop and picks him up like a stray dog. John, who's lost all his money gambling to pay for his mother's funeral, is deeply suspicious of Sydney at first, but lightens up as it becomes clear that Sydney loves him like a son. Professional gambler Sydney shows John the ropes in the Reno casinos; John's life is forever transformed for the better and he grows to love Sydney like a father. Two years pass. John falls in love with a waitress named Clementine (Gwyneth Paltrow). Sydney loves her like a daughter and treats her like a princess. But Clementine moonlights as a hooker and Sydney disapproves of that. And John has a friend named Jimmy (Samuel L. Jackson) and Sydney disapproves of him even more. Jimmy knows things about Sydney and John and Clementine and he doesn't love any of them like a son or a father or a daughter. Sydney knows what Jimmy knows, but John and Clementine don't. That's the set-up in this jewel of a movie by Paul Thomas Anderson, who made *Boogie Nights* the following year. It's dominated by the mesmerizing performance of Philip Baker Hall. Hall gives Sydney the star power of Bogie or Cagney or Edward G. Robinson and the resonance of a man who's seen, heard, felt, tasted, and been it all and is gambling on his own redemption. We trust him and, what's more, Anderson makes us trust him as much as John and Clementine do. In his follow-up film, Anderson looked at the pornographic movie business through non-judgmental eyes. This splendidly acted film noir, on a much smaller canvas than *Boogie Nights,* is equally non-judgmental and every bit as

“You know the first thing they should've taught you at hooker school? You get the money up front!”

—Sydney (Philip Baker Hall) in *Hard Eight*.

fascinating. You'll remember Hall as Sydney in *Hard Eight* long after the film is over. If you want to check out more of his work on video, look for him in *The Last Reunion, Secret Honor* (as Nixon), *Three O'Clock High, Blue Desert, Air Force One, The Truman Show, Sour Grapes, Rush Hour* and, of course, *Boogie Nights*. John C. Reilly is also in *Boogie Nights,* as well as *Missing Pieces, Touch and Go, We're No Angels, Casualties of War, State of Grace, Days of Thunder, Out on a Limb, Hoffa, The River Wild, Dolores Claiborne, Georgia, Boys, Nightwatch,* and *What's Eating Gilbert Grape?* Household names Jackson and Paltrow continue to skid towards Oscar night with every new role they play. ***AKA:*** Sydney. 🦴🦴🦴

1996 (R) 101m/C Philip Baker Hall, John C. Reilly, Gwyneth Paltrow, Samuel L. Jackson, F. William Parker, Philip Seymour Hoffman, Nathanael Cooper, Wynn White, Robert Ridgely, Michael J. Rowe, Kathleen Campbell, Peter D'Allessandro, Steve Blane, Xaleese, Melora Walters, Jean Langer; ***D:*** Paul Thomas Anderson; ***W:*** Paul Thomas Anderson; ***C:*** Robert Elswit; ***M:*** Michael Penn, Jon Brion. Nominations: Independent Spirit Awards '98: Best Actor (Hall), Best Cinematography, Best First Feature, Best Supporting Actor (Jackson). **VHS, LV, Closed Caption**

Hard Traveling

Alvah Bessie (1904–85) wrote *Bread and a Stone* in 1941 and then watched his promising career as an Oscar-nominated screenwriter turn to ashes when he was interrogated by the House Un-American Activities Committee as a member of the Hollywood Ten. He went to jail for contempt of Congress and continued to write, although not in Hollywood. (He did adapt his novel *The Symbol* for Columbia's 1974 Connie Stevens vehicle, *The Sex Symbol.*) Before his death in 1985, Bessie got to see the completed version of *Hard Traveling,* which was adapted and directed by his son Dan. This well-intentioned effort is a movie out of its time. The life-and-death Depression issues that made *Bread and a Stone* so gripping to read apparently meant less to audiences in the Reaganomics era. J.E. Freeman, Ellen Geer, Barry Corbin, James Gammon, and Jim Haynie are all fine character actors, but none of them has the sort of onscreen charisma that makes us care vitally about every breath s/he takes. Even the extras in a courtroom sequence are too representative of the mid-'80s in look and manner for us to get lost in the story and transport ourselves to the times of hard traveling. I tried turning off the color and watching this in black and white once and it helped somewhat, but not entirely. While at Warner Bros., Alvah Bessie tried to persuade Bette Davis to use her influence so that the studio would buy the book. Davis seemed interested until she asked if the downbeat ending could be changed, and he told her that he wanted the ending to remain intact. That was that. In the 1940s, they didn't buy the book for the screen, and in the 1980s, they didn't have the look for the screen. 🦴🦴🦴

1985 (PG) 99m/C J.E. Freeman, Ellen Geer, Barry Corbin, James Gammon, Jim Haynie; ***D:*** Dan Bessie; ***W:*** Dan Bessie; ***C:*** David Myers. **VHS**

Having a Wild Weekend

The Dave Clark Five, as anyone knows who devoured *16* magazine between the spring of 1964 and the summer of 1967, were the leading proponents of the Tottenham Sound, which meant that the group had been formed there (in 1960) instead of Liverpool. After the obligatory stint on *The Ed Sullivan Show* they recorded a series of hit songs, including “Glad All Over,” “Bits and Pieces,” “Do You Love Me,” “Can't You See That She's Mine,” “Because,” “Everybody Knows,” “Any Way You Want It,” “Come Home,” “Reelin' and Rockin',” “I Like It Like That,” “Catch Us If You Can,” “Over and Over,” “At the Scene,” “Try Too Hard,” “Please Tell Me Why,” “You Got What It Takes,” and “You Must Have Been a Beautiful Baby.” Ring any bells? *Having a Wild Weekend,* released 10 months after *A Hard Day's Night* and three months prior to *Help!,* begins like a brisk Richard Lester film, but swiftly descends into cynical melancholia. Everyone is trying to have fun, but no one through the end credits really IS. Dave Clark plays Steve, a stunt man who runs off with a blonde dolly bird model named Dinah (Barbara Ferris). The other four members of the band are glorified extras in assorted outfits, who comment on their trek. The advertising executives who employ Dinah claim she's been kidnapped, thus keeping her in the headlines she's trying to escape. Steve and Dinah run into a dopers' den, in which drug use looks dreary instead of fun, and then bump into a dull couple in the country, who clearly want to play a few rounds of partner swapping. Clark is movie star handsome, but has no discernible acting abilities whatever. Ferris is better, but her part is stupid. What if "dead grotty Susan" had been the focus of *A Hard Day's Night*? *Having a Wild Weekend* gives you an inkling. Fledgling director John Boorman's career could only go UP after this curio. P.S.: The costumes by Sally Jacobs are ghastly. ***AKA:*** Catch Us If You Can.

1965 91m/B *GB* Dave Clark, Barbara Ferris, Lenny Davidson, Rick Huxley, Mike Smith, Dennis Payton, Clive Swift, Hugh Walters, Robin Bailey, Yootha Joyce, David de Keyser, Robert Lang, Michael Blakemore, Marianne Stone, Julian Holloway, Susan Hanson; ***D:*** John Boorman; ***W:*** Peter Nichols; ***C:*** Manny Wynn; ***M:*** Dave Clark Five.

Hawks

In 1969, Timothy Dalton outraged everyone with the statement that he intended to be an even better actor than Laurence Olivier. *Hawks* is the first time I've been able to agree that Dalton might finally be on the way to achieving that goal. Anthony Edwards and Dalton play two dying patients who escape from a British hospital and steal an ambulance. They flee to the Netherlands for a holiday where they plan to spend their dying days in an Amsterdam whore house. Instead, they meet two English girls in pursuit of a Dutch character who made one of them pregnant. A fine screenplay by Roy Clarke makes *Hawks* a surprising delight and Robert Ellis Miller's steady, sure direction keeps the whole thing in balance. Anthony Edwards is excellent as the American football player sidelined by illness, but Dalton's performance is a true star turn, packed with charisma, tenderness, vitality, anguish, and humor. It's by far the best thing he's done onscreen. Janet McTeer is wonderful as the awkward unwed mother who towers over and captivates Dalton, and Sheila Hancock is very good as her best friend. Because it's really about life with no holds barred, *Hawks* is one of the very few films about death that I actually enjoyed and would be willing to see again.

1989 (R) 105m/C *GB* Anthony Edwards, Timothy Dalton, Janet McTeer, Jill Bennett, Sheila Hancock, Connie Booth, Camille Coduri; ***D:*** Robert Ellis Miller; ***W:*** Roy Clarke; ***C:*** Doug Milsome. **VHS, LV, 8mm, Closed Caption**

He Ran All the Way

A 19-year-old guy asked me who John Garfield was the other day and I nearly died! There must be at least 15 of the movies he made between 1938 and 1948 on the shelves of most neighborhood video outlets. Unfortunately, *Nobody Lives Forever, The Breaking Point,* and his swan song, *He Ran All the Way,* are not among them. Garfield, who began his career with the Group Theatre, was like a breath of fresh air when he first arrived in Hollywood. He wasn't a completely bad guy, but he hated fuss and pretense. He hated to be manipulated, too, but that didn't stop men and women alike from trying to use him for their own purposes. When he fell, he fell hard, and his naked face revealed every conflicting emotion that ran across it. In *He Ran All the Way,* Garfield plays a thief named Nick who becomes involved in a robbery with Al (Norman Lloyd). Al is wounded in the attempt and Nick shoots a guard, then flees to the neighborhood swimming pool. He meets a girl (Shelley Winters as Peggy Dobbs) and follows her home. At first, her parents (Wallace Ford and Selena Royle) and little brother (Bobby Hyatt) welcome Nick into their home, even leaving him alone with Peggy while they catch a movie. But Al's fears escalate when the family returns home. His guilty conscience convinces him that they've heard about the robbery, and he takes them hostage. When he learns that he killed the guard in the robbery, he feverishly makes plans to run away with Peggy. This independent production was the only job Garfield could get in the last year of his life. Berry and Butler were under inves-

"You close your eyes. You cast your mind back 30 years, and you see and hear what you want to hear."

—Grandma Ryan (Gladys Sheehan) in *Hear My Song.*

tigation by the House Committee on Un-American Activities and Garfield's turn was next. He was due to appear before the Committee and, during the grueling wait, he died of a heart attack, aggravated by emotional strain and sleep deprivation. The fear that Garfield projects in his final performance onscreen had never been this intense before; he looks like he's gnawing a part of himself away in order to escape. Winters, then 29, is believable as the girl who's torn between her family and a desperate man for the first time in her life. No one knows what sort of a career or life Garfield might have had if he'd lived, but during his too-brief time in Hollywood, he gave the working class a recognizable face and voice with which to identify, and gave each role a no-nonsense approach, almost as if he weren't acting at all. Other noir films starring Garfield include *The Postman Always Rings Twice, Body and Soul,* and *Force of Evil.* Based on the novel by Sam Ross.

1951 77m/B John Garfield, Shelley Winters, Wallace Ford, Selena Royle, Bobby Hyatt, Gladys George, Norman Lloyd, Jimmy Ames; ***D:*** John Berry; ***W:*** Guy Endore, Hugo Butler; ***C:*** James Wong Howe; ***M:*** Franz Waxman.

Hear My Song

The career of actress Shirley Anne Field says a great deal about the motion picture industry in Britain. The beautiful and talented Field began playing small roles in the mid-'50s while still a teenager. Within a few years, she was attracting attention in international hits like *The Entertainer* with Laurence Olivier and *Saturday Night and Sunday Morning* with Albert Finney. She seemed to be all over the place in the early 1960s, but with the waning of the British vogue in films, her career faded by the end of the decade. With 1985's *My Beautiful Laundrette,* Field reemerged as a stunning character actress of enormous skill, and she went on to play vivid supporting roles in *Shag, Setting It Right,* and *The Rachel Papers.* Field is not the centerpiece of Peter Chelsom's *Hear My Song,* but her appearance in this charming film about the resurrection of real-life Irish tenor Josef Locke was certainly an inspired casting decision. *Hear My Song* revolves around the efforts of young concert promoter Micky O'Neill (played by screenwriter Adrian Dunbar), who is trying to make a mint by presenting a return engagement of the great Locke. He hires a look-a-like (William Hootkins) who has done fairly well with small-time gigs by trading on his resemblance to Locke. But when the fake Locke makes a pass at one Cathleen Doyle (played with conviction by Field) who was, as a former Miss Dairy Goodness of 1958, in love with the real Locke, the jig is up. Since Doyle is the mother of Micky's girlfriend and both women are furious with him, he has no choice but to comb the countryside looking for Locke. When he finally locates him, there's another stumbling block: Locke is a tax fugitive and has no interest in making a comeback that will attract as much attention from the police (including David McCallum!) as from a nostalgic audience. For those who enjoy watching vintage Ealing comedies on the Late Show, *Hear My Song* compares favorably with many of the best efforts from that enchanted studio. Ned Beatty does a delicious job as Locke, even if he was born in Kentucky! Although *Hear My Song* is certainly not a film for cynics, it offers an affectionate and funny view of some engaging characters and, of course, a terrific role for Shirley Anne Field. Peter Chelsom's film is well worth a look on video.

1991 (R) 104m/C *GB* Ned Beatty, Adrian Dunbar, Shirley Anne Field, Tara Fitzgerald, William Hootkins, Gladys Sheehan, David McCallum; ***D:*** Peter Chelsom; ***W:*** Peter Chelsom; ***C:*** Sue Gibson; ***M:*** John Altman. **VHS, Closed Caption**

Heartland

Conchata Ferrell is quite wonderful as a widow in her 30s who accepts a position as Rip Torn's housekeeper in Wyoming in the year 1910. Torn is rather a Gloomy Gus, but the two of them get used to each other over the course of the film. The unconventional casting added to the realism of Richard Pearce's film, as did the fact that the screenplay was based on the journals of a real-life pioneer woman, Elinore Randall Stewart. If you love Torn on *The Larry Sanders Show,* here's a chance to see him in a very different part. 🦴🦴🦴

1981 (PG) 95m/C Conchata Ferrell, Rip Torn, Barry Primus, Lilia Skala, Megan Folson; ***D:*** Richard Pearce; ***W:*** Beth Ferris; ***C:*** Fred Murphy. Sundance Film Festival '81: Grand Jury Prize. **VHS**

Heat and Dust

In the summer of 1963, there were few 22-year-old actresses on the planet with more charisma than Julie Christie when she popped up as Liz, luring Tom Courtenay's *Billy Liar.* Sparkling with health and *joie de vivre*, Christie starred in a dozen major films over a 15-year span, then was offscreen for nearly five years, an eternity for an actress in her 40s. *Heat and Dust* was the vehicle she selected for her return. She was still lovely, delightful, and charming as a researcher named Anne, but the script was stacked in favor of a NEW 22-year-old actress who was playing her Great Aunt Olivia: Greta Scacchi. The contemporary investigations of the free-spirited Anne simply didn't carry the narrative weight of her rambunctious ancestor of the 1920s. Olivia is an eager young bride when she first comes to India to join her husband, Douglas Rivers (Christopher Cazenove), a civil servant. Both Olivia and Anne are caught up in the spell of India, but neither is ever fully accepted there. Olivia has an affair with Nawab (Shashi Kapoor), a local ruler, and Anne, too, has a brief romance with a young man. But their restless, rebellious personalities keep them isolated and alone, at odds with the country they both love, and never quite fitting in anywhere. *Heat and Dust* launched Scacchi's international career and over the next decade she played more than 15 major roles that took full advantage of her stunning looks before she settled into secondary character parts by the time she was 34 (!). The intriguing script for this beautifully made Merchant/Ivory production is based on the novel by Ruth Prawer Jhabvala. 🦴🦴🦴🦴

1982 (R) 130m/C *GB* Julie Christie, Greta Scacchi, Shashi Kapoor, Christopher Cazenove, Nickolas Grace, Julian Glover, Susan Fleetwood, Patrick Godfrey, Jennifer Kendal, Madhur Jaffrey, Barry Foster, Amanda Walker, Sudha Chopra, Sajid Khan, Zakir Hussain, Ratna Pathak, Charles McCaughan, Parveen Paul; ***D:*** James Ivory; ***W:*** Ruth Prawer Jhabvala, Saeed Jaffrey, Harish Khare; ***C:*** Walter Lassally; ***M:*** Richard Robbins. British Academy Awards '83: Best Adapted Screenplay; Nominations: Cannes Film Festival '83: Best Film. **VHS**

Heat and Sunlight

This boring improvisational exercise won the Grand Jury Prize at the Sundance Film Festival in 1988. Thanks to a clever advertising campaign ("BANNED BY DISTRIBUTORS!" which does sound a whole lot better than "REJECTED BY DISTRIBUTORS!" doesn't it?), Rob Nilsson was able to attract a few more audience members into the few theatres that agreed to carry it. To cut costs, Nilsson transferred 1/2-inch Betacam video to 35mm film. It's about jealousy and sex, sex and jealousy, zzzzz.... Nilsson's previous credits include *Northern Lights, Signal 7,* and *On the Edge.* **woof!**

1987 98m/B Rob Nilsson, Consuelo Faust, Bill Bailey, Don Bajema, Ernie Fosselius; ***D:*** Rob Nilsson; ***W:*** Rob Nilsson; ***C:*** Tomas Tucker; ***M:*** Mark Adler. Sundance Film Festival '88: Grand Jury Prize. **VHS, LV**

Heathers

Three years before *Heathers,* Winona Ryder only had eyes for Corey Haim as *Lucas. Heathers* turned Ryder and Christian Slater into full-fledged teen stars, although Slater's Jack Nicholson imitation wore thin for this viewer by his second line of dialogue. Ryder is wonderful, though, running the full gamut of teen angst, first as the virtual slave of the three nastiest Heathers in high school, then as the can't-live-with-him/can't-live-without-him accomplice of Slater, who determines to rid the world of Heathers once and for all. Shannen Doherty is one of the Heathers, reportedly catching the attention of Tori ("Donna Martin") Spelling, who urged father Aaron to consider casting her as Brenda Walsh on *Beverly Hills 90210.* Screenwriter Daniel Waters and director Michael Lehmann reunited for the ill-fated *Hudson Hawk.* Otherwise, Lehmann directed quirky

The Hound Salutes:
ORSON WELLES AND *TOUCH OF EVIL*
Four Big Bones!

The length of time between Orson Welles' halting apology for the national panic he ignited with his *War of the Worlds* radio broadcast and the release of his 1958 Universal film noir *Touch of Evil* was less than 20 years—not long in real time, but light years in the entertainment world. In the interim, he evolved from a dynamic, sad-eyed boy genius with a limitless future to a grizzled, life-worn fat man who seemed a skillion years old. He was just 43. Reviewers were underwhelmed by the sleazy plot line of *Touch of Evil,* with its dope fiends, sexual deviates, corrupt authority figures, and ersatz "Mexican" narc, Charlton Heston, and Welles' masterpiece was buried in its own time by all but his loyal worshippers. Time has been kinder to the film than to its detractors. They are not remembered, but when today's audiences see the fascinating, attenuated opening shot, they shake their heads at all those myopic judgments from another era.

***Touch of Evil* is simply breathtaking. Based on *Badge of Evil,* a Whit Masterson novel, Welles' adaptation is resonant with the small-time horrors in a small Mexican bordertown that's bla-**

comedies *(The Applegates, Airheads,* and the very funny *Truth About Cats and Dogs)* and Waters wrote scripts for films like *The Adventures of Ford Fairlane, Batman,* and *Demolition Man.* But *Heathers* remains the most prominent achievement on both their resumes; with its bracing satirical edge and a fearless disregard for good taste, *Heathers* is unlike any teen flick seen before or since. 🦴🦴🦴🦴

1989 (R) 102m/C Winona Ryder, Christian Slater, Kim Walker, Shannen Doherty, Lisanne Falk, Penelope Milford, Glenn Shadix, Lance Fenton, Patrick Laborteaux, Jeremy Applegate, Renee Estevez; ***D:*** Michael Lehmann; ***W:*** Daniel Waters; ***C:*** Francis Kenny; ***M:*** David Newman. Independent Spirit Awards '90: Best First Feature. **VHS, LV, Closed Caption**

Heavenly Creatures

Peter Jackson's remarkable film tells the true crime story of Pauline Parker, 16, and Juliet Hulme, 15, two schoolgirls who beat Pauline's mother to death with bricks wrapped in stockings after visiting a tea shop with her in Canterbury, New Zealand. The motive: Pauline and Juliet were about to be separated and they believed that the murder would keep them together forever. For some reason, they chose the parent with the least amount of power; Juliet's parents were the chief proponents of the move. At their 1954 trial in Christchurch, they were sentenced to be detained "until Her Majesty's pleasure be made known." Parker was 20 and Hulme was 19 when they were released in 1958, but they had been forbidden contact with each other since their arrest. *The Express* (a British tabloid) finally found Parker after a diligent search, but the identity of Hulme was revealed directly after *Heavenly Creatures*' release. As mystery writer Anne Perry, she had established an international following. Perry did say, that as a result of a serious illness, she had been prescribed mind-altering drugs that might have unduly influenced her actions at the time of the murder. Jackson takes the girls back in time a

tantly immune from ethical law enforcement. Everyone HAS something on someone else and everyone DESERVES what s/he gets. When a millionaire is blown up with a gorgeous blonde (the ill-fated Joi Lansing), the crooked Hank Quinlan (Welles) tries to frame a young Mexican for the crime. Heston as Mike Vargas is supposed to be on a honeymoon with Janet Leigh as his wife Susan, but he's determined to make Quinlan accountable for this corruption of justice. Quinlan is an old hand at framing suspects, so he calls on Akim Tamiroff as Uncle Joe Grandi, a mobster with a grudge against Vargas. They connive to set up Susan as a drug addict.

For 105 dizzy minutes, Welles is our tour guide into hell and we never know who's going to turn up next, whether it's Marlene Dietrich as the blowsy Tanya or Zsa Zsa Gabor as a nightclub owner or Mercedes McCambridge as a lesbian delinquent or Dennis Weaver as a motel night manager or Joseph Cotten as a detective. Henry Mancini's grimy score is eons away from *Moon River* and Russell Metty's stunning black-and-white cinematography is an eternity away from his work on frothy Doris Day comedies. (Metty had, after all, worked with Welles a dozen years before on *The Stranger.*) The factor that keeps us returning to *Touch of Evil* again and again and always discovering something new in it is the astonishing vision of Orson Welles. To jaded industry hacks of 1958, Welles may have seemed little more than a has-been, but no one then or now could tell a story quite the way he could. The restored *Touch of Evil* (with Universal-ordered re-takes by Harry Keller deleted and Welles' original editing choices reinstated) is the ultimate tribute to the father of independent film: Orson Welles.

couple of years before the trial, when Parker was 14 and Hulme was 13. They get caught up in a wild fantasy life, not too dissimilar from the teenaged protagonists of 1964's *The World of Henry Orient.* And it does look like quite a lot of fun, until it gets out of hand. Because of their extreme youth, it's hard to say whether the two girls were actually lesbians as their parents feared or were just great friends play acting anything and everything in sight. When Hulme becomes ill and must go to hospital for her health, their association becomes obsessive. Could this murder have been prevented? Jackson mostly concerns himself with the friends and their interior world, which he renders in a very appealing, non-judgmental way. Melanie Lynskey looks just like old news photos of Pauline, and Kate Winslet became a first-time Oscar nominee in 1995 for *Sense and Sensibility.* ☠☠☠☠

1994 (R) 110m/C *NZ* Melanie Lynskey, Kate Winslet, Sarah Pierse, Diana Kent, Clive Merrison, Simon O'Connor; ***D:*** Peter Jackson; ***W:*** Peter Jackson, Frances Walsh; ***C:*** Alun Bollinger. Nominations: Academy Awards '94: Best Original Screenplay; Australian Film Institute '95: Best Foreign Film. **VHS, LV, Closed Caption**

Heavy

One hundred and nineteen minutes is a long time to spend at a pizzeria where you'd normally get a meal to go because you don't want to eat it there. But since James Mangold put a lot of thought into this one, here's the story. Victor (Pruitt Taylor Vince) is fat, shy, and lives with his mother, Dolly. Dolly (Shelley Winters) is ailing, in her early 70s, and also fat. Dolores (Deborah Harry) is a waitress in her late 40s. She's been around the block more than once but never looked twice at Vince. Leo (Joe Grifasi) is a regular in his 50s. Joining this exciting group is, yes, LIV TYLER as Callie, the new 17-year-old waitress! Her boyfriend is a mechanic named Jeff (Evan Dando of the Lemonheads) and Victor is more than twice Callie's age, but he's inspired to start a weight loss pro-

"You don't miss your tonsils, do ye?"

—Paul McCartney tries to convince Ringo Starr to cut off his finger in *Help!*

gram, anyway. It took a long time for this subtle, well-acted, slow movie to find a distributor. Tyler, naturally, received most of the attention. Her track record to date has been just fair, though: *Silent Fall, Empire Records, Inventing the Abbotts,* and her breakthrough film, *Stealing Beauty.*

1994 (R) 104m/C Pruitt Taylor Vince, Shelley Winters, Liv Tyler, Deborah Harry, Evan Dando, Joe Grifasi; ***D:*** James Mangold; ***W:*** James Mangold; ***C:*** Michael Barrow; ***M:*** Thurston Moore. Sundance Film Festival '95: Special Jury Prize. **VHS, Closed Caption**

Heavy Petting

Heavy Petting is a dry hump of a movie, with all the assets and liabilities of early sex: the promotional teaser might be a turn-on, but the experience itself is something of a let-down. Obie Benz's shapeless movie is strongly reminiscent of Philippe Mora's *Brother, Can You Spare a Dime,* a 1975 documentary that attempted to reveal the 1930s with period newsreels and movie clips but without a narrative thrust. Working without a script, Benz cross-edited old educational films and movie clips together, showing the results every so often to his friends to see if he had a movie yet. He worked hard for seven years and his friends and many audiences may well love *Heavy Petting.* I found myself losing interest after half an hour, though, and the last 45 minutes were somewhat less than enthralling. Benz asked a dozen men and eleven women to describe their early attitudes about sex. Not all of their commentary is particularly enlightening or perceptive, but Ann Magnuson is funny at least, and the late Abbie Hoffman looks like the jolliest and least likely candidate for suicide ever. I don't even want to think about the last time William Burroughs and Allen Ginsberg, 75 and 63 when the movie first came out in 1989, indulged in heavy petting and neither looks like he wants to be in the movie. Also, were the 1950s the sole province of white teens? Sidney Poitier only shows up once in a *Blackboard Jungle* clip. This tired celebration of over-obvious cultural symbols obviously wasn't my movie, but if you think it might be yours, video is the best way to see it.

1989 75m/C David Byrne, Josh Mostel, Sandra Bernhard, Allen Ginsberg, Ann Magnuson, Spalding Gray, Laurie Anderson, John Oates, Abbie Hoffman, Jacki Ochs; ***D:*** Obie Benz; ***C:*** Sandi Sissel. **VHS, LV**

Helen's Babies

I have yet to see this movie, but not for lack of trying. When I heard that a print had surfaced in a Moscow archive, I sent letter after letter, trying to track it down. I tried asking a film archive if there was any way it could be shown there. No dice! But I WILL see this movie some day. *Helen's Babies* first surfaced as a very funny children's book by John Habberton, focusing on the trials and tribulations of a Victorian bachelor (circa 1875) who, due to circumstances beyond his control, must temporarily care for his sister's two small children. In the book, Toddie and Budge were little boys, but for the independent film production, the story was redesigned as a vehicle for child star Baby Peggy and co-star Jean Carpenter. Surviving stills suggest that the time frame may have been updated by 40 years, as well. Director William A. Seiter (1892–1964) went on to direct the Shirley Temple classics *Dimples, Stowaway,* and *Susannah of the Mounties.* Cinematographer William Daniels (1895–1970) shot such MGM classics as *Anna Christie, Cat on a Hot Tin Roof,* and *How the West Was Won,* and won the Oscar for *The Naked City.* Edward Everett Horton (1886–1976), one of the drollest character actors ever, played Uncle Harry, and lovely Clara Bow (1905–65) appeared as his romantic interest, Alice Mayton. Baby Peggy grew up to be writer Diana Serra Cary, author of such carefully researched and beautifully written books as *The Hollywood Posse, Hollywood's Children,* and *Whatever Happened to Baby Peggy? Helen's Babies* may or may not be a comedy classic, but with that cast and that crew, I hope that Grapevine Video or some other kind distributor will put me out of my misery and let us see this one soon!

1925 m/B Baby Peggy, Jean Carpenter, Clara Bow, Edward Everett Horton, Claire Adams, Richard Tucker, George Reed, Mattie Peters; ***D:*** William A. Seiter; ***W:*** Hope Loring, Louis Leighton; ***C:*** William H. Daniels.

Help!

Help! was Great Britain's top moneymaker of 1965, but over the years, there's been some grumbling over the fact that the plot was contrived, that it was in garish color, and that it wasn't *A Hard Day's Night.* Well, you can only do something for the first time once and, as pop musicals go, the Beatles could have done much worse than *Help!* How many times have you seen *Ferry Cross the Mersey* or *Having a Wild Weekend* or *Mrs. Brown, You've Got a Lovely Daughter* lately? The supporting cast is great in this one and has much more to do than in *A Hard Day's Night.* Victor Spinetti (Professor Foot) and Roy Kinnear (Algernon) would be hilarious no matter which movie they were in together; Leo McKern (Clang), Eleanor Bron (Ahme), and Warren Mitchell (Abdul) create vivid and memorable characters; and Patrick Cargill is perfection as a snide superintendent. With the exception of Ringo Starr, the most natural comedy talent of the four, it's far more evident this time around that his fellow band mates are really guest stars in their own films. Richard Lester keeps things moving briskly, giving the fans what they want and need, and perhaps looking forward to making *How I Won the War,* released in April 1967. What might have happened if Lester and the Beatles had taken the major artistic risk of filming Joe Orton's unproduced (but since published) screenplay, *Up Against It*? The deaths of Orton and the Beatles' manager Brian Epstein leave that fascinating question forever unanswered. ***AKA:*** Eight Arms to Hold You.

1965 (G) 90m/C *GB* John Lennon, Paul McCartney, Ringo Starr, George Harrison, Leo McKern, Eleanor Bron, Victor Spinetti, Roy Kinnear, John Bluthal, Patrick Cargill, Alfie Bass, Warren Mitchell, Peter Copley, Bruce Lacey; ***D:*** Richard Lester; ***W:*** Charles Wood, Marc Behm; ***C:*** David Watkin; ***M:*** The Beatles. **VHS, LV, DVD**

Hester Street

When *Hester Street* was first released, major stardom was predicted for its star, Carol Kane, and a glorious future as a world-class director awaited Joan Micklin Silver...I'll be back after I beat up a few pillows to spare everyone the institutional sexism rant. This beautiful film knocked everyone sideways in the mid-'70s. Carol Kane's look was so right for this period film, like she'd just stepped out of a daguerrotype. As it turns out, Kane's look is right for every time. She can be a flapper, a babysitter, a hippie, a mom...but she's been typed, somehow, as a wild child, so we see her in many marginal roles in many marginal films where she steals everything in her scattered sequences that isn't nailed down and then drifts out of the plot. Like a lovely wraith, we can't forget her. Micklin, who went on to make several more fine films (but not enough for this longtime admirer), carefully observes the dilemma faced by every immigrant who comes to America. As a nation of immigrants, do we reject the values of the country we left behind and embrace our adopted country on its own terms, or do we try preserve our unique identity and share it with those who come after us? Steven Keats, who plays Kane's husband, has already made his choice. By pursuing the flirtatious Dorrie Kavanaugh, he rejects both his bride and her Old World customs. (Sadly, both Keats and Kavanaugh died relatively young in real life. He committed suicide in 1994 at the age of 49 and she died at 38 in 1983, after switching from acting to a career as an opera singer.)

1975 92m/B Carol Kane, Doris Roberts, Steven Keats, Mel Howard, Dorrie Kavanaugh, Stephen Strimpell; ***D:*** Joan Micklin Silver; ***W:*** Joan Micklin Silver; ***C:*** Kenneth Van Sickle; ***M:*** William Bolcom. Nominations: Academy Awards '75: Best Actress (Kane). **VHS**

Hidden Children

Oral histories about the Holocaust are offered by John Walker's *Hidden Children,* a 1994 Canadian documentary. Walker's visits with six Jewish survivors of World War II supply a painful reminder of what it is like for small children to be torn away from their families and adjust to new names and completely different lives. The participants (from Belgium, Hungary, and Poland) all had to change their identities in

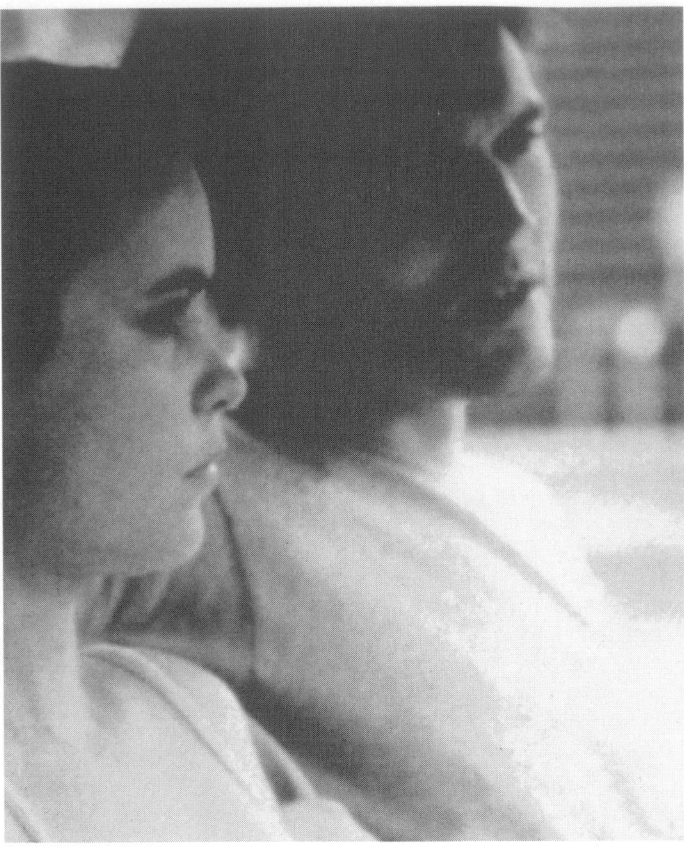

Syd (Radha Mitchell) and Arnie (William Sage) in *High Art.* October Films; courtesy of the Kobal Collection

order to live; one woman posed as a Catholic, and one man is still a Catholic priest.

1994 52m/C *CA* ***D:*** John Walker.

The Hidden Room

Naunton Wayne turns detective in this war of nerves between Dr. Clive Riordan (Robert Newton) and his lovely wife's American lover, Bill Kronin (Phil Brown). Clive wants to dissolve Bill in an acid bath, but he wants to choose just the right moment when he's under the least suspicion. Meanwhile, Clive's lovely wife Storm (lovely Sally Gray) wants to know what the heck is going on, although she never considers the acid bath. The only ones who keep their cool here are Wayne as kindly Supt. Finsbury and (though it ain't easy) Bill, who has A Plan. Everyone's good in what feels like a Victorian melodrama updated to post-war London. Wonder if Levinson and Link watched this Brit noir while germinating Lt. Columbo? ***AKA:*** Obsession.

1949 98m/B *GB* Robert Newton, Sally Gray, Naunton Wayne, Phil Brown, Olga Lindo, Russell Waters, James Harcourt, Allan Jeayes, Stanley Baker; ***D:*** Edward Dmytryk; ***W:*** Alec Coppel; ***C:*** C.M. Pennington-Richards; ***M:*** Nino Rota. **VHS**

High Art

Lisa Cholodenko's *High Art* is well made, but so effing depressing that I was in tears afterwards. It was almost as sad as Brian De Palma's *Sisters* when Margot Kidder's sweet boyfriend brings her a birthday cake and she goes psycho and I ran out of my flat and hung out in the lobby until the rental video was Off The Premises. I can't be objective about movies that are done so effectively that you can imagine turning off the movie and walking into *Sisters* or *High Art* in real life. Radha Mitchell is Syd, who is way more intimidated than she should be about the pond scum who are her colleagues at *Frame,* a trendy rag celebrating Photography as Art. Meanwhile, the receptionist eyes her enviously—what the heck did Syd ever do to become an associate editor instead of me? For one thing, Syd is still a gopher, despite the promotion to the new title. Syd lives with James (Gabriel Mann), who is a decent guy, but not right for her. A leaky ceiling leads Syd to photographer Lucy Berliner (Ally Sheedy) and her German lover Greta (Patricia Clarkson). Both are heroin addicts, and Syd is tolerant, like so many uncomprehending outsiders are. In her subsequent visits, she even participates in their scene, but recreationally. Lucy eyes Syd like catnip and Greta picks up on it and is jealous. We also see Lucy's visits to her mother (Tammy Grimes), who talks about Greta as if she were a Nazi. Syd tries to get Lucy's work into *Frame* magazine and both the pond scum and Lucy reluctantly acquiesce. It all leads to the inevitable clinch between Syd and Lucy, which changes both their lives way too much right away and, ultimately, not enough over the long haul. There is still the heroin issue to be resolved, as well as Greta. And the clueless receptionist continues to be envious of Syd. Sheedy and Clarkson certainly look sad and strung out, as if they'd been stranded at a depot where the buses don't come or go anymore. In contrast, the apple-cheeked Syd looks straight off the farm. Great acting and writing all around, but almost as nihilistic as *Sisters* AND *On the Beach* on the same double bill! I cheered myself up with Adrienne Shelly in *Teresa's Tattoo* TWICE after *High Art* was over. ℰℰℰ

1998 (R) 102m/C Radha Mitchell, Ally Sheedy, Patricia Clarkson, Tammy Grimes, Gabriel Mann, William Sage, David Thornton, Anh Duong; ***D:*** Lisa Cholodenko; ***W:*** Lisa Cholodenko; ***C:*** Tami Reiker; ***M:*** Shudder to Think. Independent Spirit Awards '99: Best Actress (Sheedy); Los Angeles Film Critics Association Awards '98: Best Actress (Sheedy); National Society of Film Critics Awards '98: Best Actress (Sheedy); Sundance Film Festival '98: Best Screenplay; Nominations: Independent Spirit Awards '99: Best Cinematography, Best First Feature, Best Supporting Actress (Clarkson), First Screenplay. **VHS, Closed Caption**

High Heels

Pedro Almodovar's early films had so many outrageous trappings that it was easy for many to overlook the fact that his scripts have always been fairly conventional. His concerns as a storyteller are pretty basic: who did what, who loves whom, how do we get from here to there? It is because of Almodovar's genius for exploring the raw emotions that ignite many gnarled relationships, that his simple plot lines seem to take on a surreal quality. His ninth film, *High Heels,* received some lukewarm reviews, undoubtedly because it is stripped of some of the wilder elements that first put Almodovar on the map. But for those who take *High Heels* on its own terms, there are genuine rewards in this overlooked 1991 release. *High Heels* examines the troubled relationship between a television anchor woman (Victoria Abril) and her much more famous mother (Marisa Paredes). The two are in not-so-subtle competition with each other, but they are also very much in need of each other's love. They share the same name ("Rebecca") and they also share the same lover (Feodor Atkine), whom the daughter is unlucky enough to marry. The daughter is also best friends with a drag queen who impersonates her mother onstage. The drag queen has several other identities in the film and serves as something of a catalyst for the relationship between the two women. Miguel Bose also appears as a not-so-mysterious judge who investigates the murder of the younger Rebecca's husband. Since the identity of the killer is never in doubt, Almodovar focuses steadily on how the murder affects the relationships of the characters. In that respect, Almodovar does his usual clinical yet passionate job. If you want the same movie from the director every time, rent one of your old favorites on video. If you want to see what Pedro Almodovar was up to in 1991, *High Heels* is an absorbing, well-crafted film that's definitely worth a look. ***AKA:*** Tacones Lejanos. ℰℰℰ

1991 (R) 113m/C *SP* Victoria Abril, Marisa Paredes, Miguel Bose, Feodor Atkine, Bibi Andersen, Rocio Munoz; ***D:*** Pedro Almodovar; ***W:*** Pedro Almodovar; ***C:*** Alfredo Mayo; ***M:*** Ryuichi Sakamoto. Cesar Awards '93: Best Foreign Film. **VHS, Closed Caption**

High Season

Admirers of Jacqueline Bisset will be pleased at the fact that the actress has finally been cast in a well-above-average movie, *High Season.* This fine comedy is the first feature directed by writer Clare Peploe, who works with husband Bernardo Bertolucci. It's about survival on a Greek island, which is not the same as survival on Skid Row. The scenery is gorgeous enough to make anyone forget about finances. Bisset plays a broke photographer who wants to sell a vase she received from her old friend Sebastian Shaw. The buyer is Robert Stephens (1931–95), who definitely has been around the block a few times since he played Sherlock Holmes in 1970. Stephens wants art historian Shaw to claim that the vase is fake. Shaw doesn't mind, especially since the vase is not exactly what it seems to be. But then,

"I *believe* this movie. A dude could jump off a mountain and not hurt himself, cause he did brace himself. And knew something about the levels of gravitivity and polarity."

—Robert Townsend in the "Sneakin' into the Movies" segment of *Hollywood Shuffle*.

neither is Shaw. And neither is the obnoxious English tourist couple who hang around Bisset's house. *High Season* gets its laughs from what we know about the characters and their relationships with each other. The humor is mostly English, although Irene Papas and Paris Tselios have some good scenes as the Greek mother and son who have to cope with all these weird people. And this group is definitely daffy, in a careless, uncontrived way. At one point, Bisset yells at her artist husband (James Fox) for being too lazy to patch up their relationship problems. Meanwhile, his bed partner casually gets dressed and makes her exit, scarcely noticed by either of them. The film is filled with "hold on now, this is really serious" sequences, which are punctured by a reality that refuses to recognize the finality of any single moment. After all, when was the last time you saw a woman plunge into passionate sex with a strange fellow simply because he fixed the flushing mechanism on her toilet? 🦴🦴🦴

1988 (R) 95m/C *GB* Jacqueline Bisset, James Fox, Irene Papas, Sebastian Shaw, Kenneth Branagh, Robert Stephens, Leslie Manville, Paris Tselios; ***D:*** Clare Peploe; ***W:*** Clare Peploe, Mark Peploe; ***C:*** Chris Menges; ***M:*** Jason Osborn. **VHS, LV, 8mm**

High Stakes

Without that cast, *High Stakes* would be just fair. It's the old story (by Amos Kollek, son of Teddy, then Jerusalem's mayor) of a hooker named Bambi (Sally Kirkland) who meets a John (Robert LuPone) who falls in love with her and helps her break free from her pimp, Slim (Richard Lynch). But it does have that cast, which elevates this film a full notch. Sally Kirkland is a superb actress who has been marginalized within the industry, because of the many blue plays and movies on her resume, and then, even after she won an Academy Award nomination for best actress in *Anna,* because of her age. It is so unfair it makes me want to scream!... Thanks, I needed that. The range of emotions on Kirkland's face gives much, much more to this film than is in the script. We see her as a victim, a mother fighting like a tigress for her cub, a seductress, and, throughout it all, a human being who isn't afraid to act on her feelings, despite a staggeringly unlucky life. Robert LuPone gives a terrific performance as John Stratton, lucky at work, unlucky at everything else. His best moments come when, with a frozen face and every emotion melting out of his pores, he initiates a deadly game of Russian Roulette. Richard Lynch, who once played the Vampire Anton Voytek, is creepier than ever, and he really earns his paycheck here by injecting stock dialogue with menacing conviction. Plus! As an extra added bonus for *Buffy* and *Misery* devotees: Sarah (Michelle) Gellar, then small for her age at 12, plays Karen, Bambi's brown-haired eight-year-old daughter with the same wide-eyed appeal that would make her a '90s icon as an Emmy winner and a Vampire Slayer. Kathy Bates, a year away from a Best Actress Oscar, plays Jill, the sort of loyal, straight-talking secretary that was once Eve Arden's specialty. Kirkland pours herself into the skin tight costumes of Ida Gearon that somehow seem superfluous when she unleashes her magnetic charisma as an actress. Note: The Trimark video I watched appears to have been cut by 16 minutes, based on the original running time. ***AKA:*** Melanie Rose. 🦴🦴🦴

1989 (R) 102m/C Sally Kirkland, Robert LuPone, Richard Lynch, Sarah Michelle Gellar, Kathy Bates, W.T. Martin, Eddie Earl Hatch, Betty Miller, Maia Danzinger, Jesse Corti, Samantha Louca, Larry Block, June Stein, Michael Steinhardt, Maggie Warner, William Kennedy; ***D:*** Amos Kollek; ***W:*** Amos Kollek; ***C:*** Marc Hirschfeld; ***M:*** Bob Dylan, Mira Spektor. **VHS, LV**

His Picture in the Papers

Movie lore has it that Anita Loos sold a script to D.W. Griffith for the Biograph film *The New York Hat* (starring Mary Pickford and Lionel Barrymore) while she was still a teenager. Since Loos was just four foot eleven, it wouldn't have been that hard to convince Mr. Griffith that she was only 19 in 1912, unless he'd picked up a copy of San Francisco's *Sunday Call* on February 16, 1902, when Loos, then at the Denham School on Bush Street, wrote, "What

I Hope to Be When I Grow Up: Having not fully made up my mind as to what I shall become when I am a woman, the answer to that question will be difficult for me to give. So far in my life, my ambitions have inclined toward being a ship architect. The idea of taking up this profession was given to me by Longfellow's poem 'The Building of the Ship,' which we had as literature work in the seventh grade. My choice for being a ship architect rather than the architect of a house or other buildings is because the city is overrun with the latter, while there are comparatively few people who draw the plans of ships. I think also that the occupation which I so far have intended to take up is a quiet and refined business for a woman. If I had any talent at all in drawing or painting, I would like to be an artist, but as the only drawing I can do is mechanical, the occupation of an architect suits me. I will not think too seriously over this subject as I am only 12 years old." Okay, so Loos was 23, not 19 when she first broke into films, but it was a close call for movie fans. We might never have HEARD of *Gentlemen Prefer Blondes* or Lorelei Lee had her creator toiled instead on blueprints for ships instead of scripts for the silver screen! Loos wrote well over 150 screenplays between 1912 and 1942, including several for Douglas Fairbanks. *His Picture in the Papers* ran 68 minutes and focused on Peter Prindle, who does all sorts of wild stunts (driving his car over a cliff, boxing with a pro, diving from a ship and swimming all the way to shore, jumping from trains), just to get his picture in the papers. Without Loos' sparkling titles, the film might have been shorn down to two reels; luckily the critics screened it before the editor started splicing away and the movie, Fairbanks, and Loos ALL got their pictures in the papers! It was a happy teaming of a supremely confident star and a very clever screenwriter and it set the standard for all future Fairbanks vehicles (he went on to star in 45 films from 1915 to 1934). ፟፟፟

1916 68m/B Douglas Fairbanks Sr., Clarence Handysides, Rene Boucicault, Jean Temple, Charles Butler, Homer Hunt, Loretta Blake, Helena Rupport; ***D:*** John Emerson; ***W:*** John Emerson, Anita Loos. **VHS, 8mm**

Hollywood on Trial

Hollywood on Trial is the story behind *The Front*. It doesn't make for pleasant watching or listening, yet it is certainly a long-overdue account. In October 1947, Alvah Bessie, Herbert Biberman, Lester Cole, Edward Dmytryk, Ring Lardner Jr., John Howard Lawson, Albert Maltz, Samuel Ornitz, Adrian Scott, and Dalton Trumbo were among the top writers and directors in Hollywood. One month later, no one in Hollywood would hire them. All went to prison. Dmytryk later removed himself from the blacklist by testifying against former Communists. Trumbo (1905–76) was able to remove himself from the blacklist when Otto Preminger (1906–86) hired him to write the screenplay for *Exodus*. (He had won two pseudonymous Academy Awards for 1953's *Roman Holiday* and 1956's *The Brave One*.) Lardner's blacklist lasted 17 years, until he wrote *The Cincinnati Kid*. By 1978, he would win his second Academy Award for *M.A.S.H.* (the first was for 1942's *Woman of the Year*). For others, like Bessie and Cole (both 1904–85), Biberman (1900–71), Lawson (1894–1977), Ornitz, and Scott (1912–73), death would come before they were hired to work on another Hollywood film. Only Maltz (1908–85) was credited with *Two Mules for Sister Sarah* in 1970. Hollywood is filled with hard-luck yarns, yet the history of Hollywood has rarely been adequately developed. With *Hollywood on Trial*, it finally was, due to the efforts of producer James C. Gutman, director David Helpern Jr., and screenwriter Arnie Reisman. The story they have to tell about Hollywood is far from flattering, but it deserves telling and re-telling. As a 100-minute documentary, *Hollywood on Trial* barely scratches the surface, yet, even in 1976, Helpern suggested that this may be due to the many people who were and are still reluctant to discuss the period during which the House Committee on UnAmerican Activities had free reign over the lives and destinies of many American citizens. ፟፟፟፟

Lloyd Bridges, James Edwards, Frank Lovejoy, and Steve Brodie in *Home of the Brave.*
United Artists; courtesy of the Kobal Collection

1976 100m/C John Huston, Lester Cole, Gary Cooper, Howard da Silva, Edward Dmytryk, Ring Lardner Jr., Albert Maltz, Zero Mostel, Otto Preminger, Ronald Reagan, Gale Sondergaard, Dalton Trumbo, Alvah Bessie; ***D:*** David Helpern; ***W:*** Arnie Reisman; ***C:*** Barry Abrams. **VHS, LV**

Hollywood Shuffle

Hollywood Shuffle created quite a splash when it was first released in 1987. Not only did it offer a funny and accurate perspective of what it's like to be a young black actor eking out a living in the film business, but it also supplied other wannabe directors with tremendous inspiration. Robert Townsend, who wrote, directed, and starred in the film, had previously played a supporting role in *A Soldier's Story.* He put his salary for that film, plus every line of credit he could max out from his credit cards, and somehow assembled the $100,000 to produce *Hollywood Shuffle.* (Well, how had John Cassavetes started out? By using his salary for the television series *Johnny Staccato.*) Townsend's film looks more expensive than it is, because of the cleverness of the concept and because of the talented cast, including the Wayans Brothers, Damon and co-writer Keenen Ivory, plus Townsend himself. One of the best satirical sequences gives us a glimpse of the Black Actors School in which white teachers show black actors how to be black actors and to play such exciting, fully dimensional characters as pimps, whores, rapists, and other stereotypical criminals. Townsend became a hot property overnight, subsequently directing *Eddie Murphy: Raw* and *B.A.P.S.* and writing, directing, and starring in *The Five Heartbeats* and *The Meteor Man.* The Wayans Brothers became household names and opportunities for black actors on film increased dramatically over the next decade.

1987 (R) 81m/C Robert Townsend, Anne-Marie Johnson, Starletta DuPois, Helen Martin, Keenen Ivory Wayans, Damon Wayans, Craigus R. Johnson, Eugene Glazer; ***D:*** Robert Townsend; ***W:*** Robert Townsend, Keenen Ivory Wayans; ***C:*** Peter Deming; ***M:*** Patrice Rushen, Udi Harpaz. **VHS, LV**

Homage

They don't give Academy Awards to little gems like *Homage,* but if they did, Blythe Danner would most assuredly deserve one. Danner, who's been quietly working her magic in indies and quality television specials over the last 25 years, steals great blocks of screen time away from co-stars Sheryl Lee, Frank Whaley, Bruce Davison, and the breathtaking landscapes of New Mexico. A low-key study of fanatical celebrity worship at its most deadly, *Homage* draws its greatest strength from the complexity of its three central characters. Blythe Danner is Elizabeth, a great teacher and a far-from-ideal mother, who lives alone on her ranch. When she's in need of a handyman, leave it to Frank Whaley as Archie to fulfill her every wish. Archie is the most dangerous sort of psycho—brilliant, charming, and deceptively vulnerable. When Elizabeth's troubled, alcoholic, semi-famous daughter Lucy comes home for a visit, Archie shifts into stalking gear. Lucy (played to the hilt by Sheryl Lee) slips easily into the "go away closer" routines that work for her in Tinseltown. She teases Archie by walking braless around the house, by drinking and flirting, and by letting him hold her hand a moment or two before wrenching it away. Archie, it seems, has a screenplay for his idol, but she doesn't like it. In two fairly graphic sequences, he masturbates to her naked image on a video monitor and while reading about her sex life in a purloined journal. To his credit, Frank Whaley doesn't pull any punches in this extremely difficult role. He could have sweetened his character with eroticism, with genuine poignance, or with an eyelash flicker of sanity, but he does none of the above. Whaley's Archie is always playing the angles to the bitter end. Mother and daughter have a brief moment of redemption by allowing each other to see their very worst sides before they accept the bond of trust each has always dreamed about. None of Archie's pitiless manipulations can rob them of that. And Danner's Elizabeth, finally, triumphs over her flawed impulses and deliberate misunderstandings to emerge from her exile into life. Writer Mark Medoff and director Ross Kagen Marks take Hollywood's ultimate violent cliche and turn it inside out in *Homage,* a little-known wonder that merits a better fate. 🦴🦴🦴

1995 (R) 100m/C Frank Whaley, Blythe Danner, Sheryl Lee, Bruce Davison, Danny Nucci; ***D:*** Ross Kagen Marks; ***W:*** Mark Medoff; ***C:*** Tom Richmond; ***M:*** W.G. Snuffy Walden. **VHS**

Hombres Armados

Like *Lone Star, Hombres Armados* wound up on quite a few lists of Ten Best Films. As always, the filmmaker's heart is in the right place. Federico Luppi (*Time for Revenge, Funny, Dirty Little War, Mayalunta, Killing Grandpa, A Place in the World, Cronos*) plays widowed old Dr. Humberto Fuentes, who has spent his life teaching young doctors to go out into the villages of his (fictional) Latin American country and save people's lives. He decides to pay a visit to his students to see how they're faring. His kids tell him not to do it; a patient who's an army general tells him not to do it—but Fuentes is determined. He meets a ditzy American tourist couple (Mandy Patinkin as Andrew, who can't speak Spanish, and Kathryn Grody as Harriet, who can barely say a few Spanish phrases out of a guidebook) who ask about the newspaper reports of violence in his country. Fuentes says that there is no violence, the newspaper reports are exaggerations, and they will be perfectly safe. The clueless sightseers, who aren't looking for trouble and don't find it, are safe; Dr. Fuentes is the one in danger. At the end of his long life, he learns that he has spent his whole life training his students to be killed by "hombres armados" (men with guns: government soldiers and/or guerrilla fighters). The critique here is that Dr. Fuentes should have made it his business to learn what sort of world his innocent students were entering. So he could have done what? When? Where? To whom? I found myself thinking about Sidney Poitier as Dr. Luther Brooks and Richard Widmark as Roy Biddle in 1950's *No Way Out,* written and directed by Joseph L. Mankiewicz. The

"A woman's place is in the home... making money!"

—Patty Terwilliger (Maggie Smith) in *Hot Millions.*

bigoted Biddle tries to kill Dr. Brooks and becomes his critically injured patient instead. Doctors save lives. They rarely have time to do anything else. When bullets are flying around them, they save the lives they can. They don't have time to investigate who the men with guns are, why the men have guns, where the men got guns, or who gave the men guns. In extreme situations, doctors don't know the histories and identities of their patients. Dr. Fuentes judges himself without mercy as he sees what his country has become and how he has unwittingly played a role in the destruction of people's lives. The more he sees, the more he feels that his life and work are worthless. Then, overexerted by his depressing journey, he dies. Who wouldn't? As John Sayles films become progressively more ambitious, their escalating thematic demands seem too large for the small, intimate pictures he chooses to make. *Hombres Armados* isn't a Dog, like *Closet Land*—John Sayles is too good a writer; but both films are riddled with humanist guilt leading nowhere. Let Dr. Fuentes (and us) off the hook for the erosion of his (fictional) Latin American homeland. Let him (and us) die in peace with the faint satisfaction that he did the best he could (as most of us try to do the best we can) on violent Planet Earth. Nuke the guns, not the spirit of the men and women who try to make the world a better place than it is. ***AKA:*** Men with Guns. 🦴🦴

1997 (R) 128m/C Federico Luppi, Damian Delgado, Dan Rivera Gonzalez, Tania Cruz, Damian Alcazar, Iguandili Lopez, Nandi Luna Ramirez, Rafael De Quevedo, Mandy Patinkin, Kathryn Grody, Roberto Sosa; ***D:*** John Sayles; ***W:*** John Sayles; ***C:*** Slawomir Idziak; ***M:*** Mason Daring. Nominations: Golden Globe Awards '99: Best Foreign Film. **VHS**

Home of the Brave

After his death in 1998, everyone remembered Lloyd Bridges fondly, but I heard distinct rumbles that there was no such thing as a Lloyd Bridges movie. *Home of the Brave* comes damn close, though. This tough look at racial prejudice in an army unit during World War II was an adaptation of Arthur Laurents' 1945 Broadway play. Onstage, the target of the abuse had been Jewish, but in the 1949 film, he was the only black member of a platoon based on a Pacific island. James Edwards played the role with an unflinching, smoldering anger that was quite rare at that time. His one friend is his old school pal, played by Bridges with deep and unforced affection. Douglas Dick is a youthful Major for whom the job is way over his head, Steve Brodie is an abrasive, prejudiced soldier who makes Edwards' life hell, and Frank Lovejoy is a seasoned G.I. who appears unprincipled at the outset. The sequences focusing on the friendship between Edwards and Bridges are the best in the film, and blacklisted screenwriter Carl Foreman's gritty script (excluding a series of "charming" and "delightful" exchanges that I can't imagine any guy saying outside of a 19th century drawing room) and Mark Robson's sensitive direction make *Home of the Brave* the best of the postwar films of its type (and far superior to the 1947 RKO release, *Crossfire*). Bridges went on to become an Emmy-nominated television star, but Edwards, despite his early fame and enormous talent, last played a bit role in *Patton* in 1970 before he died at 48. 🦴🦴🦴🦴

1949 86m/B Lloyd Bridges, James Edwards, Frank Lovejoy, Jeff Corey, Douglas Dick, Steve Brodie, Cliff Clark; ***D:*** Mark Robson; ***W:*** Carl Foreman; ***C:*** Robert De Grasse; ***M:*** Dimitri Tiomkin. **VHS, LV**

The Homecoming

Vivien Merchant (1929–82) was a wonderful actress who left behind far too few examples of her brilliant work on film. She met her future husband, Harold Pinter, in repertory and they were married in 1956. A full decade later, Merchant, then 37, first attracted the attention of international audiences as Lily, opposite Michael Caine's *Alfie.* Merchant was seen the following year as Rosalind in the Joseph Losey film *Accident,* scripted by Pinter. More prominently, she starred on Broadway as Ruth in *The Homecoming.* Her costars Paul Rogers and Ian Holm as Max and Lenny, playwright Pinter, and director

Peter Hall all received Tony awards at the first televised ceremony, and Merchant received a nomination. When *The Homecoming* was produced by the American Film Theatre six years later, most of the creative personnel who made the play a success were signed on for the movie (including Terence Rigby as Joey, but excluding John Normington as Sam and Michael Craig as Teddy, who were replaced by Cyril Cusack and Michael Jayston), a decision that should have been made for some of the other compromised A.F.T. productions. You can't take your eyes off Merchant when she's onscreen, and her delivery of Pinter's dialogue here makes me wish that they had preserved more of their work together onscreen. Merchant's Broadway triumph in *The Homecoming* was one of the high points of her much-too-brief career. By 1980, Pinter had left her for Lady Antonia Fraser, and Merchant spent the next two years drinking herself to death. Her obituary notices made sad reading for those who had seen her as Mrs. Pugh in *Under Milkwood,* as the delightful Mrs. Oxford preparing inedible gourmet meals and offering sensible advice to Alec McCowen's straightforward Inspector Oxford in *Frenzy,* and as Queen Maria Theresa in the Richard Chamberlain swashbuckler *The Man in the Iron Mask,* directed by Mike Newell. Hers was a rare and delicate talent and it's sad to think of the delicious Merchant performances we've missed over the last two decades. (*The Homecoming* was released theatrically overseas in 1976.)

1973 114m/C *GB CA* Cyril Cusack, Ian Holm, Michael Jayston, Vivien Merchant, Terence Rigby, Paul Rogers; ***D:*** Peter Hall; ***W:*** Harold Pinter; ***C:*** David Watkin; ***M:*** Thelonious Monk.

Hoop Dreams

Hoop Dreams is nearly three hours long, but the men and women who made it spent nearly five years on it, accumulating an average of an hour's worth of footage every week. It focuses on William Gates and Arthur Agee, two black Chicago teenagers, and their heartrending efforts to become professional basketball players. When you think of the obstacles that must have occurred during a project of this scope, you wonder how Gates and Agee were able to stand such close observation for such an extended length of time. You also wonder about the filmmakers; when setbacks occurred (and there were plenty), did anyone consider scrapping this picture? The intimacy of 1973's *An American Family* was almost too extreme; to see a marriage break up in front of cameras both parties knew were there became the topic of a national debate. Did we really need to watch such intensely personal moments on television? *Hoop Dreams* is even more unsparing of the privacy of its subjects; one of the boys (and the audience) sees his own father buying drugs to support his crack habit. There are other family difficulties and financial problems and injuries and corrective surgery and a hold-up and more. No kid should have to grow up with this much stress, and yet half a million high school kids hope to be among the 25 who are drafted annually to become professional basketball players. *Hoop Dreams* tells the true story of two kids who tried to buck those tremendous odds and how their lives changed as a result.

1994 (PG-13) 169m/C Arthur Agee, William Gates; ***D:*** Steve James; ***C:*** Peter Gilbert. Los Angeles Film Critics Association Awards '94: Best Feature Documentary; MTV Movie Awards '95: Best New Filmmaker Award (James); National Board of Review Awards '94: Best Feature Documentary; New York Film Critics Awards '94: Best Feature Documentary; National Society of Film Critics Awards '94: Best Feature Documentary; Sundance Film Festival '94: Audience Award; Nominations: Academy Awards '94: Best Film Editing. **VHS, LV**

Hot Millions

This very funny sleeper came and went in the summer of 1968. Within six months Maggie Smith would become an international star, but no one knew that yet. Those who did see *Hot Millions* in theatres or who catch it now on cable television can see what stage buffs knew very early on: that Maggie Smith is among the funniest comediennes of her generation. She certainly has plenty of chances to show her flair for comedy here as Patty, a hopeless muddler who screws up one job after an-

“I can’t help it; I’m out of control.”

—Psychotherapist Margaret Ford (Lindsay Crouse) in *House of Games.*

other. She is befriended by Marcus Pendleton (Peter Ustinov), who gets her a job where he works, but she muffs that, too. Fellow office worker Gnatpole (Bob Newhart) has an eye on Patty, too, but she only has eyes for the kindly Marcus and they get married. Marcus has big plans involving computers, none of which are legal, and Klemper (Karl Malden) is on his trail. But Patty has a few big (and extremely clever, considering her employment history) plans of her own, all of which she keeps to herself. Robert Morley and Cesar Romero are on hand for the fun, and Ustinov co-wrote the screenplay. Well worth a hunt and/or setting the alarm for Red Eye Theatre. 🦴🦴🦴

1968 106m/C *GB* Peter Ustinov, Maggie Smith, Karl Malden, Bob Newhart, Robert Morley, Cesar Romero, Melinda May, Ann Lancaster, Margaret Courtenay, Lynda Baron, Billy Milton, Peter Jones, Raymond Huntley, Kynaston Reeves; ***D:*** Eric Till; ***W:*** Ira Wallach, Peter Ustinov; ***C:*** Ken Higgins. **VHS, Closed Caption**

The Hours and Times

Die-hard Beatles fans may quibble with the historical accuracy of Christopher Munch's 1992 movie, but *The Hours and Times* is in fact inspired by an authentic 1963 incident in the lives of John Lennon and Brian Epstein while they were on a Barcelona holiday. It has attracted rave reviews all over the world, and the look of the film is exactly right for the period. But since both Lennon and Epstein are long dead, why make THIS movie, rather than any other, about their long professional association? Well, if the film had been about a well-dressed fictional man of the world and his young, gifted, and fictional client, would *The Hours and Times* have attracted the attention it has? No, it would not. Ethical considerations aside, incomplete forward passes generally occupy a minute, not an hour, of screen time. Very well acted by David Angus as Brian and by Ian Hart as John, though. (Hart played the role a second time in 1994's more elaborate *Backbeat.*) 🦴🦴🦴

1992 60m/B David Angus, Ian Hart, Stephanie Pack, Robin McDonald, Sergio Moreno, Unity Grimwood; ***D:*** Christopher Munch; ***W:*** Christopher Munch. Sundance Film Festival '92: Special Jury Prize. **VHS**

A House in the Hills

Chances are that you missed *A House in the Hills* on the big screen. I'm still trying to figure out whether or not I would have liked it if I'd seen it in a theatre instead of on video. Like many contemporary thrillers, it deals with the menace of everyday phenomena in 20th century life. In *A House in the Hills,* the very appealing Helen Slater is a waitress by day and an actress in her dreams. She accepts a position as a house-sitter for strangers and, sure enough, it's the job from hell. There was a murder next door, the somewhat hostile lady of the house tells her. (Does Slater quit? Of course not!) The man of the house is weird, too; as soon as they meet, he compares the petals of his precious roses to female genitalia. (WHY doesn't she quit? I DON'T KNOW!) Anyway, they split and Helen immediately starts rummaging through closets and trying on clothes when burglar Michael Madsen shows up. But they Fall in Love for the weekend, so that's okay. Nope, the guy you got to watch out for is the lumpy next-door neighbor, Jeffrey Tambor, who looks like he should be playing the sort of roles that the late Richard Deacon used to get, but whose career has taken a much odder turn. *A House in the Hills* succeeds in spite of its predictable self; Slater is brave and resourceful, especially when she's swinging shovels, and Madsen has the sort of lived-in charm that has made him an always pleasant discovery on the video shelf. 🦴🦴½

1993 (R) 91m/C Helen Slater, Michael Madsen, Jeffrey Tambor, James Laurenson, Elyssa Davalos, Toni Barry; ***D:*** Ken Wiederhorn; ***W:*** Ken Wiederhorn; ***C:*** Josep Civit; ***M:*** Richard Einhorn. **VHS, LV, Closed Caption**

House of Cards

Rule Number One for today's screenwriters is "Write lean." You'd think that a

109-minute movie like *House of Cards* would be long enough to say just about everything it had to say about the efforts of a mother and a psychiatrist to help a troubled child recover from the trauma of her father's sudden death. But let's say they cut—oh—11 minutes from that lean screenplay, minutes when they might have explained why a presumably caring mother barely notices when her daughter Sally clicks off to the outside world. Minutes when they might have explained why Mom continues to appear cavalier as her little girl's deep distress becomes more and more obvious. Or minutes when they might have explained why Mom could expose Sally to a high architectural structure when the kid has nearly fallen to her death twice. All these missing minutes turn what could have been a consistently absorbing story into one that grinds to a halt every so often as you ask yourself, "Why the heck did they do that?" Screenwriter Michael Lessac was the director on this one, so the film's flaws and virtues can fairly be attributed to his vision or lack of same. The Mom in *House of Cards* was originally supposed to be a Dad, but when Kathleen Turner heard that Lessac wanted William Hurt for the lead, she said, "Hey, what about me?" and the role was hers. Would it have made more sense if a FATHER was the clueless parent? Maybe, because we expect mothers to be the caretakers. Since Turner's character, very definitely, is established as the parent responsible for raising Sally, her laissez-faire behavior makes us question both her inclinations and her ability to help her kid. Dr. Tommy Lee Jones is brought into the plot to strike a few subterranean sexual sparks with Mom (they never ignite) and to drag Sally into a clinical setting where autistic and other troubled kids remain in their own irretrievable inner worlds. Mom resists this approach and tries another, with the aid of a recently ubiquitous cinematic tool: virtual reality. The device is mostly hooey, but works at the level of science fiction. In fact, the entire movie plays well enough, in fits and starts, to make you realize that a few more drafts would have turned *House of Cards* into the thoughtful, lovely film it deserved to be.

1992 (PG-13) 109m/C Kathleen Turner, Asha Menina, Tommy Lee Jones, Shiloh Strong, Esther Rolle, Park Overall, Michael Horse, Anne Pitoniak; ***D:*** Michael Lessac; ***W:*** Michael Lessac; ***C:*** Victor Hammer. **VHS, LV, Closed Caption**

House of Games

Writer David Mamet made his directorial debut with *House of Games* starring his then-wife Lindsay Crouse. The sequences with Crouse in action as a psychiatrist really do not work, but once she starts investigating the world of con artists, the plot really starts to hum. Screenwriter Mamet seems more interested in the psychiatrist's dark side than he is in her professional veneer. Crouse is ideally cast opposite Joe Mantegna as the weirdly paired couple who need each other like a coffin needs nails. Both are cool customers who know how to turn on the heat when it serves their purposes. There's rarely been a film with such a perfect middle and such unsatisfactory opening and closing scenes. Still, from the moment Crouse enters the House of Games until she leaves Charlie's Tavern for the last time, you may find yourself as hypnotized by sleaze as she is.

1987 (R) 102m/C Joe Mantegna, Lindsay Crouse, Lilia Skala, J.T. Walsh, Meshach Taylor, Ricky Jay, Mike Nussbaum, Willo Hausman; ***D:*** David Mamet; ***W:*** David Mamet; ***C:*** Juan Ruiz-Anchia; ***M:*** Alaric Jans. **VHS, LV**

The House of the Spirits

Readers with warm memories of Isabel Allende's classic 1982 novel, *La Casa de los Espiritus,* are well advised to treasure them and skip Miramax's ILL-advised screen translation with an award-winning international cast. From the moment you see the horrifyingly miscast Jeremy Irons trying to look like a poor suitor from Chile, you KNOW that every second of this 138-minute mess is going to be a DOOZY! I may be the only person who saw *Reversal*

Tori Spelling, Josh Hamilton, and Parker Posey in *The House of Yes.*
Miramax; courtesy of the Kobal Collection

of Fortune who was convinced that Irons won the 1990 Oscar as Claus Von Bulow by neglecting to blow his nose before he said his lines, and he's even worse here: "Hey, everybody, I'm not really from the Isle of Wight, check out the wig, check out the makeup, and check out the weird voice; all right, so it wouldn't fool anyone in Chile, but you'll never guess how I did it!" I can guess, though, and it's grisly to listen to his phlegm-ridden delivery for two hours and eighteen minutes. Next on the miscast list is Glenn Close as Jeremy Irons' sister. Maybe it's the fact that the film spans 50 years and she never ages or even changes her clothes. Close is hung up on her sister-in-law Clara, played by Meryl Streep, who is the only member of the cast who escapes looking downright silly. Vanessa Redgrave is seen briefly as Streep's mother, and the narration is supplied by the very American Winona Ryder as the daughter of Irons and Streep. It IS within the realm of possibility that even this cast might have been credible with a different script and a different director, but the script and direction here are both supplied by Bille August. Rarely has such impressive source material wound up in the hands of someone so totally out of touch with it. Where Allende's book is non-judgmental and compassionate, August's interpretation is laughable. How else can one explain a sequence in which Irons rapes Sarita Choudhury, that is followed immediately by Ryder's off-camera line, "My father earned everything he got by his own work?" Jeremy Irons and Meryl Streep age on camera, except that Streep's hands are as smooth as a baby's on her deathbed. Maria Conchita Alonso is supposed to be Irons' contemporary, but the older he gets, the younger she looks; C'MON, NO ONE NOTICED THIS IN CONTINUITY? Or was this stifled by the fact that August won an Oscar so he HAD to know what he was doing? August telegraphs every relationship shift, every plot development, every chuckle, every impending tragedy—did I mention that this thing was

138 minutes long? Cast Note: Besides Armin Mueller-Stahl, Antonio Banderas, Miriam Colon, Vincent Gallo, Jan Niklas, Teri Polo et al, the beautiful little girl who plays Clara as a child is Meryl Streep's real-life 10-year-old daughter, Mary Willa Gummer, billed here as Jane Gray. **woof!**

1993 (R) 109m/C Meryl Streep, Jeremy Irons, Glenn Close, Winona Ryder, Antonio Banderas, Armin Mueller-Stahl, Vanessa Redgrave, Sarita Choudhury, Maria Conchita Alonso, Vincent Gallo, Miriam Colon, Jan Niklas, Teri Polo, Jane Gray; ***D:*** Bille August; ***W:*** Bille August; ***C:*** Jorgen Persson; ***M:*** Hans Zimmer. **VHS, LV, Letterbox, Closed Caption**

The House of Yes

Parker Posey is an indie diva, and deservedly so, for few actresses worked harder to secure a niche in low-budget American movies of the '90s than she did. But *The House of Yes*? I can only wonder at the ventilation systems at the Sundance Film Festival for this gloppy mess to have been such a crowd pleaser. Lucretia Garfield and Ida McKinley were spared the indignity of becoming sexual icons after their husbands were assassinated in 1881 and 1901. But Jacqueline Kennedy spent her last 30 years enduring just about everything after witnessing the assassination of her husband in 1963. To her credit, she kept her sanity. Although *The House of Yes* emerged on film after her death, the original Wendy MacLeod play was a hit at San Francisco's Magic Theatre during her lifetime. Unsurprisingly, the play didn't travel well, but now we have Parker Posey as Jackie-O, preserved forever through the magic of the movies. If you want the plot, this is it: Marty Pascal (Josh Hamilton) brings his fiancee Lesly (Tori Spelling) home to meet Mom (Genevieve Bujold), brother Anthony (Freddie Prinze Jr.), and nutty twin sister Jackie-O. Marty resists and Lesly denies the obvious family games. If Marty had stayed away or remained resistant, there wouldn't be a 90-minute movie. Jackie-O tries to drag Marty into long-standing erotic re-enactments of November 22nd. Why not July 2nd or September 6th? Because there aren't any movies of Guiteau or Czolgosz in action! *The House of Yes* was clearly designed to be a smart comedy about incest. Scrub the flashbacks to the Kennedys and what's left is a dull look at five handsome but stupid characters. The fact that they're well played by the earnest cast, including Spelling, indicates that the talents of everyone would be better applied to less threadbare material. **woof!**

1997 (R) 90m/C Parker Posey, Josh Hamilton, Tori Spelling, Freddie Prinze Jr., Genevieve Bujold, Rachel Leigh Cook; ***D:*** Mark Waters; ***W:*** Mark Waters; ***C:*** Michael Spiller; ***M:*** Jeff Rona. Nominations: Golden Raspberry Awards '97: Worst New Star (Spelling). **VHS, LV, Closed Caption**

The House on Carroll Street

The House on Carroll Street is an old-fashioned political thriller directed by Peter Yates, who began his career directing television episodes of *Danger Man* and *The Saint*. There is very little gore in the film and much more emphasis on the tension created by soft sounds, shadows, and atmosphere. Yates' approach actually suits the material quite well, giving the film the look and feel of the 1951 era in which it was set. Viewers who did not live through the McCarthy era might not understand the terror faced by ordinary people with decent political convictions who were absolutely dominated and, sometimes, driven out of their professions, by the hysteria ignited by Senator Joseph McCarthy. His fictional equivalent here, played to the hilt by Mandy Patinkin, may seem the most unsubtle of villains to those who never knew McCarthy, but at the height of his powers, between 1950 and 1954, even those who saw through him couldn't stop him. Screenwriter Walter Bernstein was blacklisted in 1948 after working on one Burt Lancaster film noir, and he didn't work in Hollywood for another 11 years. His script captures the fear of that illogical time, and he has written nicely shaded roles for the principals. Kelly McGillis is an interesting heroine, capturing the gutsiness shared by many who lost their jobs

A comedy with serious relief.

—Tagline from the movie *Hugo Pool*.

through blacklisting. Remember Kent Smith in the '40s *Cat People* movies on the late show? Jeff Daniels may be his closest cinematic equivalent today, slightly stupid, sorta sweet, and the perfect leading man for a stunning female star. Jessica Tandy has a good bit as McGillis' new employer after she is fired from her magazine job. The whole thing is well edited and photographed, with a romantic score by Georges Delerue. The plot, for all its realistic background details, is pure fiction. In real-life, McGillis would have cooled her heels for a decade working at poverty-level jobs, but Bernstein gives her an exciting mystery to solve and a government agent as an ally. For those who want more lowdown on the Communist witch hunt years, watch *The Front. The House on Carroll Street* makes fine use of its 111-minute running time in an intriguing blend of politics and suspense.

1988 (PG) 111m/C Kelly McGillis, Jeff Daniels, Mandy Patinkin, Jessica Tandy; ***D:*** Peter Yates; ***W:*** Walter Bernstein; ***C:*** Michael Ballhaus; ***M:*** Georges Delerue. **VHS, LV, Closed Caption**

House Party

Any comedy about a party without grownups is my idea of a fun flick. *House Party* features a likeable cast, great dance numbers, and suspense, as in Will-Kid (Christopher Reid) Make-It-to-the-Party-Even-Though-His-Dad-Grounded-Him? *House Party* was so popular that two sequels followed in the next four years, but neither matched the spontaneity of Reginald Hudlin's original film.

1990 (R) 100m/C Christopher Reid, Christopher Martin, Martin Lawrence, Tisha Campbell, Paul Anthony, A.J. Johnson, Robin Harris; ***D:*** Reginald Hudlin; ***W:*** Reginald Hudlin; ***C:*** Peter Deming; ***M:*** Marcus Miller. Sundance Film Festival '90: Best Cinematography. **VHS, LV**

Household Saints

I can see why *Household Saints* intrigued non-Catholic audiences, but for me, it fell into the "Oh, Those Crazy Catholics!" file. Actually, it reminded me of the morbid stories the nuns used to tell us in Catholic school, which we were almost positive Never Happened. We heard the grisliest one from our second grade teacher and I have to admit we egged her on. Two nurses put an amputated arm in the bed of a third nurse, just to play a trick on her. When they check in on her later, she is completely mad and sucking the fingers of the amputated arm. What a nice story for seven-year-old kids.... Lili Taylor nails it as Teresa, who thinks she sees Jesus (Sebastien Roche) in her apartment and wants to be a saint when she dies. Creepy. The rest of the cast is quite good, especially Vincent D'Onofrio as Joseph Santangelo, but director Nancy Savoca's *True Love* and *Dogfight* are better. Based on a novel by Francine Prose.

1993 (R) 124m/C Tracey Ullman, Vincent D'Onofrio, Lili Taylor, Judith Malina, Michael Rispoli, Victor Argo, Michael Imperioli, Rachael Bella, Illeana Douglas, Joe Grifasi, Sebastien Roche; ***D:*** Nancy Savoca; ***W:*** Nancy Savoca, Richard Guay; ***C:*** Bobby Bukowski; ***M:*** Stephen Endelman. Independent Spirit Awards '94: Best Supporting Actress (Taylor); Nominations: Independent Spirit Awards '94: Best Actor (D'Onofrio), Best Screenplay. **VHS, Closed Caption**

How to Get Ahead in Advertising

Once upon a time, Bruce Robinson was an actor. He played Benvolio in *Romeo and Juliet* and co-starred with Isabelle Adjani in *The Story of Adele H....* Many years later, he won an Oscar nomination for writing *The Killing Fields* and in 1987 he directed his first movie, *Withnail and I,* starring Richard E. Grant. That film, like *How to Get Ahead in Advertising,* was produced by George Harrison. If his scripts are any indication, Robinson's eclectic life has served him well. The intensity of his dialogue suggests years of angry simmering and he wastes no time now getting straight to the point: advertising is the root of all evil. The less said about how Robinson develops this theme, the better, since I nearly took a pass on the film when I heard the plot. As Robinson showed with his debut feature, though, he knows exactly where and how he's going, most of the time. *How to Get Ahead* would make an insane double bill with a similarly themed Cary Grant comedy from 1948, *Mr. Blandings Builds His Dream House.* The frustration of both ad men elicits hilarity, but where Mr. Blandings is lulled into security with Myrna Loy's Mrs. Blandings in post-war Connecticut, Richard E. Grant's character is so consumed by his profession that even the compassionate Rachel Ward is unable to retrieve him. Robinson's script is a raging polemic by film's end, which is a visual drag especially since the force of his argument has already been conveyed so well by the ad man's internal struggle for his own soul. Still, the sharpness of Robinson's language as well as Richard E. Grant's dazzling transformation make *How to Get Ahead in Advertising* one of the most original and bracing British comedies of the late 1980s. 🦴🦴🦴

1989 (R) 95m/C *GB* Richard E. Grant, Rachel Ward, Susan Wooldridge, Mick Ford, Richard Wilson, John Shrapnel, Jacqueline Tong; ***D:*** Bruce Robinson; ***W:*** Bruce Robinson; ***C:*** Peter Hannan; ***M:*** David Dundas, Rick Wentworth. **VHS, LV**

Hu-Man

Hu-Man may call itself a "visual feast," but it's SOOO boring. It wastes the talents of Terence Stamp and Jeanne Moreau; director Jerome Lapperrousaz gives them little to do but say about 15 lines of dialogue in his 93-minute screenplay. It's an Orpheus re-tread. Stamp's an actor from the future who's decided to be the first time traveler. His ex-mistress Moreau wants him to be on her television show before he begins his travels. *Hu-Man* seems little more than a massive stage for a mysterious concept, the exact nature of which is never revealed. **woof!**

1976 93m/C *FR* Terence Stamp, Jeanne Moreau, Agnes Stevenin, Frederik Van Pallandt; ***D:*** Jerome Lapperrousaz; ***W:*** A. Ruellan, G. Lapperrousaz; ***C:*** Jimmy Glasberg.

Hugo Pool

Hugo Pool is a mess. There are moments during the 92-minute flick, especially when Thelonious Monk is on the soundtrack, that you wish it were in black and white so you wouldn't have to see in crystal clear Foto-Kem color what a fool so many professional actors are making of themselves. Take Malcolm McDowell as Henry Dugay, complete with lookalike hand puppet, trying to kick his heroin habit. On top of this, he seems to be doing a take-off on Jimmy Durante, for god knows what reason. Maybe he just thought it would be neat. On this planet, he would not be married to Cathy Moriarty as a gambling junkie named Minerva, but in this movie, he is, even though they are so NOT each other's types. Their daughter, Hugo Dugay, is played by the always delightful Alyssa (*Charmed*) Milano, who enlists their help to clean 44 L.A. pools in a single day. One client is Robert Downey Jr. as Franz Mazur, whose performance is way out of control, ditto his so-called Hungarian accent. Richard Lewis does another client, Chick Chicalini, either as Al Pacino in *Scarface* or as Will Jordan doing Ed Sullivan (I couldn't tell), but at least he's consistent. And then there's Patrick Dempsey as Floyd Gaylen, a man dying of ALS who's also dying to go outside. He joins Hugo and Minerva on their rounds and an unexpected and very touching romance evolves between Floyd and Hugo. In a film crawling with at least three confirmed overactors, Dempsey steals the picture with his eyes and his smile. It helps that his lines (co-scripted by Laura Downey, who died of ALS in 1994) are among the best in the film. Speaking through a voice box as Stephen Hawking does, Floyd makes the most of his day in the sun with a pretty girl. A movie with a performance as fine as Dempsey's Floyd (beautifully balanced by Milano's Hugo) deserves a look on video, even if you do yield to the temptation (I didn't, but I THOUGHT about it) to fast forward through the moments featuring his less-disciplined co-stars. 🦴🦴½

1997 (R) 92m/C Alyssa Milano, Patrick Dempsey, Robert Downey Jr., Malcolm McDowell, Cathy Moriarty, Sean Penn, Richard Lewis, Bert Remsen, Chuck Barris, Ann Magnuson; ***D:*** Robert Downey; ***W:*** Laura Downey; ***C:*** Joe Montgomery; ***M:*** Danilo Perez. **VHS, LV**

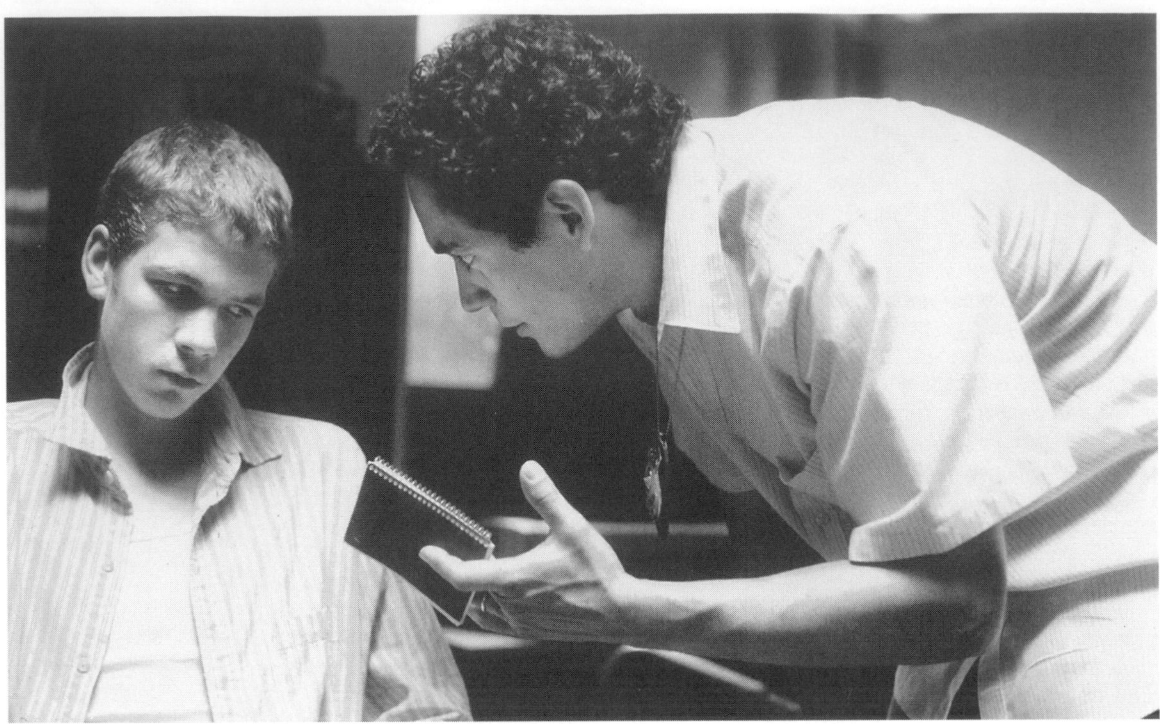

Marcus (Brendan Sexton III) is interrogated by Detective Kramer (Jose Zuniga) in *Hurricane Streets.* United Artists; courtesy of the Kobal Collection

Hundred Per Cent

It's too late now, but if Eric Koyanagi wanted to make a film worthy of its title, he'd scrap two of its three segments and keep the focus on the plight of Asian actor Troy Tashima (*Star Trek: Voyager*'s Garrett Wang) and his girlfriend Cleveland (*BH90210*'s Lindsay Price). As it is, *Hundred Per Cent* looks, sounds, and feels like three different movies and once you're caught up in Troy's story, you'll want to stay with it. Troy auditions as an actor for a variety of different roles, but sooner or later, stereotypical preconceptions about his ethnicity come into play. It's frustrating, because he's a fine actor and the auditions seem painfully real, as if they were drawn from life. Flipping to the marijuana-fueled life of Slim Kim (Darion Basco) as a Bob Marley wannabe and to the slacker dreams of Dustin Nguyen's Isaac just doesn't have the same impact. Moreover, the segments differ in pace, style, and tone, and not to the advantage of the film as a whole. *Hundred Per Cent* looks great, the cast is very good, and Koyanagi CAN write and direct. The 102-minute hodgepodge here simply isn't the best showcase for this assembly of considerable talents.

1998 102m/C Garrett Wang, Lindsay Price, Darion Basco, Dustin Nguyen, Tamlyn Tomita, Adam Collis, Keiko Agena, Francois Giroday, Stan Egi; ***D:*** Eric Koyanagi; ***W:*** Eric Koyanagi; ***C:*** Michael Goi; ***M:*** John Keane.

The Hungarians

Zoltan Fabri tries to make *The Hungarians* a more substantial film than it really is. He focuses on some migrant farm workers who go to Germany, partly for the money and partly to avoid fighting in World War II. The weak script seems to make the statement that everyone picks on the Hungarians and it's a shame, really, because they're such nice people. Unfortunately, neither the dramatic situations nor any of the characters are developed very well. The best thing about this movie is Gyorgy Illes' fine cinematography. ***AKA:*** Magyarok. 🦴🦴

1978 m/C *HU* Andras Ambrus, Noemi Apor, Jozsef Bihari, Gabor Koncz, Sandor Szabo, Zoltan Gera; ***D:*** Zoltan Fabri; ***W:*** Zoltan Fabri; ***C:*** Gyorgy Illes.

Hurricane Streets

This intensely sad film shows how quickly a young boy's life can turn to ashes when he lacks love and guidance from anyone. Marcus (wonderfully played by Brendan Sexton III) is only 15, but his father is dead, his mother is in prison, and his grandmother has to work. He thinks he knows how his dad died and why his mom's in prison, but he's mistaken, and when he realizes why, he has no foundation on which he can build any sort of life. All that's left are the daily hustles with his friends, who are planning to make the leap from misdemeanor theft to grand theft auto and other felonies. Some of the children he runs with can barely keep their eyes open on their assorted rounds, but when they break and enter a house, what seems like a highly charged game at first evolves into something much more serious. Marcus' life is further complicated by the love he feels for Melena (Isidra Vega), who's just 14. Like Marcus, Melena's life is more than she can handle. Her biggest problem is her father, who snaps his kindly act on and off at will. Her mother left because of the beatings and now Melena's stuck with them. What are two children on *Hurricane Streets* to do? The first film of Morgan J. Freeman (the director, not the actor) supplies some powerful insights. ***AKA:*** Hurricane. 🦴🦴🦴

1996 89m/C Brendan Sexton III, Isidra Vega, David Roland Frank, L.M. Kit Carson, Jose Zuniga, Lynn Cohen, Edie Falco, Shawn Elliot, Heather Matarazzo; ***D:*** Morgan J. Freeman; ***W:*** Morgan J. Freeman; ***C:*** Enrique Chediak. Sundance Film Festival '97: Best Cinematography, Best Director (Freeman), Audience Award. **VHS**

I Am Cuba

Agitprop Russian-Cuban co-production illustrates different aspects of the Cuban revolution from the toppling of Batista's decadent Havana to idealistic soldiers and student revolutionaries. Lots of oratory and deliberate artificiality combined with cinematographer Sergei Urusevsky's stunning high-contrast photography. A 1996 Independent Spirit Award nominee for Best Foreign Film. 🦴🦴

1964 141m/B *CU RU* Luz Maria Collazo, Jose Gallardo, Sergio Corrieri, Jean Bouise, Raul Garcia, Celia Rodriguez; ***D:*** Mikhail Kalatozov; ***W:*** Yevgeny Yevtushenko, Enrique Pineda Barnet; ***C:*** Sergei Urusevsky; ***M:*** Carlos Farinas. Nominations: Independent Spirit Awards '96: Best Foreign Film. **VHS**

I Bury the Living

Richard Boone (1917–81) was born to be an independent filmmaker at a time when few ventured into Indie Land. He did his best, though: 1963–64's *The Richard Boone Show* was a noble attempt to create a stock company (Boone, Robert Blake, Lloyd Bochner, Laura Devon, June Harding, Bethel Leslie, Harry Morgan, Jeanette Nolan, Ford Rainey, Warren Stevens, and Guy Stockwell) for a weekly dramatic anthology series and although it is less well-remembered than *Medic* (1954–56), *Have Gun Will Travel* (1957–63), or *Hec Ramsey* (1972–74), Boone's indie spirit was clearly in the right place at the wrong time. And then there is THIS strange little flick, which came and went in the summer of 1958, but still survives on video. Boone is Robert Kraft, who's just taken over as chairman of the town cemetery. For most of the 76-minute running time, he's convinced he's losing his mind, because when he accidentally puts a black pin in the cemetery map of pre-sold burial sites, the owner winds up dead. (Unoccupied grave sites are supposed to be represented by white pins!) Under Albert Band's guidance, Boone successfully manages to pull off this creepy tale until the inevitable logical explanation, which rather ruins it. Before that, Boone's haunted performance, Frederick Gately's remarkable camera work, and Gerald Fried's spooky score ignite some genuine terror. A script doctor would have helped *I Bury the Living,* but a larger budget would have scuttled it. As it stands, the film's

“Goodbye, Jennifer—be a bad girl.”

—Warlock Daniel (Cecil Kellaway) bids farewell to his daughter, Jennifer (Veronica Lake), in *I Married a Witch.*

cheap sincerity gives it a look and tone unlike anything else made at the time. ☙☙☙

1958 76m/B Richard Boone, Theodore Bikel, Peggy Maurer, Herb Anderson, Howard Smith, Robert Osterloh, Russ Bender, Matt Moore, Ken Drake, Glenn Vernon, Lynn Bernay, Cyril Delevanti; ***D:*** Albert Band; ***W:*** Louis Garfinkle; ***C:*** Frederick Gately; ***M:*** Gerald Fried. **VHS**

I Have Killed

It wasn't easy sustaining a career as a Japanese matinee idol, yet Sessue Hayakawa (1889–1973) was able to avoid the stereotypical roles that most Asian actors of his generation had to play. Even when he was assigned to a part in which the racism was taken for granted, Hayakawa invested the role with such strong sensuality that the racist message was subverted through sheer charisma. Take 1915's *The Cheat:* the unstated text is that Fannie Ward's branding by Hayakawa is A Fate Worse Than Death. But clearly there were many female audience members who were attracted to Hayakawa, and they turned out in droves to make him one of the top stars in 1915. Four years later, Hayakawa starred in *The Tong Man,* torn between his love (for Helen Jerome Eddy) and duty. In spite of his obvious box-office appeal, especially to women, jobs in Hollywood were not as plentiful as they might have been and Hayakawa signed on to make *I Have Killed* in France. Once again, he is torn; the wife (Huguette Duflos) of a close friend with a bad heart is being blackmailed by a slime and Hayakawa comes gallantly to her rescue. Maybe a little TOO gallantly, for even in France, he couldn't cruise off into the sunset with her, only alone. To stack the deck even more, her child gets along famously with Hayakawa. Isn't it amazing, what a great husband and father he might have been, if only...? (things were different, of course!). In 1931, Hayakawa as Scotland Yard investigator Ah Kee starred opposite Anna May Wong as Ling Moy in *Daughter of the Dragon,* with Swedish character actor Warner Oland as Fu Manchu. Hayakawa picked up a whole new generation of fans when he became a character actor himself in such films as *Tokyo Joe, Three Came Home, The Bridge on the River Kwai* (for which he won an Oscar nomination), *The Geisha Boy, Green Mansions, Hell to Eternity,* and Walt Disney's *The Swiss Family Robinson. I Have Killed* is vintage Hayakawa; his underplaying wipes out everyone else's histrionics and you'll be seeing his eyes in your dreams long after the movie's over. ***AKA:*** J'ai Tué. ☙☙☙

1924 90m/B *FR* Sessue Hayakawa, Huguette Duflos, Max Maxudian, Maurice Sigrist, Pierre Daltour, Denise Legeay, Jules De Spoly, Andre Volbert; ***D:*** Roger Lion; ***W:*** Roger Lion; ***C:*** Maurice Defassiaux.

I Just Wasn't Made for These Times

The Beach Boys dominated international music charts between 1962 and 1969 as living proof that the California sun, the Pacific ocean, and non-stop “Good Vibrations” could keep five Hawthorne surfer boys frozen in time as teenagers forever. Dennis Wilson's 1983 drowning and Brian Wilson's 1991 autobiography *Wouldn't It Be Nice* revealed that, long before their rise and fall and resurrection, life was far from happy-go-lucky for the group. *I Wasn't Made for These Times,* a 70-minute documentary by filmmaker Don Was, takes a look at Brian Wilson today, with brief appearances by mother Audree, brother Carl, daughters Carnie and Wendy, and even ex-wife Marilyn. Dr. Eugene Landy, the controversial therapist whom Brian Wilson credited with saving his life, is nowhere in evidence, although Wilson refers to him somewhat dismissively just once. Despite the decision to make the film in timeless black and white, Was' film is not even remotely nostalgic, nor is there any attempt to examine the Beach Boys' career in scholarly fashion. This appears to be how Brian Wilson wants to be seen and remembered at the age of 52, clearly ravaged by his youthful excesses, but still eager for audience acceptance and attention as a solo artist. ***AKA:*** Brian Wilson: I Just Wasn't Made for These Times. ☙☙☙

1994 70m/B Brian Wilson, Carnie Wilson, Wendy Wilson; ***D:*** Don Was; ***C:*** Wyatt Troll.

I Like It Like That

I Like It Like That is not an indie, but deserves inclusion here as the first feature written and directed by a black woman (Darnell Martin) for a major studio (Hail Columbia!) in Hollywood. There are only two well-known stars in it, Griffin Dunne as Stephen Price, a recording industry executive, and Rita Moreno as Rosario Linares, a nagging mother-in-law. The best performances in the movie are given by little-known actors, mainly Lauren Velez as the female protagonist, Lisette Linares. Lisette and her yucky husband, Chino (Jon Seda), have three kids (Tomas Melly as Li'l Chino, Desiree Casado as Minnie, and Isaiah Garcia as Pee Wee). Chino is busted for stealing a stereo and Lisette has to get a job FAST. Price hires her as his assistant, but soon the neighborhood is gossiping that Lisette only got the job because she's having sex with him. When Chino is out of jail and hears the false gossip, he has sex with neighborhood girl Magdalena Soto (Lisa Vidal). By this point, you may wonder why Lisette doesn't leave Chino. (I sure the hell would!) Life, this film suggests, doesn't work that way. Although Martin's sympathy is clearly with Lisette, she has a humorous take on the problems faced by the rest of the Linares clan, including Lisette's transsexual brother, Alexis (Jesse Borrego). But the humor renders tolerable stuff that really shouldn't be, not for Lisette, and certainly not for her kids. Nonetheless, it's a promising cinematic start for Martin and for Velez.

1994 (R) 106m/C Lauren Velez, Jon Seda, Lisa Vidal, Jesse Borrego, Griffin Dunne, Rita Moreno, Tomas Melly, Desiree Casado, Isaiah Garcia; ***D:*** Darnell Martin; ***W:*** Darnell Martin; ***C:*** Alexander Grusynski; ***M:*** Sergio George. Nominations: Independent Spirit Awards '95: Best Actor (Seda), Best Actress (Velez), Best Cinematography, Best First Feature. **VHS, LV, Closed Caption**

I Love You, I Love You Not

For 19 hours between August 25, 1994, and January 26, 1995, Claire Danes had the role of a lifetime. As moody Angela Chase in *My So-Called Life,* she created a role so on target that those 19 hours are still played constantly on MTV and they even received their own video release in 1998. Since 1995, Danes has kept busy onscreen, but is mainly a "cool teen" star on magazine covers with yucky hair styles and clothes that stubbornly refuse to become pace-setting fashions. Danes began well as Beth in 1994's *Little Women,* then played bits in *How to Make an American Quilt* and *Home for the Holidays.* The weepy *To Gillian on Her 37th Birthday* followed and then *William Shakespeare's Romeo and Juliet,* which attained hit status largely because Romeo was Leonardo DiCaprio. *U-Turn* was barely released, her role in John Grisham's *The Rainmaker* was wimpy and unpersuasive, and she was lost in the large cast of *Les Miserables.* And then there is *I Love You, I Love You Not,* which might have looked terrific in the planning stages before it required the participation of investors in four different countries only to wind up as a straight-to-video release in America after a short run in a few European theatres. Danes is Daisy, a Manhattan schoolgirl who loves Ethan (Jude Law), but he doesn't love her back because she's Jewish. (James Van Der Beek is Tony, another classmate who's mean to Daisy for the same reason.) Danes also plays her Nana (Jeanne Moreau) as a young girl, who survived Auschwitz OFFSCREEN. This movie seems unfinished and disjointed as it's missing all the elements that would make it affecting and real. It feels like they shot footage, raised money, shot footage, raised money, ad infinitum. Somewhere in the process, the whole point of the movie got lost. Do we believe that Daisy and Nana are related? Not for a second. What made *My So-Called Life* work so well was the fact that the writers knew Angela Chase inside and out and spent a lot of time and care ensuring that she looked and sounded just right. Now Claire Danes is on a career track with jobs that look impressive on her resume, but are not specifically good for her. She's way too young to be the McLean Stevenson of the 1990s, but her career needs a lot more thought and considerably more

Daisy (Claire Danes) and Nana (Jeanne Moreau) in *I Love You, I Love You Not.* Columbia; courtesy of the Kobal Collection

focus than she and/or her advisers are giving it.

1997 (PG-13) 92m/C *FR GE GB* Claire Danes, Jeanne Moreau, Jude Law, James Van Der Beek, Robert Sean Leonard, Kris Park, Lauren Fox, Emily Burkes-Nossiter, Carrie Slaza; ***D:*** Billy Hopkins; ***W:*** Wendy Kesselman; ***C:*** Maryse Alberti; ***M:*** Gil Goldstein. **VHS, Closed Caption**

I Married a Witch

One of the coolest movie stars between 1941 and 1947 was...Veronica Lake (1919–73) AND *I Married a Witch* is one of her coolest movies. Along with her father, Daniel (Cecil Kellaway, 1893–1973), she is burned at the stake during the Puritan era. For their part in this nefarious deed, the male descendants of the Wooley family are doomed forever to be the most miserable married men on Earth. Cut to the early 1940s: Wallace Wooley (Fredric March, 1897–1975) is about to be married to Estelle Masterson (Susan Hayward, 1917–75), a real shrew. Not if Jennifer (Lake) can help it! Wooley also wants to be Governor with the support of his future father-in-law, J.R. (Robert Warwick, 1878–1964). He "rescues" Jennifer from a fire (well, she IS a witch!), and she proceeds to bewitch him, as only she can. Estelle and J.R. don't like it one bit. Tough. Jennifer and Daniel make mischief in Wooley's life, until she falls in love with him and loses her magic powers. (There's a lesson here!) French director Rene *(The Ghost Goes West)* Clair (1898–1981) keeps things moving at a merry clip, and Robert Benchley (1889–1945) is a delight as always as Dr. Dudley White. His Algonquin Round Table crony Marc Connelly (1890–1980) contributed to the splendid adaptation of Thorne Smith's *The Passionate Witch.* Look for exquisite five-year-old Ann Carter as Jennifer's daughter, soon to receive rave reviews as Amy for Val Lewton's *The Curse of the Cat People* and as Beatrice for Mark Hellinger's *The Two Mrs. Carrolls.* P.S. Ten years after what turned out to be the highlight of her career, Lake accepted a television assignment on an episode of *Tales of Tomorrow* entitled "Flight Overdue." Her glorious blonde mane had been hacked away in favor of a butch cut suitable for an aviatrix. The primitive video lighting was harsh on a young woman of 32, and so were the ghastly costumes. But the saddest thing about the show is the script. Lake speaks forcefully of her right to live her life as she chooses and, after her Amelia Earhart-style disappearance, Walter Brooke as her icky husband says, "I'm glad she's gone and at last I'm free." This horrifying bit of sexual propaganda from the spring of 1952 nearly broke my heart. ♪♪♪♪

1942 77m/B Veronica Lake, Fredric March, Susan Hayward, Robert Benchley, Cecil Kellaway, Elizabeth Patterson, Robert Warwick, Eily Malyon, Mary Field, Nora Cecil, Emory Parnell, Helen St. Rayer, Aldrich Bowker, Emma Dunn, Harry Tyler, Ralph Peters, Ann Carter; ***D:*** Rene Clair; ***W:*** Robert Pirosh, Marc Connelly; ***C:*** Ted Tetzlaff; ***M:*** Roy Webb. Nominations: Academy Awards '42: Best Original Score. **VHS, LV**

I Met a Murderer

James Mason was years away from achieving international stardom when he made *I Met a Murderer* in 1939 with Roy Kellino as director and cinematographer and his future wife Pamela Kellino as co-star. All three produced the low-budget film and the two stars collaborated on adapting Mrs. Kellino's short story for the screen. This excellent early showcase for James Mason focuses on a fugitive who wanders around the country with a writer; the film benefits from the on-location filming. Its sympathetic depiction of a man who shoots his wife (Sylvia Coleridge) only after she shoots his dog provided the film with a noir atmosphere that was unusual for British movies of that era. ♪♪♪

1939 79m/B James Mason, Pamela Kellino, Sylvia Coleridge, William Devlin, Esma Cannon, James Harcourt; ***D:*** Roy Kellino; ***W:*** Roy Kellino; ***C:*** Roy Kellino. **VHS**

I Shot Andy Warhol

Valerie Solanas is not a historical figure for whom one automatically feels a great deal of sympathy. Until I saw Lili Taylor's take on her, I always thought she was a precursor of would-be assassins like Squeaky Fromme or Sara Jane Moore. If you compare her story with the one told in *Basquiat,* you wonder why she would even want to solicit Warhol's approval, every card in his deck was so stacked against her. But she did want his approval, and her mental health steadily declined as a result. There is one rather sad sequence in which Solanas carefully chooses just the right outfit to meet a would-be publisher. She is so excited by what she hopes will be her big break and she tries so hard to create a dignified impression. Most of the time, though, she lugs around deep hostility toward everyone, while hoping that her work will win acceptance in spite of her behavior. As in every film that revolves around Andy Warhol (played here by Jared Harris), there are the usual eccentric roles that actors wanting to give their careers a jump start would do anything to play. Stephen Dorff is Candy Darling, a Warhol superstar who died at 26 in 1974. Jamie Harrold is Jackie Curtis, a Warhol superstar who died at 38 in 1985. Michael Imperioli is Ondine, a Warhol superstar who died at 51 in 1989. On the other hand, Reginald Rodgers, Miriam Cyr, and Tahnee Welch are living legends Paul Morrissey, Ultra Violet, and Viva. The filmmakers try hard to show that Solanas wanted to do more with her life than shoot Andy Warhol, but as she antagonizes every single one of her supporters, her manifesto shrinks in importance compared to the one act of violence that got her in the history books. ♪♪♪

1996 (R) 100m/C Lili Taylor, Jared Harris, Stephen Dorff, Martha Plimpton, Donovan Leitch, Tahnee Welch, Michael Imperioli, Lothaire Bluteau, Anna Thompson, Peter Friedman, Jill Hennessey, Craig Chester, James Lyons, Reginald Rodgers, Jamie Harrold, Edoardo Ballerini, Lynn Cohen, Myriam Cyr, Isabel Gillies, Eric Mabius; ***D:*** Mary Harron; ***W:*** Mary Harron, Daniel Minahan; ***C:*** Ellen Kuras; ***M:*** John Cale. Nominations: Independent Spirit Awards '97: Best First Feature. **VHS**

The Hound Salutes: ANG LEE
Director, *The Ice Storm*

I think it's really the emotions in *The Ice Storm* towards the end of the book that got me. To me, it's more than unjustified retribution, it's Greek tragedy. It's very disturbing. It's examining emotions that are really strong and spiritually self evoking. What does it take to go to that emotional point? What sort of movie would that be? That interested me, very much. Finally, in the morning, when the family in *The Ice Storm* pick up the narrator Paul (Tobey Maguire) at the train station, you can say all sorts of nasty things about family, but that moment really makes family worthwhile. I was very touched by it. I wanted to make an interesting textural movie, somehow foreign to me, but which emotionally really hit home. I hope the movie hits people so the audience doesn't know what hit them. That's my wishful thinking.

"The Hood family in *The Ice Storm* is pretty much the flip side of how I was brought up. I'm probably closest to Ben Hood, the character played by Kevin Kline. I think I relate to him very much.

I Think I Do

If we watch too many movies, we might believe that the boy we left behind is our soul mate, destined to run off into the sunset with us where we'll live happily ever after. For most of us, he isn't, of course, and we know exactly why (or think we do). But suppose we're wrong? That's the premise of Brian Sloan's *I Think I Do,* or, as the Internet Movie Database cleverly subtitles it: *One Wedding. No Funerals.* Carol Gonzales (Lauren Velez) is getting married to Matt (Jamie Harrold). All their friends are coming to the ceremony, including soap opera writer Bob (Alexis Arquette) and his unofficial fiancee, soap opera star Sterling Scott (Tuc Watkins). So are college buddies Beth (Maddie Corman), Eric (Guillermo Diaz), Sarah (Marianne Hagan), and Brendan (Christian Maelen). Bob used to be madly in love with Brendan, but Brendan beat him up when he realized the depth of Bob's feelings for him, thus ending their friendship. Years later, Brendan realizes that he, too, was madly in love with Bob and flirts with him through all the preliminaries leading up to Carol and Matt's wedding. Bob is confused, Brendan is insatiable, Sterling is clueless, and everyone else is looking for action. Filmed mostly in New York, the film is supposed to take place in Washington, D.C. (36 hours of second-unit photography takes care of that discrepancy.) The relationships of most of the characters feel real, fresh, and funny. Arquette is effective as Bob, Corman once again shows what an adroit comedienne she is, Velez is a riot as the reluctant bride who hates the fuss and every aspect of her wedding except the groom, and Watkins does a clever satire of daytime's deceptively boyish idol. Marni Nixon appears in a funny bit as Aunt Alice and Dechen Thurman (a ringer for Uma) holds his own with Corman as a lusty photographer. But newcomer Maelen brings dark eyes and lustrous lashes to the key role of Brendan and little else. We can accept a fairy tale like *I Think I Do,* but we need a little help in the suspension of reality department and Maelen needs more film experience to supply it. Otherwise, if

He grew up in America in the '50s, I grew up in Taiwan of the '70s, both quite traditional, socially conservative times. And then we're fathers in the modern world, trying to level with the kids, trying to adapt to a new way of dealing with wife and children. Inside, we're just big boys, but we have to behave in such a way that's adult. It was like a dream, working with Tobey Maguire, Christina Ricci, and Elijah Wood. They're totally professional. They have less idea than I have about 1973, because they weren't born yet. They had no idea what lines like 'a political re-education' meant. I think what the kids have to offer is their innocence. The audience will see a certain image and I tried not to interfere with that. Actually, I was quite scared. It was the first time I worked with American teenagers, so I didn't know what sort of monsters they might be or what it was going to be like, but having that group—they're very natural to work with, they're not influenced by television—they just do film. I thought they could relate to the material of the kids' situation, except today when kids rebel against their parents, they're much more confident. We had to set them back in 1973 when the rebellion's just happened. They have to say those rebellion lines in a much edgier, more nervous fashion. They weren't as sure about themselves then. Today's kids are much more matter-of-fact about rebellion."

ANG LEE also directed *Sense and Sensibility, Eat Drink Man Woman, The Wedding Banquet,* and *Pushing Hands.*

not quite the 1997 screwball comedy Sloan wants it to be, *I Think I Do* is a painless fantasy of what might be...IF! 𝒥𝒥𝒥

1997 92m/C Alexis Arquette, Christian Maelen, Maddie Corman, Guillermo Diaz, Lauren Velez, Jamie Harrold, Marianne Hagan, Tuc Watkins, Marni Nixon, Dechen Thurman; ***D:*** Brian Sloan; ***W:*** Brian Sloan; ***C:*** Milton Kam; ***M:*** Gerry Gershman.

The Ice Storm

How do you make an absolutely riveting movie about the colossal boredom of life in a small town, circa 1973? Ask Ang Lee, director of *The Ice Storm*! All of the ingredients of suburban malaise are here, from anesthetizing affairs to children's doctor games, from distracted and/or deliberate shoplifting to Thanksgiving gatherings that no one really wants to attend. It's cold in Connecticut and that applies to relationships as well as the weather. Ben and Elena Hood (Kevin Kline and Joan Allen) are going through the motions of marriage, a fact of life not missed by their kids, Paul and Wendy (Tobey Maguire and Christina Ricci). Ben is having an affair with Janey Carver (Sigourney Weaver). Because the affair means nothing to her, it means something to him and both his sense of discretion and his wife suffer as a result. Icy Janey is also married (to Jamey Sheridan as husband Jim) with children (Adam Hann-Byrd and Elijah Wood as Sandy and Mikey). The affair leads to tragedy in a slow and indirect fashion. The teenaged kids learn a little about sexual electricity from each other but nothing from the grown-ups about the consequences of actual electricity, a lesson ideally learned by the age of three. Was life in 1973 really this grim? For the Hoods and the Carvers it is, ditto the participants in the world's unsexiest mate swapping party ever. Sensitive direction by Ang Lee and fine acting by all, especially the kids, keep you tuned into an emotional climate you'd only want to visit with a 113-minute return ticket. After playing Pat Nixon in the White House, Elisabeth Proctor in Salem, Elena Hood in New Canaan, and Betty Parker in *Pleasantville,* Joan Allen

Wendy Hood (Christina Ricci) and her father Ben (Kevin Kline) in *The Ice Storm.* Fox Searchlight; courtesy of the Kobal Collection

would definitely benefit from a tourist visa to Screwball Comedy Land at this stage of her career. Katie (Joey Potter on *Dawson's Creek*) Holmes made her first screen appearance here as Libbets Casey. ☙☙☙☙

1997 (R) 113m/C Kevin Kline, Sigourney Weaver, Joan Allen, Christina Ricci, Tobey Maguire, Elijah Wood, Katie Holmes, Henry Czerny, Adam Hann-Byrd, David Krumholtz, Jamey Sheridan, Maia Danzinger; ***D:*** Ang Lee; ***W:*** James Schamus; ***C:*** Frederick Elmes; ***M:*** Mychael Danna. British Academy Awards '97: Best Supporting Actress (Weaver); Nominations: Australian Film Institute '98: Best Foreign Film; British Academy Awards '97: Best Adapted Screenplay; Golden Globe Awards '98: Best Supporting Actress (Weaver); Writers Guild of America '97: Best Adapted Screenplay. **VHS, LV, Closed Caption**

The Iceman Cometh

The idea for the American Film Theatre was laudable: the very best American plays, interpreted by the very best American actors, and helmed by the very best American directors. Season tickets would be sold in advance to subscribers who presumably cared about the preservation of American theatrical classics on film... whoa, let me stop right there. It sounds rather elitist, doesn't it? And PAY for eight movies all at once? (Well, okay, there WAS a special rate for students.) The ordering information said that only subscribers would ever be able to see these movies, which seems to be true, because *The Iceman Cometh,* the personal favorite of its director John Frankenheimer, didn't appear to turn up anywhere after its original screenings in 1973. Two-thirds of its cast members are now deceased and it did provide Frederic March, Robert Ryan, and Martyn Green with fitting swan songs to their long careers. There are many memorable moments in this ensemble piece, but it also gave this audience member my one and only movie hangover. It's 17 minutes LONGER than *Gone with the Wind,* and it all takes place in one bar where the mostly male patrons discuss their need for illusions. For example, Harry Hope (March) can't leave the bar—he'll get run over by a car if he does. Some reviewers in 1973 felt that Jason Robards, as the greatest actor of his generation to interpret Eugene O'Neill, should have played Hickey instead of Lee Marvin. Oscar-winner Marvin wound up being okay instead of great in the role, which compromises the film's value to scholars AND audiences, then and now. The acting by everyone else (especially by March, Ryan, and Jeff Bridges, with two Oscars and seven nominations between them) is remarkable, but it's still very heavy going and undoubtedly benefits writers of O'Neill theses the most. 🦴🦴🦴

1973 239m/C Lee Marvin, Fredric March, Robert Ryan, Jeff Bridges, Martyn Green, George Voskovec, Moses Gunn, Tom Pedi, Evans Evans, Bradford Dillman, Sorrell Booke, John McLiam; ***D:*** John Frankenheimer; ***W:*** Thomas Quinn Curtiss; ***C:*** Ralph Woolsey.

If...

I was so desperate to see a movie one winter in Venice that I watched a revival screening of *If...,* dubbed in German and with Italian subtitles (neither of which I can understand or read). It was still every bit as subversive as I remember, and a bracing antidote to so many schoolboy sagas, where the status quo is rigidly maintained at any cost. Malcolm McDowell is pretty scary here as Mick Travers, but nowhere near as scary as he would become as Alex De Large in 1972's *A Clockwork Orange.* (It would be several YEARS before I could look at a McDowell picture again after that.) *If...* is a product of its time in that all paths lead to the revolution, but no paths lead from it. Mick and his mates succeed in bringing down the headmaster, but what then? Outside of this movie, there was Labour Leader Harold Wilson (1916–95, who DIDN'T go to public school), Conservative Edward Heath, Wilson again, Labour Leader James Callaghan, Conservatives Margaret Thatcher and John Major, and Labour Leader Tony Blair. But Conservatives and Labour Leaders alike try to woo the opposite party these days, and the most moderate Conservatives may well be more liberal than Tony Blair; not exactly the stuff of which anarchists and revolutions are made. Still, the energy and intensity of the revolt in *If...* is what sticks in your memory, not the middle-aged character actor that Malcolm McDowell has become. Based on John Howlett's *Crusaders.* 🦴🦴🦴🦴

1969 (R) 111m/C *GB* Malcolm McDowell, David Wood, Christine Noonan, Richard Warwick, Robert Swann, Arthur Lowe, Mona Washbourne, Graham Crowden, Hugh Thomas, Guy Rose, Peter Jeffrey, Geoffrey Chater, Mary MacLeod, Anthony Nicholls, Ben Aris, Charles Lloyd Pack, Rupert Webster, Brian Pettifer, Sean Bury, Michael Cadman; ***D:*** Lindsay Anderson; ***W:*** David Sherwin; ***C:*** Miroslav Ondricek; ***M:*** Marc Wilkinson. Cannes Film Festival '69: Best Film. **VHS, LV**

If I Had It to Do Over Again

Who's going to believe that Anouk Aimee, attractive as ever at 44, would fall for the 14-year-old son of her best friend, especially with the shady past her character has had? Moreover, Catherine Deneuve (at 33, but looking much younger) is absolutely unbelievable as a woman who's been in prison for 16 years. Expository sequences are omitted and all the characters are unevenly developed in Lelouch's flimsily constructed screenplay here. Needless to say, though, Aimee and Deneuve make *If I Had It to Do Over Again* a most pleasant film to watch. ***AKA:*** Second Chance; Si C'Était à Refaire. 🦴🦴🦴

1976 94m/C *FR* Anouk Aimee, Catherine Deneuve, Charles Denner, Francis Huster; ***D:*** Claude Lelouch; ***W:*** Claude Lelouch; ***C:*** Jacques Lefrancois.

Impact

Ella Raines (1921–88) was a cool, green-eyed brunette (with auburn highlights) who twice made the cover of *Life* magazine when she starred in two '40s noir films for Universal, *Phantom Lady* and *Criss Cross.* Two

The Hound Salutes:

CAROL LYNLEY

Actress, *In Possession*

I'm a graduate of St. Eugene's, St. Joseph's, and Good Shepherd, and that was all before I started in show business at the age of 10. My mother was a Catholic convert, so I became a Catholic by accident, actually. I just started going back to Mass regularly several years ago and I'm very happy that I did. I recommend it highly. I don't know why my character wound up the way she did in Otto Preminger's *The Cardinal.* It was a book and I know that Otto was involved with Cardinal Spellman at the time [1963] and we met Cardinal Cushing, but the actors had nothing to do with how their characters evolved. That was all Otto and his dealings with the political hierarchy of the Church.

"It was the only time in my life that I played two parts, a mother and her daughter. As an actress, I'm a blonde; as a mother, I'm a brunette and I give birth to myself as a redhead. Weird! I did the play *Blue Denim* on Broadway and won a Theatre World award for it and then I did the movie with Brandon de Wilde in 1959. For 1965's *Harlow,* I rehearsed for three weeks with Judy Garland, who was in very good shape at the time. She was wonderful to hang out with and very, very funny. We were going to start shooting the next day in something new called Electronovision. Right before our final rehearsal was over, Judy came to me and said, 'Carol, you won't see me tomorrow.' 'Oh, Judy!' 'No, I'm leaving! This is a piece of sh—!' 'Judy, no! Please don't leave!' 'I just want you to know, because they're going to say that I'm nuts because I'm Judy Garland, but this really is a piece

years before her 1943 film debut, a stove exploded in her face, fortunately resulting in just temporary damage to her hair and eyebrows. (The experience later added to the realism of her performance when she played a woman whose face had been scarred in *The Second Face.*) Raines' career started out strong and she always gave good performances, but her films declined in quality and importance during her five-year contract. 1949's *Impact* was made independently in San Francisco, making fine use of both the city itself and the surrounding Bay area, including Sausalito and Larkspur. With better distribution, it might have picked up the reputation it deserves, for rarely has a film noir been as expertly convoluted as this one has. It has everything! Infidelity, attempted murder, accidental death, amnesia, false imprisonment, exciting courtroom sequences, missing evidence, a missing witness...what more could anyone ask for at three in the morning? Ella Raines plays a resourceful garage mechanic who stops at nothing to free the man she loves (Brian Donlevy). The excellent cast also features Charles Coburn as a tenacious inspector, lovely Helen Walker as the wife from hell, Anna May Wong as the loyal employee who holds they key to the mystery, and Mae Marsh as Raines' mom. Only a few of Raines' films are available on video (including some episodes of her 1954 television series, *Janet Dean, Registered Nurse*). Luckily, *Impact* is among them.

1949 83m/B Brian Donlevy, Ella Raines, Charles Coburn, Helen Walker, Anna May Wong, Philip Ahn, Art Baker, Tony Barrett, Harry Cheshire, Lucius Cooke, Sheilah Graham, Tom Greenway, Hans Herbert, Linda Johnson, Joe Kirk, Clarence Kolb, Mary Landa, Mae Marsh; ***D:*** Arthur Lubin; ***W:*** Dorothy Reid, Jay Dratler; ***C:*** Ernest Laszlo; ***M:*** Michel Michelet. **VHS**

of sh—!' I went home and thought, 'Well, I know she's eccentric. She's just testing me.' Sure enough, the next day—no Judy, and Ginger Rogers was standing there and she did the whole thing with no rehearsals. Ginger brought her mother with her, which was astounding, but she was a trouper. She just went in there and did it. She did a wonderful job, but I was glad I got to spend three weeks with Judy Garland. She's a very funny lady with a wonderful sense of humor. I told Liza Minnelli this story, because she collects Judy Garland stories and she said, 'Yeah, that's Mama.'

"I was astonished by the whole thing that happened at San Francisco's Castro Theatre for *The Poseidon Adventure* AIDS benefit. For a 2,000-seat house to be sold out really surprised me! I was waiting for my cue to go on and I heard a roar! It was such a wild party with such a wild crowd on such a wild night! I was astounded! The onstage interview was hysterical! I was kidding around about it being such a tough crowd to work and the audience went crazy!

"1984's *In Possession* was a movie about the paranormal I did with Christopher Cazenove. (He's such a sweetheart.) We play husband and wife and we go to bed together and we share a mutual nightmare and the movie's about that. Is the nightmare the reality or is the reality the nightmare?.... The whole thing ends with me screaming (I happen to have a very good operatic scream) and the camera moving in closer and closer and closer! I enjoyed spending all that time with Christopher Cazenove. We were in every scene together and we became very close friends. We're still very close friends today."

CAROL LYNLEY also appeared in *Blue Denim, The Cardinal, Harlow,* and *The Poseidon Adventure.*

Impromptu

It's holiday time in the 1830s and the Duke and Duchess d'Antan (Anton Rodgers and Emma Thompson) have invited a glittering array of guests to their mansion: Frederic Chopin (1810–49, Hugh Grant), Franz Liszt (1811–86, Julian Sands), Marie d'Agoult (Bernadette Peters), and Eugene Delacroix (1798–1863, Ralph Brown). Who should crash the house party but George Sand (1804–76, Judy Davis)? This dynamo winds up with the crush to end all crushes on Chopin, whom Grant plays as a twit (duh!). Also on hand is Sand's current lover Felicien Mallefille (Georges Corraface) and future (?) lover Alfred de Musset (Mandy Patinkin), but so what? It's a delight to see these venerable artists so young and high-spirited here and having such a rattling good time in the romantic department, with passionate minglings galore. Another view of Sand's romance with Chopin is 1975's *Notorious Woman* with Rosemary Harris and George Chakiris (and Jeremy Irons as Liszt). 🦴🦴🦴🦴

1990 (PG-13) 108m/C Judy Davis, Hugh Grant, Mandy Patinkin, Bernadette Peters, Julian Sands, Ralph Brown, Georges Corraface, Anton Rodgers, Emma Thompson, Anna Massey, John Savident, Elizabeth Spriggs; ***D:*** James Lapine; ***W:*** Sarah Kernochan; ***C:*** Bruno de Keyzer. Independent Spirit Awards '92: Best Actress (Davis). **VHS, LV**

In a Wild Moment

In a Wild Moment is Claude Berri's view of a March-September affair. This light and enjoyable comedy benefits from a terrific cast and Berri's above-average screenplay. Middle-aged male movie critics at that time were staggered that teenage girls

Aaron Eckhart and Matt Malloy in *In the Company of Men.* Sony Pictures Classics; courtesy of the Kobal Collection

and middle-aged males HAD affairs. When *In a Wild Moment* was remade in 1984 as Stanley Donen's *Blame It on Rio* (with a terrific cast including Michael Caine, Michelle Johnson, Joseph Bologna, Demi Moore, and Valerie Harper) middle-aged male movie critics at THAT time were staggered that teenage girls and middle-aged males HAD affairs. *La plus ça change, la plus ça même....* ***AKA:*** One Wild Moment; Un Moment d'Égarements.

1978 m/C *FR* Jean-Pierre Marielle, Agnes Soral, Victor Lanoux, Christine Dejoux, Martine Sarcey; ***D:*** Claude Berri; ***W:*** Claude Berri; ***C:*** Andre Neau.

In Celebration

Three successful brothers return to the old homestead for their parents' 40th wedding celebration. With that cast and that director, audiences expected more from *In Celebration* than this walled-in, slightly above average American Film Theatre production. (*In Celebration* was released theatrically overseas in 1976.) Based on a play by David Storey.

1975 (PG) 131m/C *GB CA* Alan Bates, James Bolam, Brian Cox, Constance Chapman, Gabrielle Daye, Bill Owen; ***D:*** Lindsay Anderson; ***W:*** David Storey; ***C:*** Dick Bush. **VHS**

In Possession

In Possession was one of a series of 26 self-contained films that legendary Hammer Films made between 1980 and 1984. Although the pictures were lensed in Britain, they often teamed an American star with a British star to intrigue audiences on both sides of the Atlantic. (Simon McCorkindale and Kathryn Leigh Scott in *A Visitor from the Grave,* David Carradine and Stephanie Beacham in *A Distant Scream,* Christina Raines and Simon Williams in *The Late Nancy Irving,* Season Hubley and Leigh Lawson in *Black Carrion,* Deborah Raffin and David Langton in *Last Video and Testament,* Dirk Benedict and Jenny Seagrove in *Mark of the Devil,* Michelle Phillips and James

Laurenson in *Paint Me a Murder,* etc.) Many directors from Hammer's glory days were signed for the series, including Val Guest, who began at Hammer in 1954 and made such classics as *The Creeping Unknown* and *When Dinosaurs Ruled the Earth.* Here, Guest has the unusual challenge of keeping *In Possession*'s two story lines running simultaneously. Carol Lynley and Christopher Cazenove are Sylvia and Frank Daly, who experience nightmares (flashbacks? premonitions?) in the house where they're staying. When they go downstairs, other people who neither see nor hear them are inhabiting their rooms and going on about their lives. The Dalys don't know whether the people are ghosts or if THEY ARE! (Ta-dah!) Very well written by Michael J. Bird, the tale moves along at a suspenseful clip and Lynley and Cazenove have good chemistry together. The psychological creepiness escalates in intensity and there is, mercifully, no copout conclusion. *In Possession* is not yet available on video, alas, but does air every so often on the Sci Fi Channel.

1984 90m/C *GB* Carol Lynley, Christopher Cazenove, David Healy, Judy Loe, Bernard Kay, Vivienne Burgess, Brendan Price, Peter Bland, Hugh Sullivan, Marianne Stone; ***D:*** Val Guest; ***W:*** Michael J. Bird.

In the Company of Men

Two women I know went to see *In the Company of Men.* One seemed to like it, the other came back spitting cotton. I was prepared for the worst, but wound up liking all but one sequence of Neil LaBute's biting first film, and I especially appreciated its ironic conclusion. *In the Company of Overgrown Infants* would be a more accurate description of the friendship between Chad (Aaron Eckhart) and Howard (Matt Malloy). To identify these two creeps as misogynists would be to miss the depth and scope of their hatred. Chad and Howard set the record for what they actually are: Misanthropes! They hate everybody: males, females, minorities, the handicapped, younger colleagues...the list goes on and on. After checking out Howard's injured ear (inflicted by a woman, Grrr...) in a public bathroom for men, Chad comes up with the ultimate revenge. Why don't they both go out with the same insecure, vulnerable woman, treat her like crap, and then, when they've done enough damage to last her entire lifetime, bust up with her?! And so they do. (Has this ever happened to me? Yeah, once—by one misanthrope, and that was enough, Ouch!) Chad and Howard find Christine, a lovely, shy, deaf colleague (Stacy Edwards, who's outstanding) and start to chat her up and date her up, one week at a time. During the title cards announcing every new week, Ken Williams' pulsating score escalates in intensity and volume. Of course, Christine, who isn't in on their brilliant scheme, changes all the rules and all the strategies. There is a subtle yet significant difference between a movie which is misogynistic and a movie about misogynistic characters. LaBute treads a dangerous line here, but his artistic vision is mature enough for careful viewers to realize that he is, in fact, busting Chad and Howard on their language, their attitudes, and their behavior. The one sequence where LaBute overstacks the deck occurs when Chad asks a black male colleague to unzip so he can check out whether he has the necessary equipment for the job. Yeah, yeah, we know that Chad is the lowest form of life on Earth, but he really shouldn't be in one piece after making a request like that. Guillotine splicer to the rescue, please! Aside from that, *In the Company of a Men* is satire most savage.

1996 (R) 93m/C Matt Malloy, Aaron Eckhart, Stacy Edwards, Mark Rector, Jason Dixie, Emily Cline, Michael Martin, Chris Hayes; ***D:*** Neil LaBute; ***W:*** Neil LaBute; ***C:*** Anthony P. Hettinger; ***M:*** Ken Williams. Independent Spirit Awards '98: Debut Performance (Eckhart); Sundance Film Festival '97: Filmmakers Trophy; Nominations: Independent Spirit Awards '98: Best Actress (Edwards), Best First Feature. **VHS, Closed Caption, DVD**

In the Name of the Father

If U.S. audiences have a difficult time understanding the paternalistic relationship between Northern Ireland and Great Britain, *In the Name of the Father* reveals

"I would never have believed that a professional prostitute could be so boring."

—Roger Flan (Peter Falk) on Crystal (Jeannie Berlin) in *In the Spirit.*

the deadlock in sharp relief. While huge land masses like Australia and Canada are successfully and peacefully breaking away from the British Empire, tiny Northern Ireland remains painfully tied to a government determined to keep it under control. That control is a key issue in Jim Sheridan's 1993 film, based on Gerry Conlon's autobiography *Proved Innocent*. As a very young and rebellious man, Conlon (beautifully played by Daniel Day-Lewis here) was constantly getting in minor skirmishes with the law. None were particularly serious, but all contributed to making him vulnerable to the far more serious charge of blowing up two pubs as a terrorist. Conlon and his equally devil-may-care friend Paul Hill (portrayed by John Lynch) are innocent, but they are hounded around the clock without legal representation by British authorities, determined to secure speedy convictions. Finally, while they are both half-mad from sleep deprivation and relentless interrogations, they make false confessions, and squirm through their subsequent trial. ("We were bored out of our minds," Day-Lewis as Conlon intones on the soundtrack.) The grim results: not only were both innocent men imprisoned, but their friends and families as well, including Conlon's father, Guiseppe (Pete Postlethwaite, in an Oscar-nominated performance). It is in prison that Conlon gradually becomes politicized by meeting one of the terrorists who was actually responsible for the bombings. He also learns to love and respect his father, a frail but overwhelmingly decent man who retains his deep faith despite the hardships of prison life. Enter Emma Thompson, just right as Gareth Peirce, the Conlons' new attorney who works tirelessly for their release. She is able to prove what the British authorities knew all along, that not only were the Conlons and their associates entirely innocent, but that crucial evidence was suppressed, and all were kept in prison many years after the real terrorists revealed their identities. Strong stuff and still a sore point among many officials of the British crown, so don't expect *In the Name of the Father* to be the honored film at the next Royal Command Performance. Director Sheridan packs an incredible amount of information into his 127-minute film, spanning the mid-'70s through the early '90s. His powerful economy with images is demonstrated from the very first sequence when the horror of the first bombing takes place in mid-gesture, as it would in real life. By keeping the evolving relationship of father and son in strong focus and by making sure that all the period details are dead on center, Sheridan says more about the tortured Irish-British bond than dozens of other films on the subject. 🦴🦴🦴🦴

1993 (R) 127m/C *GB IR* Daniel Day-Lewis, Pete Postlethwaite, Emma Thompson, John Lynch, Corin Redgrave, Beatie Edney, John Benfield, Paterson Joseph, Marie Jones, Gerard McSorley, Frank Harper, Mark Sheppard, Don Baker, Britta Smith, Aidan Grennell, Daniel Massey, Bosco Hogan, Daniel Massey; ***D:*** Jim Sheridan; ***W:*** Jim Sheridan, Terry George; ***C:*** Peter Biziou; ***M:*** Trevor Jones, Bono, Sinead O'Connor. Berlin International Film Festival '94: Golden Berlin Bear; Nominations: Academy Awards '93: Best Actor (Day-Lewis), Best Adapted Screenplay, Best Director (Sheridan), Best Film Editing, Best Picture, Best Supporting Actor (Postlethwaite), Best Supporting Actress (Thompson); British Academy Awards '93: Best Actor (Day-Lewis), Best Adapted Screenplay; Golden Globe Awards '94: Best Actor—Drama (Day-Lewis), Best Film—Drama, Best Song ("(You Made Me the) Thief of Your Heart"), Best Supporting Actress (Thompson). **VHS, LV, Letterbox, Closed Caption, DVD**

In the Soup

Adolpho Rollo (Steve Buscemi) wants to be a filmmaker in the worst way. Scam maestro Joe (Seymore Cassel) says HE'LL be the producer! For the next 93 minutes, Joe shows Adolpho how to con his way through life and into feature film production. Buscemi and Cassel are great together, and Cassel's splashy role recalls his glory days of 1971 when he co-starred opposite Gena Rowlands in *Minnie and Moskowitz* for John Cassavetes. Jennifer Beals (who is married to director Alexandre Rockwell) is charming as Angelica, the object of Adolpho's affection. Many indie legends also contribute to the fun in assorted cameos. For the record, *In the Soup* was not colorized by computer. It was filmed on color stock and released in black and white. For those who can only watch a color movie, *In the Soup* is available on video in color. Happily, it's also available on video in scrumptious black and white. ♪♪♪

1992 (R) 93m/B Steve Buscemi, Seymour Cassel, Jennifer Beals, Will Patton, Pat Moya, Stanley Tucci, Sully Boyar, Rockets Redglare, Elizabeth Bracco, Ruth Maleczech, Debi Mazar, Steven Randazzo, Francesco Messina; ***Cameos:*** Jim Jarmusch, Carol Kane; ***D:*** Alexandre Rockwell; ***W:*** Tim Kissell, Alexandre Rockwell; ***C:*** Phil Parmet; ***M:*** Mader. Sundance Film Festival '92: Grand Jury Prize. **VHS, LV, Closed Caption**

In the Spirit

In the Spirit's inept promotion campaign must have killed it at the boxoffice. It probably didn't help that Peter Falk, who is terrific in the first half of the film, vanishes mysteriously and never comes back. He is so good that you wish he would return for a line or two at film's end, but no! Jeannie Berlin, playing the world's most boring hooker, wrote an often-hilarious script for her mother, Elaine May, and Marlo Thomas, who work surprisingly well together under Sandra Seacat's brisk direction. May only needs to raise an eyebrow or lower her voice to get a laugh, thus supplying the perfect counterpoint for Thomas' kinetic energy. Melanie Griffith and Olympia Dukakis have cameo roles in this nicely paced crime caper, which does a delicious job of satirizing Had-I-But-Known mysteries and phony New Ageism. ♪♪♪

1990 (R) 94m/C Elaine May, Marlo Thomas, Jeannie Berlin, Peter Falk, Melanie Griffith, Olympia Dukakis, Chad Burton, Thurn Hoffman, Michael Emil, Christopher Durang, Laurie Jones; ***D:*** Sandra Seacat; ***W:*** Jeannie Berlin, Laurie Jones; ***C:*** Dick Quinlan; ***M:*** Patrick Williams. **VHS**

The Incident

The first 10 minutes of Larry Peerce's *The Incident* draw us into the grim world of two sadistic jerks played by 31-year-old Tony Musante and 27-year-old Martin Sheen in their film debuts. Then we meet a series of couples who are about to board a New York subway. Diana Van der Vlis wants to take a taxi but her husband (Ed McMahon, in a surprisingly effective performance) grumbles about the expense and insists on a less expensive route home. A couple in their 60s (Thelma Ritter and Jack Gilford) bicker all the way to the station. Ruby Dee tries to calm down her angry husband, black activist Brock Peters. Robert Fields makes an attempt to pick up Gary Merrill, who seems interested at first, then terrified at the implications. Mike Kellin is convinced that his wife Jan Sterling had been making passes at everyone at a cocktail party. A young couple, Victor Arnold and 23-year-old Donna Mills, make out before boarding the subway car. And local soldier Bob Bannard introduces an Oklahoma soldier with a broken arm (brilliantly played by 25-year-old Beau Bridges) to New York City night life. Director Peerce had made his remarkable directing debut in 1964 with the award-winning interracial love story *One Potato, Two Potato,* also beautifully filmed in black and white. Peerce's early, more personal works placed extremely complex characters against sharply critiqued contemporary American landscapes and *The Incident* is no exception. Once everyone is settled on the subway for the ride home, Musante and Sheen proceed to terrorize everyone on the train. They seize on the passengers' most obvious fears (sexuality, race, age) and strip away every illusion of pride or courage in all but one person. *The Incident* has few flattering observations to make about this group of strangers on the subway. It's hardly an advertisement for public transportation, and there are no feel-good remedies for the internal and actual violence ignited by Musante's and Sheen's characters. *The Incident* reveals the urban despair and dissolving community ties of the late '60s as few films of that era did. Musante and Sheen played archetypical punks; we had seen their like before and would see them again. But *The Incident* showed something far more disturbing. No one was going to make our private worlds all better again with homilies and heroism. Private solutions might be found to combat the evils in the night, but the social order and harmony would not be restored by them. *The Incident* is a timeless and eerie look into the world of the future made as the once-mighty Hollywood studios of the past were collapsing.

Writer Nicholas E. Baehr adapted his screenplay for *The Incident* from his 1963 teleplay "Ride with Terror" that aired on NBC's *Dupont Show of the Month.* Gene Hackman, then 33, and Tony Musante, then 22, starred. 🦴🦴🦴🦴

1967 99m/B Martin Sheen, Tony Musante, Beau Bridges, Ruby Dee, Jack Gilford, Thelma Ritter, Brock Peters, Ed McMahon, Gary Merrill, Donna Mills, Jan Sterling, Mike Kellin, Bob Bannard, Diana Van Der Vlis, Victor Arnold, Robert Fields; ***D:*** Larry Peerce; ***W:*** Charles Fox, Nicholas E. Baehr; ***C:*** Gerald Hirschfeld; ***M:*** Charles Fox. **VHS, LV**

Independent's Day

When media rags pick up on the bright lights of any arena, they usually give three white guys three full-color pages plus a lot of words, and women and minorities get "The Best of the Rest" sidebars. I once watched a verrry depressing documentary about Sundance; it looked like the Boy Scouts. I know it isn't because Sundance helps both male and female filmmakers, but that was the thrust of the documentary. *Independent's Day* is Marina Zenovich's view of Sundance, but it's more about the carnival atmosphere that surrounds the annual festival, where Everyone is simultaneously a Somebody and a Nobody. Neil LaBute talks about people who ask if he gets paid, how much he gets paid, if his movie was successful, and if it was as successful as *The Brothers McMullen.* (Etiquette note: Please don't ask your Filmmaker Friends these harsh questions. I never hear THEM ask people how much they're making at THEIR day jobs.) Steven Soderbergh makes refreshing sense; he keeps his focus on what most interests him and he does the best he can no matter what budget he has. Zenovich interviews actors and directors on the run, all of whom are afflicted with varying degrees of festival fever: Too Much to See, Too Little Time, and Is That What's-His-Name Over There? There's the usual Art vs. Business blather, as well as chatter about whoever "THEY" are. Filmmakers do all the Right/Wrong things and then they Fail/Succeed. *Independent's Day* is either free-form or shapeless, bustling or claustrophobic, depending on your mood when you see it. For casual viewers only; if you really want to be an independent filmmaker, you won't have the time and/or energy and/or inclination to watch documentaries about how Other People make indies. *Independent's Day* played at San Francisco's Indie Fest in 1999. 🦴🦴½

1997 54m/C Neil LaBute, Steven Soderbergh, Kevin Smith, Sydney Pollack, Roger Ebert, Greg Mottola; ***D:*** Marina Zenovich; ***W:*** Marina Zenovich; ***C:*** Laurent Basset, Neil Colligan, Ed Nachtrieb, Jeffrey L. Weaver.

The Innocents

The Innocents lingers in your mind long after you see it. We are used to being on Deborah Kerr's side whenever she's cast in a film, but HERE, well, she's high-strung and obsessive as Miss Giddens, the new governess. Is it because her little charges Miles and Flora are playing with lascivious ghosts or is it because she's in love with their Uncle (Michael Redgrave), and hasn't had much of an outlet in her sheltered life for lascivious fantasies of any description? Why was little Miles expelled from school? Why does she kiss little Miles on the mouth like a lover? (Or is HE kissing HER on the mouth like a lover?) Why does little Miles talk like the ghost of a man named Quint (Peter Wyngarde)? Why does Miss Giddens see the ghost of Miss Jessel (Clytie Jessop) at the lake? Why doesn't the housekeeper Mrs. Grose (Megs Jenkins) know ANYTHING? The children get weirder and weirder, and Miss Gidden gets more and more paranoid about the ghosts, and although we SEE ghosts, we see them through the increasingly unreliable eyes of the governess. And as for the precocious behavior of the children, isn't it a childhood obligation to drive any new authority figure out of her mind? Director Jack Clayton meticulously re-creates the Victorian world, and his superb cameraman Freddie Francis employs filmmaking techniques popularized during the silent era, e.g. extended dissolves. The unusual look of the film unsettles us as viewers, and we go back and forth between our sympathy for Miss Giddens and our increasing fears that she's doing more harm to her charges than any ghost ever could. Compounding the conflict is the fact that Martin Stephens (Miles) had already played the devil child of George Sanders and Barbara Shelley in Wolf Rilla's *Village of the Damned* the previous year. Plus! Newcomer Pamela Franklin (Flora) had the spookiest look in her wide eyes. Those eyes would help to make her a horror film staple for the next 15 years. *The Innocents* has great repeat value. Depending on your mood, it becomes an entirely different story each time you see it. (Megs Jenkins played Mrs. Grose again in a 1974 color telefeature starring Lynn Redgrave.) ₰₰₰₰

1961 85m/B *GB* Deborah Kerr, Michael Redgrave, Pamela Franklin, Martin Stephens, Peter Wyngarde, Megs Jenkins, Clytie Jessop, Isla Cameron, Eric Woodburn; ***D:*** Jack Clayton; ***W:*** Truman Capote, William Archibald, John Mortimer; ***C:*** Freddie Francis; ***M:*** Georges Auric. **VHS, Closed Caption**

Inside Monkey Zetterland

Surprise: Monkey Zetterland (Steve Antin) is the son of a Jewish smother mother (Katherine Helmond as Grace). I can't imagine Helmond being married to Bo Hopkins (who plays Monkey's rarely seen father, Mike), but she is, and her other kids are hairdresser Brent (Tate Donovan), and Grace (Patricia Arquette), who just broke up with pregnant Cindy (Sofia Coppola). But wait, there's more, namely Monkey's friends: Sandra Bernhard as Imogene, who never shuts up; Debi Mazar as his Mean Girlfriend Daphne; and political terrorists Sophie and Sasha. (I can't imagine Martha Plimpton being married to Rupert Everett, either, but she is.) Hey guys, let's get together and make a movie. Okay!...About what? How wacky we all are, of course. Okay...And then what? Well, isn't that enough? If it is, this is your movie. ₰₰

1993 (R) 92m/C Steve Antin, Patricia Arquette, Sandra Bernhard, Sofia Coppola, Tate Donovan, Katherine Helmond, Bo Hopkins, Debi Mazar, Martha Plimpton, Rupert Everett, Ricki Lake, Lance Loud, Frances Bay, Luca Bercovlcl; ***D:*** Jefery Levy; ***W:*** John Boskovich, Steve Antin; ***C:*** Christopher Taylor; ***M:*** Rick Cox, Jeff Elmassian. Nominations: Independent Spirit Awards '94: Best Supporting Actor (Donovan). **VHS, LV**

Interlude

The interesting thing about *Interlude,* released within a couple of months of the Summer of Love, was that it showed a couple being passionate, rather than casual, about love; it made at least as persuasive a case for romance in 1967 as *When Tomorrow Comes* (with Irene Dunne and Charles Boyer) had in 1939 or the first *Interlude* (with June Allyson and Rosanno Brazzi) had in 1957. Stefan Zeiter (Oskar Werner) is a 45-year-old world-class conductor (and married) and Sally (Barbara Ferris) is a 27-year-old dolly bird journalist (and single). Her assignment is to interview him, and she makes mistakes right and left and her flakiness enchants him. Until Stefan's gorgeous and gracious wife, Antonia, arrives on the scene (Virginia Maskell, and yes, that IS Patrick McGoohan's co-star in "The Arrival," the first episode of *The Prisoner* series), Stefan and Sally are obsessed with each other. The supporting cast includes Alan Webb (1906–82) as Andrew, and Nora Swinburne, then 65, as Mary (in the penultimate role of a career that began in 1920). Also in the cast are Donald Sutherland, then 33, as Lawrence, and John Cleese, 28, in his very first role as a television public relations man. All the elements of the future Basil Fawlty are in place: the nervous energy, the twittiness, the fathomless desire to impress everyone in sight, and that odd blend of ingratiating abrasiveness that only Cleese can convey with a shift of expression or tone. Werner was a 1965 Oscar nominee for his exquisitely tortured performance as a dying doctor in love with a doomed passenger (fellow nominee Simone Signoret) in *Ship of Fools* and few could convey erotic anguish as well as he. Ferris, too, hits all the right notes as Sally. She had been Dinah, the Dave Clark Five's leading lady in 1965's *Catch Us If You Can/Having a Wild Weekend,* John Boorman's first film. *Interlude* accurately reflects the discrepancy between the devil-

Vanessa Redgrave is *Isadora.* Universal; courtesy of the Kobal Collection

may-care atmosphere of its era and the timeless ache of the human heart for a life filled with some meaning. Timi ("Hurt") Yuro sings the title song. 𝅘𝅥𝅘𝅥𝅘𝅥

1967 113m/C *GB* Oskar Werner, Barbara Ferris, Virginia Maskell, John Cleese, Bernard Kay, Robert Lang, Geraldine Sherman, Donald Sutherland, Nora Swinburne, Alan Webb; ***D:*** Kevin Billington; ***W:*** Hugh Leonard, Lee Langley; ***C:*** Gerry Fisher.

The Interrogation

As always, 1990's Mill Valley Film Festival was jam-packed with the sort of movies that help to make it my favorite of all the festivals I go to each year. One Polish entry you won't want to miss is *The Interrogation.* Krystyna Janda plays Tonia, a nightclub performer and good-time girl who's taken in for questioning by the security police and winds up with a grueling five-year prison rap. She is drunk when she's first brought into custody and even the next day, she does not understand how serious her plight is. She willingly reveals that she went to bed with a guy that the police are looking for, but so what, what's the big deal? Gradually, she learns more about her position, her true friends, and the complexity of her relationship with one of her guards. A film with none of the easily identifiable prison stereotypes, *The Interrogation* is brilliantly written, directed, and acted. It was finally released after an eight-year ban (1982–90). ***AKA:*** Przesluchanie. 𝅘𝅥𝅘𝅥𝅘𝅥

1982 118m/C *PL* Krystyna Janda, Janusz Gajos, Adam Ferency, Agnieszka Holland, Anna Romantowska; ***D:*** Richard Bugajski; ***W:*** Richard Bugajski, Janusz Dymek; ***C:*** Jacek Petrycki. **VHS**

The Intimate Stranger

Blacklisted director Joseph Losey (1909–84) seemed to dodge the issue of blacklisting when he made *The Intimate Stranger* in the relative safety of Britain in 1956. In it, Reggie Wilson, the filmmaker played by Richard Basehart (1914–84), is blacklisted by a spiteful colleague for something he didn't do. Although the guilty culprit is eventually discovered, Basehart's character finally arrives at the astonishing realization that it was right for him to be blacklisted, because he's sure he did other bad things for which he was never punished! The running time below is the original length of *The Intimate Stranger.* To attract an American distributor, this ethically murky crime drama was re-edited and oddly retitled *Finger of Guilt.* Perhaps the uncut British film made more sense, but the version that crops up on late night television is missing 24 minutes. Even the truncated movie is an attention grabber and the expert cast does their best with the script, based on Howard Koch's novel, *Pay the Piper.* Now that Losey's and Koch's contributions have been officially acknowledged, I hope the complete movie will be made available for critical reappraisal. ***AKA:*** Finger of Guilt. 𝅘𝅥𝅘𝅥𝅘𝅥

1956 **95m/B** *GB* Richard Basehart, Mary Murphy, Constance Cummings, Roger Livesey, Mervyn Johns, Faith Brooks, Vernon Greeves, Andre Mikhelson, Basil Dignam, David Lodge, Grace Denbigh-Russell; ***D:*** Joseph Losey; ***W:*** Howard Koch; ***C:*** Gerald Gibbs; ***M:*** Trevor Duncan.

Iphigenia

At the risk of sounding facile, Agamemnon emerges as a real clod in Michael Cacoyannis' *Iphigenia.* Your sympathy will be with Clytemnestra (Irene Papas) and Iphigenia (Tatiana Papamoskou, then 12) all the way, as they are the real heroes in this vigorously rendered re-telling of Euripides' tragedy. Yorgos Arvanitis' camera work injects excitement into the longish narrative. But how could Agamemnon (Costa Kazakos) even THINK of sacrificing such an adorable daughter as Tatiana's Iphigenia? ꝏꝏꝏ

1977 130m/C *GR* Irene Papas, Costa Kazakos, Tatiana Papamoskou, Costas Carras, Christos Tsangas, Panos Michalopoulas; ***D:*** Michael Cacoyannis; ***W:*** Michael Cacoyannis; ***C:*** Yorgos Arvanitis; ***M:*** Mikis Theodorakis. Nominations: Academy Awards '77: Best Foreign Film; Cannes Film Festival '77: Best Film. **VHS**

Isadora

Isadora, quite literally, saved my life. The sequence in which Isadora Duncan meets her death when her scarf wraps around the spokes of her car wheel is so final, so graphic, and so horrifying that I remembered it when MY scarf wrapped around a piece of metal as I was going up an underground escalator. One word, *Isadora,* raced through my brain and I tore off the scarf in an instant, grateful to be alive. The thing that made Isadora Duncan's death in 1927 at age 49 even sadder is that she had, prior to her last moment, seemed so grateful to be alive. Isadora Duncan, born in San Francisco in 1878, discovered, like many a local girl, that she was insufficiently appreciated in her own country. Undaunted, she took the dances that she had interpreted from classical Greek art and brought them to Budapest, where, in 1903, she was the toast of the town at age 25. She met with an equally feverish response in Berlin the following year. A triumphant engagement in London followed, and by the time she showed New York City audiences what she could do in 1908, her reputation had preceded her and she became, at age 30, a household name across the country that had ignored her five years earlier. For the next 19 years, Duncan WAS modern dance personified. She toured; she established modern dance schools in Berlin, London, Paris, and Moscow; she was always surrounded by men, and she even married some of them. There was no better casting choice for the charismatic Isadora than the charismatic Vanessa Redgrave. You can see why Duncan was the darling of her era; like other darlings of other eras, she brought life into every room she entered. There was much that was tragic in Isadora's life, including the drowning of her two beautiful children in her presence. Under Karel Reisz's brilliant direction, Redgrave reveals the griefs and joys of the barefoot artist as a living, breathing woman, rather than as an ethereal, unearthly legend in her time. James Fox is British actor/producer/designer Gordon Craig (1872–1966), one of Duncan's many lovers, and Ivan Tchenko is Russian poet Sergei Essenin (1895–1925), who married Duncan, left her to marry Leo Tolstoy's granddaughter, and later killed himself. Based on *My Life* (Duncan's autobiography) and on *Isadora Duncan, An Intimate Portrait* by Sewell Stokes, *Isadora* succeeds in capturing the riveting personality of a passionate woman who first made her mark on the dance world of 1903 and whose influence has been felt ever since. And, unlike many Hollywood biographies in which ALL celebrities seem to lead interchangeable lives, *Isadora* shows how irreplaceably unique Duncan really was and how impossible it is to imagine the 20th century without her. ***AKA:*** The Loves of Isadora. ꝏꝏꝏꝏ

1968 138m/C *GB* Vanessa Redgrave, Jason Robards Jr., James Fox, Ivan Tchenko, John Fraser, Bessie Love, Cynthia Harris, Libby Glenn, Tony Vogel, Wallace Eaton, John Quentin, Nicholas Pennell, Ronnie Gilbert, Alan Gifford, Christian Duvaleix; ***D:*** Karel Reisz; ***W:*** Clive Exton; ***C:*** Larry Pizer; ***M:*** Maurice Jarre. Cannes Film Festival '69: Best Actress (Redgrave); National Society of Film Critics Awards '69: Best Actress (Redgrave); Nomi-

"I have seen the devil in my microscope, and I have chained him."

—Dr. Moreau (Marlon Brando) in *The Island of Dr. Moreau.*

nations: Academy Awards '68: Best Actress (Redgrave). **VHS**

The Island of Dr. Moreau

The Hawaiian island antics in the lightweight *A Very Brady Sequel* are far more cerebral than anything I saw in the 1996 remake of *The Island of Dr. Moreau,* directed by John Frankenheimer. Although Burt Lancaster and Michael York did their best in 1977 to re-create the terror of H.G. Wells' 1896 novel, nothing since 1933 has come along to surpass or even equal the chills in *Island of Lost Souls* starring Charles Laughton and Bela Lugosi. The stars this time are Marlon Brando as Dr. Moreau (who gets a laugh every time he tries on a new costume designed by Norma Moriceau, complete with hair styling by Vera Mitchell and chalky makeup by Philip Rhodes) and Val Kilmer as Dr. Montgomery (who gets a laugh when he tries to imitate Brando, complete with a Norma Moriceau creation of his very own and the obligatory chalky makeup by John Elliott and Leonard Engleman). Both actors dabble with British accents, Brando all the time and Kilmer when he's aping Brando. With David Thewlis in the film as castaway Edward Douglas, why did they even bother? Fetching Fairuza Balk is on hand as Aissa, the most successful of Moreau's experiments in gene splicing. (She's unhappy with her looks, though: "I want to look like you!" she wails on Brando's shoulder, supplying the narrative with yet another laugh.) Moreau is a Nobel Prize winner chafing in the island heat, Montgomery is a brilliant neurosurgeon gone to seed on drugs, but they're both such dim bulbs that you wonder how either of them managed to pass Surgery 101. A crash course in Systems Analysis might have helped, too. As it is, when Moreau's experiments turn on their master, he tries to soothe them with a few bars of Gershwin's *Rhapsody in Blue* on the piano. Most of the principals are out of the picture 20 minutes before it's over, although Ron Perlman does get to wave to David Thewlis and spout something philosophical before the credits. Buy the book. Rent the earlier videos. This Moreau is for Brando and Kilmer completists only. **woof!**

1996 (PG-13) 91m/C Marlon Brando, Val Kilmer, David Thewlis, Fairuza Balk, Marco Hofschneider, Temuera Morrison, Ron Perlman; ***D:*** John Frankenheimer; ***W:*** Richard Stanley, Ron Hutchinson; ***C:*** William A. Fraker. Nominations: Golden Raspberry Awards '96: Best Director (Frankenheimer), Worst Picture, Worst Supporting Actor (Kilmer, Brando), Worst Screenplay. **VHS, LV, Closed Caption, DVD**

Island of the Lost

I spent forever trying to figure out the family relationships in this movie. Richard Greene (1914–85) is Josh MacRae, the father of Sharon (who looks 30), Stu (Luke Halpin, then 21), and Lizzie (Robin Mattson, 12). There is no mother. No one talks about Mother. There is, however, a lovely assistant named Judy Hawilani (Irene Tsu, 25) who doesn't appear to be involved with anyone in the family. Another assistant, Gabe Larsen (Mart Hulswit), appears out of nowhere, expressing incredulity about Josh's anthropological skills. Sharon and Gabe soon appear to be hitting on each other. There is also a native islander named Tupuna, played by dancer Jose De Vega (1934–90), one of *West Side Story*'s Sharks. Tupuna and Judy soon appear to be hitting on each other. Josh, who fathered three kids (one every nine years), doesn't get to hit on anyone and neither do Stu and Lizzie. The family have "adventures" on an island. They look like stock footage adventures, but one of the credits says that Ralph Helfer was in charge of animal sequences. Does this mean that he pored over stock footage or actually coached a people-eating ostrich? The credits don't say. The credits do say that underwater sequences were directed in the Bahamas by producer Ricou Browning and photographed by Lamar Boram and Jordan Klein. Executive producer Ivan Tors worked on the story with Richard Carlson and Carlson received credit for the final screenplay. THE Richard Carlson (1912–77)? So why isn't he IN this movie? The whole shebang was filmed at Palm

Beach Gardens and in Miami, Florida. I rented this thing when I was desperate on Thanksgiving Day, 1988. Was it ever released to theatres or broadcast on television? I haven't a clue, but learn from my mistake and DON'T RENT THIS TURKEY ON THANKSGIVING DAY! **woof!**

1968 92m/C *GB* Richard Greene, Luke Halpin, Mart Hulswit, Jose De Vega, Robin Mattson, Irene Tsu, Sheilah Wells; ***D:*** John Florea, Ricou Browning; ***W:*** Richard Carlson, Ivan Tors; ***C:*** Howard Winner; ***M:*** George Bruns. **VHS**

It Takes Two

My Chauffeur wasn't seen by too many people when it was released to theatres in 1986, but it introduced me to the films of director David Beaird, who seems attracted to conventional comedy plots, although he approaches them in a decidedly offbeat way. *It Takes Two,* for example, tells the old story of the kid who suffers from prewedding jitters and who pours all his anxieties into symbolic escape, in this case, an expensive Italian car and its braless saleswoman. There's an insistent theme that marriage will be the end of the line for him as a free spirit and that afterward his life will be an endless series of concessions to his wife and sacrifices to society. Although that theme isn't really explored in depth, it's always there, eroding whatever joy the kid allows himself to feel. His final surrender to convention is bathed in cuteness, but there's an underlying thud because he never has stood up for himself and his luck in finding others to help him obviously won't last forever. Except for the protagonist, most of the film's characters lack dimension and Beaird permits pointless racist "jokes" to gum up the uneven script. The cast of *It Takes Two,* especially Anthony Geary in a colorful featured role, is capable and the slight film does have some interesting moments. ♪♪♪

1988 (PG-13) 79m/C George Newbern, Leslie Hope, Kimberly Foster, Barry Corbin, Anthony Geary; ***D:*** David Beaird; ***W:*** Thomas Szollosi, Richard Christian Matheson; ***C:*** Peter Deming; ***M:*** Carter Burwell. **VHS, Closed Caption**

It's All True

"On my desk in a script of the film was a long steel needle. It had been driven entirely through the script and to the needle was attached a length of red wool. This was the mark of the voodoo...." Yep, that was Orson Welles describing one of the many disasters that made the 1942 film *It's All True* impossible to complete in his own lifetime. If Welles were alive today, according to his daughter Beatrice, "He would never restore one of his old films. He would say, 'Hey, give me the money and I'll make a movie NOW!'" In the absence of the unrealized Orson Welles projects we will never get to see, his *It's All True* collaborators rescued the original raw footage and then edited a tantalizing 22-minute segment into a full-length documentary about the making of the entire film. The "Four Men on a Raft" segment reveals the truth about what Welles and his crew were able to accomplish on this ill-fated South American film. It also supplies compelling evidence that Welles' reputation was destroyed, not by artistic extravagance or undisciplined work habits, but by studio executives who needed an excuse to get rid of him. Both Welles and Walt Disney were recruited by the ambitious Nelson Rockefeller to promote Pan American relations during separate trips to South America in the early days of World War II. Disney, who was one of RKO's greatest assets and also politically sympathetic to Rockefeller, delivered two crowd-pleasing entertainments, *Saludos Amigos* and *Three Caballeros.* Welles was a maverick, no friend of Rockefeller, and his splashy film debut, *Citizen Kane,* had attracted critical raves, but was essentially a money-loser for RKO. (It lost $160,000 in its original release.) But Welles was only 26, eager for a new challenge and politically naive, and he accepted studio assurances that he would be able to edit *The Magnificent Ambersons* in South America. Disney, then 40 and the survivor of many setbacks in his 22-year career, knew how to play the studio game. Welles didn't. The loss was ours, since Welles did know how to make movies. *It's All True* would never

Pam Grier is *Jackie Brown.*
Miramax; courtesy of the Kobal Collection

have been a travelogue blockbuster in the Disney style and RKO knew it. But the "Four Men on a Raft" segment is a beautifully made story of discovery, loss, resourcefulness, and courage, considerably enhanced by contemporary sound technicians. Welles wrung such exceptional performances out of a non-professional cast that it's easy to understand why he tried so long and so hard to finish *It's All True.* Unlike *The Epic that Never Was,* about the making of Josef von Sternberg's *I, Claudius,* enough remains of *It's All True* to make the restoration of Welles' "Legendary Lost Classic" survive on its own merits. Any filmmaker worth his or her salt would die to make a movie as good as this one, and unfortunately Welles is no longer here to say that he could have told us that long ago. Recommended: 1995's *Orson Welles: The One-Man Band.*

1993 (G) 85m/C Miguel Ferrer; ***D:*** Richard Wilson, Bill Krohn, Myron Meise, Orson Welles; ***W:*** Richard Wilson, Bill Krohn, Myron Meise; ***C:*** George Fanto, Gary Graver; ***M:*** Jorge Arriagada. **VHS, LV**

It's My Party

Yes, there are parties like the one in this movie; I know folks with enough stamina to handle that much grief. Eric Roberts plays Nick Stark, a young man dying of AIDS, who decides to throw a party "celebrating" his own suicide. His former lover Brandon Theis (Gregory Harrison) turns up, much to the resentment of Nick's other friends who feel that Brandon abandoned Nick when he needed him most. Nick's supportive best friend (Margaret Cho) is on hand, as well as his inconsolable mother (Lee Grant), uncomfortable father (George Segal), and even Roddy McDowall as a by-the-book gay Catholic in his late 60s who tells all and sundry that suicide is illegal, and a mortal sin, to boot. The weekend-long party continues anyway, and a star-studded guest list (Marlee Matlin, Bronson Pinchot, Bruce Davison, Devon Gummersall, Paul Regina, Olivia Newton-John, Christopher Atkins, Dennis Christopher, Ron Glass) pay their last farewells to Nick, who's determined to check out in his own way, in his own time. Written and directed by Randal Kleiser, *It's My Party,* along with 1990's superior (and shorter) *Longtime Companion* by Norman Rene, will be a time capsule for the AIDS era, when young people all over the world watched the long, lingering deaths of the best and brightest of their own generation. Before they lose each other forever, and Nick and Brandon discover what made them fall in love to begin with, audiences are advised to have an entire box of Kleenex within reach. (Try not to watch this one alone at night or on a double bill with *Dark Victory.*)

1995 (R) 120m/C Eric Roberts, Gregory Harrison, Marlee Matlin, Lee Grant, George Segal, Bronson Pinchot, Bruce Davison, Devon Gummersall, Roddy McDowall, Margaret Cho, Paul Regina, Olivia Newton-John, Christopher Atkins, Dennis Christopher, Ron Glass; ***D:*** Randal Kleiser; ***W:*** Randal Kleiser; ***C:*** Bernd Heinl; ***M:*** Basil Poledouris. **VHS, LV, Closed Caption**

Jackie Brown

Pam Grier took no guff during her glory days as an action queen onscreen, nor does she here as *Jackie Brown.* The difference now is that she's been around the block so many times, she knows the drill all too well. It is ennui more than adrenaline that separates her from the low lifes who would use her for their own reasons. The startling element in *Jackie Brown* is a long, slow, sweet romance between stewardess Jackie and bail bondsman Max Cherry (Robert Forster). It surprises them both and their attachment adds unpredictability to the rest of the story. We know how everyone else is going to act: Ordell Robbie (Samuel L. Jackson) will continue to be his shameless rotten self; Melanie (Bridget Fonda) will continue to play dumb, until alas, out of force of habit, she truly IS dumb; Michael Keaton does everything but wear a billboard as federal agent Ray Nicolette; Robert De Niro kills time until he kills; and so forth. But the unguarded expression of a man head over heels in love and Jackie's cautious response tend to knock all the other shenanigans out of the ball park. When the other characters twiddle their thumbs in Quentin Tarantino's 155-minute adaptation of Elmore Leonard's *Rum Punch,* that's all they do. But when Grier and Forster play it slow, their every moment together is a skillful dance on fire and ice. You can't just be gorgeous, you have to be damn good to play it as well as they do and they both have Oscar nominations and career revivals to prove it.

1997 (R) 155m/C Pam Grier, Robert Forster, Samuel L. Jackson, Robert De Niro, Bridget Fonda, Michael Keaton, Michael Bowen, Chris Tucker, Lisa Gay Hamilton, Tommy (Tiny) Lister, Hattie Winston, Aimee Graham; ***D:*** Quentin Tarantino; ***W:*** Quentin Tarantino; ***C:*** Guillermo Navarro. Nominations: Academy Awards '97: Best Supporting Actor (Forster); Golden Globe Awards '98: Best Actor—Musical/Comedy (Jackson), Best Actress—Musical/Comedy (Grier); MTV Movie Awards '98: Best Male Performance (Jackson); Screen Actors Guild Award '97: Best Actress (Grier). **VHS, LV, Closed Caption**

Jack's Back

Jack's Back is a well-made "B" film, with surprisingly little violence for a tale about a latter-day Jack the Ripper. James Spader, who paid his dues playing one-dimensional villains in a succession of teen flicks, is quite good in a dual role as twins caught up in the case. *Salvador's* Cynthia Gibb plays an interesting, resourceful heroine in this promising effort by writer/director Rowdy Herrington. Chris Mulkey, a likable actor in 1988's abysmal *Patti Rocks,* is seventh-billed as a police detective and he gives considerable texture to the small role. The script takes the time to provide a context for each character and every plot twist, which makes it stand out from other films of the genre. An understated, low-key entry like *Jack's Back* had difficulty attracting an audience during its brief theatrical run, but it's a pleasure to see Spader and Gibb show what they can do with some decent material at this stage of their careers. Note: Herrington's future efforts would include *Road House, Gladiator,* and *Striking Distance.*

1987 (R) 97m/C James Spader, Cynthia Gibb, Rod Loomis, Rex Ryon, Robert Picardo, Jim Haynie, Chris Mulkey, Danitza Kingsley, Wendell Wright; ***D:*** Rowdy Herrington; ***W:*** Rowdy Herrington; ***C:*** Shelly Johnson. **VHS, LV, Closed Caption**

Roberto Benigni in *Johnny Stecchino.* New Line; courtesy of the Kobal Collection

Jacques Brel Is Alive and Well and Living in Paris

Jacques Brel Is Alive and Well and Living in Paris features dozens of deeply moving song-stories about love, death, loneliness, bullfighting, old age, war, and bittersweet romance. "Carousel" perhaps best illustrates Brel's style. The tune begins cheerfully, with a sense of magic. We hear of cotton candy. The lovely, gay mood of the song shifts. The rhythm speeds up. The carousel is no longer pleasant but dizzy. It becomes a metaphor for life, a mad whirl from which there is no escape. The song ends in terror. The theme of beautiful, bright things turning ugly and frightening is developed in other song-stories; in "The Bulls," there is cheering at the beginning. Gradually, the glories of past wars are lauded, along with the matador. Finally, he cries, "Saigon!" No cheers this time. The score for the original cast show album is a classic; it was awarded a Grammy nomination in 1968. In an intimate, cabaret-style setting, song-stories like "If You Go Away," "The Middle Class," "Marieke," "Funeral Tango," and "Brussels" can be seen and heard to best advantage. But not even the participation of Jacques Brel himself could recapture a delightful evening in the theatre on film. This American Film Theatre Production is an unimaginative transfer, and viewers of the future may well wonder why the work of Jacques Brel was loved so much by the audiences of his own time.

1975 98m/C *FR* Elly Stone, Mort Shuman, Joe Masiell, Jacques Brel; ***D:*** Denis Heroux; ***W:*** Eric Blau; ***C:*** Rene Verzier; ***M:*** Jacques Brel.

Jane Eyre

When we want to see *Jane Eyre,* we can buy the 1934 version from Sinister Cinema or we can rent the 1944 all-star classic from Fox Video or we can watch the 1970 telefeature that turns up every so often on double-digit UHF channels or we can plow through all six hours of the 1983 PBS miniseries. Clearly, there is no shortage of Jane Eyres and Edward Rochesters in this century. Does this 1847 saga by Charlotte Brontë have anything new to say to the audiences of 1996? Director Franco Zeffirelli clearly thinks so, and his latest movie is a fairly faithful adaptation marred by serious miscasting. William Hurt may look like the subject of an early daguerreotype, but the instant he opens his mouth, we get to hear a Mr. Rochester who owes more to Elmer Fudd than Orson Welles. His interpretation throws the film off balance; aside from a self-conscious scowl, he seems entirely disinterested in Jane or Thornfield or anything. Charlotte Gainsbourg's Jane speaks with a constant lisp, which may not be as detectable in her many French film assignments, but it clearly eliminates the possibility of Jane's extended narrations. (The charismatic Amanda Root has a small role as Miss Temple; why couldn't SHE have played Jane opposite someone like Gabriel Byrne?) Elle Macpherson's Blanche Ingram is reduced to a walk-on bit, ditto Maria Schneider as Rochester's mad first wife. Joan Plowright is wonderful as Mrs. Hudson and Billie Whitelaw has a few splendid, but all-too-brief sequences as Grace Poole. This *Jane Eyre* sounds like it will be better than it looks until you're watching it and then it looks better than it sounds. Do we care a fig for THESE repressed lovers? Not this time; bring back Orson Welles and Joan Fontaine and Hillary Brooke! 🦴🦴

1996 (PG) 116m/C William Hurt, Anna Paquin, Charlotte Gainsbourg, Joan Plowright, Elle Macpherson, Geraldine Chaplin, Fiona Shaw, John Wood, Amanda Root, Maria Schneider, Josephine Serre, Billie Whitelaw; ***D:*** Franco Zeffirelli; ***W:*** Franco Zeffirelli, Hugh Whitemore; ***C:*** David Watkin; ***M:*** Alessio Vlad, Claudio Capponi. **VHS, LV, Closed Caption**

John and Julie

Whatever became of Colin Gibson and Lesley Dudley? They were the two adorable stars of *John and Julie,* who go all the way to London to see the coronation of Queen Elizabeth II. (Actual footage of the Queen and her family waving from the balcony at Buckingham Palace appears in the film.) Needless to say, there's an uproar when their families learn out about it. Peter Sellers has a funny early role as befuddled Police Constable Diamond who tries to help them find their six-year-old children and Wilfrid Hyde-White is his usual impeccable, congenial self as Sir James. Richard Dimbleby, whose son Jonathan would grow up to write about the failed marriage of Prince Charles, repeats his famed commentary on the Coronation. 🦴🦴🦴

1955 82m/C *GB* Moira Lister, Noelle Middleton, Constance Cummings, Wilfrid Hyde-White, Sidney James, Joseph Tomelty, Colin Gibson, Lesley Dudley, Megs Jenkins, Patric Doonan, Peter Sellers, John Stuart, Vincent Ball, Colin Gordon, Peter Jones, Katie Johnson, Cyril Smith, Andrew Cruikshank, Winifred Shotter, Richard Dimbleby, Wynfold Vaughn Thomas; ***D:*** William Fairchild; ***W:*** William Fairchild. **VHS**

Johnny Stecchino

Roberto Benigni has a huge following in Italy and America, but I missed the membership drive. Benigni plays both Dante the bus driver and Johnny the mafioso in this 100-minute comedy that's written and directed by himself. If you've seen two Maurice Chevaliers in *Folies Bergere* or two Don Ameches in *That Night in Rio* or two Danny Kayes in *On the Riviera,* two Roberto Benignis might seem like two too many. His charm escaped me, at any rate; I didn't laugh once. As Miss Jean Brodie says, "For those who like that sort of thing, that is the sort of thing they like." If you enjoy Benigni in this one, you may also want to see his work in *The Monster* and *Life Is Beautiful.* 🦴🦴

1992 (R) 100m/C *IT* Roberto Benigni, Nicoletta Braschi, Paolo Bonacelli, Ignazio Pappalardo, Franco Volpi; ***D:*** Roberto Benigni; ***W:*** Roberto Benigni, Vincenzo Cerami; ***C:*** Giuseppe Lanci; ***M:*** Evan Lurie. **VHS, LV**

johns

A few minutes into *johns* I deduced that a particular character was not going to make it out of the movie alive and I was wrong: *johns* deliberately keeps us off bal-

The Hound Salutes:
WILSON CRUZ
Actor, *johns, All Over Me,*

I started onstage when I was much younger than I already am—because I'm very young—I was dancing by the age of eight and I started singing soon after that. Acting was a natural progression from that, so I started when I was 10. I acted in junior high school and did some theatre in New York and Los Angeles. I lived on both coasts when I was a teenager. In high school, I started doing a lot more serious drama and right out of high school, I got my agent and started auditioning for good. It didn't go very smoothly at all.

"Rickie Vasquez on *My So-Called Life* was one of the first roles that I got. I did a series called *Great Scott* for six episodes on the Fox network. As soon as that was canceled, I auditioned for *My So-Called Life* the following pilot season. It was a long journey, but I'm still here. When I went in for the first call, they said that they wanted someone who was willing to play (I loved the wordage) a half-black, half–Puerto Rican 15-year-old boy who was sexually ambiguous like the Audrey character played by Jodie Foster in Martin Scorsese's *Alice Doesn't Live Here Anymore.* That's what they said. Jodie Foster played the little person who you couldn't tell was a boy or a girl who was a friend of Alice's son. I remember watching the movie and I couldn't tell if she was a boy or girl at that young age, so I knew what they were talking about when they said that.

"Rickie Vasquez was a special part and even though any audition is difficult, they made it as easy as possible. I always become a nervous wreck right before I walk in the door including, needless to say, this audition, because I really wanted that part. I remember going in to the first call and

ance in a way that adds to our fascination with its sad story. It's about kids who turn tricks by hanging out on Santa Monica Boulevard in Los Angeles, with the emphasis on John (David Arquette) and Donner (Lukas Haas). John wakes up on Christmas Eve to harsh reality: all his cash has been stolen as well as the lucky sneakers in which he hid his money. His plans to spend Christmas (and his birthday) in an expensive hotel are finito; he'll have to spend the day turning tricks instead. His best friend Donner wants John to leave the Boulevard and travel to the Midwest with him where they can work as lifeguards at Camelot Theme Park. John, who hates the water, is none too thrilled with the idea, but as the day drags on, it grows on him. There are two wistful sequences at the expensive hotel where John pretends to be a filmmaker and the gracious desk clerk is human enough not to challenge the pretense. There's also John's goofy visit with a family man (played with relish by Elliott Gould) who only wants love while John only wants a loan. Meanwhile, Donner seems to only attract tricks who want to hit him, and when he's done, he talks about tricks who want to hit him. (One of Donner's fellow Johns on the street is Wilson Cruz as Mikey. He's been so good in a such a variety of smallish roles, I keep hoping he'll get a part into which he can really sink his teeth.) After sunset, depression sets in, the tricks get stranger, and the vulnerable Johns are vic-

meeting the casting director and saying, 'I really want this, but if you don't want to give it to me, it's O.K.' I had this aggressive edge at the time, but I'd always pull back, because you never know what casting directors are looking for, you never know exactly what they want. Sometimes, it has nothing to do with your talent, it's really what you look like and how you look with the rest of the cast. Luckily, producer Winnie Holzman and I spoke afterwards and she said that when I walked in the door, I was the person she had pictured as Rickie Vasquez. She said that happened all the time, with all of us in the cast (Bess Armstrong, Claire Danes, Devon Gummersall, A.J. Langer, Jared Leto, Devon Odessa, Lisa Wilhoit, Tom Irwin). We would walk in the door and she would see that this was the person that she wanted and she hoped we could act. We didn't let her down. She'll tell you over and over again that she got her dream cast for *My So-Called Life* and that always makes me feel good.

"I'm not naive and I did feel the responsibility playing the first gay teen hero on a continuing series on network television, but I think it's sad when you think about the fact that Rickie Vasquez was the first one; it was past due by 1994–95. I get a lot of letters from teenagers around the country and they wanted to see this, and not only the lesbian/gay/bisexual/transgender/transsexual teens, but also the straight kids. They had kids in their classes that were like Rickie Vasquez. When they saw him on the show, it reaffirmed the fact that *My So-Called Life* was real and that we were really trying to show them their lives on television. Because of the show and because of my own life, I go on in my personal life doing as much as I possibly can to further the cause and enlighten people about the fact that these kids are in trouble and it's our responsibility as adults to do something about it."

WILSON CRUZ appeared in *Nixon* opposite Bob Hoskins as J. Edgar Hoover and Brian Bedford as Clyde Tolson and in the indie flicks *johns, All Over Me,* and *Joyride.*

timized by tricks who hate the fact that they need a john at all. It's at night when *johns* is saddest, and fledgling writer/director Scott Silver shows us why in a clear, restrained way. Arquette and Haas dive into the roles of John and Donner as if their lives depended on the decisions their desperate characters have to make, and Arliss Howard as a character named Cardoza delivers his specialty: another carefully textured performance. *johns* is a fine first effort for Silver, who achieves a great deal on this sharply focused, modestly budgeted film. ℒℒℒ

1996 (R) 96m/C David Arquette, Lukas Haas, Arliss Howard, Keith David, Elliott Gould, Christopher Gartin, Joshua Schaefer, Wilson Cruz, Terrence DaShon Howard, Nicky Katt, Alanna Ubach; ***D:*** Scott Silver; ***W:*** Scott Silver; ***C:*** Tom Richmond; ***M:*** Charles D. Brown. **VHS**

Jonah Who Will Be 25 in the Year 2000

Alain Tanner's *Jonah Who Will Be 25 in the Year 2000* was among the best of the entries at 1976's San Francisco International Film Festival. Tanner tries to convey depth in superficial terms, but with imagination, humor, and insight. The results are awesome. The stories—of eight people connected to one another by the political events of 1968—swirl in and around each other. Tanner's sure, sensitive touch

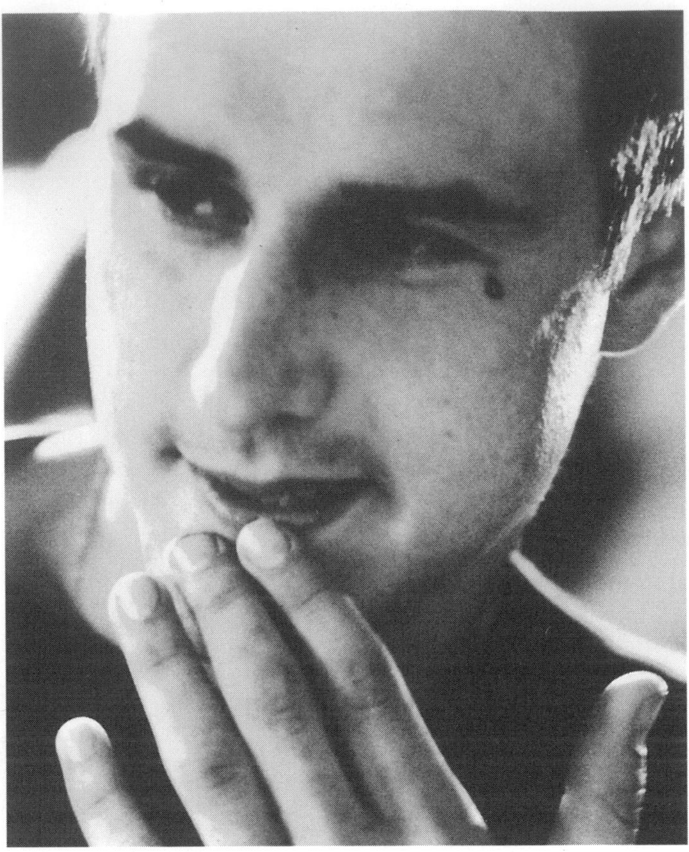

David Arquette in *johns.* First Look Pictures; courtesy of the Kobal Collection

blends and balances his study into a solidly constructed film, despite its lack of a conventional plot. The sequences involving an inventive high school teacher and his class convey Tanner's deep wonder at the world, as well as his hope for a future that values the opinions of young and old alike. ***AKA:*** Jonas—Qui Aura 25 Ans en l'An 2000. 𝄢𝄢𝄢

1976 110m/C *SI* Jean-Luc Bideau, Myriam Meziere, Miou-Miou, Jacques Denis, Rufus, Dominique Labourier, Roger Jendly, Miriam Boyer, Raymond Bussieres, Jonah; ***D:*** Alain Tanner; ***W:*** Alain Tanner; ***C:*** Renato Berta; ***M:*** Jean-Marie Senia. National Society of Film Critics Awards '76: Best Screenplay. **VHS**

Joyless Street

When Greta Garbo came to Hollywood with director Mauritz Stiller, she was streamlined, plucked, garbed, and coiffured to MGM perfection, whether or not it suited the role she was playing. This was not the case in G.W. Pabst's *Joyless Street,* where Garbo looked exactly like what she was supposed to be: a gauche and rather awkward young woman, still living at home with her father Josef (Jaro Furth) and little sister Rosa (Loni Nest). Greta gets a job, but soon finds herself fighting off the advances of her employer. Under such circumstances, she begins to consider prostitution at the urging of Frau Griefer (Valeska Gert). Much of the narrative focuses on the character played by Asta Nielsen (1883–1972), then seven films away from her 1932 swan song after a career that began in 1910. Fed up with unemployment, she HAS become a prostitute, but becomes dangerously obsessed with one of her clients, who eventually discards her. Meanwhile, hefty butcher Josef Geiringer (Werner Krauss) refuses to serve the long line of hungry people who wait in vain for a scrap of meat to bring home to their families. ("I have meat," he taunts them, "But not for you!") Audiences of the late 1920s (the film didn't reach America until 1927 when Garbo was already an international star) found Pabst's vision of post-war Vienna to be too decadent and too grim. Over the years, the picture has acquired a reputation among Pabst admirers who consider *Joyless Street* to be one of his finest films. It certainly shows why Vienna would be so vulnerable to a German takeover the following decade. Ground down by World War I, Vienna was no longer the glittering capitol it had been in the 19th century. It had become a city of contrasts: newly rich men and women courtesy of the black market versus poverty-stricken families devastated by the war. Pabst lays bare that contrast by cutting from bold images of booze-soaked nightclubs to close-ups of starving people in doorways, shivering in the cold night air. We may have been on a collision course with a worldwide Depression, but no one wanted to face it in a movie theatre yet. Edited by Anatol Litvak and based on a novel by Hugo Battauer. ***AKA:*** Street of Sorrow; Die Freudlosse Gasse. 𝄢𝄢𝄢𝄢

1925 96m/B *GE* Greta Garbo, Werner Krauss, Asta Nielson, Jaro Furth, Loni Nest, Max Kohlhase, Silva Torf, Karl Ettlinger, Ilka Gruning, Agnes Esterhazy, Alexander Musky, Valeska Gert; ***D:*** G.W. Pabst; ***W:*** Willi Haas; ***C:*** Guido Seeber, Curt Oertel, Walter Robert Lach. **VHS, LV**

Ju Dou

Ju Dou was the first Chinese film to be nominated for an Academy Award. The Chinese government fought the nomination for the film, which had effectively been banned in its own country. *Ju Dou* is sharply critical of the traditional rural customs that prevailed in the 1920s. Ju Dou, the title character, is purchased as the third wife of Jinshan, an abusive old man who beats her when she fails to produce an heir. The young woman enters into an affair with Tianquing, her husband's nephew, but they must pretend that their baby is the son of Ju Dou's husband. The husband is soon the victim of an accident, which paralyzes him and leaves him helpless. Ju Dou and her lover make no attempt to hide their affair in front of him, although they conceal the affair from the villagers on penalty of death. The triangle becomes progressively more and more tortured and, without giving too much of the plot away, it's no wonder that Tianbai, Ju Dou's baby, evolves into rather a strange child. Director Zhang Yimou's interpretation of Liu Heng's novel-based screenplay is masterful; it was his wonderfully cinematic decision to transplant the story into a dye factory. The colorful dye factory serves the function of a fifth character and is symbolic of everything the lovers have to gain and lose. Beautifully acted and photographed, *Ju Dou* lingers in the mind, both for its compelling narrative and its deeply disturbing emotional landscape. Although the film is set entirely in the '20s, the hopelessness of Ju Dou's situation persisted in China of the '90s, where women could still be bought and sold for as little as $400. ✂✂✂✂

1990 (PG-13) 98m/C *CH* Gong Li, Li Bao-Tian, Li Wei, Zhang Yi, Zheng Jian; ***D:*** Zhang Yimou; ***W:*** Liu Heng; ***C:*** Gu Changwei, Yang Lun; ***M:*** Xia Ru-jin, Jiping Zhao. Nominations: Academy Awards '90: Best Foreign Film. **VHS, LV**

Julia and Julia

Here's a word of advice to filmmakers who plan to shave production costs by shooting your major motion pictures in the new, improved high-definition video process: DON'T! If Oscar-nominated cinematographer Giuseppe Rotunno couldn't pull it off in *Julia and Julia,* you won't be able to either at this stage of the game. The process looks okay, better then a kinescope, anyway, if every single one of your actors doesn't move a muscle. Once you yell "action," though, there's no such thing as a fluid motion onscreen, and if you're working with pigeons as extras, forget it. You may as well substitute Dramamine for Jujubes because you'll need it after 96 minutes. The closest equivalent to the high-definition video experience is the stretch printing process used by film preservationists when they restore silent films. The headache you get from watching that process is almost worth it when you're screening a rare treasure from 1903. But even if you weren't bombarded by *Julia and Julia*'s excruciating aesthetic problems, you still would be stuck with director Peter Del Monte's loco script. *Julia and Julia* is about a woman (Kathleen Turner) on her honeymoon with her husband (Irish actor Gabriel Byrne, with an all-purpose Spanish-Italian accent), whose car explodes after she's made her narrow escape. Widowed, she leads a solitary life as a travel agent in Trieste, Italy, until she drives through a tunnel one night and enters a time warp. Maybe her husband Paolo wasn't killed. Maybe she's really been married to him all those years, and maybe they even have a little boy named Marco (Alexander Van Wyk, who spends more time in bed than most of the grown-ups do). Wouldn't that be nice? But wait. There's a snag. What is Julia going to do about her lover Daniel, deftly played by Sting? In a mysterious shift back to her former life, Julia sells Sting a ticket to Dubrovnik. A flight to Dubrovnik would write him out of the script too easily, though. What's a poor traveler in a time warp to do? Have no fear, "Life is wonder-

"When you first meet people, all you notice are the differences between you and them, but as time passes you start noticing the similarities. I guess that's how all friendships begin."

—Brian Kessler (David Duchovny) in *Kalifornia.*

ful," as a blissful Julia informs us before film's end. ***AKA:*** Guilia e Guilia. **woof!**

1987 (R) 98m/C *IT* Kathleen Turner, Sting, Gabriel Byrne, Gabriele Ferzetti, Angela Goodwin, Alexander Van Wyk; ***D:*** Peter Del Monte; ***W:*** Peter Del Monte; ***C:*** Giuseppe Rotunno; ***M:*** Maurice Jarre. **VHS, LV, Closed Caption**

Just Another Girl on the I.R.T.

Seventeen-year-old Chantel (Ariyan Johnson) dreams about zapping through high school and going on to medical school. Then she meets Tyrone (Kevin Thigpen), has sex with him, fritters away the abortion money he gives her, and her options and dreams scatter like commuters on the I.R.T. Leslie Harris makes a promising directorial debut, newcomer Johnson's portrait of a tough Brooklyn teen is energetic and convincing, and Thigpen is also memorable as sexy Tyrone. A raw, bleak look at a mouthy character who thwarts her own best interests at every turn.

1993 (R) 96m/C Ariyan Johnson, Kevin Thigpen, Ebony Jerido, Jerard Washington, Chequita Jackson, William Badget; ***D:*** Leslie Harris; ***W:*** Leslie Harris; ***C:*** Richard Conners. Sundance Film Festival '93: Special Jury Prize; Nominations: Independent Spirit Awards '94: Best Actress (Johnson). **VHS, LV**

Just Like a Woman

If *Just Like a Woman* had originated in Hollywood story conferences, it would have emerged as a broad farce crammed with puns and sight gags and stripped of any real insight. But, just like in 1987's *Personal Services,* wonderful Julie Walters is our sympathetic tour guide into another world. Based on Monica Jay's book, *Geraldine,* Christopher Monger's film takes a look at Gerald Tilson (Adrian Pasdar), drawn to transvestism since childhood. He keeps this part of his life private (although one does wonder how he manages with a wife and two children). The wife discovers Geraldine's wardrobe, thinks it belongs to another woman, and files for divorce. Gerald acquiescently agrees to end his marriage, convinced that his wife would never believe, much less understand, the truth. He rents a room in Monica's (Julie Walters) house and, warmed by her kind and jolly nature, falls in love with her and confides in her for the first time in his life. The truth, which is complex and not undemanding of considerable adjustment, winds up setting them both free. Nick Evans' script is quite good and Walters and Pasdar are terrific together.

1992 (R) 102m/C *GB* Adrian Pasdar, Julie Walters, Paul Freeman, Susan Wooldridge, Gordon Kennedy, Ian Redford, Shelley Thompson; ***D:*** Christopher Monger; ***W:*** Nick Evans; ***C:*** Alan Hume; ***M:*** Michael Storey. **VHS**

Just Like in the Movies

Just Like in the Movies is a likable independent feature from the directing/screenwriting team of Bram Towbin and Mark Halliday. It also provides an extremely fine role for Jay O. Sanders as Ryan Legrand, private eye. The film is hardly a recruiting movie for those with dreams of exciting and dangerous undercover assignments. Legrand's job strictly involves following husbands and wives who suspect infidelity; a more sordid job is hard to imagine. Legrand is also a definite creep, the world's worst date, and embarrassingly awkward on divorced dad days with his son as well. Somehow, the film invests its protagonist with a few appealing qualities; maybe it has something to do with the fact that he tries so hard and everyone else in the film despises him so thoroughly. Perennial celluloid sidekick Alan Ruck once again plays Legrand's droll sidekick: "Just Like in the Movies!"

1990 98m/C Jay O. Sanders, Alan Ruck, Katherine Borowitz, Michael Jeter, Alex Vincent; ***D:*** Bram Towbin, Mark Halliday; ***W:*** Bram Towbin, Mark Halliday; ***C:*** Peter Fernberger; ***M:*** John Hill.

Kafka

This is not the film the cognoscenti were expecting from Steven Soderbergh after *sex, lies and videotape,* so they raked it and him over the coals. I thought it was pretty interesting and definitely the work of

a free spirit. It's set in 1919 Prague and Kafka (1883–1974, Jeremy Irons) is leading a pretty drab life, clerking by day, scribbling by night. He gets mixed up in a strange tale of terror, culminating in a trip to the Castle of Dr. Murnau (Ian Holm as the villain of the piece). It's all in creepy black and white, except for the castle segment that is in color. And look at that mouth-watering cast (Joel Grey, Jeroen Krabbe, Armin Mueller-Stahl, Alec Guinness)! What do you want from a second movie: "more sex, more lies and more videotape?" Get over it!

1991 (PG-13) 100m/C Jeremy Irons, Theresa Russell, Joel Grey, Ian Holm, Jeroen Krabbe, Armin Mueller-Stahl, Alec Guinness, Brian Glover, Robert Flemyng, Keith Allen, Simon McBurney; ***D:*** Steven Soderbergh; ***W:*** Lem Dobbs; ***C:*** Walt Lloyd; ***M:*** Cliff Martinez. Independent Spirit Awards '92: Best Cinematography. **VHS, LV, Letterbox, Closed Caption**

Kalifornia

The flat voiceover narration gives us the road map for *Kalifornia.* A writer (David Duchovny) and his photographer girlfriend (Michelle Forbes) are en route to California, doing a word-and-picture tour of the locales of famous American murders along the way. To share expenses, they accept, sight unseen, the companionship of serial killer Brad Pitt and his deliberately oblivious girlfriend, Juliette Lewis. At first glance, Forbes observes that Pitt and Lewis are dumb, and Lewis decides that Duchovny and Forbes are strange. The two men, however, form an inexplicable bond, so all four hit the road. The writer (shades of silly Geraldine Chaplin searching for symbolism with her tape recorder in *Nashville* here) feels that by visiting murder sites and recording his observations, he will understand how and why people kill. And, of course, all the time, Pitt is wiping people out in men's restrooms and service stations; it takes the others half the movie to get a firm grasp of the obvious. Screenwriter Tim Metcalfe finds this situation amusing; the old educated-hicks-want-to-experience-real-life-but-fall-to-pieces-when-they-do formula. The film works best when the focus is on Juliette Lewis, clearly one of the best actresses of her generation and absolutely fearless about exposing the truth of her characters, without a flicker of self-protective reserve. Like all great actors, she works from the inside out; director Dominic Sena gives her props and bits of business to work with, but she works equally well with the force of her naked emotions. We might split a gut if anyone else summed up a serial killer with an inadequate description like "mean," but Lewis breaks your heart with the sequence. There ain't a question in your mind that while she's raging at Pitt, she means it. Unfortunately, none of the rest of the cast is in Lewis' league. Forbes is a good actress; she might very well wrap up another movie, but not 1994's *Swimming with Sharks,* for reasons beyond her control. In *Kalifornia,* she is an excellent foil for Lewis, and the two women share some of the film's best moments. The sequences with Pitt and Duchovny work less well. Both actors work from the outside in, and the impact of their performances is nowhere near as intense as the basic narrative would have you believe. *Kalifornia* is mostly an absorbing film and it looks great. The film would have done even better if it had taken its emotional cue from the unforced honesty of Juliette Lewis, instead of trying to wring existential mileage out of the unanswerable questions posed by its dippy protagonist.

1993 (R) 117m/C Brad Pitt, Juliette Lewis, David Duchovny, Michelle Forbes, Sierra Pecheur, Lois Hall, Gregory Mars Martin; ***D:*** Dominic Sena; ***W:*** Tim Metcalfe; ***C:*** Bojan Bazelli; ***M:*** Carter Burwell. **VHS, LV, Letterbox, Closed Caption, DVD**

Kama Sutra: A Tale of Love

For reasons that are beyond me, *Kama Sutra* received a critical roasting. It's a Tale of Love—well, 16th century sexual politics, really—through the eyes of women who are trained from childhood to please men. Sarita Choudhury is Princess Tara, fated to marry a king, Raj Singh (*The English Patient*'s Naveen Andrews). But Tara is cruel to her maid Maya (Indira Varma), who seduces the king before the wedding night in revenge, and is exiled

"One day you are your father's property. One day you are your husband's property. It must be difficult."

—Raj Singh (Naveen Andrews) in *Kama Sutra: A Tale of Love.*

from her village by Tara. Needless to say, the union of the princess and the king begins badly and goes downhill from there. Maya lands on her feet, though, and soon attracts the professional attention of Jai, a handsome sculptor (Ramon Tikaram). When Jai learns that he can't focus on his work and the lovely Maya, too, she embarks on a crash course in Kama Sutra, winding up as Raj Singh's favorite palace courtesan. Mira Nair focuses on how the women of the 16th century develop the only power they are permitted to wield and how the men in their lives, more often than not, would rather die than deal with that power on its own terms. Filmed in spectacular Technicolor, *Kama Sutra* is a feast for the eyes, and Indira Varma makes an appealing first impression. *Kama Sutra: A Tale of Love* works wonderfully well on the level of an adult fairy tale. It doesn't even try to be a 16th century documentary. If Nathaniel Hawthorne could speculate about 17th century colonial America in 1850's *The Scarlet Letter,* what's the big deal about Mira Nair creating a compelling fantasy about the women of another time? For a bunch of middle-aged male movie critics who got all hot and bothered about *Kama Sutra*'s "historical accuracy," it seemed to be a VERY big deal. Hey, guys, if that's all you want, read a history book! 🦴🦴🦴

1996 117m/C *IN* Indira Varma, Sarita Choudhury, Ramon Tikaram, Naveen Andrews, Devi Rekha; ***D:*** Mira Nair; ***W:*** Mira Nair, Helena Kriel; ***C:*** Declan Quinn; ***M:*** Mychael Danna. **VHS, LV, Closed Caption, DVD**

Kansas City

Robert Altman and Jennifer Jason Leigh are like the little girl with the curl in the middle of her forehead; when they are good, they are very, very good, but when they are bad, they are horrid. For *Kansas City,* both are at their worst: Altman rambling and out of control, Leigh meticulously creating a role from all the non-essential externals and losing the heart and soul of her character in the process. The threadbare plot, set in 1934, has Leigh kidnapping Miranda Richardson, as the strung-out wife of a presidential advisor, so that her husband will be forced to influence crooked nightclub owner Harry Belafonte into freeing the larcenous love of Leigh's life. (Who else but Dermot Mulroney, who only gets to talk in one sequence? And Michael Murphy is all-but-invisible as the FDR crony.) Leigh's idol is supposed to be Jean Harlow, but she seems to have obsessed on early Warner Bros. talkies starring Glenda Farrell and Joan Blondell without learning a thing about the secret of their appeal. Watching Leigh's face twist into actressy mannerisms and listening to her fake her way through gun-moll slang is, to put it kindly, excruciating. Blessedly, Richardson is on hand as the so-called victim. Richardson's subterranean mysteries offer welcome counterpoint to Altman's banal script and Leigh's tedious contortions. I was stunned to see the gushing praise that Jack Kroll gave this mess in *Newsweek;* the entire review could be splashed verbatim on *Kansas City* advertisements. But 1996 was the summer of serious fawning for deeply flawed films, like *Lone Star,* that might be politely dismissed in a season less saturated with computer wizardry. There has to be more to a movie than that it NOT have special effects. Altman thinks he's found it in the Hey Hey nightclub sequences where Ron Carter, Craig Handy, Joshua Redman, and James Carter are meant to evoke jazz legends like Coleman Hawkins and Lester Young. However, the structure here is basically Leigh talking out of the side of her mouth, cut to jazz, back to Leigh, back to more jazz, and so on with little connecting detail. Altman even admits that the screenplay was knitted together from two separate yarns. When Altman is at the peak of his form, as in *M.A.S.H.* and *Nashville,* no one can tell a story with more brilliance or greater precision. But *Kansas City*—sadly—is way down there at the bottom, along with *Popeye* and *Pret-a-Porter.* 🦴

1995 (R) 110m/C Jennifer Jason Leigh, Miranda Richardson, Harry Belafonte, Michael Murphy, Dermot Mulroney, Steve Buscemi, Brooke Smith, Jane Adams; ***D:*** Robert Altman; ***W:*** Frank Barhydt, Robert Altman; ***C:*** Oliver Stapleton; ***M:*** Hal Willner. New York Film Critics Awards '96: Best Supporting Actor (Belafonte). **VHS, LV, Closed Caption**

Kids

A very grim look at the lives of depressingly young children. Telly (Leo Fitzpatrick) is terminally incapable of zipping it up. He will succumb to AIDS eventually but he doesn't know it yet. However, Jennie (Chloe Sevigny), who's tested HIV positive, DOES know it. She was among a long line of virgins who had sex for the first time with Telly. Telly seduces a very young blonde (Sarah Henderson) at the start of *Kids,* and picks up Darcy (Yakira Peguero) by picture's end. The tragic irony is Telly probably enjoys bragging about his virginal conquests to his friend Gasper (Justin Pierce) even more than he digs the sex. *Kids* shows a parentless world where a gang of homophobic, racist kids drift through the streets of Manhattan, and where children of 10 turn on and/or drink themselves into a stupor. Harmony Korinc was just 19 when she wrote *Kids,* and Larry Clark was over 50 when he directed it.

1995 90m/C Leo Fitzpatrick, Justin Pierce, Chloe Sevigny, Rosario Dawson, Sarah Henderson, Harold Hunter, Yakira Peguero, Joseph Knafelmacher; ***D:*** Larry Clark; ***W:*** Harmony Korine; ***C:*** Eric Alan Edwards; ***M:*** Louis Barlow. Independent Spirit Awards '96: Debut Performance (Pierce); Nominations: Independent Spirit Awards '96: Best First Feature, Best Supporting Actress (Sevigny). **VHS, LV, Closed Caption, DVD**

Kika

Pedro Almodovar thrived in the post-Franco era, directing a series of nine films that challenged our ideas of how sexuality, violence, comedy, and tragedy could be conveyed onscreen. His tenth film, premiering at 1994's San Francisco International Film Festival, reveals evidence of an unmistakable and, I hope, temporary decline. Almodovar's best films have always dealt with his own concerns and his own culture. In *Kika,* he drew his inspiration from the media feeding frenzy that surrounded the William Kennedy Smith rape trial. How humiliating, perhaps more humiliating than the rape itself, Almodovar observed, that the alleged victim's underwear was shown on U.S. television. And, although tabloid television has invaded Spain as well, his source material is essentially external. His understanding of the lives of the people who are affected by tabloid television is not terribly profound; in *Kika,* for the first time, Almodovar fails to get inside the skin of his characters. The title role is well played by Veronica Forque as a distaff version of Candide, but her relentless cheerfulness makes no sense, especially in a rape sequence. She may be uncomfortable, but for the most part, she takes the act for granted. To her, the true villain is not her rapist, but Andrea Scarface (Victoria Abril), who obtains footage of the rape and televises it. In the entire 115-minute film, Kika only expresses outraged sensibilities for an instant, and the moment passes very quickly. All of the stock Almodovar ingredients are in place: the dry wit in moments of high drama, the sheer speed of Almodovar's storytelling style, even the zany fringe characters who would add ironic contrast to a more compelling central premise. With his latest strained effort at grabbing the attention of international audiences, Almodovar strays further and further from his greatest artistic gift: the ability to see all the way down to the darkness of the human soul with clarity and compassion. *Kika* is only a tourist's eye view of serial killings, voyeurism, and the contemporary media. Rent *Matador* or *Law of Desire* on home video instead and look forward to better things from Almodovar on the big screen in the future.

1994 115m/C *SP* Veronica Forque, Peter Coyote, Victoria Abril, Alex Casanovas, Rossy de Palma; ***D:*** Pedro Almodovar; ***W:*** Pedro Almodovar; ***C:*** Alfredo Mayo; ***M:*** Enrique Granados. **VHS, DVD**

Kill Me Again

She is a "greedy, two-faced bitch." He is a member in good standing of the Dumb Dicks of America. As played by Joanne Whalley and Val Kilmer, they are a match made in a casting director's heaven. I first saw *Kill Me Again* at San Francisco's Geneva Drive-in on a double bill with the Judd Nelson movie *Relentless,* a film which makes *Kill Me Again* look like *The Maltese Falcon.* Actually, *Kill Me Again* brings to mind quite a few noir classics, including

The Hound Salutes:

PETER COYOTE

Actor, *Kika*

It started with a phone call from Pedro Almodovar. I was in New York, en route to France. I was going to shoot a Chanel commercial written by Joe Eszterhas and directed by Roman Polanski like a one-minute movie, then I was going to be a judge at a sci-fi/horror film festival in the mountains of Switzerland. So I met with Pedro in Paris and we had a very nice chat. Pedro asked, 'Can you speak any Spanish?' 'Buenos dias,' I answered blithely. He said, 'I think you can do *Kika* in Spanish.' I was dubbed, anyway, but I did actually learn Spanish for the film. I did the whole thing in Spanish, but Pedro is a very stylistic director and he directs at the speed of Billy Wilder. My Spanish was not up to that. At first, I was quite hurt for about 20 minutes, but when I saw the movie I realized that Pedro was right, then it didn't bother me because he got a very good actor to dub me and I WAS speaking Spanish, so the lip-synching matched. Let's just say that my character in *Kika* has secrets and the film is about secrets and what happens when secrets are revealed. What went into my character is what goes into every actor's work: I researched, I got ideas, I put stuff together, but even if I knew exactly how I did it, I couldn't explain it to you. I think what's more important is the function a character plays in the script, since actors are there to serve the script. Each character is created to tell a part of the story, so my character was cre-

Double Indemnity and *Out of the Past.* When Whalley takes it off and turns it on, you want to believe every single one of her lies. The film is saturated with sleaze and violence, and it's never boring (which is more than I can say for *Relentless*). Michael Madsen plays a great old-fashioned psycho and writer/director John Dahl makes interesting use of fire, water, and the rest of the limited resources in this tightly budgeted yarn. If you don't expect *Murder My Sweet,* you'll have fun. 🦴🦴🦴

1989 (R) 93m/C Val Kilmer, Joanne Whalley, Michael Madsen, Jonathan Gries, Bibi Besch; ***D:*** John Dahl; ***W:*** John Dahl, David Warfield; ***C:*** Jacques Steyn. **VHS, Closed Caption**

Killer Flick

This one-joke movie deserves a single bone for the script, but the acting and cinematography elevate it another bone. Director Rome (Zen Todd), Cinematographer One Eye (Christian Leffler), Scriptwriter Max (Emmett Grennan), and Musician Buzz (Creighton Howard) would and do kill to make a movie. Love Interest Tess (Kathleen Walsh) doesn't like the sexism in the script, but she shares their philosophy and M.O. about enforcing it, so she's immediately inducted into the gang. "The world's greatest character actor" Virgil Morgan (who?) played by Fred Dennis (who?) is forced to act at gunpoint. At least WE aren't forced to watch at gunpoint, so what's our excuse? After 93 minutes, our patience with these adventures in guerrilla filmmaking is finito! *Killer Flick* "introduces" Walsh, but I couldn't find credits for her four co-stars, either, so who knows? According to the closing credits, *Killer Flick* was filmed in and around Apple Valley, Barstow, Rancho Cucamonga, and Victorville. 🦴🦴

1998 93m/C Zen Todd, Christian Leffler, Emmett Grennan, Creighton Howard, Kathleen Walsh, Fred Dennis, Kareem Oliver, Kyle Van Horne, Virgil Frye,

ated to have secrets and they're very dangerous secrets and they're secrets that, if revealed, would cause great damage.

"When I played Michael in *Outrageous Fortune,* I really wanted to warn people how easy it is to fool them by making the perfect person. It was me taking the mickey out of a lot of my women friends to say, 'I know the sort of guy you want. Watch—here he is: Mr. Perfect. Butch and sensitive. Caring and rugged. Diapering the baby while he's watching sports. And Ha-Ha. Michael is a murderer.' So there's a little bit of that in the character I play in *Kika.* He's a writer, he looks sincere, and we're all easy to fool. That's part of the joke we need to know about ourselves. As for *Bitter Moon,* I have nothing but great things to say about it and about working with Roman Polanski. I loved Oscar, the character I got to play. Making *Bitter Moon* was like throwing a chocolate addict into a chocolate factory. Oscar's character is so large and reprehensible and eager and fun and wicked. I couldn't get enough of him. I could make a career out of playing that guy."

PETER COYOTE on video: *Baja Oklahoma, Best Kept Secrets, Bitter Moon, The Blue Yonder, Breach of Conduct, Buffalo Girls, Crooked Hearts, Cross Creek, Dalva, Die Laughing, Echoes in the Darkness, Endangered Species, E.T., Exposure, Heart of Midnight, Heartbreakers, Hitchhiker 2, Jagged Edge, Keeper of the City, Legend of Billie Jean, A Man in Love, The Man Inside, Moonlight and Valentino, Out, Outrageous Fortune, The People Vs. Jean Harris, Seeds of Doubt, Slayground, Southern Comfort, Sphere, Stacking, Stranger's Kiss, Tell Me a Riddle, That Eye, the Sky, Timerider, Two for Texas,* and *Unforgettable.*

Scott Jaicks; ***D:*** Mark Weidman; ***W:*** Mark Weidman; ***C:*** Robert Stenger; ***M:*** Kyle Van Horne.

The Killer inside Me

Ever since the Creative Arts Book Company in Berkeley began re-printing Jim Thompson's novels in its Black Lizard series, I've been trying to track down the movies that were inspired by his books, and it hasn't been easy. 1979's *Serie Noire* based on *A Hell of a Woman,* for example, was made in France by Alain Corneau, and if it's shown up on cable or at a video outlet or on the revival circuit, I must have been out of town. Burt Kennedy's *The Killer inside Me* was released by Warner Bros. in 1976, and even though it features an all-star cast (Stacy Keach, Susan Tyrell, Tisha Sterling, Don Stroud, Julie Adams, and the late character actors Keenan Wynn, Charles McGraw, John Dehner, Royal Dano, and John Carradine), this one is hard to see, although well worth waiting for. Berkeley alumnus Keach gives a crisp, controlled performance as the sheriff whose violent core is obscured by his nice guy facade. The film perfectly captures the Thompson atmosphere of frightening undercurrents of emotion, which are set in motion by seemingly innocuous sights, sounds, and gestures. The only irritating sequences in *Killer* (although perhaps they were meant to be irritating) are the colossally dull relationship spats between Keach and Sterling. Keach's moments with Stroud and Carradine are played with very dark, very weird humor. Along with *Serie Noire, The Killer inside Me* tops my wish list of film noir double bills I'd most like to see on the big screen.

1976 (R) 99m/C Stacy Keach, Susan Tyrrell, Tisha Sterling, Keenan Wynn, John Dehner, John Carradine, Don Stroud, Charles McGraw, Julie Adams,

The Hound Salutes:
JOHN CARRADINE
(1906–88)

John Carradine began making films in 1930, specializing in horror movies. You may remember seeing him as a mad doctor in *Captive Wild Woman,* as a Nazi spy in *Waterfront,* or as Count Dracula in *House of Frankenstein* and *House of Dracula.* Carradine was in San Francisco in the spring of 1988 for a tribute honoring his work in the 1939 mystery, *The Hound of the Baskervilles,* the first of 14 movies starring Basil Rathbone as Sherlock Holmes and Nigel Bruce as Dr. Watson. In 1939, no one could have played a more suspicious-looking butler than John Carradine in *The Hound of the Baskervilles.* As the last surviving member of the cast, Carradine was inducted into the Persian Slipper Society of Holmes scholars at Baskerville Hall in San Francisco.

"Basil was a very incisive man. That's why he was so wonderful as Sherlock Holmes. I was supposed to play a character named Barrymore, but the Barrymores didn't like the idea and so I had to change the name to Berryman."

John Carradine was born Richmond Reed Carradine in Greenwich Village on February 5, 1906. His mother was a surgeon and his father was a lawyer, a poet, and an artist. One of Carradine's early careers was making quick sketch portraits of people, and he financed his 1927 trip to Hollywood by doing just that and by hitchhiking. He later drew on his experiences when he created a memorable portrait of a homicidal artist in 1944's *Bluebeard,* a film directed by Edgar Ulmer, which co-starred Jean Parker.

"As a matter of fact, Edgar Ulmer, who was the director, let me direct one scene...I was playing a painter and painting a portrait of a gal...and then I strangle her and drop her in a subterranean stream."

While still a teen Carradine worked with a Shakespearean stock company, and when he didn't find work in the movies right away, he polished his craft on the stage. He later worked with many great film directors, including John Ford on *The Grapes of Wrath* and Cecil B. De Mille

Royal Dano; ***D:*** Burt Kennedy; ***W:*** Robert Chandlee; ***C:*** William A. Fraker. **VHS**

The Killing

After 1955's *Killer's Kiss,* Stanley Kubrick received $200,000 to make *The Killing* for United Artists. There were only two strings attached: he had to cast a star as Johnny Clay and U.A. had to like his script. Sterling Hayden turned out to be perfect as a grizzled small-time convict in hot pursuit of the big time and who WOULDN'T like the masterful screenplay by Kubrick and Jim Thompson? *The Killing* examines crime and sexuality with a laser-like beam that looked and sounded like nothing else in the Fidgety '50s. Listen to the dialogue

on *The Ten Commandments,* but it was after his performance in *The Merchant of Venice* that he received one of his favorite compliments for his acting from a pioneer filmmaker with whom he never worked.

"I remember there was a knock on the door and I opened it. There stood David Wark Griffith, who had never directed me, but he had just seen my performance as Shylock and he told me, 'It's the best Shylock I've ever seen'. I said, 'Sir, that is praise from Caesar.'

In his later years, John Carradine continued to delight audiences in horror movies like *The Howling.* Seven months before his death he had another challenging project in the works: the role of Jeeter Lester in a new stage production of *Tobacco Road.*

"In *Tobacco Road,* I play a character named Jeeter Lester who's an old farmer and the thing about this play is that he's trying to raise a crop on worn-out old soil and he's a worn-out old man himself, so that's a milestone in his career as a farmer."

He was a tired man of 82 when I finally met him, but he was filled with humor, ambition, and boundless affection for his work as an actor. Carradine was often criticized for wasting his time and talent on what he freely admitted was crap, but he was never a rich man and he needed to support his five sons, four of whom became actors. For every memorable effort like *The Grapes of Wrath,* there were multiples of movies like his least favorite, *Billy the Kid Vs. Dracula.* Carradine's career endured partly because of his accessibility to independent producers, but mostly because of his scene-stealing abilities. Carradine may often have been over-the-top, but he never telephoned in his roles and he was capable of fine work even in the '80s, when he won an Emmy award for his sensitive portrayal of *Umbrella Jack.* The *Hound of the Baskervilles* star being honored by Sherlock Holmes scholars in San Francisco was a happy man, looking forward to playing *Tobacco Road* in North Carolina. I suspect that Carradine died a happy man, eager to share his work with film buffs at a Milan movie tribute. John Carradine left behind hundreds of movies, both good and bad, and countless memories of one of Hollywood's most enthusiastic and best-loved character actors.

JOHN CARRADINE's indies on video include *The Hurricane, Stagecoach, Isle of Forgotten Sins, Waterfront, Bluebeard, It's in the Bag, Captain Kidd, The Private Affairs of Bel Ami, C-Man, The Kentuckian, The Incredible Petrified World, Big Foot,* and *The House of Long Shadows.*

between Elisha Cook and Marie Windsor as George and Sherry Peatty. Was any guy ever whipped as graphically as George was by Sherry? Watch the classic racetrack sequence with Timothy Carey as vicious hood Nikki Arane and James Edwards as the parking attendant. Ever see racism delivered with such a startling flick of rattlesnake venom? The presence of fresh-faced Coleen Gray and the voice-of-God narration are reassuring throwbacks to film noir of the '40s, and then the evil implodes, in bright sunshine as well as in dark shadows, in a way that is raw, real, ugly, and cruel. All the hoods are human and stupid; their doomed schemes may be intricately planned, but their intrinsic flaws are blurred by the sheer speed of

The Hound Salutes:
ELISHA COOK
(1903–95)

Movie nostalgia became big business in the early '70s, and swept in with the new boom was a revival of *Liberty Magazine,* which, during its five-year run, devoted entire issues to the Golden Age of Hollywood. The cover of one such issue listed dozens of luminaries including Elisha Cook. "Who was Elisha Cook?" a reader asked in the next issue, and a photograph was duly published. Nearly everyone who loves movies knows who Elisha Cook is, but, as with many unsung character actors, they don't know that they know him. But think Wilmer, the resentful henchman of genial Casper Gutman, who kicked Sam Spade in the head simply because Spade wouldn't stop riding him. THEN Cook's face and voice swim into focus. For many years, Cook was the sole surviving cast member of *The Maltese Falcon*; the other characters treated him like a kid, even though he was well into middle age by then. But Cook was short, with a youthful face, so audiences accepted him in adolescent and young adult roles for many years. Cook appreciated but resisted nostalgic inquiries about his long career; if you asked him how he prepared for his greatest roles, he was likely to answer, "I don't know. I read the script." He might recall his dialogue from a Boris Ingster classic like 1940's *Stranger on the Third Floor,* but nothing else about making the first true film noir. "Whatever they write, that's what I portray, the best I can," Cook would say, not with slightly disowned vanity, but with absolute conviction.

the narrative drive. Stanley Kubrick blasted his way into the movies with an unsparing frankness about the undercurrents of reality no one else was willing to acknowledge and an originality that audiences continue to experience with all five senses. 🦴🦴🦴🦴

1956 83m/B Sterling Hayden, Marie Windsor, Elisha Cook Jr., Jay C. Flippen, Vince Edwards, Timothy Carey, Coleen Gray, Joseph Sawyer, Ted de Corsia, James Edwards, Jay Adler, Kola Kwarian, Joe Turkel; ***D:*** Stanley Kubrick; ***W:*** Stanley Kubrick, Jim Thompson; ***C:*** Lucien Ballard. **VHS, LV**

The Killing of a Chinese Bookie

How does a single act of violence, executed on a grand scale, fit into the fabric of people's lives, why does it happen, and what sort of person commits such an act? These are some of the questions explored in John Cassavetes' 1976 film, *The Killing of a Chinese Bookie.* The main source of Cosmo Vitelli's validation is his strip club, the "Crazy Horse West." When faced with the loss of his club, Vitelli realizes that the value of his life can not be regained with the same slow measures he used to build it. After incurring an enormous gambling debt, he freely chooses to pay back his losses by killing a man he never met. Cassavetes tells his story in a deliberate, leisurely style, carefully selecting his cast so that each moment rings true. Ben Gazzara makes every one of Vitelli's moves seem as if he were contemplating their expense to him. Virginia Carrington, a real-life waitress at the Hamburger Hamlet discovered by Cassavetes in 1973, delivers another excellent performance. Murder in this film is simply a price tag, a disturbing concept, but one that Cassavetes reveals with brilliant distinction. 🦴🦴🦴

1976 (R) 109m/C Ben Gazzara, Jean-Pierre Cassel, Zizi Johari, Soto Joe Hugh, Robert Phillips, Tim-

According to Cook, his trade secret for playing a good onscreen villain was "Good writing and directing. If you don't have those things, forget it, you've got nothing. I don't care how good you are." It was more than that for this lifelong admirer, though. Franchot Tone was billed way above Cook in Robert Siodmak's *Phantom Lady,* but who can forget the famous drumming sequence when Cook risked 1943 Production Code censors to show how he really felt about Ella Raines? Although Cook gave all the credit for a breath-taking night sequence to his 1947 director Robert Wise and fellow players Lawrence Tierney and Esther Howard, *Born to Kill*'s moral dilemma was more consistently revealed by Claire Trevor and Elisha Cook.

Sterling Hayden and Coleen Gray did a good job in 1956's *The Killing,* but for me the real stars of this vintage Stanley Kubrick noir are Marie Windsor and Elisha Cook. Cook explained that he liked playing shady characters or bums, which may explain why he didn't sweeten them—he fully accepted their values while the cameras were rolling and returned to his own modest, hard-working self offscreen. Towards the end of his life, he didn't even live in Hollywood, but that didn't stop producers from calling; in the '80s, he played Ice Pick opposite Tom Selleck on *Magnum, P.I.* Who was Elisha Cook? For many years he was my favorite living character actor and along with Humphrey Bogart and Sydney Greenstreet, he's gonna live forever...on film. Elisha Cook's first film for Windsor Picture Plays ("Oh, God! What a film! We made *Her Unborn Child* in a garage basement in 1929.") was followed by more than 100 others over more than half a century.

His indies on video include *Dark Waters, The Indian Fighter, Electra Glide in Blue,* and his favorite picture, *The Killing.*

othy Carey, Morgan Woodward, Virginia Carrington; ***D:*** John Cassavetes; ***W:*** John Cassavetes; ***C:*** Frederick Elmes. **VHS, Closed Caption, DVD**

The Killing of Sister George

When the industry makes gazillions of movies about nothing but straight characters, it can afford to show many of them in a negative light without upsetting anyone too much, because there are positive images to counterbalance all those Up Close and Personal portraits of Sexual Numbskulls. But in the few flicks made about uncoded gay characters through 1968, most of the onscreen images we saw seemed weird and strange. Gay folks had to pay rent and taxes, earn paychecks, and buy groceries just like everyone else, but what films told us was that the gay subculture was obsessed with sexuality, that it pervaded every activity, and that homosexuality often led to Misery, Death, and the Destruction of Society As We Know It. *The Killing of Sister George* is overblown and hypnotic as so many of Robert Aldrich's films are (*Autumn Leaves, Whatever Happened to Baby Jane?, Hush, Hush, Sweet Charlotte*), but when the directorial gaze is on lesbians, viewers are stuck with his (and the writers') oddball visions of their marginalized lives. Beryl Reid, then 50 (whose performance is worthy of an Oscar nomination), plays soap opera star June Buckridge. Her character, Sister George, is being phased out of the show, and she knows it. Her private life is in no better shape, and she knows that, too. Her much younger longtime companion (Alice "Childie" McNaught, 32, played by Susannah York, 29) is losing interest in her. The disintegration of June's personal and professional life is set against the landscape of the Lesbian Community As Seen By Aldrich. (At one social function,

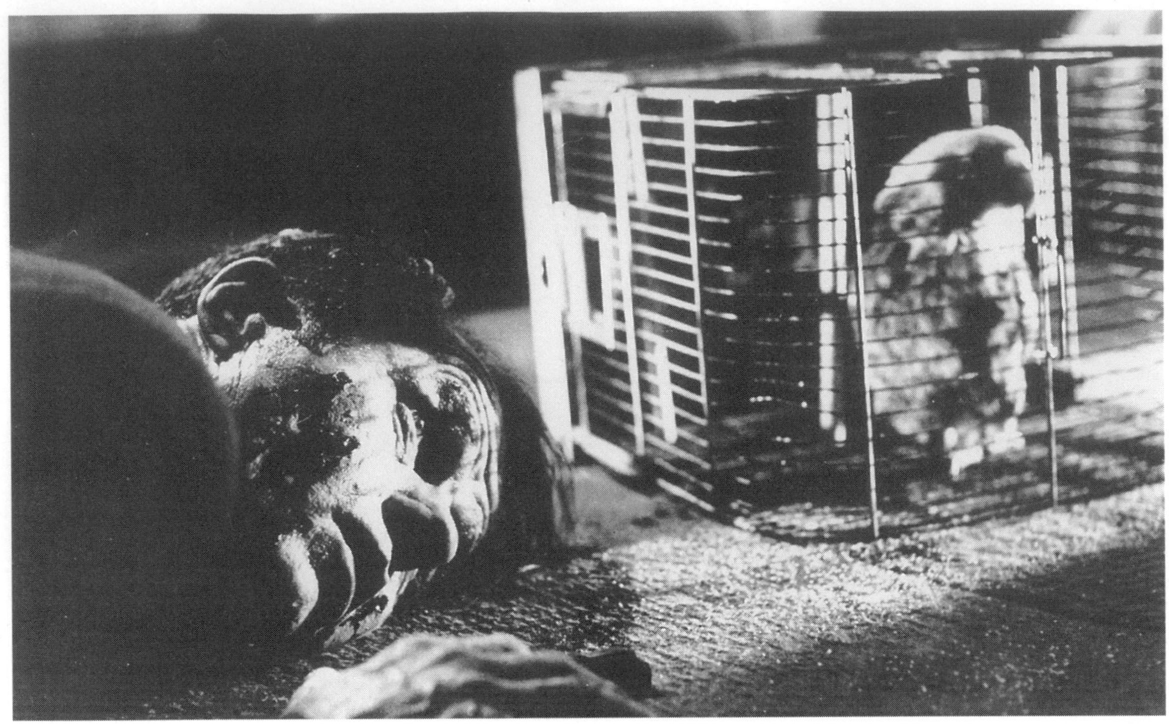

George Peatty (Elisha Cook Jr.) in *The Killing.*
United Artists; courtesy of the Kobal Collection

June and Childie dress up as Laurel and Hardy.) Lurking in the wings and lusting after Childie is Coral Browne, 55, as Mercy Croft, who is finally left alone with the object of her desire in a then-explicit sequence that earned this picture an "X" certificate. Although both June and Mercy seem to prefer the same type in women (baby-faced blondes), "The child," as June roars, "is 32! She's bloody near old enough to be a grandmother!" Childie appears to be a spiritual descendant of Tennessee Williams' *Baby Doll,* a full-grown woman who acts like a baby. June, a spiritual descendant of John Osborne's "Jimmy Porter" in *Look Back in Anger,* commands our attention and our understanding because she's so blunt and so real. The overall effect of the emotional game-playing in *The Killing of Sister George* is quite sad. The always elegant Patricia Medina is seen as Betty Thaxter, although, as she wistfully recalled in 1998, her best sequence was deleted from the final print, sniff....

1969 (R) 138m/C Beryl Reid, Susannah York, Coral Browne, Ronald Fraser, Patricia Medina, Hugh Paddick, Cyril Delevanti, Brandan Dillon, Sivi Aberg, William Beckley, Elaine Church, Mike Freeman, Maggie Paige, Jack Raine, Dolly Taylor; ***D:*** Robert Aldrich; ***W:*** Lukas Heller, Frank Marcus; ***C:*** Joseph Biroc; ***M:*** Gerald Fried. **VHS**

Kind Hearts and Coronets

Kind Hearts and Coronets is a cynical comedy about money, beautifully narrated by Dennis Price as Louis Mazzini, who would do anything to get it. He murders one member of the d'Ascoyne family after another, all played by Alec Guinness. Unfortunately, Louis is tried for a crime he didn't do—killing the boring husband of his longtime sweetheart, Sibella (Joan Greenwood). He records his homicidal activities in his prison cell and hopes for a pardon. Another Ealing masterpiece, and a sure-fire antidote for run-of-the-mill blues. Lovely Valerie Hobson is Edith, the one d'Ascoyne Louis longs to marry.

June (Beryl Reid) and Childie (Susannah York) in ***The Killing of Sister George.***

Courtesy of the Kobal Collection

Based on the Roy Horniman novel *Israel Rank.* 🦴🦴🦴🦴

1949 104m/B *GB* Alec Guinness, Dennis Price, Valerie Hobson, Joan Greenwood, Audrey Fildes, Miles Malleson, Clive Morton, Cecil Ramage, John Penrose, Hugh Griffith, John Salew, Eric Messiter, Anne Valery, Arthur Lowe, Jeremy Spenser; ***D:*** Robert Hamer; ***W:*** Robert Hamer, John Dighton; ***C:*** Douglas Slocombe; ***M:*** Ernest Irving. **VHS, LV**

Kiss Me Deadly

Robert Aldrich's *Kiss Me Deadly* succeeds in creating such a grimy atmosphere that you want to take a bath after seeing it. When Ralph Meeker as Mickey Spillane's Mike Hammer leaves a room, tough guys say, "Open a window." Yet Hammer is the HERO in this violent 1955 blend of hard-boiled detective yarn and atomic bomb paranoia, plus all the corny poetic ramblings Spillane liberally injects into the plot. Except for Cloris Leachman, most of the babes in the film sank from sight after making the picture. Meeker, too, an excellent actor, never again received such a flashy part, although he continued to deliver solid performances in character roles through the 1970s. The physical ordinariness of the stars fits in perfectly with the anonymity most of us are reduced to when dealing with our radioactive fears. Serving as counterpoint for the rough, scary stuff with which Hammer must deal, A.I. Bezzerides' script for *Kiss Me Deadly* is bitingly funny, and Aldrich's never-subtle directing style is well suited to Mickey Spillane's volcanic world. 🦴🦴🦴🦴

1955 105m/B Ralph Meeker, Albert Dekker, Paul Stewart, Wesley Addy, Cloris Leachman, Strother Martin, Marjorie Bennett, Jack Elam, Maxine Cooper, Gaby Rodgers, Nick Dennis, Jack Lambert, Percy Helton; ***D:*** Robert Aldrich; ***W:*** A. I. Bezzerides; ***C:*** Ernest Laszlo. **VHS, LV, Closed Caption**

Kiss of the Spider Woman

Molina (William Hurt) and Valentin (Raul Julia) are cellmates in a South American prison. Only his fantasies of grade-Z Holly-

The Hound Salutes:
RALPH MEEKER
(1920–88)

Ralph Meeker. Not exactly a household name. Meeker had the talent to become one, however, as he proved in 1955 when he played Mike Hammer in Robert Aldrich's film noir classic, *Kiss Me Deadly.* Meeker first attracted national attention in 1947 when he replaced Marlon Brando as Stanley Kowalski in *A Streetcar Named Desire* on Broadway. At that time, every young actor was compared to Brando, whether the comparison fit or not. Upon his arrival in Hollywood, Meeker found himself working in projects like a Betty Hutton musical (1952's *Somebody Loves Me*) and a Jimmy Stewart western (1953's *The Naked Spur*). He reclaimed his critical stature after starring on Broadway in William Inge's *Picnic,* but William Holden played his part in the movie version. Meeker then turned to character roles in films. One of his best 1957 movies was Stanley Kubrick's masterful antiwar film, *Paths of Glory,* in which Meeker convincingly portrayed a condemned soldier. A decade later, Robert Aldrich cast him in *The Dirty Dozen,* one of the most successful movies about prisoners ever made. Meeker worked with Frank Sinatra on 1968's *The Detective,* with Gregory Peck on John Frankenheimer's *I Walk the Line,* with Sean Connery in Sidney Lumet's *The Anderson Tapes,* and with John Huston and an all-star cast on 1979's *Winter Kills.* Well respected within the industry for his ability to create convincing characters, Meeker was less well known to the public, perhaps for the same reason. His most striking role by far, and the role for which he will be best remembered, was as Mickey Spillane's sleazy private eye in *Kiss Me Deadly.*

RALPH MEEKER's films on video include *Four in a Jeep, Kiss Me Deadly, Run of the Arrow, Battle Shock, Paths of Glory, The St. Valentine's Day Massacre, The Dirty Dozen, The Detective, The Night Stalker, The Anderson Tapes, Mind Snatchers, Birds of Prey, Cry Panic, Johnny Firecloud, The Dead Don't Die, Brannigan, Food of the Gods, The Alpha Incident, Hi-Riders, My Boys Are Good Boys,* and *Winter Kills.*

wood flicks keep Molina going over the long haul. At first, revolutionary Valentin disdains the gay Molina, but gradually, the Spider Woman (smoldering Sonia Braga) becomes absolutely real to them both. Hurt won an Oscar and Julia (1940–94) was equally deserving of a nomination as well. He was a thoughtful, charismatic actor of incredible range and, as I think of all the meaty roles he could have made his own well into the next century, I miss him terribly. Based on a novel by Manuel Puig and dynamically directed by Hector Babenco.

1985 (R) 119m/C *BR* William Hurt, Raul Julia, Sonia Braga, Jose Lewgoy, Milton Goncalves, Nuno Leal Maia, Denise Dumont; ***D:*** Hector Babenco; ***W:*** Leonard Schrader; ***M:*** John Neschling, Wally Badarou. Academy Awards '85: Best Actor (Hurt); British Academy Awards '85: Best Actor (Hurt); Cannes Film Festival '85: Best Actor (Hurt); Independent Spirit Awards '86: Best Foreign Film; Los Angeles Film Critics Association Awards '85: Best Actor (Hurt); National Board of Review Awards '85: Best Actor (Hurt), Best Actor (Julia); Nominations: Academy Awards '85: Best Adapted Screenplay,

Best Director (Babenco), Best Picture. **VHS, LV, 8mm, Closed Caption**

A Kiss to This Land

Daniel Goldberg's *A Kiss to This Land* shows how Jewish immigrants of the 1920s and 1930s were able to build new lives in Mexico. Crammed with seldom-seen archival footage, Goldberg's documentary reveals the process of starting over with a nuts and bolts approach; all the interviewees are wonderfully eloquent and candid about their experiences. ***AKA:*** Un Beso a Esta Tierra.

1994 93m/C *MX* ***D:*** Daniel Goldberg.

The Krays

We were glutted with gangster movies in the fall of 1990, a fact of life certain to affect the reception of a film like *The Krays,* starring Gary and Martin Kemp of Spandau Ballet fame. The Kray Twins owned a succession of nightclubs in the '60s. They made it their business to be seen and photographed with the right people, some of whom ironically appear in this film. Portions of a 1963 British film called *Sparrows Can't Sing* were filmed at one of their clubs and the Krays mingled with the cast at the opening night party. But, as Ronald Kray's character aptly points out in this film, "Glamour is fear." London's East End certainly had abundant reasons to fear the Krays. When they weren't hanging out with Judy Garland and other international celebrities, the Krays were brutal homicidal thugs. They thought nothing of sustaining their empire through murder and did so on several occasions, some of which are horrifyingly reenacted in their movie biography. In contrast, the rest of their lives were painfully ordinary. Both were devoted to their mother, Violet, who obligingly served them tea and biscuits as they plotted their assorted gangland strategies. Ronald's private life was filled with a succession of attractive young boys while Reginald doggedly pursued a young woman named Frances Shea (renamed Dawson in the film). It is the film's perspective on Frances that sets *The Krays* apart from most other gangster films. Frances descended into madness and suicidal despair after she married Reginald Kray. Her freedom of mobility began and ended with their relationship, and no material benefits could compensate for the terror she experienced when her life was no longer her own. The cliche, that women are attracted to and blinded by money and power, is shattered by Philip Ridley's sharply observed account of Frances Kray. Billie Whitelaw does a superb turn as Violet Kray and the Kemp brothers are quite good as the twins. Show business veteran Jimmy Jewel (1909–93) has fun with a grandfather role and even gets a chance to perform "Balling the Jack." Kate Hardie does a touchingly sensitive job as Frances, and Tom Bell is slimily venal as always as a vicious but gutless hood. Victor Spinetti and Barbara Ferris, one-time show business acquaintances of the twins, have one good sequence as Frances' parents. Peter Medak, who was an assistant director on *Sparrows Can't Sing,* knew the Kray twins in the heady early '60s, long before their criminal careers crashed to a halt. (Ronald died at 61 in 1995). Because of Medak's exceptional feeling for the period and for his subjects, *The Krays* may be the sort of film that will linger in your mind weeks and months after you've seen it.

1990 (R) 119m/C *GB* Gary Kemp, Martin Kemp, Billie Whitelaw, Steven Berkoff, Susan Fleetwood, Charlotte Cornwell, Jimmy Jewel, Avis Bunnage, Kate Hardie, Alfred Lynch, Tom Bell, Steven Berkoff, Victor Spinetti, Barbara Ferris, Julia Migenes-Johnson, John McEnery, Sadie Frost, Norman Rossington, Murray Melvin; ***D:*** Peter Medak; ***W:*** Philip Ridley; ***C:*** Alex Thomson; ***M:*** Michael Kamen. **VHS, LV, 8mm, Letterbox, Closed Caption**

Kurt and Courtney

Nick Broomfield has a lot of nerve calling *Kurt and Courtney* a documentary. Without a budget, however small, he would be standing on a street corner, telling all and sundry the "conspiracy" theories even he doesn't believe about the "murder" of Nir-

Jeanne (Isabelle Huppert) and Sophie (Sandrine Bonnaire) in *La Ceremonie.* New Yorker Films; courtesy of the Kobal Collection

vana's Kurt Cobain (1967–94). What "evidence" does Broomfield offer to support the notion of a murder conspiracy? One private eye. One alcoholic who died after staggering into a train. Oh, and Hank Harrison, Courtney Love's father, who no longer sees her for obvious reasons. After this "primary source material," there are "character witnesses" like Cobain's best friend and one of Love's old boyfriends. Then Broomfield crashes the stage of the ACLU awards to demand an explanation from Love about why she harasses reporters before security people give him the hook. All of this was watched enthusiastically by a Roxie Cinema crowd of Kurt Cobain fans who dislike Courtney Love because she's alive, thriving, and still famous. Love's lawyers yanked *Kurt and Courtney* from the Sundance Film Festival because of Broomfield's unauthorized use of Nirvana music. There was still some legal squabbling about the film's content at the time of the Roxie engagement, but eventually Courtney's "people" left the film alone to live and die on its own terms. The one credible participant here is Cobain's Aunt Mari Earl, who talks fondly about her talented nephew and plays some of little Kurt's very early recordings. It's a small but real comfort to know that he had a few moments of happiness before the rot of fame, drugs, and a gun shot ended his short life.

1998 (R) 100m/C *GB* Courtney Love, Kurt Cobain; ***D:*** Nick Broomfield; ***C:*** Joan Churchill. **VHS**

La Ceremonie

Don't, whatever you do, watch *La Ceremonie* the night before the entire family cozies up to watch Mozart's *Don Giovanni* OR just before you go to bed (you'll be staring at the dark ceiling all night). *La Ceremonie* is among the select few chillers that top all the other chillers trying to do the same thing. Jacqueline Bisset is Catherine Lelievre, a nice, well-to-do lady of the house whose most difficult task is finding a decent live-in housekeeper. At last she finds a treasure named Sophie (Sandrine Bonnaire), who cooks and cleans like everybody's dream servant out of a story book. Husband Georges (Jean-Pierre Cassel) dislikes Sophie, however, but when he suggests to his wife that their new employee might be happier elsewhere, Catherine reminds him how hard it was to hire someone in the first place. So: The status quo is preserved. The Lelievre family, including the kids Miranda and Gilles, are genuinely good people. They are not by any means dysfunctional; they talk to each other and enjoy sharing their evenings together. The reserved Sophie is very much left to her own devices and her friend of choice is Jeanne (Isabelle Huppert), the nutty local postmistress. Georges dislikes Jeanne even more than Sophie and insists that she not set foot in the house as a guest. So: We have two of society's cast-offs, appreciated only for their work and not for themselves, AND a charming, civilized family, living comfortably in a beautiful home. Novelist Ruth Rendell's here and Claude Chabrol's got her, so SOMETHING'S got to give, and voila! It does. Depending on your circumstances and viewpoint, the payoff here is either the result of a mere culture clash or a case of a sympathetic Society accommodating the most psychotic denominator at the ultimate expense of—Society, of course! In any event, the splendid acting and Chabrol's expert command of the material will have you gnawing on your fingernails all movie long. Based on Rendell's 1977 novel *A Judgment in Stone.* Cast Note: Bisset and Cassel also co-star in 1978's delightful *Who Is Killing the Great Chefs of Europe?* Save that one for another evening in another mood. ***AKA:*** A Judgment in Stone. 🦴🦴🦴

1995 109m/C *FR GE* Sandrine Bonnaire, Isabelle Huppert, Jacqueline Bisset, Jean-Pierre Cassel, Virginie Ledoyen, Valentine Merlet, Julien Rochefort, Dominique Frot, Jean-Francois Perrier; ***D:*** Claude Chabrol; ***W:*** Claude Chabrol, Caroline Eliacheff; ***C:*** Bernard Zitzermann; ***M:*** Matthieu Chabrol. Cesar Awards '96: Best Actress (Huppert); Los Angeles Film Critics Association Awards '96: Best Foreign Film; National Society of Film Critics Awards '96: Best Foreign Film; Nominations: Cesar Awards '96: Best Actress (Bonnaire), Best Director (Chabrol), Best Film, Best Supporting Actor (Cassel), Best Supporting Actress (Bisset), Best Writing. **VHS**

La Femme Nikita

For the record, Anne Parillaud IS *La Femme Nikita* in a well-made, solidly constructed French thriller that also features the legendary Jeanne Moreau. So leave it to Hollywood to co-opt, distort, and screw up a huge international hit. Question: What is the difference between the 1990 indie *La Femme Nikita* and the 1993 Warner Bros. release *Point of No Return*? Answer: *Point of No Return* is in English. I'm trying to imagine the extent of director John Badham's professional pride, although I suppose at his shameless level it must be easy to face himself in the mirror since he was paid a whopping salary for plagiarizing Luc Besson's directing style. I'm not kidding; *Point of No Return* not only has the same directorial slant and dialogue PLUS near-identical reconstruction of all the original sequences, but it ALSO has the same damn camera angles on many of the shots. After all the time that John Ritter and the late Michael Landon spent shoving the "Where there's a will, there's an A" philosophy down everyone's throats, you'd think there'd be a better way to spend zillions of dollars than redoing French movies because Americans can't read subtitles. The whole point of the re-make seems to be that if a dame puts on a little lipstick and fluffs up her hair, she has most of what she needs as the ideal professional assassin. But of course, all those cosmetics also supply her with a conscience, so U.S. audiences are treated to dilemmas on the order of "Oh gee whiz, should I shoot that guy or go to bed with my boyfriend?" Apparently 1993 audiences were expected to respond in droves to that burning ethical quandary, because Warner Bros. wanted *Point of No Return* to be an even huger international hit than the superior French flick. Bridget Fonda, Gabriel Byrne, Dermot Mulroney, Miguel Ferrer, and Anne Bancroft round out the cast of Badham's overproduced photocopy. There are SOME differences between *La Femme Nikita* and the re-make. You see, Nikita and her boyfriend went to Venice on holiday, while Fonda and

The year is 1962. The place is Willow-point Falls. Nobody talks about what happened in the school cloakroom 10 years ago. Now, in the dead of night, Frankie Scarlatti is going to find out why.

—Tagline from the movie *The Lady in White*.

Mulroney went to New Orleans; and the fistfights and gunshots sounded real in the original, while Hollywood SFX cranked them up to drown out nuclear explosions; and Fonda listened to Nina Simone and Nikita didn't and...on Monday, January 13, 1997, *La Femme Nikita* (with 26-year-old Australian Peta Wilson making her television debut) became a weekly series on the USA cable network. On the small screen, in a fundamental corruption of Luc Besson's enigmatic character, Nikita was not a killer, but a wronged woman, and an innocent! The original Nikita created by Besson was AMORAL to the core; in John Badham's photocopy, her amorality is muted. In the USA variation, it's nonexistent. See *The Third Man* for the sweetening of Harry Lime, transformed from a big-screen bad guy to a small-screen hero! ☠☠☠

1991 (R) 117m/C *FR* Anne Parillaud, Jean-Hugues Anglade, Tcheky Karyo, Jeanne Moreau, Jean Reno, Jean Bouise; ***D:*** Luc Besson; ***W:*** Luc Besson; ***C:*** Thierry Arbogast; ***M:*** Eric Serra. Cesar Awards '91: Best Actress (Parillaud). **VHS**

Lacombe, Lucien

In this 1974 film by Louis Malle, we are presented with an unlikely object of audience sympathy. Lucien (Pierre Blaise) smashes little birds with slingshots, finks on the village schoolmaster who's a member of the French resistance, and forces himself on his Jewish girlfriend immediately after her father has been picked up by the Nazis. Through it all, newcomer Blaise gives an accurate performance as the detached, dispassionate, even dumb farmboy-turned-German cop, except when he repeatedly narrows his eyes just like the bad guys in old Hollywood movies. It's a tricky topic for a 130-minute picture, especially one as leisurely paced as this one. Malle de-emphasizes Lucien's every action. Even when Lucien helps his girl and her granny flee from the Nazis, Malle gives him a plausible motivation: the arresting officer has just ripped off Lucien's stolen watch. Naturally, Lucien has a characteristic plan to get it back, and, only incidentally, get his friends off the hook. Because of Lucien's predictability, there are few genuine surprises in the film, but one of the best plot strands shows the relationship Lucien develops with his tailor (Holger Lowenadler) and his daughter (Aurore Clement). Grudgingly, and for individual reasons, the three learn to accept or, at least, get used to one another as human beings, despite considerable underlying tension. Lucien has the choice of turning them in or not, the girl can use Lucien to get her to Spain and, sadly, the tailor comes to realize that his family's safety depends entirely on his daughter's acceptance of Lucien's attentions. Clement does a graceful, touching job as the girl, and Lowenadler's portrait of the tailor is a perfect blend of restrained anger and opportunistic dignity. Stunningly photographed by Tonino Delli Colli, *Lacombe, Lucien* is an absorbing movie on many levels. (Cast Note: Pierre Blaise died at 24, the year after *Lacombe, Lucien* was released; Aurore Clement later starred in 1983's *Paris, Texas* for Wim Wenders.) ☠☠☠

1974 130m/C *FR* Pierre Blaise, Aurore Clement, Holger Lowenadler, Therese Giehse; ***D:*** Louis Malle; ***W:*** Louis Malle, Patrick Modiano; ***C:*** Tonino Delli Colli; ***M:*** Django Reinhardt, Andre Claveau.

The Lady Confesses

Yes, Hugh Beaumont did have an acting career long before he became Ward Cleaver, but you can't see him in a movie in a revival theatre without hearing a near-deafening buzz: "Oh-my-God! That's-Beaver's-father!" *The Lady Confesses* is fun because Beaumont's wholesome appeal has a sinister twist here. And Mary Beth Hughes IS front and center all the way through, trying to solve the mystery. You may remember Edmund MacDonald and Claudia Drake from the cast of *Detour.* Cheap-cheap-cheap, but never dull. ☠☠

1945 66m/B Mary Beth Hughes, Hugh Beaumont, Edmund MacDonald, Claudia Drake, Emmett Vogan, Barbara Slater, Edward Howard, Dewey Robinson, Carol Andrews; ***D:*** Sam Newfield; ***W:*** Helen Martin, Irwin H. Franklyn; ***C:*** Jack Greenhalgh; ***M:*** Lee Zahler. **VHS**

The Lady in White

Writer/director Frank LaLoggia clearly spent a great deal of time and care to make his movie exactly the way he wanted it: *Lady in White* is a lovely, gentle film that really understands childhood terrors on their own terms. Lukas Haas, whose large brown eyes were so memorable in 1986's *Witness,* plays 10-year-old writer Frank Scarlatti. Frankie's vivid imagination scares his classmates when he reads *The Beast that Destroyed London* to them on Halloween Day, 1962. Two of them, Donald and Louie, decide to scare Frankie by locking him in the school cloakroom overnight. While there, Frankie has intense nightmares about his dead mother and wakes up to watch the re-enactment of the 1951 murder of Melissa, a beautiful little red-haired ghost, by her invisible slayer. She asks for Frankie's help, but then he is nearly strangled by the same child-killer who murdered Melissa. Frankie is shown astrally projecting, and, in a beautifully photographed sequence, agreeing to help Melissa. When LaLoggia sticks with Frankie, he never makes a false step. There are suggestions that he may not have had faith in his basic material. He wants to make a social statement about civil rights, too. He also strains to pump comedy and nostalgia into the proceedings by making buffoons of Frankie's elderly grandparents and by oversweetening some of the family scenes. None of these strategies is particularly effective or necessary. Frankie's nightmares, his meetings with Melissa, his search for her mother, and his discovery of the killer are quite chilling enough for any horror movie. Instead of padding the plot with extranea, time could either have been shaved or better spent exploring the personality of the killer, since his identity is no surprise. Eerie use is made of the 1933 Bing Crosby hit, "Did You Ever See a Dream Walking?," but if that were the killer's favorite song, Frankie would have known who he was right away, not after 92 minutes. The acting by Lukas Haas as Frankie, Jason Presson as his brother Gene, Joelle Jacob as the haunting Melissa, and by Len Cariou, Alex Rocco, and Katherine Helmond as the grown-ups is sensitive and convincing. LaLoggia and his cousin raised the production money from 4000 investors in upstate New York where this film was made. The results? Even though *Lady in White* only has a PG-13 rating, it was the first horror movie in ages that genuinely frightened me. ☙☙☙

1988 (PG-13) 92m/C Lukas Haas, Len Cariou, Alex Rocco, Katherine Helmond, Jason Presson, Renata Vanni, Angelo Bertolini, Jared Rushton, Joelle Jacob; ***D:*** Frank LaLoggia; ***W:*** Frank LaLoggia; ***C:*** Russell Carpenter; ***M:*** Frank LaLoggia. **VHS, LV, Letterbox, Closed Caption, DVD**

The Lady Vanishes

The Lady Vanishes was Alfred Hitchcock's ticket to Hollywood. When I got a Eurailpass in 1975 and took Amtrak cross-country in 1977, I was disappointed that I didn't meet any cool passengers like Iris Henderson (Margaret Lockwood) or Gilbert Redman (Michael Redgrave) or Charters and Caldicott (Basil Radford and Naunton Wayne) or a high-heeled nun (Catherine Lacey) or Miss Froy (May Whitty). *The Lady Vanishes* revealed how a variety of personalities react to international conflict. The pacifist played by Cecil Parker is portrayed as a pompous fool, a not-so-subtle indication of the British mood 12 months before the invasion of Poland. As for production values, Hitchcock didn't even try to conceal the fact that he was saving shillings by using a miniature train for exteriors. (A lifelong penny pincher, Hitchcock continued to use painted sets and rear-screen projection throughout his long career.) Nor was he unduly concerned by the fact that a frail old lady with a tune in her head was the ONLY one who could save the day. As it turned out, international audiences didn't mind, either. They loved the wit, style, and speed of *The Lady Vanishes,* and especially the veddy British Charters and Caldicott (Radford and Wayne made 10 films as a team throughout the 1940s). The lovely and talented Margaret Lockwood received an invi-

"I've been every-where and done everything —what's left for me except marriage."

—Iris Henderson (Margaret Lockwood) resigns herself in *The Lady Vanishes.*

tation to Hollywood, but, after playing third fiddle to Shirley Temple and Randolph Scott in 1939's *Susannah of the Mounties,* she made a fast trip back; Lockwood became Great Britain's most popular female star. Americans wanted every British import to be as great as *The Lady Vanishes.* That wasn't possible, of course, so the Hitchcock family had to come to us. Hitchcock's cameo occurs in a London train station. Kathleen Tremaine plays Miss Froy's impostor. Googie Withers (who isn't on the train) was in 1996's *Shine* along with Redgrave's daughter, Lynn.

1938 99m/B *GB* Margaret Lockwood, Paul Lukas, Michael Redgrave, May Whitty, Googie Withers, Basil Radford, Naunton Wayne, Cecil Parker, Linden Travers, Catherine Lacey; ***Cameos:*** Alfred Hitchcock; ***D:*** Alfred Hitchcock; ***W:*** Sidney Gilliat, Frank Launder; ***C:*** Jack Cox; ***M:*** Louis Levy. New York Film Critics Awards '38: Best Director (Hitchcock). **VHS, LV, DVD**

Ladybird, Ladybird

Poor Cow is a British flick that I've always wanted to see, but have never been able to find. It starred the late Carol White (1941–91) as Joy in the title role, and Terence Stamp, then 28, as Dave. Adapted (from Neil Dunn's novel) and directed by Kenneth Loach, 31, this 1967 drama explored the life of a woman who moved in with her incarcerated husband's best friend. The sympathetic concern that Loach showed for the poor cow of the late 1960s is now focused on single mother of four-going-on-five, Maggie Conlan (Crissy Rock in a fact-based character). The not-so-hidden-agenda of the film is to show how the Social Service System in Great Britain harms rather than helps the people it seeks to benefit (this was also D.W. Griffith's message to the world in 1916's *Intolerance*). Maggie has had an ugly history. The victim of childhood abuse from her Dad, she grew up to be the victim of a horrific beating from a lover. Just as things seem to be looking up for Maggie (she meets Vladimir Vega as nice Jorge Arellano from Paraguay in a bar), she gets pregnant again. Social Services people take her baby away and Immigration Services people try to kick Jorge out of the country. It all looks pretty hopeless, and then we learn what happened to the real Maggie. Because of the violence and despair of the narrative, the film sometimes seems as if it'll go on forever, even though it's only 102 minutes. Loach guides Rock through a difficult, award-winning performance, and the performances by the other cast members, especially Chilean actor Vega, are vividly rendered.

1993 (R) 102m/C *GB* Crissy Rock, Vladimir Vega, Ray Winstone, Sandie Lavelle, Mauricio Venegas, Clare Perkins, Jason Stracey, Luke Brown, Lily Farrell; ***D:*** Ken Loach; ***W:*** Rona Munro; ***C:*** Barry Ackroyd; ***M:*** George Fenton. Berlin International Film Festival '94: Best Actress (Rock); Nominations: Independent Spirit Awards '95: Best Foreign Film. **VHS**

The Ladykillers

Katie Johnson was WAY down on the cast list of most of the movies that she made, but in *The Ladykillers,* she was the star, and high time, too. She's absolutely terrific as Mrs. Wilberforce, a sweet little old lady who outwits a bunch of crooks who plan to murder her. Alec Guinness, looking his all-time seediest, was "Professor" Marcus, the leader of the gang; Cecil Parker WAS the "Major"; Herbert Lom was Louis; chubby Peter Sellers was Harry; and Danny Green was One-Round, who adores Mrs. Wilberforce on sight. They all pretend to be members of a string quintet so they can hole up in her place while figuring out what to do with the loot from a bank heist. The contrast between darling Mrs. Wilberforce and these thugs is hilarious, particularly as they try to fit into her genteel world with catastrophic results. Ealing at its all-time zenith! ***AKA:*** The Lady Killers.

1955 87m/C *GB* Alec Guinness, Cecil Parker, Katie Johnson, Herbert Lom, Peter Sellers, Danny Green, Jack Warner, Kenneth Connor, Edie Martin, Jack Melford; ***D:*** Alexander MacKendrick; ***W:*** William Rose; ***C:*** Otto Heller; ***M:*** Tristram Cary. British Academy Awards '55: Best Actress (Johnson), Best Screenplay. **VHS**

Lair of the White Worm

Ken Russell's *Lair of the White Worm* just may be the only film you'll ever see in which an archaeologist in kilts wards off a vampire cop by playing the bagpipes. It also functions as a cautionary tale to Boy Scouts who may be tempted to accept a lift from a ravishing lady vampire in a Jaguar. And, like Hillaire Belloc, Victorian author of such Cautionary Verses as *Jim, Who Ran Away from His Nurse, and Was Eaten by a Lion* and *Matilda, Who Told Lies, and Was Burned to Death,* Russell adapted a little-known Bram Stoker work with tongue in cheek and both eyes and ears receptive to humor. There are more groan jokes about sex in the script than there is sex, and there are, of course, the obligatory British digs at Class, the Police, and Hospitals. Fetching Amanda Donohoe portrays evil vampire Lady Sylvia Marsh, who kidnaps first the Trent parents and then their innkeeper daughters, Eve and Mary (Catherine Oxenberg and Sammi Davis). Will Lord James (Hugh Grant) and Angus Flint (Peter Capaldi) reach the girls in time? We can at least rest assured that, along the way, Russell will use every item in his usual bag of tricks. The acting from all four leads is funny and sincere, and Oxenberg, traditionally cast as princesses-in-waiting, is quite good as a working class damsel-in-distress. Too silly to be scary and an eyelash too smug to be entirely clever, *Lair of the White Worm* will nonetheless please horror fans too young to remember the early serials to which Russell owes his greatest debt. 🦴🦴🦴

1988 (R) 93m/C *GB* Amanda Donohoe, Sammi Davis, Catherine Oxenberg, Hugh Grant, Peter Capaldi, Stratford Johns, Paul Brooke, Christopher Gable; ***D:*** Ken Russell; ***W:*** Ken Russell; ***C:*** Dick Bush; ***M:*** Stanislas Syrewicz. **VHS, LV, DVD**

Lamerica

Gino (Enrico Lo Verso) and Fiore (Michele Placido) are Italian partners who dream up what they believe is a sure-fire scheme to make some money in Albania, now that its Communist system is out of power. They're not allowed to run a company because they're not Albanians, so they hustle an old man (Carmelo Di Mazzarelli as Spiro) to be the figurehead of a bogus shoe factory. Spiro is a longtime political prisoner, so he has no desire to remain in Albania an instant longer than necessary after his release, and he makes a quick escape to Italy with Gino in hot pursuit. The apolitical Gino, who only wants to make a quick buck with Fiore, is forced to learn more about political survival than he had planned when he finally catches up with Spiro. This film by Gianni Amelio *(Open Doors, Stolen Children)* won an Academy Award nomination as 1995's Best Foreign-Language Film, as well as an Independent Spirit Award nomination. 🦴🦴🦴

1995 120m/C *IT* Enrico Lo Verso, Michele Placido, Carmelo Di Mazzarelli, Piro Milkani; ***D:*** Gianni Amelio; ***W:*** Gianni Amelio, Andrea Porporati, Alessandro Sermoneta; ***C:*** Luca Bigazzi; ***M:*** Franco Piersanti. Nominations: Academy Award '95: Best Foreign-Language Film; Independent Spirit Awards '97: Best Foreign Film. **VHS, Letterbox**

L'Amour en Herbe

L'Amour en Herbe is wonderfully written and directed by Roger Andrieux. Andrieux coaxes terrific performances out of an inexperienced cast, including Pascal Meynier and Guilhaine Dubos as Marc and Martine, a 16-year-old boy and 17-year-old girl who fall in love. The simple love story emphasizes the more complicated background against which it develops: are lovestruck children the only ones who never make concessions to life? In one disturbing sequence, Andrieux focuses on a personal/professional conflict faced by Marc's adored older brother (Bruno Raffaelli). The choice he makes stuns and disillusions Marc, a reality that changes forever the lives of the innocent young lovers. Andrieux next directed 1980's *La Petite Sirene/The Little Mermaid.* ***AKA:*** Budding Love; Tender Love. 🦴🦴🦴

1977 100m/C *FR* Pascal Meynier, Guilhaine Dubos, Michel Galabru, Francoise Prevost, Alix Mahieux; ***D:*** Roger Andrieux; ***W:*** Roger Andrieux, Jean-Marie Benard; ***C:*** Ramon Suarez; ***M:*** Maxime Le Forestier. **VHS**

"She ain't pregnant, she's just fat."

—Big Joe (Burt Young) tries to deny his daughter's (Ricki Lake) delicate condition in *Last Exit to Brooklyn.*

Lancelot of the Lake

Lancelot of the Lake was a smash hit at the Cannes Film Festival; I wonder why. It's such a bloody, boring picture with little to recommend it besides Pasqualino De Santis' immaculate cinematography (unless you get some sort of a kick out of frozen acting styles and blood flowing out of helmets at a rapid clip). Robert Bresson's re-working of the Camelot mythology includes the search for the Holy Grail (hmmm...was 1975's funnier but equally bloody *Monty Python and the Holy Grail* a SATIRE of this movie?), Lancelot's romance with Guinivere, and the ill-fated joust that brought an end to the legendary Round Table. ***AKA:*** Lancelot du Lac; The Grail; Le Graal. 🦴

1974 85m/C *FR* Luc Simon, Laura Duke Condominas, Vladimir Antolek-Oresek, Humbert Balsan, Patrick Bernard, Arthur De Montalembert; ***D:*** Robert Bresson; ***W:*** Robert Bresson; ***C:*** Pasqualino De Santis; ***M:*** Philippe Sarde. **VHS**

The Land That Time Forgot

The Land that Time Forgot is inspired by one of Edgar Rice Burroughs' non-Tarzan books. Starring the late Doug McClure (1935–95) as Bowen Tyler, it deals with the age-old story of a crew of men (plus Susan Penhaligon as a character named Lisa Clayton thrown in for good measure) who accidentally stumble on a mysterious territory, jam-packed with cave men and prehistoric beasts. It's basically a pretty good flick, but the dinosaurs, ship models, and special effects ALL look fake. And why does someone always have to be carried away by that prehistoric predecessor of the vaudevillian hook, the pterodactyl? John McEnery gives dignity to his role as the German Captain Van Schoenvorts and Bobby Parr looks less ridiculous than most actors who wind up playing cavemen named Ahm. 🦴🦴🦴

1975 (PG) 90m/C *GB* Doug McClure, John McEnery, Susan Penhaligon, Keith Barren, Anthony Ainley, Godfrey James, Bobby Parr, Declan Mulholland, Colin Farrell, Ben Howard, Roy Holder, Andrew McCulloch, Ron Pember, Steve James; ***D:*** Kevin Connor; ***W:*** James Cawthorn, Michael Moorcock; ***C:*** Alan Hume; ***M:*** Douglas Gamley. **VHS**

The Last Days of the Last Tsar

There was no time to grieve for the last of the Romanovs after Nicholas II, Alexandra, and their five children were massacred at Ekaterinburg in 1918. The Soviet Union, then in its infancy, did not permit such a threatening luxury. Yet the sense of loss must have been intense to endure through nearly 75 years of repression. When the collapse of the Soviet Union made it safe to express such emotions, the Russian people recalled the Romanovs with affection and nostalgia. Director Anatoli Ivanov captures the sadness of the final rituals of the doomed Romanovs in his 1992 film, *The Last Days of the Last Tsar.* Ivanov blends archival footage with some of the most skillful re-enactments I've ever seen. In many cases, the look and tempo of the new footage so precisely matches the original films that it is only the fact that we know certain events would never have been recorded for posterity that allows us to tell the difference between them. 1971's *Nicholas and Alexandra* gave us the chocolate box version of the Tsar's demise. Ivanov's deeply poetic account is a far more eloquent and illuminating examination of the Romanov tragedy and its aftermath. 🦴🦴🦴

1992 m/C ***D:*** Anatoli Ivanov. **VHS**

Last Exit to Brooklyn

Welcome to Hell, circa 1952. The Korean War is still going on, as we can see from the young men who depart from the nearby Navy yards. Closer to home, a factory strike has been going on for six months, with no end in sight. Harry Black (Stephen Lang) has been stealing from the strike funds so that he can have an extramarital affair with his gay lover (Alexis Arquette as Georgette). Fired by his boss Boyce (Jerry Orbach), Harry's dumped by the lover, makes a pass at a kid, and is nearly beaten to death by a street gang for same. Meanwhile, Jennifer Jason Leigh, with her usual courage for taking huge artistic risks, is Tralala, a hooker who entices tricks with fat wallets into the clutches of the violent gang. But Tralala is picked up by one soldier who falls in love with her and, hoping that his wallet will belong exclusively to her, she plays his girlfriend for a few days, receiving nothing but a "My Darling Tralala" letter for her efforts. She invites a bar full of rough trade to have sex with her; at this point, the book and the movie part company, although both are so horrific you'll wind up feeling like you've been hit by a truck. Leigh, light years away from the wholesome waitress she played in 1982's *Fast Times at Ridgemont High,* is absolutely riveting as the lost Tralala. *Last Exit to Brooklyn* is tough, grim material, filmed on location by a West German film company. Director Uli Edel's other credits include *Christiane F., Body of Evidence,* and *Tyson,* and screenwriter Desmond Nakano went on to write *American Me* and *White Man's Burden.* Based on the 1964 novel by Hubert Selby Jr., who appears briefly as the driver of a car.

1990 (R) 102m/C Jennifer Jason Leigh, Burt Young, Stephen Lang, Ricki Lake, Jerry Orbach, Maia Danzinger, Stephen Baldwin, Peter Dobson, Jason Andrews, James Lorinz, Sam Rockwell, Camille Saviola, Cameron Johann, John Costelloe, Christopher Murney, Alexis Arquette; ***D:*** Uli Edel; ***W:*** Desmond Nakano; ***C:*** Stefan Czapsky, Stefan Czapsky; ***M:*** Mark Knopfler. New York Film Critics Awards '89: Best Supporting Actress (Leigh). **VHS, LV, Letterbox**

The Last of the High Kings

If anyone decides to do another homage to *The Cabinet of Dr. Caligari,* let me suggest Jared Leto for the part of Cesare the somnambulist. With those luminous blue eyes, he's sure to get viewer's pulses racing and he won't even have to pretend to be awake. As Jordan Catalano on *My So-Called Life,* he was easily the most laid-back member of the cast, but so cute that no one minded his leisurely delivery and pacing. In *The Last of the High Kings,* his low-key style as Frankie Griffin is totally eclipsed by Catherine O'Hara's dynamic performance as his Ma. Someone who isn't Irish watched this with me and, while raving about O'Hara, said he thought Ma was insane! "Nah, she's just a wild Irish rose," I kept insisting. Ma used to be an actress, but now she's concerned with raising her brood, rooting for her favorite political darlings, and yelling at "Protestant" outsiders. The stage would really be the best outlet for her extraordinary energy, but circumstances have led her to the inevitable alternative: turning her life into a melodrama. Ma overreacts; she does nothing by halves and she wastes no lavish compliments on her kids that might lead them to believe that life is easier than it is. O'Hara walks into a room and all eyes are chained to her every move; she leaves and it feels like 10 people left with her. And then there is Frankie. Should he have a Beach Party like they do in America? Should he sleep with Jane (Lorraine Pilkington) or try for something more meaningful with Romy (Emily Mortimer)? Christina Ricci appears all too briefly as Erin, an American visitor who tries to loosen Frankie up a bit. He doesn't really come to life until the last 20-odd minutes or so. Executive Producer Gabriel Byrne is actor Jack Griffin, Frankie's Da, Colm Meaney is a lusty politician, and Stephen Rea is a cab driver gabbing for a tip, even when he puts the fare to sleep. Since *The Last of the High Kings* is set in 1977, the last summer of Elvis Presley's short life, excerpts from his screen test are included in a touching wake on the Beach where the Party was meant to be. David Keating's warm, funny first feature has been re-titled *Summer Fling* for video, which doesn't suit it at all. Based on the novel by Ferdia Mac Anna. ***AKA:*** Summer Fling.

1996 (R) 103m/C *IR GB DK* Catherine O'Hara, Jared Leto, Christina Ricci, Gabriel Byrne, Stephen Rea, Colm Meaney, Lorraine Pilkington, Jason Barry, Emily Mortimer, Karl Hayden, Ciaran Fitzgerald, Darren Monks, Peter Keating, Alexandra Haughey, Renee Weldon, Amanda Shun; ***D:*** David Keating; ***W:*** David Keating, Gabriel Byrne; ***C:*** Bernd Heinl; ***M:*** Michael Convertino. **VHS, Closed Caption**

Gabriel Byrne as Jack and Jared Leto as Frankie in *The Last of the High Kings.*
Miramax; courtesy of the Kobal Collection

The Last Seduction

Suzy Amis in *Blown Away.* Anne Archer in *Patriot Games* AND *Clear and Present Danger.* Linda Hamilton in *Silent Fall.* What do all these actresses have in common? Wimpo women's parts! They're there for hugging and kissing. They wait while the HERO fights in all sorts of dangerous situations. They may even be brain surgeons! But so what? They have NO meaningful moments onscreen. And then there's Linda Fiorentino as Bridget Gregory in John Dahl's *The Last Seduction.* Now there's our kind of screen queen. Her husband (Bill Pullman?!) hits her and she runs off with their heist money. Love it! Then she runs away and has sex with this small town guy played by Peter Berg. He wants to get to know her better, she doesn't. Not unless he plays her games her way. And she plays rough. Not since *Double Indemnity*'s Phyllis Dietrichson have we seen such a remorseless manipulator. Steve Barancik's screenplay goes from strength to strength; every time you start to wonder what Bridget could possibly do after a string of dastardly deeds, she pulls off a nasty string of encores with ease. Bridget MOSTLY lays her cards upon the table. She may not let the guys in on all the details, but at least the outlines of every single one of her traps are visible to the naked eye. Linda Fiorentino is the only actress I know who's able to elicit sympathy even when we spend most of a movie convinced she's a cold-blooded killer, as in 1993's *Acting on Impulse.* But that was just a warm-up for her expert work in *The Last Seduction.* After watching movie after movie in which the good guys blow away 292 people, I can't see why 1994 audiences would have a problem with a small-scale, if full-blown villainess. And I hope Fiorentino decides to stay mean; anyone can pour coffee and whine about the hero's job, but NO ONE ever gave scenes with a plate of cookies or a can of mace such a sinister edge! ♪♪♪♪

1994 (R) 110m/C Linda Fiorentino, Peter Berg, J.T. Walsh, Bill Nunn, Bill Pullman; ***D:*** John Dahl; ***W:*** Steve Barancik; ***C:*** Jeffrey Jur; ***M:*** Joseph Vitarelli. Independent Spirit Awards '95: Best Actress (Fiorentino); New York Film Critics Awards '94: Best Actress (Fiorentino). **VHS, LV, Closed Caption**

Last Summer

Last Summer focuses on a beautifully photographed but threatening shift of circumstances: a family facing relocation. Christo Christov's style has undeniable conviction. Sometimes, he splashes his intense visions all over the screen, flecked with sharp images of passion and brutality. The elements can destroy people (as when a cow kicks an old man to death), but they can also save them (as when another man finds shelter on a river raft). *Last Summer* was a departure for Christov, who has achieved greater fame as an artist of spectacular creations. ♪♪

1974 90m/C Grigor Vachkov, Bogdan Spasov, Lili Metodieva, Dimiter Ikonomov, Vesko Zehirev; ***D:*** Christo Christov; ***W:*** Yordan Radichov; ***C:*** Tsevetan Chobanski.

Law of Desire

In Pedro Almodovar's *Law of Desire,* the great Carmen Maura invests her role as transsexual actress Tina Quintero with such extremes of fire and ice, both beautifully controlled, that you can watch nothing else when she is onscreen. The plot structure, which caves in at key points, is quite similar to Clint Eastwood's 1971 thriller *Play Misty for Me.* However, Almodovar's sexual and political concerns extend far beyond showing obsession and possession between two young men in Spain's gay community against the backdrop of a dazzling theatrical atmosphere (an earlier collaboration by Almodovar and Maura was 1985's *What Have I Done to Deserve This?*). ***AKA:*** La Ley del Deseo. ♪♪♪♪

1986 100m/C *SP* Carmen Maura, Eusebio Poncela, Antonio Banderas, Bibi Andersson, Miguel Molina, Manuela Valasco, Nacho Martinez; ***D:*** Pedro Almodovar; ***W:*** Pedro Almodovar; ***C:*** Angel Luis Fernandez. **VHS, LV**

Le Grand Chemin

France's *Le Grand Chemin/The Grand Highway* shows how the visit of a shy little boy throws the lives of a group of villagers into high relief. In revealing his all-too-human characters, writer/director Jean-Loup Hubert says something about the good and bad that is in all of us and how we must accept both in order to grow up. The acting, especially by youngsters Antoine Hubert and Vanessa Guedj, is fresh and truthful and the Britanny village, circa 1959, is beautifully photographed. ***AKA:*** The Grand Highway. ♪♪♪

1987 107m/C *FR* Anemone, Richard Bohringer, Antoine Hubert, Vanessa Guedj, Christine Pascal, Raoul Billerey, Pascale Roberts; ***D:*** Jean-Loup Hubert; ***W:*** Jean-Loup Hubert; ***C:*** Claude Lecomte; ***M:*** Georges Granier. Cesar Awards '88: Best Actor (Bohringer), Best Actress (Anemone). **VHS, LV**

Le Sexe des Étoiles

Les Sexe des Etoiles is a film without a neat wrap-up. Marianne Mercier plays a young girl who longs for the love of her transsexual father, played by Denis Merrier. After her parent's bitter split, she tries to draw him back into her lonely life (leading to moments like the one in which he is being cruised at a diner and she walks in with a cheery, "Hi, Dad!"). When she is forced to make a choice, she acknowledges for the first time the very real difference between her real "Dad" and the idolized father of her fantasies. Director Paule Baillargeon played the curator in Patricia Rozema's *I've Heard the Mermaids Singing.* ***AKA:*** The Sex of the Stars. ♪♪♪

1993 100m/C *CA* Marianne-Coquelicot Mercier, Denis Mercier, Tobie Pelletier, Sylvie Drapeau; ***D:*** Paule Baillargeon; ***W:*** Monique Proulx; ***C:*** Eric Cayla. Genie Awards '93: Best Sound. **VHS**

Leather Boys

Before he moved to America in 1966, Sidney J. Furie *(The Ipcress File)* was considered a remarkable director, and 1963's *The Leather Boys* represents some of his finest work. This thoughtful film is an interesting study of latent homosexuality clashing against the more conventional life envisioned by Rita Tushingham as a young bride named Dot. Dot is in love with a biker named Reggie (Colin Campbell) who, prior to his marriage, spent most of his time hanging out with his best friend Pete (Dudley Sutton). Domestic life quickly takes its toll on Dot and Reggie as he turns more and more to Pete to relieve the crushingly familiar routine of adult life. Dot, too, finds herself forced into playing an increasingly unattractive role in Reggie's life, basically because she doesn't know what else to do. As their relationship founders, Dot suspects that Reggie and Pete may have more in common than their passion for motorcycles. It's all very understated and bittersweet, in common with many "kitchen sink" Brit flicks of the late '50s

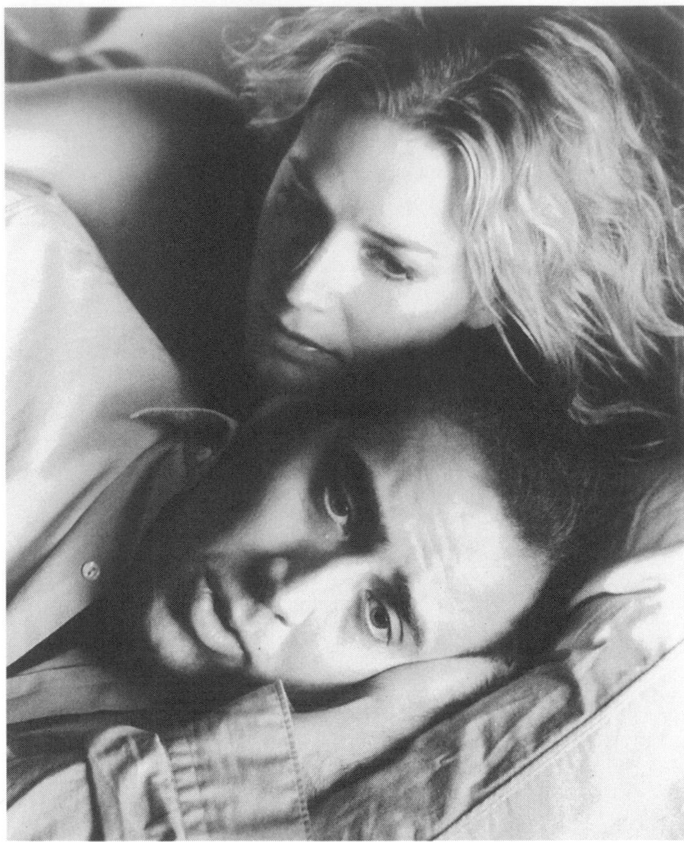

Sera (Elisabeth Shue) and Ben (Nicolas Cage) in *Leaving Las Vegas.* United Artists; courtesy of the Kobal Collection

and early '60s. Yet the superb performances and Furie's gritty approach to Gillian Freeman's sensitive screenplay give *The Leather Boys* a unique quality that resonates far beyond the obvious title and inevitable conclusion.

1963 103m/C *GB* Rita Tushingham, Dudley Sutton, Gladys Henson, Colin Campbell, Avice Landon, Lockwood West, Betty Marsden, Johnny Briggs, Geoffrey Dunn, Dandy Nichols; ***D:*** Sidney J. Furie; ***W:*** Gillian Freeman; ***C:*** Gerald Gibbs. **VHS**

Leaving Las Vegas

As Miss Jean Brodie would say, "For those who like that sort of thing, that is the sort of thing they like." Before I'd re-evaluate this downer, I'd do the following, and all on the same day: (1) take care of that root canal, (2) squirm through a tetanus shot, and (3) look up that kid from fourth grade who used to pull up his eyelids to show us what was underneath. Note: Nicolas Cage and Elisabeth Shue are the healthiest, most athletic-looking dissolutes we've seen to date. (Check out their shoulder blades.)

1995 (R) 120m/C Nicolas Cage, Elisabeth Shue, Julian Sands, Laurie Metcalf, David Brisbin, Richard Lewis, Valeria Golino, Steven Weber; ***D:*** Mike Figgis; ***W:*** Mike Figgis; ***C:*** Declan Quinn; ***M:*** Mike Figgis. Academy Awards '95: Best Actor (Cage); Golden Globe Awards '96: Best Actor—Drama (Cage); Independent Spirit Awards '96: Best Actress (Shue), Best Cinematography, Best Director (Figgis), Best Film; Los Angeles Film Critics Association Awards '95: Best Actor (Cage), Best Actress (Shue), Best Director (Figgis), Best Film; National Board of Review Awards '95: Best Actor (Cage); New York Film Critics Awards '95: Best Actor (Cage), Best Film; National Society of Film Critics Awards '95: Best Actor (Cage), Best Actress (Shue), Best Director (Figgis); Screen Actors Guild Award '95: Best Actor (Cage); Nominations: Academy Awards '95: Best Actress (Shue), Best Adapted Screenplay, Best Director (Figgis); British Academy Awards '95: Best Actor (Cage), Best Actress (Shue), Best Adapted Screenplay; Directors Guild of America Awards '95: Best Director (Figgis); Golden Globe Awards '96: Best Actress—Drama (Shue), Best Director (Figgis), Best Film—Drama; Independent Spirit Awards '96: Best Actor (Cage), Best Screenplay; Screen Actors Guild Award '95: Best Actress (Shue); Writers Guild of America '95: Best Adapted Screenplay. **VHS, LV, Closed Caption, DVD**

Legacy

The print was not a good one. At first, the movie seemed slow when it wasn't offensive and offensive when it wasn't slow. Yet gradually, this study of the crack-up of a frustrated woman of 40 proved to be a moving and affecting experience. *Legacy* was all the more remarkable in that it was virtually a four-person operation, made on an $18,000 budget and filmed in eight days. Not only did Karen Arthur and company finish the project with flair, they even reported that filmmaking under such severe limitations was altogether worthwhile and that other would-be filmmakers should go and do likewise. After making *Legacy,* Arthur went on to work fairly steadily, directing movies for television.

1975 90m/C Joan Hotchkis, Sean Allan, George McDaniel, Dixie Lee; ***D:*** Karen Arthur; ***W:*** Joan Hotchkis; ***C:*** John Bailey; ***M:*** John Kellaway. **VHS**

Legacy of the Hollywood Blacklist

Legacy of the Hollywood Blacklist, Judy Chaikin's concise, well-edited documentary, focuses on the widows and children of the men who were blacklisted half a century ago, all of whom are still coping with the pain of the past. For those interested in seeing the work of some of the blacklisted artists who had to go underground, *Salt of the Earth,* a deeply moving 1954 film of a Chicano mine workers strike, is highly recommended. 🦴🦴🦴

1987 60m/C Burt Lancaster; ***D:*** Judy Chaikin; ***W:*** Judy Chaikin, Eve Goldberg; ***C:*** Rick Rosenthal, Cathy Zheutlin, Kristin Glover; ***M:*** Michael Andreas. **VHS**

Let Him Have It

Without wallowing in nostalgia, Peter Medak attempts to understand the world in which he grew up with an admirably low-key directing style. Medak's view of post-war Britain is far from flattering, and it may be hard for Americans to understand the toll that extended rationing placed on Brits until 1954 for food and 1957 for petrol. The 1950s were not a good time for Britain, and the country lost a great deal in international prestige as the decade wore on and its inflexible leaders continued to make one error in judgment after another. *Let Him Have It* tries to re-create some of the feeling of that era by showing the tattered rituals as the strong sources of comfort they represented to a country of bewildered men, women, and children. Medak also casts striking images from the "kitchen sink" school of filmmaking like Tom Courtenay, who has never been better, as an agonized father, and the scene-stealing Murray Melvin as a school master who demands the hidden arsenal of guns that his students have brought to class, and the usually unsympathetic James Villiers as a compassionate but ineffectual barrister. *The Krays,* filmed by Medak in 1990, is a film about vicious criminals who were still alive and well (at least through 1995, when Ronnie died of natural causes at 61), if segregated from a society which no longer believed in the death penalty at the time of their crimes. The wrongful executions of Timothy Evans, Ruth Ellis, and Derek Bentley (this film's protagonist, who never killed anyone) reflected the values of an era that has long since passed, but it would be false to show that era without revealing why those values were once important. Medak clearly extends measured sympathy for people who acted out against what they saw as a dreary and changeless way of life. If only for the splendid acting, both *The Krays* and *Let Him Have It* are well worth seeing, and it is Medak's thoughtful voice as a filmmaker that gives even sharper poignance to his well-crafted studies of how Britain grudgingly entered the 20th century, well over 50 years too late. In 1998, Derek Bentley finally received a posthumous pardon 45 years after his execution. Also recommended for Britain's shifting position on the death penalty: 1971's *10 Rillington Place,* and 1985's *Dance with a Stranger.* 🦴🦴🦴🦴

1991 (R) 115m/C *GB* Christopher Eccleston, Paul Reynolds, Tom Bell, Eileen Atkins, Clare Holman, Michael Elphick, Mark McGann, Tom Courtenay, Ronald Fraser, Michael Gough, Murray Melvin, Clive Revill, Norman Rossington, James Villiers; ***D:*** Peter Medak; ***W:*** Neal Purvis, Robert Wade; ***C:*** Oliver Stapleton. **VHS, LV**

Let's Get Lost

Let's Get Lost was nominated for an Oscar and *The Thin Blue Line* wasn't. As callous as it sounds, that may be because at least the Academy members knew who the late Chet Baker was, unlike Randall Dale Allan. Twenty minutes into Bruce Weber's sluggish study of a jazz artist in decline, my question was not "What's going to happen next?" but "Do I have to watch all this?," a fatal response to a documentary that will drag on for over two long hours. Will it keep you on the edge of your seat to observe that a man of 57 with a history of drug and alcohol abuse does not look 24 years old? It seems to come as news to Bruce Weber: "Do you know how much it hurts me to see you looking like this?" he asks the star of his film. "Well, Bruce,"

"Buongiorno, Principessa!"

—Guido (Roberto Benigni) courts his wife-to-be (and real-life wife, Nicoletta Braschi) in *Life Is Beautiful.*

Baker drawls, "I AM 57 years old." Weber started out as a fashion photographer and it's obvious from the images he chooses: See Chet looking great. See Chet looking like hell. He even "casts" young Chet Baker lookalikes in his "documentary": See what Chet would look like if...; who cares but Weber? And the rest of his documentary choices play like raw filler for the tabloids. We hear from no less than one mother, three children, one ex-wife, and three past and present girlfriends, all of whom bicker about their relationship with Chet Baker. Weber to Baker's mother: "Did he disappoint you as a son?" Vera Baker doesn't want to answer but is too polite to tell the man with the camera to buzz off. "Yes," she says finally. "But don't let's go into that." If Vera Baker won't come across with the dirt, Weber asks Baker himself about the time he was beat up and lost his teeth. Then he cuts to a girlfriend. ("Chet lied about the way that happened.") When an ex-wife tells Weber that Baker's girlfriend is evil and then asks him to cut something out, he leaves everything in, including her request. Unsurprisingly, the Baker family could no longer stand Weber by the time of the film's release. What happens in *Let's Get Lost* is that we learn more about Bruce Weber than Chet Baker. Thirty to forty minutes could be edited from this picture with no harm done, but we'd still be stuck with Weber's vision of Chet Baker as well as his one-of-a-kind insight that a great trumpet player could be a real creep. If you want to know the trumpet player, listen to Baker's Complete Pacific Jazz Live Recordings from 1953–57 and skip *Let's Get Lost.* ☙☙

1988 125m/B Chet Baker; ***D:*** Bruce Weber. Nominations: Academy Awards '88: Best Feature Documentary. **VHS**

Letters from the Park

Letters from the Park is about two shy young people who hire a clerk for the purpose of a romance by mail. The clerk falls in love with the romance and pours all his energies into the correspondence. The graceful narrative is enhanced with delicate humor and charming performances by the three leads. *Letters from the Park,* Tomas Gutierrez Alea's beautifully directed tale about love and longing, was co-scripted by its original author, Gabriel Garcia Marquez. ***AKA:*** Cartes del Parque. ☙☙☙

1988 85m/C *CU* Victor Laplace, Ivonne Lopez, Miguel Paneque; ***D:*** Tomas Gutierrez Alea; ***W:*** Gabriel Garcia Marquez, Tomas Gutierrez Alea; ***C:*** Mario Garcia Joya. **VHS**

Licensed to Kill

Filmmaker Arthur Dong was the victim of a hate crime in the 1970s. Since his assailants were all juveniles, their criminal records were sealed. Long after coming to terms with the attack, Dong wanted to understand how and why hate crimes continue to occur, from the perspective of seven murderers of gay men. Donald Aldrich, the only one of the seven on death row, murdered a 23-year-old male victim the month he turned 29. Prior to that, Aldrich had been looking for gay men he could hurt and rob. Corey Burley, sentenced to life in prison for the murder of a 29-year-old male victim, smiles broadly and talks like a stand-up comic. Without a voice track, you might think this engaging young man (he was only 21 at the time of the murder) was describing his thriving career. Sad-eyed William Cross was raped by a family friend as a child and was sentenced to 25 years in prison for killing a 51-year-old fellow resident of a Chicago hotel. Then 28, he had never recovered from the rape and didn't recall that he had stabbed his victim seven times. Raymond Childs, who also received a sentence of 25 years, was also 28 when he stabbed a well-known lawyer 27 times. Sgt. Kenneth French was 22 when he killed a woman and three men while shooting up a family restaurant. French, who had just consumed a fifth of whiskey during a screening of Clint Eastwood's *The Unforgiven* (with its saloon massacre finale), was angered by President Clinton's position about gays in the military. Personable and articulate Jay Johnson, who is gay himself, came from the proverbial good family and once wanted to enter politics. When he learned that he was HIV-positive at 23, he decided to achieve fame as a serial killer instead. He was sentenced to two life terms after killing two men, including a Minnesota state senator. And Jeffrey Swinford, the least remorseful of a generally remorseless group and the first due for release, was 22 when he murdered a young male acquaintance. He was sentenced to 20 years, but may be paroled much earlier than that. *Licensed to Kill* is a difficult picture to watch because Dong humanizes his victims by giving them a chance to tell their stories without a debate. Police video footage of an actual confession, news clips, and films of crime scenes are also included. Arthur Dong's film tells us ugly truths about America and its mass perception of gays that tend to reinforce individual acts of violence. We may not want to face these truths, but clearly Dong's searing study is long overdue.

1997 80m/C *D:* Arthur Dong; ***W:*** Arthur Dong; ***C:*** Robert Shepard; ***M:*** Miriam Cutler. Sundance Film Festival '97: Best Director (Dong), Filmmakers Trophy (Dong).

Life Is Beautiful

The surprise among 1998's Oscar nominees was to see this $6.5 million Italian import receive seven Academy Award nominations, including Best Picture, Best Actor (Roberto Benigni), Best Director (Benigni), Best Foreign Film, Best Screenplay (by Benigni and Vincenzo Cerami), Best Dramatic Score (by Nicola Piovani), and Best Editing (by Simona Paggi). *Life Is Beautiful* is a 122-minute comedy about a decidedly unbeautiful topic: the effect of the Holocaust on Guido (Benigni) and his little boy, Giosue (Giorgio Cantarini). The first half of the film is devoted to Guido's romantic pursuit of Dora (Nicoletta Braschi, Mrs. Benigni). Dora's Mama (Marisa Paredes) doesn't feel that Guido's good enough to be her son-in-law, et cetera. The film's second half is set five years later during World War II, after Guido and Dora have married and become the parents of little Giosue. Guido and Giosue are sent to a concentration camp; Dora hopes to remain with her family, but is sent to another camp. In order to elevate Giosue's spirits and his own, Guido does his best to make their life in camp seem like one big game. If you've done any reading about Holocaust atrocities (e.g. *Anne Frank,* Melissa Muller's masterful 1998 biography), it's very hard to accept Benigni's concept and the accompanying lightness of tone, even for the sake of little Giosue. NOT for all tastes, including mine, frankly; if *Stalag 17* led to *Hogan's Heroes,* how will *La Vita E Bella* be corrupted for mass consumption in the 21st century? Another question for further discussion: After the reception of this film, will Jerry Lewis' *The Day the Clown Cried,* deemed unreleasable since 1971 because of the controversial treatment of ITS Holocaust theme, ever see the light of day? As 1998's Academy Award competition heated up, *Globe* and *People* ran stories about the actual Bergen-Belsen experiences of Benigni's father, Luigi, that inspired *Life Is Beautiful.* Yet Luigi Benigni was unable to turn concentration camp life into a game while he was in one. It was only after he was free that Luigi was able to come to terms with the horrors of the war with the aid of humor. Clearly, *Life Is Beautiful* has struck a nerve with audiences in no small part because it shows the triumph of the human spirit over the unimaginable suffering endured by victims of the Holocaust. It is clearly a dream in which many people want to believe. In this lifetime, I simply can't. ***AKA:*** La Vita E Bella.

1998 (PG-13) 122m/C *IT* Roberto Benigni, Nicoletta Braschi, Giustino Durano, Sergio Bustric, Horst Buchholz, Marisa Paredes, Giorgio Cantarini; ***D:*** Roberto Benigni; ***W:*** Vincenzo Cerami, Roberto Benigni; ***C:*** Tonino Delli Colli; ***M:*** Nicola Piovani. Academy Awards '98: Best Actor (Benigni), Best Foreign Film, Best Original Dramatic Score; Cannes Film Festival '98: Grand Jury Prize; Cesar Awards '99: Best Foreign Film; Screen Actors Guild Award '98: Best Actor (Benigni); Broadcast Film Critics Association Awards '98: Best Foreign Film; Nominations: Academy Awards '98: Best Director (Benigni), Best Film Editing, Best Original Screenplay, Best Picture; British Academy Awards '98: Best Actor (Benigni), Best Foreign Film, Best Original Screenplay; Directors Guild of America Awards '98: Best Director (Benigni); Screen Actors Guild Award '98: Cast. **VHS**

"The simple plan is, no one in this room is going to have sex with anyone else in this room. We'll be platonic... like our parents."

—Vivian (Eszter Balint) in *The Linguini Incident.*

Life Is Cheap... But Toilet Paper Is Expensive

Wayne Wang appears to be an artist struggling for his own voice in his fifth effort, *Life Is Cheap...But Toilet Paper Is Expensive.* Like Pedro Almodovar, director of *Tie Me Up! Tie Me Down!,* Wang is using an inferior product to battle a censorship issue. It's hard to render much enthusiasm for a movie when its denouement consists of a wisecrack delivered while the protagonist is eating a pile of manure. Earlier in the film, Wang shows a man on a toilet, complete with sound effects. There is also an eight-minute long chase with no real resolution and with the chasee often chasing the chaser. Accident or design? Hard to tell, since Wang, in a six-item statement then released to the press, admitted that he went with a crew to Hong Kong "with no particular perspective or commercial interest in mind." Wang combines documentary footage of ducks being slaughtered for market with a next-to-nothing plot involving the delivery of a suitcase filled with junk. The cast consists of actors with variable abilities. Executive producer John K. Chan impersonates an anthropologist, but not as well as Bonnie Ngai portrays his unwilling bride. Mr. and Mrs. Kai-Bong Chau, complete with the punk coats and car which attracted the attention of Robin Leach and *Lifestyles of the Rich and Famous,* appear as themselves. Character actor Victor Wong is great as always, but why is he in this movie? Well, Wayne Wang "wanted to take a critical and sardonic look at...contemporary Hong Kong society," so he assembled a screenplay with his director of photography, Amir M. Mokri (who shoots better than he writes). The resulting 89 minutes gave him "a better understanding of the world" although bewildered audiences may have some trouble with that. *Life Is Cheap* did not receive a rating when it was released theatrically, so the director identified it as an "A" picture: for Adults. Wang insists that the project is neither the "technical drill" IT appears to be nor the "business venture" HE appears to be trying to hype with a ratings issue. Wayne's GOOD films include *Chan Is Missing, Dim Sum: A Little Bit of Heart, Eat a Bowl of Tea,* and *The Joy Luck Club.* As for this butt-wiper wannabe, is it cutting edge art or is it pretentious trash? You decide!!! **woof!**

1990 89m/C Victor Wong, John K. Chan, Bonnie Ngai, Kai-Bong Chau; ***D:*** Wayne Wang; ***W:*** Wayne Wang, Amir M. Mokri; ***C:*** Amir M. Mokri.

Lightning Jack

Watching *Lightning Jack* is like spending an hour and a half with a well-meaning but boring uncle who thinks he's cute and clever and funny and demands every conceivable chance to prove all three. At a social gathering, you'd be sitting there with a smile chained to your face, waiting for someone, anyone, to change his needle. But no one has that excuse at the neighborhood bijou, which made the $5.5 million dollars *Lightning Jack* raked in at the boxoffice in its opening week rather a mystery. It's the story of an Australian outlaw and his mute sidekick, played by Paul Hogan and 1996 Oscar winner Cuba Gooding Jr. Their interaction with outsiders is minimal, which means audiences get to sit through one sequence after another in which Lightning Jack explains to his partner what a cool mate he is. Either you have a taste for this sort of thing or you don't. If you don't, you can look at the scenery or wait for the few short moments when Beverly D'Angelo and/or Roger Daltrey are onscreen or play "Who Is That?" with the old-time character actors in the cast (including Pat Hingle, Ben Chapman, and L.Q. Jones). Cuba Gooding Jr. does his best in a role that, as written by 1986 Oscar-nominee Hogan, plumbs the depth of bad taste. Hogan also produced *Lightning Jack* by charming the socks off 5,860 private Australian investors. Next time, they'll probably demand *Crocodile Dundee III* AND *IV* and insist that he film them in the outback. Now if someone could just convince Paul Hogan that guys over 55 don't HAVE to be so dang cute...in the meanwhile, there's always pre-sold works-for-hire like 1996's *Flipper.* **woof!**

1994 (PG-13) 93m/C Paul Hogan, Cuba Gooding Jr., Beverly D'Angelo, Kamala Dawson, Pat Hingle, Richard Riehle, Frank McRae, Roger Daltrey, L.Q. Jones, Max Cullen; ***D:*** Simon Wincer; ***W:*** Paul Hogan; ***C:*** David Eggby; ***M:*** Bruce Rowland. **VHS, LV**

Like Water for Chocolate

Like Water for Chocolate is one of Mexico's biggest hits and it did equally well here, thanks to an excellent cast, lush cinematography, and its frank exploration of sexual tensions within the family. That said, the film is not be to everyone's taste and it certainly wasn't mine, dealing as it does with every imaginable stomach disorder for many of its 126 minutes. ***AKA:*** Como Agua para Chocolate. 🦴🦴

1993 (R) 105m/C *MX* Lumi Cavazos, Marco Leonardi, Regina Torne, Mario Ivan Martinez, Ada Carrasco, Yareli Arizmendi, Caludette Maille, Pilar Aranda; ***D:*** Alfonso Arau; ***W:*** Laura Esquivel; ***C:*** Steven Bernstein; ***M:*** Leo Brower. Nominations: British Academy Awards '93: Best Foreign Film; Independent Spirit Awards '94: Best Foreign Film. **VHS, LV**

The Linguini Incident

Despite lackluster returns at the boxoffice, *The Linguini Incident* is notable for several reasons. It is the first Rosanna Arquette movie I can recall in which she wears clothes in every single scene. It is also the first romantic comedy Cor David ("Oh well, there's always Bowie—HE'LL play a Martian") Bowie. *The Linguini Incident* is also an hilarious spoof of Manhattan trendsetters, best exemplified by Eszter Balint, an appealing fresh talent who plays Vivian, a guntoting underwear designer. Arquette has never been funnier or more charming as Lucy, who works nights as a waitress and auditions for radical feminist touring troupes during the day. Lucy's goal is to fill the footsteps of escape artist Harry Houdini so she can feed her collecting habit: buying Houdini memorabilia. (The late, great Viveca Lindfors has a couple of nice sequences as a memorabilia dealer named Miracle who just happens to have Mrs. Houdini's wedding ring in stock for a mere five grand.) Bowie is Monte, a new bartender at the restaurant Dali, where Lucy also works. He hits on one waitress after another, hoping to marry one of them, ostensibly to earn his green card. His mysterious involvement with Dante and Cecil, the restaurant Dali's fey owners (played by Andre Gregory and Buck Henry) isn't explained until well into the plot, but he and Lucy manage to connect in a quirky sort of way. The screenplay was written by first-time director Richard Shepard in collaboration with Oakland writer Tamar Brott, who based much of *The Linguini Incident* script on her early experiences as a New York waitress. It would be easy for a film like this to have a brittle, cynical feel, but largely because of the affection Shepard and Brott feel for each and every character, they have done a good job reinventing all the conventions they satirize and/or romanticize. Many of the restaurant details are just right, from the good-cop/bad-cop style of the Dali's owners to the enormous contrast between the lush dining room and the far from glamorous kitchen the patrons never get to see. Marlee Matlin (in her first theatrical feature since 1987's ill-fated *Walker*) has a delightful character bit as the cashier at the Dali; and Julian Lennon, Iman, and even the 1940s Warner Bros. starlet Andrea King make brief appearances as dinner patrons. A photograph of the charismatic Houdini appears, too, but anyone who has had the bad luck to see Harry in 1921's *The Man from Beyond* knows that the even more charismatic David Bowie, with one blue eye, one brown eye, and a mouthful of crooked teeth, can act rings around this dreamy icon from another time. 🦴🦴🦴

1992 (R) 99m/C Rosanna Arquette, David Bowie, Eszter Balint, Andre Gregory, Buck Henry, Viveca Lindfors, Marlee Matlin, Lewis Arquette, Andrea King; ***Cameos:*** Julian Lennon, Iman; ***D:*** Richard Shepard; ***W:*** Tamar Brott, Richard Shepard; ***C:*** Robert Yeoman; ***M:*** Thomas Newman. **VHS, LV, Closed Caption**

Lisa

Lisa is the first film I rented just because I liked the clip they were playing in the video store. (We don't recall seeing ANY other advertisements for this movie, which is a

The erotic, exotic, electrifying rock fantasy...it out-Tommys *Tommy.*

—Tagline from the movie *Lisztomania.*

1990 variation on 1965's *I Saw What You Did* theme). Karen Clark's screenplay clearly has some first-hand understanding of what it's like to be an isolated 14-year-old girl. Lisa and her best friend start out by playing casual games with the telephone. Lisa's friend, complete with obnoxious kid brother and idealized parents who let her go out on dates, soon loses interest in the games. Lisa, the daughter of an overly protective single working mother, continues playing a dangerous telephone game with a serial killer. While he stalks his victims, she stalks him with considerable skill but without a clue as to the real implications of the game. Television actresses Staci Keanan and Cheryl Ladd are convincing as Lisa and her mother and the conclusion, without a male rescuer in sight, provides a satisfying payoff to this overlooked theatrical release. 🦴🦴🦴

1990 (PG-13) 95m/C Staci Keanan, Cheryl Ladd, D.W. Moffett, Tanya Fenmore, Jeffrey Tambor, Julie Cobb; ***D:*** Gary Sherman; ***W:*** Karen Clark. **VHS, Closed Caption**

Lisztomania

Lisztomania is a movie to avoid, with a score by Rick Wakeman that would horrify Liszt. The conceit here is that Franz Liszt (Roger Daltrey) was the first pop star. If you can handle that, you won't have any trouble seeing Ringo Starr as the Pope, either. Director Ken Russell is way out of control with this tasteless schlock. He would next tackle the life of Rudolph Valentino. **woof!**

1975 (R) 106m/C *GB* Roger Daltrey, Sara Kestelman, Paul Nicholas, Fiona Lewis, Ringo Starr, Veronica Quilligan, Nell Campbell, John Justin, Andrew Reilly, Anulka Dziubinska, Rick Wakeman, Rikki Howard, Felicity Devonshire, Aubrey Morris, Kenneth Colley, Ken Parry, Otto Diamont, Murray Melvin, Andrew Faulds, Oliver Reed; ***D:*** Ken Russell; ***W:*** Ken Russell; ***C:*** Peter Suschitzsky; ***M:*** Rick Wakeman. **VHS, LV, Letterbox**

Little Dorrit, Film 1: Nobody's Fault

The Charles Dickens the 20th century prefers to remember is the man who wrote about the Ghosts of Christmas Past, Present, and Future. Dickens also wrote about the boys David and Oliver who evolved, at least on film, into nostalgic symbols of wretched childhoods whose lives were sweetened by sudden charity. Yet Dickens was also a severe critic of a 19th century society that lionized apparent success and imprisoned economic failures. *Little Dorrit* was originally published as a monthly serial between 1855 and 1857, and it might be easier on contemporary admirers to see Christine Edzard's splendid film in one- or two-hour portions. However, seeing all six hours in one day will allow you to indulge yourself in the full cumulative power of the narrative as well as the sheer beauty of Edzard's skillful interpretation. Also, the parallel structures of parts one and two, both with subtle but definite variations in points of view, provide treats best appreciated in single day viewings. You won't find any of the things which are usually so wrong with today's movies about the past in *Little Dorrit;* no garish lighting, no bright lipsticks, no synthetic fabrics. What you will find is a vivid, unsentimental look at London from another time. Forty years after he played Herbert Pocket in David Lean's *Great Expectations,* Alec Guinness is magnificent as William Dorrit, whose poverty is only made bearable by constant self-deception. It's a complex, fascinating role, and Guinness makes the most of it. Another stunning character, played by Miriam Margolyes, offers a detailed portrait of Flora, a coquette who never grew up but instead grew out (and out and out). She is reminiscent of Dora, the delicate child bride of *David Copperfield* and for good reason. Both Dora and Flora are based on Maria Beadnell, with whom Dickens fell in love as a young man. In real life, she didn't die as a beautiful girl, but married another man and became, in her own words, "fat, old, and ugly." We see Flora fluttering about and are saddened, as Dickens must have been, by the realization that such a surfeit of charm is only bearable in the very young. Also worth watching are the sharp exchanges between the late Joan Greenwood as Mrs.

Clennam and Max Wall as her wily steward Flintwich, plus the bitchy competition between Amelda Brown as Fanny Dorrit and Eleanor Bron as a banker's snobbish wife.

1988 180m/C *GB* Alec Guinness, Derek Jacobi, Cyril Cusack, Sarah Pickering, Joan Greenwood, Max Wall, Amelda Brown, Daniel Chatto, Miriam Margolyes, Bill Fraser, Roshan Seth, Michael Elphick, Eleanor Bron, Patricia Hayes, Robert Morley, Sophie Ward; ***D:*** Christine Edzard; ***W:*** Christine Edzard; ***C:*** Bruno de Keyzer; ***M:*** Giuseppe Verdi. Los Angeles Film Critics Association Awards '88: Best Film, Best Supporting Actor (Guinness); Nominations: Academy Awards '88: Best Adapted Screenplay, Best Supporting Actor (Guinness). **VHS, LV, Closed Caption**

Little Dorrit, Film 2: Little Dorrit's Story

Nineteenth century London was not quite as rosy as it appears in contemporary storybooks. Typhoid ran rampant among rich and poor alike, debtor's prisons were a fact of life, and work was often synonymous with unrelieved drudgery. And then there was something called a government bureaucracy that first engulfed and finally drained those who tried to grapple with it. In *Little Dorrit,* named 1988's picture of the year by the National Board of Review, director Christine Edzard is scrupulously faithful to Charles Dickens' critical view of the period. Both *Nobody's Fault* (AKA *Poverty*), focusing on Derek Jacobi as Arthur Clennam, and *Little Dorrit's Story* (AKA *Riches*), told from Amy Dorrit's perspective, are compulsively watchable, the cinematic equivalent of a book you can't put down. What Clennam lacks in drive and imagination, he makes up for in kindness and decency. Clennam wanders through a world of far more colorful characters than himself, but as portrayed by the innately charismatic Jacobi, his low-key demeanor constantly seems on the edge of some sort of private revolution. Interestingly, it is Amy Dorrit, even more low-key than himself, who provides the catalytic change. When Clennam looks at Little Dorrit, played by 20-year-old newcomer Sarah Pickering, she appears more delicate than glass, but Amy actually proves to be a diamond in the rough. Little Dorrit certainly doesn't see herself as frail while she resourcefully makes her own way in the world. Producers for this Dickensian epic are Richard Goodwin and John Brabourne (the late Lord Mountbatten's son-in-law), who showed us another glimpse of an eroding Empire with *A Passage to India.* It's actually possible to catch the entire epic of *Nobody's Fault* and *Little Dorrit's Story* in one day. Allow an hour for dinner and you may find that you'll spend the most memorable day of the season in another time and place, courtesy of your VCR. Despite its length, *Little Dorrit* is well worth making a special point to see. Christine Edzard and company have certainly provided me with six hours that I'll never forget.

1988 189m/C *GB* Alec Guinness, Derek Jacobi, Cyril Cusack, Sarah Pickering, Joan Greenwood, Max Wall, Amelda Brown, Daniel Chatto, Miriam Margolyes, Bill Fraser, Roshan Seth, Michael Elphick, Patricia Hayes, Robert Morley, Sophie Ward, Eleanor Bron; ***D:*** Christine Edzard; ***W:*** Christine Edzard; ***C:*** Bruno de Keyzer; ***M:*** Giuseppe Verdi. Los Angeles Film Critics Association Awards '88: Best Film, Best Supporting Actor (Guinness). **VHS, LV, Closed Caption**

The Little Girl Who Lives down the Lane

Jodie Foster could have been a film noir heroine of the '40s and '50s, but she was born too late, my darlings! Instead, we get to see her in a great movie like *The Little Girl Who Lives down the Lane,* which would never have been made prior to 1976. Jodie plays a brilliant little girl who lives alone with her equally brilliant "father" and is persistently harassed by the mean landlady Mrs. Hallet (Alexis Smith) and her creepy son (Martin Sheen). Mrs. Hallet doesn't like little girls, and her son likes them too much. Yes, Jodie knows exactly what he has in mind, but she has an idea or two up her sleeve, too. We never forget how young (13) Jodie is, but we never cease to wonder how she's become way too wise way

Frank Hallet (Martin Sheen) and Rynn (Jodie Foster) in *The Little Girl Who Lives Down the Lane.* AIP; courtesy of the Kobal Collection

too young. Her very isolation and lack of emotional protection command our sympathy, even when we witness the lengths to which she will go to keep outsiders at arm's length. She opens herself up to one person, a frail, sweet magician with a limp (the excellent Scott Jacoby) and the contrast between her childlike delight with him and her frosty regality with everyone else is a key element of her meticulously crafted character. Alexis Smith actually had DONE film noir at Warner Bros. in the '40s, but usually in the wrong roles, as idealized ingenues. In the meaty part of evil Mrs. Hallet, Smith reveals what an underappreciated actress she had been throughout her career. And Martin Sheen as the lethal, loco son? His sequences with Jodie are saturated with menace and tension. Despite the late release date, *The Little Girl Who Lives down the Lane* is vintage AIP. It'll wrap you in its own unique spell, wake you up in the middle of the night and dare you not to scream. ✂✂✂✂

1976 (PG) 90m/C *CA FR* Jodie Foster, Martin Sheen, Alexis Smith, Scott Jacoby, Mort Shuman, Dorothy Davis, Hubert Noel, Jacques Famery, Mary Morter, Judie Wildman; ***D:*** Nicolas Gessner; ***W:*** Laird Koenig, Richard Lochte; ***C:*** Rene Verzier; ***M:*** Christian Gaubert. **VHS, LV**

The Little Kidnappers

Watch Charlton Heston's 1996 Canadian re-make if you must, but the original movie is far superior. Duncan MacRae didn't have to impersonate a stern Scottish Grandaddy, he lived and breathed the role of Jim MacKenzie. Anyway, the focus rightfully belongs on the kids: Jon Whiteley, then eight, and Vincent Winter, six, deservedly won Oscars as Harry and Davy, who really want a dog, but when Grandaddy says no, they start doting on a "babby" of their very own. Director Philip Leacock showed such sensitivity and skill on the film that a bright future was predicted for him. He made a few more good films with kids *(Escapade, The*

Spanish Gardener with Whiteley, *Hand in Hand),* but after 1960, his career veered toward telefeatures, none of them particularly distinguished. Whiteley appeared in a few more films, including *Moonfleet* with Stewart Granger. Winter appeared in *The Dark Avenger* with Errol Flynn, *Time Lock* with Sean Connery, *Gorgo* with Bill Travers, and a string of Disney films: *Greyfriars Bobby, Almost Angels, The Horse Without a Head,* and *The Three Lives of Thomasina.* Bring back special Oscars for best juvenile actors, so they don't have to compete with adult stars! ***AKA:*** The Kidnappers. 🦴🦴🦴🦴

1953 95m/B *GB* Duncan MacRae, Adrienne Corri, Jon Whiteley, Vincent Winter, Jean Anderson, Theodore Bikel, Francis De Wolff, James Sutherland, John Rae, Jack Stewart, Jameson Clark, Howard Connell; ***D:*** Philip Leacock; ***W:*** Neil Paterson; ***C:*** Eric Cross.

Little Nemo: Adventures in Slumberland

Little Nemo: Adventures in Slumberland has quite a few things going for it. Ray Bradbury created the concept for Chris Columbus' screenplay and the animation effectively blends a fluid Disney-style animation with the charm of the original artwork by Winsor McCay. The thing that didn't work for me was the overpowering soundtrack. It was distracting to hear vocalists (including Melissa Manchester) blasting numbers reminiscent of Broadway show tunes when I were trying to focus on the story. The plot revolves around Little Nemo's vivid dreams, especially his valiant efforts to free the residents of Slumberland from the terrifying control of Nightmareland. Mickey Rooney is the voice of Flip the Frog, a character more mischievous than evil, even though he is responsible for most of the disasters that threaten the good guys. Rene Auberjonois plays Professor Genius, who is not much of a help to Nemo (Gabriel Damon) and his pet squirrel Icarus in a crisis. The whole thing is directed by Disney veteran William T. Hurtz. *Nemo* may be overcute for adult audiences, lacking the sly wit that makes the best of children's animation absorbing to adult viewers. (This is something that Disney himself would have made sure was the object of extensive research and development before the cameras ever rolled.) But, except for those songs and a dull teach-the-kiddies-a-lesson-in-responsible-values sub-theme, it's a painless way to pass 85 minutes and it even succeeded in giving me a nightmare or two when I got home. 🦴🦴🦴

1992 (G) 85m/C ***D:*** William T. Hurtz, Masami Hata; ***W:*** Chris Columbus, Richard Outten; ***M:*** Tom Chase, Steve Rucker; ***V:*** Gabriel Damon, Mickey Rooney, Rene Auberjonois, Daniel Mann, Laura Mooney, Bernard Erhard, William E. Martin. **VHS, LV, Letterbox**

Little Odessa

After 1992's *Reservoir Dogs,* Tim Roth could have played a killer in his sleep. As hitman Joshua Shapira, he goes back to Brighton Beach (where he grew up) to kill his next target. The situation of a killer being sheltered within an American family was previously explored in 1943's *Shadow of a Doubt,* but in that film, the Merry Widow Killer returns to a bright, glistening home in Santa Rosa, California, filled with a mostly happy, mostly loving family whose sole problem seems to be an occasional twitch of small town boredom. In *Little Odessa,* Joshua faces father Arkady (Maximilian Schell) who hates his guts, mother Irina (Vanessa Redgrave) who is close to death, and kid brother Reuben (Edward Furlong) who loves him, in spite of the fact that he knows Joshua is rotten all the way down to the bone. For his first film, James Gray, 24, has written and directed a dark, unrelieved downer. 🦴🦴🦴

1994 (R) 98m/C Tim Roth, Edward Furlong, Moira Kelly, Vanessa Redgrave, Maximilian Schell, Paul Guilfoyle, Natasha Andreichenko, David Vadim, Mina Bern, Boris McGiver, Mohammed Ghaffari, Michael Khumrov, Dmitry Preyers, David Ross, Ron Brice, Jace Kent, Marianna Lead, Gene Ruffini; ***D:*** James Gray; ***W:*** James Gray; ***C:*** Tom Richmond; ***M:*** Dana Sano. Nominations: Independent Spirit Awards '96: Best Actor (Roth), Best Cinematography, Best First Feature, Best Supporting Actress (Redgrave). **VHS, LV, Closed Caption, DVD**

The Little Prince

The Little Prince was a major disappointment in 1974, and still is, for those who

"What is essential is invisible to the eye. It's only with the heart that one can see clearly."

—The Fox (Gene Wilder) to the Pilot (Richard Kiley) in *The Little Prince.*

would like to see a decent adaptation of Antoine De Saint-Exupery's (1900–44) delicate little book. Every time the orchestra begins to play another awful song in the terrible score, you'll shudder with embarrassment. Director Stanley Donen seems to have the unerring knack for making his cast look ridiculous here. Occasionally, he permits the book's wise, gentle themes to slip into the film, but most of the time, he's far more concerned with how big and expensive he can make everything look. I have never heard one kid ask to see this one on video, but for the record: Richard Kiley is the Pilot, Steven Warner is the title character, the late Bob Fosse has his moments as the Snake, Gene Wilder steals a few more moments as the Fox, Joss Ackland is the King, Clive Revill is the Businessman, Victor Spinetti is the Historian, Graham Crowden is the General, and Donna McKechnie is Rose. Avoid this cinematic massacre and read the 1943 book instead. 🦴🦴

1974 (G) 88m/C *GB* Richard Kiley, Bob Fosse, Steven Warner, Gene Wilder, Joss Ackland, Clive Revill, Victor Spinetti, Graham Crowden, Donna McKechnie; ***D:*** Stanley Donen; ***W:*** Alan Jay Lerner; ***C:*** Christopher Challis; ***M:*** Frederick Loewe, Alan Jay Lerner. Golden Globe Awards '75: Best Score; Nominations: Academy Awards '74: Best Song ("Little Prince"), Best Original Score. **VHS, LV**

A Little Princess

The Little Princess is the most frequently televised of all the Shirley Temple vehicles made by 20th Century Fox between 1934 and 1940, and with good reason. Someone forgot to renew the film's 1939 copyright and it lapsed into the public domain in 1967. It is among the best of Temple's childhood movies with a strong storyline, great supporting cast, and the obligatory dream sequence which ensured that the Ideal Toy Corporation would market yet another Shirley doll in lavish princess costume. But the one element of the picture that strayed from Francis Hodgson Burnett's 1888 novel *Sara Crewe* was an unrealistic insistence that Sara's search for her father, reported dead in action, be given a fairy tale ending. The 1995 version of *A Little Princess* retains the fairy tale ending with a slightly more plausible twist. Even those who are sated by the Temple version will be pleasantly surprised by director Alfonso Cuaron's update. The setting has been transferred to America and the period moved up a bit in time to the First World War. Liesel Matthews, the new Sara, neither sings nor dances, but she does tell magical stories about India (beautifully interpreted by Cuaron). Eleanor Bron, also seen in 1994's *Black Beauty,* adopts an American accent to play mean schoolmistress Miss Amelia Minchin, although the script here suggests a reason for her relentless nastiness. Adorable Vanessa Lee Chester plays Sara's friend Becky this time (Chester would play *Harriet the Spy*'s best friend the following year) and all the other kids are well cast and appealingly believable. Sara's sunny personality and some colorful sight gags take the edge off grim plot turns. All in all, *A Little Princess* still has something to say to the kids who were born over a century after its creation. And think about this, parents: no singing, no dancing, and no Queen Victoria! 🦴🦴🦴🦴

1995 (G) 97m/C Liesl Matthews, Eleanor Bron, Liam Cunningham, Rusty Schwimmer, Arthur Malet, Vanessa Lee Chester, Errol Sitahal, Heather DeLoach, Taylor Fry; ***D:*** Alfonso Cuaron; ***W:*** Richard LaGravenese, Elizabeth Chandler; ***C:*** Emmanuel Lubezki; ***M:*** Patrick Doyle. Nominations: Academy Awards '95: Best Art Direction/Set Decoration, Best Cinematography. **VHS, LV, Closed Caption, DVD**

Little Shots of Happiness

Bonnie Dickenson has just enough of an onscreen personality to keep you watching her performance as the offbeat Frances in *Little Shots of Happiness.* By day, she works at a collection agency for a credit card company until 5 p.m. By night, anything goes, including massive consumption of alcohol. Frances wakes up where she wakes up, which could be just about anywhere. Still, except for one morning when she calls in sick, she's always at her desk by 9 a.m. Director/cinematographer Todd Verow came up with the story for *Lit-*

tle Shots of Happiness and apparently the actors improvised the dialogue according to Verow's outline. It isn't slow or boring, it's sporadically surprising and funny—but it needed tweaking at some point prior to release and it didn't get it. Filmed in Boston. Played at San Francisco's Indie Fest in 1997.

1997 85m/C Bonnie Dickenson, Todd Verow, Linda Ekoian, Rita Gavelis, P.J. Marino, Castalia Jason, Leanne Whitney, Bill Dwyer, Eric Sapp, Maureen Picard, Eric Romley; ***D:*** Todd Verow; ***W:*** Todd Verow; ***C:*** Todd Verow.

Living in Oblivion

Tom DiCillo's *Living in Oblivion* began life as *Scene 6, Take 1* (manically well acted by Steve Buscemi as director Nick Reve), all about the technical nightmares that occur on a low-budget film where the six-day-old milk is the most experienced member of the crew. The 17-minute segment, shown at the San Francisco International Film Festival, wound up as the first sequence in the finished film. The second sequence, interestingly, is about an egotistical, not very bright star (James LeGros as Chad Palomino), who tries to manipulate the shoot and everyone on the set to his own advantage. Watch this on a double bill with 1992's *Johnny Suede* and connect the dots: Brad Pitt starred in that first directorial effort by DiCillo, along with Catherine Keener, who's also in *Oblivion* as Chad's co-star Nicole. The third segment involves Nicole, a dwarf, and Nick's mother. *Oblivion* is a very funny flick about what it's like to make an indie, with great work by Dermot Mulroney as the cinematographer with an eye patch, and by Rica Martens as a motherly looking actress delivering sharp asides re: the mise-en-scene between takes. Rent it and laugh till you cry.

1994 (R) 92m/C Steve Buscemi, Catherine Keener, James LeGros, Dermot Mulroney, Danielle von Zerneck, Robert Wightman, Rica Martens, Hilary Gilford, Peter Dinklage, Kevin Corrigan, Matthew Grace, Michael Griffiths, Ryna Bowker, Francesca DiMauro; ***D:*** Tom DiCillo; ***W:*** Tom DiCillo; ***C:*** Frank Prinzi; ***M:*** Jim Farmer. Sundance Film Festival '95: Best Screenplay; Nominations: Independent Spirit Awards '96: Best Film, Best Screenplay, Best Supporting Actor (LeGros). **VHS, LV, Closed Caption**

Loch Ness

Loch Ness deserved an art house run instead of the world premiere on network television that it finally received. But the title suggests a monster movie, which it isn't. And Ted Danson's television-style emoting, unlike the performances of the rest of the cast, shrieks "TELEFEATURE!" Danson is Dr. Jonathan Dempsey, searching for Nessy in the Highlands with his helper Adrian Foote (James Frain). Lovely Joely Richardson is his innkeeper, Laura MacFetteridge, who gradually (very gradually) learns to appreciate Jonathan's well-hidden charms. Her delightful daughter Isabel (Kirsty Graham) likes him right away, though she's the only one in town who does. Andy MacLean (Nick Brimble) is downright jealous, because he's convinced Jonathan means to spirit Laura away from him. Ian Holm is on hand as the Water Bailiff. *Loch Ness,* which sat on John Fusco's shelf for a full decade before it was finally filmed, is ideal indie material. In its own gentle way, it shows why leaving an idyllic small town exactly the way it is might be far more important than reviving an old legend which may or may not be real. I'd love to see this on a movie screen some day.

1995 (PG) 101m/C *GB* Ted Danson, Ian Holm, Joely Richardson, Kirsty Graham, James Frain, Harris Yulin, Keith Allen, Nick Brimble; ***D:*** John Henderson; ***W:*** John Fusco; ***C:*** Clive Tickner; ***M:*** Trevor Jones. **VHS**

Lolita

I first read Vladimir Nabokov's classic novel *Lolita* late at night with a flashlight when I was way too young for it—12. At that age, the idea of any middle-aged man slobbering all over a kid was the ultimate gross-out, although I must confess that I couldn't put down the book all night long. The idea of returning to the original source material has always made me squeamish, but Stanley Kubrick's 1962 screen adaptation has been a kick to watch over and over again. In spite of

some rather unfair reviews at the time of the film's original release, James Mason IS Humbert Humbert, the ideal incarnation of elegant sleaze. In real life, Mason was a fairly down-to-earth guy, but only a few of his directors, like Kubrick and *Georgy Girl*'s Silvia Narizzano, captured his authentic self-deprecating charm. You rarely think of sensuous, brooding Mason discussing junky American cultural symbols with crushing familiarity, but as Humbert Humbert, he is obsessed not only with a seductive child but also with the cheap trappings that surround her. To get the kid, he even pursues her mother, portrayed, with her usual egoless desire for the truth, by Shelley Winters, then just 40. Winters, who had not then acquired the padding that sustained the illusion that she was many years older than she really was, nevertheless stuffs herself into a series of outfits that are several sizes too small. Even better, she is absolutely merciless at exposing the intense sexual competition at the heart of many mother-daughter relationships. The sequences in which Winters' character tries to entice Humbert wearing low-cut leopard pajamas while Lolita ignites his ardor with a sullen request for a mayonnaise-ridden sandwich are both painful and hilarious to watch. For many original audience members, Peter Sellers as Claire Quilty wrapped up the picture, and the role gave the inventive Sellers a chance to lose himself in many memorable roles-within-the-role. The movie was shot in England, providing a comfortable distance between Kubrick and the native land he lampoons so relentlessly for two and a half hours. Kubrick lets none of his fantasizing characters off the hook, not the lust-driven Humbert, not the treacherous Lolita and her unlucky Mama, and certainly not the devilish Quilty. A 1996 movie of *Lolita* with Jeremy Irons and Dominique Swain is reportedly on the shelf; see the Kubrick version first for his unforgettable vision of America as an endless succession of highways and hotel rooms. They all may promise incredible sex, but they actually lead to a far more credible nowhere. 🦴🦴🦴🦴

1962 152m/B *GB* James Mason, Shelley Winters, Peter Sellers, Sue Lyon, Gary Cockrell, Jerry Stovin, Diana Decker, Lois Maxwell, Cec Linder, Bill Greene, Shirley Douglas, Marianne Stone, Marion Mathie, James Dyrenforth, C. Denier Warren, Terence Kilburn, John Harrison; ***D:*** Stanley Kubrick; ***C:*** Oswald Morris; ***M:*** Nelson Riddle. Nominations: Academy Awards '62: Best Adapted Screenplay. **VHS, LV, Letterbox**

Lolita

I wasn't supposed to read *Lolita* when I was 12, but I did, anyway, mostly because I wasn't supposed to read *Lolita* when I was 12. It's a very troubling book for a kid that age and I felt miserable the whole time I was reading it (with a homemade *Heidi* cover to fool the Sisters of the Holy Cross at Holy Rosary Convent School). Watching Adrian Lyne's *Lolita* on a hot Sunday evening in early August, I felt drenched with waves of sadness and the waves didn't subside after the movie was over; poor little Lolita with her dolls and her braces and her long nights alone crying for her lost mother. The very middle-aged Humbert Humbert claims to love her but he has no real use for her when he isn't having sex with her, and he slaps her and tries to control her at every turn. Somehow, because he's convinced himself he's in love with her, he affects a nauseating tone of ethical purity which is all the more irritating when delivered by the plummy voice of Jeremy Irons. It's an evocative reminder of his performance as Charles Ryder in *Brideshead Revisited* when he drooled endlessly over Sebastian and Julia Flyte. But Sebastian and Julia are grown-ups and Lolita is a child. ("I really do wish she would take a bath once in a while," Vladimir Nabokov commented in the original novel.) The delusion here is that the child is the sexual aggressor even though she hasn't a clue about what her actions mean. I've actually heard guys say that if the kid wants it and the adult wants it, that's O.K., isn't it? It isn't, of course, for either of them, as Lyne's direction and Stephen Schiff's screenplay makes clear. Humbert falls into a malaise that's saturated with decay and Lolita (played with astonishing brilliance by Dominique Swain) correctly learns that sex equals power, but

Ted Danson, Kirsty Graham, and Joely Richardson in *Loch Ness.* Gramercy; courtesy of the Kobal Collection

Dominique Swain and Jeremy Irons in *Lolita.* Courtesy of the Kobal Collection

the only other things she learns are how to lie, scheme, and manipulate. The villain of the piece is meant to be Frank Langella as Clare Quilty, who's quite proud of his degeneracy, as opposed to Humbert and his non-stop torture wallow. Melanie Griffith (who used to play onscreen nymphets herself in her early teens) is Lolita's mother, who has the bad luck to imagine herself in love with Humbert. In Stanley Kubrick's 1962 interpretation of *Lolita* as a black comedy, each of the four key characters was played on a very arch note by James Mason, Sue Lyon, Peter Sellers, and Shelley Winters. Lyne's emphasis on the jugular exposes Lolita's corrupted childhood as the tragedy it really is—poor little Lolita, crying alone for her lost mother because the man in the next room is too lust-ridden to comfort her or to acknowledge his systematic destruction of her life. (The score by Ennio Morricone, available on compact disc, is outstanding.) 🦴🦴🦴

1997 (R) 137m/C Jeremy Irons, Melanie Griffith, Frank Langella, Dominique Swain, Suzanne Shepherd, Keith Reddin, Erin J. Dean; ***D:*** Adrian Lyne; ***W:*** Stephen Schiff; ***C:*** Howard Atherton; ***M:*** Ennio Morricone. **VHS**

London Kills Me

Hanif Kureishi has written some fine screenplays for director Stephen Frears, but left to his own devices, the best he can come up with is *London Kills Me,* a shapeless film about the down-and-out residents of Ladbroke Grove. Beware of movies where the synopsis and the auteur's explanation of why he had to make the movie fill up six pages of the press kit! If it ain't on the screen, fergeddit! The plot (such as it is) revolves around a street person named Clint who resolves to find a pair of shoes so he can get a job as a waiter. This 105-minute odyssey takes place among a low-life crowd from which Clint is trying to escape. Unless aristocratic cheekbones make you go weak in the knees, no one emerges as a character you can care about one way or the other. Most of the film's few laughs were for a pudgy bit player who's obsessed by Elvis Presley and when a bit player overshadows the so-called leading characters, you KNOW the script is in trouble. There's also a character who swallows prescription drugs by the handful and ingests harder drugs in an assortment of grisly ways, but I can't tell you much else about her. Jon Pertwee's son Sean plays a tiny role as a gullible German tourist along with Pippa Hinchley, who starred in a *Fergie and Andrew* movie in the fall of 1992. Roshan Seth is wasted in an ill-defined, peripheral role, and poor Gordon *(My Beautiful Laundrette)* Warnecke is seen briefly as a sort of a henchman. *London Kills Me*? No, but this movie did, all 105 minutes of it.

1991 (R) 105m/C *GB* Justin Chadwick, Steven Mackintosh, Emer McCourt, Roshan Seth, Fiona Shaw, Brad Dourif, Gordon Warnecke, Sean Pertwee, Pippa Hinchley; ***D:*** Hanif Kureishi; ***W:*** Hanif Kureishi; ***C:*** Edward Lachman. **VHS, LV, Closed Caption**

Lone Star

John Sayles is perhaps the most thoughtful and individualistic of today's independent filmmakers. He could easily cross over to make a mass audience action flick, but he never has and very likely never will, knock wood. His 1996 project, *Lone Star,* is an ambitious movie about a lot of different stuff, but the dots aren't always connected. The script has a first-draft feel that suggests those dots could easily have been connected with a few more revisions. My feeling is that the actors were ready when the script wasn't, and Sayles figured that he could compensate for the uneven screenplay with careful direction, which just kills me when I think about other meticulously crafted Sayles classics like *City of Hope* and *Passion Fish.* The fact that a full-page director's statement PLUS a diagram (to explain the 10 major characters) were actually included in the press kit says a lot. The fact that we have to watch the whole dang 137-minute movie to discover something that's been collecting dust in the sheriff's ex-wife's garage for-like-ever says even more. Considering its denouement, *Lone Star* might be a more compelling yarn if it were a comedy or a satire instead of a star-crossed romance grafted onto a murder mystery. Chris Cooper does a nice, understated job as Sheriff Sam Deeds, and Elizabeth Pena is a strong presence as Pilar, his lost love, but they're playing with a sucker deck in a no-nonsense style; both are way too smart for us to believe that THEY believe their material. Kris Kristofferson is mean Sheriff Charley Wade from the 1950s and Matthew McConaughey plays Buddy Deeds, his enigmatic replacement. Both are seen in sketchy flashbacks, remembered by marginal older characters who are then played by younger actors who don't exactly look or sound like them. (Who would, after 40 years? It really does get awfully confusing.) When we find out who killed Wade, does it matter? When we see the generational ripples created by his slaying, do they matter? And then Sayles comes up with a weird ending that only a daft critter from another planet would find acceptable; what can we say except, "Did they run out of blue pencils on location?" and "Weren't there any B.S. detectors on the payroll?" Sayles' idea, to say something about how history affects the present, isn't terrible, but how he says it in *Lone Star* is sort of a mess. You may wind up talking to yourself after watching *Lone Star:* "WHY in tarnation did he wrap it up like that? Was he bitten by a rattlesnake or what?" Who knows? Perhaps because Sayles is practically worshipped by his admirers, his *Lone Star* screenplay was nominated for an Oscar, which says more about the state of the art in 1996 than it does about the best efforts of this always intriguing artist.

1995 (R) 137m/C Chris Cooper, Matthew McConaughey, Kris Kristofferson, Elizabeth Pena, Joe Morton, Ron Canada, Clifton James, Miriam Colon, Frances McDormand; ***D:*** John Sayles; ***W:*** John Sayles; ***C:*** Stuart Dryburgh; ***M:*** Mason Daring. Independent Spirit Awards '97: Best Supporting Actress (Pena); Nominations: Academy Awards '96: Best Writing; British Academy Awards '96: Best Original Screenplay; Golden Globe Awards '97: Best Screenplay; Independent Spirit Awards '97: Best Actor (Cooper), Best Film, Best Screenplay; Writers Guild of America '96: Best Original Screenplay. **VHS, LV, Closed Caption**

Jimmy (Richard Burton) and Alison (Mary Ure) in *Look Back in Anger.*
Woodfall Films; courtesy of the Kobal Collection

The Lonely Passion of Judith Hearne

It took 33 years and producer George Harrison to bring Brian Moore's classic novel, *The Lonely Passion of Judith Hearne,* to the screen. But it was well worth the long wait. Thanks, George! This is the Catholic critique to end all Catholic critiques, and now that I've seen Maggie Smith as Judy and Bob Hoskins as Jim, I can't imagine any other actors who could have played them half as well. Marie Kean and Ian McNeice are perfect too as Judy's unbelievably seedy landlady and her repellent son. Under Jack Clayton's careful direction, Judy is not good and Jim is not bad. Peter Nelson's masterful screenplay scrutinizes many crises of conscience that Catholics still struggle to understand on a daily basis. For those who may feel that John Huston's *The Dead* is essentially a mausoleum piece, check out how Clayton and Nelson capture a living, breathing chunk of the seductive Irish Catholic culture. It may not always make sense and, yes, it is often a very lonely life, yet *The Lonely Passion of Judith Hearne* succeeds in showing how powerful its grip really is. ♪♪♪

1987 (R) 116m/C *GB* Maggie Smith, Bob Hoskins, Wendy Hiller, Marie Kean, Ian McNeice, Alan Devlin, Rudi Davies, Prunella Scales; ***D:*** Jack Clayton; ***W:*** Peter Nelson; ***C:*** Peter Hannan; ***M:*** Georges Delerue. British Academy Awards '88: Best Actress (Smith). **VHS**

The Long Good Friday

The Mirror Crack'd (set in The Coronation Year 1953) and *The Long Good Friday* (set in The Wedding of the Century Year 1981) were both released the same month that Prince Charles and Lady Diana announced their engagement to the world. I can't think of two films that better revealed the dissolution of Things Past and the destiny of Things to Come. *The Long Good Friday* focused on Brit gangster Harold Shand (Bob Hoskins), who despaired at the erosion of the Great Britain that once was, at the same time he was scrambling to make a deal with the American Mafia, represented by a tough guy named Charlie (Eddie Constantine, 1917–93). But wait. IRA bombings are destroying Harold's lifelong dream. What's a patriotic thug to do? *The Long Good Friday* is doom-laden from Reel One to its final incredible sequence featuring some of the best acting (by Hoskins) you'll ever see. At an earlier point in the story, Hoskins must slaughter a trusted colleague in spectacularly bloody fashion, AND, at the same time reveal the anguish he feels for killing a friend. No one else in 1980 could quite touch Hoskins as an actor, which makes his later work in fluff like *Sweet Liberty, Hook,* and *Super Mario Bros.* a source of anguish for this longtime admirer. Helen Mirren co-stars as Victoria, George Coulouris (1903–89) makes one of his last film appearances, and Pierce Brosnan has one of his first small roles in this classic Brit film noir (Pierce Brosnan also plays a small role in *The Mirror Crack'd,* but THAT, like Charles and Diana, is another story). Produced by George Harrison's Handmade Films. 🦴🦴🦴🦴

1980 109m/C *GB* Bob Hoskins, Helen Mirren, Dave King, Bryan Marshall, George Coulouris, Pierce Brosnan, Derek Thompson, Eddie Constantine, Brian Hall, Stephen Davies, P. H. Moriarty, Paul Freeman, Charles Cork, Paul Barber, Patti Love, Ruby Head, Dexter Fletcher, Roy Alon; ***D:*** John MacKenzie; ***W:*** Barrie Keefe; ***C:*** Phil Meheux; ***M:*** Francis Monkman. **VHS**

Longtime Companion

Longtime Companion shows how a happy, creative, close-knit group of friends are decimated by the AIDS virus throughout the '80s. First to go is John (Dermot Mulroney), then David's lover, Sean (Mark Lamos), a television writer. Bruce Davison deservedly won an Oscar nomination as David for an achingly restrained performance reflecting the real-life role that lovers continue to play all over the world. *Longtime Companion* transcends the terminal illness genre because of its funny, perceptive, timely script and because of its strong cast, including Campbell Scott as Willy, Stephan Caffrey as Fuzzy, and the luminous Mary-Louise Parker as Fuzzy's sister Liza. The most wrenching moment occurs on the beach where everyone enjoyed the sand, the sun, and the surf in the early '80s. We revisit it at decade's end with the sad knowledge that nearly everyone has died since then. There is a heartbreaking fantasy where the ghosts of the characters we have come to know and love are laughing on the beach again, while Blondie sings, "The tide is high and I'm moving on...." 🦴🦴🦴🦴

1990 (R) 100m/C Stephen Caffrey, Patrick Cassidy, Brian Cousins, Bruce Davison, John Dossett, Mark Lamos, Dermot Mulroney, Mary-Louise Parker, Michael Schoeffling, Campbell Scott, Robert Joy, Brad O'Hara; ***D:*** Norman Rene; ***W:*** Craig Lucas; ***C:*** Tony Jennelli. Golden Globe Awards '91: Best Supporting Actor (Davison); Independent Spirit Awards '91: Best Supporting Actor (Davison); New York Film Critics Awards '90: Best Supporting Actor (Davison); National Society of Film Critics Awards '90: Best Supporting Actor (Davison); Sundance Film Festival '90: Audience Award; Nominations: Academy Awards '90: Best Supporting Actor (Davison). **VHS**

Look Back in Anger

By the time *Look Back in Anger* arrived on the big screen, only three years had elapsed since its theatrical nod had created a sensation, but it seemed much longer. At age 27, John Osborne had forever changed the look and sound of British theatre, but his Angry Young Man had aged prematurely. In its own grouchy way, Osborne's hatred of the status quo seemed to echo the civilized rantings of previous generations of writers who detested anything that flourished after the Victorian era and during their own lifetimes. Richard Burton at 33 had the well-fed look of personal prosperity, which undercut the savagery of Jimmy Porter's

“The sign says ‘thank you for not smoking.’ As I *am* smoking, I don’t expect to be thanked.”

—Giles De’Ath (John Hurt) in *Love and Death on Long Island.*

rantings and ravings against The System. Kenneth Haigh, who originated the role at London’s Royal Court Theatre, had not only been a much younger Jimmy Porter at 27, but there was also an ambiguity about his sexuality that Burton doesn’t project. Why do Porter’s feelings for his wife Alison (Mary Ure) vacillate between childlike obsession and casual cruelty? Why is Cliff Lewis (Alan Bates onstage, Gary Raymond in the film) always hanging around, asserting his love for both Jimmy and Alison? And the cool Helena Charles (Helena Hughes onstage, Claire Bloom onscreen) adores Alison and despises Jimmy, who despises her just as much in return. (This doesn’t stop them from becoming sexually obsessed with each other.) The play had just these four characters plus the smallish part of Colonel Redfern played by John Welsh onstage and by Glen Byam Shaw onscreen. But in the film, old Mrs. Tanner isn’t just described by Jimmy Porter, she’s fleshed out by the formidable Edith Evans, which knocks the violent sexual tension off balance and rather dissipates the impact of Osborne’s intricately crafted games for a one-room flat. It is a good adaptation of a landmark play, instead of a great one, and a small splash in the wave of Great Britain’s “kitchen sink” flicks instead of a standard bearer, even though its brilliant theatrical director Tony Richardson stayed on to helm the picture. Burton and Bloom were more successfully teamed in 1965’s *The Spy Who Came in from the Cold* and Ure and Burton co-starred in 1968’s *Where Eagles Dare* opposite Clint Eastwood. By that point, Osborne (1929–94) was firmly entrenched in The System he never ceased to assail. Audiences who watched other actors attempt to update *Look Back in Anger* in the ’80s (Malcolm McDowell) and ’90s (Kenneth Branagh) realized how deeply its rage was rooted in the 1956 malaise that ignited it. 🦴🦴🦴

1958 99m/B *GB* Richard Burton, Claire Bloom, Mary Ure, Edith Evans, Gary Raymond, Glen Byam Shaw, George Devine, Donald Pleasence, Phyllis Neilson-Terry; ***D:*** Tony Richardson; ***W:*** John Osborne, Nigel Kneale; ***C:*** Oswald Morris; ***M:*** John Addison. **VHS, LV**

Lost Highway

Lost Highway takes its time getting started; nearly a third of the running time creeps by before anything remotely approaching a narrative thrust turns up. Fred and Renee Madison (Bill Pullman and Patricia Arquette) keep finding videotapes on their doorstep. Then, blink-and-you’ll-miss-it, Fred is in a death row jail cell, awaiting his execution via the electric chair for Renee’s murder. (There IS no electric chair in California, where this story appears to be set, but so what?) Somehow, Fred changes places with Pete Dayton (Balthazar Getty). Since Pete isn’t Fred, he is sent home to Mom and Dad (Pete’s dad is none other than Gary Busey). Pete continues going out with the girl down the block (Natasha Gregson Wagner) and working as a garage mechanic for his boss Arnie (Richard Pryor). One of the clients at the garage is Mr. Eddy (Robert Loggia), who has a bad-news/half-his-age girlfriend. (Surprise! Patricia Arquette IS Alice Wakefield, only now she resembles a washed-out version of the late blonde starlet Joyce Jameson.) Faster than you can say “Mr.-Eddy-will-kill-us-if-he-ever-finds-out,” Pete and Alice are looking for trouble and finding it. Among the other characters who pop up is a weird Mystery Man with an ominous aura (Robert Blake). And so this movie goes—on and on until it’s over. Like Lynch’s *Twin Peaks* series, *Lost Highway* is flecked with interesting touches amidst long stretches of total boredom. Yeah, this looks, sounds, and feels like a rough draft, but David Lynch fans won’t mind. 🦴🦴

1996 (R) 135m/C Bill Pullman, Patricia Arquette, Balthazar Getty, Robert Loggia, Robert (Bobby) Blake, Gary Busey, Jack Nance, Richard Pryor, Natasha Gregson Wagner, Lisa Boyle, Michael Massee, Jack Kehler, Henry Rollins, Gene Ross, Scott Coffey; ***D:*** David Lynch; ***W:*** David Lynch, Barry Gifford; ***C:*** Peter Deming; ***M:*** Angelo Badalamenti. **VHS, LV, Closed Caption**

Lost in the Stars

This is one of the few American Film Theatre productions I wouldn’t mind seeing again. It’s based on Alan Paton’s *Cry the*

Beloved Country, detailing a minister's search for his son in Johannesburg, South Africa. Brock Peters and a strong supporting cast benefited from on-location filming in Jamaica and the West Indies under the direction of Daniel Mann. ☙☙☙

1974 114m/C Brock Peters, Melba Moore, Raymond St. Jacques, Clifton Davis, Paula Kelly; ***D:*** Daniel Mann; ***W:*** Maxwell Anderson; ***M:*** Kurt Weill.

Love and a .45

After 1994's *Natural Born Killers* exploited the illusion that violence is sexy, follow-up clones were inevitable. Case in point: *Love and a .45,* directed by C.M. Talkington. Or maybe no one directed this thing. Maybe C.M. just pointed cameras at the actors and told them to ham it up. And they do; every single one of them, without exception, overacts his or her little heart out. The leader of the pack in this department is Rory Cochrane, so good as the stoned Slater in *Dazed and Confused* when he was directed by Richard Linklater. As Billy the Psycho here, he never shouts when he can scream and never screams when he can blow someone's head off. I assume we're supposed to root for the idiotic runaway lovers Watty and Starlene Watts, who are played by Gil Bellows and Renee Zellweger. After all, they never would have gotten into trouble if it weren't for Billy the Psycho, it's all HIS fault. But Watty and Starlene are, for all their wildly overplayed mugging on camera, a deeply boring couple. Her parents are two over-the-hill hippies played by Ann Wedgeworth and Peter Fonda. Starlene's dad tore his throat out while under the influence of something or other in the 1960s, so he has to communicate with a voice box. The cameo is humiliating enough for *Easy Rider*'s Peter Fonda, but it's downright painful to see the excellent, underrated character actress Ann Wedgeworth in such a throwaway role. Well, you can always listen to Jesus and Mary Chain, Meat Puppets, Butthole Surfers, Kim Deal, and Johnny Cash on the soundtrack and wonder why the onscreen zeroes get to be media stars and how many more movie clones will ask the same damn thing over and over again. **woof!**

1994 (R) 101m/C Gil Bellows, Renee Zellweger, Rory Cochrane, Ann Wedgeworth, Peter Fonda, Jeffrey Combs, Jace Alexander; ***D:*** C.M. Talkington; ***W:*** C.M. Talkington; ***C:*** Tom Richmond; ***M:*** Tom Verlaine. Nominations: Independent Spirit Awards '95: Debut Performance (Zellweger). **VHS, LV, Closed Caption**

Love and Death on Long Island

The title of the movie is *Love and Death on Long Island,* or is it *Love and De'Ath on Long Island,* as in Giles De'Ath, drolly played by the delightful John Hurt? De'Ath is an obscure Brit writer and a distinguished looking gent in his late 50s who deplores anything developed in his own lifetime or, indeed, at any time throughout the 20th century. And then he's persuaded to see a film adaptation of that young whippersnapper E.M. Forster (1879– 1970), so off he trots to the multiplex to see it. Alas, he winds up at a screening for *Hotpants College 2,* which most definitely owes nothing to Forster. As Giles tries to slip out of the theatre, his eyes behold the image of the one and only Ronnie Bostock (Jason Priestley), and it's love at first sight. Soon, Giles finds himself doing all sorts of 1998 things: purchasing a videocassette recorder (although he hasn't a clue that a television monitor is required), renting such previous Ronnie Bostock titles as *Skid Marks* and *Tex Mex,* and pinching fan magazines so that he can scour them and cut out Ronnie Bostock's pictures for a series of scrapbooks he stores in a locked filing cabinet labeled "Bostockiana." Giles' literary agent persuades him to take a rest and what better place for a holiday than Chesterton, Long Island—where, as the fan magazines reveal, Ronnie Bostock actually resides? The stylish Giles is warmly received by the female owner of the motel in Chesterton and by Irving Buckmiller (Maury Chaykin), the proprietor of Irv's coffee shop. In search of Ronnie Bostock, Giles strolls through neighborhoods, stalks the postman, and makes friends with Ronnie Bostock's girlfriend Audrey (Fiona

Thomas Gibson in *Love and Human Remains.*
Sony Pictures Classics; courtesy of the Kobal Collection

Loewi) and dog. It isn't long before he's finally shaking the hand of Ronnie Bostock himself. Flattered that he's "so big in England," Ronnie listens attentively to every word he says, especially when Giles recommends inserting Walt Whitman's *Untold Want* into a funeral sequence for *Hotpants College 3.* You see, Ronnie Bostock wants to be a serious actor and if Giles develops a meaningful script for him, he may very well BE one someday. Audrey, however, recognizes the lust in De'Ath's heart and develops an idea or two of her own about the future of Ronnie Bostock. Richard Kwietniowski's *Love and Death on Long Island,* a very clever adaptation of Gilbert Adair's novel, is a delicious, hilarious experience; it's sad to think that *Beverly Hills 90210* fans, who watch Jason Priestley as Brandon Walsh everyday, won't go near this movie, ditto the grown-ups who look down on his career and thus missed his sharp 1994 satire as an assassin opposite Peter Reigert in M. Wallace Wolodarsky's *Coldblooded.* If you take yourself and the world very seriously, *Love and Death on Long Island* may not do it for you. Otherwise, you'll have an absolute ball!

1997 (PG-13) 93m/C *GB CA* John Hurt, Jason Priestley, Fiona Loewi, Sheila Hancock, Maury Chaykin, Gawn Grainger, Elizabeth Quinn; ***D:*** Richard Kwietniowski; ***W:*** Richard Kwietniowski; ***C:*** Oliver Curtis; ***M:*** Richard Grassby-Lewis. **VHS, Closed Caption**

Love and Duty

At the time of her suicide at 25, Ruan Ling-Yu was China's leading actress and the sudsy *Love and Duty* shows why. As Yang Naifan, Ling-Yu ages from a sheltered school girl to a chic matron to a runaway lover to an old-before-her-time seamstress, raising her illegitimate daughter without the support of her long-dead lover. Ling-Yu worked from the inside out, so her evolution is persuasively achieved with very little makeup. (Only her front tooth is blacked out as the seamstress, something no Western star of comparable magnitude would ever dare to do!) With a minimalist, deeply moving acting style, Ling-Yu skillfully interprets Yang Naifan's many transformations, and, interestingly, her inner turmoil is revealed in a series of fantasies that show the intense psychological pressures that crush her spirit at every turn. *Love and Duty* gives us a fascinating glimpse at a China that appears both ultramodern and saturated with tradition. Our sympathy for Yang Naifan's lover is lost when he insists that she abandon her small children, our interest in her absent-minded husband increases as we see what a tender and considerate father he is to their son and daughter. But Ruan Ling-Yu's greatest gift as an actress was her ability to dig into the soul of a character so that her many fans could set aside whatever troubling questions they may have had about WHY someone like Yang Naifan made such incomprehensible life choices. We don't DARE drag our eyes away from her face for a single second, because Ruan Ling-Yu solves mysteries of the heart with such subtle expressions and simple gestures. The greatest mystery of all, of course, is why, until quite recently, a jewel like Ruan Ling-Yu was known only to the audiences of her own time and country. She died just as the Chinese film industry was launching sound films, leaving behind a note, "Gossip is a dreadful thing." Among her few extant films are 1931's *The Peach Blossom Weeps Tears of Blood* plus *The Goddess* and *New Women,* both filmed in 1934. ***AKA:*** Lian'ai Yu Yiwu. 🦴🦴🦴

1931 152m/B *CH* Ruan Ling-Yu, Jin Yan, Chen Yanyan, Li Yi; ***D:*** Bu Wancang; ***W:*** Zhu Shilin; ***C:*** Huang Shaofen.

Love and Human Remains

Canada's *Love and Human Remains* supplies a quirky look at the romantic rituals of two roommates; he's gay and she's straight, sort of. They both want to meet a nice guy but they're afraid, and why not? There's a serial killer on the loose. She succumbs to a one-night stand with a romantic lesbian at her gym and then falls for a bartender before she discovers he's married. He waits tables at age 30, and tries to be responsible by side-stepping a fling with a 17-year-old bus boy who had a crush on him when he was a television child star. Meanwhile, his psychic friend senses danger from the serial killer, who continues to terrorize the women of Montreal. With a well-chosen cast of unknowns and brisk direction from Denys Arcand, Brad Fraser's script is on target more often than not, with humor and affection to spare for each and every character (except, of course, the serial killer, who remains a marginal figure throughout). 🦴🦴🦴

1993 (R) 100m/C *CA* Thomas Gibson, Ruth Marshall, Cameron Bancroft, Mia Kirshner, Joanne Vannicola, Matthew Ferguson, Rick Roberts; ***D:*** Denys Arcand; ***W:*** Brad Fraser; ***C:*** Paul Sarossy. Genie Awards '94: Best Adapted Screenplay. **VHS, LV**

Love Jones

A contemporary Chicago nightclub, the Sanctuary, is the gathering spot for middle-class black urbanites looking for romance. Would-be writer/poet Darius (Larenz Tate) spouts provocative verse to beautiful photographer Nina (Nia Long), who's not too happy with men at the moment (she's just been dumped). But they make a connection, with both protesting a little too much that's it just a "sex thing." Funny what happens when love clearly enters the picture. Theodore Witcher's directorial debut features fine lead performances. 🦴🦴🦴

1996 (R) 105m/C Larenz Tate, Nia Long, Isaiah Washington, Lisa Nicole Carson, Khalil Kain, Bill Bellamy, Leonard Roberts, Bernardette L. Clarke; ***D:*** Theodore Witcher; ***W:*** Theodore Witcher; ***C:*** Ernest Holzman; ***M:*** Darryl Jones. Sundance Film Festival '97: Audience Award. **VHS, LV, Closed Caption**

Love unto Waste

Stanley Kwan's *Love Unto Waste* is a flashy existential film about love and friendship in Hong Kong of the 1980s. The strong performances by its young cast (Tony Leung would later make a strong im-

Robert Shaw and Liam Redmond in *The Luck of Ginger Coffey.* Continental Distributing, Inc.; courtesy of the Kobal Collection

pression in Kwan's *Centre Stage/The Actress,* released in 1992) should have won this exceptional import wider U.S. distribution than it initially received. 🦴🦴🦴

1986 97m/C *HK* Tony Leung Chiu-Wai, Chow Yun-Fat, Irene Wan, Elaine Jin, Tsai Chin; ***D:*** Stanley Kwan; ***W:*** Lai Kit, Chiu Tai An-Ping. **VHS**

Lover Girl

I didn't know what to make of this odd little indie, which I picked up on an impulse from a video shelf, but it's been lingering in my mind ever since. Jake (extremely well played by Tara Subkoff) is a little homeless girl who tries to move in with her mean older sister, Darlene (Kristy Swanson). Darlene won't let Jake crash with her, not even for one night, so Jake wanders around and then drifts back to Darlene's vicinity. Marti (Sandra Bernhard) lives down the passage from Darlene, so Jake begs to stay with her. After some grumbling, Marti says O.K., for one night. It turns out that Marti works in a massage parlor where most of the male clients don't even expect her to have sex with them, they just play with themselves while she dances around. That sounds easy, Jake thinks, so she asks if she can stay with Marti and pay her own way by being a masseuse, too. No, she's underage, absolutely no and definitely no. So Jake does it anyway when none of the other masseuses are around. Well, she doesn't actually do it, she just hangs out with a young male client who seems as inexperienced as she is and who pays her almost $200. Marti and the other masseuses figure they can make some extra money as long as the madame/manager doesn't find out. Since Jake is so young, the job does get to her after a while. She doesn't want to do ANYTHING with the clients. "Who does?" shrugs Coco, another masseuse (Loretta Devine). Then Darlene wants in on the action—she wants to be a sister act with Jake, actually, which Jake doesn't dig at all. She's becoming so morose that she doesn't even care when Darlene blows the whistle on Jake's part-time job. Nor, it seems, do the other masseuses, who quit en masse, except for mean Darlene. Jake drifts away, only to be rescued once again by Marti, whose maternal impulses seem to have kicked into gear somehow. Or have they? That's why *Lover Girl* lingers in my mind. Lisa Addario and Joe Syracuse's view of prostitution is so non-judgmental and so free of eroticism and so sympathetic to the women who toil as sex industry workers that I had to wonder after a while what they were saying in *Lover Girl.* No matter how cordial or kind the female masseuses are to Jake, she is a child and being with male clients is hurting her. After such a mercenary start with Marti, could they really adjust to a surrogate mom/kid relationship? This troubling picture asks more questions than it ever tries to answer, but the acting is very good (Bernhard is exceptional as Marti and Renee *Fun* Humphrey is also around as Teddy) and the absence of Sunday school morality made the story seem heartbreakingly real. Allison Anders was executive producer. The soundtrack includes songs by Cibo Matto ("Sugar Water," "Aquas De Marco"), Bellatone, Land of the Loops, Team Dresch, Containe, Surf Maggots, Go Sailor and the Murmurs.

1997 (R) 87m/C Tara Subkoff, Sandra Bernhard, Kristy Swanson, Loretta Devine, Renee Humphrey, Susan Barnes, Sahara Lotti, Tim Griffin; ***D:*** Lisa Addario, Joe Syracuse; ***W:*** Lisa Addario, Joe Syracuse; ***C:*** Dean Lent; ***M:*** Mark Kilian. **VHS**

The Luck of Ginger Coffey

More people saw Lotte Lenya as Rosa Klebb punch Robert Shaw as Red Grant in the stomach than will ever see a frame of this move, which is a pity really, because *The Luck of Ginger Coffey* contains one of Shaw's finest performances. Shaw is Ginger Coffey, who moves to Canada with his family, dreaming of a better life. Instead, he slides deeper and deeper into alcoholism. A strong cast gives meaning to Ginger's story. Irvin Kershner previously directed the well-regarded *Hoodlum Priest* and went on to direct offbeat films like *Flim-Flam Man* and *Up the Sandbox.* Between *The Empire Strikes Back* and *Robocop 2,* he directed Sean Connery and Kim Basinger in *Never Say Never Again* (the least generic James Bond film), and 1989's *Traveling Man,* an underrated return to his offbeat roots with John Lithgow, Jonathan Silverman, Margaret Colin, and John Glover. Kershner's indie debut, 1958's *Stake-Out on Dope Street* (shot when he was 25 on a $30,000 budget), and his best movie, 1970's *Loving,* are not yet available on video. Sadly, the hard-living Robert Shaw and Mary Ure were both dead by 1975. Based on Brian Moore's novel and filmed in Montreal.

1964 100m/B *CA* Robert Shaw, Mary Ure, Liam Redmond, Tom Harvey, Libby McClintock, Leo Leyden, Tom Kneebone; ***D:*** Irvin Kershner; ***W:*** Brian Moore; ***C:*** Manny Wynn; ***M:*** Bernardo Sagall. **VHS**

The Luckiest Man in the World

Who could resist a movie premise like this one? A rich jerk named Sam is 10 minutes late for a plane that crashes on take-off with no survivors. At the airport, the victims' heartbroken relatives scream at Sam: "Why you?" In the men's room, Sam ponders his escape from certain death and determines to be kinder to the people in his life. The only problem is, they're all used to Sam being a jerk and won't accept him any other way. Pulitzer Prize–winning playwright Frank D. Gilroy directs his own screenplay for *The Luckiest Man in the World,* a wise and funny satire revolving around one creep's response to the randomnesss of fate. Philip Bosco is ideally cast as Sam, bringing a sharp comic bite to his unbearable character. The rest of the cast is populated with little-known but well-chosen New York actors and the production values are rock-bottom adequate. Gilroy's dialogue is so good and the direction is so on target that I can't help feeling that the whole point of *The Luckiest Man in the World* might have been buried under an expensive Hollywood budget and a distracting stellar lineup.

"What do you know about it? What are you saying? If it comes to that, who are you? What right do you have to speak?"

—Child murderer Hans Becker (Peter Lorre) defies a criminal crowd in *M.*

1989 82m/C Philip Bosco, Doris Belack, Joanne Camp, Matthew Gottlieb, Arthur French, Stan Lachow; ***D:*** Frank D. Gilroy; ***W:*** Frank D. Gilroy.

Lucky Jim

"Oh, Lucky Jim, how I envy him..." Well, who wouldn't, when he's played by the delightful Ian Carmichael, long before he inherited the role of Lord Peter Wimsey? The thing is, university lecturer Jim Dixon is far from lucky, although he'd certainly like to be. This wonderfully played, deftly directed vintage Britcom is a good one to rent when you're home sick with a head cold; it will have you laughing your way to health in no time. Cast Notes: Canadian actress Sharon Acker, then 22, makes her debut here; she would later star in three short-lived U.S. television series of the 1970s, including the ill-fated *Perry Mason* show in which she—ahem—TRIED to inherit Barbara Hale's role as Della Street. Kenneth Griffith turned up in 1994's *Four Weddings and a Funeral* and John Welsh (1905–85) was dear old Merriman in *The Duchess of Duke Street.* 🦴🦴🦴

1958 91m/B *GB* Ian Carmichael, Terry-Thomas, Hugh Griffith, Sharon Acker, Jean Anderson, Maureen Connell, Clive Morton, John Welsh, Reginald Beckwith, Kenneth Griffith, Jeremy Hawk, Harry Fowler; ***D:*** John Boulting, Roy Boulting; ***W:*** Jeffrey Dell, Patrick Campbell; ***C:*** Mutz Greenbaum; ***M:*** John Addison. **VHS**

Lullaby

At first, *Lullaby* offers a child's-eye view of sheer loveliness unclouded by foreboding. But then the little girl is kidnapped and not returned to her family for so long that she recognizes nothing of her former life. The sequences where her mother tries everything to wring a memory from her lost daughter are truly heart wrenching. The beautiful surroundings mean nothing to her without her child's love, a point made with conviction by director Nana Janelidze. ***AKA:*** Ivnana. 🦴🦴🦴

1994 70m/C Nata Murvanidze, Nine Abuladze, Maya Bagrationi; ***D:*** Nan Janelidze; ***W:*** Nino Natroshvili; ***C:*** Georgi Beridze; ***M:*** Jansug Kakhidze, Vakhtang Kakhidze.

Lumière

Jeanne Moreau assembled an impressive cast (including Keith Carradine, who has very little to do here) and technical crew, but the result is a carefully wrought film in every respect except one: Moreau, clearly wanting to reveal the strong ties that bind women together, gets sidetracked by (and overwhelmed with) the superficial ways in which her characters express their concern for one another. She never takes her characters one step further. In one sequence, a lady invites her male seducer to join her for a tryst. She has, in fact, dumped two other men so that she may be alone with this guy, and never at any point does she suggest to her pursuer that she wants anything from him other than casual sex. When he follows through on her invitation, she wriggles away from him, and Moreau's direction implies criticism that he would even begin to construe such an idea. Moreau casually sprinkles this sort of skin-deep critique throughout her script. Only one female character in *Lumière* is fully dimensional, and that seems to be due more to the skill of Lucia Bose than to the insubstantial part Moreau wrote for her. François Simon and Francis Huster are quite moving as two men whom Moreau discards in her onscreen role as Sarah. The four women Moreau attempts to capture with such complexity emerge as selfish drips, and not very interesting selfish drips at that. 🦴🦴

1976 (R) 101m/C *FR* Jeanne Moreau, Lucia Bose, Francine Racette, Caroline Cartier, Keith Carradine, Francois Simon, Francis Huster, Bruno Ganz, Rene Feret, Niels Arestrup, Jerome Lapperrousaz; ***D:*** Jeanne Moreau; ***W:*** Jeanne Moreau; ***C:*** Ricardo Aronovich; ***M:*** Astor Piazzolla. **VHS**

Luther

An earnest but dull look at Martin Luther (Stacy Keach), as seen by John Osborne. It don't mean a thing if it ain't got that swing. (*Luther* was released theatrically overseas in 1976.) An American Film Theatre Production. 🦴🦴

1974 (G) 112m/C Stacy Keach, Patrick Magee, Hugh Griffith, Robert Stephens, Alan Badel, Julian Clover, Judi Dench, Leonard Rossiter, Maurice Denham, Peter Cellier, Thomas Heathcote, Malcolm

Stoddard, Bruce Carstairs; ***D:*** Guy Green; ***W:*** Edward Anhalt, John Osborne; ***C:*** Frederick A. (Freddie) Young; ***M:*** John Addison. **VHS**

M

M made Peter Lorre (1904–64) immortal and rightly so; by humanizing a monstrous killer, he changed forever how we would perceive such characters. There really was a child murderer; his name was Peter Kurten (1883–1931), and he had not yet been executed at the time of *M*'s release. Unlike the tormented Hans Becker played by Lorre, Kurten felt no remorse for his many crimes, only a clinical fascination with them afterward. Otto Wernicke (1893–1965) gives a superb performance as Inspector Lohmann, who tracks down Becker. Fritz Lang, who had spent considerable time at Berlin Alexanderplatz closely observing the police in action, used his in-depth knowledge of their methods to add to the realism of the narrative. There actually were criminal characters among the thugs who judge Becker for his crimes, one of whom asked Lang to speed up the shooting as the police were expected in an hour. Gustav Grundgens (1899–1963), who played Schranker, the underworld chief, was the real-life model for the central character of Klaus Mann's *Mephisto.* Mann (1906–49), who was Grundgens' brother-in-law, killed himself because he couldn't publish *Mephisto.* Grundgens, whose career flourished during the Third Reich, was unable to achieve real professional acceptance after the war, and he, too, killed himself. *M* seems like a different movie every time you see it. There is the horror of knowing what victim Elsie Beekman is too young to realize, and then there is deep empathy for her mother. Even so, there is intense compassion for her murderer. You cannot hate him, because of Lang's and Thea von Harbou's exceptionally written address to the underworld, and because of the deep complexity of Lorre's interpretation of a man who kills because he must. Peter Lorre explained his approach to his most famous role by saying, "My only concern was to understand WHY. I did understand." Unsurprisingly, *M* is Fritz Lang's own favorite of all his films. 🦴🦴🦴🦴

1931 99m/B *GE* Peter Lorre, Ellen Widmann, Inge Landgut, Gustav Grundgens, Otto Wernicke, Ernest Stahl-Nachbaur, Franz Stein, Theodore Loos, Fritz Gnass, Fritz Odemar, Paul Kemp, Theo Lingen, Georg John, Karl Platen, Rosa Valetti, Hertha von Walther, Rudolf Blumner; ***D:*** Fritz Lang; ***W:*** Fritz Lang, Thea von Harbou; ***C:*** Fritz Arno Wagner, Gustav Rathje; ***M:*** Edvard Grieg. **VHS, DVD**

Ma Vie en Rose

Seven-year-old Ludovic (Georges DuFresne) wants nothing better from life than to be a little girl, to dress like a fairy princess, to play with his doll Pam, and to marry his playmate Jerome (Julien Riviere). His parents pray it's just a phase. But the neighbors in their new suburban home, who had seemed so nice at first, treat Ludovic's entire family—including his two brothers and teenaged sister—like pariahs. Mother Hanna (Michele Laroque) and Father Pierre (Jean-Philipe Ecoffey) love their little boy, but are deeply distressed at being placed in Coventry, particularly since Jerome's dad Albert (Daniel Hanssens) is Pierre's new boss. How do they solve a problem like Ludovic? Alain Berliner sympathetically examines Ludovic's world and shows how what seems simple and reassuring for very young children (to be themselves) is complex and threatening for the grown-ups in their lives. Jerome is more than happy to be part of the fantasy wedding envisioned by Ludovic so why does Albert regard it as some sort of Satanic ritual? DuFresne is so convincing and sweet as the determined Ludovic that you'll root for him all the way. The picture-perfect Parisian suburb takes quite a hit, though. Are newcomers only entitled to a serene life in attractive surroundings if they accept what the existing community perceives as natural and healthy? Berliner asks this question and others with gentle humor. *Ma Vie en Rose* is a charmer from start to finish, and young DuFresne is a real find. ***AKA:*** My Life in Pink. 🦴🦴🦴

1997 (R) 90m/C *BE FR GB* Georges DuFresne, Jean-Philippe Ecoffey, Michele Laroque, Daniel Hanssens, Julien Riviere, Helene Vincent, Laurence Bibot, Jean-Francois Galotte, Caroline Baehr, Marie Bunuel; ***D:*** Alain Berliner; ***W:*** Alain Berliner, Chris

Ludovic (Georges DuFresne) in *Ma Vie en Rose.* Sony Pictures Classics; courtesy of the Kobal Collection

Vander Stappen; ***C:*** Yves Cape; ***M:*** Dominique Dalcan. Golden Globe Awards '98: Best Foreign Film; Nominations: British Academy Awards '97: Best Foreign Film. **VHS**

Mac

John Turturro's film about three Italian brothers was far more effective with this viewer than Edward Burns' movie about *The Brothers McMullen.* Perhaps this is because the inspiration (Turturro's late father) feels more real. Turturro gets inside the bickering and the fighting to show the genuine love and strong bonds beneath the surface in the Vitelli family. He plays the title role, also known as Niccolo; Michael Badalucco and Carl Capotorto are his younger siblings Vico and Bruno; Katherine Borowitz (Mrs. John Turturro) is Mac's wife, Alice; and Ellen Barkin is Oona, a '50s-style kook. The wonderful acting by all more than compensates for the fact that the low budget clearly didn't cover authentic period details. In a family saga like this one, the authentic expression of feelings is clearly far more vital. 𝒮𝒮𝒮

1993 (R) 118m/C John Turturro, Carl Capotorto, Michael Badalucco, Katherine Borowitz, John Amos, Olek Krupa, Ellen Barkin, Joe Paparone, Nicholas Turturro, Dennis Farina, Steven Randazzo; ***D:*** John Turturro; ***W:*** Brandon Cole, John Turturro; ***C:*** Ron Fortunato; ***M:*** Richard Termini, Vin Tese. Nominations: Independent Spirit Awards '94: Best Director (Turturro), Best First Feature. **VHS, LV, Letterbox, Closed Caption**

Madeleine

Madeleine Smith was a Victorian murderess...or was she? Director David Lean wanted audiences of the 1950s to have a question in their minds after seeing his film. Apparently, Madeleine (played by Lean's wife, Ann Todd) had a lusty relationship with Emile L'Angelier (Ivan Desny). Her father (Leslie Banks) wanted her to marry a man named Minnoch (Norman Wooland) who was more suited to her station in life. Scenting either hush money or a lucrative alliance, L'Angelier threatened

to show Madeleine's letters to Mr. Smith. Not long after, Madeleine entered a chemist's shop, purchased a bottle of arsenic from a Mr. Murdoch (Ivor Barnard), and soon L'Angelier was writhing in agony from a fatal dose of arsenic. Who done it? We won't be able to tell from the Scottish court transcripts; Madeleine's guilt was "not proven." Madeleine herself never discussed her guilt or innocence after she was dismissed by the court. It's an unsolved mystery, and, nearly 150 years after the fact, it's liable to remain one forever. With so many unyielding participants, Lean reveals how everyone's strict code of behavior led directly to murder. For all Lean's meticulous attention to every historical detail, the film's one flaw was inevitable. These are the most passionless of people; indeed, if there had been one spark of genuine passion, Lean might be making a film about a legendary elopement or a shocking rebellion, instead of a cool, conscienceless disposal of a human impediment to a rigid way of life. Recommended for further research: Mary S. Hartman's superb 1977 Pocket Book, *Victorian Murderesses* (including Miss Smith)! ***AKA:*** The Strange Case of Madeleine. 🦴🦴🦴

1950 114m/B Ann Todd, Leslie Banks, Ivan Desny, Norman Wooland, Barbara Everest, Susan Stranks, Patricia Raine, Elizabeth Sellars, Edward Chapman, Jean Cadell, Eugene Deckers, Amy Veness, John Laurie, Henry Edwards, Ivor Barnard, Barry Jones, David Morne, Andre Morell, Douglas Barr; ***D:*** David Lean; ***W:*** Nicholas Phipps, Stanley Haynes; ***C:*** Guy Green; ***M:*** William Alwyn. **VHS**

The Madness of King George

When *Edward and Mrs. Simpson* first hit international television screens in 1978, the actor playing Walter Monckton, a bespectacled advisor to the King, nearly stole the entire show. Nigel Hawthorne continued to play supporting roles in films and on television, but onstage, he was recognized as the star his enormous talent ought to have made him on big and small screens alike. Finally, Hawthorne has been given the chance to show movie fans just what theatrical audiences have been raving about. In *The Madness of King George,* Hawthorne achieves the impossible; who other than Prince Charles has ever extended a shred of sympathy to George III? But Hawthorne succeeds in making us care about the mad monarch of 1788. At best, His Majesty was, by many accounts, not a bad sort and well meaning, but was easily led by self-serving advisors much brighter than he was. For most of Alan Bennett's retelling of George's nervous breakdown, we do not see him at his best, but wracked with a disease later suspected to be porphyria, then diagnosed as madness by the king's advisors. After assorted barbaric attempts to treat his illness, the King is referred to a Doctor Willis (splendidly played by Ian Holm), who proposes a radical cure. Meanwhile, his dissipated and profligate son (Rupert Everett is ideally cast as the future King George IV) schemes to wrest power away from his daft father so that he may be appointed Regent. The loyal Queen Charlotte (Oscar nominee Helen Mirren) and her lady-in-waiting (Amanda Donohoe) have other ambitions, AND crafty approaches for achieving them. Bennett nails down all the political intrigues with wit and humor and with a sharp understanding of who the real players are. Being on the wrong side at an inconvenient time can lead to royal banishment even faster than outright treachery. You may need to make deals with the traitors, but it's easier to sacrifice a friend who's too intimately familiar with regal fallibility. One of Hawthorne's best moments as the recovering King comes in a garden sequence when he tries to show a courtier how much better he is by reading from Shakespeare. Alas, after picture's end, the King finally did lose his mind, and George IV's regency and reign considerably eroded the prestige and influence of the monarchy until his niece Victoria acceded to the throne, but that's another story. (Oscar nominee Hawthorne's other films on video include *S*P*Y*S, Holocaust, A Tale of Two Cities, The Hunchback of Notre Dame, A Woman Called Golda, Firefox, Pope John Paul II, Jenny's War, Tartuffe, Demolition Man,* and *Richard III.* Mirren, of course, can be

"My grandmother always said, 'Why buy the cow...when you get the sex for free.'"

—Brodie (Jason Lee) in *Mallrats.*

seen in dozens of films on video dating all the way back to 1968's *A Midsummer Night's Dream.*) ⟡⟡⟡⟡

1994 (R) 110m/C *GB* Nigel Hawthorne, Helen Mirren, Ian Holm, Rupert Everett, Amanda Donohoe, Rupert Graves, Julian Wadham, John Wood, Julian Rhind-Tutt; ***D:*** Nicholas Hytner; ***W:*** Alan Bennett; ***C:*** Andrew Dunn; ***M:*** George Fenton. Academy Awards '94: Best Art Direction/Set Decoration; British Academy Awards '95: Best Actor (Hawthorne); Cannes Film Festival '95: Best Actress (Mirren); Nominations: Academy Awards '94: Best Actor (Hawthorne), Best Adapted Screenplay, Best Supporting Actress (Mirren); British Academy Awards '95: Best Actress (Mirren), Best Adapted Screenplay, Best Cinematography, Best Director (Hytner), Best Film, Best Supporting Actor (Holm), Best Score. **VHS, LV, Closed Caption**

The Maids

In spite of the cast, *The Maids* is one of the least imaginative productions in the American Film Theatre series, and that's saying something. Skip this film version of Jean Genet's play and see 1994's *Sister My Sister* instead. It isn't perfect, but it won't bore you like this one will. *The Maids* was released theatrically overseas in 1976. ⟡

1975 95m/C *GB CA* Glenda Jackson, Susannah York, Vivien Merchant, Mark Burns; ***D:*** Christopher Miles; ***W:*** Christopher Miles, Robert Enders; ***C:*** Douglas Slocombe; ***M:*** Laurie Johnson. **VHS**

The Making of "A Hard Day's Night"

The Making of "A Hard Day's Night" unravels one mystery I've been trying to solve for-absotively-ever: if Phil Collins, then 14, made his film debut in it, where the heck WAS he? Collins himself answers the question and shows us a crowd shot in which only his family could recognize him screaming along with all the other teenaged extras. This new documentary, produced by and featuring Walter Shenson (who made the original film), reveals other little-known facts about the world's most famous rock musical: Ringo's choice of reading material in the movie was *Anatomy of a Murder;* John WASN'T in the fondly remembered field sequence; and the title song over the credits was—literally—written overnight, after the rest of the movie was already completed. Also included is the "You Can't Do That" number, shaved from the final release, as well as an informal trailer the Beatles shot to promote the picture. The surprise for producer Walter Shenson and director Richard Lester was that the Beatles were such naturals in their very first movie. Alun Owen's Oscar-nominated screenplay was deliberately composed of very short bits of dialogue so that none of its four stars would have to say or do anything that would expose their lack of training as actors. Surprise, surprise; under the expert guidance of Lester, they turned out to be so engaging onscreen that Owen wrote extra sequences to highlight George Harrison and Ringo Starr. Moreover, at least a dozen of John Lennon's ad-libs remained in the finished movie. (Charitably unmentioned is the fact that one of Paul McCartney's solo moments wound up on the cutting room floor due to his self-conscious performance.) The years have been kind to actor Victor Spinetti, who recalls his work in the film with obvious pride and pleasure. Clearly, *A Hard Day's Night,* made thousands of miles away from executive busy mitts in Hollywood, was a happy experience for its fortunate creators. *The Making of "A Hard Day's Night"* is an affectionate look back at the musical classic helmed by the man MTV has long identified as its father. The great Richard Lester accepts the compliment, but characteristically, insists on a blood test. ⟡⟡⟡⟡

1994 60m/C Phil Collins, The Beatles, Victor Spinetti, Alun Owen, Richard Lester, Peter Noone; ***W:*** David Leaf. **VHS**

Mallrats

Clerks wasn't a smash hit or anything, but the black-and-white debut film did well enough in art houses for Gramercy Pictures to lure its young writer/director into making a color movie about *Mallrats.* After watching the rushes, did Kevin Smith wonder for an instant about giving all the credit to Alan Smithee? We may never know the answer to that one, but it would have

been a kinder gesture to his promising career if he had. Although this dreadful film was supposedly written after *Clerks,* it feels like the first draft of something that was written in high school, stashed in a closet, and forgotten until Hollywood started panting for a follow-up project. You want a funny mall movie, rent *Fast Times at Ridgemont High.* You want excruciating jokes, lousy acting, lame sight gags, and a plotline that should have been tossed in a dumpster at the very first story conference, *Mallrats* is the scum de la scum, BENEATH the pile of ultra-bad teen movies, in fact. Anyway, Shannen Doherty was pushing 25 at the time, way too old to be lusting after a guy (execrable newcomer Jason Lee) who sticks his fist up his butt and then shakes hands with his best friend's future father-in-law for a laugh. Are you beginning to get the level of the agony factor here? Marvel Comics veteran Stan Lee appears as himself. Game show maestro Art James and Priscilla Barnes (in a particularly humiliating cameo) are also in this piece of crap. Even if there's nothing else on the video shelf, don't talk yourself into seeing *Mallrats* even if someone else is paying. (Smith apologized to the critics who hated *Mallrats* in the end credits of his much better follow-up film, 1997's *Chasing Amy,* and Jason Lee's acting had even improved by then, too.) **woof!**

1995 (R) 95m/C Shannen Doherty, Jeremy London, Jason Lee, Claire Forlani, Michael Rooker, Renee Humphrey, Ben Affleck, Joey Adams, Jason Mewes, Brian O'Halloran, David Brinkley, Kevin Smith; ***Cameos:*** Priscilla Barnes, Stan Lee, Art James; ***D:*** Kevin Smith; ***W:*** Kevin Smith; ***C:*** David Klein; ***M:*** Ira Newborn. **VHS, LV, Closed Caption**

The Man in the Glass Booth

The Man in the Glass Booth is unique among the 13 American Film Theatre productions because its star, Maximilian Schell, won an Academy Award nomination for Best Actor in the title role, the only participant to be so honored. Aside from that, we're looking at another stagey filmed play, a common failing among all but one of these movies (that would be Lord Laurence Olivier's *Three Sisters,* made in 1970). Actor/playwright Robert Shaw was so angered by this interpretation of his play that he demanded his name be removed from the film credits. Donald Pleasence had originated the Broadway role (somewhat modeled after Adolf Eichmann) under Harold Pinter's direction.

1975 (PG) 117m/C Maximilian Schell, Lois Nettleton, Luther Adler, Lawrence Pressman, Henry Brown, Richard Rasof; ***D:*** Arthur Hiller; ***W:*** Edward Anhalt; ***C:*** Sam Leavitt. Nominations: Academy Awards '75: Best Actor (Schell). **VHS**

The Man Who Knew Too Much

The 1956 re-make of *The Man Who Knew Too Much* is big and expensive and it has "Que Sera, Sera," but the little kid in it drives me nuts, and I hate it when Jimmy Stewart gives Doris Day a sedative before he tells her about the kidnapping and she doesn't even return his volley with a left hook—she just goes into hysterics. Everything I detest about the 1950s is tossed into that one: bad clothes, bad dialogue, and bad manners. But the 1934 version is an altogether different story. Nova Pilbeam is a genuinely appealing kid and we do worry about her welfare in the hands of a slime like Peter Lorre. And Leslie Banks and Edna Best are a witty and sophisticated couple with individual interests and a lightly bantering style well suited to their free and easy marriage. We don't want anything to hurt their family and we're with them all the way as they draw on their own ingenious resources to save their daughter. The sheer speed of the narrative makes this sparkling ORIGINAL Hitchcock classic the one to look for on the video shelf. Bigger isn't always better and the story doesn't need another 45 minutes of singing and yakking, anyway.

1934 75m/B *GB* Leslie Banks, Edna Best, Peter Lorre, Nova Pilbeam, Pierre Fresnay, Frank Vosper, Hugh Wakefield, Cicely Oates, D. A. Clarke-Smith, George Curzon, Henry Oscar, Wilfrid Hyde-White; ***D:*** Alfred Hitchcock; ***W:*** Emlyn Williams, Charles Bennett, A.H. Rawlinson, Edwin Greenwood, D. B. Wyndham-Lewis; ***C:*** Curt Courant. **VHS, DVD**

Frank Vosper, Peter Lorre, and Leslie Banks in *The Man Who Knew Too Much.*
Gaumont-British; courtesy of the Kobal Collection

The Man Who Loved Women

Love can be both sweet and fatal, the late François Truffaut (1932–84) says in his 1977 film, *The Man Who Loved Women.* Charles Denner plays a man who sneers at Don Juans, but behaves just like them. He's so obsessed with romance that he gets hit by a car and falls out of a hospital bed just because he wants to get a better look at all the pretty girls there are in the world. Chasing women delights him and dooms him, and he has his choice of the prettiest woman in France, including Brigitte Fossey and Leslie Caron. At one point, Truffaut starts to say, yes, lasting love IS important, repetitive trysts ARE meaningless, but he drops these ideas very quickly by cutting to yet another brief affair lovingly photographed by Nestor Almendros. Whatever Truffaut wants to say about love here, he has said it better many times before. Despite its provocative subject matter and Truffaut's expert handling of same, *The Man Who Loved Women* remains essentially a fluff piece. ***AKA:*** L'Homme Qui Aimait les Femmes.

1977 119m/C *FR* Charles Denner, Brigitte Fossey, Leslie Caron, Nelly Borgeaud, Genevieve Fontanel, Nathalie Baye, Sabine Glaser; ***D:*** Francois Truffaut; ***W:*** Francois Truffaut, Suzanne Schiffman, Michel Fermaud; ***C:*** Nestor Almendros; ***M:*** Maurice Jaubert. **VHS, LV, Closed Caption**

The Man with the Movie Camera

Dziga Vertov's *The Man with the Movie Camera* was made over 75 years ago, but it might well put many of today's avant-garde efforts to self-conscious shame. It is pure cinema, by a director madly in love with the medium, and like any delirious lover, he tries to capture life at a breathless pace. Vertov's fast-paced 66-minute movie is filled with fun and wit. ***AKA:*** Chelovek S Kinooapparatom. 🦴🦴🦴🦴

1923 66m/B *RU* ***D:*** Dziga Vertov; ***W:*** Dziga Vertov; ***C:*** Mikhail Kaufman. **VHS**

The Manchurian Candidate

Among the best movies released in 1988 was a 26-year-old film noir directed by John Frankenheimer. *The Manchurian Candidate* boasts a beautifully constructed script by Frankenheimer and George Axelrod, a terrific cast headed by Frank Sinatra, Laurence Harvey, and Angela Lansbury, and a dark premonitory vision that reveals all the horrors of the late '60s in embryo. Those who would like to remember 1962 as an innocent year can look elsewhere for nostalgia. *The Manchurian Candidate* is grim, gripping entertainment. Filmed within five years of Senator Joe McCarthy's death, the movie makes use of the paranoid Cold War era, and also reveals the slickness of the characters who marketed our national fears. Angela Lansbury was only 37 when she played 34-year-old Laurence Harvey's villainous mother, but she gets away with it and steals every scene she's in. Lithuanian-born Harvey never was convincing in American roles, although he certainly played enough of them, yet he is otherwise sympathetic and restrained in the pivotal role. Frank Sinatra could be a fine actor when he wanted to be, and he plays with cool, crisp authority here. Not many people remember an attractive, talented starlet named Leslie Parrish, but she is shown to good advantage opposite Harvey. One bit of miscasting is Puerto Rican Henry Silva as a Korean, an especially odd choice in a picture which also features Khigh Deigh. There's also a weak love interest bit for Janet Leigh opposite Sinatra. *The Manchurian Candidate* was made in the midst of the Kennedy years and yet it's atypical of films of that era in that it's genuinely noir and genuinely prophetic. It runs rings around most of today's thrillers. 🦴🦴🦴🦴

1962 126m/B Frank Sinatra, Laurence Harvey, Angela Lansbury, Janet Leigh, James Gregory, Leslie Parrish, John McGiver, Henry Silva, Khigh Deigh; ***D:*** John Frankenheimer; ***W:*** George Axelrod, John Frankenheimer; ***C:*** Lionel Lindon; ***M:*** David Amram. Golden Globe Awards '63: Best Supporting Actress (Lansbury); National Board of Review Awards '62: Best Supporting Actress (Lansbury); Nominations: Academy Awards '62: Best Film Editing, Best Supporting Actress (Lansbury). **VHS, LV, Closed Caption, DVD**

Manny & Lo

Amanda/Manny, 11 (Scarlett Johansson), and Laurel/Lo, 16 (Aleksa Palladino), are sisters, but they were adopted by different parents. They run away together, but Lo finds out she's expecting a baby, so they kidnap Elaine (Mary Kay Place), who works in a baby store. What's Elaine's story? They don't know, but Lo knows she needs help, so Manny, Lo, and Elaine are off to the woods until the baby comes. This offbeat first feature written and directed by Lisa Krueger is filled with warmth, charm, and good acting by the kids. And wonderful Mary Kay Place is an absolute treasure as Elaine. 🦴🦴🦴

1996 (R) 90m/C Mary Kay Place, Scarlett Johansson, Aleksa Palladino, Paul Guilfoyle, Glenn Fitzgerald, Cameron Boyd, Novella Nelson, Angie Phillips; ***D:*** Lisa Krueger; ***W:*** Lisa Krueger; ***C:*** Tom Krueger; ***M:*** John Lurie. Nominations: Independent Spirit Awards '97: Best Actress (Johansson), Best First Feature, Best Supporting Actress (Place). **VHS, LV, Closed Caption**

The Mark

The recidivism rate for child molesters is so high that no one in his or her right mind would want to place a child in the unsupervised care of a known pedophile. That said, *The Mark* plans a unique form of violence on the viewer. Stuart Whitman gives the finest performance of his career as convicted child molester Jim Fuller. Fuller has served his time in prison, and has also received intensive therapy from Dr. McNally (Rod Steiger). He wants to become a useful member of society, but his past has shattered .him, drained his confidence, and

Ernest Borgnine and Betsy Blair in *Marty.* United Artists; courtesy of the Kobal Collection

turned him into a haunted, hesitant man, terrified of nearly every emotional impulse. (God, what a part this must have been for Whitman to play!) He meets Ruth Leighton (Maria Schell) at his new job and they become friends. Ruth, a single mother with a young daughter named Janie (Amanda Black), is aware that Fuller has experienced deep unhappiness, but so has she, and she knows nothing about his conviction for child molestation. Janie, starved for a father figure in her life, adores Fuller, but he distances himself from her need for affection. Meanwhile, his friendship with her mother evolves into a romance. Well, you can see where all this is leading—it's only a matter of time before Fuller's past and present collide, and they do, thanks to an investigative reporter. The underlying theme is that since Jim Fuller has been "cured," Society should give him another chance to lead a normal life. This was a kindly perspective for 1961, but it's also gobbledygook. The viewpoint here is that if Ruth is really in love with him, she must trust him alone with her daughter because he's "cured." They can all be a normal family and Fuller can forget his past. Well, it's only a movie, and the filmmakers meant well, but that may explain why you don't see *The Mark* too often on television. Maria Schell and Rod Steiger are ideally cast as Ruth and Dr. McNally, and Stuart Whitman's moving performance as Jim Fuller cannot be faulted (he won an Oscar nomination for it, but lost to Maximilian Schell). Based on a novel by Charles Israel. ☆☆☆☆

1961 127m/B *GB* Stuart Whitman, Maria Schell, Rod Steiger, Brenda de Banzie, Maurice Denham, Donald Wolfit, Paul Rogers, Donald Houston, Amanda Black, Russell Napier, Marie Devereux; ***D:*** Guy Green; ***W:*** Sidney Buchman, Raymond Stross; ***C:*** Dudley Lovell; ***M:*** Richard Rodney Bennett. Nominations: Academy Awards '61: Best Actor (Whitman). **VHS**

The Marquise of O

Eric Rohmer's *The Marquise of O* is based on a 17th century book by Heinrich von

Kleist and very much evokes the paintings of that time; every sequence of this beautifully photographed story would be suitable for framing. Rohmer paces his tale in a leisurely, deliberate manner; it is extraordinary that he injects passion and down-to-earth fun in such a staid subject. He is able to achieve this partly by his scrupulous attention to period details of the early 1800s, and mainly by the ease with which he renders his heroine's strength. 𝄞𝄞𝄞

1976 102m/C *FR GE* Edith Clever, Bruno Ganz, Peter Luhr, Edda Seipel, Otto Sander, Ruth Drexel; ***D:*** Eric Rohmer; ***W:*** Eric Rohmer; ***C:*** Nestor Almendros.

The Marriage

The Marriage may just be the most vicious movie ever made regarding that particular institution, yet Arnaldo Jabor's ability to scrape close to the very core of human feelings is not only dazzling, it's right on the money. The neurotic, tempestuous music of Astor Piazzola emphasizes to perfection the feverish emotions in Jabor's film. Jabor's flamboyant style, given full rein in *The Marriage,* is never gratuitous, being well balanced by the presence of leading man Paulo Porto. Porto seems perpetually bewildered by his own responses to events as much as he does by the wild circumstances which tend to surround him. Jabor also directed 1973's *All Nudity Will Be Punished,* a dark love story. Less successful was Jabor's 1981 film, *I Love You,* with Sonia Braga. ***AKA:*** O Casamento. 𝄞𝄞𝄞

1976 113m/C *GB* Adriana Prieto, Paulo Porto, Camila Amado, Nelson Dantas, Erico Vidal, Fregolente, Maria Rubia; ***D:*** Arnaldo Jabor; ***W:*** Arnaldo Jabor; ***C:*** Dib Lufti; ***M:*** Astor Piazzolla.

Martha and I

Martha and I was warmly received at the San Francisco International Film Festival in 1991 but after its distributor went bankrupt, it sat on the shelf for three years until this beautifully made German entry acquired a new distributor. Based on the childhood experiences of Czech director Jiri Weiss, the film stars Michel Piccoli and Marianne Saegebrecht in two exceptional performances as a Jewish doctor and German cook who confound their families by marrying and living happily ever after together, or at least until the imminent Nazi invasion of Czechoslovakia. Longtime admirers of Weiss, Piccoli, and Saegebrecht won't want to miss this one. 𝄞𝄞𝄞

1991 107m/C *GE* Marianne Saegebrecht, Michel Piccoli, Vaclov Chalupa, Ondrej Vetchy; ***D:*** Jiri Weiss; ***W:*** Jiri Weiss; ***C:*** Viktor Ruzicka; ***M:*** Jiri Stivin. **VHS**

Marty

Marty gave the little independent film stature and prestige at a time when the motion picture industry was trying to be BIG in order to attract the millions who were enjoying entertainment on the small screen. *Marty* also stunned movie studio executives with the realization that what people were watching on television for free could be every bit as good as or better than lavish films with high-priced stars like *Love Is a Many Splendored Thing, Mister Roberts, Picnic,* and *The Rose Tattoo. Marty* first appeared as a television drama on the May 24, 1953, broadcast of NBC's Kraft Theatre, starring 28-year-old Rod Steiger in the title role and Nancy Marchand, then 25, as his wallflower date Clara. For the movie version also directed by Delbert Mann, Ernest Borgnine, 38, played Marty and Betsy Blair, 32, was Clara. Paddy Chayefsky's screenplay of his original teleplay so infiltrated the consciousness of 1950s audiences that its influence continues to be felt many decades later. Leading men prior to *Marty* knew what they wanted to do; they didn't have trouble getting dates and they didn't look like Ernest Borgnine. But indecision and insecurity are intrinsic to real life and when Chayefsky tapped into that, the audience identification with Marty was pervasive. Lonely, middle-aged men recognized and understood Marty and felt validated by him. Although Chayefsky's portrait of Clara is harsher in many ways, it does show that a woman doesn't have to be movie-star pretty to find love and happiness. Clara is seen in isolation; all we know about her is that she's a schoolteacher who's been rejected by a blind date. We learn about her goodness and kindness as she blossoms

Marcy (Janeane Garofalo) and Sean (David O'Hara) in *The Matchmaker.*
Gramercy; courtesy of the Kobal Collection

through Marty's sympathetic attention. We know more about Marty's world—about his mother, his aunt, his brother, his sister-in-law, and most of all, his friends, Angie, Ralph, The Kid, and Joe. ("What do you feel like doing tonight?" "I don't know. What do you feel like doing?") Divided, they might have a chance at a real life, but united they are losers with a capital "L." In their world, nothing worth having is here, it has to be somewhere else, but they haven't a clue where that might be. For Marty to break away from these guys is difficult—they're all he knows, but his leap of courage is accomplished in a poignant, bittersweet way, considerably enhanced by Borgnine's kind eyes and his big, homely face. Pioneer indie producers Harold Hecht and Burt Lancaster made *Marty* for $343,000, only to strike gold with the Academy voters. With its unfussy presentation and simple truths, *Marty* had touched everyone's heart. 🦴🦴🦴🦴

1955 91m/B Ernest Borgnine, Betsy Blair, Joe Mantell, Esther Minciotti, Jerry Paris, Karen Steele, Augusta Ciolli, Frank Sutton, Walter Kelley, Robin Morse; ***D:*** Delbert Mann; ***W:*** Paddy Chayefsky; ***C:*** Joseph LaShelle; ***M:*** Roy Webb, Harry Warren. Academy Awards '55: Best Actor (Borgnine), Best Director (Mann), Best Picture, Best Screenplay; British Academy Awards '55: Best Actor (Borgnine), Best Actress (Blair); Directors Guild of America Awards '55: Best Director (Mann); Golden Globe Awards '56: Best Actor—Drama (Borgnine); National Board of Review Awards '55: Best Actor (Borgnine), National Film Registry '94;; New York Film Critics Awards '55: Best Actor (Borgnine), Best Film; Nominations: Academy Awards '55: Best Art Direction/Set Decoration (B & W), Best Black and White Cinematography, Best Supporting Actor (Mantell), Best Supporting Actress (Blair). **VHS, LV, Closed Caption**

Matador

Matador begins with its male lead masturbating to splatter videos. Then the female lead stabs a sexual partner as she climaxes. The rest of the movie shows how these two perfectly matched people meet and prepare for their mutual idea of the ultimate orgasm: simultaneous death. Writer/director Pedro Almodovar doesn't regard all this as aberrant or tragic, nor does he pass any moral judgments on his characters. Things like this happen all the time, his film says, and the main ones who get hurt are those who can't believe that there are people who freely choose to play it this way. The guy has another girlfriend, for example, with relentless faith that her love can save him from what he wants most. It can't, of course, but she tortures herself as he happily dashes off to screw his Doppelganger. Then there's the guy's student, who faints at the sight of blood, but who shares a strange psychic connection with his teacher, which forces him to claim guilt for the other's crimes. Almodovar, a post-Franco director with a vengeance, has clearly freed himself from the self-censorship that was inevitable for Spain's filmmakers during the repressive fascist regime. He has a way of plunging all the way to the bottom of the worst nightmares and examining each and every aspect in a way that is both clinical and passionate. His exhaustive explorations, far from destroying the enchantment of obsession, confront fatal charms on their own terms and render them plausible and even erotic. It is because he is so unsparing in his pursuit of truth that he can reveal the darkest human behavior and not be offensive, as a lesser artist surely would be with some of the huge risks Almodovar takes in *Matador.* ♦♦♦♦

1986 90m/C *SP* Assumpta Serna, Antonio Banderas, Nacho Martinez, Eva Cobo, Carmen Maura, Julieta Serrano, Chus Lampreave; ***D:*** Pedro Almodovar; ***W:*** Pedro Almodovar, Jesus Ferrere; ***C:*** Angel Luis Fernandez; ***M:*** Bernardo Bonazzi. **VHS, LV, Letterbox**

The Matchmaker

The plot for *The Matchmaker* is straight out of a screwball comedy. Senator John McGlory (Jay O. Sanders) sends his assistant Marcy Tizard (Janeane Garofalo) to Ireland in search of his relatives. His re-election campaign in Massachusetts is in trouble and his strategy is to evoke John F. Kennedy's trip to Ireland in 1963. A few video clips of the Senator with his "cousins" and he'll be a living legend in Boston, just like you know who. That's the plan, anyway. Marcy lands in Ballinagra in the middle of the annual Matchmaking Festival. A great way to meet McGlory "cousins," right? Wrong, never wronger. Lots of guys want to propose to Marcy, but the "cousins" are elusive. Never mind, says cynical campaign manager Nick (Denis Leary). We'll hire them! That doesn't work, either, since the paid "cousins" clearly don't know how to behave when they're being videotaped in the same room as a would-be living legend who's trying to pull off an election scam. Politicians being politicians, a pragmatic solution is soon found. Meanwhile, Marcy falls in love with a local bloke named Sean (David O'Hara) and vice versa. Three screenwriters (script doctors?) receive credit for working on Greg Dinner's original screenplay, and the results are flaky. A genuine screwball comedy plays fast but writes slow because it demands such precise craftsmanship. It's a good thing that Garofalo is front and center for most of the running time, because her intuitive understanding of screwball comedy is what makes *The Matchmaker* work. Except for some sparkling work by Milo O'Shea as Dermot the Matchmaker and Jimmy Keogh as a local nut named O'Hara, it is mainly Garofalo's personality that makes this movie funny. She's working in a minefield of quirky, cute, and quaint cliches, but she nimbly works around them. One arched eyebrow or radiant smile or dry riposte from her and we care what happens to Marcy and forget about everything else. For that reason alone, *The Matchmaker* is a pleasant, painless way to spend a rainy Saturday afternoon. ♦♦½

1997 (R) 97m/C Janeane Garofalo, Milo O'Shea, David O'Hara, Denis Leary, Jay O. Sanders, Rosaleen Linehan, Maria Doyle Kennedy, Saffron Burrows, Paul Hickey, Jimmy Keogh; ***D:*** Mark Joffe; ***W:*** Louis Nowra, Karen Janszen, Graham Linehan, Greg Dinner; ***C:*** Ellery Ryan; ***M:*** John Altman. **VHS, Closed Caption**

Matewan

Matewan is the sort of picture that illustrates why independent film production is so necessary. John Sayles wrote the screenplay in the '70s, but no Hollywood studio was remotely interested in making a movie about a real-life massacre in which a dozen coal miners were murdered in West Virginia during the '20s. Sayles made it anyway, and it is among the most powerful works of his memorable career. Ah, Hollywood studios; how could any hotshot iceberg turn down a script with lines like these: "You want to be treated like men? You want to be treated fair? Well, ya ain't men to the coal company, you're equipment. They'll use you till you wear out or break down or you're buried under a slate fall, and then they'll get a new one, and they don't care what color it is or where it comes from." Chris Cooper is labor organizer Joe Kenehan, who tries to form a union in Mingo County, West Virginia. The threatened coal company then hired the Baldwin Felts detective agency to evict the coal miners from their homes. The agency had previously carried out an illegal 1914 eviction order in Colorado where gunmen

"I'm an unspeakable...of the Oscar Wilde sort."

—Maurice (James Wilby) confesses his sexual preference in *Maurice.*

murdered 20 people, including a dozen women and children who were burned alive. The eviction order was just as illegal in Mingo County, and Police Chief Sid Hatfield (David Straithairn) and the coal miners knew it. Hatfield became a hero to the coal miners by killing agency gunmen Al Felts (Frank Hoyt Taylor), but it didn't stop the massacre. Moreover, Hatfield himself was murdered (with his wife watching) by agency gunman C.E. Lively (Bob Gunton) within 15 months of the Matewan massacre. This harsh, brutal historical incident was little remembered by anyone outside the UMWA until Sayles and his brilliant cast and crew made this film. A movie like *Matewan* should be as important to motion-picture history and our understanding of U.S. history as *The Grapes of Wrath.* Perhaps, over time, it will be. 🦴🦴🦴🦴

1987 (PG-13) 130m/C Chris Cooper, James Earl Jones, Mary McDonnell, William Oldham, Kevin Tighe, David Strathairn, Jace Alexander, Gordon Clapp, Mason Daring, Joe Grifasi, Bob Gunton, Jo Henderson, Jason Jenkins, Ken Jenkins, Nancy Mette, Josh Mostel, Michael B. Preston, Maggie Renzi, Frank Hoyt Taylor; ***Cameos:*** John Sayles; ***D:*** John Sayles; ***W:*** John Sayles; ***C:*** Haskell Wexler; ***M:*** Mason Daring. Independent Spirit Awards '88: Best Cinematography; Nominations: Academy Awards '87: Best Cinematography. **VHS, LV, Closed Caption**

Maurice

Maurice continues Berkeley-born director James Ivory's exploration of the English upper crust's high-class worries. Based on E.M. Forster's novel, the 139-minute film would not be hurt if it were half an hour shorter. It should come as no shock that there is a class structure in England and that schoolboys run off at the mouth, but it is tedious to watch long sequences convincing us of these kindergarten truths. The film works best when it shows the loneliness of the closet homosexual at the turn of the century. In a world which celebrates heterosexuality, the loneliness can only be relieved by an expression of sexuality, but even for the privileged in Great Britain, the consequences once included imprisonment. We see how two young men face their sexuality, one burying it in convention, the other acquiring strength by accepting himself as he is. It takes enormous reserves of courage to see through fear and disarm it. Very few can risk the social disapproval such an effort requires, which lends a rosy cast to the idealistic conclusion. The usual Ivory production values prevail, including gorgeous sets and costumes. *Maurice* is blessed with a top-notch cast, including then-ubiquitous Denholm Elliott and Ben Kingsley as an oddly accented American hypnotist who has the film's best line, "England has always been disinclined to accept human nature." 🦴🦴🦴

1987 (R) 139m/C *GB* James Wilby, Hugh Grant, Rupert Graves, Mark Tandy, Ben Kingsley, Denholm Elliott, Simon Callow, Judy Parfitt, Helena Bonham Carter, Billie Whitelaw, Phoebe Nicholls, Barry Foster; ***D:*** James Ivory; ***W:*** James Ivory, Kit Hesketh-Harvey; ***C:*** Pierre Lhomme; ***M:*** Richard Robbins. Nominations: Academy Awards '87: Best Costume Design. **VHS, LV, Closed Caption**

Medicine River

Medicine River is a captivating romance from Canada directed by Stuart Margolin. Oscar nominee Graham Greene plays Will, an international photojournalist who reluctantly returns to his native Blackfoot home for the first time in 20 years. He arrives late for his mother's funeral and finds himself unable to leave right away. A small-time hustler named Harlan Big Bear (Tom Jackson) wants to raise money for basketball uniforms and insists that Will take a series of portrait photographs that will form the basis of a fund-raising calendar and book. Will puts his career and sophisticated life on hold as he becomes intensely caught up in the activities of small-time life and a free-spirited accountant named Louise (beautifully played by Sheila Tousey). Under Margolin's sensitive direction, Greene delivers a wonderfully appealing performance as the world-weary journalist who changes his entire life when he falls in love with the Medicine River community that he abandoned long ago. Filmed in Alberta. 🦴🦴🦴

1994 (PG) 96m/C *CA* Graham Greene, Tom Jackson, Sheila Tousey, Jimmy Herman, Raoul Trujillo, Byron Chief-Moon, Janet-Laine Green; ***D:*** Stuart Margolin. **VHS**

Medium Cool

At the time of its release, *Medium Cool* received rave reviews all over the world and its reputation remains undiminished over 30 years later. The first time I tried to reassess it in late 1997, I found myself mysteriously unmoved. The second time I tried, in late 1998, the mystery cleared up: As a writer/director, Haskell Wexler is a world-class cinematographer. I suspect that *The Making of "Medium Cool"* would be a far more fascinating story than the film itself. Shot on location in Chicago at the Democratic National Convention in 1968, *Medium Cool* follows the career of John (Robert Forster, then in his pin-up days at age 27) as a television news photographer. The first shot of the film (eerily echoed at the end) shows cameramen John and Gus (Peter Bonerz, 30) shooting a grisly auto accident in matter-of-fact style. Only after they have all their footage does Gus mention anything about an ambulance. John's life, as can be seen in a sequence with well-endowed Marianna Hill as Ruth, is hedonistic, unblinking, and unthinking. While covering a routine human interest story, he is confronted by members of the black community who tell him that television films are being scanned by the Chicago police department and used to harass and arrest people. (Duh!) The uncomprehending John doesn't know anything about that, he's just doing his job, Honey, Dear. (Don't call me Honey! Don't call me Dear!) Then John is fired. It turns out that the Chicago police department IS scanning his television films and using them to harass and arrest people. (Duh-Squared!) John the robot cameraman is John the human being again and he becomes involved with a 13-year-old kid named Harold (Harold Blankenship) and his mother Eileen (Verna Bloom, then 29). John's story is grafted onto the riot footage that Wexler shot during the convention. (At one point, someone yells, "Look out, Haskell, it's real'" as the police attempt to control protesters with a canister of tear gas.) Bloom wanders through the crowds, long hair neatly combed, wearing a short bright yellow dress with a white belt and high heels, not your basic riot gear. She's looking for Harold in all the wrong places. Why doesn't she stay home where Harold is sure to find her? Because she has to be grafted into the riot footage. She's wearing that atypical outfit so that we can spot her in a crowd, like the Queen of England. She gets in a car with John and there's a flash forward voiceover. No matter what, her face NEVER changes expression. (I pressed the pause button a lot.) And that is the problem with grafting a fictional story onto a much more exciting true story—unless you're a genius writer as well as a genius cinematographer, there's no way a made-up story can compete with reality. The problem is compounded by the fact that *Medium Cool* is populated with TERRIBLE actresses, not to mention one excruciating dance band! (There are so many great actresses and bands in Chicago, why not use some of them?) Moreover, the film is riddled with bland images of women and bland language for and about them. The guys are the real story, Honey, Dear, and so much more important. Over apply that makeup and wait your turn like a good girl. *Medium Cool* will continue to remain an important document because Wexler is a cinematography god. And the years, previously unkind, have become kind to Robert Forster. His 1997 performance in *Jackie Brown* is a text on what a great character actor can do with a role. As picture perfect as Forster is in *Medium Cool,* his eyes are a vacant lot, lacking the texture and density only real life could give them.

1969 111m/C Robert Forster, Verna Bloom, Peter Bonerz, Marianna Hill, Peter Boyle, Harold Blankenship, Charles Geary, Sid McCoy, Christine Bergstrom, William Sickingen; ***D:*** Haskell Wexler; ***W:*** Haskell Wexler; ***C:*** Haskell Wexler; ***M:*** Michael Bloomfield. **VHS, Closed Caption**

Meier

Meier is an enjoyable West German entry written and directed by Peter Timm. Its working-class hero, played with considerable charm by Rainer Grenkowitz, tries to have the best of both worlds, East and West. The film gets considerable mileage

Dr. Moira Sullivan on
MAYA DEREN
Meshes of the Afternoon

Maya Deren [1917–61] is considered to be the mother of independent film and she made her own films, distributed them, talked about them, and went to colleges and universities across the United States and Canada. We could say our film appreciation courses come directly from Maya Deren, because she was one of the first people to bring films to colleges so that everyday people could see them. She was one of the first persons, if not *the* first person, involved in non-commercial film distribution. Maya used to say, 'I spend on my films what Hollywood spends on lipstick.' And it's true. Maya was before any of the funding organizations existed, like the American Film Institute, etc. She actually started an organization called the Creative Film Foundation and funded filmmakers with grants, like Shirley Clarke, and she was right there from the very beginning. She could have worked in Hollywood if she wanted to. She chose not to and she used to write articles for amateur filmmakers. She called amateur filmmaking the great fortés for filmmakers: The word 'amateur' meaning 'lover' in Latin, a lover of one's craft. And she would write articles so that people would learn how to make independent films simply, to make creative films without narratives, which was the way Hollywood made movies.

"Her first film, *Meshes of the Afternoon,* was made in Hollywood as a kind of a spoof film. Maya Deren went to Haiti. She was the first person to receive a scholarship to film the so-called

out of situations that do not ordinarily lend themselves to comedy. 🦴🦴🦴

1987 98m/C *GE* Rainer Grenkowitz, Nadja Engelbrecht, Alexander Hauff, Thomas Bestvater; ***D:*** Peter Timm; ***W:*** Peter Timm; ***C:*** Karl Eichhamer.

Men in Love

Men in Love is reportedly the first feature film to be shot on BETA-SP and digitally mastered on D1-component before being transferred to 35mm. Producer/actor Scott Catamas believes that his $350,000 movie looks like it was shot on a budget of $2 million. A cast of inexperienced, mostly nonprofessional actors do their best with a sentimental and self-conscious story about safe sex in the era of AIDS. Long shots and action sequences instantly reveal the picture's video origins, despite Fawn Yacker's expert camera work. *Men in Love,* directed by Marc Huestis, rates an "A" for its intentions but barely squeaks by with a "C" for the results. 🦴🦴

1990 93m/C Doug Self, Joe Tolbe, Emerald Starr, Kutira Decosterd, Scott Catamas; ***D:*** Marc Huestis; ***W:*** Emerald Starr, Scott Catamas; ***C:*** Fawn Yacker. **VHS**

Menace II Society

In the first few minutes of *Menace II Society,* a teenaged boy named Caine (Tyrin Turner) watches as O-Dog (Larenz Tate) guns down a Korean couple who run a

Haitian dances during the late '40s. She found out when she went there these weren't dances, they were part of rituals. She shot over 20,000 feet of film in Haiti, which was virtually unprecedented. What many people don't know about Maya Deren is that she also was a brilliant ethnologist and tried to have these films accepted as documentary footage in archives and tried to sell them, etc. There was this problem in Maya's time where she couldn't wear two hats. Either she was a filmmaker or she was an ethnographer, but not both. Maya Deren was really successful building a bridge between the two art forms. I think what Maya Deren would say to filmmakers today is to plan your films meticulously and carefully.

"Maya was making films also at the time where there was a crossover into improvisational work, spearheaded by directors like John Cassavettes. She vehemently opposed this kind of unplanned filmmaking. She felt that film had to have a form and without it having a form, it had no meaning. So I would say that Maya would say, plan your films well. Try to create original motion pictures through editing. Don't just try to tell stories. Try to use editing principles and camera techniques to make your own films in non-narrative form. We could say that Maya Deren was definitely ahead of her time. She is contemporary, she's never grown old, and she has relevance to today's audience. In the compilation package of Maya Deren's films, there is an interesting quote of her saying something like, 'I'm not greedy. I don't wish to possess the major portion of your days. I will be content if only some of my images inspire you.' I think it's amazing that somebody working in the '40s is so contemporary and vivid and meaningful to audiences in the year 2000. It's very interesting to see this classic filmmaker survive through time and if you really want to see something very different, see Maya Deren's films. She's a woman that you should know about."

DR. MOIRA SULLIVAN teaches film history and is the author of *An Anagram of the Ideas of Filmmaker Maya Deren*; she also manages the official Maya Deren web site (http://www.algonet.se/~mjsull/).

shop in Watts, California. Unlike O-Dog, Caine Lawson wants to leave this way of life, but he can't see a way out. Fellow gang member Sharif (Vonte Sweet) is the son of a teacher, Mr. Butler (Charles S. Dutton), who lets Caine know that education is one way out. Another gang member, Stacy (Ryan Williams), receives a college scholarship to play football in Kansas, and he asks Caine to go with him. And Caine's girlfriend, Ronnie (Jada Pinkett), tries to persuade Caine to move to Atlanta with her. Despite these possibilities, Caine has been worn down by a life filled with guns and drugs, violence and death. Unsurprisingly, he's fatalistic about his life, if he ever has a chance to HAVE a future. The Hughes brothers, who are twins, were only 21 when they made their directorial debut. Both *Menace II Society* and their equally compelling follow-up film, 1995's *Dead Presidents* starring Tate, are filled with disturbing images of realistic bloodletting and the raging, urban sound of raw language. The core of their films, a deep understanding of each and every character, more than justifies their take-no-prisoners approach to filmmaking. We really NEED directors with such penetrating insights into contemporary society.

1993 (R) 104m/C Tyrin Turner, Larenz Tate, Samuel L. Jackson, Glenn Plummer, Julian Roy Doster, Bill Duke, Charles S. Dutton, Jada Pinkett Smith, Vonte Sweet, Ryan Williams; ***D:*** Allen Hughes, Albert Hughes; ***W:*** Tyger Williams; ***C:*** Lisa Rinzler. Independent Spirit Awards '94: Best Cine-

"Rick Von Slonecker is tall, rich, good looking, stupid, dishonest, conceited, a bully, liar, drunk and thief, an ego-maniac, and probably psychotic. In short, highly attractive to women."

—Nick Smith (Christopher Eigeman) in *Metropolitan.*

matography; MTV Movie Awards '94: Best Film; Nominations: Independent Spirit Awards '94: Best Actor (Turner), Best First Feature. **VHS, LV, Closed Caption, DVD**

Meshes of the Afternoon

The first thing you appreciate when you watch the films of Maya Deren is how unreflective of their own time they are. Deren made her first film, *Meshes of the Afternoon,* in 1943 when she was 26, but the visuals look like they might have been dreamed up 25 years later or more. Don't look for a plot. Traditional film narratives didn't interest her in the least. Maya Deren's avant-garde films were visual poetry, defying description or analysis (although many have tried). The beautiful woman with lots of soft, fluffy hair is Maya Deren herself, who appeared in most of her own films. Many of Deren's cinematic techniques continue to receive homage from filmmakers born many years after her early death in 1961. She is called the mother of independent film, and for good reason. Deren's beautiful, meticulously crafted films reflect her ideas and her interests and she made them to express herself as an artist, not to attract the attention of Hollywood executives at commercial studios. Deren would have been miserable in Hollywood, anyway. She had artistic control on her short films, which include 1944's *At Land* and *A Study in Choreography for Camera,* 1946's *Ritual in Transfigured Time,* 1948's *Meditation on Violence,* and *Divine Horsemen,* filmed in Haiti between 1947 and 1951. Why would such a maverick want to trade all that to work on other people's movies? She wouldn't, and only a truly independent artist can answer the question that way without a moment's hesitation and no regrets. Her films survive on a compilation video and are highly recommended for those who want to see the world as they've never experienced it before. 🦴🦴🦴🦴

1943 18m/B Maya Deren; ***D:*** Maya Deren; ***C:*** Alexander Hamid.

Message to Love: The Isle of Wight Festival, the Movie

It took Murray Lerner a quarter of a century to raise completion funds for *Message to Love,* his film of the 1970 Isle of Wight concert. Part of the problem was the TYPE of film he wanted to make. He wanted to show the sturm und drang that surrounded the concert, while most of the money folks wanted to skip all that and keep the focus on the music. Yet the behind-the-scenes conflict says a great deal about the atmosphere that surrounded the concert. Only 60,000 of the 600,000 fans paid for their three pound tickets; among the 540,000 crashers there were rumblings that music should be free and for the people and even if it were free, it had to be great and not a rip-off and all the usual parasitic caca of that era. To humor the crowds, some of the entertainers paid lip service to the notion of free concerts, but Tiny Tim, for one, demanded his performance fee in advance. This is the concert in which Joni Mitchell scolded the crowd for "acting like tourists!" Jimi Hendrix, a dozen days before his death, sings "Foxy Lady." Jim Morrison sings "The End." *Message to Love* reveals the cranky side of peace and harmony. It's a period piece, but it isn't nostalgic because of the undercurrents Lerner chose to show and the dissonant details he selected. 🦴🦴🦴

1970 126m/C Jim Morrison, Roger Daltrey, John Entwhistle, Keith Moon, Ian Anderson, Pete Townshend, Tiny Tim, John Sebastian, Donovan, Kris Kristofferson, Joni Mitchell, Miles Davis, Leonard Cohen, Jimi Hendrix, Joan Baez; ***D:*** Murray Lerner; ***C:*** Jack Hazan, Nicholas D. Knowland, Norman G. Langley, Andy Carchrae, Richard Stanley, Charles Stewart, Mike Whittaker. **VHS, DVD**

Metamorphosis

Metamorphosis offers a striking visualization of the Franz Kafka story, set in Prague, circa 1900. In this first filmed version of the story, we finally SEE Gregor Samsa being turned into a bug, much to the revulsion of his family. A U.S. version released 15 years later didn't fly. ***AKA:*** Förvandlingen. 🦴🦴🦴

1975 90m/C *SW* Ernst Gunther, Gunn Wallgren, Peter Schildt, Inga-Lili Carlsson, Per Oscarsson; ***D:*** Ivo Dvorak; ***W:*** Ivo Dvorak, Lars Forssell; ***C:*** Jiri Tirl.

The Method

The Method is clearly a well-intentioned effort by Joseph Destein and 13 other men who worked on the film with him. It's the old story about the middle-aged woman who leaves home and family to find herself by taking acting lessons and by playing hookers on film. The filmmakers try to solve plot problems by picking up the slack with undeveloped sub-plots involving minor characters. Remember the pompous white teachers in the Black Actors School sketch in Robert Townsend's *Hollywood Shuffle*? *The Method*'s pompous white male teachers show women how to be women, but their lessons, like this film, present a false vision lacking any real depth or understanding. Taylor Gilbert had previously appeared in *Torment* and *Alone in the T-Shirt Zone.* Rob Nilsson's writing and directing credits include *Northern Lights, Signal 7, On the Edge,* and *Heat and Sunlight.* 🦴🦴

1987 100m/C Melanie Dreisbach, Kathryn Knotts, Deborah Swisher, Taylor Gilbert, Anthony Cistaro, Richard Arnold, Rob Reece, Jack Rikess, Robert Elross, Jean Shelton; ***D:*** Joseph Destein; ***W:*** Rob Nilsson, Joseph Destein, Joel Adelman; ***C:*** Stephen Lighthill; ***M:*** Ray Obiedo.

Metropolis

Metropolis was set 74 years in the future in the year 2000. Fritz Lang "detested it after it was finished"; he wanted it to include elements of magic and the occult, ghosts and ghouls, instead of the notion that "human beings were nothing but part of a machine." Lang credits Thea von Harbou with the original concept ("She had foresight and was right"), but the execution was all his ("I was wrong"). But Lang's view of the film is not shared by those who have seen the film over the years. The effect of all that photogenic machinery on an audience is visceral in the extreme. Even contemporary science-fiction flicks would benefit from the lavish art direction of Lang's epic. The amazing Brigitte Helm, only 21, plays both kindly Maria and the evil robot. The electricity between the robot and the 30,000 extras pre-dates every political rally/revival meeting/rock concert one can possibly imagine! And the fact that all those thousands would willingly follow the robot to their doom gives *Metropolis* an eerily premonitory quality, considering so many things that were to come between 1927 and the year 2000. *Metropolis* provides a timeless view of an ever-timely theme. (Note: The original score by the Clubfoot Orchestra, performed at San Francisco's Castro Theatre, is far superior to the score composed by Giorgio Moroder.) 🦴🦴🦴🦴

1926 115m/B *GE* Brigitte Helm, Alfred Abel, Gustav Froehlich, Rudolf Klein-Rogge, Fritz Rasp, Heinrich George, Theodore Loos, Erwin Biswanger, Olaf Storm, Hans Leo Reich, Heinrich Gotho; ***D:*** Fritz Lang; ***W:*** Fritz Lang, Thea von Harbou; ***C:*** Karl Freund, Gunther Rittau, Eugene Schufftan; ***M:*** Gottfried Huppertz. **VHS, LV, DVD**

Metropolitan

Christopher Eigeman looks and sounds like he's out of another time, like you'd find him at one of Jay Gatsby's garden parties immaculately tailored, supplying Scott AND Zelda Fitzgerald with literary inspiration for dozens of short stories. He was in Whit Stillman's first two pictures and Noah Baumbach's debut film, but I only see him in Pacific Bell commercials these days. Even though he's great in them, I'd rather see him at the movies. Edward Clements as Tom Townsend runs into a group of young socialites who need an extra male. Even though he's out of their league, he joins them and, through guarded responses, wins their acceptance. Eigeman as Nick shows Tom the ropes and he's in. The lives of the socialites really do seem as if they belong to an earlier era, but Stillman's dialogue is so bright and witty (especially as delivered by Eigeman) that most of the 98 minutes whizzes by, until Nick drops out of the plot. I had to wait four years to see Eigeman again, co-starring with Taylor Nichols in Stillman's *Barcelona.* What's the matter with movie producers these

Real badge. Real gun. Fake cop.

—Tagline from the movie *Miami Blues.*

days, anyway? Don't they recognize a star when they see one? Eigeman was scheduled to appear in a weekly television series by the spring of 1999. 🦴🦴🦴

1990 (PG-13) 98m/C Carolyn Farina, Edward Clements, Taylor Nichols, Christopher Eigeman, Allison Rutledge-Parisi, Dylan Hundley, Isabel Gillies, Bryan Leder, Will Kempe, Elizabeth Thompson; ***D:*** Whit Stillman; ***W:*** Whit Stillman; ***C:*** John Thomas; ***M:*** Mark Suozzo. Independent Spirit Awards '91: Best First Feature; New York Film Critics Awards '90: Best Director (Stillman); Nominations: Academy Awards '90: Best Original Screenplay. **VHS, LV**

Miami Blues

How often have you watched a movie and wondered: "How in the world were they able to get this project past the story board?" In the case of *Miami Blues,* I have a pretty good hunch which sequences attracted Jonathan Demme to produce it, but that doesn't necessarily mean that YOU have to blow your entertainment allowance on it. *Miami Blues* is your basic home movie with a budget. Although the direction by Roger Corman alumnus George *(Private Duty Nurses, Hot Rod)* Armitage is described (by the press kit) as "precise," he pretty much lets stars Alec Baldwin and Jennifer Jason Leigh overact their little hearts out. The characters they play are generic psycho and generic ditz, complete with accompanying stock mannerisms. This permits executive producer Fred Ward to steal the film with his usual roguish charm and easy underplaying. The plot (Will Sgt. Ward catch the insane Baldwin?) is so predictable that the minor shocks in the movie are supplied by its very occasional gross-outs. Shirley Stoler and Charles Napier are on hand for the hard core film buffs. And in the "So-that's-how-they-get-away-with-it" department, writer/director George Armitage pulled into the first convenience store he could find while scouting for movie locations. He went up to the owner and said, "I'm with a film company and we'd like to drive a truck through your front door." The store owner, who'd already been held up several times, said "yes" without batting an eye. Believe it or don't! (After *Miami Blues,* Armitage went on to co-script 1996's *The Late Shift,* a Golden Globe winner for actress Kathy Bates.) 🦴🦴

1990 (R) 97m/C Fred Ward, Alec Baldwin, Jennifer Jason Leigh, Nora Dunn, Charles Napier, Jose Perez, Paul Gleason, Obba Babatunde, Martine Beswick, Shirley Stoler; ***D:*** George Armitage; ***W:*** George Armitage; ***C:*** Tak Fujimoto; ***M:*** Gary Chang. New York Film Critics Awards '90: Best Supporting Actress (Leigh). **VHS, LV, Closed Caption**

Michael Collins

Galway-born actor George Brent used to be a dispatch rider for Michael Collins. He escaped Ireland with a price on his head and eventually wound up in Hollywood at the Warner Bros. studio. Had the future of Ireland not been his preeminent concern, Michael Collins could have torn up the silver screen. Check out the newsreels of the early 1920s; Collins appears onscreen and you can't look at anything else. His skin, like that of many great stars, photographs so vividly you feel you can reach out and feel it, and his style, gestures, and charisma would be timeless in any era. Michael Collins had more important things on his mind than newsreel cameramen, namely an Irish Republic free of British control. Neil Jordan scrupulously charts the IRA's campaign of that time and, despite his finest efforts to create a movie that is both historically accurate and dramatically gripping, *Michael Collins* came under heavy attack from international political scholars who charged that considerable liberties had been taken with the truth. Well, you can plow through history books or you can see this film, starring the well-chosen Liam Neeson. For the record, Harry Boland (Aidan Quinn) and Collins did indeed fight together, but not in the Easter Uprising of 1916. Boland was killed in a hotel room instead of a sewer. Informer Ned Broy (Stephen Rea) was not executed by the British; he is a composite of two other fighters who WERE tortured and killed by the British. Collins did not actually see the hanging of Tom Cullen (Stuart Graham), although hangings of Irish rebels did, in fact, occur. Joe O'Reilly (Ian Hart) was not with Collins when he was assassinated. And no, Kitty Kiernan (Julia Roberts) and Collins didn't meet like THAT. So now you know. It is difficult to show a pure political power struggle onscreen without some fidgety nitpickers asking when we get to hear some humor or see some sex. Despite all this, Jordan's epic is a masterful one and will likely find a more receptive audience on video than it did in theatrical release. And the tension between Collins and future Irish Prime Minister Eamon De Valera (1882–1975, played here by Alan Rickman) is revealed with chilling economy. If he had lived, Collins probably would not have joined George Brent in Hollywood at the Warner Bros. studio, but current affairs in the Irish Republic might be very different today. (Cast Note: Neeson and Roberts previously co-starred in 1988's *Satisfaction*.)

1996 (R) 117m/C Liam Neeson, Aidan Quinn, Alan Rickman, Stephen Rea, Julia Roberts, Ian Hart, Sean McGinley, Gerard McSorley, Stuart Graham, Brendan Gleeson, Charles Dance, Jonathan Rhys Myers; ***D:*** Neil Jordan; ***W:*** Neil Jordan; ***C:*** Chris Menges; ***M:*** Elliot Goldenthal. Los Angeles Film Critics Association Awards '96: Best Cinematography; Venice Film Festival '96: Golden Lion, Best Actor (Neeson); Nominations: Academy Awards '96: Best Cinematography, Best Original Dramatic Score; British Academy Awards '96: Best Supporting Actor (Rickman); Golden Globe Awards '97: Best Actor—Drama (Neeson), Best Score. **VHS, DVD**

Mina Tannenbaum

At first, *Mina Tannenbaum* evokes memories of the 1991 British comedy, *Antonia and Jane,* although director Martine Dugowson's incisive reflections on a 25-year friendship are in no way softened by humor. Instead, we see two young women sustained and strengthened by the friendship each wishes she had, rather than what's actually there. Mina, the more sensitive and artistic of the two, yearns for a friend that would listen to her for hours as she describes a deep crush. Mortally bored and mostly deceptive with Mina, Ethel is far more adaptable and willing to settle for what she can get. The friendship limps along for many years, always meaning more to Mina than to Ethel, until the inevitable break. *Mina Tannenbaum* is a real button pusher; maybe you'd better see it with anyone EXCEPT an old friend in shaky standing!

1993 128m/C *FR* Romane Bohringer, Elsa Zylberstein, Nils Tavernier, Florence Thomassin, Jean-Philippe Ecoffey, Stephane Slima; ***D:*** Martine Dugowson; ***W:*** Martine Dugowson; ***C:*** Dominique Chapuis. **VHS**

The Miracle

A storm of controversy erupted when Roberto Rossellini's *The Miracle* was released with *The Human Voice* in 1948 as a two-part film, *L'Amore.* Cardinal Spellman in New York was particularly outraged at this tale of a simple woman who sleeps with a bum (portrayed by screenwriter Federico Fellini) under the impression that he is Saint Joseph. The next item on her agenda is giving birth to Jesus Christ, a plan that is greeted with derision by the people of her village. Blasphemous or not, *The Miracle* and *The Human Voice* gave Anna Magnani a superb showcase, and she made the most of it. She began her career in small parts like the maid she played in *Deadline,* a 1934 Vittorio De Sica comedy. Magnani's enormous talent might well have been consigned to servant roles for the rest of her life on film had it not been for Rossellini's and her own willingness to give the movies a realism they had never had before. ***AKA:*** Ways of Love.

1948 43m/B *IT* Anna Magnani, Federico Fellini; ***D:*** Roberto Rossellini; ***W:*** Federico Fellini; ***C:*** Aldo Tonti. **VHS**

Miracle Mile

When *Miracle Mile* was first released, some reviewers commented on the improbability of a ringing pay telephone alerting protagonist Harry (Anthony Edwards) to a nuclear nightmare. But how did we learn about Chernobyl in 1986, anyway? And doesn't Death sometimes (in 1997, actually) arrive in the form of two drops of dimethyl-mercury that leak through latex gloves? *Miracle Mile* begins as a sweet, romantic story about Harry and Julie (Mare Winningham), with no premonitory warning shots. And then Harry picks up the telephone and hears a terrified voice describing the ultimate nuclear war, due globally within the hour. You have 60 minutes to live: what would you do? Harry

The Hound Salutes:
BILLY CONNOLLY
Actor, *Mrs. Brown*

Queen Victoria's *Highland Diaries* exist, except they've been edited by the government of that time. Judi Dench read them, but I've never read them. John Brown's diaries went missing completely (absolutely destroyed, I suspect), so very little is known about his side of the story at all. The biggest constitutional uproar is the fact that Victoria didn't really enjoy being Queen. She took to the job, but she didn't really like the duties: marching around and pomp and circumstance. Her husband Prince Albert had showed her the importance of being part of the government and she didn't mind doing that, but she wasn't at all mad on being the Queen. She felt as if it was an imposition that she didn't ask for. People today who think that she was stiff and starchy keep mistaking Victoria for the Victorian era. She was nothing like the era she lived in. She adored her husband and had nine children with him. She was sexy, warm, and sensual, with a good sense of humor.

"I think that Victoria and John Brown might have had a physical relationship; Judi Dench thinks not. But I'm a Scotsman and Judi's English, you see. Going to bed with the Queen is like getting a home run for a Scotsman. Why not? And we don't let you know what we think happened between them. It's none of anyone's damn business but theirs. And if you want it to be your business, make up your own mind about it. Their backgrounds were so ludicrously different. She was never al-

goes looking for Julie. Along the way, Harry sees people doing what they normally do: hanging out in an all-night diner, working out in a health club. Julie has taken Valium to help her sleep and Harry doesn't tell her at first about the inevitable. He tells her estranged folks, though (wonderfully played by John Agar and Lou Hancock) and the two resolve many year's worth of conflicts in an instant and drive off into the night together. What Harry decides to do with his last hour doesn't exactly appear to be shared by Julie, especially since she doesn't know what the heck is going on at first. The soundtrack by Tangerine Dream is strikingly similar to their score for 1983's *Risky Business,* only here the persistent theme leads, literally, Nowhere, instead of to a Party. Steve DeJarnatt evokes the escalating tension of 1950's *D.O.A.* for 1988, in a way that the actual remake of *D.O.A.,* also filmed in 1988, does not. Existentially well acted by Edwards and Winningham. O-lan Jones can also be seen in *Shelf Life,* directed by Paul Bartel in 1994. 🦴🦴🦴

1989 (R) 87m/C Anthony Edwards, Mare Winningham, John Agar, Denise Crosby, Lou Hancock, Mykelti Williamson, Kelly Jo Minter, Kurt Fuller, Robert DoQui, Danny De La Paz, O-lan Jones, Alan Rosenberg, Claude Earl Jones; ***D:*** Steve DeJarnatt; ***W:*** Steve DeJarnatt; ***C:*** Theo van de Sande; ***M:*** Tangerine Dream. Nominations: Independent Spirit Awards '90: Best Screenplay (DeJarnatt), Best Supporting Actress (Winningham). **VHS, LV, Closed Caption**

The Missing Reel

The history of the motion picture industry has always been shrouded in mystery. Take the very first filmmaker, for example. In November of 1888, Louis Aime Augustin Le Prince patented his camera, and some

lowed to say what she meant and he never did anything else but say exactly what he meant. She came from a severely formal background. His countryside background was much looser: mountains and rivers and Highland walks—he's looking after salmon and deer and all that. He didn't care about formality; he found it pretentious and boring. He liked to get drunk on whiskey. So did his brother. He was very ambitious as well. He wanted to get on in life. All of these things (the drunkenness, the ambition, the Queen as royalty) somewhat cloud the issue of their romance/friendship/royal connection. He tried to protect her all the time. He was overprotective, he was like a wall between the Queen and her family. There's a lovely argument he has with her—'All the things I've done for you, I've kept your children away from you'—like it was a big favor, because she didn't particularly like her family. She loved them as babies, but she lost interest in them when they grew up. A wild rough man like John Brown was exactly what she needed. She was surrounded by all those pale-skinned men in frock coats who whispered all around her and when asked anything, would say yes-yes-yes-yes-yes, to keep up the status quo. John Brown came along and told her she looked terrible, she needed to get some color in her cheeks: 'Let's ride horses!' 'Let's go for a swim!' 'Let's have a picnic!' 'Let's live a little!' She loved Brown for the rough way he spoke to her.

"Antony Sher's breathtaking as Benjamin Disraeli, as is Judi Dench as Queen Victoria. They're both real heavyweights to act with and achieved tremendous reality as their characters. As a result, the lovely thing about them is that, when you're working with them, the scene becomes very real and you react in a very real way as well."

of the films he made in October of that year still survive. One shows the Yorkshire garden of his British father-in-law, the other records traffic crossing Leeds Bridge. The following year, Le Prince used perforated film for the first time. Why don't we remember Le Prince as well as we do Thomas Edison today? On September 16, 1890, Le Prince planned to demonstrate a brand new movie projector for the Secretary of the Paris Opera. He was last seen carrying the projector and his films as he boarded a Paris-bound train at Dijon. The inventor, his equipment, and all of his films vanished without a trace, and Le Prince became a mere footnote in film history, barely acknowledged throughout the first century of the cinema. Then writer Christopher Rawlence became intrigued by the unsolved mystery and also by the role Le Prince had played in the evolution of film. His research made both a compelling 321-page book, published by Atheneum, as well as a fine feature-length documentary. Rawlence speaks with members of the Le Prince family, reconstructs events from Le Prince's life, and does some solid investigative work to show what led up to the disappearance and why. Great viewing for neophytes AND scholars! 🦴🦴🦴🦴

1990 90m/C John Hart-Dyke, Mona Bruce, Steve Shill, Alison Skilbeck, William Whymper, George Malpas, Vincent Marzello, Ron Berglas, Billy Le Prince Huettel; ***D:*** Christopher Rawlence; ***W:*** Christopher Rawlence; ***C:*** Chris Morphet; ***M:*** Francis Shaw.

Mrs. Brown

When Queen Victoria's doctor told her that her days of bearing children were over, she cried, "Oh, Doctor, can I have no more fun in bed?" Despite this reported incident, and many examples in the Queen's own writing of her deep physical attraction to Prince Albert and their sensual love life,

Billy Connolly as John Brown and Judi Dench as Queen Victoria in *Mrs. Brown.*
Miramax; courtesy of the Kobal Collection

the Victorians and their era have acquired an undeserved reputation for prudishness. John Madden's movie *Mrs. Brown,* scripted by Jeremy Brock, shows that Victoria did not spend the last 40 years of her life mourning the death of her young husband without consolation. Judi Dench, then 62, plays Victoria between the ages of 45 and 64 and Billy Connolly, 54, ages from 38 to 57 as her beloved servant, John Brown. Victoria seems to have been the only person who DID think that Brown was beloved. Everyone else at Court hated him cordially, especially the Queen's son Bertie, the future Edward VII, who was between the ages of 23 and 42 during Brown's era of enormous influence over his mother. Bertie had his own problems during those years. He was involved in no less than three major scandals at ages 27, 34, and 39, but Madden's film simply shows him chafing at the bit for the long-distant days when he, too, can tell everyone what to do. (At 30, Bertie inadvertently stemmed the Republican tide by nearly dying of typhoid. Victoria came out of seclusion to celebrate his recovery and a grateful nation forgot about overturning the monarchy for the rest of the Queen's reign.) John Brown was a rough, wild character, who spoke his mind without hesitation, and won Victoria's adoration. Although the film doesn't suggest any bedtime frolics (which were highly unlikely, actually), it does make it clear that Victoria was head over heels in love with Brown and his feelings for her bordered on worship. This did not prevent him from bluntly ordering her about all the time, which seems to have been part of the attraction. Dench, a wonderful stage star too little seen in films, makes a splendid Victoria, and Connolly gives Brown a certain ragged charm. One isolated incident suggests that his reputation for fighting and drunkenness was engineered by others and THAT is highly unlikely, actually. There are too many documented incidents of his feisty personality and alcoholic intake for the filmmakers to embroider a terribly persuasive new legend that Victoria and Brown were star-crossed lovers, torn apart by others. One of the best performances is delivered by Antony Sher as Benjamin Disraeli (1804–81). Sher, 48, who once played Ringo Starr on stage, nails the consummate politician as an alert listener, always telling the right people at the right time exactly what they need to hear. If *Mrs. Brown* looks and sounds like a Masterpiece Theatre production, that's because it IS, released in the heart of the very commercial summer of 1997 for reasons best known to its distributor. U.S. audiences fell head over heels in love with it and Dench won an Oscar nomination.

1997 (PG) 103m/C *GB* Judi Dench, Billy Connolly, Geoffrey Palmer, Anthony Sher, Richard Pasco, Gerard Butler, David Westhead; ***D:*** John Madden; ***W:*** Jeremy Brock; ***C:*** Richard Greatrex; ***M:*** Stephen Warbeck. British Academy Awards '97: Best Actress (Dench), Best Costume Design; Golden Globe Awards '98: Best Actress—Drama (Dench); Nominations: Academy Awards '97: Best Actress (Dench), Best Makeup; British Academy Awards '97: Best Actor (Connolly), Best Film, Best Original Screenplay; Screen Actors Guild Award '97: Best Actress (Dench), Best Supporting Actor (Connolly). **VHS, LV, Closed Caption**

Mrs. Parker and the Vicious Circle

Dorothy Parker (1893–1967) left behind a few recordings of her voice, which Jennifer Jason Leigh listened to over and over again, trying to get every inflection just right. Audiences either loved or hated Leigh's voice as Parker; it was the centerpiece of her interpretation. Let's see—if Parker only made a few recordings, she could not have been very comfortable making them, and her personality might well have been...lost in the process? Uhm... maybe, but she WAS nominated for a Grammy in 1961 for the *World of Dorothy Parker* album she recorded for the Verve label. Voice aside, Leigh plays Parker as a chronically unhappy woman, obsessed with Robert Benchley (1889–1945) when her real-life obsession appears to have been with her husband and *Star Is Born* collaborator Alan Campbell (they were both nominated for Oscars for their screenplay and Parker was a nominee again in 1947 for *Smash Up*). It's unlikely that if the real Parker had been half as miserable as Leigh's Parker, she would have been drinking lunch with the guys everyday at the Algonquin Round Table. Then and now, guys may prefer lunch with wine, but seldom with a whiner. Campbell Scott was much praised for his performance as Benchley, and he would be bloody marvelous if he were playing anyone BUT Benchley. As anyone who is addicted to Benchley's short films knows, no one could look at Benchley without smiling, and no one could read his books or listen to him at the movies without laughing (check out 1928's original *Sex Life of a Polyp!* OR *How to Sleep,* a 1935 Oscar winner!). Scott plays Benchley as sensitive, concerned, lean, and humorless. In trying to include every one of the Algonquin wits, Rudolph does justice to no one, really. Everyone passes into the frame for a second before s/he's gone. And there's still identity fudging. Some of the female characters are composites, probably for legal reasons. At least Rudolph waited until Helen Hayes (1900–93) died before painting her husband Charles MacArthur (1895–1963) as a faithless jerk. As a fiction flick, this one ain't half bad, but I'd rather watch Sally Kellerman and John Lithgow in Parker's *The Big Blonde* or Robert Benchley delivering his own dialogue in Hitchcock's *Foreign Correspondent.* ***AKA:*** Mrs. Parker and the Round Table.

1994 (R) 124m/C Jennifer Jason Leigh, Matthew Broderick, Andrew McCarthy, Campbell Scott, Jennifer Beals, Tom McGowan, Nick Cassavetes, Sam Robards, Rebecca Miller, Wallace Shawn, Martha Plimpton, Gwyneth Paltrow, Peter Gallagher, Lili Taylor; ***D:*** Alan Rudolph; ***W:*** Rudolph Coburn, Randy Sue Coburn; ***C:*** Jan Kiesser; ***M:*** Mark Isham. National Society of Film Critics Awards '94: Best Actress (Leigh); Nominations: Golden Globe Awards '95: Best Actress—Drama (Leigh); Independent Spirit Awards '95: Best Actor (Scott), Best Actress (Leigh), Best Director (Rudolph), Best Film, Best Screenplay. **VHS, LV, Closed Caption**

Mr. North

Mr. North is a 1988 movie that, except for the color and the sound, is virtually indistin-

"I believe my mental situation is extremely illegal."

—Morgan (David Warner) in *Morgan!*

guishable from any Cinderella yarn of 1928. Ah, for the good old days when integration meant marriage between the immigrant Irish and the third generation Irish, when amusing the rich provided the poor with access to their privileged world, and when every young dreamer enjoyed a fairytale ending. Set in Newport, Rhode Island, in 1926, the plot revolves around Theophilus North (Anthony Edwards, then 26), who yearns to be a free man and begins his quest by reading to the rich. He makes friends with Robert Mitchum (too young at 71 in a role intended for the late John Huston) by supplying him with candy and diapers, panaceas for incontinence. He makes friends with lovely Virginia Madsen and unrecognizable Mary Stuart Masterson by reassuring one of her worth with a kiss on the mouth and curing the other of her migraine with a tap on the forehead. Theophilus makes enemies, too: Tammy Grimes doesn't like the uppity young man and neither does Dr. David Warner, who's losing patients to this amateur quack. But, with a little help from Harry Dean Stanton and Lauren Bacall, Mr. North wins the day and control of Mitchum's money, dancing off into the night with Anjelica Huston. Madsen's character is happy: she winds up married to the grandson of an Irish mogul, played by (who else?) Joe Kennedy's grandson, Christopher Lawford. Everyone is happy except for the characters played by Grimes and Warner and the audience members who swallow this confection, yearning for satire as a mild antidote. Adapted by John Huston from Thornton Wilder's old-fashioned 1973 novel, *Mr. North* was directed by Danny Huston without a trace of irony. The clothes and the locations are beautiful, the cast is fun to look at, but *Mr. North* is little more than a foggy memory of an era that seems to exist only in the never-neverland of yellowing rotogravures. 🦴🦴

1988 (PG) 90m/C Anthony Edwards, Robert Mitchum, Lauren Bacall, Harry Dean Stanton, Anjelica Huston, Mary Stuart Masterson, Virginia Madsen, Tammy Grimes, David Warner, Hunter Carson, Christopher Durang, Mark Metcalf, Katharine Houghton, Christopher Lawford; ***D:*** Danny Huston; ***W:*** John Huston, Janet Roach, James Costigan; ***C:*** Robin Vidgeon; ***M:*** David McHugh. **VHS, LV, Closed Caption**

A Modern Affair

A Modern Affair is a first directorial effort by Vern Oakley, working with a script by Paul Zimmerman. The plot is your basic telefeature about the female executive who goes to a sperm bank to have a baby and then wants to know who the father is. This one could be sold to the Lifetime channel as is, but it has a nice performance by the criminally underrated Lisa Eichhorn and not a bad co-star in Stanley Tucci, previously seen stealing Bridget Fonda's Macadamia nuts in *It Could Happen to You*. ***AKA:*** Mr. 247. 🦴🦴

1994 (R) 91m/C Lisa Eichhorn, Stanley Tucci, Caroline Aaron, Tammy Grimes, Robert Joy, Wesley Addy, Cynthia Martells, Mary Jo Salerno; ***D:*** Vern Oakley; ***W:*** Paul Zimmerman; ***C:*** Rex Nicholson; ***M:*** Jan Hammer. **VHS, Closed Caption**

Mommy

What you notice first about *Mommy* is how good an actress Patty McCormack was and still is. Since McCormack never relied on the tricks of most kiddie stars (baby talk, cuteness, innocence, OR sweetness), she didn't miss them when she moved into adult roles. As the title character, McCormack projects skin-deep politeness, but we all know what's underneath her mask: a sociopathic murderer! This time, it's her daughter (Rachel Lemieux) who's at her wit's end, trying first to protect Mommy from herself and eventually, to protect herself from Mommy! *Mommy* appears to have been shot on high-definition video (the sequel will be on film, rather than tape), but lit for film. One has to admire the ingenuity of Max Allan Collins: his script is great, his directing style pushes all the right buttons, and he's assembled an astonishingly fine cast, considering the fact that he probably had to stretch every dollar into doing the job of five. 🦴🦴🦴

1995 89m/C Patty McCormack, Majel Barrett, Jason Miller, Brinke Stevens, Rachel Lemieux, Mickey Spillane, Michael Cornelison, Sarah Jane Miller; ***D:*** Max Allan Collins; ***W:*** Max Allan Collins; ***C:*** Phillip W. Dingeldein; ***M:*** Richard Lowry. **VHS**

Mona Lisa

Bob Hoskins gets out of prison and asks slimy gangster Michael Caine for a job. He winds up driving around an expensive call girl (Cathy Tyson). Hoskins keeps a pretty tight lid on his loneliness and desperation, but by caring about his nightly charge, he's in over his head. Neil Jordan would later re-work and satirize some of the themes here in 1992's *The Crying Game,* but *Mona Lisa* is emotion at its most raw; Hoskins works without a net as only he can. Tyson delivers a lovely performance in her first film. Sadly, for those who admire her work here, she's made few pictures since: Wes Craven's *The Serpent and the Rainbow,* Lezli-Ann Barrett's *Business As Usual,* a small role in Nigel Finch's *The Lost Language of Cranes,* and another brief appearance in Antonia Bird's *Priest.* One nice touch puts Jordan leagues in front of noir pretenders who allow bloodletting and machismo to speak for them because they have nothing to say, really. A rabbit enters the frame at one point in the story. In any other neo-noir flick of the '80s or '90s, that rabbit would have a life expectancy of five or ten minutes, max. But the rabbit survives everything—you don't have to worry about that rabbit. Keep watching. The rabbit isn't a Player; there's no reason to rub him out. Not everyone in Hoskins' world gets off that lightly and as he prepares to stand up to Caine and his henchmen, you hope that this time, things will work out for him. The odds are against him (remember that lonely ride at the conclusion of *The Long Good Friday?*), but he's going to go down fighting till the bitter end.

1986 (R) 104m/C *GB* Bob Hoskins, Cathy Tyson, Michael Caine, Clarke Peters, Kate Hardie, Robbie Coltrane, Zoe Nathenson, Sammi Davis, Rod Bedall, Joe Brown, Pauline Melville; ***D:*** Neil Jordan; ***W:*** David Leland, Neil Jordan; ***C:*** Roger Pratt; ***M:*** Michael Kamen. British Academy Awards '86: Best Actor (Hoskins); Cannes Film Festival '86: Best Actor (Hoskins); Golden Globe Awards '87: Best Actor—Drama (Hoskins); Los Angeles Film Critics Association Awards '86: Best Actor (Hoskins), Best Supporting Actress (Tyson); New York Film Critics Awards '86: Best Actor (Hoskins); National Society of Film Critics Awards '86: Best Actor (Hoskins); Nominations: Academy Awards '86: Best Actor (Hoskins). **VHS, LV**

Money Madness

Here's Hugh Beaumont in another "B" movie for *Leave It to Beaver* fans who just HAVE to see Ward Cleaver acting like a real rat once in a while. He's a fiend in this one as "Steve Clark" (it's an alias). In one sequence, he asks Julie (Frances Rafferty) to turn up the radio so the neighbors won't be disturbed while he rubs out someone who rubs him the wrong way. And watch what he does to Julie's Aunt Cora (Cecil Weston); is this where Eddie Haskell learned his exclusive tips on supercilious courtesy? Meanwhile, Donald (Harlan Warde) waits patiently for Julie to come to her senses and notice HIM once in a while. An ultra cut-rate exploration of *amour fou.* Don't look at the wallpaper and set decorations too closely!

1947 ?m/C Hugh Beaumont, Frances Rafferty, Harlan Warde, Cecil Weston, Ida Moore, Danny Morton, Joel Friedkin, Lane Chandler; ***D:*** Peter Stewart, Sam Newfield; ***W:*** Al Martin; ***C:*** Jack Greenhalgh. **VHS**

Morgan!

From his breakthrough appearance in the 1966 Karel Reisz classic *Morgan: A Suitable Case for Treatment* right on up to the present day, David Warner has specialized in playing strange dudes, each role progressively weirder than the one that preceded it. His body of work provides a feast for fans of offbeat cult films, although I can think of no other actor of his stature who is such a shy enigma offscreen. *Morgan!* is a stylish study of an nutty anarchist who does everything in his power to regain his delectable ex-wife's affections, including kidnapping her, trying to blow up her future mother-in-law, and harassing her current lover on the job. Clips from *King Kong* and old Tarzan movies reinforce Morgan's ultimate fantasy: to carry off the very sophisticated, very urban Vanessa Redgrave into the jungle where they can be free of society's restraints. Since Morgan's unsympathetic rival Robert Stephens (1931–95) deserves no better fate than to be shoved face first into a wedding cake, Morgan

"Marriage is like a dull meal, with the dessert at the beginning."

—Toulouse-Lautrec (Jose Ferrer) in *Moulin Rouge.*

grabs our interest and sympathy from the very first reel. *Morgan!* was a dream role for a young, little-known actor and Warner made the most of it. One of Warner's unique qualities as an actor is to drag the viewer into an assortment of twisted minds, by projecting intense vulnerability and contrasting it with cool, crisp control. Follow-up roles included fat parts in prestige films that were little seen outside of his native Britain and, more typically, a long line of villains and psychos. Watching vintage David Warner performances, you may wonder why such a nutcase is allowed to move undisturbed through civilized society. Warner is definitely not the guy you'd want to meet in a dark alley, and audiences can never quite trust him in ordinarily trustworthy professions. David Warner's name on a cast list generally means that you can have fun watching him, if no one else, for even after nearly 35 years onscreen, he's always a fascinating, unpredictable presence. ***AKA:*** Morgan: A Suitable Case for Treatment; A Suitable Case for Treatment.

1966 93m/B *GB* Vanessa Redgrave, David Warner, Robert Stephens, Irene Handl, Bernard Bresslaw, Arthur Mullard, Newton Blick, Nan Munro, Graham Crowden, John Rae, Peter Collingwood, Edward Fox; ***D:*** Karel Reisz; ***W:*** David Mercer; ***C:*** Larry Pizer. British Academy Awards '66: Best Screenplay; Cannes Film Festival '66: Best Actress (Redgrave); Nominations: Academy Awards '66: Best Actress (Redgrave), Best Costume Design (B & W). **VHS, LV**

Morgan's Cake

San Francisco Bay area filmmaker Rick Schmidt is the author of *Feature Filmmaking at Used Car Prices* and he isn't kidding about that title. The press kit for *Morgan's Cake* begins with a list of virtually every dollar that was spent on the movie, as well as informative tips on how he was able to make the best use of his time and money. Roughly, production expenses cost $3,700, salaries added up to $2,900, and post-production at Palmer and Monaco film labs totaled $8,400. Three investors contributed to the movie's $15,000 budget. The 87-minute feature took nine days to shoot and the plucky Schmidt wrote, directed, filmed, edited, and produced it all by himself. The results are occasionally touching and amusing but always lacking the creative energy and original insights that characterize the best rock bottom efforts. Morgan Schmidt-Feng, the director's son, is a cute kid, but both his story and his personality wear thin after 20 minutes. Ultimately, reading about the making of *Morgan's Cake* is much more interesting than watching the movie itself. Schmidt, who had made four films by 1990, admitted at the time that he hadn't found his voice as a director yet and I wouldn't care to argue with him. You can see *Morgan's Cake* if you can find it (it doesn't appear to be available on video) or buy *Feature Filmmaking at Used Car Prices* at used bookstores and make your own movie!

1988 87m/B Morgan Schmidt-Feng, Willie Boy Walker, Rachel Pond, M. Louise Stanley, Aaron Leon Kenin, Eliot Kenin, John Claudio; ***D:*** Rick Schmidt; ***W:*** Rick Schmidt; ***C:*** Rick Schmidt, Kathleen Beller; ***M:*** Gary Thorp.

Mother Küsters Goes to Heaven

This successful West German effort by Rainer Werner Fassbinder focuses on the title character, played by Brigitte Mira. Mother Küsters is a woman who finds herself drawn into politics after her husband's suicide; she acquires our sympathy slowly, but relentlessly. At first, she appears to be a woman unfairly hanging on to her grown children and her memories. Gradually, however, her awareness of the world grows with her knowledge of herself. Her speech before the members of a political group who exploit her husband's story for their own purposes provides the film with its most moving moments. Fassbinder and Mira brilliantly show us Mother Küsters' growth with sensitive compassion for both her position and her predicament. A bonus is the presence of Karl Boehm, better known for his work in *Unnatural, The Wonderful World of the Brothers Grimm,* and *Peeping Tom.* Boehm also worked with Fassbinder on *Fox and His Friends.* ***AKA:*** Mutter Küsters Fahrt Zum Himmel.

1976 108m/C *GE* Brigitte Mira, Ingrid Caven, Armin Meier, Irm Hermann, Gottfried John, Margit Carstensen, Karl-Heinz Boehm; ***D:*** Rainer Werner Fassbinder; ***W:*** Rainer Werner Fassbinder; ***C:*** Michael Ballhaus. **VHS**

Mother's Boys

Mother's Boys, deemed to be unworthy of an advance press screening and therefore destined for automatic boxoffice failure, is, in fact, not a bad little film. It stars Jamie Lee Curtis as Jude, a deeply disturbed woman who's already abandoned her family twice and is now back for a third stab at re-engaging their affections. Her husband, Peter Gallagher, has finally adjusted to her departure and is trying to build a new life with Joanne Whalley, the assistant principal at the school attended by his three little boys. But 12-year-old Kes, the oldest son (extraordinarily well played by Luke Edwards), still yearns for the mother he adored as a small child. He acts out, sulks, and withdraws from the new life his father and brothers seem all too eager to lead. Kes is a sitting duck for the expert game player who knows how to manipulate his emotions better than anyone: Jude. We haven't seen much of Jamie Lee Curtis in the movie villain department, and she makes the most of her star turn here. She's smart, sexy, and cunning, but there's clearly something vital missing at the core of her personality. We don't know why she split for three years and neither does she. She invents reasons for her behavior that only SEEM to make sense; dig a little deeper and they're gobbledygook. Her mother, the wonderful Vanessa Redgrave, gives us a clue dating back to Jude's childhood, and considering all the grief Jude puts her kids through, it's more than evident that she's re-enacting painful rituals from her past. With enough well-acted Sturm und Drang for several movies, *Mother's Boys* plays quite well with an audience, including the one in your living room on a lazy Sunday afternoon.

1994 (R) 96m/C Jamie Lee Curtis, Peter Gallagher, Joanne Whalley, Luke Edwards, Vanessa Redgrave, Colin Ward, Joss Ackland, Paul Guilfoyle, John C. McGinley, J.E. Freeman, Ken Lerner, Lorraine Toussaint, Joey Zimmerman, Jill Freedman; ***D:*** Yves Simoneau; ***W:*** Richard Hawley, Barry Schneider; ***C:*** Elliot Davis; ***M:*** George S. Clinton. **VHS, LV, Closed Caption, DVD**

Motorama

Motorama is a shapeless travelogue about a 10-year-old boy whose big dream is to collect all eight letters in the title so that he can compete for $500 million in a national contest. It turns out that the contest is full of hot air and so is the movie, in spite of all its stellar cameos (Shelley Berman, Martha Quinn, Michael J. Pollard, Drew Barrymore, etc.). The chief problem with *Motorama* is that its small protagonist doesn't get a chance to do much more than function as a mouthpiece for some half-baked observations about society by the so-called grown-ups who wrote and directed this mess.

1991 (R) 89m/C Jordan Christopher Michael, Martha Quinn, Flea, Michael J. Pollard, Meat Loaf, Drew Barrymore, Garrett Morris, Robin Duke, Sandy Baron, Mary Woronov, Susan Tyrrell, John Laughlin, John Diehl, Robert Picardo, Jack Nance, Vince Edwards, Dick Miller, Allyce Beasley, Shelley Berman; ***D:*** Barry Shils; ***W:*** Joe Minion; ***C:*** Joseph Yacoe; ***M:*** Andy Summers. **VHS**

Moulin Rouge

This is the movie that started me on a lifelong love affair with Henri De Toulouse-Lautrec (1864–1901), and once again, it was John Huston who ignited the affair, just as he had with Sam Spade and *The Maltese Falcon* on his very first assignment as a young director. *Moulin Rouge* was a nominee the year that Cecil B. De Mille's *The Greatest Show on Earth* won the Academy Award for Best Picture of 1952, even though Huston's re-creation of the Paris art scene of the 1890s is a far superior film. Jose Ferrer was also nominated for the physically painful role of the aristocratic Toulouse-Lautrec, who captured the gaiety of Montmartre night life, while moving through life with a sad, resigned dignity. Huston got a wonderful performance out of Colette Marchand, playing Marie Charlet, the young model who tormented Toulouse-Lautrec more out

Emma Thompson and Kenneth Branagh as Beatrice and Benedick in *Much Ado about Nothing.* Samuel Goldwyn Company; courtesy of the Kobal Collection

of personal desperation than any real malice. However, Toulouse-Lautrec's friendship with Myriamme Hayem (Suzanne Flon) seems to owe more to Pierre la Mure's novel than it does to reality. Certainly, some of the other colorful characters here played far more authentic roles in the artist's life. There really was a La Goulue (Katherine Kath), of course; her real name was Louise Weber (1870–1929), and Toulouse-Lautrec's posters of the dancer will long outlive them both. Jane Avril (1868–1943) survived a difficult childhood to become one of the great entertainers of her day. Zsa Zsa Gabor delivers one of her better performances as the charming dancer immortalized in Toulouse-Lautrec's posters. Toulouse-Lautrec's friend Maurice Joyant (1864–1930, played by Lee Montague) wrote one of the first biographies of the artist. Like Toulouse-Lautrec, Huston was well born, and both artists shared a deep passion for the truth plus a strong determination to establish their own reputations quite separate and apart from the circumstances of their birth. Both succeeded, although Toulouse-Lautrec undoubtedly paid the higher price. Huston lovingly re-creates the Moulin Rouge in all its garish splendor, paying meticulous attention to the Technicolor process, trying to get every detail just right. (*Moulin Rouge* did win the Oscar for art direction and set decoration that year.) It's a sad, exquisite film of an irretrievably vanished era that still has the power to lure us into its spell, if only in our dreams. 🦴🦴🦴🦴

1952 119m/C Jose Ferrer, Zsa Zsa Gabor, Christopher Lee, Peter Cushing, Colette Marchand, Katherine Kath, Michael Balfour, Eric Pohlmann, Suzanne Flon, Claude Nollier, Muriel Smith, Mary Clare, Walter Crisham, Harold Kasket, Jim Gerald, George Lannes, Lee Montague, Maureen Swanson, Tutte Lemkow, Jill Bennett, Theodore Bikel; ***D:*** John Huston; ***W:*** John Huston, Anthony Veiller; ***C:*** Oswald Morris. Academy Awards '52: Best Art Direction/Set Decoration (Color), Best Costume Design (Color); Nominations: Academy Awards '52: Best Actor (Ferrer), Best Director (Huston), Best Film Editing, Best Picture, Best Supporting Actress (Marchand). **VHS, LV**

Mountains of the Moon

Mountains of the Moon, like many movies about explorers, raises an inevitable question: how would these sagas emerge if they had been told from the point of view of the natives rather than the outsiders who invaded their homelands? British explorers of the past were a stubborn lot, determined to impose inappropriate values and customs on uncharted territories even when it when meant the loss of lives and limbs. To his credit, director Bob Rafelson takes scrupulous care not to romanticize the conflicts and adventures of Richard Burton and John Speke, who sought a passage to the Nile in 1857. Rafelson's honest depiction of the physical hardships endured during the expedition is painfully real, especially during several intense and quite explicit sequences. Patrick Bergin and Iain Glen pull out all the stops as Burton and Speke, and Richard E. Grant delivers another riveting performance as an Iago-like character who tries to drive them apart. Fiona Shaw creates a strong impression as Isabel Burton and Bernard Hill has a splendid cameo as Dr. Livingstone. I'm still waiting for that movie from the natives' point of view, but in the meanwhile, *Mountains of the Moon* offers a masterful behind-the-scenes account of the dark and dazzling lives of 19th century explorers. Put Rafelson's epic on a triple bill with *Scott of the Antarctic* and *Burke and Wills* and you may wonder how Great Britain ever won a reputation as an empire builder. 🦴🦴🦴🦴

1990 m/C Patrick Bergin, Iain Glen, Richard E. Grant, Fiona Shaw, John Savident, James Villiers, Adrian Rawlins, Peter Vaughan, Delroy Lindo, Bernard Hill; ***D:*** Bob Rafelson; ***W:*** Bob Rafelson, William Harrison; ***C:*** Roger Deakins; ***M:*** Michael Small.

Much Ado about Nothing

Kenneth Branagh wanted to breathe life into the works of William Shakespeare, and that he definitely has. This rambunctious romantic comedy is filled with fun and high spirits, not to mention four glittering American stars. Well, if Branagh had filled EVERY role with moonlighting actors from *Masterpiece Theatre,* you'd be looking at a movie that was at Cannes on April 15th and on PBS by April 22nd! Branagh and Emma Thompson are the battling Benedick and Beatrice and Robert Sean Leonard and Kate Beckinsale are the young lovers Claudio and Hero. Add Michael Keaton as Dogberry, Keanu Reeves as Don John, Denzel Washington as Don Pedro and then we can play! All this and the sunny scenery of Tuscany, too! 🦴🦴🦴

1993 (PG-13) 110m/C *GB* Kenneth Branagh, Emma Thompson, Robert Sean Leonard, Kate Beckinsale, Denzel Washington, Keanu Reeves, Michael Keaton, Brian Blessed, Phyllida Law, Imelda Staunton, Gerard Horan, Jimmy Yuill, Richard Clifford, Ben Elton, Richard Briers; ***D:*** Kenneth Branagh; ***W:*** Kenneth Branagh; ***C:*** Roger Lanser; ***M:*** Patrick Doyle. Nominations: Golden Globe Awards '94: Best Film—Musical/Comedy; Independent Spirit Awards '94: Best Actress (Thompson), Best Film. **VHS, LV, Closed Caption, DVD**

Murder on the Orient Express

Until *Murder on the Orient Express* was released, big screen adaptations of the works of Agatha Christie (1890–1976) were few and far between. And then came this sumptuous production with a cast headed by 11 Oscar winners and/or nominees. Set in 1930, the plot focuses on a group of highly suspicious-looking passengers aboard the Orient Express (from the classy, gum-chewing Lauren Bacall to the nervous, newly married young Count played by Michael York). The real fun of this leisurely whodunit is guessing which screen legend will next appear. Albert Finney's makeup as Hercule Poirot was such a shock to 1974 audiences that it undoubtedly contributed to the Oscar nomination he won for his interpretation. One of the wittiest wisecracks belongs to John Gielgud, perfecting his persona as a butler seven years before he won an Oscar for it in *Arthur.* Occasionally, it all gets to be a bit much; the late Ingrid Bergman won her third Oscar as a neurotic missionary, but who could believe her for one second in that role? Sidney Lumet's direction and Geoffrey Unsworth's cinematography add to the overall elegance, and mysterious,

The Hound Salutes:
P.J. HOGAN
Director, *Muriel's Wedding*

The inspiration for *Muriel's Wedding* was desperation. I was trying to get films made in the early '90s—it had been that way for quite a long time and it just didn't look like it was going to happen. I was feeling like, 'I think I should give this up and try something else.' At the time, I spent a lot of time in this coffee shop near my house. Across the road from the coffee shop was a bridal wear store. As I was writing down ideas and drinking coffee, I watched the women on the street go into this bridal wear store and they'd appear in the window transformed as brides. At that time in my life, I was very interested in transformation. I wanted to transform myself into a film director. I thought this bridal wear store was a lot like the film industry. It looks open to everyone, but it's really an exclusive club you have to be invited to join and sometimes it just doesn't happen. So I began to think, 'What if one of these women was an imposter? What if she were someone who wanted the experience of dressing up as a bride, but didn't have the fiance or maybe didn't even want to get married?' That's where the idea of Muriel came from. I thought, 'What kind of a character would this girl be?' I worked on it a bit more and came up with the idea of Muriel, the serial bride, someone who wanders from bridal wear store to bridal wear store in the city, dressing up and fantasizing about fiances. I linked the character of Muriel with the things that I was going through during that time, the need to achieve my dreams, and that's how it all started.

"ALL Australian films are independent; we don't have a studio system. The government has an investment fund, so we have government financing and if you're lucky, the government panel will choose your film. It's a small industry, so it can be a real closed shop. It can be very much along the lines of who you know. From what I hear, Hollywood is exactly the same, but I think there are a little bit more opportunities for independent filmmakers outside of the studio system. In Australia, there are very few opportunities and you have to be very lucky. The terrible thing is writing a good script isn't any guarantee, because there are very few people who can spot it. So it really is hard. There's this saying in Australia that it's easier to get a film made if you're a director who's made

creepily shot flashbacks are used to focus on details relevant to the crime-solving. Followed by another adaptation of a Poirot novel by Christie, 1978's *Death on the Nile,* with Peter Ustinov assuming the role of the Belgian detective. 🦴🦴🦴

1974 (PG) 128m/C *GB* Albert Finney, Martin Balsam, Ingrid Bergman, Lauren Bacall, Sean Connery, Richard Widmark, Anthony Perkins, John Gielgud, Jacqueline Bisset, Jean-Pierre Cassel, Wendy Hiller, Rachel Roberts, Vanessa Redgrave, Michael York, Colin Blakely, George Coulouris, Denis Quilley, Vernon Dobtcheff, Jeremy Lloyd; ***D:*** Sidney Lumet; ***W:*** Paul Dehn; ***C:*** Geoffrey Unsworth; ***M:*** Richard Rodney Bennett. Academy Awards '74: Best Supporting Actress (Bergman); British Academy Awards '74: Best Supporting Actor (Gielgud), Best Supporting Actress (Bergman); Nominations: Academy Awards '74: Best Actor (Finney), Best Adapted Screenplay, Best Cinematography, Best Costume Design, Best Original Score. **VHS, LV**

three bombs in a row than if you're a first-time director who's made one very good short film, because the investors and the funding bodies would rather invest in someone who's failed on a big budget.

"Working on the film *Proof* and in Australian television certainly helped me when I was directing *Muriel's Wedding,* but it didn't help much when I was raising the money, because I wasn't the director of *Proof,* that was Jocelyn Moorhouse, and my television experience wasn't very satisfying. It took about three or four years to get the financing and when we did, we just moved straight into casting.

"I always thought the key to the film working was Toni Collette as Muriel, so I set aside a great deal of time to find the right actress for that character. The producers and I would have very serious conversations. We'd sit around and they'd say, 'This film won't work unless we have a brilliant actress as Muriel' and other sage things. Toni Collette came in the first day to audition. I wasn't prepared for someone that good to be there on the first day, because I had all this time to look. When you cast the lead role, it really is like falling in love. It took me about a month before I realized it was Toni who had all the qualities that Muriel needed. I look back on it and think, 'Well, that was the best decision I made.' And it was Rachel Griffith's first film and the moment I saw her, that was really love at first sight. Rachel came in to audition and I thought she was Rhonda. The interesting thing is that the character of Rhonda was very different in the script. She was written as much more like Muriel, particularly physically. When Rachel came in, she was so tall and beautiful, I thought, 'Well, she's not right for this part. What makes her an outsider?' And when she did the audition scene for me, I realized she could capture Rhonda's abrasive personality and the need to tell the truth. So I knew it had to be Rachel in that part. And Bill Hunter is one of Australia's best actors and he's marvelous. I wrote the part of Bill the Battler, Muriel's father, especially for Bill Hunter, and I was very pleased he said yes, because I didn't know who was going to do it if he turned it down."

TONI COLLETTE (Muriel) can be seen in *The Efficiency Expert, The Pallbearer, Lilian's Story, Cosi, Emma,* and *Clockwatchers.* RACHEL GRIFFITHS (Rhonda) can be seen in *Cosi, Children of the Revolution, Jude, My Best Friend's Wedding,* and 1998's *Hilary and Jackie,* for which she received an Academy Award nomination as best supporting actress in the role of Hilary. Both Collette and Griffiths won Australian Academy Awards for *Muriel's Wedding.*

Muriel's Wedding

An unusual friendship is explored in the Australian entry by P. J. Hogan, *Muriel's Wedding.* Muriel (Toni Collette) is a chunky young woman who dreams of a lavish wedding and warm acceptance from a clique who reject her at every opportunity. Muriel is also a compulsive liar and a thief who thinks nothing of feeding her unrealistic dreams with a string of deceptions. While on holiday, she meets the hedonistic, chain-smoking Rhonda (newcomer Rachel Griffiths), who thinks nothing of blasting the exclusive clique with the truth, and who clearly adores Muriel on sight. Of course, Truth wins the day in this extreme-

> "Take my advice. There's money in muck."
>
> **—Nasser (Saeed Jaffrey) counsels his nephew (Gordon Warnecke) in *My Beautiful Laundrette.***

ly uneven film; key sequences appear to have wound up on the cutting room floor, diminishing the overall dramatic impact, and even fine acting by Collette can't make Muriel a truly riveting central character. The scene stealer in this one is the luminous Griffiths; I found myself wishing that the movie had revolved around Rhonda instead of Muriel, and missed her every second she was offscreen. International filmmakers, take note! 🦴🦴🦴

1994 (R) 105m/C *AU* Toni Collette, Bill Hunter, Rachel Griffiths, Jeanie Drynan, Gennie Nevinson Brice, Matt Day, Daniel Lapaine, Sophie Lee, Rosalind Hammond, Belinda Jarrett; ***D:*** P.J. Hogan; ***W:*** P.J. Hogan; ***C:*** Martin McGrath; ***M:*** Peter Best. Australian Film Institute '94: Best Actress (Collette), Best Film, Best Sound, Best Supporting Actress (Griffiths); Nominations: Australian Film Institute '94: Best Director (Hogan), Best Screenplay, Best Supporting Actor (Hunter), Best Supporting Actress (Drynan); British Academy Awards '95: Best Original Screenplay; Golden Globe Awards '96: Best Actress—Musical/Comedy (Collette); Writers Guild of America '95: Best Original Screenplay. **VHS, LV, Closed Caption**

Murmur of the Heart

You can make a comedy about any subject, but getting audiences to watch it is a whole other problem. In 1971, Louis Malle wrote and directed *Murmur of the Heart,* about a young boy with a heart condition who winds up in bed with his ravishing mother. The French Movie Commission wanted to ban the film, but later decided to restrict attendance to adult audiences. Those who actually saw the movie in France and America loved it, but *Murmur* was then, and remains today, a classic seen by very few people. Only an artist like the late Louis Malle could attempt such a tricky project, much less get away with it. The director wisely decides to stick with the kid and we see his life through his eyes. Because of his delicate condition, he is an outsider. Because his mother is an Italian married to a Frenchman, her status is also that of an outsider. When they go off to the country together for his health, their shared isolation forces him to see her as a person rather than as only his mother. His charming Mama (wonderfully played by Lea Massari) is pretty much a mystery, but it's obvious that she's a good soul and so is her son. Nothing very tragic is going to come of anything that happens between these two. The director knows exactly when enough is enough, throughout the entire narrative. There isn't an image, a gesture, or a line that's even mildly gratuitous. The first time you see *Murmur,* you may watch the proceedings wondering when the director is going to stumble. He never does. The second time you see it, it'll be obvious that all Malle's skill went into developing his likable characters and their unusual situation. The comic outcome, improbable in real life, works beautifully as a film fantasy. ***AKA:*** Dearest Love; Le Souffle au Coeur. 🦴🦴🦴🦴

1971 (R) 118m/C *FR* Benoit Ferreux, Daniel Gelin, Lea Massari, Corinne Kersten, Jacqueline Chauveau, Marc Wincourt, Michael (Michel) Lonsdale; ***D:*** Louis Malle; ***W:*** Louis Malle; ***C:*** Ricardo Aronovich; ***M:*** Charlie Parker. Nominations: Academy Awards '72: Best Story & Screenplay; Cannes Film Festival '71: Best Film. **VHS, LV**

Mushrooms

Alan Madden's *Mushrooms* shows how two dotty best friends cover up the accidental death of their lodger. They absolutely HAVE to do that with a cop in the house as their other lodger. The cop's in love with one of them, but that won't help them unless they can cook up a sure-fire scheme...that's it! How could it fail to work? This dark comedy from Australia is a gem. 🦴🦴🦴

1995 93m/C *AU* Julia Blake, Simon Chilvers, Lynette Curran, Christina Andersson; ***D:*** Alan Madden; ***W:*** Alan Madden; ***C:*** Louis Irving; ***M:*** Paul Grabowsky.

My Beautiful Laundrette

My Beautiful Laundrette was a landmark film for Daniel Day-Lewis, Stephen Frears, and Hanif Kureishi, but not alas, for the appealing Gordon Warnecke, who plays Omar, the central character. (He would make an appearance, along with Fergie impersonator Pippa Hinchley, in Kureishi's *London Kills Me* six years later.) Omar re-

models a seedy laundry with his friend Johnny (Day-Lewis) and they turn it into a stylish moneymaker. The stunner for international audiences of 1985 was that Frears revealed the expression of Omar's and Johnny's sexuality in such unstressed fashion. And because it is unstressed, its impact on gay cinema was enormous. Prior to *Laundrette,* a gay relationship in a movie was either A Joke or A Big Deal. In *Laundrette,* it was neither. It was simply a part of the story. Kureishi's screenplay pays far more attention to how and where Pakistani workers fit into the conservative British economy that endured from 1979–97. (By stunning coincidence, it was a time when the Royal Family acted out the most, perhaps functioning as distracting national jesters for Mrs. Thatcher and Mr. Major?) Also included is a demonstration of how magic affects the affair of Omar's married uncle and his lady friend Rachel (Shirley Anne Field), who sighs, "Your wife is a very clever woman." A rich, meticulously rendered film with a marvelous cast. Cast Note: Day-Lewis, the son of Poet-Laureate Cecil Day-Lewis and actress Jill Balcon, made his film debut at age 14 in *Sunday Bloody Sunday.* He married writer/director Rebecca (1994's *Angela*) Miller after appearing in the 1996 film of playwright Arthur Miller's *The Crucible.* ♫♫♫♫

1985 (R) 93m/C *GB* Gordon Warnecke, Daniel Day-Lewis, Saeed Jaffrey, Roshan Seth, Shirley Anne Field, Derrick Branche, Rita Wolf, Souad Faress, Richard Graham, Dudley Thomas, Garry Cooper, Charu Bala Choksi, Neil Cunningham, Walter Donohue, Stephen Marcus, Badi Uzzaman; ***D:*** Stephen Frears; ***W:*** Hanif Kureishi; ***C:*** Oliver Stapleton; ***M:*** Ludus Tonalis, Stanley Myers. National Board of Review Awards '86: Best Supporting Actor (Day-Lewis); New York Film Critics Awards '86: Best Screenplay, Best Supporting Actor (Day-Lewis); National Society of Film Critics Awards '86: Best Screenplay; Nominations: Academy Awards '86: Best Original Screenplay. **VHS, LV, Closed Caption**

My Family

I first became aware of filmmakers Anna Thomas and Gregory Nava in 1981 when I saw Thomas' *The Haunting of M,* a Scottish ghost story starring Shelagh Gilbey as Marianna and Nina Pitt as her sister. I haven't been able to get the film out of my head, although sadly, I've never been able to find it on cable or video. The idea then was that Thomas and Nava would alternate as writers and directors. The following year, they both wrote *End of August,* which IS on video, but not in my neck of the woods. I'd like to see it if only to compare it with 1992's *Grand Isle,* since they're both based on Kate Chopin's *The Awakening. El Norte* was their breakthrough film (which Nava directed), then came (yuck) *A Time of Destiny* (which Nava directed) and THEN came *My Family* (which Nava directed). My question is: when am I going to see a movie by Anna Thomas, reflecting HER experiences and HER interests? Yes, she's been a screenwriter on all of the above movies, but *The Haunting of M* had a look and feel quite different from any of the projects she's worked on since. *My Family* is a good, well-acted, multi-generational saga, but the emphasis is on the patriarchal, rather than the matriarchal line of the Sanchez family. First we see Jose (Jacob Vargas, Eduardo Lopez Rojas), then we see Jose's son Chucho (Esai Morales), then we see Jose's younger son Jimmy (Jonathan Hernandez, Jimmy Smits), then we see yet another son, Memo (Enrique Castillo), and so on.... Their trials and tribulations dominate the 126-minute running time. AND it's narrated by a writer named Paco (Edward James Olmos). Who are the women in this story? There's Jose's wife Maria (Jennifer Lopez, Jenny Gago), who has six kids. There's daughter Irene (Maria Canals, Lupe Ontiveros), who gets married and runs a restaurant, and daughter Toni (Constance Marie), who becomes a nun and a political activist. There's Jimmy's wife Isabel (Edpidio Carillo) who has his son. But the only moments of any real drama in their lives occur when Maria and baby Chucho survive the river rapids on a raft, and when Toni protects Isabel from the death squads of El Salvador. Otherwise, whether the Sanchez boys are good or bad, the story line remains focused on THEM and the melodramatic twists and turns of THEIR lives. In that respect, *My Family* is evocative of the long-running radio soap

Bonnie (Amber Denyse Austin), Jack (Crispin Glover), and Bobby (Matt Lattanzi) in *My Tutor.* Courtesy of the Kobal Collection

opera *One Man's Family,* which ran for 27 years. (PLEASE direct another movie, Ms. Thomas!) ***AKA:*** Mi Familia. 🦴🦴🦴

1994 (R) 126m/C Jimmy Smits, Esai Morales, Eduardo Lopez Rojas, Jenny Gago, Elpidia Carrillo, Lupe Ontiveros, Jacob Vargas, Jennifer Lopez, Scott Bakula, Edward James Olmos, Michael De Lorenzo, Maria Canals, Leon Singer, Jonathan Hernandez, Constance Marie, Enrique Castillo, Mary Steenburgen; ***D:*** Gregory Nava; ***W:*** Gregory Nava, Anna Thomas; ***C:*** Edward Lachman; ***M:*** Pepe Avila, Mark McKenzie. Nominations: Academy Awards '95: Best Makeup; Independent Spirit Awards '96: Best Actor (Smits), Best Supporting Actress (Lopez). **VHS, LV, Closed Caption**

My Left Foot

Daniel Day-Lewis was a sure bet for an Academy Award from the instant audiences first saw him as Christy Brown. *My Left Foot,* a splendid film written and directed by Jim Sheridan, is based on the book by Brown, who refused to let a major obstacle like cerebral palsy prevent him from achieving recognition as an artist and a writer. The key to Brown's success, the film makes clear, is largely due to the efforts of his loving, no-nonsense Irish mother, briskly played by Oscar winner Brenda Fricker. Brown grew up in a large, rambunctious family who included him in every group activity. The Browns are dirt poor, headed by a boozy and often harsh father (subtly played by the late Ray McAnally). Nonetheless, Brown receives constant encouragement and plenty of love until finally he finds a way to communicate with his left foot. Later, he receives speech lessons and artistic encouragement from Dr. Eileen Cole (sympathetically portrayed by Fiona Shaw) who helps to organize his first one-man show. Later, he initiates a wholehearted romantic pursuit of his attractive nurse Mary (Ruth McCabe, in a devilish performance). The whole story, which might have been pure goo in the hands of a sentimental director, is presented with matter-of-fact vigor by Day-Lewis and director Sheridan. Many of the best and funniest lines in this delightful movie are unquotable and you'll want to discover them for yourselves, anyway. 🦴🦴🦴🦴

1989 (R) 103m/C *IR* Daniel Day-Lewis, Brenda Fricker, Ray McAnally, Cyril Cusack, Fiona Shaw, Hugh O'Conor, Adrian Dunbar, Ruth McCabe, Alison Whelan; ***D:*** Jim Sheridan; ***W:*** Shane Connaughton, Jim Sheridan; ***C:*** Jack Conroy; ***M:*** Elmer Bernstein. Academy Awards '89: Best Actor (Day-Lewis), Best Supporting Actress (Fricker); British Academy Awards '89: Best Actor (Day-Lewis), Best Supporting Actor (McAnally); Independent Spirit Awards '90: Best Foreign Film; Los Angeles Film Critics Association Awards '89: Best Actor (Day-Lewis), Best Supporting Actress (Fricker); Montreal World Film Festival '89: Best Actor (Day-Lewis); New York Film Critics Awards '89: Best Actor (Day-Lewis), Best Film; National Society of Film Critics Awards '89: Best Actor (Day-Lewis); Nominations: Academy Awards '89: Best Adapted Screenplay, Best Director (Sheridan), Best Picture. **VHS, LV, Closed Caption, DVD**

My Life As a Dog

This sweet little film is about a boy of 12 (Anton Glanzelius) who is sent to stay with relatives during his mother's illness. It's set in 1950s Sweden and is filled with colorful village characters and an irresistible tomboy with whom he tumbles into as much puppy love as he can handle at that age. The unexpected success of *My Life As a Dog* stunned exhibitors and woke up U.S. producers; Lasse Hallstrom was welcomed to Hollywood to make *Once Around, What's Eating Gilbert Grape?,* and *Something to Talk About.* ***AKA:*** Mitt Liv Som Hund. 🦴🦴🦴🦴

1985 101m/C *SW* Anton Glanzelius, Tomas Van Bromssen, Anki Liden, Melinda Kinnaman, Kicki Rundgren, Ing-mari Carlsson; ***D:*** Lasse Hallstrom; ***W:*** Lasse Hallstrom, Per Berglund, Brasse Brannstrom; ***C:*** Jorgen Persson, Rolf Lindstrom. Golden Globe Awards '88: Best Foreign Film; Independent Spirit Awards '88: Best Foreign Film; New York Film Critics Awards '87: Best Foreign Film; Nominations: Academy Awards '87: Best Adapted Screenplay, Best Director (Hallstrom). **VHS, LV, DVD**

My Own Private Idaho

Zzzzzz... Of course, I didn't know at the time that I was watching self-destruction in action, I thought I was just watching a couple of actors delivering dialogue that was written for them by the director. Even if I had known what was going to happen in front of the Viper Club in the wee hours of Halloween, 1993, my reaction to *My Own Private Idaho* would still be zzzzzz.... There's a very long, very boring gay version of Shakespeare's *Henry IV* here that you have to fidget through or leave. Major critics raved about the performance of River Phoenix, then 21, as a narcoleptic gay hustler, but any of his performances from 1985's *Explorers* through 1991's *Dogfight* are better. Reportedly, his serious involvement with drugs began with this picture and in two of his last three films his performances were way out of control. In any event, both Keanu Reeves and River Phoenix had the burden of bringing Gus Van Sant's screenplay to life, and it couldn't have been easy. This will remain a cult film no matter what anyone says about it, like James Dean's auto safety spot with Gig Young and Tyrone Power's public service message about preventing heart disease. 🦴🦴

1991 (R) 105m/C River Phoenix, Keanu Reeves, James Russo, William Richert, Rodney Harvey, Michael Parker, Flea, Chiara Caselli, Udo Kier, Grace Zabriskie, Tom Troupe; ***D:*** Gus Van Sant; ***W:*** Gus Van Sant; ***C:*** John Campbell, Eric Alan Edwards. Independent Spirit Awards '92: Best Actor (Phoenix), Best Screenplay; National Society of Film Critics Awards '91: Best Actor (Phoenix). **VHS, LV, Letterbox, Closed Caption**

My Teacher Ate My Homework

This modest entry in the *Shadow Zone* series created by J.R. Black represents a comeback of sorts for a nearly unrecognizable Margot Kidder as a character named Sol. It also stars Shelley Duvall as a teacher named Mrs. Fink whose fate is linked to that of a spooky-looking doll. Sheila McCarthy and John Neville are in it, too, as a Mom and as a mysterious shopkeeper. Young protagonist Jesse brings home the doll despite the admonitions of the shopkeeper and discovers that anything that happens to the doll happens to his classroom nemesis, too. Unaddressed is the fact that the kid is under a tremendous amount of parental pressure and his folks only refer to his escalating responsibilities by increasing his allowance. The solution to his dilemma doesn't come from grown-ups, naturally, but from his

James LeGros as Cezanne and Julianne Moore as Mia in *The Myth of Fingerprints.* Sony Pictures Classics; courtesy of the Kobal Collection

best friend Cody's sister Geneva, a wise little girl who knows how to cast spells. Acting by the kids (Gregory Smith, Dara Perlmutter, Edwin Hodge, Dan Warry-Smith, and Diana Theodore) is winning throughout and its good to see Duvall and Kidder again. This may be too intense for younger children, but older kids will probably like it. The creepy doll with an amazing resemblance to Duvall is hauntingly lifelike. ***AKA:*** Shadow Zone: My Teacher Ate My Homework. 🦴🦴🦴

1998 (PG) 91m/C *CA* MacKenzie Gray, Gregory Smith, Shelley Duvall, Dara Perlmutter, Tim Progosh, Sheila McCarthy, Edwin Hodge, Dan Warry-Smith, Diana Theodore, John Neville, Karen Robinson, Margot Kidder, Damon D'Oliveira; ***D:*** Stephen Williams; ***W:*** Garfield Reeves-Stevens, Judith Reeves-Stevens; ***C:*** Curtis Petersen; ***M:*** John McCarthy. **VHS, LV, DVD**

My Tutor

Believe it or don't, *My Tutor* is among the top 50 indie moneymakers of all time. Why? My own theory is that the cast and the script helped to give it good word-of-mouth. Hunky Matt Lattanzi needs a tutor so Dad Kevin McCarthy hires pretty Caren Kaye for the job. So far, it's standard. In fact, the plot line continues to be standard (GUY MEETS TUTOR, TUTOR LIKES GUY, GUY LOSES TUTOR), but the many different acting styles give *My Tutor* a skewed edge. For example, Crispin Glover, whom I'd never seen before, makes an early appearance as Matt's buddy. Even in 1982, Glover could take a conventional part and twist every line of dialogue inside out. At first, I thought he was doing an imitation of Stu Erwin, but it soon became obvious that Glover's wild internal energy was all his own. When he turned up later in *River's Edge, Twister,* and *Wild at Heart,* audiences knew what to expect from the moment they laid eyes on him: ANYTHING and EVERYTHING! Matt Lattanzi was such a cute puppy that no one really cared whether he could act or not, Caren Kaye (later seen in 1990's *Satan's Princess* and 1994's *Pumpkinhead 2: Blood Wings*)

COULD act, thus giving her character an aura of intelligence and common sense, and one-time Oscar nominee Kevin McCarthy just played Dad like a villain and it worked. A painless, and sometimes funny, way to spend 97 minutes at an airport hotel between planes. 𝄞𝄞𝄞

1982 (R) 97m/C Caren Kaye, Matt Lattanzi, Kevin McCarthy, Clark Brandon, Bruce Bauer, Arlene Golonka, Crispin Glover, Shelley Taylor Morgan, Amber Denyse Austin, Francesca "Kitten" Natividad, Jewel Shepard, Marilyn Tokuda; ***D:*** George Bowers; ***W:*** Joe Roberts; ***C:*** Mac Ahlberg; ***M:*** Webster Lewis. **VHS, LV**

Mystery of the Last Tsar

This watchable but sketchy film arrives on the heels of two superior documentaries, *Last of the Tsars* and *The Last Days of the Last Tsar;* it incorporates footage from *Days* that reconstructs the slaughter of the Romanov family at Ekaterinburg. The screenwriter is Peter Kurth, author of the well-written but now debunked *Anastasia: The Riddle of Anna Anderson.* Kurth got caught up in the long-running fantasy that the child of a Polish factory worker was actually the youngest daughter of Nicholas and Alexandra. (His book, which may now be filed under the F for Fiction section of your neighborhood library, was the basis for NBC's 1986 fairy tale, *Anastasia: The Mystery of Anna* starring Amy Irving as the would-be Grand Duchess and Olivia De Havilland as Marie, Claire Bloom as Alexandra, Omar Sharif as Nicholas, Rex Harrison as Cyril, and Christian Bale as Alexei.) It's a legend that refuses to die, even after the Romanov family's remains have been found. However, since *The Mystery of the Last Tsar* identifies itself as a documentary, one might wish that facts AND speculations were not given equal (and confusing) weight. But then, even the surviving Romanovs cannot agree about who the "real" successor to Nicholas II is or is not. The most engaging moments are supplied by family members who bicker about what "roles" they should play in contemporary Russia and who are most "qualified" to play those roles. Playwright Edvard Radzinsky describes the death scene as if he were hyping a lavish theatrical production. Historian Robert Massie and forensic pathologist Dr. William H. Maples offer more reflective and sober commentary, but there's no getting around the fact that this is a bit of a re-hash, designed for casual viewers with only the mildest interest in the subject matter. On a more compelling note, an animated version of *Anastasia* was released in 1997, with accompanying doll and other assorted tie-in merchandise especially for little would-be grand duchesses everywhere. 𝄞𝄞𝄞

1997 77m/C Maggie Britton; ***D:*** Victoria Lewis; ***W:*** Peter Kurth; ***C:*** Michael Anderson, Chris Li; ***M:*** Caleb Sampson, John Kusiak.

Mystic Pizza

This charming story about three teenage girls growing up in Mystic, Connecticut, won its director a Best First Film prize at 1989's Independent Spirit Awards. With that sort of encouragement, better movies were expected of director Donald Petrie than *Opportunity Knocks, The Favor, Grumpy Old Men,* and *Richie Rich.* But back in Mystic, the characters played by Annabeth Gish, Julia Roberts, and Lili Taylor are protected in a time capsule as best friends forever. There are wonderful performances, too, from Vincent D'Onofrio as Taylor's boyfriend, William R. Moses as the quintessential married man who's playing both ends against the middle (and who's Such A Nice Guy to Gish's naive babysitter), and from the great character actress Conchata Ferrell. The perceptive script by Amy Holden Jones (who went on to write *Beethoven, Indecency, The Getaway,* and *Indecent Proposal*—hmm...do we see a trend here when fine indie artists go to Hollywood?) nails down the restless atmosphere of young women itching to leave the over-familiar surroundings in which they grew up, but filled with nostalgia for the associations that made their childhood bearable. 𝄞𝄞𝄞

1988 (R) 101m/C Annabeth Gish, Julia Roberts, Lili Taylor, Vincent D'Onofrio, William R. Moses, Adam Storke, Conchata Ferrell, Joanna Merlin, Matt Damon; ***D:*** Donald Petrie; ***W:*** Amy Holden Jones, Perry Howze, Alfred Uhry; ***C:*** Tim Suhrstedt; ***M:***

The Hound Salutes: SAMUEL FULLER (1911–97)

The other night, I rented 1987's *Return to Salem's Lot,* which is not a sequel to 1979's so-so *Salem's Lot* miniseries, really, just a cheap chance to cash in on that title. But the talents involved happened to be writer/director Larry Cohen with a fantastic cast: Michael Moriarty, June Havoc, Andrew Duggan, Evelyn Keyes, Ronee Blakley and, best of all, the late director Samuel Fuller as the HERO! Fuller only shows up in the last 45 minutes or so, but while he's there, just try dragging your eyes away from him; and when he's not there, you can't stop thinking about him. As a self-described vampire killer, Fuller knows and *uses* every acting trick in the book. It's the sort of role Bogie might have been great in, if he'd stuck around another 30 years. Samuel Fuller didn't stick around for 86 years without learning that you can be gnarled and scuzzy and still wrap an audience around your baby finger; Fuller could play wily codgers in his sleep and and you'd STILL root for him over everyone else in the movie. As a director, Fuller made such classics as *I Shot Jesse James, The Steel Helmet, Baron of Arizona, Pickup on South Street, Run of the Arrow, China Gate, Verboten! Underworld, U.S.A., Merrill's Marauders, Shock Corridor, Naked Kiss, Dead Pigeon on Beethoven Street,* and *The Big Red One* (all on video), but his feisty vigilante in *Return to Salem's Lot* is the way I'll always remember this crusty mutt who gave us so many great moments over the last half century. For a terrific double bill, see *Return to Salem's Lot* with *Q,* a 1982 Cohen/Moriarty vintage chiller. Samuel Fuller isn't in that one, but David Carradine *is.* Trust brand names!

David McHugh. Independent Spirit Awards '89: Best First Feature. **VHS, LV, Closed Caption**

The Myth of Fingerprints

Terrific title, fair flick. Why do families who don't get along get together for the holidays? This dreary gathering of relatives is like 91 minutes in Hell. The only interesting part occurs when Mia (Julianne Moore) splits in search of the ending of a book and meets Cezanne (James LeGros) who used to send her Valentines when they were little. Their moments together are like a blast of fresh air in an otherwise stale story. Does Noah Wyle LIKE home-for-the-holidays flicks? Is that why *Crooked Hearts* and this downer are both on his resume? Watch them together and open a vein. (He even served as associate producer on this one!) Wait a few years and then use that title on a delectable MYSTERY! 🦴🦴

1997 (R) 91m/C Blythe Danner, Roy Scheider, Julianne Moore, Noah Wyle, Michael Vartan, Laurel Holloman, Hope Davis, Brian Kerwin, James LeGros; ***D:*** Bart Freundlich; ***W:*** Bart Freundlich; ***C:*** Stephen Kazmierski; ***M:*** David Bridie, John Phillips. Nominations: Independent Spirit Awards '98: Best Supporting Actor (Scheider). **VHS, Closed Caption**

Nadja

Abel Ferrara's *The Addiction* flops because he wanted to make a movie about vampires that wasn't a vampire movie. Doncha just hate filmmakers who consider that genre to be beneath them? (Hey, anyone who makes a frozen turkey like *Fear City* has no right to sneer at time-honored bloodsuckers.) Michael Almereyda's *Nadja* is another story. *Nadja* is fun! Let's face it, any movie that was partly shot in Pixelvision with a Fisher Price toy camera AND casts Professor Peter Fonda as Dr. Van Helsing (in the venerable tradition of Edward van Sloan) has got to be a kick. When a drained Lucy (Galaxy Craze) explains that she ate a bag of M & M's except for the yellow ones and Fonda vigorously intones to his nephew, "Let's face it, Jim, she's a zombie!," it can't help being a kick and a half. The title character (played by Elina Lowensohn) looks sorta like Gale Sondergaard, Gloria Holden, and Frida Kahlo all rolled into one. Her twin brother Edgar (Jared Harris) is one of those nice vampires who only wants to get married to his nurse Cassandra (Suzy Amis) and live happily ever after. Clearly made on the cheap, *Nadja* is nonetheless impressively atmospheric and saucily respectful to vampires. 🦴🦴🦴

1995 (R) 92m/B Elina Lowensohn, Suzy Amis, Galaxy Craze, Martin Donovan, Peter Fonda, Karl Geary, Jared Harris; ***Cameos:*** David Lynch; ***D:*** Michael Almereyda; ***W:*** Michael Almereyda; ***C:*** Jim Denault; ***M:*** Simon Fisher Turner. Nominations: Independent Spirit Awards '96: Best Actress (Lowensohn), Best Cinematography, Best Director (Almereyda). **VHS**

Naked

For Mike Leigh fans, *Naked* is a Must-See Movie. For yours truly, it is 131 minutes of talking, only 11 minutes less than *Secrets and Lies.* It's the story of a man named Johnny (David Thewlis) who talk-talk-talks his way through the flick and eventually is beaten up. See *Secrets and Lies* review for the reason why I am the Last Person on Earth to be writing one syllable about ANY Mike Leigh movie (although Thewlis is no less an actor here than he is in *Black Beauty, Restoration, The Island of Dr. Moreau,* etc.). ***AKA:*** Mike Leigh's Naked. 🦴🦴½

1993 (R) 131m/C *GB* David Thewlis, Lesley Sharp, Katrin Cartlidge, Greg Cruttwell, Claire Skinner, Peter Wight, Ewen Bremmer, Susan Vidler, Deborah MacLaren, Gina McKee; ***D:*** Mike Leigh; ***W:*** Mike Leigh; ***C:*** Dick Pope; ***M:*** Andrew Dickson. Cannes Film Festival '93: Best Actor (Thewlis), Best Director (Leigh); New York Film Critics Awards '93: Best Actor (Thewlis); National Society of Film Critics Awards '93: Best Actor (Thewlis); Nominations: British Academy Awards '93: Best Film; Independent Spirit Awards '94: Best Foreign Film. **VHS, LV**

Naked Kiss

The Naked Kiss is a genuinely schizophrenic film noir. Kelly (Constance Towers) is a sympathetic character, but capable of extreme violence. She makes a career change from hooker to nurse and wavers between two men, Officer Griff (Anthony Eisley) and a rich guy named Grant (Michael Dante). Griff knows about her, Grant doesn't. When she tells Grant about her career change, he kisses her and asks her to marry him. She likes the proposal, but not the kiss. When she discovers that Grant is a child molester, he tells her that they were made for each other. Turning tricks equals fondling kids? Kelly is enraged by his rationale and acts on it with a vengeance. The movie flips back and forth between hokey sequences of Kelly as a nurse, singing hokey songs with handicapped children, and surrealistic depictions of Kelly fighting with her pimp, fighting with a madam, and fighting with Grant. In spite of Griff's compassion towards her, Kelly doesn't belong in small-town America and she goes through Hell and Back before she accepts the fact. As always, Sam Fuller stirs the viewer's emotions at the visceral level. At times, he's such a cornball that you may actually find yourself blushing. A beat later, he'll shift to savagery, which makes *The Naked Kiss* the edgiest of viewing experiences. Cast Note: Virginia Grey (Candy) played Little Eva in 1927's *Uncle Tom's Cabin* and Betty Bronson (Miss Josephine) played the title role in 1924's *Peter Pan.* ***AKA:*** The Iron Kiss. 🦴🦴🦴

1964 92m/B Constance Towers, Anthony Eisley, Michael Dante, Virginia Grey, Patsy Kelly, Betty Bronson, Edy Williams, Marie Devereaux, Karen Conrad, Linda Francis, Barbara Perry, Walter Matthews, Betty Robinson; ***D:*** Samuel Fuller; ***W:*** Samuel Fuller; ***C:*** Stanley Cortez; ***M:*** Paul Dunlap. **VHS, LV, Letterbox, DVD**

The Nasty Girl

The Nasty Girl is an irreverent film about a serious (and true) subject: how one Bavarian town reacted when a young girl tried to investigate its history during the Third Reich. Lena Stolze is an enchanting presence as Sonja, a much-loved and much-honored young scholar who is vilified when

> **"Regrets? I've got no regrets... except that I was born a woman instead of a man."**
>
> —Nico in *Nico Icon.*

she starts digging into her hometown's past. Initially, she believes her community to be filled with citizens who resisted National Socialism, but her research indicates otherwise. The people who seem to be most concerned by her investigation are her parent's generation, her husband, and teenagers. All of them are too young to be much threatened by old scandals, but threatened they definitely are, and Sonja is the recipient of bureaucratic harassment, family pressures, and anonymous persecution. Director Michael Verhoeven adds many unsettling touches, some which work, some which don't. The backgrounds for many of the sequences are black-and-white stills from the wartime period or color footage of the town itself, presumably to remind us of the emotional landscapes Sonja is revealing. Sonja's childhood, of course, is shot in crisp black and white until she falls in love and her world is seen in vivid colors. (Filmmakers tend to see the past in black and white even though Technicolor has been around since 1917!) Lena Stolze plays Sonja from the years 1976 to 1990 when she ages from the oldest-looking 12 year old in the world to an extremely young-looking woman in her middle 20s. In fact, Sonja's chief adversary is supposed to have been a clergyman in 1936, when the actor playing the role looks like HE might have been all of 12 years old! Because of Verhoeven's excellent intentions, terrific pacing, and quirky viewpoint, the film can be forgiven for a confusing time line and narrative lapses. The enormously appealing personality of Stolze is what you'll remember most about *The Nasty Girl,* especially in Sonja's scenery-chewing finale. ***AKA:*** Das Schreckliche Madchen. 𝔚𝔚𝔚

1990 (PG-13) 93m/C *GE* Lena Stolze, Monika Baumgartner, Michael Gahr; ***D:*** Michael Verhoeven; ***W:*** Michael Verhoeven; ***C:*** Axel de Roche. British Academy Awards '91: Best Foreign Film; New York Film Critics Awards '90: Best Foreign Film; Nominations: Academy Awards '90: Best Foreign Film. **VHS**

Nenette and Boni

This festival favorite tells the story of teenage cook Boni (Gregoire Colin), who sublimates his sexual fantasies about La Boulangere (Valeria Bruni-Tedeschi) by kneading pizza dough as if it were the object of his desire. She's married to Vincent Gallo as Le Boulanger (once again leaving me mystified regarding whatever spell Gallo is supposed to have on women). But Boni has an even more serious concern, his pregnant kid sister, Nenette (Alice Houri), who turns up unannounced. Nenette doesn't want the baby, but Boni does. Well acted, but way too cute for its own good. For those who like cuteness for its own sake, here it is, Marseille-style. If *Nenette and Boni* is ever re-made as a U.S. flick, expect it to be even cuter. 𝔚𝔚𝔚

1996 103m/C *FR* Gregoire Colin, Alice Houri, Valeria Bruni-Tedeschi, Jacques Nolot, Vincent Gallo, Gerard Meylan, Alex Descas, Jamila Farah, Christine Gaya; ***D:*** Claire Denis; ***W:*** Claire Denis, Jean-Pol Fargeau; ***C:*** Agnes Godard. Nominations: Independent Spirit Awards '98: Best Foreign Film. **VHS, Letterbox**

Never Take Candy from a Stranger

This low-key little film was released without fanfare and has no reputation whatever, but it offers an intelligent look at child molestation, especially for its era. Janina Faye and Frances Green play Jean and Lucille, two nine-year-old girls who dance naked for Mr. Olderberry after he promises to give them candy. When Jean tells her mother (Gwen Watford) about it that night, her father (Patrick Allen) tries to resolve the matter with the old man's son (Bill Nagy). But then Jean has a nightmare and her father reports the incident to Captain Hammond (Bud Knapp), who refuses to do anything because, even though the old man is a chronic offender, he IS the town founder. The captain even suggests that the family might be happier elsewhere. The movie reveals that resolving such matters in court is of little avail, at least in 1960. Lucille's parents spirit her out of town for the duration, so Jean is all alone on the stand. Jean's parents finally agree that they WOULD be happier elsewhere and decide to move. But first, Jean goes over to Lucille's house to say goodbye and the two little girls stroll over to Moon Lake. The chilling conclusion leaves the viewer in no doubt whatever about the severity of child molestation. The fact that the molester is played by the venerable Felix Aylmer (1889–1979), who usually plays judges and other benign authority figures, drives home the point that the molester MUST be dealt with directly, not tolerated, regardless of his community standing. This is still strong stuff now; in the Eisenhower era, *Never Take Candy from a Stranger* didn't have a chance. I've yet to meet anyone who's ever seen it, even though it IS on video. Freddie Francis, who won the Oscar that year for *Sons and Lovers* and who would photograph *The Innocents* the following year, does a superb job here, especially in the gripping Moon Lake sequence. Faye, Watford, and Allen are very good as Jean and her parents, and Aylmer is downright spooky! Based on Roger Caris' play, *The Pony Cart.* 🦴🦴🦴

1960 81m/B *GB* Gwen Watford, Patrick Allen, Felix Aylmer, Niall MacGinnis, Alison Leggatt, Bill Nagy, MacDonald Parke, Michael Gwynn, Bud Knapp, Janina Faye, Frances Green, James Dyrenforth, Estelle Brody, Robert Arden, Vera Cook; ***D:*** Cyril Frankel; ***W:*** John Hunter; ***C:*** Freddie Francis; ***M:*** Elizabeth Luytens. **VHS**

New Jersey Drive

Another depressing movie about a youth gang. This group steals cars. Although praised for its realism, the film depicts all the cops as (white, male) villains and all the car thieves as unrepentant criminals, so there's no one you can really root for. The acting is good (Gabriel Casseus received a nomination for his debut performance as Midget at the Sundance Film Festival), but the pervasive mood is one of total despair, unrelieved by any remedy except LEAVING. Spike Lee served as executive producer. 🦴🦴

1995 (R) 98m/C Sharron Corley, Gabriel Casseus, Saul Stein, Andre Moore, Donald Adeosun Faison, Conrad Meertin Jr., Deven Eggleston, Gwen McGee, Koran C. Thomas, Samantha Brown, Christine Baranski, Robert Jason Jackson, Roscoe Orman, Dwight Errington Myers, Gary DeWitt Marshall; ***D:*** Nick Gomez; ***W:*** Nick Gomez, Michel Marriott; ***C:*** Adam Kimmel; ***M:*** Wendy Blackstone. Nominations: Independent Spirit Awards '96: Debut Performance (Casseus). **VHS, LV, Closed Caption, DVD**

Nico Icon

While watching Susanne Ofteringer's *Nico Icon,* I kept asking myself, "Why the heck did she make a documentary about THIS thumping bore of a mannequin whose chief distinction was looking good in designer originals and whose toneless singing voice appealed mainly to audiences who must have been as strung out on heroin as she was?!" If you're going to make a movie about a one-time junkie, why not an interesting and outrageous one like Marianne Faithfull, who could and can act and sing rings around Nico, and is still alive!? Hmmm...maybe that's it. Maybe the fact that Nico DIED after falling off a bicycle in the south of France made the storyline simple: "Beautiful Selfish Model Sleeps with Famous Men (Alain Delon, Jim Morrison, Jackson Browne) and Goes to Hell, But Not Before She Shares Her Legacy with Her Son by Turning Him on to Heroin." Four of the voices in Jean Stein's biography of Edie Sedgwick are also in *Nico Icon* (Danny Fields, Paul Morrisey, Billy Name, Viva). Does that mean we can expect more unriveting movies on all the other non-luminaries in Andy Warhol's Factory? Hope not! At least this story of a woman who loved no one (and vice versa) is short. And the archival footage may be of some interest if you happen to be a '60s clipaholic. Yeah, if I get to vote on a movie about a '60s icon, please make a great one about super diva Marianne Faithfull and let Rosanna Arquette be the star! Faithfull's live concerts (with songs from Noel Coward, Harry Nilsson, and Kurt Weill) are something to see, hear, and treasure well into the 21st century! 🦴🦴

1995 (R) 75m/C *GE* ***D:*** Susanne Ofteringer; ***W:*** Susanne Ofteringer; ***C:*** Judith Kaufmann. **VHS, DVD**

The Night of the Hunter

If you see *Night of the Hunter* when you're too young, you'll have recurring night-

Pearl (Sally Jane Bruce) and the Preacher (Robert Mitchum) in *The Night of the Hunter.* United Artists; courtesy of the Kobal Collection

mares for the rest of your life. Robert Mitchum, who'd been so sexy and heroic in most of the 53 movies he made prior to this one, IS Preacher Harry Powell, one of the scariest bad men of all time. (Mitchum would return to the well of evil seven years later when he played a chilling Max Cady in 1962's *Cape Fear.*) Mitchum played right into a primal terror that so many kids have, that their caretakers will kill them. At the start of the film, young John Harper (Billy Chapin) sees his real father Ben (Peter Graves) dragged away to prison by the police. Entrusted with the care of his mother Willa (Shelley Winters) and little sister Pearl (Sally Jane Bruce), John grows up fast. When Powell (who'd shared a cell with the doomed Ben) swings into Willa's life, John doesn't trust him. Willa drifts towards her second marriage like a subject under hypnosis, learns on her wedding night that her handsome new husband will not have sex with her, and subsequently slides into a religious haze. When she finally faces the truth about him, he has no further use for her and John is thrust into a life-and-death game with the Preacher, complicated by Sally's adoration of their stepfather. John knows where his late father's money is hidden and the Preacher knows that he knows. Stanley Cortez's beautiful cinematography follows the children into the night as they make their escape from the Preacher, who stalks them tenaciously. Everyone here (especially Lillian Gish as the kindly Rachel who helps John and Pearl) is ideally cast and Charles Laughton, who never directed another movie, sustains the mood of horror for 93 minutes. Mitchum relayed directorial instructions to the children since Laughton detested working with kids. (In that light, *The Night of the Hunter,* with so many youngsters in the cast, is an odd directing choice for Laughton.) Nevertheless, it's an unforgettable picture with beautiful and haunting imagery and a literate screenplay by James Agee. ℒℒℒℒ

1955 93m/B Robert Mitchum, Shelley Winters, Lillian Gish, Don Beddoe, Evelyn Varden, Peter Graves,

James Gleason, Billy Chapin, Sally Jane Bruce, Gloria Castillo, Mary Ellen Clemons, Cheryl Callaway, Corey Allen, Paul Bryar; ***D:*** Charles Laughton; ***W:*** James Agee; ***C:*** Stanley Cortez; ***M:*** Walter Schumann. National Film Registry '92. **VHS, LV**

Night of the Living Dead

Until 1995, rental videos of this classic horror movie were dupey, contrasty, grimy copies of the original film. That's when Anchor Bay Entertainment released a special collector's edition that was digitally remastered from the 35mm negative. Don't even think about buying or renting anything else! This was the way George A. Romero intended *Night of the Living Dead* to be seen. Made in Pittsburgh during the last year of the Johnson era, the story explored our very real fears of the unknown during that violent, tense time. Why are the dead walking around and attacking the living? Who cares? Get through the night as best you can! Duane Jones, then 31, stars as Ben, who is trying to fortify a farmhouse against the flesh-eating zombies. He's courageous, decisive, and smart, all worthy qualities for the triumphant hero he would be in a less nihilistic tale. (Jones, a fine actor who later appeared in *Black Vampire, Beat Street,* and *Fright House,* died at 51 a year before 1989's *To Die For* was released; he is sixth-billed as a very gaunt Simon Little and the film is dedicated to his memory. Jones also taught literature at Antioch College and directed theatrical productions.) Ben's nemesis is (producer) Karl Hardman as Harry Cooper, who wants to hide in the cellar with his wife Helen (Marilyn Eastman) and injured daughter. Blowhard Harry fights Ben every step of the way, but he doesn't impress Helen for an instant. The peacemaker of the group is Keith Wayne as Tom, who respectfully addresses Harry as "Mr. Cooper," although his sympathies clearly lie with Ben. Judith O'Dea is cast to type as Barbra, who acts like a zombie, even though she isn't one yet, and Judith Ridley as Tom's girlfriend Judy must have gone to the same acting school as O'Dea. Everyone else is quite good and the existential quality of their fate, plus the steps they take to circumvent it, will suck you in for the duration. If you want to see what Romero looked like in 1968, check out that television interviewer from the nation's capital. And don't watch this one alone! ***AKA:*** Night of the Flesh Eaters; Night of the Anubis. 🦴🦴🦴🦴

1968 90m/B Judith O'Dea, Duane Jones, Karl Hardman, Marilyn Eastman, Keith Wayne, Judith Ridley, Russell Streiner, Bill "Chilly Billy" Cardille; ***Cameos:*** George A. Romero; ***D:*** George A. Romero; ***W:*** George A. Romero, John A. Russo; ***C:*** George A. Romero. **VHS, LV, DVD**

Night on Earth

Jim Jarmusch shows five different taxi drivers and their passengers in Los Angeles, New York, Paris, Rome, and Helsinki, all on the same night on Earth. Winona Ryder as Corky the cabbie and Gena Rowlands as Victoria Snelling the Los Angeles casting agent work extremely well together in their segment, as do Giancarlo Esposito as YoYo the Brooklyn cabbie and Armin Mueller-Stahl as his East German passenger, Helmut. Highly recommended for Jarmusch fans, pretty good for everyone else. 🦴🦴🦴

1991 (R) 125m/C Winona Ryder, Gena Rowlands, Giancarlo Esposito, Armin Mueller-Stahl, Rosie Perez, Beatrice Dalle, Roberto Benigni, Paolo Bonacelli, Matti Pellonpaa, Kari Vaananen, Sakari Kuosmanen, Tomi Salmela, Lisanne Falk, Isaach de Bankole, Alan Randolph Scott, Anthony Portillo, Richard Boes, Pascal Nzonzi, Emile Abossolo-M'Bo; ***D:*** Jim Jarmusch; ***W:*** Jim Jarmusch; ***C:*** Frederick Elmes; ***M:*** Tom Waits, Kathleen Brennan. Independent Spirit Awards '93: Best Cinematography. **VHS, LV, Letterbox**

Night Tide

If the '60s had been the '40s and Curtis Harrington had had his way, he would have become a film director in the dark, brooding style of his idol, Val Lewton. With the explosion of color film in the mid-'60s, that didn't quite happen, and Harrington did the best he could with television movies like *How Awful About Allan, The Cat Creature,* and *Killer Bees,* plus the occasional offbeat theatrical feature. But in 1963, he was permitted one chance to make a black-and-white classic: *Night Tide.* Clearly inspired by *The Cat People,*

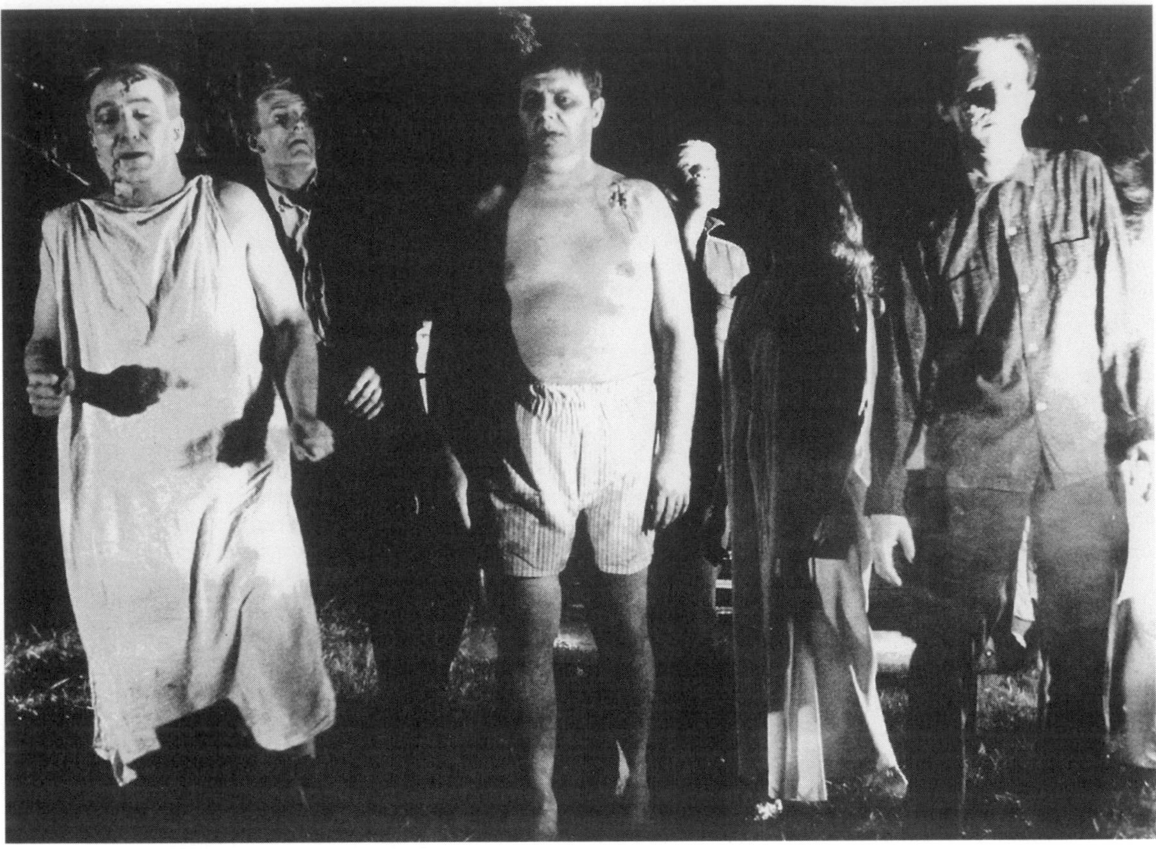

Zombies walk the earth on the *Night of the Living Dead.*
Courtesy of the Kobal Collection

this haunting love story stars an impossibly young-looking Dennis Hopper as a naive sailor who falls in love with a mysterious mermaid at a seaside carnival. Hopper not only looks like a baby here, he's so painfully vulnerable, that it's hard to believe that he could play a grungy, lived-in *Easy Rider* within six years of this film. The late Luana Anders, another future cast member of *Easy Rider,* is the nice normal girl who supplies chilling commentary on Hopper's dark-eyed seductress Linda Lawson. While Harrington is deeply sympathetic to the dilemma faced by his central characters, he effectively contrasts their romance with graphic nightmare fantasies. *Night Tide* is THE perfect film to watch on a dark and stormy night. 🦴🦴🦴

1963 84m/B Dennis Hopper, Gavin Muir, Linda Lawson, Luana Anders, Marjorie Eaton, Tom Dillon; ***D:*** Curtis Harrington; ***W:*** Curtis Harrington; ***C:*** Vilis Lapenieks. **VHS**

A Night to Remember

Eva Hart (1905–96) thought that of all the movies made about the Titanic, *A Night to Remember* came the closest to capturing those last few hours aboard the "unsinkable" ship, and Miss Hart ought to know; as a seven-year-old child, she was saved from drowning by her no-nonsense mother, Esther, but her father Benjamin went down with the ship. The large cast is upstaged by the White Star liner, but there are some unforgettable moments here by some very fine actors. Michael Goodliffe (1914–76) as Titanic designer Thomas Andrews gives a performance of such agonized restraint that it's almost impossible to believe that he's acting. Courteous and gracious nearly to the end, only a flicker of his dark eyes betrays the horror that he takes such pains to conceal. George Rose (1920–88) as Charles Joghlin does absolutely everything wrong, yet he is said to have survived his many hours paddling in the Atlantic because the massive quantities of alcohol he consumed served as a sort of anti-freeze. (Remember that if you're ever on the world's "safest" cruise.) Honor Blackman was still an English rose at this stage of her career (no leather on A-deck), but acquits herself admirably as a first-class passenger who must confront the reality of instant widowhood. Kenneth More (1914–82) was at the height of his popularity, so who better to play Herbert Lightoller, who enforced the policy of "women and children first" and then managed to swim to safety? If there were villains of the piece besides arrogance, carelessness, and neglect, Bruce Ismay (played as "The Chairman" by Frank Lawton, 1904–69), who urged that the Titanic beat some sort of speed record through the icy waters, Phillips (Kenneth Griffith), who ignored ice warning after ice warning all day Sunday, and Captain Lord (Laurence Naismith, 1908–92), who went to bed early while the Titanic sent repeated distress signals less than 10 miles away, top the list of the usual suspects. *A Night to Remember,* with its contracting perspectives of useless opulence and imminent mortality, makes April 15, 1912, seem like yesterday, not over 85 years in the past. 🦴🦴🦴🦴

1958 119m/B Kenneth More, David McCallum, Anthony Bushell, Honor Blackman, Michael Goodliffe, George Rose, Laurence Naismith, Frank Lawton, Alec McCowen, Jill Dixon, John Cairney, Joseph Tomelty, Jack Watling, Richard Clarke, Ralph Michael, Kenneth Griffith; ***D:*** Roy Ward Baker; ***W:*** Eric Ambler; ***C:*** Geoffrey Unsworth. Golden Globe Awards '59: Best Foreign Film. **VHS, LV, DVD**

Night Train to Munich

The essence of the very British *Night Train to Munich* is captured in the comic performances of Basil Radford and Naunton Wayne, reprising their roles in *The Lady Vanishes* as Charters and Caldicott. Working with a tight script by Frank Launder and Sidney Gilliat, Carol Reed skillfully reveals how ordinary people react to war. Faced with an international crisis, Charters tries to call Berlin to retrieve the golf clubs he loaned to a friend. Charters and Caldicott then find themselves caught up in a world of spies, which they resist at first. It is not until they are insulted by a Gestapo officer that the realities of war penetrate their consciousness and they make an effort to help their old school chum, played by Rex Harrison. Radford and Wayne were to brighten 10 British films together during their dozen years as a team, satirizing the old school boys who never grew up. Obsessed with cricket and other sports, touchingly convinced that everyone in the world knows that British is best, innately decent, terrified of women and forthright action, Charters and Caldicott were enormously appealing representatives of a type that vanished when the British empire shriveled. Oh, yes, there IS an all-star cast in this one, headed by Margaret Lockwood and Paul Henreid, plus plenty of political tension AND sexual tension, but to character actor devotees, Charters and Caldicott are practically the whole story. You can see Radford and Wayne at their best in this fast-paced 1940 thriller. Recommended for further viewing: 1945's *Dead of Night,* 1946's *A Girl in a Million,* and 1949's *Passport to Pimlico.* ***AKA:*** Night Train; Gestapo. 🦴🦴🦴🦴

1940 93m/B *GB* Margaret Lockwood, Rex Harrison, Paul Henreid, Basil Radford, Naunton Wayne, James Harcourt, Felix Aylmer, Roland Culver, Raymond Huntley, Austin Trevor, Keneth Kent, C.V. France, Frederick Valk, Morland Graham, Wally Patch, Irene Handl, Albert Lieven, David Horne; ***D:*** Carol Reed; ***W:*** Frank Launder, Sidney Gilliat; ***C:*** Otto Kanturek. **VHS**

Nina Takes a Lover

There's a very old joke that bartenders still tell sometimes about the real identities of their weekend clientele. If by some extraordinary chance you haven't heard the joke, *Nina Takes a Lover* may seem

The Hound Salutes:
LINDA LAWSON
Singer, Actress, *Night Tide*

When I first came to Hollywood, I was in an elevator one day with a pile of stuff to deliver and these two men were looking at me and whispering. One of them said, 'Are you an actress?' I said, 'Of course!' (I had never done any acting in my life.) He said, 'Do you have an agent?' And I said, 'No.' That's how it started. Then I got into acting. I was walking down Sunset Boulevard one day and the horn beeps and it was Blake Edwards. He had just started *Peter Gunn* and Henry Mancini's amazing theme song had just zoomed to the top of the charts. Hank had mentioned to Blake that I was a terrific singer and that he was one of my biggest fans. I adored him. He was great. Blake said. 'Let me give you a lift home. I want to talk to you about something. I've written a script for you.' I was 21 and so cynical already, I thought, 'Yeah, sure you have, Blake.' And he said, 'I'll have it sent over this afternoon.' And the script arrived and it was called *Lynn's Blues* and I auditioned and he said 'Yeah, we can make this work.'

"I lied to get the part of Mora the mermaid in *Night Tide.* I told them I could swim. I never lied again. ('Can you ride a horse?' 'NO!') They did a Curtis Harrington retrospective and he didn't remember this. I have my calendar book from 1960 and I have the *Night Tide* schedule in there. Dennis Hopper was always weird. Shall I tell a story out of school? I went to a barbecue and there were six or seven of us there, among them Dennis Hopper. I left my bathing suit at the barbecue, so Dennis called me and said, 'You left your bathing suit at the barbecue and I have it. Can I bring it by?' 'If you wouldn't mind, it would be terrific.' 'O.K.' So he came over with my bathing suit and I was ironing in the kitchen of my little single room apartment. He walked around and looked at everything, even though there wasn't anything to look at. I didn't own anything except my clothes and a few books. He crawled under the kitchen table. 'What are you doing under there?' 'It's really neat under here. I like it.' 'Do you? O.K.' And I got my purse and I left. I don't know how long he sat there without an audience. When I came back, he was gone."

LINDA LAWSON also appeared in *Sometimes a Great Notion, Let's Kill Uncle, Apache Rifles,* and *The Threat.*

like a fresh take on the ancient concept of the wife having a fling while her husband is out of town. The title character tries to explain to a nosy journalist that "it's more complicated than that." But it isn't—it's exactly that and no more, except for the always beautiful San Francisco locations (with Oakland doubling for its neighboring city in a few sequences). One might wonder about the direction of Laura San Giacomo's career which was sizzling hot at the time she made *sex, lies and videotape,* but lost steam fast in a succession of supporting roles in films that took a dive or showcased other players. From being "devastatingly erotic" at age 27 in her breakthrough film to looking like a little girl playing dress-up (at age 30!) in *Under Suspicion,* San Giacomo's cinematic identity seems distressingly out of focus. (In fact, she had signed on for episodic television by 1997.) As Nina, she delivers the sort of low-key performance suitable for a telly feature of the week, entirely in keeping with both the spirit and the execution of writer/director Alan Jacobs' first feature. Brit Paul Rhys is an agreeable presence as the enigmatic photographer who pursues her and beyond that, what can we say? If it's a new joke to you and you enjoy the scenery, *Nina Takes a Lover* may be just the video ticket for a wistful spring evening. 🦴🦴

1994 (R) 100m/C Laura San Giacomo, Paul Rhys, Michael O'Keefe, Cristi Conaway, Fisher Stevens; ***D:*** Alan Jacobs; ***W:*** Alan Jacobs; ***C:*** Phil Parmet; ***M:*** Todd Boekelheide. **VHS, LV, Closed Caption**

Nine Days a Queen

Here's irony for you—in the year of three kings (Edward VIII plus Georges V and VI), British producer Michael Balcon (Daniel Day-Lewis' grandfather, by the way) assembled this lavish production set in 1553, ALSO the year of three monarchs (Edward VI, Lady Jane Grey, and Mary I). Did Balcon (and the Americans) know something four months into the uncrowned king's reign that loyal monarchists did not? Probably. If Lord Beaverbrook (1879–1964) of the *Daily Express and Evening Standard* knew, Balcon MUST have known. Enough of 20th century gossip! Let's get back to historical...gossip...of the 16th century. *Nine Days a Queen* boasts touching performances by Nova Pilbeam as Lady Jane Grey (1537–54), and by Desmond Tester as the frail Edward VI (1537–53). Before his death of tuberculosis at 15, Edward was persuaded by the Earl of Warwick (Cedric Hardwicke) to change the order of succession in Lady Jane's favor. Jane, also 15, was too young and naive to present any serious challenge to the ascendancy of Mary I (1516–58), played by Gwen Francon-Davies. Jane's father was a much greater threat, so both were beheaded, along with Jane's young husband, Lord Guilford Dudley (John Mills). It's a very sad tale, well and economically told; it's a good 64 minutes shorter than the sumptuous 1985 re-make starring Helena Bonham Carter. Miles Malleson, who plays Lady Jane's father, co-scripted with director Robert Stevenson. ***AKA:*** Lady Jane Grey; Tudor Rose. 🦴🦴🦴

1936 80m/B *GB* John Mills, Cedric Hardwicke, Nova Pilbeam, Sybil Thorndike, Leslie Perrins, Felix Aylmer, Miles Malleson, Frank Cellier, Desmond Tester, Gwen Francon-Davies, Martita Hunt, John Laurie, Roy Emerton, John Turnbull, J.H. Roberts; ***D:*** Robert Stevenson; ***W:*** Robert Stevenson, Miles Malleson; ***C:*** Mutz Greenbaum. **VHS**

Nine Months

Marta Meszaros is a fine writer and director who makes a number of important universal statements in *Nine Months.* Widely praised for her award-winning 1975 movie, *The Adoption,* Meszaros has a sharp eye for the details that determine the direction of her character's lives. Why does her strong, brave, self-reliant heroine (Lili Minori) fall for the violent tactics of the foreman who wants to marry her? She resists him up to the point when he breaks into her room and tears her clothing, then she undresses him tenderly and feeds him from a bowl filled with bread and vegetables. Meszaros shows us how a woman can break out of a trap in which she finds herself, but not why she would choose such a fascist dork to begin with. Minori is plain and pudgy, yet she seems quite lovely as she struggles to maintain her work, her studies, her child, and her dignity. Jan Nowicki plays the role of the stubborn fiance to the hilt, his piercing blue eyes expressing his feelings better than reams of dialogue. And Janos Kende's exceptional cinematography makes the drab factories, laboratories, and train stations in and around Budapest seem almost beautiful. 🦴🦴🦴

1977 93m/C *HU* Lili Monori, Jan Nowicki, Dzsoko Roszics; ***D:*** Marta Meszaros; ***W:*** Marta Meszaros, Gyula Hernadi, Ildiko Korodl; ***C:*** Janos Kende; ***M:*** Gyorgy Kovacs.

The Hound Salutes:
LAURA SAN GIACOMO AND PAUL RHYS
Nina Takes a Lover

Laura San Giacomo: "I really loved the script for *Nina Takes a Lover* and I really loved the characters Paul Rhys and I were to play, and I wanted to know if they were meant to be together and why. We shot so much, though, that I didn't get any time to go shopping in San Francisco or to explore the city at all. But also, every place we shot was continuously noisy—well, any place you shoot on location is just planes, trains, and automobiles. One location that we shot in where there was a train, I remember standing around and waiting for *six hours!* There was nothing we could do. We just had to stop half a day every day.

"I don't see myself as a femme fatale at all. I consider myself a normal person with normal insecurities, so I see Nina as probably closer to who I am than anything else that I've done. It wasn't such a huge bridge to cross between who I thought she was and how to make that happen onscreen. From my perspective, I believe that Nina and the photographer are supposed to be together and that they *could* be together and really move forward."

Paul Rhys: "I thought my character as the photographer was a complex person and I was interested in telling his story. Because he goes back and forth in time, his emotional truths change. It

1984

To make a movie like *1984* IN 1984, as Michael Radford did, is to make a quaint period piece by default. It's bleak, it's interesting, but the whole *raison d'etre* for the film (to scare us out of our wits at what COULD happen!) is missing. When the novel was written in 1948, fears about the future had many people wondering if any of us would survive until 1984. Seven years later, in an edgy, Cold War–ridden world, Orwell's dark visions were still quite persuasive to 1950s audiences. A film noir atmosphere pervades the original film by Michael Anderson in 1956, enhanced by the casting of American noir icons like Edmond O'Brien as Winston Smith and Jan Sterling as Julia. Smith's great fear of rats is successfully exploited in the creepy Orwellian universe presided over by Michael Redgrave as O'Connor. Julia, too, is confronted with her greatest fear, and each betrays the other and their mutual dreams of love. They know that Big Brother is always watching. And WE know there are always more rats in the dark, the better to give us nightmares, My Dears...no 1980s special effects can compete with our terrorized imaginations...definitely worth a reissue on video! 🦴🦴🦴🦴

1956 90m/B *GB* Edmond O'Brien, Jan Sterling, Michael Redgrave, David Kossoff, Mervyn Johns, Donald Pleasence, Carol Wolveridge, Ernest Clark, Ronan O'Casey, Kenneth Griffith; ***D:*** Michael Anderson Sr.; ***W:*** William Templeton, Ralph Gilbert Bettinson; ***C:*** N. Peter Rathvon.

1999

The difference between a Jerk and a Good Guy is not a Heartbeat, but a Decision. That's what Rufus Wild (Dan Futterman) discovers in an end-of-the-millennium party and that's what all self-deceptive Jerks

was intriguing for me to play so many levels of reality at the same time. We were told daily that we were shooting this scene here or there because there's this beautiful bridge or something. I used to play devil's advocate and say that San Francisco was the most overrated place I'd ever been in, but I do like it a lot, even though we were always stopping because there was this huge train in the warehouse district where my studio was meant to be. I agree with Laura: I feel that the couple we play definitely have a future together. It's so easy to be trite and overly simplistic about it—I mean, I've never come across a perfect relationship, marital or otherwise, but this is a story about two people who overcome an obstacle to reach a place where they'll come across *other* obstacles! Through the lesson of this film, I hope their strength has made them deal with future obstacles—god knows what they are—in a better way."

LAURA SAN GIACOMO can be seen in *Miles from Home, sex, lies and videotape, Vital Signs, Quigley Down Under, Pretty Woman, Once Around, Under Suspicion, Stuart Saves His Family, The Stand, The Right to Remain Silent, The Apocalypse,* and *Suicide Kings.*

PAUL RHYS' films include *Vincent and Theo, Chaplin, Becoming Colette,* and *Gallowglass.*

Writer/director ALAN JACOBS went on to direct *Diary of a Serial Killer* with Gary Busey and Michael Madsen.

(and you know who you are) have to learn, the hard way, more often than not. We can change jobs and friends (girlfriends and boyfriends) and families and drugs and cocktails and cities until we get it. Interchangeable life choices change nothing. Realizing that we are who we are and we have to make the best (as opposed to the worst) of who we are makes us Good Guys. And who wouldn't be riddled with confusion for 25 years with a moniker like Rufus Wild? A pox on his parents for giving him that name. Rufus the Jerk is going with Annabell (Jennifer Garner), who's cool, but he's also attracted to a colleague with lots of hair and teeth (Amanda Peet as Nicole), so he (foolishly) breaks up with Annabell just before they attend 1999's New Year's Eve party at which Nicole will be present. Andrew Goldman (Matt McGrath) is the host and his father Harold (Buck Henry) shows up with the line, "Guess what I found?" as he produces a gun. Andrew hides it in the bathroom hamper; a kid finds the gun and Andrew hides it again. Two teenage boys watch the guests use the bathroom, especially the female guests. Two grown-up boys bring hallucinogenic fruit redolent with its own special rotting corpse fragrance, enough for dozens of guests to share. Sylvia (Margaret Devine) tells girlfriend Suki (Sandrine Holt) that she'd rather be an ear doctor than a singer. Harry tells a distraught Andrew that he's not his real father. Suki comforts Andrew. Unattractive guest Goat Man (Steven Wright) blathers non-stop whenever we see him. Nicole does a striptease for Rufus, who's wearing a party card that says "Lutheran." Writer/director Nick Davis has wicked eyes and ears, especially for silly party behavior and all those stupid end of millennium lists (greatest presidents,

"Is this your wife? What a lovely throat."

—Orlok (Max Schreck) knows his necks in *Nosferatu*.

greatest writers, etc.) compiled by idiots: Lincoln is *18th?* Shakespeare is *3rd?* Davis is the grandson of Herman Mankiewicz of *Citizen Kane* fame and he has plotted his 92-minute slice of our very own fin de siecle with great care, abundant wit, and a unique sense of humor, even evoking the spirit of radio drama when he examines Rufus Wild's crisis of conscience. I wonder what *1999* would look like on a double bill with *Withnail and I*? *1999* opened San Francisco's indie fest in January 1999. If only 15 of the 16 features that followed had been as good as this one. We can't have everything we want, shucks! 🦴🦴🦴

1998 92m/C Dan Futterman, Jennifer Garner, Matt McGrath, Amanda Peet, Steven Wright, Sandrine Holt, Buck Henry, Margaret Devine, Daniel Lapaine, David Gelb, Nick Davis; ***D:*** Nick Davis; ***W:*** Nick Davis; ***C:*** Howard Krupa.

Ninth Street

Two old men (Don Washington and Kevin Willmott as Bebo and Huddie) reminisce about how Junction City, Missouri, went downhill from a thriving jazz mecca during World War II to a dilapidated, crime-ridden street during the Vietnam War. *Ninth Street* took seven years to make on a rock-bottom budget and its intentions are nobler than the final product. There are some intriguing actors and fine dialogue here, but *Ninth Street* does not transcend its origins as a stage play, even with pros like Isaac Hayes and Martin Sheen in the cast. The drama escalates a bit in the last third of the film, if you can stick with it beyond the talky first hour. Queen Bey is excellent as Mama Butler. Played at San Francisco's Indie Fest in 1999. 🦴🦴

1998 98m/B Don Washington, Kevin Willmott, Nadine Griffith, Byron Myrick, Isaac Hayes, Queen Bey, Kaycee Moore, Martin Sheen; ***D:*** Tim Rebman, Kevin Willmott; ***W:*** Kevin Willmott; ***C:*** Troy Paddock; ***M:*** Wayne Hawkins.

Nobody's Fool

Love hurts, and Cassie (Rosanna Arquette) is finding out just how much it hurts as *Nobody's Fool* begins. She hates her job as a waitress in a bar (except for her friend Pat, nicely played by Mare Winningham), she hates being dumped by her boyfriend Billy (Jim Youngs) when she told him she was pregnant, she hates that she had to give the baby up for adoption, and she hates the fact that she's tried so many times to kill herself without success. She's making yet another unsuccessful suicide bid in the opening sequence, and it's clear from her energy, humor, and vitality that she doesn't really want to die. Then an engaging technician named Riley (Eric Roberts) comes to town with a touring theatrical troupe. Cassie starts to perk up a bit, but the part of her that feels good feeling bad still casts longing glances in Billy's direction. Evelyn Purcell does a fine job showing how disconnected a girl like Cassie can feel in a small town like Buckeye. Ironically, *Nobody's Fool* was released on the same day as ex-husband Jonathan Demme's *Something Wild.* It's a lovely, much underappreciated film, and Rosanna Arquette and Eric Roberts are delightful as Cassie and Riley. 🦴🦴🦴

1986 (PG-13) 107m/C Rosanna Arquette, Eric Roberts, Mare Winningham, Louise Fletcher, Jim Youngs, Gwen Welles, Stephen Tobolowsky, Charlie Barnett, Lewis Arquette; ***D:*** Evelyn Purcell; ***W:*** Beth Henley; ***C:*** Misha Susov; ***M:*** James Newton Howard. **VHS, LV, Closed Caption**

Non-Stop New York

Non-Stop New York was directed by Robert Stevenson, who went on to direct many of Walt Disney's greatest hits. Its star, Anna Lee (Mrs. Stevenson), wasn't much of an actress in 1937 and her onscreen teaming with John Loder produced no sparks. Also in the cast as a musical prodigy is 18-year-old Desmond Tester, heartily disliked by so many male audience members that you might mistake him for the villain of the film. The real star of *Non-Stop New York* is an incredible airliner that zips across the Atlantic, in spite of the fact that it is weighed down by massive staterooms and a convenient observation deck for passengers. The plane is, in fact, more like a luxury ocean liner, but by the time that contraption is up in the air, Stevenson has guided the characters into so many preposterous situations with such giddy results, that you won't mind going along for a far-from-real ride. 🦴🦴🦴

1937 71m/B Anna Lee, John Loder, Francis L. Sullivan, Frank Cellier, Desmond Tester, Athene Seyler, William Dewhurst, Drusilla Wills, Jerry Verno, James Pirrie, Ellen Pollock, Arthur Goullet, James Carew, Alf Goddard, Danny Green; ***D:*** Robert Stevenson; ***W:*** Curt Siodmak, Roland Pertwee, Derek Twist, J.O.C. Orton, E.V.H. Emmett; ***C:*** Mutz Greenbaum. **VHS**

Normal Life

When Dylan McKay came back to *Beverly Hills 90210* in November 1998, the show's devoted followers were thrilled, but the more cynical looked at his return and said, "Ah Hah! If he were Number One at the Boxoffice he wouldn't even consider episodic television." Now who's saying this? Certainly no one who actually IS Numero Uno. Superstars are more aware than anyone of what a roller-coaster ride show business is. Nope, it's the voices of the countless observers who never will be on a magazine cover saying that if someone with Luke Perry's looks and talent has to make a bow-wow like *American Strays* (see review), what chance does anyone else have? Unlike *American Strays, Normal Life,* which first played at the Sundance Film Festival, is a good film, with excellent performances by Perry and co-star Ashley Judd. Based on fact and feeling like classic noir, *Normal Life* tells the story of Officer Chris Anderson and his wife Pam, who are on a fast track to Hell. She is Trouble and he knows it, but from the moment he first rescues her from a fight in a bar (a clear hint of trouble for any guy who actually wants a normal life), Chris is hooked. It isn't sex that chains Chris to Pam, but a deep emotional bond that defies logic and reason. He robs banks to give her a better life and when she finds out, she's revved up and ready to join him on a heist. Whenever Chris tries to set limits with Pam that might extend their life expectancy, she threatens divorce and he acquiesces to her every destructive demand. It isn't a pretty story and Perry and Judd don't play it pretty, which may be why this intriguing tale eventually played on cable television rather than in theatres. The Andersons are too dependent on the good life to make effective rebels and too whacked out as a couple to represent a cautionary fable about the American Dream. Like most of life, they make little sense, and Perry and Judd wisely tackle their characters from the gut so that, at least for 108 minutes, we can experience their ride, even if we don't understand it. 🦴🦴🦴

1996 (R) 108m/C Luke Perry, Ashley Judd, Bruce A. Young, Jim True, Dawn Maxey, Penelope Milford, Tom Towles; ***D:*** John McNaughton; ***W:*** Bob Schneider, Peg Haller; ***C:*** Jean De Segonzac. **VHS, LV, Closed Caption**

Nosferatu

Why do we love *Nosferatu,* F.W. Murnau's German classic from the year 1922? Let us TRY to count the ways: When we see the captain's records for the doomed ship, the Demeter, we always get a shiver at this chilling indication of the blood-sucking horrors yet to come. And when the horrible-looking vampire played by Max Schreck gazes at the bleeding hand of Jonathan Harker, he leers, "Blood! Your precious blood!" as only Schreck can. And THIS Nosferatu is PURE evil; there's no feeling sorry for his character as we sometimes do for the charming Draculas later played by Bela Lugosi, Christopher Lee, and Louis Jourdan. The film itself, even by 1922 standards, is clearly drawn larger than life, especially when compared with the subtlety of such other F.W. Murnau classics as *The Last Laugh* and *Sunrise.* Alexander Granach, who would one day star in *Ninotchka* with Greta Garbo, portrays Renfield as a caricature. The rest of the cast, including hordes of rats plus Gustav Von Wangenheim and Greta Schroder as the Harkers, are also in over-the-top gear. The overacting suits this particular *Symphony of Horrors,* which Murnau himself revamped for sound in 1930, the year before his death on a California highway. ***AKA:*** Nosferatu, Eine Symphonie des Grauens; Nosferatu, A Symphony of Terror; Nosferatu, A Symphony of Horror; Nosferatu, The Vampire. 🦴🦴🦴🦴

The Hound Salutes:
F.W. MURNAU
Director, *Nosferatu*

All of Friedrich Wilhelm Murnau's films between 1919 and 1926 were independently made in Berlin, far away from Hollywood. The enormous international success of such pictures as 1921's *The Haunted Castle,* 1922's *Nosferatu,* 1926's *Faust,* and in particular, 1924's *The Last Laugh* (which told its story without a single intertitle), attracted Fox Film Studios, who invited Murnau to work his magic in Hollywood. By strict definition, 1927's *Sunrise* is not an independent film. Murnau had the run of the Fox lot and the best resources that an American film studio could extend to him. Yet *Sunrise,* as the loveliest silent movie ever made, is far more representative of Berlin than Hollywood. It is one of those rare stories that captures the magic of what might still be possible within the context of a marriage.

Based on Hermann Suderman's novel *A Trip to Tilsit, Sunrise* first focuses on a farmer whose life is being torn apart by his obsession with a chain-smoking woman from the city. He steals away from his wife and child at night so he can make love to her and even considers her suggestion that he drown his wife and run away with her. In the daylight, his young wife eagerly joins him on a boat excursion and he very nearly gives in to the dark side of his nature by strangling her to death. His innate decency takes over and what we see next of the couple's

1922 63m/B *GE* Max Schreck, Alexander Granach, Gustav von Wagenheim, Greta Schroder, John Gottowt, Ruth Landshoff, G.H. Schnell; ***D:*** F.W. Murnau; ***W:*** Henrik Galeen; ***C:*** Fritz Arno Wagner, Gunther Krampf. **VHS, LV, DVD**

Not Fourteen Again

Gillian Armstrong's *Not Fourteen Again* is rather a distaff version of Michael Apted's acclaimed *7-14-21-28-35 Up* series of documentaries. So far, the director has filmed her three subjects at 14, 18, 26, and 33. With a spritely soundtrack, she shows the evolving lives of Carrie, Josie, and Diana, all of whom raised girls of their own, and whom Armstrong films as well. One of the women faces the eternal dilemma: should she continue a rewarding career or have a baby? We get an answer the next time Armstrong returns to film her. She's happy that she had the baby, happy in general, but she's BORED. How can you be happy AND bored? We suspect that you'd have to film every second of someone's life, and even then, you might blink and miss that answer.

1996 110m/C ***D:*** Gillian Armstrong; ***W:*** Gillian Armstrong; ***C:*** Steve Arnold; ***M:*** Peter Dasent.

Not of This Earth

Remember *Not of This Earth,* the 1957 Roger Corman movie about an alien vampire? Well, the movie you tried to forget is also the movie Jim Wynorski was born to re-make. Following in Beverly Garland's footsteps is Traci Lords, reportedly writing a cautionary book about her experiences making adult films in real life. In the movie, she plays a nurse and Arthur Roberts inherits the role that shot the late Paul Birch to obscurity. Dick Miller is not re-cast in the new movie, but Lenny Juliano, a young actor with a flair for comedy,

complicated day together is achieved without a word of a dialogue and very few subtitles. She must overcome her fear of him; he must remember why he first fell in love with her, and he must seek her love and forgiveness. Then the two spend an exhilarating day together, climaxed by the dark irony of their return home during a dangerous storm.

Along the way, we are treated to Murnau's impeccable pictorial sense. Never will the streets of a city, or a barber shop or a carnival or a dance hall, look as exquisite as they do in *Sunrise.* Murnau had a special gift for contrasting moments of extreme emotion with a playful sense of mischief, and this is what helps to give *Sunrise* so much of its charm. Its one concession to American morality lies in its ecstatic ending. *Sunrise* emerged as a perfect romantic date movie, but Murnau himself had envisioned a downbeat conclusion more in keeping with its overall tone of a paradise lost thanks to an evil seductress. Murnau's second Fox film, 1929's *Four Devils,* is apparently lost, but 1930's *City Girl,* also for Fox, survives on video, as does another Murnau masterpiece, 1931's *Tabu,* made for Paramount. Murnau died before its premiere, a wrenching loss of the dazzling films he would certainly have made had he survived the car crash that killed him. There is an eerie moment in *Sunrise* when two lovers kiss on a bustling street, oblivious to the traffic that swirls around them. As his films clearly show, Murnau was not much of an optimist, yet he found oases of beauty in the grimmest tales. Wherever and however he made films, F.W. Murnau was the most independent of artists. His genius will prevail as long as other independent artists make movies in the 21st century and beyond.

has some good sequences as the alien's chauffeur. The acting of the nurse's cop-boyfriend is nothing to write home about, but luckily he has little to do. *Not of This Earth* would be fun to watch with other "great" horror films like *Cat Women of the Moon* starring Marie Windsor and the late Sonny Tufts. **woof!**

1988 (R) 92m/C Traci Lords, Arthur Roberts, Lenny Juliano, Rebecca Perle, Ace Mask, Roger Lodge; ***D:*** Jim Wynorski; ***W:*** Jim Wynorski, R.J. Robertson; ***C:*** Zoran Hochstatter. **VHS**

Nothing but a Man

A sincere, well-meant film about a black worker in Alabama, *Nothing but a Man* was among the first 250 American films selected for preservation by the National Film Registry. It is still an important film for its era, but if you turned down the sound, you might mistake it for a British kitchen-sink drama. The characters are SOOO serious, like they've got the weight of the world on their shoulders 24 hours a day. Michael Roemer's perspective feels like that of an outsider, as if whatever real-life characters he observed couldn't afford to relax their company manners and let their hair down in front of a stranger. The one moment when the protagonist Duff (Ivan Dixon) expresses his hostility at the system that's doing a good job breaking his spirit, he lashes out at his nice, sympathetic wife, Josie (Abbey Lincoln). She understands; he's under a lot of pressure. Even though things seem to work out for them at the fade-out, I still didn't feel as if I really got to know either of them over the course of 95 minutes. Earnestly made on a tiny budget of $230,000, *Nothing but a Man* showcases some fine actors, arty cinematography by co-scripter Robert Young, and a great Motown soundtrack.

Ivan Dixon, Gloria Foster, and Julius W. Harris in *Nothing but a Man.* Cinema 5; courtesy of the Kobal Collection

1964 95m/B Ivan Dixon, Abbey Lincoln, Gloria Foster, Julius W. Harris, Martin Priest, Yaphet Kotto, Leonard Parker, Stanley Greene, Helen Lounck, Helene Arrindell; ***D:*** Michael Roemer; ***W:*** Michael Roemer, Robert M. Young; ***C:*** Robert M. Young. National Film Registry '93. **VHS**

Number One

At 42 minutes, *Number One* just barely qualifies as a feature film, but Dyan Cannon packs quite a number of astute observations about kids and sex into the brief running time. One sequence, in which a little boy is chastised at the dinner table, is almost unbearable to watch. As writer/director/composer, Cannon shows more understanding and compassion for her characters than she did with any of the acting roles she tackled between 1970 and 1977. Working with a nominal budget, Cannon (and cameraman Fred Elmes) elicited strong performances from a cast of young children and she received an Oscar nomination for her first directorial effort.

1976 42m/B Nan Martin, Allen (Goorwitz) Garfield, Gary Lockwood; ***D:*** Dyan Cannon; ***W:*** Dyan Cannon; ***C:*** Frederick Elmes; ***M:*** Dyan Cannon.

Nuns on the Run

Nuns on the Run with Eric Idle and Robbie Coltrane is pretty funny, although any movie with that title and those stars deserves to be VERY funny. One reason it isn't is because *Nuns on the Run* is set up almost exactly the same way as the great Billy Wilder's *Some Like It Hot.* In that movie, Tony Curtis and Jack Lemmon play two characters who hide out from gangsters by pretending to be members of an all-girls band. In *Nuns on the Run,* Idle and Coltrane play two characters who hide out from gangsters by pretending to be nuns in a convent. There's even a dizzy blonde (Camille Coduri) who has the same plot functions as Marilyn Monroe did in *Some Like It Hot.* She even walks into things when she isn't wearing her glasses, just like Monroe did in *How to Marry a Millionaire.* The comedies that make us laugh the loudest are the ones that make us laugh when we don't expect to laugh. But when we know the plot, no matter how silly Eric and Robbie look in nun's clothes, no gag can be that much of a surprise. Janet Suzman is as good as she can be in the skimpy supporting role that director Jonathan Lynn wrote for her, but it IS odd to see Eric Idle hand scenes to other cast members on a platter. He is so low-key in *Nuns on the Run* that Robbie Coltrane gets most of the laughs. Still, watching these two impersonate Sister Euphemia of the Five Hounds and Sister Inviolata of the Immaculate Conception is good for a few giggles, especially if you ever went to Catholic school. And Coltrane dancing in a nun's outfit is definitely a sight to see.

1990 (PG-13) 95m/C Eric Idle, Robbie Coltrane, Janet Suzman, Camille Coduri, Robert Patterson, Tom Hickey, Doris Hare, Lila Kaye; ***D:*** Jonathan Lynn; ***W:*** Jonathan Lynn; ***C:*** Mike Garfath. **VHS, LV**

The Obsessed

If you're merely looking for a whodunit, *The Obsessed* will disappoint you. There's no suspense in it. What I think is funny about this movie is the way that Gregory Black (David Farrar) and Elizabeth the housekeeper (Geraldine Fitzgerald) are always yelling at each other when they're not having sex. At least I THINK they have sex; maybe they yell each other to sleep in bed, too. Anyway, it's 1890 and Gregory's wife Edwina is dead. The unthinkable starts to occur to the lovers. Maybe she/he done her in?! A kindly inspector (Roland Culver) snoops around, asking the maid (Jean Cadell as Ellen) to answer his questions about poison and such, and Gregory and Elizabeth have to account for themselves, too, of course. But even THIS doesn't stop them from fighting with each other! Farrar and Fitzgerald give this one everything they've got, poor dears, since Maurice Elvey doesn't seem to give anyone much help. Culver is wonderful, as always. Based on a play by William Dinner and William Morum. ***AKA:*** The Late Edwina Black.

1951 77m/B *GB* David Farrar, Geraldine Fitzgerald, Roland Culver, Jean Cadell, Mary Merrall, Harcourt Williams, Charles Heslop, Ronald Adam, Sydney Monkton; ***D:*** Maurice Elvey; ***W:*** Charles Frank, David Evans; ***C:*** Stephen Dade. **VHS, LV**

The Odessa File

This untidy, overlong potboiler didn't do much for Jon Voight's career; in fact, except for 1976's *End of the Game,* he vanished from the big screen until his Oscar-winning performance in 1978's *Coming Home.* Frederick Forsyth wrote the bestselling novel (about a 1963 Nazi conspiracy based in Hamburg) that inspired it and Ronald *(The Poseidon Adventure)* Neame directs with his usual melodramatic style. Every cliche you can possibly imagine is recycled in this "thriller." There is the obligatory sequence when the heroine whines to the hero "I may not be here when you get back," before he sets off for Adventures Unknown. On the other hand, there is the obligatory sequence when the villain asks the hero if he can smoke and—voila!—the cigarette and his gun just happen to be in the same drawer. And, as the *pièce de résistance,* there is the obligatory sequence when some crazy Nazi screams about ruling the world. The best thing about *The Odessa File* is Maria Schell's cameo appearance. In five vivid moments, Schell reveals more about the tragic consequences of war than the lumbering 128 minutes that surround her all-too-brief appearance. (If you have a problem accepting Maria Schell, 48, as the mother of Jon Voight, 36, though, you're not alone!)

1974 (PG) 128m/C *GB GE* Jon Voight, Mary Tamm, Maximilian Schell, Maria Schell, Derek Jacobi, Peter Jeffrey, Klaus Lowitsch, Kurt Meisel, Hannes Meesember, Garfield Morgan, Shmuel Rodensku, Ernst Schroder, Noel Willman, Hans Canineberg, Towje Kleiner, Gunnar Moiler; ***D:*** Ronald Neame; ***W:***

He said it was a lesson. She said it was sexual harassment. Whichever side you take, you're wrong.

—Tagline from the movie *Oleanna.*

Kenneth Ross, George Markstein; ***C:*** Oswald Morris; ***M:*** Andrew Lloyd Webber. **VHS, LV, Closed Caption**

Old Enough

Slow-moving coming-of-age comedy on the rich kid-poor kid friendship theme. Director Marisa Silver's directing debut won the 1984 Sundance Grand Jury Prize; she went on to make *Permanent Record, Vital Signs, He Said, She Said,* and *Indecency.*

1984 (PG) 91m/C Sarah Boyd, Rainbow Harvest, Neill Barry, Danny Aiello, Susan Kingsley, Roxanne Hart, Alyssa Milano, Fran Brill, Anne Pitoniak; ***D:*** Marisa Silver; ***W:*** Marisa Silver; ***C:*** Michael Ballhaus. Sundance Film Festival '84: Grand Jury Prize. **VHS**

Oleanna

Let me preface this by mentioning that *House of Games, Things Change,* and *Homicide* are among my favorite movies of 1987–91. And then there's...*Oleanna.* When I was in my first year at UCD, I was stuck with a professor who couldn't stand being a professor. And I couldn't stand him. He wrote nice things on my papers and he spoke well of me to others, but whenever we were in the same room, he was whiny and belligerent, and finally I went to his office to ask him what I had to do to pass his class without having to see him anymore. Without looking up from his desk, he said, "Three papers. Any subject. I don't care." And that ended it. (It also meant I wound up getting my degree and credential by NEVER going to any class if writing papers were the option instead of showing up.) I thought about this professor when I saw a professor named John in David Mamet's *Oleanna.* How do these guys get tenure? They're so clueless about their effect on others and teaching is all about the effect that someone who knows has on a student who doesn't know. John is a windbag, in love with the sound of his own voice. His student Carol (let me put this charitably) is unfinished and easily led. She doesn't know her own mind yet and she simmers through harangues she doesn't want to hear when she COULD (a) speak up for herself or (b) split. When these two get together, *Oleanna* becomes a LOOONG (90 minutes) polemical rant. William H. Macy, a fine actor, and Debra Eisenstadt do what they can with their unplayable, slogan-driven parts. Somehow, Mamet's heart does not seem to be in *Oleanna* since there's nothing in the text to show that he cares about either character. For a writer who cares vitally about every character in *House of Games, Things Change,* and *Homicide,* this is sad. **woof!**

1994 90m/C William H. Macy, Debra Eisenstadt; ***D:*** David Mamet; ***W:*** David Mamet; ***C:*** Andrzej Sekula; ***M:*** Rebecca Pidgeon. Nominations: Independent Spirit Awards '95: Best Actor (Macy). **VHS, LV, Closed Caption**

Oliver Twist

Filmgoers today mainly remember Jackie Coogan for two roles: 1921's *The Kid* with Charlie Chaplin and 1964's Uncle Fester on *The Addams Family* television series. Coogan, however, made many movies as a child and even more as an adult character actor. Until its rediscovery some years back, one of his earliest and best silent files was long feared lost. Coogan was barely eight when *Oliver Twist* was released, a bit young for the part that is usually played by boys of nine or ten, but his small size makes his character even more lovable. Lon Chaney's makeup as Fagin is somewhat overwhelming and he has so few close-ups (most of those seem reserved for his young co-star!) that although he looks the part, his performance does not have quite the same impact as later Fagins of the sound era. However, George Siegmann is truly frightening as the vicious Bill Sykes and Gladys Brockwell creates a vivid impression as the terrified Nancy. The film was adapted and directed in workman-like style by Glasgow-born Frank Lloyd. This thrifty but thoroughly respectable version of the Charles Dickens classic was independently produced by Sol Lesser, who went on to make a dozen *Tarzan* pictures. Like many other silent features, *Oliver Twist* was preserved not in Hollywood but in Czechoslovakia, where it was finally located in the late 1970s. Blackhawk Films then restored the film with the help of Lesser and Coogan, who reconstructed its missing intertitles. This *Oliver* is well worth seeing, not only for comparison purposes with the later British classics by David Lean, Carol Reed, and Clive Donner, but also for the wonderfully appealing work of Jackie Coogan, whose brimming eyes would melt the heart of ANY curmudgeon in frozen storage. ♪♪♪

1922 77m/B Jackie Coogan, Lon Chaney Sr., Gladys Brockwell, George Siegmann, Esther Ralston, James Marcus, Aggie Herring, Nelson McDowell, Lewis Sargent, Joan Standing, Carl Stockdale, Edouard Trebaol, Lionel Belmore; ***D:*** Frank Lloyd; ***W:*** Frank Lloyd, Henry Weil; ***C:*** Glen MacWilliams, Robert Martin. **VHS**

On Approval

This rare jewel of a film gives us a chance to see Tony-winning Beatrice Lillie (1895–1989) at her sparkling best. How does she manage to play a character who's simultaneously insufferable AND endearing? As rich Maria Wislack in *On Approval,* Lillie is a social brute who doesn't know she's a social brute. There's no individual malice behind her verbal barbs; her meanness toward everyone is only exceeded by her unconsciousness of same. Watching Lillie in action is rather like studying the effect of a laser beam; her sharp yet subtle humor is achieved by focused intensity on a person, place, or thing. She sticks to the point, sincerely believing she can do no wrong, ever. Meanwhile, she's surrounded by chaos, the direct result of virtually everything she says and does. Lillie didn't think much of Hollywood, yet she tried to become a star there four times for four different studios. In 1926, she made *Exit Sailing* opposite Jack Pickford. It's extremely funny to watch today, but apparently MGM executives felt otherwise. In 1929, she appeared in the Warner Bros. musical *Show of Shows;* the following year, she starred as Lady Diana in the Fox musical *Are You There?* (widely appreciated at a recent revival screening); and in 1938 she made the Paramount musical *Doctor Rhythm* opposite Bing Crosby. Except for a cameo bit as a revivalist in 1956's *Around the World in 80 Days* and a sixth-billed role as Mrs. Meers in the 1967 Universal musical *Thoroughly Modern Millie, On Approval* is Lillie's only film on video. Luckily it's also the best. Producer/director/screenwriter/star Clive Brook (1887–1974) re-vamped the 1926 play by Frederick Lonsdale (1881–1954) by setting it in the Edwardian era, adding a tongue-in-cheek prologue and a zany dream sequence. His dream cast included himself as the always-broke George, Duke of Bristol; Roland Culver (1900–84) as the equally broke Richard Halton; and Googie Withers, then 27, as millionairess Helen Hale. Along with Lillie's Maria, they agree to spend time alone together in a Scottish castle..."On Approval." The Herculean efforts involved in making this one-of-a-kind cinematic treat must have exhausted Brook; he retired after a successful career spanning 25 years, re-emerging onscreen just once for Universal's *The List of Adrian Messenger* in 1963. Culver continued making films right up through Michael Palin's *The Missionary* in 1983. Withers appeared most recently in the 1996 Australian release, *Shine.* A 1980s version of *On Approval,* set in the 1920s, aired on *Masterpiece Theatre* starring the late Jeremy Brett in a rare comic role as George, Penelope Keith as Maria, Benjamin Whitrow as Richard, and Lindsay Duncan as Helen. ♪♪♪♪

1944 80m/B *GB* Clive Brook, Beatrice Lillie, Googie Withers, Roland Culver, O.B. Clarence, Lawrence Hanray, Elliot Mason, Hay Petrie, Marjorie Munks, Molly Munks; ***D:*** Clive Brook; ***W:*** Terence Young, Clive Brook; ***C:*** Claude Friese-Greene. **VHS**

Once upon a Time in the East

Canadian theatrical director Andre Brassard's little-known movie debut was one of the most enjoyable entries at 1974's San Francisco International Film Festival. Transvestites, an alcoholic, a hash slinger, a down-and-out singer, a troubled pregnant girl, and others share their lives and make the best of what they can get from their respective situations. The ending is a downer, as it drains the humor and energy out of the 100 minutes that went before it. Perhaps Brassard, who also scripted, didn't know how to wrap up this rich slice of life. (Great shot: The hash slinger shoves every object she can get her hands on into her restaurant's soup du jour, then storms out, resigning in full glory to every diner in the joint.) ***AKA:*** Il Etait une Fois dans l'Est. 🦴🦴🦴

1974 100m/C *CA* Denise Filatrault, Michele Rossignol, Frederique Colin, Sophie Clement, Andre Montmorency, Jean Archambault, Gilles Renaud, Manda Parent, Claude Gai, Rita Fontaine, Beatrice Picard, Amulette Garneau, Denis Drouin; ***D:*** Andre Brassard; ***W:*** Andre Brassard, Michel Tremblay; ***C:*** Attila Dory.

One False Move

One False Move represents a promising directing debut for Carl Franklin and a chance to see some fine actors at work, notably Cynda Williams and Bill Paxton. The film begins with an extended and quite graphic bloodletting sequence, but nothing else in the narrative, not even the climax is anywhere that explicit. Paxton plays Sheriff Dale "Hurricane" Dixon, seemingly an eager beaver small-town hick who tags along after a couple of big city cops until he realizes that the execution-style drug murders they are investigating hit very close to home. Five years earlier, he and Lila Walker (Williams), a young black teenage shoplifter, had a baby son before she left town. Dixon later married and started a family of his own, who know nothing about his relationship with Lila or his little boy. Lila changes her name to Fantasia and winds up on drugs in Los Angeles with two bad dudes named Ray and Pluto. Unfortunately, Ray is played by screenwriter Billy Bob Thornton, who writes much better than he acts, and Pluto, although effectively played by Michael Beach, is only identified by his 150 I.Q. and his fondness for knives. (If he'd switched roles with Beach, would Billy Bob have written a better part for Pluto? Maybe, but nothing would have helped his acting!) This casting decision hurts because Fantasia is supposed to be dominated by the homicidal Ray and she looks as if she could eat him for breakfast. Cynda Williams does a beautiful job with the material she is given, although she is too glowingly healthy and alert to make a completely convincing strung-out junkie. *One False Move* suffers from a storyline that zaps all over the place with secondary characters and then drags for long stretches, especially when Billy Bob as Ray has to spend much time onscreen. It works best when it focuses on the relationship between Lila and the Sheriff, especially as they wait out a long night attempting to trap Ray and Pluto. Since Billy Bob Thorton's writing and acting skills improved enormously by the time he directed 1996's *Sling Blade, One False Move* is well worth a look on video for an early portrait of the artist as a young man. 🦴🦴🦴

1991 (R) 105m/C Bill Paxton, Cynda Williams, Michael Beach, Jim Metzler, Earl Billings, Billy Bob Thornton, Natalie Canderday, Robert Ginnaven, Robert Anthony Bell, Kevin Hunter; ***D:*** Carl Franklin; ***W:*** Billy Bob Thornton, Tom Epperson; ***C:*** James L. Carter. Independent Spirit Awards '93: Best Director (Franklin); MTV Movie Awards '93: Best New Filmmaker Award (Franklin). **VHS, LV, Closed Caption, DVD**

100 Days after Childhood

This beautifully photographed tribute to youthful romance in a summer camp is lovely to look at. It's episodic; each segment shows different teenagers learning to meet life's challenges by working within their limitations. Wonder what all those cute kids are up to these days? ***AKA:*** Sto Dnei rossle Detstwa. 🦴🦴

1975 93m/C *RU* Boris Tokarev, Tatiana Drubich, Irina Malysheva, Nina Menschikova, Serge Shakurov; ***D:*** Sergei Solovjov; ***W:*** Sergei Solovjov, Alexander Alexandrov; ***C:*** Leonid Kalaschnikov; ***M:*** Isaak Schvarts.

101 Nights

Agnes Varda pays tribute to the centenary of the cinema with *101 Nights.* Monsieur Cinema is played by Michel Piccoli, only 70, as a 100-year-old movie fan confined to a wheelchair. The film is packed with international stars at their most charming

(Belmondo, Delon, Deneuve, De Niro, Depardieu, Mastroianni), and its slender premise is bolstered by Varda's sheer love of movie lore, past and present. ***AKA:*** Les Cent et Une Nuits.

1995 125m/C *FR GB* Michel Piccoli, Marcello Mastroianni, Henri Garcin, Julie Gayet, Mathieu Demy, Emmanuel Salinger; ***D:*** Agnes Varda; ***W:*** Agnes Varda; ***C:*** Eric Gautier.

One Night Stand

Do you ever wonder what might happen if an international critic decided to make a movie? Okay, we all know whatever became of François Truffaut. Pierre Rissient was a likable critic/film publicist who secured a screening for his first feature film at the San Francisco International Film Festival. Rissient might have done himself some good by consulting a script doctor first. The screenplay is ludicrous. *One Night Stand* should have been run out of Hong Kong, where it was filmed, during PRE-production. Degrading to women, and even more degrading to the leading actor who degrades them (the late Richard Jordan has this thankless role), the movie drew extended hisses and numerous boos from unappreciative audience members. **woof!**

1976 102m/C *HK FR* Richard Jordan, Ting Pei, Tien Ni, Mei Fang, Tsang Kong, Ken Wayne, Marie Daems; ***D:*** Pierre Rissient; ***W:*** Pierre Rissient, Kenneth White; ***C:*** Alain Derobe.

One Sings, the Other Doesn't

One Sings, the Other Doesn't is a so-so look at a pair of feminists who stay in touch over a 15-year period. Apple, the singer (Valerie Mairesse), repeats the same dumb lyrics over and over: "I am woman, I'm me," as her quiet friend Suzanne (Therese Liotard) works at a family planning clinic to support her two fatherless children. Charlie Van Damme photographs the story attractively and the two leads give strong performances. Yet Agnes Varda's screenplay is, at least sporadically, inane. At one point, she has Apple offer her Iranian husband a deal. He can leave her and take their baby if he gives her another child, thus relegating him to the role of a functional accessory in her existence. In every previous sequence, their love had seemed real enough. If Varda is suggesting that men assume the shadowy roles once played by women, she's indicating a reactionary trend every bit as disagreeable as the one it's replacing. At least in THIS screenplay, Varda is persistent, but fairly cagey about ideologies, at the expense of a more substantial story. Her other films include *Cleo from 5 to 7, Le Bonheur, Vagabond, Le Petit Amour,* and *Jacquot.* ***AKA:*** L'Une Chante, l'Autre Pas.

1977 105m/C *FR BE* Valerie Mairesse, Therese Liotard, Robert Dadies, Ali Affi, Jean-Pierre Pellegrin, Francois Wertheimer; ***D:*** Agnes Varda; ***W:*** Agnes Varda; ***C:*** Charlie Van Damme; ***M:*** Francois Wertheimer. **VHS**

The Only One

The Only One provides a compassionate look at a marital breakup, seen from the husband's point of view. Nikolai and Tanya are an attractive, deeply in love, dream-filled couple, who divorce and go their separate ways after a misunderstanding. Still, there is a bond between them that their different directions cannot dissolve. Josef Heifetz treats this familiar situation with deep understanding and sharply rendered knowledge of the forces that link the lovers to each other. The performances by the three leading players here are well worth seeing.

1976 95m/C *RU* Elena Proklova, Valery Zolothuhin, Ludmila Gladunko, Vladimir Vyssozki; ***D:*** Josef Heifetz; ***W:*** Josef Heifetz, Pavel Nilin; ***C:*** Heinrich Marandzhjan; ***M:*** Nadeshda Simonian.

Open Season

Sometimes films play at festivals and are never seen again, unless the filmmaker makes a deal with a cable network or a video distributor. *Open Season* poses the rather esoteric question: what would happen if all the television shows we THOUGHT had low ratings (like the ones on PBS) suddenly were declared THE top-rated shows? Bet you've really stayed awake nights worrying about that one,

Lucia (Lisa Kudrow) and Bill (Martin Donovan) in *The Opposite of Sex.*
Sony Pictures; courtesy of the Kobal Collection

huh? Well, in Robert Wuhl's 1995 film, it's a mistake, but the whole country thinks it's reality and our entire society changes as a result. I guess you might call this a high-concept flick. The best thing about this movie is Maggie Han, who plays Wuhl's wife. Otherwise, good actors like Taylor and Shaver are wasted as nitwit television executives. Wuhl later played one of the nitwit movie executives in Mario Puzo's *The Last Don* for CBS.

1995 (R) 97m/C Robert Wuhl, Rod Taylor, Gailard Sartain, Maggie Han, Joe Piscopo, Helen Shaver, Dina Merrill, Saul Rubinek, Steven C. White, Timothy Arrington, Barry Flatman, Tom Selleck, Alan Thicke, Jimmie Walker; ***D:*** Robert Wuhl; ***W:*** Robert Wuhl; ***C:*** Stephen Lighthill; ***M:*** Marvin Hamlisch. **VHS, Closed Caption**

The Opposite of Sex

Dedee Truitt is a Bitch with a Capital B. Christina Ricci, on the other hand, is an enormously likeable actress, no matter who she's playing (Kate Flax in *Mermaids,* Bonnie in *The Hard Way,* Wednesday in *The Addams Family/Values,* Jessica in *The Cemetery Club,* Kat in *Casper,* Roberta in *Now and Then,* Beth Easton in *Gold Diggers: The Secret of Bear Mountain,* Dee Dee in *Bastard Out of Carolina,* Erin in *Last of the High Kings/Summer Fling,* Wendy Hood in *The Ice Storm,* Patti in *That Darn Cat,* Shelly in *Pecker,* Lucy in *Fear and Loathing in Las Vegas*).... For a girl who turns 20 in the year 2000, Ricci gets around! For every career break Ricci's received, she's earned THREE. *The Opposite of Sex* opens with Dedee leaving home after the death of her much-hated stepfather. She proceeds to make the life of her sweet gay older brother Bill (Martin Donovan) an absolute nightmare. Bill is mourning the death of his sweet gay lover Tom (Colin Ferguson) and living with stupid-but-gorgeous Matt Mateo (Ivan Sergei). Dedee needs a father for her forthcoming son because her boyfriend Randy, the actual father (William Lee Scott), is a complete lunatic, so she seduces Matt and convinces him that HE'S going to be a Daddy. To further complicate matters, Matt's OTHER boyfriend Jason (Johnny Galecki) is still carrying a torch for him, Tom's sister Lucia (Lisa Kudrow) thinks she's in love with Bill, and Sheriff Carl Tippett (Lyle Lovett) believes he's in love with Lucia. The key word in that last sentence is "complicate," because that's precisely what EVERYONE, especially narrator Dedee, does with everyone else's lives for 105 minutes. Dedee is so much more than a defective narrator, she's an absolute MENACE! If she were telling me a campfire tale, I'd throw a batch of s'mores at her! But the wise, sly performance of Ricci keeps reminding me that whatever happens, I won't be disappointed and I'm not. Donovan is the master of the slow burn. There are ZILLIONS of things going on in his interior world and he only lets one or two of them surface. Through my eyes, this makes him one of THE most fascinating actors of his generation. Watch him with a scene thief like Adrienne Shelly in *Trust* or with Ricci and Kudrow here—this man is an underrated genius! (But do siblings arrive 23 years apart? Skip it!) As for Kudrow, what can I say? Side-splitting, yes. Mistress of timing, yes. An actress who's funny as opposed to a shtick comedienne, yes, yes, yes. All of the above. To date, there seems no limit to what this talented jewel can do, on small OR large screens. Johnny Galecki, who more than held his own as Ira Reder opposite Christopher Walken in *The Suicide Kings,* creates another vivid character out of whole cloth. You'll scarcely believe you're watching the same actor. And Lovett is MY idea of a sheriff. However, Los Angeles is no one's idea of Louisiana or Indiana, where *The Opposite of Sex* takes place. (It reminds me of the Hyde Street cable car in San Francisco identified as New York City in *Attack of the Killer Tomatoes,* actually.) Naturally, no one IN Los Angeles would be as odd as this bunch. Premiered at Sundance, 1998. 𝄞𝄞𝄞

1998 (R) 105m/C Christina Ricci, Martin Donovan, Lisa Kudrow, Ivan Sergel, Lyle Lovett, Johnny Galecki, William Lee Scott, Colin Ferguson; ***D:*** Don Roos; ***W:*** Don Roos; ***C:*** Hubert Taczanowski; ***M:*** Mason Daring. Independent Spirit Awards '99: Best First Feature, Best Screenplay; National Board of Review Awards '98: Best Supporting Actress (Ricci); New York Film Critics Awards '98: Best Supporting Actress (Kudrow); Nominations: Golden Globe Awards '99: Best Actress—Musical/Comedy (Ricci); Independent Spirit Awards '99: Best Actress (Ricci), Best Supporting Actress (Kudrow); Writers Guild of America '98: Best Screenplay. **VHS, Closed Caption, DVD**

The Orders

The Orders is directed with thought and care by Michel Brault, who also did the screenplay. It's about the unjust suspension of civil liberties in Quebec during 1970. Told entirely from the viewpoint of the victims, *The Orders* stars many of the people who were actually arrested, although they take on different roles. Acting by the nonprofessionals, though low-key, is heartbreakingly affecting. If it could happen to them in Quebec, it could happen to anyone, anywhere. What would you do if the police came in the middle of the morning and took you away to jail, forcing you to leave your children and never once explained why? Brault shows us what THEY did, making us angry, making us think. *The Orders* deservedly won the Director's Prize at the Cannes Film Festival. ***AKA:*** Les Ordres. 𝄞𝄞𝄞𝄞

1975 107m/C *CA* Helene Louiselle, Jean Lapointe, Guy Provost, Claude Gauthier, Louise Forestier; ***D:*** Michel Brault; ***W:*** Michel Brault; ***C:*** Michel Brault, Francois Protat; ***M:*** Phillipe Gagnon.

Orlando

This unique adaptation of Virginia Woolf's 1928 novel is about the title character (Tilda Swinton), who lives for 400 years. Orlando starts out as a man and, "in the fullness of time," becomes a woman. The conceit allows us to see how women are treated over the centuries, courtesy of Orlando's extraordinary perspective. There are many treats in store for Woolf fans—the marvelous casting of Quentin Crisp as old Queen Elizabeth I, for one, and the appearance of *Lovejoy*'s Dudley Sutton as King James I, for another. It was partly filmed on location in St. Petersburg and Uzbekistan. And writer/director Sally Pot-

> "She's lived for 400 years and hardly aged a day; but because this is England, everyone pretends not to notice."
>
> —The narrator speaks in *Orlando.*

ter, who must be a whirlwind of energy, even wrote some of the songs. (And it's a refreshing 93 minutes long!) 🦴🦴🦴

1992 (PG-13) 93m/C *GB RU FR NL* Tilda Swinton, Charlotte Valandrey, Billy Zane, Lothaire Bluteau, John Wood, Quentin Crisp, Heathcote Williams, Dudley Sutton, Thom Hoffman, Peter Eyre, Jimmy Somerville; ***D:*** Sally Potter; ***W:*** Sally Potter; ***C:*** Alexei Rodionov; ***M:*** Bob Last. Nominations: Academy Awards '93: Best Art Direction/Set Decoration, Best Costume Design; Independent Spirit Awards '94: Best Foreign Film. **VHS, LV, Letterbox, Closed Caption**

The Orphans

Nikolai Goubenko made an extraordinary U.S. debut as a director with *The Orphans,* partly based on his own childhood experiences after World War II. The picture introduced little A. Tscherstvov, the best child actor at the San Francisco International Film Festival since six-year-old Ana Torrent appeared in 1973's *Spirit of the Beehive.* Young Tscherstvov grabs our attention so completely that dialogue is nearly unnecessary, though he does quite well with Goubenko's sensitive screenplay. His expressive blue eyes lend poignance to every sequence of this tale about a group of war orphans who attend school in 1945 Russia. Goubenko, too, is effective as a teacher who is unable to cope with the needs of the children in his care. Beautifully photographed, *The Orphans* also features strong supporting performances by Y. Boudraitis and E. Bourkov. ***AKA:*** Podranki. 🦴🦴🦴

1977 97m/C *RU* Nikolai Gubenko, Y. Boudraitis, A. Tcherstvov, A. Kaliaguine, E. Bourkov, J. Bolotova, R. Bikov, E. Evstigneev; ***D:*** Nikolai Gubenko; ***W:*** Nikolai Gubenko; ***C:*** Alexander Kniajinsky. **VHS**

Orson Welles: The One Man Band

For Orson Welles' fans, this movie is a MUST. It opens with the credit "A Film Made Possible by Oja Kodar." Kodar lived with Welles from the mid-'60s until his death at age 70 in 1985 and she appears with him in his swan song, Henry Jaglom's *Someone to Love.* As this documentary makes clear, Welles was constantly busy making movies during his last 20 years, even if none of his efforts saw the light of day until they were compiled for this documentary. Why are all of these projects unfinished? (*The Merchant of Venice,* for example, ends in the middle of Welles' speech as Shylock when he ran out of film.) By age 50, Welles had lost none of his creative energy, but most of his patience with financing. He was always broke, but usually hustled sufficient funds to start filming. And then a film was stolen or another was tied up in legalities or he tried to raise completion money and an actor died. Welles was a renegade who did what he wanted to do and although he appreciated honors like Academy Awards and the AFI Life Achievement Award, he never became an industry type who talked the talk and walked the walk. Even in the age of the indie, he might well have had just as rough a time as he did during Hollywood's so-called Golden Age. Welles wanted to be the baby at every christening, the groom at every wedding, and the ONLY kid in the candy store. (He directs himself playing ALL the roles in *Moby Dick* in one film fragment.) Welles could always find world-class stars to play with him. In the late '60s, he worked with Laurence Harvey and Jeanne Moreau on *The Deep,* AKA *Dead Reckoning.* The surviving footage of haunting imagery tantalizes us in every way and Welles, Harvey, and Moreau have it all over Sam Neill, Billy Zane, and Nicole Kidman in Phillip Noyce's 1989 potboiler, *Dead Calm.* The treasure trove in *Orson Welles: The One Man Band* shows that even though his films remained incomplete, Welles' own life was whole and complete, rich in activity, and filled with fun and friendship. 🦴🦴🦴🦴

1995 90m/C *GE SI FR* Orson Welles, Oja Kodar; ***D:*** Vassili Silovic; ***W:*** Vassili Silovic, Roland Zag; ***C:*** Thomas Mauch; ***M:*** Simon Cloquet.

Ossessione

Four years before Tay Garnett made MGM's *The Postman Always Rings Twice,* James M. Cain's grim tale of adultery starring Lana Turner and John Garfield, Luchi-

no Visconti directed Clara Calamai and Massimo Girotti in 1942's *Ossessione.* The film ran into censorship difficulties in fascist Italy and copyright problems everywhere else. A key element in the Visconti version is the erosion of Calamai's desirability as she becomes more vulnerable to Girotti. John Garfield can not free himself from his fix on Lana Turner, even though he tries with Audrey Totter. Although Girotti doesn't shrink from engulfing Calamai, he is terrified by her reciprocal attentions. The same woman he once wanted fills him with fear and revulsion, and it is painful to watch as her eroticism begins to disgust him. *Ossessione* is a more uncomfortable film than 1946's glossy *Postman,* but Visconti spells out some unpleasant truths about the differing effects of passion on men and women. 🦴🦴🦴🦴

1942 135m/B *IT* Massimo Girotti, Clara Calamai, Juan deLanda, Elio Marcuzzo; ***D:*** Luchino Visconti; ***W:*** Guiseppe de Santis, Mario Alicata; ***C:*** Aldo Tonti, Domenico Scala. **VHS**

Our Daily Bread

1934's *Our Daily Bread* was King Vidor's most direct statement to date on how he perceived the American dream. Never again would he be as self-revealing about his personal solutions to the grim realities of life. He cast Karen Morley, a sensitive and deeply political actress, in the role of Mary Sims, a young woman grappling with poverty. For the co-starring role of Mary's husband John, Vidor chose Tom Keene, a limited but sincere actor who rather resembled Vidor himself. In an unsuccessful concession to boxoffice realities, Vidor assigned the bad girl role of Sally to Barbara Pepper. (She liked to listen to jazz and we all know what THAT means.) The cast was rounded out by fine character actors John Qualen as an influential farmworker named Chris and Addison Richards as Louie, a taciturn but memorable convict. The script, written by Vidor with his then-wife Elizabeth Hill, is the dewy-eyed rural equivalent of any Warner Bros. or Fox musical starring Ruby Keeler or Shirley Temple. To lick the Depression, Mr. and Mrs. Sims take over a beat-up farm. When they realize they can not handle the place alone, they enlist the services of other down-and-out Depression victims. Individually, they are nothing, but working shoulder-to-shoulder, everyone digs in together to make the farm a growing cooperative concern. (Shades of *42nd Street* and *Stand Up and Cheer*!) And then sex arrives in the person of a bleached blonde to threaten Mr. Sims as well as everyone else's efforts. After watching the films Vidor made between 1925 and 1959, one might become convinced that the director regarded sex as the root of all evil. A Good Woman like Mrs. Sims treats her manchild with maternal affection and functions as a reliable emotional pillow. Men realize their true potential with the support of such Good Women, but they also chomp at the bit and run off to play with Tramps whenever they appear. It's always the Tramp's fault (naturally) and a Good Woman invariably takes her disloyal manchild back. In Vidor's earlier works, his other artistic statements provide a welcome relief from such tiresome Sunday school lessons. When *Our Daily Bread* emerged as a boxoffice flop, Vidor was faced with a difficult decision. He could make his artistic statements about the power of the common man more accessible to mass audiences or he could switch to commercial melodramas. He made the latter choice, and it's sometimes hard to believe that the same man who directed *Our Daily Bread*'s final inspiring irrigation sequence would also be responsible for the sudsy *Stella Dallas* three years later. ***AKA:*** Miracle of Life. 🦴🦴🦴🦴

1934 80m/B Karen Morley, Tom George Duryea Keene, John Qualen, Barbara Pepper, Addison Richards; ***D:*** King Vidor; ***W:*** Elizabeth Hill, King Vidor; ***C:*** Robert Planck. **VHS, LV**

Out of the Loop

Perhaps you have to be a dedicated follower of Chicago's independent rock scene to make head or tails out of *Out of the Loop.* From my perch in San Francisco's Laurel Heights, I saw and heard the following: (1) Musicians in Chicago don't think much of rock critic Bill Wyman. (2) A female rock singer thinks that the business practices

Russ (Vincent Gallo), Jerry (Adam Trese), and Sid (William Forsythe) in *Palookaville.*
Samuel Goldwyn Company; courtesy of the Kobal Collection

of indie labels can be just as "evil" as those of the major labels. (3) A Chicago band on the road was housed in a student dormitory at an unnamed Jesuit university in Northern California and when a female student walked in on a male singer in the shower, they both screamed. (4) Chicago musicians don't necessarily hang out together just for fun. (5) A feminist critic blistered a female vocalist for applying lipstick onstage. (6) Indie label producers are usually "fans," while major labels are mainly business people. There's a lot of kvetching on this tape, actually, and not enough context to suit yours truly. Participants in the documentary include Steve Albini (producer of Big Black, Rapeman, and Shellac), Die Warzau, the Jesus Lizard, Seam, Sister Machine Gun, and Veruca Salt. If you like the bands, you might appreciate Scott Peterson's documentary a bit more than this Laurel Heights martian did! Played at San Francisco's Indie Fest in 1999.

1997 86m/C ***D:*** Scott Peterson.

Padre Padrone

Padre Padrone is a very hard film that makes no compromises with its bleak story, which is based on the true experiences of Gavino Ledda, who wrote the book that inspired Paulo and Vittorio Taviani's screenplay. The Tavianis also directed this low-budget study of a young shepherd and the bitter relationship he endures with his cruel father, who shapes, but does not define his life. The son's adult solution to make his life his own is extraordinary, yet utterly convincing. ***AKA:*** Father Master; My Father, My Master.

1977 113m/C *IT* Omero Antonutti, Saverio Marconi, Marcella Michelangeli, Fabrizio Forte; ***D:*** Paolo Taviani, Vittorio Taviani; ***W:*** Paolo Taviani, Vittorio Taviani; ***C:*** Mario Masini; ***M:*** Egisto Macchi. Cannes Film Festival '77: Best Film. **VHS, DVD**

Palookaville

What do you call three characters who watch *Armored Car Robbery* (Richard Fleischer's 1950 film noir classic starring

William Talman, Douglas Fowley, and Gene Evans) on television and use it as a blueprint for their own heist in 1995? How about unemployed losers? Sid, Russ, and Jerry (William Forsythe, Vincent Gallo, and Adam Trese) are certainly underqualified for a life of crime. When they try to hit a jewelry shop, they only succeed in breaking and entering the adjacent bakery where they nab a few pastries and the petty cash. When they try to rob an armored car, they fail, but try again after buying toy guns in a grocery store and then CLOSELY watching the aforementioned movie. None of the three stars in this indie are comedians, which makes their life of crime in New Jersey slightly more possible than it would be if they were going for Three Stooges–caliber yucks. They look exactly like what they're meant to be, with Forsythe and Trese having a decided edge on Gallo, whose charm escapes me. Gallo was a model in the heroin chic ads for a Calvin Klein fragrance in 1996. I couldn't imagine why anyone would be inspired to spend money on HIS cologne, but then *Palookaville* was released and I heard women describing him as GORGEOUS! Say what?! Forsythe shines in a sequence where he tries to launch a cab company for senior citizens and finds out they won't share a taxi with his much-loved pooch. Trese is great in a sequence he shares with Robert (*High Stakes*) LuPone as his wife's lecherous boss Ralph, later learning that HE has to apologize for getting mad at Ralph or his wife won't get her job back. And Gallo turns on those bulging blue eyes and swipes everyone's heart in the audience but mine. But *Palookaville* works, anyway. Unlike Louis Malle's *Crackers,* Alan Taylor's *Palookaville* succeeds both as a homage to Mario Monicelli's *Big Deal on Madonna Street* AND as an enjoyable flick in its own right. It's dedicated to Italo Calvino, who inspired David Epstein's screenplay.

1995 (R) 92m/C William Forsythe, Vincent Gallo, Adam Trese, Lisa Gay Hamilton, Frances McDormand, David Boulton, James David Hilton, Gareth Williams, Bridget Ryan, Kim Dickens, Suzanne Shepherd, Robert LuPone; ***D:*** Alan Taylor; ***W:*** David Epstein; ***C:*** John Thomas; ***M:*** Rachel Portman. **VHS, Closed Caption**

Pandora's Box

Pandora's Box stars the late great Louise Brooks as Lulu and Francis Lederer (still alive well into his 90s, nearly 70 years after he co-starred opposite Brooks) as Alva Schon. In 1925's *Joyless Street,* G.W. Pabst revealed a Germany of harsh extremes: decadent jazz clubs near food lines where people wait hours at a time for a piece of butcher's meat. Innocent Lulu lives in the ugly world of 1928, but she cannot understand how she unwittingly contributes to that world. She loves guys of all sizes, shapes, and ages, except that sometimes they get mad at her and turn on her and then she gets into a whale of a lot of trouble. Like Dr. Ludwig Schon, who starts acting like he's too good for her once he gets engaged to another woman. And when he shows up with the other woman at Lulu's revue on opening night, what girl wouldn't get mad and refuse to go on with the show until she'd gotten even? And then, after she'd worked the angles so that Dr. Schon had to marry her, it wasn't her fault if he got mad at her for flirting with a Countess or for fooling around with her old pals before her wedding night. The world believes that Lulu is a femme fatale, dragging every man down to her level, but Lulu is her own greatest victim, representing much too much to much too many. Like every great director, Pabst exploited the actor's feelings toward each other to their onscreen advantage. He seduced a striking lesbian performance out of Alice Roberts as the Countess; he used Brooks' attraction to Gustav Diesl as Jack the Ripper to inject poignance into their brief but vivid moments together. And Fritz Kortner's real-life dislike of Brooks was ideal for Dr. Schon's obsessive hatred of Lulu. In her beautifully written reminiscences of working with Pabst, Brooks frankly admits that she never thought of herself as much of an actress. But her flickering image remains powerful today. And *Pandora's Box* yields a legion of treasures for first-time viewers and for longtime admirers who've memorized every frame of Pabst's masterpiece. ***AKA:*** Die Buechse der Pandora; Lulu.

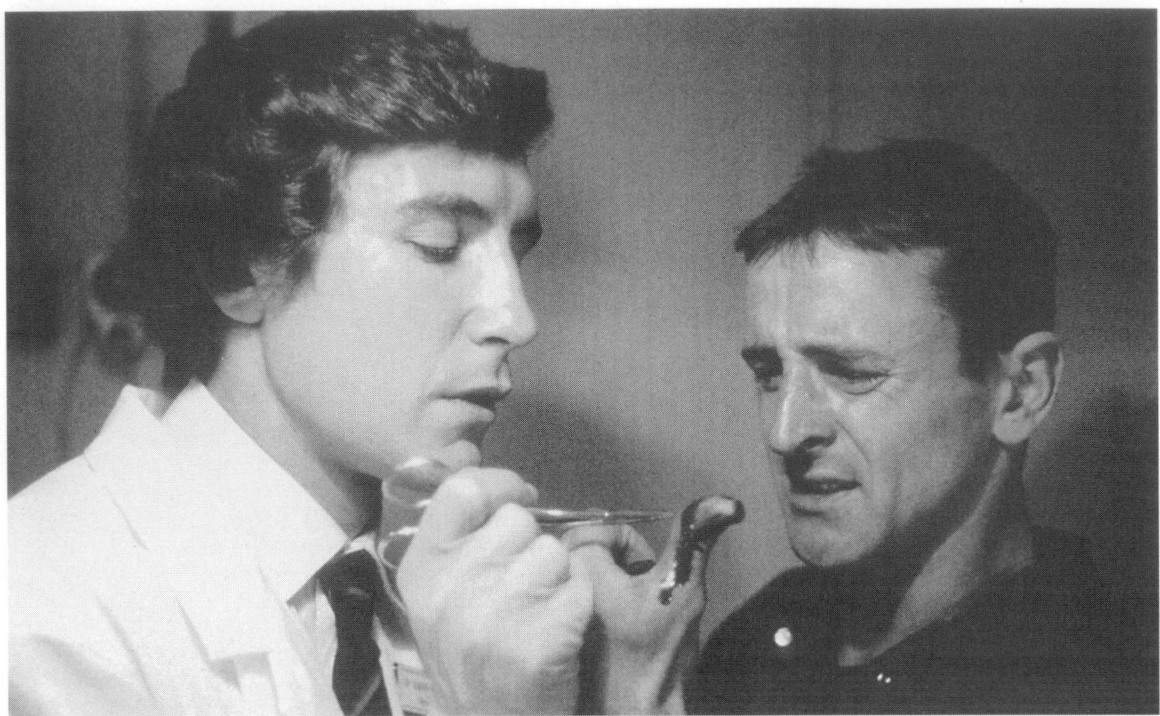

Would-be doctor Matthew Harris (Paul McGann) in *Paper Mask.*
Film Four; courtesy of the Kobal Collection

1928 110m/B *GE* Louise Brooks, Fritz Kortner, Francis Lederer, Carl Goetz, Alice Roberts, Gustav Diesl; ***D:*** G.W. Pabst; ***W:*** G.W. Pabst; ***C:*** Gunther Krampf. **VHS**

Paper Mask

Matthew Harris (Paul McGann) is chafing at the bit. He's a hospital orderly with an unexciting future until Dr. Simon Hennessy is killed in a car crash and Matthew, with the help of the doctor's papers, decides to take over his identity. He gets a job meant for Hennessy and winds up in the emergency room of another hospital during a medical crisis. Even though he's a bungler, he gets away with it. What clever psycho Matthew lacks in medical skills, he makes up for in cunning. He carefully observes the flaws of his colleagues and they, with their own guilty secrets to hide, explain away and fail to assign proper blame for his deadly surgical errors. Matthew quickly enlists an ally in Christine Taylor (Amanda Donohoe), a fine nurse with low self-esteem. She helps the new doctor in and out of scrapes and when he incompetently administers too much anesthesia and kills a patient, Christine takes the heat and rescues him. (That old Black Magic called Low Self-Esteem! It's a tribute to screenwriter John Collee, who adapted his own novel, that he's able to make a plausible case revealing how Matthew might actually be able to deceive a knowledgeable staff of doctors and nurses. Christopher Morahan's crisp direction and the terrific cast do the rest.) The hospital turns out to be just as determined to preserve its reputation as Matthew is to protect himself and so he's in the clear for the wrongful death. And then...someone recognizes "Dr. Simon Hennessy" as Matthew the orderly! Does one dead patient, a nurse who knows the truth, and a potential whistle blower faze Matthew? Rent *Paper Mask* after *E.R.* one night and find out!

1991 (R) 105m/C *GB* Paul McGann, Amanda Donohoe, Frederick Treves, Barbara Leigh-Hunt, Jimmy Yuill, Tom Wilkinson; ***D:*** Christopher Morahan; ***W:*** John Collee; ***C:*** Nat Crosby; ***M:*** Richard Harvey. **VHS**

Paradise Lost: The Child Murders at Robin Hood Hills

Paradise Lost: The Child Murders at Robin Hood Hills is a deeply sobering film experience. Joe Berlinger and Bruce Sinofsky *(Brother's Keeper)* had astonishing access to the Arkansas case, from the discovery of the children's bodies to client-lawyer discussions, from the tearful anguish of the victim's families to chilling rationalizations by the convicted killers. Some segments are eerily myopic as when the West Memphis townspeople are advised not to talk to the media while Berlinger and Sinofsky record the whole thing on video. (Weren't THEY part of the media?) Later, Berlinger and Sinofsky even supply the court with crucial evidence obtained directly from a witness. The grisly details and straightforward presentation contribute to the feeling that you're watching a docuDRAMA, not the matter-of-fact documentary that it is. 🦴🦴🦴

1995 150m/C *D:* Joe Berlinger, Bruce Sinofsky; ***C:*** Robert Richman. **VHS, Closed Caption**

Paradise Place

Paradise Place sounds like it ought to be better than it is. After all, Ingmar Bergman produced it and Gunnel Lindblom, a leading actress in many of his movies, directed it. It features fine performances by Birgitta Valberg and Sif Ruud as a pair of old friends, and by Agneta Ekmanner, an exceptionally pretty child who plays Valberg's granddaughter. And the Swedish countryside couldn't be lovelier. Yet Lindblom tries so hard to make her thematic points that she sacrifices a sense of drama (as the grown-ups drone on about how society has corrupted their children, one of their own kids is quietly going mad, to their complete indifference). Much of her story takes the form of chatty philosophizing, and by the time action crawls into the final reel, the audience is lost in zzz's and/or a coffee break. ***AKA:*** Summer Place; Paradistorg. 🦴🦴

1977 112m/C *SW* Birgitta Valberg, Sif Ruud, Margaretha Bystrom, Agneta Ekmanner, Inga Landgre, Solveig Ternstrom, Dagny Lind, Goran Stangertz, Holger Lowenadler; ***D:*** Gunnel Lindblom; ***W:*** Gunnel Lindblom, Ulla Isaakson; ***C:*** Tony Forsberg; ***M:*** George Riedel.

Pariah

Pariah was far and way the most disturbing entry at San Francisco's Indie Fest in January, 1999. It is a difficult film to watch, but an extremely rewarding one. It begins with a date between Steve (Damon Jones), who is white, and Sam (Elexa Williams), who is black. They are pounced upon by a gang of neo-Nazi skinheads who subject Sam to gang rape and force Steve to watch. Neither Sam nor Steve can handle the incident. Shattered by the rape Steve was powerless to prevent, Sam kills herself that same night. Steve's life and plans come to a virtual halt. Finally, he decides to infiltrate the racist gang and avenge Sam and himself. What happens, naturally, is that by seeing the gang members at close range, Steve begins to understand the conditions that fuel their senseless crimes. Angela Jones is outstanding as a drug addict who hangs with the gang, but seeks some compassion from Steve that he cannot give her—he's simply too broken up inside with rage and grief. *Pariah* was inspired by real-life events in the filmmakers' lives; if reality was anything like this movie, it's astonishing that Randolph Kret's powerful gangland nightmare is as controlled and as balanced as it is. 🦴🦴🦴

1998 105m/C Damon Jones, Dave Oren Ward, David Lee Wilson, Aimee Chaffin, Angela Jones, Anna Padgett, Dan Weene, Anne Zupa, Brandon Slater, Jason Posey, Elexa Williams; ***D:*** Randolph Kret; ***W:*** Randolph Kret; ***C:*** Nils Erickson; ***M:*** Scott Grusin.

Paris, France

I wonder whether *Paris, France* would seem better if I'd seen it as a silent movie. As it was, I kept wondering how in the world its small cast was able to talk so much during their complicated physical routines without hyperventilating or passing out or something. It's a long movie,

The Hound Salutes:
JENNIE LIVINGSTON
Director, Paris Is Burning

I met some people in Washington Square Park who were vogueing. I thought the dancing was great, but didn't really know what it was about. So I began to go to some balls in Harlem and to talk to people. The more I went to balls and spoke to people, the more I thought that here was a world that has so much to say about American culture, about race, about class, about gender, about consumerism, and about all the things that drive us to be what we are. I really didn't have any problem filming *Paris Is Burning*; people were very nice. People who have been spat upon because of their race, class, and sexual orientation aren't about to turn on someone who comes to the ball in a spirit of fun and say, 'Get out of here, who are you? You're white, you're female.' A ball isn't like that. A ball is fun. A ball is all-embracing. So I would go and always have a good time. People would be very nice to me. I made it very clear from the start I wanted to make a film. I never said, 'Hey, I'm going to make you a star,' but I did say, 'I want to know what you have to say.' I didn't say *Paris Is Burning* would have big distribution someday, because I never thought that it would, but I did say, 'I want to bring your opinions and your views to the outside world.' That's an appealing idea, particularly for people involved in a sub-culture which is all about pretending to address the media."

too, 111 minutes worth of blathering and gymnastics, during which the characters rant and rave about John Lennon, sexual etiquette, and each other. Halfway through all this, I found myself reflecting on how the producers of Shannon Tweed movies are able do this sort of thing in a much more entertaining way. Whatever her profession (sexual therapist, anthropologist, chat show host) Shannon Tweed is always self-possessed, with an unerring knack for knowing what to do, whom to do it with, and when. She's strong and interesting and her crisply delivered dialogue is reserved for the moments she needs it most. Back to *Paris, France:* Leslie Hope, who bears a slight resemblance to Debra Winger, is never allowed to shut up for an instant. For those of you who are looking for a plot, this is it: Hope is married to a publisher who thinks he's going to die in three days. Meanwhile, she has an affair with the poet who's living with her husband's business partner. Harsh words are exchanged about everyone's techniques, obsessions, and manners until the credits roll. All you'll see of Paris is the Eiffel Tower, but you can't have everything in an NC-17 movie. Now, in *Cannibal Women in the Avocado Jungle of Death* (only 90 minutes and PG-13), you get Shannon Tweed as a feminist professor AND Karen Mistal as her worst student, Bunny, who never can decide whether being wrapped up in red licorice is anti-feminist or not, PLUS Adrienne Barbeau, and ALL in the jungles of San Bernardino! It's what we call a Guilty Pleasure, as opposed to a Film-As-Pain entry like *Paris, France.* **woof!**

1994 (NC-17) 111m/C *CA* Leslie Hope, Peter Outerbridge, Victor Ertmanis, Raoul Trujillo, Dan Lett; ***D:*** Gerard Ciccoritti; ***W:*** Tom Walmsley; ***M:*** John McCarthy. **VHS**

Paris Is Burning

Why is a documentary about vogueing at New York drag balls called *Paris Is*

Burning? Heck if I know, but Jennie Livingston's documentary is a valuable record of its era, filmed at the Paris Ballroom in the Bronx between 1985–89. The contestants, mostly black or Hispanic gay males, get to be stars for as long as they're in costume. Except for the postscript, it's funny and nonjudgmental and at 71 minutes in length, it won't wear out its welcome. ☙☙☙

1991 (R) 71m/C Dorian Corey, Pepper Labeija, Venus Xtravaganza, Octavia St. Laurant, Willi Ninja, Anji Xtravaganza, Freddie Pendavis, Junior Labeija; ***D:*** Jennie Livingston; ***C:*** Paul Gibson. National Society of Film Critics Awards '91: Best Feature Documentary; Sundance Film Festival '91: Grand Jury Prize. **VHS**

Parting Glances

Within four years of the release of this intensely sad film, writer/director Bill Sherwood was dead, leaving behind *Parting Glances* as his sole cinematic legacy to the world. It's about how two gay men react to the positive diagnosis, subsequent illness, and then-inevitable death of their friend, wonderfully played by Steve Buscemi. The versatile Buscemi (who looked a bit like Peter Lorre, but without Lorre's up-and-down weight problems) gave AIDS a human face. His role in *Parting Glances* was a star-making part and he made the most of it, becoming the best character actor of his generation. If you can't stop crying after *Parting Glances,* rent *The Wedding Singer* and watch it twice, once for the story, and then to appreciate Buscemi's terrific comic performance as David. Buscemi makes up to five movies a year, just like Golden Age character actors, and his many fans consider him an acting god. ☙☙☙

1986 (R) 90m/C John Bolger, Richard Ganoung, Steve Buscemi, Adam Nathan, Patrick Tull; ***D:*** Bill Sherwood; ***W:*** Bill Sherwood. **VHS, Closed Caption**

Party Girl

The onscreen presence of Parker Posey is among the bright spots of moviegoing in the 1990s. Posey poured gallons of energy into many indie flicks of the decade; *Party Girl* was her chance to break out of background roles into genuine leading status. The success of the *Party Girl* movie led to a very short-lived television series starring Christine ("Marcia") Taylor of *The Brady Bunch* films. So whatever her critics may say about Parker Posey, she gave Daisy von Scherler Mayer's debut film a stylish edge that definitely lingers in the mind. As Mary, Posey is broke and headed nowhere fast when her godmother (played by Sasha von Scherler, the director's mum) reluctantly gives her a chance in a library job. Mary learns the Dewey Decimal System as if her life depended on it. Ditzy characters, sharp dialogue, and the eccentric party scene all contribute to the lively ambiance, but it's Parker Posey's high-voltage performance that makes filing books and picking up Mustafa the falafel vendor (Omar Townsend) seem vital. Very good repeat value on this one. ☙☙☙

1994 (R) 94m/C Parker Posey, Omar Townsend, Anthony De Sando, Guillermo Diaz, Sasha von Scherler, Liev Schreiber; ***D:*** Daisy von Scherler Mayer; ***W:*** Harry Birckmayer, Daisy von Scherler Mayer; ***C:*** Michael Slovis; ***M:*** Anton Sanko. **VHS, LV, Closed Caption**

Pas Tres Catholique

Tonie Marshall's *Pas Tres Catholique* is an intriguing study of a private detective, thoughtfully played by Anemone. The mysteries she has to resolve mostly have to do with her own life, and especially the young son who is a stranger to her (Gregoire Colin is an attractive presence as teenaged Baptiste). What the film lacks in genuine narrative drive is more than compensated for by Anemone's remarkably shaded performance. ***AKA:*** Something Fishy. ☙☙½

1993 100m/B *FR* Anemone, Christine Boisson, Michel Didym, Gregoire Colin, Denis Podalydes, Roland Bertin, Bernard Verley, Michel Roux; ***Cameos:*** Micheline Presle; ***D:*** Tonie Marshall; ***W:*** Tonie Marshall; ***C:*** Dominique Chapuis. Nominations: Cesar Awards '95: Best Actress (Anemone). **VHS**

Burkley, Glenn Withrow, Richard Paul; ***D:*** David Beaird; ***W:*** Neil Cohen, Joel Cohen; ***M:*** Carter Burwell. **VHS, LV**

Passion Fish

Passion Fish is an example of what John Sayles can do without a net, the net being all the stuff people think they want to see in a movie. It's like falling in love with someone who isn't your type. If you care about someone, what the heck does your so-called type matter? May-Alice used to be a soap opera star on television, but while on the way to a leg waxing in Manhattan, she was in an accident with a cab and the lower half of her body became paralyzed. So May-Alice (Mary McDonnell) becomes a Louisiana recluse, chain-drinking and chain-watching the telly until Nurse Chantelle (Alfre Woodard) arrives on the scene. Chantelle tosses the liquor, determined to make good on this job so that she can prove she's worthy of her daughter's custody. (There's drug addiction in Chantelle's past.) May-Alice starts getting interested in old flame Rennie (David Straithairn) again, and Chantelle has a glint in her eye for Sugar LeDoux (Vondie Curtis-Hall). The fact that these guys have 15 kids between them is academic, considering the rarefied life that May-Alice and Chantelle are leading. Both deliver exceptional performances, and Sayles' gentle, easy-going script and direction open a viewer's heart just as the onscreen characters are trying to open theirs. 🦴🦴🦴

1992 (R) 136m/C Mary McDonnell, Alfre Woodard, David Strathairn, Vondie Curtis-Hall, Nora Dunn, Sheila Kelley, Angela Bassett, Mary Portser, Maggie Renzi, Leo Burmester, Shauntisa Willis, John Henry, Michael Laskin; ***D:*** John Sayles; ***W:*** John Sayles; ***C:*** Roger Deakins; ***M:*** Mason Daring. Independent Spirit Awards '93: Best Supporting Actress (Woodard); Nominations: Academy Awards '92: Best Actress (McDonnell), Best Original Screenplay. **VHS, LV, Letterbox, Closed Caption, DVD**

Passionate Thief

It is New Year's Eve in Rome and the 52-year-old movie extra played by Anna Magnani is filled with hope for the night. She longs for romance, adventure, and excite-

Steve Buscemi in *Parting Glances.* Cinecom; courtesy of the Kobal Collection

Pass the Ammo

Pass the Ammo, another recent effort by David Beaird, is a televangelism spoof starring Tim Curry and Annie Potts as a pair of preachers who are kidnapped on camera by a gang that includes Linda Kozlowski, a disgruntled victim of their media pitching. The effectiveness of the satire is variable, and some of the screenwriter's ideas may have looked better on paper than they do onscreen. Curry is believably charismatic, Potts is quite fetching as his glamorous wife, Anthony Geary is wonderful as their subversive engineer, and the sheer force of their personalities plus the *Pass the Ammo*'s obvious critique of the Bakker empire may propel the whole thing along with sympathetic viewers. 🦴🦴🦴

1988 (R) 93m/C Bill Paxton, Tim Curry, Linda Kozlowski, Annie Potts, Anthony Geary, Dennis

ment and finds all three, though not in the way she had anticipated. She runs into a drunk middle-aged American businessman played by Fred Clark. She keeps running into another Cinecitta bit actor portrayed by Toto, then 62. And finally she meets Ben Gazzara, then 30, the title character of *The Passionate Thief,* directed by Mario Monicelli. In this 1960 film, Monicelli captures all the tension that traditionally accompanies New Year's Eve, a night when we think of our progress as human beings, our ability to attract and sustain love, and our own mortality. To stave off such cosmic musings, there are parties and celebrations and endless glasses of champagne. Magnani's character is forever in pursuit of The Ultimate Party, but there are obstacles wherever she turns. She is late for a bash with co-workers, who leave the rendezvous point without her. She spends much precious time alone on public transportation after being ditched by Gazzara and Toto. She is spared the knowledge that the hot-fingered Gazzara, her romantic target for the night, has no interest in her and only wants to pick up some stolen loot, with Toto as a reluctant accomplice. With Magnani in the role, the adolescent longings of this small-time actress are quite contagious. She believes in love, in the future, and in herself. She is not jaded by life's many setbacks, although she certainly has plenty of reasons. She is willing to pay for her mistaken dreams and she seems invulnerable to despair. Magnani's and Toto's *tour-de-force* performances contribute to make *The Passionate Thief* a very funny, immensely touching story. ***AKA:*** Risate de Gioia; Joyous Laughter. 🦴🦴🦴

1960 100m/C *IT* Anna Magnani, Ben Gazzara, Fred Clark, Toto, Edy Vessel; ***D:*** Mario Monicelli; ***C:*** Leonida Barboni. **VHS**

Pastime

A bittersweet baseball elegy set in the minor leagues in 1957. A boyish 41-year-old pitcher can't face his impending retirement and pals around with the team's pariah, a 17-year-old black rookie. Splendidly written and acted, it's a melancholy treat whether you're a fan of the game or not, and safe for family attendance. Shot at Chicago's Comiskey Park (now leveled). Note major league cameos. ***AKA:*** One Cup of Coffee. 🦴🦴🦴

1991 (PG) 94m/C William Russ, Scott Plank, Glenn Plummer, Noble Willingham, Jeffrey Tambor, Deirdre O'Connell, Ricky Paull Goldin; ***Cameos:*** Ernie Banks, Harmon Killebrew, Duke Snider, Bob Feller, Bill Mazeroski, Don Newcombe; ***D:*** Robin B. Armstrong; ***W:*** Robin B. Armstrong; ***C:*** Tom Richmond. Sundance Film Festival '91: Audience Award. **VHS, LV**

Pecker

Pecker: It's not what you think. Edward Furlong's character is called Pecker because he pecked at his food as a little boy. Pecker is nutty about photography. He takes pictures of anyone and everyone in his much-loved Baltimore, Maryland, neighborhood. Pecker's grandmother is Memama (Jean Schertler), who believes that her Virgin Mary statue can really talk (even though her own lips are moving). Pecker's mom is Joyce (Mary Kay Place), a thrift shop owner who sells clothes to the homeless for quarters and dimes. Pecker's older sister is Tina (Martha Plimpton), who works at a gay bar called the Fudge Palace. Pecker's younger sister is Little Chrissy (Lauren Hulsey), a sugarholic. Pecker's girlfriend is Shelly (Christina Ricci), a laundromat manager. Pecker's best friend is Matt (Brendan Sexton III), a shoplifter. Everyone in Baltimore, Maryland, is happy and then Pecker decides to exhibit his work in a burger shop. A real, live art dealer from New York City (Lili Taylor as Rorey Wheeler) loves Pecker's pictures so much that she buys one for $30 and decides to show the rest in her Manhattan gallery. The whole clan goes to the opening and finds out that Pecker's pictures have taken on a life of their own. They all become instantly famous and everyone who is anyone (including Patty Hearst!) lionizes them. With fame comes notoriety and other problems—people don't want Pecker to take their pictures anymore. People can see Memama's lips moving when her Virgin Mary statue talks. Bess Armstrong as child welfare worker Dr. Klompus puts Little Chrissy on Ritalin. Tina is fired. Shelly is angry at her media tag as

The Hound Salutes:
MICHAEL POWELL
(1905–90)

In 1960, one of Great Britain's finest directors made a movie which was panned by virtually every major British critic. Michael Powell's career never really recovered from the heated response to *Peeping Tom,* although today this compassionate study of a homicidal sex maniac is one of his most highly regarded films (and a perennial favorite at revival theatres). Michael Powell entered the British motion picture industry in 1931 at the age of 26 and spent most of the decade shooting, editing, writing, and directing a string of "quota quickies" (cheaply made domestic features which were far from a threat to the lavish and much more popular American imports). In 1940, he co-directed *The Thief of Bagdad,* an outstanding Technicolor fantasy starring Sabu, who also appeared in 1947's Oscar-winning *Black Narcissus,* co-directed by Powell with Emeric Pressburger (1902–88). This intense exploration of the violent emotions that threaten to destroy an order of nuns is perhaps Powell's most memorable film, although ballet fans will never forget Moira Shearer's passionate involvement with *The Red Shoes,* an Oscar nominee for Best Picture in 1948.

In 1985, Powell made a special appearance in San Francisco to introduce a screening of *Peeping Tom.* Then in his 80th year, he instantly developed a rapport with the audience, even though his voice was frail and he had not been provided with a microphone. Powell had no regrets about making the film which brought an abrupt halt to his once-dazzling career and he spoke of his work on the picture with great pride. In fact, Michael Powell was a master at examining the dark side of human nature, although the stunning pictorial qualities of his films often distracted audiences from the sharpness of his observations. The troubling images in *Black Narcissus* are in some ways even more subversive than *Peeping Tom* ever was. If you want to give yourself a cinematic jolt, rent *Black Narcissus* on video and watch what Powell and Pressburger were able to achieve with two great actresses (Deborah Kerr and Kathleen Byron) plus one tube of lipstick.

Other MICHAEL POWELL films on video include *The Phantom Light, Edge of the World, Spy in Black, The Lion Has Wings, One of Our Aircraft Is Missing,* and *The 49th Parallel*; and with Emeric Pressburger: *The Life and Death of Colonel Blimp, A Canterbury Tale, I Know Where I'm Going, Stairway to Heaven, The Small Black Room, The Elusive Pimpernel, The Tales of Hoffman, Pursuit of the Graph Spree,* and *Night Ambush.*

a "stain goddess" and even angrier when she sees Rorey making a pass at Pecker. Matt can't shoplift anymore. Fame: Who needs it? For all his reputation as an oddball, director John Waters is just a hometown boy at heart. He's made all 13 of his movies in Baltimore and he's never turned into an intellectual Gotham snob or a La La Land fake. He is in his creative heart and soul an innocent riveted by subjects that are basic and simple: Suburbia, Love, Family, and Bad Taste continue to obsess him as a filmmaker. The point of *Pecker* is so heartwarmingly artless it could be taught in Sunday School if it weren't for the Fudge Palace and the lesbian strip club and Little Chrissy snorting green peas like crack. *Pecker* is a sweet hoot of a flick, Furlong and Ricci are charming together, and Mary Kay Place, the hardest working and most underrated character actress of the late 20th century, turns in another gem of a performance.

1998 (R) 87m/C Edward Furlong, Lili Taylor, Christina Ricci, Martha Plimpton, Mary Kay Place, Brendan Sexton III, Mark Joy, Mink Stole, Bess Armstrong, Patty Hearst, Mary Vivian Pearce, Lauren Hulsey, Jean Schertler; ***D:*** John Waters; ***W:*** John Waters; ***C:*** Robert Stevens; ***M:*** Stewart Copeland. National Board of Review Awards '98: Best Supporting Actress (Ricci). **VHS, DVD**

Peeping Tom

Peeping Tom was made in 1960, the same year as Alfred Hitchcock's *Psycho,* but Powell's film was much kinkier and demanded far more from its audiences than the wildly successful *Psycho* did. It is not hard to sympathize with the shy, softspoken innkeeper played by Anthony Perkins and to wonder if maybe he and Janet Leigh will have a romance, but you want to warn innocent Anna Massey to stay away from the obsessed photographer portrayed by Karl Boehm. *Peeping Tom* was panned upon release by critics who had apparently thought Michael Powell was the maker of staid and genteel films. They must have gone out for popcorn when Kathleen Byron's insane nun applied her lipstick in *Black Narcissus,* for Powell had slipped in a hint of the dark side of human nature in many of his films. He doesn't pull any punches in *Peeping Tom,* and the film emerges as one of the most fascinating character studies of a killer ever put on film. That's Powell, by the way, in the old home movies showing the photographer's father.

1960 88m/C Karl-Heinz Boehm, Moira Shearer, Anna Massey, Maxine Audley, Esmond Knight, Shirley Anne Field, Brenda Bruce, Pamela Green, Jack Watson, Nigel Davenport, Susan Travers, Veronica Hurst, Martin Miller, Miles Malleson; ***Cameos:*** Michael Powell; ***D:*** Michael Powell; ***W:*** Leo Marks; ***C:*** Otto Heller. **VHS, LV**

Perfect Friday

This escapist caper yarn stars Stanley Baker as Bank Deputy Under Manager K.G. Graham, who decides to break out of his dull life by robbing the National Metropolitan Bank Ltd. of 300,000 pounds. His comrades-in-crime are David Warner as the impoverished Lord Nicholas Dorset and Ursula Andress as his wife, Lady Britt. Baker's sensuous, intelligent brown eyes tend to subvert the unexciting personality he is presumed to have; why did he wait so long to escape his humdrum life? Lady Britt promptly tumbles into bed with him, but never addresses him as anything other than Mr. Graham, which eliminates the need for explanations to her husband when she cries out her lover's name in her sleep. Warner, in a blonde wig, is a hoot as the aristocrat who sulks in the House of Lords for lack of anything better to do. Baker, Andress, and Warner are practically the whole show, although the presence of Masterpiece Theatre regulars David Waller as Bank Manager H.L. Williams, T.P. McKenna as Bank Under Manager R. Smith, and Joan Benham as Miss Welsh enriches the atmosphere of the piece. And the caper? Very stylish indeed, under the guidance of director Peter Hall, with swinging-'60s costumes to match by Kiki Byrne plus another great soundtrack by Johnny Dankworth.

1970 95m/C *GB* Ursula Andress, Stanley Baker, David Warner, Patience Collier, T.P. McKenna, David Waller, Joan Benham, Julian Orchard, Trisha Mortimer, Ann Tirard, Carleton Hobbs; ***D:*** Peter Hall; ***W:*** Scott Forbes, Anthony Greville-Bell; ***C:*** Alan Hume; ***M:*** John Dankworth.

Performance

Mick Jagger tried to launch a movie career in a big way in 1970. In May, he played the title role in *Ned Kelly* under the direction of Tony Richardson (a stretch) and in October, he starred as rich rock star Turner in Nicolas Roeg's *Performance* (not a stretch). James Fox, on the other hand, had had it with a screen career that began in 1950 on MGM's *The Miniver Story* (when he was billed as William Fox) and ended 20 years later with this decadent

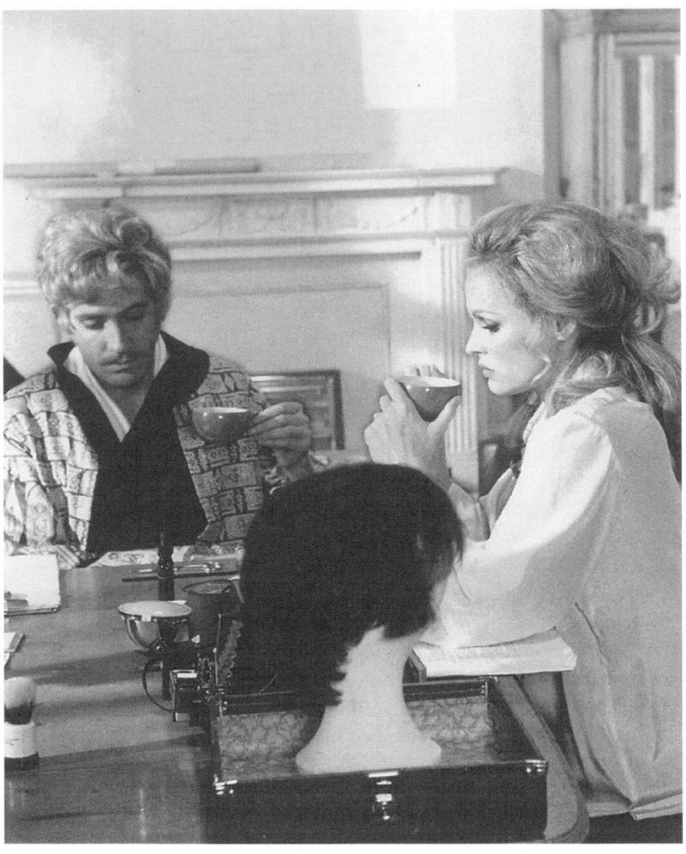

Lord Nicholas Dorset (David Warner) and Lady Britt (Ursula Andress) in *Perfect Friday.*
Courtesy of the Kobal Collection

flick. Once one of the most conspicuous party goers in the swinging '60s, Fox gave up alcohol, became a born-again Christian and a missionary and, by 1983, a born-again actor. Think about that when you see him in 1963's *The Servant* and 1986's *Absolute Beginners*! Here, he's gangster Chas Devlin, complete with a juggler's wild orange wig and sunglasses, who's killed the wrong man and is hiding out in Turner's basement. Like many films of that era, The Scene is more important than the participants' past. Anita Pallenberg and Michele Breton are Pherber and Lucy, two women who, along with Turner and Chas, engage in bisexuality, sadistic violence, masochism, and magic mushrooms. *Performance* was difficult to find on video for a good many years. I guess that it finally qualifies as a quaint period piece for classes that study 20th century Archaeology, Culture, and Customs. Nicolas Roeg made the timeless *Walkabout* with Jenny Agutter in Australia the following year, Donald Cammell went on to make *Demon Seed* with Julie Christie in 1977, and Mick Jagger never did become a superstar in the movies, although I doubt that he loses any sleep over it and he does give a fine rendition of "Memo from Turner" here. Recommended for further research (but only for the tenacious): Mick Jagger and the Rolling Stones are the "stars" of Robert Frank's 1972 documentary, *C*cks*ck*r Blues/CS Blues.* For legal reasons, the chances of Frank's film ever surfacing on video are nada. You'll have to keep track of its rare screenings, at which the filmmaker is always present. If you think Turner and Chas give Pherber and Lucy rough trade in *Performance,* wait till you see what happens to real-life groupies backstage with the Stones: It's dead kinky and a little sad. 🦴🦴🦴

1970 (R) 104m/C *GB* James Fox, Mick Jagger, Anita Pallenberg, Michele Breton, Ann Sidney, John Bindon, Stanley Meadows, Allan Cuthbertson, Antony Morton; ***D:*** Donald Cammell, Nicolas Roeg; ***W:*** Donald Cammell; ***C:*** Nicolas Roeg; ***M:*** Jack Nitzsche. **VHS, LV**

Permanent Midnight

I may have missed three masterpieces of the small screen, but I've never seen *ALF* or *thirtysomething* and the only episode of *Moonlighting* I managed to catch was the black-and-white film noir tribute featuring an appearance by Orson Welles shortly before his death in 1985. Therefore, the name of television writer Jerry Stahl means nothing to me. His autobiography, *Permanent Midnight,* might as well have been a novel, and his adapted screenplay feels fake and fictional for most of its running time. If the real Stahl is anything like the slick-skinned jerk that Ben Stiller plays in this 85-minute drugalogue, I can't help feeling that spilling his guts onscreen about his own substance abuse is just another career move. The celluloid Stahl is so full of his own B.S. that I wanted to toss kitty litter at the screen instead of

tomatoes. What do we know about him? Well, he helps his buddy look for the stash he ripped off from him and encourages him to build a case against someone else. And he doesn't like the British because they're British, but he marries the lovely "Sandra" (Elizabeth Hurley) anyway, because she needs a green card and she pays him for the favor. She even gets him a job on a television show (thinly disguised as *ALF*), but is he grateful? NO. Projecting his own mean-spirited core onto her, he decides that she only wants him to be half of a Power Couple. (One look at the spineless Stiller, whose leather pants split when he bends over, ought to dispel anyone's illusions about THAT.) We're supposed to feel sorry for Stahl because he squanders year after year, job after job, and paycheck after paycheck on drugs, but we don't because there isn't a glint of an actual emotion anywhere in this zombie. He mops up his mother's blood like a pod person, he obsesses power agent Jana Farmer for reasons even the wonderful Janeane Garofalo can't make plausible, and he takes his own baby on an extended shopping expedition for MORE STUFF! And then we're supposed to believe that he gets clean, works at a fast-food restaurant, and goes on chat shows out of the sheer goodness of his so-called heart? What heart? Drug addicts don't watch chat shows about other drug addicts, but development deal makers do. C'mon, it's a TRUE STORY! Who wouldn't be moved? Well, me for one. Stiller is drawing raves for growing a five o'clock shadow and rolling his eyeballs, but a persuasive junkie he ain't. The extremely likeable Hurley, Garofalo, Cheryl Ladd (as "Pamela Verlaine"), and *E/R*'s Maria Bello (as "Kitty") are required to say and do dumb things as some of the women in Stahl's life. The two girls who walked out as I walked in clearly weren't being quizzed on *Permanent Midnight* Monday morning, because they asked for a refund and wandered away, looking for something better to do on a Friday night.

Mick Jagger, Anita Pallenberg, and Michele Breton in *Performance.*
Warner Bros.; courtesy of the Kobal Collection

"I made a decision about that. I decided to write about my own experiences. I like my own experiences, all in all."

—M.G. (Michelle Meyrink) in *Permanent Record.*

1998 (R) 85m/C Ben Stiller, Elizabeth Hurley, Maria Bello, Owen C. Wilson, Lourdes Benedicto, Peter Greene, Cheryl Ladd, Fred Willard, Charles Fleischer, Janeane Garofalo, Jerry Stahl; ***D:*** David Veloz; ***W:*** David Veloz; ***C:*** Robert Yeoman; ***M:*** Daniel Licht. **VHS, DVD**

Permanent Record

In *Permanent Record,* Marisa Silver's excellent film on teen suicide, Alan Boyce is so appealing as a troubled young composer that his death is genuinely horrifying; we never stop thinking about him or missing him for the rest of the movie. His best friend is wonderfully played by Keanu Reeves, so good in 1987's *River's Edge.* The well-written script neither glamorizes suicide nor betrays the believability of its characters. Although the suicide in the film appears inevitable, the resulting trauma could have resulted in a chain reaction, which wasn't helped by the moralistic approach of heavy authority figures and was only circumvented by other adults who were able to identify and cope with the kids' grief. 🦴🦴🦴

1988 (PG-13) 92m/C Alan Boyce, Keanu Reeves, Michelle Meyrink, Jennifer Rubin, Pamela Gidley, Michael Elgart, Richard Bradford, Barry Corbin, Kathy Baker, Dakin Matthews; ***D:*** Marisa Silver; ***W:*** Jarre Fees, Alice Liddle, Larry Ketron; ***C:*** Frederick Elmes; ***M:*** Joe Strummer. **VHS, LV, Closed Caption**

Persuasion

Admirers of Jane Austen won't want to miss *Persuasion,* starring Amanda Root as a selfless Austen heroine swayed from the course of true love by family considerations. This delicately played study of English country life circa 1814 features a spirited performance by Root and a fine supporting cast: Corin Redgrave and Sophie Thompson from *Four Weddings and a Funeral,* Phoebe Nicholls from *Brideshead Revisited,* and the late Susan Fleetwood from *Heat and Dust.* 🦴🦴🦴

1995 (PG) 104m/C *GB* Amanda Root, Ciaran Hinds, Susan Fleetwood, Corin Redgrave, Fiona Shaw, John Woodvine, Phoebe Nicholls, Samuel West, Sophie Thompson, Judy Cornwell, Felicity Dean, Simon Russell Beale, Victoria Hamilton, Emma Roberts; ***D:*** Roger Mitchell; ***W:*** Nick Dear, Jeremy Sams; ***C:*** John Daly. **VHS, LV, Closed Caption**

Phantom of Liberty

Even at 74, Luis Buñuel (1900–83) could still romp with his audiences with an appreciation of playfulness at its deepest and purest levels, jesting here, poking there. *The Phantom of Liberty* is a delicious film: warm, humorous, and delightful. Stories of pornography, violence, death, Catholicism, and convention all wind into each other, and each and every subject is ribbed to bits by film's end. (Only Buñuel could direct a dinner sequence as wild as the one you'll see in this film!) Buñuel's next film, 1977's *That Obscure Object of Desire,* was his swan song. ***AKA:*** Le Fantôme de la Liberté; The Specter of Freedom. 🦴🦴🦴🦴

1974 104m/C *FR* Adriana Asti, Jean-Claude Brialy, Michel Piccoli, Adolfo Celi, Monica Vitti, Milena Vukotic, Michael (Michel) Lonsdale, Claude Pieplu, Julien Bertheau, Paul Frankeur, Paul Leperson, Bernard Verley; ***D:*** Luis Bunuel; ***W:*** Luis Bunuel, Jean-Claude Carriere; ***C:*** Edmond Richard. **VHS, LV**

Phobia

Phobia, John Dingwall's riveting movie from Australia, is a good bet for inclusion in a list of the 10 best first films ever made. The film stars Polish actress Gosia Dobrowolska as Renate Simmons, whose naked face reveals her progressive recognition of the depth of her agoraphobia. This paralyzing fear of open spaces thwarts her efforts to heal herself at every turn. Renate's husband and "phobic companion" is played by Sean Scully, whose multi-layered performance as Bob won him an Australian Academy Award nomination. Scully starred in the Walt Disney classics *The Prince and the Pauper, Almost Angels,* and *The Scarecrow of Romney Marsh* between 1962 and 1964 and also in 1981's *Sara Dane.* Scully has surpassed his early promise and now, with his preternatural knack for zooming in on the heart of sexual frustration, he has the potential to become one of the leading actors of his generation. (Grown-ups may not have been aware of the underlying sexual tension in Scully's juvenile work, but pre-teen girls certainly were!) Dingwall's *Phobia* script is a dizzying blend of terror and comedy, of love and loathing, of compassion and scrutiny. To suggest both the brighter days and the gradual disintegration of this tortured couple, the director uses the effective device of old home videotapes, Bob's obsessive preoccupation. Dingwall also makes marvelous use of his own suburban home in Newport, New South Wales, although one hopes that the place is more fun for him to live in than this searing film suggests. 🦴🦴🦴🦴

1988 85m/C *AU* Sean Scully, Gosia Dobrowolska; ***D:*** John Dingwall; ***W:*** John Dingwall. **VHS**

Photographing Fairies

FairyTale: A True Story is for kids. *Photographing Fairies* isn't. Until a miscast Ben Kingsley as Reverend Templeton turns up, it's an intriguing story about photographer Charles Castle (Toby Stephens, then 28), who gets married in Switzerland in 1912 and then takes a honeymoon hike with his lovely bride Anne-Marie (Rachel Shelley). She is swallowed alive by a snow fissure and he is a disconsolate widower. All he can remember her by is an out-of-focus picture of the wedding. He doesn't even know her favorite color. He becomes a cool craftsman, taking battlefield pictures during The Great War and studio portraits after the Armistice (but no weddings). While distributing his business cards at a Theosophical Society meeting, he analyzes a photograph of the Cottingley Fairies and concludes that it's a mere trick of the light, with accessories purchased in shops to complete the illusion. Castle impresses Sir Arthur Conan Doyle (worthily interpreted by Edward Hardwicke, who once played Dr. Watson) while remaining completely unimpressed himself. Then the mother of two other little girls who photograph fairies turns up at his studio one day. She is the soft-voiced, ethereal Beatrice Templeton (Frances Barber). He follows her to her country home and meets her children Clara (Hannah Bould) and Ana (Miriam Grant) and their lovely governess, Linda (Emily Woof). It seems that the fairies convene most often around a craggy old tree that lures Beatrice, the children and, finally Charles himself. For Charles Castle, as for Conan Doyle, a belief in fairies meant that perhaps it was possible to contact loved ones, perhaps they weren't only a dream and/or a mere trick of the light, perhaps they still lived and could communicate with us. This delicate material is not helped by Kingsley's ham-handed approach to it, nor could a rumored 23 drafts of the screenplay have done much more than confuse the film-making team, as well as the audience. There are some good performances here (along with one that's way over the top), some attractive rural scenery, and several VERY interesting ideas that desperately needed a fine script doctor to showcase them to full advantage. Based on the novel by Steve Szilagyi. (Mike Newell is among the executive producers.) 🦴🦴½

1997 (R) 107m/C *GB* Toby Stephens, Frances Barber, Ben Kingsley, Emily Woof, Philip Davis, Rachel Shelley, Edward Hardwicke, Hannah Bould, Miriam Grant, Clive Merrison; ***D:*** Nick Willing; ***W:*** Nick Willing, Chris Harrald; ***C:*** John de Borman; ***M:*** Simon Boswell. **VHS**

Pi

Pi is a first film and Darren Aronofsky worked hard on it and even received a Best Director award at 1998's Sundance Film Festival. But if you've ever gone out with a genius with a touching belief in the infallibility of mathematics and science, you may have the less-than-touching belief that, when it comes to listening to him discuss the objects of his compulsive obsessions, a little goes a long way. Sean Gullette is the obsessive-compulsive Max Cohen, who goes daft and weird in his pursuit of impenetrable imponderables. *Pi* is only 85 minutes long, the same as *A Brief History of Time,* but it feels longer. For those who like this sort of thing, there won't be enough hours in the day to watch it. Already a cult movie. 🦴🦴

1998 (R) 85m/B Sean Gullette, Mark Margolis, Ben Shenkman, Pamela Hart, Stephen Perlman, Samia Shoaib; ***D:*** Darren Aronofsky; ***W:*** Darren Aronofsky; ***C:*** Matthew Libatique; ***M:*** Clint Mansell. Independent Spirit Awards '99: First Screenplay; Sundance Film Festival '98: Best Director (Aronof-

Fernando Ramos Da Silva in Hector Babenco's *Pixote.*
Unifilm/Embrafilme; courtesy of the Kobal Collection

sky); Nominations: Independent Spirit Awards '99: Best First Feature. **VHS, DVD**

The Piano

The Piano is a long, brooding story about sexual politics circa 1850. Oscar winners Holly Hunter and Anna Paquin play Ada and Flora McGrath, who leave Scotland in order to settle in New Zealand with Ada's new husband, Stewart, whom neither of them has ever seen. After a rough voyage, they are confronted with the stark loneliness of their new home and the loss of Ada's most treasured belonging, her piano; Stewart (Sam Neill) won't carry it to his house. He gives what is not his to give to George Baines (Harvey Keitel), another settler. Ada pines for her piano and George pines for her; they soon make an arrangement where she can buy it back from him with escalating erotic favors. Mother and daughter, who have always been close, find themselves at opposite ends of Stewart's power struggle. All Flora can see is that Stewart appears to be doing his best and they are, after all, living with him. Ada, who is mute, cannot explain the complexities of her situation to her daughter, who is too young to know how she is placing her mother in grave danger. Nothing is simple in Jane Campion's artfully woven screenplay (also an Oscar winner), which evolves in increasingly strange and disturbing ways. The strong imagery here is the stuff that nightmares are made of, especially the final shot. Hunter turned up later in David Cronenberg's *Crash* as a crash survivor strung out on crash-related sex; Paquin next played young *Jane Eyre* for Franco Zeffirelli and then made kiddie matinee movies in Hollywood. 🦴🦴🦴

1993 (R) 120m/C *AU* Holly Hunter, Harvey Keitel, Sam Neill, Anna Paquin, Kerry Walker, Genevieve Lemon; ***D:*** Jane Campion; ***W:*** Jane Campion; ***C:*** Stuart Dryburgh; ***M:*** Michael Nyman. Academy Awards '93: Best Actress (Hunter), Best Original Screenplay, Best Supporting Actress (Paquin); Australian Film Institute '93: Best Actor (Keitel), Best Actress (Hunter), Best Cinematography, Best Costume Design, Best Director (Campion), Best Film, Best Film Editing, Best Screenplay, Best Sound, Best Original

Score; British Academy Awards '93: Best Actress (Hunter); Cannes Film Festival '93: Best Actress (Hunter), Best Film; Golden Globe Awards '94: Best Actress—Drama (Hunter); Independent Spirit Awards '94: Best Foreign Film; Los Angeles Film Critics Association Awards '93: Best Actress (Hunter), Best Cinematography, Best Director (Campion), Best Screenplay, Best Supporting Actress (Paquin); National Board of Review Awards '93: Best Actress (Hunter); New York Film Critics Awards '93: Best Actress (Hunter), Best Director (Campion), Best Screenplay; National Society of Film Critics Awards '93: Best Actress (Hunter), Best Screenplay; Writers Guild of America '93: Best Original Screenplay; Nominations: Academy Awards '93: Best Cinematography, Best Costume Design, Best Director (Campion), Best Film Editing, Best Picture; British Academy Awards '94: Best Director (Campion), Best Film, Best Original Screenplay, Best Original Score; Directors Guild of America Awards '93: Best Director (Campion); Golden Globe Awards '94: Best Director (Campion), Best Film—Drama, Best Screenplay, Best Supporting Actress (Paquin), Best Original Score. **VHS, LV, Closed Caption, DVD**

Picnic at Hanging Rock

1975's *Picnic at Hanging Rock,* Peter Weir's exquisitely lensed Australian film, is something of a cautionary tale about the conflict between nature and civilization. Three girls and their teacher persist in imposing themselves on a threatening landscape about which they know nothing except its age. They fail, and the one girl who does return can't remember why. Even before they leave the picnic, their attachments to the others are loose, and they are riddled with a sense of their own mortality. Unlike most contemporary treatments of the past which thrust current sensibilities on an earlier time, Weir's international classic reveals Valentine's Day 1900 on its own terms, with the exception of one new twist on the old chestnut of separated twins. The sweet-voiced Helen Morse perfectly illustrates the interior strength and surface gentleness that survived best in that era. The faces, especially the hauntingly lovely Anne Lambert, are straight out of an old photograph album and the dialogue betrays no ironic premonitions of how the new century will disrupt the Victorian world. Based on a novel by Joan Lindsay, who never revealed whether her chiller was inspired by a true story—or not! 🦴🦴🦴🦴

1975 (PG) 110m/C *AU* Margaret Nelson, Rachel Roberts, Dominic Guard, Helen Morse, Jacki Weaver, Vivean Gray, Anne Lambert; ***D:*** Peter Weir; ***W:*** Clifford Green; ***C:*** John Seale; ***M:*** Bruce Smeaton. **VHS, Closed Caption, DVD**

Picture Bride

It is 1918. Seventeen-year-old Riyo arrives in Hawaii from Yokohama. She is marrying Matsuji (Akira Takayama) and they only know each other through the exchange of photographs. When she learns that Matsuji sent her a 25-year-old picture, she feels tricked and will not let him sleep with her. She has no money to go home, but determines to do so as soon as she earns the $300 return fare by working on a sugar plantation at 65 cents a day. If only Riyo had gone on to show the gumption that she proved she already had when she first arrived in Hawaii, *Picture Bride* would he a much more gripping film. Instead, we get female bonding, tragedy, submission, and acquiescence. We don't know what Riyo feels and the emotional territory that Kayo Hatta covers here is awfully familiar. Better films about the immigrant experience include 1979's *Gaijin* by Tiruka Yamasaki and 1991's *1000 Pieces of Gold* by Nancy Kelly. Toshiro Mifune makes a cameo appearance as a benshi (narrator) of a silent movie. 🦴🦴

1994 (PG-13) 95m/C *JP* Yoko Sugi, Youki Kudoh, Akira Takayama, Tamlyn Tomita, Cary-Hiroyuki Tagawa; ***Cameos:*** Toshiro Mifune; ***D:*** Kayo Hatta; ***W:*** Kayo Hatta, Mari Hatta, Diane Mark; ***C:*** Claudio Rocha; ***M:*** Cliff Eidelman. Sundance Film Festival '95: Audience Award; Nominations: Independent Spirit Awards '96: Best First Feature. **VHS, LV, Closed Caption**

Pink String and Sealing Wax

Googie Withers came within an eyelash of giving Britain's top female star (Margaret Lockwood, with whom she'd appeared in 1938's *The Lady Vanishes*) a run for her money at the boxoffice. This examination of a Victorian murderess (set in Brighton, circa 1880) is a fine vehicle for Withers, who clearly knows the secret that any great screen villain knows, namely that her

The Hound Salutes:
ANDRE DE TOTH

When I made *House of Wax,* I didn't make a three-dimensional film. I made a story of a man—a human being—who wanted to give beauty to the world, and because of filthy money, he has been robbed of his chance to do this, because his partner burned down his dreamland. To make the wax figures of Phyllis Kirk and Carolyn Jones look real, there was no difficulty at all, there was just a certain care and concern and aim and YOU have to know what you're doing. It was simple. The sequence with the ping pong ball was not done specially as a 3-D gimmick. That was a barker, calling attention to the wax museum. There are no 3-D gimmicks in *House of Wax.* I was telling a story and the story called for a man calling your attention to walk into the wax museum.

"I feel humble when people ask me about my movies, because I really wanted to please people. I'm embarrassed when something I said and did makes people happy. My first book, *Fragments: Portraits from the Inside,* was not an autobiography—it was a memoir, it was a traveling book, really, going through a certain section of life I lived through. I witnessed the years between the '30s till 1980. The book's not finished there, because it's still going in the '90s. The second book is *Put the Drama in Front of the Camera* (with Antony Slide). Buy the books. I need the money. God bless you."

ANDRE DE TOTH also directed *Pitfall, Dark Waters, Ramrod, Man in the Saddle, Springfield Rifle, Last of the Comanches, The Stranger Wore a Gun, Crime Wave, The Indian Fighter, The Mongol,* and *Morgan the Pirate.*

character can do no wrong. Gordon Jackson is the youth who is seduced into her plans for homicide and Mervyn Johns does an excellent job as a father who nearly loses his family because of his rigid views on right and wrong. John Carol is as much of a dirty rat as you'll ever see in this sort of melodrama, and Mary Merrall, Jean Ireland, and Sally Ann Howes are appealing as the mother and daughters who learn how to manipulate an impossible family situation to their advantage. The minor characters are effective too, especially Catherine Lacey as Miss Porter, a tipsy but genteel barfly. The title refers to a catch phrase of the era and has nothing to do with the story. Based on the play by Roland Pertwee.

1945 89m/B *GB* Mervyn Johns, Mary Merrall, Gordon Jackson, Googie Withers, Sally Ann Howes, Catherine Lacey, Garry Marsh, Frederick Piper, Don Stannard, Valentine Dyall; ***D:*** Robert Hamer; ***W:*** Robert Hamer; ***C:*** Richard S. Pavey. **VHS**

Pitfall

Pitfall is the second of three noir films Andre de Toth directed between 1944 and 1954. Only four years after *Murder My Sweet,* Dick Powell isn't Philip Marlowe anymore, he's insurance agent John Forbes, Sue's (Jane Wyatt) husband and Tommy's (Jimmy Hunt) father. Forbes once nurtured an adolescent fantasy that his life would be more interesting and more rewarding, but now the years of domestic rituals and insurance claims stretch ahead

Chiropractor Tom Mason gets his big break as a Bela Lugosi stand-in walking among cardboard gravestones in Ed Wood's *Plan 9 from Outer Space.* DCA; courtesy of the Kobal Collection

of him in all their yawning dullness. Forbes and a private investigator named Mack MacDonald (Raymond Burr) are trying to recover goods purchased with robbery loot. They meet model Mona Stevens (Lizabeth Scott), the robber's girlfriend, retrieve the goods, and the credits roll. Whoa, rewind! Well, what do you THINK happens? Frustrated agent and frustrated detective meet gorgeous blonde Mona, they all become pals (Sue and Tommy, too), and the credits roll. NOPE, this is Noirville. If John and Mona have an affair, all hell will break loose and it does. Remember: Mack is frustrated, too. Mona has a boyfriend in jail (Byron Barr as Bill Smiley). Sue doesn't know about Mona, which means she'll HAVE to know about Mona, and life will never be the same. The moral? Don't choke on your adolescent fantasies! We're practically in the 1950s, boys and girls, domestic rituals and insurance claims are GOOD for you, sex with the cool blonde who hates the detective who wants to have sex with the cool blonde instead of you is BAD for you. Again, wife and work: GOOD; affair with Mona: BAD. De Toth shows how the crushing weight of the familiar would drive a guy like John Forbes to go wild. He also shows that the familiar is equally crushing to Sue Forbes, and only her faith in a faithless partner makes it any more bearable for her. And de Toth gets a really sick and twisted performance out of Burr, who's aces as Mack! Look for de Toth's *Dark Waters* and *Crime Wave,* also on video. Based on the novel by Jay Dratler.

1948 85m/B Dick Powell, Jane Wyatt, Lizabeth Scott, Raymond Burr, John Litel, Byron Barr, Ann Doran, Jimmy Hunt, Selmer Jackson, Margaret

The Hound Salutes:
CONRAD BROOKS
Actor, *Plan 9 from Outer Space*

When I met Ed Wood back in 1948, I had no intention of ever working as a motion picture actor. He told me then that he would make films eventually, and he said that whenever he got to do his first film, he would use me. I told him I wasn't an actor, but that didn't mean a damn thing with Ed Wood. He was very ambitious and he was going to make films, which he did. It took him four years, but he kept his promise and he did use me in a 1953 film called *Glen or Glenda?* That was my first film for Ed Wood. It was a sexy little story. I was surprised at the type of subject it was, but knowing Ed Wood (Ed liked me very much, he sort of adopted me)—it was a big thrill for me to work for Ed Wood, regardless of the type of film it was. The most surprising thing about it all was the film starred Bela Lugosi—I was going to appear in a picture with Bela, who was my idol. He was a fine gentleman and a wonderful person and I also worked as a stand-in for him—I wasn't just an actor in the film. Between takes, I'd hold his cigar and bring him a glass of water. It was a pleasure to be there with this man. I kept looking at him thinking, 'That's not Bela, that's Dracula!' I couldn't get that out of my mind. We also had Lyle Talbot [1902–96] as Police Inspector

Wells, Dick Wassel; ***D:*** Andre de Toth; ***W:*** Karl Kamb; ***C:*** Harry Wild; ***M:*** Louis Forbes. **VHS, LV**

Pixote

Both 1981's *Pixote* by Hector Babenco and 1984's *Streetwise* by Martin Bell offer a harsh portrait of the lives led by street children. Both *Streetwise* and *Pixote* (a horrifying fictional saga of a 10-year-old murderer) raise disturbing questions for which neither film provides answers. Bell and Babenco attracted considerable reputations for their honesty in showing the toll of street hustling on the very young. The children are clearly no better off, and in the case of *Pixote*'s young star, the doors to acting which were opened by his appearance in an international hit were quickly slammed. Young Fernando Ramos Da Silva eventually returned to the street life he shared with three million children in Sao Paulo. He was killed in a shootout with the police early in 1987. ***AKA:*** Pixote: A Lei do Mais Fraco. 🦴🦴🦴🦴

1981 127m/C *BR* Fernando Ramos Da Silva, Marilia Pera, Jorge Juliao, Gilberto Moura, Jose Nilson dos Santos, Edilson Lino; ***D:*** Hector Babenco; ***W:*** Hector Babenco; ***C:*** Rodolfo Sanchez; ***M:*** John Neschling. Los Angeles Film Critics Association Awards '81: Best Foreign Film; New York Film Critics Awards '81: Best Foreign Film; National Society of Film Critics Awards '81: Best Actress (Pera). **VHS**

Plan 9 from Outer Space

It's hard to put a WOOF! by this movie, because I enjoy it so much. I have this six-hour tape that includes the following: (1) *Queen of Outer Space,* (2) *Attack of the 50 Ft. Woman,* (3) this movie, and (4) *Bait.* Put this tape in the VCR at midnight and Voila! Auf Wiedershen, Insomnia! Tor Johnson couldn't do dialogue, Vampira wouldn't do dialogue, and Mona McKinnon shouldn't do dialogue, EVER! Ask Gregory Walcott about this movie and he'll tell you about co-starring with Claudette Colbert in 1955! Ask Conrad Brooks about this movie and he'll tell you everyone got paid! Tom Keene (who looks absolutely shell-shocked as Col. Edwards) starred in 1934's *Our Daily Bread* under the direc-

Warren (he'd made over 30 films, including 1933's *20,000 Years in Sing Sing* with Spencer Tracy, at Warner Bros. between 1932 and 1960 and he was also a very pleasant man).

"Ed Wood was a terrible director, but he had good taste. *Plan 9 from Outer Space* was condemned and crucified for many reasons. They said it was shot on 8mm film in someone's back yard in the town of San Fernando for $3,000 and the acting and direction were bad and it was lucky if the actors even got paid and all that. But I got news for all these people: *Plan 9 from Outer Space* was shot on 35mm film on a Hollywood sound stage. All the actors got paid scale. It was a union film and Ed had to do the film in five days and that was it. If he went over five days he was in trouble, but he did it. Of course, it was made in 1956 and 24 years later when the book *The Golden Turkey Awards* came out, I read the reviews and thought, 'Uh-oh. It'll be another 24 years before I get to see it again.' But, believe it or not, when it hit a Los Angeles television station, *Plan 9 from Outer Space* got the royal treatment. It played three times a day in prime time one weekend. I couldn't believe that a low-budget film like that could get that sort of treatment. I'm a lucky guy; after playing Patrolman Jamie, I went on to make at least 99 other bad motion pictures, like *A Polish Vampire in Burbank* and *Misfit Patrol.* I always knew they'd make a movie about Ed Wood, but the real shocker is, the young Conrad Brooks is in Tim Burton's 1994 film, too!"

tion of King Vidor! Joanna Lee won a 1974 Emmy as a writer! I have a hunch that many contemporary young directors are oddly inspired by Ed Wood and his films. (Wood also wrote and/or directed *Jail Bait, Female, Revenge of the Dead, Hellborn, Glen or Glenda?,* and *Bride of the Monster.*) They can't all be the greatest director of all time and they know it. That inner voice that nags even the greatest artists into feeling that the projects into which they've poured all their energies, may turn out to be nothing after all, is far more prevalent than, say, crushing self-confidence. It's hard to resist an optimistic soul like Ed Wood who tried his very hardest and who did, in fact, entertain people, if not in the way he'd always dreamed of doing. ***AKA:*** Grave Robbers from Outer Space. **woof!**

1956 78m/B Bela Lugosi, Tor Johnson, Lyle Talbot, Vampira, Gregory Walcott, Tom George Duryea Keene, Dudley Manlove, Mona McKinnon, Duke Moore, Joanna Lee, Bunny Breckinridge, Criswell, Carl Anthony, Paul Marco, Norma McCarty, David DeMering, Bill Ash, Conrad Brooks, Edward D. Wood Jr.; ***D:*** Edward D. Wood Jr.; ***W:*** Edward D. Wood Jr.; ***C:*** William C. Thompson. **VHS, LV**

Platoon

I saw plenty of movies between 1978 and 1985, but never the Best Picture of the Year, by choice. As I listened to people drone on and on about their favorite sequences from these films, I really didn't think I was missing anything and still don't. My own favorites were movies I watched over and over again and still do, stuff like *Dinner for Adele, Escape from Alcatraz, Somewhere in Time, True Confessions, Fast Times at Ridgemont High, Heat and Dust, Another Country,* and *Dance with a Stranger.* Now that I've established my qualifications as a bit of a Philistine, I have to say that what burns in my memory about *Platoon* is that goofball moment from one of the *Naked Gun* pictures when a deliriously happy Leslie Nielsen and Priscilla Presley come bounding out of the movie theatre where *Platoon* is playing as Herman's Hermits sing "Something Tells Me I'm into Something Good." I was dragged to see *Platoon* by a guy who predicted that it would be the Best Picture of

"Somebody once wrote, 'Hell is the impossibility of reason.' That's what this place feels like—hell. I don't even know what I'm doing."

—Chris (Charlie Sheen) in *Platoon.*

the Year. All I knew was that I'd already seen the Best Picture of the Year and that was *Salvador*! But you can resign yourself to anything, even a 113-minute war movie with no female characters in it. Based on the true experiences of its filmmaker, *Platoon* is graphic and well acted, especially by Willem Dafoe. It launched a wave of other Vietnam war movies that I didn't see. Once you've been scared to bits by *On the Beach* and *Fail-Safe,* what's the point? I give it four bones for the cognoscenti, and two bones for fans of Leslie Nielsen and/or James Woods, for an average of 🦴🦴🦴

1986 (R) 113m/C Charlie Sheen, Willem Dafoe, Tom Berenger, Francesco Quinn, Forest Whitaker, John C. McGinley, Kevin Dillon, Richard Edson, Reggie Johnson, Keith David, Johnny Depp; ***D:*** Oliver Stone; ***W:*** Oliver Stone; ***C:*** Robert Richardson; ***M:*** Georges Delerue. Academy Awards '86: Best Director (Stone), Best Film Editing, Best Picture, Best Sound; British Academy Awards '87: Best Director (Stone); Directors Guild of America Awards '86: Best Director (Stone); Golden Globe Awards '87: Best Director (Stone), Best Film—Drama, Best Supporting Actor (Berenger); Independent Spirit Awards '87: Best Cinematography, Best Director (Stone), Best Film, Best Screenplay; Nominations: Academy Awards '86: Best Cinematography, Best Original Screenplay, Best Supporting Actor (Berenger, Dafoe). **VHS, LV, Closed Caption**

The Player

The Player did for Robert Altman's career at the age of 67 what *Prizzi's Honor* had done for John Huston's career seven years earlier at the age of 79—it turned him into a hot young director all over again. This savage satire of Hollywood, informed by a myriad of details that could only be assembled via thorough scrutiny over the long haul, is every bit as brilliant a depiction of Hollywood in the '90s as *Sunset Boulevard* was of Hollywood in the '50s. The less said about this masterwork the better, because a large share of the fun comes from not knowing who or what's going to pop up next. If it's a textbook scenario, Heaven help Hollywood in the 21st century. The first shot is a jaw dropper, ditto Tim Robbins' and Vincent D'Onofrio's performances as the symbol and sacrificial lamb of the industry. And, if you really want to blow your mind, watch *The Player* on a double bill with 1957's *The Delinquents,* Altman's very first movie! 🦴🦴🦴🦴

1992 (R) 123m/C Tim Robbins, Greta Scacchi, Fred Ward, Whoopi Goldberg, Peter Gallagher, Brion James, Cynthia Stevenson, Vincent D'Onofrio, Dean Stockwell, Richard E. Grant, Dina Merrill, Sydney Pollack, Lyle Lovett, Randall Batinkoff, Gina Gershon; ***Cameos:*** Michael Tolkin, Louise Fletcher, Dennis Franz, Malcolm McDowell, Ray Walston, Rene Auberjonois, David Alan Grier, Jayne Meadows, Michael Bowen, Steve James, Brian Tochi, Burt Reynolds, Cher, Nick Nolte, Jack Lemmon, Lily Tomlin, Marlee Matlin, Julia Roberts, Bruce Willis, Anjelica Huston, Elliott Gould, Sally Kellerman, Steve Allen, Richard Anderson, Harry Belafonte, Shari Belafonte, Karen Black, Gary Busey, Robert Carradine, James Coburn, Cathy Lee Crosby, John Cusack, Brad Davis, Peter Falk, Teri Garr, Leeza Gibbons, Scott Glenn, Jeff Goldblum, Joel Grey, Buck Henry, Kathy Ireland, Sally Kirkland, Andie MacDowell, Martin Mull, Mimi Rogers, Jill St. John, Susan Sarandon, Rod Steiger, Joan Tewkesbury, Robert Wagner; ***D:*** Robert Altman; ***W:*** Michael Tolkin; ***C:*** Jean Lepine; ***M:*** Thomas Newman. British Academy Awards '92: Best Adapted Screenplay; Cannes Film Festival '92: Best Actor (Robbins), Best Director (Altman); Golden Globe Awards '93: Best Actor—Musical/Comedy (Robbins), Best Film—Musical/Comedy; Independent Spirit Awards '93: Best Film; New York Film Critics Awards '92: Best Cinematography, Best Director (Altman), Best Film; Writers Guild of America '92: Best Adapted Screenplay; Nominations: Academy Awards '92: Best Adapted Screenplay, Best Director (Altman), Best Film Editing. **VHS, LV, Letterbox, Closed Caption, DVD**

Point of Order

For anyone interested in the McCarthy era, *Point of Order* is a must-see movie! The filmmakers had to pore over 188 hours of kinescopes in order to make their selections and still retain all the salient points of the hearings; editing down this gargantuan amount of footage to a reasonable running time must have been a formidable task indeed. Joseph McCarthy, who died of alcoholism within three years of the 1954 hearings, was a political careerist and not particularly interested in Communism until he discovered (after a speech) that he could use the issue to build a power base for himself. His pugnacious techniques were not universally admired in the Senate, but as one more cultured colleague put it, sometimes you needed someone like McCarthy to shake things up. While McCarthy was making political hash out of his opponents, his days were numbered, and it took sharp, folksy

Joseph Welch just a few exchanges to make political hash out of HIM in front of millions of television viewers. Welch was so good and so concise at the job that Otto Preminger hired him to play a judge in 1959's *Anatomy of a Murder.* See why your grandparents and great grandparents raced home everyday to watch a middle-aged bully with a gin blossom nose (and with young bully Roy Cohn always at his side) dominate the air waves. McCarthy set the standard for ruthless investigatorial tenacity, made his opponent's lives hell for a while, and finally lost his career and his reputation when he tried to bully the wrong man at the wrong time while the whole nation was watching. 🦴🦴🦴🦴

1964 97m/B *D:* Emile DeAntonio, Daniel Talbot.

Poison

A film in three segments, inspired by three Jean Genet stories: "Hero," a comedy set in Suburbia, shows how a seven-year-old boy's Mom, teacher, and friends try to explain why he killed Dad. In "Horror," another comedy, a mad scientist drinks this sex-drive fluid and looks and acts like a homicidal monster afterward. "Homo," not a comedy, shows the mutual seduction of a couple of French prisoners. There's masturbation, anal intercourse, sadomasochism, plus a sequence where a bunch of guys spit into a kid's mouth. Not for all tastes, including mine. 1995's *Safe* by director Todd Haynes is better. I give *Poison* three bones for the hipsters, but for me, just 🦴

1991 (R) 85m/C Edith Meeks, Larry Maxwell, Susan Norman, Scott Renderer, James Lyons, Millie White, Buck Smith, Anne Giotta, Al Quagliata, Michelle Sullivan, John R. Lombardi, Tony Pemberton, Andrew Harpending; ***D:*** Todd Haynes; ***W:*** Todd Haynes; ***C:*** Maryse Alberti; ***M:*** James Bennett. Sundance Film Festival '91: Grand Jury Prize. **VHS**

Popcorn

As horror movies go, *Popcorn* is about what you'd expect from a story that takes place at the fictitious Oceanview campus of the University of California but is filmed entirely on location in Jamaica. With the money the seven producers saved hiring non-union crews, they were able to cast Ray Walston in a take-a-leak-and-you'll-miss-him cameo PLUS Tony Roberts for a badly played feature role as a professor. In the film-as-pain division, *Popcorn* is more fun than a root canal, but not half as enjoyable as renting an old American International video (or even *Cannibal Women in the Avocado Jungle of Death!*). The least painful segments of the film are the re-creations of old horror movies from the '50s and '60s. There are no 3-D movies called *The Mosquito,* no *Attack of the Electrified Man* complete with wired theatre seats, no aromatic stinkers entitled *The Stench.* But someone associated with *Popcorn* obviously has fond memories of the gimmickry that helped to sell similar films in the past and there is genuine enthusiasm in these all-too-brief sequences. Unfortunately, the actual narrative of *Popcorn* has something to do with the legend of a terrible homicidal filmmaker, history repeating itself, characters trusting the wrong people, et cetera. Jill Schoelen, who turned in a fairly decent performance in *The Stepfather,* squeaks her way through *Popcorn* with negligible help from director Mark Herrier. Also wasted is Dee Wallace Stone, who presumably got to spend some time soaking up the Jamaican sun during the long stretches of the film when she is nowhere in sight. *Popcorn* might actually have been a much better movie if it had more of a visceral connection with the genre. After watching *Andy Hardy from Carvel meets Freddy from Elm Street in the Bahamas,* you may be groaning but not from fright. 🦴🦴

1989 (R) 93m/C Jill Schoelen, Tom Villard, Dee Wallace Stone, Derek Rydell, Elliott Hurst, Kelly Jo Minter, Malcolm Danare, Ray Walston, Tony Roberts, Karen Witter; ***D:*** Mark Herrier; ***W:*** Alan Ormsby; ***C:*** Ronnie Taylor. **VHS, LV, 8mm**

The Postman

The Postman wrapped on June 3, 1994. Its star, Massimo Troisi, long overdue for a heart transplant, was killed by a heart attack within 24 hours. When he died, very few American audiences knew who Troisi was, but within a year, the whole world had fallen in love with Mario, the self-effacing title character in Michael Radford's *The*

Betty Garrett Parks, author of *Betty Garrett and Other Songs,* on

THE HOLLYWOOD BLACKLIST

[The Hollywood Blacklist] was a dark period of history in our country. It was a bad time. I think all young people as they come up see injustices around them and the world and want to do something about it. The Communist Party seemed to be the only organization doing anything about it, and I and many other young people my age all joined and were all very active in things that I still feel strongly about—things like anti-discrimination, poor people and housing, and all the ills of the world I still would like to take care of if I could. So at one point in our history, they created the House Un-American Activities Committee, later egged on by people like Joseph McCarthy (who actually was a Senator so he had nothing to do with the House Un-American Activities Committee because that committee had been part of the House of Representatives since 1938). But he certainly stirred up a kettle of fish, and the Committee, I will always feel, was a very opportunistic thing.

"They picked on my husband [Larry Parks], who at that time was probably the biggest star at that moment after doing *The Jolson Story,* and everybody else were writers or directors, people who were not known to the public, but of course, Larry's name got them headlines. I'm bitter about it, but life goes on and we were able to make a wonderful life for ourselves. I'm not sure if people can find out [via the Freedom of Information Act] that Larry Parks just read a list of names given to him, because I notice it's never mentioned that that's what happened in this private session that he was drawn into. However, I do know that he desperately protested and tried not to name names and felt very humiliated by the whole experience. He was the first to stand up and say 'Yes, I was a member of the Communist Party and the reason I was is that I felt as I did,' and in a way it was nobody's business.

Postman/Il Postino. When exiled Chilean poet Pablo Neruda (1904–73, wonderfully portrayed by Phillipe Noiret) comes to stay on Isla Negra in 1952, Mario volunteers to be his postman. They become friends, and Mario asks Neruda if he will help him win Beatrice, the object of his desire (played by the absolutely gorgeous Maria Grazia Cucinotta). Troisi's beautifully sustained performance received a posthumous Academy Award nomination, and heartfelt tears from millions of moviegoers who were moved both by Mario and by the 41-year-old actor who sacrificed his life to play the role. Troisi can also be seen in 1983's *Hotel Colonial,* co-starring Robert Duvall, John Savage, and Rachel Ward. Just don't expect as perfectly realized a film as *The Postman/Il Postino.* **AKA:** Il Postino. 🦴🦴🦴🦴

1994 (PG) 115m/C *IT* Massimo Troisi, Philippe Noiret, Maria Grazia Cucinotta, Linda Moretti, Renato Scarpa, Anna Buonaiuto, Mariana Rigillo; ***D:*** Michael Radford; ***W:*** Massimo Troisi, Michael Radford, Furio Scarpelli, Anna Pavignano, Giacomo Scarpelli; ***C:*** Franco Di Giacomo; ***M:*** Luis Bacalov. Academy Awards '95: Best Original Dramatic Score; British Academy Awards '95: Best Director (Radford), Best Foreign Film, Best Score; Broadcast Film Critics Association Awards '95: Best Foreign Film; Nominations: Academy Awards '95: Best Actor

"I'm very familiar with the play *Are You Now or Have You Ever Been?* and at the time it made me very angry because I know all Larry and I wanted to do was to get on with our lives and have people forget about that. However, my two boys saw it. I've never really felt the courage to see it. I think it would be very hard for me to see an actor going through what Larry went through—the great humiliation and the deep agony that he went through. However, my boys told me, they said 'Ma, you would be proud of dad,' and the actor who did it originally out here and my boys became friendly and the actor was very sympathetic to Larry and admired him and evidently did a wonderful job.

"I have this incredible story: We were playing in Las Vegas, which is kind of interesting—there was no blacklist in Las Vegas. You could play there and make a nice amount of money, which we needed at the time. And all of a sudden, the maitre'd came back one night after a show and said, 'Senator Joe McCarthy would like to buy you a drink.' Larry looked at me and said, 'What do you want to do?' And I said, 'I don't want to have a drink with the old S.O.B.' But Larry had that kind of curiosity and he wanted to see what made this man tick. We went out and he was sitting in this big leather booth, just swacked to the gills. And he put his arm around Larry and said, 'Are they giving you a tough time, kid?' Larry looked at him and said, 'You're asking me?' And McCarthy said, 'Let me give you a motto to live by: Don't let the bastards grind you down.' Well, we got out of there as fast as we could. The next morning we came out, and my mother had brought my two boys up there out to Vegas—and there were my two little boys, like [ages] three and four, in the swimming pool and Senator McCarthy was teaching them to swim. So we got them out of the pool as fast as we could. They never could understand why they had to take a bath right after getting out of the swimming pool."

BETTY GARRETT appeared in several classic musicals of Hollywood's Gilded Age, including *Words and Music, Take Me Out to the Ball Game, On the Town, Neptune's Daughter,* and *My Sister Eileen.* The films of LARRY PARKS (1914–75) include *Harmon of Michigan, You Were Never Lovelier, Destroyer, The Jolson Story, Her Husband's Affairs, Down to Earth, Jolson Sings Again,* and *Love Is Better Than Ever.*

(Troisi), Best Adapted Screenplay, Best Director (Radford), Best Picture; British Academy Awards '95: Best Actor (Troisi), Best Adapted Screenplay; Cesar Awards '97: Best Foreign Film; Directors Guild of America Awards '95: Best Director (Radford); Screen Actors Guild Award '95: Best Actor (Troisi). **VHS**

Powwow Highway

Gary Farmer is Philbert Bono, a Cheyenne Indian en route to New Mexico, who gives a ride to his activist friend Buddy Red Bow (A. Martinez). Their eye-opening travels give them and us a grim picture of Native American reservations, where living conditions and employment opportunities are poor. Under such day-to-day hardships, it becomes nearly impossible to maintain a sense of pride in past accomplishments and customs. Based on David Seals' novel. The large, mostly Native American cast includes Graham Greene as a Vietnam veteran. ♪♪♪

1989 (R) 105m/C Gary Farmer, A. Martinez, Amanda Wyss, Rene Handren-Seals, Graham Greene; ***D:*** Joanelle Romero, Jonathan Wacks; ***W:*** Janet Heaney, Jean Stawarz; ***C:*** Toyomichi Kurita; ***M:***

"Please try to do as I say and not as I do. Remember, you are a child, Sandy, and far from your prime."

—Jean Brodie (Maggie Smith) in *The Prime of Miss Jean Brodie.*

Barry Goldberg. Sundance Film Festival '89: Filmmakers Trophy. **VHS**

Priest

For reasons which escape me, the 1994 movie *Priest* made the hierarchy of the Catholic Church far more nervous than 1993's *The Boys of St. Vincent,* a superior telefeature eventually broadcast in prime time on the Arts and Entertainment network. There were NO effective role models on that disturbing study of sexual abuse and its subsequent cover-up by Catholic brothers in a Canadian orphanage for young boys. No clergy member in *Priest* remotely approaches the evil villainy of St. Vincent's Brother Lavin, chillingly played by Henry Czerny. Antonia Bird's 1994 film reveals the ongoing moral dilemma faced by many Catholic priests today and suggests that the Church remains stubbornly out of touch with the tormented souls it professes to care for. Father Greg (Linus Roache) is a young Catholic priest determined to play by the book. "Sin is sin," he snaps at Father Matthew (Tom Wilkinson) when he discovers that the latter is sleeping with Maria the housekeeper (Cathy Tyson). But both Father Matthew and Maria are unrepentant about their living situation and tell Father Greg to mind his own business. For Father Greg, that includes a secret life in gay bars where he picks up Graham (Robert Carlyle). It also includes his self-doubts about the secrecy of the confessional when Lisa, a 14-year-old parishioner tells him about her incestuous relationship with her father. (Here's a tip for kids watching the film who are lucky enough to find a sympathetic priest who'll listen to their complaints about parental sex and/or violence; if you tell them outside of the confessional, great priests—and they do exist—can do something to help.) Father Greg feels powerless about his lover, especially when Graham shows up in Church on Sunday for Communion, and about Lisa, especially when her sociopathic father threatens him. Filmmakers before Bird (including Alfred Hitchcock with *I Confess* and Mike Hodges with *A Prayer for the Dying*) have had difficulty explaining the secrecy of the confessional to general audiences. But Father Greg, for all of Roache's fine acting, would be a dim bulb about his life choices even if he weren't a priest. For example, if you want to have a private sex life AND be a dogmatic theologian, don't have sex on a public beach. It all gets very melodramatic after that, and *Priest,* unlike *The Boys of St. Vincent,* never quite escapes its television origins. But it asks some searching questions, many at least as agonizing as those raised by Peter, the Church's first Pope, on a grim Good Friday almost two thousand years ago. (Cast Note: Tom Wilkinson, who gets all the best, most compassionate, and sanest lines as Father Matthew in *Priest,* later played the irate Marquess of Queensbury opposite Stephen Fry as Oscar and Jude Law as Lord Alfred "Bosie" Douglas in the 1997 film *Wilde.*)

1994 (R) 98m/C *GB* Linus Roache, Tom Wilkinson, Cathy Tyson, Robert Carlyle, James Ellis, John Bennett, Rio Fanning, Jimmy Coleman, Lesley Sharp, Robert Pugh, Christine Tremarco; ***D:*** Antonia Bird; ***W:*** Jimmy McGovern; ***C:*** Fred Tammes; ***M:*** Andy Roberts. Nominations: Australian Film Institute '95: Best Foreign Film. **VHS**

The Prime of Miss Jean Brodie

The Prime of Miss Jean Brodie was my favorite movie of 1969. For a kid raised on the often baffling rules of Holy Rosary Convent School in Woodland, California, Jean Brodie seemed to me to be the coolest teacher in the universe. Charismatic, idiosyncratic, fearless, and funny, Jean Brodie (Maggie Smith, then 34) was worshipped by her students, adored by her very married lover Teddy Lloyd (Robert Stephens, then 37 and Smith's real-life husband), and cordially hated by Headmistress Miss Mackay (Celia Johnson, then 60). I can't count how many times I watched the movie and then tried to fill in the blanks of the original novel by Muriel Spark. Spark freely admitted that she only found her true voice as a writer after she converted to Catholicism. Now what did THAT mean? Spark's satire of the sexually obsessed Catholic art teacher played by Stephens could not have been more biting. Teddy Lloyd was a breeder whose "unfortunate affiliation with the Church of Rome" (Jean Brodie's words) led him to sire masses of kids with Mrs. Lloyd while not-so-secretly lusting after the radiant Jean Brodie. And when she wearied of the dance, she actually selected a successor from among her young students to replace her in his bed. Lloyd and one of Brodie's OTHER students (the dependable and much-overlooked Sandy, played by Pamela Franklin, then 18) had other ideas, however, a reality that would present *The Prime of Miss Jean Brodie* with its gravest threat. The critics of 1969 raved about the powerful acting of Maggie Smith (who deservedly won her first Oscar that year). They sighed wistfully about the dozens of years that separated Celia Johnson's superb work here from her affecting performance as Laura in *Brief Encounter.* And Pamela Franklin, who had first captivated international audiences as Flora in 1961's *The Innocents,* seemed on the verge of major stardom. (Franklin nearly turned down the role because she didn't want to play another schoolgirl, but was persuaded otherwise and tore into the role of Sandy, who evolves from worshipful naivete into resentful treachery.) Stephens, too, added genuine poignance to the deceptively lightweight predicament of the mediocre painter with delusions of superiority. And Gordon Jackson, then 48, who would later achieve his greatest fame on *Upstairs, Downstairs* as Hudson, the quintessential butler, is just right as music teacher Gordon Lowther, yearning to marry Jean Brodie and settling for a semi-discreet affair. Jay Presson Allen's powerful screenplay and Ronald Neame's meticulous direction made the political and sexual concerns of 1930's Edinburgh seem immediate and timeless. (Sadly for her admirers, Franklin made just five more films, and only 1973's *The Legend of Hell House* is worth staying up late to see. Jane Carr as Mary MacGregor, the least likely to succeed among Jean Brodie's set, went on to star opposite Judd Hirsch in NBC's *Dear John* from 1988 to 1992.)

1969 (PG) 116m/C *GB* Maggie Smith, Pamela Franklin, Robert Stephens, Celia Johnson, Gordon Jackson, Jane Carr; ***D:*** Ronald Neame; ***W:*** Jay Presson Allen; ***C:*** Ted Moore. Academy Awards '69: Best Actress (Smith); British Academy Awards '69: Best Actress (Smith), Best Supporting Actress (Johnson); Golden Globe Awards '70: Best Song ("Jean"); National Board of Review Awards '69: Best Supporting Actress (Franklin); Nominations: Academy Awards '69: Best Song ("Jean"); Cannes Film Festival '69: Best Film. **VHS, Closed Caption**

Princess and the Goblin

My niece Emma, then two years old, had severe reservations about 1994's *Thumbelina,* so I wasn't quite sure how she would react to *The Princess and the Goblin.* Who knows what will or won't frighten very small children? This time around, Emma wasn't even mildly alarmed, not by dark caverns or subterranean creatures or a ghost in the castle tower. The three-year-old boy in the row behind us, though, screamed bloody murder at a huge close-up of one of the goblins. *The Princess and the Goblin* is based on George MacDonald's fairy tale from the year 1872. It revolves around the Princess Irene and her efforts to save the kingdom from an evil scheme hatched by the Froglip, the Goblins' leader. Irene is helped by the spirit of her magical grandmother, by her faithful cat Turnip, and by her young friend Curdle. Most of the grown-ups are fairly ineffectual; they're forever riding off somewhere or falling asleep or simply not paying attention. So it's the kids to the rescue for most of the narrative's 82 minutes. The artwork is nicely done and the voice artists (including Claire Bloom as Irene's grandmother and Joss Ackland as the King) are well chosen. Yet there seems to be a remote quality at the core of this movie as if the filmmakers felt they were skating on thin ice and were trying maybe a bit too hard to keep MacDonald's delicate allegory in balance: scary but not too horrifying, instructive but not too preachy, lighthearted but don't forget that Irene has to confront her own fears in order to allay those of everyone else. Well, *The Princess and the Goblin* is a brave effort and Turnip

The Hound Salutes: IDA LUPINO (1914–95)

Hollywood obituaries are generally written at the time of a movie star's greatest fame, and a series of updated facts, unilluminated by analysis, are then grafted onto the original article. In the case of Ida Lupino, such cobbling led to a mess of a report. Lupino's contributions both as an actress and as an independent filmmaker were enormous. She entered the industry in her native Britain where her father and uncle were stars, and after making several films there in the early '30s, she moved to Southern California and dutifully paid her dues as a bleached blonde ingenue. Two of her 1939 efforts changed all that.

In William Wellman's *The Light That Failed,* she played the vindictive brunette model of an artist with failing eyesight. Working opposite the legendary Ronald Colman, who did not want her in the role, Lupino didn't pull a single punch or try to soften her character in any way. Her notices were spectacular, and after making a striking impression opposite Basil Rathbone and Nigel Bruce in *The Adventures of Sherlock Holmes,* she was signed to a long-term contract at Warner Bros. where Bette Davis was queen of the lot. Lupino's first assignment, in fact, was *They Drive by Night,* Raoul Walsh's 1940 remake of the 1935 Davis classic, *Bordertown.* In many ways the remake, and Lupino, were superior to the original version, but Davis-type roles were harder to come by in the '40s than they had been during the Great Depression. For one

the cat is a charming distraction, at least. If it does well, MacDonald also wrote *Irene and Curdle* in 1882, supplying ample source material for a sequel. ***AKA:*** A Hercegno es a Kobold. 🦴🦴

1992 (PG) 82m/C *D:* Jozsef Gemes; ***V:*** Glenda Jackson, Joss Ackland, Claire Bloom, William Hootkins, Rik Mayall, Peggy Mount, Victor Spinetti. **VHS**

Private Hell 36

Private Hell 36 has one of my all-time favorite lines of dialogue, deftly delivered in a bar by Ida Lupino (who also wrote the screenplay). I won't spoil its impact by telegraphing it here, but in a few short words, it tells you everything you need to know about what sort of gal nightclub singer Lilli Marlowe is, right down to her toenails. The rest of the noir script is also terrific, interpreting the deep malaise of 1954 Los Angeles as only a sharp, perceptive insider can observe it. Detectives Cal Bruner (the underrated Steve Cochran, 1917–65) and Jack Farnham (Howard Duff, 1913–90) hate risking their lives on cop's salaries, but Jack has the outlets of a wife (Dorothy Malone as Francey) and baby (Lupino's and Duff's real-life daughter Bridget, then two), while Cal can only seal up his feelings of anger and resentment. When they investigate a robbery that ended in homicide, the partners meet Lilli, who received some of the stolen money as a tip. Cal and Lilli strike sparks, but she thinks she wants a guy with dough and he doesn't have any. By the time Lilli realizes that the guy might be more important than the dough, Cal's in a fatalistic tailspin. Cochran is great at portraying twisted characters who try like hell to convince themselves they can do no wrong. The materialistic yearnings shared by Jack and Francey are nowhere near as intriguing as the feverish passions that ignite Cal and Lilli, but this IS 1954 and convention-

thing, strong onscreen women were less of a threat when their offscreen counterparts had a negligible chance of becoming anything like them. For another, both Bette Davis and Olivia De Havilland had to sue Warner Bros. for better parts.

Ida Lupino did her supernatural best with the retread jobs she was given to do (check her out in *High Sierra* or *The Hard Way* or ANY movie she had to make with Joan Leslie, for example), but her meatiest characters were usually offered to her on loan-out. In *Ladies in Retirement,* she stripped her face of makeup and played a cold-blooded killer devoted to her two daft sisters. In *Roadhouse* and *Lust for Gold,* she played intriguing variations of women gone wrong because of the need for men or money. But even as she was delivering some of her finest performances, Lupino had her eye on a director's hat and although she wore it most often on television, she also made seven theatrical features as a director, producer, writer, and sometimes all three. There was no American Film Institute to support her dream, which made its fulfillment with low-budget gems like *Not Wanted* and *The Hitchhiker* all the more remarkable. Lupino herself credited her own strong stomach. There had never been anyone quite like her in Hollywood before she arrived, and the fact that she was able to achieve so much helped to pave the way for women who wanted to be taken seriously in a town where most of the guys only wanted to look at them.

IDA LUPINO's work on video includes *The Ghost Camera, One Rainy Afternoon, Sea Devils, The Sea Wolf, Thank Your Lucky Stars, Forever and a Day, Hollywood Canteen, The Man I Love, Escape Me Never, On Dangerous Ground, Beware My Lovely, The Bigamist* (also directed), *The Big Knife, While the City Sleeps, Junior Bonner, Devil's Rain, Food of the Gods,* and *My Boys Are Good Boys.*

al morality is GONNA prevail. Lupino's tight script and Donald Siegel's brisk direction manage to keep this clash of ethics on the boil and we get to hear Lupino as Lilli sing, too. A crisp, much-overlooked indie with Ida Lupino at the top of her game.

1954 81m/B Ida Lupino, Howard Duff, Steve Cochran, Dean Jagger, Dorothy Malone, Bridget Duff, Jerry Hausner, Dabbs Greer, Chris O'Brien, Kenneth Patterson, George Dockstader, Jimmy Hawkins, King Donovan; ***D:*** Donald Siegel; ***W:*** Ida Lupino; ***C:*** Burnett Guffey; ***M:*** Leith Stevens. **VHS, LV**

The Private Life of Henry VIII

International audiences (and especially Hollywood industry types) started paying attention to British films after they saw *The Private Life of Henry VIII.* Charles Laughton and Elsa Lanchester were welcomed to California with outstretched arms, and so were Binnie Barnes, Merle Oberon, and Wendy Barrie. Laughton created such an indelible impression as Henry VIII that every actor who portrays the much-married monarch has had to cope with the everlasting influence of his Oscar-winning interpretation. The film focuses on the subject of most concern to 1933 audiences: not politics, not religion, but WIVES, the last five of them, anyway. The most prominent one here is Binnie Barnes as Catherine Howard. Elsa Lanchester is the funniest as Anne of Cleves, since she is trying her darndest to look ghastly, because Henry isn't her type and she doesn't want to lose her head. We only get a quick look at lovely Merle Oberon as Anne Boleyn before she DOES lose her head, but Wendy Barrie is a zestier Jane Seymour than most of the pale young things who have to die giving birth to King Edward VI. Robert Donat is so attractive and kind as Thomas Culpepper and SO necessary since Laughton's Henry is such

Susan Gilvray (Evelyn Keyes) and Webb Garwood (Van Heflin) in *The Prowler.* United Artists; courtesy of the Kobal Collection

an oaf. The sixth wife? That would be Everley Gregg as Catherine Parr, a good woman, and consequently of no interest to this lively narrative! 🦴🦴🦴🦴

1933 97m/B *GB* Charles Laughton, Binnie Barnes, Elsa Lanchester, Robert Donat, Merle Oberon, Miles Mander, Wendy Barrie, John Loder, Lady Tree, Franklin Dyall, Claud Allister, William Austin, Gibb McLaughlin, Sam Livesey, Lawrence Hanray, Everley Gregg, Judy Kelly, John Turnbull, Frederick Culley, Hay Petrie, Wally Patch; ***D:*** Alexander Korda; ***W:*** Arthur Wimperis, Lajos Biro; ***C:*** Georges Perinal. Academy Awards '33: Best Actor (Laughton); Nominations: Academy Awards '33: Best Picture. **VHS, LV**

The Private Life of Sherlock Holmes

Peter O'Toole and Peter Sellers as Sherlock Holmes and Doctor Watson? It sounded great to director Billy Wilder in the early '60s, too. Unfortunately, the working relationship between the three never made it to the starting gate. Wilder apparently felt that O'Toole's demands were in the prima donna league and he made the mistake of calling Sellers an "unprofessional rat fink." Harsh words for a man who'd already had one heart attack during a Wilder movie. (Sellers was replaced by Ray Walston on 1964's *Kiss Me Stupid.*) So *The Private Life of Sherlock Holmes* was released in 1970 starring stage actors Robert Stephens and Colin Blakely in the leads (who come very close to playing Holmes and Watson as a well-adjusted gay couple, especially Holmes, who looks like he's wearing mascara, rouge, and lipstick). Although both were extremely good actors, the resulting film was still far from the masterpiece Wilder hoped it would become. The main problem, according to Wilder, is that United Artists insisted that nearly an hour be trimmed from its three-hour running time. Edited to 125 minutes, all the flashbacks to Holmes' earlier life (actually Wilder's own past) are eliminated, including crucial sequences that contain Wilder's main reasons for making the picture. Even though we learn more about

Wilder's sexual humor than we do about the great detective, *The Private Life of Sherlock Holmes* is a lavish contribution to the canon with an intriguing script and genuine affection for the late Victorian era (circa 1887). ☙☙☙☙

1970 (PG-13) 125m/C *GB* Robert Stephens, Colin Blakely, Genevieve Page, Irene Handl, Stanley Holloway, Christopher Lee, Clive Revill, Catherine Lacey, Tamara Toumanova, Mollie Maureen, Michael Balfour; ***D:*** Billy Wilder; ***W:*** Billy Wilder, I.A.L. Diamond; ***C:*** Christopher Challis; ***M:*** Miklos Rozsa. **VHS, LV**

Professor Mamlock

Professor Mamlock would be a remarkable film no matter when it was made. The fact that it was a Soviet attack on National Socialism so threatened American audiences that it was originally banned in several states. Nazi characters are shown as ordinary human beings, still capable of shifting allegiance, as one sympathetic female character does. The film's thrust is softened by the position that Jews must rely on help from outsiders rather than themselves, but it does show why Professor Mamlock's apoliticism helped to make him an easy target. *Professor Mamlock* is not available on video, although it should be! Not to be confused with the 1961 East German re-make with the same title, which was written and directed by Konrad Wolfe. ☙☙☙

1938 100m/B *RU* S. Mezhinski, Y. Kochurov, M. Timofeyev, E. Nikitina, Otto Zhakov, V. Chesnokov, B. Svetlov, N. Shaternikova; ***D:*** Adolph Minkin, Herbert Rappaport; ***W:*** Adolph Minkin, Herbert Rappaport; ***C:*** G. Filatov.

The Profiteer

For reasons that escape me, *The Profiteer* played just twice at the Cannes Film Festival before it was banned in Italy. The film is successful on many levels: as comedy, as satire, as a portrait of the opportunist as a young man. The scenes from a funeral and a procession at Lourdes are both apt and hilarious. Giancarlo Marinangeli makes a devilish debut as a mean little man who befriends the title character. Sergio Nasca's remarkably impressive first film builds to a surprising, highly dramatic finish. Of the cast, only Al Cliver, Janet Agren, and Leopoldo Trieste are familiar to video buffs. Cliver and Agren haven't made any other unbad movies as far as I know, but character actor Trieste has worked with Fellini, Germi, Campanile, Petri, Bellochio, Rossi, Coppola, and Tornatore. ***AKA:*** Il Saprofita. ☙☙☙☙

1974 97m/C *IT* Al Cliver, Janet Agren, Leopoldo Trieste; ***D:*** Sergio Nasca; ***W:*** Sergio Nasca; ***C:*** Giuseppe Aquari.

Project A: Part 2

Jackie Chan came to America in 1987 as the honored guest of the San Francisco International Film Festival. At that time, despite the failure of 1985's *The Protector,* co-starring Danny Aiello, he was eager to be as big a star in the U.S. as he was in Hong Kong. It was not until 1996's *Rumble in the Bronx* that he finally broke into the American consciousness with a splash, and by then he was the biggest movie star in the world everywhere BUT in the U.S. In *Project A: Part 2,* stunts look like a snap, but don't try them at home! As he meticulously explained to the international press corp assembled at the festival, even Chan is vulnerable to an aching back, sore ankles, and a skull fracture. This action-packed spectacle is fast and funny, featuring an irresistible performance by Chan as Dragon Ma, an honest Hong Kong cop, circa 1900. There IS a *Project A: Part 1,* starring Samo Hung, but *Project A: Part 2* is a self-contained story, and extremely entertaining for international audiences on its own unique terms. ☙☙☙

1987 101m/C *CH* Jackie Chan, Maggie Cheung, Carina Lau, David Lam; ***D:*** Jackie Chan; ***W:*** Edward Tang, Jackie Chan. **VHS**

The Prowler

Sometimes, Van Heflin could melt into the wallpaper and sometimes he could creep up on you and demand your attention as no one else could. The overlooked Evelyn Keyes was capable of superb performances, too, and both were at their best

"That's thirty minutes away. I'll be there in ten."

—Winston Wolf (Harvey Keitel) in *Pulp Fiction.*

in *The Prowler,* under Joseph Losey's expert direction. In her autobiography, Keyes says that then-blacklisted Dalton Trumbo had a hand in the script. Heflin is a cop investigating a prowler at Keyes' home. It's as good a way to meet as any and it isn't long before he's pretending to be after a prowler so he can shoot Keyes' husband, an impotent disc jockey, and run away with the widow. That's his plan, anyway. The unwitting femme fatale isn't in on the plan, nor is she aware of the next unexpected development. *The Prowler* is a caustic portrait of the horrors of the early '50s, with the smallest of canvases, in very sharp relief. ♪♪♪♪

1951 92m/B Van Heflin, Evelyn Keyes, Katherine Warren, John Maxwell, Emerson Treacy, Madge Blake, Wheaton Chambers, Sherry Hall, Robert Osterloh, Matt Dorff; ***D:*** Joseph Losey; ***W:*** Hugo Butler, Dalton Trumbo; ***C:*** Arthur C. Miller; ***M:*** Lyn Murray. **VHS**

Public Access

Bryan Singer's *The Usual Suspects* won two Academy Awards (Best Screenplay and Best Supporting Actor) in 1995. *Public Access* is not in the same league, but it's an interesting first effort by a filmmaker who clearly learned a great deal from the experience. Whiley Pritcher (Ron Marquette) arrives in the small town of Brewster, and launches a public access call-in show with the theme: "What's wrong with Brewster?" A question more to the point might be: "What's wrong with Whiley Pritcher?" but we never hear the answer to that one (maybe he's an underachieving relative of Keyser Soze!). Pritcher becomes as much of a celebrity as one can be in a backwater community like Brewster, and then...oh, watch it for yourself! Christopher McQuarrie collaborated with Michael Feit Dougan and Singer on the script (when he worked alone on *Suspects,* he won an Oscar). A promising start to what I hope will be long and increasingly fascinating careers for both Singer and McQuarrie. ♪♪♪

1993 (R) 90m/C Ron Marquette, Dina Brooks, Burt Williams, Charles Kavanaugh, Larry Maxwell, Brandon Boyce; ***D:*** Bryan Singer; ***W:*** Bryan Singer, Christopher McQuarrie, Michael Feit Dougan; ***C:*** Bruce Douglas Johnson; ***M:*** John Ottman. Sundance Film Festival '93: Grand Jury Prize. **VHS**

Pulp Fiction

Pulp Fiction is a dizzying ride through the violent Los Angeles that exists in the mind of its creator, Quentin Tarantino. It is a world of lethal small-time and not particularly brilliant thugs who exhaustively discuss the differences between American and French-style McDonald's as they kill time before a hit. It is a world where the time-worn cliche of Mr. Big's sexy wife being taken for a date by his henchman is turned inside out with terrifying and hilarious results. It is a world where even the awesome Mr. Big finds himself in a situation where no one knows that he is Mr. Big and none of his faithfully honored rules apply. Although the whole point of the film is to pay twisted tribute to the conventions of film noir, the 154-minute script might have become a silly and long-winded mess if anyone but Tarantino had been at the helm. Nowhere is this more clear than in one of the funniest segments in which Mr. Big's problem-solver (crisply played by Harvey Keitel) must step in to resolve a situation caused by a clueless hit man (John Travolta). As genuine pulp fiction, this essentially banal yarn might barely have passed muster on the printed page. But onscreen, under Tarantino's sure guiding hand (the director also plays a central role in this segment), it's a priceless demonstration of gangland hygiene; the segment's humor and wit are driven by the sheer banality of the situation. Moreover, it leads directly into the brilliant wrap-up of the circular narrative. The film opens and closes in a ubiquitous L.A. diner with Pumpkin and Honey Bunny (Tim Roth and Amanda Plummer), but we don't know what the pair have to do with the rest of the story until film's end. The powerhouse ensemble cast includes folks who are normally above-the-title stars in any other movie: Bruce Willis and Maria de Medeiros, Eric Stoltz and Rosanna Arquette, Samuel L. Jackson, Christopher Walken, and Frank Whaley. John Travolta may not be the obvious choice as Vincent Vega, the world's dumbest hit man, but he acquits himself admirably in the role he describes as his sixth comeback. He even gets a chance to be a heroin-ridden twist contestant in a surrealistic nightclub. His dancing partner is Uma Thurman as Mia, AKA Mrs. Marsellus Wallace (this film's Mr. Big). Thurman is provocative and appealing as the seductive former starlet who imbibes $5 milkshakes and lines of coke with equal conviction. And check out the incredible retro-style club with James Dean, Buddy Holly, Marilyn Monroe, and Mamie Van Doren as the waiters and waitresses and real 1950s convertibles as the booths! *Pulp Fiction* deservedly won the best picture prize at 1994's Cannes Film Festival. The film shows what those who grumbled about *True Romance,* scripted but not directed by Tarantino, subliminally realized: that his films need his vision as well as his ear. Luckily for audiences, *Pulp Fiction* is vintage Tarantino from breathless start to breathtaking finish. ♪♪♪♪

1994 (R) 154m/C John Travolta, Samuel L. Jackson, Uma Thurman, Harvey Keitel, Tim Roth, Amanda Plummer, Maria De Medeiros, Ving Rhames, Eric Stoltz, Rosanna Arquette, Christopher Walken, Bruce Willis, Frank Whaley, Steve Buscemi, Quentin Tarantino; ***D:*** Quentin Tarantino; ***W:*** Roger Roberts Avary, Quentin Tarantino; ***C:*** Andrzej Sekula. Academy Awards '94: Best Original Screenplay; British Academy Awards '94: Best Original Screenplay, Best Supporting Actor (Jackson); Cannes Film Festival '94: Best Film; Golden Globe Awards '95: Best Screenplay; Independent Spirit Awards '95: Best Actor (Jackson), Best Director (Tarantino), Best Film, Best Screenplay; Los Angeles Film Critics Association Awards '94: Best Actor (Travolta), Best Director (Tarantino), Best Film, Best Screenplay; MTV Movie Awards '95: Best Film, Best Dance Sequence (John Travolta/Uma Thurman); National Board of Review Awards '94: Best Director (Tarantino), Best Film; New York Film Critics Awards '94: Best Director (Tarantino), Best Screenplay; National Society of Film Critics Awards '94: Best Director (Tarantino), Best Film, Best Screenplay; Nominations: Academy Awards '94: Best Actor (Travolta), Best Director (Tarantino), Best Film Editing, Best Original Screenplay, Best Picture, Best Supporting Actor (Jackson), Best Supporting Actress (Thurman); Australian Film Institute '95: Best Foreign Film; Directors Guild of America Awards '94: Best Director (Tarantino); Golden Globe Awards '95: Best Actor—Drama (Travolta), Best Director (Tarantino), Best Film—Drama, Best Supporting Actor (Jackson), Best Supporting Actress (Thurman); Independent Spirit Awards '95: Best Supporting Actor (Stoltz); MTV Movie Awards '95: Best Male Performance (Travolta), Best Female Performance (Thurman), Best On-Screen Duo (John Travolta/Samuel L. Jackson), Best Song ("Girl, You'll Be A Woman Soon"); Screen Actors Guild Award '94: Best Actor (Travolta). **VHS, LV, Closed Caption, DVD**

Pygmalion

You need an iron bottom to sit through all 170 minutes of *My Fair Lady,* notwithstanding Rex Harrison, Stanley Holloway, Wilfrid Hyde-White, Theodore Bikel, Mona Washbourne, Jeremy Brett, Robert Coote, Gladys Cooper, Lerner and Loewe's score, Cecil Beaton's costumes, et cetera, et cetera, et cetera. But the original *Pygmalion* starring Leslie Howard, Wendy Hiller, Wilfrid Lawson, and Marie Lohr clocks in at a brisk 96 minutes WITH Shaw's blessing (he won an Oscar for collaborating on the screenplay). With his consent, a prologue and 14 additional sequences were included to make the story more like a movie and less like a play. Hiller was Shaw's personal choice as Eliza Doolittle. He would have preferred, however, to see Charles Laughton as Professor Henry Higgins, insisting that *Pygmalion* was NOT a love story and that Leslie Howard was hopelessly wrong (!) for the part. However, Shaw agreed to let the film close with a hint that Eliza will remain with Higgins, since he did have a shrewd understanding of Howard's enormous popularity at the boxoffice. The original *Pygmalion* is crisp and cool, the perfect blueprint for the hit Broadway musical of 1956 (*My Fair Lady* was based on this movie, not Shaw's 1913 play). Leslie Howard and Anthony Asquith co-directed with skill and assurance, in spite of the fact that producer Gabriel Pascal was breathing down their necks throughout filming. Moreover, leading lady Hiller had a real-life toothache during the ballroom sequence (especially written for the movie, at Asquith's insistence), which could not have been easy on a 26-year-old newcomer in a Schiaparelli gown with only one prior screen credit. None of the production woes show up in the shimmering finished product; *Pygmalion* was Britain's top moneymaker of the year, Howard went on to make an even bigger moneymaker in Hollywood *(Gone with the Wind)* and Hiller next starred in another Shaw adaptation, *Major Barbara.* Here's a trivia question for die-hard buffs. Q: Who was the cinematographer for both *Pygmalion* and *My Fair Lady?* A: Harry

The Hound Salutes:

DAVID CARRADINE

Q (The Winged Serpent)

"Actually, it's true that I've made more films than any person alive. Ned Beatty's right behind me, but I'm the winner. I've made 20 films in a one- to two-year stretch. *Psychotronic Magazine* missed one title and left it out of my credits. There's only about 79 theatrical movies, though. My father, John Carradine [1906–88], was certainly a big influence on every aspect of my life. I was born and bred to be an actor. I went to high school in Berkeley and college at San Francisco State. I started acting onstage when I was 20, playing Tybalt in Shakespeare's *Romeo and Juliet.* My favorite movie, aside from *Americana,* would be *Bound for Glory.* It was the greatest experience I ever had making a movie. We worked 19 weeks on it and no one wanted it to end. We just wanted to keep on doing it forever and it was an awful lot of fun for me. All I did was play the guitar, jump on and off trains, and pretend I was drunk. It was a great time. I don't know how to phone in a part. Everything I do is personal for me, unless I'm playing a hatchet murderer. Then I tell a joke everytime they turn off the camera. Nowadays I stretch every day, and I have some guys I get together with and we practice kung fu on Sundays. I'm still making movies, hand over fist. If you can find work, don't leave San Francisco. That's why I left, otherwise I'd still be there."

DAVID CARRADINE's indies on video include *Macho Callahan, Old Boyfriends, The Long Riders, Americana, Safari 3000, Q,* and *Sonny Boy.*

Stradling, Oscar winner for *The Picture of Dorian Gray* and *My Fair Lady.* ☙☙☙☙

1938 96m/B *GB* Leslie Howard, Wendy Hiller, Wilfred Lawson, Marie Lohr, Scott Sunderland, David Tree, Everley Gregg, Leueen McGrath, Jean Cadell, Eileen Beldon, Frank Atkinson, O.B. Clarence, Esme Percy, Violet Vanbrugh, Iris Hoey, Viola Tree, Irene Browne, Kate Cutler, Cathleen Nesbitt, Cecil Trouncer, Stephen Murray, Wally Patch, H.F. Maltby; ***D:*** Anthony Asquith, Leslie Howard; ***W:*** W.P. Lipscomb, Anatole de Grunwald, Cecil Lewis, Ian Dalyrymple, George Bernard Shaw; ***C:*** Harry Stradling. Academy Awards '38: Best Adapted Screenplay; Venice Film Festival '38: Best Actor (Howard); Nominations: Academy Awards '38: Best Actor (Howard), Best Actress (Hiller), Best Picture. **VHS, LV**

Q (The Winged Serpent)

Q is a great movie to scream through in a huge revival theatre on a Saturday afternoon, but it would still be a hoot to see at home on video with your friends. Michael Moriarty isn't the first actor to come to mind as Jimmy Quinn, former addict, current petty criminal, and musician wannabe, but he's terrific in the role. Larry Cohen's direction and screenplay are pretty terrific, too, and the rest of the cast is top-notch: David Carradine (yes, David Carradine) and Richard Roundtree as detectives and Candy Clark as Jimmy's girlfriend. The plot revolves around the aforementioned winged serpent Q (for Quetzacoatl) who's nesting in New York's Chrysler Building. Except for priests who are skinning people as sacrifices (and construction workers, just before Q lops off their heads), only Jimmy knows where Q resides. Can he and detectives Carradine and Roundtree save Manhattan in time?

Cohen's sharp storytelling skills reveal all. Catch it if you can! ***AKA:*** Q: The Winged Serpent. 🦴🦴🦴

1982 (R) 92m/C Michael Moriarty, Candy Clark, David Carradine, Richard Roundtree, Malachy McCourt; ***D:*** Larry Cohen; ***W:*** Larry Cohen; ***C:*** Fred Murphy; ***M:*** Robert O. Ragland. **VHS, DVD**

Queen Kelly

Queen Kelly is one of the great might-have-beens in movie history. Directed by the great Erich von Stroheim and starring the legendary Gloria Swanson, fresh from her Oscar-nominated triumph as *Sadie Thompson, Queen Kelly* promised to be yet another mouth-watering excursion into the world of the rich and decadent. It was. But Swanson, who was then in the midst of an affair with its married producer, Joseph Kennedy, was convinced that von Stroheim's sexy epic would be censored by Will Hays. About a third of the film had been made when Swanson walked off the set without warning to tattle on von Stroheim to Kennedy and *Queen Kelly* ended production that very day. She made an effort to release a truncated version of the film in the early '30s and even included a segment in 1950s *Sunset Boulevard,* in which von Stroheim made an ironic appearance as her butler. What remains of *Queen Kelly* is tantalizing: it draws on all our fantasies of one night of romance between a star-struck schoolgirl and the handsome prince. Von Stroheim is entirely sympathetic to the plight of young Patricia Kelly and makes her situation even more poignant by supplying her with an unforgettable nemesis. Seena Owen is mesmerizing as the possessive Queen who wants to have the wild prince Wolfram all to herself, whether or not he loves her. In one breathtaking sequence, after the Queen has caught the two of them in bed together, she banishes her rival from the palace, whipping her unmercifully as amused male courtiers laugh at the spectacle. This is the sort of sequence that might be unplayable, or at the very least diminished, in a sound film, but von Stroheim stages the primal conflict between the two women in such a lavish operatic style that it's almost impossible not to get caught up in the underlying emotions. With such a remarkable start, what's missing from the film may be even sadder than all those missing reels of *Greed.* At least we can read *McTeague,* the Frank Norris novel on which *Greed* was based. But *Queen Kelly* is a pure von Stroheim screen original from start to finish and his interpretation of the African brothel where the disgraced Kelly is forced to live in exile is filled with a sexual candor rarely seen on the screen before or since. Granted, von Stroheim's vision of the brothel is over the top, but the surviving footage still offers fascinating and unique insights into the sexual politics that informed his every film. Even in its incomplete form, *Queen Kelly* is still something to see; catch it if you can! 🦴🦴🦴½

1929 113m/B Gloria Swanson, Walter Byron, Seena Owen, Tully Marshall, Madame Sul Te Wan; ***D:*** Erich von Stroheim; ***W:*** Erich von Stroheim; ***C:*** Paul Ivano, Gordon Pollock. **VHS, LV, 8mm**

Queens Logic

Screenwriter-turned-actor Tony Spiridakis asks us to believe that the inhabitants of Queens are more real than anyone else and that no one in the neighborhood is full of crap. That, believe it or don't, is the payoff for *Queens Logic,* about five lifelong buddies who are still the most important people in each other's lives. This may very well represent new territory for its young writer, but the material will be awfully familiar to any cable subscriber with a VCR. Federico Fellini examined five Adriatic buddies in the 1953 classic, *I Vitelloni* and George Lucas explored many similar rite-of-passage themes in 1973's *American Graffiti.* More recently, Nancy Savoca directed 1989's no-star but fun-to-watch *True Love,* an unpretentious little film that showed rather than explained pre-wedding jitters in the Bronx. Most of the characters in this 1991 re-tread by Spiridakis have little to do and are very sketchily drawn. Ken Olin is a frustrated artist who doesn't know what he wants. Kevin Bacon is a frustrated Hollywood actor (you can tell by the pink sunglasses) who hates phonies. Tony Spiridakis is a frustrated Manhattan actor (you can tell by the terrible Brando

> "Very beautiful and wonderful things do happen, and we live in the hope of them, don't we?"
>
> **—Old Gentleman William Mervyn in *The Railway Children.***

imitation) who wants a woman who will howl at the moon. And John Malkovich is a frustrated but choosy gay man (he says so often enough) who prefers his straight childhood friends to anyone he might pick up in a bar. Tom Waits has a cameo as a Queens weirdo and Jamie Lee Curtis has a cameo as a rich weirdo. Spiridakis is a not-terribly original writer who has a sporadically good ear for dialogue and is also the least colorful onscreen presence in the film. Luckily for audiences, Joe Mantegna is the star of *Queens Logic.* No matter how many cliched situations Mantegna is stuck in, he packs them all with an intense vitality that's hard to resist. Chloe Webb also works wonders with the thankless role of a long-suffering hairdresser who waits patiently for her much-adored fiance to grow up. And deep-voiced Linda *(The Last Seduction)* Fiorentino creates a vivid impression as a young mother of two who clearly has had it waiting for her childlike husband. The action takes place on the weekend of Chloe Webb's wedding to Ken Olin. Will they get married and remain true to Queens or not? (Hint: "I Fooled Around and Fell in Love" is on the soundtrack.) *Queens Logic* is directed by Steven Rash, who began his career making *The Buddy Holly Story* and *Can't Buy Me Love* and later went on to direct Pauly Shore in *Son-in-Law* and Whoopi Goldberg in *Eddie* (Spiridakis went on to write the poorly received *If Lucy Fell.*) 🦴🦴

1991 (R) 116m/C John Malkovich, Kevin Bacon, Jamie Lee Curtis, Linda Fiorentino, Joe Mantegna, Ken Olin, Tom Waits, Chloe Webb, Ed Marinaro, Kelly Bishop, Tony Spiridakis; ***D:*** Steve Rash; ***W:*** Tony Spiridakis; ***C:*** Amir M. Mokri; ***M:*** Joe Jackson. **VHS, LV, Closed Caption**

The Railway Children

If you're looking for a movie on video with a little more respect for its subject than, say, 1991's *Hook* has for Peter Pan, 1970's *The Railway Children* is a fine example. Director Lionel Jeffries wisely tackles this much-loved children's book on its own terms. The story opens when the police arrive to take Father Charles Waterbury into custody straight after a holiday performance of *Peter Pan.* We know right away that this Father is a decent, free-spirited man. His three children clearly adore him and he yells louder than anyone to save Tinkerbell's life. But he spends Christmas night and most of the film in prison (unfairly, it turns out), while his wife quietly works for his release. (Mother is beautifully played by Dinah Sheridan with the sly humor that helped to make *Genevieve* such a gem in the early '50s.) The three children include Jenny Agutter, who at 18 was an eyelash too mature for her role as Bobbie, but she's wonderful anyway in a delicately shaded performance. Along with her younger siblings Phyllis and Peter, she is given no real information about their predicament as the family leaves the city and struggles to survive in the Yorkshire countryside. Mother writes magazine stories and her offspring make new friends by hanging about a nearby railway line. By not minding their own business they are able to combat their loneliness and isolation, and they develop a great deal of empathy for others in the process. Ultimately they are able to free themselves from their greatly reduced circumstances. Making *The Railway Children* demanded tremendous discipline on Jeffries' part. He could easily have torn the whole thing by mucking about with material for which he clearly had enormous affection to spare. Jeffries chose to honor the sheer simplicity of *The Railway Children,* and let the story tell itself. *The Railway Children* was filmed in Technicolor by one of the world's finest cinematographers, Arthur Ibbetson. Intricate attention was paid to period detail, not only with the sets and the costumes, but also with the atmosphere and the attitudes of 1905. When grown-ups return to the world of childhood, we really need to tread lightly, for we remember good and bad alike without real precision. *The Railway Children* offers a gentle, understated view of another time that may be even more appealing today than it was to the first-time readers of E. Nesbit's Edwardian classic. 🦴🦴🦴🦴

1970 104m/C *GB* Jenny Agutter, William Mervyn, Bernard Cribbins, Dinah Sheridan, Iain Cuthbertson, Sally Thomsett, Peter Bromilow, Ann Lancaster, Gary Warren, Gordon Whiting, David Lodge; ***D:*** Lionel Jeffries; ***W:*** Lionel Jeffries; ***C:*** Arthur Ibbetson. **VHS**

Rambling Rose

Martha Coolidge is among the best working directors in America today, and she should have received an Oscar nomination for *Rambling Rose.* One of the drags of the pre-Oscar media buzz is seeing a bunch of guys sitting around a table yakking about how fine directors like Coolidge aren't "ready" to be an Oscar nominee because it's Demme's "turn" this year (or Levinson's or Stone's) or anyone's but a smashingly talented, perceptive female director like Coolidge. Laura Dern and Diane Ladd WERE nominees for this extraordinary film that takes a sensitive look at Rose, a randy teenaged nanny who is threatened with a hysterectomy because a couple of men (Robert Duvall and the doctor played by Kevin Conway) are threatened by her sexuality. A sequence where Ladd's character stands up for Rose's right to be free of these judgmental meddlers is a highlight. Another is a very delicately handled sequence in which Rose's 13-year-old charge (Lukas Haas) learns more about what makes his nanny happy than he really has the right to know. Screenwriter Calder *(The Strange One)* Willingham adapted his own autobiographical novel. Filmed in Wilmington, North Carolina.

1991 (R) 115m/C Laura Dern, Diane Ladd, Robert Duvall, Lukas Haas, John Heard, Kevin Conway, Robert John Burke, Lisa Jakub, Evan Lockwood; ***D:*** Martha Coolidge; ***W:*** Calder Willingham; ***C:*** Johnny E. Jensen; ***M:*** Elmer Bernstein. Independent Spirit Awards '92: Best Director (Coolidge), Best Film, Best Supporting Actress (Ladd); Nominations: Academy Awards '91: Best Actress (Dern), Best Supporting Actress (Ladd). **VHS, LV, DVD**

Random Encounter

Showgirls was a mess from start to finish, but anyone who spent years enjoying Elizabeth Berkley as intellectual feminist Jessie Spano opposite Mario Lopez as A.J. Slater isn't going to give up on her after one terrible movie. (Who'd give up on Kyle MacLachlan or Gina Gershon or Robert Davi or director Paul Verhoeven?) *Random Encounter* is a much more low-key and far less-hyped affair, a Canadian indie by Doug Jackson with plot holes (by Matt Dorff) the size of the Grand Canyon, plus a yucky co-star. Berkley plays Alicia, an up-and-coming professional woman who loves her parents and is fiercely loyal to her business mentor. She meets a guy with too many teeth at a company party and goes to bed with him! A mistake, naturally. Soon, Alicia is embroiled in a murder and is linked to the one-night stand by her inexplicable attraction to him, as well as a more believable sense of self-preservation. Berkley, who did well in small roles in *First Wives Club* and *The Real Blonde,* does her sincere best in the leading role, but her seedy nemesis, whose performance is all over the map, fails to supply crucial sizzle and support. I once read that there's nothing as irrelevant as the score at half time; Berkley's only in her 20s, so I hope she finds a project that does her career and her talent (which she does have) some good by the 21st century. Update: Berkley's Saturday morning colleagues are all still gainfully employed, although Screech and Mr. Belding (Dustin Diamond and Dennis Haskins) received their pink slips in 1998 after many years at Bayside High School. Zack Morris (Mark Paul Gosselaar), Kelly Kapowski (Tiffani-Amber Thiessen), and Slater (Lopez) went on to prime time television (*Hyperion Bay, Beverly Hills 90210,* and *Pacific Blue*) and Lisa Turtle (Lark Voorhees) continued in daytime television and commercials.

1998 100m/C *CA* Elizabeth Berkley, Joel Wyner, Frank Schorpion, Barry Flatman, Mark Walker, Ellen David, Susan Glover, Frank Fontaine; ***D:*** Douglas Jackson; ***W:*** Matt Dorff; ***C:*** Georges Archambault; ***M:*** Daniel Scott. **VHS**

The Real Blonde

An hour and 45 minutes into Tom DiCillo's *The Real Blonde,* I noted with gratitude that it was over and I could go home. To

Dee Dee is a hard-as-nails agent, straight out of a cookie cutter. And Tina (not a real blonde) is a Madonna double who just wants to be loved. Even if these stereotypical characters were funny (and they aren't), none of the situations in which they find themselves are worth watching for as long as it takes to sit through four or five situation comedies on television. *The Real Blonde* feels like (a) the script was sitting in Tom DiCillo's closet for several years, (b) it's been seen by too many script doctors, or (c) both of the above. It stars all the folks you'd expect to turn up in an indie these days (Matthew Modine, Catherine Keener, Maxwell Caulfield, Bridgette Wilson, Daryl Hannah, Buck Henry, Marlo Thomas, Christopher Lloyd, Kathleen Turner, Denis Leary, and Elizabeth Berkley), but all their best efforts can't breathe life into this movie. Steve Buscemi puts in a cameo as a director (duh!) of a music video. He's so self-assured and confident here; he looks like he's slumming and he is. The best indies aren't just studio wannabes. They're infused with a free spirit and a fresh way of looking at life. Alas, the only free, fresh thing about *The Real Blonde* is the exit.

1997 (R) 105m/C Matthew Modine, Catherine Keener, Daryl Hannah, Maxwell Caulfield, Elizabeth Berkley, Marlo Thomas, Buck Henry, Bridgette Wilson, Christopher Lloyd, Kathleen Turner, Denis Leary; ***Cameos:*** Steve Buscemi; ***D:*** Tom DiCillo; ***W:*** Tom DiCillo; ***C:*** Frank Prinzi; ***M:*** Jim Farmer. **VHS, Closed Caption, DVD**

Bob (Maxwell Caulfield) and Kelly (Daryl Hannah) in *The Real Blonde.*
Paramount; courtesy of the Kobal Collection

be grateful to leave a film by the writer/director of indie classics *Living in Oblivion* and *Box of Moonlight* is indeed a sad realization, but the grim fact is that there isn't a whole lot going on in *The Real Blonde.* Joe and Mary have been living together for six years and are experiencing lukewarm relationship problems. Bob and bottle blonde Sahara started out as a one-night stand, but he wants to marry a real blonde, if he can ever find her, and she wants to get married. Kelly IS a real blonde, alright, but that's about it. Dr. Leuter, not-so-secretly lusting after Mary, diagnoses her problem as "hostility towards men" and recommends a self-defense class. Blair is a fashion photographer who likes male models with chunky abdominal muscles. Ernest is an old-school gay man who trains his all male staff to be scrupulously correct waiters.

Reasons of State

This film about a hypocritical Latin American dictator was co-produced in Mexico, Cuba, and France. Despite a skimpy budget of $2 million, Chilean director Miguel Littin has made a film of epic dimensions, shooting in all three countries and employing a huge cast. Unhappily, *Reasons of State* suffers from sluggish pacing and a 145-minute run time. Too many cooks, perhaps?

1978 145m/C *MX FR CU* Katy Jurado; ***D:*** Miguel Littin.

Reckless

The Christmas season terrifies me more than anything that could possibly go bump in the night. The only reason I saw *Reckless* at THAT time of year was because, with Craig Lucas as the screenwriter and Mia Farrow as the star, I were reasonably sure that it would supply a strange and skewed take on the holidays. And it does. Mia Farrow is a blissful housewife with a wonderful life except for one thing: her husband has taken a contract out on her life. Guilt-stricken, he confesses the whole thing to his wife and urges her to jump out the window before the hired killer turns up. Farrow wanders around in the snow until she hitches a ride from Scott Glenn, who takes her home to his disabled wife, Mary-Louise Parker. Parker also pretends to be a deaf-mute so that Glenn will stay with her (no, I didn't get it either!), and the sweet couple adopt Farrow and make her feel right at home. So, Farrow creates a new life for herself at the non-profit organization where Glenn gets her a job and all is well until the next Christmas.... Poor Mia Farrow. Talk about the Perils of Pauline; this sweet, gentle lady has to put up with everything! She's great in the role, retaining the doll-like sense of innocent wonder that kept audiences rooting for her in *Rosemary's Baby* and *The Purple Rose of Cairo.* Scott Glenn, too, does a nice job in a rather whacked-out role (for him). And Stephen Dorff makes a brief but affecting appearance as Farrow's long-lost son. *Reckless* travels its own weird one-of-a-kind route with the prolific Lucas as tour guide. It isn't exactly a foolproof antidote for the cheery warmth we're supposed to be feeling the last six weeks of the year, but *Reckless* beats being anesthetized by the 10,000th broadcast of *It's a Wonderful Life.* 🦴🦴🦴

1995 (PG-13) 91m/C Mia Farrow, Scott Glenn, Mary-Louise Parker, Tony Goldwyn, Stephen Dorff, Eileen Brennan, Giancarlo Esposito, Deborah Rush; ***D:*** Norman Rene; ***W:*** Craig Lucas; ***C:*** Frederick Elmes; ***M:*** Stephen Endelman. **VHS, LV, Closed Caption**

The Red House

Independent producer Sol Lesser was pleased when *The Red House* played to packed houses, but whether that was due to the tremendous performances by Edward G. Robinson and Judith Anderson or to the passionate make-out sequences between gorgeous Tibby (Julie London, 21) and strapping Teller (Rory Calhoun, 29), the boxoffice receipts don't say. *The Red House* is an unusual film noir, because it takes place in a rural, rather than an urban setting. Robinson is Pete Morgan, a disabled farmer with a secret, plus a phobia about anyone going near The Red House on his property. Lon McCallister is Nath Storm, Pete's hired hand and the so-called love interest in the story. He's sort of a nerd, actually, pining over the always occupied Tibby, and only acquiescing to the gentle affection of Allene Roberts as Meg Morgan. But Pete's secret and his phobia don't go away—they fester and elicit attention in spite of his resistance. Moreover, the horrors of his own past creep up on him. In an urban setting, there would be plenty of distractions, but here, there are constant reminders of what happened in The Red House, and Miklos Rosza's score going into hysterics everytime Pete even THINKS about The Red House....Yes, it IS very melodramatic, but Robinson gives the role everything he's got. Everyone in the cast is good with the exception of McCallister, who looks like a cheerful soul, even though he can barely act at all. Also that year, Delmer Daves went subjective with Humphrey Bogart, Lauren Bacall, and his own adaptation of David Goodis' urban noir novel, *Dark Passage. The Red House* is based on the novel by George Agnew Chamberlain. 🦴🦴🦴

1947 100m/B Edward G. Robinson, Lon McCallister, Judith Anderson, Allene Roberts, Rory Calhoun, Ona Munson, Julie London, Harry Shannon, Arthur Space, Walter Sande, Pat Flaherty; ***D:*** Delmer Daves; ***W:*** Delmer Daves; ***C:*** Bert Glennon; ***M:*** Miklos Rozsa. **VHS**

The Red Poster

The Red Poster tells the story of 23 members of the French Underground who were killed by the Nazis in 1944. Director/writer Frank Cassenti shifts uneasily back and forth between cinematic and theatrical styles as if he is grasping for the best

"Do you know what I am doing, Miss Kenton? I am placing my mind elsewhere while you chatter away."

—Stevens (Anthony Hopkins) to housekeeper Miss Kenton (Emma Thompson) in *The Remains of the Day.*

structure to support the meaning of the narrative. Cassenti was once Constantin Costa-Gavras' assistant, but seems to have no other credits of note. ***AKA:*** L'Affiche Rouge. 🦴🦴

1976 90m/C *FR* Roger Ibanez, Pierre Clementi, Laszlo Szabo, Anicee Alvina; ***D:*** Frank Cassenti; ***W:*** Rene Richen, Frank Cassenti; ***C:*** Philippe Rousselot; ***M:*** Cuarteto Cedron.

Red Ribbon Blues

When my friend John lay dying a dozen summers ago, he wasn't interested in any disease-of-the-weak movies. He'd yell, "Get me *Modesty Blaise!*" or "Get me *Fantastic Voyage!*" or "Get me *The Wizard of Oz!*" The more escapist the fare, the better he liked it. I think that John would have liked *Red Ribbon Blues,* though. It's a very broad satire about the difficulties the very indigent face in obtaining expensive drug cocktails that fight the HIV virus. Paul Mercurio, who entered films as a sexy dancer in *Strictly Ballroom,* went on to star in the Garry Marshall flop *Exit to Eden,* and to play Joseph in TNT's Biblical mini-series, has kept busy in six or seven films since 1995; *Red Ribbon Blues* is the best of the follow-up projects I've seen. He doesn't dance in this one; he's an artist named Troy, who's just received a positive diagnosis. His best friend is Debi Mazar as Darcy, a tough drug addict with a fondness for bottles of Percodan. She's first seen shooting up underneath her fingernail. Like Troy, she's positive, as are their friends RuPaul as Duke and Lypsinka as Harold. Neither RuPaul nor Lypsinka appear in their world-famous drag personas here—in fact, Lypsinka is billed as John Epperson. All are depressed, appearing fitfully at support groups conducted by Troy, since none of them have a chance to buy effective medication. And then the idea hits them: Why not rob and distribute the drug to those who can't afford it, including themselves? Faster than you can say "Robin Hood," Paul Bartel as Fred the Pharmacist is handcuffed to his desk as they help themselves to the medication. They soon acquire a media rep as the Red Ribbon bandits and detectives David Spielberg and Lisa Waltz are hot on their trail. Everyone wants to know who they are, AIDS activists and price clubs support them, the pharmaceutical company vindictively raises its prices, and sickly Harold is ironing his own shirt—not very well, but at least he isn't bedridden anymore. Even Deb is less bombed than usual and no one is in imminent danger of fearing the reaper. Bright performances by all and Charles Winkler's clever writing and direction lift *Red Ribbon Blues* above most lugubriously themed AIDS yarns. Mercurio and Mazar make a great team, even if they don't dance. (Note: Mercurio dances a little bit in *Back of Beyond* as a ghost named Tom, but at least he's alive and kicking here and improving as an actor all the time.) 🦴🦴🦴

1995 97m/C Paul Mercurio, Debi Mazar, RuPaul, John (Lypsinka) Epperson, Alan Boyce, Leland Orser, David Spielberg, Lisa Waltz, Paul Bartel; ***D:*** Charles Winkler; ***W:*** Charles Winkler; ***C:*** Larry Blanford; ***M:*** John Frizzell.

Red Rock West

Red Rock West went nowhere until San Francisco's Roxie Cinema picked it up for an extended run. (1990's *Kill Me Again,* another good film noir by John Dahl, only played in the San Francisco Bay area at the Geneva Drive-In.) With an appreciative audience, its sharp script and on-target performances became obvious. Nicolas Cage IS Mike, who tries to get out of Red Rock West, Wyoming, but no dice. Wayne (who else but J.T. Walsh?) wants to kill his wife Suzanne (Lara Flynn Boyle), and mistakes Mike for the hired killer (who else but Dennis Hopper as Lyle?). Oh, and Suzanne has some ideas of her own; soon Mike is in Noir-ville up to his eyeballs. Invite some friends over for this one! 🦴🦴🦴

1993 (R) 98m/C Nicolas Cage, Dennis Hopper, Lara Flynn Boyle, J.T. Walsh, Timothy Carhart, Dan Shor, Dwight Yoakam, Bobby Joe McFadden, Craig Reay, Vance Johnson, Robert Apel, Dale Gibson, Ted Parks, Babs Bram, Robert Guajardo, Sarah Sullivan; ***D:*** John Dahl; ***W:*** John Dahl, Rick Dahl; ***C:*** Marc Reshovsky; ***M:*** William Olvis. Nominations: Independent Spirit Awards '95: Best Director (Dahl), Best Screenplay. **VHS, LV, Closed Caption**

The Refrigerator

A crowd pleaser at 1991's Mill Valley Film Festival is *The Refrigerator,* a movie that will strike terror into the hearts of anyone who's ever walked into a kitchen. Julia *(The Unbelievable Truth)* McNeal plays Eileen, a young actress married to Steve (David *Amateur* Simonds), the biggest jerk in Manhattan. They move into a dump on the Lower East Side, expecting to fix it up, but the apartment soon possesses them both, day and night. The worst culprit is the refrigerator from Hell, an unlikely but photogenic fiend. Nicholas A.E. Jacobs' low-budget film is laced with horror and humor and benefits from a strong cast, including some devastating performances from the inanimate actors. 🦴🦴🦴

1991 86m/C David Simonds, Julia McNeal, Angel Caban, Nena Segal, Jaime Rojo, Michelle DeCosta, Phyllis Sanz; ***D:*** Nicholas A.E. Jacobs; ***W:*** Nicholas A.E. Jacobs; ***C:*** Paul Gibson. **VHS**

The Remains of the Day

Upstairs Downstairs and *The Duchess of Duke Street* became television classics for a variety of reasons. Each was a sharply observed examination of an irretrievable time with a very definite bias: that the working classes learned to adjust to a changing world in a way that the aristocracy could not. This perspective, along with appealing characters, nostalgic detail, and beautifully crafted scripts, charmed audiences all over the world. Each series had a reliable male staff member who took every aspect of his work very seriously, but who was always an object of affection and respect. We would trust our lives with Hudson (Gordon Jackson) or Starr (John Cater). At times, the quiet dignity of these men took on heroic, larger than life dimensions. Kazuo Ishiguro's slender novel, *The Remains of the Day,* had a different perspective on Stevens, the faithful family retainer of one Lord Darlington. She saw him as an essentially tragic figure, so mired in empty household rituals that he is unable to attract or accept love from those who are only too willing to give it to him. The Merchant Ivory team has supplied the usual candy box trappings to this character study. In trying to have it BOTH ways (oh, wasn't it great AND awful in the 1930s!), Stevens emerges as a pathetic joke and the centerpiece of the most boring prestige film of 1993. Since at least a dozen people walked out of the screening that I attended and we cast several impatient glances at our wristwatches over the course of 135 minutes, it's only fair to mention that not one real thing happens to Stevens in the whole movie. What? Aren't there a lot of big stars in *The Remains of the Day* like Oscar winners Anthony Hopkins and Emma Thompson, plus James Fox, Christopher Reeve, Peter Vaughan, Hugh Grant, Michael Lonsdale, and Tim Pigott-Smith? Sure, but even the greatest actors need SOME directorial guidance. Even the most indulgent audiences need a payoff. How riveted are we going to get by a man who spends an entire film on the verge of feeling a single honest emotion? How much will we root for a woman who gets so caught up in the drab routines of this dweeb that she regards their working life together as the happiest time in her life? And how enthralled will we be by the fact that every major event over a 20-year span happens OFF camera? On the edge of our seats?...NOT!!! And then, four years after *The Remains of the Day* won a stupefying quantity of awards, I saw Christopher Guest's hilarious *Waiting for Guffman,* and now, go figure, I WANT MY *REMAINS OF THE DAY* LUNCHBOX! 🦴🦴

1993 (PG) 135m/C *GB* Anthony Hopkins, Emma Thompson, James Fox, Christopher Reeve, Peter Vaughan, Hugh Grant, Michael (Michel) Lonsdale, Tim Pigott-Smith; ***D:*** James Ivory; ***W:*** Ruth Prawer Jhabvala; ***C:*** Tony Pierce-Roberts; ***M:*** Richard Robbins. British Academy Awards '93: Best Actor (Hopkins); Los Angeles Film Critics Association Awards '93: Best Actor (Hopkins); National Board of Review Awards '93: Best Actor (Hopkins); Nominations: Academy Awards '93: Best Actor (Hopkins), Best Actress (Thompson), Best Adapted Screenplay, Best Art Direction/Set Decoration, Best Costume Design, Best Director (Ivory), Best Original Screenplay, Best Picture; British Academy Awards '94: Best Actress (Thompson), Best Adapted Screenplay, Best Director (Ivory), Best Film; Directors Guild of America Awards '93: Best Director (Ivory); Golden Globe Awards '94: Best Actor—Drama (Hopkins), Best Actress—Drama (Thompson), Best Di-

The Hound Salutes:

LAWRENCE TIERNEY

Reservoir Dogs, Tough Guys Don't Dance, City of Hope

The business has done well by me and I've done well by the business. I've been in and out of the business. I quit for a long time and went back to New York when things got tough. Now, I'm still making pictures. In 1987, I enjoyed working with Norman Mailer on *Tough Guys Don't Dance.* He's a funny guy and I loved that part as Ryan O'Neal's father, Dougie. That movie and *Dillinger* are my favorites. In 1992, I played Joe Cabot, another part I liked very much, in a film which was a big success, *Reservoir Dogs.* Quentin Tarantino, a very talented young man, is a wonderful writer with a great sense of humor and a great sense of film. I expect great things from him. In 1993 and 1994, they made films from two of his scripts, *True Romance* and *Natural Born Killers* and in 1994, he directed *Pulp Fiction.* I'm not in them, but one of the actors I liked working with very much is a good man and a wonderful actor named Chris Penn, and he's in *True Romance* and in *Short Cuts.* I expect great things from him, too. He's a nice person.

"It's sort of a funny thing how I became a tough guy in the movies. I was under contract to RKO studios in 1945 and I heard about *Dillinger* over at Monogram, so I went in and on a fluke, I

rector (Ivory), Best Film—Drama, Best Screenplay. **VHS, LV, 8mm, Letterbox, Closed Caption**

Reno's Kids: 87 Days Plus 11

Reno's Kids: 87 Days Plus 11 is the first documentary feature by actress Whitney (Dorothy Baxter on NBC's *Hazel,* 1961–65) Blake. The director is justifiably proud of her film, which shows a semester in the life of Daly City teacher Reno Taini and his life-toughened students, who learn how to confront the system head-on and win. Blake has selected some extraordinary footage of the class at work and at play, a technique which serves the film's purpose far better than the traditional talking-heads format. ☠☠☠

1987 99m/C *D:* Whitney Blake; ***C:*** Frances Reid.

Repulsion

Most films about madness glamorize the subject or shift the point of view to a sane observer. Roman Polanski's 1965 British film *Repulsion* provides a rare screen examination of insanity from the perspective of the person who is going mad. Twenty-one-year-old Catherine Deneuve portrays Carol Ledoux, a quiet manicurist who loses her grip on the most fundamental aspects of her routine life. Bridget, a sympathetic colleague (played by Helen Fraser), tries to cure her blues with a Charlie Chaplin imitation, but Carol is beyond help. When her much-older sister (Yvonne Furneaux, then 37) takes a holiday with her lover (Ian Hendry), she leaves Carol all alone. Sexual repression is the most obvious symptom of her mental anguish, but left to her own devices, Carol plummets into an irreversible nightmare. Deneuve's glacial face and expressive eyes serve her well here; her love-

got the part. After that, because *Dillinger* did so well and became a big overnight success, it broke all world records for the most money recouped and earned by a film in that budget class. It only cost $60,000 to make and it earned millions all over the world. So then RKO studios thought they had a good thing, so they started putting me in one bad guy role after another, like Sam Wild in *Born to Kill,* and *San Quentin* and *The Devil Thumbs a Ride.* People liked that horror stuff in *Born to Kill,* but I don't like playing that kind of a character. Preparing for tough guy parts is the same as getting ready for any other parts: I just read the script, get the idea, listen to the director and go in and give it hell.

"Turner Network Television threw a nice celebration for my 74th birthday on March 15, 1993. They talked to me, had me do some imitations and do some kidding around. I had fun doing that. They say the older you get, the more you dislike having birthdays. What the hell? If you don't have birthdays, you know what you have instead of them: the sound of a shovel scraping dirt. Mr. and Mrs. America, stop smoking before smoking stops you!"

LAWRENCE TIERNEY's films on video include *Dillinger, Back to Bataan, Those Endearing Young Charms, The Devil Thumbs a Ride, Born to Kill, Best of the Badmen, The Hoodlum, The Greatest Show on Earth, The Bushwackers, The Female Jungle, Abduction, Never Pick Up a Stranger, The Prowler, Midnight, Silver Bullet, Prizzi's Honor, Murphy's Law, The Offspring, Why Me?, The Death Merchant, City of Hope, Casualties of Love, Wizards of the Demon Sword,* and *A Kiss Goodnight.*

ly mask conceals the festering psychosis within and an ordinary flat becomes her prison as she grows progressively more ill. Her landlord (Patrick Wymark) can't read her, a well-meaning suitor (John Fraser) can't read her, and household objects take on a deeply sinister quality. This one will make you want to sleep with the lights on for a MONTH. 🦴🦴🦴🦴

1965 105m/B *GB* Catherine Deneuve, Yvonne Furneaux, Ian Hendry, John Fraser, Patrick Wymark, James Villiers, Renee Houston, Helen Fraser, Mike Pratt, Valerie Taylor; ***D:*** Roman Polanski; ***W:*** Roman Polanski, Gerard Brach, David Stone; ***C:*** Gilbert Taylor. **VHS, LV**

Reservoir Dogs

While recognizing that American cinema in the 1990s would not be what it is today without Quentin Tarantino and acknowledging his originality and talent AND being forever grateful that he cast Lawrence Tierney in such a terrific role here as Joe Cabot, *Reservoir Dogs* is not the sort of flick I can watch over and over again. Many guys of my acquaintance can and do—I can't and don't. I have also been asked why I didn't think the bloody torture scenes in the warehouse were funny. How can I answer a question like that? Because I didn't. Except for Cabot's son, Nice Guy Eddie (Christopher Penn), most of the characters are named after colors: White (Harvey Keitel), Orange (Tim Roth), Pink (Steve Buscemi), Blonde (Michael Madsen), Brown (Tarantino), and Blue (Eddie Bunker). The extremely well-acted plot revolves around a diamond heist gone wrong. *Variety*'s Todd McCarthy said it best when the picture was first shown at the Sundance Film Festival: "*(Reservoir Dogs)* is about nothing other than a bunch of macho guys and how big their guns are." I give it four bones for the guys, but for me, just 🦴🦴🦴

1992 (R) 100m/C Harvey Keitel, Tim Roth, Michael Madsen, Steve Buscemi, Christopher Penn,

Dr. Michele Wolf (Ingrid Thulin), Stanislas Pilgrin (Maximilian Schell), and Dr. Charles Bovard (Herbert Lom) in *Return from the Ashes.* United Artists; courtesy of the Kobal Collection

Lawrence Tierney, Kirk Baltz, Quentin Tarantino, Eddie Bunker, Randy Brooks; ***D:*** Quentin Tarantino; ***W:*** Quentin Tarantino; ***C:*** Andrzej Sekula. Independent Spirit Awards '93: Best Supporting Actor (Buscemi). **VHS, LV, Letterbox, Closed Caption, DVD**

Return from the Ashes

For the world's worst chess player, movies about chess are catnip for my soul. This one's my favorite. Ingrid Thulin is so beautiful and so haunted as Dr. Michele Wolf, a concentration camp survivor who endures the nightmare of Dachau only to return to Stanislas Pilgrin, the sociopathic chess champion played by Maximilian Schell. He's in the middle of a hot and heavy affair with her brilliant stepdaughter Fabi, played with nasty conviction by stunning Samantha Eggar. Neither experiences a twinge of guilt as they connive, with systematic care, to do away with Thulin's character. Wracked with profound guilt about her stepdaughter and worn away with passion for what she believes is the last love of her life, Thulin struggles with the gnawing realization that both are faithless. Dismissed at the time of its release, *Return from the Ashes* (based on a Hubert Monteilhet novel) is the only film I've seen that deposits a Holocaust survivor in such a grim end game. The direction by J. Lee Thompson is gripping, and it's well worth a reappraisal by thoughtful viewers. Yes, that is Herbert Lom in a change-of-pace role as Dr. Charles Bovard, Thulin's colleague. The exquisite Talitha Pol, then 25, appears as Claudine. Within a year, she would marry Jean Paul Getty II and spend the last five years of her life as one of the richest flower children on the planet. Three years before her early death from a drug overdose in 1971, she became the mother of her only child, Tara Gabriel Galaxy Gramophone. 🦴🦴🦴🦴

1965 104m/B *GB* Maximilian Schell, Samantha Eggar, Ingrid Thulin, Herbert Lom, Talitha Pol, Vladek Sheybal, Jacques Brunius, Andre Maranne, Yvonne Andre, John Serret; ***D:*** J. Lee Thompson; ***W:*** Julius J. Epstein, Charles Blair; ***C:*** Christopher Challis; ***M:*** John Dankworth.

Return of the Secaucus 7

I watched *Return of the Secaucus 7* with a devotee who treasured every frame, every expression, every line of this film. I, alas, found it dull, dreary, and depressing, and its running time of 110 minutes barely endurable. In real life, I would deliberately lose an invitation to such a reunion. As a viewer, all I could think was how sad life can be, that anyone could look forward to such a gathering. A lot of thought and care and time went into *Return of the Secaucus 7* and it's such a highly regarded film that it's part of the National Film Registry. *Return of the Secaucus 7* is considered by many to be superior to *The Big Chill* (which left me equally cold). The high point of the movie was seeing what David Strathairn looked like 17 years before I watched him four times in *L.A. Confidential.* To each his (or her) own! 🦴🦴

1980 110m/C Mark Arnott, Gordon Clapp, Maggie Cousineau-Arndt, David Strathairn, Adam LeFevre, Bruce MacDonald, Maggie Renzi, Jean Passanante, Karen Trott, John Sayles; ***D:*** John Sayles; ***W:*** John Sayles; ***C:*** Austin De Besche; ***M:*** Mason Daring. Los Angeles Film Critics Association Awards '80: Best Screenplay, National Film Registry '97. **VHS**

The Return of Tommy Tricker

Tommy, his sister, and their friends work their magic to free Charles Meriweather from the Bluenose sailing ship stamp he's been imprisoned in for 60 years. But when they try to bring Charlie back, they rescue his younger sister Molly instead. But Molly suddenly begins aging and it's up to Tommy to figure out how to save her (and still rescue Charlie). 🦴🦴🦴

1994 100m/C *CA* Michael Stevens, Joshawa Mathers, Heather Goodsell, Paul Nocholls, Andrew Bauer-Gador, Adele Gray; ***D:*** Michael Rubbo; ***W:*** Michael Rubbo; ***C:*** Thomas Vamos. **VHS**

Rhinoceros

Zero Mostel won the 1961 Tony for *Rhinoceros*—so who better to re-create his original Broadway role on film? And who better to turn Eugene Ionesco's play into a fun, wacky movie than Tom O'Horgan, the original director of *Hair*? Reunite Mostel with Gene Wilder, his Oscar-nominated co-star for *The Producers,* add Oscar nominee Karen Black and Tony nominee Joe Silver to the ensemble, and voila! Who says theatre on film has to be dull? It was inept misfires like this one that contributed to the demise of the American Film Theatre. Why subscribe to lousily executed movies like *Rhinoceros* when real Gene Wilder movies were playing down the block—*Blazing Saddles* and *Young Frankenstein,* not to mention other 1974 gems like *Chinatown, The Conversation,* and *Day for Night*? **woof!**

1974 101m/C *GB CA* Zero Mostel, Gene Wilder, Karen Black, Robert Weil, Joe Silver, Marilyn Chris; ***D:*** Tom O'Horgan; ***W:*** Eugene Ionesco; ***C:*** James A. Crabe. **VHS**

Rhythm Thief

Simon (Jason Andrews) bootlegs dubs of New York's underground bands to sustain his grungy life. Musicians in the bands hate his guts. His one-time girl friend Marty (Eddie Daniels) turns up and disrupts his low-life existence with the information that she and Simon's mother were in a mental institution together. Simon spends some time with Marty in Far Rockaway, but then he returns to New York to bootleg once again. Good acting and writing shine through this rock-bottom indie, which deserves wider distribution at video outlets. 🦴🦴

1994 88m/B Jason Andrews, Eddie Daniels, Kimberly Flynn, Kevin Corrigan, Sean Haggerty, Mark Alfred, Paul Rodriguez, Cynthia Sley; ***D:*** Matthew Harrison; ***W:*** Matthew Harrison, Christopher Grimm; ***C:*** Howard Krupa; ***M:*** Danny Brenner. Sundance Film Festival '95: Special Jury Prize; Nominations: Independent Spirit Awards '96: Debut Performance (Andrews). **VHS**

Rich and Strange

Rich and Strange is an early Hitchcock film that's widely available, but rarely discussed. It's a comedy and just what the title says it is. Joan Barry (1902–89) had previously dubbed the voice for Anny Ondra in 1929's *Blackmail.* She has very

"I had a girlfriend once. I loved her. And I killed her."

—Feck (Dennis Hopper) in *River's Edge.*

little onscreen chemistry with actor Henry Kendall (1892–1967), who was reportedly gay. Except for *The Lodger, Blackmail,* and *Murder,* Hitchcock's pre-1934 films are a mixed bag; he had yet to be typed as a master of the macabre. As in the 1941 screwball comedy *Mr. and Mrs. Smith,* Hitchcock added darkly humorous touches here and there to *Rich and Strange* that carry his unique signature. If you don't demand that your spine be tingled by this one, you'll have fun with it. ***AKA:*** East of Shanghai. 🦴🦴🦴

1932 92m/B *GB* Henry Kendall, Joan Barry, Betty Amann, Percy Marmont, Elsie Randolph; ***D:*** Alfred Hitchcock; ***W:*** Alfred Hitchcock, Alma Reville; ***C:*** Jack Cox, Charles Martin. **VHS, LV**

Ricochets

Ricochets evolved from an Israeli army training film into the theatrical release it became. It transcends its modest start, but simplifies the conflict between Israel and Lebanon by examining the problems of one small fighting unit. Still, since it never claims to show anything other than war from the Israeli soldier's point of view, the amount of military criticism in this effort is surprising, considering its origins. ***AKA:*** Shtei Etzbaot Mi'Tzidon. 🦴🦴🦴

1987 91m/C *IS* Roni Pinovich, Shaul Mizrahi, Dudu Ben-Ze'ev, Alon Aboutboul; ***D:*** Eli Cohen; ***W:*** Eli Cohen, Baruch Nevo, Zvi Kretzner; ***C:*** Yechiel Ne'eman; ***M:*** Benny Nagari.

Ripe

Ripe is a seedy-looking film about two screwed-up sisters. Monica (*Dawson's Creek*) Keena and Daisy Eagan are Violet and Rosie, who exit from the family car seconds before their parents are burned to death following an accident. The opening flashbacks suggest that the "14"-year-old girls may have been abused as children, so they take off for Kentucky without a backwards glance. They wind up at an army base where, instead of being turned over to children's protective services, they become quasi-mascots on base instead. And they stay with a grungy handyman named Pete (Gordon Currie), with whom Violet becomes sexually involved. The story makes less and less sense as Violet and Daisy go through the motions of weirdness, each in her own way. The only possible reasons for renting this turkey are (a) if you want to see Keena after she was cast as Oksana Baiul on CBS and before she evolved into bad girl Abby on the WB and (b) if you really must see why *Saturday Night Fever*'s Karen Lynn Gorney is in this flick as randy "Janet Wyman." All others, beware. 🦴

1997 (R) 93m/C Monica Keena, Daisy Eagan, Gordon Currie, Ron Brice, Karen Gorney, Vincent Laresca; ***D:*** Mo Ogrodnik; ***W:*** Mo Ogrodnik; ***C:*** Wolfgang Held; ***M:*** Anton Sanko. **VHS**

Rita, Sue & Bob Too

There is probably no subject that both men and woman lie about as much as sex, but moments into *Rita, Sue & Bob Too* it seems that the filmmakers are out to set some sort of a record for sexual dishonesty. Just for starters, we are asked to accept that the line "Can either of you put a rubber johnny on?" would trigger unbridled lust in two 16-year-old babysitters when their 40-year-old employer drives them home at his wife's suggestion. Since he has a track record with babysitters, it's hard to believe that any 27-year-old woman would set herself up like that, as well as the two girls, but the incredulity continues. Although Rita and Sue are both virgins, they experience no pain whatever from their first sexual experience. Sex with each takes one minute flat, he's ready to roll without a break, and both girls share a simultaneous climax with Bob. If viewers have gotten this far, then they may have no problem accepting the fact that Bob's attractive wife is frigid due to her hatred of French kisses and sterilization, not because she's married to a faithless jerk who lies to her, then blames her for his problems. The script was written by a talented teenager named Andrea Dunbar (1961–). She writes of Northern England in an observant, uninterpretive style: "If it's put there on a plate, he's going to take it. He wouldn't be much of a man if he didn't" is the sort of sexual propaganda that her female characters can and do swallow. Other instructive lyrics: "We're having a gang bang. It's the thing to do. We'd like to give you one." The women in the film are punished not only for having sex, but also for being sexual fantasies. *Rita, Sue & Bob Too* hardens prejudices rather than challenges them: a cute boy from Pakistan, whom Sue sees for a while, is shown as violent, manipulative, and mercenary. He is written out of the plot when a white neighbor telephones the police the minute he enters his neighborhood. Although teens Rita and Sue are obviously played by women in their 20s, the cast of unknowns is talented, the Bradford scenery is attractive, and there is a gritty quality to director Alan Clarke's (1935–90) vision of the drabness of these characters' lives. **woof!**

1987 (R) 94m/C *GB* Michelle Holmes, George Costigan, Siobhan Finneran, Lesley Sharp, Willie Ross, Patti Nicholls, Kulvinder Ghir; ***D:*** Alan Clarke; ***W:*** Andrea Dunbar; ***C:*** Ivan Strasburg; ***M:*** Michael Kamen. **VHS, LV**

River of Grass

No-budget noirish crime/romance set in the swampy, low-rent Florida area between Miami and the Everglades. Uncaring and frankly dumb housewife/mom Cozy (Lisa Bowman) hooks up with the boozing Lee Ray (Larry Fessenden) and the dim duo take an illegal dip in a private pool. Cozy manages to fire off Lee's gun and thinks she hit a man who suddenly appeared. Not bothering to find out if this is true, they decide to hole up in a motel until they can figure out what to do. You won't really care but director Kelly Reichardt does have a way with visuals, so things aren't a total loss.

1994 80m/C Lisa Bowman, Larry Fessenden, Dick Russell; ***D:*** Kelly Reichardt; ***W:*** Jesse Hartman, Kelly Reichardt; ***C:*** Jim Denault. Nominations: Independent Spirit Awards '96: Best First Feature, Debut Performance (Bowman). **VHS**

River's Edge

River's Edge was one of the most disturbing movies of 1987. Tim Hunter's study of how a high school gang reacts to the murder of one of their friends showed a conscience-free group, easily led by the always stoned Crispin Glover. The only one with any feeling for the dead girl seems to be Keanu Reeves, who went on to deliver impressive performances in *Permanent Record* and *Dangerous Liaisons.* Dennis Hopper, who co-stars as a lunatic (again), also appeared in 1955's *Rebel Without a Cause,* directed by Nicholas Ray. The original ad for *Rebel* could describe both films: "Teenage terror torn from today's headlines!"

1987 (R) 99m/C Keanu Reeves, Crispin Glover, Daniel Roebuck, Joshua Miller, Dennis Hopper, Ione Skye, Roxana Zal, Tom Bower, Constance Forslund, Leo Rossi, Jim Metzler; ***D:*** Tim Hunter; ***W:*** Neal Jimenez; ***C:*** Frederick Elmes; ***M:*** Jurgen Knieper. Independent Spirit Awards '88: Best Film, Best Screenplay; Sundance Film Festival '87: Special Jury Prize. **VHS, LV, 8mm, Closed Caption**

Road Games

Steven Spielberg first attracted critical attention in 1971 when he directed a television movie called *Duel* starring Dennis Weaver. It's a suspenseful little saga about a battle to the death between a compact car and a truck, but there's very little character development, so *Duel* doesn't have much in the way of repeat value. A similar film with a lesser reputation emerged in Australia a decade later and the best thing about *Road Games* is the richness of its characters, which are played to perfection by American actors Stacy Keach and Jamie Lee Curtis. The director, Richard Franklin, like Brian De Palma, is an avid fan of Alfred Hitchcock. Unlike De Palma, Franklin's sense of humor is suggestive, rather than graphic, and more in tune with what Hitchcock himself might enjoy. Keach's character insists that "just because (he) rides a truck, it doesn't make (him) a truck driver." Keach talks to himself a lot, or rather he talks to his partner, a dog whom he thinks is a wild dingo. It's a dream part for an actor, and Keach makes the most of it. Curtis has less to do, but her comparatively few onscreen moments show why she was later able to steal *A Fish Called Wanda* and *Fierce Creatures.* The plot hinges

The story of a rebel and his mike.

—Tagline from the movie *Roger & Me.*

around a daft killer whom everyone thinks is Keach, so he has to prove his innocence by finding the real madman. There's an interesting exploration of Keach's own assumptions about women which trip him up, as well as them. *Road Games* on video is an ingratiating 100-minute ride. If you check out *The Killer Inside Me* at the same time, you may wonder why Stacy Keach isn't approached more often with roles that are worthy of his considerable talent. Franklin later went on to direct *Psycho 2, Cloak and Dagger, FX 2,* and *Sorrento Beach.* 🦴🦴🦴

1981 (PG) 100m/C *AU* Stacy Keach, Jamie Lee Curtis, Marion Edwards, Grant Page, Bill Stacey, Thaddeus Smith, Alan Hopgood; ***D:*** Richard Franklin; ***W:*** Everett De Roche; ***C:*** Vincent Monton; ***M:*** Brian May. **VHS**

Roads to the South

Yves Montand, Laurent Malet, and Miou-Miou dignify a watery script about a political father and son who clash in the aftermath of Franco's death. As with 1968's *Secret Ceremony,* the director (1909–84) seems awfully detached from both the story and the characters. When Montand came to the San Francisco International Film Festival to "plug" the film, he kvetched about Joseph Losey's direction, Jorge Semprun's screenplay, and Michel Legrand's blasting score. Montand said that Bobby Roth's *The Boss' Son* was a far superior movie, then returned home to immerse himself in French politics until his death in 1991 at age 70. ***AKA:*** Les Routes du Sud. 🦴🦴

1978 100m/C *FR* Yves Montand, Miou-Miou, Laurent Malet, Mario Gonzalez, Jose Luis Gomez, Jeannine Mestre, Roger Planchon, Didier Sauvegrain; ***D:*** Joseph Losey; ***W:*** Jorge Semprun; ***C:*** Gerry Fisher; ***M:*** Michel Legrand. **VHS, LV**

Robert et Robert

Robert et Robert is Claude Lelouch's valentine to the so-called losers of the world, and it would be difficult to find a more heartfelt salute. Based largely on the history of actor Jacques Villeret, who plays a real-life character based on himself, *Robert et Robert* shows the warm and funny friendship shared by a pair of bachelors seeking wives through a computer dating service. They never do find lasting ceremonial bliss, but both blossom from knowing each other. Lelouch clearly cares about his characters and he translates that caring to audiences with great sweetness and a lovely visual style. (Villeret and Charles Denner are perfect as the two Roberts, and Jacques Lefrançois' photography is excellent.) 🦴🦴🦴

1978 105m/C *FR* Charles Denner, Jacques Villeret, Jean-Claude Brialy, Macha Meril, Germaine Montero, Regine; ***D:*** Claude Lelouch; ***W:*** Claude Lelouch; ***C:*** Jacques Lefrancois. Cesar Awards '79: Best Supporting Actor (Villeret). **VHS**

Rock Hudson's Home Movies

Unless it's spoofing old educational short subjects, *Mystery Science Theater 3000* drives me nuts. I don't care if that guy and the robots want to yak through *Dating Do's and Don'ts,* but I want to HEAR Beverly Garland and Marie Windsor, not THEM, okay? I don't think I'd mind watching movies with Mark Rappaport, though. He does his homework, he knows how to read a film, and he's funny. How many people can sit through a marathon of Rock Hudson movies, anyway? But this 63-minute study, drily narrated by Eric Farr, shows the films in the context of the time in which they were made. Even at kiddie matinees, I used to wonder why Rock Hudson's he-man status was the joke of so many films, like he was such a hunk that he couldn't possibly be a mama's boy or pregnant or even an indoor guy!!! In film after film, these same themes would sneak up again and again, until 1966's *Seconds,* still one of the scariest movies I've ever seen. But as Rappaport's illuminating commentary reveals, *Seconds,* too, was more of the same, only in a threatening rather than comedic vein. The clips are well chosen and Rappaport's thoughtful, witty analysis is interesting to hear, whether or not you agree with all of it. Rappaport would go on to examine the career of another ill-fated star in *From the Journals of Jean Seberg* (narrated by Mary Beth Hurt). At press time, an exploration of Howard Hughes was in the planning stages.

1992 63m/C Eric Farr; ***D:*** Mark Rappaport; ***W:*** Mark Rappaport. **VHS**

Rockers

Rockers, helmed with assurance by Theodoros Bafaloukos, is a fascinating first film, both for its lively reggae music, and for its intriguing variation on the Robin Hood theme. Leroy Wallace makes an engaging appearance as a broke drummer named Horsemouth, who takes on a batch of rich crooks, with some help from his friends. *Rockers* is subtitled, rendering comprehensible the deeply accented English spoken in Jamaica. The soundtrack album is now a collector's item.

1979 100m/C *JM* Richard Hall, Gregory Isaacs, Marjorie Norman, Leroy Wallace, Jacob Miller, Monica Craig; ***D:*** Theodore Bafaloukos; ***W:*** Theodore Bafaloukos; ***C:*** Peter Sova; ***M:*** Bunny Wailer, Burning Spear, Gregory Isaacs. **VHS**

Roger & Me

Have Nick (*Kurt and Courtney*) Broomfield and Michael (*Roger & Me*) Moore ever met? Just asking! Although they both have in-your-face interviewing techniques, *Roger & Me* is a much weightier documentary than *Kurt and Courtney.* After all, 30,000 people found themselves unemployed when General Motors left Flint, Michigan. For GM chairman Roger Smith to turn his back on the Flint community after its truck plant closed is a far more meaningful subject for investigation than the incoherent alcoholic ramblings of Kurt Cobain's wannabe hit man who wound up staggering into a train. If the so-called Gilded Age of the late 19th century had ever been examined by a documentarian of Michael Moore's caliber, a few myths about the Good Old Days would have been demolished. Moore contrasts the rosy babblings of Flint's rich citizens with the statements of former auto workers who know firsthand how devastating GM's departure really is. Moore can't get a meeting with Roger Smith for most of the movie and when he finally does encounter him, Smith's sole response is to decline to return to Flint. *Roger & Me* is hilarious, but also horrifying because it reveals how little power we have over our individual destinies when they're controlled by profit-loss statements. One of the more controversial interviews is with Bob Eubanks, a local boy who made good as host of *The Newlywed Game.* His sexist, racist comments seem extraneous unless you appreciate their context. Eubanks got his by getting out of town: You're on your own in Flint, folks! In that vein, pep talks by Pat Boone, Anita Bryant, and Robert Schuller are oblivious to the obvious: that the harsh lives of Flint residents are not due to a lack of optimism, but a very real fiscal depression, a direct result of a cold business decision in which they had no voice. Michael Moore, whose dad was a GM employee for 33 years, is a model of documentarians at their finest. He forces society to see and hear unpleasant truths that are everyone's business.

1989 (R) 91m/C Michael Moore, Anita Bryant, Bob Eubanks, Pat Boone; ***D:*** Michael Moore; ***W:*** Michael Moore; ***C:*** Kevin Rafferty, Chris Beaver, John Prusak, Bruce Schermer. **VHS, LV, Closed Caption**

The Rolling Stones Rock and Roll Circus

Well, It just goes to show that artists can be their own worst critics. This film remained unreleased until 1996 because the Rolling Stones were concerned that they had been upstaged by the Who. In fact, *Rock and Roll Circus* was a great show then and would be a great show today with no qualifications. It's fun to watch John Lennon at his goofiest, to hear *Sympathy for the Devil* with the original Stones lineup, and to experience so many of the very best rock acts of 1968. To watch this film on a triple bill with David Maysles' *Gimme Shelter* and Lindsay-Hogg's *Let It Be* would be a wistful reminder of how much the world had...and lost...in a chillingly brief passage of time. *Rock and Roll Circus* was

"I have no profession. My attitude is quite an indefensible one, that as long as I'm no trouble to anyone, I have the right to do as I like. It is, I dare say, an example of my decadence."

—Cecil Vyse (Daniel Day-Lewis) in *A Room with a View.*

filmed in December 1968, the Beatles' last concert on a rooftop was filmed the following month, Brian Jones drowned on July 3, 1969, and by December 1969, the Stones (with new member Mick Taylor) were the centerpiece of the deadly concert at Altamont, California, that ended the decade with a harsh aftertaste. *Rock and Roll Circus* is such a great rediscovery, it makes me wonder: how many more filmed records of vintage concerts are collecting dust in vaults? 🦴🦴🦴

1968 65m/C *GB* Rolling Stones, Marianne Faithfull, John Lennon, Yoko Ono, Eric Clapton, Taj Mahal; ***D:*** Michael Lindsay-Hogg. **VHS, LV**

Room at the Top

Laurence Harvey (1928–73) is such a snide cad. He could have been the new George Sanders, except he didn't outlive him by very long. As Joe Lampton, he is an opportunistic slime, heartlessly seducing a rich man's daughter to advance himself. The woman Joe really wants is Alice (Simone Signoret, 1921–85), unhappily married to a twit named George Aisgill (Allan Cuthbertson, 1920–88). Why Alice wants a transparent hustler like Joe is a mystery, but want him she does and she is devastated when he leaves her to marry well. Joe is beaten brutally before the so-called "happy ending," actually a grim resignation to a much grimmer fate, since his bride Susan (Heather Sears, 1935–94) knows that they can never be happy. There was a follow-up film in 1965: Joe Lampton, his in-laws, and George Aisgill are all back in *Life at the Top,* but Jean Simmons has replaced Heather Sears and Honor Blackman plays Joe's new sexual diversion when he isn't playing local politics. The stakes had been reduced, because Lampton had already sold his soul and his humanity in the first film. By 1973's *Man at the Top,* Kenneth Haigh was Joe Lampton, dealing with unfamiliar characters in another game altogether. What made *Room at the Top* so special was the moral tension between Joe and Alice as each sees a different sort of life reflected in the other's eyes. When Simone Signoret won the Best Actress Oscar, it would be 37 years before another French actress (Juliette Binoche for *The English Patient*) would bring home the Academy Award. Based on the novel by John Braine. 🦴🦴🦴🦴

1959 118m/B *GB* Laurence Harvey, Simone Signoret, Heather Sears, Hermione Baddeley, Avril Ungar, Donald Wolfit, Wendy Craig, Allan Cuthbertson, Ian Hendry, Donald Houston, Raymond Huntley, Miriam Karlin, Wilfred Lawson, Richard Pasco, Mary Peach, Prunella Scales, Beatrice Varley, John Westbrook; ***D:*** Jack Clayton; ***W:*** Neil Paterson; ***C:*** Freddie Francis; ***M:*** Mario Nascimbene. Academy Awards '59: Best Actress (Signoret), Best Adapted Screenplay; British Academy Awards '58: Best Actress (Signoret), Best Film; Cannes Film Festival '59: Best Actress (Signoret); Nominations: Academy Awards '59: Best Actor (Harvey), Best Director (Clayton), Best Picture, Best Supporting Actress (Baddeley). **VHS**

A Room with a View

Here's the deal: Helena Bonham Carter is in love with Julian Sands, but she settles for Daniel Day-Lewis (who isn't cute like he was in *My Beautiful Laundrette,* but rather resembles a gopher). What on Earth is that unhappy lovesick girl going to do? This is the central story of E.M. Forster's *A Room with a View,* along with the usual meticulous examination of Edwardian England that is *de rigeur* for all three of the Merchant-Ivory films based on the works of E.M. Forster. (The others are *Maurice* and *Howard's End.*) Bonham Carter and Sands are the quintessential romantic couple, circa 1908, and Venice has never been so photogenic. An Oscar winner for its screenplay, art direction, and costumes, *A Room with a View* also received nominations for Best Picture, for director James Ivory, and for Denholm Elliott and Maggie Smith (Smith is a hoot as always as Carter's aunt). Two other Forster adaptations are David Lean's *A Passage to India* and Charles Sturridge's *Where Angels Fear to Tread.* 🦴🦴🦴🦴

1986 117m/C *GB* Helena Bonham Carter, Julian Sands, Denholm Elliott, Maggie Smith, Judi Dench, Simon Callow, Daniel Day-Lewis, Rupert Graves, Rosemary Leach; ***D:*** James Ivory; ***W:*** Ruth Prawer Jhabvala; ***C:*** Tony Pierce-Roberts. Academy Awards '86: Best Adapted Screenplay, Best Art Direction/

Set Decoration, Best Costume Design; British Academy Awards '86: Best Actress (Smith), Best Film, Best Supporting Actress (Dench); Golden Globe Awards '87: Best Supporting Actress (Smith); Independent Spirit Awards '87: Best Foreign Film; National Board of Review Awards '86: Best Supporting Actor (Day-Lewis); New York Film Critics Awards '86: Best Cinematography, Best Supporting Actor (Day-Lewis); Writers Guild of America '86: Best Adapted Screenplay; Nominations: Academy Awards '86: Best Cinematography, Best Director (Ivory), Best Picture, Best Supporting Actor (Elliott), Best Supporting Actress (Smith). **VHS, LV, Closed Caption**

The Rosary Murders

The Rosary Murders does an admirable job of tackling one of film's most unyielding subjects. It is extremely difficult for non-Catholics and Catholics alike to understand the vow of silence taken by Catholic confessors when human lives are at stake. Perhaps only another priest can identify with the agony faced by Father Donald Sutherland when he hears the confession and learns the identity of a murderer who has every intention of murdering again. Unlike many recent crime sagas, the film makes its victims real and it does not sweeten the character of the killer by showing him as a nice guy flawed with sexual and psychological quirks. It does fall prey to the movie cliche of the pretty woman who falls for the priest, and it also drags in the bombastic Detroit pastor with a mind lock on arbitrary problem solving, which clouds his understanding of church law. As portrayed by Charles Durning, this egomaniac is to Catholic priests what Shelley Winters is to Jewish mothers. The stereotype does exist, but in a film that strains away from the obvious in so many other ways, its inclusion is both unimaginative and regrettable. The acting is otherwise quite good, Elmore Leonard's complex script based on William Kienzle's novel is directed with subtlety by Fred Walton, and the details that give the film its density are very well chosen.

1987 (R) 105m/C Donald Sutherland, Charles Durning, Belinda Bauer, Josef Sommer, James Murtaugh, John Danelle, Addison Powell, Janet Smith, Kathleen Tolan; ***D:*** Fred Walton; ***W:*** Fred Walton, Elmore Leonard; ***C:*** David Golia. **VHS, LV, Closed Caption**

Rouge

Stanley Kwan's *Rouge* is an extremely interesting ghost story about a lovely wraith who returns to Hong Kong in the 1980s searching for her lover, with whom she had made a suicide pact over half a century before. The fine acting by Anita Mui as the ghost and by Alex Man and Emily Chu as the young couple who try to help her, plus Bill Wong's excellent camera work, helped to make *Rouge* an award winner in Taiwan. Anita Mui was Kwan's first choice to play the late legendary actress Ruan Ling-Yu in 1992's *Centre Stage/The Actress* (she was replaced by Maggie Cheung). ***AKA:*** Yanzhi Kou.

1987 99m/C *HK* Anita Mui, Leslie Cheung, Alex Man, Emily Chu; ***D:*** Stanley Kwan; ***W:*** Lei Bik Wah, Chiu Tai An-Ping; ***C:*** Bill Wong; ***M:*** Michael Lai. **VHS**

Ruby in Paradise

At the risk of sounding cranky...forget it, I don't care...*Ruby in Paradise* DOES make me cranky! Ashley Judd is a wonderful actress, and I hope she wins an Academy Award some spring night in the not-too-distant future, but watching *Ruby in Paradise* is like watching (1) grass grow, (2) paint dry, (3) writers write, AND (4) pigeons sleep ALL AT THE SAME TIME! Put some meat on the bones of this script! Give Ruby something to DO into which she can really sink her teeth! Never mind, there are too many folks who love *Ruby in Paradise* exactly the way it is to adjust its sluggish pace at this point. Now I've seen what Judd can do with a juicy role, like Pam Anderson in *Normal Life* and Norma Jean in *Norma Jean and Marilyn,* watching her wander through a plotless flick like this one simply isn't MY idea of Paradise.

1993 (R) 115m/C Ashley Judd, Todd Field, Bentley Mitchum, Allison Dean, Dorothy Lyman, Betsy Dowds; ***D:*** Victor Nunez; ***W:*** Victor Nunez; ***C:*** Alex Vlacos; ***M:*** Charles Engstrom. Independent Spirit Awards '94: Best Actress (Judd); Sundance Film Festival '93: Grand Jury Prize; Nominations: Independent Spirit Awards '94: Best Cinematography, Best Director (Nunez), Best Film, Best Screenplay, Best Supporting Actor (Field). **VHS, LV, Closed Caption**

Jean Renoir's *The Rules of the Game.* Nouvelle Editions; courtesy of the Kobal Collection

The Rules of the Game

Remember this when you read a book of reviews or even a single review, really. When *The Rite of Spring* was first performed in 1913, with its composer in attendance, it was BOOED! Quite rightly, Igor Stravinsky, then 31, said, "Go to Hell!" and kept right on being Igor Stravinsky for another 58 years. When *The Rules of the Game* first premiered in 1939, it, too, was booed! Even worse, it was banned for 20 years. Only when it was politically safe for the world to appreciate *The Rules of the Game* was it finally recognized as Jean Renoir's masterpiece. What do audiences and reviewers know about cutting edge art that addresses the world in a way that is new, uncomfortable, and even threatening? We're none of us omniscient prophets. After the rise to power of the National Socialists in 1933 and the signing of the Munich Pact in the fall of 1938, you didn't have to be an omniscient prophet to see what was happening in Europe. No one wanted war, and Jean Renoir (1894–1979) was not a politician, but a deeply concerned writer and director. He decided to address the pre-war atmosphere in a film with satire, violence, comedy, and death. Marcel Dalio, who played the croupier in *Casablanca* four years later, is the amiable Marquis de la Chesnaye, who presides over the aristocratic game players at the Chateau la Coliniere, and a lying, cheating lot they are, too. Empty courtesies are paramount in this amoral playground where truth and honor have no place. Only a few conduct themselves according to clashing ethical codes that are clearly outdated. French audiences resented Renoir's social critique and they detested *The Rules of the Game.* Renoir, who had made an honest film in an essentially dishonest era, tried hard to edit and revise the film, but nothing would have helped at that point. The film was finally banned and the negative was destroyed when the laboratory in which it

was stored was hit by allied bombers. Jacques Durand and Jean Gaborit painstakingly restored the film, which is why we're lucky enough to enjoy this unique treasure today. ***AKA:*** Le Regle du Jeu.

1939 110m/B Marcel Dalio, Nora Gregor, Jean Renoir, Mila Parely, Julien Carette, Gaston Modot, Roland Toutain, Paulette Dubost, Odette Talazac; ***D:*** Jean Renoir; ***W:*** Jean Renoir. **VHS, LV, 8mm**

The Runaway Bus

The late comic Frankie Howerd (1921–92) was a great favorite in Great Britain, but he's still an acquired taste for many Americans. He was in excellent company for *The Ladykillers, Mouse on the Moon,* and *Carry on Doctor,* and his co-stars here give him terrific support for this first film. The premise is that the bad guys have hidden 200,000 pounds on the airport bus (this is before the devaluation of the pound when such an amount represented a cool million bucks in 1954 money) and the oblivious Percy Lamb (Howerd) is driving. What's more, the fog is thicker than pea soup. Who are the bad guys? It could be any of the usual suspects: Margaret Rutherford (1892–1972) as Miss Cynthia Beeston (halfway between her days as Madame Arcati and as Miss Jane Marple) OR Petula Clark as coach hostess Miss Lee Nichols OR delightful Belinda Lee (1935–61) as crime buff Miss Janie Grey OR George Coulouris (1903–89) as Edward Schroeder OR Toke Townley (1912–84) as gardening expert Henry Waterman OR Terence Alexander, then 31, in uniform as Peter Jones. All play their roles with obvious zest and the inevitable solution to the mystery clearly takes a back seat to the comedy. The wildly different styles of Rutherford and Lee are especially fun to watch. The less-challenging English rose part played by Clark, then 22, was one of the reasons she abandoned the movie career she began at age 12 for the more lucrative status of popular recording artist by 1964.

1954 78m/B *GB* Frankie Howerd, Margaret Rutherford, Petula Clark, George Coulouris, Belinda Lee, Reginald Beckwith, Terence Alexander, Toke Townley, John Horsley, Anthony Oliver, Stringer Davis, Lisa Gastoni, Frank Phillips; ***D:*** Val Guest; ***W:*** Val Guest; ***C:*** Stanley Pavey; ***M:*** Ronald Binge. **VHS**

Sabotage

Remember when Hitchcock played a cameo in *Blackmail* as a subway passenger being bothered by a little boy? In *Sabotage,* he created considerable suspense by showing a young boy as he dawdled through the city streets while carrying a bomb timed to explode. By creating tension through rapid cross-cutting and then relieving it with horror, Hitchcock tried to do something that was quite a few decades ahead of its time. The audiences of his own time were horrified and outraged, and he decided never to do THAT again. Only he did, many times—he just played with the audience's sense of morality; it was perfectly all right, he found, to relieve tension with horror if the character was a mean lesbian (Judith Anderson in *Rebecca*), a treacherous spy (Edmund Gwenn or Herbert Marshall in *Foreign Correspondent* or Norman Lloyd in *Saboteur*), a Merry Widow killer (Joseph Cotten in *Shadow of a Doubt*), a hired poseur (Kim Novak in *Vertigo*), a thief (Janet Leigh in *Psycho*), or a barmaid (Anna Massey) just dumb enough to trust Barry Foster. Only make sure that Doris Day sings "Que Sera, Sera" until her kid is rescued! *Sabotage* has a good performance by Sylvia Sidney, who resolves to Do Something about the boy's death, plus the usual menacing turn by Oscar Homolka, and the usual masculine turn by the powerfully built John Loder. As for Desmond Tester, who played the unlucky Steve, *Sabotage* was the fourth of nine films he made between 1935 and 1939. His next character as a child prodigy was so obnoxious that the future cast and crew of 1937's *Non-Stop New York* (including John Loder) might have reacted with cynicism if he'd taken a flying leap into the stratosphere without benefit of a parachute. ***AKA:*** A Woman Alone; Hidden Power.

1936 81m/B Oscar Homolka, Sylvia Sidney, John Loder, Desmond Tester, Joyce Barbour, Matthew Boulton, S. J. Warmington, William Dewhurst, Austin Trevor, Torin Thatcher, Aubrey Mather, Peter Bull,

The Hound Salutes:
SYLVIA SIDNEY
Sabotage, You Only Live Once, Dead End

Sylvia Sidney picked up a whole new generation of fans when she played a harried case worker in 1988's *Beetlejuice.* Sharp and wry, with a gravelly voice and impeccable timing, Sidney proved that she was just as magnetic a screen presence in 1988 as she had been in 1931 when she first electrified Depression-era audiences in films like *City Streets, An American Tragedy,* and *Street Scene.* With her dahlia-like face and soft, sweet voice, Sidney looked small and extremely delicate. Her fragile appearance was definitely deceptive, as Alfred Hitchcock realized when he hired Sidney to drive a knife into Oscar Homolka's stomach in 1936's *Sabotage*! Sidney also starred in the Fritz Lang classics *Fury* and *You Only Live Once,* playing women who were driven to consider violent extremes when the men they loved were trapped by an unjust society. Sidney also created a vivid impression in William Wyler's *Dead End* as a Depression-weary heroine struggling to make a better life for herself.

Sidney made dozens of films during the '30s. Unfortunately, she was so identified with the decade that she found it hard to find work after it was over. She appeared opposite tough guys Humphrey Bogart, James Cagney, George Raft, and John Hodiak in the '40s and made just three films in the '50s. Luckily, television was able to provide her with over 30 meaty roles, and she won an Emmy nomination in 1962 for her work in a two-part *Defenders* episode. She went on to make 15 more movies for television between 1971 and 1985, so she was in no way retired when she emerged as an Oscar contender in 1973 for *Summer Wishes, Winter Dreams.* She later appeared in *I Never Promised You a Rose Garden* and other big-screen projects, including 1996's *Mars Attacks,* her latest film. Sylvia Sidney, who is not in the least bit nostalgic over her former career as a major star, is famous for her remark: "What's the use of talking about a favorite role if you can't get it? The role you're doing ought to be your favorite."

SYLVIA SIDNEY on video: *The Trail of the Lonesome Pine, You and Me, One Third of a Nation, Blood on the Sun, Mr. Ace, Love from a Stranger, Death at Love House, Demon, Snowbeast, Rain on Entebbe, Damien: Omen 2, The Shadow Box, A Small Killing, Having It All, Hammett, Finnegan Begin Again, Corrupt, Come along with Me, An Early Frost, Pals,* and *Used People.*

Charles Hawtrey, Martita Hunt, Hal Walters, Frederick Piper; ***D:*** Alfred Hitchcock; ***W:*** Charles Bennett, Ian Hay, Alma Reville, E.V.H. Emmett, Helen Simpson; ***C:*** Bernard Knowles. **VHS, LV, 8mm**

Safe

Safe is an unforgettable viewing experience in a theatre. I don't know that I'd want to see it on the small screen, though. Writer/director Todd Haynes makes no concession to his film's eventual release on video. Protagonist Carol is frequently shown in extreme long shots, the better to emphasize how engulfed she is by the threatening environment. This perspective works wonderfully well as Carol's health is drained away from her and she seeks increasingly radical solutions over the course of two hours. Do try to see *Safe* in a theatre so you can catch Julianne Moore's outstanding performance (AND her paranoia) without binoculars! 🦴🦴🦴

1995 (R) 119m/C Julianne Moore, Peter Friedman, Xander Berkeley, Susan Norman, James LeGros, Mary Carver, Kate McGregor Stewart, Jessica Harper, Brandon Cruz; ***D:*** Todd Haynes; ***W:*** Todd Haynes; ***C:*** Alex Nepomniaschy; ***M:*** Ed Tomney. Nominations: Independent Spirit Awards '96: Best Actress (Moore), Best Director (Haynes), Best Film, Best Screenplay. **VHS, LV, Closed Caption**

Salmonberries

k.d. lang wants to be an actor in the worst way. And she's succeeding...in the worst way. Anyone catch her on ABC's historic *Ellen* episode April 30, 1997? Okay, so that was a bit. But she had entire sequences in Mario Puzo's *The Last Don* on May 13–14, 1997, yelling about art as Daryl Hannah's movie director. (CBS claimed a national audience of 30 million for this small-screen *Godfather.*) lang's reactions reminded me of someone. Could it possibly be Madonna in the 1987 bow-wow, *Who's That Girl?* Yes, and it also reminded me of k.d. lang in the little-seen Percy Adlon film *Salmonberries.* Adlon, who'd enjoyed considerable success with *Celeste, The Last Five Days, Sugar Baby, Bagdad Cafe, Rosalie Goes Shopping,* and *Younger and Younger,* could NOT attract a U.S. distributor for *Salmonberries!* Finally, San Francisco's Roxie Cinema agreed to screen it in early 1994. Co-starring Rosel Zech (so good as *Veronika Voss* for Fassbinder in 1982) and Chuck Connors (perhaps hoping that this flick would do for his career what *Bagdad Cafe* had done for Jack Palance), *Salmonberries* is listed as a 1989 credit in at least one Chuck Connors filmography. The Berlin Wall had already been opened by that time, a reality that dates the story since Zech had tried to escape Berlin with her lover, who was killed in the attempt. Somehow, Zech carries on and winds up in Alaska with lang as her lover. It is odd to watch a fine actor like Zech play sequences with someone who can barely act at all; not exactly fascinating, but...weird. lang sings the same song over and over again on the soundtrack. Connors (1921–92) has very little to do. I wonder if they actually had to go to Alaska to shoot this thing. Anyway, lang's agent has undoubtedly been instructed to look for other parts to diversify lang's career. Think of the possibilities.... 🦴

1991 (R) 94m/C *GE CA* Rosel Zech, k.d. lang, Chuck Connors, Jane Lind, Oscar Kawagley, Wolfgang Steinberg, Wayne Waterman, Christel Merian; ***D:*** Percy Adlon; ***W:*** Percy Adlon, Felix Adlon; ***C:*** Tom Sigel. **VHS**

Salut Victor!

Salut Victor! was a wonderfully appealing opening night entry at 1989's San Francisco's Lesbian and Gay Film Festival. The plot revolves around two elderly men in a rather posh health care facility. Both are gay, but Philippe Lanctot (Jean-Louis Roux) is restrained and a bit of a prude, while Victor Laprade (Jacques Godin) is a flamboyant hedonist. Although the two men could not be less alike, they become friends and Philippe realizes that he is enjoying life for the first time in many years. A visit to Philippe's club/restaurant becomes an exciting adventure with the rambunctious Victor as company, and their plans to take a balloon ride together are as much fun as the ride itself would have been. Very well acted and directed. ***AKA:*** Bye Bye Victor. 🦴🦴🦴

1989 84m/C Jean-Louis Roux, Jacques Godin; ***D:*** Anne Claire Poirier; ***W:*** Marthe Blackburn; ***C:*** Michel Brault; ***M:*** Joel Vincent Bienvenue. **VHS**

Salvador

If for no other reason than the hilarious sequence where James Woods as Richard Boyle pays his first visit to the confessional in 32 years, *Salvador* would be ingrained in my consciousness forever. But *Salvador,* co-written by Boyle and based on his own experiences as a photojournalist in El Salvador, gets underneath my skin for its entire 123-minute running time. Boyle is unsparing of his own flaws, and Woods may have missed out on an Oscar because he didn't try to weaken its searing honesty in any way. James Belushi is also very good as Doctor Rock, and if you want your heart tugged all the way down to your toes, check out Cynthia Gibb's perfor-

"You've got to think of the people first. In the name of human decency, something we Americans are supposed to believe in, you got to at least try to make something of a just society here."

—Richard Boyle (James Woods) in *Salvador.*

mance as Cathy Moore. Woods as Boyle develops a conscience in spite of himself in this gritty account of life in El Salvador in 1980–81.

1986 (R) 123m/C James Woods, James Belushi, John Savage, Michael Murphy, Elpidia Carrillo, Cynthia Gibb, Tony Plana, Colby Chester, Will MacMillan, Jose Carlos Ruiz, Jorge Luke, Juan Fernandez, Valerie Wildman; ***D:*** Oliver Stone; ***W:*** Oliver Stone, Richard Boyle; ***C:*** Robert Richardson; ***M:*** Georges Delerue. Independent Spirit Awards '87: Best Actor (Woods); Nominations: Academy Awards '86: Best Actor (Woods), Best Original Screenplay. **VHS, LV, Closed Caption**

Sammy & Rosie Get Laid

Stephen Frears' *Sammy & Rosie Get Laid* is every bit as unsettling to viewers as its title was to theatrical exhibitors. This is a densely plotted story about a London couple whose unconventional life is changed when the husband's father arrives on the scene from Pakistan. The father, played by Indian star Shashi Kapoor, is responsible for atrocities back home, but he is unprepared for the war zone he finds in London, following the real-life killing of a black woman by a policeman. American viewers will also find screenwriter Hanif Kureishi's visions of riot-torn streets disturbing. The world of the Queen and her Prime Ministers is one that can be entered only by the most privileged of blacks and Pakistanis, or by the children who offer them flowers. The rest live in a world where violence is always near and where sex is an acceptable escape. *Sammy & Rosie* is so complex it would benefit from repeated viewings, but the performances by Kapoor, Claire Bloom, and newcomers Ayub Khan Din and Frances Barber are as clear as a bell.

1987 97m/C *GB* Shashi Kapoor, Frances Barber, Claire Bloom, Ayub Khan Din, Roland Gift, Wendy Gazelle, Meera Syal; ***D:*** Stephen Frears; ***W:*** Hanif Kureishi; ***C:*** Oliver Stapleton; ***M:*** Stanley Myers. **VHS, LV**

Saraband for Dead Lovers

Forget H.R.H. Charles, The Prince of Wales, and return to the days when H.R.H. Prince George-Louis of Hanover was so mean to his wife Sophie-Dorothea that he divorced her 20 years before he ever became H.M. King George I and imprisoned her in the castle of Ahlden for the last 32 years of her life. She was forbidden to see her children after the divorce, and her ex-husband hated the future King George II just because he looked like his mother. Strong stuff, and who better to play George-Louis and Sophie-Dorothea than Peter Bull (1912–84, one of Britain's best heavies from 1934 on) and Joan Greenwood (1921–87, one of Britain's most regal leading ladies from 1940 on)? *Saraband for Dead Lovers* was released a couple of months before Prince Charles' birth in 1948, and like it or don't, he owes his very existence to the sad and lonely woman so rarely mentioned in the history books. As a vivacious teen, Sophie-Dorothea didn't want to marry a cold fish like George-Louis, and she frequently asked her father if a divorce were ever possible. After 11 years of this so-called marriage, she fell in love with Count Philip Koenigsmark of Sweden (who better than eminently attractive Stewart Granger, 1913–93?). The lovers planned to run away together, and then...in agreement with many scholars, *Saraband* speculates on what happened next. *Saraband* is an intelligent historical romance, with colorful court schemers (Flora Robson is outstanding as Countess Platen) and well-mounted spectacle. And Greenwood and Granger strike considerable sparks as the dead lovers from another time. Over three centuries later, when will the descendants of the Hanoverians ever learn?

1948 96m/C *GB* Stewart Granger, Joan Greenwood, Francoise Rosay, Flora Robson, Frederick Valk, Peter Bull, Anthony Quayle, Megs Jenkins, Michael Gough, David Horne, Miles Malleson, Allan Jeayes, Guy Rolfe; ***D:*** Basil Dearden; ***W:*** John Dighton, Alexander MacKendrick; ***C:*** Douglas Slocombe. **VHS**

Scandal

Even more so than the Americans, the British seem particularly vulnerable to sex scandals. Sex is essential for producing heirs, but the preservation of appearances often seems to be far more essential. Not that it matters, but the Profumo scandal of 1963 has always seemed like much ado about nothing. It certainly didn't deserve to lead to suicide, betrayal, exile, social ostracism, and political disgrace. The centerpiece of the scandal was an artistic, name-dropping osteopath named Dr. Stephen Ward, sensitively portrayed in *Scandal* by John Hurt. Ward liked to surround himself with "good time girls" (prostitutes is too strong a word) and never seemed to get laid himself. The best that Ward could hope for was to increase his sphere of influence by encouraging the liaisons of his protegees with potential dukes and lords. One big mystery in the scandal is why Christine Keeler was worth (as she claims) even a five-night stand when Mrs. Profumo was the beautiful and elegant Valerie Hobson. Hobson, star of such classics as *Bride of Frankenstein, Great Expectations,* and *Kind Hearts and Coronets,* had given up a long and successful film career to marry Profumo in 1954, and she remained loyal to him before, during, and after the scandal. One hot Saturday night on July 8, 1961, the couple attended a party at the Cliveden estate of Lord and Lady Astor where they met Ward, Keeler, and Eugene "Honey Bear" Ivanov, a Soviet attache. *Scandal* fudges on certain details. A wife would have to be brain dead not to see the sexual games between Profumo and Keeler as they are shown in the film. In real life, Keeler's friend Mandy Rice-Davies named Valerie Hobson's former co-star, Douglas Fairbanks Jr., as one of her lovers. His name is changed to David Fairfax Jr. in the film. The actual son-in-law of Fairbanks, Richard Morant, appears in *Scandal* as a playboy. Britt Ekland, described by her former husband, the late Peter Sellers, as "a professional girlfriend and an amateur actress" is sixth-billed as a party hostess at an orgy. *Scandal* is mostly Hurt's film, although Joanne Whalley is quite good as Christine. As Mandy Rice-Davies, Bridget Fonda extends her family's onscreen charisma to the third generation. Ian McKellen isn't given much to say or do with the role of Profumo. The film solicits intense sympathy for Keeler and Ward and largely succeeds, thanks to Hurt and Whalley. Director Michael Caton-Jones films the first half of the picture rather like a comedy. All the childish games appear to be great fun, which they probably were while they lasted. Even in 1963, the notion of a War Minister sharing military secrets with a five-night stand must have seemed fantastic to anyone but a Big Mouth with a vivid imagination like Stephen Ward. But there's no compassionate grown up around to protect these adult youngsters from hurting themselves, and hurt themselves they did, until revisionist filmmakers romanticized them for 1989 audiences. 🦴🦴🦴🦴

1989 (R) 105m/C *GB* John Hurt, Joanne Whalley, Ian McKellen, Bridget Fonda, Jeroen Krabbe, Britt Ekland, Roland Gift, Daniel Massey, Leslie Phillips, Richard Morant; ***D:*** Michael Caton-Jones; ***W:*** Michael Thomas; ***C:*** Mike Molloy; ***M:*** Carl Davis. **VHS, LV**

The Scarlet Pimpernel

The Scarlet Pimpernel must have been Margaret Truman's favorite film while her father Harry was President; she arranged for it to be screened no less than 16 times, according to *Guinness' Movie Facts and Feats.* This picture has absolutely everything. Leslie Howard is exactly what a stylish dandy AND a shrewd renegade should be. Even with all the swashbuckling, Howard as Sir Percival Blakeney comes up with some astonishingly subtle moments, like when he must conceal that he's madly in love with his wife (gorgeous Merle Oberon), whom he believes to be a traitor. Raymond Massey is rather a one-note Chauvelin, though. If you want to see how the part can be played to perfection, see the 1982 version with Ian McKellen in which lust, jealousy, rage, and revenge are brilliantly conveyed with the simplest of gestures and with slight, vivid shifts of expression. *The Scarlet Pimpernel* consolidated the enormous impact producer Alexander Korda had made on American audiences with 1933's *The Private Life of Henry VIII,* starring the Oscar-winning

"Just because it happened to you does not make it interesting."

—Dr. Waxling (Dennis Hopper) in *Search and Destroy.*

Charles Laughton. In many ways, this is a richer, more complex yarn, but the Motion Picture Academy members, still reeling from the previous year, only nominated domestic productions in 1934. ♥♥♥♥

1934 95m/B *GB* Leslie Howard, Joan Gardner, Merle Oberon, Raymond Massey, Anthony Bushell, Nigel Bruce, Bramwell Fletcher, Walter Rilla, O.B. Clarence, Ernest Milton, Edmund Breon, Melville Cooper, Gibb McLaughlin, Morland Graham, Allan Jeayes; ***D:*** Harold Young; ***W:*** Robert Sherwood, Arthur Wimperis, Lajos Biro; ***C:*** Harold Rosson. **VHS, DVD**

Scenes from a Marriage

The runaway hit of 1974's San Francisco International Film Festival was this searing entry by Ingmar Bergman, originally made for Swedish television. In spite of its length (168 minutes, cut down from 360 minutes), Bergman uses every second, exploring the hardest of truths about the relationship between two people. Sven Nykvist's flawless camera work doesn't let us leave Liv Ullman and Erland Josephson for very long, and everything else blends beautifully in this masterful film. Ullman's gem of a performance will haunt you for years. ♥♥♥♥

1973 (PG) 168m/C *SW* Liv Ullmann, Erland Josephson, Bibi Andersson, Jan Malmsjo, Anita Wall; ***D:*** Ingmar Bergman; ***W:*** Ingmar Bergman; ***C:*** Sven Nykvist. Golden Globe Awards '75: Best Foreign Film; New York Film Critics Awards '74: Best Actress (Ullmann), Best Screenplay; National Society of Film Critics Awards '74: Best Actress (Ullmann), Best Film, Best Screenplay, Best Supporting Actress (Andersson). **VHS**

Scenes from the Class Struggle in Beverly Hills

Viewers who see Paul Bartel's *Scenes from the Class Struggle in Beverly Hills* will either love it or hate it. I hated it, even though it wasn't worth hating. There's a mean-spirited streak to this self-styled "restoration comedy," something that might seem hilarious to Bartel and his aficionados. And for all Bartel's efforts to outrage, stale situations are recycled, old stereotypes are revived, and talented actors are wasted. Jacqueline Bisset's performance, for example, seems like an audition for a *Dynasty* revival, since Joan Collins' character has presumably been killed off with a back flip off a balcony. Sample dialogue, Bisset to servant: "You're not supposed to think, you're supposed to wrap brussel sprouts in bacon." Robert Beltran and real-life AIDS victim Ray Sharkey make a bet that whoever goes to bed with his employer first, wins. Sharkey's prize is anal intercourse with Beltran and no condoms in sight. Beltran rides off with Mary Woronov; this is happily ever after? A bad writer played by Ed Begley Jr. arrives with bride Arnetia Walker, who's mistaken for a servant at first because she's black. She has anal intercourse with one of the men, and fools around with a leukemia-ridden teen. Et cetera. There's also a young girl (real-life murder victim Rebecca Schaeffer) who winds up traipsing off with the diet doctor played by Paul Bartel (who looks something like three and a half times her age), a dog named Bojangles (don't get too attached to him...), a fat ghost played by Paul Mazursky, a womanizing gynecologist played by Wallace Shawn, and a Mexican maid played by Edith Diaz. Sexual chemistry between any two of these characters chosen at random is ZERO. There is one funny bit in which a porn video is recreated, complete with bad acting and fractured pronunciations. But the humor in the sequence is stifled by the fact that we have to watch it with the dying (and masturbating) kid. Another false note is struck when Bartel shows a journalist running away in horror after listening to the frank language of Bisset and her friends at the breakfast table. Oh, please...journalists are more likely to react in horror to the size of their paychecks. It would take far more than rude behavior at breakfast to shock them, much less horrify them. Watching *Scenes from the Class Struggle in Beverly Hills* is like being a four a.m. straggler at a very dull party. Check out 1982's much funnier *Eating Raoul* with Bartel, Woronov, and Beltran instead. **woof!**

1989 (R) 103m/C Jacqueline Bisset, Ray Sharkey, Mary Woronov, Robert Beltran, Ed Begley Jr., Wallace Shawn, Paul Bartel, Paul Mazursky, Arnetia Walker, Rebecca Schaeffer, Edith Diaz; ***Cameos:*** Little Richard; ***D:*** Paul Bartel; ***W:*** Bruce Wagner; ***C:*** Steven Fierberg; ***M:*** Stanley Myers. **VHS, LV**

Search and Destroy

Once again, I'm giving a movie an extra half bone for the presence of Illeana Douglas, because she's such a scene-stealing treat to watch. (And that's no mean feat in a flick that co-stars Dennis Hopper, Christopher Walken, and John Turturro.) Until 1996's *Grace of My Heart* was released, I combed the video shelves for ANY movie with Douglas in it: 1991's *Cape Fear,* 1993's *Alive* and *Household Saints,* 1994's *Grief,* 1995's *To Die For,* and this flick by David Salle, which might have been even wilder if Michael *(Twister, Nadja)* Almereyda had directed his own screenplay. Someone, PUH-LEEZE make the terrific Illeana Douglas a name above the title STAR!!!

1994 (R) 91m/C Griffin Dunne, Dennis Hopper, Rosanna Arquette, Christopher Walken, John Turturro, Illeana Douglas, Ethan Hawke; ***Cameos:*** Martin Scorsese; ***D:*** David Salle; ***W:*** Michael Almereyda; ***C:*** Michael Spiller, Bobby Bukowski; ***M:*** Elmer Bernstein. **VHS, LV, Closed Caption**

Seclusion near a Forest

Seclusion is about a family and their efforts to obtain a summer cottage. It is also the story of how people adjust to their own needs for territory and how they reconcile themselves to other people's morality. At first, the family waits for their old landlord to go away or die so they can have the place to themselves. Later, they grow to depend on his strength and common sense. Josef Kemr is wonderful as the old man and Jiri Menzel *(Closely Watched Trains)* explores the gentle themes here with humor and insight. ***AKA:*** Na Samote u Lesa.

1976 92m/C *CZ* Zdenek Sverak, Jan Triska, Josef Kemr, Ladislav Smoljak; ***D:*** Jiri Menzel; ***W:*** Zdenek Sverak, Ladislav Smoljak; ***C:*** Jaromir Sofr; ***M:*** Jiri Sust.

The Second Awakening of Christa Klages

This West German film is essentially a simplistic fairy tale, but so well acted, scripted, and directed that its many implausibilities can be forgiven. Tina Engel, in the title role, commits a "political" robbery with a pair of male cohorts when her kindergarten becomes strapped for funds. The rest of the film shows how she deals with the consequences of her crime. Her colleagues refuse to accept the money and a female witness pursues her, in this feminist variation on *Les Miserables.* Engel, a plain and chunky yet attractive actress, is excellent as Christa, her performance enhanced by a superb supporting cast, including the entrancing Peter Schneider in a romantic role. Margarete von Trotta does a forceful job directing her own script (co-written with Luisa Francia). Franz Rath's expert camera work and Klaus Doldinger's effective score add to the suspense. ***AKA:*** Das Zweite Erwachen der Christa Klages.

1978 90m/C *GE* Tina Engel, Sylvia Reize, Marius Muller-Westernhagen, Peter Schneider, Katharina Thalbach; ***D:*** Margarethe von Trotta; ***W:*** Margarethe von Trotta, Luisa Francia; ***C:*** Franz Rath; ***M:*** Klaus Doldinger. **VHS**

Second Coming of Suzanne

When I saw *Second Coming* (with its creator in attendance), it was a total embarrassment, wasting its talented cast, and deserving of every BOO it got. If you don't mind being exploited by self-indulgent, chest-beating harangues against exploitation, enjoy! Inspired by the Leonard Cohen song and made in the San Francisco Bay area, the film's executive producer was Michael's proud father, Gene Barry.

1980 90m/C Sondra Locke, Richard Dreyfuss, Gene Barry, Paul Sand, Jared Martin; ***D:*** Michael Barry; ***W:*** Michael Barry; ***C:*** Isidore Mankofsky. **VHS**

Michael Lally and Jeni Courtney in *The Secret of Roan Inish.* First Look Pictures; courtesy of the Kobal Collection

Secret Honor

As a woman without much money or power, I confess to more than mild curiosity about what happens when rich and powerful men gather in the Bohemian Grove and do whatever it is they do. In an era when tabloid scribes scavenge celebrity dust bins in search of gossip, the Bohemian Grove remains a secret. No one crawls on his or her stomach with precious cameras and recording devices to violate the inviolate. I mention this because a fictional Richard Milhous Nixon in *Secret Honor* describes what he had to do to a fictional Nelson Aldrich Rockefeller in the Bohemian Grove on the way to the White House. Nowadays, government secrets are as accessible as ants at a picnic, but I suspect that the secrets of the Bohemian Grove are meant for a lifetime beyond my own. Despite my admiration for director Robert Altman, I wouldn't have rented *Secret Honor* to learn more about the aforementioned fictional R.M.N. I rented it because I watched Philip Baker Hall play Sydney in *Hard Eight* and I wanted to see more of Hall's work. Sydney is a man with a secret, but he knows where he's been, what he's done, and who he is. The fictional R.M.N. doesn't. It is not only his loss, but ours as well. Throughout the course of *Secret Honor,* we observe the regret that R.M.N. feels when he has tried to curry favor with someone who can't stand him. He admires, respects, even likes the people who subsequently became his personal and political enemies. Hall's approach to the role is an extension of what anyone who lived during all or part of R.M.N.'s lifetime (1913–94) could not fail to observe. He always looked like the kid an authority figure might force you to hang out with. You'd be whispering with your friends and then..."SSSHHH! There's Dick Nixon again. I'll tell you more LATER!" A big fake smile would appear in his eyes and on his mouth, but not on the rest of his face. That's how you could tell his smile wasn't real. He gave the impression of being an underdog, and, if you were dumb enough to believe that impression, he took fierce advantage of you. He seemed to count on his fingers the times that he was wrong, but his elaborate rationales showed that he never ever BELIEVED he was wrong. Hall captures all this and more: the choked impulses, the fury that lashes out in jagged fragments of incoherence, the reverence for his mother, his awe for the beauty of Helen Gahagan Douglas (whom he still attacked in his campaign like a savage pit bull), the venom he felt for the charm and elegance of Alger Hiss (and the pragmatism with which he made use of Whittaker Chambers). There's only one man onscreen in *Secret Honor,* but it feels like much more. Philip Baker Hall paints this fictional Richard Milhous Nixon in broad, furious strokes, creating a fictional portrait that may be truer to life than any 900-page tome with footnotes. Filmed with the (lucky!) students at the University of Michigan. ***AKA:*** Lords of Treason; Secret Honor: The Last Testament of Richard M. Nixon; Secret Honor: A Political Myth. 🦴🦴🦴

1985 90m/C Philip Baker Hall; ***D:*** Robert Altman; ***W:*** Donald Freed, Arnold Stone; ***C:*** Pierre Mignot; ***M:*** George Burt. **VHS, LV**

The Secret of Roan Inish

Based on Rosalie K. Fry's novel, *Secret of the Ron Mor Skerry, The Secret of Roan Inish* is a charming and gentle fable, featuring a delightful performance by newcomer Jeni Courtney as 10-year-old Fiona. Fiona is enchanted by her grandfather's stories about her baby brother, Jamie, who once drifted out to sea, and about the lovely selkie Seal/Lady, who once came on land to live with Fiona's family. Mason Daring's atmospheric score adds to the mood and tone of the piece, which represents a point of departure for writer/director John Sayles. Set in County Donegal, it's the perfect movie for St. Patrick's Day or anytime you feel like being wrapped in the spell of another time and place. 🦴🦴🦴

1994 (PG) 102m/C Jeni Courtney, Michael Lally, Eileen Colgan, John Lynch, Richard Sheridan, Susan Lynch, Cillian Byrne; ***D:*** John Sayles; ***W:*** John Sayles; ***C:*** Haskell Wexler; ***M:*** Mason Daring. Nominations: Independent Spirit Awards '96: Best Director (Sayles), Best Film, Best Screenplay. **VHS, LV, Closed Caption**

Secrets and Lies

Mike Leigh became the darling of international film festivals and archives in 1986. I dutifully attempted to watch a selection of the Leigh oeuvres at that time. 1976's *Nuts in May* was nothing special, but okay; at least I could make out the dialogue in that one. Then, in rapid succession, I found myself chain-drinking endless cups of tea and coffee after walking out on a string of Leigh flicks: 1980's *Grown Ups,* 1982's *Home Sweet Home,* 1983's *Meantime,* 1984's *Four Days in July.* The thick dialects were impossible for me to decipher without benefit of subtitles. With *Secrets and Lies,* Mike Leigh became a world-class, Oscar-nominated film director. And I still had trouble plowing through the dialects, at least during a LOOONG series of introductory sequences (some extraneous) that set the plot in motion. I like the late character actress Irene Handl (1900–87) just fine, but if she were the central character in any of the movies in which I saw her, I'd reach for the mute button. THIS is my dilemma with the Oscar-nominated Brenda Blethyn, a fine actress, with a face that wells up with enough raw emotion to ignite a dozen soap operas, and a (cultivated) screechy voice like Handl's that is painful to listen to during the course of two hours and 22 minutes. Blethyn as Cynthia lives out her dreary life with her sullen daughter Roxanne (Claire Rushbrook). Cynthia sees less of her brother Maurice (Timothy Spall) than she would like because she can't stand his wife Monica (Phyllis Logan) and vice-a versa. Into this cozy group, a sophisticated optometrist (renamed Hortense by her adopted parents) comes looking for Cynthia, her birth mother. Marianne Jean-Baptiste is quite wonderful as the well-read, soft-spoken young woman who is determined to get to know her mother after the deaths of the parents who raised her.

> **"I've never met an ordinary person. To me, all people are extraordinary. I meet all sorts here, you know, in my job, and the one thing I've learnt in five years is that the word 'normal,' applied to any human being, is utterly meaningless. In a sort of way it's an insult to our Maker, don't you think, to suppose that He could possibly work to any set pattern?"**
>
> **—Pat Cooper (Wendy Hiller) to Sibyl Railton-Bell (Deborah Kerr) in *Separate Tables.***

There's a wrap-up which is, for all the surface grit, deeply false and way too pat. In real-life families, the revelation of secrets and the exposure of lies don't get resolved in a few moments of hugs and tears. They invariably lead to violent brawls and long years of silence between emerging family factions. Even though it's a pseudo-depiction of life rather than an honest one, *Secrets and Lies* IS the breakthrough film for which Leigh will be best remembered. The clothes, as always in a Leigh film, are ghastly. ♪♪♪

1995 (R) 142m/C *GB* Brenda Blethyn, Marianne Jean-Baptiste, Timothy Spall, Claire Rushbrook, Phyllis Logan, Lee Ross, Ron Cook, Leslie Manville, Irene Handl; ***Cameos:*** Alison Steadman; ***D:*** Mike Leigh; ***W:*** Mike Leigh; ***C:*** Dick Pope; ***M:*** Andrew Dickson. Cannes Film Festival '96: Best Actress (Blethyn), Best Film; Golden Globe Awards '97: Best Actress (Blethyn); Independent Spirit Awards '97: Best Foreign Film; Los Angeles Film Critics Association Awards '96: Best Actress (Blethyn), Best Director (Leigh), Best Film; Nominations: Academy Awards '96: Best Actress (Blethyn), Best Director (Leigh), Best Picture, Best Supporting Actress (Jean-Baptiste), Best Writing; British Academy Awards '96: Best Actor (Spall), Best Actress (Blethyn), Best Director (Leigh), Best Film, Best Original Screenplay, Best Supporting Actress (Jean-Baptiste); Cesar Awards '97: Best Foreign Film; Directors Guild of America Awards '96: Best Director (Leigh); Golden Globe Awards '97: Best Film—Drama, Best Supporting Actress (Jean-Baptiste); Screen Actors Guild Award '96: Best Actress (Blethyn); Writers Guild of America '96: Best Original Screenplay. **VHS**

Separate Tables

British playwright Terrence Rattigan specialized in intricately crafted dramas about ordinary men and women whose interior worlds were shattered when they were forced to face themselves truthfully for the first time. Unsurprisingly, many of his plays, like *The Winslow Boy* and *The Browning Version,* became splendid film vehicles for Britain's finest actors and actresses. When *Separate Tables* was first performed onstage as two one-act plays, Margaret Leighton and Eric Portman played different leading characters for each act, gimmickry that probably would not have worked in a movie. Independent producers Burt Lancaster, Harold Hecht, and James Hill hired Laurence Olivier and Vivien Leigh to play an estranged couple, and cast David Niven and Deborah Kerr against type as a phony war hero and the mousy spinster who adores him from afar. Lancaster and Olivier soon realized that they would not be able to work together and both Olivier and Leigh withdrew from the project. Lancaster decided to play the part that Olivier had vacated and Delbert Mann stepped in as director. Rita Hayworth, then engaged to marry co-producer James Hill, was quickly signed to play the estranged wife. These (mis)casting decisions resulted in half of a great movie, and even the half that isn't great is redeemed by the Oscar-winning performance of Wendy Hiller as Lancaster's discarded mistress. The more interesting half revolves around the self-styled Major Pollock, who faces social castigation after misbehaving in a movie theatre. The *West Hampshire Weekly News* details the facts of the case as well as his military career, and the first reaction of his fellow residents at the Beauregard Hotel is to throw him out. David Niven, usually smooth, elegant, and charming, shed all of these mannerisms to create a new character, filled with uncertainty and doubt. It was far and away the most challenging role of Niven's long career, and he won an Oscar for the part, considerably helped by Deborah Kerr's touching performance as his disillusioned admirer. Gladys Cooper once again played a domineering mama to the hilt, and other recognizable British types were sharply observed by Cathleen Nesbitt, Felix Aylmer, and May Hallatt. Rattigan firmly believed that "British is best" and that even his country's greatest flaws could be compensated for by individual acts of kindness and decency. There may have been a great deal of wishful thinking in Rattigan's world view, but it's hard not to get caught up in the plight of poor Major Pollock and the lonely souls who surround him. ♪♪♪

1958 98m/B Burt Lancaster, David Niven, Rita Hayworth, Deborah Kerr, Wendy Hiller, Rod Taylor, Gladys Cooper, Felix Aylmer, Cathleen Nesbitt, Rod Taylor, Audrey Dalton, May Hallatt, Priscilla Morgan, Hilda Plowright; ***D:*** Delbert Mann; ***W:*** John Gay; ***C:***

Charles B(ryant) Lang; ***M:*** David Raksin. Academy Awards '58: Best Actor (Niven), Best Supporting Actress (Hiller); Golden Globe Awards '59: Best Actor—Drama (Niven); New York Film Critics Awards '58: Best Actor (Niven); Nominations: Academy Awards '58: Best Actress (Kerr), Best Adapted Screenplay, Best Black and White Cinematography, Best Picture, Best Original Score. **VHS**

Serial Mom

There comes a time in every femme fatale's movie life when she looks at the scripts she's being offered and realizes, "Hey, no one's offering me parts where I get to say lines like, 'I never forget a face once I've sat on it.' I'd better start thinking about my next career move." In the case of Kathleen Turner, then 39, 1994's *Serial Mom* was it. When she made her screen debut in *Body Heat* in 1981, John Waters was just beginning to think in terms of conventional casting; Divine alone might not have lured mallrats into multiplexes to see *Polyester,* but DIVINE AND TAB HUNTER?! Times change and now even Sam Waterston, who ordinarily plays candidates for canonization, is on hand as a latter-day Carl Betz to Turner's twisted Donna Reed. Also in *Serial Mom* are Ricki Lake and Matthew Lillard as the kids, Misty and Chip; Mink Stole, Patty Hearst, and Mary Jo Catlett as the Serial Mom's nemeses; L7 as the house band; and even Traci Lords, Joan Rivers, and Suzanne Somers in cameo roles. For the most part, *Serial Mom* is a sick and cynical film about the sick and cynical homage mass murderers receive in our society. But, since Waters admittedly reads the books and sees the films about assorted lunatics who inspired this film, he makes no effort to supply an antidote to the media's obsession with them. Instead, his perspective flips back and forth between the ultra-correct Serial Mom AND her poor victims who have the bad taste to watch Chesty Morgan videos under the blankets or to sing along with lousy Hollywood musicals while eating meat. When Serial Mom isn't stalking prey, she's shown in a flattering, if extreme light. After all, garbage men, uh, sanitation engineers adore her. With a few exceptions (the Chesty Morgan fanatic and Patty Hearst as Juror #8, who commits the blunder of wearing white shoes after Labor Day), the nicest thing you can say about Serial Mom's targets is that, uh, sanitation engineers DON'T adore them. And that too dovetails into society's worship of living psychos as magazine pin-ups. Very rarely does the media focus on naming, much less characterizing, the ghosts they leave behind. *Serial Mom,* in Waters' own demented way, is a film of deep moral intensity, with a solemn respect for homespun values. Just rent Alfred Hitchcock's *Shadow of a Doubt* afterward for an in-your-face clue to its satirical roots. (Cast Note: Turner next joined the ensemble cast of 1995's *Moonlight and Valentino,* Waterston went on to make John Duigan's *The Journey of August King,* Lake re-made the 1950 Barbara Stanwyck film noir *No Man of Her Own* as 1996's *Mrs. Winterbourne,* and Lillard signed on for the 1995 Iain Softley flick, *Hackers,* as well as the blockbusters *Scream* and *Scream 2.*)

1994 (R) 93m/C Kathleen Turner, Ricki Lake, Sam Waterston, Matthew Lillard, Justin Whalin, Mink Stole, Mary Jo Catlett, Traci Lords; ***Cameos:*** Suzanne Somers, Joan Rivers, Patty Hearst; ***D:*** John Waters; ***W:*** John Waters; ***M:*** Basil Poledouris. **VHS, LV, Letterbox, Closed Caption**

Servant and Mistress

Bruno Gantillon focuses on a sadomasochistic relationship between a housekeeper-turned-heiress and a diplomat-turned-butler. *Servant and Mistress* is a seamlessly constructed film; not a word or a gesture between the two leads is wasted. With careful direction and a tasteful screenplay, this strong story of cruelty and humiliation is woven into another, more subtle romantic theme. It's a tricky balance, and Gantillon and cast handle it quite well. This fascinating, disturbing portrait of shifting power via the strange games this couple plays is definitely worth a look. ***AKA:*** Servante et Maîtresse.

1977 90m/C *FR* Victor Lanoux, Andrea Ferreol, David Pontremoli, Jean Rougerie; ***D:*** Bruno Gantillon; ***W:*** Dominique Fabre.

"I want to live, though it's been a disgusting life so far. I've been miserable with it, but I don't want it to come to an end. I'm not going to let them end it."

—Pasqualino Frafuso (Giancarlo Giannini) speaks of the Nazi guards in *Seven Beauties.*

Set It Off

Stony (Jada Pinkett), Cleo (Queen Latifah), single mom Tisean (newcomer Kimberly Elise), and bank teller Frankie (Vivica Fox) have shared similar miserable experiences with bosses, boyfriends, and the police. They decide to team up and pursue a life of crime by robbing banks. Their internal friction is complicated by the constant threat of the police, as well as banker Keith's (Blair Underwood) attraction to one of the women. Well acted by the four leads, but reviewers have learned to watch out for movies about robbing banks where the director says stuff in the press kits like "This movie is not about robbing banks, it's about personal sacrifice and commitment to friendship...robbing banks is a means to an end." As opposed to all those other movies where robbing banks is what? NOT a means to an end? 🦴🦴

1996 (R) 121m/C Jada Pinkett Smith, Queen Latifah, Vivica A. Fox, Kimberly Elise, Blair Underwood, John C. McGinley, Anna Maria Horsford, Ella Joyce, Charles Robinson, Chaz Lamas Shepard, Vincent Baum, Van Baum, Tom Byrd, Samantha MacLachlan; ***D:*** F. Gary Gray; ***W:*** Kate Lanier, Takashi Bufford; ***C:*** Marc Reshovsky; ***M:*** Christopher Young. Nominations: Independent Spirit Awards '97: Best Supporting Actress (Queen Latifah). **VHS**

Seven Beauties

A single act of violence executed on a grand scale—how does it fit into the fabric of people's lives? Why does it happen? What manner of person commits the act? Lina Wertmuller demonstrates the foolishness of such a killing in *Seven Beauties.* Her protagonist (Giancarlo Giannini) kills his sister's pimp to avenge his honor, but makes the mistake of improperly setting the death scene. He is too impatient to wait for the pimp to defend himself. Consequently, he must serve time in an insane asylum and later in World War II. Then he is faced with different sorts of life choices: with so many killings in the concentration camps, does it matter who does the killing? Isn't he guilty everytime he looks the other way? Finally he is faced with his life and his life only, for he has nothing else. *Seven Beauties,* already hailed as Wertmuller's masterpiece, is a sizzling account of the solutions one man accepts for himself as a reaction to the senseless patterns of life. Considering its content, it's amazing that Wertmuller is so successful at injecting a quality of comic zaniness into the grim proceedings. She moves swiftly from one insanity to the other with dizzying speed, yet she skillfully blends all the imagery so that the point of this cutting edge satire is strong and clear. Note: At press time, Lina Wertmuller and Jane Campion remain the only women in the entire history of the Academy Awards to receive Oscar nominations as Best Director. ***AKA:*** Pasqualino Settebellezze; Pasqualino: Seven Beauties. 🦴🦴🦴🦴

1976 116m/C *IT* Giancarlo Giannini, Fernando Rey, Shirley Stoler, Elena Fiore, Enzo Vitale; ***D:*** Lina Wertmuller; ***W:*** Lina Wertmuller; ***C:*** Tonino Delli Colli. Nominations: Academy Awards '76: Best Actor (Giannini), Best Director (Wertmuller), Best Foreign Film, Best Original Screenplay. **VHS, LV**

sex, lies and videotape

No question about it, *sex, lies and videotape* is an impressive first feature for writer/director Steven Soderbergh, then 26. The movie was lionized at the 1989 Cannes Film Festival, where it won two major awards. I can't help feeling, though, that there was an "Oh, those funny Americans" factor about its lavish reception. Spike Lee's *Do the Right Thing,* a far more threatening view of American society, was virtually ignored by the same festival. James Spader as Graham illustrates what ruthless seducers have known forever: that if a man tells a potential conquest he's normally impotent around women and then shows her that he isn't around her, he's practically assured of another notch on his belt. And this is late-breaking news? Meanwhile, across town, Peter Gallagher as John learns another astonishing lesson: that if a man fools around with his wife's sister, he's going to lose them both. Soderbergh is so wrapped up in these two urgent social statements that he ignores minor details. For example, Spader has a car and a place to live and an extensive video collection of assorted women discussing their sex lives on camera. At one point, he says that he supports himself with money under the mattress. One helpful sentence about where he gets his grocery money would have dissolved the notion that he might be a blackmailing slime instead of the film's only candidate for a romantic prince. The movie gets off to a slow start with an endless sequence between Andie MacDowell as Ann and her therapist. (Surprise: the therapist is a dope!) The rest of the film consists of sequences between Ann and husband John, Ann and sympathetic Graham, Ann and sister Cynthia, Cynthia and brother-in-law John, Cynthia and sympathetic Graham, and finally, dishonest John and honest Graham. The movie was made in Baton Rouge, Louisiana, on $1.2 million, which included the salary of my favorite actress in the film: Laura San Giacomo as Cynthia. When San Giacomo snarls "You are scum" to John and then hops into bed with him, she gives an understanding to these contradictory acts that isn't in the script. Despite his best actor award, Spader basically has three expressions: asleep, constipated, and adorable. *sex, lies and videotape* leaves unanswered the burning question of why it takes some men forever to realize what burns out many women long before they finish high school. 🦴🦴🦴

1989 (R) 101m/C James Spader, Andie MacDowell, Peter Gallagher, Laura San Giacomo, Ron Vawter, Steven Brill; ***D:*** Steven Soderbergh; ***W:*** Steven Soderbergh; ***C:*** Walt Lloyd; ***M:*** Cliff Martinez. Cannes Film Festival '89: Best Actor (Spader), Best Film; Independent Spirit Awards '90: Best Actress (MacDowell), Best Director (Soderbergh), Best Film, Best Supporting Actress (San Giacomo); Los Angeles Film Critics Association Awards '89: Best Actress (MacDowell); Sundance Film Festival '89: Audience Award; Nominations: Academy Awards '89: Best Original Screenplay. **VHS, LV, Letterbox, Closed Caption, DVD**

Shack Out on 101

You haven't LIVED until you've seen the ultimate sleazeball classic of 1955: Ed Dein's *Shack Out on 101.* Yep, the Commies are it again and who is their recruit of choice but grungy Lee Marvin, cast to type as a slob, and warming up for his Academy Award acceptance speech some 10 years later? Female viewers can admire the gutsiness of Terry Moore's character as a waitress named Kotty (now THERE is a dame who knows how to handle sexual harassment!). Meanwhile, male viewers can sympathize with the dilemma of all those poor lonely men onscreen who have to live with the fact that the only women for miles around can't stand them. The climax of *Shack Out* is beyond belief; your jaw will either be nailed to your chin or you'll be in such uncontrollable hysterics that you may have to slap yourself. (Thanks, I needed that!) If the late, great Tex Avery had ever made a live-action feature, it might have looked like this one. Don't miss *Shack Out,* co-starring Frank Lovejoy as the Professor, Keenan Wynn as George, and the ubiquitous Whit Bissell as Eddie. 🦴🦴🦴

1955 80m/B Lee Marvin, Terry Moore, Keenan Wynn, Frank Lovejoy, Whit Bissell, Jess Barker, Donald Murphy, Frank De Kova, Len Lesser, Fred Gabourie; ***D:*** Edward Dein; ***W:*** Edward Dein, Mildred Dein; ***C:*** Floyd Crosby; ***M:*** Paul Dunlap, Louis Prima. **VHS**

Shades of Doubt

Deeply troubled teenagers were the focus of quite a number of the entries at 1995's Mill Valley Film Festival. Aline Issermann's *Shades of Doubt* accurately reflects the confusion a 12-year-old victim of incest experiences when she tries to bring the truth out into the open. Alexandrine's story begins in the most idyllic of settings: a family outing in beautiful surroundings. But the first of a series of brief encounters occurs with her father (off camera), and her life is forever changed. A sensitive teacher tries to help her come forward in order to stop the abuse, but Alexandrine buckles under family pressure, retracts her charges, and the abuse continues. When she runs away with her small brother, her family and the authorities finally listen to her. If *Shades of Doubt* had been a telefeature on American television, the issues would have been simplified with all battle lines clearly drawn. But this French-made drama gains

The Hound Salutes:
TERRY MOORE
Shack Out on 101

In February 2000, I'll celebrate my 60th year in movies. A neighbor of mine sent my picture to a casting agency and they called me to play Walter Brennan's granddaughter in a 1940 movie called *Maryland,* which was a follow-up to 1938's *Kentucky,* for which he won an Oscar. I went into Fox studio with 500 other little girls. They picked six of us, we screen-tested, I got the role, and that started me at age 11. I worked in that movie under the name Helen Koford, and then the Paramount studio changed my name to Judy Ford and then PRC changed my name to Jan Ford and then King Cohn [the head of Columbia studio, Harry Cohn, 1891–1958], changed my name again for *The Return of October,* which co-starred Glenn Ford, so I've been Terry Moore since I was a teenager. The reason he changed my name from Jan Ford is because he didn't want two Fords in the same movie.

"I loved the Terry Ramsey role I played in that picture. It's one of my favorites. Right after I did that, I went over to RKO studios and played Jill in 1949's *Mighty Joe Young.* It was a wonderful movie to make because I adored Ben Johnson [1918–96], he was a very dear friend, and the director, Ernest B. Schoedsack, was my best friend until the day he died in 1979. He was 6'5" and he co-produced and co-directed *Chang* and *King Kong* with Merian C. Cooper. When he directed *Mighty Joe Young,* he was 56 and legally blind. He was very dear and quite wonderful as all the people on that movie were to me. One day, I asked Ben Johnson how he got into the movies and he said he started as a horse wrangler on 1943's *The Outlaw.* I thought he was cute. He was a real cowboy

its strength from the subtlety of Issermann's script and direction as well as from the strikingly colorless camera work by Darius Khondji. And the acting, especially by the young protagonist, is frighteningly real. ***AKA:*** L'Ombre du Doute; Shadow of a Doubt. 🦴🦴🦴

1993 105m/C *FR* Mireille Perrier, Alain Bashung, Sandrine Blancke, Emmanuelle Riva; ***D:*** Aline Issermann; ***W:*** Aline Issermann, Martine Fadier-Nisse, Frederique Gruyer; ***C:*** Darius Khondji; ***M:*** Reno Isaac.

Shag: The Movie

Shag is a pleasant summer comedy about four teenage girls enjoying a fling in Myrtle Beach, South Carolina, circa 1963, a plot only its English producers would consider "a rarity." Phoebe Cates, a star of high school films since 1982, finally graduates in this one. She's clearly had some theatrical training: her performance as a future bride attracted to a one-night stand named "Buzz" is her most restrained to date. Daryl Hannah's sister Page, then 25, plays the plain daughter of a Senator who has a crush on Cates' strict boyfriend, Tyrone Power Jr., 30. Bridget Fonda, another 26-year-old teenager, gives her role of a preacher's wild daughter a poignant blend of self-mocking humor and desperation. Perhaps the only real teenager in the bunch is high school junior Annabeth Gish, who is charming as always. Carol Bur-

and he was the world champion calf roper from Oklahoma. Mighty Joe Young himself was very small and Mr. Schoedsack promised to give me the original, but his wife died first and one of the maids stole it from their house. She probably thought it was just a toy rather than something so valuable. It's just heartbreaking to think that the original Mighty Joe Young was lost like that and it was supposed to be mine!

"I received an Academy Award nomination for playing Marie Buckholder in 1952's *Come Back, Little Sheba* when I was just 23 and I received a film festival award for a 1960 movie called *Why Must I Die?* It was very nice, and maybe one day I'll get that Oscar. Everyone loves to say that they don't care about it, but I do; I think it would be marvelous to have. I've had a lot of fun making movies. Another favorite role I loved very much is the part of Tereza Cernik. I played opposite Fredric March [1897–1975] in 1953's *Man on a Tightrope* [AKA *Der Mann auf dem Drahtseil*]. He was the best actor I ever worked with, and the kindest, sweetest, most glamorous man in the whole world. That same year, I also enjoyed being Susan Maitland in *King of the Khyber Rifles* opposite Tyrone Power [1913–58] as Captain King and, again in 1953, I loved playing Gwyneth Rhys opposite Robert Wagner on *Beneath the 12-Mile Reef,* but it wasn't my favorite movie, because it was a location picture and very hard to make since I did my own stunts in all my movies. And it was the wrong season for Florida and there were a lot of barracuda and sharks swimming around. I adored Robert Wagner, though, and we're still good friends. I talk to him and Glenn Ford nearly every week."

TERRY MOORE can also be seen on video in *The Howards of Virginia, Since You Went Away, Gaslight, Son of Lassie, Summer Holiday, The Great Rupert, Daddy Long Legs, Postmark for Danger* (as Alison Ford), *Between Heaven and Hell* (as Jenny opposite Robert Wagner), *Peyton Place, Platinum High School, Kill Factor, Hellhole, Death Blow,* and *Beverly Hills Brats* (as Veronica in a 1989 indie Moore also co-wrote and produced).

nett's lookalike daughter Carrie Hamilton is also around to provide competition for Fonda in their star-struck pursuit of a teen idol who thinks Elvis Presley is pathetic. Beautiful British actress Shirley Anne Field, who once played a delinquent in 1960's *Beat Girl,* plays Page's Southern belle mama. Speaking of which, do all Southern beauty pageants require Scarlett's vomit scene at Tara plus American flag dance routines as part of their talent competitions? The film is your basic retread of the old "Beach Party" movies where the only black faces you'll see on the beach belong to "The Voltage Brothers" singing "Sixty Minute Man," where the emphasis on innocence evokes 1963 media caca rather than reality, and where a group of talented newcomers somehow manage to give the non-stop cliches a fresh twist. *Shag* is directed by Zelda *(Secret Places)* Barron. 🦴🦴🦴

1989 (PG) 96m/C Phoebe Cates, Annabeth Gish, Bridget Fonda, Page Hannah, Scott Coffey, Robert Rusler, Tyrone Power Jr., Jeff Yagher, Carrie Hamilton, Shirley Anne Field, Leilani Sarelle Ferrer; ***D:*** Zelda Barron; ***W:*** Robin Swicord, Lanier Laney, Terry Sweeney; ***C:*** Peter Macdonald. **VHS, LV**

Shakespeare in Love

If Tom Stoppard had written nothing else in his life but *Arcadia* (a brilliant play about my two least favorite subjects, mathematics and gardening), his name would be en-

Reiko Kusamura and Koji Yakusho in *Shall We Dance?* Miramax; courtesy of the Kobal Collection

graved on my heart forever. He has, of course, written much more than that, including *Night and Day* (starring Diana Rigg, John Thaw, and David Langton), which I, despite being the world's worst airline passenger, flew all the way from San Francisco to London's Phoenix Theatre to see in 1978. One of the lines from that play, "Information is light," became a sort of mantra with me, helping me to examine unpleasant truths I didn't even want to glimpse. On March 21, 1999, Stoppard and co-scripter Marc Norman were among the many worthy Oscar recipients for *Shakespeare in Love* (the film won in seven categories, including best picture). Was *Shakespeare in Love* such an eccentric choice for Picture of the Year when everyone was expecting *Saving Private Ryan* to do what *Titanic* had done the previous year? I don't think so. War movies, however well written, well directed, well produced, et cetera, are hard on an audience—not as hard as war itself, but the voters may have been needled by the Oscar campaign for *Saving Private Ryan* when its anti-war statement appeared to be transmogrified into jingoism. Look at the Academy's choices in 1998: three big war movies, *Elizabeth,* and THIS high-spirited entertainment, filled with wit and romance, not to mention enchanting Gwyneth Paltrow as Viola de Lesseps. What sort of a churl could anyone be not to fall in love with her? And the narrative isn't fluff by any means. It's about all the heart-wrenching experiences that writers go through so that the best part of themselves will live forever. There are so many wonderful little touches in this film that make it rich and wonderful: Judi Dench as Queen Elizabeth, who's so droll and wry in her eight minutes onscreen that her presence is felt all the way through the other 114 minutes; Ben Affleck as Ned Alleyn, who has just the right egotistical swagger for an actor who thinks that Mercutio is the star of *Romeo and Juliet*; Colin Firth, so romantic as Darcy in 1995's *Pride and Prejudice* and such a earringed creep as Lord Wessex,

Viola's husband-to be; Geoffrey Rush as a broke and jittery producer; Tom Wilkinson as Hugh Fennyman, whose personality is forever changed when he gets to play the tiny part of the apothecary onstage; Anthony Sher as Dr. Moth, sort of a 16th-century shrink to Will Shakespeare; Joe Roberts as John Webster, a nasty little boy who feeds rats to a cat (and later became a playwright himself, specializing in tales of revenge); and Rupert Everett as legendary playwright Kit Marlowe. *Shakespeare in Love*'s credentials as an indie are not impeccable, since both Universal and Disney helped with the financing. But Miramax, which also made 1996's *The English Patient,* continues to insist that it IS independent. Although Miramax film budgets stretch every dollar, the movies always look more expensive than they actually are and the Miramax ballyhoo for Academy Award nominations rivals that of the old-time studios. If I can make one—okay, two—quibbles: (1) My esteemed colleague Heather Clisby thinks that Joseph Fiennes as Will looks just like Prince in *Purple Rain* (and he does, which is a tad jarring, especially since he has nowhere near the passion or charisma of Paltrow's Viola), and (2) That hokey title. Think about it! Playwrights in Love, Composers in Love, Statesmen in Love, Philosophers in Love, Chihuahuas in Love....

1998 (R) 122m/C *GB* Joseph Fiennes, Gwyneth Paltrow, Ben Affleck, Geoffrey Rush, Colin Firth, Judi Dench, Simon Callow, Tom Wilkinson, Imelda Staunton, Jim Carter, Rupert Everett, Martin Clunes, Anthony Sher, Joe Roberts; ***D:*** John Madden; ***W:*** Marc Norman, Tom Stoppard; ***C:*** Richard Greatrex; ***M:*** Stephen Warbeck. Academy Awards '98: Best Actress (Paltrow), Best Art Direction/Set Decoration, Best Costume Design, Best Original Screenplay, Best Picture, Best Supporting Actress (Dench), Best Original Musical/Comedy Score; Golden Globe Awards '99: Best Actress—Musical/Comedy (Paltrow), Best Film—Musical/Comedy, Best Screenplay; New York Film Critics Awards '98: Best Screenplay; National Society of Film Critics Awards '98: Best Supporting Actress (Dench); Screen Actors Guild Award '98: Best Actress (Paltrow), Cast; Writers Guild of America '98: Best Original Screenplay; Broadcast Film Critics Association Awards '98: Best Screenplay; Nominations: Academy Awards '98: Best Director (Madden), Best Film Editing, Best Makeup, Best Sound, Best Supporting Actor (Rush); British Academy Awards '98: Best Actor (Fiennes), Best Actress (Paltrow), Best Cinematography, Best Costume Design, Best Director (Madden), Best Film, Best Film Editing, Best Original Screenplay, Best Sound, Best Supporting Actor (Rush, Wilkinson), Best Supporting Actress (Dench), Best Score; Directors Guild of America Awards '98: Best Director (Madden); Golden Globe Awards '99: Best Director (Madden), Best Supporting Actor (Rush), Best Supporting Actress (Dench); Screen Actors Guild Award '98: Best Actor (Fiennes), Best Supporting Actor (Rush), Best Supporting Actress (Dench). **VHS**

Shall We Dance?

In 1992's *Strictly Ballroom,* competitive dancing was an obsession for its amateur contestants. In 1996's *Shall We Dance,* it functions as a key to unlock deeply hidden dreams and emotions. Shohei Sugiyama (Koji Yakusho) is a middle-aged married businessman with an adolescent daughter. His spirit has been ground down by years of repetitive routines. And then he sees the silhouette of a graceful dancer (Tamiyo Kusakari as Mai Kishikawa) through the window of a dancing school. Impulsively, he enrolls in classes, keeping his attendance a secret from his wife, his daughter, and all but one male colleague (who's also a dance student). Like his colleague, Shohei isn't much of a dancer at first, but he sticks with it. His wife is convinced that he's having an affair and she hires a private detective to investigate. (The detective becomes an enthusiastic and knowledgeable ballroom buff.) Shohei is rebuffed by Mai when he pays her a compliment, but as she helps him prepare for a competition, she learns again through him her own deep love of dance, something she thought she'd lost during her early days as an unhappy competitor. Naturally, Shohei can't keep his obsession with dance a secret forever, and there is the inevitable encounter between the people in his two separate and very compartmentalized lives. *Shall We Dance?* struck a nerve with international audiences, who made it an art house hit. Expect an American remake, *sans* subtitles, but it would have to go a long way to capture anywhere near the sweetness, the mystery, and the seductive charm of Masayuki Suo's original film. ***AKA:*** Shall We Dansu?

"I've never seen a dead body before. I saw my grand-mother of course, but I don't think that counts. I mean, she was alive at the time."

—David Stephens (Christopher Eccleston) in *Shallow Grave.*

1996 118m/C *JP* Koji Yakusho, Tamiyo Kusakari, Naoto Takenaka, Akira Emoto, Eriko Watanabe, Yu Tokui, Hiromasa Taguchi, Reiko Kusamura; ***D:*** Masayuki Suo; ***W:*** Masayuki Suo; ***C:*** Naoke Kayano; ***M:*** Yoshikazu Suo. National Board of Review Awards '97: Best Foreign Film; Broadcast Film Critics Association Awards '97: Best Foreign Film. **VHS, LV, Closed Caption**

Shallow Grave

Shallow Grave is a nasty little tale about three flatmates looking for a fellow occupant to share their living space. As they grill prospective tenants, we learn that Juliet, David, and Alex have the sort of darkly humorous relationship that excludes nearly everyone else. Until Hugo arrives on the scene. He creates an interesting and rather charming first impression. And then they discover his body in his new room plus a million dollars in his suitcase. At this point, some logical viewers might have a best possible scenario all worked out for the three buddies. But anyone who's seen *The Treasure of Sierra Madre, Ocean's Eleven, Perfect Friday,* or countless other sure-fire heist movies knows that best possible scenarios never work out once greed kicks into gear. So we get to watch as Juliet turns crafty, David turns weird, and Alex turns, well, just a bit gallant. And screenwriter John Hodge plays fair with the outcome. Danny Boyle, too, directs the comedic moments with broad strokes and underplays the escalating violence with fast cuts of real gore and artfully composed long shots that look far more grisly than they really are. *Shallow Grave* may not be the sort of movie police procedural buffs will care to examine too carefully, but as a psychological chiller, it supplies splendid value. Best of all, the expert ensemble work in *Shallow Grave* is a treat to watch; Kerry Fox, Christopher Eccleston, and Ewan McGregor are ideally cast as the best friends who know way too much and far too little about each other. (You may remember Fox from Jane Campion's *An Angel at My Table* and Eccleston from Peter Medak's *Let Him Have It.* McGregor would share the spotlight with the worst toilet in Scotland in another film by Boyle and Hodge, 1996's *Trainspotting.*) ♛♛♛

1994 (R) 91m/C *GB* Kerry Fox, Christopher Eccleston, Ewan McGregor, Keith Allen, Ken Stott, Colin McCredie, John Hodge; ***D:*** Danny Boyle; ***W:*** John Hodge; ***C:*** Brian Tufano; ***M:*** Simon Boswell. **VHS, DVD**

Shelf Life

Shelf Life bears the surprising imprint of director Paul Bartel. Fans of Bartel's more outrageous works such as *Eating Raoul, Lust in the Dust,* and *Scenes from the Class Struggle in Beverly Hills* may not know what to make of this modest stage-to-screen transfer of the play written by its three stars, the story of what would happen to the kids in a family that were whisked into a bomb shelter straight after the assassination of President Kennedy. Thirty years later, the parents are dead, but the grown-up children live on, entrenched in long-established rituals. It may not be life as you or I would know it, but it is life as they know it, take it or leave it. The idea of escape never seriously occurs to them, so the rituals are all they have, really. The three leads are excellent, especially O-lan Jones, who would make a terrific onscreen vampire. Along with co-stars Jim Turner and Andrea Stein, the three have the comedic timing of a highly polished vaudeville team. If you can accept the reality that, like the participants, you're stuck in a hermetically sealed environment for the duration, *Shelf Life* ain't a bad little way to spend 83 minutes. But then, at the very end, The Great Bartel makes a brief appearance. The larger-than-life Bartel, who can generate a laugh without even trying, had the effect of making me wish that the movie had started with his entrance. Such mutinous thoughts aside, *Shelf Life* is best watched on its own quirky terms and may be more widely enjoyed as a cult video item. ♛♛½

1994 83m/C O-lan Jones, Jim Turner, Andrea Stein, Paul Bartel; ***D:*** Paul Bartel; ***W:*** O-lan Jones, Jim Turner, Andrea Stein.

She's Gotta Have It

Nola Darling (Tracy Camilla Johns) is having an affair with Jamie Overstreet (Tommy

Redmond Hicks), who thinks he can tell her what to do. Nola is also having an affair with Greer Childs (John Canada Terrell), a rich male model who's more in love with himself than with her. And finally, Nola is seeing Mars Blackmon (Spike Lee), a bit of a clown, who's young for his age. Jamie, Greer, and Mars are all jealous of each other and want Nola to settle down with one of them. Nola, a genuinely free spirit, resists the idea of being forced to make such a decision. *She's Gotta Have It* introduced the multi-talented Lee to the world. Within a decade, we would see 10 of this fiercely free spirit's exciting, thoughtful films. His influence on the industry remains enormous, and he continues to create once-in-a-lifetime characters and to support the emergence of other new filmmakers. By 1992, cinematographer Ernest R. Dickerson was directing his own projects. Johns can be seen in Lee's *Mo' Better Blues* and in Mario Van Peebles' *New Jack City.* A milestone film in every respect, *She's Gotta Have It* is also fresh, beautifully shot and scored, and very, very funny. ℒℒℒ

1986 (R) 84m/B Tracy C. Johns, Spike Lee, Tommy Redmond Hicks, Raye Dowell, John Canada Terrell, Joie Lee, Epatha Merkinson, Bill Lee, Cheryl Burr, Aaron Dugger, Stephanie Covington, Renata Cobbs, Cheryl Singleton, Monty Ross, Lewis Jordan, Erik Dellums, Reginald Hudlin, Eric Payne, Marcus Turner, Gerard Brown, Ernest R. Dickerson; ***D:*** Spike Lee; ***W:*** Spike Lee; ***C:*** Ernest R. Dickerson; ***M:*** Bill Lee. Independent Spirit Awards '87: Best First Feature. **VHS, LV, Closed Caption**

She's the One

Edward Burns, Mike McGlone, and newcomer Maxine Bahns return in the so-so follow-up to Burns' so-so breakthrough film, *The Brothers McMullen.* This time, they're surrounded by familiar television faces (John Mahoney from *Frasier,* whose career will neither be helped nor hindered by this picture, and Jennifer Aniston from *Friends,* who might do well to consider a new movie agent), PLUS clever Cameron Diaz, who runs away with the flick's only rave reviews. Expectations for *She's the One* were huge, never an auspicious climate for a second feature. Burns used to go with Diaz, who worked her way through college as a call girl, but now he's married to Bahns and driving a cab. McGlone (as his brother—yes, again) is fooling around with Diaz (now supporting herself as a broker), who doesn't think much of his technique. Meanwhile, wife Aniston tries her darndest to look sexy, but settles for a vibrator in the bathroom when McGlone ignores her. Mom Anita Gillette is supposed to be praying for her overgrown infants in Church, but she's actually...oh well, never mind.... Dad John Mahoney takes the brothers fishing and explains the facts of Catholic life to them, but he's actually...oh well, never mind.... Catholicism is (yes, again) a major motif. Diaz has an older lover (offscreen) whom she prefers to McGlone. Bahns has a lesbian admirer (onscreen) whom she doesn't prefer to Burns. I guess it would hurt worse to BE in this family than to watch them for 95 minutes. *She's the One* is no better and no worse than any average telefeature except that Robert Redford is one of the executive producers. ℒℒ

1996 (R) 95m/C Edward Burns, Mike McGlone, Jennifer Aniston, Cameron Diaz, Maxine Bahns, John Mahoney, Leslie Mann, George McCowan, Leslie Mann, Amanda Peet, Anita Gillette, Frank Vincent; ***D:*** Edward Burns; ***W:*** Edward Burns; ***C:*** Frank Prinzi; ***M:*** Tom Petty. **VHS, LV, Closed Caption**

She's Vintage

I rarely meet anyone in San Francisco who bores the hell out of me, but—in *She's Vintage,* I spent 100 minutes with the four staggeringly dull flat mates whose less-than-spellbinding lives make up Mulan Chan's narrative for Peter M. Wilson's indie. All four are the subjects of rambling interviews that seem to lead nowhere. Sam (Danyel Roberts) is a blond bike messenger, Dahlia (Sally Dana) is an unemployed "dancer" who haunts garage sales, Isaac (Samuel Sheng) is a non-smoking, gay Asian writer who wants to write a book about Mammy Pleasant, and Beth (Tishan Waymire) bakes cakes. After 85 minutes of Nothing, they get robbed by drug dealers who are after the TV/VCR plus the $85 grand that was stashed in an old couch Dahlia picked up at a street sale. But: She found the money and stashed it in a cup-

The Hound Salutes: SCOTT HICKS
Director, *Shine*

Shine came about because I happened to see David Helfgott one day in recital in Adelaide, in South Australia where I live. I was fascinated by his extraordinary, eccentric personality and the amazing virtuoso he becomes when he sat down at the piano. He seemed like two completely different people and I felt that in that gap there must be an amazing story, so I set about finding out what that was, working closely with David and his wife Gillian to find out. So it was very much a project that I initiated and developed over what turned into a 10-year period to get it made.

"Casting is one of the fundamental things of directing a film. It's both a fascinating and a frustrating process, but you'd better get it right, otherwise it's never going to work, especially when you have to have three actors portray the character at three different ages. It presents a very particular challenge, especially this type of character. David Helfgott is absolutely unique. He talks in a gushing torrent of words that tumble and bounce and jump and clash and clang off each other; puns and jokes and ideas all ripple and riff along in his dialogue in the most extraordinary way. His speeches are all written in the screenplay. There is nothing improvised by Geoffrey Rush, who plays David

board and then Beth stashed it on a shelf and then let's just say that it's an awfully long set-up for an eight-second punch line. Waymire and Dana are the only cast members who can actually act. Played at San Francisco's Indie Fest, January 1999.

1998 100m/C Danyel Roberts, Tishan Waymire, Samuel Sheng, Sally Dana, Devon West, Andrew Piccone, Peter M. Wilson, Mulan Chan; ***D:*** Peter M. Wilson; ***W:*** Mulan Chan; ***C:*** Andrew Piccone.

Shine

Geoffrey Rush deservedly won a Golden Globe and an Academy Award for his full-throttle performance as David Helfgott, and Noah Taylor really deserved a nod, too, as adolescent David. Armin Mueller-Stahl was SO creepy as Helfgott's control freak father that he probably freaked out the Academy members who voted for Cuba Gooding Jr. instead. *Shine* basked in a 90 something–day glow until some nasty music critics said that Helfgott was no Van Cliburn. Man, they were mean! The credits clearly state that *Shine* was never meant to be a documentary and that many situations had been fictionalized, but the folks who bet on the Oscars actually said that there would be a backlash because Helfgott wasn't a better piano player. All of this had zip to do with Rush or *Shine,* but that didn't stop musical cognoscenti from buzzing about both as if they were investigative reporters! Even after the Oscars, critics continued to gun for Helfgott as if it weren't enough that he'd conquered madness, he had to be a genius, too. (Oh, get a life/a heart/a grip...GRR!!!) John Gielgud is so animated as one of young David's teachers, it's hard to believe that you're watching someone who made his movie debut at age 20 in 1924's *Who Is the Man?* It's a treat to see Googie Withers again as another influential teacher and friend. And Lynn Redgrave is radiant as the delightful lady who sees past David's mumbling straight into

Helfgott as an adult in a monumental performance. It was something that was always going to require a really particular sort of actor to realize this role. With the adolescent David played by Noah Taylor, who's a better-known film actor from Australia, Geoffrey is an actor with almost exclusively stage experience in theatre; Noah has been in a number of well-known Australian films over the years (*The Year My Voice Broke, Flirting, The Nostradamus Kid, One Crazy Night*). Noah plays the character moving through the process of disintegration as a young teenager into a young man. It's about character and about where those funny little points of character creep in between the two ages of David. And then the child, again, is like another person altogether. If you look at a photograph of yourself as a five- or six- or seven-year-old, that's a different person. So, again, the physical similarity's not the point, its about the character. And that was the driving element for me in making those three choices. I cast Geoffrey Rush in 1992, so he met David Helfgott a number of times in the intervening time between then and 1995 when Geoffrey actually got in front of a film camera, but neither of us were really interested just in mimicry or party tricks. It was a matter of Geoffrey having to find something in himself that could bring out this character as completely as he does. There was a lot of material that I had gathered in lengthy conversations or dialogues I'd had with David Helfgott over the years, because you don't interview David in a conventional way. Geoffrey Rush certainly made use of those in coming to understand the rhythms of David's speech. He totally possessed that dialogue."

his heart. That's sort of the point of the film, actually.

1995 (PG-13) 105m/C *AU* Geoffrey Rush, Noah Taylor, Armin Mueller-Stahl, Lynn Redgrave, John Gielgud, Googie Withers, Chris Haywood, Sonia Todd, Randall Berger, Alex Rafalowicz; ***D:*** Scott Hicks; ***W:*** Jan Sardi; ***C:*** Geoffrey Simpson; ***M:*** David Hirschfelder. Academy Awards '96: Best Actor (Rush); Australian Film Institute '95: Best Actor (Rush), Best Cinematography, Best Director (Hicks), Best Film, Best Film Editing, Best Screenplay, Best Sound, Best Supporting Actor (Mueller-Stahl), Best Score; Golden Globe Awards '97: Best Actor—Drama (Rush); Los Angeles Film Critics Association Awards '96: Best Actor (Rush); National Board of Review Awards '96: Best Film; New York Film Critics Awards '96: Best Actor (Rush); Screen Actors Guild Award '96: Best Actor (Rush); Broadcast Film Critics Association Awards '96: Best Actor (Rush); Nominations: Academy Awards '96: Best Director (Hicks), Best Film Editing, Best Picture, Best Supporting Actor (Mueller-Stahl), Best Writing, Best Original Dramatic Score; Australian Film Institute '95: Best Actor (Taylor); British Academy Awards '96: Best Actor (Rush), Best Director (Hicks), Best Film, Best Original Screenplay, Best Supporting Actor (Gielgud), Best Supporting Actress (Redgrave); Directors Guild of America Awards '96: Best Director (Hicks); Golden Globe Awards '97: Best Director (Hicks), Best Film—Drama, Best Screenplay, Best Score; Screen Actors Guild Award '96: Best Supporting Actor (Taylor), Cast; Writers Guild of America '96: Best Original Screenplay. **VHS, LV, Closed Caption, DVD**

The Shining

The 1997 miniseries may have had Stephen King's seal of approval, but nothing beats the eyes and ears of a world-class filmmaker. As I was nearly driven into a coma while Steven Weber and Rebecca DeMornay had a LOOONG chat about whether or not they should have sex, I knew that this would never happen in the original Stanley Kubrick movie starring Jack Nicholson and Shelley Duvall. They won't let us conk out on them. They grab our attention and they keep it for, okay, nearly two and a half hours. Yeah, that's a generous running time, but at least they have a legitimate claim on our interest the whole time (which is more than I can say for the remake). The quality that audiences have always responded to in Jack Nicholson is

"It's a good thing we're not having soup, else I'd stick my face in it and drown myself."

—Shirley (Pauline Collins) is really bored in *Shirley Valentine.*

that he gives a role everything he has; that guy never reigns it in. When he loses his mind, he doesn't fool around. When he turns homicidal, he puts all those HOW TO BE SUBTLE instruction pamphlets in the shredder. And Shelley Duvall (although it is difficult imagining the two of them doing anything together that would result in the birth of Little Danny) is the ideal foil for Nicholson and his what-the-hell style. She lives in her own little world until her antibodies start warning her about life-threatening danger and then there's no stopping her; she knows how to fight! *The Shining* is not a movie about restraint or about an ordinary family battling the forces of darkness in the lonely Overlook Hotel. It's about three oddballs, one of whom was born to wind up in a haunted setting like this one, and the other two who will fight their apparent destiny to the death. The one flaw is Dick Halloran's (Scatman Crothers) exhaustively illustrated flight to save Danny. Crothers is excellent in the part, but we don't want to leave the hotel to watch a guy on a plane or a receptionist or a forest ranger. We want to see Jack and that weird bartender and those odd little twins in the hall and.... 🦴🦴🦴½

1980 (R) 143m/C Jack Nicholson, Shelley Duvall, Scatman Crothers, Danny Lloyd, Joe Turkel, Barry Nelson, Philip Stone, Lia Beldam, Billie Gibson, Barry Dennan, David Baxt, Lisa Burns, Alison Coleridge, Kate Phelps, Anne Jackson, Tony Burton; ***D:*** Stanley Kubrick; ***W:*** Stanley Kubrick, Diane Johnson; ***C:*** John Alcott. **VHS, LV, Closed Caption**

Shirley Valentine

Surprise! Thanks to writer Willy Russell and actress Pauline Collins, *Shirley Valentine* emerges as one of the most charming midlife crisis sagas ever. The plot revolves around a 42-year-old Liverpudlian housewife who's tired of talking to her kitchen wall. She leaves her husband with two weeks of frozen dinners and flies away to Greece with a friend. On the sunny island of Mykonos, Shirley confronts her fears of the unknown and successfully resists sliding back into her safe, predictable world. The best thing about Shirley's new adventures is the way the writer shows that she isn't running away from herself, only unpeeling the layers of muck that have separated her from her own bright, rebellious spirit. A delightful young actress named Gillian Kearney portrays Shirley as an impish schoolgirl alienated from the class kissy, Marjorie (also well played by Catherine Duncan). Years later, Shirley meets Marjorie, now a high-class call girl played by Joanna Lumley, and is surprised to note how well they get along. It's one of the film's best moments, perfectly capturing the pointless mutual envy that circumvents many friendships between women. Shirley has detached sympathy for the snobbish neighbor Julia McKenzie, for Greek native Tom Conti (?!), who always uses the same pickup lines, and even for her husband Bernard Hill. In fact, the only person who seems to be under major attack in Willy Russell's script is the self-styled feminist portrayed by Alison Steadman. This "feminist" has her politically correct lingo down cold, but her rhetoric has nothing to do with what she feels or does. Shirley wisely recognizes a B.S. artist when she sees one and shoves her in the direction of the most boring tourists on the island. With "friends" like that, it's best to make friends with yourself, says Russell. In her first major feature, Pauline Collins fulfills the promise of her early performance as the feisty Sarah in the *Upstairs, Downstairs* television series. She has an honest face and an honest body (for once, no one asked the leading lady to go on a diet). Russell's sharp script is a blessing, but Pauline Collins is the main reason why this movie will remain a glowing memory long after you see *Shirley Valentine.* 🦴🦴🦴

1989 108m/C *GB* Pauline Collins, Tom Conti, Alison Steadman, Julia McKenzie, Joanna Lumley, Bernard Hill, Sylvia Syms, Gillian Kearney, Catherine Duncan; ***D:*** Lewis Gilbert; ***W:*** George Hadjinassios, Willy Russell; ***C:*** Alan Hume; ***M:*** Willy Russell. British Academy Awards '89: Best Actress (Collins); Nominations: Academy Awards '89: Best Actress (Collins), Best Song ("The Girl Who Used to Be Me"). **VHS, LV, 8mm, Closed Caption**

A Shock to the System

There are actors who reach the stage in their careers when they telephone in their

performances. Then there is Michael Caine, who tackles each new role with the hunger of a beginner whose career depended on every movie he makes. Jan Egleson's *A Shock to the System* is vintage Caine. Surrounded by an excellent supporting cast, he outacts everyone on screen with fine character shadings and total attention to detail. He's the only actor I know who even seems to act with the nerve endings of his teeth! Andrew Klavan's clever screenplay is based on a novel by Simon Brett, the only flaw being its logical, but rather flat conclusion. This may be partly due to the competent but not especially sizzling performance of Will Patton as Caine's nemesis. The rest of the well-chosen cast includes Elizabeth McGovern, Peter Riegert, Swoosie Kurtz, Jenny Wright, John McMartin, and the late, great Barbara Baxley. WITHOUT Michael Caine, this wicked tale of a frustrated businessman's cool plan to eliminate all the obstacles to his success might seem like a padded mystery of the week for television. But Michael Caine's hypnotic performance gives *A Shock to the System* its claustrophobic atmosphere and charges the narrative with its driving force.

1990 (R) 88m/C Michael Caine, Elizabeth McGovern, Peter Riegert, Swoosie Kurtz, Will Patton, Jenny Wright, John McMartin, Barbara Baxley; ***D:*** Jan Egleson; ***W:*** Andrew Klavan; ***C:*** Paul Goldsmith; ***M:*** Gary Chang. **VHS, LV, Closed Caption**

Short Cuts

There is probably no filmmaker alive who is more expert at capturing the pulse of a community than Robert Altman. He examined the world of country music in *Nashville* with humor and affection, and the motion picture industry with savagery and wit in *The Player.* Now, in *Short Cuts,* he casts a dark gaze at the sunny world of Los Angeles where sex is plentiful and joyless, where wrongful death is taken for granted, and where love never ever hits the right target. Despite the superficial milk-and-honey surroundings, the Los Angeles of *Short Cuts* is a bleak landscape, populated by losers waiting for Armageddon. There is Jennifer Jason Leigh's wonderfully drawn white trash housewife who feeds her baby while paying the bills with phone sex. There is the idiotic mother, played with feeling by Andie MacDowell, who insists that her child not speak to strangers, but allows him to slip into a coma after a serious head injury. There are three good old boys (Fred Ward, Buck Henry, and Huey Lewis) who continue to fish at their favorite watering hole after discovering the dead body of a young woman. There is the estranged grandfather, played to the hilt by Jack Lemmon, who tells wildly inappropriate stories of his past escapades in a hospital waiting room. There are the two jerks played by Robert Downey Jr. and Chris Penn, who look for women to ravish while on a picnic with their wives and kids. There is the doctor (Matthew Modine) and his wife (Julianne Moore) who make much ado about nothing (her long ago drunken indiscretion), and then hiss at each other over a game of Jeopardy and a hot tub with another couple. And that's just for starters. For 189 minutes, Altman weaves his way through nine different plot threads, and through it all, nothing, nothing, nothing is anyone's fault. If someone dug up *Short Cuts* out of a time capsule in 500 years, it might be like watching the last days of Pompeii. Anne Archer as Fred Ward's wife goes through a temporary transformation where you think, "Oh, my God, is SOMEONE in this movie actually going to give a damn about someone else?" But the transformation is over in a flash, and she dutifully joins her husband for barbecued fish and that hot tub. Lily Tomlin's hit-and-run driver rationalizes her mistake. Annie Ross dismisses her suicidal daughter one too many times. Tim Robbins' character ditches the family dog, then tears it away from the new owners. Lyle Lovett feeds muffins to Andie MacDowell after harassing her on the phone over an unpaid bill while her son is dying. In *Short Cuts,* the sun sparkles brightly on the dark ugliness of a world where a game show host like Alex Trebek is God and only an 8.6 earthquake can put everyone out of their misery. Until then, courtesy of Robert Altman, it's hard to tear our eyes away from the ants under the rock.

Huey Lewis, Fred Ward, and Buck Henry in *Short Cuts.* Fine Line; courtesy of the Kobal Collection

1993 (R) 189m/C Annie Ross, Lori Singer, Jennifer Jason Leigh, Tim Robbins, Madeleine Stowe, Frances McDormand, Peter Gallagher, Lily Tomlin, Tom Waits, Bruce Davison, Andie MacDowell, Jack Lemmon, Lyle Lovett, Fred Ward, Buck Henry, Huey Lewis, Matthew Modine, Anne Archer, Julianne Moore, Lili Taylor, Christopher Penn, Robert Downey Jr., Jarrett Lennon, Zane Cassidy; ***D:*** Robert Altman; ***W:*** Frank Barhydt, Robert Altman; ***C:*** Walt Lloyd; ***M:*** Mark Isham. Independent Spirit Awards '94: Best Director (Altman), Best Film, Best Screenplay; National Society of Film Critics Awards '93: Best Supporting Actress (Stowe); Venice Film Festival '93: Best Film; Nominations: Academy Awards '93: Best Director (Altman); Golden Globe Awards '94: Best Screenplay; Independent Spirit Awards '94: Best Supporting Actress (Moore). **VHS, LV, Closed Caption**

Shy People

Andrei Konchalovsky strikes out with *Shy People,* a witless film about *Cosmopolitan* writer Jill Clayburgh, who drags teenage daughter Martha Plimpton off to the backwoods to visit their cousins for the purpose of a magazine article about families. The cousins are presided over by Barbara Hershey, whose husband is an omnipresent ghost, whose sons are violent and strange, and whose pregnant daughter-in-law (Mare Winningham, wasted again) wants a battery-operated television set. There's a Biblical quote from Revelations to "explain" all the nonsense onscreen, only it doesn't. Before that, the married son nearly rapes Plimpton while Hershey is away shooting the hand of a man who hit her son in the head. She shoots him in the strip joint operated by yet another son who later chats with Clayburgh. Inexplicably, Clayburgh has left her daughter alone with the other three boys while she "helps" Hershey, and Winningham, too, of course. (Remember the television set?) Well, when Clayburgh finds out what happened to Plimpton, she goes looking for her with the help of the ghost and then Hershey explains that even though her dead husband pistol whipped her while she was pregnant, he still helped the family survive. Clayburgh learns the appropriate lesson and tells Plimpton that she's going to be a stricter mother to her in the future. The strip joint owner returns to the fold and breaks the television set right away, which must be yet another lesson on something or other. If *Shy People* represents the clash between urban and rural values in America to Soviet writer/director Konchalovsky, then perhaps some time away from the Cannon group might provide him with fresh understanding of the people about whom he will be making films in the future. His next three projects *(Homer and Eddie, Tango and Cash,* and *The Inner Circle)* were far from acclaimed for any startling insights into these films' characters. 𝒮𝒮

1987 (R) 119m/C Jill Clayburgh, Barbara Hershey, Martha Plimpton, Mare Winningham, Merritt Butrick, John Philbin, Don Swayze, Pruitt Taylor Vince; ***D:*** Andrei Konchalovsky; ***W:*** Gerard Brach, Marjorie David; ***C:*** Chris Menges; ***M:*** Tangerine Dream. Cannes Film Festival '87: Best Actress (Hershey). **VHS, LV, Closed Caption**

Sidewalks of London

This tribute to the sidewalk entertainers who performed outside London theatres is a good early showcase for Vivien Leigh as Libby. The lion's share of the attention goes to Charles Laughton as a street performer who befriends Libby and makes her part of his act. Libby has greater ambitions for herself. She wants to be a star and, through her connection with the young songwriter played by Rex Harrison, she becomes one. She also insults Charles when he proposes to her, but then thinks better of it and sets up an audition for him. Charles, needing the attention that he can only get by being a street performer, returns to his pals outside the theatre. Reportedly, Leigh didn't much enjoy the experience of making this picture. There is only one star in a Charles Laughton movie, and she wasn't it. After *Gone with the Wind* was released, British theatres, hungry for any Vivien Leigh vehicles, re-released this one in 1940. It wasn't up to the glossy MGM standards of 1940's *Waterloo Bridge,* but the feisty Libby was certainly a lot closer to Scarlett O'Hara than the doomed ballerina Leigh played opposite Robert Taylor. ***AKA:*** St. Martin's Lane. 𝒮𝒮𝒮

1938 86m/B *GB* Charles Laughton, Vivien Leigh, Rex Harrison, Larry Adler, Tyrone Guthrie, Gus McNaughton, Bart Cormack, Edward Lexy, Maire O'Neill, Basil Gill, Claire Greet, David Burns, Cyril Smith, Ronald Ward, Romilly Lunge, Helen Haye, Jerry Verno; ***D:*** Tim Whelan; ***W:*** Clemence Dane; ***C:*** Jules Kruger; ***M:*** Arthur Johnson. **VHS**

Silent Tongue

The conclusion of *Silent Tongue* is abrupt for a reason; reportedly, the original ending was scrapped because of the uneven quality of some of the performances. Watching the rest of the film, it isn't too difficult to identify the weakest cast members: Dermot Mulroney and River Phoenix, both of whom acquitted themselves with distinction in many other ensemble showcases. Mulroney is simply inept, but even Phoenix's most worshipful admirers will wince at his lack of focus here. He is supposed to be a grief-crazed widower, but in his eyes we see nothing but an artistic athlete dying young, and not appearing to care one way or another. But there are many other rewards to be found in Sam Shepard's western ghost story, namely the strong, deeply felt performances of Alan Bates, Richard Harris, Sheila Tousey, and Jeri Arrendondo. 𝒮𝒮

1992 (PG-13) 101m/C River Phoenix, Sheila Tousey, Richard Harris, Alan Bates, Jeri Arredondo, Dermot Mulroney, Tantoo Cardinal; ***Cameos:*** Bill Irwin, David Shiner; ***D:*** Sam Shepard; ***W:*** Sam Shepard; ***C:*** Jack Conroy; ***M:*** Patrick O'Hearn. **VHS, LV, Closed Caption**

Silent Witness

Oral histories about the Holocaust are offered by Harriet Wichins' *Silent Witness,* a 1994 Canadian documentary. Wichins' study of the death camps at Dachau and Auschwitz is deliberately low-key. 𝒮𝒮½

1994 74m/C *CA* ***D:*** Harriet Wichins.

The Silver Screen: Color Me Lavender

If you've never seen *Rock Hudson's Home Movies* or *From the Journals of Jean Seberg, The Silver Screen: Color Me Laven-*

"You can give birth to an excuse so easily, you will believe it's always been there."

—Lauren Bell (Sonja Sohn) in *Slam.*

der isn't a bad introduction to the films of Mark Rappaport. But if you have, watching Rappaport's latest effort is like sitting through movies you've already seen with the person you've seen them with—you know all the observations, punch lines, and witticisms in advance. This time around, Rappaport looks at the relationship between male characters in the movies: butlers, desk clerks, and gigolos as played by Eric Blore, Franklin Pangborn, and Erik Rhodes. Comedy teams like Hope and Crosby, Martin and Lewis, Danny Kaye and Danny Kaye. Murder suspect Clifton Webb receiving detective Dana Andrews in his bathtub. Massimo Girotti all by himself in *Ossessione.* Wendell Corey hanging out with anybody, especially John Hodiak in *Desert Fury.* Randolph Scott and, again, anybody, especially Cary Grant, in *My Favorite Wife.* Walter Brennan, of all people, and anybody, anywhere, anytime. Rappaport devotes considerable screen time to Brennan, not because he was the best character actor of his day, but because he's so, you know, attached to all the male leads. What does it mean? Not that the hero is a strong silent type who says about eight words to the heroine, so we need SOME exposition in there somewhere delivered as painlessly as possible to a scene-stealing sidekick! It had to be the unimaginable, that Gary Cooper (or even Humphrey Bogart) and Walter Brennan were GOING together! Well, it's a thought. But, like so many ideas expressed in this 103-minute compilation, it's a surface perception. Unlike *The Celluloid Closet,* which digs a little deeper for its insights and expresses a variety of viewpoints from actual participants, *The Silver Screen: Color Me Lavender* has just one joke, re-told again and again and again. If you (a) like the joke and (b) enjoy the clips, have fun. 🦴🦴

1997 103m/C *D:* Mark Rappaport; ***W:*** Mark Rappaport; ***C:*** Nancy Schreiber; ***M:*** Dan Butler. **VHS**

Sirens

It's been so long since I've seen contemporary movies with sexual themes free of violence or devastating consequences that I was beginning to wonder if they were still being made. *Sirens* is certainly the most low-key sexual fantasy film that you're likely to see from the year 1994. It's partly based on the life of Australian artist Norman Lindsay, who died in 1968 at the age of 90. For most of Lindsay's career, his explicit works shocked the people of his own time. John Duigan's fictional film takes a look at a 1930s weekend in the life of the Lindsay family and three of their models. Anthony and Estella Campion, a fictitious twit of a minister and his repressed wife, come to pay a call in order to persuade the artist to withdraw his profane works from a major exhibition. The twit is played by the devilishly attractive Hugh Grant, with tongue firmly in cheek ("Call me Tony"), and his wife by the sultry Tara Fitzgerald, last seen in *Hear My Song.* True to the artist's code of never putting an amorous hand on a model, Sam Neill's Lindsay is far from the lecherous hedonist expected by the Campions. He is, rather, a devoted husband, kindly father, and disciplined worker. His feelings are expressed entirely in his art, whereas the women who pose for him express their sexuality in their own lives. (They're played by supermodels Elle MacPherson, Kate Fischer, and Portia de Rossi, by far the best actress of the three.) The entire Lindsay clan are looked on with suspicion by the townspeople, but there is no predictable clash. Menacing snakes and spiders crawl through the film, but they do not destroy the Lindsays' Garden of Eden, either. Instead, we read about their mischief in the newspapers where they're presumably harming the good people who predict disaster for the Lindsays. *Sirens,* seen from Estella's perspective, reveals how she is seduced into having a rollicking good time, and, surprise, no one gets punished, goes mad, or brandishes a weapon. Beautifully photographed eroticism for its own sake, a few rattled conceptions about Bohemians, and the prevailing social order is all you will get from *Sirens,* and that's just fine, thank you. For doom and gloom, you will have to choose another movie from the umpteen thousands that occupy the SEX=TROUBLE file. 🦴🦴🦴

1994 (R) 96m/C *AU GB* Hugh Grant, Tara Fitzgerald, Sam Neill, Elle Macpherson, Kate Fischer, Portia de Rossi, Pamela Rabe, Ben Mendelsohn, John Polson, Mark Gerber, Julia Stone, Ellie MacCarthy, Vincent Ball; ***Cameos:*** John Duigan; ***D:*** John Duigan; ***W:*** John Duigan; ***C:*** Geoff Burton; ***M:*** Rachel Portman. **VHS, LV, Closed Caption**

Sister My Sister

While it's by no means flawless, *Sister My Sister* has it all over *The Maids.* Based on a true French murder case, set in Le Mans, the story revolves around the Papin sisters, Christine, 28 (Joely Richardson), and Lea, 21 (Jodhi May). The two maids are treated like dirt by their employer Madame Lancelin, changed to Ranzard for the film (Julie Walters). With no other allies, they depend on each other for everything until the domestic situation reaches the boiling point, then it's Au Revoir, Madame, and Mademoiselle, too. Mademoiselle was Genevieve Lancelin, 27, changed to Isabelle Danzard for the film (Sophie Thursfield). Both were found brutally murdered on the evening of February 2. Their maids were found huddled together in bed, naked. The case fascinated intellectuals of 1933, who read Christine's confession in the newspapers: "I'd rather have had the skin of my mistresses than that they should have had mine or my sister's. I did not plan my crime and I didn't feel any hatred toward them." The sisters were both found to be sane and guilty. Christine was originally sentenced to death, then to a life of hard labor. Instead, she went mad and was dead within four years. Lea was sentenced to 10 years of hard labor, was released, and then lived a life of quiet obscurity. Director Nancy Meckler and screenwriter Wendy Kellelman show how the nerves of all four women were at the breaking point. Madame was used to dominating her daughter, Christine was used to dominating her sister. Madame expected her orders to be obeyed, it did not occur to her that by only obsessing on the maids' faults and never on their accomplishments, she was contributing to a toxic atmosphere which, tragically, could only be relieved with violence. By focusing on the emotional landscape of Madame's house, we see the Maids of Le Mans as the sad, neglected, futureless creatures they really were.

1994 (R) 89m/C *GB* Julie Walters, Joely Richardson, Jodhi May, Sophie Thursfield; ***D:*** Nancy Meckler; ***W:*** Wendy Kellelman; ***C:*** Ashley Ropwe; ***M:*** Stephen Warbeck. **VHS**

Slacker

Slacker is the sort of movie that will either make you laugh hysterically or switch theatres when the manager isn't looking. It made me laugh hysterically. There is something about people talking to themselves (in a movie, NOT in real life) that gives me the giggles. I had to scrape myself off the floor after one windbag (Richard Linklater) droned on and on about alternate realities to a priceless taxi driver and another explained how the U.S. and Russia have already set up colonies on the moon. Even better, *Slacker* led directly to 1993's *Dazed and Confused,* one of my all-time favorite movies, and I've never quite been able to scrape myself off the floor after that one.

1991 (R) 97m/C Richard Linklater, Rudy Basquez, Jean Caffeine, Jan Hockey, Stephan Hockey, Mark James, Samuel Dietert; ***D:*** Richard Linklater; ***W:*** Richard Linklater; ***C:*** Lee Daniel. **VHS**

Slam

A prison film with a difference: poetry, not violence, can set you free. The fact that two of the cast members are poets in their own right gives *Slam* a sincere, eloquent quality, enhanced by the documentary skills of director Marc Levin, making his fictional feature film debut here. Saul Williams is Ray Joshua, a small-time pot peddler who is present when his supplier Big Mike is shot. Ray is sent to prison for two years for possession of marijuana. While in prison, he resists joining the various factions, but becomes friends with one of the leaders, Bonz Malone as Bopha. Ray joins a writing workshop and is encouraged by Lauren Bell, the volunteer teacher. Bopha helps Ray obtain bail and Ray discovers that Big Mike was blinded by the shooting, but still alive. Having po-

Ray and Lauren (Saul Williams and Sonja Sohn) in *Slam.* Trimark Pictures; courtesy of the Kobal Collection

etry as an outlet makes Ray keenly aware that there is another way to deal with his life than with revenge and gangland warfare and Lauren is around to support his change of heart and mind. Naturally, if Ray and Lauren were mediocre poets, *Slam* wouldn't work, but Williams' and Sonja Sohn's rousing poetry slam really strikes a nerve with an audience.

1998 (R) 100m/C Saul Williams, Sonja Sohn, Bonz Malone; ***D:*** Marc Levin; ***W:*** Marc Levin, Saul Williams, Sonja Sohn, Richard Stratton; ***C:*** Mark Benjamin. Sundance Film Festival '98: Grand Jury Prize; Nominations: Independent Spirit Awards '99: Debut Performance (Sohn), Debut Performance (Williams). **VHS, DVD**

The Sleazy Uncle

In 1963, Vittorio Gassman starred as Bruno Fortuna, a jerk who introduces a kid portrayed by Jean-Louis Trintingnant to *The Easy Life.* In spite of the fact that Bruno had virtually no redeeming qualities, he gave Roberto the kid the best time he ever had in his life, and with the charismatic Vittorio Gassman as his guide, the reasons why were abundantly clear. In 1989's *The Sleazy Uncle,* Gassman plays another lovable rogue, but Uncle Lucca, like all of Gassman's unique characters, is created out of whole cloth. Uncle Lucca, an obscure but genuine poet, is adored by a small group of devoted fans, but he drives his responsible nephew Ricardo crazy. Lucca lies, steals, and carries his medical history with him at all times to facilitate one-night stands. The exasperated Ricardo finally takes his old uncle to court, where Lucca wins everyone's sympathy by crying his eyes out. Since Lucca's history is truly reprehensible, no one but a great actor like Vittorio Gassman could carry off such a sequence, but get away with it, he does. He sits there and cries like a baby and it works. Giancarlo Giannini, an actor who usually steals every picture he's in, is a wonderful foil for his co-star, handing most of their moments together to Gassman on

a platter. Franco Brusati's *The Sleazy Uncle* would make a memorable double bill on video along with Dino Risi's *The Easy Life.* An even more intriguing triple bill would include 1975's *Scent of a Woman* with Gassman originating the role that won Al Pacino the 1992 Oscar. This Italian classic, which won Gassman the Best Actor Award at the Cannes Film Festival, is, alas, not yet released on video, so in the meanwhile don't miss Vittorio Gassman's *tour-de-force* performance in 1989's *The Sleazy Uncle.* ***AKA:*** Lo Zio Indegno.

1989 104m/C *IT* Giancarlo Giannini, Vittorio Gassman, Andrea Ferreol, Stefania Sandrelli; ***D:*** Franco Brusati; ***W:*** Franco Brusati, Leo Benvenuti, Piero De Bernardi; ***C:*** Romano Albani. **VHS**

Sling Blade

It's been a while since Billy Bob Thornton wrote and starred in 1992's *One False Move.* At the time, his dialogue was better than his acting. But in *Sling Blade,* Thornton has written himself a role that any actor worth his salt would walk barefoot on ground glass to play, and son of a gun if he doesn't make the most of the chance. Thornton IS Karl Childers, a mentally disabled man (and a Capricorn) with terrible posture who sounds like the late Edgar Buchanan and who's spent most of his life in a state hospital for killing his mother and a young man many years before. Now, Karl is well, and he can't stay in hospital anymore as much as he'd like to. The hospital administrator (James Hampton) helps him get a job as a repairman, and Karl befriends Frank Wheatley, a fatherless little boy who lives with his mother Linda, and, sometimes, her alcoholic and abusive boyfriend, Doyle Hargraves. Linda's best friend is Vaughan Cunningham, a gay co-worker and a Virgo. Vaughan is played by a nearly unrecognizable John Ritter, in a startling, fully shaded performance. Vaughan wants to leave town, but he has a boyfriend and he cares about Frank and Linda, particularly when Doyle starts drinking and hitting people. Frank attaches himself to Karl, even when he finds out why his new friend was in the state hospital, and Linda (Natalie Canerday) invites him to stay in their garage, even though she also knows he was in the state hospital. She doesn't ask Karl to leave when she finds about what he did to his mother and the young man or even when he comes into her bedroom in the night, holding a hammer and asking to be baptized. (Frank and Linda are both Cancers, maybe that's why.) Doyle (played right on target by Dwight Yoakam as an Aries with Scorpio rising) gets drunker and meaner and life in the Wheatley home gets more and more tense. Karl tries to confront his past, both by going to see his no-account Dad (Robert Duvall in a cameo) and by talking about his crummy childhood with Frank. The 134-minute film moves at a deliberate pace; we know where the plot is going, but we're in no real hurry to get there, with all those rich characters and quirky humor and the tremendous star turns by Thornton and by Lucas *(American Gothic)* Black as Frank. *Sling Blade* is a pure American original—filled with tenderness and understanding, but also with a sense of the harsh measures needed to fight evil when it's destroying the lives of the only folks you've ever loved.

1996 (R) 134m/C Billy Bob Thornton, Dwight Yoakam, John Ritter, Lucas Black, Natalie Canerday, James Hampton, Robert Duvall, J.T. Walsh, Rick Dial, Brent Briscoe, Christy Ward, Col. Bruce Hampton, Vic Chesnutt, Mickey Jones, Jim Jarmusch, Ian Moore; ***D:*** Billy Bob Thornton; ***W:*** Billy Bob Thornton; ***C:*** Barry Markowitz; ***M:*** Daniel Lanois. Academy Awards '96: Best Adapted Screenplay (Thornton); Independent Spirit Awards '97: Best First Feature (Thornton); Writers Guild of America '96: Best Adapted Screenplay; Nominations: Academy Awards '96: Best Actor (Thornton); Screen Actors Guild Award '96: Best Actor (Thornton), Cast. **VHS, LV, Closed Caption, DVD**

The Slipper and the Rose

Not too many people know about *The Slipper and the Rose* and that's a shame. To be sure, there's a surfeit of *Cinderella* movies on video shelves competing for our attention, but this version has always been among my favorites. It was originally released at 146 minutes, an uncomfortable length for children, and reissued in 1980

Archbishop Geoffrey Bayldon is flanked by Gemma Craven as Cinderella and Richard Chamberlain, the Prince, in *The Slipper and the Rose.* Universal; courtesy of the Kobal Collection

at 127 minutes. The late 1970s were not a particularly receptive time for musicals, unless they reinvented the genre, like *Saturday Night Fever, Grease, Rock 'n' Roll High School, All That Jazz, The Blues Brothers,* or *Fame. The Slipper and the Rose* was definitely a musical out of its time. There's much to appreciate in Bryan Forbes' valentine to the classic fairy tale, though. For one thing, there's Richard Chamberlain as Prince Edward. Then in the swashbuckling phase of his long career, Chamberlain is clearly having a rattling good time in the role of a Prince Charming. Cinderella herself (Gemma Craven) is lovely, if a bit subdued, but the best British character actors in the business keep things moving along with energy to spare. Annette Crosbie, often cast as British Queens, is the Fairy Godmother, trying to bring a bit of fun into Cinderella's grim life with her mean stepmother (Margaret Lockwood in her swan song) and nasty stepsisters Palatine (Sherrie Hewson) and Isabella (Rosalind Ayres). The King (Michael Hordern) is eager to find a bride for Edward and suggests that he make his selection at the Grand Ball. Edward doesn't much like the idea ("It's like being a judge at a cattle show"), but reluctantly submits to the event where he expects to be bored out of his mind. And bored he is until Cinderella makes her entrance. We all know the drill after that. The Sherman Brothers, clearly influenced by Gilbert and Sullivan, composed a score of new songs designed to set the tone and advance the plot. So we hear Chamberlain singing "Why Can't I Be Two People?" and Craven doing a duet ("Suddenly It Happens") with Crosbie. The closest thing to a patter song is the "Protocoligorically Correct" number the King does with Lord Chamberlain Kenneth More, General Peter Graves, and the Palace Ministers. It's all great fun to watch (the costumes by Julie Harris are stunning) and listen to—a soundtrack album was even issued. At another point in movie history, *The Slipper and the Rose* might have been appreciated on its own terms. If you catch it on late night cable, it still can be, but there's no video release in sight yet. (Rating based on 127-minute version.) 🦴🦴🦴

1976 127m/C *GB* Richard Chamberlain, Gemma Craven, Annette Crosbie, Edith Evans, Christopher Gable, Michael Hordern, Margaret Lockwood, Kenneth More, Julian Orchard, Lally Bowers, Sherrie Hewson, Rosalind Ayres, John Turner, Keith Skinner, Polly Williams, Norman Bird, Roy Barraclough, Peter Graves, Bryan Forbes; ***D:*** Bryan Forbes; ***W:*** Robert B. Sherman, Richard M. Sherman, Bryan Forbes; ***C:*** Tony Imi; ***M:*** Robert B. Sherman, Richard M. Sherman.

Small Change

François Truffaut's movies are filled with sweet observations, invariably from a detached viewpoint. *Small Change* is a delightful romp with a group of school children. At one point, a small child topples from a high building, lands on his fanny in some soft bushes, then laughs his head off. Kids bounce back from life at its hardest, Truffaut says. They live through experiences that would shatter adults, pick themselves up and go right on living, all the more resilient for their brushes with hardship. If only it really were that simple.... 🦴🦴🦴🦴

1976 (PG) 104m/C *FR* Geory Desmouceaux, Philippe Goldman, Jean-Francois Stevenin, Chantal Mercier, Claudio Deluca, Frank Deluca, Richard Golfier, Laurent Devlaeminck, Francis Devlaeminck, Sylvie Grezel, Pascale Bruchon, Nicole Felix; ***D:*** Francois Truffaut; ***W:*** Francois Truffaut, Suzanne Schiffman; ***C:*** Pierre William Glenn; ***M:*** Maurice Jaubert. **VHS, LV**

The Smallest Show on Earth

This charming Basil Dearden comedy focuses entirely on the management of a dilapidated movie theatre. The elderly ticket taker (Margaret Rutherford as Mrs. Fazackerlee) is used to accepting barter as the price of admission from many of the patrons, the elderly projectionist is an alcoholic named Percy Quill who occasionally muddles the reels (Peter Sellers was only 32 at the time), and the sweet young couple (Virginia McKenna and Bill Travers) who inherit this beat-up bijou haven't a clue about how to whip the place in shape. This affectionate look at the days before mall multiplexes is scripted with obvious affection by William Rose and John Eldridge, who really capture the essence of why the neighborhood theatre meant so much to those who still remember them. ***AKA:*** Big Time Operators. 🦴🦴🦴

1957 80m/B *GB* Bill Travers, Virginia McKenna, Margaret Rutherford, Peter Sellers, Bernard Miles, Leslie Phillips, Stringer Davis, Francis De Wolff, Sidney James, June Cunningham; ***D:*** Basil Dearden; ***W:*** William Rose, John Eldridge; ***C:*** Douglas Slocombe. **VHS**

Smoke

Movies change our lives, for better and worse. *Smoke* is the movie that broke my heart after I saw it with a male viewer I respected and considered a friend. We got a lift from someone who asked me what I thought of the movie, so I told him. For the guy who saw the movie with me, the friendship ended right there, although it took me three years to believe it. I'm a fatalist, so I'm convinced it would have ended anyway. But over a movie? *Smoke* takes place in and around Auggie Wren's Brooklyn Cigar Store. The stars are Harvey Keitel as Auggie and William Hurt as Paul Benjamin, a sad writer whose wife was killed before the movie begins; Harold Perrineau Jr. as Thomas (Rashid) Cole, a troubled kid whom Paul tries to help; and Forest Whitaker as Cyrus, the kid's father. Jared Harris, Giancarlo Esposito, and Victor Argo are Jimmy Rose, Tommy, and Vinnie, some of the other sketchily drawn characters in the orbit of Auggie's cigar shop. Unlike my companion, I was extremely unmoved by 112 minutes of well-acted hot air. In a feature-length study of guys where the only women with screen time of any consequence are (1) killed and not heard, (2) in a few sequences to flesh out a guy, namely Stockard Channing as Ruby, Auggie's ex-wife, and (3) in one sequence only, namely Ashley Judd as Ruby's strung-out daughter, I'd just as soon the male screenwriter blue-penciled them from the flick's first draft. If women don't serve any real function in a story about men (AND vice versa, naturally), they don't need to be there at all. I tried to explain this in the car and un-

"I look into your eyes and all I see are trashy dreams."

—Katherine (Mary Kay Place) to her daughter (Laura Dern) in *Smooth Talk.*

wittingly blue-penciled myself out of AND derailed The Friendship, Ouch.

1995 (R) 112m/C Harvey Keitel, William Hurt, Stockard Channing, Forest Whitaker, Harold Perrineau Jr., Ashley Judd, Mary Ward, Victor Argo, Jared Harris, Giancarlo Esposito, Mel Gorham; ***D:*** Wayne Wang; ***W:*** Paul Auster; ***C:*** Adam Holender; ***M:*** Rachel Portman. Nominations: Independent Spirit Awards '96: Best Supporting Actor (Perrineau); Screen Actors Guild Award '95: Best Supporting Actress (Channing). **VHS, LV, Closed Caption**

Smoke Signals

Smoke Signals played at the Bridge theatre on my block for MONTHS. Not since *Strictly Ballroom* did I recall seeing such long lines, lured mostly by enthusiastic word-of-mouth praise rather than print advertising. It's a road movie about two mismatched traveling companions from the Coeur d'Alene Indian reservation. Victor Joseph (Adam Beach) isn't thrilled by the idea of traveling from Idaho to Arizona with a nerd like Thomas (Evan Adams), but the trip is necessary, Victor can't afford it, and Thomas is paying for everything as long as he can tag along. The taciturn Victor tries to instruct Thomas in a few social skills and dress tips, but the sad nature of their trip (bringing home the remains of Victor's father Arnold) gives Sherman Alexie's screenplay a resonance and density beyond the depiction of a mere personality clash. Arnold Joseph (Gary Farmer) rescued baby Thomas from a fire that killed both his parents. But Victor hasn't seen his father since Arnold deserted his family in a drunken rage 10 long years ago. Victor's feelings about Arnold are understandably complex at the outset, and the trip helps him to come to terms with his father. Even as he examines deeper relationship issues, director Chris Eyre maintains a light comedic tone throughout. Thus audiences who watch *Smoke Signals* always leave in a great mood, and many viewers see it several times. This sleeper's a charmer!

1998 (PG-13) 88m/C Adam Beach, Evan Adams, Irene Bedard, Gary Farmer, Tantoo Cardinal, Michelle St. John, Robert Miano, Molly Cheek, Elaine Miles, Michael Greyeyes, Chief Leonard George, John Trudell, Cody Lightning, Simon Baker; ***Cameos:*** Tom Skerritt, Cynthia Geary; ***D:*** Chris Eyre; ***W:*** Sherman Alexie; ***C:*** Brian Capener; ***M:*** E. C. Smith. Independent Spirit Awards '99: Debut Performance (Adams); Sundance Film Festival '98: Audience Award, Filmmakers Trophy; Nominations: Independent Spirit Awards '99: Best Supporting Actor (Farmer), First Screenplay. **VHS, LV, Closed Caption**

Smooth Talk

When *Smooth Talk* first played at Wheeler Auditorium at the University of California at Berkeley, the resounding hisses and boos were heard clear across campus; it was politically incorrect for a movie to show a teenage girl (Laura Dern) apparently asking to be raped by a stranger (Treat Williams). A closer look reveals that this is neither the point of Joyce Chopra's film, nor of the original story by Joyce Carol Oates. It's one thing to goof around in the safety of a shopping mall with girlfriends, quite another to be confronted with a psychotic adult male who threatens both his target and her family. There is nothing particularly seductive about Williams' approach, and Dern does nothing to encourage him once she realizes the extreme danger of her situation. However, she IS playing a kid, and her perceptions and decisions are not as savvy as an adult's might be in the same predicament. The most memorable aspect of the film, which won the Grand Jury Prize at the Sundance Film Festival in 1986, is Dern's heartrending performance; the picture certainly did NADA for Williams' career! Chopra later made *The Lemon Sisters,* plus the telefeatures *Murder in New Hampshire: The Pamela Smart Story* and *Danger of Love.* Dern and Mary Kay Place worked together again in *Citizen Ruth.*

1985 (PG-13) 92m/C Laura Dern, Treat Williams, Mary Kay Place, Levon Helm, William Ragsdale, Margaret Welsh, Sarah Inglis; ***D:*** Joyce Chopra; ***W:*** Tom Cole; ***C:*** James Glennon. Sundance Film Festival '86: Grand Jury Prize. **VHS, LV**

So Long at the Fair

You may have vague memories of *The Vanishing Lady,* a 1955 *Alfred Hitchcock Presents* episode starring his daughter Pat. Originally titled *Into Thin Air,* it was reportedly based on a true story of 1889's Paris World Exposition: a young woman checks into a hotel with a relative who immediately becomes quite ill. A doctor is called, he sends her to fetch the medication and when she comes back, the relative is gone, and absolutely no one recalls who they are. She thinks she's going mad, but there IS a rather horrible explanation. Well, there's only so much that can be done in 30 minutes and Hitchcock himself didn't direct, so try to find *So Long at the Fair,* an outstanding British drama co-directed by Anthony Darnborough and Terence Fisher. Jean Simmons and David Tomlinson are Victoria and John Barton, who check into the hotel run by Mme. Herve (Cathleen Nesbitt). Brother John gets sick, Victoria sends for Dr. Hart (Andre Morell, a future Professor Quatermass) and then the mystery begins. It's a beautifully done interpretation of Anthony Thorne's novel (Thorne co-scripted), and the acting throughout is first rate. And who could wish for a more attractive and kind ally than Dirk Bogarde's George Hathaway. Honor Blackman, then in her English rose period, is in it too, and so is another future Bond girl, Zena Marshall. 🦴🦴🦴

1950 86m/B *GB* Jean Simmons, Dirk Bogarde, David Tomlinson, Honor Blackman, Cathleen Nesbitt, Felix Aylmer, Marcel Poncin, Austin Trevor, Andre Morell, Zena Marshall, Betty Warren; ***D:*** Terence Fisher, Anthony Darnborough; ***W:*** Hugh Mills, Anthony Thorne; ***C:*** Reg Wyer.

Sois Belle et Tais-Toi

A title like *Look Beautiful and Shut Up* won't win *Sois Belle et Tais-Tois* a rampaging horde of female fans, although there is much of interest for both men and women who discover this by chance on a video shelf. When this flick was first released in the summer of 1958, Jean-Paul Belmondo, then 25, and Alain Delon, 22, somehow escaped critical attention, although they're both quite good here and it's a treat to see them in the early days of their careers. The film is a vehicle for sexy Mylene Demongeot, who'd turned in a memorable performance the previous summer as Abigail in *The Witches of Salem* opposite Yves Montand and Simone Signoret. Five screenwriters including Roger Vadim worked on the plot, which blends a lively action caper with a more conventional romantic comedy. The cast is better than the material which, however lightweight, is at least entertaining. Demongeot worked in many European (including British) films, but did not attract international frenzy as Brigitte Bardot had in the early 1950s. Bardot was a straightforward sex kitten, however, and Demongeot's characters tended to be more calculating, deliberate, and practical in their erotic decision-making: Demongeot would never merely look beautiful and shut up. Still, *Sois Belle et Tais-Tois* is a fascinating curio of its era. ***AKA:*** Look Beautiful and Shut Up; Be Beautiful but Shut Up; Be Beautiful and Shut Up; Blonde for Danger. 🦴🦴½

1958 110m/B *FR* Henri Vidal, Mylene Demongeot, Jean-Paul Belmondo, Alain Delon, Hugh Brooks, Roger Hanin; ***D:*** Marc Allegret; ***W:*** Roger Vadim, Odette Joyeux, William Benjamin, Jean Marsan, Gabriel Arout; ***C:*** Armand Thirard. **VHS**

Song of the Siren

My particular favorite at 1995's Jewish Film Festival was Eytan Fox's *Song of the Siren,* based on Irit Linur's best-selling novel. *Siren* takes place during the days of Operation Desert Storm, but Talila Katz, its wry and funny protagonist, pretty much ignores the conflict, the news bulletins, and all the precautions she's supposed to be taking in order to outlive the war. Instead, she's concerned with finding a husband, and not just any husband. Her choice is Noah, a food engineer so cute that violins play when she first lays eyes on him. But things get in the way, as they often do during 91-minute love stories. The intense focus on the personal at a time when the media focused an nothing but the war seems very real. ***AKA:*** Shirat Ha'Sirena. 🦴🦴🦴

1994 91m/C *IS* Dalit Kahan, Boaz Gur-Lavi, Yair Lapid, Avital Dicker; ***D:*** Eytan Fox; ***C:*** Avi Koren.

Sorceress

Sorceress, directed by longtime François Truffaut–collaborator Suzanne Schiffman,

They wanted meat so they ate the Flower Children.

—Tagline from the movie *Sore Losers.*

is an immaculate film about a 13th century French village and the priest who confronts their "heretical" superstitions. Co-written by art history professor Pamela Berger, the story never lets you forget for an instant that it is told through 20th century eyes. For that reason, this rather remote film lacks one crucial ingredient: the element of surprise. Even so, *Sorceress* is well worth watching for the superb acting and fine period details. ***AKA:*** Le Moine et la Sorcière. 🦴🦴🦴

1988 98m/C *FR* Tcheky Karyo, Christine Boisson, Jean Carmet, Raoul Billerey, Catherine Frot, Feodor Atkine; ***D:*** Suzanne Schiffman; ***W:*** Pamela Berger, Suzanne Schiffman; ***C:*** Patrick Blossier. **VHS**

Sore Losers

Another one-joke movie with a weird-looking cast and cinematography to match PLUS comic book ambiance, substandard sound to match the level of the dialogue, and uniformly wretched acting by everybody. Even pharmaceuticals might not enhance your tolerance for this one, although seeing it on a double bill with Ray Dennis Steckler's 1966 opus *Rat Pfink and Boo Boo* might. Will probably come to its final resting place on a Le Bad Cinema video shelf. The closing credits, transcribed from the screen, were in a strange type that I did my best to decipher, although I gave up when the credits began to crawl for seven FBI agents and 14 hippy partygoers. Played at San Francisco's Indie Fest in 1999. 🦴🦴

1997 69m/C Jack Oblivian, Kerine Elkins, Mike Maker, D'lana Tunnell, Hugh Brooks, Ghetty Chasun; ***D:*** John Michael McCarthy; ***W:*** John Michael McCarthy; ***C:*** Darin Ipema.

Sorrento Beach

The three Moynihan sisters grew up in Sorrento Beach, but only Hilary (Caroline Gillmer) stays there as an adult, raising the adolescent Troy (Ben Thomas) and tending to her dad, Wal (Ray Barrett). Pippa (Tara Morice) lives in New York, and Meg (Caroline Goodall), who lives in London, is the acclaimed author of *Melancholy,* an ill-disguised novel about the sisters and a book which touches a responsive chord in reader Marge Morrissey (Joan Plowright). When Wal dies, the sisters are reunited, and although young Troy is filled with questions for his aunt, neither Hilary nor Pippa will discuss the book with Meg. She's hurt ("All those people out there are talking about it and not my own sisters!?"), but the Moynihan women share a painful secret from the past—involving Hilary's late husband—that has estranged them for many years. With such undercurrents, why don't Pippa and Meg fly back to New York and London straight after Dad's funeral? Instead they talk around subjects for 112 minutes and Marge's magazine editor friend Dick Bennett (John Hargreaves) chips in with HIS opinion that Meg's recent press interviews are doing Australia no favors. For all this illuminating chatter, my favorite characters are Marge (Plowright is wonderful here); Troy (appealingly played by Thomas), who yawns whenever the grown-ups warm up to snap at one another; and the poor beautiful housecat, who is forever being shoved off HER furniture! What's a mistress of her domain to do?: "That's right, I'll eat all this lovely fish they expect to have for dinner. Everyone is so busy chatting, NO ONE will notice!" ***AKA:*** Hotel Sorrento. 🦴🦴🦴

1995 (R) 112m/C *AU* Caroline Goodall, Caroline Gillmer, Tara Morice, Joan Plowright, John Hargreaves, Ray Barrett, Ben Thomas, Nicholas Bell; ***D:*** Richard Franklin; ***W:*** Richard Franklin, Peter Fitzpatrick, Hannie Rayson; ***C:*** Geoff Burton; ***M:*** Nevida Tyson-Chew. Australian Film Institute '95: Best Adapted Screenplay, Best Supporting Actor (Barrett); Nominations: Australian Film Institute '95: Best Actress (Gillmer), Best Actress (Goodall), Best Director (Franklin), Best Film. **VHS**

S.O.S. Titanic

Why include this ABC telefeature that aired in a 180-minute time slot in the fall of 1979 before it was released theatrically overseas in the spring of 1980? How many more movies do we need to see about this maritime catastrophe, anyway? Except for *A Night to Remember,* they all have the same plot: two-thirds fictional dramatizations of the lives of characters who may or may not have existed in real life, one-third rescue operations, with a moment or two at the end for someone to say something about

The Folly of Man. As these make-believe yarns go, *S.O.S. Titanic* is pretty good. It's nearly the end of the line for David Janssen as the doomed John Jacob Astor. (Janssen's only 49 here, but looks much older and he died before an edited version played in theatres.) Susan St. James does a nice job in the role of a passenger whose name isn't on any of the Titanic lists. David Warner is quite effective in one of his more restrained roles as Laurence Beesley, a survivor who wrote an account of the disaster. Helen Mirren is on hand as May Sloan, another survivor, and Ian Holm is perfect as always as the self-important Bruce Ismay. James Costigan's script, while not in the same league as Eric Ambler's 1958 adaptation of Walter Lord's classic book, is intelligently low-key. But the question remains for filmmakers of the future: what else needs to be said about the Titanic? With all the time, energy, and money that have been spent since April 15, 1912, every microbe on the Titanic could have had a lifeboat of its very own. Historical Note: The very first movie about the Titanic starred actress Dorothy Gibson, a surviving first-class passenger who wears the same clothes in the 10-minute movie that she was wearing when she was rescued. Her co-stars include Alex Francis, Jack Adolfi, and Guy Oliver. *Saved from the Titanic* was released on May 14, 1912, and is considered a lost film so if anyone is hoarding it in an attic (and you know who you are), contact your nearest archive!

1979 102m/C *GB* David Janssen, Cloris Leachman, Susan St. James, David Warner, Ian Holm, Helen Mirren, Harry Andrews, David Battley, Ed Bishop, Peter Bourke, Shevaun Briars, Nick Brimble, Jacob Brooke, Catherine Byrne, Tony Caunter, Warren Clarke, Nicholas Davies, Deborah Fallender; ***D:*** Billy Hale; ***W:*** James Costigan; ***C:*** Christopher Challis; ***M:*** Howard Blake. **VHS**

Spanking the Monkey

This is a good guy's movie, which is not damning it with feint praise. It's just that guys who dig this movie do so with such passion that it's clearly primal for them in a way that it isn't for me. *Spanking the Monkey* put David O. Russell on the map as an indie filmmaker and made it easier for him to assemble a big-name cast for his next project, *Flirting with Disaster.* I'd like to think that Russell simply has a vivid imagination than to guess about the inspiration for this one-of-a-kind flick.

1994 (R) 99m/C Jeremy Davies, Alberta Watson, Benjamin Hendrickson, Carla Gallo, Matthew Puckett; ***D:*** David O. Russell; ***W:*** David O. Russell; ***C:*** Mike Mayers. Independent Spirit Awards '95: Best First Feature; Sundance Film Festival '94: Audience Award; Nominations: Independent Spirit Awards '95: Best Supporting Actress (Gallo), Debut Performance (Davies). **VHS, LV**

Sparrows

Mary Pickford was the only woman among the original founders of United Artists. (Her three co-founders were D.W. Griffith, Douglas Fairbanks, and Charlie Chaplin.) Since all four wanted to make movies free of studio interference, their original goal in 1919 was to release movies they produced themselves. *Sparrows,* for which Pickford served as star AND producer, was one of several attempts to change the image of Little Mary. At 34, she had every right, but audiences cherished the notion of her remaining a child with golden curls forever, and boxoffice receipts for *Sparrows* suffered as a result. Director William Beaudine has a miserable reputation today, but he did a credible job on *Sparrows.* The appealing element about *Sparrows* is that Pickford singlehandedly rescued a batch of abused children from Grimes, a villainous farmer (vividly interpreted by Gustav von Seyffertitz, who had played a memorable Moriarty in 1920's *Sherlock Holmes* opposite John Barrymore and Roland Young). Pickford could afford the best, so the children's escape through the swamplands of Louisiana was convincingly and eerily photographed by the great Charles Rosher, Karl Struss, and Hal Mohr. The eloquent portrayal of Mrs. Grimes by Charlotte Mineau reveals the stark desperation of a woman who knows there is no escape from her marriage to a brute. (Pickford wears braids throughout most of *Sparrows.*)

1926 81m/B Mary Pickford, Gustav von Seyffertitz, Charlotte Mineau, Roy Stewart, Mary Louise Miller,

Spec O'Donnell and Mary Pickford in *Sparrows.* United Artists; courtesy of the Kobal Collection

"Spec" O'Donnell, Mary Frances McLean, Camilla Johnson, Seeseell Ann Johnson; ***D:*** William Beaudine; ***W:*** C. Gardner Sullivan, Winifred Dunn; ***C:*** Charles Rosher, Karl Struss, Hal Mohr; ***M:*** William Perry. **VHS, LV**

A Special Day

They can do anything to Sophia Loren: strip her of makeup, stuff her in dumpy dresses, rip her stockings, frazzle her hair—anything, and she'll still take your breath away. In *A Special Day,* she plays an unappreciated housewife who befriends a disgraced homosexual (played by the late Marcello Mastroianni in an imaginative casting coup that led straight to an Oscar nomination). Ettore Scola films Ruggero Maccari's script rather like a play, with the two characters providing a dash of reality against the unreal backdrop of an unseen Hitler/Mussolini parade. The stars, as usual, make 105 minutes seem like ten and a half. ***AKA:*** Una Giornata Speciale; The Great Day. 🦴🦴🦴

1977 105m/C *IT* Sophia Loren, Marcello Mastroianni, John Vernon, Francoise Berd; ***D:*** Ettore Scola; ***W:*** Ettore Scola, Ruggero Maccari, Maurizio Costanzo; ***C:*** Pasqualino De Santis; ***M:*** Armando Trovajoli. Golden Globe Awards '78: Best Foreign Film; Nominations: Academy Awards '77: Best Actor (Mastroianni), Best Foreign Film. **VHS, LV, Letterbox**

Special Effects

I can never tell whether director Larry Cohen is putting everyone on or not. Just when I'm convinced he's made one of the funniest FBI movies of all time (1977's *The Private Files of J. Edgar Hoover* starring the late Broderick Crawford), he'll come up with a genuinely scary film like 1982's *Q* starring Michael Moriarty. 1985's *Special Effects* falls somewhere between these two pictures in terms of quality. It's also filled with Cohen's weird sense of humor. Zoe Tamerlis plays a dual role as a doomed would-be actress and the Good Will employee who's hired to impersonate her. Tamerlis is no great shakes in either role, but maybe she isn't supposed to be. Eric Bogosian stars as a porno movie director who plans to make a film of the dead actress in order to trap the Killer. Yes, there is a catch. (Of course.) Cohen has a good time showing how the movie industry swallows everything it touches, including police detective Kevin J. O'Connor. Cohen also has fun with the victim's boring husband (and the most likely suspect) who wants to drag back his first wife and later the Good Will employee to take care of him and the baby, a fate worse than anything anyone can imagine. Along with the *It's Alive* trilogy and most of Larry Cohen's other camp classics, *Special Effects* is great fun to watch. It is also interesting to observe Bogosian's emerging charisma, long before he made 1988's *Talk Radio.*

1985 (R) 103m/C *GB* Zoe Tamerlis, Eric Bogosian, Kevin J. O'Connor, Brad Rijn, Bill Oland, Richard Greene; ***D:*** Larry Cohen; ***W:*** Larry Cohen. **VHS**

Spice World: The Movie

As a preview screening of *Spice World* made abundantly clear, it doesn't really matter what's on the silver or small screen OR on the tweaked soundtrack as long as the five Spice Girls themselves can be seen and heard by millions of their rampaging fans. The fact that only Sporty and Scary (the two Melanies, Chisholm, then 24, and Brown, then 22) can really sing, dance, and act is beside the point. The fact that the filmmakers are clearly trying to conceal that Victoria ("Posh") Adams, then 23, has no talent whatsoever (her speaking voice even sounds as if it's been dubbed by another actress in several sequences that require real emotion) is equally irrelevant. And the painful reality that Kim Fuller's screenplay would be dead on arrival in any other film has obviously been dismissed by Spicemaniacs, who bring their own movie to the theatre anyway. In that movie, they too can sing, dance, and hang out with the Spice Girls forever and ever. Patterned after *A Hard Day's Night, Spice World* follows the Spice Girls in their pursuit of Girl Power despite the Forces of Evil that would attempt to crush them and distort their message. These include tacky tabloid publisher Kevin McMaxford (Barry Humphries), his evil minion Damien (Richard O'Brien), Piers, a daft documentarian played by Alan Cumming, and Clifford, their maladjusted manager (Richard E. Grant, who was more believable wrangling with his very own talking boil in 1989's *How to Get Ahead in Advertising* than he is here). The Forces of Good are represented by Naoki Mori as Nicola, their best friend and a mother-to-be. (They don't romp in a field here, that's Boy Power; instead they hold hands and lend moral support in a delivery room.) $25 million was spent on this extravaganza, which includes massive Foley artistry and about five bucks for a toy bus in an action sequence on London Bridge. Brit stars galore turn up in cameos that scarcely do them justice, although Stephen Fry as a judge and Hugh Laurie as Hercule Poirot fare the best, and Jennifer Saunders and Roger Moore seem rather embarrassed evoking their past triumphs in *Absolutely Fabulous* and the Bond flicks. Ab/Fab director Bob Spiers, also responsible for Disney's abysmally unfunny 1996 remake of *That Darn Cat,* is content to tread carefully in the footsteps of Richard Lester without, of course, sharing Lester's impeccable sense of taste, timing, and sheer comedy. Emma ("Baby") Bunton, then 22, and Geri ("Ginger") Halliwell, who photographs ten years older than her 25-plus years, plus Sporty, Scary, and Posh, share the spotlight for all 92 minutes of *Spice World,* which opened in the United States colonies on January 23, four short months before Halliwell left the group on May 31 to become a health care activist and United Nations Ambassador! Her sudden departure before the group's first American tour in the summer of 1998 and the subsequent pregnancies of Scary and Posh made *Spice World* an instant period piece, which it virtually was even prior to its

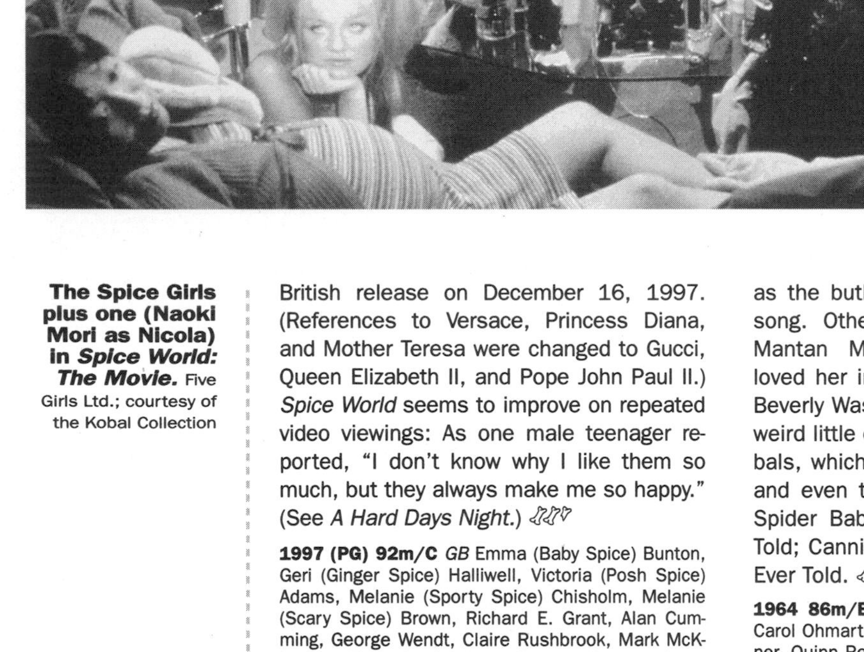

The Spice Girls plus one (Naoki Mori as Nicola) in *Spice World: The Movie.* Five Girls Ltd.; courtesy of the Kobal Collection

British release on December 16, 1997. (References to Versace, Princess Diana, and Mother Teresa were changed to Gucci, Queen Elizabeth II, and Pope John Paul II.) *Spice World* seems to improve on repeated video viewings: As one male teenager reported, "I don't know why I like them so much, but they always make me so happy." (See *A Hard Days Night.*)

1997 (PG) 92m/C *GB* Emma (Baby Spice) Bunton, Geri (Ginger Spice) Halliwell, Victoria (Posh Spice) Adams, Melanie (Sporty Spice) Chisholm, Melanie (Scary Spice) Brown, Richard E. Grant, Alan Cumming, George Wendt, Claire Rushbrook, Mark McKinney, Richard O'Brien, Roger Moore, Barry Humphries, Jason Flemyng, Meat Loaf, Bill Paterson, Stephen Fry, Richard Briers, Michael Barrymore, Naoki Mori, Hugh Laurie, Jennifer Saunders; ***Cameos:*** Elvis Costello, Bob Geldof, Bob Hoskins, Elton John; ***D:*** Bob Spiers; ***W:*** Kim Fuller, Jamie Curtis; ***C:*** Clive Tickner; ***M:*** Paul Newcastle. **VHS, LV, Closed Caption, DVD**

Spider Baby

Spider Baby is a movie to cure anyone's blues. For starters, Lon Chaney Jr. stars as the butler and he also sings the title song. Other horror movie veterans like Mantan Moreland, Carol Ohmart (you loved her in *House on Haunted Hill*), and Beverly Washburn are also on hand in this weird little comedy about a family of cannibals, which must be seen to be believed, and even then.... ***AKA:*** The Liver Eaters; Spider Baby, or the Maddest Story Ever Told; Cannibal Orgy, or the Maddest Story Ever Told.

1964 86m/B Lon Chaney Jr., Mantan Moreland, Carol Ohmart, Sid Haig, Beverly Washburn, Jill Banner, Quinn Redeker, Mary Mitchell; ***D:*** Jack Hill; ***W:*** Jack Hill; ***C:*** Alfred Taylor. **VHS**

Spirit of the Beehive

Little Ana Torrent has a wistful, appealing quality, with sinister undertones. She and her sister are so enthralled by the *Frankenstein* movie that they begin to act it out in their own lives. Victor Erice directs in a tense, if leisurely style, and the cinematography, featuring extended dissolves, effectively captures Erice's haunting story of childhood. Torrent went on to star in 1976's *Cria!* for Carlos Saura, 1980's *The Nest* for Jaime De Arminian, and 1989's *Blood and Sand* for Javier Elorrieta. ***AKA:*** El Espiritu de la Colmena. 🦴🦴🦴

1973 95m/C *SP* Fernando Gomez, Teresa Gimpera, Ana Torrent, Isabel Telleria, Laly Soldevilla; ***D:*** Victor Erice; ***W:*** Victor Erice; ***C:*** Luis Cuadrado; ***M:*** Luis De Pablo. **VHS, LV**

The Spitfire Grill

Alison Elliott may not be my first choice for Peter Gallagher's femme fatale in *The Underneath,* but she is THE best possible Percy Talbott in Lee David Zlotoff's *The Spitfire Grill.* Actually, there are three breathtaking performances here. Ellen Burstyn does a beautiful job as Hannah Ferguson, the owner of the Spitfire Grill, and Marcia Gay Harden turns the role of an unsophisticated small-town wife and mother inside out in her portrayal of Shelby Goddard. The weak link here is Will Patton as Shelby's mean husband Nathan. By playing the same cookie cutter villain in most of his films over the last 15 years, Patton has remained steadily employed. Except for the Maine "accent" he uses here, Nathan is basically the same bad guy you saw in *No Way Out,* without the subtle shading a John Mahoney or J.T. Walsh would give an ambiguous character. Fortunately, Patton's not in every other sequence here. Percy has just been released from prison on a manslaughter rap and Nathan has it in for her. She finds a home working at the Grill and soon becomes fast friends with Hannah and Shelby. She also wanders through the beautiful countryside that surrounds the town of Gilead and befriends a silent reclusive loner (John M. Jackson) she dubs Johnny B., after the song. Shelby then comes up with an idea to help Hannah; Shelby's for it, Nathan's against it, and a deliberately paced character study evolves into a full-fledged melodrama. The sterling work of Elliott, Burstyn, and Harding undoubtedly helped to make this one an Audience Award winner at 1996's Sundance Film Festival. ***AKA:*** Care of the Spitfire Grill. 🦴🦴🦴

1995 (PG-13) 117m/C Alison Elliott, Ellen Burstyn, Marcia Gay Harden, Will Patton, Kieran Mulroney, Gailard Sartain, Louise De Cormier, John M. Jackson; ***D:*** Lee David Zlotoff; ***W:*** Lee David Zlotoff; ***C:*** Rob Draper; ***M:*** James Horner. Sundance Film Festival '96: Audience Award. **VHS, LV, Closed Caption**

Squeeze

I saw three movies in a row where kids were well along on the road to self-destruction before the closing credits. *Squeeze* looked like it was going to be the fourth variation on the same thing, only it wasn't. Director Robert Patton-Spruill is an acting teacher in Boston and he wrote the screenplay specifically for three young actors who star in the film, including Eddie Cutanda as Hector and Phuong Duong as Boa. Because the movie ends on an upbeat note, it may strike some viewers as being less "honest" than a picture that focuses on lives that are over by age 12. Still, there are kids who used to run with gangs and they managed to grow up anyhow and *Squeeze* shows one possible way to do that. The most talented of the kids is Tyrone Burton as Tyson, and the cinematography by Richard Moos is especially noteworthy. The script for *Squeeze* could have benefited from a few more drafts, but the film does represent a promising start for the future career of Robert Patton-Spruill. 🦴🦴½

1997 (R) 105m/C Tyrone Burton, Eddie Cutanda, Phuong Duong, Geoffrey Rhue, Russell Jones, Leigh Williams; ***D:*** Robert Patton-Spruill; ***W:*** Robert Patton-Spruill; ***C:*** Richard Moos; ***M:*** Bruce Flowers. Nominations: Independent Spirit Awards '98: Debut Performance (Burton), Debut Performance (Cutanda, Duong). **VHS, LV, Closed Caption**

Stacking

In *Stacking,* Megan Follows, Christine Lahti, Frederic Forrest, Peter Coyote, and Jason Gedrick turn in remarkable performances, but this low-key film failed to find its proper audience. It's a shame because Victoria Jenkins' wise, cliche-free screenplay reveals that she knows her rural characters through and through. Sensitively directed by Martin Rosen and shot by

Phuong Duong, Eddie Cutanda, and Tyrone Burton in *Squeeze.* Miramax; courtesy of the Kobal Collection

Richard Bowen, the film takes a great many chances with its material and succeeds most of the time. A decade later, most of the cast were earning their bread and butter on television. The gifted Follows, after a strong, prolific start between 1984 and 1991, all but faded from view, except in a one-shot *Outer Limits* episode or in endless encore airings of *Anne of Green Gables/Anne of Avonlea*. ***AKA:*** Season of Dreams.

1987 (PG) 95m/C Christine Lahti, Megan Follows, Frederic Forrest, Peter Coyote, Jason Gedrick; ***D:*** Martin Rosen; ***W:*** Victoria Jenkins; ***C:*** Richard Bowen, Paul Elliott, Richard Bowen; ***M:*** Patrick Gleeson. **VHS, LV**

Stand and Deliver

Stand and Deliver began life as *Walking on Water* when it was first shown at 1987's Mill Valley Film Festival. Jaime Escalante (Edward James Olmos) is a mathematics teacher at an East Los Angeles high school where half the students fail to graduate. Knowing that education is the only way that his students can escape a lifetime of low-paying jobs, Escalante is tough and demanding with his class as he inspires them to pass the California Advanced Placement Calculus Test with distinction. Olmos won an Oscar nomination for his impassioned performance and the kids (including Lou Diamond Phillips in the role of Angel) are totally believable as they prepare for the Olympic-style challenge of the test.

1988 (PG) 105m/C Edward James Olmos, Lou Diamond Phillips, Rosana De Soto, Andy Garcia, Will Gotay, Ingrid Oliu, Virginia Paris, Mark Eliot; ***D:*** Ramon Menendez; ***W:*** Ramon Menendez, Tom Musca; ***C:*** Tom Richmond; ***M:*** Craig Safan. Independent Spirit Awards '89: Best Actor (Olmos), Best Director (Menendez), Best Film, Best Screenplay, Best Supporting Actor (Phillips), Best Supporting Actress (De Soto); Nominations: Academy Awards '88: Best Actor (Olmos). **VHS, LV, 8mm, Closed Caption**

Star Kid

Star Kid is the movie I watched to cheer myself up after *The Sweet Hereafter.* It's a

Spencer (Joseph Mazzello) and Turbo (Joey Simmrin) in *Star Kid.* Trimark Pictures; courtesy of the Kobal Collection

wonderful kiddie flick about Spencer Griffith (Joseph Mazzello), a sweet little boy who's constantly tormented at school by Turbo Bruntley (Joey Simmrin). Spencer and his sister Stacey (Ashlee Levitch) have been rather neglected by their workaholic dad Rolan (Richard Gilliland, Laurie in 1978's *Little Women*) since the sad death of their beautiful Mom (Heidi Lotito). All Spencer wants to do is become friends with a pretty little girl in his class and dodge Turbo. In the meanwhile, his sympathetic teacher Janet Holloway (Corinne Bohrer) has to intervene whenever he's being pulverized. Spencer's life takes an unexpected turn when he meets an alien Cyborsuit (Alex Daniels, with voice by Arthur Burghardt). The object is for Spencer to get INSIDE the Cyborsuit and fight the forces of evil: Turbo, nasty aliens, et cetera. Only Turbo turns out to be not such a bad guy once he develops a bit of respect for Spencer after an above-average licking. The nasty aliens are something else again. Mazzello is easy to root for and a great screamer; the Cyborsuit's face and voice are expressive and appealing; the screenplay is bright, funny, and even poignant (as when Spencer asks the Cyborsuit if he can see his mother again for just one more moment); and writer/director Manny Coto keeps the whole thing rolling along with just the right amount of spills and chills. Apparently the first *Star Kid* did well enough for *Star Kid 2* to begin production in 1999. ***AKA:*** The Warrior of Waverly Street.

1997 (PG) 101m/C Joseph Mazzello, Alex Daniels, Richard Gilliland, Joey Simmrin, Brian Simpson, Danny Masterson, Corinne Bohrer, Arthur Burghardt, Ashlee Levitch, Heidi Lotito; ***D:*** Manny Coto; ***W:*** Manny Coto; ***C:*** Ronn Schmidt; ***M:*** Nicholas Pike. **VHS, LV, DVD**

Star Maps

We all know that parents don't want their kids to grow up to be wannabe movie stars, but here's a switch: Pimp Pepe (Efrain Figueroa) doesn't want his son Carlos (Douglas Spain) to take a small acting

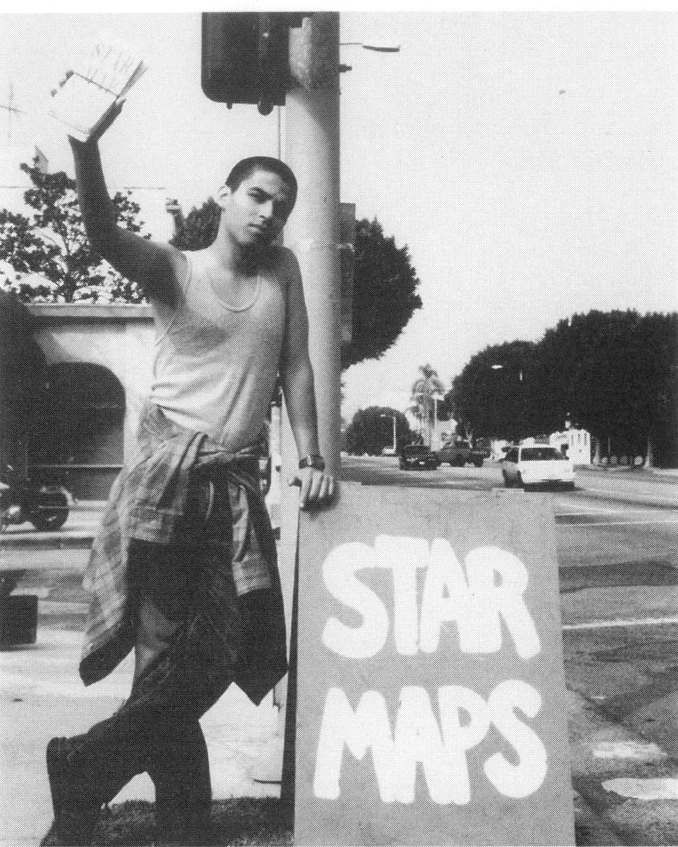

Carlos (Douglas Spain) peddles *Star Maps.* Fox Searchlight; courtesy of the Kobal Collection

role because it will interfere with his real job, turning tricks. Is *Star Maps* meant to be a heartbreaker, a side splitter, or both? If it's both, there's something hollow about seeing everyone's dreams shattered in the course of this 80-minute family saga that often plays like a comedy. Carlos' sexual mentor is Pepe's mistress (Annette Murphy); at one point, they act out a sexual fantasy for a May-December couple who clearly need some help in the ignition department. Carlos' sister can't bring a boy home, because Pepe asks her dates to pay for her sexual favors. And she isn't even in the family business—she's taking care of their sick Mama (Martha Velez). And then there's the brother (Vincent Chandler) who dresses up like a wrestler and is a wanker at the dinner table, even when there's company. This is a first film that feels like a first draft from writer/director Miguel Arteta. It's interesting and clever, but not as well thought out as it might be. Pepe definitely buys his own B.S. and unfortunately, so does everyone in this movie; its hard to care all that much about this brute and his all-too-willing victims. 🦴🦴

1997 (R) 80m/C Douglas Spain, Efrain Figueroa, Lysa Flores, Kandeyce Jensen, Martha Velez, Annette Murphy, Vincent Chandler, Al Vincente, Herbert Siguenza, Robin Thomas, Jeff Michalski; ***D:*** Miguel Arteta; ***W:*** Miguel Arteta; ***C:*** Chuy Chavez; ***M:*** Lysa Flores. Nominations: Independent Spirit Awards '98: Best First Feature, Best Supporting Actor (Figueroa), Debut Performance (Spain, Flores). **VHS, LV, Closed Caption**

Stardust

So you want to be a rock and roll star? Jim MacLaine (David Essex) starts out broke and happy and winds up rich and alienated. He doesn't want it that way, but isn't offered any other real alternatives. His pay-off in the back of an ambulance, being yelled at by his manager for his habitual selfishness, is wrenching to watch. *Stardust* could be the story of the Beatles and it resembles it in many ways, yet Ray Connolly's fascinating screenplay doesn't dwell on the obvious similarities. His attention to character detail is one of the best things about the film. Women, usually ignored or relegated to the roles of groupies in most scrutinies of rock stars, are intriguing in their own right here. Ines Des Longchamps is so affecting as MacLaine's girlfriend, Danielle, that her absence is keenly felt whenever she's off-screen. Rosalind Ayres as MacLaine's neglected wife, Jeanette, only has one sequence, but it's a gem. Larry Hagman is remarkable as Porter Lee Austin, the man who handles MacLaine's career and eventually dominates his life. Adam Faith as MacLaine's road manager, Mike Menary, starts out as a sweet, sincere hustler circa 1965, and winds up totally dependent on MacLaine to the extent that he must cut everyone out of his life. Even Edd "Kookie" Byrnes does well here as a television interviewer. Michael Apted directs a complex subject with sensitivity and originality. *Stardust* sustains its detached view without once losing its compassion. The music is produced by Dave Edmunds, who also appears as Alex and performs some of the songs, along with Essex and the Stray Cats. The excellent soundtrack is a fine time capsule of its era. (Essex, Ayres, and Moon played the same roles in 1973's *That'll Be the Day,* set in 1959 and also scripted by Connolly.) 🦴🦴🦴🦴

1974 111m/C *GB* David Essex, Adam Faith, Larry Hagman, Ines Des Longchamps, Rosalind Ayres, Marty Wilde, Edd Byrnes, Keith Moon, Dave Edmunds, Paul Nicholas, Karl Howman, Rick Lee Parmentier, Peter Duncan, John Normington, James Hazeldine, David Daker, Anthony Naylor, Charlotte Cornwell, Rose Marie Klespitz, David Jacobs; ***D:*** Michael Apted; ***W:*** Ray Connolly; ***C:*** Tony Richmond. **VHS**

Start the Revolution without Me

What a difference nearly 30 years makes. When 1970's *Start the Revolution Without Me* was reviewed by Clive Hirschhorn in *The Warner Bros. Story,* he dismissed it as "a disappointing farce which squandered the talents of its two leading players." Hmmph.... Well, it made me laugh hysterically in 1970 and it makes me laugh in 1999. My wise, witty, and wonderful friends Clinton and Raymond treasure the memories of the year they first saw this movie, which may explain why I became such kindred spirits with them when we met in the 1990s. "Revolution" must be one of those 10-letter words in movie marquees (like the seven-letter word "M-cb-th" spoken aloud in the theatre) that ensures bad luck at the boxoffice. Rent it, anyway. You won't be sorry. Presumably inspired by Alexandre Dumas' *The Corsican Brothers,* Donald Sutherland and Gene Wilder play Philippe and Pierre, two snobby members of the nobility as well as Claude and Charles, two grubby members of the French revolution. Orson Welles' booming voice accompanies the written clarification that it is 1789 and STILL 1789 every time there's a scene change. It's fated that the two sets of twins will meet and that when they do, a mess will ensue. Hugh Griffith is a gentle cuckold as King Louis; wearing the wrong outfit to a ball, he explains to all and sundry, "I thought it was a costume party!" Billie Whitelaw is the voluptuous Queen Marie, who invites her lovers to share her bed, even when Louis is occupying it. Victor Spinetti is the scheming Duke d'Esgargot and Helen (*Repulsion*) Fraser is Claude's girlfriend, who's convinced that the ethereal Princess Christina (Ewa *Candy* Aulin) is her sister. Jack MacGowran is Jacques the revolutionary, Murray Melvin is a blind man who really IS a blind man, Wilder pulls out all the stops as the twins who can't control their ambitions or their tempers ("I SHALL BE KING!"), and Sutherland tries a fey approach with his characters ("AND I SHALL BE QUEEN!"). The 91 minutes go by very fast and there's even a Dadaesque denouement to add to the fun. A guaranteed side splitter. Produced by Norman Lear. 🦴🦴🦴🦴

1970 (PG) 91m/C *GB* Gene Wilder, Donald Sutherland, Orson Welles, Hugh Griffith, Jack MacGowran, Billie Whitelaw, Victor Spinetti, Ewa Aulin, Denise Coffey, Helen Fraser, Murray Melvin; ***D:*** Bud Yorkin; ***W:*** Lawrence J. Cohen, Fred Freeman; ***C:*** Jean Tournier; ***M:*** John Addison. **VHS**

Starving Artists

Allan Piper certainly had his work cut out for him when he decided to write, direct, edit, and produce *Starving Artists* PLUS play a klutz named Zach. For some reason, Joy (Bess Wohl) is wildly attracted to Zach. She'd have to be, because in his pursuit of her, he accidentally breaks her nose, burns her, insults her, sets the dinner table on fire, nukes their romantic chicken dinner...we're just scratching the surface here, actually, but you get the idea. Meanwhile Jay (Joe Smith) and Doris (Sandi Carroll) are making a movie next door and everything they do wrong is lionized by the Boston cognoscenti, as well as their backers. (I think the backers call themselves Frozen Yoga and their financing is dependent on blatant product placement in the final print.) Zach's delusional roommate Bob (John De Vore) is convinced their neighbors are murderers. Zach tells him to take out the trash and mind his own business, which doesn't help Bob be-

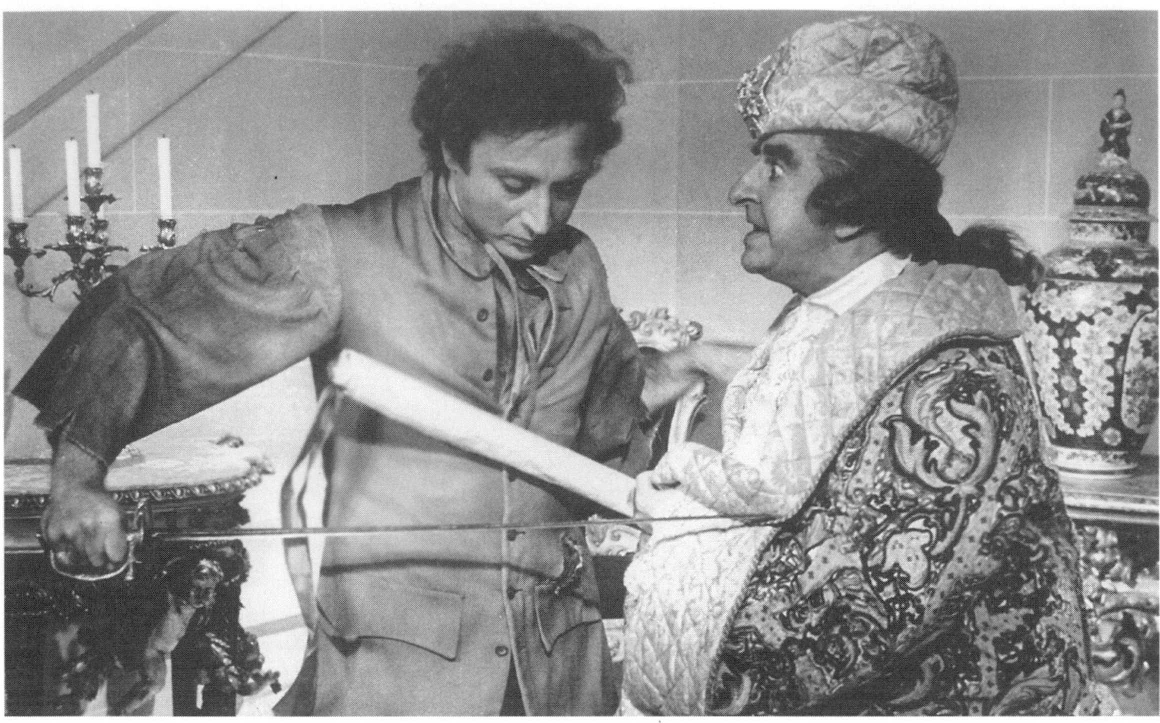

Pierre (Gene Wilder) and King Louis (Hugh Griffith) in *Start the Revolution without Me.*
Warner Bros.; courtesy of the Kobal Collection

come any less delusional. *Starving Artists* doesn't try to look expensive or sound politically correct, but does incorporate all the universal fears that every artist shares. There are some solid yucks here, and a mostly attractive, appealing cast. *Starving Artists* played at San Francisco's Indie Fest in January 1999. ☙☙☙

1997 85m/C Sandi Carroll, Joe Smith, Bess Wohl, Allan Piper, John De Vore, Geoff Gladstone; ***D:*** Allan Piper; ***W:*** Allan Piper; ***C:*** Robert Ball; ***M:*** Claire Harding.

Steppenwolf

Steppenwolf is a visually striking and disturbing film, but admirers of Herman Hesse (1877–1962) will probably loathe it; it has a bubble gum quality that undercuts its impact. Film novice Fred Haines jazzes up his first movie with stylistic tricks, animation, and special effects, in an effort to come to terms with Hesse's 1927 novel. Haines runs the risk of becoming absurd, and he loses more often than not. Magnifique Dominique Sanda's work as Hermine here is both ethereal and complex, but Max von Sydow seems merely pathetic as Herr Haller. Occasionally amusing (especially in the 25-minute Magic Theatre sequence), the overall impact is unsatisfying. ☙☙

1974 (PG) 105m/C *SI* Max von Sydow, Dominique Sanda, Pierre Clementi, Carla Rominelli, Roy Bosier; ***D:*** Fred Haines; ***W:*** Fred Haines; ***C:*** Tomislav Pinter; ***M:*** George Gruntz. **VHS, LV**

Sticky Fingers

Sticky Fingers represents the directing debut of actress Catlin Adams, so perhaps Adams' intrusive "Look Ma, I'm directing" style will acquire more discipline on future projects. Adams wrote the script with actress Melanie Mayron, who co-stars in the movie with Helen Slater and a cast of mostly women: Shirley Stoler and the late Gwen Welles plus Oscar nominees Eileen Brennan and Carol Kane. The plot hinges around a bag that Mayron agrees to keep for Slater's drug connection. It turns out that the bag contains nearly a million dollars, which horrifies the roommates at first and later hypnotizes them into a $240,000 shopping binge. Along the way, we see a world frequently shot in extreme close-up through pale green or blue filters. We also hear self-conscious statements about relationships between women as well as some labored concessions to straight audiences who might be threatened by the suggestion that any of the major characters could be gay. Despite the obvious feminist sentiments of the filmmakers, it is irritating to observe how carelessly and how often the roommates lose money and how passive these two are about most of the circumstances in their lives. When the pair takes action, it is usually a dumb move. If a film history of female buddy movies is ever written, I predict that *Sticky Fingers* will warrant a small footnote as one of many attempts to repeat the success of 1987's *Outrageous Fortune,* a film which isn't worth imitating. It's a pity, because a lot of time and talent went into the film. (Mayron went on to direct 1995's *The Baby-Sitter's Club.*) 🦴

1988 (PG-13) 89m/C Melanie Mayron, Helen Slater, Eileen Brennan, Carol Kane, Christopher Guest, Danitra Vance, Gwen Welles, Stephen McHattie, Shirley Stoler; ***D:*** Catlin Adams; ***W:*** Catlin Adams, Melanie Mayron; ***C:*** Gary Thieltges; ***M:*** Gary Chang. **VHS, LV**

The Story of Fausta

The Story of Fausta is a sexy, hilarious romp from Bruno Barreto and Betty Faria, his *Bye, Bye Brazil* star. Brandao Filho has a ball with one of the best senior citizen's parts ever; this Brazilian entry may well leave you breathless with laughter. ***AKA:*** Romance da Empregada. 🦴🦴🦴

1988 (R) 90m/C *BR* Betty Faria, Daniel Filho, Brandao Filho; ***D:*** Bruno Barreto; ***M:*** Ruben Blades. **VHS**

The Story of Qui Ju

Peasant Qui Ju (Gong Li) is expecting a baby, but nonetheless fights for justice when her husband Liu (Liu Pei Qui) is kicked in the groin by their village head (Lei Lao Sheng). Arbitrators say the chief must compensate Qui Ju's husband, but she wants him to say he's sorry for what he's done, even when it appears that her relationship with her husband is being damaged by her tireless efforts on his behalf. This well-directed look at Chinese village life benefits from powerful acting by Gong Li and from stunningly real cinematography, occasionally achieved with a concealed camera. ***AKA:*** Qui Ju Da Guansi. 🦴🦴🦴

1991 (PG) 100m/C *CH* Gong Li, Lei Lao Sheng, Liu Pei Qu, Ge Zhi Jun, Ye Jun, Yang Liu Xia, Zhu Qanging, Cui Luowen, Yank Huiquin, Wang Jianfa, Lin Zi; ***D:*** Zhang Yimou; ***W:*** Liu Heng; ***C:*** Chi Xiaonin, Yu Xaioqun; ***M:*** Zhao Jiping. National Society of Film Critics Awards '93: Best Foreign Film; Venice Film Festival '92: Best Actress (Li), Best Film; Nominations: Independent Spirit Awards '94: Best Foreign Film. **VHS, LV**

Straight out of Brooklyn

This would be a fair movie for an adult director, but Matty Rich was only 19 when he made *Straight out of Brooklyn,* reportedly based on his own life. It's a depressing look at a Brooklyn family who live in the Red Hook Housing Project. Ray Brown (George T. Odom) beats his wife Frankie (Ann D. Sanders). Their kids Dennis (Laurence Gilliard) and Carolyn (Barbara Sanon) are desperate. Although girlfriend Shirley (Reana E. Drummond) tries to talk him out of it, Dennis and friends Larry (Rich) and Kevin (Mark Malone) plan a robbery to escape the poverty and the abuse. Generally shot with one camera and inadequate sound, *Straight out of Brooklyn*'s painful narrative is often hard to watch. Still, for a teenager to raise the money, finish a whole movie, and get it released was such an accomplishment that Rich was overpraised (23-year-old John Singleton's Oscar-nominated *Boys N the Hood* was far superior). Rich's next film was 1994's *The Inkwell.* I give *Brooklyn* two bones for content and four bones for effort, for an average of 🦴🦴🦴

Two sisters are about to meet the man of every woman's dreams. He's wealthy, sexy, and incredibly romantic. Something's got to be wrong.

—Tagline from the movie *Strapless.*

1991 (R) 91m/C George T. Odom, Ann D. Sanders, Lawrence Gilliard, Mark Malone Jr., Reana E. Drummond, Barbara Sanon, Matty Rich; ***D:*** Matty Rich; ***W:*** Matty Rich; ***C:*** John Rosnell; ***M:*** Harold Wheeler. Independent Spirit Awards '92: Best First Feature; Sundance Film Festival '91: Special Jury Prize. **VHS**

The Stranger's Hand

Since Graham Greene wrote the stories for both *The Fallen Idol* and *The Stranger's Hand,* it might be interesting to see them both on a double bill for comparison purposes. Each involves a little boy lost (no parents in sight) who attaches himself to a guilty-looking couple who don't care half as much about him as he cares about them. Roger Court (Richard O'Sullivan, then 11) is in Venice to meet his father (Trevor Howard). But Dad is kidnapped and drugged by bad guy Dr. Vivaldi (Eduardo Ciannelli), who, coincidentally, also buys Roger some ice cream. Roger wanders around, waiting for Dad, and starts hanging out with Roberta (Alida Valli). Roberta's hung up on Joe Hamstringer (Richard Basehart), who has to make a fast getaway. Roger can't find Dad, he's scared of the authorities, and clings to Roberta and Joe because he doesn't know what else to do. O'Sullivan's large eyes and expressive face made him one of Great Britain's most sought-after juvenile actors, and he continued his career on television as an adult. Valli and Basehart are upstaged by their little co-star here, but the film's best performances are delivered by Howard and Ciannelli (did either of them ever do a less than sterling job EVER?). ***AKA:*** La Mano del Straniero. 🦴🦴🦴

1954 85m/B *GB IT* Trevor Howard, Alida Valli, Richard Basehart, Eduardo Ciannelli, Richard O'Sullivan, Stephen Murray, Giorgio Constantini; ***D:*** Mario Soldati; ***W:*** Guy Elmes, Georgino Bassani; ***C:*** Enzo Serafin.

Strapless

A few minutes into David Hare's *Strapless,* I realized that I would be sitting through yet another long, pretentious movie in which a dense guy tries to explain how women feel (sigh). I suspect that some people think that Hare is cute when he tries to be clever, but he's not THAT cute, not with 99 minutes of my time. Blair Brown plays a 40-year-old doctor who goes on and on about how OLD she is. Although we see her in hospital wards, neither Hare's screenplay nor his direction give us an indication of any real emotional investment in her work. She lives with her flaky younger sister, Bridget Fonda. (We know that Bridget is a flake, because she enjoys fashion and parties and sex. Right.) According to the press kit, Blair "meets a mysterious, elegant stranger who is immediately taken with her." Who else but Bruno Ganz, who looks like he was scraped out of a gutter and sounds like Thug Number Three in an old gangster movie? Faster than you can say "plot device" or "deus ex machina" or whatever, Blair is obligingly writing checks for this slime, draining away her life savings and even marrying him. When Bruno arrives home one night with an expensive car as a gift for her, Blair tells him that she wants to be ordinary, so Bruno disappears into the night. Meanwhile, Bridget is pregnant by a drifter named Carlos and Blair yells at her because she's a slob. You can watch *The Hard Way* with Ida Lupino and Joan Leslie on the late movie or you can watch *Strapless* with Blair Brown and Bridget Fonda on video. *Strapless* will probably put you to sleep faster, especially David Hare's idea of a *pièce de résistance:* Bridget Fonda designs a line of strapless gowns that are held in place with no visible means of support. And guess what? (nudge-nudge) Women hold their lives in place with no visible means of support EITHER. Give us a BREAK! 🦴🦴

1990 (R) 99m/C *GB* Blair Brown, Bridget Fonda, Bruno Ganz, Alan Howard, Michael Gough, Hugh Laurie, Suzanne Burden, Camille Coduri, Alexandra Pigg, Billy Roch, Gary O'Brien; ***D:*** David Hare; ***W:*** David Hare; ***C:*** Andrew Dunn; ***M:*** Nick Bicat. **VHS, LV**

Street Music

The elderly people living in an old hotel join forces with a young couple to organize a protest that may save their building. Well-directed comedy drama; good location shooting in San Francisco's Tenderloin.

1982's Grand Jury Prize winner at the Sundance Film Festival. 🦴🦴🦴

1981 88m/C Larry Breeding, Elizabeth Daily, Ned Glass, Marjorie Eaton, D'Alan Moss, David Parr; ***D:*** Jenny Bowen, H. Anne Riley; ***W:*** Jenny Bowen, H. Anne Riley; ***C:*** Richard Bowen. Sundance Film Festival '82: Grand Jury Prize. **VHS**

Street Smart

To be a great actor, you have to be able to project real emotion any which way you can. Morgan Freeman is a great actor. Kathy Baker is a great actor. After a dozen movies in ten years, the empirical evidence that Christopher Reeve, then turning 35, was not a great actor was too compelling to be ignored. The same year that Robert Townsend was lampooning how black actors were invariably cast as pimps in *Hollywood Shuffle,* Morgan Freeman played the ultimate pimp in *Street Smart.* Like Bette Davis in 1935's *Dangerous,* Freeman defied you to ignore the alchemy in a no-holds-barred performance and made a stock part real. Baker took another favorite Hollywood stock part, that of a hooker, and turned it inside out. No matter what else was onscreen, Baker forced you to see what she saw, hear what she heard, feel what she felt. Needless to say, there were kudos galore for Freeman and Baker, and *Street Smart* is well worth watching for them alone, but *Street Smart* is not much of a movie. The story revolves around a fake scoop that ignites an authentic investigation. Reeve was unable to transform his essentially rigid role as a dishonest reporter, and the plot goes into slow motion whenever Freeman or Baker are offscreen. (The same thing occurred in 1995's *Above Suspicion* when Reeve was cast in an actor's dream role, brilliantly scripted by Jerry Lazarus, W.H. Macy, and director Steven Schachter. It's an eerily premonitory picture in light of actual events in Reeve's life, but he can't breathe life into his character as fellow cast members Joe Mantegna and William H. Macy can with their parts. Reeve's acclaimed debut as director of 1997's *In the Gloaming* suggests a career shift that might have been inevitable, anyway.) 🦴🦴🦴

1987 (R) 97m/C Christopher Reeve, Morgan Freeman, Kathy Baker, Mimi Rogers, Andre Gregory, Jay Patterson, Anna Maria Horsford; ***D:*** Jerry Schatzberg; ***W:*** David Freeman; ***C:*** Adam Holender; ***M:*** Miles Davis. Independent Spirit Awards '88: Best Supporting Actor (Freeman); Los Angeles Film Critics Association Awards '87: Best Supporting Actor (Freeman); New York Film Critics Awards '87: Best Supporting Actor (Freeman); National Society of Film Critics Awards '87: Best Supporting Actor (Freeman), Best Supporting Actress (Baker); Nominations: Academy Awards '87: Best Supporting Actor (Freeman). **VHS, LV, Closed Caption**

Streetwise

Both 1981's *Pixote* by Hector Babenco and 1984's *Streetwise* by Martin Bell offer a harsh portrait of the lives led by street children. *Streetwise* has deglamorized the runaway life for many young people who have seen Bell's movie, but for the Seattle children who appear in the film, life continues to run downhill. Erin, also known as Tiny, was one of the few participants who revealed genuine depth of feeling for the people in her life, but the pain reportedly led to more than one drug overdose. The others whistle in the dark by "pulling dates" between jail terms. We already know that Dewayne's imprisoned father loves him, but he can do nothing for his kid and Dewayne knows it. At another point, we see a mother excusing her husband's sexual abuse of her daughter ("Well, he isn't doing it anymore, is he?"). All the kids hear well-meaning, BandAids-over-gangrene solutions to their problems. Bell and Babenco attracted considerable reputations for their honesty in showing the toll of street hustling on the very young. 🦴🦴🦴🦴

1984 92m/C ***D:*** Martin Bell; ***C:*** Cheryl McCall; ***M:*** Tom Waits. **VHS, LV**

Strictly Ballroom

Old-time film buffs describe their primal experiences at local Bijous of the '30s with such intense passion: "And I paid my dime every day and went to see *42nd Street* or *Golddiggers of 1933* or *Flying Down to Rio* over and over and over again; it was magic." Although movies with that

"A life lived in fear is a life half lived."

—Fran (Tara Morice) in *Strictly Ballroom.*

sort of repeat value are indeed rare, we have found one, and so, apparently, have other romance-starved film buffs. *Strictly Ballroom* made its first U.S. appearance at the Mill Valley Film Festival in the fall of 1992. Not even a surfeit of critical euphoria prepared me for the night I first saw *Strictly Ballroom,* a classic example of the picture that F. Scott Fitzgerald once described as "the-little-girl-wanting-a-piece-of-candy original; our attention must be called with sharp novelty to the fact that she wants it." The girl in *Strictly Ballroom* is Fran, the inexpressibly plain dance student played by Tara Morice, and the candy is her big chance to turn into a swan and compete with a sexy open amateur at the Pan Pacific dance competition. The open amateur is Paul Mercurio as Scott Hastings, who is, quite literally, the most exciting dance personality to emerge onscreen since the Golden Age of the Hollywood musical. Unfortunately for film buffs, Mercurio headlines the Sydney Dance Company in Australia and is unlikely to leave it for a movie genre that has no real future. (He was wasted in *Exit to Eden,* and fared better in TNT's *Joseph,* but the Australian-made *Back of Beyond* went straight to cable.) It's a shame, because Mercurio is also a remarkable actor, ideally conveying his character's conflicting emotions. He wants to win, but he wants to dance his own steps; and he wants to win with flashy Tina Sparkle, but he wants to dance HIS way with the adoring Fran; and he doesn't want to wind up like his whipped father, but his father's approval is the only thing that can set him free. Who cares about the shenanigans that obsess all these ballroom fanatics? Thanks to director Baz Luhrmann and a superb cast (the late Pat Thomsen and Barry Otto are especially memorable as Scott's parents), WE care, even if we can't dance to save our lives. Luhrmann's wry understanding of the impact of every frame of his film is breathtaking. At one point, when Scott's shrill partner Liz screams that she wants Ken Railings to walk into the studio to say that HIS partner (Pam Short) has broken both her legs and he wants to dance with HER, Luhrmann with two quick, sure cuts, shows us both the stylized accident and Ken Railings' word-for-word delivery of Liz's implausible projection. That Luhrmann is able to reinvent and revitalize this technique throughout the film, even in dance sequences that are already saturated with highly charged energy, is one of the reasons why *Strictly Ballroom* is as much of a delight to watch the twelfth time around as the first. 🦴🦴🦴🦴

1992 (PG) 94m/C *AU* Paul Mercurio, Tara Morice, Bill Hunter, Pat Thomsen, Barry Otto, Gia Carides, Peter Whitford, John Hannan, Sonia Kruger-Tayler, Kris McQuade, Pip Mushin, Leonie Page, Antonio Vargas, Armonia Benedito; ***D:*** Baz Luhrmann; ***W:*** Baz Luhrmann, Craig Pearce; ***C:*** Steve Mason; ***M:*** David Hirshfelder. Australian Film Institute '92: Best Costume Design, Best Director (Luhrmann), Best Film, Best Film Editing, Best Supporting Actor (Otto), Best Supporting Actress (Thomsen), Best Writing; Nominations: Golden Globe Awards '94: Best Film—Musical/Comedy. **VHS, LV, Closed Caption**

Strongman Ferdinand

One of the more amusing releases of 1976 failed to win much in the way of audience acceptance. It's a shame, really, because West Germany's *Strongman Ferdinand* had a great deal to say about the sort of mentality that may have made the Watergate break-in possible. Ferdinand (convincingly played by Heinz Schubert) is the security officer for a large corporation. He soon discovers that the continuation of his job is dependent on frequent states of emergency. When they fail to occur, he creates them, thus "proving" that his services are needed. Law and order carried to its logical end, director/screenwriter Alexander Kluge suggests, leads to probable sabotage and destruction. Ferdinand's rationale may be extreme, but it had its parallels in many political acts of the 1970s. *Ferdinand* is absorbing, yet so subtle that many audience members at 1976's San Francisco International Film Festival screening seemed to miss altogether the wry humor in the German voiceover statements. The inadequate subtitles did not quite provide the essential ironic counterpoint that Kluge clearly

intended for them to have. ***AKA:*** Der Starke Ferdinand.

1976 98m/C *GE* Heinz Schubert, Verena Rudolph, Gert Gunther Hoffman, Heinz Schimmelpfennig, Siegfried Wischnewski, Joachim Hackethal; ***D:*** Alexander Kluge; ***W:*** Alexander Kluge; ***C:*** Thomas Mauch.

Struggle

Movie pioneer D.W. Griffith (1875–1948) couldn't get ARRESTED in 1931, so he financed his $300,000 swan song himself and released it through United Artists, the independent releasing corporation he founded with Charlie Chaplin (1889–1977), Douglas Fairbanks (1883–1939), and Mary Pickford (1892–1979). Even by 1931 standards, *The Struggle* is out of touch with its own era. King Vidor's version of Elmer Rice's *Street Scene,* starring Sylvia Sidney and William Collier Jr., produced by Samuel Goldwyn and released by United Artists the same year, dealt with strong social issues in a harsh, realistic way, AND managed to achieve critical and audience acceptance. But Goldwyn did his job as producer, Vidor did his job as director, and both let Rice adapt his own screenplay. Griffith, by that time more than a little desperate, fiddled with Anita Loos' and John Emerson's screenplay until his whole reason for making this anti-Prohibition film was lost; *The Struggle* voices all the arguments for temperance that led to Prohibition in the first place. The first audience at New York's Rivoli Theatre (on December 10, 1931) giggled all through the picture, a painful reality for Griffith, who hoped that viewers would break into spontaneous applause as they had for his early silent masterpieces. Viewers of the 1990s may not feel that *The Struggle* is as bad as all that, but remember, this was Griffith, not some hack director churning out a Depression era quickie. The cast, except for Zita Johann (the future object of the *The Mummy*'s desire and then Mrs. John Houseman), is undistinguished, the grim visual realism is unmatched by the shrill aural melodramatics. *The Struggle* promptly went into exhibition limbo. Griffith lost two-thirds of his investment and, worse yet, wandered around Hollywood for the next 17 years, bitter and bewildered, until a cerebral hemorrhage killed him on July 23, 1948.

1931 87m/B Hal Skelly, Zita Johann, Evelyn Baldwin, Charlotte Wynters, Helen Mack, Kate Bruce, Jackson Halliday, Edna Hagan, Claude Cooper, Arthur Lipson, Charles Richman, Dave Manley; ***D:*** D.W. Griffith; ***W:*** D.W. Griffith, Anita Loos, John Emerson; ***C:*** Joseph Ruttenberg; ***M:*** D.W. Griffith, Philip A. Scheib. **VHS**

Stubby

Bo Widerberg's *Stubby* is such a dear, sweet movie. So how come I don't like it any better than 1967's *Elvira Madigan,* also by Widerberg? The title character is a precocious youngster, played by a cute kid named Johan Bergman, who plays for Sweden's national soccer team. Monica Zetterlund gives a nice, winning performance as his teacher and John Olsson tenderly photographs little kitties and pretty kiddies. Widerberg also edited and produced. Soccer fans may dig it, but cranky cynics, beware!

1974 90m/C *SW* Johan Bergman, Monica Zetterlund, Magnus Harenstam, Ernst-Hugo Jaregard, Swedish National Soccer Team; ***D:*** Bo Widerberg; ***W:*** Bo Widerberg; ***C:*** John Olsson.

SubUrbia

It's a day in the life of *SubUrbia,* as seen by Eric Bogosian! How boring can its inhabitants be? You'll have 118 ennui-packed minutes to find out. The suburbs, at their best and at their worst, are always the cheapest shots and easiest targets in the world. Even with Richard Linklater at the helm, Bogosian's screenplay crawls at its own stagey pace. Kids hanging out at a convenience store, duh! Local boy makes good and meets them there so they can all squirm with loser-like envy, duh-squared! Guns are produced and lives threatened. Don't worry, this is cinematic *SubUrbia,* nothing ever happens there. Jayce Bartok is Pony, a nice, well-protected young rock star who's clueless about the effect he's having on his former friends and neighbors. Erica (Parker Posey) is the most congenial L.A. publicist on the planet. Sooze (Amie Carey) has aspirations to become an artist and hopes

Sooze (Amie Carey) and Jeff (Giovanni Ribisi) in *SubUrbia.*
Castle Rock Entertainment; courtesy of the Kobal Collection

Pony and Erica can help her. Tim (Nicky Katt) is just as brilliant as anyone would be who sliced off a finger tip to get away from the Air Force. Nazeer and Pakeesa (Ajay Naidu and Samia Shoaib) run their 24-hour market accompanied by an endless barrage of racism. Jeff (Giovanni Ribisi) is never undepressed or unmiserable. He needs a good old boy like Buff (Steve Zahn) to cheer him out of his doldrums, although Buff never succeeds. And Bee-Bee (Dina Spybey) is an apple-cheeked alcoholic who drinks herself into a stupor whenever she gets the chance. One hundred and eighteen minutes with these charming people in the inviting atmosphere of a convenience store parking lot! When was the last time you spent 118 SECONDS there? Enjoy!

1996 (R) 118m/C Giovanni Ribisi, Steve Zahn, Nicky Katt, Jayce Bartok, Amie Carey, Dina Spybey, Parker Posey, Ajay Naidu, Samia Shoaib; ***D:*** Richard Linklater; ***W:*** Eric Bogosian; ***C:*** Lee Daniel. Nominations: Independent Spirit Awards '98: Best Supporting Actor (Naidu). **VHS, Closed Caption**

Sudden Manhattan

A quirky entry at 1996's Mill Valley Film Festival, *Sudden Manhattan* is nicely written and directed by Adrienne Shelly, who also stars as Donna. This appealing black comedy is filled with goofy supporting characters (Roger Rees, Louise Lasser) and an oddball story line. Like Shelly herself, it all looks effortless and spontaneous, but clearly some very careful craftsmanship went into it.

1996 80m/C Adrienne Shelly, Tim Guinee, Roger Rees, Louise Lasser, Hynden Walch; ***D:*** Adrienne Shelly; ***W:*** Adrienne Shelly; ***C:*** Jim Denault; ***M:*** Pat Irwin.

Suicide Kings

There must be few things more satisfying for a great actor than to play a character who is sedated, inebriated, tied up, and bleeding to death AND to know that he's stealing every frame of the movie from five ambulatory young actors. The part of Carlo ("Charles Barrett") Bartolucci is a piece of cake for Christopher Walken and the subsequent careers of his young co-stars can only benefit from THE acting lesson of their lives they receive in *Suicide Kings.* Lisa Chasten (Laura Harris) has been kidnapped, and brother Avery (Henry Thomas) decides to abduct mobster Bartolucci with the help of Lisa's boyfriend Max (Sean Patrick Flanery) and their friends Brett (Jay Mohr) and T.K. (Jeremy Sisto). The four hold him hostage in the summer house of their friend, Ira Reder (the terrific Johnny Galecki), who doesn't know about the plan, but arrives home unexpectedly. All Ira does is kvetch about how he's going to get in trouble with his parents, a minor point after T.K. has cut off one of the hostage's fingers. The plan is to get Lisa back with Bartolucci's influence. A call to his lawyer Marty (Cliff DeYoung) initiates the $2 million ransom raising process, and a second call to his henchman Lono Vecchio (Denis Leary) starts the operation to locate Lisa. Even a bombed and disabled Bartolucci is still the ultimate shrewd operator, and he quickly discerns that one of his abductors was also involved in Lisa's kidnapping. He plays the friends off against each other, which isn't terribly hard to do. The captors screw up left and right, Bartolucci simmers with calculated deadliness, and we can't wait to see what's going to happen next. *Suicide Kings* is an absorbing, satisfying, very funny way to spend a Friday night. And Christopher Walken is nothing less than Movieland's quintessential Magician. Who needs a zillion dollar action sequence when Walken can take our breath away with a subtle glint in his eyes? 🦴🦴🦴🦴

1997 (R) 106m/C Christopher Walken, Jay Mohr, Henry Thomas, Sean Patrick Flanery, Denis Leary, Jeremy Sisto, Johnny Galecki, Cliff DeYoung, Laura San Giacomo, Nina Siemaszko, Frank Medrano, Brad Garrett, Lisanne Falk, Laura Harris; ***D:*** Peter O'Fallon; ***W:*** Josh McKinney, Gina Goldman, Wayne Rice; ***C:*** Christopher Baffa; ***M:*** Graeme Revell, Tim Simonec. **VHS, DVD**

A Summer Story

When young men play fast and loose with young women, they're only being human, according to the movies. This is the theme of *A Summer Story.* (When young women play fast and loose with young men, they're invariably monsters, but that's another story.) Upper-class English twit James Wilby shows his bad manners: (1) by falling in love with fetching country lass Imogen Stubbs, (2) by ditching her for aristocratic Sophie Ward, and (3) by later returning to the country with his childless wife to learn whatever became of his first love. His worst offense, according to another upper-class twit, was in promising to marry the poor girl at all. This Piers Haggard film has nothing new to say about class differences, but the Somerset and Devon locations are pretty, and Imogen Stubbs makes a strong impression as the jilted farm girl. Susannah York, who specialized in playing bewitching heroines circa 1963, has a few brief scenes as a protective relation of Miss Stubbs. During the final credits, the period film breaks into a Moody Blues song for no apparent reason. It's the only unpredictable element in this dusty romance based on John Galsworthy's *The Apple Tree. A Summer Story* focuses on a spineless and irritating character who doesn't deserve sympathy and who certainly doesn't rate an entire movie. 🦴🦴

1988 (PG-13) 97m/C *GB* James Wilby, Imogen Stubbs, Susannah York, Sophie Ward, Kenneth Colley, Jerome Flynn; ***D:*** Piers Haggard; ***W:*** Penelope Mortimer; ***M:*** Georges Delerue. **VHS, Closed Caption**

Suture

Suture is all about two guys who are almost identical twins, the "almost" being the centerpiece of another one-joke movie although it most certainly does not qualify as a deliberate comedy (at least I don't think so). In any event, I didn't get the joke. The film's conceit is that no one notices the extremely obvious difference between the two of them. I'd give *Suture* one bone for its concept and three bones for its look, which is impressive, thanks to superb black-and-white cinematography by Greg Gardiner. The presence of elegant Dina Merrill in the cast adds a touch of class to this very weird flick. 🦴🦴

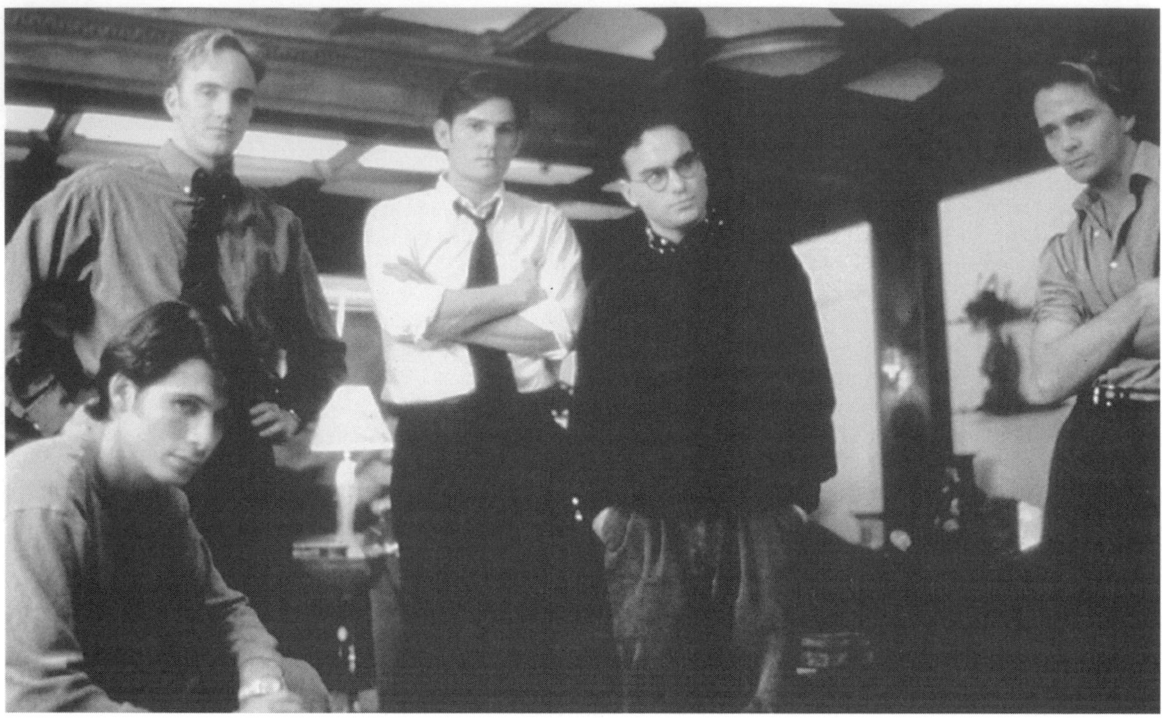

Jeremy Sisto, Jay Mohr, Henry Thomas, Johnny Galecki, and Sean Patrick Flanery in *Suicide Kings*, co-starring Christopher Walken. Live Entertainment; courtesy of the Kobal Collection

1993 96m/B Dennis Haysbert, Sab Shimono, Mel Harris, Michael Harris, Dina Merrill, David Graf, Fran Ryan; ***D:*** Scott McGehee, David Siegel; ***W:*** Scott McGehee, David Siegel; ***C:*** Greg Gardiner; ***M:*** Cary Berger. Sundance Film Festival '94: Best Cinematography; Nominations: Independent Spirit Awards '95: Best Cinematography, Best First Feature. **VHS**

Swastika

It is hard to imagine that anyone could recall the Third Reich with affection and nostalgia, but this 1973 British film by Philippe Mora did infuriate many who first saw it at the Cannes Film Festival that year. The most stunning portions of the film feature color home movies shot by Eva Braun at Berchtesgaden. Mora retained a lip reader to determine what Hitler and his friends were saying to each other and then found an actor who could mimic the Fuhrer's style of social chatter. The conversation is completely banal, and so are most of the activities on the terrace at Berchtesgaden. It was this very banality that disgusted the audiences who first saw the confiscated films, one referring to "the appalling normality of Hitler's home life." *Swastika* also includes propaganda movies extolling the virtues of National Socialism as well as segments of the infamous *Jud Suess,* a film that so horrified Ferdinand Marian, its guilt-ridden star, that he later committed suicide. Mora's objective in revealing Hitler and his cronies in all their boring blandness was to render them comprehensible as human beings rather than as monsters. But to watch Eva Braun preening in front of the camera to the tune of Helen Morgan's "What Wouldn't I Do for That Man" and to hear Hitler blather about how all the women present would prefer a screening of *Gone with the Wind* with Clark Gable is an absolutely surreal experience. How could Auschwitz and Bergen-Belsen and Dachau have existed with these numbskulls at the helm? *Swastika,* the sort of documentary that makes you want to crawl under your seat when you see it theatrically, is

also available for private appraisal on home video. 𝅘𝅥𝅮𝅘𝅥𝅮𝅘𝅥𝅮

1973 ?m/C *GB* ***D:*** Philippe Mora. **VHS**

The Sweet Hereafter

I got no sleep the night I saw *The Sweet Hereafter.* It's an immeasurably sad movie about the aftermath of a tragic bus accident and it demands tremendous concentration, so this is not the movie to watch while doing taxes, homework, or crossword puzzles. Attorney Mitchell Stephens (Ian Holm) is on the job after 14 Canadian children are killed when their bus swerves off the road and crashes into a frozen pond, drowning the kids in the icy waters beneath the surface. He's pressing for a lawsuit so the grieving families can be compensated for their pain. There is a witness—the proud father of two of the kids, Billy Ansell (played by Bruce Greenwood, who deserved to be, but unaccountably wasn't, an Oscar nominee for this one). There is also a paralyzed survivor, Nicole Burnell (*Tales of Avonlea*'s Sarah Polley). Prior to the accident, Nicole was the recipient of sexual attentions from her father, Sam (Tom McCamus). Reportedly, the original novel by Russell Banks showed that the attentions were unwanted and that Sam was far from the conscience-plagued character he appears to be here. But Polley reveals Nicole's internal rage with blazing clarity, especially in a deposition sequence with both Stephens and her father present. There are some incredible shots in *The Sweet Hereafter*: We flash back to the bus on the icy roads of British Columbia, and, without a cut, the camera seems to pan the plane in the sky on which Stephens is flying. Extensive pressing of the pause button suggests that some optical printing was involved, but however the effect was done, it's an impressive achievement. A sub-plot involves Stephens' drug-riddled daughter, Zoe (Caerthan Banks), and Nicole's narration draws an analogy be-

Mitchell Stephens (Ian Holm) and Nicole Burnell (Sarah Polley) in *The Sweet Hereafter.* Fine Line; courtesy of the Kobal Collection

The Hound Salutes:
BUZZ HAYES
Co-Producer, *Swimming with Sharks*

Our budget was less than any major studio's catering budget. We set out to make an independent film; we knew it's very tough being an independent filmmaker, we had nothing going for us at all, so we really tried hard. Writer/director George Huang came up with a very good story that involved only three characters—we knew that was a manageable number—and mostly interior locations. So then we started mostly banging on doors, trying to raise money. The script was actually written with Frank Whaley in mind as Guy, a character who works for Buddy, the Hollywood Boss from Hell, played by Kevin Spacey. We gave the script to Frank Whaley, he read it; he and Kevin had worked on a project a few years earlier, so Frank offered to get the script to Kevin, who was working on a play in London at the time. We didn't expect to hear back from him anytime soon, but he read the script; he really liked it a lot and he wanted to know if this was something we were really serious about. He got right back to us, for which we were really thankful.

"It was worth it for us to know that Kevin was intimately involved in the production, to make sure that people knew we existed. Look at the number of people in Hollywood, working in industries

tween the children of her town and the youngsters who followed *The Pied Piper of Hamelin.* It's all very lugubrious and depressing, so wait until you're in the mood for it, but when you do catch up with *The Sweet Hereafter,* you will appreciate both the superb acting and the complexity of the issues in this extremely well-made film by Atom Egoyan. Scratch half a bone for prettying up Sam's and Nicole's father-daughter romance. 🦴🦴🦴🦴

1996 (R) 110m/C *CA* Ian Holm, Sarah Polley, Bruce Greenwood, Tom McCamus, Arsinee Khanjian, Alberta Watson, Gabrielle Rose, Maury Chaykin, David Hemblen, Earl Pastko, Peter Donaldson, Caerthan Banks, Brook Johnson, Stephanie Morgenstern; ***D:*** Atom Egoyan; ***W:*** Atom Egoyan; ***C:*** Paul Sarossy; ***M:*** Mychael Danna. Cannes Film Festival '97: Grand Jury Prize; Genie Awards '97: Best Actor (Holm), Best Cinematography, Best Director (Egoyan), Best Film, Best Film Editing, Best Sound, Best Score; Independent Spirit Awards '98: Best Foreign Film; Toronto-City Award '97: Best Canadian Feature Film; Nominations: Academy Awards '97: Best Adapted Screenplay, Best Director (Egoyan); Genie Awards '97: Best Actor (Greenwood), Best Actress (Polley, Rose), Best Screenplay. **VHS, LV, Closed Caption, DVD**

Sweet Sweetback's Baadasssss Song

Fledgling filmmakers generally throw everything they know, including the kitchen sink, into their early movies, and so does Melvin Van Peebles. When he plays around with what he can do visually on film, the results are striking and unforgettable; four bone potential, actually. The Black Community (billed just like that) generally deliver strong, gritty performances, considerably enhanced by Van Peebles' editing. All the white actors in this movie are terrible, though, as in they can barely deliver their lines, much less pack any emotion into them. The lopsided quality of the performances makes for a schizophrenic viewing experience. Who are we going to root for: Melvin Van Peebles as Sweetback who CAN act up a storm, or subprofessional white actors as cops who com-

unrelated to film who have written a script, who want to direct or act, who know full well what the process is all about—how it's like a giant meat grinder and it's easy to get spit out, and yet they're lining up to jump into this big machine. It's just part of human nature, maybe a part that's buried really deep within, so it's ironic that we would attempt to make a film like this as independent filmmakers, knowing that our first film could easily be our last film. Our take on it is that this is how people are willing to try to get a film job—it's sad and it's funny, and we tried to incorporate all of that into the film.

"The development of the swimming with sharks theme was very important to us as we created Buddy's and Guy's relationship. George struggled with it in his screenplay, because we knew that the situation could easily come across as not a very fair treatment of women in any industry. With George's own personal experiences in the film industry, he observed that there were very few roles for women in the film world's corporate structure. A lot of that has to do with the bravado nature of the industry. Buddy is certainly modeled after the more notorious yelling screamers in Hollywood, where it seems that the squeaky wheels definitely get the grease. It's certainly tougher for women because the ones who have emulated that model, who have kicked and scratched and fought their way to the top, are dismissed as cranky bitches who don't fit in with the rest of the team. It's ironic that the boys can play that way, but the girls can't do it. The film business has always been a good old boy network. There are plenty of positions for women in independent film, but the feature film industry is very tough for anyone to break into, let alone women."

mit vicious, merciless acts of violence? Van Peebles' shockingly premonitory film reveals what black Americans have always understood and what white Americans needed empirical evidence to realize (the 1991 videotape of Rodney King being beaten by LAPD members). The strong story swims in and out of focus because of the variable production values. Young Mario Van Peebles plays Sweetback as a 14-year-old child having sex with an adult female hooker. Renaissance Father Melvin Van Peebles also wrote, directed, and scored *The Story of a Three Day Pass,* directed and scored *Watermelon Man* and *Tales of Erotica,* wrote *Greased Lightning, Sophisticated Gents,* and *Panther,* and directed *Identity Crisis* and *Gang in Blue.* Renaissance Son Mario Van Peebles grew up to direct *New Jack City, Posse, Panther,* and *Gang in Blue,* and to write *Identity Crisis* and *Los Locos Posse.* ☞☞☞

1971 97m/C Melvin Van Peebles, Simon Chuckster, Hubert Scales, John Dullaghan, Rhetta Hughes, John Amos, West Gale, Niva Rochelle, Nick Ferrari, Mario Van Peebles, Megan Van Peebles; ***D:*** Melvin Van Peebles; ***W:*** Melvin Van Peebles; ***C:*** Robert Maxwell; ***M:*** Melvin Van Peebles. **VHS**

Swept Away...

If anyone had told me what this movie was about before I saw it, I wouldn't have made it past the popcorn stand. Gorgeous Giancarlo Giannini and Mariangela Melato are stuck together on a Mediterranean island; he treats her terribly, even beats her up—and she loves it, and him, and doesn't want to leave. In anyone else's hands but Lina Wertmuller's, it would have been unbearable for me to squirm through, much less sit through it. Yet Wertmuller's touch is deft and sure, savagely funny and deeply human, and the results are a sheer delight. Wertmuller's statements about sexual politics are well under her artistic control here, much as Pedro Almodovar's were at the time he made 1986's *Matador.* The acting by the two leads is wise and artful, and Julio Battiferri's cinematography is ex-

"You are nothing! If you were in my toilet I wouldn't bother flushing it. My bathmat means more to me than you!"

—Buddy Ackerman (Kevin Spacey) to hapless assistant Guy (Frank Whaley) in *Swimming with Sharks.*

quisite. ***AKA:*** Swept Away...By an Unusual Destiny in the Blue Sea of August. 🦴🦴🦴🦴

1975 (R) 116m/C *IT* Giancarlo Giannini, Mariangela Melato; ***D:*** Lina Wertmuller; ***W:*** Lina Wertmuller; ***C:*** Julio Battiferri; ***M:*** Piero Piccioni. **VHS, Letterbox**

Swimming with Sharks

Once upon a time when a writer like William Somerset Maugham wanted to write about the games guys play with each other, he'd turn one of the guys, like Mildred Rogers in *Of Human Bondage,* into a girl. *Swimming with Sharks* explores the S&M relationship between a Hollywood executive named Buddy (Kevin Spacey), and Guy, his assistant (Frank Whaley). There's a girl in the picture, but Michelle *(Kalifornia)* Forbes plays her like an alley tomcat who's been in one fight too many. The previous assistant is so clearly gay and Guy and Buddy employ so many bitchy mannerisms and expressions that there's no real point addressing the issue of how deeply women are hated in this movie. Consider the source and all that. *Swimming with Sharks* admittedly owes a debt to *Sunset Boulevard* and *The Player,* and maybe writer/director George Huang will be in Billy Wilder's and/or Robert Altman's league someday. But not yet. He telegraphs the ending way too early with a sob story that doubles as character rationale and plot contrivance. All the admittedly clever observations about the master/servant relationship just hang in dead air when they're forced to support an artificially cynical climax that, frankly, belongs in the So What? Department. How wrapped up can we be in a situation that goes on for a year, and that two words would have ended at any time? (For contrast, think four words: "Death and the Maiden.") And then there's supposed to be a generational clash between Buddy and Guy that doesn't work because Kevin Spacey is a very healthy-looking 35 and Frank Whaley seems rather old and frail before his time at 32. Spacey is the film's producer and he's having such a rattling good time playing a creep that I can't help enjoying myself whenever he's onscreen. Whaley is a fine actor, but he's played an assassin one too many times and needs to develop a lighter touch for satire (although the script's deck is clearly stacked in Spacey's favor). So, "A" for the director's efforts, his sharp ears, and for choosing a situation that virtually everyone can identify with, "C" for originality and for sexual circumspection, and "F" for spelling "accountant" in the credits with three Cs. ***AKA:*** The Buddy Factor. 🦴🦴

1994 (R) 93m/C Kevin Spacey, Frank Whaley, Michelle Forbes, Benicio Del Toro; ***D:*** George Huang; ***W:*** George Huang; ***C:*** Steven Firestone. New York Film Critics Awards '95: Best Supporting Actor (Spacey); Nominations: Independent Spirit Awards '96: Best Actor (Spacey). **VHS, LV, Closed Caption, DVD**

Switchblade Sisters

Quentin Tarantino dug this Jack Hill oldie a lot, so he re-released it for audiences of the 1990s to reappraise. The plot revolves around the lives of girl gang members. The leader of the Debs is Lace (Robbie Lee). Maggie (Joanne Nail) gets into the gang, but Patch (Monica Gayle) is jealous and tries to diss her to Lace. The Debs get into a rumble with the Silver Blades, who are all guys, and Lace winds up in hospital. (You ought to see the guys, though.) Maggie takes over the gang and calls them the Jezebels, and then there's a merging with an even tougher girl gang, and so forth and so on. It's way violent, obviously; the acting isn't bad; and Lenny Bruce's then-chubby daughter Kitty, then 21, plays a gang member aptly named Donut. Asher Brauner, who went on to make 1979's well-received *The Boss' Son* with director Bobby Roth (Yves Montand dug THAT one a lot), plays Dominic, and Kate Murtagh IS Prison Warden Moms Smackley. Leonard Klady of *Variety* kvetched about why the "marginal" *Switchblade Sisters* was revived "while truly great films are neglected and decomposing." However, the Museum of Modern Arts' Eileen Bowser wisely observed that Charlie Chaplin was once widely regarded as "a low, vulgar comedian." Preserve and revive everything, if we can; what the heck does any one of us know about what's worth saving and seeing? *Switchblade Sisters* is a genuine artifact! Thank you, Mr. Tarantino! ***AKA:*** The Jezebels; Playgirl Gang. 🦴🦴🦴

1975 90m/C Robbie Lee, Joanne Nail, Monica Gayle, Kitty Bruce, Asher Brauner, Chase Newhart, Marlene Clark, Janice Karman, Don Stark, Kate Murtagh, Bill Adler; ***D:*** Jack Hill; ***W:*** F.X. Maier; ***C:*** Stephen M. Katz; ***M:*** Les Baxter, Medusa, Chuck Day, Richard Person. **VHS, DVD**

Swoon

Swoon is an irritating intellectual exercise allowing filmmaker Tom Kalin to say in his movie what Richard Fleischer and Alfred Hitchcock didn't say in *Compulsion* and *Rope,* that Nathan Leopold and Richard Loeb were homosexuals. Fleischer and Hitchcock didn't have to SAY it, they SHOWED it. How can there be any doubt when you watch the interactions of the two fictional but clearly fact-based characters played by Farley Granger and John Dall in *Rope*? Any question in your mind as you check out the gnarled relationship of Dean Stockwell and Bradford Dillman in *Compulsion*? It wasn't sexual politics that the real names and actual orientations of Leopold and Loeb couldn't be included onscreen; it was the fact that a reformed Leopold was very much alive and litigant right up to his death in 1971. *Swoon* is the cinematic equivalent of sitting through a dull lecture from a windbag, except for Ellen Kuras' black-and-white cinematography, which is outstanding. I give it three bones for the cognoscenti, but for me, just 🦴

1991 95m/B Daniel Schlachet, Craig Chester, Ron Vawter, Michael Kirby, Michael Stumm, Valda Z. Drabla, Natalie Stanford; ***D:*** Tom Kalin; ***W:*** Tom Kalin; ***C:*** Ellen Kuras; ***M:*** James Bennett. Sundance Film Festival '92: Best Cinematography. **VHS, LV, Closed Caption**

Ted

It was inevitable that SOMEONE would make a movie about the Unabomber and his troubled relationship with his family and the world. What was less inevitable was that a flick with a rock-bottom budget like *Ted* would attract the likes of Edie McClurg, 47, as Ted's mother, Jeff Corey, 84, as his professor, and Andy Dick as a sheriff. *Ted* looks like it was shot on short ends of 16mm film stock and then tossed into a vat of yellow dye to disguise its humble origins. Director Gary Ellenberg, star Daniel Passer, and producer A. J. Peralta all worked on the script, which looks, feels, and sounds like it was meant to be funny. This Ted (no last names here) is idolized by his brother and actually goes out on dates with girls in his pre-scraggly days. He is peculiar, but appears to be making somewhat of an effort to find a niche within society. The real Ted remains a mystery, especially when we compare the photograph of him as a young man at the Berkeley campus of the University of California and the press pictures taken on the day of his arrest. What happened? Don't look for answers here! Played at San Francisco's Indie Fest in 1999. 🦴

1998 85m/C Daniel Passer, Edie McClurg, Paul Provenza, Jeff Corey, Richard Fancy, Megan Cavanaugh, Kaitlin Hopkins, Andy Dick; ***D:*** Gary Ellenberg; ***W:*** Gary Ellenberg, A. J. Peralta, Daniel Passer; ***C:*** John Wolfenden; ***M:*** Evan Eder.

Teenage Gang Debs

Diane Conti, where are you? The guy I saw the movie with wants to know! Diane Conti IS Terry (she's from Manhattan) who moves to Brooklyn and quickly moves in on the leader of the pack. When he tells her he has to brand her (it's a rule), she decides to have him killed! So she moves in on the second-in-command and entices him to Take Over with herself as bait. She soon has him whipped into shape, but then, she starts picking on the Wrong People in the Gang: The Women. Hasn't this girl read ANY plays by Shakespeare? They're practically a blueprint of what not to do when you Take Over a Gang. Terry looks so cool that first time she walked into the bar, I thought she was a detective working undercover. Sande N. Johnson does some interesting directorial-type stuff on a rock-bottom budget. There's a terrible group dance that was evidently meant to ignite a craze, so everyone at San Francisco's Roxie Cinema applauded charitably. All the rumbles are "choreographed" (someone gets a credit), which basically means that, while the cam-

The Hound Salutes:
RICHARD FLEISCHER
Director, *10 Rillington Place*

The '40s and the '50s were a wonderful experimental period for me. I was very lucky. I had tolerant bosses who pretty much let me do what I wanted and I was in an experimental period of my career, so I tried things in 'B' pictures that I don't think they let other 'B' directors try. It was a great break for me because as I experimented, I gradually evolved a whole technique that I used for myself and I ended up with *The Narrow Margin,* a watershed picture for me. That was the culmination of my career as a 'B' picture career, and a very good culmination it was. The whole production cost about $200,000 (which buys Kleenex for a regular movie today) and I shot it in 13 days. It turned out to be a very important film for me and it's survived up to now. It still runs very frequently on television and is considered a cult film of its kind.

"*20,000 Leagues under the Sea* was very exciting and very tough to make. It was a really difficult picture, because I had to learn to scuba dive and I'm not a great lover of the water, nor does the water love me very much, so I threw up a lot during the filmmaking. It was a big film, grand in scope, with wonderful actors [Kirk Douglas, James Mason, Peter Lorre, Paul Lukas, Carleton Young] and my first directing job with real stars. It was a big step up for me, and of course, working with Walt Disney [1901–66] on a daily basis was also very instructive and we got along beautifully.

"*Fantastic Voyage* was a pretty fantastic film to make. The great challenge was to show the majesty of the human body, when looked at from a microscopic point of view; to make a beautiful

era's all over the place, you never get to see what's actually going on. I wonder if the cast members ever get together for reunions these days.

1966 77m/B Diana Conti, Linda Gale, Eileen Scott, Sandra Kane, Robin Nolan, Linda Cambi, Sue McManus, Geri Tyler, Joey Naudic, John Batis, Tom Yourk, Thomas Andrisano, George Winship, Doug Mitchell, Tom Eldred, Frank Spinella, Alec Primrose, Gene Marrin, Lyn Kennedy, Janet Banzet; ***D:*** Sande N. Johnson; ***W:*** Hy Cahl. **VHS**

10 Rillington Place

The execution of Timothy John Evans for the 1949 murder of his wife Beryl and daughter Baby Geraldine eventually led to the abolition of the death penalty in England, but it would be another four years until the real murderer was brought to justice. That was Evans' neighbor, John Reginald Christie, who murdered eight times over a 13-year stretch, which finally ended with his capture at the age of 55. Evans had, in fact, identified Christie as the killer, but no one listened. Christie was even commended by the judge at Evans' trial, because he offered evidence to the court in such a clear way. Evans was neither a bright nor an honest defendant, and his contrived confession led directly to the hangman, thus freeing Christie to end the lives of other victims. In his long career,

film—a surrealistic, artistic experience, and to have it be nothing like what you think it's going to be (blood, gore, guts, livers, and all of that stuff). Instead of building miniatures, we were building what I called macrotures. In terms of what's going on in science today with gene splicing and miniature cameras and motors, *Fantastic Voyage* is actually becoming true now. If you're going to make movies, you're going to have problems; there's no such thing as an easy picture to make, and if there is, it's very, very seldom.

"In my long career of 47 features, I've probably had only three or four pictures that I considered easy to make and, oddly enough, they turned out to be the pictures I liked best and I think they're really my best films: *The Happy Time* (with Charles Boyer, Marsha Hunt, Louis Jourdan, Linda Christian, Kurt Kasznar, Marcel Dalio, and Bobby Driscoll), *Compulsion* (based on the story of Nathan Leopold and Richard Loeb with Orson Welles, E.G. Marshall, Dean Stockwell, Bradford Dillman, Martin Milner, and Diane Varsi), *10 Rillington Place* (a British indie based on the story of John Christie and Timothy Evans with Richard Attenborough, John Hurt, Bernard Lee, Judy Geeson, and Pat Heywood), and *The New Centurions* (with George C. Scott, Stacy Keach, Jane Alexander, Rosalind Cash, Scott Wilson, Erik Estrada, Clifton James, Isabel Sanford, James B. Sikking, Ed Lauter, William Atherton, and Roger E. Mosley). Those pictures I found easy to make and I got them right; that's the main thing."

RICHARD FLEISCHER on video: *Amityville 3: The Demon, Armored Car Robbery, Ashanti: Land of No Mercy, Barrabas, Between Heaven and Hell, The Boston Strangler, The Clay Pigeon, Compulsion, Conan the Destroyer, Doctor Dolittle, The Don Is Dead, Fantastic Voyage, Follow Me Quietly, The Incredible Sarah, The Jazz Singer, Mandingo, Million Dollar Mystery, Mr. Majestyk, The Narrow Margin, The New Centurions, The Prince and the Pauper, Red Sonja, See No Evil, Soylent Green, 10 Rillington Place, Tora! Tora! Tora!, Tough Enough, Trapped, 20,000 Leagues under the Sea,* and *The Vikings.*

Richard Attenborough has played everything from cold-blooded killers to Kris Kringle, but in *10 Rillington Place,* he bears an uncanny resemblance to the soft-spoken, unassuming Christie. He manipulates the dim Evans (hauntingly played by John Hurt) into an unimaginably incriminating position and takes the life of the swee-faced Bery (Judy Geeson) and her baby without a flicker of regret or a twinge of mercy. This is a grim, unpleasant tale, and altogether different in tone and scope from Richard Fleischer's prior fact-based entries, 1959's *Compulsion* and 1968's *The Boston Strangler.* There is no attempt to explain or excuse Christie, and the sheer matter-of-factness of his crimes is the most terrifying aspect of this film. Adding to the horror is the fact that *10 Rillington Place* was shot, complete with meticulous period detail, on location at the actual address where Christie committed his dastardly deeds. In 1972, the building and the street (renamed Ruston Close) were leveled to make way for a parking lot for trucks. Christie's image is preserved in Madame Tussaud's Wax Museum. Based on the book by Ludovic Kennedy, a tireless crusader for the abolition of the death penalty in England.

1970 (PG) 111m/C *GB* Richard Attenborough, John Hurt, Bernard Lee, Judy Geeson, Gabrielle Daye, Andre Morell, Isobel Black, Pat Heywood; ***D:***

Margaret Hamilton, Bonita Granville, and Catherine Dorcet in *These Three.* United Artists; courtesy of the Kobal Collection

Richard Fleischer; ***W:*** Clive Exton; ***C:*** Denys Coop; ***M:*** John Dankworth. **VHS, LV**

Teresa's Tattoo

Teresa's Tattoo is a zany 1994 comedy directed by Julie Cypher and starring Adrienne Shelly in a dual role. First, she's Gloria whose earrings are encoded with NASA secrets and who doesn't know she's been abducted by two bozos. They eat Cheerios while she accidentally drowns in a pool. To cover up their mistake, they abduct look-alike Teresa who "voluntarily went to a party of lesbian prostitutes where three men drugged her. She woke up with a new hairdo and a tattoo, was fed greasy freezer treats and drugged (again) after which she was driven to a dark, scary place where additional bad men chased her and threatened to cut off her fingers before wrecking their own car!" Teresa's police statement is read in a hilarious deadpan by Diedrich Bader, whose only other big-screen credit was as Jethro and Jethrine in 1993's *The Beverly Hillbillies.* He's very funny here, and so is Shelly, who appears to be gorgeously vague but whose comedy is rooted in a very precise and specific style. Others contributing to the fun are Majel Barrett and Nanette Fabray as a pair of ditzy friends; Anthony Clark, C. Thomas Howell, Lou Diamond Phillips, and Casey Siemaszko as the bad men; Tippi Hedren as Evelyn, Teresa's newlywed mother; k.d. lang as a religious nut; Nancy McKeon as Sara Pond, Teresa's best friend; Mary Kay Place as Nora, a straight-talking new in-law; Joe Pantoliano as Bruno; Jonathan Silverman as Rich, Teresa's would-be date who forgot to show up; Kiefer Sutherland as a cop; and Mare Winningham in a bit as a singer. This serious side-splitting remedy for the blues was written by Georgie Huntington, and five of the songs are written by Melissa Etheridge, who has a cameo as a hooker. *Teresa's Tattoo*'s reputation is zero, but it made me laugh for 88 minutes. When you absolutely NEED a laugh, this silly flick with a great cast may offer a welcome respite from grim reality. 𝓛𝓛𝓛

1994 88m/C Adrienne Shelly, C. Thomas Howell, Nancy McKeon, Lou Diamond Phillips, Casey Siemaszko, Jonathan Silverman, Diedrich Bader; ***Cameos:*** Majel Barrett, Anthony Clark, Nanette Fabray, Tippi Hedren, k.d. lang, Joe Pantoliano, Mary Kay Place, Mare Winningham, Kiefer Sutherland, Melissa Etheridge; ***D:*** Julie Cypher; ***W:*** Georgie Huntington; ***C:*** Sven Kirsten; ***M:*** Melissa Etheridge. **VHS**

Terminal Bliss

Another outstanding first feature at 1990's Mill Valley Film Festival was *Terminal Bliss,* scripted by its 22-year-old director Jordan Alan, when he was only 18 years old. Alan's drama of young friendships curdled by drugs and betrayal is not only keenly observed, it is also filled with a deep understanding rare in this type of film. Alex the protagonist appears to be a flip, wisecracking kid, but he is not so wrapped up in himself that he is unaffected by other people's sorrows. Alex's best friend from childhood is John, who grows progressively weirder under the influence of drugs. John is used to having everything all his own way and in one miserable sequence he casually rapes a girl. Alan manages to convey the girl's intense pain and John's blurry detachment without a suggestion of the eroticism that far more experienced filmmakers often employ. The cast of unknowns (including Luke "Dylan McKay" Perry in his first starring role) is excellent, but it is Jordan Alan's steady control of his material that will linger in your memory. 𝓛𝓛𝓛

1991 (R) 94m/C Luke Perry, Timothy Owen, Estee Chandler, Sonia Curtis, Micah Grant, Alexis Arquette; ***D:*** Jordan Alan; ***W:*** Jordan Alan; ***C:*** Greg Smith; ***M:*** Frank Becker. **VHS, LV, Closed Caption**

That'll Be the Day

This is Part One of Jim MacLaine's (David Essex) meteoric rise and fall as a rock and roll star. As the story opens in 1959, Jim is dissatisfied with his drab existence and hopes that rock and roll will lead to a better life. The presence of Ringo Starr in a dramatic role adds to the film's authenticity. Neil Aspinall and Keith Moon supervise the music and David Essex and Billy Fury perform. The great soundtrack by early rock greats was clearly chosen with great care, not just slapped together. The sequel, *Stardust,* directed by Michael Apted, is even better (Essex, Ayres, and Moon played the same roles). 𝓛𝓛𝓛

1973 (PG) 91m/C Ringo Starr, Keith Moon, David Essex, Rosemary Leach, James Booth, Billy Fury, Rosalind Ayres, Robert Lindsay, Brenda Bruce, Verna Harvey, James Ottoway, Deborah Watling, Beth Morris, Daphne Oxenford, Kim Braden, Ron Hackett, Johnny Shannon, Susan Holderness, The Debonairs; ***D:*** Claude Whatham; ***W:*** Ray Connolly; ***C:*** Peter Suschitzsky. **VHS, LV**

These Three

If the Independent Spirit Awards had existed in 1936, *These Three* would definitely have been a contender. The fact that this film was made at all is a tribute to Samuel Goldwyn's free spirit as a producer. Even though *The Children's Hour* had been a huge hit on Broadway, lesbians were not allowed to appear in ANY American movies due to censorship by the Hays Office. Goldwyn bought the movie rights knowing he couldn't use the title or the story onscreen or in publicity. What he could do was hire Lillian Hellman (who had scripted *The Dark Angel* for him in 1935) to write the screenplay. Hellman felt that the real point of *The Children's Hour* was not whether or not its two central characters were lesbians, but that a lie has the power to shatter people's lives and livelihoods. Therefore, instead of showing how two schoolteachers were ruined when one of their students accused them of an "unnatural (lesbian) affair," *These Three* showed the teachers being accused of an "unnatural affair" with the same man. The teachers, Martha Dobie and Karen Wright, are played by Miriam Hopkins and Merle Oberon, and the man is Joel McCrea as Dr. Joseph Hardin. Hopkins plays Martha as a cool woman, unable to express her

A softcore movie, Dr. Death, a chocolate milkshake, a nosey blonde, and *The Carol Burnett Show.* Solving this mystery is going to be murder.

—Tagline from the movie *The Thin Blue Line.*

love for Doctor Joe or to attract him. She is exactly the sort of standoffish teacher that schoolgirls do make up stories about all the time. In contrast, Merle Oberon's Karen is sweet, sympathetic, and head over heels in love with Doctor Joe, who is equally head over heels in love with her. Why would Martha, who does not like her nasty, gossipy Aunt Lily Mortar (Catherine Doucet), hire her as a teacher? Maybe it's a family thing, but the aunt turns out to be her downfall, as well as Karen's and Joe's. The centerpiece of *These Three* is Bonita Granville as Mary Tilford, who won a nomination as Best Supporting Actress for her interpretation. In a year when Shirley Temple was the number one star at the boxoffice with films like *Captain January, Poor Little Rich Girl, Dimples,* and *Stowaway,* the undiluted menace of Bonita Granville was electrifying to 1936 audiences. Mary Tilford is a merciless bully, who terrorizes her younger classmate Rosalie Wells (Marcia Mae Jones) into backing up her story about the "unnatural affair" (based solely on Aunt Lily's gossip and Doctor Joe's constant presence). Soon, the students are leaving in droves. Martha and Karen sue for libel, but without the crucial testimony of Aunt Lily who's conveniently left town, they lose. If Doctor Joe marries Karen, his career is over, too. Under the meticulous direction of William Wyler, *These Three* is a story you can't tear your eyes away from for a single instant. He keeps the focus on the relentless course of the gossip as it spreads from Aunt Lily to Mary to Rosalie, to Mary's snobbish, influential grandmother (Alma Kruger). Martha, Karen, and Joe are paralyzed by the sheer speed of their destruction. *These Three* wound up packing as much of a wallop onscreen as *The Children's Hour* had done onstage. Samuel Goldwyn shrewdly sidestepped the Hays Office and, in the process, made one of the best films of the 1930s. ♪♪♪♪

1936 92m/B Miriam Hopkins, Merle Oberon, Joel McCrea, Bonita Granville, Marcia Mae Jones, Walter Brennan, Margaret Hamilton, Catherine Doucet, Alma Kruger, Carmencita Johnson, Mary Ann Durkin, Frank McGlynn; ***D:*** William Wyler; ***W:*** Lillian Hellman; ***C:*** Gregg Toland; ***M:*** Alfred Newman. Nominations: Academy Awards '36: Best Supporting Actress (Granville). **VHS, LV**

They Drive by Night

In 1987, the late film historian William K. Everson contributed an important new article on British film noir to *Films in Review,* hoping that it might lead to a pioneering book on the subject. That it has not (so far) is every film noir fan's loss. In a later interview, Everson admitted that to most publishers, noir means American noir, period; ironic, considering that the roots of film noir are in France. Moreover, British noir directors were far more influenced by French films than were American directors (who often looked to German films for their inspiration). Leave it to Sinister Cinema to fill an important gap in film scholarship by releasing *They Drive by Night,* the film that Everson considers the first ever British noir. Released by Warner Bros. in December 1938 for British home consumption only, *They Drive by Night* stars Emlyn Williams, then 35, as Shorty Matthews, an ex-convict wrongly accused of murdering a former lover upon his release from prison. With the help of Molly O'Neill, a friend of the deceased (played by the little-known Anna Konstam), Shorty tries to prove his innocence, an exercise in frustration until they bump into Mr. Walter Hoover, an erudite sex maniac played by that magnificent ham, Ernest Thesiger (loved by all as the immortal Dr. Pretorius in *The Bride of Frankenstein*). Directed in no-nonsense style by Arthur Woods from a script by Derek Twist, *They Drive by Night* scrupulously avoids what Alfred Hitchcock was so fond of doing: depicting the lower social orders of Britain with sly and often patronizing humor. For there is no humor in the life of Shorty Matthews; his life is played out against a grimy background of pubs, back roads, and dance halls. *They Drive by Night* may not have the reputation of Renoir's *La Bete Humaine,* also made in 1938, but it is an altogether worthy addition to the noir canon. *They Drive by Night* may also have been an important influence on the future screenplays of Graham Greene; he praised the virtues of this realistic quota quickie as a young movie reviewer the same day that he panned the falseness of mighty MGM's overproduced version of *Idiot's Delight* by Pulitzer Prize–winner Robert Sherwood. Sinister Cinema admits that their print of the extremely rare *They Drive by Night* is soft in comparison with their normally crisp video transfers, but we are lucky to have the film at all; many of the movies released by British Warner Bros. in the '30s and '40s no longer exist. 🦴🦴🦴½

1938 84m/B Emlyn Williams, Ernest Thesiger, Anna Konstam, Allan Jeayes, Antony Holles, Ronald Shiner, Yolande Terrell, Julie Barrie, Kitty De Legh; ***D:*** Arthur Woods; ***W:*** Derek Twist; ***C:*** Basil Emmott. **VHS**

The Thin Blue Line

The Thin Blue Line was among the best entries at international film festivals in 1988. This Errol Morris movie is documentary filmmaking at its finest: it entertains and informs, magnetizes audiences, and stirs their emotions. It even helped to free a convicted man who was wrongly convicted for murder. How can a man be wrongly convicted for murder in this day and age? Morris shows us how in 101 absorbing minutes. It's frightening to watch how the man who is probably the real killer was able to fool so many people with his carefully cultivated attitude of innocence and respectfulness. Morris conducted the interviews of many subjects in shadows, evoking a film noir mood. A memorable score by Philip Glass enhances the suspense. Although Errol Morris admitted that much of the investigative work he had to do was boring, *The Thin Blue Line* is absolutely original, and with a pace and style like no other documentary ever made. 🦴🦴🦴🦴

1988 101m/C *D:* Errol Morris; ***W:*** Errol Morris; ***C:*** Robert Chappell, Stefan Czapsky; ***M:*** Philip Glass. **VHS, LV, Closed Caption**

The Thing Called Love

Let's try for just a moment to ignore some of the media ca-ca of the last few years. Before he died on Halloween morning 1993, River Phoenix made a couple of movies that failed to attract wide distribution: Sam Shepard's *Silent Tongue* and Peter Bogdanovich's *The Thing Called Love.* If Phoenix were still alive, one would be forced to confess that his acting was going through a bad patch. The way things turned out, neither film offers much in the way of an enduring legacy. In *Silent Tongue,* Phoenix's performance is completely out of control; he mugs furiously, and, it must be said, artificially, in the role of a grief-stricken young widower. The same actor who acquitted himself with such distinction in many other ensemble showcases is entirely out-acted by Alan Bates, Richard Harris, Sheila Tousey, and Jeri Arrendondo. In *The Thing Called Love,* we see an ashen-faced Phoenix, old beyond his years, delivering a mannered performance by what appears to be rote. His expressions and gestures seem cluttered; he isn't feeling his way through the part, he's just passing through, with only the most perfunctory investment in the trip. Phoenix' artistic decline is all the more striking when contrasted with the glowing work of his co-star Samantha Mathis, who approaches her role with intelligent assurance. Even Dermot Mulroney, who was just as inept as Phoenix in *Silent Tongue,* does a pretty credible job under the guidance of Bogdanovich. The story of hopeful young singers looking for love with all the wrong partners is so slow and so slight that its eventual distributor deliberately kept the movie away from the claws of big city reviewers. Maybe they hoped *The Thing Called Love* would strike gold on video, but on its first day at our neighborhood outlet where ALL new releases are ripped off the shelves, every single copy was still in the store at five minutes to midnight. Overlooked at the time of release was Sandra Bullock, microseconds away from superstardom via *Speed.* 🦴🦴

1993 (PG-13) 116m/C River Phoenix, Samantha Mathis, Sandra Bullock, Dermot Mulroney, K.T. Oslin, Anthony Clark, Webb Wilder; ***Cameos:*** Trisha Yearwood; ***D:*** Peter Bogdanovich; ***W:*** Allan Moyle, Carol Heikkinen; ***C:*** Peter James. **VHS, LV, Closed Caption**

The Third Man

The Third Man is a vintage Graham Greene/Carol Reed collaboration about a

"In Italy for 30 years under the Borgias, they had warfare, terror, murder, and bloodshed. But they produced Michelangelo, Leonardo Da Vinci, and the Renaissance. In Switzerland, they had brotherly love. They had five hundred years of democracy and peace. And what did they produce? The cuckoo clock."

—Harry Lime (Orson Welles) rationalizes his own actions in *The Third Man.*

serious subject. Harry Lime is no good (he distributes bad penicillin that results in brain-damaged children) and only Western hack writer Holly Martins can stop Harry IF he can find him. Actress Anna Schmidt (Alida Valli) is in love with Harry, but she isn't much interested in helping Holly find Harry, either. Mr. Crabbin (Wilfrid Hyde-White) is VERY interested in Holly; he wants him to speak for the Viennese literary society. After Holly flops there, he tells Major Calloway that he'll help him find Harry if the Major will let Anna get away. After hearing about Harry Lime for most of the movie, we can't wait to see him, and he turns out to be an even better bad guy than we could have imagined. Orson Welles wrote his own dialogue and added some interesting directorial flourishes that Greene and Reed graciously kept in the finished film. Reportedly, most of the fighting on this movie was between producers Alexander Korda and David O. Selznick, who wound up in a lawsuit. Joseph Cotten made such a pleasant, self-deprecating impression as Holly that he extended his career for another 35 years playing mostly pleasant, self-deprecating characters, and Trevor Howard's immaculate performance as the wry Major was followed by nearly 40 more years of wonderfully shaded characters. Alida Valli didn't make nearly as nearly as many movies as her admirers would have liked, but *Senso, Eyes Without a Face, Oedipus Rex, The Spider's Strategem, 1900, Suspiria,* and *A Month by the Lake* are among her more memorable appearances after *The Third Man.* Anton Karas' zither became famous and Harry Lime was reincarnated as the hero (!) of Michael Rennie's 1960 television series. 🦴🦴🦴🦴

1949 104m/B Joseph Cotten, Orson Welles, Alida Valli, Trevor Howard, Bernard Lee, Wilfrid Hyde-White, Ernst Deutsch, Erich Ponto, Siegfried Breuer, Hedwig Bleibtreu, Paul Hoerbiger, Frederick Sehreicker, Herbert Halbik, Jenny Werner, Nelly Arno, Alexis Chesnakov, Leo Bieber, Paul Hardtmuth; ***D:*** Carol Reed; ***W:*** Graham Greene; ***C:*** Robert Krasker; ***M:*** Anton Karas. Academy Awards '50: Best Black and White Cinematography; British Academy Awards '49: Best Film; Cannes Film Festival '49: Best Film; Directors Guild of America Awards '49: Best Director (Reed); Nominations: Academy Awards '50: Best Director (Reed), Best Film Editing. **VHS, LV, 8mm**

32 Short Films about Glenn Gould

32 Short Films about Glenn Gould was well received when it was first released, but for the uninitiated (yours truly), the structure of the film was too broken up for me to get a clear portrait of its subject. It's a decidedly different approach to film biography, but I left the film with the famed piano player (1932–82) being as much of a mystery as ever. 🦴🦴🦴

1993 94m/C *CA* Colm Feore, Gale Garnett, David Hughes, Katya Ladan, Gerry Quigley, Carlo Rota, Peter Millard, Yehudi Menuhin, Bruno Monsaingeon; ***D:*** Francois Girard; ***W:*** Don McKellar, Francois Girard; ***C:*** Alan Dostie. Genie Awards '93: Best Cinematography, Best Director (Girard), Best Film, Best Film Editing; Nominations: Independent Spirit Awards '95: Best Foreign Film. **VHS, LV**

35 Up

I can think of few things I would LESS like to do than be interviewed every seven years for a movie between the ages of seven and thirty-five. That said, there are few series that are more compelling to watch than Michael Apted's superb *7-14-21-28-35 Up* collection. It all began when the director spent a day with 14 English schoolchildren in 1963. There was pug-nosed Paul, and Tony who dreamed of being a disc jockey, and a bright-eyed little girl named Suzy, and a soft-spoken idealist named Bruce. Then there were two groups of three that he interviewed together: three insufferably stuck-up upper-class twits (John, Andrew, and Charles), and three children of the working class (Jackie, Lynn, and Sue). Symon, the only black child on the program, was also interviewed, as well as Nick, and a cheerful, charismatic little boy named Neil. Like most children, the kids were blessed with elastic, expressive faces, and—except for the twits—with fresh, original views of the world and themselves. When Apted returned to talk with them in 1970, 1977, 1984, and 1991, he, and movie audiences, discovered how each child survived the process of growing up. The most riveting story, of course, is Neil. At the age of

14, his cheerful face seemed enormously sad. He no longer talked about being an astronaut, but still thought he would make a good coach driver. At 21, he looked even sadder, and by 28 he was not only sad, but downright unhealthy and homeless as well. His inexorable descent into mental illness is wrenching to watch, especially since, unlike the others, he believes that his condition is entirely due to something inside of him. He never discusses relatives or any other close relationships, and he fears that if he were ever to marry, his kids would wind up like him rather than his wife, however outgoing she might be. Nick, who lives in America, suggests that the process of making the series and accounting for one's life to an international audience every seven years can't help but change a person. His wife Jackie, who received tremendous criticism for the way she came off in *28 Up,* refuses to appear in the series anymore, and neither Nick nor Jackie will let their child participate. Nick, who now has an American accent, seems well, happy, and fairly philosophical about his many years under media scrutiny. He discusses the low-key British personality which may strike U.S. audiences as dull, and suggests that his and Jackie's frankness in *28 Up* was misinterpreted by many viewers as a sign that their marriage was on the rocks. As a viewer who did feel that way, I might point out that things may not always be what they seem, even in a wonderfully revealing documentary like *35 Up.* ☙☙☙☙

1991 128m/C *GB* ***D:*** Michael Apted; ***W:*** Michael Apted; ***C:*** George Jesse Turner. **VHS**

The 39 Steps

Robert Donat, then 30, looks so hale and hearty in this key Alfred Hitchcock film, it's sad to realize that all his performances were a major triumph of mind over matter. A lifelong sufferer of asthma, which finally killed him in 1958, the 1939 Oscar winner had to schedule movie roles around his delicate health. Donat is the quintessential Hitchcock hero: funny, charming, a bit of a flake, and completely unprepared for life as a fugitive. Splendid chemistry with beautiful Madeleine Carroll (1906–87) certainly helped, as did the exciting screenplay. Wylie Watson as Memory is to this one what May Whitty as Miss Froy is to *The Lady Vanishes* (only SHE gets more to do). The McGuffin is basically twaddle, but NO one is glued to a Hitchcock classic for the McGuffin; how he shows the way ordinary men and women behave in a crisis burns into our memory far longer than whatever set them spinning in the first place. Elizabeth Inglis (AKA Earl, Sigourney Weaver's mum) and Wilfrid Brambell (making his film debut at 23) are supposed to be in this one, but I've yet to do a frame-by-frame check to find them, or even to see Hitchcock himself in a street sequence. ☙☙☙☙

1935 81m/B *GB* Robert Donat, Madeleine Carroll, Godfrey Tearle, Lucie Mannheim, Peggy Ashcroft, John Laurie, Wylie Watson, Helen Haye, Frank Cellier, Gus McNaughton, Jerry Verno, Peggy Simpson, Hilda Trevelyan, John Turnbull, Elizabeth Inglis, Wilfrid Brambell; ***D:*** Alfred Hitchcock; ***W:*** Charles Bennett, Alma Reville, Ian Hay; ***C:*** Bernard Knowles; ***M:*** Louis Levy. **VHS, LV, 8mm**

This Happy Breed

The name of director David Lean conjures up images of blistering heat, frozen tundra, sand dunes, and thousands of extras. From 1957–1984, with one exception, Lean was a director of lavish epics. But there was a time when Lean made small, intimate films like *This Happy Breed.* It's hard to imagine Robert Newton in an UNDER-the-top role, but that's who Frank Gibbons is and that's how he plays him. Celia Johnson plays his no-nonsense wife, Ethel, their cat Percy plays himself (I guess), and Kay Walsh is their dissatisfied daughter, Queenie. She's meant to marry Billy Mitchell (John Mills), the son of Frank's friend, Bob (Stanley Holloway). But Queenie wants more from life, and she leaves home and hearth to find it; Ethel is determined never to forgive her. In the meanwhile, Frank's sister (Alison Leggatt) and Ethel's mother (Amy Veness) bait each other day in and out, each to deflect their unhappiness with their lot in life. They feel lonely and unwanted and if they

"This is your neighbor speaking. I'm sure I speak for all of us when I say that something must be done about your garbage cans in the alley here. It is definitely second-rate garbage! Now, by next week, I want to see a better class of garbage. I want to see champagne bottles and caviar cans. I'm sure you're all behind me on this, so let's snap it up and get on the ball."

—Murray Burns (Jason Robards) preaches from his window to the neighbors in *A Thousand Clowns.*

didn't needle each other, they wouldn't have much else. A milestone occurs when Reg Gibbons (John Blythe) marries a girl named Phyllis (Betty Fleetwood), and another, sadder milestone occurs soon after, beautifully conveyed by Lean in a sequence without dialogue. Time passes, and people and their circumstances change. Noel Coward, who did not grow up like this, has a tendency to satirize the working classes. Lean, who might have grown up on the same block as the Gibbons and Mitchell families, paid his dues going for the director's tea. His interpretation here is filled with empathy, insight, and generosity of spirit. 🦴🦴🦴🦴

1947 114m/C *GB* Robert Newton, Celia Johnson, John Mills, Kay Walsh, Stanley Holloway, Amy Veness, Alison Leggatt, Eileen Erskine, John Blythe, Guy Verney, Betty Fleetwood, Merle Tottenham; ***D:*** David Lean; ***W:*** David Lean, Noel Coward, Ronald Neame; ***C:*** Ronald Neame; ***M:*** Noel Coward, Muir Mathieson. **VHS**

Thomas Jefferson: A View from the Mountain

When President Kennedy honored a group of Nobel Prize winners at a White House dinner, he quipped, "I think this is the most extraordinary collection of talent and human knowledge that has ever been gathered together at the White House, with the possible exception of when Thomas Jefferson dined alone." Jefferson's memory has been burnished brightly into our national consciousness; any discussion of our greatest presidents (Lincoln, Washington, FDR, Wilson) always embraces the Virginia-born genius who drafted the Declaration of Independence at age 33 and won the presidency 25 years later. But according to *Thomas Jefferson: A View from the Mountain,* both Jefferson's life and his philosophy reveal a long series of contradictions that historians have been arguing about for over 170 years. Why, for example, if he believed that "all men are created equal," did he free only three of his own slaves during his lifetime? And why, if he truly believed in an agrarian democracy, did he maintain the paternalistic view that slaves were better off under his care and protection than they would be if he paid them a living wage and then threw in the care and protection as a bonus? The huge plantations of the South would not have survived intact if ALL the slaves were paid a living wage, and Jefferson and his fellow agrarian Democrats knew it. The same man who fought successfully to abolish the paternalistic system of primogeniture that still exists in Great Britain today, the same man who fought tirelessly for religious freedom, maintained the status quo of the slave-run plantation system during his own lifetime. There were deeply personal factors at work here, too, although genealogists are still wrangling about them as well. Did Jefferson father children by the mulatto daughter of his own father-in-law? Was Sally Hemings really his late wife's half-sister, and was his fear of disclosing their true origins the reason why he was so reluctant to free his own children? Well-spoken historians of every persuasion thrash it out and the answers may continue to be elusive for many viewers. The documentary is taped in many historical locations and a wide-ranging selection of primary source materials from the era is also shown. Tackling yet another president among his gallery of statesman is Edward Herrmann as the voice of Jefferson, Sissy Spacek is daughter Martha, and Danny Glover reads the words of Jefferson's slave, Isaac. *Thomas Jefferson: A View from the Mountain* is a thoughtful point of departure for further research and is well worth seeing for its rigorous questioning and fresh perspectives on the Jefferson legend. 🦴🦴🦴

1995 114m/C ***Host:*** Martin Doblmeier; ***W:*** Martin Doblmeier; ***V:*** Edward Herrmann, Sissy Spacek, Danny Glover, Robert Prosky. **VHS**

A Thousand Clowns

One of the best movies of 1965 is Fred Coe's *A Thousand Clowns,* written by Herb

Gardner. Jason Robards plays Murray Burns, the sort of parent every kid would love to have: funny, flexible, free, and fearless. The only problem is, he isn't the sort of parent who receives grown-up approval. In fact, he isn't even a parent, although you wouldn't know it from the warm relationship he has built with his nephew Nick, precociously played by Barry Gordon. Social worker Barbara Harris enters their lives with antiseptic William Daniels in tow. Daniels is a grown-up with a capital "G," but Harris recognizes fellow free spirits when she sees them. Unfortunately, concessions to reality must be made and they drain a bit of the fearlessness from both Murray and his nephew. For his performance as Murray's brother, a New York businessman with "a gift for surrender," Martin Balsam (1914–96) won an Oscar, and future director Gene Saks set the standard for nauseating kiddie show hosts with his lacerating performance as Chuckles the Chipmunk. A thoughtful and hilarious film, *A Thousand Clowns.* 🦴🦴🦴🦴

1965 118m/B Jason Robards Jr., Barry Gordon, William Daniels, Barbara Harris, Gene Saks, Martin Balsam; ***D:*** Fred Coe; ***W:*** Herb Gardner; ***C:*** Arthur Ornitz. Academy Awards '65: Best Supporting Actor (Balsam); Nominations: Academy Awards '65: Best Adapted Screenplay, Best Picture, Best Original Score. **VHS**

Thousand Pieces of Gold

Among the impressive domestic entries at 1990's Mill Valley Film Festival was Nancy Kelly's *Thousand Pieces of Gold,* starring Rosalind Chao as Lalu, a reluctant immigrant to America during the 1880s. Even though her father sells her to a marriage broker, she is filled with nostalgia for her family and her homeland. Her first stop on the West Coast is San Francisco's Chinatown, where she is bought and paid for by a Chinese agent named Jin, who delivers her to Oregon saloon keeper Hong King. To avoid the life of a whore, Lalu works hard around the saloon, still dreaming that she can return home one day. She becomes infatuated with the agent who promises that he will earn the money to rescue her from Hong King. Instead, Hong King loses Lalu in a card game and she moves in with the winner, Charlie. Although she insists that their relationship remain platonic, she loses the respect of the agent who assumes the worst and rejects her. Lalu, with her new American name of Polly, is forced to fend for herself. Filmed entirely in Nevada City, Montana, *Thousand Pieces of Gold* accomplishes wonders with its small budget and straightforward narrative. Rosalind Chao gives such a remarkable performance as Lalu that you'll wish that she were offered more such roles instead of the supporting roles she normally plays in films like *Chinese Web, The Big Brawl, Twirl, Slamdance, White Ghost,* and *Memoirs of an Invisible Man.* (She got her chance in *The Joy Luck Club,* featuring Michael Paul Chan.) Equally good is John Sayles regular Chris Cooper *(Matewan, City of Hope, Lone Star)* in the beautifully written role of Charlie. Dennis *(The Last Emperor)* Dun and Michael Paul Chan do a good job revealing the negative aspects of Chinese assimilation into the get-rich-quick society of the Victorian era. Anne Makepeace's well-shaded screenplay for *Thousand Pieces of Gold* is based on Ruthanne Lum McCann's biographical novel. 🦴🦴🦴

1991 (PG-13) 105m/C Rosalind Chao, Dennis Dun, Michael Paul Chan, Chris Cooper, Jimmie F. Skaggs, William Oldham, David Hayward, Beth Broderick; ***D:*** Nancy Kelly; ***W:*** Anne Makepeace; ***C:*** Bobby Bukowski; ***M:*** Gary Remal Malkin. **VHS, LV, Closed Caption**

Three Lives and Only One Death

Raul Ruiz is much loved by devotees of international film festivals and not particularly well known outside the festival circuit. The presence of the late Marcello Mastroianni in this 1996 movie may attract a few more viewers, but it's still a typical film festival entry, the details of which tend to blur, not over time, but the instant the closing credits start to roll. It is Mastroianni's ever-wise, always humble face that gives the three tales their momentum. International audiences have trusted the naked honesty of that face since 1947,

Laurence Olivier and Louise Purnell in *Three Sisters.* British Lion; courtesy of the Kobal Collection

and wherever Marcello Mastroianni wants to take us, we will go, at least for the length of a movie. ***AKA:*** Trois Vies et Une Seule Mort. 𝅘𝅥𝅮𝅘𝅥𝅮

1996 124m/C *FR* Marcello Mastroianni, Anna Galiena, Marisa Paredes, Melvil Poupaud, Chiara Mastroianni, Arielle Dombasle, Feodor Atkine, Jean-Yves Gautier, Pierre Bellemare, Lou Castel, Jacques Pieller; ***D:*** Raul Ruiz; ***W:*** Raul Ruiz, Pascal Bonitzer; ***C:*** Laurent Machuel; ***M:*** Jorge Arriagada. **VHS**

Three Sisters

The best of 1974's American Film Theatre productions had actually been waiting for U.S. release since 1970. Joan Plowright and Laurence Olivier starred as Masha Prosorov and Dr. Chebutikin, Derek Jacobi and Alan Bates were Andrei Prosorov and Col. Vershinin, and Ronald Pickup and Daphne Heard were Baron Tusenbach and Anfissa. Most of the rest of the cast were unknown to American audiences. *Three Sisters* had received several notable Broadway stagings over the years: Eva Le Gallienne, Josephine Hutchinson, and Beatrice Terry starred in a 1927 production; 15 years later, Katherine Cornell, Gertrude Musgrove, and Judith Anderson were the *Three Sisters;* and Geraldine Page, Kim Stanley, and Shirley Knight revived the play for 1964 audiences. As much as I wish that fragments of moving pictures of these revivals still existed, it's hard to imagine how anyone could have made a better film version of Anton Chekhov's play then Olivier. He sees straight into the heart of each character and brings every story to life in a fresh and startling way. The look of the film may have been accomplished more by accident than design, but the delicate color cinematography makes it appear that we are watching the lives of the Prosorov sisters through a mist. Plowright gives a wonderfully real performance as Masha. This one may be hard to find, but it's well worth the search. 🦴🦴🦴🦴

1970 (PG) 165m/C *GB* Jeanne Watts, Joan Plowright, Louise Purnell, Derek Jacobi, Alan Bates, Laurence Olivier, Kenneth Mackintosh, Sheila Reid, Ronald Pickup, Frank Wylie, Daphne Heard; ***D:*** Laurence Olivier; ***W:*** Moura Budberg; ***C:*** Geoffrey Unsworth. **VHS**

Through the Olive Trees

Mohamad Ali Keshavarz tells us that he is really an actor playing a movie director and everyone else in the picture is an amateur. Mrs. Shivah is his assistant director and she wants everything to be just right. Taherek the star (Taherek Ladanian) won't address lines to Hossein (Hossein Rezai) because she turned down his marriage proposal. He confides in the director who changes the script. Taherek still won't talk to Hossein. Obligingly, the director changes the script again. This is part of a trilogy, but you don't need to see *Where Is My Friend's Home?* or *And Life Goes On* to appreciate Abbas Kiarostami's ingenious concept here and its thoughtful execution. ***AKA:*** Under the Olive Trees; Zire Darakhtan Zeyton. 🦴🦴🦴🦴

1994 (G) 104m/C Zarifeh Shivah, Hossein Rezai, Mohamad Ali Keshavarz, Taherek Ladania; ***D:*** Abbas Kiarostami; ***W:*** Abbas Kiarostami; ***C:*** Hossein Jafarian, Farhad Saba. Nominations: Independent Spirit Awards '96: Best Foreign Film. **VHS**

Thursday's Child

Sally Ann Howes made a dozen films in the 1940s and '50s, long before director Ken Hughes tried to turn her into another Julie Andrews opposite Dick Van Dyke in the 1968 musical dud, *Chitty Chitty Bang Bang.* She was, in fact, an enormously appealing juvenile actress, as evidenced by her debut in *Thursday's Child.* Howes, then 12, plays Fennis Wilson, who has a scholarly life in mind for her future. Circumstances bring her into a film studio, where she is cast in a movie. Her new career leads to all sorts of family problems, a reality rarely addressed in Hollywood flicks where supposedly well-adjusted kiddie stars then reigned supreme. Howes steadily improved as an actress, but as Nova Pilbeam discovered before her, great teen roles weren't consistently there in Great Britain between 1934–59. (Hayley Mills was England's first really big teen star and even she had to go to Hollywood to sustain her career.) Stewart Granger, then 29, appears as David Penley, a grown-up sensitive to Fennis' true interests and ambitions. 🦴🦴🦴½

1943 95m/B *GB* Stewart Granger, Sally Ann Howes, Wilfred Lawson, Kathleen O'Regan, Eileen Bennett, Marianne Davis, Gerhard Kempinski, Felix Aylmer, Margaret Yarde, Vera Bogetti, Percy Walsh, Ronald Shiner; ***D:*** Rodney Ackland; ***W:*** Rodney Ackland, Donald Macardle; ***C:*** Desmond Dickinson. **VHS**

Thy Kingdom Come, Thy Will Be Done

Among the more intriguing entries at 1987's Mill Valley Film Festival was Antony Thomas' excellent documentary, *Thy Kingdom Come, Thy Will Be Done.* Originally intended as a *Frontline* special, but canceled prior to its May 1987 telecast, the film focuses on the significant relationship between Christian fundamentalists and right-wing politicians. Thomas' film provides a rich, detailed investigation of his controversial subjects, and his soft-spoken, veddy British interviewing style clearly soothes the fundamentalists into revealing themselves in ways they never would if his approach were more combative. (Antony Thomas is also credited as director on 1990's *Code Name: Chaos.*) 🦴🦴🦴

1987 107m/C ***D:*** Antony Thomas; ***W:*** Antony Thomas; ***C:*** Curtis Clark.

Ticket to Heaven

Most movies about cults fall into the realm of propaganda, as in, hey kids, don't try this at home with your friends. *Ticket to Heaven* digs deeper than that, and be-

cause it does, it's an intensely frightening film to watch. Nick Mancuso plays a young man who's at a turning point in his life. He's just broken up with someone, he's miserable, he could go one way or the other. At the exact moment of his greatest vulnerability, he becomes attracted to some women in a cult who make it seem as if it's perfectly safe and cozy to be with them. Initially hoping to get laid, he sticks around the cult long enough to get sucked in and then he can't leave. Saul Rubinek (as the best friend in the whole world) takes a leave from his job to get his buddy back. The cult members try to suck him in, too, and he escapes, determined to try another (illegal) strategy: hiring a deprogrammer and kidnapping Mancuso's character from the cult. Director Ralph L. Thomas wisely focuses on the central character's emotional landscape, which is so isolated that the claustrophobic togetherness of cult life seems appealing in comparison. Anne Cameron's perceptive script, too, reveals that cult members are made, not born; severe sleep deprivation, non-stop programming, and constant supervision might turn any strong personality into a compliant recruit under the wrong circumstances. Mancuso and Rubinek deservedly won Genie awards for their sensitive, driven performances, and the film itself won a Genie as well. The two leads went on to make dozens of films in the 1980s and 1990s, while Thomas' next projects were 1983's Genie-winning *The Terry Fox Story* and 1988's *Apprentice to Murder.* 🦴🦴🦴

1981 (PG) 109m/C *CA* Nick Mancuso, Meg Foster, Kim Cattrall, Saul Rubinek, R.H. Thomson, Jennifer Dale, Guy Boyd, Paul Soles; ***D:*** Ralph L. Thomas; ***W:*** Anne Cameron; ***C:*** Richard Leiterman; ***M:*** Micky Erbe. Genie Awards '82: Best Actor (Mancuso), Best Film, Best Supporting Actor (Rubinek). **VHS, DVD**

Tie Me Up! Tie Me Down!

When Sigmund Freud asked "What do women want?," he, like many men, probably wasn't listening to the answer. We watched most of *Tie Me Up! Tie Me Down!* with clenched teeth. Pedro Almodovar's eighth movie deserves its NC-17 rating and I dread its effects on grown-up weirdos who might be inspired by it. Ricky is an escaped mental patient who falls in love with a drug-addicted prostitute named Marina and vows to return as her husband. When Ricky is finally released from the institution, his true love has abandoned her former wild ways and is working hard to improve her life as an actress. Ricky kidnaps Marina, punches her in the face, gags her, ties her up, and keeps her a prisoner until she falls in love with him. Even though Marina swears this will NEVER, NEVER happen, Ricky the psycho obviously knows his willing female better than she knows herself. The gay version of this story, 1987's *Law of Desire,* made Almodovar a household name in America. Why did that film work while *Tie Me Up! Tie Me Down!* emerges as the uninspired retread that it is? Well, for one thing, Carmen Maura isn't around to distract us from the lameness of the central plot. Also, I suspect that Marina is really supposed to be a gay male who's into bondage, but Almodovar turned the character into a defenseless woman so it would look like he'd dreamed up a brand new plot. Without the wonderful Maura as his hilarious interpreter, Almodovar's humor seemed forced, corny, and misogynistic. Almodovar even throws away a promising subplot involving some amusing shenanigans on a movie set. Victoria Abril is lovely and poignant as Marina, but Antonio Banderas, once again, is completely unbearable as an obsessive lover. Almodovar has complained about the American ratings system, comparing it to France's repressive regime. But restricting access to adult patrons of *Tie! Me Up! Tie Me Down!* in the U.S. is hardly the same as the internal censorship Almodovar would have faced if he were making films in Franco's Spain. If Almodovar's latest is not the huge international hit that *Women on the Verge of a Nervous Breakdown* was, his shaky sense of proportion and faltering artistic balance is largely to blame this time around. ***AKA:*** Atame. 🦴🦴

1990 (NC-17) 105m/C *SP* Victoria Abril, Antonio Banderas, Loles Leon, Francesco Rabal, Julieta Serrano, Maria Barranco, Rossy de Palma; ***D:*** Pedro

Victoria Abril and Antonio Banderas in *Tie Me Up! Tie Me Down!* Courtesy of the Kobal Collection

"You know Mr. Gorbachev, the guy that ran Russia for so long? I am a firm believer that he would still be in power today if he had had that ugly purple thing taken off his head."

—Suzanne (Nicole Kidman) in *To Die For.*

Almodovar; ***W:*** Pedro Almodovar; ***C:*** Jose Luis Alcaine; ***M:*** Ennio Morricone. **VHS, LV, Letterbox**

The Tie That Binds

It's always a treat when an underhyped thriller that slips into theatres without the benefit of a press screening turns out to be better than expected. *The Tie that Binds,* dumped on unsuspecting audiences with the threadbare tagline that it's from the producers of *The Hand that Rocks the Cradle,* is actually pretty good. It boasts terrific performances by Keith Carradine as a psycho, Vincent Spano and Moira Kelly as the well-rounded heroes, and remarkable acting by a little girl named Julia Devin. Wesley Strick's direction pushes all the right suspense buttons and only Daryl Hannah is a wash-out as Carradine's zombie-like partner in psychosis. Carradine and Hannah are irredeemable bad guys, dragging their small daughter along as they engage in sadistic crimes. When they're nearly busted, they manage to slip away from the cops who take their troubled child into custody. She winds up being adopted by Spano and Kelly, a nice, interesting couple who are hep enough to recognize her underlying sadness. Devlin captures all the nuances of a deeply frightened child so well that it's tough to believe she's only acting. She's a little young yet to compare to Lillian Gish, but her terror of violence does evoke memories of *Broken Blossoms,* not that the film as a whole is anywhere near that league. The script slides in and out of focus (as does Hannah's character), which doubtless explains the skittishness of its eventual distributor. But *The Tie that Binds* earns most of its chills fairly and is worth a look on the small screen.

1995 (R) 98m/C Daryl Hannah, Keith Carradine, Moira Kelly, Vincent Spano, Julia Devin, Ray Reinhardt, Cynda Williams; ***D:*** Wesley Strick; ***W:*** Michael Auerbach; ***C:*** Bobby Bukowski; ***M:*** Graeme Revell. **VHS, LV, Closed Caption**

Tiger Bay

At the end of the '50s, director J. Lee Thompson wanted to make an offbeat crime film showing the tender relationship between a young killer and a little boy who witnesses his crime. He found himself in the garden of John and Mary Mills one day and watched their 12-year-old daughter at play. Thompson observed what international audiences would soon discover to their delight: that young Hayley Mills had a riveting, elastic face and that you never wanted to take your eyes off her for fear that you'd miss what she might do next. Thompson assembled the usual sterling British cast along with a young German discovery, Horst Buchholz. The resulting film, *Tiger Bay,* was well-scripted and briskly paced, but as anticipated, Hayley Mills as the mischievous Gillie stole every scene she was in, even the ones she played with the police inspector portrayed by her father John. Watching *Tiger Bay* many years later, it is easy to see why Hayley Mills became a major star with this film. To be sure, the plot revolves around her, and later when she found herself upstaged by special effects, animals, and nuns, her popularity plummeted. As Hayley Mills became more of an actress, she tailored her work to meet the demands of each part and her strong personality became less evident. Parts like Gillie clearly come along once in a lifetime and Hayley Mills, soon to inherit the Little Miss Fixit roles that were once *de rigueur* for child stars, clearly made the most of her appealing role.

1959 107m/B *GB* John Mills, Horst Buchholz, Hayley Mills, Yvonne Mitchell, Megs Jenkins, Anthony Dawson, Kenneth Griffith, Michael Anderson Jr.; ***D:*** J. Lee Thompson; ***W:*** John Hawkesworth; ***C:*** John Hawkesworth; ***M:*** Laurie Johnson. **VHS, DVD**

Time Lock

It probably happens all the time: A little boy traps himself in a Canadian Bank vault with a 63-hour time-lock and everyone spends the better part of 73 minutes trying to get him out before he suffocates to death. When Robert Beatty as Vault Expert Dawson is on the case, you know you've got a rollicking chance for a happy ending. And who IS that actor, 13th on the cast list? Why, it's Sean Connery as a powerfully built acetylene welder, a full five years before he was "Bond, James Bond." This tightly scripted, tensely directed, unpretentious suspense yarn is everything it should be. You care about the unfortunate lad played by Vincent Winter (four years after his Oscar-winning performance in *The Little Kidnappers*) and hope he will be safely returned to his folks. You might wish his folks (Betty McDowall and Lee Patterson) had kept a closer watch on their kid, but you can't help sympathizing with their plight. After all, kids WILL get trapped in bank vaults, especially in the movies. Over 40 years after *Time Lock*'s release, Connery and Winter (1947–98) were among the prestigious assembly of Academy Award winners on Oscar night, 1998. 🦴🦴🦴

1957 73m/B *GB* Robert Beatty, Betty McDowall, Vincent Winter, Lee Patterson, Sandra Francis, Alan Gifford, Robert Ayres, Victor Wood, Jack Cunningham, Peter Mannering, Gordon Tanner, Larry Cross, Sean Connery; ***D:*** Gerald Thomas; ***W:*** Peter Rogers; ***C:*** Peter Hennessy; ***M:*** Stanley Black. **VHS**

Tito and Me

Yugoslavia's *Tito and Me* has a great deal of the charm of the early "Our Gang" comedies, showing childhood on its own unique terms. Its protagonist is a little boy named Zoran who idolizes Marshall Tito. He wins a school essay competition in which he explains why he loves Tito so much and then finds himself in the midst of a group pilgrimage to visit the dictator's place. Confronted with the authoritarian nature of the group's leader, Zoran's personality asserts itself again and again and his worship of uniformed authority gradually dissolves. *Tito and Me* is a delight to watch from start to finish and child actor Dimitrie Vojnov is excellent as 10-year-old Zoran. ***AKA:*** Tito and I; Tito i Ja. 🦴🦴🦴

1992 104m/C *YU* Dimitrie Vojnov, Lazar Ristovski, Anica Dobra, Predrag Manojlovic, Olivera Markovic; ***D:*** Goran Markovic; ***W:*** Goran Markovic. **VHS**

To Cross the Rubicon

My favorite of all the films I had a chance to see at 1991's On Screen: A Celebration of Women in Film Festival was *To Cross the Rubicon*. Shot on a very low budget, it is not a perfect film and there are no name stars in it, but it does such a superb job revealing the best friendship of two very different women that I wish it had been chosen for the opening night film (instead of Mary Lambert's *Grand Isle*)! Lorraine Devon and Patricia Royce co-wrote their starring roles for the film and Royce co-produced *Rubicon* with director Barry Caillier. The dialogue between the two women is very real, fresh, and funny. *Rubicon* shows how women have the power to make each other feel better and worse than anyone else, and often both in the blink of an eye. Devon and Royce are an extremely appealing team and J.D. Souther and Billy Burke are excellent as two of the men in their lives. The Seattle-based *To Cross the Rubicon* also benefits from judicious editing. When the film was first screened six months before the festival, it was an unwieldy two and a half hours in length; it was later trimmed to a far more manageable 120 minutes. 🦴🦴🦴

1991 120m/C Patricia Royce, J.D. Souther, Lorraine Devon, Billy Burke; ***D:*** Barry Caillier; ***W:*** Patricia Royce, Lorraine Devon. **VHS**

To Die For

Gus Van Sant's *To Die For* is indeed a movie to die for. With a fine-tuned screenplay by the great Buck Henry (who appears in a side-splitting cameo as a high school teacher), *To Die For* takes an up close and personal look at a cable TV weather girl who will do anything (well, almost anything) to be a network anchorwoman with a household name. Just one thing; she is initially attracted to the good-looking Italian lug played by Matt Dillon. But when Matt becomes her husband, he wants her to help out with the family restaurant and intends to fill her up with little bambinos. What's a future national celebrity to do? That's right, go to the local high school and enlist the three most dazed and confused kids there to rub out Dillon. How? Well, one chunky kid (Alison Folland) absolutely idolizes her and does anything her heroine asks her to do. And Joaquin Phoenix is so sexually obsessed with her that he lets himself be dragged into mur-

The Hound Salutes:
LORRAINE DEVON AND PATRICIA ROYCE
Writers/actresses, *To Cross the Rubicon*

Lorraine Devon: "Pat and I started talking a lot about our lives and cracking ourselves up to no end and decided, heck, let's write a film that encompasses some of what we've experienced in our script. So I'd be sitting at the computer and Pat would be literally acting out the scenes in my dining room and I'd be cracking up and putting them on paper. We wrote the first draft together in five days, locked up in my apartment. It was a piece of cake. We never left except to get Egg McMuffins."

Patricia Royce: "Both Lorraine and I have written other screenplays before. This project was magical in the sense that our two energies came together and there was nothing to do BUT write a screenplay together. We were creating two characters that we intended all along to play ourselves. And the character played by J.D. Souther was based on a wonderful guy we both know, but who is very committed to not being committed."

der just to keep her in bed with him. Only the audience and the wonderfully snide Illeana Douglas as Dillon's sister see through this self-absorbed temptress played to the hilt by Nicole Kidman. The last time they filmed this variation on the Pamela Smart story, adorable Helen Hunt played it straight in 1991's *Murder in New Hampshire,* the obligatory "fact-based" television movie. But novelist Joyce Maynard, Buck Henry, and Gus Van Sant took the bare bones of the case and ran with it in a bold effort to shred our tattered visions of the media to a pulp. It won't, of course; this is Kidman's breakthrough movie, the one that she will always be identified with, even when she is wheeled out for cameo roles in the 21st century. I do worry about Joaquin Phoenix, though. River's kid brother looks so strung out in every single sequence that his presence feels like a cruelly evocative in-joke. Matt Dillon sheds his sexual charisma to play Kidman's worshipful schnook. And newcomer Folland is impressive as the clunky fan who, like the ill-fated Barbara Bates in *All About Eve,* fragments into many images of herself, even more than her role model. Slap this movie and the Simpson trial in a time capsule for centuries, and wonder what the future will think about our time. 🦴🦴🦴🦴

1995 (R) 103m/C Nicole Kidman, Matt Dillon, Joaquin Rafael (Leaf) Phoenix, Casey Affleck, Alison Folland, Illeana Douglas, Dan Hedaya, Wayne Knight, Kurtwood Smith, Holland Taylor, Maria Tucci, Susan Traylor; ***Cameos:*** George Segal, Buck Henry; ***D:*** Gus Van Sant; ***W:*** Buck Henry, Johnny Burne; ***C:*** Eric Alan Edwards; ***M:*** Danny Elfman. Golden Globe Awards '96: Best Actress—Musical/Comedy (Kidman); Broadcast Film Critics Association Awards '95: Best Actress (Kidman); Nominations: British Academy Awards '95: Best Actress (Kidman); MTV Movie Awards '96: Most Desirable Female (Kidman). **VHS, LV, 8mm, Closed Caption, DVD**

To Have and to Hold

I had been looking forward to another Rachel Griffiths movie ever since her award-winning performance as Rhonda in 1994's *Muriel's Wedding. To Have and to Hold,* sadly, is a depressing bore. Tcheky Karyo used to be married to Anni Finster-er, and is now trying to turn Griffiths into a facsimile of his first wife. If we gave a damn about any of the characters, this might make an intriguing minor noir entry, but we don't. Griffiths is a jewel, but *To Have and to Hold* isn't, and her innate intelligence is in conflict with the incomprehensible choices of her character. Watching this flick is like walking into the screwed-up household of a stranger where all you can do is fidget and wonder, "Why do I have to be here? May I go now, please?" **woof!**

1996 98m/C *AU* Tcheky Karyo, Rachel Griffiths, Steve Jacobs, Anni Finsterer, David Field, Robert Kunsa; ***D:*** John Hillcoat; ***W:*** Gene Conkie; ***C:*** Andrew de Groot.

To Hell with Love

The day after the deadline for this book, Karl Kozak sent me an unsolicited video of his first film by priority mail. It's about a guy in San Diego named Alan Rigatelli (nicely played by David Coburn) who's always a little late. He gets fired and robbed on the same day and, worse yet, his girlfriend leaves him and he leaves the only copy of his first novel in a taxi. His married brother Andrew (Michael McCafferty) is always running Alan down, but what does HE do with a pretty paralegal (who's also an ex-hairdresser and an ex-telepsychic) as soon as he arrives at San Francisco's Fairmont hotel for a legal convention? And Alan's cousin Nick (Corey Michael Blake) is alone in San Diego for a day and already he has a job as a head cook and a date with a girl named Maria (Julie McKee)! Life has dealt Alan a dirty deal, as we can tell from the nicely constructed black-and-white home movies of one of his childhood birthday parties. Random stuff happens to all three guys, a bit far-fetched maybe, but you can't always make up this stuff. Sometimes, life's just unfair and funny and strange. Karl Kozak can write and direct on a budget, his cast (which also includes Natalie Williams as Julie, Alan's infamous girlfriend who splits with ALL the dishes, and Kate Parselle as taxi rider Sarah Franklin) can really act and *To Hell with Love* is really funny. Within six months of its premiere at Santa Monica's Dances with Films Festival of the Unknowns, *To Hell with Love* attracted a domestic distributor (Panorama Entertainment) for theatrical release in April 1999 and a foreign distributor (PorchLight Entertainment) as well. Fairy tales can come true, they can happen to you.... (And thanks, Karl, for using Coit Tower, not the Golden Gate Bridge, in your establishing shot of San Francisco!) 🦴🦴🦴

1998 98m/C Karl Kozak, Corey Michael Blake, Kate Parselle, Michael McCafferty, Julie McKee, David Coburn, Natalie Williams; ***D:*** Karl Kozak, David Coburn; ***W:*** Karl Kozak, David Coburn; ***C:*** Victor Lou; ***M:*** Scott Harper.

To See Paris and Die

Award-winning actress Tatyana Vasilyeva stars in Alexander Proshkin's *To See Paris and Die.* Orekhova (Vasilyeva) and her adult son, Yuri, live together in a room in an apartment shared with many neighbors who are incapable of minding their own business. Orekheva hopes that Yuri will receive a prize in an upcoming music contest, so she tells him that he cannot marry Katya, his Jewish fiancee. A fierce anti-Semite, Orekhova firmly believes that Katya will destroy any chance Yuri may have to achieve success. This Russian entry suggests that talent only appears to transcend the perennial challenge of a Jewish identity, and its downbeat conclusions indicate that, drawn to its most illogical extremes, belief in such an apparition leads to tragic consequences. By some startling coincidence, Leonid Gorovets' *Coffee with Lemon,* made in Israel in 1994 and also starring Vasilyeva, had pretty much the same theme. ***AKA:*** Uvidet Parizh i Umeret. 🦴🦴

1993 100m/C *RU* Tatyana Vasilyeva, Dimitry Malikov, Stanislav Lyubshin, Vladimir Steklov, Nina Usatova; ***D:*** Alexander Proshkin; ***W:*** Georgi Branev; ***C:*** Boris Brozhovsky. **VHS**

To Sleep with Anger

One of the many exceptional entries at 1990's Mill Valley Film Festival was *To*

The Hound Salutes:
KARL KOZAK
Writer/director/producer/actor, *To Hell with Love*

In order to make an independent film, you need a certain kind of mindset going in, and it's the kind of a mindset where you tell yourself—at least for me it was—that nothing's going to stop me. I'm going to get this done no matter what. [After writing the script for *To Hell with Love*] I contemplated going the studio route and it seemed too formidable. It just seemed too long. I'm much too impatient for that, so I just decided that I would do it on my own. Besides, really, when I started writing *To Hell with Love,* I wrote it with the budgetary concerns in mind, and locations in mind, and things like that. I knew I'd be a bit limited but I thought I'd make up for that with some resourcefulness and creativity. I sold a company that I owned. However, I did run out of money right on the last week of the shoot. Then I turned to some people that I had met several months prior and they were financial people who were raising money for independent films. Since I had completed the film, they were willing to look at it, look at dailies and everything. We put some 15 minutes of film together for them, rough cut. They liked it and said, 'Hey, we think you've got something here,' so they started raising extra money for me and they got the money to allow me to finish the post-production.

"You really have to want to be in this business because the worst part about being a director is you only get to be a director every other year, I think, or something like that, for a month, I think if you are lucky. Once we got the film all done, we started submitting the rough cut—actually, before

Sleep with Anger. It is a wonderfully layered tale of family tensions, magic, and mystery set in a deceptively down-to-earth black neighborhood in Los Angeles. Refreshingly free of stereotypes, the film focuses on the disturbing effect of an intruder named Harry on the basically healthy family who offer him their hospitality. Who is Harry? No one seems to know, although they shared some stormy experiences together in their younger days. But Harry has changed over the years and so have they. Gradually he begins to chip away at their collective strengths, creating disharmony wherever he goes. Harry has cultivated a fairly delightful shell, however, so it takes a while before his friends realize why their lives have become so chaotic in his crafty presence. Although it is difficult to tear your eyes away from the spellbinding Danny Glover as Harry, the supporting cast is outstanding. Paul Butler and Mary Alice deliver warm, rich performances as Gideon and Suzie, the kindly couple who agree to take Harry on as a guest. Carl Lumbly and Vonetta McGee have such charisma in supporting roles that you wish you could see more of them. Ethel Ayler is also excellent in a scene-stealing role as a tough cookie who sees all the way through Harry's shenanigans and Davis Roberts is a treasure as one of Suzie's old but still hopeful suitors. Writer/director Charles Burnett has exceptional skill at sustaining suspense and then almost, but not quite, relieving it with humor, so even as you laugh, you're waiting for the tension to start building again. Gideon's family is an imperfect group who seemed to have made peace with an imperfect world until Harry arrived on their doorstep. Producer Glover, Charles Burnett, and company deserve credit for

we even cut the negative—to several film festivals. We tried to hit as many as we could and then we started getting accepted to several, and we cut the negative and went. At Santa Monica's Dances with Films Festival of the Unknowns we got a lot of people from the industry to come down and take a look and I actually got a producer's rep through that festival. Someone came down and saw the film, and really enjoyed it and decided to rep the film. I got a lot of good coverage and *Variety* gave us a real nice write-up from that festival, and the reviewer really liked the film quite a bit. Having the review helped, but there are so many independent films out there right now and I think there will probably be even more in the future because of digital video and things like that. The distributor's rep we had had just signed a film to Lion's Gate. So they picked up our film and took it through the process and PorchLight seemed the most interested. PorchLight produces children's shows. They do a lot of international business. This year they decided to get into independent films so they picked up about 10 films, I believe, and ours is one of them. We found our domestic distributor, Panorama Entertainment, through PorchLight.

"Sometimes [seeing *To Hell with Love* with an audience] is great and other times it can be excruciating. Usually, it's technical problems, though. When I started the casting process I had some open calls and after being deluged with people who had little or no experience, I decided to go with theatre actors. So I got people who had the most extensive resumes that I could possibly find and got them together and started auditioning them. We just worked with them a bit to bring their performances down a bit. A lot of them were trying to project to the last row in the house. We worked with them and it worked out terrifically, and we went through rehearsals several weeks in advance and I think that did it."

sustaining their unique vision throughout *To Sleep with Anger* and for bringing such a rare gem to the attention of movie audiences everywhere.

1990 (PG) 105m/C Danny Glover, Mary Alice, Paul Butler, Richard Brooks, Carl Lumbly, Vonetta McGee, Sheryl Lee Ralph, Ethel Ayler, Davis Roberts; ***D:*** Charles Burnett; ***W:*** Charles Burnett; ***C:*** Walt Lloyd. Independent Spirit Awards '91: Best Actor (Glover), Best Director (Burnett), Best Screenplay, Best Supporting Actress (Ralph); National Society of Film Critics Awards '90: Best Screenplay; Sundance Film Festival '90: Special Jury Prize. **VHS, Closed Caption**

Tommy

Tommy boasts a number of fine rock stars, as well as Oliver Reed (Frank Hobbs) and (Doctor) Jack Nicholson, who don't let their lack of vocal talent bother them too much. And (Preacher) Eric Clapton is outstanding as always. You'll either love *Tommy* or hate it, depending on how you feel about Ken Russell as a movie director. Russell's style is uniquely his own: wild, excessive, and gooey. He gets extravagant performances out of Ann-Margret as Nora Walker and Tina Turner as the Acid Queen, makes Roger Daltrey look good as Tommy Walker, and blasts everyone within six blocks of the movie theatre with Quintaphonic Sound, a system he reportedly adored in the 1970s. *Tommy*'s themes are charged with energy and pizzazz. They are also, as interpreted by Russell, bigger than life, predictable, and completely obvious. Russell overindulges audiences, stuffs them to the gills, in fact. So how come so many viewers tend to feel so empty afterward?

1975 (PG) 108m/C Ann-Margret, Elton John, Oliver Reed, Tina Turner, Roger Daltrey, Eric Clapton, Keith Moon, Pete Townshend, Jack Nicholson, Robert

"You haven't anything to hide, have you? ... No, I can see you haven't."

—Danny Fuller (Dan Duryea) to Jane Palmer (Lizabeth Scott) after she crosses her legs, in *Too Late for Tears.*

Powell, Paul Nicholas, Barry Winch, Victoria Russell, Ben Aris, Mary Holland, Jennifer Baker, Susan Baker, Arthur Brown, John Entwhistle; ***D:*** Ken Russell; ***W:*** Ken Russell, Keith Moon, John Entwhistle; ***C:*** Dick Bush; ***M:*** Pete Townshend. Golden Globe Awards '76: Best Actress—Musical/Comedy (Ann-Margret); Nominations: Academy Awards '75: Best Actress (Ann-Margret), Best Original Score. **VHS, LV**

Tommy Tricker & the Stamp Traveller

The owner of a stamp store gives Ralph a 60-year-old stamp album that happens to include a letter and an enchanted rhyme that will send him (in stamp form) to Australia, China—you name it! Ralph and mischievous 12-year-old Tommy (Anthony Rogers) then begin an international treasure hunt to find a fabulous stamp collection in a mystery location. This wonderfully imaginative kid's flick was followed in 1994 by an equally good sequel, *The Return of Tommy Tricker* with Michael Stevens as Tommy.

1987 101m/C *CA* Lucas Evans, Anthony Rogers, Jill Stanley, Andrew Whitehead; ***D:*** Michael Rubbo; ***W:*** Michael Rubbo; ***C:*** Andreas Poulsson; ***M:*** Kate & Anna McGarrigle. **VHS**

Tomorrow the World

Skippy Homeier was all of 13 years when he stunned Broadway audiences with his electrifying performance as Emil Bruckner, a Hitler youth transplanted into the midwestern American home of his uncle, Professor Michael Frame (Ralph Bellamy), where he soon launches a verbal assault on his Jewish aunt-to-be, Leona Richards (Shirley Booth). Independent producer Lester Cowan rushed *Tomorrow the World* into production the following year with Homeier re-creating his original role, but Bellamy and Booth were replaced by Fredric March and Betty Field for the movie. As the screenplay makes clear, the little Nazi has been conditioned by the circumstances of his life into rejecting the values of his late parents, including his American mother Mary. His German father Karl, a Nobel prize-winning opponent of National Socialism, died in a concentration camp, and the child was then raised to believe he was the son of a traitor. Uncle Michael believes that love and kindness will work wonders on the little Nazi in his home, but quickly learns that the damage done to his nephew may be irreparable. A series of incidents with the neighborhood children and Emil's potentially fatal fight with his cousin Patricia (Joan Carroll, replacing nine-year-old Joyce Van Patten) almost make Michael and Leona give up on the boy, just as he is beginning to learn how to feel. The theme of *Tomorrow the World* was both provocative and tricky. How do you persuasively show this kid's transformation into a human being capable of living peacefully with other human beings? Fine acting by the three leads and by Agnes Moorehead (replacing Dorothy Sands as Aunt Jessie, Michael's unmarried sister) certainly helped. One-time actor Leslie Fenton, whose forte as a director lay in action pictures (mysteries, westerns) ventilated the script's philosophical concerns with a sharp sense of what it feels like to be a kid in an unfamiliar environment. And, despite his age, Homeier had already had plenty of practice; he began his acting career at age six in live radio dramas. As veteran radio actress Moorehead once said, "You had to work to make the audience visualize you and that isn't easy to do. Many stage actors fall by the wayside because of their inability to make an audience 'see.'" Homeier made audiences see, all right, and luckily his early work has been preserved in this rarely revived (and therefore ideal!) candidate for home video release. Based on the play by James Gow and Armand D'Usseau.

1944 86m/B Fredric March, Betty Field, Agnes Moorehead, Skip Homeier, Joan Carroll, Boots Brown, Edit Angold, Rudy Wiesler, Marvin Davis, Patsy Ann Thompson, Mary Newton, Tom Fadden; ***D:*** Leslie Fenton; ***W:*** Ring Lardner Jr., Leopold Atlas; ***C:*** Henry Sharp.

Too Beautiful for You

Long before the 1996 divorce of T.R.H. Charles and Diana, The Prince and

Princess of Wales (with frumpy Camilla Parker-Bowles unnamed, but widely believed to be THE contributing factor), Bertrand Blier explored a similar mystery in this 1988 French film. Why does Gerard Depardieu (hey—has anyone said anything mean about HIS stomach lately?) prefer his frumpy secretary to his meltingly lovely wife (Carole Bouquet)? The line that the late Richard Jordan (courtesy of Woody Allen) springs on Mary Beth Hurt in 1978's *Interiors* comes to mind: "It's been so long since I've made love to a woman that I didn't feel inferior to." Is that it? Depardieu clearly doesn't feel worthy of his wife who suffers agonies while he trots off to share a bed with Josiane Balasko. (Fact of life: Even some of the most beautiful women in the world NEVER really believe it and being strung along by just one underwhelmed guy can make them feel hideous.) Well, the premise IS primal and writer/director Blier develops it in a promising way...at first. But then, he diddles it. Where do you take a situation like this? The three characters don't know because Blier doesn't, either. Maybe he feels that identifying the issue is enough. The truth may be larger and more ugly than one romantic melodrama can contain. Anyway, it's very well acted by the three principals and it won four Cesar awards in France, before U.S. viewers like yours truly started kvetching about trivialities like the denouement. ***AKA:*** Trop Belle pour Toi.

1988 (R) 91m/C *FR* Gerard Depardieu, Josiane Balasko, Carole Bouquet, Roland Blanche, Francois Cluzet; ***D:*** Bertrand Blier; ***W:*** Bertrand Blier; ***C:*** Philippe Rousselot. Cannes Film Festival '89: Grand Jury Prize; Cesar Awards '90: Best Actress (Bouquet), Best Director (Blier), Best Film, Best Writing. **VHS**

Too Late for Tears

The next time you get in a fight with your spouse and drive your convertible off the road, whatever you do, DON'T BLINK THE LIGHTS. Not only is your marriage probably doomed anyway, but some guys in another car might think it's a signal and throw $60 grand (the root of all evil) in your car. This is the lesson NOT learned by Jane and Alan Palmer (Lizabeth Scott and Arthur Kennedy). Jane wants to keep it, but Alan wants to turn it in, so Jane keeps it. Then, Danny Fuller (Dan Duryea) shows up at Jane's door, saying it's HIS money, but it's okay with him if she wants to share it. (Did I forget to mention that Jane is beautiful?) Jane temporizes, then puts an idea of her own in motion. (Did I forget to mention that Jane is greedy?) Lizabeth Scott was one of the great femme fatales of the silver screen between 1946 and 1951, starting with *The Strange Love of Martha Ivers* opposite Van Heflin, moving up in the world to *Dead Reckoning* opposite Humphrey Bogart, then *Pitfall* with Dick Powell AND Raymond Burr, and then *I Walk Alone* with Burt Lancaster AND Kirk Douglas. *Too Late for Tears* was followed by *Two of a Kind,* in which she crushed Edmond O'Brien's finger in a car door, and *The Racket,* in which she is a nightclub singer and a police informer, with Robert Mitchum as a police captain. But in none of these bad girl roles was she as vicious as Jane Palmer. Scott's really something to see as she sweet-talks and murders her way to the bottom. *Too Late for Tears* was among Dan Duryea's many noir films. He specialized in playing tough guys (good, bad, and in-between) with mushy centers. For such a low-budget indie, the location sequences are impressive. ***AKA:*** Killer Bait.

1949 99m/B Lizabeth Scott, Don DeFore, Dan Duryea, Arthur Kennedy, Kristine Miller, Barry Kelley, Denver Pyle, Jimmy Ames, Billy Halop, Jimmie Dodd; ***D:*** Byron Haskin; ***W:*** Roy Huggins; ***C:*** William Mellor; ***M:*** Dale Butts. **VHS**

Tough Guys Don't Dance

Watching Norman Mailer's *Tough Guys Don't Dance* is like being chained to a blind date with a 14-year-old motor mouth. You know his batteries will run down eventually, but in the meanwhile you find yourself entertaining the stray fantasy that Godzilla will turn up and flatten the kid. Mailer wanted his film noir to be "a murder mystery, a suspense tale, a film of horror—and a comedy of manners." That's

"We would have injected vitamin C if only they had made it illegal!"

—Renton (Ewan McGregor) in *Trainspotting.*

nice. Lots of little boys want to do five different things when they grow up. By the time they hit their 60s, they might wish for their film to be in a better league than *Tough Guys Don't Dance.* Mailer writes as if he spent most of his life running away from women whose sole aim is to chop off his "pride and joy" with a machete. Mailer thinks that life is like this film. He seems obsessed with the suspicion that any man anywhere might be abusing more women than he is. And if the man is black, or gay, or a preacher, or a policeman, the script takes especially vindictive turns. Much of the plot runs like something like this: A woman shoots a man. A woman shoots a woman. A man shoots a woman. A man shoots himself. Another woman shoots another man for calling her "small potatoes." And so on. In a contrapuntal casting decision, Ryan O'Neal, arguably the most constipated actor in Hollywood, mouths Mailer's dialogue. Isabella Rossellini is around, presumably to lend an international panache to the proceedings, but she seems to be slumming. Clarence Williams III, who's done good work in bad films, has one entrance, which is also his exit from the plot. Veteran film heavy Lawrence Tierney is the only cast member who seems at ease in his tough guy role. The rest of the players do the best they can with what they have been given to do. The most revealing line in the film is, "I'm not a good enough writer to delineate how I really feel." *Tough Guys* is crammed with Mailer dialogue so excruciatingly bad that the best possible marketing ploy for this mess would have been to slap it on a Golden Turkey triple bill so its filmmakers could nurse their hurt feelings all the way to the bank. **woof!**

1987 (R) 110m/C Ryan O'Neal, Isabella Rossellini, Wings Hauser, Debra Sandlund, John Bedford Lloyd, Lawrence Tierney, Clarence Williams III, Penn Jillette, Frances Fisher; ***D:*** Norman Mailer; ***W:*** Norman Mailer; ***C:*** John Bailey; ***M:*** Angelo Badalamenti. Golden Raspberry Awards '87: Worst Director (Mailer). **VHS, LV, Closed Caption**

Traces of Red

Jim Belushi is a good actor, but I've never really thought of him as Mr. Sex. Nevertheless, he has two sex scenes in the first 18 minutes of *Traces of Red,* a so-called thriller with a great beginning, a great ending, and an absolute mess of a middle. The movie looks like it was shot one way and then re-edited and re-mixed in a patch job. (For starters, most of the film is a flashback, but the flashback doesn't go back far enough, so we hear about characters dealing with stuff that we NEVER get to see. That's cheating!) This is one of those movies where we can tell instantly what all the relationships are from the way that everyone glances at each other, and we're talking about from scene one. Moreover, from scene two it's easy to spot who's going to get it next and when, another sure sign of an inexperienced director, which Andy Wolk definitely is; this is his first movie. The worst thing that Wolk achieves is something that I didn't think was possible: a mediocre performance from Lorraine Bracco as a high society tramp. Since Wolk had Bracco's great husky voice and strong personality to work with, why would he, or anyone, want to encourage her to adopt Melanie Griffith's voice and mannerisms? There's a poorly developed subplot involving Belushi's police partner; in fact, there are long stretches when we don't know which partner is the actual focus of the movie. Since the partner is played by Tony Goldwyn, grandson of Samuel Goldwyn, and *Traces of Red* IS a Goldwyn release, it might make career-track sense, but it sure makes the plot hard to follow. Some viewers may just want to give up on this one and laugh at the mind-boggling ineptness of it all; it's a textbook!

1992 (R) 105m/C James Belushi, Lorraine Bracco, Tony Goldwyn, William Russ, Michelle Joyner, Joe Lisi, Jim Piddock; ***D:*** Andy Wolk; ***W:*** Jim Piddock; ***C:*** Tim Suhrstedt; ***M:*** Graeme Revell. **VHS, LV, Closed Caption**

Tracks

Tracks, seen from the perspective of a Vietnam veteran, took the Cannes Film Festival by storm, and it certainly offers some fine ensemble acting. The movie was filmed on a train without permission, and it's more than obvious. Paul Glickman tries hard with the camera work, but the overall picture has a hurried, jerky quality. Maybe Henry Jaglom was trying to emphasize how honest his screenplay was by interspersing overlong sequences with swiftly edited shots. But as a dramatic device, it's way too transparent to be successful. There is an internal integrity to *Tracks,* which is not altogether diminished by its inadequate attempts at technical flash. Jaglom should have had enough faith in his material and his cast to let the veteran's story emerge without artificial emphasis.

1976 (R) 90m/C Dennis Hopper, Dean Stockwell, Taryn Power, Zack Norman, Michael Emil, Barbara Flood; ***D:*** Henry Jaglom; ***W:*** Henry Jaglom; ***C:*** Paul Glickman. **VHS, Closed Caption**

Trading Favors

The previews for *Trading Favors* make it look like one of Brian Krakow's wet dreams: Nerd Lincoln Muller (Devon Gummersall) links up with Bad Girl Alex Langley (Rosanna Arquette) and they do wild and wacky things all the way to sunset...and beyond! If you rent this one expecting a comedy, you'll note that it plays like one until things turn ugly and it becomes something else altogether. Arquette is electrifying as always and Gummersall more than holds his own opposite her. Chad Lowe pops up in a funny bit as Marty, the convenience store clerk, and George Dzundza, who's never been light as a feather, looks dangerously over the scale as Lincoln's sad dad, Wallace. (I pray that he's padded.) Peter Greene is a mean brutal sicko incongruously named Teddy. In a sisterhood-is-powerful stroke of casting, Frances Fisher is a librarian! Note the director, who does a bang-up job. (I mention this only because some of the coolest women I've ever met also went with some of the uncoolest jerks I ever went with, so it's good to see that Fisher and Sondra Locke are working together. For the benefit of 21st century readers, the initials of their Oscar-winning, change-the-locks-without-notice jerk in common are C.E. Look it up!) If you've ever rented Mitchell Leisen's 1940 Paramount film *Remember the Night* (scripted by Preston Sturges) with Barbara Stanwyck as the Bad Girl and Fred MacMurray as the Sweet Schnook who falls for her, you might think that *Trading Favors* is a skewed update. It isn't quite, but it often plays that way for large chunks of the running time.

1997 (R) 103m/C Rosanna Arquette, Devon Gummersall, George Dzundza, Peter Greene, Julie Ariola, Alanna Ubach, Jason Hervey, Craig Nigh, Mary Jo Catlett, Lin Shaye, Richard Riehle, William Frankfather, Frances Fisher, Chad Lowe; ***D:*** Sondra Locke; ***W:*** Timothy Albaugh, Tag Mendillo; ***C:*** Jerry Sidell; ***M:*** Jeff Rona. **VHS**

Trainspotting

If I were to list even a fraction of the grim things that occur during the course of *Trainspotting,* it wouldn't sound anything like much of a laugh. But neither did the bald plot of John Osborne's *Look Back in Anger,* or its protagonist Jimmy Porter. The spiritual descendant of 1956's Angry Young Man may well be Mark Renton, who lives, in 1996 fashion, by slipping in and out of Edinburgh's shooting galleries. "Who needs reasons when you've got heroin?" Renton asks no one in particular. Maybe US, sitting in a movie trance, watching him dive into the worst toilet in Scotland in search of opium suppositories. The sequence, like many others in Danny Boyle's hypnotic film, drags us into squalor, and gives us a glimpse of the euphoria on the other side. But *Trainspotting* is more than a full-color drugalogue for naive and foolish neophytes. It captures the flip side, too; the horrors of cold turkey, the self-deception of hanging out with your old mates while trying to kick the habit, the screwed-up drug deals that seem like such a great idea after you've had a free sample. The lethargy that has always been so intrinsic to every drug movie ever made (with the exception of 1916's *The Mystery of the Leaping Fish*) has been replaced here by John Hodge's hyperkinetic screenplay and by the fluidity of Boyle's direction. If you try reading the original novel by Irvine Welsh, you're going to need more than a glossary, even if you see the far more lucid film adaptation first. If ever a yarn with

The Hound Salutes: DEVON GUMMERSALL

Actor, *It's My Party, Trading Favors*

I'd always wanted to be an actor. My dad's an artist, so he was always very supportive. I didn't live in Los Angeles until I was 10 and that was when I really started. I got an agent just by sending out photographs and doing interviews and then I auditioned and auditioned, using the auditioning process as part of my training. I always looked at auditions as an excuse to act rather than as a disappointment if I didn't get the part. I did small parts on television and commercials for two or three years, then I tried out for 'geeky, soulful, diamond-in-the-rough' Brian Krakow on *My So-Called Life* and got the job. The role was sort of made for me and I was in love with the part from the first time I read the script. Parts of me were Brian and parts of Brian were me, but there were also a lot of parts that were different. The fun part of playing Brian is that he's an extension of everyone that's both sincere and insecure at the same time. He's honest and he tries really hard to know what to say and do, but he never quite gets it right. When I got Jason Katims' script for 1994's *Life of Brian,* it read like a self-contained film or like another pilot, only from from Brian's viewpoint.

"Tons of people told me that they locked themselves in their houses and watched *My So-Called Life* marathons on Music Television. MTV treated the show with respect and showed how it should have been promoted during its initial run on network television. They didn't try to promote the show as something that it wasn't. The support that we received from viewers was amazing. It meant everything to the people who worked on the show and the support wasn't invalidated because the show didn't continue past the 19th episode. We miss it, too; we did it hoping that people would be touched by it and they were."

DEVON GUMMERSALL appeared in *My Girl 2* and *Beethoven's 2nd* and in the indie flicks *It's My Party* and *Trading Favors.*

thick Scottish dialects and obscure drug references screamed out for graphic visual context, it's this one. Acting by skinny Ewan McGregor (he's more chubby in *Emma,* also released in 1996) is excellent and *Hackers*' Jonny Lee Miller is also first-rate as his larcenous crony, Sick Boy. Robert Carlyle is everybody's nightmare as the terrifying Bregbie, and more benign—if misguided—spirits are played by Ewan Bremner as Spud and Kevin McKidd as Tommy. The undercurrents here are both wise and amoral, a heady mix for the Iggy Pop-heads who will flock to see *Trainspotting.* Add the fact that Irvine Welsh only dabbled with heroin before writing his account in the early 1980s, and you have a tale that reveals the best and the worst of drug times, told by a tourist, and interpreted by the manic Scottish talent who reinvented the concept of a *Shallow Grave.* 🦴🦴🦴🦴

1995 (R) 94m/C *GB* Ewan McGregor, Ewen Bremmer, Jonny Lee Miller, Robert Carlyle, Kevin McKidd, Kelly Macdonald, Shirley Henderson, Pauline Lynch; ***D:*** Danny Boyle; ***W:*** John Hodge; ***C:*** Brian Tufano. British Academy Awards '95: Best Adapted Screenplay; Nominations: Academy Awards '96: Best Adapted Screenplay; Australian Film Institute '96: Best Foreign Film; British Academy Awards '95: Best Film; Independent Spirit Awards '97: Best Foreign Film; Writers Guild of America '96: Best Adapted Screenplay. **VHS, LV, Closed Caption, DVD**

Trees Lounge

Trees Lounge marks Steve Buscemi's debut as an indie filmmaker after making dozens of films for other indie filmmakers. He wrote the main part of Tommy Basilio for himself, of course. Tommy is a 31-year-old screw-up, only he looks several years older than that. It's an important distinction, because he makes out with 17-year-old Debbie (Chloe Sevigny), the daughter of his former sister- and brother-in-law (Mimi Rogers and Daniel Baldwin). Debbie's dad is none too pleased about that, but...ah, well...only in the movies. But wait, there's more. Tommy had a girlfriend (Elizabeth Bracco), but then he took $1500 from his boss' till (Tommy MEANT to return it, of course), so now he isn't best friends with his former boss (Anthony LaPaglia) anymore, and, even worse, his girlfriend's having a baby with the guy! But there's hope: Tommy's Uncle Al, the Good Humor Man (Seymour Cassel), died at the wheel of his ice cream truck and Tommy can take his place! Debbie can be his little helper (and future make-out partner). When it all gets to be too much, Tommy can always go over to his favorite watering hole, Trees Lounge, to drink and pick up women and drink and pass out on women and wake up and drink some more. Connie (Carol Kane) serves the drinks. Sound like fun? The press kit included the following: one Trees Lounge mini poster, one Trees Lounge coaster, one Trees Lounge shot glass, one 50 ml. sample bottle of 80 proof Austin Nichols Wild Turkey Kentucky Straight Bourbon Whiskey, one set of lyrics for the Trees Lounge theme song, plus one audio cassette of Hayden singing same. There was also a Trees Lounge comedy web site at www.treeslounge.com. Talk about good, old-fashioned promotional ballyhoo. *Trees Lounge* isn't exactly a fidget-proof experience, but, as *Movie Magazine* staffer Mary Weems puts it, "I guess a drunken mechanic is less tragic than a drunken writer." Well, maybe, but that doesn't mean I want to watch him drink for 94 minutes while listening to deathless lyrics like, "I need something to forget what got me in this mess...." 🦴🦴🦴

1996 (R) 94m/C Steve Buscemi, Chloe Sevigny, Daniel Baldwin, Elizabeth Bracco, Anthony LaPaglia, Debi Mazar, Carol Kane, Seymour Cassel, Mark Boone, Eszter Balint, Mimi Rogers, Kevin Corrigan, Samuel L. Jackson; ***D:*** Steve Buscemi; ***W:*** Steve Buscemi; ***C:*** Lisa Rinzler; ***M:*** Evan Lurie. Nominations: Independent Spirit Awards '97: Best First Feature. **VHS, DVD**

The Trip to Bountiful

Unhappy living with her whipped son (John Heard) and nagging daughter-in-law (Carlin Glynn), an elderly woman (Geraldine Page) makes the trip to Bountiful, Texas, which no longer exists except in her happy memories. Her traveling companion is Rebecca DeMornay, who responds to her in an empathetic way that her family does not. The much-honored Geraldine Page (1924–87) won her only Oscar for her beautiful performance here. When first telecast in 1953, Lillian Gish, Eva Marie Saint, John Beal, and Eileen Heckart had the roles later played by Page, DeMornay, Heard, and Glynn. Based on the play by Horton Foote. 🦴🦴🦴

1985 (PG) 102m/C Geraldine Page, Rebecca DeMornay, John Heard, Carlin Glynn, Richard Bradford; ***D:*** Peter Masterson; ***W:*** Horton Foote; ***C:*** Fred Murphy. Academy Awards '85: Best Actress (Page); Independent Spirit Awards '86: Best Actress (Page), Best Screenplay; Nominations: Academy Awards '85: Best Adapted Screenplay. **VHS, LV, 8mm, Closed Caption**

Trois Couleurs: Blanc

Although *White* is highly regarded by admirers of Krzysztof Kieslowski's trilogy, for me, it was the least involving segment of the three. The story revolves around Karol, a Polish hairdresser (Zbigniew Zama-

"A little bit of everyone belongs in hell, Lieutenant."

—Hawk (Kris Kristofferson) to Lt. Gunther (George Kirby) in *Trouble in Mind.*

chowski) whose marriage to gorgeous French wife Dominique (Julie Delpy) is dissolving. Dominique wants Karol out of her life, out of their Paris hairdressing salon (she sets it on fire), and out of France. Isn't it always the way?—Karol still wants Dominique back after all that! After a brief period of insolvency, he goes to Warsaw, restores his lost fortune, and then comes up with a sure-fire scheme. *White* was the favorite installment of many followers of the series. ***AKA:*** White; Three Colors: White. ☙☙☙

1994 (R) 92m/C *FR SI PL* Zbigniew Zamachowski, Julie Delpy, Janusz Gajos, Jerzy Stuhr, Aleksander Bardini, Grzegorz Warchol, Cezary Harasimowicz, Jerzy Nowak, Jerzy Trela, Cezary Pazura, Michel Lisowski, Philippe Morier-Genoud; ***Cameos:*** Juliette Binoche, Florence Pernel; ***D:*** Krzysztof Kieslowski; ***W:*** Krzysztof Kieslowski, Krzysztof Piesiewicz; ***C:*** Edward Klosinski; ***M:*** Zbigniew Preisner. Berlin International Film Festival '94: Best Director (Kieslowski). **VHS**

Trois Couleurs: Bleu

The life of Julie de Caurcey (Juliette Binoche) is shattered. Her composer husband Patrice (Hugues Quester) and five-year-old child Anna have been killed in a car accident. She decides to withdraw from life and all her former associations and possessions (except for a blue crystal lamp) and live alone. Needless to say, her friends have things to say and do about the decision she made in a moment of deep depression and gradually, Julie works through her grief. A *tour de force* for Binoche, who won a Cesar for her performance. ***AKA:*** Three Colors: Blue; Blue. ☙☙☙½

1993 (R) 98m/C *FR* Juliette Binoche, Benoit Regent, Florence Pernel, Charlotte Very, Helene Vincent, Phillipe Volter, Claude Duneton, Hugues Quester, Florence Vignon, Isabelle Sadoyan, Yann Tregouet, Jacek Ostaszewski; ***Cameos:*** Emmanuelle Riva; ***D:*** Krzysztof Kieslowski; ***W:*** Krzysztof Kieslowski, Krzysztof Piesiewicz, Slawomir Idziak, Agnieszka Holland, Edward Zebrowski; ***C:*** Slawomir Idziak. Cesar Awards '94: Best Actress (Binoche), Best Film Editing, Best Sound; Los Angeles Film Critics Association Awards '93: Best Score; Venice Film Festival '93: Best Actress (Binoche), Best Film; Nominations: Golden Globe Awards '94: Best Actress—Drama (Binoche), Best Foreign Film, Best Original Score. **VHS, LV, Letterbox**

Trois Couleurs: Rouge

Valentine (Irene Jacob) hits a dog with her car. When she returns the injured animal to its owner, she meets a retired judge (Jean-Louis Trintignant, who has a ball with the role). The judge enjoys listening in while his neighbors whisper sweet nothings to their lovers on the telephone. Valentine isn't exactly crazy about the hobby of her new acquaintance, but she does like HIM. (And the judge's dog doesn't die.) Krzysztof Kieslowski wraps up the trilogy in this absorbing installment, which won a Cesar for best score. ***AKA:*** Three Colors: Red; Red. ☙☙☙☙

1994 (R) 99m/C *FR PL SI* Irene Jacob, Jean-Louis Trintignant, Frederique Feder, Jean-Pierre Lorit, Samuel Lebihan, Marion Stalens, Teco Celio, Bernard Escalon, Jean Schlegel, Elzbieta Jasinska; ***Cameos:*** Juliette Binoche, Julie Delpy, Benoit Regent, Zbigniew Zamachowski; ***D:*** Krzysztof Kieslowski; ***W:*** Krzysztof Kieslowski, Krzysztof Piesiewicz; ***C:*** Piotr Sobocinski; ***M:*** Zbigniew Preisner. Cesar Awards '94: Best Score; Independent Spirit Awards '95: Best Foreign Film; Los Angeles Film Critics Association Awards '94: Best Foreign Film; New York Film Critics Awards '94: Best Foreign Film; National Society of Film Critics Awards '94: Best Foreign Film; Nominations: Academy Awards '94: Best Cinematography, Best Director (Kieslowski), Best Original Screenplay; Cesar Awards '94: Best Actor (Trintignant), Best Actress (Jacob), Best Director (Kieslowski), Best Film; Golden Globe Awards '95: Best Foreign Film. **VHS, LV**

Trouble in Mind

Trouble in Mind has one of the lushest, most evocative scores ever, with a fine rendering of the title song by Marianne Faithfull. The cinematography and the soundtrack give the film what Alan Rudolph fails to supply as writer/director: a mood straight out of 1940s film noir. Rudolph, always an intellectual tease, uses the aura of other times and places to play Games with Time and Place. You either worship the guy (I don't) or you just sit there wondering what in tarnation is going on. *Trouble in Mind* is set in "The Near Future," which helps to explain Coop the Thief's (Keith Carradine) weird curly hairstyle and loud yucky clothes. Kris Kristofferson is Hawk, a one-time cop just released from prison for killing a Bad

Dude—a Mobster. Wanda (Genevieve Bujold), who used to be his lover, runs the Rain City Diner. Hawk, about 50, gets hung up on Coop's wife Georgia (Lori Singer), about 24. Coop, already bizarre, gets MORE bizarre. Divine as (male) gangster Hilly Blue is almost worth the rental fee. Almost, because Rudolph seems determined to do everything but tell the story. A very frustrating movie, filmed in Seattle. P.S. If I ever see *Vortex* (with another one of my all-time favorite scores) and it turns out to be anything like *Trouble in Mind,* I will be SO disillusioned! It could be even worse, I suppose. I could be looking at Carradine in THIS movie and LISTENING to the music Richard Baskin wrote for *Welcome to L.A.*

1986 (R) 111m/C Kris Kristofferson, Keith Carradine, Genevieve Bujold, Lori Singer, Divine, Joe Morton, George Kirby, John Considine, Dirk Blocker, Gailard Sartain, Tracy Kristofferson; ***D:*** Alan Rudolph; ***W:*** Alan Rudolph; ***C:*** Toyomichi Kurita; ***M:*** Mark Isham. Independent Spirit Awards '86: Best Cinematography. **VHS, LV, 8mm, Closed Caption**

The Trouble with Dick

There's plenty of trouble with this adolescent would-be comedy. An ambitious young science-fiction writer's personal troubles (which include being involved with several over-sexed women) begin to appear in his writing. This 1987 Grand Jury Prize Winner at Sundance is basically a genre-movie reworking of *The Secret Life of Walter Mitty,* but nowhere near as charming as that description might suggest. The story (what there is of it) gets very tedious after the first five minutes.

1988 (R) 86m/C Tom Villard, Susan Dey, Elaine Giftos, Elizabeth Gorcey, David Clennon, Marianne Muellerleile; ***D:*** Gary Walkow; ***W:*** Gary Walkow; ***C:*** Daryl Studebaker; ***M:*** Roger Bourland. Sundance Film Festival '87: Grand Jury Prize. **VHS**

The Troublemaker

Three years before *The Graduate,* Buck Henry, then 34, wrote and co-starred in this quirky early indie about naive young Jack Armstrong (played by stage actor Tom Aldredge, then 36), who comes to The Big City and gets taken advantage of by just about everyone in Manhattan. Henry plays the role of T.R. Kingston with wicked glee, and Joan Darling, then 29, is most appealing as the city girl with whom country boy Jack forms an attachment. Industry support for indies at this time was not what it would become in the late 20th century, which makes this pioneering effort an impressive harbinger of Things to Come. Joan Darling paid her dues as secretary Frieda Krause in *Owen Marshall, Counselor at Law* between 1971 and 1974, then received a chance to direct a theatrical feature for Paramount, 1977's *First Love* (with Susan Dey, William Katt, Beverly D'Angelo, John Heard, Swoosie Kurtz, and Robert Loggia). She returned to the big screen after helming *Doc, Phyllis,* Part V of *Rich Man, Poor Man* AND after winning two Emmy nominations for directing, one for "Chuckles Bites the Dust," a 1975 episode of *The Mary Tyler Moore Show,* and another in 1977 for "The Nurses" episode of *MASH.* Even so, industry support for women directors at that time was not what it would become in the late 20th century, either: the so-so film sank at the boxoffice, and the excited buzz about Darling faded quickly. Theodore J. Flicker, 34 in 1964, worked with Darling and the late Godfrey Cambridge again when he wrote and directed Paramount's *The President's Analyst* for James Coburn in 1967. (He also wrote and directed AIP's *Three in the Cellar* for Joan Collins and Larry Hagman in 1970 and directed *Soggy Bottom USA* for Don Johnson in 1982.) And Al Freeman Jr., who'd torn the screen apart in 1967's *Dutchman* opposite Shirley Knight, went on to collect Emmy nominations for *My Sweet Charlie* opposite Patty Duke and *Roots: The Next Generation* before finally winning for daytime drama *One Life to Live.* Buck Henry, with enough talent and energy for several careers in several lifetimes, remained close to his indie roots and played the role of the gun-toting Harold Goldman with wicked glee in Nick Davis' first indie, *1999. The Troublemaker,* filled with mischievous fun and youthful high spirits, has yet to be released on

"I had a bad day at work. I had to subvert my principles and kow-tow to an idiot. Television makes these daily sacrifices possible. Deadens the inner core of my being."

—Matthew (Martin Donovan) explains to Maria (Adrienne Shelly) why he can't shut off the T.V. in *Trust*.

video, but it often surfaces on the Bravo cable network. 🦴🦴🦴

1964 80m/B Tom Aldredge, Godfrey Cambridge, Joan Darling, Al Freeman Jr., Buck Henry; ***D:*** Theodore J. Flicker; ***W:*** Buck Henry.

True Confessions

True Confessions, a United Artists release with Robert De Niro and Robert Duvall giving two of the best performances you'll ever see, was barely noticed when it first hit theatres, for reasons which escape me—it's a great movie! Like *Cutter's Way,* another 1981 United Artists release, it is quintessential neo-noir, a re-invention of the genre for the '80s. Loosely based on the unsolved Black Dahlia murder of Elizabeth Ann Short in 1947, the film targets the corruption that would allow such a murder to occur. De Niro is ambitious Father Des Spellacy; Duvall is his brother Tom, a tough police detective. The killer is due to be named "Catholic layman of the year" at a lavish banquet and Tom's investigation eventually leads him to Father Des, who knows the killer but hasn't yet connected the dots (watch the movie!). The murder (and subsequent cover-up) changes both the brothers' lives forever. Joan Didion and John Gregory Dunne's screenplay is sharp and incisive, and Owen Roizman's camera work is a classic evocation of the era. Director Ulu Grosbard, who made his film debut with *The Subject Was Roses,* is enormously skillful at conveying the complex, tangled relationship of siblings; he would make *Georgia* with Jennifer Jason Leigh and Mare Winningham in 1995. 🦴🦴🦴🦴

1981 (R) 110m/C Robert De Niro, Robert Duvall, Kenneth McMillan, Charles Durning, Cyril Cusack, Ed Flanders, Burgess Meredith, Louisa Moritz, Rose Gregorio, Dan Hedaya, Jeanette Nolan, Pat Corley, Matthew Faison, Richard Foronjy, James Hong; ***D:*** Ulu Grosbard; ***W:*** John Gregory Dunne, Joan Didion; ***C:*** Owen Roizman; ***M:*** Georges Delerue. **VHS, LV**

True Love

Donna (Annabella Sciorra) and Michael (Ron Eldard) are getting married. She's down-to-earth, he's kind of a baby, and writer/director Nancy Savoca follows them all the way from their engagement to the wedding. The two leads are absolutely convincing, and the details of this Italian wedding in the Bronx are shown with plenty of humor and razor-sharp insight. 🦴🦴🦴

1989 (R) 104m/C Annabella Sciorra, Ron Eldard, Aida Turturro, Roger Rignack, Michael J. Wolfe, Star Jasper, Kelly Cinnante, Rick Shapiro, Suzanne Costallos, Vinny Pastore; ***D:*** Nancy Savoca; ***W:*** Nancy Savoca, Richard Guay; ***C:*** Lisa Rinzler. Sundance Film Festival '89: Grand Jury Prize. **VHS, LV, Closed Caption**

Trust

If you liked Adrienne Shelly in *The Unbelievable Truth,* you'll enjoy seeing her as Maria Coughlin in *Trust.* Both Maria and her newfound friend (Martin Donovan as Matthew Slaughter) supply *Trust* with a quirky view of the roots of all evil, Suburbia and Families. Maria's father John (Marko Hunt) dies of a heart attack when she tells the folks she's having a baby, courtesy of her ex-boyfriend, the high school quarterback. On the other hand, Matthew's mother died in the delivery room. PLUS: Both Maria's mother Jean (Merritt Nelson) and Matthew's father Jim (John MacKay) are MEAN. Only in Hal Hartleyland! 🦴🦴🦴

1991 (R) 107m/C Adrienne Shelly, Martin Donovan, Merritt Nelson, Edie Falco, John MacKay, Marko Hunt; ***D:*** Hal Hartley; ***W:*** Hal Hartley; ***C:*** Michael Spiller; ***M:*** Phil Reed. Sundance Film Festival '91: Best Screenplay. **VHS, LV, Closed Caption**

Try and Get Me

It was the last Saturday night in November, 1933, exactly one month before Christmas. The body of one of the best and brightest young men in San Jose had just been found, and his two confessed killers were in jail, awaiting trial. Only there was no trial. The town's angry citizens tried and executed the defendants that night, and California governor Sunny Jim Rolph praised their actions as he justified his own decision not to send in additional protection for the prisoners. This may sound like the plot for more than one movie, and it has, in fact, been filmed at least twice. (German emigre director Fritz

Lang first chose the story for his 1936 American film debut, *Fury.*) The San Jose lynching of 1933 was never interpreted better than by the soon-to-be-blacklisted director Cy Endfield in 1950. *Try and Get Me* is a little-known film noir classic, focusing on Frank Lovejoy as an ordinary man with no money and no prospects. His wife and child don't mind, they love him anyway, but he turns out to be an absolutely vulnerable target for Lloyd Bridges' smooth-talking con man. Before long, they have pulled several small town robberies, but their big score arrives in the form of a rich young man whom they kidnap and rob. On a casual, but deliberate, impulse, Bridges kills his victim, sickening Lovejoy, whose conscience, too late, kicks into gear. The two men "celebrate" their newfound riches by taking in a nightclub with two goodtime girls, but the fundamental decency of Lovejoy's character won't permit him to deny his horror and nausea over the killing. He pours out a confession to his pickup and then staggers home while she summons the police. Richard Carlson plays a newsman whose articles on the killing stir up the emotions of the townspeople to the point where he feels guilty for his part in the ultimate fate of the prisoners. However, director Endfield reinforces this point far more effectively by sticking with Frank Lovejoy, who conveys anguish with such conviction that he forces audiences to identify with his feelings, if not his actions. Lloyd Bridges never got a part that demanded more of him than he did as Lovejoy's amoral partner in crime. It was a real loss for American audiences that Endfield, who got his start making *Our Gang* comedies, was forced to leave the country as a result of the Hollywood red scare of that era. There are some movies that almost defy the term, they seem so real that you'd swear you were tailing real people and eavesdropping on them. (And the superb, offbeat, black-and-white camera work by Guy Roe certainly contributes to that illusion.) Endfield would later make some excellent British adventure films like *Mysterious Island,* but *Try and Get Me* forces viewers to confront their feelings about retribution in a way that no other film, then or now, has quite been able to match. ***AKA:*** Sound of Fury. 𝒦𝒦𝒦𝒦

1950 91m/B Lloyd Bridges, Kathleen Ryan, Richard Carlson, Frank Lovejoy, Katherine Locke; ***D:*** Cy Endfield; ***W:*** Cy Endfield, Jo Pagano; ***C:*** Guy Roe. **VHS**

Tune in Tomorrow

Writers are seldom captured well on the silver screen. Either we get Gregory Peck slumming his way through F. Scott Fitzgerald's drunken escapades in *Beloved Infidel* or we get the agonies but not the ecstasies of *The Brontë Sisters.* Leave it to Peter Falk to deliver a full-blooded interpretation of a radio writer in *Tune in Tomorrow,* a delightful homage to the soap operas that dominated the radio air waves in 1951. This is just about the first movie I've seen that captures how much fun the interior world of a writer really is, in and of itself. Falk portrays Pedro, an insatiable eavesdropper who uses anything and everything he sees and hears as material for a wildly convoluted soap opera serial. Two of Pedro's favorite subjects are his colleague Martin and his Aunt Julia, who fall head over heels in love with each other, despite unbelievable obstacles. Pedro plays games with their lives in order to flesh out his fictional creations, but no movie with this much fondness for its characters is going to betray their aspirations by passing judgment on their weaknesses. Keanu Reeves does a credible job as Martin and his performance picks up steam as he gets more and more caught up in Pedro's tangled web and his complicated affair with his aunt by marriage. Barbara Hershey is irresistible as Aunt Julia, and her nicely textured performance does much to lend density to her young co-star's performance as well. The sequences that re-create the charm and excitement of radio drama are beautifully edited, contrasting Pedro's lavish fantasies with the ordinary men and women who help to make those fantasies real for their captive audiences. William Boyd's *Tune in Tomorrow* script is based on Mario

"Eat—or be eaten!"

—Pedro Carmichael (Peter Falk) in *Tune in Tomorrow.*

Vargas Llosa's novel *Aunt Julia and the Scriptwriter,* which was in turn based on Llosa's own early marriage to his Aunt Julia. We've seen so many contemporary movies that dance skittishly around the possibilities of authentic involvement that it's a pleasure to see a film in which the characters plunge wholeheartedly into life. It's good, too, to see a mercurial love affair in which the participants are crazy out of their minds in love with each other, consequences be hanged. As directed by Jon Amiel, *Tune in Tomorrow* approaches nostalgia for the 1950s at a devilishly skewed angle and the results are pretty exhilarating for audiences of the 1990s, too.

1990 (PG-13) 90m/C Barbara Hershey, Keanu Reeves, Peter Falk, Bill McCutcheon, Patricia Clarkson, Peter Gallagher, Dan Hedaya, Buck Henry, Hope Lange, John Larroquette, Elizabeth McGovern, Robert Sedgwick, Henry Gibson; ***D:*** Jon Amiel; ***W:*** William Boyd; ***C:*** Robert Stevens; ***M:*** Wynton Marsalis. **VHS, LV, Closed Caption**

Turnabout

Carole Landis (1919–48) was one of the loveliest starlets who ever tried to make a splash in Hollywood. She deserved a better legacy than to be chiefly remembered for her morgue photograph in *Hollywood Babylon* (a persuasive argument AGAINST suicide if you've even achieved a flashlight beam's worth of fame!). *Turnabout* is brought to us through the courtesy of the vivid imagination of humorist Thorne *(Topper)* Smith, who, along with James Thurber and Robert Benchley, is on my "A" list for a heavenly cocktail party in the year 2050. *Turnabout* may not be the greatest sexual farce ever made, but it's pretty funny if you're in the right mood. Sally (Landis) and Tim Willows (John Hubbard, 1914–88) are discontented with their respective lots in life. She thinks that she'd make a better advertising executive and he thinks he'd have a swell time doing HER job at home. Mr. Ram, the genie in their bedroom (Georges Renavent, 1894–1969) is tired of hearing their brawls and changes Sally into Tim and Tim into Sally overnight. She wakes up butch, sort of, and he wakes up VERY effeminate (which Landis never was—real women don't need to be effeminate!) Sally has Tim's voice and mannerisms, and Tim has Sally's voice. Landis is really better at this sort of thing, but Hal Roach (1892–1992) probably couldn't afford someone like Cary Grant as Tim. The household help—wonderful character actors Donald Meek (1880–1946) as Henry, and Marjorie Main (1890–1975) as Nora—know there's definitely been a change in their eccentric employers, but somehow, everyone muddles through the day. Unsurprisingly, Sally does a terrific job as the "new" Tim, but Tim bungles things at home as Sally. This screwball comedy gets wilder and nuttier until...but that would be telling. *Turnabout* was and still is considered tasteless, and the presence of the unfunny Hubbard (always best when he was being upstaged by Abbott and Costello or Roy Rogers and Dale Evans or Adolph Menjou or the Mummy!) is a severe blow, since audiences don't worry about taste when they're laughing hysterically. But it has a great supporting cast (Mary Astor, Adolphe Menjou, Verree Teasdale, William Gargan, Joyce Compton, Berton Churchill, Inez Courtney, Yolande Donlan) AND, lest we forget, Franklin Pangborn (1893–1958) as Mr. Pingboom! They might be able to re-make this with better writers and a much more appealing Tim, and I hope they go back to Thorne Smith's novel for inspiration; it's a gem. Other Landis movies on video: *One Million B.C., Dance Hall, I Wake Up Screaming, Moon over Miami, Road Show, Topper Returns, Orchestra Wives, Wintertime, Having Wonderful Crime,* and *Out of the Blue.*

1940 83m/B Carole Landis, John Hubbard, Mary Astor, Adolphe Menjou, Verree Teasdale, William Gargan, Joyce Compton, Donald Meek, Inez Courtney, Polly Ann Young, Berton Churchill, Franklin Pangborn, Marjorie Main, Yolande Donlan, Miki Morita, Georges Renavent, Norman Budd, Ray Turner, Murray Alper, Eleanor Riley, Margaret Roach; ***D:*** Hal Roach; ***W:*** Rian James, John McClain, Berne Giler, Mickell Novack; ***C:*** Norbert Brodine.

Twenty Bucks

A concept-driven movie about a $20 bill and the people who hold it, however briefly. Nothing special, but it gives us a chance to see some of our favorite actors at work, like Elisabeth Shue as waitress Emily Adams, who aspires to be a writer. Steve Buscemi and the award-winning Christopher Lloyd have fun as Frank and Jimmy, a couple of hold-up men. Made in Minneapolis. ☠☠

1993 (R) 91m/C Linda Hunt, David Rasche, George Morfogen, Brendan Fraser, Gladys Knight, Elisabeth Shue, Steve Buscemi, Christopher Lloyd, Sam Jenkins, Kamal Holloway, Melora Walters, William H. Macy, Diane Baker, Spalding Gray, Matt Frewer, Concetta Tomei, Nina Siemaszko; ***D:*** Keva Rosenfeld; ***W:*** Leslie Bohem, Endre Bohem; ***C:*** Emmanuel Lubezki; ***M:*** David Robbins. Independent Spirit Awards '94: Best Supporting Actor (Lloyd). **VHS, Closed Caption**

Twenty-One

Patsy Kensit wants to be a movie star in the worst way. *Twenty-One* is a skin-deep study of a skin-deep character involved in skin-deep relationships. Kensit is in virtually every scene, unlike *Lethal Weapon 2* or the ill-fated *Chicago Joe and the Showgirl* or *Absolute Beginners* in which she drifted in and out of the protagonists' lives. Kensit's character Katie has sex with a married man she doesn't love because she doesn't have sex with the single junkie she does love. Got that? Later on Katie marries her best friend (appealingly played by Maynard Eziashi), then leaves him so that she can play the field with American men. In between men, Katie is nice to her Dad, mean to her Mum, and has dreary luncheon discussions with her girl friend Sophie. All this is shown without a shred of insight by *Twenty-One*'s "color-by-numbers" writer/director Don Boyd. You can always tell when Boyd knows that the action is leading nowhere; the direction gets very arty and tense. Key plot shifts occur offscreen as if it would be uncool to reveal Katie's life for the melodramatic mess it is. But at least showing the melodrama would be a choice, and *Twenty-One* avoids making choices for most of its 90-odd minute running time. The ambitious Ms. Kensit is not without talent, but she is definitely without a decent showcase here. She would fare a bit better in 1995's *Angels and Insects.* ☠☠

1991 (R) 92m/C *GB* Patsy Kensit, Jack Shepherd, Patrick Ryecart, Maynard Eziashi, Rufus Sewell, Sophie Thompson, Susan Wooldridge, Julia Goodman; ***D:*** Don Boyd; ***W:*** Don Boyd; ***C:*** Keith Goddard; ***M:*** Michael Berkeley. **VHS, LV**

25 Fireman's Street

Hungary's official entry in 1974's San Francisco International Film Festival was *25 Fireman's Street,* a puzzling, disturbing movie directed by Istvan Szabo. This beautifully photographed movie focuses on the residents of a soon-to-be-demolished building. Their memories, dreams, and fears are shown in unsparing detail, as well as their uncertain daily lives: a young girl jumps off the building to her death, a woman swims in the air of her room, an old man chews thoughtfully on broken glass. Piles of junk, old photographs, and used furniture are regretfully abandoned in the streets. The actors are all blessed with fascinating, well-lined faces that any good cinematographer would sell his or her shirt to shoot, and every line tells a different story. Rita Bekes as the landlady and Lucyna Winnicka as a resident are especially memorable. Szabo successfully exposes the terror and vulnerability of the inhabitants of *25 Fireman's Street* and both his surrealistic style and his unconventional approach italicize the brutality repeated relocations inflict on the human spirit. ***AKA:*** Almok a hazrol; Tuzolto utca 25. ☠☠☠

1973 97m/C *HU* Rita Bekes, Peter Muller, Lucyna Winnicka, Andras Balint; ***D:*** Istvan Szabo; ***W:*** Istvan Szabo, Luca Karall; ***C:*** Sandor Sara. **VHS**

Twilight of the Cockroaches

Twilight of the Cockroaches/Gokiburi is anthropomorphism at its most extreme. Japanese animator Hiroaki Yoshida creates plenty of sweet little creatures with highly appealing faces in the hope that we will identify with a kingdom of humanized cockroaches. If you can accept that premise, you may not have any problem with the rest of the film, including the following line from a "roachette" named Naomi, torn between her poetic boyfriend Ichiro and Hens the warrior: "I'm pregnant. I don't think the lit-

the synopsis for *Twilight of the Cockroaches* (with Yoshida's comments) didn't even help the press all that much. It's hard for me to imagine an American filmmaker getting away with a film that depicts Japanese industrialists as greedy cockroaches. Yoshida's cautionary tale strains to fit his good intentions, and the results, even for diehard animation fans, may be bewildering. ***AKA:*** Gokiburi. **woof!**

1990 105m/C *JP* ***D:*** Hiroaki Yoshida; ***V:*** Kaoru Kobayashi, Setsuko Karamsumarau. **VHS, LV**

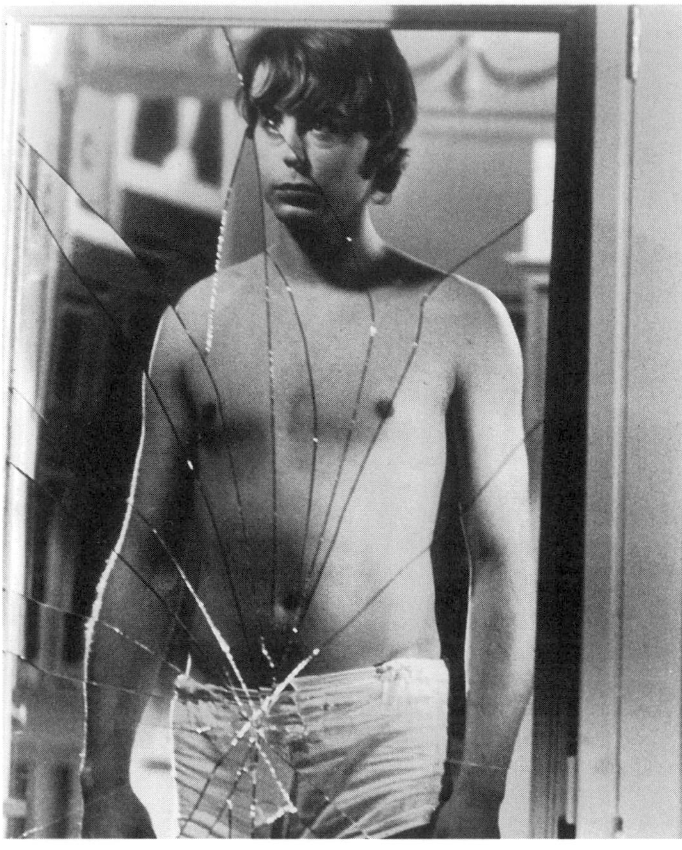

Martin (Hywel Bennett) in *Twisted Nerve.*
National General Pictures; courtesy of the Kobal Collection

ter is Ichiro's." According to the press kit, the director "fear(s) that Japan will be treated like loathsome cockroaches by the rest of the world if it continues to aggravate other countries with unfair trade practices.... (He) hopes everyone will see a little of himself or herself in the cockroaches who thought the high life would go on forever." Small children may not understand the sophistication of Yoshida's theme and they may overidentify with real-life roaches when their parents try to protect their food supply from invasion. Yoshida's concept may be a bit far-fetched for adult audiences, too. You may not be crazy about the idea of peaceful coexistence with cockroaches, or feel guilty about evicting them from your living space. If there is one type of movie that demands dubbing, rather than subtitles, it is the animated film. Many of the backgrounds are too light to read the English subtitles, and

Twisted Nerve

Hayley Mills was Walt Disney's top teen star in six films made between 1960 and 1965, but by 1968, she was scrambling to create a new cinematic identity for herself. It didn't help the fans who wanted her to stay a child forever that she was madly in love with 54-year-old director Roy Boulting. Her career choices from 1966–69 compounded the difficulty. Although Mills' talents as an actress had not diminished, her roles during this crucial period were unshowy parts that were unlikely either to reveal range or to please the admirers who'd followed her career since she was 12. (Actually, Mills made her 1947 film debut as a BABY in her father's *So Well Remembered,* which also featured her sister Juliet, then five.) Boulting's *Twisted Nerve* is the best of this sorry bunch of career-scuttling flicks, but co-stars Hywel Bennett and Billie Whitelaw have the showy parts, not Mills. Moreover, the film is rarely shown, either in England or in the U.S., because of its X rating, its flash of Bennett's bare butt, and its tricky subject matter. Before the opening credits, we see a blank screen for 20 seconds while a plummy male voice intones on the soundtrack: "Ladies and gentleman, because of the controversy already aroused, the producers of this film wish to re-emphasize what is already stated in the film, that there is no established scientific connection between Mongolism and psychotic or criminal behavior." Okay...so then we see Bennett acting like a psycho for the next couple of hours. The top-billed Mills tries hard, but she doesn't get the lines or the sequences to compete with Bennett. Anyone could have played her part and it would have made no difference to the finished film. In spite of the extraneous nature of her character and *Twisted Nerve*'s muddled psychological insights, it's still an intriguing film to watch today, with flashes of the controlled mania that Bennett would later convey so brilliantly in 1981's *Malice Aforethought.* By the time Mills and Bennet made their third picture together, in 1972's *Endless Night* by Agatha Christie, she had played just one small supporting role in three years (in the John Hurt film, *Cry of the Penguins*), and the Hayley Mills phenomenon was long over. Mills is the proud mother of Crispian MILLS (not Boulting), leader of the hot Brit rock band Kula Shaker. 🦴🦴🦴

1968 118m/C *GB* Hayley Mills, Hywel Bennett, Billie Whitelaw, Phyllis Calvert, Frank Finlay, Barry Foster, Salmaan Peer, Gretchen Franklin, Christian Roberts, Thorley Walters, Timothy West, Russell Napier, Robin Parkinson, Timothy Bateson, Brian Peck, Richard Davies, Basil Dignam, Mollie Maureen; ***D:*** Roy Boulting; ***W:*** Roy Boulting, Roger Marshall, Jeremy Scott, Leo Marks; ***C:*** Harry Waxman; ***M:*** Bernard Herrmann.

Twister

Twister is THE movie to watch the night that the cable system blitzes out and you're NOT in the mood to watch *A Man for All Seasons.* Writer/director Michael Almereyda keeps a cool grip on the antics of an oddball family headed by Harry Dean Stanton. Crispin Glover is part of the clan, so that should tell you something. At the time of its San Francisco engagement, I kept asking if Glover could make a personal appearance with the film, but more than one theatre manager patiently explained that anyone who made that many strange flicks just had to be strange himself. And then there was that one night with David Letterman...well, BIG deal and so WHAT, dudes?! This very enjoyable weirdomesticomedy ought to send anyone with a pulse straight to the floor, doubled up with laughter. 🦴🦴🦴

1989 (PG-13) 93m/C Dylan McDermott, Crispin Glover, Harry Dean Stanton, Suzy Amis, Jenny Wright, Lindsay Christman, Lois Chiles; ***D:*** Michael Almereyda; ***W:*** Michael Almereyda; ***C:*** Renato Berta; ***M:*** Hans Zimmer. **VHS, LV**

2 by 4

I used to go to a theatre that showed a lot of international flicks without subtitles. I figured it would be my only chance to see some of these things, so I'd show up anyway and plow through a single-spaced four-page synopsis and try to struggle through the movies as best I could. Jimmy Smallhorne, who founded the Irish Bronx Theatre, has assembled an impressive cast for his first film as director, screenwriter, and star, but *2 by 4* needs subtitles or a single-spaced four-page synopsis or something; thick Irish brogues all over the place plus heavy consumption of alcohol means that you're always missing some line or other. It's about construction foreman Johnnie (Smallhorne), complete with wretched childhood, drunken uncle (Chris O'Neill as Trump), and nice girlfriend (Kimberly Topper as Maria). Faster than you can sing "Johnnie, Are You Queer?," Johnnie's looking for action with Christian, a flirtatious hustler (Bradley Fitts). *2 by 4* does nothing to allay the conventional wisdom that the Irish are an unhappy, messed-up, pugnacious lot, whatever their sexual inclinations may be. The gifted Declan Quinn won an award for *2 by 4*'s cinematography. 🦴🦴

1998 90m/C Jimmy Smallhorne, Chris O'Neill, Bradley Fitts, Joe Holyoake, Terrence McGoff, Michael Liebman, Ronan Carr, Leo Hamill, Seamus McDonagh, Kimberly Topper; ***D:*** Jimmy Smallhorne; ***W:*** Fergus Tighe, Jimmy Smallhorne, Terrence McGoff; ***C:*** Declan Quinn. Sundance Film Festival '98: Best Cinematography. **VHS**

Two for the Road

True confession: I was no great admirer of Audrey Hepburn's unreal screen image throughout the '50s and most of the '60s. Born into quasi-royalty, she was, for a time, everyone's idea of a fairy princess, forever teaming up with male stars who were old enough to be her dad or even granddad, admittedly starving herself to remain 35 pounds underweight as a Givenchy mannequin her entire adult life, and always, always, in need of physical and emotional protection from a guy, any

Jon Voight and Sean Penn in *U-Turn.* Tri-Star Pictures; courtesy of the Kobal Collection

guy. And then, Hepburn got a chance to play women who could eat food and take care of themselves, in *Wait Until Dark* and *Two for the Road.* She won her fifth Oscar nomination for *Dark,* and she got to call her husband a bastard in *Road.* Stranger things were happening in 1967, but for Hepburn, who even gave up her Givenchy wardrobe to make the film, there was really nothing a 38-year-old symbol of frailty could do after two such groundbreaking performances but retire and so she did. Stanley Donen's *Two for the Road* is the story of a marriage, seen in a series of brilliantly edited flashbacks. The flashbacks are not seen in a linear fashion, but here, there, and everywhere, as a real married couple would review their life together. Mark Wallace is played by the wonderfully appealing Albert Finney, then 31, just seven years younger than Hepburn, a minor age gap dissolved by their great chemistry together. For once, Hepburn is in a relationship that has, thanks to Frederic Raphael's superb screenplay, some basis in reality. In the present, they bicker, but then we return to their far-from-romantic meeting and they bicker then, too. Mark doesn't want her at first, anyway—he wants Jacqueline Bisset, then 23, but Jackie gets the measles, so he's stuck with Joanna (Hepburn). Somehow, they manage to have an idyllic day at the beach, with passion-killing sunburn as the capper. Flash forward, flash back—we see problems at every stage of their marriage: to marry or not to marry, other women, other men, money, no money, another couple's child, their own child, and on and on. Underneath the waves of hostility are wit, humor, and a strong sense that these two belong together, and that no one else in their lives creates the sort of sparks that they do together. The romance in *Two for the Road* is intensified by the fact that the couple's feelings for each other are often rough and tangled, and always visceral. *Two for the Road,* featuring the once-in-a-lifetime magic created by Audrey Hepburn and Albert Finney, also stars the very

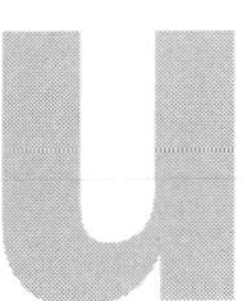

funny Eleanor Bron, 33, and William Daniels, 40, as Cathy and Howard Manchester, the parents of an obnoxious brat named Ruthie, the most persuasive argument ever for adult holidays in France without the kiddies!

1967 112m/C *GB* Audrey Hepburn, Albert Finney, Eleanor Bron, William Daniels, Claude Dauphin, Nadia Gray, Jacqueline Bisset, Georges Descrieres, Gabrielle Middleton, Judy Cornwell, Irene Hilda, Roger Dann, Libby Morris, Yves Barsac; ***D:*** Stanley Donen; ***W:*** Frederic Raphael; ***C:*** Christopher Challis; ***M:*** Henry Mancini. Nominations: Academy Awards '67: Best Story & Screenplay. **VHS, LV, Letterbox**

Two Small Bodies

Fred Ward and Suzy Amis do their best to bring Neal Bell's ultra-contrived play to life onscreen. It's a gallant effort, but the 85-minute running time feels MUCH longer. Beth B had previously co-scripted and co-directed (with Scott B) the 1981 Lydia Lunch vehicle *Vortex,* and made her solo writing and directing debut with 1987's *Salvation!* starring Stephen McHattie.

1993 85m/C *GE* Fred Ward, Suzy Amis; ***D:*** Beth B; ***W:*** Beth B, Neal Bell; ***C:*** Phil Parmet. **VHS**

U-Turn

This movie would get a "WOOF!" if Jennifer Lopez weren't in it. If you want to see a neo-noir entry that's done right, watch John Dahl's *Red Rock West.* If you want to watch Roadrunner cartoons, by all means watch them. And if you want *le bad* noir and live-action cartoons scrambled together for 125 minutes, this is your movie. Both Oliver Stone and Jon Voight (as a blind man) EARNED their Golden Raspberry nominations for this one. I'd have nominated Claire Danes for running around in a "Don't Bug Me" T-shirt and shrieking in a bad Southern accent that she wants to have Sean Penn's love child when she's already going with Joaquin Phoenix. Someone: Get this girl a map and show her that Arizona is not in the Deep South. Sean Penn struggles along with a "Who do I have to sleep with to get out of this movie?" expression, only lightening up when he gets to do an update of *Duel in the Sun* with Lopez. Ah, Jennifer Lopez...when she's onscreen you may actually think that *U-Turn* isn't THAT bad, but whenever she goes away, YOU KNOW. Julie Hagerty has a bit as a haggard waitress, Bo Hopkins has a bit, Liv Tyler has a bit, Powers Boothe is the sheriff...oh, and Nick Nolte gets to be one of those guys who wants his wife dead, then she wants him dead, then they make up, then he wants her dead, then she wants him dead, then you'll lose count. And guess what? "She's my wife! She's my daughter! She's my wife and my daughter!" (Sound familiar?) Billy Bob Thornton goes through the whole movie without a bath, even when he's getting ready to play a game of Twister with a girl. Like Otto Preminger's *Skidoo, U-Turn*'s a mess, but you just may be in the mood for a mess some night. ***AKA:*** Stray Dogs.

1997 (R) 125m/C Sean Penn, Jennifer Lopez, Claire Danes, Nick Nolte, Joaquin Rafael (Leaf) Phoenix, Powers Boothe, Billy Bob Thornton, Jon Voight, Abraham Benrubi, Julie Hagerty, Bo Hopkins, Valery Nikolaev, Aida Linares, Laurie Metcalf, Liv Tyler; ***D:*** Oliver Stone; ***W:*** John Ridley; ***C:*** Robert Richardson; ***M:*** Ennio Morricone. Nominations: Golden Raspberry Awards '97: Worst Supporting Actor (Voight), Worst Director (Stone). **VHS, LV, Closed Caption, DVD**

Ulee's Gold

This was a comeback vehicle (of sorts) for Peter Fonda, because (surprise!) he's never been away, he's just been making the sort of pictures that don't win Golden Globes or Oscar nominations. He's always been good even when the rest of the flick isn't. In point of fact, Victor Nunez movies are slow, subtle films, so they need the best actors in the world (Ashley Judd in *Ruby in Paradise,* Peter Fonda in *Ulee's Gold*) to keep your eyes chained to the screen instead of your wristwatch. Ulee is a Florida beekeeper presiding over the lives of his grandchildren Casey and Penny (Jessica Biel and Vanessa Zima). Their father (Tom Wood as Ulee's son Jimmy) is incarcerated and their drug-addicted mother (Christine Dunford as Jimmy's wife Helen) has just come back into their lives along with a couple of thugs. The thugs are wild and crazy so Ulee doesn't have to be. His

Peter Fonda in *Ulee's Gold.* Orion Pictures Corporation; courtesy of the Kobal Collection

internal mechanism is working all the time, though; we can see it and feel it. Fonda is so good that we're more than happy just to watch him work for 111 minutes, especially when he inhabits a character who rarely speaks, but whose silences are so expressive. No one delivers this beautifully shaded a performance simply by showing up and saying lines. Take a look at Fonda's work since 1964's *Lilith,* like 1968's *Spirits of the Dead* or 1969's *Easy Rider* or 1974's *Dirty Mary, Crazy Larry* or 1976's *92 in the Shade* or 1982's *Split Image* or his hilarious turn as Dr. Van Helsing in 1995's *Nadja.* I suspect that the cinematic prime of Professor Peter Fonda may well occur in the 21st century, far more than in the century of his birth (on February 23, 1939).

1997 (R) 111m/C Peter Fonda, Tom Wood, Vanessa Zima, Jessica Biel, Christine Dunford, Patricia Richardson, Steve Flynn, Dewey Weber, J. Kenneth Campbell; ***D:*** Victor Nunez; ***W:*** Victor Nunez; ***C:*** Virgil Marcus Mirano; ***M:*** Charles Engstrom. Golden Globe Awards '98: Best Actor—Drama (Fonda); New York Film Critics Awards '97: Best Actor (Fonda); Nominations: Academy Awards '97: Best Actor (Fonda); Independent Spirit Awards '98: Best Actor (Fonda), Best Director (Nunez), Best Film, Best Screenplay, Best Supporting Actress (Richardson); Screen Actors Guild Award '97: Best Actor (Fonda). **VHS, Closed Caption**

The Unbearable Lightness of Being

Daniel Day-Lewis plays Czech surgeon Tomas, who makes love with Sabina (Lena Olin) and falls in love with Tereza (Juliette Binoche). The backdrop is Prague, 1968. Just before Russia invades Czechoslovakia, Tomas and Tereza escape to Switzerland. Tomas has spent his entire adult life avoiding politics and serious involvements; now events beyond his control require him to confront both. *Being* launched Binoche, then 24, as a very romantic international star, culminating in the Academy Award she received for 1996's *The English Patient. Being* also added to the universal perception that there was NO part that was beyond the range of Day-Lewis, as he demonstrated in his Oscar-winning interpretation of Christy Brown in 1989's *My Left Foot.* Philip Kaufman's previous films *(The Great Northfield Minnesota Raid, The White Dawn, Invasion of the Body Snatchers, Wanderers, The Right Stuff)* gave little indication of the masterpiece that he would make by the time he was 52. Many seemed shocked that an American director (oh, come now!) could make such a sensitive, sensual picture. His follow-up movie, 1990's *Henry and June,* virtually invented the NC-17 rating, but 1993's *Rising Son* was more like the popular entertainment Kaufman had made earlier in his career. Unlike *What Happened Was, The Unbearable Lightness of Being* is ideal for a romantic video date. Hmmm...maybe not on the very FIRST date.... Based on the novel by Milan Kundera.

1988 (R) 172m/C Daniel Day-Lewis, Juliette Binoche, Lena Olin, Derek De Lint, Erland Josephson, Pavel Landovsky, Donald Moffat, Daniel Olbrychski, Stellan Skarsgard, Tormek Bork, Bruce Myers, Pavel Slaby, Pascale Kalensky, Jacques Ciron, Anne Lonnberg, Laszlo Szabo, Vladimir Valenta, Clovis Cornillac, Leon Lissek, Consuelo de Haviland; ***D:*** Philip Kaufman; ***W:*** Jean-Claude Carriere, Philip Kaufman; ***C:*** Sven Nykvist; ***M:*** Mark Adler, Ernie Fosselius, Leos Janacek. British Academy Awards '88: Best Adapted Screenplay; Independent Spirit Awards '89: Best Cinematography; National Society of Film Critics Awards '88: Best Director (Kaufman), Best Film; Nominations: Academy Awards '88: Best Adapted Screenplay, Best Cinematography. **VHS, LV, Closed Caption**

The Unbelievable Truth

This may be one of the best movies ever made on an 11-day shooting schedule; I rarely stopped laughing at the onscreen antics which is not to say that it will have that effect on everyone. What is Robert *(Robocop 3)* Burke doing back in town after serving hard time? Everyone wants to solve this strange enigma, but the wonderfully appealing Adrienne Shelly finds out. (Her dad thinks she should go to school, even though she really doesn't see the point since the world is going to end, after all.) After enlivening several other indies, Shelly later wrote, directed, and starred in her own indie, 1996's *Sudden Manhattan.* Julia McNeal later battled *The Refrigerator,* an underrated 1993 chiller. Hal Hartley went on to make *Surviving Desire, Trust* (with Shelly), *Simple Men* (with Mark Bailey), *Amateur,* and *Flirt.* ☙☙☙

1990 (R) 100m/C Adrienne Shelly, Robert John Burke, Christopher Cooke, Julia Mueller, Julia McNeal, Mark Bailey, Gary Sauer, Kathrine Mayfield; ***D:*** Hal Hartley; ***W:*** Hal Hartley; ***C:*** Michael Spiller; ***M:*** Jim Coleman. **VHS, LV**

Under Suspicion

Under Suspicion may look pretty good on cable television at one o'clock in the morning. But on the huge screen, well, there's nothing wrong with *Under Suspicion* that a good script doctor and/or a decent director couldn't have fixed. Simon Moore is the director of this British made-for-television "thriller" starring Liam Neeson and Laura San Giacomo. Neeson is cast as the traditional "wrong man" and plays the entire role that way. But there is one sequence when he whispers in San Giacomo's ear and another when he ignites a cigarette lighter that look just like the director told him, "Just do these shots and I'll explain why later." As any good thriller writer will tell you, you can use sleight of hand all you want, but the clues have got to be there or the audience will feel cheated. I wonder if Liam Neeson will feel cheated if he ever gets around to seeing *Under Suspicion.* I was eager to see Laura San Giacomo in a lead, since she's done some wonderful work in supporting roles, but alas, she'll have to wait for another lead to do her career some good. San Giacomo CAN play a femme fatale—I've seen her do it—but Simon Moore is no Steven Soderbergh or Lasse Hallstrom; San Giacomo looks and sounds like a little kid playing dress-up. This is the sort of movie that tries to evoke silent serials, film noir, kitchen sink dramas, and even the suspense-building style of Alfred Hitchcock, but fails on every count. Why is there a 1957 flashback? (It's a red herring.) Why is a stuck-up barrister in bed with a young boy? (That's a double red herring.) Why does most of the story take place on the eve of the '60s? (Well, partly to explain '50s British attitudes toward divorce and homosexuality, but mostly because Moore has a neat line about the passing of the decade. He seems to think it's neat, anyway.) This movie is so out of touch that a character has to say out loud twice "I'll never make it in time" when he's racing to save a man from the gallows. And GUESS what happens after that? One saving grace: Kenneth Cranham does a fine job in an incomprehensible character role. ☙☙

1992 (R) 99m/C *GB* Liam Neeson, Laura San Giacomo, Alphonsia Emmanuel, Kenneth Cranham, Maggie O'Neill, Martin Grace, Stephen Moore; ***D:*** Simon Moore; ***W:*** Simon Moore; ***C:*** Vernon Layton; ***M:*** Christopher Gunning. **VHS, LV, Closed Caption**

The Underneath

Recovering gambling addict Michael Chambers (Peter Gallagher) returns home after

"The greatest trick the devil ever pulled was convincing the world he didn't exist."

—Verbal Kint (Kevin Spacey) in *The Usual Suspects.*

skipping out on his debts and his wife Rachel (sultry newcomer Alison Elliot) several years before. Old passions ignite in more ways than one, and Michael's lust for his ex, now married to a hot-tempered hoodlum, leads him to risk it all for a final big score. Moody and tense study of the complexities of emotion is capped by smart lead performances but style wins out over substance and the finale definitely leaves more questions than answers. Remake of the 1949 film noir classic *Criss Cross,* based on Don Tracy's novel of the same name. 🦴🦴🦴

1995 (R) 99m/C Shelley Duvall, Richard Linklater, Dennis Hill, Peter Gallagher, Alison Elliott, William Fichtner, Elisabeth Shue, Adam Trese, Paul Dooley, Joe Don Baker, Anjanette Comer, Harry Goaz, Vincent Gaskins, Tony Perenski, Helen Cates, John Martin, David Jensen, Joseph Chrest; ***D:*** Steven Soderbergh; ***W:*** Daniel Fuchs, Sam Lowry; ***C:*** Elliot Davis; ***M:*** Cliff Martinez. Nominations: Independent Spirit Awards '96: Best Cinematography. **VHS**

Uneasy Terms

Two Slim Callaghan movies were made between 1948 and 1954, this one and *Meet Mr. Callaghan,* based on *The Urgent Hangman* starring Derrick de Marney as Slim, Delphi Lawrence as Effie, and Trevor Reid as Inspector Gringall. The first film starred Michael Rennie as Slim, Joy Shelton as Effie, and Barry Jones as Inspector Gringall. Peter Cheyney's original novels attempt to transplant most of the characteristics of the hard-boiled American detective into a smooth-talking British equivalent. Rennie's Slim is disrespectful, shifty, and a bit of a skirt chaser, but he does get results. Moira Lister gives another trademarked acid performance as Corinne, one of three sisters who hire Slim and his sidekick Windy (Paul Carpenter) to figure out who killed their stepfather; Faith Brook and Patricia Goddard are Viola and Patricia, the other sisters. Effie does research from the office and fends off Windy's advances, Gringall issues daily bulletins about how many laws Slim and Windy are breaking, and Nigel Patrick does an intriguingly twisted job as one of the murder suspects. A dozen years later, Rennie played Harry Lime on *The Third Man* television series, but he still seemed a lot like Slim Callaghan. He's not a serious threat to Sam Spade or Philip Marlowe, but if you can't find *The Day the Earth Stood Still* on the video shelf, Rennie's cool, dapper approach to *Uneasy Terms* makes this entry a fairly easy way to spend 91 minutes. 🦴🦴½

1948 91m/B *GB* Michael Rennie, Moira Lister, Faith Brook, Joy Shelton, Patricia Goddard, Barry Jones, Nigel Patrick, Paul Carpenter, Marie Ney, Sydney Tafler, J.H. Roberts, John Robinson; ***D:*** Vernon Sewell; ***W:*** Peter Cheyney; ***C:*** Ernest Palmer. **VHS**

The Unfinished Sentence in 141 Minutes

The Unfinished Sentence is a long, complicated study about the efforts of an industrialist's son to better understand the workers' world, despite his own privileged position. Based on a long, complicated novel by Tibor Dery. ***AKA:*** 141 Perc a Befejezetlen Mondatbal; 141 Minutes from the Unfinished Sentence. 🦴

1975 141m/C *HU* Andras Balint, Zoltan Latonovits, Mari Csomos, Aniko Safar, Laszlo Mansaros, Maria Bisztray, Lujza Orosz; ***D:*** Zoltan Fabri; ***W:*** Zoltan Fabri; ***C:*** Gyorgy Iles; ***M:*** Gyorgy Vukan.

Unzipped

Fashion designer Isaac Mizrahi is the whole show in this crowd-pleasing documentary that won the 1995 Audience Award at the Sundance Film Festival. The film focuses on Mizrahi's preparations for the showing of his 1994 collection. It also touches on how he reads fashion in classic Hollywood movies, like 1935's *Call of the Wild* starring a dressed-to-the-nines Loretta Young: "If you're going to freeze to death in the Yukon, this is the way to do it." Perhaps because of the surprise success of this movie, another film about fashion—*Catwalk*—was rushed into 1996 release, also featuring Mizrahi but to a lesser extent. If you can only see one movie about the trials and tribulations of assembling a fashion show, *Unzipped* is the one to see. It's unpretentious, it's stylish, and it's FUN! 🦴🦴🦴

1994 (R) 76m/C ***D:*** Douglas Keeve; ***C:*** Ellen Kuras. Sundance Film Festival '95: Audience Award. **VHS, LV, Closed Caption**

The Usual Suspects

The Usual Suspects was one of the best movies of 1995, featuring a dazzling, tautly constructed screenplay by Oscar winner Christopher McQuarrie and a star-making performance by Kevin Spacey. The less you know about the film in advance, the better, because the story will put you through more twists and turns than a roller coaster ride, and half the fun is the sheer unexpected inventiveness of it all. McQuarrie and director Bryan Singer had previously worked together on *Public Access,* 1993's Grand Jury Prize winner at the Sundance Film Festival. Spacey had been toiling in Hollywood since 1987 and steadily attracting a legion of admirers who believe there's nothing this brilliant actor can't play.

1995 (R) 105m/C Kevin Spacey, Gabriel Byrne, Chazz Palminteri, Kevin Pollak, Stephen Baldwin, Benicio Del Toro, Giancarlo Esposito, Pete Postlethwaite, Dan Hedaya, Suzy Amis, Paul Bartel, Peter Greene; ***D:*** Bryan Singer; ***W:*** Christopher McQuarrie; ***C:*** Newton Thomas Sigel; ***M:*** John Ottman. Academy Awards '95: Best Original Screenplay, Best Supporting Actor (Spacey); British Academy Awards '95: Best Original Screenplay; Independent Spirit Awards '96: Best Screenplay, Best Supporting Actor (Del Toro); National Board of Review Awards '95: Best Supporting Actor (Spacey); New York Film Critics Awards '95: Best Supporting Actor (Spacey); Broadcast Film Critics Association Awards '95: Best Supporting Actor (Spacey); Nominations: Academy Awards '95: Best Screenplay; British Academy Awards '95: Best Film; Golden Globe Awards '96: Best Supporting Actor (Spacey); Independent Spirit Awards '96: Best Cinematography; Screen Actors Guild Award '95: Best Supporting Actor (Spacey). **VHS, LV, Closed Caption, DVD**

Valentino

Whenever I admit that I actually enjoy this flick, I get this uncomprehending LOOK, followed by, "And you call yourself a FILM CRITIC?" No, I call myself Monica. Under threat of social torture, I will confess to being a movie reviewer, but that's a full step away from what I really am, a movie buff who doesn't care a hoot whether my opinion on a flick is shared or not. I didn't put any MONEY into *Valentino*'s escrow account, I just dig its operatic excesses, that's all. Once, when Rudolf Nureyev came to dance in San Francisco, his foot was hurt and after listening to a doctor's gobbledygook, he took a swig of vodka and sailed through a scheduled performance without a hitch; I didn't even realize he was in pain until I read the newspapers the next day. Nureyev was exactly the sort of guy who should have been playing *Valentino!* NOT Anthony Dexter! NOT Franco Nero! As always, Ken Russell doesn't even try to make a scrupulously researched dramatic documentary. He has always been more intrigued in the emotional landscapes of his famous subjects (Tchaikovsky, Mahler) than in accurate detail. Here, he is interested in the mythology of fame and how it helped to destroy the life of the living legend that Rodolfo Guglielmo became between 1921 and 1926. The casting all the way down the line is eccentric for anyone else, but on the mark for Russell. Who could be a zanier Alla Nazimova (1879–1945) than Leslie Caron? Who was more adept at playing bitches than Michelle Phillips as Natasha Rambova (1897–1969)? And who else would you cast as Jesse Lasky (1880–1958)? (NO, not Milton Berle, that's for Aaron Spelling's 1975 telefeature!) *Dead End* kid Huntz Hall, of course! Russell's vision of the '20s undoubtedly exists only in his imagination, but his depiction of the truths about the pervasiveness of fame applies throughout the 20th century. Valentino had been a beggar, a gardener, and a taxi dancer, but nothing prepared him for his mass worship by women and derisive baiting by men. In an aria-like sequence, Russell flashes back and forth between Valentino's disintegrating personal life and screaming Rudymaniacs. There's an abundance of sex and cynicism in *Valentino,* with Nureyev vividly recreating the naive, terror-stricken title character at the maelstrom's core. This surprisingly moral picture received an "X" certificate in Great Britain. Based on the Brad Steiger book, *Valentino: An Intimate Expose.*

1977 (R) 127m/C *GB* Rudolf Nureyev, Leslie Caron, Michelle Phillips, Carol Kane, Felicity

The First All-Drag Queen Sci-Fi Musical Ever!

—Tagline from the movie *Vegas in Space.*

Kendal, Seymour Cassel, Peter Vaughan, William Hootkins, Huntz Hall, David DeKeyser, Alfred Marks, Anton Diffring; ***D:*** Ken Russell; ***W:*** Mardik Martin, Ken Russell, John Byrum; ***C:*** Peter Suschitzsky; ***M:*** Ferde Grofe Jr. **VHS**

Vampyr

The films of Danish director Carl Theodor Dreyer require considerable patience from audiences, even horror film devotees. To a certain extent, Dreyer anticipates the viewers' perceptions and plays with them. (In a slow way.) (Very slow.) *Vampyr,* AKA *The Strange Adventure of David Gray,* stars the film's backer, Baron Nicholas de Gunzberg, AKA Julien West. The vampire in this film is an old woman in a village, a fact the hero may not comprehend but is forced to accept when he sees what happens to her fellow villagers. Dreyer shows that ordinary surroundings take on a different atmosphere when we know that vampires are in the vicinity. Many Dreyer aficionados consider this to be his masterpiece. My rating reflects the boredom/fidget factor. Note: The sad real-life story of leading lady Sybille Schmitz inspired Rainer Werner Fassbinder to make 1982's *Veronika Voss.* ***AKA:*** Vampyr, Ou l'Etrange Aventure de David Gray; Vampyr, Der Traum des David Gray; Not against the Flesh; Castle of Doom; The Strange Adventure of David Gray; The Vampire.

1931 75m/B *GE* Julian West, Sybille Schmitz, Harriet Gerard, Maurice Schutz, Rena Mandel, Jan Hieronimko, Albert Bras; ***D:*** Carl Theodor Dreyer; ***W:*** Carl Theodor Dreyer, Christen Jul; ***C:*** Rudolph Mate, Louis Nee; ***M:*** Wolfgang Zeller. **VHS, DVD**

The Vanishing

The Vanishing is one of the saddest, most chilling movies ever made. The first part of the plot focuses on a young Dutch couple embarking on a holiday. Their relationship has slid into one of easy intimacy. They talk of inconsequentials, they bicker, they get separated for part of an evening because of car trouble. We learn that Saskia (charmingly portrayed by Johanna Ter Steege) is frightened of the dark and that Rex (played with intensity by Gene Bervoetes) tends to be dogged once he's started on a course of action. When they are reunited, they snap at each other, make up quickly, and resume their holiday with fresh enthusiasm. They stop at an all-purpose rest station and she runs an errand. They play on the lawn. These unstressed details will haunt both the audience and Rex the protagonist when he later searches for Saskia. She is like a playful, endearing kitten, and we begin to wish that the mystery of the film would fully engage them both, that maybe they would discover buried treasure together. Instead, the mystery haunts and torments Rex, and stakes a terrifying claim on our imaginations. I haven't been this spooked by a film with such understated visual information since I first caught up with the films of Val Lewton on the late, late show. *The Vanishing* shows us things that we don't fully understand until several reels later. They work extremely well as individual sequences, but when we finally realize what we've actually seen long after the fact, the initial panic and underlying sadness are incredibly powerful. Screenwriter Tim Krabbe and director George Sluizer obviously knew exactly what they were doing. Like the protagonist, you may find yourself replaying similar episodes in your own life, and you may also overidentify with Rex's obsession for real answers as he pursues Saskia. In any event, it'll be impossible to predict your exact response to the film's startling conclusion or to its final visual tag. After making *Utz* in Great Britain, Sluizer was lured by Fox to America to duplicate his indie success in 1993, but the studio insisted on a happy ending, infuriating admirers of the classic original. Sluizer then began the ill-fated *Dark Blood* with Jonathan Pryce and River Phoenix, a film left unfinished when Phoenix died on Halloween, 1993. ***AKA:*** Spoorloos.

1988 107m/C *NL FR* Barnard Pierre Donnadieu, Johanna Ter Steege, Gene Bervoets, Gwen Eckhaus, Bernadette Le Sache, Tania Latarjet, Lucille Glenn, Roger Souza; ***D:*** George Sluizer; ***W:*** George Sluizer, Tim Krabbe; ***C:*** Toni Kuhn; ***M:*** Henny Vrienten. **VHS, DVD**

Vanya on 42nd Street

If you wanted to send away for *My Dinner with Andre* action figures when you saw *Wait-*

ing for Guffman, you'll probably find *Vanya on 42nd Street* an equally rewarding experience. Louis Malle's swan song shows a 1993 rehearsal at New York's New Amsterdam theatre of Anton Chekhov's *Uncle Vanya,* adapted by David Mamet. Wallace Shawn acquits himself admirably in the title role, Julianne Moore is Yelena, Brooke Smith is Sonya, Larry Pine is Dr. Astrov, George Gaynes is Serybryakov, Lynn Cohen is Maman, Phoebe Brand is Nanny, Jerry Mayer is Waffles, Madhur Jaffrey is Mrs. Chao, and Andre Gregory appears as himself. (Phoebe Brand was a member of the influential Group Theatre, appearing in 1933's *Men in White* with Margaret Barker, Elia Kazan, Alexander Kirkland, and Sanford Meisner; in 1935's *Awake and Sing* with Luther and Stella Adler, Roman Bohnen, J. Edward Bromberg, Morris Carnovsky, Art Smith, John Garfield, and Meisner; in *Weep for the Virgins* with Marie Hunt, Tony Kraber, Paula Miller, Ruth Nelson, William Nicholas, Dorothy Patten, Hilda Reis, Virginia Stevens, Eunice Stoddard, Mildred Van Dorn, Evelyn Varden, Barker, Bromberg, Kirkland, Smith, and Garfield; in 1936's *The Case of Clyde Griffiths* with Barker and Kirkland; and in 1937's *Golden Boy* with Luther Adler, Harry Bratsburg, Lee J. Cobb, Bert Conway, Charles Crisp, Howard da Silva, Frances Farmer, Michael Gordon, Robert Lewis, Karl Malden, Charles Niemeyer, John O'Malley, Martin Ritt, Bohnen, Carnovsky, Kazan, and Garfield. If the list sounds like a Who's Who of 1930s stage legends, it IS; what a wealth of theatrical lore this durable stage actress must have!) ƒƒƒ

1994 (PG) 119m/C Wallace Shawn, Julianne Moore, Brooke Smith, Larry Pine, George Gaynes, Lynn Cohen, Madhur Jaffrey, Phoebe Brand, Jerry Mayer, Andre Gregory; ***D:*** Louis Malle; ***W:*** Andre Gregory, David Mamet; ***C:*** Declan Quinn; ***M:*** Joshua Redman. Nominations: Independent Spirit Awards '95: Best Supporting Actor (Pine), Best Supporting Actress (Smith). **VHS, LV**

Variety Lights

1950's *Variety Lights* is often overlooked and underrated by Federico Fellini buffs, partly because he shared directing credit on this maiden effort with Alberto Lattuada. But it is a jewel of a film to discover on a video shelf. Carla Del Poggio is its beautiful but not particularly talented protagonist. She wants to be a star and the terribly smitten Peppino de Felippo wants her. Giulietta Masina is his long-suffering love, ready to scrape him out of the gutter after the inevitable moment when Carla breaks his heart. Besides this oh-so-familiar triangle, we have the joy and vitality of small-time show business, best appreciated on its own ephemeral terms. One of the best sequences involves a rich guy who wines and dines the entire theatrical troupe just so he can have his way with Carla. Everyone knows the game but him: eat first, then protect your virtue. Masina was to become Fellini's eternal gamine, but in this film she is well able to take care of herself. *Variety Lights* is Fellini's early tribute to Masina's unique ability to project a love that helps her to survive life's painful realities, and make her partner's grandiose visions possible. ***AKA:*** Luci del Varieta; Lights of Variety. ƒƒƒƒ

1951 93m/B *IT* Giulietta Masina, Peppino de Filippo, Carla Del Poggio, Folco Lulli; ***D:*** Federico Fellini, Alberto Lattuada; ***W:*** Alberto Lattuada, Federico Fellini, Tullio Pinelli, Ennio Flaiano; ***C:*** Otello Martelli; ***M:*** Felice Lattuada. **VHS**

Vegas in Space

The making of *Vegas in Space* reveals how difficult assembling a truly independent film really is. The enormously talented, much-missed Doris Fish (1952–91) spent the last nine years of his life helping writer/director Philip R. Ford complete the project, three years before its premiere. It may have seemed like a fun thing to do after a successful party given by future cast member Ginger Quest, but raising even a tiny budget like $60,000 meant that Fish/Ford films had to shoot film, stop, make money, edit film, stop, make money, mix film, stop, make money...for many years. Under these trying circumstances, Ford was able to accomplish wonders and he assembled a lively cast of San Francisco drag queens who paid affectionate homage to the colorful science-fiction epics of the early '60s. Fish and Miss X, who also wrote the screenplay with Ford, have the film's most prominent roles as Captain Dan Tracey/Tracey Daniels and Vel Croford, Empress of Earth/Veneer, Queen of Police. Also worth noting are the late "Tippi" as the petulant Princess Angel and Lori Naslund in a brisk performance as Lieutenant Steve/Debbie Dane. Executive producer/production designer Fish worked hard on the film's makeup and wigs, costumes, and miniatures; not bad for the extremely skilled, very funny Fish, who could work droll wonders with the simplest dialogue. Although *Vegas in Space* IS the "easy-to-understand-no-hidden-meaning-entertainment" that its filmmakers hoped it would be, it is, sadly, NOT the camp classic it might have been. The rollicking, unforced humor of the live stage appearances of drag queens Fish, "Tippi," and Miss X has not been effectively captured on film. *Vegas in Space* is a time capsule of the year 1982 in the same way that a daguerreotype preserves people's images from the year 1842. We can see what everyone looked like, but not the unique undercurrents that made them precious beyond their own era. Note: *Vegas in Space* received some technical support from San Francisco's Film Arts Foundation and was virtually complete when Troma Films picked it up for "distribution." Aside from its premiere at San Francisco's Castro Theatre, this seems to have consisted mainly of late night USA telecasts and its Troma Team Video release. Composer Timmy Spence sings the title song with Katie Guthorn.

1994 85m/C Doris Fish, Miss X, Ginger Quest, Ramona Fischer, Lori Naslund, Timmy Spence, Silvana Nova, Sandelle Kincaid, Tommy Pace, Arturo Galster, Jennifer Blowdryer, Freida Lay, Tippi; ***D:*** Phillip R. Ford; ***W:*** Phillip R. Ford, Doris Fish, Miss X; ***C:*** Robin Clark; ***M:*** Ramona Fischer, Timmy Spence. **VHS**

The Very Edge

Among my favorite not-so-guilty pleasures is watching the early films of television's most iconographic heroes. Before his image congealed into sterling saintliness on the small screen, Raymond Burr was one of the toughest thugs you could ever find on the late, late, late show. And you haven't lived until you've seen William Talman play a vicious killer or a religious maniac. Although it sickened him to play the role, Basil Rathbone was chillingly effective as mean Mr. Murdstone, brutalizing little Freddie Bartholomew and delicate Elizabeth Allan in *David Copperfield.* Rathbone's successor as Sherlock Holmes, Jeremy Brett (1935–95), was the most monastic of Victorian sleuths. Not even a marginal hint of attraction to the opposite sex crept into his interpretation. Like a chess master at the top of his form, he was rather dry, brittle, precise, and obsessed. What a surprise, then, to discover *The Very Edge,* a dark little British film from the year 1963 in which Brett, then 27, played a full-fledged sexual psychopath, terrorizing gorgeous Anne Heywood. She is "happily" married to Richard Todd until Brett, who has been stalking her for some time, attacks her in her home while her husband fiddles helplessly with the latch key. She loses the baby she is expecting, and tries hard both to cooperate with the police and to rebuild her shattered marriage. Her wonderful husband, it seems, expects her to instantly recover from the incident without a mark. If she can't, well, there's always Nicole Maurey, his stunning French secretary, lurking in the wings. The intriguing element about *The Very Edge,* under Cyril Frankel's assured direction, is that Heywood has more of a psychic bond with her attacker than she does with her own husband. It isn't that she wants him or anything like that, but she has compassion for his illness, and she is, ironically, less of a victim around Brett than she is around Todd. Both men desire her for their own reasons, but in a life-and-death situation, her fighting spirit emerges with her obsessed stalker in a way that it never does within her marriage. Brett is riveting as the tortured psycho, and your real hisses will be reserved for Todd and the so-called normal life to which Heywood must return again and again; it is a tribute to her expert performance that you can appreciate why her struggle with Brett gives her such an authentic grip on life. The ending, in which the police ignore the poor tied-up handyman played by Patrick Magee, and focus their energies on the folks from a higher social order, is VEDDY, VEDDY British. 𝄞𝄞𝄞

1963 90m/B *GB* Anne Heywood, Richard Todd, Jeremy Brett, Jack Hedley, Barbara Mullen, Maurice Denham, William Lucas, Gwen Watford, Patrick Magee; ***D:*** Cyril Frankel; ***W:*** Elizabeth Jane Howard; ***C:*** Robert Huke. **VHS**

Victim

Victim was an important film in 1961 when homosexuality was still illegal in Great Britain. Actor Dirk Bogarde was then famous as everybody's favorite Dr. Simon Sparrow in a series of four medical comedy films he made between 1954 and 1963. At the time, his decision to play a gay barrister might have called a halt to his thriving career. It didn't, but it certainly marked a professional turning point for him. In order to increase *Victim*'s impact, director Basil Dearden made the decision to show most of the gay characters not as drag queens but as dedicated professionals, vulnerable to violence and blackmail. *Victim* rates high marks for its pioneering efforts to confront previously unexplored issues with honesty and compassion. The title, which locks the film in an early '60s time capsule, says it all, though: for all his hard work, intelligence, and stature, Bogarde's character faces a sad and lonely life, isolated from frightened gays and cautious heterosexuals alike. 𝄞𝄞𝄞𝄞

1961 100m/C *GB* Dirk Bogarde, Sylvia Syms, Dennis Price, Peter McEnery, Nigel Stock, Donald Churchill, Anthony Nicholls, Hilton Edwards, Norman Bird, Derren Nesbitt, Alan McNaughton, Noel Howlett, Charles Lloyd Pack, John Barrie, John Bennett; ***D:*** Basil Dearden; ***W:*** John McCormick, Janet Green; ***C:*** Otto Heller; ***M:*** Philip Green. **VHS**

Victory March

Victory March, filmed in Italy, is a savage examination of military life. Although there are no deaths until the final moment, it drew extended hissing at 1976's San Francisco International Film Festival, largely because director/screenwriter Marco Bellocchio also dabbles with another theme: the greatest enforcers of violence may be its greatest victims. He draws back from exploring this theme on any real depth, but one of the film's most revealing sequences occurs when a captain, played with feeling by Franco Nero, realizes that the tyranny he inflicted on his wife is exactly what drove her away. No one else in the movie emphasizes this as well, and 118 moments of brutality are in no way dismissed with this brief insight. This may be what Bellocchio intended, but by then he has spent a great deal of screen time preparing us for emotional connections between people that never pay off. Bellocchio later made *The Eyes, The Mouth, Henry IV,* and *Devil in the Flesh.* **AKA:** Marcia Trionfale. 𝄞𝄞½

1976 118m/C *IT FR GE* Franco Nero, Miou-Miou, Michele Placido, Patrick Dewaere; ***D:*** Marco Bellocchio; ***W:*** Marco Bellocchio, Sergio Bazzini; ***C:*** Franco Di Giacomo; ***M:*** Nicola Piovani.

Village of the Damned

Wolf Rilla's vintage 1960 chiller, *Village of the Damned,* based on John Wyndham's novel, *The Midwich Cuckoos,* was shot in creepy black and white and focused on the efforts of an unlikely married couple to humanize their weird offspring. (Well, if you were 27 years old, gorgeous, brilliant, and sensitive like Barbara Shelley, would 54-year-old GEORGE SANDERS be on YOUR short list of husbands?) The opening shots are beautifully done; the inhabitants of the quiet village of Midwich simply fall asleep mid-activity. The military gets wind of the unexpected afternoon siesta and, predictably, botch the investigation. Nine months later, any woman who's capable of bearing an infant delivers a precocious baby who quickly evolves into a genius demon child with straight blonde hair and spooky eyes. Spookiest of the bunch is Martin Stephens as David, Shelley's son. Stephens made a dozen films in his 12-year career, becoming progressively less frightening as he entered his teens, but luckily for horror fans, *Village of The Damned* and 1961's *The Innocents* were filmed when Stephens was still at his blood-curdling best. You didn't need to have a bunch of great child actors with Stephens as the ringleader. In the film's finest moments, the grown-ups fight a losing war of nerves with their cool, well-spo-

Violette Noziere (Isabelle Huppert) and Jean Dabin (Jean-François Garreaud) in *Violette.* Courtesy of the Kobal Collection

ken, would-be conquerors. The smash status of Rilla's film is partly due to the universal mutual distrust between adults and kids, but mostly because he stuck to basics and kept things simple. *Village of the Damned* is well worth a look on video, especially for 10- or 11-year-old fantasists who'd love to terrify their caretakers into doing everything they say with the help of one cold lethal stare. 🦴🦴🦴

1960 78m/B *GB* George Sanders, Barbara Shelley, Martin Stephens, Laurence Naismith, Michael C. Goetz, Michael Gwynn, John Phillips, Richard Vernon, Jenny Laird, Richard Warner, Thomas Heathcote, Charlotte Mitchell, John Stuart, Bernard Archard; ***D:*** Wolf Rilla; ***W:*** Wolf Rilla, Stirling Silliphant, George Harley; ***C:*** Geoffrey Faithfull. **VHS, LV**

Violette

The trial of Violette Noziere was among the most notorious in French legal history. On August 23, 1934, 19-year-old Violette poisoned her father's coffee with 20 tablets of Veronal. After she gave her mother six tablets, she took a nap until two the following morning, turned on the gas stove, stole 1,000 francs from her mother and yelled for help, adding that the pipe attached to the stove must have burst. As she had intended, her father died and her mother survived. The police soon discovered what had actually occurred and issued a warrant for Violette. By October 13, less than six weeks later, Violette was condemned to death by guillotine. The story of the homicidal teen intrigued Claude Chabrol, who immortalized her in his 1978 film starring Isabelle Huppert as Violette and Stephane Audran as Madame Noziere, both of whom received well-deserved awards for their performances; each interprets her real-life character with rich detail and a full range of emotion. Because of the notoriety of the case, we know what's going to happen—what we don't know is why. Violette lives with her strict parents in a small bourgeoisie apartment. It is so tiny that we wonder why they didn't rub each other's nerves raw many years before. Violette has evolved into a subtle manipulator, with the coolest lying technique you'll ever see. Monsieur Noziere (Jean Carmet) appears to be a harmless, ineffectual man and quite fond of both Violette and his wife. As we watch them go through their domestic routines, we wonder why a 19-year-old woman is still so involved with her parents. We've seen her turning tricks by day—why doesn't she move out? Although the motive for Violette's crime is suggested in broad brush strokes, Chabrol reveals the facts in flashes. The most significant of all the facts is revealed in one raised veil and a single line exchange, so pay attention and stick with this one until the very end. It's worth it! ***AKA:*** Violette Noziere. 🦴🦴🦴

1978 (R) 122m/C *FR* Isabelle Huppert, Stephane Audran, Jean Carmet, Jean-Francoise Garreaud, Bernadette LaFont; ***D:*** Claude Chabrol; ***W:*** Odile Barski, Frederic Grendel; ***C:*** Jean Rabier; ***M:*** Pierre Jansen. Cannes Film Festival '78: Best Actress (Huppert); Cesar Awards '79: Best Supporting Actress (Audran). **VHS**

A Virgin Named Mary

A Virgin Named Mary is an effective and amusing religious satire by Sergio Nasca, who also made 1974's *The Profiteer.* The title says it all, with the contemporary twist that those who believe in the Virgin Birth the most are the village atheists. ***AKA:*** Virgine, E Di Nome Maria. 🦴🦴½

1975 102m/C *IT* Turi Ferro, Andrea Ferreol, Cinzia de Carolis, Renato Pinciroli, Clelia Matania, Leopoldo Trieste, Tino Carraro, Marino Mase, Jean Louis, Sandra Dori; ***D:*** Sergio Nasca; ***W:*** Sergio Nasca; ***C:*** Giuseppe Acquari; ***M:*** Santa Maria Romitelli.

Vortex

Punk/film noir style in which a female private eye becomes immersed in corporate paranoia and political corruption. Its soundtrack, by cast members Lydia Lunch and Adele Bertei, is one of my all-time favorites. Co-scripter and co-director Beth B later scripted and directed 1993's *Two Small Bodies* starring Fred Ward and Suzy Amis, which was just fair, in spite of that cast. 🦴½

1981 87m/C Lydia Lunch, James Russo, Bill Rice, Richard France, Ann Magnuson, Haoui Montaug, Adele Bertei, Bill Landis; ***D:*** Scott B, Beth B; ***W:*** Scott B, Beth B; ***M:*** Lydia Lunch, Adele Bertei. **VHS**

Voyage of the Damned

This extremely sad film is based on one of the most disgraceful episodes of World War II. In 1939, the S.S. *St. Louis,* a ship full of Jewish refugees, left Germany for asylum in Cuba. When they reached their destination, they were not allowed to disembark. Refugee organizations tried to intercede on their behalf, but no country would permit them to land, including the United States. Many passengers, refusing to return to Germany, discussed mass suicide by jumping into the sea, before a compromise was reached in which they would sail to a European harbor and be assigned to refugee camps throughout the continent. Six hundred of the nine hundred passengers faced death in concentration camps and the three hundred who were spared owed their fate to the most arbitrary of bureaucratic decisions. Stuart Rosenberg's film, based on the novel by Gordon Thomas and Max Morgan-Witts, deals with the passage itself and the growing horror of the passengers as they come to realize that their journey is meant to be Germany's example to the world that no one really cared about the plight of Jewish refugees. It turned out to be a chillingly effective example, regretfully not fully understandable until long after the war was over. The top-billed Faye Dunaway gives her usual high-strung performance as Denise Kreisler, with the great Oskar Werner as her faithless husband Dr. Egon Kreisler and Max von Sydow handling the complex role of Captain Gustav Schroeder. But the heart of the tragedy is most eloquently conveyed by the doomed lovers Max Gunther and Anna Rosen. What starts out as an innocent shipboard romance transforms them both into anguished symbols of the passage. Given more time, they might have married and had a family or broken up and married others and had families. But there is no more time for the couple, sensitively played by Malcolm McDowell and Lynne Frederick. Also worth noting in the cast are Sam Wanamaker and Lee Grant as Carl and Lili, Anna's par-

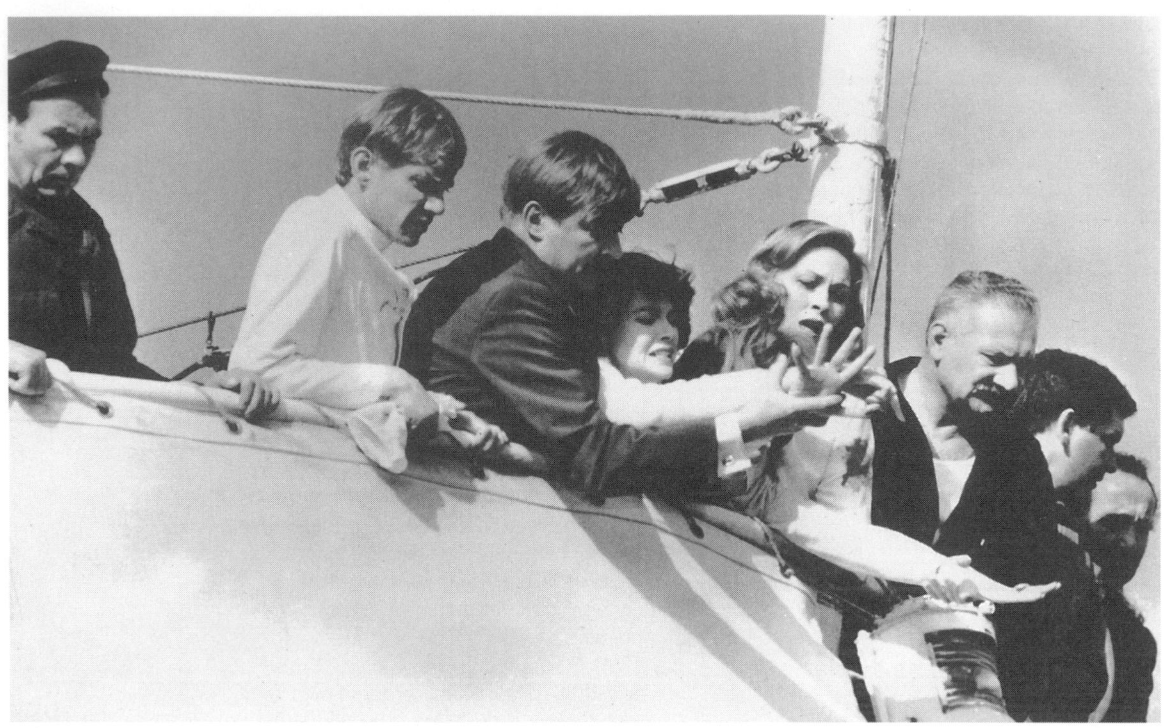

Malcolm McDowell, Oskar Werner, Lynne Frederick, and Faye Dunaway on the *Voyage of the Damned.*
Associated General; courtesy of the Kobal Collection

ents, and a haunted and rather gaunt Jonathan Pryce in his first theatrical feature as Joseph Manasse. Katharine Ross plays a smallish role as a beautiful courtesan who tries to buy freedom for her parents (Nehemiah Persoff and Maria Schell are the improbably cast pair.) 𝄢𝄢𝄢

1976 (G) 155m/C *GB* Faye Dunaway, Max von Sydow, Oskar Werner, Malcolm McDowell, Orson Welles, James Mason, Lee Grant, Katharine Ross, Ben Gazzara, Lynne Frederick, Wendy Hiller, Jose Ferrer, Luther Adler, Sam Wanamaker, Denholm Elliott, Nehemiah Persoff, Julie Harris, Maria Schell, Jonathan Pryce, Janet Suzman, Helmut Griem, Michael Constantine, Victor Spinetti; ***D:*** Stuart Rosenberg; ***W:*** Steve Shagan, David Butler; ***C:*** Billy Williams; ***M:*** Lalo Schifrin. Golden Globe Awards '77: Best Supporting Actress (Ross); Nominations: Academy Awards '76: Best Adapted Screenplay, Best Supporting Actress (Grant), Best Original Score. **VHS**

Waiting for Guffman

Although Christopher Guest and Eugene Levy receive screenwriting credit for *Waiting for Guffman,* cast member Fred Willard says in interviews that the actors were given the outline of each sequence and that all the dialogue was improvised. Believe it or don't! (Who can ever tell whether Fred Willard is kidding or not?) Even though Guest and wife Jamie Lee Curtis are now Lord and Lady Haden-Guest, he really nails what it's like to do an All-American small town show. I remember one nameless town where three local girls made a small splash lip-synching a Broadway show tune and danged if it didn't go to their heads. Corky St. Claire (Guest) USED to live and work in New York theatre (he says), and a real Broadway producer is coming to see *Red, White, and Blaine,* his amateur extravaganza. The stars are Ron and Sheila Albertson (Willard and Catherine O'Hara), dentist Allan Pearl (Levy), and Libby Mae Brown (Parkey Posey) from the local Dairy Queen. When Corky receives the note from the Broadway producer, he does let it go to his head and becomes full of himself, even though the actors are totally dependent on him! The Blaine town council (annual Blaine budget: $15,000) refuses to give Corky $100,000 to produce the show and he goes on a one-day strike! Et cetera! Since the satire here is more affectionate than condescending, *Waiting for Guffman* improves on repeat viewings; I've seen it three times. (See *The Remains of the Day* review.)

1996 (R) 84m/C Christopher Guest, Eugene Levy, Catherine O'Hara, Parker Posey, Fred Willard, Lewis Arquette, Matt Keeslar, Paul Dooley, Paul Benedict, Bob Balaban, Larry Miller, Brian Doyle-Murray; ***D:*** Christopher Guest; ***W:*** Christopher Guest, Eugene Levy; ***C:*** Roberto Schaefer; ***M:*** Michael McKean, Harry Shearer, Christopher Guest. Nominations: Independent Spirit Awards '98: Best Actor (Guest), Best Film, Best Screenplay. **VHS, Closed Caption**

Waiting for the Moon

Were Linda Hunt and Andrew Lloyd Webber separated at birth? Just curious. Hunt is Alice B. Toklas and Linda Bassett is writer Gertrude Stein (1874–1946) in this dreary American Playhouse telecast about their lives which inexplicably won the Grand Jury Prize at 1987's Sundance Film Festival. Try watching it on PBS sometime: zzzzzz.... **woof!**

1987 (PG) 88m/C Linda Hunt, Linda Bassett, Andrew McCarthy, Bruce McGill, Jacques Boudet, Bernadette LaFont; ***D:*** Jill Godmilow; ***W:*** Mark Magill; ***C:*** Andre Neau. Sundance Film Festival '87: Grand Jury Prize. **VHS, Closed Caption**

Walk on the Wild Side

The BBC has always been fascinated by American pop iconography, and *Walk on the Wild Side* might easily qualify to be a segment on A&E's *Biography* series. This portrait of the drag queens in Andy Warhol's factory is chockful of clips about what went wrong and when and why. Many of Warhol's superstars are no longer around; did his films provide valuable documentation for losers who would have died anyway, without leaving a trace, or was there something about the starmaking process itself that sped up their destruction? Don't look for the answers here, although Joe Dallesandro's appearance at 45 lends validity to Howard Hawks' assertion that real stars walk on the set thinking that everyone wants to lay them. Time has definitely been unkind to *Trash*'s once baby-faced star.

1993 40m/C *GB* ***D:*** James Marsh.

Christopher Guest as Corky St. Clair in *Waiting for Guffman.* Castle Rock Entertainment; courtesy of the Kobal Collection

Walking and Talking

One provincial critic recently expressed enormous concern for the career of Anne Heche, now that everyone knows that she and Ellen DeGeneres are an item; will audiences be able to accept a gay woman in a straight role? Well, why not? We've been accepting gay actors and actresses in straight roles since the movies began, the only difference is that the gossip and whispers have been replaced with dialogue and

They changed the way campaigns are won.

—Tagline from the movie *The War Room.*

information. Anyway, the answer is, yeah, sure. If you caught *Walking and Talking* in theatres and saw Heche doing an absolutely credible job as a young woman in love, her performance hasn't changed since the video release. *Walking and Talking* is a sharp and funny look at the friendship of two women as they adjust to new men and new interests in their lives. It also shows what ought to be the very first etiquette guideline about what NOT to leave on a best friend's answering machine! And then there is a well-observed vignette on the pointless nature of obsession: Amelia (Catherine Keener) finds herself following a guy around when she'd felt nothing for him prior to their one-night stand. She needs to know why she was frozen out more than she needs him, although the distinction escapes her during her dogged pursuit of this virtual stranger. Laura (Heche) has her share of self doubts masquerading as crises; she focuses on her boyfriend Frank's (Todd Field) mole until it takes on gigantic dimensions and she wakes up screaming bloody murder in the middle of the night. She gets a mild crush on another guy after a casual meeting. Nicole Holofcener's quirky study of how friendships evolve over time feels authentic; contrast the one-dimensional role Liev Schreiber has in Greg Mottola's *Daytrippers* with the fleshed-out character he has as Andrew here. *Walking and Talking* is a small yet altogether sparkling jewel of a movie.

1996 (R) 86m/C Anne Heche, Catherine Keener, Liev Schreiber, Todd Field, Kevin Corrigan, Randall Batinkoff, Joseph Siravo, Vinny Pastore, Lynn Cohen, Andrew Holofcener; ***D:*** Nicole Holofcener; ***W:*** Nicole Holofcener; ***C:*** Michael Spiller; ***M:*** Billy Bragg. Nominations: Independent Spirit Awards '97: Best Actress (Keener), Best Supporting Actor (Corrigan). **VHS, LV, Closed Caption**

Wanda

It is easy for us to see the humanity in characters who DO things in their lives, who show subtle acts of courage, who make small gestures of kindness. But what about a character who is completely passive, who lets her life and her family drift away from her? Welcome to the world of Wanda, whom we first see on the couch of her sister and brother-in-law, sleepily getting ready for what turns out to be a custody hearing for her children. She arrives late to court and puts up no resistance to her husband's demand for custody, saying that the kids would be better off with him. She has a one-night stand in a motel with a traveling salesman who tries to leave without her. Later, while using the bathroom in a bar, she encounters Mr. Dennis (Michael Higgins, then 48) the most inept thief imaginable. Wanda hooks up with him, sleeps with him, and grudgingly accompanies him on jobs. Later, she wanders off by herself and, in one solitary struggle for self preservation, Wanda fights off a rapist in a car. We last see her sitting alone in a bar. Aside from a few words of dialogue here and there ("Don't you like onions? I do"), Wanda doesn't have a whole lot to say for herself, nor does the uptight Mr. Dennis, except to bark orders at her. Yet the story is told simply and well, without the intrusions of stylish flourishes or cinematic razzle dazzle. It is hard to imagine how anyone could BE Wanda, but it's clear that she doesn't spend much time wondering about that. *Wanda* won the International Critic's Prize at the Venice Film Festival in 1971, and director Barbara Loden (1932–80), who played Wanda, appeared on *The Mike Douglas Show* in 1972 as the guest of Yoko Ono and John Lennon. Aside from two supporting roles in *Wild River* and *Splendor in the Grass* and some stills of her Tony-winning performance in *After the Fall*, *Wanda* and the one television appearance are all that survive of stage director Loden's legacy to the world. Yet she had an influence on independent filmmakers who followed her. She made up her own rules as she went along and *Wanda*'s unself-conscious realism continues to startle audiences today. It IS a tough film to find; I finally saw it on a PAL transfer from a video issued by the British Film Institute. Good luck tracking it down, though. *Wanda* is well worth watching.

1970 (PG) 100m/C Barbara Loden, Michael Higgins, Dorothy Shupenes, Peter Shupenes, Jerome Their, Marian Their, Rotell Anthony; ***D:*** Barbara Loden; ***W:*** Barbara Loden; ***C:*** Nicholas T. Proferes.

The War Room

The Clinton team had been in the White House for less than a year when *The War Room* was released, but in many ways, the campaign and election of 1992 seemed incredibly far away, even then. P. F. Bentley's striking photographs for his book on the campaign, *Portrait of Victory,* were shot entirely in black and white, and these timeless yet pleasantly dated images are the ones we remember best. *The War Room,* the 1993 documentary by D.A. Pennebaker and Chris Hegedus, is further dated since Clinton's campaign team gave the press such generous access to behind-the-scenes strategy-making that we somehow took for granted how unique that was. In this film, the Clintons and Gores are seen largely through news footage, and Pennebaker and Hegedus focus instead on the efforts of James Carville and George Stephanopoulos to orchestrate the attack on George Bush. There are the inevitable segues: a *Star Magazine* representative stands between the now-famous splashy tabloid cover and Gennifer Flowers, trying vainly to pretend that the circus is a dignified press conference. In fact, hardly anything is an accident in a political campaign; the press reports every "disclosure" in the form of late-breaking news, as if all the campaign teams didn't repeatedly feed these so-called leaks until they catch fire. Sometimes, they never do. Carville tried to make something out of a report on Portuguese television that Bush-Quayle campaign materials were printed south of the border with cheap labor. But the story couldn't be nailed down with enough corroborative detail, and eventually it fizzled. Carville was luckier with his efforts to add key phrases to a major campaign speech. Meanwhile, Mary Matalin defended her candidate, George Bush, and 21st century audiences might wish that the personal relationship between Carville and Matalin had been made a little more clear. (How many details do we remember about individual members of past campaign teams, anyway?) As election day approached, both Carville and Stephanopoulos resorted to eerie gallows humor, presumably to stave off last-minute doubts and superstitions. The July 1993 suicide of longtime Clinton associate Vince Foster revealed a dark side to the political landscape that we didn't see in the glory days of November 1992. *The War Room* supplies counterpoint to the old myth of smoke-filled rooms behind closed doors, while fueling a new myth about the folksy value of apparent candor; clearly, all the candor in the world won't blunt the brutality of contemporary politics. 🦴🦴🦴

1993 (PG) 93m/C *D:* Chris Hegedus, D.A. Pennebaker; ***C:*** D.A. Pennebaker, Kevin Rafferty. National Board of Review Awards '93: Best Feature Documentary; Nominations: Academy Awards '93: Best Feature Documentary. **VHS, LV, Closed Caption, DVD**

Warm Nights on a Slow-Moving Train

Wendy Hughes is among the most gifted actresses in the world today, yet her last two Australian films, *Shadows of the Peacock* and *Warm Nights on a Slow-Moving Train,* are romantic fluff pieces in which travel represent sexual fulfillment. I can actually see very little difference between *Warm Nights* and the Sigourney Weaver flop *Half Moon Street.* In both films, we are asked to believe that intelligent, well-educated women can only achieve a fair rate of exchange for their work if they moonlight as hookers. For all their independent chatter, they make stupid mistakes, act against their stated principles in pursuit of sexual highs, and live out every male fantasy in the book. Two questions: Do you have any trouble with the idea that a woman would willingly become a political assassin at the request of a man with terrific staying power she's bedded only twice? Would this concept seem even more ridiculous if a man agreed to kill a stranger just because a great two-night stand asked him to do it? In a popular film like *Body Heat,* William Hurt is seen as a sexually obsessed schmuck for doing everything femme fatale Kathleen Turner commands. In *Warm Nights,* Wendy Hughes is just another woman in love. 🦴🦴

The Hound Salutes:

D(ONN) A(LAN) PENNEBAKER AND CHRIS HEGEDUS

Directors, *The War Room*

D.A. Pennebaker: "James Carville is an overwhelming figure. He looks like he's about to explode, like a detonated hand grenade. He's not without a certain irreverence for the normal laws that bind us together as a society. On the other hand, George Stephanopoulos is very calm. As things get wilder and wilder around him, he tends to get calmer and calmer; but when he's speaking at his lowest, you know you'd better be careful and mind your ways. They're like a whole group of people, even though there's only two of them. James Carville really is the unauthorized biography of the 1992 campaign. If you're going to go into theatres with a film, it had better be entertaining, whatever that means. What's entertaining to Albert Einstein is probably not going to entertain me much, but for him it's the same thing. It's got to be something he goes to willingly and enjoys. It isn't an instruction, it isn't homework, and it's something that he wants to do. When you're in the business, I think that you have to consider that, so that if frills make it more entertaining, you have to consider putting frills on it. Our frills are a little different from those of other documentary filmmakers. We don't make the same films they do. We decorated *The War Room* a little bit. We put fireworks at the beginning. We can have fun, too. You really need to enjoy what you do, which means you can't get used to it. You want to surprise yourself, too, or you get moldy."

Chris Hegedus: "Mary Matalan calls James Carville 'serpent head.' The War Room is James Carville's creation and it's a perfect setting for him, because he loves to get feedback for all of his ideas. He functions almost like a performance artist in that room. The War Room was basically

1987 (R) 90m/C *AU* Wendy Hughes, Colin Friels, Norman Kaye, John Clayton, Peter Whitford; ***D:*** Bob Ellis; ***W:*** Bob Ellis, Denny Lawrence; ***C:*** Yuri Sokol. **VHS, LV**

The Wash

The Wash is a wise, gentle film about the death of love and its rebirth. Nobu McCarthy portrays a woman who is leaving her husband after 40 years, yet who continues to care about him even though she is no longer in love with him. After watching film after film in which the Japanese male is portrayed as cold and unfeeling and wondering how he could stand such loneliness, viewers finally have an opportunity to see and hear Asian-American writer Philip Kan Kotanda expose the truth about such characters: maybe they cannot stand it any more than the women who love them. The Oscar-nominated actor Mako does a masterful job of revealing all the underlying cracks in the armor. Sab Shimono plays a very different type of man, the one Nobu's character has been yearning for all her life. When she is finally confronted with his kindness and sensitivity, all the old habits that bind her to her husband no longer mean anything. It is rare for a film to wring such extraordinary mileage out of very simple truths about relationships, but Philip Kan Kotanda is a

'Strategy Central' for the 1992 campaign. It was an idea that James Carville and George Stephanopoulos went to Bill and Hillary Clinton with after all the primaries. They said they would like to continue in Little Rock with a headquarters that had a strategy room where they could instantly respond to anything that came up during the 1992 campaign. It should have all the latest technology and be something that goes 24 hours a day so they could react to the news that now is able to go for 24 hours a day. It isn't like two newspapers being put out anymore. Hillary Clinton said, 'Great! I think it's a fabulous idea. We should do it—but if we're going to do it, I think we should call it the War Room, because we want to get beyond the wimpy Democratic idea to show that we have the power to fight back in the same way as the Republicans have had the image of doing over the past two administrations.' At the very end of our film, the night before and election night, Ted Koppel arrived in the War Room, and before that no one was ever allowed in the War Room. We always had little tags on us that said 'Guests,' rather than 'Press.' So when he came, it was almost like David and Goliath and I was totally upset, because Ted Koppel had money to be everywhere. He had a crew on the plane with Bill Clinton, he was in the War Room with us, he was in the room downstairs, and it seemed like ABC was everywhere. And I thought, 'Here we've got to the very end of our story and it's totally co-opted.' But at the same time, the film that they were trying to do was really a very different film because they're making a television program that's based around the personality of Ted Koppel as much as it was about the 1992 campaign. We got a little fix of doing something with frills one summer when we did a music video with a band called Soul Asylum for a compilation album for Victoria Williams. And we did a little pun on 1967's *Don't Look Back* on the sign scene that everybody loves to pun themselves. It was quite fun to do; we did a very fancy blue screen effect in it. I edited it on a computer editing system and we got to play with all the other toys."

D.A. PENNEBAKER and CHRIS HEGEDUS also directed *Depeche Mode 101, The Music Tells You, Keine Zeit,* and *Moon over Broadway.*

writer with a unique ability to dig beneath rituals and structures. Deeply enhanced by Michael Toshiyuki Uno's intimate direction, *The Wash* provides a memorable and unusual film experience.

1988 94m/C Mako, Nobu McCarthy, Sab Shimono; ***D:*** Michael Toshiyuki Uno; ***W:*** Philip Kan Kotanda; ***C:*** Walt Lloyd. **VHS, LV**

The Waterdance

Neal Jimenez, who was paralyzed in a 1984 accident, wrote and co-directed *The Waterdance,* an exceptional film about the trials and tribulations of adjusting to paralysis. Eric Stoltz is wisely cast as Joel, the central character, and Helen Hunt delivers her usual beautifully understated performance as his girlfriend Anna. Wesley Snipes is a flamboyant scene stealer as Ray, who becomes the unlikely friend of Bloss, the bitter white hiker played by William Forsythe. Realistic and funny details make *The Waterdance* a fine video pick. Unaccountably, there were no long lines at the box office for this winning film, co-directed by Michael Steinberg.

1991 (R) 106m/C Eric Stoltz, Wesley Snipes, William Forsythe, Helen Hunt, Elizabeth Pena, Grace Zabriskie; ***D:*** Neal Jimenez, Michael Steinberg; ***W:*** Neal Jimenez; ***C:*** Mark Plummer; ***M:*** Michael Con-

The Hound Salutes:
NOBU MCCARTHY
Actress, *The Wash*

I think my character in *The Wash* is the person with the contradictions. I think all of us are, in many different ways. We seem to seek freedom, but we are the ones blocking our own freedom. For my character to wash her husband's [Mako] laundry is one thing, but I don't think she is really doing his wash for his sake. She is doing his wash for herself, to still her feelings of guilt and indecision for lingering 40 years in her marriage. Over the last generation, the separation of older Asian-American couples is becoming very apparent, I think. That has a lot to do with changes in our society and a lot to do with Asian women's awareness of being Americans. It might have taken my character at least 30 of the 40 years of her marriage to consider those changes.

"The brilliance of Philip Kan Kotanda's screenplay is that through the characters played by Mako and Sab Shimono, he shows the two extreme aspects of the Asian-American male. The man played by Sab Shimono signifies the integrated Asian American that my character really wants. I began my career as a model in a very early stage of my life, at 20, and I always felt that there must be something

vertino. Independent Spirit Awards '93: Best First Feature, Best Screenplay; Sundance Film Festival '92: Best Screenplay, Audience Award. **VHS, LV, Closed Caption**

Way Down East

Way Down East was severely dated when D.W. Griffith spent the extravagant sum of $175,000 for the rights to turn it into a movie in 1920. Its star, Lillian Gish, was not the only one who wondered about the wisdom of acquiring a creaky piece of Americana which had been familiar to audiences since 1898. Clearly, Griffith realized that the tale of a country girl led astray by a rich adventurer had visceral appeal, and indeed it had and still does, even today. Viewers from other cultures wondered why the fragile Miss Lillian (or even a less virtuous heroine) had to be cast out into the snow by so-called good Christians. And contemporary viewers, realizing the physical dangers Griffith demanded from his cast and crew during a painfully realistic blizzard sequence, still wonder why anyone would put up with such sacrifices for the sake of a movie. But *Way Down East,* with all its flaws, is absolutely spellbinding, especially when Lillian Gish is onscreen. In the course of the story, she is transformed from a gauche poor relation, to an eager young bride, to a grief-stricken mother, to a hard-working family retainer. Like Hester Prynne (a role Miss Gish would later play), this discarded woman grows in strength and character by dealing directly with her limited lot in life, which is far more than can be said for those who ill-treat her. There is nice work by the ensemble players, too, notably the impossibly beautiful Richard Barthelmess as a farm boy who worships Miss Lillian from afar, but it is Gish's and Griffith's triumph all the way. An added bonus on some video transfers is a glistening toned and tinted 35mm print, plus a lovely score, personally approved by Griffith. 🦴🦴🦴🦴

1920 107m/B Lillian Gish, Richard Barthelmess, Lowell Sherman, Creighton Hale, Burr McIntosh, Kate Bruce, Florence Short; ***D:*** D.W. Griffith; ***W:***

more to my life than beauty that lies perched on the edge. Through my life, I've found that a true sense of beauty comes from within. When I was a teenaged actress, I really didn't know how stereotypical my roles were. I'd just come from Japan, and I was chosen by Paramount Studios in Hollywood and I starred in one film after another. No one was even making an issue about typecasting then, simply because there was no such thing as consciousness about Asian-American stereotypes on film. I thought that was the way Hollywood looked at us, so that was the way they wanted me to look at and present an Asian-American woman. At the same time, I'd just come from Japan, so I was, in a very true sense, a stereotypical woman in certain ways, now that I look back. I didn't speak English, I only knew Japanese culture, I only knew how to act as a Japanese woman in a very stereotypical way. When I played those early roles, I didn't add to the stereotype, I just played myself as I was then. I have no regrets, because I understand how I learned from that point to now."

NOBU MCCARTHY played opposite Jerry Lewis in 1956's *The Geisha Boy* and also appeared in 1986's *The Karate Kid: Part 2* and 1990's *Pacific Heights.* She co-starred with Richard Long in 1959's *Tokyo After Dark,* and was in Fox's *Five Gates to Hell* the same year, followed by Fox's *Wake Me When It's Over* in 1960 and MGM's *Two Loves* in 1961. She participated in the documentary *Slaying the Dragon* along with James Shigeta, her co-star from the 1960 Jack Lord western *Walk Like a Dragon.*

D.W. Griffith, Joseph R. Grismer; ***C:*** Billy Bitzer, Hendrik Sartov. **VHS, LV, DVD**

The Wedding Banquet

The Wedding Banquet is a charade for the benefit of Wai-Tung's parents. He's really gay and living happily with Simon. When tenant Wei-wei (May Chin) suggests marriage to Wai-Tung (Winston Chao) so she can get a green card, he says sure and so does Simon (Mitchell Lichtenstein). And then Wai-Tung's parents (Sihung Lung and Ah-Leh Gua as Mr. and Mrs. Gao) insist on attending the wedding. Ang Lee *(Pushing Hands, Eat Drink Man Woman)* works miracles with a tiny budget; *The Wedding Banquet* is a warm, funny flick, made two years before Lee's Oscar nomination as Best Director for *Sense and Sensibility.* ***AKA:*** Xiyan; Hsi Yen. 🦴🦴🦴

1993 (R) 111m/C *TW* Winston Chao, May Chin, Mitchell Lichtenstein, Sihung Lung, Ah-Leh Gua, Michael Gaston, Jeffrey Howard; ***D:*** Ang Lee; ***W:*** Ang Lee, Neil Peng, James Schamus; ***C:*** Jong Lin. Nominations: Academy Awards '93: Best Foreign Film; Golden Globe Awards '94: Best Foreign Film; Independent Spirit Awards '94: Best Actor (Lichtenstein), Best Actress (Chin), Best Director (Lee), Best Film, Best Screenplay, Best Supporting Actress (Gua). **VHS, LV, Closed Caption**

Welcome to the Dollhouse

This hilarious view of junior high as seen by 11-year-old Dawn Wiener is Todd Solondz' second film. (His first, 1989's *Fear, Anxiety and Depression* starring himself and Stanley Tucci, was generally panned for being unduly influenced by Woody Allen.) So we don't need to concern ourselves here with the Second Film Syndrome experienced by hot (overpraised) newcomers. Solondz' identification with the plight of his young heroine is total and so is ours. Dawn wears glasses and hair balls and is outshone in every way by her nauseatingly precious little sister, who whirls around in a ballerina costume. When Dawn refuses to apologize to the

sister for something or other, her parents order her to remain at the table until she does. The soundtrack goes into a rebellious riff; hours later, Dawn is still sitting there. Then Dawn gets a crush on one of her older brother's no-good study partners (we know he's no good, because we catch him stealing when he comes to the house), and her life is transformed. She grills a former girlfriend of this guy, and when she discovers that they only did things to each other with their fingers, Dawn stares at her own fingers in wonder. It's an 11-year-old moment, something an older, superficially stunning adolescent would never be able to carry off. Dawn's world is dark, miserable, and seemingly endless. We know it isn't, but she doesn't, and Todd Solondz keeps the focus on Dawn's perceptions of events, where it belongs. It is this innocence of the vast future beyond junior high school that distinguishes *Welcome to the Dollhouse* from other coming-of-age stories about children. What 11-year old girl is blessed with ironic detachment, anyway? 𝒥𝒥𝒥𝒥

1995 (R) 87m/C Heather Matarazzo, Brendan Sexton III, Daria Kalinina, Matthew Faber, Angela Pietropinto, Eric Mabius; ***D:*** Todd Solondz; ***W:*** Todd Solondz; ***C:*** Randy Drummond; ***M:*** Jill Wisoff. Independent Spirit Awards '97: Debut Performance (Matarazzo); Sundance Film Festival '96: Grand Jury Prize; Nominations: Independent Spirit Awards '97: Best Director (Solondz), Best Film, Best Supporting Actor (Faber), Debut Performance (Sexton). **VHS, LV, Closed Caption**

Went to Coney Island on a Mission from God...Be Back by Five

The cast is good, but the story leads nowhere. The narrative goes back and forth and forth and back, in quest of a friend (Rafael Baez as Richie) and the meaning of the friendship he shared with the two men who are looking for him (Jon Cryer as Daniel and Rick Stear as Stan). The friends encounter distractions along the way, but both the distractions and the back story are like road scenery glimpsed from a car window. The events mean something to the people who are living them, but nothing to the strangers who observe them. *Went to Coney Island* might have meant more if the incidents in the screenplay by Cryer and Richard Schenkman had been selected with greater care and developed with more oomph. Cryer and Schenkman, who previously collaborated on *The Pompatus of Love,* co-produced the film, which played at San Francisco's Indie Fest in 1999. 𝒥𝒥

1998 94m/C Jon Cryer, Rick Stear, Rafael Baez, Ione Skye, Frank Whaley, Peter Gerety, Akili Prince, Aesha Waks, Dominic Chianese; ***D:*** Richard Schenkman; ***W:*** Richard Schenkman, Jon Cryer; ***C:*** Adam Beekman; ***M:*** Midge Ure.

Wes Craven's New Nightmare

Wes Craven's New Nightmare is a work of imagination and wit from the man who's been scaring us for over 25 years. In this film, he's written nice roles for himself and three participants in 1984's *The Nightmare on Elm Street*—Heather Langencamp, Robert Englund, and John Saxon, plus producers Marianne Maddalena, Robert Shaye, and Sara Risher. They all play themselves, caught up in a new nightmare that's much worse than Freddy Krueger circa 1984. Heather, now a wife and mom, doesn't want to make another horror movie, but bad things start happening, and she's dragged into another bout with Freddy to save her son Dylan (Miko Hughes) and herself. Hughes is a good little actor, and Tracy Middendorf is wonderfully effective as Julie the babysitter. But it's Langencamp's show and she holds our interest and attention for all 112 minutes of this enthralling yarn. In addition to the horrific aspects of the plot, Craven does a clever job scraping past our jaded response to cinematic terrors and jabbing at a much more basic source of fear. 𝒥𝒥𝒥

1994 (R) 112m/C Heather Langenkamp, Robert Englund, Miko Hughes, David Newsom, Tracy Middendorf, Fran Bennett, John Saxon, Wes Craven, Robert Shaye, Sara Risher, Marianne Maddalena; ***D:*** Wes Craven; ***W:*** Wes Craven; ***C:*** Mark Irwin; ***M:*** J. Peter Robinson. Nominations: Independent Spirit Awards '95: Best Film. **VHS, LV, Closed Caption**

Heather Matarazzo as Dawn Wiener in *Welcome to the Dollhouse.* Sony Pictures Classics; courtesy of the Kobal Collection

The Hound Salutes:
LILLIAN GISH
(1893–1993)

When Mary Pickford, then Queen of the Biograph lot, first saw Lillian Gish, she observed that the delicate young actress was "not long for this world." Indeed, Miss Gish always looked as if she could be carried away by the mildest breeze. If you compared her to the one-time matinee idol Harold Lockwood during the 1918 influenza epidemic, for example, you would have thought that the hale and hearty Lockwood had a much better chance of survival than the deceptively fragile Miss Gish. But although both were ravaged during the epidemic, Lillian Gish survived virtually every major star of the silent era, while few today remember Lockwood over 80 years after his death.

During Miss Gish's long movie career (1912–87), she specialized in playing gentle heroines who were tougher than they looked. She ignited a gang war in 1912's *Musketeers of Pig Alley* and resisted the attentions of brawny gang leader Elmer Booth, who shrugged off his disappointment with such anti-heroic grace that the young James Cagney must surely have taken note and transformed the style into his very own nearly 20 years later. It was perhaps the only time that Miss Gish was to be upstaged by a fellow player.

Her decade-long association with D.W. Griffith continued through his two early epics *Birth of a Nation* and *Intolerance* and she became a life-long defender of Griffith when audiences of later eras attacked her mentor as racist, as a sentimentalist, and as an old-school pioneer unable to adjust to a rapidly changing industry. But Miss Gish could and did adjust to Hollywood, the

The Whales of August

Lindsay Anderson's *The Whales of August* features one luminous piece of work by Miss Lillian Gish, then in her 95th year, and four excellent performances by Bette Davis, then 79, Harry Carey Jr., 66, and Vincent Price and Ann Sothern, both 78. The script by playwright David Berry is not so hot, with a confusing timeline and a fuzzy psychological grasp of its elderly characters. Berry offers a younger person's view of how older people see life. As two sisters bound by blood, finances, and circumstances, Davis' blind character might well wind up a crabby whiner, but Miss Lillian would not be blamed for giving Sis a good shaking instead of serenely waiting on her hand and foot. Price is so irresistible as a charming scrounge who tries to horn in on this pair that when he makes his graceful exit from the plot with resignation, he takes much of the film's lightness of tone with him. Ann Sothern, too, is seen to good effect as a well-meaning Maine friend. But Miss Lillian, defying every assumption about what a woman in her tenth decade should be, acts rings around all these outstanding pros, drawing every bit of emotion from each line, gesture, and expression, in a subtle yet richly textured portrayal that's as powerful as anything she did on film since her 1912 debut.

1987 91m/C Lillian Gish, Bette Davis, Vincent Price, Ann Sothern, Mary Steenburgen, Harry Carey Jr., Tisha Sterling, Margaret Ladd; ***D:*** Lindsay Ander-

town she wryly referred to as an "emotional Detroit." Under Griffith's direction, she suffered and suffered and suffered in such silent classics as *Broken Blossoms, Orphans of the Storm,* and *Way Down East.* After she broke with Griffith, she made several films for MGM, including two gems with Victor Seastrom, *The Scarlet Letter* and *The Wind.*

When the movies began to talk, Miss Gish's film career faltered, although as a stage-trained actress, there was no real reason why her career had to be limited to just 20 films over a 60-year period. Miss Gish always turned in immaculate, beautifully crafted performances, and, of course, stole every scene she was in; was that why the giants of the sound era were skittish about working with her? She was philosophical about her exalted, yet often underappreciated, position in a so-called art form that was first and foremost a business. How many terrorized children who saw *Night of the Hunter* longed for an angel like Miss Gish to protect them from their tormentors, real or imagined? And when her luminous work in *The Whales of August* was not even recognized with an Academy award nomination, she merely said, "Oh, good. Now I won't have to lose to Cher." She had already lost to Anne Baxter over 40 years earlier, but did receive an honorary Oscar in 1970 as well as the AFI's Life Achievement Award in 1984. The belated honors were a very small way of acknowledging the foremost and certainly most irreplaceable actress of the silent era.

LILLIAN GISH films on video include *Battle of Elderbush Gulch, Judith of Bethulia, Home Sweet Home, Hearts of the World, True Heart Susie, The Greatest Question, The White Sister, Romola, His Double Life, Commandos Strike at Dawn, Duel in the Sun, Portrait of Jennie, The Cobweb, The Unforgiven, Follow Me Boys, The Comedians, A Wedding, Hobson's Choice, Hambone and Hillie, Sweet Liberty, The Adventures of Huckleberry Finn, The Night of the Hunter,* and *The Whales of August.*

son; ***W:*** David Berry; ***C:*** Mike Fash. National Board of Review Awards '87: Best Actress (Gish); Nominations: Academy Awards '87: Best Supporting Actress (Sothern). **VHS, LV, 8mm**

What Happened Was...

Co-workers Jackie and Michael discover that neither is what s/he appears to be on the first date from Hell. Well acted and well observed, but EXCRUCIATINGLY detailed. Not a good video bet on anyone's first date.

1994 (R) 92m/C Tom Noonan, Karen Sillas; ***D:*** Tom Noonan; ***W:*** Tom Noonan; ***C:*** Joe DeSalvo; ***M:*** Lodovico Sorret. Sundance Film Festival '94: Best Screenplay, Grand Jury Prize; Nominations: Independent Spirit Awards '95: Best Actress (Sillas), First Screenplay. **VHS**

When the Cat's Away

Chloe (Garance Clavel) wants to go on a seaside holiday but her gay roommate Michel (Olivier Py) won't accept responsibility for her sweet little black cat Gris-Gris. Madame Renee (Renee Le Calm) agrees to make a home for Gris-Gris while Chloe is away. Chloe returns to every cat lover's nightmare—Madame Renee is in despair! Chloe is lost! The rest of the movie shows Chloe's search for Gris-Gris and her subsequent discovery of her own neighborhood, which she'd known only superficially before Gris-Gris' disappearance. My favorite of all

Garance Clavel in *When the Cat's Away.* Sony Pictures Classics; courtesy of the Kobal Collection

her neighbors is Djamel (Zinedine Soualem) who never stops searching for Gris-Gris, even when it means risking his life on a roof. When teased about it, Djamel cries, which just broke me up. He's so determined and so kind and so vulnerable. Meanwhile, Chloe goes to a club in a nice dress looking for romance, but finding attention only from the nastiest of creeps. Then, Chloe believes she has found a kindred spirit in a drummer and she has a fling with him. (He can't get rid of her fast enough afterwards.) Chloe keeps looking both for Gris-Gris and for a good guy. Cat lovers won't rent this movie unless they know whether Gris-Gris makes it all the way through the picture, so the answer is, as a cat lover, I made it all the way through this delicate flick and I only cried when Djamel cried. ***AKA:*** Chacun Cherche Son Chat. 🦴🦴🦴

1996 (R) 91m/C *FR* Garance Clavel, Zinedine Soualem, Olivier Py, Renee Le Calm, Romain Duris; ***D:*** Cedric Klapisch; ***W:*** Cedric Klapisch; ***C:*** Benoit Delhomme. **VHS**

Where Angels Fear to Tread

Where Angels Fear to Tread was E. M. Forster's first novel and it is filled with all the ambitious flaws of a 26-year-old writer who wants to say something important but doesn't quite know how to say it yet. His subsequent novels, *A Room with a View, Maurice,* and *A Passage to India,* reflected Forster's greater understanding of human nature, but when he wrote *Angels,* he was still struggling to understand people. Charles Sturridge's movie, sticking reverently to the text as it does, is therefore just as flawed as its original source material. *Angels* attempts to show how silly the British are to pre-judge the Italian culture, so we get 112 minutes of assorted twits thinking like fools and behaving like beasts. The wonderful Helen Mirren appears, all too briefly, as a rich widow who marries a broke Italian (Giovanni Guidelli). Judy Davis and Rupert Graves play Mirren's in-laws, who dash off to Italy to bring

Mirren's Italian baby back to England, whether the father likes it or not. Helena Bonham Carter is on hand as a much-interested bystander and is the voice of reason in the film. A lot of melodramatic stuff happens in the film and there are plenty of discussions where people explain themselves and the world around them. 1905 readers probably read *Where Angels Fear to Tread* and hoped for better things from its talented young author. But today's Forster buffs and filmmakers seem to regard every Forster work, even this uneven effort, as a masterpiece. *Where Angels Fear to Tread* will not play well on video, as many of the sequences are darkly lit and hard to see. The soundtrack is also muddy, and some of Forster's elegant language is difficult to hear. That said, the cast, especially Davis and Mirren, is splendid, and you're unlikely to see a more sympathetic portrait of a twit than the one played by Rupert Graves. 🦴🦴

1991 (PG) 112m/C *GB* Rupert Graves, Helena Bonham Carter, Judy Davis, Helen Mirren, Giovanni Guidelli, Barbara Jefford, Thomas Wheatley, Sophie Kullman; ***D:*** Charles Sturridge; ***W:*** Charles Sturridge, Tim Sullivan, Derek Granger; ***C:*** Michael Coulter; ***M:*** Rachel Portman. **VHS, LV, Closed Caption**

Which Way, Por Favor?

Which Way, Por Favor? is an inexpensive travelogue that looks like it was more fun to make than it is to watch. The premise is that American tourists are looking for the meaning of life and who better to give it to them than the Mexican residents of Velapa? If nothing else, it provided the cast members with attractive take-home souvenirs for their video scrapbooks. Shot on video and shown at San Francisco's Indie Fest in 1999. 🦴🦴

1998 107m/C ***D:*** Mick Diener; ***W:*** Mick Diener, Nathaniel Eaton; ***C:*** Mick Diener; ***M:*** Paul Scriver.

The Whistle Blower

The British are fascinated with members of its upper classes who continue to enjoy their positions of privilege while betraying Queen and country as Soviet spies. This obsession has evolved into plays and films like *Another Country* and *Blunt,* and many books, one of which, by John Hale, was released as *The Whistle Blower,* starring Michael Caine in the title role. The most intriguing question, why does a pampered aristocrat turn traitor?, is one that screenwriter Julian Bond does not really try to answer in depth. There is still plenty of meat, however, in this gripping story of an agonized father's attempts to uncover the mystery behind the death of his much-loved son. Espionage is shown as a venomous game, mostly populated by players who neither know nor understand its true rules. As always, Michael Caine is excellent as Frank Jones, the businessman whose unquestioning faith in England is shattered by what he learns about her intelligence agencies. He is surrounded by an outstanding cast. James Fox portrays a chilling agent who euphemizes his deadliest work as "assessing the damage." Nigel Havers, in a slender but memorable role, turns in an appealing performance. Barry Foster's over-the-top style is well suited to his portrait of a man way out of his league. John Gielgud, in a part clearly fashioned after Sir Anthony Blunt, remains a charming puzzle. Intelligence agent Gordon Jackson shares a brief, classy sequence with David Langton. It is stylishly directed, as is the entire movie, by David's son, Simon Langton, in his feature film debut after a long apprenticeship on British television, including *Upstairs, Downstairs.* One character observes that "the secret world" of British intelligence is "beyond the law." It is revealing that the Royal Family serves as the film's framing device; royalty has always been an attractive smokescreen for political shenanigans. As Frank Jones, Michael Caine lends an individual's conscience to the cold-blooded spying activities of today. If innocents are murdered when they stumble onto the truth and their bereaved families are neutralized with charges of insanity when they question the wisdom of such policies, if treacherous courtiers have tea with the Queen while intelligence agencies "assess the damage" they have done, the division between good

Arthur Blakely (Alan Bates), Nan Bostock (Diane Holgate), and Kathy Bostock (Hayley Mills) in *Whistle down the Wind.*
Allied Film Makers/Beaver Films; courtesy of the Kobal Collection

and evil blurs. *The Whistle Blower* makes a penetrating stab at showing who the enemy might really be. ☠☠☠

1987 98m/C *GB* Michael Caine, Nigel Havers, John Gielgud, James Fox, Felicity Dean, Gordon Jackson, Barry Foster, David Langton; ***D:*** Simon Langton; ***W:*** Julian Bond; ***C:*** Fred Tammes; ***M:*** John Scott. **VHS, LV, Closed Caption**

Whistle down the Wind

The big Hayley Mills movie of July 1961, the one that everyone remembers, is *The Parent Trap,* a primal flick for every child of divorce during that era. Mills' contract for six Disney movies was non-exclusive, meaning that she could continue to make small British films like this one. At 15, Mills was too mature for the part of Kathy, a little girl (obviously pre-sexual) who believes that Jesus Christ "Himself" (Alan Bates, then 27, as Arthur Blakey, a homicidal fugitive from justice) has found sanctuary in the family barn. Mills' open face and honest eyes are persuasive, but she really needs the thick coat and bulky scarf she wears throughout the narrative and most of the other children in the cast are half as tall as she is. Nevertheless, Kathy, little sister Nan (Diane Holgate), seven-year-old brother Charlie (Alan Barnes), and nine neighborhood kids are overwhelmed by the prospect of caring for "Him" by fetching provisions and begging for stories. Obligingly, "He" reads His Disciples the tale of *Ruth Lawrence, Air Hostess,* straight out of the newspaper. There's only one way this story can end, naturally; the fascination here rests mainly on the effect Blakey has on the youngsters and vice versa. As the leading child star of the

'60s, Mills wielded even more power in her films than Shirley Temple did in her vehicles of the '30s. In the course of nine movies, Hayley Mills redeemed a homicidal fugitive from justice twice, brought joy to an entire town, reunited her estranged parents, braved danger to find her missing father, saved her insolvent family, tangled with Greek gangsters and a governess who was an ex-convict AND solved a kidnapping case too tough for the FBI! No wonder her fans were let down when her sole plot function in her early adult pictures was to lose her virginity. If the delicate *Whistle down the Wind* yarn was overstretched in 1961, it was too little too late in the summer of 1998 when a musical version opened at London's Aldwych Theatre. For that adaptation, Andrew Lloyd Webber transported the story to the U.S. Bible Belt, circa 1959, only to be greeted with blistering critical reviews. (Filmed on location in Lancashire, produced by Richard Attenborough, and based on the novel by Hayley Mills' mother, Mary Hayley Bell.)

1961 99m/B *GB* Hayley Mills, Bernard Lee, Alan Bates, Norman Bird, Elsie Wagstaff, Diane Holgate, Alan Barnes, Roy Holder, Barry Dean, Diane Clare, Patricia Heneghan; ***D:*** Bryan Forbes; ***W:*** Keith Waterhouse, Willis Hall; ***C:*** Arthur Ibbetson; ***M:*** Malcolm Arnold. **VHS**

White Mischief

White Mischief is a tale of lust and violence in the Happy Valley region of Kenya. It is based on a true story, and what a story it is: in 1940, Sir Henry Delves Broughton, known as Jock, arrived in Kenya with his beautiful wife Diana. At 27, Diana was 30 years younger than her rich new husband, and it took her all of one day in Nairobi to become attracted to jock's friend Lord Erroll, a dashing 39-year-old peer. The meeting led to an affair, a murder, and a mystery, which writer James Fox claims to solve in his book about the seamy side of Kenya's aristocratic night life. The couple who stir up all the fuss are portrayed by Greta Scacchi and Charles Dance, two physically perfect specimens who, oddly enough, have no sexual chemistry between them at all. Their characters share decidedly earthbound passions: she wants sex and money, he wants money and sex. Michael Radford's script also defines them as a deeply stupid pair, completely lacking in imagination or depth. Our interest shifts, therefore, to the lady's aristocratic husband played with understanding and irony by Joss Ackland, a fine character actor. He is the sort of chap who has been denying reality for nearly 60 years and would probably continue to lead a boring, uneventful life were he not forced to confront his true feelings about his young wife's affair with a cad. Facing himself proves catastrophic for all three, although the film's final blood-letting is a melodramatic shuck. In real life, Sir Jock ended his days alone in a Liverpool hotel room with an overdose of medinal. Well, the director obviously wanted to say some something about the self-indulgent and self-destructive aspects of the idle classes. Imagine them lolling around on polo grounds and in orgies and on the beaches while Britishers at home were squaring their shoulders against the blitz! John Hurt, Geraldine Chaplin, and Trevor Howard (1916–88) are in it, too. And yet, except for Sarah Miles' sly performance as perhaps the worst woman in Kenya, Radford's concept of decadence is rather too carefully staged, and his understanding of his female characters is nil. If Radford had told the story with simple economy and psychological precision, his moral concerns would still be apparent and have a far greater impact than they do now. In 1994, Radford directed his finest work to date, *The Postman.*

1988 (R) 108m/C Greta Scacchi, Charles Dance, Joss Ackland, Sarah Miles, John Hurt, Hugh Grant, Geraldine Chaplin, Trevor Howard, Murray Head, Susan Fleetwood, Alan Dobie, Jacqueline Pearce; ***D:*** Michael Radford; ***W:*** Michael Radford; ***C:*** Roger Deakins; ***M:*** George Fenton. **VHS, LV, 8mm**

White Nights

When Maria Schell, then 31, and Marcello Mastroianni, then 34, played Natalia and Mario in *White Nights* in 1957, they were both too mature and worldly to play a pair of innocents. Feodor Dostoevsky's 1848 story, published when he was 27, makes

Why with everybody else—why with every slob...and not with me?

—Tagline from the movie *Who Killed Teddy Bear?*

sense for a girl of 17 and a lonely dreamer of 26 in cold St. Petersburg in the midst of the 30-year-reign of Tsar Nicholas I. For all the visual loveliness of the film, there is no getting around the fact that a beautiful, strong-willed woman of Venice in the reign of Elvis Presley is not going to be intimidated by her blind old grandmother who pins their skirts together to protect her. Nor would she wait an entire year for a man (icily played by Jean Marais) who embraced her once and never once wrote to her after he went away. Visconti tries to tackle the implausibility of his updated script by focusing on Mario's incredulous reaction. But if Natalia is in love with a fantasy, Mario's obsession with her fantasy is an absolute fetish. In her 1986 study of *Fascism in Film,* Marcia Landy suggests that in *Ossessione,* Visconti shows that "romantic aspirations are a source of repression, not liberation," and certainly this is true of *White Nights.* Locked into their romantic dreams, Natalia's and Mario's characters remain childlike and powerless in their efforts to control their destinies. Unfortunately, the results seem forced, contrived, and empty. *White Nights* is enhanced by Giuseppe Rotunno's beautiful camerawork, and by the sincerity of its cast, yet ultimately Visconti's emotional distance from the material limits our participation in his self-conscious fairy tale. ***AKA:*** Le Notti Bianche. 🦴🦴

1957 107m/C *IT FR* Maria Schell, Jean Marais, Marcello Mastroianni, Clara Calamai, Helmut Woudenberg; ***D:*** Luchino Visconti; ***W:*** Luchino Visconti, Suso Cecchi D'Amico; ***C:*** Giuseppe Rotunno; ***M:*** Nino Rota. **VHS**

Who Am I This Time?

I discovered this treasure on a library shelf where you can check out "educational" tapes like this one for a whole week for free! Even Christopher Walken aficionados who follow his every professional move may not know about *Who Am I This Time?* Susan Sarandon is Helene Shaw, who is cast in a local production of *A Streetcar Named Desire* and is immediately attracted to Harry Shaw (Walken), the actor playing Stanley Kowalski. When they play scenes together, she can feel that he is receptive to her interest in him, but without a script, the crushingly shy Harry says nothing, Helene is frustrated, and they get nowhere. Eventually, she is able to find the key that will solve the riddle; he is responsive, and the whole town is ecstatic that Harry has found happiness at last. The splendid direction by Jonathan Demme does full justice to the original source material by Kurt Vonnegut Jr; in one short hour, this gentle tale will creep up on you. It also makes you wonder why Walken, who can play sweeties as deftly as he does psychos, has been cast in so few good guy roles over his long career. 🦴🦴🦴

1982 60m/C Susan Sarandon, Christopher Walken, Robert Ridgely, Mike Bacarella, Aaron Freeman, Caitlin Hart; ***D:*** Jonathan Demme; ***M:*** John Cale. **VHS, LV**

Who Are the DeBolts and Where Did They Get 19 Kids?

I wonder what's happened to Dorothy and Bob DeBolt and their large and enchanting family in the 20-something years since filmmaker John Korty won both an Oscar and an Emmy for making a documentary about their lives in Piedmont, California. Until it won the Oscar and ABC picked it up, television networks shied away from the project. They claimed it was depressing because many of the DeBolt kids are physically disabled war orphans, and Korty made no attempt to conceal how they adjust to the serious problems they face getting around the world. Two of the littlest girls sat next to me at the San Francisco International Film Festival screening, clearly UNdepressed, and giggling in delight at their movie antics. Korty, who won his first Oscar at 23 in 1964 for *Breaking the Habit,* has made some of television's best movies over the years: *The People, Go Ask Alice, Class of '63, The Autobiography of Miss Jane Pittman* (winner of nine Emmies), *Farewell to Manzanar* (an Emmy nominee), *Forever, The Haunting Passion,*

Second Sight, The Ewok Adventure, A Deadly Business, Resting Place (another Emmy nominee), *Baby Girl Scott, They Watch,* and *Redwood Curtain.*

1978 72m/C Sydney Walker; ***D:*** John Korty; ***W:*** John Korty; ***C:*** John Else; ***M:*** Ed Bogas. Academy Awards '77: Best Feature Documentary. **VHS**

Who Done It?

You either love Benny Hill or you don't. If you do, you'll get a kick out of seeing him in his first movie. Hill is Hugo, a mystery buff who reads *Date with Death* when he's supposed to be working at his job at an ice show. He wins money in a contest for amateur detectives and decides to use it to make himself a real private eye. Only in the movies! He gets mixed up in some gobbledygook with spies and scientists and the lovely Belinda Lee as Frankie. Anyone who sees the late comic star on television knows that he has the sexual maturity of Mr. Dick in *David Copperfield,* which is to say ZERO! When we see him with a gorgeous blonde who's much tougher physically than he is, he seems like an overgrown schoolboy who can't believe his luck. I miss Benny Hill (1925–92), whose comic routines are considered too low-brow by everyone but the millions who continue to laugh at his shows on videotape. I'm not putting him in the same artistic league as Charlie Chaplin, but when early film archivists began to think about what to save, Chaplin's flickers were considered by some to be too low-brow for preservation. Luckily, they were saved, anyway. And luckily for Benny Hill buffs and those with fond memories of the Ealing comedies of the '40s and '50s, the silly goofiness of *Who Done It?* has been saved as well.

1956 85m/B *GB* Benny Hill, Belinda Lee, David Kossoff, Ernest Thesiger, Garry Marsh, George Margo, Denis Shaw, Fred Schiller, Jeremy Hawk, Thorley Walters, Philip Stainton, Stratford Johns; ***D:*** Basil Dearden; ***W:*** T.E.B. Clarke; ***C:*** Otto Heller; ***M:*** Philip Green. **VHS, Closed Caption**

Who Killed Teddy Bear?

Surviving pre-code film festivals provide a forcible reminder of just how much we missed onscreen between 1934 and 1969 when the Production Code had a stranglehold on major studio releases. But occasionally, independent filmmakers of "B" movies were able to slip a little something extra into their pictures that sailed clean past the censors. While moral guardians remained fixated on Anita Ekberg's neckline in 1958's *Screaming Mimi,* director Gerd Oswald revealed a straightforward lesbian relationship in an entirely unstressed manner; it was just there. Seven years later, Phoebe Cates' father Joseph turned out an arty, low-budget study of a Peeping Tom called *Who Killed Teddy Bear?* The star was 26-year-old Sal Mineo, on the verge of a ten-year career slide, despite winning two Oscar nominations by the time he was 21. This grim little story is crammed with homoerotic and autoerotic references throughout, but they're grafted onto a traditional boy-stalks-girl plotline. THAT the censors got, and since the outcome satisfied all the Code requirements, they let everything else go. Contemporary viewers should have a field day with this one; most of Mineo's wardrobe consists of snug underwear, skimpy swim briefs or form-fitting tee shirts and skin-tight jeans. He's a shirtless body builder and porno book browser, too. In contrast, the object of his attentions is almost demure. Athletic Juliet Prowse, long past her glory days in Frank Sinatra and Elvis Presley musicals, only gets one dance number with Mineo, but most of the time she's bundled up in nightgowns, bathrobes, god-awful coats, and other terrible fashions and hairstyles of the mid-'60s. (Except she has a full-length mirror in her bedroom reflecting onto the street and she doesn't hang up when she hears heavy breathing on her telephone line.) Cates occasionally strays from the seamy side of obsession with lyrical visual interludes, suggesting the childlike innocence that is destroyed by twisted fantasies. Maybe these are efforts to distract us from the cheaper-than-cheap nightclub where Mineo and Prowse work, as well as from the wretched soundtrack. (They couldn't afford real 1965 chart-toppers, so they hired a couple of guys to

Natasha Richardson, Jim Broadbent, and Mia Farrow in *Widow's Peak.*
Fine Line; courtesy of the Kobal Collection

write some inadequate approximations.) But for blatant marginal subversions of the dying Code, you can't beat *Teddy Bear:* detective Jan Murray listens to recorded confessions of perverts while his real-life daughter Diane Moore tries to sleep in the next room; nightclub owner Elaine Stritch protests too much when Prowse accuses her of a lesbian advance; and then there's the definitely weird relationship Mineo has with his sister. For a catalog of sexual paranoia circa 1965, *Who Killed Teddy Bear?* has it all. Don't miss it if you get the chance to see it! 🦴🦴🦴

1965 91m/B Juliet Prowse, Sal Mineo, Jan Murray, Elaine Stritch, Daniel J. Travanti, Diane Moore; ***D:*** Joseph Cates.

The Whole Wide World

Renee Zellweger and Ann Wedgeworth last worked together in *Love and a.45,* not exactly my favorite movie of 1994. This time, they have a better vehicle for their talents, and the Oscar-worthy Vincent D'Onofrio, one of the outstanding character stars of his generation, gets a rare chance to be front and center for the length of a movie. Fans of Conan the Barbarian, Red Sonja, Solomon Kane, King Kull, and Black Turlough aren't going to rush out to rent *The Whole Wide World* simply because it describes a little-known incident in the life of their creator, pulp fiction writer Robert E. Howard. But *The Whole Wide World* will appeal to audiences looking for a thoughtful study of quiet passion, tentatively offered and desperately received. As usual there is a major obstacle: Howard is deeply dependent on his frail mother who, in turn, is frighteningly dependent on him. Their arrangement has worked out just fine for a long time and, as Wedgeworth makes threateningly clear to Zellweger's Novalyne Price, she will brook no interference from outsiders. But the force of Price's feelings for Howard has given her great reserves of courage. She fights for her happiness, and his, all the while knowing it's an uphill battle. Although Howard, who had lived in his own interior world most of his life, wants to love Price, he can only open his heart to her so far. *The Whole Wide World* will give you a lump in your throat the next time you open your beat-up collector's edition of *Weird Tales.* Based on the book *One Who Walked Alone* by Novalyne Price Ellis. ☙☙☙

1996 (PG) 120m/C Renee Zellweger, Vincent D'Onofrio, Ann Wedgeworth, Harve Presnell, Helen Cates, Benjamin Mouton, Michael Corbett, Marion Eaten, Leslie Berger, Chris Shearer, Sandy Walper, Dell Aldrich, Libby Villari, Antonia Bogdanovich, Elizabeth D'Onofrio, Stephen Marshall; ***D:*** Dan Ireland; ***W:*** Michael Scott Myers, Novalyne Price Ellis; ***C:*** Claudio Rocha; ***M:*** Hans Zimmer, Harry Gregson-Williams. Nominations: Independent Spirit Awards '97: Best Actress (Zellweger). **VHS, LV, Closed Caption**

Why Not!

Coline Serreau made her vivid directorial debut with *Why Not!* The former actress explores the relationships of two men and a woman who live happily together in a house in the suburbs. This idyllic *menage a trois* is disrupted by the presence of a young girl who falls in love with one of the inhabitants, but doesn't know how to accept the living arrangements he obviously has no desire to change. In less capable directorial hands, *Why Not!* might be heavy going indeed, but Serreau's picture is blessed with delightful humor and a wonderfully daffy cast. Serreau also LIKES most of her characters, and this lends greatly to her film's overall appeal. In the 1980s, Serreau ignited a cottage industry on both sides of the Atlantic with the domestic comedy, *Three Men and a Cradle.* (An American re-make and a sequel followed.) Her next project was *Mama, There's a Man in Your Bed.* ***AKA:*** Pourquoi Pas!. ☙☙☙

1978 93m/C *FR* Sami Frey, Christine Murillo, Mario Gonzales, Michel Aumont, Nicole Jamet, Mathe Souverbie; ***D:*** Coline Serreau; ***W:*** Coline Serreau; ***C:*** Jean-Francois Robin.

Wicked Woman

Wicked Woman is a grade-Z movie with a vengeance, starting with the grungy title song, belted with conviction by some cheesy male vocalist, circa 1954. Beverly Michaels IS the Wicked Woman, a gigantic blonde who destroys every life she touches, sort of. Her grubby neighbor down the hall is Percy Helton who'll do ANYTHING for the promise of a cheap thrill with her. Of course, NO ONE in this wonderfully sleazy movie really gets a cheap thrill, but happily, *Wicked Woman* escaped the attention of vigilant Hollywood censors: no one is punished for the film's many violations of the then-strict production code, not even Richard Egan as the bartender who is tempted to bump off his wife after ONE glance at Beverly! The sequence where the beefy Richard Egan is actually jealous of poor little Percy Helton is priceless!!! ☙☙☙

1954 77m/B Beverly Michaels, Richard Egan, Evelyn Scott, Percy Helton, Robert Osterloh; ***D:*** Russel Rouse; ***W:*** Russel Rouse, Clarence Greene; ***C:*** Eddie Fitzgerald.

Widow's Peak

Hugh Leonard originally wrote *Widow's Peak* for the late Maureen O'Sullivan and her daughter Mia Farrow. O'Sullivan was to play Miss O'Hare and Farrow would be Edwina Broome. When *Widow's Peak* finally went into production, Farrow inherited the role of Miss O'Hare and Natasha Richardson wound up playing Edwina Broome. The story takes place in Kilshannon in the 1920s. Mrs. Doyle O'Counihan (Joan Plowright) is the town's grand dame. She has a son, Godfrey (Adrian Dunbar), who falls madly in love with the elegant American widow Broome. Miss O'Hare detests Mrs. Broome on sight and she soon spreads the gossip that Edwina wants to murder her. Sure enough, Miss O'Hare suddenly vanishes and Edwina is arrested for her "murder." Mysteries pile up on mysteries, but, fear not, all will ultimately be revealed. The pleasure here is watching three terrific actresses doing star turns as only they can. Farrow, lovely as ever, starts out by persuasively making Miss O'Hare seem as mad as a hatter. Plowright is her usual droll self and Richardson is a perfectly radiant Edwina. Even though Jim Broadbent (as Clancy) and Plowright were both in 1992's *Enchanted April,* the charm of *Widow's Peak* is quite different and

"This whole world's wild at heart and weird on top."

—Lula (Laura Dern) in *Wild at Heart.*

much darker in tone. It's the ideal film to rent on a rainy Saturday afternoon when there's nothing worth seeing at the neighborhood multiplex. Filmed on location in County Wicklow, Ireland. 🦴🦴🦴

1994 (PG) 102m/C *GB* Mia Farrow, Joan Plowright, Natasha Richardson, Adrian Dunbar, Jim Broadbent, John Kavanagh, Gerard McSorley, Anne Kent, Rynagh O'Grady, Michael James Ford, Garrett Keogh; ***D:*** John Irvin; ***W:*** Hugh Leonard; ***C:*** Ashley Rowe; ***M:*** Carl Davis. **VHS, LV**

Wild at Heart

At the start of 1947's *The Hucksters,* one of Sidney Greenstreet's sharply etched villains spits on a table. As he was quick to admit, it was a disgusting gesture, but he wanted to make sure that people would remember him. In the opening sequence of David Lynch's *Wild at Heart,* Nicolas Cage's character commits an act so violent and so grisly that you're unlikely ever to forget it. The act also has much the same effect as a shot of Novocaine. If you don't bag the movie at that point, you've already been anesthetized for everything that follows and everything certainly does. *Wild at Heart,* believe it or don't, is a comedy about Sailor Ripley and Lula Pace Fortune, two mixed-up kids who want to be wild at heart together, only her mean old mama Marietta won't leave them alone. Marietta hires killer Marcello Santos to kill Sailor, but he arranges to kill her boyfriend Johnnie Farragut instead. Sailor and Lula have a good time being wild at heart on the road together until they stumble across a fatal accident, which Lula interprets as a bad omen. They move into a crummy motel where she promptly gets sick and doesn't clean up after herself the whole time they are there. At the motel, they meet up with Bobby Peru, a born trouble maker. (You can tell by just by looking at his teeth.) After the trouble, Mariette takes Lula home with her until the climax of the movie when the Good Fairy brings Sailor and Bobby back together again—just like in the movies! (Or maybe just like in David Lynch movies.) Only in *Wild at Heart* will you see Nicolas Cage do a movie-long Elvis Presley impersonation in his very best Rattlesnake skin jacket. (Yes, he sings "Love Me Tender," too.) Only in *Wild at Heart* will you see the most amazing collection of bric-a-brac from hell. (Where DOES Lynch find all these radios with big bronze horses on top?) Only in *Wild at Heart* will you see a vision of an absolutely insane world accompanied by Lynch's crushing self-confidence and his equally crushing Sunday school morality. But *Wild at Heart* MOVES, it's funny, it's never boring, and it won't remind you of anyone else in the universe, except of course, David Lynch, trying to top himself in true Busby Berkeley fashion: tossing everything into this movie except for phallic bananas. And who NEEDS phallic bananas when you have Nicolas Cage, Laura Dern, Diane Ladd, Willem Dafoe, Isabella Rossellini (in a bad wig), Harry Dean Stanton, Crispin Glover, Grace Zabriskie, J.E. Freeman, Freddie Jones, Sherilyn Fenn, PLUS Sheryl Lee chewing up the scenery? 🦴🦴🦴🦴

1990 (R) 125m/C Nicolas Cage, Laura Dern, Diane Ladd, Willem Dafoe, Isabella Rossellini, Harry Dean Stanton, Crispin Glover, Grace Zabriskie, J.E. Freeman, Freddie Jones, Sherilyn Fenn, Sheryl Lee; ***D:*** David Lynch; ***W:*** David Lynch; ***C:*** Frederick Elmes; ***M:*** Angelo Badalamenti. Cannes Film Festival '90: Best Film; Independent Spirit Awards '91: Best Cinematography; Nominations: Academy Awards '90: Best Supporting Actress (Ladd). **VHS, LV, Letterbox, Closed Caption**

The Wild Party

Immediately after delivering his second Oscar-winning performance in *Lust for Life,* Anthony Quinn made two independent films for Oscar-winning art director Harry Horner. *The Wild Party,* made for Security Pictures, was the second. Horner directed several films between 1952 and 1956 before returning to art direction. (He would be nominated again in 1969 for *They Shoot Horses, Don't They?*) Imagine, if you can, Quinn, Jay Robinson, Kathryn Grant, and Nehemiah Persoff as...Beatniks. Quinn, then 41, is an over-the-hill football hero (uh-oh) named Big Tom Kupfen. Robinson, then 26, plays Gage Freeposter as a coded, but unmistakably gay hotel hustler. The future Mrs. Bing Crosby, then 23, plays Honey in some sort of a drug haze, although chemicals other than alcohol are nowhere in sight. And Persoff, 36, is Kicks Johnson, the piano playing narrator, who's strung on Honey, who's strung on Tom, who's strung on rich Erica London (Carol Ohmart, then 28) who ISN'T strung on her rich fiance Lt. Mitchell (Arthur Franz, 36) but on Tom, although she doesn't want to be. Sounds sudsy, and the script IS, but Horner's interpretation isn't, and Quinn and Ohmart (who are both excellent) DEFINITELY aren't. Their characters strike genuine sexual sparks together in spite of themselves. (Tom's lamenting his long-lost past and the Lady Erica just wants to be turned ON for a change.) Paul Stewart and Barbara Nichols appear in, alas, just one sequence. Nestor Paiva is his usual colorful self as a club owner named Branson, and even the expository role of an articulate wino is deftly played by William Phipps. The brooding cinematography is by the great Sam Leavitt (Oscar winner for *The Defiant Ones* and nominee for *Anatomy of a Murder* and *Exodus*). The critics blasted *The Wild Party* and it went absolutely nowhere, but at least it isn't smug and complacent as so many 1956 flicks are. Moreover, it contains enough fascinating elements to warrant a video release. The television prints appear to have been shorn by at least 10 minutes, and considering the direction of Quinn's and Ohmart's psychosexual tango, I'm more than a little curious about what's missing.

1956 91m/B Anthony Quinn, Carol Ohmart, Arthur Franz, Jay Robinson, Kathryn Grant, Nehemiah Persoff, Paul Stewart, Barbara Nichols, Jana Mason, William Phipps, Maureen Stephenson, Nestor Paiva; ***D:*** Harry Horner; ***W:*** John McPartland; ***C:*** Sam Leavitt; ***M:*** Ruddy Bregman.

Wild West

Wild West: Cute idea, dumb execution. Not everything that comes out of the hallowed halls of London's Channel Four is an instant classic on the level of *My Beautiful Laundrette.* Three Pakistani brothers form a Country Western band called the Honky Tonky Cowboys. Their ultimate destination is Nashville, but on the road to fame and fortune, the oldest brother Zaf (Naveen Andrews) falls for Rifat (Sarita Choudhury), a beautiful woman married to a real churl. Strictly on the basis of his strong attraction to her, Zaf decides, without ever hearing her sing a note, that Rifat is the ideal leader for the band. She is. But the money men only want her, not the brothers. In a staggeringly cliched sequence that's right in keeping with everything else in *Wild West,* Rifat, Zaf, and the brothers all do the right thing, the credits roll, and that's that. *Wild West* is a cute movie to watch at home on a foggy London night, but it's pretty thin stuff on the big screen. *Mississippi Masala* fans may want to catch it for the always watchable Sarita Choudhury.

1993 83m/C *GB* Naveen Andrews, Sarita Choudhury, Ronny Jhutti, Ravi Kapoor, Bhasker; ***D:*** David Attwood; ***W:*** Harwant Bains; ***C:*** Nicholas D. Knowland. **VHS**

Wilde

Oscar Wilde became such a dearly loved character in the latter half of the 20th century that his fall from grace at the height of his fame in 1895 seems almost surreal to his loyal legion of devoted admirers. His much-trampled grave at the Pere Lachaise cemetery in Paris was, until its 1992 restoration, nearly as filled with graffiti as that of Jim Morrison. The constant revival of his plays and a series of films successfully restored his once-lustrous reputation, although his descendants still carry his wife Constance's maiden name of Holland, not his own. In 1960, two filmed biographies were released, one in color starring Peter Finch, the other in black and white with Robert Morley. Fine actors both, neither was quite right for the role, and both scripts tread cautiously into his private life. A 1985 BBC production with a tremendous performance by Michael Gambon was, until now, the best of the movies about Wilde, but, although available on home video, it was little seen when first telecast and still has yet to receive the attention it richly deserves. In *Wilde,* we finally have an Oscar so close to the original that he looks as if he stepped out of an original 19th century photograph. He is Stephen Fry, best known for *A Bit of Fry and Laurie* and for being the ideal Jeeves to Hugh Laurie's Wooster. Julian Mitchell's screenplay doesn't tiptoe into Wilde's life—it shows in graphic detail

The Hound Salutes:
STEPHEN FRY
Actor, *Wilde*

The great thing about [Oscar] Wilde, of course, is that he didn't live into what we think of as the 20th century. He died in 1900, which I suppose technically is the 19th century rather than the 20th century, and he never became corrupted by our age. He was a saint without being a myth, a secular saint. He had that quality—an almost messianic quality of attracting disciples, you could call it. He even told parables. The reason he has lasted, the reason he has been so validated by time, I think, is that there is nothing showy or shallow about him. He played with those ideas of superficiality, but he was deeply profound and his profundities are revealed more and more the more one reads him, and I think he speaks more to our age now than he did to his own. Very few figures truly retain a kind of authenticity or integrity across that time, and one of the few a hundred years back is Wilde, who looms over this, and I think he's become in a vulgar sense, you could say, the great tee-shirt of his age. He is a great icon, perhaps only along with someone like Einstein as a symbol, for students, for people who wish to resist the bourgeoisification, if you like, the sort of inevitable journey into a world of mortgages and houses and cars and career structures and families and so on. They wish to show a kind of allegiance to the idea of art and the freedom of the individual to express himself as he is to find out who he or she is. To realize ourselves if you like, to fulfill ourselves, to be what we were meant to be or to find out. To taste, as Wilde said, 'The fruit of every tree, of every garden in the world.'

"There is everything he could have done to have staved it off [Reading Jail], that is the awful nature of his tragedy. It is worth remembering that he was quite deliberately given some days' grace

how this charming genius, who was equally at home in a Colorado mining camp or at a London soiree, came to understand his true nature. A devoted husband and family man, he only stares at young men until he tumbles into a sexual relationship with his lifelong friend, Robert Ross. Although the affair is a brief one, the friendship endures and Wilde embarks on a double life, one at home, the other in rented lodgings with a series of male prostitutes. His downfall, of course, is Lord Alfred ("Bosie") Douglas, the nasty son of the nastier Marquess of Queensbury (Tom Wilkinson). Bosie is played by Jude (the doomed gay hustler in *Midnight in the Garden of Good and Evil*) Law. Bosie and Oscar, it seems, haven't much of a sex life together. Bosie uses Oscar to get back at Daddy and Oscar puts up with Bosie's abuse because he can't help himself. It's a match made in Hell and leads Wilde straight to Hell on Earth, AKA Reading Gaol. As mentioned, the story has been told before, but Fry and Mitchell give it a timeless resonance. What happened to Oscar Wilde over a century ago could happen now to anyone

to escape to France. It's what the Attorney General wanted, who is ultimately responsible for these sort of prosecutions, the equivalent of a sort of national D.A. over here. It's what he wanted. It's what the police wanted. It's what Parliament wanted. Nobody wanted to see Wilde in the dock. He had made an idiot of himself trying to sue the Marquess of Queensbury, his lover's [Bosie's] father and that had collapsed. He stayed for two days in the hotel in London, and then eventually a warrant was issued because he had broken a very clear law, a very recent law, incidentally. So Wilde stayed.

"It was extraordinary to think of this gentle giant, this extremely sweet-natured and remarkably gifted man being crushed beneath the remorseless wheels of Victorian society, being felled to his knees, to change metaphors mid-stream. He could have done something about it. W.B. Yeats, the Irish poet, said that for all that we would have accepted and understood if Wilde had escaped to France, he somehow wouldn't have been Oscar. It is quite extraordinary what the suffering did to him and how well he took it is to understate it. He was ennobled by it, and that sounds an awful cliche, but he truly was ennobled by his suffering. He blamed no one but himself. And we live in an age in which people can blame a termite or a United States president or the CEO of a company or their wife, their children, their mother, their lover, their television presenters. Anybody but themselves. For anything that happens to them. It is the absolute crime of the latter part of the 20th century that nobody has ever taken responsibility for their own actions. The only thing that's going to help is to look inside ourselves. And Wilde was capable of doing that. He did not recriminate, he did not blame others, he didn't look for some psychological explanation. He didn't look for some political explanation. He wanted to learn and be better for what had happened to him. Yes, we can all learn from that."

STEPHEN FRY also appeared in *A Civil Action, Spice World, The Wind in the Willows, Cold Comfort Farm, I.Q., Peter's Friends,* and *A Fish Called Wanda*; he was also the best Jeeves ever in the *Jeeves and Wooster* series co-starring Hugh Laurie.

trapped in a similarly deadly erotic web. Los Angeles–based Dove Books came up with a handsome coffee table book of Michell's screenplay, introduced by Fry and lavishly illustrated with many evocative color stills from the film. ƒƒƒ

1997 (R) 115m/C *GB* Stephen Fry, Jude Law, Vanessa Redgrave, Jennifer Ehle, Michael Sheen, Zoe Wanamaker, Tom Wilkinson, Gemma Jones, Judy Parfitt; ***D:*** Brian Gilbert; ***W:*** Julian Mitchell; ***C:*** Martin Fuhrer; ***M:*** Debbie Wiseman. Nominations: British Academy Awards '97: Best Supporting Actress (Ehle), Best Supporting Actress (Wanamaker); Golden Globe Awards '99: Best Actor—Drama (Fry). **VHS, Closed Caption**

Wildflower

This beautiful indie first turned up on the Lifetime Cable Network. The story, set in the South during the Great Depression, focuses on Reese Witherspoon, then 15, as motherless Ellie Perkins, who lives with her grandmother Bessie (Collin Wilcox Paxton), alcoholic father Jack (Beau Bridges), and teen brother Sammy (William McNamara, then 26). In spite of her own less-than-ideal situation, Ellie discovers 17-year-old Alice Guthrie (the superb Patricia Arquette, then 23), and determines to save the

Stephen Fry in *Wilde.* Sony Pictures Classics; courtesy of the Kobal Collection

epileptic, partly deaf girl from her cruel stepfather. (Believing that Alice is "possessed," he has shut her away like an animal.) Sara Flanigan adapted the script from her novel *Alice,* and director Diane Keaton gives this sad and deeply moving story a wonderfully lyrical look. Note the excellent performances of Witherspoon and Arquette several years before they made their mark as true indie divas. 🦴🦴🦴

1991 94m/C Patricia Arquette, Beau Bridges, Susan Blakely, William McNamara, Reese Witherspoon, Collin Wilcox Paxton, Norman (Max) Maxwell, Heather Lynch, Allison Smith, Richard Olsen, Mary Page; ***D:*** Diane Keaton; ***W:*** Sara Flanigan; ***C:*** Janusz Kaminski; ***M:*** Jon Gilutin, Ken Edwards. **VHS, Closed Caption**

The Windsors: A Royal Family

Four more hours on *The Windsors*? What is there left to be said about what may be the most chronicled family of all time? A great deal, actually, as can be seen in a 1994 documentary available through MPI Home Video. What distinguishes this historical overview of Britain's royal family is an impending sense of closure. The choice of the narrator, Janet Suzman, is revealing. Suzman won an Oscar nomination for playing the doomed Czarina in *Nicholas and Alexandra,* and her sober voice is a steady reminder that the Windsors are a dying breed, one of the few dynasties permitted to retain their privileges and titles in a century when many other monarchies were swept away by wars and revolutions. Ruthlessness and shrewdness were essential at the outset. King George V refused to help his Russian cousins, fearing that their presence in his country might hasten the end of his newly retitled family's reign. His epileptic youngest son was hidden from public view until his early death. Strong ties to Germany were severed. Even George V's own premature death was orchestrated by his doctor so that it could be announced in the morning edition of the *London Times.* But nothing could be done to ease the Edward VII situation, which continued with his grandson Edward VIII and with the current Prince of Wales. The British monarchy requires that its heirs have virtually nothing to do for most of their adult lives. With no real role to play, these Prince Charmings can and do get into inevitable mischief while waiting for the King or Queen to die. It took a brush with death to restore the future Edward VII to the affections of the British people. The future Edward VIII was quoted in *Time* magazine making dark predictions about his future many years before his actual abdication. And Charles, well into middle age, continues to twiddle his thumbs and whine about Daddy. Andrew Morton observed that "When historians review the reign of Queen Elizabeth II they will point to a weakness and an overindulgence at the top that allowed an unnecessary degree of drift and damage within the family to occur." The most intriguing element of this 1994 documentary is that the Queen's friends and family candidly discuss the Windsors on camera, in addition to the usual assortment of biographers, journalists, and gadflies. Many of the carefully chosen and well-researched film clips are unfamiliar to contemporary audiences. Clearly, the producers have done their homework and do in fact develop fresh insights about their increasingly vulnerable subjects. Who are the Windsors and why are they necessary? The British people are suckers for violent threats to the Establishment, and historically, the monarchy has often been revitalized as a result of such tragedies, so who knows? 🦴🦴🦴

1994 228m/C *GB* Janet Suzman; ***D:*** Kathy O'Neill, Stephen White, Annie Fienburgh; ***M:*** Michael Bacon. **VHS**

Wings of Desire

Did you ever see a movie that everyone in the world was raving about, that won a fistful of awards, that was considered the director's masterpiece, and that did absolutely nothing for you, so you shut up about it in mixed company? And then the director made a sequel five years later, so you disqualified yourself from reviewing it, but the sequel did not become the subject of mixed company, so at least you didn't have to go into seclusion. If you deify the projector that unleashes *Wings of Desire,* you are probably right. *It's a Wonderful Life* and *2001: A Space Odyssey* are also considered by many to be the masterpieces of Frank Capra and Stanley Kubrick, directors who mean much more to me than Wim Wenders does, so I've listened to skillions of explanations about why I should love those flicks, too, and I don't. Damiel (Bruno Ganz) and Cassiel (Otto Sander) are Der Himmel uber Berlin (Angels over Berlin). Ganz' angel falls in love with Marion, a circus acrobat (Solveig Dommartin), and decides to be mortal again. Curt Bois (1900–91), who played the pickpocket in *Casablanca,* is in it, too, as Homer, and Peter Falk is sublime as himself. Combined running time of *Wings of Desire* and the sequel *Angel in the Pizza Parlor*—scratch that—*Faraway, So Close:* four and a half hours. Why do angels see the world in black and white? I give it four bones for the cognoscenti, but for myself, no comment. ***AKA:*** Der Himmel Uber Berlin. 🦴🦴🦴🦴

1988 (PG-13) 130m/C *GE* Bruno Ganz, Peter Falk, Solveig Dommartin, Otto Sander, Curt Bois; ***D:*** Wim Wenders; ***W:*** Wim Wenders, Peter Handke; ***C:*** Henri Alekan; ***M:*** Jurgen Knieper. Independent Spirit Awards '89: Best Foreign Film; Los Angeles Film Critics Association Awards '88: Best Cinematography, Best Foreign Film; New York Film Critics Awards '88: Best Cinematography; National Society of Film Critics Awards '88: Best Cinematography. **VHS, LV**

The Wings of the Dove

From *Backbeat* to *Hackers* to *The Wings of the Dove* may seem like a psychological stretch for director Iain Softley, but all three of his films focus on characters that are ahead of their time, perhaps too many steps ahead for their own good. Kate (Helena Bonham Carter) has the perfectly sensible idea of transforming her lover Merton Densher (Linus Roache) from the poor writer he is into the rich widower he will be if he marries her dying friend Millie (Alison Elliott). Well, it seems like a perfectly sensible idea to Kate in theory, but

Alison Elliott and Helena Bonham Carter in *The Wings of the Dove.* Miramax; courtesy of the Kobal Collection

it evolves into shattering reality when she and Merton and Millie play their assigned roles. Everything goes like clockwork—everything, that is, but the unpredictability of passion. *The Wings of the Dove* is based on Henry James' 1902 novel and updated a bit to the year 1910. Kate's perspective has been twisted by living with her opium-ridden father (Michael Gambon) and being used as a social pawn by her Aunt Maud (Charlotte Rampling). Merton is weak and not particularly interesting except as a blank canvas on which imaginative young women like Kate and Millie can create romantic fantasies. And the radiant Millie is too good to live. That's it, except that the acting throughout is splendid, the production is handsome, and the running time (101 minutes) is manageable. Betcha that the underused Gambon and Elizabeth McGovern had a lot of time for sightseeing in Venice. 𝒟𝒟𝒟

1997 (R) 101m/C *GB* Helena Bonham Carter, Linus Roache, Alison Elliott, Elizabeth McGovern, Charlotte Rampling, Alex Jennings, Michael Gambon; ***D:*** Iain Softley; ***W:*** Hossein Amini; ***C:*** Eduardo Serra; ***M:*** Gabriel Yared. British Academy Awards '97: Best Cinematography, Best Makeup; Los Angeles Film Critics Association Awards '97: Best Actress (Bonham Carter); National Board of Review Awards '97: Best Actress (Bonham Carter); Broadcast Film Critics Association Awards '97: Best Actress (Bonham Carter); Nominations: Academy Awards '97: Best Actress (Bonham Carter), Best Adapted Screenplay, Best Cinematography, Best Costume Design; British Academy Awards '97: Best Actress (Bonham Carter), Best Adapted Screenplay, Best Costume Design; Golden Globe Awards '98: Best Actress—Drama (Bonham Carter); Screen Actors Guild Award '97: Best Actress (Bonham Carter), Best Supporting Actress (Elliott); Writers Guild of America '97: Best Adapted Screenplay. **VHS, LV, Closed Caption**

Wired

There are lousy movies and then there is *Wired,* the film that will set the standard for bad screen biographies for years to come. Remember *Reefer Madness*? *Cocaine Fiends*? *Maniac*? *Wired* may be even more laughable than watching all three of those turkeys on a triple bill at the grungiest flea pit you can imagine. It's hard to

believe that, in 1964, Larry Peerce directed *One Potato, Two Potato,* one of the best movies about an interracial marriage ever made. And he was attracted by the Earl MacRauch SCRIPT for *Wired*? Here's the premise: Michael Chiklis as John Belushi comes back to Earth as a ghost with guardian angel Ray Sharkey. He revisits all his old haunts (yes, producer Ed *The Royal Love Story of Charles and Diana* Feldman compares *Wired* to a Frank Capra comedy so maybe the screenwriter is a public domain channel junkie hooked on *It's a Wonderful Life*). Belushi watches himself with Dan Ayckroyd, with hip wife Judy, and with Billy Preston who plays himself. Meanwhile, *Washington Post* reporter Bob Woodward is doing some SERIOUS journalism. How serious? "Well, John, I think I'll play an after-the-fact voyeur while Cathy Smith gives you the fatal injection, how about THAT?" This, and I am not kidding, is the climax of the picture. Watch Belushi plead for a hit. Watch Cathy Smith try to find a vein on her own discolored arm before she shares her stash with her groveling victim. Watch Belushi shiver, listen to his death rattle, and then, as an extra special added attraction, see and hear him scream, "How about you, Woody? Want a hit?" UNBELIEVABLE. Even if you get off on crawling into the grave with dead movie stars via the constantly updated classic *Too Stupid to Live*—sorry!—*Too Young to Die, Wired* isn't worth 112 minutes of your time. Mis-cast Michael Chiklis, who is not without talent, went on to star in the title role of ABC's *The Commish* (1991–95) opposite Theresa Saldana. Mary Lambert's *Siesta,* Alan J. Pakula's *See You in the Morning,* plus *Wired* win my nomination for a triple bill in hell. **woof!**

1989 (R) 112m/C Michael Chiklis, Ray Sharkey, Patti D'Arbanville, J.T. Walsh, Gary Groomes, Lucinda Jenney, Alex Rocco, Jere Burns, Billy Preston; ***D:*** Larry Peerce; ***W:*** Earl MacRauch; ***C:*** Tony Imi; ***M:*** Basil Poledouris. **VHS, LV**

Wish You Were Here

Considerable controversy surrounded the making of *Wish You Were Here* because of its sexual candor and because its star was then just 16 years old. Yet Emily Lloyd's performance as the emotionally battered Linda is one of the most heartfelt and authentic portraits of a teen ever seen on film. You can always tell when Linda's guts have been ripped out—her sarcasm goes into high gear. Equally good is Tom Bell's seedy portrayal of a grungy older projectionist in dark glasses who stalks her in shadowy alleys and plays busy mitts with her when Daddy's out of the room. There is no nudity and there is nothing—repeat—nothing erotic about their scenes together. What is explicit is the enormous resilience of Linda's character as she survives repeated rejections by her father and the subsequent men in her life. ***AKA:*** Too Much.

1987 92m/C *GB* Emily Lloyd, Tom Bell, Clare Clifford, Barbara Durkin, Geoffrey Hutchings, Charlotte Barker, Chloe Leland, Trudy Cavanagh, Jesse Birdsall, Geoffrey Durham, Pat Heywood; ***D:*** David Leland; ***W:*** David Leland; ***C:*** Ian Wilson; ***M:*** Stanley Myers. British Academy Awards '87: Best Original Screenplay; National Society of Film Critics Awards '87: Best Actress (Lloyd). **VHS, LV**

The Witches

I never could understand why so-called Mai Zetterling fans were always sighing about her looks because she couldn't stay 16 years old forever. To me, Mai Zetterling (1925–94), was beautiful and brilliant and never more so than in her lovely swan song as the 65-year-old grandmother in Nicolas Roeg's charming film adaptation of Roald Dahl's prize-winning fantasy, *The Witches.* As Helga, Zetterling perfectly captures the essence of everyone's favorite grandmother: she is completely tuned into her young grandson Luke, she doesn't dismiss his dreams or his nightmares, she helps him out of every imaginable scrape, and gives him a big kiss to encourage him to fight his own battles. Newcomer Jasen Fisher is equally endearing as Luke, not only as a vulnerable little seven-year-old boy but also in his transformation as a resourceful mouse, determined to protect other kids from the same fate. Anjelica Huston is appropriately flamboyant as the Grand High Witch who is-

"Witches are witches because they are extremely unhappy, viciously ugly, and hate everybody."

—Helga (Mai Zetterling) to her grandson (Jasen Fisher) in *The Witches.*

sues the order to her followers that all the children of England are to be changed into mice. By the time the Grand High Witch arrives on the scene, we've already been alerted to the tell-tale signs of every true witch: their purple eyes, their lack of toes and, most important of all, their deep aversion to children. *The Witches* was among the late Jim Henson's last projects and his influence is clear as executive producer, not only in the striking makeup for the witches, but also in the appealing transformations that occur when Luke and other little boys are changed into mice. Director Roeg retains an atmosphere of wonder throughout the film's 92-minute running time and the color work on this picture is especially lovely. Worth noting among the supporting cast are Brenda *(Secrets and Lies)* Blethyn and the very funny Rowan Atkinson (hilarious as the minister in 1994's *Four Weddings and a Funeral*). Atkinson, a great comedy favorite in Great Britain, is a genuine side-splitter, etching his portrayal of the world's slimiest hotel manager in acid. *The Witches* works effectively both as a satire and as a tale of terror and is highly recommended for free spirits of all ages. 🦴🦴🦴🦴

1990 (PG) 92m/C Anjelica Huston, Mai Zetterling, Jasen Fisher, Rowan Atkinson, Charlie Potter, Bill Paterson, Brenda Blethyn, Jane Horrocks; ***D:*** Nicolas Roeg; ***W:*** Allan Scott; ***C:*** Harvey Harrison; ***M:*** Stanley Myers. Los Angeles Film Critics Association Awards '90: Best Actress (Huston); National Society of Film Critics Awards '90: Best Actress (Huston). **VHS, LV, 8mm, Closed Caption**

With or Without You

Unless it's *Eraserhead*'s Baby Henry or *Monkey Business,* in which Ginger Rogers THINKS that Cary Grant's been rejuvenated into a baby, I tend to hit the rewind button whenever movies about babies swim into focus: planning them, having them, diapering them, feeding them, walking them, et cetera. I took my sister Alanna, who had two stunning babies—Emma and Tess—between 1992 and 1997, to the press screening of *Nine Months,* and we both hated it for the same reasons. It was boring, fake, stupid, and NOT funny, like most Hollywood baby movies are, except for the aforementioned *Monkey Business.* With this bias, *With or Without You* was unlikely to make me sit up and pay attention with the same absorption that I watch Luis Buñel slice an eyeball in *Un Chien Andalou.* It's about a six-week stand between Alex Tinkham and Zoe Welles (Kristoffer Winters and Marisa Ryan). Her boyfriend's back and he's gonna be in trouble. Oh, not literally. Zoe just blindsides Alex with the news after they have sex. Such MANNERS! Alex loves Zoe and Alex is hurt. Tough! Off Zoe trots to that churl, James (Dylan Roy). Then Zoe finds out that she and Alex are expecting a baby, which makes Alex love Zoe even more, but it doesn't transform the nasty Zoe into an ethereal Madonna, ZZZ...poor Alex; I hope this wasn't inspired by a true story. Rachel True is cute as Alex's friend Misha. Poor Alex also has an awful roommate and the nasty Zoe has a nastier mother. I just remembered another (teen) pregnancy movie (circa 1959) that's pretty good for the genre: Philip Dunne's *Blue Denim,* because Carol Lynley and Brandon de Wilde are so cute in it and Marsha Hunt and Macdonald Carey are so good as the parents. If I were really into *With or Without You,* I wouldn't even be THINKING about other movies, which ought to tell you something. Played at San Francisco's Indie Fest in 1999. 🦴🦴

1998 105m/C Kristoffer Ryan Winters, Marisa Ryan, Rachel True, Linda Cropper, Jim Lichtscheidl, Margi Simmons, Dylan Roy; ***D:*** Wendell Jon Andersson; ***W:*** Wendell Jon Andersson; ***C:*** Gregory M. Cummins; ***M:*** Michael Windemacher.

With You and Without You

This exceptional, lovely Russian film begins with abduction, then evolves into a story of love and survival. Its then-youthful director gives his characters resourcefulness, strength, and courage, and sets them against a difficult background. The two leads infuse their roles with a gutsy tenderness that is extremely effective. Based on M. Shetov's story "Stepanida Basyrina." 🦴🦴🦴

1974 86m/C *RU* Marina Nejelova, Juosas Budraitis, Stanislaw Borodkin; ***D:*** Rodion Nakhapetov; ***W:*** Alexander Popov; ***C:*** Sergei Saizev; ***M:*** Rigdan Trozjuk.

Withnail and I

There's nostalgic drek about the 1960s and then there's the bracing dark comedy *Withnail and I.* Who better to separate fantasy from reality about that era than George Harrison and Richard Starkey (AKA Ringo Starr)? As a spur to struggling creative geniuses, The Beatles' Apple was worm-ridden from Day One, but Handmade Films, Harrison's independent film company, did ensure that intriguing small films like this one saw the light of day. (The roster of Handmade Films also includes *Life of Brian, Time Bandits, Privates on Parade, Water, Track 29, Powwow Highway, How to Get Ahead in Advertising, Cold Dog Soup, Nuns on the Run,* and *The Raggedy Rawney,* demonstrating that there WAS an audience for well-made indies. In the process, Handmade Films enjoyed great success for well over a decade.) The out-of-work title characters, Richard E. Grant and Mark McGann, escape their drug-and-cockroach-ridden London apartment to spend the weekend from hell in the rainy countryside, where Withnail's chubby gay uncle Monty (Richard Griffiths) soliloquizes about vegetables and makes a pass at the totally freaked-out "I." Writer/director Bruce Robinson does a brilliant job translating his vividly detailed novel to the screen, fully aware of the significance of the last few weeks of 1969, yet skillfully avoiding the trap of syrup-laden myopia 6,570 mornings after the fact.

1987 (R) 108m/C *GB* Richard E. Grant, Paul McGann, Richard Griffiths, Ralph Brown, Michael Elphick; ***D:*** Bruce Robinson; ***W:*** Bruce Robinson; ***C:*** Peter Hannan; ***M:*** David Dundas. **VHS, LV**

The Wizard of Loneliness

The Wizard of Loneliness, a pile of nostalgic goo (although another word also comes to mind) from American Playhouse will eventually wind up on public television, interrupted by excruciating pledge breaks which will run a tight race to rival this film's boredom level. Lukas Haas, whose large brown eyes and riveting presence stole *Witness* and *The Lady in White* from award-winning adult actors, delivers a credible performance in an impossible, unsympathetic role. Lea Thompson and John Randolph, two fine and much underrated actors, also give their roles far more texture than is provided by John Nichols' novel. There was a sharply observed immediacy about 1987's British wartime valentine, *Hope and Glory,* which *The Wizard of Loneliness* lacks. Set in a Vermont small town, *Wizard* seizes on obvious and not always accurate symbols of 1944: the Prince of Wales, when none existed between 1936 and 1958, *Life* magazines, 1988-style frankness about 1944-style sexual frustrations, yellow filters over the camera lenses, and trend-setting 1934 fashions. (Even in Vermont, they received mail-order clothing catalogues.) There is the obligatory goofball escapee from the trenches whom everyone protects (for reasons best known to the screenwriter), even after he punches Lea in the stomach and smashes a glass against his little son's forehead. Hey, without this wretchedly acted character, there would be no anti-war statement. Just in case we don't get the point, there is a parallel sequence involving a large white male rabbit and his newly born offspring. (And everyone knows what fascists rabbits ran be.) Even if you ignore the sluggish pacing, the obnoxious dialogue, and the thematic falseness, you are still stuck with Jenny Bowen's leaden direction. Or then again, maybe not. **woof!**

1988 (PG-13) 110m/C Lukas Haas, Lea Thompson, John Randolph, Lance Guest, Anne Pitoniak, Jeremiah Warner, Dylan Baker; ***D:*** Jenny Bowen; ***W:*** Nancy Larson, Jenny Bowen; ***C:*** Richard Bowen; ***M:*** Michel Colombier. **VHS, LV, Closed Caption**

The Woman in Question

I've never understood why talented Jean Kent didn't become a bigger star than she did. She was attractive in an evil, insolent, menacing sort of way that was just right for noir films like this one. For that matter,

Nick and Mable Longhetti (Peter Falk and Gena Rowlands) in *A Woman under the Influence.*
Faces International Films; courtesy of the Kobal Collection

I've never understood why this fine Anthony Asquith film isn't better known than it is, either. Jean Kent is a fortune teller named Astra, who is already dead when the story begins. Who done it? Was it her sister, Catherine, and her fiance, Bob Baker (Susan Shaw and Dirk Bogarde)? Was it the charlady (Hermione Baddeley)? How about a shopkeeper named Pollard (Charles Victor) or Murray the sailor (John McCallum)? Each has a different story to tell and Astra seems to be a different person to every one of them. It's a terrific part for any actress and Kent makes the most of it. She's so good that it's stunning to realize that Kent, only 29, had just one more success with Asquith (1951's *The Browning Version*) before her career sunk into a downward slide from which it never recovered. By 1957 and 1958, she was way down on the cast list in *The Prince and the Showgirl* and *Bonjour Tristesse.* Kent kept working (she can be seen in a bit in 1976's *Shout at the Devil*) and I even saw an actress billed as Jean Kent in a *Lovejoy* episode, but she looked nothing at all like an aging fortune teller once known as Astra. Other Kent titles on video: *Man of Evil, Madonna of the Seven Moons, The Wicked Lady, The Magic Bow, Sleeping Car to Trieste, The Gay Lady,* and *The Haunted Strangler.* ***AKA:*** Five Angles on Murder. 🦴🦴🦴

1950 82m/B *GB* Jean Kent, Dirk Bogarde, Susan Shaw, Duncan MacRae, John McCallum, Hermione Baddeley, Charles Victor, Lana Morris, Vida Hope, Joe Linnane, Duncan Lament, Bobbie Scroggins, Anthony Dawson, John Boxer, Julian D'Albie, Josephine Middleton, Everley Gregg, Albert Chevalier, Richard Pearson; ***D:*** Anthony Asquith; ***W:*** John Cresswell; ***C:*** Desmond Dickinson; ***M:*** John Wooldridge. **VHS**

A Woman under the Influence

Housewife Gena Rowlands is cracking up and husband Peter Falk doesn't understand why. I'm with Peter Falk on this one. I felt like a stranger who'd stumbled into a psychodramatic household for two and a half hours. At one point, when Gena Rowlands asks everyone in the house to leave so she can make love with her husband, I actually found myself blushing with acute embarrassment. Why were all those people there? Why was I there? John Cassavetes wrote roles that actors would kill to play—the lucky beneficiaries here are his wife and best friend in real life. By the time Rowlands starred in the gritty, Oscar-nominated title role of 1980's *Gloria,* the critical elite grumbled (unfairly) about how Cassavetes had made his films more accessible for mainstream audiences, but wait till they see how Sidney Lumet has sentimentalized it as a Sharon Stone vehicle for 1999 audiences! 🦴🦴

1974 (R) 147m/C Gena Rowlands, Peter Falk, Matthew Cassel, Matthew Laborteaux, Christina Grisanti; ***D:*** John Cassavetes; ***W:*** John Cassavetes; ***C:*** Caleb Deschanel, Mitch Breit. Golden Globe Awards '75: Best Actress—Drama (Rowlands); National Board of Review Awards '74: Best Actress (Rowlands), National Film Registry '90;; Nominations: Academy Awards '74: Best Actress (Rowlands), Best Director (Cassavetes). **VHS, Closed Caption, DVD**

Women on the Verge of a Nervous Breakdown

How often have you seen an absolutely magnificent woman trash herself relentlessly over a jerk? Then you see HIM and wonder what all the fuss was about. Hollywood has supplied us with stunning examples of this phenomenon: observe Bette Davis or Joan Crawford work themselves into suicidal despair over assorted male contract players. Or watch Italy's Anna Magnani pine away because Ben Gazzara or Aldo Fabrizi doesn't care about her. Into this distinguished gallery of noble sufferers, please add Carmen Maura, the star of Pedro Almodovar's *Women on the Verge of a Nervous Breakdown.* My favorite scene in the movie is when Carmen slugs the "feminist" attorney with whom her faithless lover is running away. With his merciless eye for the truth, Almodovar has correctly identified the "oh-so-politically correct-and-oh-so-full-of crap" self-styled representative of women. She may be representing herself, but she certainly isn't speaking for women like Carmen who have to fight their battles alone with no help from phony "advocates." In spite of his feminist critique, Almodovar's love and concern for women is evident in every frame of his film. Carmen achieves strength and understanding not by analyzing the politics of her pain but by working through it. The same woman who sets her bed on fire and then resignedly hoses it down can and does save lives, including her own. Almodovar's acceptance of human problems sets him apart from filmmakers who manipulate characters to illustrate their philosophies. Take a look at people as they are, good and bad, Almodovar's films tell us. Universal statements will emerge from such honest examination, not the other way around. "Women cry better," says Almodovar. *Women on the Verge of a Nervous Breakdown* is such a terrific comedy showcase for the great Carmen Maura, it's sad that it represents her last teaming with Almodovar to date. ***AKA:*** Mujeres al Borde de un Ataque de Nervios. 🦴🦴🦴🦴

1988 (R) 88m/C *SP* Carmen Maura, Fernando Guillen, Julieta Serrano, Maria Barranco, Rossy de Palma, Antonio Banderas; ***D:*** Pedro Almodovar; ***W:*** Pedro Almodovar; ***C:*** Jose Luis Alcaine; ***M:*** Bernardo Bonazzi. New York Film Critics Awards '88: Best Foreign Film; Nominations: Academy Awards '88: Best Foreign Film. **VHS, LV, Letterbox**

The Wonderful Crook

This quiet little film is about a factory owner who steals to pay his worker's wages. The acting by Marlene Jobert and Gerard Depardieu is delightful, and Claude Goretta's direction brings out the elements of charm in his script. ***AKA:*** Pas Si Méchant que Ça. 🦴🦴🦴½

1975 115m/C *SI FR* Marlene Jobert, Gerard Depardieu, Dominique Labourier, Philippe Leotard, Jacques Debary, Michel Robin, Paul Crauchet; ***D:*** Claude Goretta; ***W:*** Claude Goretta; ***C:*** Renato Berta; ***M:*** Arie Dzierlatka.

"Solomon Martinson was one of us. What he suffered we all suffer. We do not mourn him, we honor him and we say the only true tribute to him is to pick up the spear from where it has fallen. Solomon is just one, one man, and when we defy them, when we resist in our hundreds, when we resist in our thousands, in our millions, then victory is certain."

—Priest Jude Akuwidike eulogizes Albee Lesotho in *A World Apart*

The Wonderful, Horrible Life of Leni Riefenstahl

At the age of 95, Leni Riefenstahl remains a vital, seductive ball of energy. Ray Muller's three-hour documentary about her life and career doesn't even begin to scratch the surface of this frustrating enigma. *The Wonderful, Horrible Life of Leni Riefenstahl* was somewhat hindered at the start by a major restriction; Riefenstahl would only cooperate with the filmmaker if no opposing viewpoints were presented on camera. Muller agreed, but that didn't stop him from incorporating these viewpoints into his questioning of Riefenstahl. And whenever he tried to do just that, Riefenstahl made her displeasure clear in no uncertain terms. Muller's far-from-frail subject would push him, shove him, yell at him, and, luckily for us, all these moments remain in the movie. The clips from Riefenstahl's early films, both as an actress and as a director, are crisp and clear and her filmmaking entries are razor-sharp. But when it comes to larger issues, namely her precise relationship with the leaders of National Socialism, Riefenstahl's recall softens, blurs, and becomes maddeningly selective. "I NEVER socialized with the Nazis," she insists right after Muller shows us a still of her dressed to the nines and doing just that. "I never used gypsies from concentration camps for my films," she cries, a few moments after we've seen the actual bill of lading. And what about the gushing fan letter she sent to Adolf Hitler after one of his many invasions? "Well, of course I was ecstatic, we all were, because we thought that the war was over." We know, because her surviving colleagues tell us so, that Riefenstahl would do anything, ANYTHING to make *Triumph of the Will* and *Olympia* exactly the way she wanted to make them. We've seen both her combative style with Muller as well as her skill as an actress, so we ought to be irritated when she tells us that she was an apolitical artist and that she didn't mean to glorify National Socialism with her powerful propaganda films. Empirical evidence and the weight of history contradict much of what she says. But Riefenstahl has the quality of Phyllis Dietrichson in *Double Indemnity* right after she's shot Walter Neff and tells him that she didn't mean it. There's always an element of doubt with a charming seductress. *The Wonderful, Horrible Life of Leni Riefenstahl* shows how one of the 20th century's most fascinating woman was able to play both ends against the middle in the 1930s, and was still able to do so well into the 1990s. ***AKA:*** The Power of the Image: Leni Riefenstahl; Die Macht der Bilder: Leni Riefenstahl. ♪♪♪♪

1993 180m/C *GE* ***D:*** Ray Muller; ***C:*** Michel Baudour. **VHS, DVD**

Wonderland

Wonderland was a curious choice for 1989's closing night at San Francisco's Lesbian and Gay Film Festival, an event which professes to celebrate positive gay images on film. Philip Saville's film is saturated with so many homophobic messages: If you're young, nice, and gay, prepare to die. If you're a thief, a liar, and a gay basher, you deserve to survive. Moreover, *Wonderland* exploits overly obvious gay symbols for ruthless plot advances which don't always make sense. The appealing Emile Charles plays Eddie, the film's most innocent character. Kind to his mother, who cherishes her blurry 1960s fantasy of ALMOST being cast in a bit role in *Saturday Night and Sunday Morning,* Eddie is addicted to Marilyn Monroe movies and is thrilled when he meets the famous opera star Vincent at a private buffet he crashes with his best friend Michael (played by Tony Forsyth). Earlier in the evening Eddie and Michael were the reluctant witnesses to a gangland slaying in a gay bar and their encounter with Vincent provides a temporary escape from the mob's hitman, Echo (Bruce Payne.) Eddie and Michael quickly accept an invitation to join Vincent and his manager Eve for a holiday in Brighton. Up to this point, the movie has been a colorful, mostly inoffen-

sive series of character vignettes. The rest of the movie is a mess. It's hard to decide who gets trashed more in *Wonderland*'s final reels, gays or dolphins. Even a conscienceless louse like Michael would not take all night to notice a major detail like a knife wound sustained by his best friend. And, not that it would matter to screenwriter Frank Clarke, but dolphins do not attack people, therefore the melodramatic ending is a complete shuck. "What a piece of crap," I overheard the man in back of me mutter as he left the theatre before the closing credits rolled onscreen. Even a ticket taker was knocking the film to the some of the sell-out festival crowd as they entered the theatre. There might be worse movies to see on your hard-earned entertainment budget, but there are plenty of better ones. ***AKA:*** The Fruit Machine. 🦴🦴

1988 103m/C *GB* Emile Charles, Tony Forsyth, Robert Stephens, Clare Higgins, Bruce Payne, Robbie Coltrane; ***D:*** Philip Saville; ***W:*** Frank Clarke; ***C:*** Dick Pope; ***M:*** Hans Zimmer. **VHS, LV**

Word Is Out: Stories of Some of Our Lives

The Summer of Love in the straight world occurred in 1967. For the San Francisco gay community, the Summer of Love took place in 1978. Harvey Milk was still alive and thriving on the San Francisco Board of Supervisors and AIDS, the plague that would be an epidemic by the summer of 1981 and didn't even have a name yet, had only been detected in a few scattered cases. Disco was huge that summer, only the followers of Reverend Jim Jones suspected what a monster he might be, and George Moscone, the Mayor of San Francisco and an enthusiastic movie buff, was a rising political star. It seemed to be a time of endless possibilities, and for the patrons of the Gateway Cinema on Jackson and Battery Streets, 1977 and 1978 were the years that the Mariposa Film Group four-walled Jack Tillmany's revival theatre for an exclusive engagement of *Word Is Out.* Director Peter Adair, who had been a cameraman on *Gimme Shelter,* had interviewed a large group of lesbians and gay men and then selected the most articulate 26 to speak on camera for the documentary. As the FIRST full-length documentary to study gay life in America, *Word Is Out* was and is a landmark film, designed to shatter stereotypes and clarify mysteries of misinformation. After the initial grumbling about why one film was playing at the Gateway instead of golden-oldie double bills twice weekly, *Word Is Out* became a long-running phenomenon. Gay AND straight audiences were starved for the information supplied in this funny, deeply humanistic movie. The speakers aren't all kids—they are as young as 18 and as old as 77; they live across the country from San Francisco to Boston; and their experiences reflect universal concerns shared by everyone. For the proverbial one brief shining moment, the gay community flowered in prestige and power and the resulting knowledge and understanding benefited everyone. And then the horrors of Jonestown dominated international headlines by November 1978, Milk and Moscone were assassinated 10 days later, the infamous White Night Riots at San Francisco City Hall followed the light sentence received by the assassin, and rumblings about a gay cancer were heard in the land. Harvey Milk would become the subject of a movie and an opera. AIDS would claim millions of victims—including director Peter Adair, who made another picture, 1991's *Absolutely Positive,* about his and others' experience with the virus before his death at 53 in 1996. But *Word Is Out* was the first to open many people's minds to what being gay meant in a world where the subject had rarely been addressed above a whisper. 🦴🦴🦴🦴

1977 130m/C ***D:*** Peter Adair; ***C:*** Peter Adair. **VHS, Closed Caption**

A World Apart

One of the major frustrations about being a child is that grown-ups often fail to explain matters in which kids have a very real stake. Sometimes, as in *A World Apart,* a mother can't explain what's going on to her 13-year-old daughter, even when

The Hound Salutes:
PETER ADAIR
Director, *Word Is Out: Stories of Some of Our Lives* and *Absolutely Positive*

The films I make tend to be 'talking head' films. You're never supposed to call a film a talking head film. You're supposed to do everything you cannot to call it that, and to cover all talking heads with what they call 'B Roll' (which is outside footage, people singing and dancing and doing other things). Usually that's because people who talk on television aren't saying anything very interesting. That kind of documentary has gotten a bad name for itself. I love hearing stories. I love hearing people talk, providing what they're saying is interesting and fresh and real and heartfelt. And I feel it's the best way to do portraits of people. In a way, it's almost like Victorian photography. I'm more interested in having someone pose for me and learn from the way that they pose, than so-called candid photography.

"So, this film *Absolutely Positive,* just like *Word Is Out,* is just people talking, people who have tested positive for HIV, the AIDS virus. Janet Cole, who produced it, and I assembled a team of—we call them story catchers to be cute, but they're sort of researchers and they go out with home video

it seems as if their entire world is caving in. These are the rough lessons screenwriter Shawn Slovo learned at a young age in South Africa. When her political activist mother was assassinated in 1982, Slovo developed a fictional screenplay about their early relationship. The social ostracism and psychological harassment of this white anti-apartheid family are carefully shown from a child's perspective. While her mother copes with her private nightmares in prison, young Molly suddenly finds herself without friends or guidance. The statements in *A World Apart* are not as threatening as the messages in the seldom-shown *A Place for Weeping,* which examines the black South African experience. Still, Chris Menges' film examines the unfairness of life in an observant, thoughtful way, and it is extremely well acted by Barbara Hershey as Diana and Jodhi May as her daughter, Molly. ✂✂✂

1988 (PG) 114m/C *GB* Barbara Hershey, Jodhi May, Linda Mvusi, David Suchet, Jeroen Krabbe, Paul Freeman, Tim Roth, Jude Akuwidike, Albee Lesotho; ***D:*** Chris Menges; ***W:*** Shawn Slovo; ***C:*** Peter Biziou; ***M:*** Hans Zimmer. British Academy Awards '88: Best Original Screenplay; Cannes Film Festival '88: Best Actress (Hershey), Best Actress (May, Mvusi), Grand Jury Prize; New York Film Critics Awards '88: Best Director (Menges). **VHS, LV, Closed Caption**

The World of Henry Orient

The World of Henry Orient was considerably overshadowed by another Peter Sellers release in 1964, *The Pink Panther,* but it remains one of the best films about teenagers ever made, and among the few to give anything like an accurate reading of the many crossed signals between kids and adults. Sellers portrays Henry Orient, a concert piano player of limited ability who becomes the reluctant idol of 14-year-old Elizabeth (Tippy) Walker. Sellers, who perfectly captures the personality of a not-terribly-bright, middle-aged slime, is incapable of coping with much more than one-

equipment in the field and just talk to people who are positive. It's a way of sort of extending our reach, not only just in the amount of time it takes, and the number of people that need to do it—but also my circle is somewhat limited, and I can reach out from that circle, but I can't go too far, especially in other communities. It takes a long time to establish trust and if you're not from the community you won't get the same amount of trust someone in the community may have. So we hired researchers (maybe 10 or 20, none of them were really full-time) who for many, many months did interviews around the country. Asking people who were HIV-positive what their experiences were. Then we looked at the interviews, all 120 of them, and two things happened from that. First of all, you learn a lot about the subject; it really informs you, because you listen to people talking about what matters to them. Also, you get a sense of what the film can be. You get very much a sense of who should be in the film, who are effective story tellers, whose stories fit into the sort of matrix that you are creating. The community for the two films is very different. I don't know that the world is different. I suppose it is, but I'm not sure the difference in the world is reflected in the interviews. It's more the difference of what the subject matter is. *Word Is Out* was about learning that you are gay and overcoming hostility and self-imposed prejudice. It's about opening up like butterflies and coming out, exciting things, discovering things. *Absolutely Positive* is about the opposite: It's about death."

PETER ADAIR (1943–96) also did camerawork for *Gimme Shelter* and *The Life and Times of Harvey Milk.*

night stands with married women like Paula Prentiss. Unfortunately, although the talented Walker has a good mental grasp of his failings, she is unable to free herself from this pointless obsession. Walker involves her best friend Merrie Spaeth in a dogged pursuit of the dreary activities of Henry Orient, which takes the girls all over New York City. Walker collects his discarded cigarettes and other junk as if they were priceless relics and Spaeth is unable to resist the romantic compulsion of the chase. Both girls come from unconventional homes. The affluent, musical Walker is the daughter of kind pushover Tom Bosley, who has resigned himself to life with the hard-as-nails Angela Lansbury. The decidedly middle-class Spaeth lives with her mother and a woman friend, sympathetically played by Phyllis Thaxter and Bibi Osterwald. Left to their own devices, Walker would probably drift into drugs or an early marriage while the more level-headed Spaeth would lend equally loyal support to any other best friend. Despite the difference in their fortunes, it is clear that Walker has a far more poverty-stricken life and that she needs Henry Orient to distract her from the sadness and emptiness she would otherwise feel. Walker's recognition that she must learn to grow up by seeing Henry Orient exactly as he is comprises the most painful fact of her life, circa 1964. The adults in this one, despite some fine acting, are rather shadowy figures, which is probably the way most kids see them. For a man who didn't begin directing movies until he was 40, George Roy Hill is clearly captivated by the girls' story and his enthusiasm for their adventures is contagious. Note the similarities in mood and tone between 1964's *The World of Henry Orient* and the first half of 1994's *Heavenly Creatures*. 🦴🦴🦴🦴

1964 106m/C Peter Sellers, Tippy Walker, Merrie Spaeth, Tom Bosley, Angela Lansbury, Paula Prentiss, Phyllis Thaxter, Bibi Osterwald; ***D:*** George Roy Hill; ***W:*** Nunnally Johnson, Nora Johnson; ***C:*** Boris

"You're not helping Jo by trying to keep this case alive. You know as well as I do that Eddie Taylor's been pounding on the door of the execution chamber since he was born."

—Bonnie Graham (Jean Dixon) on her brother-in-law (Henry Fonda) in *You Only Live Once.*

Kaufman; ***M:*** Elmer Bernstein. **VHS, LV, Letterbox, Closed Caption**

The World of Jacques Demy

The late Jacques Demy (1931–90) was a darling of the festival circuit for over 20 years. He was in love with Hollywood musicals and fairy tales that ended happily ever after. In *The World of Jacques Demy,* his widow Agnes Varda pays tribute to the unique filmmaker who thrived during the French New Wave without ever really being part of it. Demy's uneven career consisted of huge international successes *(Lola, The Umbrellas of Cherbourg)* and neglected follow-ups *(Model Shop, The Young Girls of Rochefort).* He left a vivid impression on the actors who worked with him and the many loyal admirers of his work, as Varda's loving homage makes crystal clear. ***AKA:*** The Universe of Jacques Demy; L'Universe de Jacques Demy. ☙☙☙

1995 91m/C *FR* Anouk Aimee, Michel Legrand, Claude Berri, Richard Berry, Danielle Darrieux, Catherine Deneuve, Jean Marais, Harrison Ford, Jeanne Moreau, Michel Piccoli, Dominique Sanda, Bertrand Tavernier; ***D:*** Agnes Varda; ***W:*** Agnes Varda; ***C:*** Stephane Krausz, Georges Strouve, Peter Pilafian.

The Yellow Ticket

Many of the films at 1995's 15th annual Jewish Film Festival reflected on the pioneering spirit necessary for survival over the long haul. The selections dated back as far as 1918 when a 24-year-old Polish actress named Pola Negri made Victor Janson's *The Yellow Ticket* in Warsaw. Her character wants to make medicine her life, but the only way the fledgling actress can afford to do that is through prostitution in a St. Petersburg brothel. Her brilliant medical future is threatened when another student (with whom she is romantically involved) discovers her source of financial aid. Negri had a long career in films: she made *Gypsy Blood, Passion,* and *One Arabian Night* for Ernst Lubitsch between 1918 and 1921; she starred in Mauritz Stiller's *Hotel Imperial* in 1927; she made the screwball comedy *Hi Diddle Diddle* for Andrew L. Stone in 1943; and she even appeared opposite Hayley Mills in the 1964 Disney film *The Moon-Spinners.* When Negri died in 1987, she had outlived most of the other stars of the silent era. ☙☙☙

1918 68m/B *GE* Pola Negri; ***D:*** Victor Janson.

You Only Live Once

Director Fritz Lang escaped Nazi Germany in the nick of time, leaving behind his considerable fortune. Upon his arrival in America, he immediately addressed OUR social problems on film, starting with *Fury*'s exploration of public lynchings. A lesser-known film, but in many ways, far more uncompromising, is 1937's *You Only Live Once,* made for independent producer Walter Wanger. Both *Fury* and *You Only Live Once* star Sylvia Sidney, the quintessential Depression-era actress whose dahlia-like appearance belied her deep emotional strength. Henry Fonda, with his gaunt, lean features, was her male equivalent, far more successful at conveying '30s angst than *Fury*'s well-fed Spencer Tracy. The perspective in *You Only Live Once* is in direct opposition to the one in *Fury,* which went out of its way to show that the system would eventually address social evils. In *You Only Live Once,* all good-intentioned liberalism is ineffectual. Fonda plays Eddie Taylor, a loser trying to buck his fate with the love and support of Jo Graham, played by Sidney. But he can NOT buck it; the couple can't even have a proper wedding night together—they are tossed out after their motel manager discovers Eddie's identity. Eddie tries to get and keep a job, but his past catches up with him and he is fired. He is unjustly accused of a crime he did not commit and cooperates with authorities upon Jo's recommendation. The attorney who is Jo's employer tries to help him, a priest tries to help him, and when Eddie rejects them, it is clear that he is rejecting a society that has always rejected him. Even as the real criminals are caught, Eddie is already in existential flight along with Jo, who abandons her well-ordered life to join him. Lang treats the couple and everyone else in his sightline with understanding and sympathy. There are no real saints or sinners in *You Only Live Once,* only an overall atmosphere of despair. In the war that was to come, Lang would show other seemingly doomed couples in *Manhunt* and *Ministry of Fear,* as they struggled, not always in vain, against their destinies. But in *You Only Live Once* we see a rare time capsule that makes it clear the New Deal will not supply Eddie and Jo's salvation, only a grim acceptance of their fate.

1937 86m/B Henry Fonda, Sylvia Sidney, Ward Bond, William Gargan, Barton MacLane, Margaret Hamilton, Jean Dixon, Warren Hymer, Chic Sale, Guinn "Big Boy" Williams, Jerome Cowan, John Wray, Jonathan Hale, Ben Hall, Jean Stoddard, Wade Boteler, Henry Taylor, Walter DePalma; ***D:*** Fritz Lang; ***W:*** C. Graham Baker, Gene Towne; ***C:*** Leon Shamroy. **VHS**

Young and Innocent

Young and Innocent turns up so often in scratched and dupey prints on public domain channels that it's easy to under-appreciate what a gem it is. For starters, there's Erica, a wonderful teen heroine (Nova Pilbeam), who trusts her own instincts and relies on her resources to save Robert, a suspected killer (handsome Derrick DeMarney). Then there's the tramp (Edward Rigby) who's vital to her search for the real killer. The wonderful Basil Radford (a year before *The Lady Vanishes*) has a delightful cameo as a sympathetic ally. And there's that dazzling camera work at a tea dance where we REdiscover the killer we met in the first reel. A children's party game of Blind Man's Bluff mid-way through the film reinforces the lighthearted, intense quality of Erica and Robert's situation. It's very British, with few concessions to an international audience, but great fun. Based on Josephine Tey's *A Shilling for Candles.* Hitchcock's cameo is as a court photographer. ***AKA:*** The Girl Was Young.

1937 80m/B *GB* Derrick DeMarney, Nova Pilbeam, Percy Marmont, Edward Rigby, Mary Clare, John Longden, George Curzon, Basil Radford, Pamela Carme, George Merritt, J.H. Roberts, Jerry Verno, H.F. Maltby, John Miller, Beatrice Varley, Syd Crossley, Frank Atkinson, Torin Thatcher; ***D:*** Alfred Hitchcock; ***W:*** Charles Bennett, Alma Reville, Gerald Savory, Antony Armstrong, Edwin Greenwood. **VHS, LV**

Zebrahead

Zebrahead was first shown less than 18 months before Ray Sharkey died of AIDS in a Brooklyn Hospital, so Richard Glass, an aggressively promiscuous character that seemed funny while Sharkey was still alive, is significantly less amusing now, especially since he wants his adolescent son to follow his example. Otherwise, *Zebrahead* is an enjoyable teen indie about a star-crossed romance between white kid/black wannabe Zack Glass (Michael Rapaport) and his best friend's cousin Nikki (N'Bushe Wright), who's black. Needless to say, Nikki's mother and everyone in school has an opinion on this couple. Similar in theme, although definitely not in approach to a better Australian teen flick, 1989's *Flirting,* directed by John Duigan and starring Noah Taylor and Thandie Newton. *Zebrahead* was filmed on location in Detroit, Michigan.

1992 (R) 102m/C Michael Rapaport, N'Bushe Wright, Ray Sharkey, DeShonn Castle, Ron Johnson, Marsha Florence, Paul Butler, Abdul Hassan Sharif, Dan Ziskie, Candy Ann Brown, Helen Shaver, Luke Reilly, Martin Priest, Kevin Corrigan; ***D:*** Tony Drazan; ***W:*** Tony Drazan; ***C:*** Maryse Alberti; ***M:*** Taj Mahal. Sundance Film Festival '92: Filmmakers Trophy. **VHS, LV, 8mm, Closed Caption**

Zohar: Mediterranean Blues

Zohar: Mediterranean Blues is the sad story of Zohar Arkov, who achieved musical stardom in Israel before his death in 1987 at the age of 32. Its content and structure are similar to 1985's *Shout,* about Australian rock legend Johnny O'Keefe (who was 43 when he died in 1978), and to *Stardust,* Michael Apted's fictional re-creation of the quintessential pop star, circa 1974. Since most filmed biographies of rock stars end with them getting torn up in a wreck or done in by drugs (in this case, it's the latter), the significance of Arkov's pioneering musical contributions is that they laid the groundwork for other Yemenite artists to achieve success on a large scale.

1993 116m/C *IS* Gabi Amrani, Dafna Dekel, Menahem Einy, Cochava Harari, Shaul Mizrahi; ***D:*** Eran Riklis; ***W:*** Amir Ben-David, Moshe Zonder; ***C:*** Amnon Alait; ***M:*** Avihu Medina.

"Indie Connections" provides both the independent film devotee and the independent filmmaker with ways to keep on top of current happenings in the industry, news and opinions from other like-minded individuals, and behind-the-scenes stories from those in the know. We tracked down web pages, magazines, books, and organizations all for and about independent film, many of them by independent filmmakers themselves. Go to it!

Web Pages

Association of Independent Video and Filmmakers
http://www.aivf.org

Canadian Independent Film Caucus
http://www.hype.com/toronto/movies/hotdocs/home.htm

Canadian Independent Film Series
http://www.cifs.ca/frames/

Cashiers du Cinemart
http://www.impossiblefunky.com

Cinemaweb: The Internet Resource for Independent Film and Video
http://www.cinemaweb.com/

Delta 9 Independent Film Resource
http://www.d9.eden.com

Feature Film Project (Canadian Independent Film)
http://www.magic.ca/ffp/index2.html

Film Arts Foundation
http://www.filmarts.org/

Film Culture: America's Independent Motion Picture Magazine
http://www.arthouseinc.com/filmculture/

Film Forum
http://www.filmforum.com

Filmgun.com
http://www.idcny.com/filmgun/

Filmmag.com: The Online Source for the Indie Filmmaker
http://www.filmmag.com

Filmmakers Foundation
http://www.filmfound.org

Film Threat Online
http://www.filmthreat.com

Film Vision
http://www.filmvision.com/

FilmDependent Cyberspot
http://www.filmdependent.com

Filmmaker: The Magazine of Independent Film
http://www.filmmag.com/

Flicker
http://www.sirius.com/~sstark/

iLINE Ltd: Indie Film Cyber Network
http://www.ilineltd.com/

IMAGE (Independent Media Artists Group)
http://www.imagesite.org/

Independent and Cult Film Page
http://www.netcom.com/

The Independent Feature Project
http://www.ifp.org

The Independent Film and Video Alliance
http://www.culturenet.ca/ifva

The Independent Film Channel
http://www.ifctv.com/

Independent Films
http://www.independentfilms.com/

the indie scene
http://www.pbs.org/independents/

IndieWIRE
http://www.indiewire.com

IndieFilms
http://www.indiefilms.com/

IndieZine
http://telluridemm.com/indizine.html

The Inside Reel
http://www.goldennyc.com/insidereel/

Kulture Void Pictures: Independent Film Web Journal
http://www.kulture-void.com

Movie Magazine International
http://www.shoestring.org

M.O.V.I.E.: Makers of Visual Independent Entertainment
http://www.moviefund.com/

MovieMaker Magazine Online
http://www.moviemaker.com

National Alliance for Media Arts and Culture (NAMAC)
http://www.namac.org

The Sundance Channel
http://www.sundancechannel.com/

Sundance Institute
http://www.cybermart.com/sundance/institute/

Surfview Entertainment
http://www.surfview.com/

Toronto International Film Festival
http://www.bell.ca/filmfest

Video Eyeball
http://www.tiac.net/users/videoeye

Virtual Film Festival
http://www.virtualfilm.com

WebCinema
http://webcinema.org/

Xenomorph Filmworks
http://www.henninger.com/staff/jodoin/home.html

Books

All I Need to Know about Filmmaking I Learned from the Toxic Avenger: The Shocking True Story of Troma Studios
Lloyd Kaufman with James Gunn; introduction by Roger Corman. 1998. Boulevard.

Almodovar on Almodovar
Pedro Almodovar. 1995. Faber & Faber.

Between Stage and Screen: Ingmar Bergman Directs
Egil Tornqvist. 1996. Amsterdam University Press.

Celluloid Mavericks: A History of American Independent Filmmaking
Greg Merritt. 1999. Thunders Mouth Press.

The Cinema of Martin Scorsese
Lawrence S. Friedman. 1997. Continuum.

Clearance & Copyright: Everything the Independent Filmmaker Needs to Know
Michael C. Donaldson. 1997. Silman-James Press.

A Critical Cinema: Interviews with Independent Filmmakers
Scott MacDonald. 1988. University of California Press.

A Critical Cinema 2: Interviews with Independent Filmmakers
Scott MacDonald. 1992. University of California Press.

A Critical Cinema 3: Interviews with Independent Filmmakers
Scott MacDonald. 1998. University of California Press.

David Lynch
Michel Chion. 1995. British Film Institute.

Fellini's Films: From Postwar to Postmodern
Frank Burke. 1996. Twayne.

Film Fatales: Independent Women Directors
Judith Redding. 1997. Seal Press Feminist Publishing.

Filmmakers and Financing: Business Plans for Independents
Louise Levison. Second edition, 1998. Focal Press.

43 Ways to Finance Your Feature Film: A Comprehensive Analysis of Film Finance
John W. Cones. 1995. Southern Illinois University Press.

Hitchcock on Hitchcock: Selected Writings and Interviews
Alfred Hitchcock; edited by Sidney Gotlieb. 1995. University of California Press.

Hitchcock's Notebooks: An Authorized and Illustrated Look inside the Creative Mind of Alfred Hitchcock
Dan Auiler. 1999. Spike.

I Wake Up Screening! Everything You Need to Know about Making Independent Films including a Thousand Reasons Not To
Frank D. Gilroy. 1993. Southern Illinois University Press.

Independent Feature Film Production: A Complete Guide from Concept through Distribution
Gregory Goodell. Revised edition, 1998. St. Martin's Press.

The Independent Film & Videomaker's Guide
Michael Wiese. Second edition, 1998. Michael Wiese Productions.

The Independent Film Channel's Guide to Cinema's New Outsiders: Breaking the Rules of Movie Making
Colin Brown. 1999. Visible Ink Press.

Making Movies: The Inside Guide to Independent Movie Production
John A. Russo. 1989. Bantam/Doubleday/Dell.

Marketing and Selling Your Film around the World: A Guide for Independent Filmmakers
John Durie, Annika Pham, Neil Watson. 1998. Silman-James Press.

Micro-Budget Hollywood: Budgeting (and Making) Feature Films for $50,000 to $500,000
Philip Gaines, David J. Rhodes. 1995. Silman-James Press.

Orson Welles: A Biography
Barbara Leaming. 1995. Limelight.

Poverty Row Studios, 1929–1940: 55 Independent Film Companies
Michael R. Pitts. 1997. McFarland & Co.

Rebel without a Crew: Or How a 23-Year-Old Filmmaker with $7,000 Became a Hollywood Player
Robert Rodriguez. 1995. Plume.

Robert Altman: Hollywood Survivor
Daniel O'Brien. 1995. Chiron.

Screen Writings: Scripts and Texts by Independent Filmmakers
Scott MacDonald, editor. 1995. University of California Press.

Shooting to Kill: How an Independent Producer Blasts through the Barriers to Make Movies That Matter
Christine Vachon with David Edelstein. 1998. Avon Books.

So You Want to Make Movies: My Life As an Independent Film Producer
Sidney Pink. 1989. Pineapple Press.

Spike, Mike, Slackers & Dykes: A Guided Tour across a Decade of American Independent Cinema
John Pierson. 1996. Hyperion.

Succeeding As an Independent Film Producer: Based on the UCLA Course
Peter McAlevey. 1999. Overlook Press.

Magazines

Cashiers du Cinemart
Mike White
PO Box 2401
Riverview, MI 48192

$5.00/3 issues.

Film Culture: America's Independent Motion Picture Magazine
Arthouse, Inc.
1 Astor Pl., Ste. 9D
New York, NY 10003
(212)979-5663

Quarterly. $25.00/year in the U.S.; $30.00 in Canada and Mexico.

Filmmaker Magazine
5455 Wilshire Blvd., Ste. 1500
Los Angeles, CA 90036-4201
(323)932-5608

Quarterly. $16.00/year in the U.S.; $19.00 in Canada; $35.00 elsewhere.

The Independent Film and Video Monthly
AIVF
304 Hudson St., 6th Fl.
New York, NY 10013
(212)807-1400

$3.95/issue. Included with membership to the Association of Independent Video and Filmmakers ($55.00/year; $35.00 for students).

MovieMaker Magazine
750 S. Euclid Ave.
Pasadena, CA 91106
(626)584-6766

$30.00/12 issues.

The New York Independent Film Monitor
IFM Publishing
244 5th Ave., Ste. 2310
New York, NY 10001
(212)865-0164

Monthly.

Reel Independence
360A Bloor St. W.
PO Box 19030
Toronto, ON, Canada M5S 1X0

$15.00/6 issues in the U.S.; $18.00 in Canada.

Video Eyeball
122 Montclair Ave.
Boston, MA 02131-1344
(617)327-1039

Quarterly. $12.00/year in the U.S.; $17.00 in Canada; $20.00 in Europe/Asia; $24.00 in Australia/New Zealand.

Organizations/ Associations

American Film Institute (AFI)
John F. Kennedy Center for the Performing Arts
Washington, DC 20566
800-774-4234

Jean Firstenberg, Director.
A nonprofit corporation dedicated to preserving and developing the nation's artistic and cultural resources in film and video.

American Film Marketing Association
10850 Wilshire Blvd., 9th Fl.
Los Angeles, CA 90024-4321
(310)446-1000

Mike Frischkorn, President.
Independent producers and distributors of feature-length theatrical films.

Association of Independent Video and Filmmakers
304 Hudson St., 6th Fl.
New York, NY 10013
(212)807-1400

Ruby Lerner, Executive Director.
Independent film and video makers, producers, writers, and others. Assists in financing and exhibiting independent work.

Black American Cinema Society
3617 Monclair St.
Los Angeles, CA 90018
(213)737-3292

Mayme Agnew Clayton, Founder and Director.
Provides financial support to independent black filmmakers. Works to create awareness of black contributions to the motion picture industry.

Canadian Independent Film Caucus
181 Carlaw Ave., Ste. 211
Toronto, ON, Canada M4M 2S1
(416)469-2596

Janice Dawe, Chair.
Promotes excellence in filmmaking; seeks to advance the economic interests of independent filmmakers.

Council of Film Organizations
334 W. 54th St.
Los Angeles, CA 90037
(213)752-5811

Dr. Donald A. Reed, President.
Provides a forum for film organizations and individuals interested in filmmaking.

Film Arts Foundation
346 9th St., 2nd Fl.

San Francisco, CA 94103
(415)552-8760

Gail Silva, Director.
Supports and encourages independent film and video makers through educational and information services.

GEN ART
145 W. 28th St., Ste. 11C
New York, NY 10001
(212)290-0312

Adam Walden, Managing Director.
Supports and showcases young emerging talent in independent film, fashion, and the visual arts.

Independent Feature Project
104 W. 29th St., 12th Fl.
New York, NY 10001-5310
(212)465-8200

Michelle Byrd, Executive Director.
Promotes the production and distribution of independent feature films.

Independent Film and Video Alliance
4550 Garnier
Montreal, PQ, Canada H2J 3S5
(514)277-0328

Promotes growth and development of the Canadian independent film industry.

Independent Film Distributors' Association
c/o Connoisseur Video Ltd.
10A Stephen Mews
London W1A 0AX, England
44-171-957-8957

Association of independent film distributors.

International Film Seminars
462 Broadway, Ste. 510
New York, NY 10013-2618
(212)925-3191

Somi Roy, Executive Director.
Sponsors the annual Robert Flaherty Seminar, an international convocation of those active in independent film and video production, distribution, and exhibition.

National Asian American Telecommunications Association
346 9th St., 2nd Fl.
San Francisco, CA 94103
(415)863-0814

Eddie Wong, Executive Director.
Promotes the interests of Asian Americans in the media. Offers financial consultation services for independent film and video productions.

Outfest
8455 Beverly Blvd., Ste. 309
Los Angeles, CA 90048
(213)951-1247

Morgan Rumpf, Director.
Individuals and organizations serving as a programming group focusing on independent film and video projects dealing with gay and lesbian situations.

Producers Alliance for Cinema and Television
Gordon House
Greencoat Pl.
London SW1P 1PH, England
44-171-331-6000

David Alan Mills, Membership Officer.
Promotes and protects the commercial interests of independent producers whose primary business is the creation of television programming and feature films.

Satellite Video Exchange Society
1695 Marine St.
Vancouver, BC, Canada VAT 1Z2
(604)872-8337

Joe Sarahan, President.
Seeks to promote independently produced film and video projects and provide access to production equipment.

Sundance Institute
PO Box 16450
Salt Lake City, UT 84116
(801)328-3456

Ken Brecher, Executive Vice-President.
Resource center for independent filmmakers and other artists.

University Film and Video Foundation
c/o Dr. John Kuiper
University of North Texas
Dept. of Radio-T.V.-Film
PO Box 13108
Denton, TX 76203-3138
(817)565-2537

Dr. Steve Craig, President.
Supports university film and video production. Coordinates international screenings, film festivals, and education. Assists in distribution of independent films.

Women in Film
6464 Sunset Blvd., Ste. 1080
Hollywood, CA 90028
(213)463-6040

Meta Williams, Director.
Supports women in the film and television industries.

Alternative Titles

Frankenstein Unbound or *Roger Corman's Frankenstein Unbound*? *L'Affiche Rouge* or *The Red Poster*? *Over Her Dead Body* or *Enid Is Sleeping*? These and other alternative title quandries are addressed here in the aptly named "Alternative Titles Index." Variant and foreign titles for the movies reviewed in this book are provided in alphabetical order (and please remember that foreign articles are NOT ignored in the alpha sort), followed by a cross-reference to the appropriate entry in the main review section.

À Bout de Souffle
See Breathless (1959)
A Hercegno es a Kobold
See Princess and the Goblin (1992)
The Actress
See Center Stage (1991)
Acts of Love
See Carried Away (1995)
Adele Hasn't Had Her Supper Yet
See Dinner for Adele (1978)
The Adventures of Chatran
See The Adventures of Milo & Otis (1989)
Aelita: The Revolt of the Robots
See Aelita: Queen of Mars (1924)
L'Affiche Rouge
See The Red Poster (1976)
Aimok a hazrol
See 25 Fireman's Street (1973)
Amerikaner Shadkhn
See American Matchmaker (1940)
Angel Street
See Gaslight (1940)
Ansikte mot Ansikte
See Face to Face (1976)
Atame
See Tie Me Up! Tie Me Down! (1990)
An Average Man
See An Average Little Man (1977)
Balans Kwartalny
See The Balance (1975)
Be Beautiful and Shut Up
See Sois Belle et Tais-Toi (1958)
Be Beautiful but Shut Up
See Sois Belle et Tais-Toi (1958)
The Beans of Egypt, Maine
See Forbidden Choices (1994)
Below Utopia
See Body Count (1997)
The Best Way to Walk
See The Best Way (1976)
The Big Bang Theory
See Bang (1995)
Big Time Operators
See The Smallest Show on Earth (1957)
Blonde for Danger
See Sois Belle et Tais-Toi (1958)
Blue
See Trois Couleurs: Bleu (1993)
The Boat
See Das Boot (1981)
Brian Wilson: I Just Wasn't Made for These Times
See I Just Wasn't Made for These Times (1994)
Bride of the Atom
See Bride of the Monster (1955)
Brutti, Sporchi e Cattivi
See Down & Dirty (1976)
Budding Love
See L'Amour en Herbe (1977)
The Buddy Factor
See Swimming with Sharks (1994)
Build a Fort, Set It on Fire
See Basquiat (1996)
Bye Bye Victor
See Salut Victor! (1989)
Camada Negra
See Black Litter (1977)
Cannibal Orgy, or the Maddest Story Ever Told
See Spider Baby (1964)
Care of the Spitfire Grill
See The Spitfire Grill (1995)
Caro Michele
See Dear Michael (1976)
Cartes del Parque
See Letters from the Park (1988)
Castle of Doom
See Vampyr (1931)
Catch Us If You Can
See Having a Wild Weekend (1965)
Caught in the Act
See Cosi (1995)

Ce Cher Victor
See Dear Victor (1975)
Chacun Cherche Son Chat
See When the Cat's Away (1996)
Chelovek S Kinooapparatom
See The Man with the Movie Camera (1923)
Cheun Gwong Tsa Sit
See Happy Together (1996)
Chicken Hawk: Men Who Love Boys
See Chicken Hawk (1994)
Clean Slate
See Coup de Torchon (1981)
Como Agua para Chocolate
See Like Water for Chocolate (1993)
Cradle of Crime
See Dead End (1937)
Cutter and Bone
See Cutter's Way (1981)
Daddy Nostalgie
See Daddy Nostalgia (1990)
Dangerous Love Affairs
See Dangerous Liaisons (1960)
Das Schreckliche Madchen
See The Nasty Girl (1990)
Das Zweite Erwachen der Christa Klages
See The Second Awakening of Christa Klages (1978)
Deadly Is the Female
See Gun Crazy (1949)
Dearest Love
See Murmur of the Heart (1971)
Dellamorte Delamore
See Cemetery Man (1995)
Der Himmel Uber Berlin
See Wings of Desire (1988)
Der Starke Ferdinand
See Strongman Ferdinand (1976)
Die Buechse der Pandora
See Pandora's Box (1928)
Die Freudlosse Gasse
See Joyless Street (1925)
Die Macht der Bilder: Leni Riefenstahl
See The Wonderful, Horrible Life of Leni Riefenstahl (1993)
Dirty, Mean and Nasty
See Down & Dirty (1976)
East of Shanghai
See Rich and Strange (1932)
Eight Arms to Hold You
See Help! (1965)
El Espiritu de la Colmena
See Spirit of the Beehive (1973)
The Enigma of Kaspar Hauser
See Every Man for Himself & God against All (1975)
Entre Tinieblas
See Dark Habits (1984)
Fabula de la Bella Palomera
See The Fable of the Beautiful Pigeon Fancier (1988)
Father Master
See Padre Padrone (1977)
Federico Fellini's 8½
See 8½ (1963)
Feldmann Saken
See The Feldmann Case (1987)
Finger of Guilt
See The Intimate Stranger (1956)
Five Angles on Murder
See The Woman in Question (1950)
Förvandlingen
See Metamorphosis (1975)
The Fruit Machine
See Wonderland (1988)
Gavre Princip Himmel Unter Steinen
See Death of a Schoolboy (1991)
Gestapo
See Night Train to Munich (1940)
The Girl Was Young
See Young and Innocent (1937)
Glen or Glenda: The Confessions of Ed Wood
See Glen or Glenda? (1953)
Gokiburi
See Twilight of the Cockroaches (1990)
The Grail
See Lancelot of the Lake (1974)
Gran Bollito
See An Average Little Man (1977)
The Grand Highway
See Le Grand Chemin (1987)
Grave Robbers from Outer Space
See Plan 9 from Outer Space (1956)
The Great Day
See A Special Day (1977)
Guilia e Guilia
See Julia and Julia (1987)
Halloween 7
See Halloween: H20 (1998)
Halloween: H20 (Twenty Years Later)
See Halloween: H20 (1998)
He or She
See Glen or Glenda? (1953)
Hidden Power
See Sabotage (1936)
Hotel Sorrento
See Sorrento Beach (1995)
Hsi Yen
See The Wedding Banquet (1993)
Hurricane
See Hurricane Streets (1996)
I Changed My Sex
See Glen or Glenda? (1953)
I Led Two Lives
See Glen or Glenda? (1953)
Il Conformist
See The Conformist (1971)
Il Etait une Fois dans l'Est
See Once upon a Time in the East (1974)
Il Postino
See The Postman (1994)
Il Saprofita
See The Profiteer (1974)
Il Sorriso del Grande Tentatore
See The Devil Is a Woman (1975)
Illumination
See FairyTale: A True Story (1997)
The Iron Kiss
See Naked Kiss (1964)
Ivnana
See Lullaby (1994)
J'ai Tué
See I Have Killed (1924)
Jeder fur Sich und Gott gegen Alle
See Every Man for Himself & God against All (1975)
The Jezebels
See Switchblade Sisters (1975)
Jonas—Qui Aura 25 Ans en l'An 2000
See Jonah Who Will Be 25 in the Year 2000 (1976)
Joyous Laughter
See Passionate Thief (1960)
A Judgment in Stone
See La Ceremonie (1995)
The Kidnappers
See The Little Kidnappers (1953)
Killer Bait
See Too Late for Tears (1949)
Koneko Monogatari
See The Adventures of Milo & Otis (1989)

La Belle et la Bête
See Beauty and the Beast (1946)
La Cité des Enfants Perdus
See The City of Lost Children (1995)
La Communion Solonnelle
See First Communion (1977)
La Jeune Fille et la Mort
See Death and the Maiden (1994)
La Ley del Deseo
See Law of Desire (1986)
La Mano del Straniero
See The Stranger's Hand (1954)
La Meilleure Façon de Marcher
See The Best Way (1976)
La Vita E Bella
See Life Is Beautiful (1998)
Lady Jane Grey
See Nine Days a Queen (1936)
The Lady Killers
See The Ladykillers (1955)
Lancelot du Lac
See Lancelot of the Lake (1974)
The Late Edwina Black
See The Obsessed (1951)
Le Chat et la Souris
See Cat and Mouse (1978)
Le Fantôme de la Liberté
See Phantom of Liberty (1974)
Le Graal
See Lancelot of the Lake (1974)
Le Moine et la Sorcière
See Sorceress (1988)
Le Notti Bianche
See White Nights (1957)
Le Pays Bleu
See Blue Country (1977)
Le Regle du Jeu
See The Rules of the Game (1939)
Le Souffle au Coeur
See Murmur of the Heart (1971)
Les Cent et Une Nuits
See 101 Nights (1995)
Les Enfants du Paradis
See Children of Paradise (1945)
Les Jeux Interdits
See Forbidden Games (1952)
Les Liaisons Dangereuses
See Dangerous Liaisons (1960)
Les Ordres
See The Orders (1975)
Les Quartre Cents Coups
See The 400 Blows (1959)
Les Routes du Sud
See Roads to the South (1978)
Les Sorcières de Salem
See The Crucible (1957)
L'Homme Qui Aimait les Femmes
See The Man Who Loved Women (1977)
Lian'ai Yu Yiwu
See Love and Duty (1931)
Lights of Variety
See Variety Lights (1951)
The Liver Eaters
See Spider Baby (1964)
Lo Zio Indegno
See The Sleazy Uncle (1989)
L'Ombre du Doute
See Shades of Doubt (1993)
Look Beautiful and Shut Up
See Sois Belle et Tais-Toi (1958)
Lords of Treason
See Secret Honor (1985)

The Lost Illusion
See The Fallen Idol (1949)
The Loves of Isadora
See Isadora (1968)
Luci del Varieta
See Variety Lights (1951)
Lulu
See Pandora's Box (1928)
L'Une Chante, l'Autre Pas
See One Sings, the Other Doesn't (1977)
L'Universe de Jacques Demy
See The World of Jacques Demy (1995)
Magyarok
See The Hungarians (1978)
Marcia Trionfale
See Victory March (1976)
Meet Ruth Stoops
See Citizen Ruth (1996)
Meet the Applegates
See The Applegates (1989)
Melanie Rose
See High Stakes (1989)
Men with Guns
See Hombres Armados (1997)
Mi Familia
See My Family (1994)
Mike Leigh's Naked
See Naked (1993)
Miracle of Life
See Our Daily Bread (1934)
Mrs. Parker and the Round Table
See Mrs. Parker and the Vicious Circle (1994)
Mr. 247
See A Modern Affair (1994)
Mitt Liv Som Hund
See My Life As a Dog (1985)
Morgan: A Suitable Case for Treatment
See Morgan! (1966)
Mujeres al Borde de un Ataque de Nervios
See Women on the Verge of a Nervous Breakdown (1988)
Mutter Kusters Fahrt Zum Himmel
See Mother Kusters Goes to Heaven (1976)
My Father, My Master
See Padre Padrone (1977)
My Life in Pink
See Ma Vie en Rose (1997)
The Mystery of Kaspar Hauser
See Every Man for Himself & God against All (1975)
Na Samote u Lesa
See Seclusion near a Forest (1976)
Neco Z Alenky
See Alice (1988)
The New China Woman
See Center Stage (1991)
Nick Carter in Prague
See Dinner for Adele (1978)
Night Legs
See Fright (1971)
Night of the Anubis
See Night of the Living Dead (1968)
Night of the Flesh Eaters
See Night of the Living Dead (1968)
Night Train
See Night Train to Munich (1940)
Nosferatu, A Symphony of Horror
See Nosferatu (1922)
Nosferatu, A Symphony of Terror
See Nosferatu (1922)
Nosferatu, Eine Symphonie des Grauens
See Nosferatu (1922)
Nosferatu, The Vampire
See Nosferatu (1922)

Not against the Flesh
See Vampyr (1931)
Nuovo Cinema Paradiso
See Cinema Paradiso (1988)
O Casamento
See The Marriage (1976)
Obsession
See The Hidden Room (1949)
Of Death, Of Love
See Cemetery Man (1995)
One Cup of Coffee
See Pastime (1991)
141 Minutes from the Unfinished Sentence
See The Unfinished Sentence in 141 Minutes (1975)
141 Perc a Befejezetlen Mondatbal
See The Unfinished Sentence in 141 Minutes (1975)
One Wild Moment
See In a Wild Moment (1978)
Orkobefogadas
See Adoption (1975)
Orlacs Hände
See The Hands of Orlac (1925)
Ost und West
See East and West (1924)
Otto E Mezzo
See 8½ (1963)
Outomlionnye Solntsem
See Burnt by the Sun (1994)
Over Her Dead Body
See Enid Is Sleeping (1990)
Paradistorg
See Paradise Place (1977)
Pas Si Méchant que Ça
See The Wonderful Crook (1975)
Pasqualino Settebellezze
See Seven Beauties (1976)
Pasqualino: Seven Beauties
See Seven Beauties (1976)
Pepita Jiminez
See Bride to Be (1975)
Phenomena
See Creepers (1985)
Pixote: A Lei do Mais Fraco
See Pixote (1981)
Playgirl Gang
See Switchblade Sisters (1975)
Po Dezju
See Before the Rain (1994)
Podranki
See The Orphans (1977)
Popiol i Diament
See Ashes and Diamonds (1958)
Pourquoi Pas!
See Why Not! (1978)
The Power of the Image: Leni Riefenstahl
See The Wonderful, Horrible Life of Leni Riefenstahl (1993)
Precious
See Citizen Ruth (1996)
Przesluchanie
See The Interrogation (1982)
Q Planes
See Clouds over Europe (1939)
Q: The Winged Serpent
See Q (The Winged Serpent) (1982)
The Quarterly Balance
See The Balance (1975)
Qui Ju Da Guansi
See The Story of Qui Ju (1991)
Red
See Trois Couleurs: Rouge (1994)
Risate de Gioia
See Passionate Thief (1960)
Roger Corman's Frankenstein Unbound
See Frankenstein Unbound (1990)
Romance da Empregada
See The Story of Fausta (1988)
Ruan Ling-Yu
See Center Stage (1991)
St. Martin's Lane
See Sidewalks of London (1938)
Season of Dreams
See Stacking (1987)
Second Chance
See If I Had It to Do Over Again (1976)
Secret Honor: A Political Myth
See Secret Honor (1985)
Secret Honor: The Last Testament of Richard M. Nixon
See Secret Honor (1985)
Servante et Maîtresse
See Servant and Mistress (1977)
Seven Waves Away
See Abandon Ship (1957)
The Sex of the Stars
See Le Sexe des Étoiles (1993)
Shadow of a Doubt
See Shades of Doubt (1993)
Shadow Zone: My Teacher Ate My Homework
See My Teacher Ate My Homework (1998)
Shadows of the Peacock
See Echoes of Paradise (1986)
Shall We Dansu?
See Shall We Dance? (1996)
Shirat Ha'Sirena
See Song of the Siren (1994)
Shtei Etzbaot Mi'Tzidon
See Ricochets (1987)
Si C'Etait a Refaire
See If I Had It to Do Over Again (1976)
Skyggen Af Emma
See Emma's Shadow (1988)
Something Fishy
See Pas Tres Catholique (1993)
Sound of Fury
See Try and Get Me (1950)
Souvenirs d'en France
See French Provincial (1975)
The Specter of Freedom
See Phantom of Liberty (1974)
Spider Baby, or the Maddest Story Ever Told
See Spider Baby (1964)
The Spiritualist
See The Amazing Mr. X (1948)
Spoorloos
See The Vanishing (1988)
Spring Brilliance Suddenly Pours Out
See Happy Together (1996)
Sto Dnei rossle Detstwa
See 100 Days after Childhood (1975)
Strah
See Fear (1975)
The Strange Adventure of David Gray
See Vampyr (1931)
The Strange Case of Madeleine
See Madeleine (1950)
Stray Dogs
See U-Turn (1997)
Street of Sorrow
See Joyless Street (1925)
A Suitable Case for Treatment
See Morgan! (1966)
Summer Fling
See The Last of the High Kings (1996)
Summer Place
See Paradise Place (1977)

Swept Away...By an Unusual Destiny in the Blue Sea of August
See Swept Away... (1975)
Sydney
See Hard Eight (1996)
Tacones Lejanos
See High Heels (1991)
Tell Her I Love Her
See Dites-Lui Que Je L'Aime (1977)
Tender Love
See L'Amour en Herbe (1977)
These Foolish Things
See Daddy Nostalgia (1990)
This Sweet Sickness
See Dites-Lui Que Je L'Aime (1977)
Three Colors: Blue
See Trois Couleurs: Bleu (1993)
Three Colors: Red
See Trois Couleurs: Rouge (1994)
Three Colors: White
See Trois Couleurs: Blanc (1994)
Tito and I
See Tito and Me (1992)
Tito i Ja
See Tito and Me (1992)
Too Much
See Wish You Were Here (1987)
The Transvestite
See Glen or Glenda? (1953)
Trois Vies et Une Seule Mort
See Three Lives and Only One Death (1996)
Trop Belle pour Toi
See Too Beautiful for You (1988)
Tudor Rose
See Nine Days a Queen (1936)
Tuzolto utca 25
See 25 Fireman's Street (1973)
Ugly, Dirty and Bad
See Down & Dirty (1976)
The Umbrella Woman
See The Good Wife (1986)
Un Beso a Esta Tierra
See A Kiss to This Land (1994)
Un Borghese Piccolo Piccolo
See An Average Little Man (1977)
Un Moment d'Égarements
See In a Wild Moment (1978)
Una Giornata Speciale
See A Special Day (1977)
Under the Olive Trees
See Through the Olive Trees (1994)
The Universe of Jacques Demy
See The World of Jacques Demy (1995)
Uvidet Parizh i Umeret
See To See Paris and Die (1993)
The Vampire
See Vampyr (1931)
Vampyr, Der Traum des David Gray
See Vampyr (1931)
Vampyr, Ou l'Etrange Aventure de David Gray
See Vampyr (1931)
A Very Little Man
See An Average Little Man (1977)
Violette Noziere
See Violette (1978)
Virgine, E Di Nome Maria
See A Virgin Named Mary (1975)
Voor een Verloren Soldaat
See For a Lost Soldier (1993)
The Warrior of Waverly Street
See Star Kid (1997)
Ways of Love
See The Miracle (1948)
White
See Trois Couleurs: Blanc (1994)
The Witches of Salem
See The Crucible (1957)
A Woman Alone
See Sabotage (1936)
Xiyan
See The Wedding Banquet (1993)
Yanzhi Kou
See Rouge (1987)
Zire Darakhtan Zeyton
See Through the Olive Trees (1994)

Cast Index

The "Cast Index" provides a complete listing of—you guessed it—cast members cited within the reviews. The actors' names are alphabetical by last name, and the films they appeared in are listed chronologically, from most recent film to the oldest (note that only the films reviewed in this book are cited). Directors get the same treatment in the "Directors Index."

Caroline Aaron
A Modern Affair *'94*

Judith Abarbanel
American Matchmaker *'40*

Alexander Abdulov
Coffee with Lemon *'94*

Umar Abdurrahman
Daughters of the Dust *'91*

Alfred Abel
Metropolis *'26*

Sivi Aberg
The Killing of Sister George *'69*

Emile Abossolo-M'Bo
Night on Earth *'91*

Alon Aboutboul
Ricochets *'87*

Victoria Abril
Kika *'94*
High Heels *'91*
Tie Me Up! Tie Me Down! *'90*

Nine Abuladze
Lullaby *'94*

Frankie Acciario
Bad Lieutenant *'92*

Sharon Acker
Lucky Jim *'58*

Joss Ackland
Citizen X *'95*
Mother's Boys *'94*
White Mischief *'88*
The Little Prince *'74*

Ronald Adam
The Obsessed *'51*

Brooke Adams
Gas Food Lodging *'92*

Claire Adams
Helen's Babies *'25*

Evan Adams
Smoke Signals *'98*

Jane Adams
Happiness *'98*
Kansas City *'95*

Joey Lauren Adams
Chasing Amy *'97*
Mallrats *'95*
Dazed and Confused *'93*

Julie Adams
The Killer inside Me *'76*

Victoria (Posh Spice) Adams
Spice World: The Movie *'97*

Frank Adamson
Daughters of the Country *'86*

Robert Addie
Another Country *'84*

Mark Addy
The Full Monty *'96*

Wesley Addy
A Modern Affair *'94*
Kiss Me Deadly *'55*

Isabelle Adjani
Camille Claudel *'89*

Barbara Adler
Chicken Hawk *'94*

Bill Adler
Switchblade Sisters *'75*

Jay Adler
Crime of Passion *'57*
The Killing *'56*

Larry Adler
Sidewalks of London *'38*

Luther Adler
Voyage of the Damned *'76*
The Man in the Glass Booth *'75*
Crashout *'55*
D.O.A. *'49*

Sade Adu
Absolute Beginners *'86*

Ali Affi
One Sings, the Other Doesn't *'77*

Ben Affleck
Shakespeare in Love *'98*
Chasing Amy *'97*
Good Will Hunting *'97*
Mallrats *'95*
Dazed and Confused *'93*

Casey Affleck
Good Will Hunting *'97*
To Die For *'95*

John Agar
Miracle Mile *'89*

Keiko Agena
Hundred Per Cent *'98*

Janet Agren
The Profiteer *'74*

Jenny Agutter
The Railway Children *'70*

Pat Aherne
Clouds over Europe *'39*

Borje Ahlstedt
Emma's Shadow *'88*

Philip Ahn
Impact *'49*

Danny Aiello
Old Enough *'84*

Yveline Ailhaud
First Communion *'77*

Anouk Aimee
The World of Jacques Demy *'95*
If I Had It to Do Over Again *'76*
8½ *'63*

Anthony Ainley
The Land That Time Forgot *'75*

Mary Akin
Charley's Aunt *'25*

Jude Akuwidike
A World Apart *'88*

Bruria Albek
Coffee with Lemon *'94*

Eddie Albert
Actors and Sin *'52*

Robert Albert
Clean, Shaven *'93*

Shari Albert
The Brothers McMullen *'94*

Lola Albright
A Cold Wind in August *'61*
Champion *'49*

Damian Alcazar
Hombres Armados *'97*

Bill Alcorn
Daughters of the Country *'86*

Cynthia Alcorn
Daughters of the Country *'86*

Alan Alda
Flirting with Disaster *'95*
And the Band Played On *'93*

Tom Aldredge
The Troublemaker *'64*

Dell Aldrich
The Whole Wide World *'96*

Frederick Alexander
Another Country *'84*

Jace Alexander
Love and a .45 *'94*
City of Hope *'91*
Eight Men Out *'88*
Matewan *'87*

Peter Alexander
Color of a Brisk and Leaping Day *'95*

Rand Alexander
Caged *'97*

Terence Alexander
The Runaway Bus *'54*

Mark Alfred
Rhythm Thief *'94*

Azad Ali
Black Joy *'77*

Mary Alice
To Sleep with Anger *'90*

Dorothy Alison
Georgy Girl *'66*

Michael Allan
Dead of Night *'45*

Sean Allan
Legacy *'75*

Frankie Allarcon
Chan Is Missing *'82*

Corey Allen
The Night of the Hunter *'55*

Joan Allen
The Ice Storm *'97*

Keith Allen
Loch Ness *'95*
Shallow Grave *'94*
Kafka *'91*

Nancy Allen
Acting on Impulse *'93*

Patrick Allen
Never Take Candy from a Stranger *'60*

Ronald Allen
Eat the Rich *'87*

Sheila Allen
Children of the Damned *'63*

Todd Allen
The Apostle *'97*

Sara Allgood
Blackmail *'29*

Claud Allister
The Private Life of Henry VIII *'33*
Bulldog Drummond *'29*

Roy Alon
The Long Good Friday *'80*

Jose Alonso
Black Litter *'77*

Maria Conchita Alonso
Caught *'96*
The House of the Spirits *'93*

Murray Alper
Turnabout *'40*

Bruce Altman
The Favor, the Watch, and the Very Big Fish *'92*

Anicee Alvina
The Red Poster *'76*

Camila Amado
The Marriage *'76*

Betty Amann
Rich and Strange *'32*

Domingo Ambriz
Alambrista! *'77*

Andras Ambrus
The Hungarians *'78*

Amedee
Forbidden Games *'52*

Jimmy Ames
He Ran All the Way *'51*
Too Late for Tears *'49*

Suzy Amis
Nadja *'95*
The Usual Suspects *'95*
The Ballad of Little Jo *'93*
Two Small Bodies *'93*
Twister *'89*

John Amos
Mac *'93*
Sweet Sweetback's Baadasssss Song *'71*

Gabi Amrani
Zohar: Mediterranean Blues *'93*

Radu Amzulrescu
Citizen X *'95*

Luana Anders
Easy Rider *'69*
Night Tide *'63*

Rudolph Anders
Actors and Sin *'52*

Tiffany Anders
Gas Food Lodging *'92*

Bibi Andersen
High Heels *'91*

Adisa Anderson
Daughters of the Dust *'91*

Herb Anderson
I Bury the Living *'58*

Ian Anderson
Message to Love: The Isle of Wight Festival, the Movie *'70*

Jean Anderson
Lucky Jim *'58*
The Little Kidnappers *'53*

Jeff Anderson
Clerks *'94*

John Anderson
Eight Men Out *'88*

Judith Anderson
The Red House *'47*

Laurie Anderson
Heavy Petting *'89*

Michael Anderson Jr.
Tiger Bay *'59*

Bibi Andersson
Law of Desire *'86*
Scenes from a Marriage *'73*

Christina Andersson
Mushrooms *'95*

Marcel Andre
Beauty and the Beast *'46*

Yvonne Andre
Return from the Ashes *'65*

Natasha Andreichenko
Little Odessa *'94*

Elvia Andreoli
Apartment Zero *'88*

Ursula Andress
Perfect Friday *'70*

Brian Andrews
Halloween *'78*

Carol Andrews
The Lady Confesses *'45*

Harry Andrews
S.O.S. Titanic *'79*
Entertaining Mr. Sloane *'70*

Jason Andrews
Federal Hill *'94*
Rhythm Thief *'94*
Last Exit to Brooklyn *'90*

Naveen Andrews
The English Patient *'96*
Kama Sutra: A Tale of Love *'96*
Wild West *'93*

Thomas Andrisano
Teenage Gang Debs *'66*

Anemone
Pas Tres Catholique *'93*
Le Grand Chemin *'87*

Jean-Hugues Anglade
La Femme Nikita *'91*

Edit Angold
Tomorrow the World *'44*

David Angus
The Hours and Times *'92*

Jennifer Aniston
She's the One *'96*

Morris Ankrum
Crashout *'55*

Ann-Margret
Tommy *'75*

Francesco Anniballi
Down & Dirty *'76*

Adam Ant
Acting on Impulse *'93*

Carl Anthony
Plan 9 from Outer Space *'56*

Mark Anthony
Big Night *'95*

Paul Anthony
House Party *'90*

Rotell Anthony
Wanda *'70*

Steve Antin
Inside Monkey Zetterland *'93*

Vladimir Antolek-Oresek
Lancelot of the Lake *'74*

Omero Antonutti
Padre Padrone *'77*

Michael "Tunes" Antunes
Eddie and the Cruisers *'83*

Robert Apel
Red Rock West *'93*

Tina Apicella
Bellissima *'51*

Noemi Apor
The Hungarians *'78*

Jeremy Applegate
Heathers *'89*

Pilar Aranda
Like Water for Chocolate *'93*

Ray Aranha
City of Hope *'91*

Jean Archambault
Once upon a Time in the East *'74*

Bernard Archard
Village of the Damned '60

Anne Archer
Short Cuts '93

Robert Arden
Never Take Candy from a Stranger '60

Niels Arestrup
Lumiere '76

Fiore Argento
Creepers '85

Victor Argo
Smoke '95
Household Saints '93
Bad Lieutenant '92

Julie Ariola
Trading Favors '97

Ben Aris
Tommy '75
If... '69

Yareli Arizmendi
Like Water for Chocolate '93

Adam Arkin
Halloween: H20 '98

Arletty
Children of Paradise '45

Nikki Arlyn
Clay Pigeons '98

Angelina Armeiskaya
The Children of Theatre Street '77

Alun Armstrong
An Awfully Big Adventure '94
Black Beauty '94

Bess Armstrong
Pecker '98

Nelly Arno
The Third Man '49

Joanne Arnold
Girl Gang '54

Richard Arnold
The Method '87

Victor Arnold
The Incident '67

Mark Arnott
Return of the Secaucus 7 '80

Alexis Arquette
I Think I Do '97
Grief '94
Death of a Schoolboy '91
Terminal Bliss '91
Last Exit to Brooklyn '90

David Arquette
johns '96

Lewis Arquette
Waiting for Guffman '96
The Linguini Incident '92
Nobody's Fool '86

Patricia Arquette
Lost Highway '96
Flirting with Disaster '95
Inside Monkey Zetterland '93
Wildflower '91

Rosanna Arquette
Trading Favors '97
Crash '95
Pulp Fiction '94
Search and Destroy '94
The Linguini Incident '92
Nobody's Fool '86
After Hours '85

Jeri Arredondo
Color of a Brisk and Leaping Day '95
Silent Tongue '92

Helene Arrindell
Nothing but a Man '64

Timothy Arrington
Open Season '95

Michael Arturo
Bang '95

Bill Ash
Plan 9 from Outer Space '56

Peggy Ashcroft
The 39 Steps '35

Jane Asher
Closing Numbers '93
Dreamchild '85
Deep End '70
Alfie '66

Elizabeth Ashley
Happiness '98

Luke Askew
Easy Rider '69

Paul Askonas
The Hands of Orlac '25

Robin Askwith
Confessions of a Window Cleaner '74

Adriana Asti
Phantom of Liberty '74

Mary Astor
Turnabout '40

William Atherton
Grim Prairie Tales '89

Harvey Atkin
Critical Care '97

Feodor Atkine
Three Lives and Only One Death '96
High Heels '91
Sorceress '88

Christopher Atkins
It's My Party '95

Eileen Atkins
Let Him Have It '91

Frank Atkinson
Pygmalion '38
Young and Innocent '37

Rowan Atkinson
Four Weddings and a Funeral '94
The Witches '90

Richard Attenborough
10 Rillington Place '70

Malcolm Atterbury
Crime of Passion '57

Rene Auberjonois
The Ballad of Little Jo '93
Cafe Nica: Portraits from Nicaragua '87

Michel Auclair
French Provincial '75
Beauty and the Beast '46

Maxine Audley
Peeping Tom '60

Stephane Audran
Coup de Torchon '81
Violette '78

Patrick Auffay
The 400 Blows '59

Ewa Aulin
Start the Revolution without Me '70

Jean-Pierre Aumont
Cat and Mouse '78

Michel Aumont
Why Not! '78

Georges Auric
Beauty and the Beast '46

Amber Denyse Austin
My Tutor '82

William Austin
The Private Life of Henry VIII '33

Brian Avery
The Graduate '67

Angel Aviles
Chain of Desire '93

Mili Avital
Dead Man '95

Rosalind Ayers
Gods and Monsters '98

Dan Aykroyd
Chaplin '92

Ethel Ayler
Eve's Bayou '97
To Sleep with Anger '90

Felix Aylmer
Never Take Candy from a Stranger '60
Separate Tables '58
So Long at the Fair '50
Thursday's Child '43
Night Train to Munich '40
Nine Days a Queen '36

Robert Ayres
Time Lock '57

Rosalind Ayres
The Slipper and the Rose '76
Stardust '74
That'll Be the Day '73

Obba Babatunde
Miami Blues '90

Baby Peggy
Helen's Babies '25

Lauren Bacall
Mr. North '88
Murder on the Orient Express '74

Mike Bacarella
Who Am I This Time? '82

Kevin Bacon
Queens Logic '91
Criminal Law '89

Michael Badalucco
Mac '93

Hermione Baddeley
Room at the Top '59
The Belles of St. Trinian's '53
The Woman in Question '50

Alan Badel
Luther '74
Children of the Damned '63

Diedrich Bader
Teresa's Tattoo '94

William Badget
Just Another Girl on the I.R.T. '93

Nuria Badia
Barcelona '94

Laurence Badie
Forbidden Games '52

Annette Badland
Angels and Insects '95

Caroline Baehr
Ma Vie en Rose '97

Joan Baez
Message to Love: The Isle of Wight Festival, the Movie '70

Rafael Baez
Went to Coney Island on a Mission from God...Be Back by Five '98

Lynne Baggett
D.O.A. '49

Maya Bagrationi
Lullaby '94

Maxine Bahns
She's the One '96
The Brothers McMullen '94

Bill Bailey
Heat and Sunlight '87

Mark Bailey
The Unbelievable Truth *'90*

Robin Bailey
Having a Wild Weekend *'65*

Dave Bair
Gun Crazy *'49*

Antony Baird
Dead of Night *'45*

Don Bajema
Heat and Sunlight *'87*

Art Baker
Impact *'49*

Betsy Baker
Evil Dead *'83*

Chet Baker
Let's Get Lost *'88*

Diane Baker
Twenty Bucks *'93*

Don Baker
In the Name of the Father *'93*

Dylan Baker
Happiness *'98*
The Wizard of Loneliness *'88*

George Baker
For Queen and Country *'88*

Jennifer Baker
Tommy *'75*

Joe Don Baker
The Underneath *'95*
Criminal Law *'89*

Kathy Baker
Permanent Record *'88*
Street Smart *'87*

Simon Baker
Smoke Signals *'98*

Stanley Baker
Bride to Be *'75*
Perfect Friday *'70*
The Hidden Room *'49*

Susan Baker
Tommy *'75*

Gary Bakewell
Backbeat *'94*

Shango Baku
Black Joy *'77*

Scott Bakula
My Family *'94*

Bob Balaban
Waiting for Guffman *'96*
Girlfriends *'78*

Josiane Balasko
Too Beautiful for You *'88*
Dites-Lui Que Je L'Aime *'77*

Balbina
The Belles of St. Trinian's *'53*

Adam Baldwin
The Chocolate War *'88*

Alec Baldwin
Miami Blues *'90*

Daniel Baldwin
Trees Lounge *'96*

Dona Baldwin
Badlands *'74*

Evelyn Baldwin
Struggle *'31*

Stephen Baldwin
The Usual Suspects *'95*
Last Exit to Brooklyn *'90*

Betty Balfour
Evergreen *'34*

Michael Balfour
The Private Life of Sherlock Holmes *'70*
Genevieve *'53*
Moulin Rouge *'52*

Marty Balin
Gimme Shelter *'70*

Andras Balint
Citizen X *'95*
The Unfinished Sentence in 141 Minutes *'75*
25 Fireman's Street *'73*

Eszter Balint
Trees Lounge *'96*
The Linguini Incident *'92*

Fairuza Balk
The Island of Dr. Moreau *'96*
Gas Food Lodging *'92*

Vincent Ball
Sirens *'94*
John and Julie *'55*

William Ballantyne
Daughters of the Country *'86*

Edoardo Ballerini
I Shot Andy Warhol *'96*

Darmora Ballet
Gaslight *'40*

Martin Balsam
Murder on the Orient Express *'74*
A Thousand Clowns *'65*

Humbert Balsan
Lancelot of the Lake *'74*

Kirk Baltz
Reservoir Dogs *'92*

Anne Bancroft
Critical Care *'97*
The Graduate *'67*

Cameron Bancroft
Love and Human Remains *'93*

Antonio Banderas
The House of the Spirits *'93*
Tie Me Up! Tie Me Down! *'90*
Women on the Verge of a Nervous Breakdown *'88*
Law of Desire *'86*
Matador *'86*

Caerthan Banks
The Sweet Hereafter *'96*

Leslie Banks
Madeleine *'50*
The Man Who Knew Too Much *'34*

Bob Bannard
The Incident *'67*

Ian Bannen
Eye of the Needle *'81*
Fright *'71*

Jill Banner
Spider Baby *'64*

Janet Banzet
Teenage Gang Debs *'66*

Li Bao-Tian
Ju Dou *'90*

Christine Baranski
New Jersey Drive *'95*

Adrienne Barbeau
Cannibal Women in the Avocado Jungle of Death *'89*

Frances Barber
Photographing Fairies *'97*
Castaway *'87*
Sammy & Rosie Get Laid *'87*

Paul Barber
The Full Monty *'96*
The Long Good Friday *'80*

Joyce Barbour
Don't Take It to Heart *'44*
Sabotage *'36*

Joel Barcellos
France, Incorporated *'74*

Trevor Bardette
Gun Crazy *'49*

Aleksander Bardini
Trois Couleurs: Blanc *'94*

Lynn Bari
The Amazing Mr. X *'48*

Charlotte Barker
Wish You Were Here *'87*

Jess Barker
Shack Out on 101 *'55*

Ellen Barkin
Mac *'93*
The Big Easy *'87*
Eddie and the Cruisers *'83*

Ray Barlow
Faster, Pussycat! Kill! Kill! *'65*

Ivor Barnard
Beat the Devil *'53*
Madeleine *'50*

Alan Barnes
Whistle down the Wind *'61*

Binnie Barnes
The Private Life of Henry VIII *'33*

Priscilla Barnes
The Crossing Guard *'94*

Susan Barnes
Lover Girl *'97*
The Applegates *'89*

Charlie Barnett
Nobody's Fool *'86*

Lynda Baron
Hot Millions *'68*

Sandy Baron
Motorama *'91*

Byron Barr
Pitfall *'48*

Douglas Barr
Madeleine *'50*

Jean-Marc Barr
Breaking the Waves *'95*

Roy Barraclough
The Slipper and the Rose *'76*

Ramon Barragan
Cabeza de Vaca *'90*

Maria Barranco
Tie Me Up! Tie Me Down! *'90*
Women on the Verge of a Nervous Breakdown *'88*

Jean-Louis Barrault
Children of Paradise *'45*

Marie-Christine Barrault
Cousin, Cousine *'76*

Keith Barren
The Land That Time Forgot *'75*

Majel Barrett
Mommy *'95*

Ray Barrett
Brilliant Lies *'96*
Sorrento Beach *'95*
Don's Party *'76*

Tony Barrett
Impact *'49*

John Barrie
Victim *'61*

Julie Barrie
They Drive by Night *'38*

Wendy Barrie
Dead End *'37*
The Private Life of Henry VIII *'33*

Chuck Barris
Hugo Pool *'97*

Bruce Barry
The Good Wife *'86*

Gene Barry
Second Coming of Suzanne *'80*

Jason Barry
The Last of the High Kings *'96*

Joan Barry
Rich and Strange *'32*

Neill Barry
Old Enough *'84*

Raymond J. Barry
Dead Man Walking *'95*

Toni Barry
A House in the Hills *'93*

Drew Barrymore
Guncrazy *'92*
Motorama *'91*

Michael Barrymore
Spice World: The Movie *'97*

Yves Barsac
Two for the Road *'67*

Paul Bartel
Basquiat *'96*
Red Ribbon Blues *'95*
The Usual Suspects *'95*
Grief *'94*
Shelf Life *'94*
Acting on Impulse *'93*
Scenes from the Class Struggle in Beverly Hills *'89*
Eating Raoul *'82*

Richard Barthelmess
Way Down East *'20*

Jayce Bartok
SubUrbia *'96*

Margaret Barton
Brief Encounter *'46*

Jack Barty
Gaslight *'40*

Darion Basco
Hundred Per Cent *'98*

Richard Basehart
The Intimate Stranger *'56*
The Stranger's Hand *'54*

Alain Bashung
Shades of Doubt *'93*

Toni Basil
Easy Rider *'69*

Rudy Basquez
Slacker *'91*

Alfie Bass
Alfie *'66*
Help! *'65*

Angela Bassett
Passion Fish *'92*
City of Hope *'91*

Linda Bassett
Waiting for the Moon *'87*

Billy Bastiani
Blood & Concrete: A Love Story *'90*

Michal Bat-Adam
Daughters, Daughters *'74*

Nikolai Batalov
Aelita: Queen of Mars *'24*

Geoffrey Bateman
Another Country *'84*

Alan Bates
Silent Tongue *'92*
In Celebration *'75*
Butley *'74*
Three Sisters *'70*
Georgy Girl *'66*
Whistle down the Wind *'61*
The Entertainer *'60*

Jeanne Bates
Eraserhead *'78*

Kathy Bates
Curse of the Starving Class *'94*
High Stakes *'89*

Michael Bates
Frenzy *'72*
Bedazzled *'68*

R. C. Bates
...And God Spoke *'94*

Timothy Bateson
Twisted Nerve *'68*

Randall Batinkoff
Walking and Talking *'96*
The Player *'92*

John Batis
Teenage Gang Debs *'66*

David Battley
S.O.S. Titanic *'79*

Patrick Bauchau
Acting on Impulse *'93*
And the Band Played On *'93*
Chain of Desire *'93*
Creepers *'85*

Belinda Bauer
The Rosary Murders *'87*

Bruce Bauer
My Tutor *'82*

Andrew Bauer-Gador
The Return of Tommy Tricker *'94*

Van Baum
Set It Off *'96*

Vincent Baum
Set It Off *'96*

Monika Baumgartner
The Nasty Girl *'90*

Barbara Baxley
A Shock to the System *'90*

David Baxt
The Shining *'80*

Anne Baxter
Guest in the House *'44*

Frances Bay
Inside Monkey Zetterland *'93*

Nathalie Baye
And the Band Played On *'93*
The Man Who Loved Women *'77*

Eduardo Bea
Bride to Be *'75*

Adam Beach
Smoke Signals *'98*

Michael Beach
One False Move *'91*

Simon Russell Beale
Persuasion *'95*

Aaron Beall
Habit *'97*

Jennifer Beals
Mrs. Parker and the Vicious Circle *'94*
In the Soup *'92*
Blood & Concrete: A Love Story *'90*

Sean Bean
Black Beauty *'94*

Allyce Beasley
Motorama *'91*

John Beasley
The Apostle *'97*

Jackie Beat
Grief *'94*

Norman Beaten
Black Joy *'77*

The Beatles
The Making of "A Hard Day's Night" *'94*

Ned Beatty
Hear My Song *'91*
The Big Easy *'87*
Alambrista! *'77*

Rick Beatty
Breakaway *'95*

Robert Beatty
Time Lock *'57*

Hugh Beaumont
Bury Me Dead *'47*
Money Madness *'47*
The Lady Confesses *'45*

Robert Beauvais
The 400 Blows *'59*

Konrad Becker
Das Boot *'81*

Kate Beckinsale
Much Ado about Nothing *'93*

William Beckley
The Killing of Sister George *'69*

Reginald Beckwith
Lucky Jim *'58*
The Runaway Bus *'54*
Genevieve *'53*

George Becwar
Bride of the Monster *'55*

Rod Bedall
Mona Lisa *'86*

Irene Bedard
Smoke Signals *'98*

Don Beddoe
The Night of the Hunter *'55*
Gun Crazy *'49*

Henry Bederski
Glen or Glenda? *'53*

John Bedford-Lloyd
Diary of a Hitman *'91*

Ed Begley Jr.
The Applegates *'89*
Scenes from the Class Struggle in Beverly Hills *'89*
Eating Raoul *'82*

Rita Bekes
25 Fireman's Street *'73*

Doris Belack
The Luckiest Man in the World *'89*

Harry Belafonte
Kansas City *'95*

Lia Beldam
The Shining *'80*

Eileen Beldon
Pygmalion *'38*

Ann Bell
Christabel *'89*

Marshall Bell
The End of Violence *'97*

Nicholas Bell
Sorrento Beach *'95*

Robert Anthony Bell
One False Move *'91*

Tom Bell
Let Him Have It *'91*
The Krays *'90*
Wish You Were Here *'87*

Rachael Bella
Household Saints *'93*

Bill Bellamy
Love Jones *'96*

Ralph Bellamy
Guest in the House *'44*

Pierre Bellemare
Three Lives and Only One Death *'96*

Melvin Belli
Gimme Shelter *'70*

Maria Bello
Permanent Midnight *'98*

Gil Bellows
Love and a .45 *'94*

Jean-Paul Belmondo
Breathless *'59*
Sois Belle et Tais-Toi *'58*

Lionel Belmore
Oliver Twist *'22*

Robert Beltran
Scenes from the Class Struggle in Beverly Hills *'89*
Eating Raoul *'82*

James Belushi
Destiny Turns on the Radio *'95*
Traces of Red *'92*
Diary of a Hitman *'91*
Salvador *'86*

Dudu Ben-Ze'ev
Ricochets *'87*

Robert Benchley
I Married a Witch *'42*

Russ Bender
I Bury the Living *'58*

William Bendix
Crashout *'55*

Billy Benedict
Bride of the Monster *'55*

Paul Benedict
Waiting for Guffman *'96*

Lourdes Benedicto
Permanent Midnight *'98*

Armonia Benedito
Strictly Ballroom *'92*

John Benfield
In the Name of the Father *'93*

Wilson Benge
Bulldog Drummond *'29*

Hubertus Bengsch
Das Boot *'81*

Joan Benham
Perfect Friday *'70*

Roberto Benigni
Life Is Beautiful *'98*
Johnny Stecchino *'92*
Night on Earth *'91*

Annette Bening
The Grifters *'90*

Floella Benjamin
Black Joy *'77*

Eileen Bennett
Thursday's Child *'43*

Fran Bennett
Wes Craven's New Nightmare *'94*

Hywel Bennett
Twisted Nerve *'68*

Jill Bennett
Hawks *'89*
Moulin Rouge *'52*

Joan Bennett
Bulldog Drummond *'29*

John Bennett
Priest *'94*
Eye of the Needle *'81*
Victim *'61*

Marjorie Bennett
Kiss Me Deadly *'55*

Abraham Benrubi
U-Turn *'97*

Fabrizio Bentivoglio
Apartment Zero *'88*

Susanne Benton
A Boy and His Dog *'75*

Daniel Benzali
The End of Violence *'97*

Luca Bercovici
Inside Monkey Zetterland *'93*

Francoise Berd
A Special Day *'77*

Kati Berek
Adoption *'75*

Tom Berenger
Betrayed *'88*
Platoon *'86*
Eddie and the Cruisers *'83*

Peter Berg
Cop Land *'97*
The Last Seduction *'94*

Tushka Bergen
Barcelona *'94*

Leslie Berger
The Whole Wide World *'96*

Randall Berger
Shine *'95*

Sidney Berger
Carnival of Souls *'62*

Patrick Bergin
Mountains of the Moon *'90*

Ron Berglas
The Missing Reel *'90*

Ingrid Bergman
Murder on the Orient Express *'74*

Johan Bergman
Stubby *'74*

Christine Bergstrom
Medium Cool *'69*

Xander Berkeley
Safe *'95*

Elizabeth Berkley
Random Encounter *'98*
The Real Blonde *'97*

Steven Berkoff
The Krays *'90*

Jeannie Berlin
In the Spirit *'90*

Shelley Berman
Motorama *'91*

Mina Bern
Little Odessa *'94*

Andre Bernard
The Crying Game *'92*

Patrick Bernard
Lancelot of the Lake *'74*

Susan Bernard
Faster, Pussycat! Kill! Kill! *'65*

Herschel Bernardi
A Cold Wind in August *'61*

Lynn Bernay
I Bury the Living *'58*

Joachim Bernhard
Das Boot *'81*

Sandra Bernhard
Lover Girl *'97*
Inside Monkey Zetterland *'93*
Heavy Petting *'89*

Claude Berri
The World of Jacques Demy *'95*

Elizabeth Berridge
Five Corners *'88*

Paul Berrones
Alambrista! *'77*

Kate Berry
Daughters of the Country *'86*

Owen Berry
Fire Maidens from Outer Space *'56*

Richard Berry
The World of Jacques Demy *'95*

Adele Bertei
Vortex *'81*

Julien Bertheau
Phantom of Liberty *'74*

Roland Bertin
Pas Tres Catholique *'93*

Jane Bertish
Dance with a Stranger *'85*

Angelo Bertolini
The Lady in White *'88*

Gene Bervoets
The Vanishing *'88*

Bibi Besch
Kill Me Again *'89*

Alvah Bessie
Hollywood on Trial *'76*

Edna Best
The Man Who Knew Too Much *'34*

Thomas Bestvater
Meier *'87*

Martine Beswick
Miami Blues *'90*

Laura Betti
Allonsanfan *'73*

Jack Betts
Gods and Monsters *'98*

Queen Bey
Ninth Street *'98*

Turhan Bey
The Amazing Mr. X *'48*

Bhasker
Wild West *'93*

Rosetta Bialis
American Matchmaker *'40*

Laurence Bibot
Ma Vie en Rose *'97*

Jean-Luc Bideau
Jonah Who Will Be 25 in the Year 2000 *'76*

Leo Bieber
The Third Man *'49*

Jessica Biel
Ulee's Gold *'97*

Ramon Bieri
Badlands *'74*

Adam Biesk
The Applegates *'89*

Nine Bignamini
Everything Ready, Nothing Works *'74*

Jozsef Bihari
The Hungarians *'78*

Theodore Bikel
I Bury the Living *'58*
The Little Kidnappers *'53*
Moulin Rouge *'52*
The African Queen *'51*

R. Bikov
The Orphans *'77*

Ashley Billard
The Boys of St. Vincent *'93*

Raoul Billerey
Sorceress *'88*
Le Grand Chemin *'87*

Earl Billings
One False Move *'91*

John Bindon
Performance *'70*

Claire Binney
Don's Party *'76*

Juliette Binoche
The English Patient *'96*
Trois Couleurs: Bleu *'93*
The Unbearable Lightness of Being *'88*

Emma Bird
The Governess *'98*

Norman Bird
The Slipper and the Rose '76
Victim '61
Whistle down the Wind '61

Richard Bird
Don't Take It to Heart '44

Jesse Birdsall
Wish You Were Here '87

Jane Birkin
Daddy Nostalgia '90
Blow-Up '66

Ed Bishop
S.O.S. Titanic '79

Kelly Bishop
Queens Logic '91
Dirty Dancing '87

Pat Bishop
Don's Party '76

Whit Bissell
Shack Out on 101 '55

Jacqueline Bisset
La Ceremonie '95
Scenes from the Class Struggle in Beverly Hills '89
High Season '88
Murder on the Orient Express '74
Two for the Road '67

Erwin Biswanger
Metropolis '26

Maria Bisztray
The Unfinished Sentence in 141 Minutes '75

Gunnar Bjornstrand
Face to Face '76

Amanda Black
The Mark '61

Isobel Black
10 Rillington Place '70

Jack Black
Bongwater '98

Karen Black
Rhinoceros '74
Easy Rider '69

Lucas Black
Sling Blade '96

Richard Blackburn
Eating Raoul '82

Honor Blackman
Fright '71
A Night to Remember '58
So Long at the Fair '50

Betsy Blair
A Delicate Balance '73
Marty '55

Lionel Blair
A Hard Day's Night '64

Nicky Blair
The Crossing Guard '94

Pierre Blaise
Lacombe, Lucien '74

Corey Michael Blake
To Hell with Love '98

Julia Blake
Mushrooms '95

Loretta Blake
His Picture in the Papers '16

Madge Blake
The Prowler '51

Robert (Bobby) Blake
Lost Highway '96

Colin Blakely
Murder on the Orient Express '74
Galileo '73
The Private Life of Sherlock Holmes '70

Susan Blakely
Wildflower '91

Michael Blakemore
Having a Wild Weekend '65

Michel Blanc
The Favor, the Watch, and the Very Big Fish '92

Francis Blanche
France, Incorporated '74

Roland Blanche
Too Beautiful for You '88

Sandrine Blancke
Shades of Doubt '93

Peter Bland
In Possession '84

Steve Blane
Hard Eight '96

Harold Blankenship
Medium Cool '69

Alessandro Blasetti
Bellissima '51

Hedwig Bleibtreu
The Third Man '49

Brian Blessed
Much Ado about Nothing '93

Brenda Blethyn
Secrets and Lies '95
The Witches '90

Newton Blick
Morgan! '66

Jason Blicker
American Boyfriends '89

Bernard Blier
Dear Victor '75

Larry Block
High Stakes '89

Dirk Blocker
Trouble in Mind '86

Claire Bloom
Sammy & Rosie Get Laid '87
Look Back in Anger '58

Verna Bloom
After Hours '85
Medium Cool '69

Lisa Blount
Box of Moonlight '96

Jennifer Blowdryer
Vegas in Space '94

Rudolf Blumner
M '31

Graeme Blundell
Don's Party '76

Lothaire Bluteau
I Shot Andy Warhol '96
Orlando '92

John Bluthal
Help! '65

Betty Blythe
Girls in Chains '43

Charlotte Blythe
Angela '94

Domini Blythe
Afterglow '97

John Blythe
This Happy Breed '47

Peter Blythe
Carrington '95

Anne Bobby
Happiness '98

Hart Bochner
Apartment Zero '88

Wolfgang Bodison
Freeway '95

Karl-Heinz Boehm
Mother Kusters Goes to Heaven '76
Peeping Tom '60

Richard Boes
Night on Earth '91

Paul Boesing
The Giving '91

Dirk Bogarde
Daddy Nostalgia '90
Victim '61
So Long at the Fair '50
The Woman in Question '50

Humphrey Bogart
Beat the Devil '53
The African Queen '51
Dead End '37

Antonia Bogdanovich
The Whole Wide World '96

Vera Bogetti
Thursday's Child '43

Eric Bogosian
Special Effects '85

Corinne Bohrer
Star Kid '97

Richard Bohringer
Le Grand Chemin '87

Romane Bohringer
Mina Tannenbaum '93

Curt Bois
Wings of Desire '88

Christine Boisson
Pas Tres Catholique '93
Sorceress '88

Svetlana Bojakvic
The Dog Who Loved Trains '78

James Bolam
In Celebration '75

Eamon Boland
Business As Usual '88

John Bolger
Parting Glances '86

J. Bolotova
The Orphans '77

Catharine Bolt
The Brothers McMullen '94

Paolo Bonacelli
Johnny Stecchino '92
Night on Earth '91

Cynthia Bond
Def by Temptation '90

James Bond III
Def by Temptation '90

Ward Bond
You Only Live Once '37

Peter Bonerz
Medium Cool '69

Ken Bones
Bellman and True '88

Helena Bonham Carter
The Wings of the Dove '97
Where Angels Fear to Tread '91
Maurice '87
A Room with a View '86

Sandrine Bonnaire
La Ceremonie '95

Priscilla Bonner
Charley's Aunt '25

Sorrell Booke
The Iceman Cometh '73

Mark Boone
Trees Lounge '96

Pat Boone
Roger & Me '89

Richard Boone
I Bury the Living '58

Katrine Boorman
Camille Claudel '89

Anthony Booth
Confessions of a Window Cleaner *'74*

Connie Booth
Hawks *'89*

James Booth
That'll Be the Day *'73*

Powers Boothe
U-Turn *'97*

Caterina Boratto
8½ *'63*

Nelly Borgeaud
The Man Who Loved Women *'77*

Ernest Borgnine
Marty *'55*

Tormek Bork
The Unbearable Lightness of Being *'88*

Gene Borkan
Bound *'96*

Stanislaw Borodkin
With You and Without You *'74*

Katherine Borowitz
Mac *'93*
Just Like in the Movies *'90*

Jesse Borrego
I Like It Like That *'94*

Maria Bosco
Down & Dirty *'76*

Philip Bosco
Critical Care *'97*
The Luckiest Man in the World *'89*

Lucia Bose
Lumiere *'76*

Miguel Bose
High Heels *'91*

Roy Bosier
Steppenwolf *'74*

Tom Bosley
The World of Henry Orient *'64*

Caitlin Bossley
Crush *'93*

Wade Boteler
You Only Live Once *'37*

Costa Botes
Forgotten Silver *'96*

Savannah Smith Boucher
The Applegates *'89*

Claude Bouchery
First Communion *'77*

Chili Bouchier
The Ghost Goes West *'36*

Patrick Bouchitey
The Best Way *'76*

Rene Boucicault
His Picture in the Papers *'16*

Jacques Boudet
Waiting for the Moon *'87*

Y. Boudraitis
The Orphans *'77*

Jean Bouise
La Femme Nikita *'91*
I Am Cuba *'64*

Daniel Boulanger
Breathless *'59*

Hannah Bould
Photographing Fairies *'97*

Gideon Boulting
Another Country *'84*

David Boulton
Palookaville *'95*

Matthew Boulton
Sabotage *'36*

Carole Bouquet
Too Beautiful for You *'88*

Michel Bouquet
France, Incorporated *'74*

Peter Bourke
S.O.S. Titanic *'79*

E. Bourkov
The Orphans *'77*

Clara Bow
Helen's Babies *'25*

Michael Bowen
Jackie Brown *'97*

David Bower
Four Weddings and a Funeral *'94*

Tom Bower
River's Edge *'87*

Lally Bowers
The Slipper and the Rose *'76*

Angie Bowie
Eat the Rich *'87*

David Bowie
Basquiat *'96*
The Linguini Incident *'92*
Absolute Beginners *'86*

Aldrich Bowker
I Married a Witch *'42*

Ryna Bowker
Living in Oblivion *'94*

Peter Bowles
Blow-Up *'66*

Lisa Bowman
River of Grass *'94*

Tom Bowman
The Frightened City *'61*

John Boxer
The Woman in Question *'50*

Sully Boyar
In the Soup *'92*

Alan Boyce
Red Ribbon Blues *'95*
Permanent Record *'88*

Brandon Boyce
Public Access *'93*

Cameron Boyd
Manny & Lo *'96*

Guy Boyd
Ticket to Heaven *'81*

Sarah Boyd
Old Enough *'84*

Stephen Boyd
Abandon Ship *'57*

Miriam Boyer
Jonah Who Will Be 25 in the Year 2000 *'76*

Lara Flynn Boyle
Happiness *'98*
Afterglow *'97*
Equinox *'93*
Red Rock West *'93*

Lisa Boyle
Lost Highway *'96*

Peter Boyle
Medium Cool *'69*

Harvey Braban
Blackmail *'29*

Elizabeth Bracco
Trees Lounge *'96*
In the Soup *'92*

Lorraine Bracco
Hackers *'95*
The Basketball Diaries *'94*
Traces of Red *'92*

Kim Braden
That'll Be the Day *'73*

Jesse Bradford
Hackers *'95*

Richard Bradford
The Crossing Guard *'94*
Permanent Record *'88*
The Trip to Bountiful *'85*

Eric (Hans Gudegast) Braeden
The Ambulance *'90*

Sonia Braga
Kiss of the Spider Woman *'85*

Jill Braidwood
The Belles of St. Trinian's *'53*

Babs Bram
Red Rock West *'93*

Wilfrid Brambell
A Hard Day's Night *'64*
The 39 Steps *'35*

Kenneth Branagh
Cinema Europe *'96*
Much Ado about Nothing *'93*
High Season *'88*

Derrick Branche
My Beautiful Laundrette *'85*

Neville Brand
D.O.A. *'49*

Phoebe Brand
Vanya on 42nd Street *'94*

Marlon Brando
The Island of Dr. Moreau *'96*

Clark Brandon
My Tutor *'82*

Betsy Brantley
Another Country *'84*

Albert Bras
Vampyr *'31*

Nicoletta Braschi
Life Is Beautiful *'98*
Johnny Stecchino *'92*

Pierre Brasseur
Children of Paradise *'45*

Asher Brauner
Boss' Son *'78*
Switchblade Sisters *'75*

Mano Breckenridge
Chameleon Street *'89*

Bunny Breckinridge
Plan 9 from Outer Space *'56*

Larry Breeding
Street Music *'81*

Jacques Brel
Jacques Brel Is Alive and Well and Living in Paris *'75*

Ewen Bremmer
Trainspotting *'95*
Naked *'93*

Eileen Brennan
Reckless *'95*
Sticky Fingers *'88*

Michael Brennan
Fright *'71*

Walter Brennan
These Three *'36*

Edmund Breon
The Scarlet Pimpernel *'34*

Bernard Bresslaw
Morgan! *'66*

Michele Breton
Performance *'70*

Jeremy Brett
The Good Soldier *'81*
The Very Edge *'63*

Siegfried Breuer
The Third Man *'49*

Jean-Claude Brialy
Robert et Robert *'78*
Phantom of Liberty *'74*
The 400 Blows *'59*

Shevaun Briars
S.O.S. Titanic *'79*

Gennie Nevinson Brice
Muriel's Wedding *'94*

Ron Brice
Ripe *'97*
Fresh *'94*
Little Odessa *'94*
Fly by Night *'93*

Beau Bridges
Wildflower *'91*
The Incident *'67*

Jeff Bridges
The Big Lebowski *'97*
American Heart *'92*
Cold Feet *'89*
Cutter's Way *'81*
The Iceman Cometh *'73*

Lloyd Bridges
Try and Get Me *'50*
Home of the Brave *'49*

Richard Briers
Spice World: The Movie *'97*
Much Ado about Nothing *'93*
A Chorus of Disapproval *'89*

Johnny Briggs
Leather Boys *'63*

Pat Briggs
All Over Me *'96*

Richard Bright
The Ambulance *'90*

Susie Bright
Bound *'96*

Fran Brill
Old Enough *'84*

Steven Brill
sex, lies and videotape *'89*

Nick Brimble
Loch Ness *'95*
Frankenstein Unbound *'90*
S.O.S. Titanic *'79*

Mark Bringleson
Dead Man *'95*

David Brinkley
Mallrats *'95*

David Brisbin
Leaving Las Vegas *'95*

Brent Briscoe
Sling Blade *'96*

Connie Britton
The Brothers McMullen *'94*

Maggie Britton
Mystery of the Last Tsar *'97*

Pamela Britton
D.O.A. *'49*

Jim Broadbent
Bullets over Broadway *'94*
Widow's Peak *'94*
The Crying Game *'92*
Enchanted April *'92*

Peter Brocco
The Balcony *'63*

Gladys Brockwell
Oliver Twist *'22*

Beth Broderick
Thousand Pieces of Gold *'91*

Matthew Broderick
Mrs. Parker and the Vicious Circle *'94*

Steve Brodie
Home of the Brave *'49*

V. S. Brodie
Go Fish *'94*

Estelle Brody
Never Take Candy from a Stranger *'60*

James Brolin
Gas Food Lodging *'92*

Josh Brolin
Flirting with Disaster *'95*

Peter Bromilow
The Railway Children *'70*

Eleanor Bron
A Little Princess *'95*
Black Beauty *'94*
Little Dorrit, Film 1: Nobody's Fault *'88*
Little Dorrit, Film 2: Little Dorrit's Story *'88*
Bedazzled *'68*
Two for the Road *'67*
Alfie *'66*
Help! *'65*

Betty Bronson
Naked Kiss *'64*

Clive Brook
On Approval *'44*

Faith Brook
Eye of the Needle *'81*
Uneasy Terms *'48*

Jacob Brooke
S.O.S. Titanic *'79*

Paul Brooke
Lair of the White Worm *'88*

Albert Brooks
Critical Care *'97*

Conrad Brooks
Plan 9 from Outer Space *'56*
Bride of the Monster *'55*
Glen or Glenda? *'53*

Dina Brooks
Public Access *'93*

Faith Brooks
The Intimate Stranger *'56*

Hadda Brooks
The Crossing Guard *'94*

Hugh Brooks
Sore Losers *'97*
Sois Belle et Tais-Toi *'58*

Louise Brooks
Pandora's Box *'28*

Randy Brooks
Reservoir Dogs *'92*

Richard Brooks
To Sleep with Anger *'90*

Pierce Brosnan
The Deceivers *'88*
The Long Good Friday *'80*

Amelda Brown
Little Dorrit, Film 1: Nobody's Fault *'88*
Little Dorrit, Film 2: Little Dorrit's Story *'88*

Andy Brown
The Daytrippers *'96*

Arthur Brown
Tommy *'75*

Blair Brown
Strapless *'90*

Boots Brown
Tomorrow the World *'44*

Bruce Brown
Eddie and the Cruisers *'83*

Bryan Brown
The Good Wife *'86*

Candy Ann Brown
Zebrahead *'92*

Georgia Brown
Galileo *'73*

Gerard Brown
She's Gotta Have It *'86*

Henry Brown
The Man in the Glass Booth *'75*

Joe Brown
Mona Lisa *'86*

Luke Brown
Ladybird, Ladybird *'93*

Melanie (Scary Spice) Brown
Spice World: The Movie *'97*

Paul Brown
Butterfly Kiss *'94*
Anne of Green Gables *'85*

Phil Brown
The Hidden Room *'49*

Philip Brown
Eye of the Needle *'81*

Ralph Brown
The Crying Game *'92*
Impromptu *'90*
Christabel *'89*
Withnail and I *'87*

Samantha Brown
New Jersey Drive *'95*

Coral Browne
Dreamchild *'85*
The Killing of Sister George *'69*

Irene Browne
Pygmalion *'38*

Brenda Bruce
That'll Be the Day *'73*
Peeping Tom *'60*

Cheryl Lynn Bruce
Daughters of the Dust *'91*

Kate Bruce
Struggle *'31*
Way Down East *'20*

Kitty Bruce
Switchblade Sisters *'75*

Mona Bruce
The Missing Reel *'90*

Nigel Bruce
The Scarlet Pimpernel *'34*

Sally Jane Bruce
The Night of the Hunter *'55*

Pascale Bruchon
Small Change *'76*

Jane Brucker
Dirty Dancing *'87*

Genevieve Brunet
The City of Lost Children *'95*

Valeria Bruni-Tedeschi
Nenette and Boni *'96*

Jacques Brunius
Return from the Ashes *'65*

Patrick Bruyere
Daughters of the Country *'86*

Dora Bryan
Apartment Zero *'88*
The Fallen Idol *'49*

Peggy Bryan
Dead of Night *'45*

Anita Bryant
Roger & Me *'89*

Paul Bryar
The Night of the Hunter *'55*

Horst Buchholz
Life Is Beautiful *'98*
Tiger Bay *'59*

Norman Budd
Turnabout *'40*

Juosas Budraitis
With You and Without You *'74*

Genevieve Bujold
The House of Yes *'97*

Trouble in Mind '86

Peter Bull
The African Queen '51
Saraband for Dead Lovers '48
Sabotage '36

Sandra Bullock
The Thing Called Love '93

Eddie Bunker
Reservoir Dogs '92

Ralph Bunker
The Ghost Goes West '36

Avis Bunnage
The Krays '90

Emma (Baby Spice) Bunton
Spice World: The Movie '97

Marie Bunuel
Ma Vie en Rose '97

Anna Buonaiuto
The Postman '94

Suzanne Burden
Strapless '90

Dorothy Burgess
Girls in Chains '43

John Burgess
Christabel '89

Vivienne Burgess
In Possession '84

Arthur Burghardt
Star Kid '97

Alfred Burke
Children of the Damned '63

Billy Burke
To Cross the Rubicon '91

James Burke
Dead End '37

Michelle Burke
Dazed and Confused '93

Robert John Burke
Rambling Rose '91
The Unbelievable Truth '90

Emily Burkes-Nossiter
I Love You, I Love You Not '97

Dennis Burkley
Pass the Ammo '88

Leo Burmester
Fly by Night '93
Passion Fish '92

David Burns
Sidewalks of London '38

Edward Burns
She's the One '96
The Brothers McMullen '94

Jere Burns
Wired '89

Lisa Burns
The Shining '80

Mark Burns
The Maids '75

Cheryl Burr
She's Gotta Have It '86

Raymond Burr
Crime of Passion '57
Pitfall '48

Coles Burroughs
Art for Teachers of Children '95

Jackie Burroughs
Careful '92
Anne of Green Gables '85

William S. Burroughs
Drugstore Cowboy '89

Saffron Burrows
The Matchmaker '97

Ellen Burstyn
The Spitfire Grill '95
Grand Isle '91
A Dream of Passion '78

Chad Burton
In the Spirit '90

Richard Burton
Look Back in Anger '58

Tony Burton
The Shining '80

Tyrone Burton
Squeeze '97

Sean Bury
If... '69

Steve Buscemi
The Real Blonde '97
The Big Lebowski '97
Fargo '96
Trees Lounge '96
Kansas City '95
Living in Oblivion '94
Pulp Fiction '94
Twenty Bucks '93
In the Soup '92
Reservoir Dogs '92
Parting Glances '86

Dennis Busch
Faster, Pussycat! Kill! Kill! '65

Gary Busey
Lost Highway '96
Carried Away '95

Anthony Bushell
A Night to Remember '58
The Scarlet Pimpernel '34

Raymond Bussieres
Jonah Who Will Be 25 in the Year 2000 '76

Sergio Bustric
Life Is Beautiful '98

Charles Butler
His Picture in the Papers '16

Gerard Butler
Mrs. Brown '97

Paul Butler
Zebrahead '92
To Sleep with Anger '90

Merritt Butrick
Shy People '87

Johnny Butt
Blackmail '29

Red Buttons
The Ambulance '90

Tom Byrd
Set It Off '96

Catherine Byrne
S.O.S. Titanic '79

Cillian Byrne
The Secret of Roan Inish '94

David Byrne
Heavy Petting '89

Eddie Byrne
Abandon Ship '57

Gabriel Byrne
The End of Violence '97
The Last of the High Kings '96
Dead Man '95
Frankie Starlight '95
The Usual Suspects '95
Julia and Julia '87

Michael Byrne
Butley '74

Edd Byrnes
Stardust '74

Kathleen Byron
Hand in Hand '60
Black Narcissus '47

Walter Byron
Queen Kelly '29

Margaretha Bystrom
Paradise Place '77

Scott Caan
Bongwater '98

Angel Caban
The Refrigerator '91

Jean Cadell
The Obsessed '51
Madeleine '50
Pygmalion '38

Michael Cadman
If... '69

Jose Maria Caffarell
Bride to Be '75

Jean Caffeine
Slacker '91

Stephen Caffrey
Longtime Companion '90

Nicolas Cage
Leaving Las Vegas '95
Red Rock West '93
Wild at Heart '90

Michael Caine
A Shock to the System '90
The Whistle Blower '87
Mona Lisa '86
Alfie '66

John Cairney
A Night to Remember '58

Clara Calamai
White Nights '57
Ossessione '42

Guiliana Calandra
Everything Ready, Nothing Works '74

Paul Calderone
The Addiction '95
Bad Lieutenant '92

Rory Calhoun
The Red House '47

Cheryl Callaway
The Night of the Hunter '55

Simon Callow
Shakespeare in Love '98
Four Weddings and a Funeral '94
Maurice '87
A Room with a View '86

Donald Calthrop
Blackmail '29

Phyllis Calvert
Twisted Nerve '68

Linda Cambi
Teenage Gang Debs '66

Godfrey Cambridge
The Troublemaker '64

Isla Cameron
The Innocents '61

Hamilton Camp
Eating Raoul '82

Joanne Camp
The Luckiest Man in the World '89

Bruce Campbell
Evil Dead '83

Colin Campbell
Leather Boys '63

J. Kenneth Campbell
Ulee's Gold '97

Judy Campbell
The Cater Street Hangman '98

Kathleen Campbell
Hard Eight '96

Nell Campbell
Lisztomania '75

Tisha Campbell
House Party '90

Ron Canada
Lone Star '95

Maria Canals
My Family '94

Natalie Canerday
Sling Blade '96
One False Move '91

Hans Canineberg
The Odessa File '74

Esma Cannon
I Met a Murderer '39

Giorgio Cantarini
Life Is Beautiful '98

Peter Capaldi
Lair of the White Worm '88

Carl Capotorto
Mac '93

Ion Caramitru
Citizen X '95

Renzo Carboni
An Average Little Man '77

Bill "Chilly Billy" Cardille
Night of the Living Dead '68

Tantoo Cardinal
Smoke Signals '98
Silent Tongue '92

Claudia Cardinale
8½ '63

Julien Carette
The Rules of the Game '39

James Carew
Non-Stop New York '37

Amie Carey
SubUrbia '96

Harry Carey Jr.
The Whales of August '87

Joyce Carey
Brief Encounter '46
Blithe Spirit '45

Timothy Carey
The Killing of a Chinese Bookie '76
The Killing '56

Patrick Cargill
Help! '65

Timothy Carhart
Red Rock West '93

Gia Carides
Brilliant Lies '96
Strictly Ballroom '92

Zoe Carides
Brilliant Lies '96

Len Cariou
The Lady in White '88

George Carl
Funny Bones '94

Richard Carlson
Try and Get Me '50
The Amazing Mr. X '48

Ing-mari Carlsson
My Life As a Dog '85

Inga-Lili Carlsson
Metamorphosis '75

Robert Carlyle
The Full Monty '96
Trainspotting '95
Priest '94

Pamela Carme
Young and Innocent '37

Jean Carmet
Sorceress '88
Violette '78

Ian Carmichael
Lucky Jim '58

Morris Carnovsky
Gun Crazy '49

Leslie Caron
Funny Bones '94
The Man Who Loved Women '77
Valentino '77

Jean Carpenter
Helen's Babies '25

Paul Carpenter
Fire Maidens from Outer Space '56
Uneasy Terms '48

Fabio Carpi
Dear Michael '76

Jane Carr
The Prime of Miss Jean Brodie '69

Ronan Carr
2 by 4 '98

David Carradine
Q (The Winged Serpent) '82

John Carradine
The Killer inside Me '76

Keith Carradine
The Tie That Binds '95
The Ballad of the Sad Cafe '91
Cold Feet '89
Trouble in Mind '86
Lumiere '76

Tino Carraro
A Virgin Named Mary '75

Costas Carras
Iphigenia '77

Ada Carrasco
Like Water for Chocolate '93

Tonia Carrero
The Fable of the Beautiful Pigeon Fancier '88

Corey Carrier
After Dark, My Sweet '90

Elpidia Carrillo
My Family '94
Salvador '86

Virginia Carrington
The Killing of a Chinese Bookie '76

Diahann Carroll
Eve's Bayou '97

Helen Carroll
The Dead '87

Joan Carroll
Tomorrow the World '44

Madeleine Carroll
The 39 Steps '35

Matthew Carroll
Dance with a Stranger '85

Sandi Carroll
Starving Artists '97

Hunter Carson
Mr. North '88

L. M. Kit Carson
Hurricane Streets '96

Lisa Nicole Carson
Eve's Bayou '97
Love Jones '96

Bruce Carstairs
Luther '74

Margit Carstensen
Mother Kusters Goes to Heaven '76

Carmen Cartellieri
The Hands of Orlac '25

Ann Carter
I Married a Witch '42

Jim Carter
Shakespeare in Love '98
Black Beauty '94

Omar Carter
Fly by Night '93

Caroline Cartier
Lumiere '76

Katrin Cartlidge
Breaking the Waves '95
Before the Rain '94
Naked '93

Mary Carver
Safe '95

Desiree Casado
I Like It Like That '94

Alex Casanovas
Kika '94

Maria Casares
Children of Paradise '45

Salvatore Cascio
Cinema Paradiso '88

Chiara Caselli
My Own Private Idaho '91

June Carter Cash
The Apostle '97

Nick Cassavetes
Mrs. Parker and the Vicious Circle '94

Jean-Pierre Cassel
La Ceremonie '95
The Favor, the Watch, and the Very Big Fish '92
The Killing of a Chinese Bookie '76
Murder on the Orient Express '74

Matthew Cassel
A Woman under the Influence '74

Seymour Cassel
Trees Lounge '96
Chain of Desire '93
In the Soup '92
Diary of a Hitman '91
Valentino '77

Gabriel Casseus
New Jersey Drive '95

Patrick Cassidy
Longtime Companion '90

Zane Cassidy
Short Cuts '93

Claudio Cassinelli
The Devil Is a Woman '75
Allonsanfan '73

Carlos Castanon
Cabeza de Vaca '90

Lou Castel
Three Lives and Only One Death '96
Dear Michael '76

Philippe Castelli
Dear Victor '75

Molly Castelloe
Clean, Shaven '93

Nino Castelnuovo
The English Patient '96

Enrique Castillo
The End of Violence '97
My Family '94

Gloria Castillo
The Night of the Hunter '55

DeShonn Castle
Zebrahead '92

John Castle
The Cater Street Hangman '98
Blow-Up '66

Nick Castle
Halloween '78

Peggy Castle
Bury Me Dead '47

Scott Catamas
Men in Love '90

Georgina Cates
Clay Pigeons '98
Frankie Starlight '95

An Awfully Big Adventure '94

Helen Cates
The Whole Wide World '96
The Underneath '95

Joe Cates
Eddie and the Cruisers '83

Phoebe Cates
Bodies, Rest & Motion '93
Shag: The Movie '89

Mary Jo Catlett
Trading Favors '97
Serial Mom '94

Kim Cattrall
Ticket to Heaven '81

Maxwell Caulfield
The Real Blonde '97

Tony Caunter
S.O.S. Titanic '79

Trudy Cavanagh
Wish You Were Here '87

Megan Cavanaugh
Ted '98

Lumi Cavazos
Like Water for Chocolate '93

Ingrid Caven
Mother Kusters Goes to Heaven '76

Robert Cawdron
The Frightened City '61

Christopher Cazenove
In Possession '84
Heat and Dust '82
Eye of the Needle '81

Daniel Ceccaldi
France, Incorporated '74

Nora Cecil
I Married a Witch '42

Adolfo Celi
The Devil Is a Woman '75
Phantom of Liberty '74

Teco Celio
Trois Couleurs: Rouge '94

Frank Cellier
Non-Stop New York '37
Nine Days a Queen '36
The 39 Steps '35

Peter Cellier
Luther '74

Virginia Cerenio
Chan Is Missing '82

Michaela Cerna
The Children of Theatre Street '77

Tom Chadbon
Dance with a Stranger '85

Justin Chadwick
London Kills Me '91

Sarah Chadwick
The Adventures of Priscilla, Queen of the Desert '94

Aimee Chaffin
Pariah '98

Julian Chagrin
Blow-Up '66

Vaclov Chalupa
Martha and I '91

Richard Chamberlain
The Slipper and the Rose '76

Wheaton Chambers
The Prowler '51

Jackie Chan
Project A: Part 2 '87

John K. Chan
Life Is Cheap...But Toilet Paper Is Expensive '90

Lester Chan
Combination Platter '93

Michael Paul Chan
Thousand Pieces of Gold '91

Mulan Chan
She's Vintage '98

Piggy Chan
Chungking Express '95

Roy Chan
Chan Is Missing '82

Estee Chandler
Terminal Bliss '91

Lane Chandler
Money Madness '47

Vincent Chandler
Star Maps '97

Lon Chaney Jr.
Spider Baby '64

Lon Chaney Sr.
Oliver Twist '22

Sylvia Chang
Eat Drink Man Woman '94

Stockard Channing
Smoke '95
The Applegates '89

Rosalind Chao
The End of Violence '97
Thousand Pieces of Gold '91

Winston Chao
Eat Drink Man Woman '94
The Wedding Banquet '93

Billy Chapin
The Night of the Hunter '55

Christopher Chaplin
Death of a Schoolboy '91

Geraldine Chaplin
Cousin Bette '97
Jane Eyre '96
Chaplin '92
White Mischief '88

Sydney Chaplin
Charley's Aunt '25

Constance Chapman
In Celebration '75

Edward Chapman
Madeleine '50

Morgan Chapman
Anne of Green Gables '85

Sean Chapman
For Queen and Country '88

Craig Charles
Business As Usual '88

Emile Charles
Wonderland '88

Josh Charles
Coldblooded '94

Ken Charlette
Daughters of the Country '86

Nigel Charnock
Closing Numbers '93

Ghetty Chasun
Sore Losers '97

Geoffrey Chater
The Good Soldier '81
If... '69

Daniel Chatto
Little Dorrit, Film 1: Nobody's Fault '88
Little Dorrit, Film 2: Little Dorrit's Story '88

Kai-Bong Chau
Life Is Cheap...But Toilet Paper Is Expensive '90

Jacqueline Chauveau
Murmur of the Heart '71

Maury Chaykin
Love and Death on Long Island '97
The Sweet Hereafter '96

Don Cheadle
Boogie Nights '97

Molly Cheek
Smoke Signals '98

Chang Chen
Happy Together '96

Joan Chen
Golden Gate '93

Lester Chen
Eat Drink Man Woman '94

Harry Cheshire
Impact '49

Alexis Chesnakov
The Third Man '49

V. Chesnokov
Professor Mamlock '38

Vic Chesnutt
Sling Blade '96

Colby Chester
Salvador '86

Craig Chester
I Shot Andy Warhol '96
Grief '94
Swoon '91

Vanessa Lee Chester
A Little Princess '95

Leslie Cheung
Happy Together '96
Rouge '87

Maggie Cheung
Center Stage '91
Project A: Part 2 '87

Albert Chevalier
The Woman in Question '50

Laureen Chew
Chan Is Missing '82

Dominic Chianese
Went to Coney Island on a Mission from God...Be Back by Five '98

Walter Chiari
Bellissima '51

Byron Chief-Moon
Medicine River '94

Michael Chiklis
Wired '89

Lois Chiles
Diary of a Hitman '91
Twister '89

Simon Chilvers
Mushrooms '95

May Chin
The Wedding Banquet '93

Tsai Chin
Love unto Waste '86

William Ching
D.O.A. '49

Nicholas Chinlund
The Ambulance '90

Melanie (Sporty Spice) Chisholm
Spice World: The Movie '97

Margaret Cho
It's My Party '95

Charu Bala Choksi
My Beautiful Laundrette '85

Bok Yun Chon
Color of a Brisk and Leaping Day '95

Sudha Chopra
Heat and Dust '82

Sarita Choudhury
Kama Sutra: A Tale of Love '96
The House of the Spirits '93

Wild West '93

Valerie Chow
Chungking Express '95

Joseph Chrest
The Underneath '95

Marilyn Chris
Rhinoceros '74

Julie Christie
Afterglow '97
Heat and Dust '82

Lindsay Christman
Twister '89

Dennis Christopher
It's My Party '95

Emily Chu
Rouge '87

Paul Chubb
Cosi '95

Simon Chuckster
Sweet Sweetback's Baadasssss Song '71

Cheung Chung
Center Stage '91

David Chung
Color of a Brisk and Leaping Day '95
The Ballad of Little Jo '93
Combination Platter '93

Elaine Church
The Killing of Sister George '69

Berton Churchill
Turnabout '40

Donald Churchill
Victim '61

Iris Churn
An Angel at My Table '89

Eduardo Ciannelli
The Stranger's Hand '54

Kelly Cinnante
True Love '89

Augusta Ciolli
Marty '55

Bruno Cirino
Allonsanfan '73

Jacques Ciron
The Unbearable Lightness of Being '88

Anthony Cistaro
The Method '87

Jennifer Claire
The Good Wife '86

Rony Clanton
Def by Temptation '90

Gordon Clapp
Eight Men Out '88
Matewan '87
Return of the Secaucus 7 '80

Eric Clapton
Tommy '75
The Rolling Stones Rock and Roll Circus '68

Christine Claravall
Hangin' with the Homeboys '91

Diane Clare
Whistle down the Wind '61

Mary Clare
Moulin Rouge '52
Young and Innocent '37

O. B. Clarence
Great Expectations '46
On Approval '44
Pygmalion '38
The Scarlet Pimpernel '34

Anthony Clark
The Thing Called Love '93

Candy Clark
Q (The Winged Serpent) '82

Cliff Clark
Home of the Brave '49
Bury Me Dead '47

Dave Clark
Having a Wild Weekend '65

Ernest Clark
1984 '56

Fred Clark
Passionate Thief '60

Jameson Clark
The Battle of the Sexes '60
The Little Kidnappers '53

Marlene Clark
Switchblade Sisters '75

Petula Clark
The Runaway Bus '54

Roger Clark
Girls in Chains '43

Bernardette L. Clarke
Love Jones '96

Jacqueline Clarke
Blithe Spirit '45

Richard Clarke
A Night to Remember '58

Warren Clarke
S.O.S. Titanic '79

D. A. Clarke-Smith
The Man Who Knew Too Much '34

Patricia Clarkson
High Art '98
Tune in Tomorrow '90

John Claudio
Morgan's Cake '88

Garance Clavel
When the Cat's Away '96

Christian Clavier
Dites-Lui Que Je L'Aime '77

Jill Clayburgh
Shy People '87

John Clayton
Warm Nights on a Slow-Moving Train '87

John Cleese
Interlude '67

Christian Clemenson
And the Band Played On '93

Aurore Clement
Dear Michael '76
Lacombe, Lucien '74

Sophie Clement
Once upon a Time in the East '74

Pierre Clementi
The Red Poster '76
Steppenwolf '74
The Conformist '71

Edward Clements
Metropolitan '90

Mary Ellen Clemons
The Night of the Hunter '55

David Clennon
The Trouble with Dick '88

Edith Clever
The Marquise of O '76

Clare Clifford
Wish You Were Here '87

Richard Clifford
Carrington '95
Much Ado about Nothing '93

Emily Cline
In the Company of Men '96

Al Cliver
The Profiteer '74

Glenn Close
The House of the Spirits '93

Julian Clover
Luther '74

Martin Clunes
Shakespeare in Love '98

Francois Cluzet
Too Beautiful for You '88

Kurt Cobain
Kurt and Courtney '98

Julie Cobb
Lisa '90

Renata Cobbs
She's Gotta Have It '86

Eva Cobo
Matador '86

Roberto Cobo
Cabeza de Vaca '90

Charles Coburn
Impact '49

David Coburn
To Hell with Love '98

James Coburn
Affliction '97

Steve Cochran
Private Hell 36 '54

Rory Cochrane
Love and a .45 '94
Dazed and Confused '93

Arlene Cockburn
The Governess '98

Gary Cockrell
Lolita '62

Camille Coduri
Nuns on the Run '90
Strapless '90
Hawks '89

Denise Coffey
Start the Revolution without Me '70
Georgy Girl '66

Elizabeth Coffey
Female Trouble '74

Scott Coffey
Lost Highway '96
Shag: The Movie '89

Leonard Cohen
Message to Love: The Isle of Wight Festival, the Movie '70

Lynn Cohen
Hurricane Streets '96
I Shot Andy Warhol '96
Walking and Talking '96
Vanya on 42nd Street '94

George Cole
Fright '71
The Belles of St. Trinian's '53

Lester Cole
Hollywood on Trial '76

Charlotte Coleman
Different for Girls '96
Four Weddings and a Funeral '94

Dabney Coleman
The Applegates '89

Jimmy Coleman
Priest '94

Patricia Coleman
Habit '97

Alison Coleridge
The Shining '80

Sylvia Coleridge
I Met a Murderer '39

Charles "Honi" Coles
Dirty Dancing '87

Eileen Colgan
The Secret of Roan Inish '94

Frederique Colin
Once upon a Time in the East '74

Gregoire Colin
Nenette and Boni '96
Before the Rain '94
Pas Tres Catholique '93

Luz Maria Collazo
I Am Cuba '64

Toni Collette
Cosi '95
Muriel's Wedding '94

Kenneth Colley
A Summer Story '88
Lisztomania '75

Patience Collier
Perfect Friday '70

Peter Collingwood
Morgan! '66

Joanne Collins
Eddie and the Cruisers '83

Pauline Collins
Shirley Valentine '89

Phil Collins
The Making of "A Hard Day's Night" '94

Robert Collins
Anne of Green Gables '85

Tara Collinson
Fright '71

Adam Collis
Hundred Per Cent '98

Ronald Colman
Bulldog Drummond '29

Miriam Colon
Lone Star '95
The House of the Spirits '93

Robbie Coltrane
Nuns on the Run '90
Wonderland '88
Mona Lisa '86

Holly Marie Combs
Chain of Desire '93

Jeffrey Combs
Love and a .45 '94

Anjanette Comer
The Underneath '95

Joyce Compton
Turnabout '40

Cristi Conaway
Nina Takes a Lover '94

Laura Duke Condominas
Lancelot of the Lake '74

Joe Conley
Crime of Passion '57

Howard Connell
The Little Kidnappers '53

Maureen Connell
Lucky Jim '58

Jennifer Connelly
Creepers '85

Sean Connery
A Good Man in Africa '94
Murder on the Orient Express '74
The Frightened City '61
Time Lock '57

Billy Connolly
Mrs. Brown '97

Kenneth Connor
The Ladykillers '55

Chuck Connors
Salmonberries '91

Karen Conrad
Naked Kiss '64

Kevin Conroy
Chain of Desire '93

John Considine
Trouble in Mind '86

Eddie Constantine
The Long Good Friday '80

Michael Constantine
Voyage of the Damned '76

Giorgio Constantini
The Stranger's Hand '54

Diana Conti
Teenage Gang Debs '66

Tom Conti
Shirley Valentine '89
Galileo '73

Kevin Conway
Rambling Rose '91

Jackie Coogan
Oliver Twist '22

Elisha Cook Jr.
The Killing '56

Peter Cook
Black Beauty '94
Bedazzled '68

Rachel Leigh Cook
The House of Yes '97

Ron Cook
Secrets and Lies '95

Vera Cook
Never Take Candy from a Stranger '60

Christopher Cooke
The Unbelievable Truth '90

Lucius Cooke
Impact '49

Camille (Cami) Cooper
The Applegates '89

Chris Cooper
Lone Star '95
City of Hope '91
Thousand Pieces of Gold '91
Matewan '87

Clancy Cooper
Girls in Chains '43

Claude Cooper
Struggle '31

Garry Cooper
My Beautiful Laundrette '85

Gary Cooper
Hollywood on Trial '76

Gladys Cooper
Separate Tables '58
Beware of Pity '46

Maxine Cooper
Kiss Me Deadly '55

Melville Cooper
The Scarlet Pimpernel '34

Nathanael Cooper
Hard Eight '96

Geoffrey Copleston
The Belly of an Architect '91

Peter Copley
Help! '65

Sofia Coppola
Inside Monkey Zetterland '93

Michael Corbett
The Whole Wide World '96

Barry Corbin
It Takes Two '88
Permanent Record '88
Hard Traveling '85

Cathleen Cordell
Gaslight '40

Dorian Corey
Paris Is Burning '91

Jeff Corey
Ted '98
The Balcony '63
Home of the Brave '49

Caris Corfman
Dreamchild '85

Charles Cork
The Long Good Friday '80

Annie Corley
Box of Moonlight '96

Pat Corley
True Confessions '81

Sharron Corley
New Jersey Drive '95

Bart Cormack
Sidewalks of London '38

Catherine Corman
Frankenstein Unbound '90

Maddie Corman
I Think I Do '97

Michael Cornelison
Mommy '95

Clovis Cornillac
The Unbearable Lightness of Being '88

Charlotte Cornwell
The Krays '90
Stardust '74

Judy Cornwell
Persuasion '95
Two for the Road '67

Georges Corraface
Impromptu '90

Michael Corrente
Federal Hill '94

Adrienne Corri
The Little Kidnappers '53

Sergio Corrieri
I Am Cuba '64

Kevin Corrigan
Trees Lounge '96
Walking and Talking '96
Living in Oblivion '94
Rhythm Thief '94
Zebrahead '92

Bud Cort
The Chocolate War '88

Julia Cortez
The Adventures of Priscilla, Queen of the Desert '94

Jesse Corti
High Stakes '89

Suzanne Costallos
True Love '89

Robert Costanzo
Delusion '91

John Costelloe
Last Exit to Brooklyn '90

George Costigan
Rita, Sue & Bob Too '87

Peter Cotes
Beware of Pity '46

Joseph Cotten
A Delicate Balance '73
The Third Man '49

James Cotton
After Dark, My Sweet '90

George Coulouris
The Long Good Friday '80
Murder on the Orient Express '74
The Runaway Bus '54

Bernie Coulson
Eddie and the Cruisers 2: Eddie Lives! '89

Suzanne Courtal
Forbidden Games '52

Margaret Courtenay
Hot Millions '68

Tom Courtenay
The Boy from Mercury '96
Let Him Have It '91

Inez Courtney
Turnabout '40

Jeni Courtney
The Secret of Roan Inish '94

Maggie Cousineau-Arndt
Return of the Secaucus 7 '80

Brian Cousins
Longtime Companion '90

Annabelle Covey
The Belles of St. Trinian's '53

Stephanie Covington
She's Gotta Have It '86

Jerome Cowan
Guest in the House '44
You Only Live Once '37

Victor Cowie
Careful '92
Daughters of the Country '86

Nicola Cowper
Dreamchild '85

Alan Cox
An Awfully Big Adventure '94
Death of a Schoolboy '91

Brian Cox
In Celebration '75

Paul Cox
Careful '92

Peter Coyote
Kika '94
Stacking '87

Charles Crafts
Glen or Glenda? '53

Monica Craig
Rockers '79

Wendy Craig
Room at the Top '59

Kenneth Cranham
Under Suspicion '92

Paul Crauchet
The Wonderful Crook '75

Gemma Craven
The Slipper and the Rose '76

Wes Craven
Wes Craven's New Nightmare '94

John Crawford
Actors and Sin '52

Galaxy Craze
Nadja '95

Francis Creighton
Barcelona '94

Bernard Cribbins
Frenzy '72
The Railway Children '70

Walter Crisham
Moulin Rouge '52

Quentin Crisp
Orlando '92

Criswell
Plan 9 from Outer Space '56

Vincenzo Crocitti
An Average Little Man '77

Jonathan Crombie
Anne of Green Gables '85

Gail Cronauer
Carried Away '95

Peter Crook
Chaplin '92

Linda Cropper
With or Without You '98

Annette Crosbie
The Slipper and the Rose '76

David Crosby
Gimme Shelter '70

Denise Crosby
Miracle Mile '89

Dennis Cross
Crime of Passion '57

Larry Cross
Time Lock '57

Syd Crossley
Young and Innocent '37

Vertamae Crosvenor
Daughters of the Dust '91

Scatman Crothers
The Shining '80

Lindsay Crouse
House of Games '87

Roger Crouzet
Blue Country '77

Graham Crowden
The Little Prince '74
If... '69
Morgan! '66

Suzan Crowley
Christabel '89

Andrew Cruikshank
John and Julie '55

Rosalie Crutchley
Four Weddings and a Funeral '94

Greg Cruttwell
Naked '93

Art Cruz
Bong '95

Brandon Cruz
Safe '95

Tania Cruz
Hombres Armados '97

Wilson Cruz
All Over Me '96
johns '96

Jon Cryer
Went to Coney Island on a Mission from God...Be Back by Five '98

Mari Csomos
The Unfinished Sentence in 141 Minutes '75

Maria Grazia Cucinotta
The Postman '94

Max Cullen
Lightning Jack '94

Frederick Culley
The Private Life of Henry VIII '33

Roland Culver
The Obsessed '51
Dead of Night '45
On Approval '44
Night Train to Munich '40

Alan Cumming
Spice World: The Movie '97

Constance Cummings
The Battle of the Sexes '60
The Intimate Stranger '56
John and Julie '55
Blithe Spirit '45

Peggy Cummins
Gun Crazy '49

Jack Cunningham
Time Lock '57

June Cunningham
The Smallest Show on Earth '57

Liam Cunningham
A Little Princess '95

Neil Cunningham
My Beautiful Laundrette '85

Alain Cuny
Camille Claudel '89
Emmanuelle '74

Lynette Curran
Mushrooms '95

Finlay Currie
Hand in Hand '60
Abandon Ship '57
Great Expectations '46

Gordon Currie
Ripe '97

Tim Curry
Pass the Ammo '88

Bill Curtis
Eating Raoul '82

Donald Curtis
The Amazing Mr. X '48

Jamie Lee Curtis
Halloween: H20 '98
Mother's Boys '94
Queens Logic '91
Road Games '81
Halloween '78

Sonia Curtis
Terminal Bliss '91

Vondie Curtis-Hall
Eve's Bayou '97
Passion Fish '92

Jacqueline Curtiss
Fire Maidens from Outer Space '56

George Curzon
Clouds over Europe '39
Young and Innocent '37
The Man Who Knew Too Much '34

Cyril Cusack
My Left Foot '89
Little Dorrit, Film 1: Nobody's Fault '88
Little Dorrit, Film 2: Little Dorrit's Story '88
True Confessions '81
The Homecoming '73

John Cusack
Bullets over Broadway '94
The Grifters '90
Eight Men Out '88

Peter Cushing
Moulin Rouge '52

Eddie Cutanda
Squeeze '97

Allan Cuthbertson
Performance '70
Room at the Top '59

Iain Cuthbertson
The Railway Children '70

Kate Cutler
Pygmalion '38

Zbigniew Cybulski
Ashes and Diamonds '58

Charles Cyphers
Halloween '78

Satya Cyprian
The Giving '91

Myriam Cyr
I Shot Andy Warhol '96

Henry Czerny
The Ice Storm '97
The Boys of St. Vincent '93

Fernando Ramos Da Silva
Pixote '81

Howard da Silva
Hollywood on Trial '76

Robert Dadies
One Sings, the Other Doesn't '77

Marie Daems
One Night Stand '76

Willem Dafoe
Affliction '97
Basquiat '96
The English Patient '96
Wild at Heart '90
Platoon '86

Elizabeth Daily
Street Music '81

David Daker
Stardust '74

Julian D'Albie
The Woman in Question '50

Jennifer Dale
Ticket to Heaven '81

Marcel Dalio
First Communion '77
The Rules of the Game '39

John Dall
Gun Crazy '49

Beatrice Dalle
Night on Earth '91

Joe Dallesandro
Guncrazy '92
Black Moon '75

Peter D'Allessandro
Hard Eight '96

Francesca D'Aloja
Apartment Zero '88

Audrey Dalton
Separate Tables '58

Timothy Dalton
Hawks '89

Pierre Daltour
I Have Killed '24

Roger Daltrey
Lightning Jack '94
Lisztomania '75
Tommy '75
Message to Love: The Isle of Wight Festival, the Movie '70

Mark Daly
The Ghost Goes West '36

Seadia Damar
The Garden '77

Matt Damon
Good Will Hunting '97
Mystic Pizza '88

Sally Dana
She's Vintage '98

Malcolm Danare
Popcorn '89

Charles Dance
Michael Collins '96
Century '94
White Mischief '88

Evan Dando
Heavy '94

John Danelle
The Rosary Murders '87

Claire Danes
I Love You, I Love You Not '97
U-Turn '97

Beverly D'Angelo
Lightning Jack '94

Mirella D'Angelo
Apartment Zero '88

Isa Danieli
Everything Ready, Nothing Works '74

Alex Daniels
Star Kid '97

Eddie Daniels
Rhythm Thief '94

Harry Daniels
Daughters of the Country '86

Jeff Daniels
The House on Carroll Street '88

Mark Daniels
Bury Me Dead '47

William Daniels
The Graduate '67
Two for the Road '67
A Thousand Clowns '65

Richard Danielson
Body Count '97

Roger Dann
Two for the Road '67

Blythe Danner
The Myth of Fingerprints '97
Homage '95

Royal Dano
The Killer inside Me '76
Crime of Passion '57

Ted Danson
Loch Ness '95

Nelson Dantas
The Marriage '76

Michael Dante
Naked Kiss '64

Maia Danzinger
The Ice Storm '97
Last Exit to Brooklyn '90
High Stakes '89

Ingeborga Dapkounaite
Burnt by the Sun '94

Patti D'Arbanville
Wired '89

Mason Daring
Matewan '87

Joan Darling
The Troublemaker '64

James Darren
Boss' Son '78

Danielle Darrieux
The World of Jacques Demy '95

Sonia Darrin
Bury Me Dead '47

Claude Dauphin
Two for the Road '67

Elyssa Davalos
A House in the Hills '93

Nigel Davenport
Peeping Tom '60

Ellen David
Random Encounter '98

Keith David
johns '96
Platoon '86

Lolita Davidovich
Gods and Monsters '98

Jaye Davidson
The Crying Game '92

Lenny Davidson
Having a Wild Weekend '65

Betty Ann Davies
The Belles of St. Trinian's '53

David Davies
The Frightened City '61

Freddie Davies
Funny Bones '94

Jeremy Davies
Spanking the Monkey '94

Nicholas Davies
S.O.S. Titanic '79

Ray Davies
Absolute Beginners '86

Richard Davies
Twisted Nerve '68

Rudi Davies
Frankie Starlight '95
The Lonely Passion of Judith Hearne '87

Stephen Davies
The Long Good Friday '80

Bette Davis
The Whales of August '87

Clifton Davis
Lost in the Stars '74

Dorothy Davis
The Little Girl Who Lives down the Lane '76

Hope Davis
The Myth of Fingerprints '97
The Daytrippers '96

Judy Davis
Where Angels Fear to Tread '91
Impromptu '90

Marianne Davis
Thursday's Child '43

Marvin Davis
Tomorrow the World '44

Miles Davis
Message to Love: The Isle of Wight Festival, the Movie '70

Nick Davis
1999 '98

Philip Davis
Photographing Fairies '97

Sammi Davis
Lair of the White Worm '88
Mona Lisa '86

Stringer Davis
The Smallest Show on Earth '57
The Runaway Bus '54

Bruce Davison
Grace of My Heart '96
Homage '95
It's My Party '95
Short Cuts '93
Longtime Companion '90

Peter Davison
Black Beauty '94

Anthony Dawson
Tiger Bay '59
The Woman in Question '50

Kamala Dawson
Lightning Jack '94

Rosario Dawson
Kids '95

Cora Lee Day
Daughters of the Dust '91

Diana Day
The Belles of St. Trinian's '53

Josette Day
Beauty and the Beast '46

Matt Day
Muriel's Wedding '94

Peter Day
Bride to Be '75

Daniel Day-Lewis
In the Name of the Father '93
My Left Foot '89
The Unbearable Lightness of Being '88
A Room with a View '86
My Beautiful Laundrette '85

Gabrielle Daye
In Celebration '75
10 Rillington Place '70

Isaach de Bankole
Night on Earth *'91*

Brenda de Banzie
The Mark *'61*
The Entertainer *'60*

Renato de Carmine
Allonsanfan *'73*

Cinzia de Carolis
A Virgin Named Mary *'75*

Louise De Cormier
The Spitfire Grill *'95*

Ted de Corsia
The Killing *'56*

Peppino de Filippo
Variety Lights *'51*

Marina De Graaf
Antonia's Line *'95*

Consuelo de Haviland
The Unbearable Lightness of Being *'88*

Jaime de Hoyos
El Mariachi *'93*

David de Keyser
Having a Wild Weekend *'65*

Frank De Kova
Shack Out on 101 *'55*

Danny De La Paz
Miracle Mile *'89*

Kitty De Legh
They Drive by Night *'38*

Derek De Lint
The Unbearable Lightness of Being *'88*

Michael De Lorenzo
My Family *'94*

Maria De Medeiros
Pulp Fiction *'94*

Arthur De Montalembert
Lancelot of the Lake *'74*

Robert De Niro
Cop Land *'97*
Jackie Brown *'97*
True Confessions *'81*

Rossy de Palma
Kika *'94*
Tie Me Up! Tie Me Down! *'90*
Women on the Verge of a Nervous Breakdown *'88*

Miranda de Pencier
Anne of Green Gables *'85*

Rafael De Quevedo
Hombres Armados *'97*

Chris De Rose
Breakaway *'95*

Portia de Rossi
Sirens *'94*

Anthony De Sando
Federal Hill *'94*
Party Girl *'94*
Grand Isle *'91*

Joe De Santis
A Cold Wind in August *'61*

Rosana De Soto
Stand and Deliver *'88*

Jules De Spoly
I Have Killed *'24*

Jose De Vega
Island of the Lost *'68*

John De Vore
Starving Artists *'97*

Elsje de Wijn
For a Lost Soldier *'93*

Francis De Wolff
The Smallest Show on Earth *'57*
The Little Kidnappers *'53*

Brent Deal
Caged *'97*

Allison Dean
Ruby in Paradise *'93*

Barry Dean
Whistle down the Wind *'61*

Erin J. Dean
Lolita *'97*

Felicity Dean
Persuasion *'95*
The Whistle Blower *'87*

Loren Dean
The End of Violence *'97*

Jacques Debary
The Wonderful Crook *'75*

Diane DeBassige
Daughters of the Country *'86*

The Debonairs
That'll Be the Day *'73*

Jean Debucourt
The Crucible *'57*

Diana Decker
Lolita *'62*

Eugene Deckers
Madeleine *'50*

Jan Decleir
Antonia's Line *'95*

Guy Decomble
The 400 Blows *'59*

Michelle DeCosta
The Refrigerator *'91*

Kutira Decosterd
Men in Love *'90*

Ruby Dee
Color Adjustment *'91*
The Incident *'67*
The Balcony *'63*

Don DeFore
Too Late for Tears *'49*

John Dehner
The Killer inside Me *'76*
Bury Me Dead *'47*

Khigh Deigh
The Manchurian Candidate *'62*

Christine Dejoux
In a Wild Moment *'78*

Dafna Dekel
Zohar: Mediterranean Blues *'93*

David DeKeyser
Valentino *'77*

Albert Dekker
Kiss Me Deadly *'55*

Carla Del Poggio
Variety Lights *'51*

Dulio Del Prete
The Devil Is a Woman *'75*

Benicio Del Toro
Basquiat *'96*
The Funeral *'96*
The Usual Suspects *'95*
Swimming with Sharks *'94*

Juan deLanda
Ossessione *'42*

Cyril Delevanti
The Killing of Sister George *'69*
I Bury the Living *'58*

Damian Delgado
Hombres Armados *'97*

Gabriel Dell
Dead End *'37*

Erik Dellums
She's Gotta Have It *'86*

Heather DeLoach
A Little Princess *'95*

Alain Delon
Sois Belle et Tais-Toi *'58*

Julie Delpy
Trois Couleurs: Blanc *'94*

Hal Delrich
Evil Dead *'83*

Gerald Delsol
Children of the Damned *'63*

Claudio Deluca
Small Change *'76*

Frank Deluca
Small Change *'76*

Derrick DeMarney
Young and Innocent *'37*

Orane Demazis
French Provincial *'75*

David DeMering
Plan 9 from Outer Space *'56*

Kristine Demers
The Boys of St. Vincent *'93*

Mylene Demongeot
Sois Belle et Tais-Toi *'58*
The Crucible *'57*

Rebecca DeMornay
Dealers *'89*
The Trip to Bountiful *'85*

Patrick Dempsey
Hugo Pool *'97*

Jeffrey DeMunn
Citizen X *'95*
Betrayed *'88*

Jacques Demy
The 400 Blows *'59*

Mathieu Demy
101 Nights *'95*

Grace Denbigh-Russell
The Intimate Stranger *'56*

Judi Dench
Shakespeare in Love *'98*
Mrs. Brown *'97*
A Handful of Dust *'88*
A Room with a View *'86*
Luther *'74*

Catherine Deneuve
The World of Jacques Demy *'95*
If I Had It to Do Over Again *'76*
Repulsion *'65*

Maurice Denham
Luther *'74*
The Very Edge *'63*
The Mark *'61*

Jacques Denis
Dites-Lui Que Je L'Aime *'77*
Jonah Who Will Be 25 in the Year 2000 *'76*

Anthony John Denison
City of Hope *'91*

Barry Dennan
The Shining *'80*

Brian Dennehy
The Belly of an Architect *'91*

Charles Denner
Robert et Robert *'78*
The Man Who Loved Women *'77*
If I Had It to Do Over Again *'76*

Fred Dennis
Killer Flick *'98*

Nick Dennis
Kiss Me Deadly *'55*

Gene Densmore
Gal Young 'Un *'79*

Walter DePalma
You Only Live Once *'37*

Gerard Depardieu
Camille Claudel *'89*
Too Beautiful for You *'88*
Dites-Lui Que Je L'Aime *'77*
The Wonderful Crook *'75*

Johnny Depp
Dead Man *'95*
Platoon *'86*

Maya Deren
Meshes of the Afternoon *'43*

Bruce Dern
After Dark, My Sweet *'90*

Laura Dern
Citizen Ruth *'96*
Rambling Rose *'91*
Wild at Heart *'90*
Blue Velvet *'86*
Smooth Talk *'85*

Ines Des Longchamps
Stardust *'74*

Gerard Desarthe
France, Incorporated *'74*

Alex Descas
Nenette and Boni *'96*

Georges Descrieres
Two for the Road *'67*

Geory Desmouceaux
Small Change *'76*

Ivan Desny
Madeleine *'50*

Louis D'Esposito
Eddie and the Cruisers *'83*

Ernst Deutsch
The Third Man *'49*

Marie Devereux
Naked Kiss *'64*
The Mark *'61*

Julia Devin
The Tie That Binds *'95*

George Devine
Look Back in Anger *'58*

Loretta Devine
Lover Girl *'97*

Margaret Devine
1999 *'98*

Francis Devlaeminck
Small Change *'76*

Laurent Devlaeminck
Small Change *'76*

Alan Devlin
The Lonely Passion of Judith Hearne *'87*

William Devlin
I Met a Murderer *'39*

Lorraine Devon
To Cross the Rubicon *'91*

Felicity Devonshire
Lisztomania *'75*

Jon DeVries
Grand Isle *'91*

Patrick Dewaere
The Best Way *'76*
Victory March *'76*

Colleen Dewhurst
Anne of Green Gables *'85*

William Dewhurst
Non-Stop New York *'37*
Sabotage *'36*

Anthony Dexter
Fire Maidens from Outer Space *'56*

Susan Dey
The Trouble with Dick *'88*

Mireille Deyglun
Daughters of the Country *'86*

Cliff DeYoung
Suicide Kings *'97*

Captain DeZita
Glen or Glenda? *'53*

Dalia di Lazzaro
Creepers *'85*

Carmelo Di Mazzarelli
Lamerica *'95*

Rodney Diak
Fire Maidens from Outer Space *'56*

Rick Dial
The Apostle *'97*
Sling Blade *'96*

Otto Diamont
Lisztomania *'75*

Cameron Diaz
She's the One *'96*

Chico Diaz
The Fable of the Beautiful Pigeon Fancier *'88*

Edith Diaz
Scenes from the Class Struggle in Beverly Hills *'89*

Guillermo Diaz
I Think I Do *'97*
Girls Town *'95*
Party Girl *'94*

Luigi Diberti
Everything Ready, Nothing Works *'74*

Leonardo DiCaprio
The Basketball Diaries *'94*

Andy Dick
Bongwater *'98*
Ted *'98*
...And God Spoke *'94*

Douglas Dick
Home of the Brave *'49*

Kim Dickens
Palookaville *'95*

Bonnie Dickenson
Little Shots of Happiness *'97*

Avital Dicker
Song of the Siren *'94*

Ernest R. Dickerson
She's Gotta Have It *'86*

George Dickerson
After Dark, My Sweet *'90*
Blue Velvet *'86*
Cutter's Way *'81*

Michel Didym
Pas Tres Catholique *'93*

Juan Diego
Cabeza de Vaca *'90*

John Diehl
The End of Violence *'97*
Color of a Brisk and Leaping Day *'95*
Motorama *'91*

Gustav Diesl
Pandora's Box *'28*

Samuel Dietert
Slacker *'91*

Anton Diffring
Valentino *'77*

Basil Dignam
Twisted Nerve *'68*
The Intimate Stranger *'56*

Stephen Dillane
Christabel *'89*

Bradford Dillman
The Iceman Cometh *'73*

Brandan Dillon
The Killing of Sister George *'69*

Kevin Dillon
Platoon *'86*

Matt Dillon
Grace of My Heart *'96*
Frankie Starlight *'95*
To Die For *'95*
Golden Gate *'93*
Drugstore Cowboy *'89*

Tom Dillon
Night Tide *'63*

Francesca DiMauro
Living in Oblivion *'94*

Richard Dimbleby
John and Julie *'55*

Ayub Khan Din
Sammy & Rosie Get Laid *'87*

Peter Dinklage
Living in Oblivion *'94*

Phillip Dinn
The Boys of St. Vincent *'93*

Divine
Trouble in Mind *'86*
Female Trouble *'74*

Jason Dixie
In the Company of Men *'96*

Beth Dixon
The Ballad of the Sad Cafe *'91*

Ivan Dixon
Nothing but a Man *'64*

Jean Dixon
You Only Live Once *'37*

Jill Dixon
A Night to Remember *'58*

Edward Dmytryk
Hollywood on Trial *'76*

Alan Dobie
White Mischief *'88*

Anica Dobra
Tito and Me *'92*

Gosia Dobrowolska
Careful *'92*
Phobia *'88*

Peter Dobson
Last Exit to Brooklyn *'90*

Vernon Dobtcheff
Murder on the Orient Express *'74*

George Dockstader
Private Hell 36 *'54*

Michal Docolomansky
Dinner for Adele *'78*

Brian Dodd
The Boys of St. Vincent *'93*

Jimmie Dodd
Too Late for Tears *'49*

John Doe
Boogie Nights *'97*
Georgia *'95*

Shannen Doherty
Mallrats *'95*
Heathers *'89*

Damon D'Oliveira
My Teacher Ate My Homework *'98*

Arielle Dombasle
Three Lives and Only One Death *'96*

Solveig Dommartin
Wings of Desire *'88*

Peter Donaldson
The Sweet Hereafter *'96*

Robert Donat
The Ghost Goes West *'36*
The 39 Steps *'35*
The Private Life of Henry VIII *'33*

Yolande Donlan
Turnabout *'40*

Brian Donlevy
Impact *'49*

Barnard Pierre Donnadieu
The Vanishing '88

Donal Donnelly
The Dead '87

Elizabeth D'Onofrio
The Whole Wide World '96

Vincent D'Onofrio
The Whole Wide World '96
Household Saints '93
The Player '92
Mystic Pizza '88

Amanda Donohoe
The Madness of King George '94
Paper Mask '91
Lair of the White Worm '88
Castaway '87

Walter Donohue
My Beautiful Laundrette '85

Donovan
Message to Love: The Isle of Wight Festival, the Movie '70

King Donovan
Private Hell 36 '54

Martin Donovan
The Opposite of Sex '98
Nadja '95
Trust '91

Tate Donovan
Equinox '93
Inside Monkey Zetterland '93

Brian Dooley
The Boys of St. Vincent '93

Paul Dooley
Waiting for Guffman '96
The Underneath '95

Patric Doonan
John and Julie '55

Robert DoQui
Miracle Mile '89

Ann Doran
Pitfall '48

Matt Dorff
The Prowler '51

Stephen Dorff
I Shot Andy Warhol '96
Reckless '95
Backbeat '94

Cliff Dorfman
Acting on Impulse '93

Sandra Dori
A Virgin Named Mary '75

Sandra Dorne
Eat the Rich '87

Diana Dors
Deep End '70

John Dossett
Longtime Companion '90

Julian Roy Doster
Menace II Society '93

Els Dottermans
Antonia's Line '95

Catherine Doucet
These Three '36

Doug E. Doug
Hangin' with the Homeboys '91

Illeana Douglas
Grace of My Heart '96
To Die For '95
Grief '94
Search and Destroy '94
Household Saints '93

Kirk Douglas
Champion '49

Shirley Douglas
Lolita '62

Suzanne Douglas
Chain of Desire '93

Brad Dourif
London Kills Me '91
Grim Prairie Tales '89
Blue Velvet '86

Ann Dowd
All Over Me '96

Betsy Dowds
Ruby in Paradise '93

Raye Dowell
She's Gotta Have It '86

Constance Dowling
Gog '54

Alan Downer
The Good Soldier '81

Robert Downey Jr.
Hugo Pool '97
Short Cuts '93
Chaplin '92

Jacqueline Doyen
Dear Victor '75

Jack Doyle
The Belles of St. Trinian's '53

Maria Doyle Kennedy
The Matchmaker '97

Brian Doyle-Murray
Waiting for Guffman '96

Valda Z. Drabla
Swoon '91

Billy Drago
Guncrazy '92

Claudia Drake
Detour '46
The Lady Confesses '45

Ken Drake
I Bury the Living '58

Sylvie Drapeau
Le Sexe des Étoiles '93

Milena Dravic
Fear '75

Alfred Drayton
Don't Take It to Heart '44

Melanie Dreisbach
The Method '87

Sonia Dresdel
The Fallen Idol '49

Ruth Drexel
The Marquise of O '76

Jean Claude Dreyfus
The City of Lost Children '95

Richard Dreyfuss
Second Coming of Suzanne '80
The Graduate '67

Carol Drinkwater
An Awfully Big Adventure '94

Minnie Driver
The Governess '98
Good Will Hunting '97
Big Night '95

Denis Drouin
Once upon a Time in the East '74

Tatiana Drubich
100 Days after Childhood '75

Reana E. Drummond
Straight out of Brooklyn '91

Jeanie Drynan
Muriel's Wedding '94
Don's Party '76

Roland Dubillard
France, Incorporated '74

Yudel Dubinsky
American Matchmaker '40

Guilhaine Dubos
L'Amour en Herbe '77

Paulette Dubost
The Rules of the Game '39

David Duchovny
Kalifornia '93
Chaplin '92

Neil Dudgeon
Different for Girls '96

Lesley Dudley
John and Julie '55

Shoshanah Duer
The Garden '77

Bridget Duff
Private Hell 36 '54

Howard Duff
Private Hell 36 '54

Jacques Dufilho
Dear Victor '75

Huguette Duflos
I Have Killed '24

Georges DuFresne
Ma Vie en Rose '97

Aaron Dugger
She's Gotta Have It '86

Olympia Dukakis
In the Spirit '90

Bill Duke
Menace II Society '93

Robin Duke
Motorama '91

David Dukes
Gods and Monsters '98

John Dullaghan
Sweet Sweetback's Baadasssss Song '71

Denise Dumont
Kiss of the Spider Woman '85

James DuMont
Combination Platter '93

Dennis Dun
Thousand Pieces of Gold '91

Faye Dunaway
Voyage of the Damned '76

Adrian Dunbar
Widow's Peak '94
The Crying Game '92
Hear My Song '91
My Left Foot '89

Catherine Duncan
Shirley Valentine '89

Peter Duncan
Stardust '74

Claude Duneton
Trois Couleurs: Bleu '93

Christine Dunford
Ulee's Gold '97

Emma Dunn
I Married a Witch '42

Geoffrey Dunn
Leather Boys '63

Harvey B. Dunn
Bride of the Monster '55

Kevin Dunn
Chaplin '92

Nora Dunn
Passion Fish '92
Miami Blues '90

Griffin Dunne
I Like It Like That '94
Search and Destroy '94
After Hours '85

Anh Duong
High Art '98

Phuong Duong
Squeeze '97

The Underneath '95

Starletta DuPois
Hollywood Shuffle '87

Philip Dupuy
Another Country '84

Chris Durand
Halloween: H20 '98

Christopher Durang
In the Spirit '90
Mr. North '88

Giustino Durano
Life Is Beautiful '98

Geoffrey Durham
Wish You Were Here '87

Romain Duris
When the Cat's Away '96

Barbara Durkin
Wish You Were Here '87

Mary Ann Durkin
These Three '36

Charles Durning
The Rosary Murders '87
True Confessions '81

Dan Duryea
Too Late for Tears '49

Ann Dusenberry
Cutter's Way '81

Charles S. Dutton
Menace II Society '93

James Duval
The Doom Generation '95

Christian Duvaleix
Isadora '68

Robert Duvall
The Apostle '97
Sling Blade '96
Rambling Rose '91
True Confessions '81

Shelley Duvall
My Teacher Ate My Homework '98
The Underneath '95
The Shining '80

Bill Dwyer
Little Shots of Happiness '97

Franklin Dyall
The Private Life of Henry VIII '33

Valentine Dyall
Brief Encounter '46
Pink String and Sealing Wax '45

James Dyrenforth
Lolita '62
Never Take Candy from a Stranger '60

Anulka Dziubinska
Lisztomania '75

George Dzundza
Trading Favors '97

Nicholas Eadie
Celia: Child of Terror '90

Daisy Eagan
Ripe '97

Elizabeth Earl
FairyTale: A True Story '97

Marilyn Eastman
Night of the Living Dead '68

Marion Eaten
The Whole Wide World '96

Marjorie Eaton
Street Music '81
Night Tide '63

Wallace Eaton
Isadora '68

Roger Ebert
Independent's Day '97

Christopher Eccleston
Shallow Grave '94
Let Him Have It '91

Aaron Eckhart
In the Company of Men '96

Gwen Eckhaus
The Vanishing '88

Jean-Philippe Ecoffey
Ma Vie en Rose '97
Mina Tannenbaum '93

Dave Edmunds
Stardust '74

Beatie Edney
In the Name of the Father '93

Richard Edson
Eight Men Out '88
Platoon '86

Annie-Joe Edwards
Bullets over Broadway '94

Anthony Edwards
Hawks '89
Miracle Mile '89
Mr. North '88

Henry Edwards
Madeleine '50

Hilton Edwards
Victim '61

James Edwards
The Killing '56
Home of the Brave '49

Luke Edwards
Mother's Boys '94

Marion Edwards
Road Games '81

Stacy Edwards
In the Company of Men '96

Vince Edwards
Motorama '91
The Killing '56

Peter Egan
The Cater Street Hangman '98

Richard Egan
Gog '54
Wicked Woman '54

Samantha Eggar
Return from the Ashes '65

Konstantin Eggert
Aelita: Queen of Mars '24

Deven Eggleston
New Jersey Drive '95

Stan Egi
Hundred Per Cent '98
Golden Gate '93

Jennifer Ehle
Wilde '97
Backbeat '94

Lisa Eichhorn
A Modern Affair '94
Grim Prairie Tales '89
Cutter's Way '81

Christopher Eigeman
Barcelona '94
Metropolitan '90

Menahem Einy
Zohar: Mediterranean Blues '93

Debra Eisenstadt
Oleanna '94

Anthony Eisley
Naked Kiss '64

Britt Ekland
Scandal '89

Agneta Ekmanner
Paradise Place '77

Linda Ekoian
Little Shots of Happiness '97

Jack Elam
Kiss Me Deadly '55

Ron Eldard
Bastard out of Carolina '96
True Love '89

Tom Eldred
Teenage Gang Debs '66

Michael Elgart
Permanent Record '88

Mark Eliot
Stand and Deliver '88

Kimberly Elise
Set It Off '96

Kerine Elkins
Sore Losers '97

Shawn Elliot
Caught '96
Hurricane Streets '96

Alison Elliott
The Wings of the Dove '97
The Spitfire Grill '95

Denholm Elliott
Maurice '87
A Room with a View '86
Voyage of the Damned '76
Alfie '66

Sam Elliott
The Big Lebowski '97

Stephen Elliott
Cutter's Way '81

Aunjanue Ellis
Girls Town '95

James Ellis
Priest '94

Robin Ellis
The Good Soldier '81

Art Ellison
Carnival of Souls '62

Michael Elphick
Let Him Have It '91
Little Dorrit, Film 1: Nobody's Fault '88
Little Dorrit, Film 2: Little Dorrit's Story '88
Withnail and I '87

Robert Elross
The Method '87

Ben Elton
Much Ado about Nothing '93

Cary Elwes
Another Country '84

Roy Emerton
Nine Days a Queen '36

Michael Emil
In the Spirit '90
Tracks '76

Daniel Emilfork
The City of Lost Children '95

Alphonsia Emmanuel
Under Suspicion '92

Takis Emmanuel
Caddie '76

Noah Emmerich
Cop Land '97

Akira Emoto
Shall We Dance? '96

Susan Engel
Butley '74

Tina Engel
The Second Awakening of Christa Klages '78

Nadja Engelbrecht
Meier '87

Robert Englund
Wes Craven's New Nightmare '94

Anthony Ennis
Chameleon Street '89

John Entwhistle
Tommy '75
Message to Love: The Isle of Wight Festival, the Movie '70

John [Lypsinka] Epperson
Red Ribbon Blues '95

Kathryn Erbe
The Addiction '95

R. Lee Ermey
Dead Man Walking '95

Eileen Erskine
This Happy Breed '47
Great Expectations '46

Victor Ertmanis
Paris, France '94

Bernard Escalon
Trois Couleurs: Rouge '94

Giancarlo Esposito
Reckless '95
Smoke '95
The Usual Suspects '95
Fresh '94
Night on Earth '91

David Essex
Stardust '74
That'll Be the Day '73

Agnes Esterhazy
Joyless Street '25

Joe Estevez
Breakaway '95

Renee Estevez
Heathers '89

Karl Ettlinger
Joyless Street '25

Bob Eubanks
Roger & Me '89

Douglas Evans
Actors and Sin '52

Edith Evans
The Slipper and the Rose '76
Look Back in Anger '58

Evans Evans
The Iceman Cometh '73

Gene Evans
Crashout '55

Lee Evans
Funny Bones '94

Lucas Evans
Tommy Tricker & the Stamp Traveller '87

Barbara Everest
Madeleine '50

Rupert Everett
Shakespeare in Love '98
Cemetery Man '95
The Madness of King George '94
Inside Monkey Zetterland '93
The Comfort of Strangers '91
Dance with a Stranger '85
Another Country '84

E. Evstigneev
The Orphans '77

Dwight Ewell
Chasing Amy '97

Peter Eyre
Orlando '92

Maynard Eziashi
Twenty-One '91

Matthew Faber
Welcome to the Dollhouse '95

Adriana Fachetti
Enchanted April '92

Tom Fadden
Tomorrow the World '44

Mary-Anne Fahey
Celia: Child of Terror '90

Douglas Fairbanks Sr.
His Picture in the Papers '16

Donald Adeosun Faison
New Jersey Drive '95

Frankie Faison
City of Hope '91

Matthew Faison
True Confessions '81

Adam Faith
Stardust '74

Marianne Faithfull
The Rolling Stones Rock and Roll Circus '68

Amina Fakir
Chameleon Street '89

Anna Falchi
Cemetery Man '95

Edie Falco
Cop Land '97
Hurricane Streets '96
The Addiction '95
Trust '91

Lisanne Falk
Suicide Kings '97
Night on Earth '91
Heathers '89

Peter Falk
In the Spirit '90
Tune in Tomorrow '90
Wings of Desire '88
A Woman under the Influence '74
The Balcony '63

Rossella Falk
8½ '63

Deborah Fallender
S.O.S. Titanic '79

Jacques Famery
The Little Girl Who Lives down the Lane '76

Richard Fancy
Ted '98

Mei Fang
One Night Stand '76

Rio Fanning
Priest '94

Sergio Fantoni
The Belly of an Architect '91

Jamila Farah
Nenette and Boni '96

Souad Faress
My Beautiful Laundrette '85

Betty Faria
The Story of Fausta '88

Carolyn Farina
Metropolitan '90

Dennis Farina
Mac '93

Gary Farmer
Smoke Signals '98
Dead Man '95
Powwow Highway '89

Mimsy Farmer
Allonsanfan '73

Virginia Farmer
Gun Crazy '49
Bury Me Dead '47

Richard Farnsworth
Anne of Green Gables '85

Eric Farr
Rock Hudson's Home Movies '92

Malik Farrakhan
Daughters of the Dust '91

David Farrar
The Obsessed '51
Black Narcissus '47

Colin Farrell
The Land That Time Forgot '75

Lily Farrell
Ladybird, Ladybird '93

Mike Farrell
The Graduate '67

Timothy Farrell
Girl Gang '54
Glen or Glenda? '53

Mia Farrow
Reckless '95
Widow's Peak '94

Andrew Faulds
Lisztomania '75

Lisa Faulkner
A Feast at Midnight '95

Consuelo Faust
Heat and Sunlight '87

Farrah Fawcett
The Apostle '97

Alice Faye
Carmen Miranda: Bananas Is My Business '95

Janina Faye
Never Take Candy from a Stranger '60

Jan Fedder
Das Boot '81

Frederique Feder
Trois Couleurs: Rouge '94

Frances Feist
Carnival of Souls '62

Nicole Felix
Small Change '76

Norman Fell
The Graduate '67

Federico Fellini
The Miracle '48

Tanya Fenmore
Lisa '90

Sherilyn Fenn
Diary of a Hitman '91
Wild at Heart '90

Lance Fenton
Heathers '89

Colm Feore
Critical Care '97
32 Short Films about Glenn Gould '93

Adam Ferency
The Interrogation '82

Rene Feret
First Communion '77
Lumiere '76

Colin Ferguson
The Opposite of Sex '98

Jay R. Ferguson
Campfire Tales '98

Matthew Ferguson
Love and Human Remains '93

Karen Fergusson
An Angel at My Table '89

Juan Fernandez
Salvador '86

Nick Ferrari
Sweet Sweetback's Baadasssss Song '71

Conchata Ferrell
Mystic Pizza '88
Heartland '81

Tyra Ferrell
Equinox '93

Andrea Ferreol
The Sleazy Uncle '89
Servant and Mistress '77
A Virgin Named Mary '75

Jose Ferrer
Voyage of the Damned '76
Moulin Rouge '52

Leilani Sarelle Ferrer
Shag: The Movie '89

Benoit Ferreux
Murmur of the Heart '71

Lou Ferrigno
...And God Spoke '94

Barbara Ferris
The Krays '90
A Chorus of Disapproval '89
Interlude '67
Having a Wild Weekend '65
Children of the Damned '63

Turi Ferro
A Virgin Named Mary '75

Gabriele Ferzetti
Julia and Julia '87

Larry Fessenden
Habit '97
River of Grass '94

William Fichtner
The Underneath '95

Betty Field
Tomorrow the World '44

David Field
To Have and to Hold '96

Mary Field
I Married a Witch '42

Sallie-Anne Field
Dance with a Stranger '85

Shirley Anne Field
Hear My Song '91
Shag: The Movie '89
My Beautiful Laundrette '85
Alfie '66
The Entertainer '60
Peeping Tom '60

Todd Field
Walking and Talking '96
Ruby in Paradise '93

Robert Fields
Anna '87
The Incident '67

Joseph Fiennes
Shakespeare in Love '98

Ralph Fiennes
The English Patient '96

Patrick Fierry
First Communion '77

Harvey Fierstein
Bullets over Broadway '94

Efrain Figueroa
Star Maps '97

Denise Filiatrault
Once upon a Time in the East '74

Audrey Fildes
Kind Hearts and Coronets '49

Brandao Filho
The Story of Fausta '88

Daniel Filho
The Story of Fausta '88

Jon Finch
Frenzy '72

Freddie Findlay
A Feast at Midnight '95

Agnes Fink
False Weights '74

Frank Finlay
Twisted Nerve '68

Siobhan Finneran
Rita, Sue & Bob Too '87

Warren Finnerty
Easy Rider '69

Albert Finney
Murder on the Orient Express '74
Two for the Road '67
The Entertainer '60

Anni Finsterer
To Have and to Hold '96

Elena Fiore
Seven Beauties '76

Kristin Fiorella
Curse of the Starving Class '94

Linda Fiorentino
The Last Seduction '94
Acting on Impulse '93
Chain of Desire '93
Queens Logic '91
After Hours '85

Colin Firth
Shakespeare in Love '98
The English Patient '96
Apartment Zero '88
Another Country '84

Peter Firth
An Awfully Big Adventure '94

Kate Fischer
Sirens '94

Ramona Fischer
Vegas in Space '94

Doris Fish
Vegas in Space '94

Frances Fisher
Trading Favors '97
Tough Guys Don't Dance '87

Jasen Fisher
The Witches '90

Jack Fisk
Eraserhead '78

Bradley Fitts
2 by 4 '98

Ciaran Fitzgerald
The Last of the High Kings '96

Geraldine Fitzgerald
The Obsessed '51

Glenn Fitzgerald
Manny & Lo '96
Flirting with Disaster '95

Tara Fitzgerald
The Englishman Who Went up a Hill But Came down a Mountain '95
Sirens '94
Hear My Song '91

Walter Fitzgerald
The Fallen Idol '49

Charles Fitzpatrick
Badlands '74

Leo Fitzpatrick
Kids '95

Lanny Flaherty
The Ballad of the Sad Cafe '91

Pat Flaherty
The Red House '47

Georges Flament
The 400 Blows '59

Ed Flanders
True Confessions '81

Sean Patrick Flanery
Suicide Kings '97

Barry Flatman
Random Encounter '98
Open Season '95

Flea
The Big Lebowski '97
Motorama '91
My Own Private Idaho '91

Erick Fleeks
Campfire Tales '98

James Fleet
Four Weddings and a Funeral '94

Betty Fleetwood
This Happy Breed '47

Susan Fleetwood
Persuasion '95
The Krays '90
White Mischief '88
Heat and Dust '82
The Good Soldier '81

Charles Fleischer
Permanent Midnight '98

Jason Flemyng
Spice World: The Movie '97

Robert Flemyng
Kafka '91

Bramwell Fletcher
The Scarlet Pimpernel '34

Dexter Fletcher
The Long Good Friday '80

Louise Fletcher
Nobody's Fool '86

Michael Fletcher
Daughters of the Country '86

Jay C. Flippen
The Killing '56

Suzanne Flon
Moulin Rouge '52

Barbara Flood
Tracks '76

Marsha Florence
Zebrahead '92

Jose Flores
Cabeza de Vaca '90

Lysa Flores
Star Maps '97

Jerome Flynn
A Summer Story '88

Kimberly Flynn
Rhythm Thief '94

Steve Flynn
Ulee's Gold '97

Arnoldo Foa
The Devil Is a Woman '75

Alison Folland
All Over Me '96
To Die For '95

Megan Follows
Stacking '87
Anne of Green Gables '85

Megan Folson
Heartland '81

Bridget Fonda
Jackie Brown '97
Grace of My Heart '96
Bodies, Rest & Motion '93
Frankenstein Unbound '90
Strapless '90
Scandal '89
Shag: The Movie '89

Henry Fonda
You Only Live Once '37

Peter Fonda
Ulee's Gold '97
Nadja '95
Love and a .45 '94
Bodies, Rest & Motion '93
Easy Rider '69

Damon Fontaine
Daughters of the Country '86

Frank Fontaine
Random Encounter '98

Rita Fontaine
Once upon a Time in the East *'74*

Genevieve Fontanel
The Man Who Loved Women *'77*

Bryan Forbes
The Slipper and the Rose *'76*

Michelle Forbes
Swimming with Sharks *'94*
Kalifornia *'93*

Francis Ford
Girls in Chains *'43*

Harrison Ford
The World of Jacques Demy *'95*

Michael James Ford
Widow's Peak *'94*

Mick Ford
How to Get Ahead in Advertising *'89*

Wallace Ford
He Ran All the Way *'51*

Louise Forestier
The Orders *'75*

Claire Forlani
Basquiat *'96*
Mallrats *'95*

Fabiana Formica
Cemetery Man *'95*

Emilio Fornet
Black Litter *'77*

Richard Foronjy
True Confessions *'81*

Veronica Forque
Kika *'94*

Frederic Forrest
The End of Violence *'97*
Stacking *'87*

Cay Forrester
D.O.A. *'49*

Constance Forslund
River's Edge *'87*

Robert Forster
Jackie Brown *'97*
Medium Cool *'69*

Tony Forsyth
Wonderland *'88*

William Forsythe
Palookaville *'95*
The Waterdance *'91*

Fabrizio Forte
Padre Padrone *'77*

Pasquale Fortunato
The Conformist *'71*

Bob Fosse
The Little Prince *'74*

Ernie Fosselius
Heat and Sunlight *'87*

Brigitte Fossey
Blue Country *'77*
The Man Who Loved Women *'77*
Forbidden Games *'52*

Barry Foster
Maurice *'87*
The Whistle Blower *'87*
Heat and Dust *'82*
Frenzy *'72*
Twisted Nerve *'68*

Gloria Foster
City of Hope *'91*
Nothing but a Man *'64*

Jodie Foster
Five Corners *'88*
The Little Girl Who Lives down the Lane *'76*

Julia Foster
Alfie *'66*

Kimberly Foster
It Takes Two *'88*

Meg Foster
Ticket to Heaven *'81*

Harry Fowler
Lucky Jim *'58*
Fire Maidens from Outer Space *'56*

Edward Fox
A Feast at Midnight *'95*
Galileo *'73*
Morgan! *'66*

Frank Fox
Clouds over Europe *'39*

James Fox
The Remains of the Day *'93*
High Season *'88*
The Whistle Blower *'87*
Absolute Beginners *'86*
Performance *'70*
Isadora *'68*

Kerry Fox
Shallow Grave *'94*
An Angel at My Table *'89*

Lauren Fox
I Love You, I Love You Not *'97*

Michael Fox
Gog *'54*

Vivica A. Fox
Set It Off *'96*

Mickey Foxx
Faster, Pussycat! Kill! Kill! *'65*

James Frain
Loch Ness *'95*

C. V. France
Night Train to Munich *'40*

Richard France
Vortex *'81*

Alec B. Francis
Charley's Aunt *'25*

Geff Francis
For Queen and Country *'88*

Linda Francis
Naked Kiss *'64*

Sandra Francis
Time Lock *'57*

Gwen Francon-Davies
Nine Days a Queen *'36*

David Roland Frank
Hurricane Streets *'96*

Paul Frankeur
Phantom of Liberty *'74*

William Frankfather
Trading Favors *'97*

Gretchen Franklin
Twisted Nerve *'68*

Pamela Franklin
The Prime of Miss Jean Brodie *'69*
The Innocents *'61*

Arthur Franz
The Wild Party *'56*

Bill Fraser
Little Dorrit, Film 1: Nobody's Fault *'88*
Little Dorrit, Film 2: Little Dorrit's Story *'88*
Eye of the Needle *'81*

Brendan Fraser
Gods and Monsters *'98*
Twenty Bucks *'93*

Helen Fraser
Start the Revolution without Me *'70*
Repulsion *'65*

John Fraser
Isadora *'68*
Repulsion *'65*

Ronald Fraser
Let Him Have It *'91*
The Killing of Sister George *'69*

Lynne Frederick
Voyage of the Damned *'76*

Scott Frederick
Bodies, Rest & Motion *'93*

Jill Freedman
Mother's Boys *'94*

Aaron Freeman
Who Am I This Time? *'82*

Al Freeman Jr.
The Troublemaker *'64*

Cheryl Freeman
Fresh *'94*

J. E. Freeman
Mother's Boys *'94*
Wild at Heart *'90*
Hard Traveling *'85*

K. Todd Freeman
The End of Violence *'97*

Mike Freeman
The Killing of Sister George *'69*

Morgan Freeman
Street Smart *'87*

Paul Freeman
Just Like a Woman *'92*
A World Apart *'88*
The Long Good Friday *'80*

Fregolente
The Marriage *'76*

Arthur French
The Luckiest Man in the World *'89*

Pierre Fresnay
The Man Who Knew Too Much *'34*

Matt Frewer
Twenty Bucks *'93*

Sami Frey
Why Not! *'78*

Brenda Fricker
My Left Foot *'89*

Gavin Friday
Creepers *'85*

Joel Friedkin
Money Madness *'47*

Peter Friedman
I Shot Andy Warhol *'96*
Safe *'95*

Colin Friels
Cosi *'95*
A Good Man in Africa *'94*
Warm Nights on a Slow-Moving Train *'87*

Paul Frison
Gun Crazy *'49*

Gustav Froehlich
Metropolis *'26*

Piotr Fronczewski
The Balance *'75*

Sadie Frost
The Krays *'90*

Catherine Frot
Sorceress *'88*

Dominique Frot
La Ceremonie *'95*

Stephen Fry
Spice World: The Movie *'97*
Wilde *'97*

Taylor Fry
A Little Princess *'95*

Virgil Frye
Killer Flick *'98*

Leo Fuchs
American Matchmaker '40

Dolores Fuller
Bride of the Monster '55
Glen or Glenda? '53

Kurt Fuller
Miracle Mile '89

Samuel Fuller
The End of Violence '97

Edward Furlong
Pecker '98
Little Odessa '94
American Heart '92

Yvonne Furneaux
Repulsion '65

Judith Furse
Black Narcissus '47

Jaro Furth
Joyless Street '25

Billy Fury
That'll Be the Day '73

Jeanne Fusier-Gir
The Crucible '57

Dan Futterman
1999 '98

Christopher Gable
Lair of the White Worm '88
The Slipper and the Rose '76

Zsa Zsa Gabor
Moulin Rouge '52

Fred Gabourie
Shack Out on 101 '55

Renee Gadd
Dead of Night '45

Marjorie Gaffney
Evergreen '34

Jenny Gago
My Family '94

Michael Gahr
The Nasty Girl '90

Claude Gai
Once upon a Time in the East '74

M. C. Gainey
Citizen Ruth '96

Charlotte Gainsbourg
Jane Eyre '96

Janusz Gajos
Trois Couleurs: Blanc '94
The Interrogation '82

Michel Galabru
L'Amour en Herbe '77

Eddra Gale
8½ '63

Linda Gale
Teenage Gang Debs '66

West Gale
Sweet Sweetback's Baadasssss Song '71

Johnny Galecki
The Opposite of Sex '98
Suicide Kings '97

Anna Gallena
Three Lives and Only One Death '96

Megan Gallagher
The Ambulance '90

Peter Gallagher
The Underneath '95
Mrs. Parker and the Vicious Circle '94
Mother's Boys '94
Short Cuts '93
The Player '92
Tune in Tomorrow '90
sex, lies and videotape '89
Dreamchild '85

Carlos Gallardo
El Mariachi '93

Jose Gallardo
I Am Cuba '64

Carla Gallo
Spanking the Monkey '94

Vincent Gallo
The Funeral '96
Nenette and Boni '96
Palookaville '95
Angela '94
The House of the Spirits '93

Jean-Francois Galotte
Ma Vie en Rose '97

Arturo Galster
Vegas in Space '94

Michael Gambon
The Wings of the Dove '97

James Gammon
Hard Traveling '85

Richard Ganoung
Parting Glances '86

Bruno Ganz
Strapless '90
Wings of Desire '88
Lumiere '76
The Marquise of O '76

Victor Garber
Exotica '94

Greta Garbo
Joyless Street '25

Andy Garcia
Stand and Deliver '88

Isaiah Garcia
I Like It Like That '94

Jerry Garcia
Gimme Shelter '70

Raul Garcia
I Am Cuba '64

Ginette Garcin
Blue Country '77
Cousin, Cousine '76

Henri Garcin
101 Nights '95
Abel '87

Jimmy Gardner
Frenzy '72

Joan Gardner
The Scarlet Pimpernel '34

Katya Gardner
Careful '92

Allen (Goorwitz) Garfield
Destiny Turns on the Radio '95
Number One '76

John Garfield
He Ran All the Way '51

William Gargan
Turnabout '40
You Only Live Once '37

Michael Garganese
Breakaway '95

Beverly Garland
D.O.A. '49

Amulette Garneau
Once upon a Time in the East '74

Jennifer Garner
1999 '98

Gale Garnett
32 Short Films about Glenn Gould '93

Janeane Garofalo
Clay Pigeons '98
Permanent Midnight '98
Cop Land '97
The Matchmaker '97
Coldblooded '94

Teri Garr
After Hours '85

Jean-Francoise Garreaud
Violette '78

Bob Garrett
Eddie and the Cruisers '83

Brad Garrett
Suicide Kings '97

Christopher Gartin
johns '96

Elizabeth Garvie
The Good Soldier '81

Vincent Gaskins
The Underneath '95

Vittorio Gassman
The Sleazy Uncle '89

Jany Gastaldi
First Communion '77

Michael Gaston
The Wedding Banquet '93

Lisa Gastoni
The Runaway Bus '54

Jill Gatsby
The Ambulance '90

Mikkel Gaup
Breaking the Waves '95

Claude Gauthier
The Orders '75

Jean-Yves Gautier
Three Lives and Only One Death '96

Rita Gavelis
Little Shots of Happiness '97

Jean Gaven
The Crucible '57

Christine Gaya
Nenette and Boni '96

Julie Gayet
101 Nights '95

Monica Gayle
Switchblade Sisters '75

George Gaynes
Vanya on 42nd Street '94

Wendy Gazelle
Sammy & Rosie Get Laid '87

Ben Gazzara
Happiness '98
The Big Lebowski '97
The Killing of a Chinese Bookie '76
Voyage of the Damned '76
Passionate Thief '60

Anthony Geary
It Takes Two '88
Pass the Ammo '88

Charles Geary
Medium Cool '69

Karl Geary
Nadja '95

Jason Gedrick
Stacking '87

Ellen Geer
Hard Traveling '85

Judy Geeson
10 Rillington Place '70

David Gelb
1999 '98

Daniel Gelin
Murmur of the Heart '71

Sarah Michelle Gellar
High Stakes '89

Minnie Gentry
Def by Temptation '90

Gladys George
He Ran All the Way '51

Heinrich George
Metropolis '26

Chief Leonard George
Smoke Signals '98

Susan George
Fright '71

Zoltan Gera
The Hungarians '78

Jim Gerald
Moulin Rouge '52

Harriet Gerard
Vampyr '31

Mark Gerber
Sirens '94

Peter Gerety
Went to Coney Island on a Mission from God...Be Back by Five '98

Nane Germon
Beauty and the Beast '46

Christopher-Michael Gerrard
Fly by Night '93

Gina Gershon
Bound '96
The Player '92
City of Hope '91

Valeska Gert
Joyless Street '25

Balthazar Getty
Lost Highway '96

John Getz
Blood Simple '85

Mohammed Ghaffari
Little Odessa '94

Marilyn Ghigliotti
Clerks '94

Kulvinder Ghir
Rita, Sue & Bob Too '87

Alice Ghostley
The Graduate '67

Giancarlo Giannini
The Sleazy Uncle '89
Seven Beauties '76
Swept Away... '75

Cynthia Gibb
Jack's Back '87
Salvador '86

Billie Gibson
The Shining '80

Colin Gibson
John and Julie '55

Dale Gibson
Red Rock West '93

Henry Gibson
Color of a Brisk and Leaping Day '95
Tune in Tomorrow '90

Thomas Gibson
Barcelona '94
Love and Human Remains '93

Pamela Gidley
Permanent Record '88

Therese Giehse
Black Moon '75
Lacombe, Lucien '74

John Gielgud
Shine '95
The Whistle Blower '87
Murder on the Orient Express '74
Galileo '73

Alan Gifford
Isadora '68
Time Lock '57

Roland Gift
Scandal '89
Sammy & Rosie Get Laid '87

Elaine Giftos
The Trouble with Dick '88

Jody Gilbert
Actors and Sin '52

Ronnie Gilbert
Isadora '68

Taylor Gilbert
The Method '87

Hilary Gilford
Living in Oblivion '94

Jack Gilford
The Incident '67

Basil Gill
Sidewalks of London '38

Anita Gillette
She's the One '96

Lawrence Gilliard
Fly by Night '93
Straight out of Brooklyn '91

Isabel Gillies
I Shot Andy Warhol '96
Metropolitan '90

Richard Gilliland
Star Kid '97

Linda Gillin
Alambrista! '77

Caroline Gillmer
Sorrento Beach '95

Jack Gilpin
Barcelona '94

Daniel Gimenez Cacho
Cabeza de Vaca '90

Teresa Gimpera
Spirit of the Beehive '73

Robert Ginnaven
One False Move '91

Allen Ginsberg
Heavy Petting '89

Rocky Giordani
After Dark, My Sweet '90

Elenora Giorgi
Creepers '85

Anne Giotta
Poison '91

Francois Giroday
Hundred Per Cent '98

Massimo Girotti
Ossessione '42

Annabeth Gish
Shag: The Movie '89
Mystic Pizza '88

Lillian Gish
The Whales of August '87
The Night of the Hunter '55
Way Down East '20

George Giudall
Golden Gate '93

Geoff Gladstone
Starving Artists '97

Ludmila Gladunko
The Only One '76

Anton Glanzelius
My Life As a Dog '85

Sabine Glaser
The Man Who Loved Women '77

Ned Glass
Street Music '81
Bury Me Dead '47

Ron Glass
It's My Party '95

Eugene Glazer
Hollywood Shuffle '87

James Gleason
The Night of the Hunter '55

Joanna Gleason
Boogie Nights '97

Paul Gleason
Miami Blues '90

Brendan Gleeson
Michael Collins '96

Iain Glen
Mountains of the Moon '90

Libby Glenn
Isadora '68

Lucille Glenn
The Vanishing '88

Scott Glenn
Reckless '95

Brian Glover
Kafka '91

Crispin Glover
Dead Man '95
Wild at Heart '90
Twister '89
River's Edge '87
My Tutor '82

Danny Glover
To Sleep with Anger '90

John Glover
The Chocolate War '88

Julian Glover
Heat and Dust '82

Susan Glover
Random Encounter '98

Carlin Glynn
Blessing '94
The Trip to Bountiful '85

Fritz Gnass
M '31

Harry Goaz
The Underneath '95

Alf Goddard
Non-Stop New York '37

Patricia Goddard
Uneasy Terms '48

Suzanne Goddard
Campfire Tales '98

Patrick Godfrey
Heat and Dust '82

Jacques Godin
Salut Victor! '89

Carl Goetz
Pandora's Box '28

Michael C. Goetz
Village of the Damned '60

Walton Goggins
The Apostle '97

Adam Goldberg
Dazed and Confused '93

Whoopi Goldberg
The Player '92

Harold Goldblatt
Children of the Damned '63

Jeff Goldblum
The Favor, the Watch, and the Very Big Fish '92

Ricky Paull Goldin
Pastime '91

Sidney Goldin
East and West '24

Philippe Goldman
Small Change '76

Bob(cat) Goldthwait
Destiny Turns on the Radio '95

Tony Goldwyn
Reckless '95
Traces of Red '92

Richard Golfier
Small Change '76

Valeria Golino
Leaving Las Vegas '95

Arlene Golonka
My Tutor '82

Robert Alan Golub
Acting on Impulse *'93*

Consuelo Gomez
El Mariachi *'93*

Fernando Gomez
Spirit of the Beehive *'73*

Jose Luis Gomez
Roads to the South *'78*

Ramiro Gomez
El Mariachi *'93*

Milton Goncalves
Kiss of the Spider Woman *'85*

Dan Rivera Gonzalez
Hombres Armados *'97*

Mario Gonzalez
Roads to the South *'78*
Why Not! *'78*

Meagan Good
Eve's Bayou *'97*

Caroline Goodall
Sorrento Beach *'95*

Cuba Gooding Jr.
Lightning Jack *'94*

Michael Goodliffe
The Battle of the Sexes *'60*
A Night to Remember *'58*

John Goodman
The Big Lebowski *'97*
The Big Easy *'87*

Julia Goodman
Twenty-One *'91*

Heather Goodsell
The Return of Tommy Tricker *'94*

Alexander Goodwin
Box of Moonlight *'96*

Angela Goodwin
Julia and Julia *'87*

Howard Goorney
Bedazzled *'68*

Elizabeth Gorcey
The Trouble with Dick *'88*

Leo Gorcey
Dead End *'37*

Barry Gordon
A Thousand Clowns *'65*

Colin Gordon
John and Julie *'55*

Mel Gorham
Smoke *'95*

Peggy Gormley
Bad Lieutenant *'92*

Karen Gorney
Ripe *'97*

Louis Gossett Jr.
Curse of the Starving Class *'94*
A Good Man in Africa *'94*

Will Gotay
Stand and Deliver *'88*

Walter Gotell
The African Queen *'51*

Heinrich Gotho
Metropolis *'26*

Matthew Gottlieb
The Luckiest Man in the World *'89*

John Gottowt
Nosferatu *'22*

Michael Gough
Let Him Have It *'91*
Strapless *'90*
Galileo *'73*
Saraband for Dead Lovers *'48*

Elliott Gould
johns *'96*

Arthur Goullet
Non-Stop New York *'37*

Anna Grace
Girls Town *'95*

Martin Grace
Under Suspicion *'92*

Matthew Grace
Living in Oblivion *'94*

Nickolas Grace
Heat and Dust *'82*

David Graf
Citizen Ruth *'96*
Suture *'93*

David Allen Graff
Bang *'95*

Todd Graff
City of Hope *'91*
Five Corners *'88*

Aimee Graham
Jackie Brown *'97*

Bill Graham
Gimme Shelter *'70*

Heather Graham
Boogie Nights *'97*
The Ballad of Little Jo *'93*
Drugstore Cowboy *'89*

John Michael Graham
Halloween *'78*

Kirsty Graham
Loch Ness *'95*

Morland Graham
Night Train to Munich *'40*
The Scarlet Pimpernel *'34*

Richard Graham
My Beautiful Laundrette *'85*

Sheilah Graham
Impact *'49*

Stuart Graham
Michael Collins *'96*

Gawn Grainger
Love and Death on Long Island *'97*

Sam Grana
The Boys of St. Vincent *'93*

Alexander Granach
Nosferatu *'22*

Stewart Granger
Saraband for Dead Lovers *'48*
Thursday's Child *'43*

Hugh Grant
The Englishman Who Went up a Hill But Came down a Mountain *'95*
An Awfully Big Adventure *'94*
Four Weddings and a Funeral *'94*
Sirens *'94*
The Remains of the Day *'93*
Impromptu *'90*
Lair of the White Worm *'88*
White Mischief *'88*
Maurice *'87*

Kathryn Grant
The Wild Party *'56*

Lawrence Grant
Bulldog Drummond *'29*

Lee Grant
It's My Party *'95*
Voyage of the Damned *'76*
The Balcony *'63*

Micah Grant
Terminal Bliss *'91*

Miriam Grant
Photographing Fairies *'97*

Richard E. Grant
Spice World: The Movie *'97*
The Player *'92*
Mountains of the Moon *'90*
How to Get Ahead in Advertising *'89*
Withnail and I *'87*

Schuyler Grant
Anne of Green Gables *'85*

Bonita Granville
These Three *'36*

Doris Grau
Coldblooded *'94*

Peter Graves
The Slipper and the Rose *'76*
Alfie *'66*
The Night of the Hunter *'55*

Rupert Graves
Different for Girls *'96*
The Madness of King George *'94*
Where Angels Fear to Tread *'91*
A Handful of Dust *'88*
Maurice *'87*
A Room with a View *'86*

Adele Gray
The Return of Tommy Tricker *'94*

Coleen Gray
The Killing *'56*

Jane Gray
The House of the Spirits *'93*

MacKenzie Gray
My Teacher Ate My Homework *'98*

Nadia Gray
Two for the Road *'67*

Sally Gray
The Hidden Room *'49*

Spalding Gray
Twenty Bucks *'93*
Heavy Petting *'89*

Vivean Gray
Picnic at Hanging Rock *'75*

Calvin Green
Exotica *'94*

Danny Green
The Ladykillers *'55*
Non-Stop New York *'37*

Rev. Ervin Green
Daughters of the Dust *'91*

Frances Green
Never Take Candy from a Stranger *'60*

Gail Green
The Giving *'91*

Janet-Laine Green
Medicine River *'94*

Marika Green
Emmanuelle *'74*

Martyn Green
The Iceman Cometh *'73*

Pamela Green
Peeping Tom *'60*

Bill Greene
Lolita *'62*

Graham Greene
Medicine River *'94*
Powwow Highway *'89*

Peter Greene
Permanent Midnight *'98*
Trading Favors *'97*
Bang *'95*
The Usual Suspects *'95*
Clean, Shaven *'93*

Richard Greene
Special Effects *'85*
Island of the Lost *'68*
Don't Take It to Heart *'44*

Stanley Greene
Nothing but a Man *'64*

Tom Greenway
Impact *'49*

Bruce Greenwood
The Sweet Hereafter '96
Exotica '94

Joan Greenwood
Little Dorrit, Film 1: Nobody's Fault '88
Little Dorrit, Film 2: Little Dorrit's Story '88
Kind Hearts and Coronets '49
Saraband for Dead Lovers '48

Dabbs Greer
Private Hell 36 '54

Claire Greet
Sidewalks of London '38

Vernon Greeves
The Intimate Stranger '56

Everley Gregg
The Woman in Question '50
Brief Encounter '46
Great Expectations '46
Pygmalion '38
The Ghost Goes West '36
The Private Life of Henry VIII '33

Virginia Gregg
The Amazing Mr. X '48

Nora Gregor
The Rules of the Game '39

Rose Gregorio
City of Hope '91
Five Corners '88
True Confessions '81

Andre Gregory
Vanya on 42nd Street '94
The Linguini Incident '92
Street Smart '87

James Gregory
The Manchurian Candidate '62

John Gregson
Fright '71
The Frightened City '61
Hand in Hand '60
Genevieve '53

Joyce Grenfell
The Belles of St. Trinian's '53
Genevieve '53

Rainer Grenkowitz
Meier '87

Emmett Grennan
Killer Flick '98

Aidan Grennell
In the Name of the Father '93

Laurent Grevill
Camille Claudel '89

Jennifer Grey
Dirty Dancing '87

Joel Grey
Kafka '91

Virginia Grey
Naked Kiss '64
Crime of Passion '57

Michael Greyeyes
Smoke Signals '98

Sylvie Grezel
Small Change '76

Helmut Griem
Voyage of the Damned '76

Pam Grier
Jackie Brown '97

Jonathan Gries
Kill Me Again '89

Joe Grifasi
Heavy '94
Household Saints '93
City of Hope '91
Matewan '87

Robert Griffin
Crime of Passion '57

Tim Griffin
Lover Girl '97

Guy Griffis
Blessing '94

Melora Griffis
Blessing '94

Hugh Griffith
Luther '74
Start the Revolution without Me '70
Lucky Jim '58
Kind Hearts and Coronets '49

Kenneth Griffith
The Englishman Who Went up a Hill But Came down a Mountain '95
Four Weddings and a Funeral '94
The Frightened City '61
Tiger Bay '59
Lucky Jim '58
A Night to Remember '58
1984 '56

Melanie Griffith
Lolita '97
In the Spirit '90
The Garden '77

Nadine Griffith
Ninth Street '98

Richard Griffith
Funny Bones '94

Michael Griffiths
Living in Oblivion '94

Rachel Griffiths
To Have and to Hold '96
Cosi '95
Muriel's Wedding '94

Richard Griffiths
Withnail and I '87

John Grillo
The Good Soldier '81

Tammy Grimes
High Art '98
A Modern Affair '94
Mr. North '88

Unity Grimwood
The Hours and Times '92

Christina Grisanti
A Woman under the Influence '74

Czeskaw Grocholski
Citizen X '95

Kathryn Grody
Hombres Armados '97

Herbert Gronemeyer
Das Boot '81

Gary Groomes
Wired '89

Gustav Grundgens
M '31

Ilka Gruning
Joyless Street '25

Ah-Leh Gua
Eat Drink Man Woman '94
The Wedding Banquet '93

Robert Guajardo
Red Rock West '93

Dominic Guard
Picnic at Hanging Rock '75

Nikolai Gubenko
The Orphans '77

Vanessa Guedj
Le Grand Chemin '87

Christopher Guest
Waiting for Guffman '96
Sticky Fingers '88
Girlfriends '78

Lance Guest
The Wizard of Loneliness '88

Giovanni Guidelli
Where Angels Fear to Tread '91

Paul Guilfoyle
Manny & Lo '96
Little Odessa '94
Mother's Boys '94
Actors and Sin '52

Fernando Guillen
Women on the Verge of a Nervous Breakdown '88

Tim Guinee
Sudden Manhattan '96
Chain of Desire '93

Alec Guinness
Kafka '91
A Handful of Dust '88
Little Dorrit, Film 1: Nobody's Fault '88
Little Dorrit, Film 2: Little Dorrit's Story '88
The Ladykillers '55
Kind Hearts and Coronets '49
Great Expectations '46

Julien Guiomar
French Provincial '75

Luis Guizar
Bang '95

Sean Gullette
Pi '98

Devon Gummersall
Trading Favors '97
It's My Party '95

Moses Gunn
The Iceman Cometh '73

Ernst Gunther
Metamorphosis '75

Bob Gunton
Matewan '87

Boaz Gur-Lavi
Song of the Siren '94

Tyrone Guthrie
Sidewalks of London '38

Lucy Gutteridge
Grief '94

Deryck Guyler
A Hard Day's Night '64

Luis Guzman
Boogie Nights '97

Michael Gwynn
Never Take Candy from a Stranger '60
Village of the Damned '60

Lukas Haas
johns '96
Rambling Rose '91
The Lady in White '88
The Wizard of Loneliness '88

Joachim Hackethal
Strongman Ferdinand '76

Ron Hackett
That'll Be the Day '73

Francois Hadji-Lazaro
Cemetery Man '95

Edna Hagan
Struggle '31

Marianne Hagan
I Think I Do '97

Julie Hagerty
U-Turn '97

Sean Haggerty
Rhythm Thief '94

Larry Hagman
Stardust '74

Sid Haig
Spider Baby '64

Leisha Hailey
All Over Me '96

Haji
Faster, Pussycat! Kill! Kill! *'65*

Herbert Halbik
The Third Man *'49*

Creighton Hale
Way Down East *'20*

Georgina Hale
Castaway *'87*
Butley *'74*

Jonathan Hale
You Only Live Once *'37*

Sonnie Hale
Evergreen *'34*

Albert Hall
Betrayed *'88*

Ben Hall
You Only Live Once *'37*

Brian Hall
The Long Good Friday *'80*

Huntz Hall
Valentino *'77*
Dead End *'37*

Lois Hall
Kalifornia *'93*

Philip Baker Hall
Boogie Nights *'97*
Hard Eight *'96*
Secret Honor *'85*

Richard Hall
Rockers *'79*

Sherry Hall
The Prowler *'51*

May Hallatt
Separate Tables *'58*

Jackson Halliday
Struggle *'31*

May Hallitt
Black Narcissus *'47*

Geri (Ginger Spice) Halliwell
Spice World: The Movie *'97*

Billy Halop
Too Late for Tears *'49*
Dead End *'37*

Luke Halpin
Island of the Lost *'68*

Charles Halton
Dead End *'37*

Leo Hamill
2 by 4 *'98*

Carrie Hamilton
Shag: The Movie *'89*

Josh Hamilton
The House of Yes *'97*

Lisa Gay Hamilton
Jackie Brown *'97*
Palookaville *'95*

Margaret Hamilton
Guest in the House *'44*
You Only Live Once *'37*
These Three *'36*

Murray Hamilton
The Graduate *'67*

Patricia Hamilton
Anne of Green Gables *'85*

Victoria Hamilton
Persuasion *'95*

Kay Hammond
Blithe Spirit *'45*

Roger Hammond
The Good Soldier *'81*

Rosalind Hammond
Muriel's Wedding *'94*

Col. Bruce Hampton
Sling Blade *'96*

James Hampton
Sling Blade *'96*

Lee Hampton
The Giving *'91*

Maggie Han
Open Season *'95*

Lou Hancock
Miracle Mile *'89*

Sheila Hancock
Love and Death on Long Island *'97*
Hawks *'89*

Irene Handl
Secrets and Lies *'95*
The Private Life of Sherlock Holmes *'70*
Morgan! *'66*
The Belles of St. Trinian's *'53*
Brief Encounter *'46*
Night Train to Munich *'40*

Rene Handren-Seals
Powwow Highway *'89*

Clarence Handysides
His Picture in the Papers *'16*

Roger Hanin
Sois Belle et Tais-Toi *'58*

Jimmy Hanley
Gaslight *'40*

Adam Hann-Byrd
Halloween: H20 *'98*
The Ice Storm *'97*

Daryl Hannah
The Real Blonde *'97*
The Tie That Binds *'95*

Duncan Hannah
Art for Teachers of Children *'95*

John Hannah
Four Weddings and a Funeral *'94*

Page Hannah
Shag: The Movie *'89*

John Hannan
Strictly Ballroom *'92*

Lawrence Hanray
On Approval *'44*
The Private Life of Henry VIII *'33*

Joachim Hansen
Anne of Green Gables *'85*

Susan Hanson
Having a Wild Weekend *'65*

Daniel Hanssens
Ma Vie en Rose *'97*

Vlastimil Harapes
Day for My Love *'77*

Cochava Harari
Zohar: Mediterranean Blues *'93*

Cezary Harasimowicz
Trois Couleurs: Blanc *'94*

Sebastian Harcombe
Carrington *'95*

James Harcourt
The Hidden Room *'49*
Night Train to Munich *'40*
I Met a Murderer *'39*

Marcia Gay Harden
The Daytrippers *'96*
The Spitfire Grill *'95*
Crush *'93*

Jamie Hardesty
Daughters of the Country *'86*

Kate Hardie
The Krays *'90*
Mona Lisa *'86*

Tonya Harding
Breakaway *'95*

Kadeem Hardison
Def by Temptation *'90*

Karl Hardman
Night of the Living Dead *'68*

Paul Hardtmuth
The Third Man *'49*

Cedric Hardwicke
Beware of Pity *'46*
Nine Days a Queen *'36*

Edward Hardwicke
Photographing Fairies *'97*

Robert Hardy
A Feast at Midnight *'95*

Doris Hare
Nuns on the Run *'90*

Magnus Harenstam
Stubby *'74*

John Hargreaves
Sorrento Beach *'95*
Don's Party *'76*

Zaharira Harifai
Daughters, Daughters *'74*

Dennis Harkin
Brief Encounter *'46*

Rufus Harley
Eddie and the Cruisers *'83*

Jamie Harold
Chain of Desire *'93*

Andrew Harpending
Poison *'91*

Frank Harper
In the Name of the Father *'93*

Jessica Harper
Safe *'95*
Eat a Bowl of Tea *'89*

Ron Harper
Body Count *'97*

Tess Harper
Criminal Law *'89*

Barbara Harris
A Thousand Clowns *'65*

Bruklin Harris
Girls Town *'95*

Cynthia Harris
Isadora *'68*

Jared Harris
Happiness *'98*
I Shot Andy Warhol *'96*
Dead Man *'95*
Nadja *'95*
Smoke *'95*

Julie Harris
Carried Away *'95*
Voyage of the Damned *'76*

Julius W. Harris
Alambrista! *'77*
Nothing but a Man *'64*

Laura Harris
Suicide Kings *'97*

Mel Harris
Suture *'93*

Michael Harris
Suture *'93*

Richard Harris
Silent Tongue *'92*

Robin Harris
House Party *'90*

Wendell B. Harris Jr.
Chameleon Street *'89*

Cathryn Harrison
A Handful of Dust *'88*
Black Moon *'75*

George Harrison
Help! *'65*
A Hard Day's Night *'64*

Gregory Harrison
It's My Party *'95*

Jimmy Harrison
Charley's Aunt *'25*

John Harrison
Lolita *'62*

Rex Harrison
Blithe Spirit *'45*
Night Train to Munich *'40*
Sidewalks of London *'38*

Jamie Harrold
I Think I Do *'97*
I Shot Andy Warhol *'96*

Lisa Harrow
The Devil Is a Woman *'75*

Deborah Harry
Cop Land *'97*
Heavy *'94*

Caitlin Hart
Who Am I This Time? *'82*

Henry Hart
D.O.A. *'49*

Ian Hart
Michael Collins *'96*
The Englishman Who Went up a Hill But Came down a Mountain *'95*
Backbeat *'94*
The Hours and Times *'92*

Pamela Hart
Pi *'98*

Roxanne Hart
Old Enough *'84*

John Hart-Dyke
The Missing Reel *'90*

Josh Hartnett
Halloween: H20 *'98*

Rainbow Harvest
Old Enough *'84*

Don Harvey
American Heart *'92*
Eight Men Out *'88*

Harold (Herk) Harvey
Carnival of Souls *'62*

Laurence Harvey
The Manchurian Candidate *'62*
Room at the Top *'59*

Rodney Harvey
Guncrazy *'92*
My Own Private Idaho *'91*
Five Corners *'88*

Tom Harvey
The Luck of Ginger Coffey *'64*

Verna Harvey
That'll Be the Day *'73*

Eddie Earl Hatch
High Stakes *'89*

Mert Hatfield
The Ballad of the Sad Cafe *'91*

Rutger Hauer
Forbidden Choices *'94*

Alexander Hauff
Meier *'87*

Alexandra Haughey
The Last of the High Kings *'96*

Cole Hauser
Good Will Hunting *'97*
All Over Me *'96*
Dazed and Confused *'93*

Wings Hauser
Tough Guys Don't Dance *'87*

Willo Hausman
House of Games *'87*

Jerry Hausner
Private Hell 36 *'54*

Richie Havens
Boss' Son *'78*

Nigel Havers
The Whistle Blower *'87*

Robin Hawdon
Bedazzled *'68*

Keeley Hawes
The Cater Street Hangman *'98*

Jeremy Hawk
Lucky Jim *'58*
Who Done It? *'56*

Ethan Hawke
Search and Destroy *'94*

Stephen Hawking
A Brief History of Time *'92*

Jack Hawkins
The Fallen Idol *'49*

Jimmy Hawkins
Private Hell 36 *'54*

Nigel Hawthorne
The Madness of King George *'94*

Charles Hawtrey
Sabotage *'36*

Colin Hay
Cosi *'95*

Sessue Hayakawa
I Have Killed *'24*

Marc Hayashi
Chan Is Missing *'82*

Harry Hayden
Gun Crazy *'49*

Karl Hayden
The Last of the High Kings *'96*

Sterling Hayden
Crime of Passion *'57*
The Killing *'56*

Helen Haye
Sidewalks of London *'38*
The 39 Steps *'35*

Chris Hayes
In the Company of Men *'96*

Isaac Hayes
Ninth Street *'98*
Acting on Impulse *'93*

Patricia Hayes
Little Dorrit, Film 1: Nobody's Fault *'88*
Little Dorrit, Film 2: Little Dorrit's Story *'88*

Tommy Haynes
Glen or Glenda? *'53*

Jim Haynie
From Hollywood to Deadwood *'89*
Jack's Back *'87*
Hard Traveling *'85*

Dennis Haysbert
Suture *'93*

James Hayter
Abandon Ship *'57*
The Fallen Idol *'49*

David Hayward
Thousand Pieces of Gold *'91*

Susan Hayward
I Married a Witch *'42*

Chris Haywood
Shine *'95*

Rita Hayworth
Separate Tables *'58*

James Hazeldine
Stardust *'74*

Murray Head
White Mischief *'88*

Ruby Head
The Long Good Friday *'80*

Lena Headey
Century *'94*

Glenne Headly
Bastard out of Carolina *'96*
And the Band Played On *'93*
Grand Isle *'91*

Anthony Heald
The Ballad of Little Jo *'93*

David Healy
In Possession *'84*

Dorian Healy
For Queen and Country *'88*

Daphne Heard
Three Sisters *'70*

John Heard
Rambling Rose *'91*
Betrayed *'88*
After Hours *'85*
The Trip to Bountiful *'85*
Cutter's Way *'81*

Patty Hearst
Pecker *'98*

Thomas Heathcote
Luther *'74*
Village of the Damned *'60*

Anne Heche
Walking and Talking *'96*

Jenny Hecht
Actors and Sin *'52*

Dan Hedaya
Freeway *'95*
To Die For *'95*
The Usual Suspects *'95*
Tune in Tomorrow *'90*
Blood Simple *'85*
True Confessions *'81*

Jack Hedley
The Very Edge *'63*

Tippi Hedren
Citizen Ruth *'96*

Van Heflin
The Prowler *'51*

Gerard Heinz
The Fallen Idol *'49*

Brigitte Helm
Metropolis *'26*

Levon Helm
Smooth Talk *'85*

Charlotte J. Helmkamp
Frankenhooker *'90*

Katherine Helmond
Inside Monkey Zetterland *'93*
The Lady in White *'88*

Percy Helton
Crashout *'55*
Kiss Me Deadly *'55*
Wicked Woman *'54*

David Hemblen
The Sweet Hereafter *'96*
Exotica *'94*

Martin Hemme
Das Boot *'81*

David Hemmings
Blow-Up *'66*

Jo Henderson
Matewan *'87*

Sarah Henderson
Kids *'95*

Shirley Henderson
Trainspotting *'95*

Benjamin Hendrickson
Spanking the Monkey *'94*

Jimi Hendrix
Message to Love: The Isle of Wight Festival, the Movie *'70*

Ian Hendry
Repulsion *'65*
Children of the Damned *'63*

Room at the Top '59

Patricia Heneghan
Whistle down the Wind '61

Jill Hennessey
I Shot Andy Warhol '96

Paul Henreid
Night Train to Munich '40

Bobby Henrey
The Fallen Idol '49

Lance Henriksen
Dead Man '95

Buck Henry
1999 '98
The Real Blonde '97
Short Cuts '93
The Linguini Incident '92
Tune in Tomorrow '90
Eating Raoul '82
The Graduate '67
The Troublemaker '64

John Henry
Passion Fish '92

Douglas Henshall
Angels and Insects '95

Gladys Henson
Leather Boys '63

Audrey Hepburn
Two for the Road '67

Katharine Hepburn
A Delicate Balance '73
The African Queen '51

Hans Herbert
Impact '49

Louis Herbert
Forbidden Games '52

Jimmy Herman
Medicine River '94

Stanley Herman
Bang '95

Irm Hermann
Mother Kusters Goes to Heaven '76

Jonathan Hernandez
My Family '94

Marcel Herrand
Children of Paradise '45

Aggie Herring
Oliver Twist '22

Edward Herrmann
Critical Care '97

Mark Herron
8½ '63

Barbara Hershey
Tune in Tomorrow '90
A World Apart '88
Shy People '87

Jason Hervey
Trading Favors '97

Charles Heslop
The Obsessed '51

David Hewlett
The Boys of St. Vincent '93

Sherrie Hewson
The Slipper and the Rose '76

Barton Heyman
Dead Man Walking '95

Anne Heywood
The Very Edge '63

Pat Heywood
Wish You Were Here '87
10 Rillington Place '70

James Hickey
The Boy from Mercury '96

Paul Hickey
The Matchmaker '97

Tom Hickey
Nuns on the Run '90

Tommy Redmond Hicks
Daughters of the Dust '91
She's Gotta Have It '86

Joan Hickson
Century '94
Don't Take It to Heart '44

Jan Hieronimko
Vampyr '31

David Anthony Higgens
Coldblooded '94

Clare Higgins
Wonderland '88

Michael Higgins
Wanda '70

Irene Hilda
Two for the Road '67

Benny Hill
Who Done It? '56

Bernard Hill
Mountains of the Moon '90
Shirley Valentine '89
Bellman and True '88

Dennis Hill
The Underneath '95

Marianna Hill
Medium Cool '69

Wendy Hiller
The Lonely Passion of Judith Hearne '87
Voyage of the Damned '76
Murder on the Orient Express '74
Separate Tables '58
Pygmalion '38

Patricia Hilliard
The Ghost Goes West '36

Candace Hilligoss
Carnival of Souls '62

Gillian Hills
Blow-Up '66

James David Hilton
Palookaville '95

Pippa Hinchley
London Kills Me '91

Earl Hindman
The Ballad of the Sad Cafe '91

Ciaran Hinds
Persuasion '95

Pat Hingle
Lightning Jack '94
The Grifters '90

Joaquin Hinojosa
Black Litter '77

Kristin Hinojosa
Dazed and Confused '93

Mary Hinton
Gaslight '40

Paul Hipp
The Funeral '96

Thora Hird
The Entertainer '60

Judith Hoag
Acting on Impulse '93

Florence Hoath
The Governess '98
FairyTale: A True Story '97

Carleton Hobbs
Perfect Friday '70

Valerie Hobson
Kind Hearts and Coronets '49
Great Expectations '46
Clouds over Europe '39

Jan Hockey
Slacker '91

Stephan Hockey
Slacker '91

Edwin Hodge
My Teacher Ate My Homework '98

John Hodge
Shallow Grave '94

Paul Hoerbiger
The Third Man '49

Iris Hoey
Pygmalion '38

Abbie Hoffman
Heavy Petting '89

Dustin Hoffman
The Graduate '67

Gert Gunther Hoffman
Strongman Ferdinand '76

Philip Seymour Hoffman
Happiness '98
The Big Lebowski '97
Boogie Nights '97
Hard Eight '96

Thom Hoffman
Orlando '92

Thurn Hoffman
In the Spirit '90

Marco Hofschneider
The Island of Dr. Moreau '96

Bosco Hogan
In the Name of the Father '93

Paul Hogan
Lightning Jack '94

Hal Holbrook
Carried Away '95

Jan Holden
Fire Maidens from Outer Space '56

Roy Holder
The Land That Time Forgot '75
Whistle down the Wind '61

Susan Holderness
That'll Be the Day '73

Diane Holgate
Whistle down the Wind '61

Agnieszka Holland
The Interrogation '82

Mary Holland
Tommy '75

Adam Hollander
Halloween '78

Antony Holles
They Drive by Night '38

Laurel Holloman
The Myth of Fingerprints '97

Julian Holloway
Having a Wild Weekend '65

Kamal Holloway
Twenty Bucks '93

Stanley Holloway
The Private Life of Sherlock Holmes '70
This Happy Breed '47
Brief Encounter '46

Ian Holm
The Sweet Hereafter '96
Big Night '95
Loch Ness '95
The Madness of King George '94
Kafka '91
Dance with a Stranger '85
Dreamchild '85
S.O.S. Titanic '79
The Homecoming '73

Clare Holman
Let Him Have It '91

Katie Holmes
The Ice Storm *'97*

Mark Holmes
The Adventures of Priscilla, Queen of the Desert *'94*

Michelle Holmes
Rita, Sue & Bob Too *'87*

Andrew Holofcener
Walking and Talking *'96*

Sandrine Holt
1999 *'98*

Joe Holyoake
2 by 4 *'98*

Skip Homeier
Tomorrow the World *'44*

Oscar Homolka
Sabotage *'36*

James Hong
True Confessions *'81*

Shin Hong
Center Stage *'91*

Heinz Honig
Das Boot *'81*

William Hootkins
Hear My Song *'91*
Valentino *'77*

Dawn Hope
Black Joy *'77*

Leslie Hope
Fun *'94*
Paris, France *'94*
It Takes Two *'88*

Richard Hope
Bellman and True *'88*

Vida Hope
The Woman in Question *'50*

Alan Hopgood
Road Games *'81*

Anthony Hopkins
The Remains of the Day *'93*
Chaplin *'92*
A Chorus of Disapproval *'89*

Bo Hopkins
U-Turn *'97*
The Ballad of Little Jo *'93*
Inside Monkey Zetterland *'93*

Kaitlin Hopkins
Ted *'98*

Miriam Hopkins
These Three *'36*

Dennis Hopper
Basquiat *'96*
Carried Away *'95*
Search and Destroy *'94*
Red Rock West *'93*
River's Edge *'87*
Blue Velvet *'86*
Tracks *'76*
Easy Rider *'69*
Night Tide *'63*

Gerard Horan
Much Ado about Nothing *'93*

Michael Hordern
The Slipper and the Rose *'76*

David Horne
Saraband for Dead Lovers *'48*
Night Train to Munich *'40*

Stephen Hornyak
The Giving *'91*

Jane Horrocks
The Witches *'90*

Michael Horse
House of Cards *'92*

Anna Maria Horsford
Set It Off *'96*
Street Smart *'87*

John Horsley
The Runaway Bus *'54*

Edward Everett Horton
Helen's Babies *'25*

Peter Horton
The End of Violence *'97*

Bob Hoskins
Cousin Bette *'97*
The Favor, the Watch, and the Very Big Fish *'92*
The Lonely Passion of Judith Hearne *'87*
Mona Lisa *'86*
The Long Good Friday *'80*

Joan Hotchkis
Legacy *'75*

Katharine Houghton
Mr. North *'88*

Alice Houri
Nenette and Boni *'96*

Donald Houston
The Mark *'61*
Room at the Top *'59*

Renee Houston
Repulsion *'65*
The Belles of St. Trinian's *'53*

Alan Howard
Strapless *'90*

Arliss Howard
johns *'96*

Arthur Howard
Another Country *'84*
The Belles of St. Trinian's *'53*

Ben Howard
The Land That Time Forgot *'75*

Creighton Howard
Killer Flick *'98*

Edward Howard
The Lady Confesses *'45*

Esther Howard
Detour *'46*

Ivor Howard
Another Country *'84*

Jeffrey Howard
The Wedding Banquet *'93*

Leslie Howard
Pygmalion *'38*
The Scarlet Pimpernel *'34*

Mel Howard
Hester Street *'75*

Rikki Howard
Lisztomania *'75*

Terrence DaShon Howard
johns *'96*

Trevor Howard
White Mischief *'88*
The Stranger's Hand *'54*
The Third Man *'49*
Brief Encounter *'46*

C. Thomas Howell
Teresa's Tattoo *'94*
Acting on Impulse *'93*

Jean Howell
Crime of Passion *'57*

Frankie Howerd
The Runaway Bus *'54*

Sally Ann Howes
Dead of Night *'45*
Pink String and Sealing Wax *'45*
Thursday's Child *'43*

Noel Howlett
Victim *'61*

Karl Howman
Stardust *'74*

Rudolf Hrusinsky
Dinner for Adele *'78*

Thomas S. Hsiung
Combination Platter *'93*

John Hubbard
Turnabout *'40*

Cork Hubbert
The Ballad of the Sad Cafe *'91*

Antoine Hubert
Le Grand Chemin *'87*

David Huddleston
The Big Lebowski *'97*

Reginald Hudlin
She's Gotta Have It *'86*

Ernie Hudson
The Basketball Diaries *'94*

Billy Le Prince Huettel
The Missing Reel *'90*

Soto Joe Hugh
The Killing of a Chinese Bookie *'76*

David Hughes
32 Short Films about Glenn Gould *'93*

Mary Beth Hughes
The Lady Confesses *'45*

Miko Hughes
Wes Craven's New Nightmare *'94*

Rhetta Hughes
Sweet Sweetback's Baadasssss Song *'71*

Wendy Hughes
Warm Nights on a Slow-Moving Train *'87*
Echoes of Paradise *'86*

Yank Huiquin
The Story of Qui Ju *'91*

Steve Huison
The Full Monty *'96*

Lauren Hulsey
Pecker *'98*

Mart Hulswit
Island of the Lost *'68*

Renee Humphrey
Lover Girl *'97*
Mallrats *'95*
Fun *'94*

Barry Humphries
Spice World: The Movie *'97*
Bedazzled *'68*

Dylan Hundley
Metropolitan *'90*

Gareth Hunt
A Chorus of Disapproval *'89*

Helen Hunt
The Waterdance *'91*

Homer Hunt
His Picture in the Papers *'16*

Jimmy Hunt
Pitfall *'48*

Linda Hunt
Twenty Bucks *'93*
Waiting for the Moon *'87*

Marko Hunt
Trust *'91*

Marsha Hunt
Actors and Sin *'52*

Martita Hunt
Great Expectations *'46*
Nine Days a Queen *'36*
Sabotage *'36*

Bill Hunter
The Adventures of Priscilla, Queen of the Desert *'94*
Muriel's Wedding *'94*
Strictly Ballroom *'92*

Harold Hunter
Kids *'95*

Holly Hunter
Crash *'95*
The Piano *'93*

Kevin Hunter
One False Move *'91*

Raymond Huntley
Hot Millions *'68*
Room at the Top *'59*
Night Train to Munich *'40*

Isabelle Huppert
La Ceremonie *'95*
Coup de Torchon *'81*
Violette *'78*

Elizabeth Hurley
Permanent Midnight *'98*
Christabel *'89*

Elliott Hurst
Popcorn *'89*

Marguerite Hurst
Forgotten Silver *'96*

Veronica Hurst
Peeping Tom *'60*

John Hurt
Love and Death on Long Island *'97*
Dead Man *'95*
Frankenstein Unbound *'90*
Scandal *'89*
White Mischief *'88*
10 Rillington Place *'70*

Mary Beth Hurt
Affliction *'97*

William Hurt
Jane Eyre *'96*
Smoke *'95*
Kiss of the Spider Woman *'85*

Zakir Hussain
Heat and Dust *'82*

Francis Huster
If I Had It to Do Over Again *'76*
Lumiere *'76*

Anjelica Huston
The Crossing Guard *'94*
The Grifters *'90*
The Witches *'90*
A Handful of Dust *'88*
Mr. North *'88*
The Dead *'87*

Michael Hutchence
Frankenstein Unbound *'90*

Geoffrey Hutchings
Wish You Were Here *'87*

Harry Hutchinson
Blow-Up *'66*

Rick Huxley
Having a Wild Weekend *'65*

Bobby Hyatt
He Ran All the Way *'51*

Wilfrid Hyde-White
John and Julie *'55*
The Third Man *'49*
The Man Who Knew Too Much *'34*

Warren Hymer
You Only Live Once *'37*

Roger Ibanez
The Red Poster *'76*

Ice-T
Body Count *'97*

Eric Idle
Nuns on the Run *'90*

Istvan Iglody
False Weights *'74*

Dimiter Ikonomov
Last Summer *'74*

Igor Illinski
Aelita: Queen of Mars *'24*

Vladimir Ilyine
Burnt by the Sun *'94*

Michael Imperioli
I Shot Andy Warhol *'96*
The Addiction *'95*
The Basketball Diaries *'94*
Household Saints *'93*

Jennifer Inch
Anne of Green Gables *'85*

Miguel Incian
Aventurera *'49*

Elizabeth Inglis
The 39 Steps *'35*

Sarah Inglis
Smooth Talk *'85*

Jeremy Irons
Lolita *'97*
The House of the Spirits *'93*
Kafka *'91*
A Chorus of Disapproval *'89*

Michael Ironside
Guncrazy *'92*

Amy Irving
Carried Away *'95*

Bill Irwin
Eight Men Out *'88*

Frances Irwin
Gun Crazy *'49*

Gregory Isaacs
Rockers *'79*

Chris Isaak
Grace of My Heart *'96*

Ryo Ishibashi
The Crossing Guard *'94*

Michael Jace
Boogie Nights *'97*

Anne Jackson
The Shining *'80*

Chequita Jackson
Just Another Girl on the I.R.T. *'93*

Freda Jackson
Beware of Pity *'46*
Great Expectations *'46*

Glenda Jackson
Business As Usual *'88*
The Devil Is a Woman *'75*
The Maids *'75*

Gordon Jackson
The Whistle Blower *'87*
The Prime of Miss Jean Brodie *'69*
Abandon Ship *'57*
Pink String and Sealing Wax *'45*

John M. Jackson
The Spitfire Grill *'95*

Robert Jason Jackson
New Jersey Drive *'95*

Rosemark Jackson
Hangin' with the Homeboys *'91*

Samuel L. Jackson
Eve's Bayou *'97*
Jackie Brown *'97*
Hard Eight *'96*
Trees Lounge *'96*
Fresh *'94*
Pulp Fiction *'94*
Menace II Society *'93*
Def by Temptation *'90*

Selmer Jackson
Pitfall *'48*

Sherry Jackson
Daughters of the Dust *'91*

Tom Jackson
Medicine River *'94*

Irene Jacob
Trois Couleurs: Rouge *'94*

Joelle Jacob
The Lady in White *'88*

Derek Jacobi
Little Dorrit, Film 1: Nobody's Fault *'88*
Little Dorrit, Film 2: Little Dorrit's Story *'88*
The Odessa File *'74*
Three Sisters *'70*

David Jacobs
Stardust *'74*

Steve Jacobs
To Have and to Hold *'96*
Echoes of Paradise *'86*

Bobby Jacoby
The Applegates *'89*

Scott Jacoby
The Little Girl Who Lives down the Lane *'76*

Madhur Jaffrey
Vanya on 42nd Street *'94*
Heat and Dust *'82*

Saeed Jaffrey
The Deceivers *'88*
My Beautiful Laundrette *'85*

Dean Jagger
Private Hell 36 *'54*

Mick Jagger
Gimme Shelter *'70*
Performance *'70*

Scott Jaicks
Killer Flick *'98*

Lisa Jakub
Rambling Rose *'91*

Brion James
American Strays *'96*
The Player *'92*

Clifton James
Lone Star *'95*
Eight Men Out *'88*

David James
Charley's Aunt *'25*

Godfrey James
The Land That Time Forgot *'75*

Hawthorne James
Campfire Tales *'98*

Mark James
Slacker *'91*

Oscar James
Black Joy *'77*

Sidney James
The Smallest Show on Earth *'57*
John and Julie *'55*
The Belles of St. Trinian's *'53*

Steve James
The Land That Time Forgot *'75*

Joyce Jameson
The Balcony *'63*

Nicole Jamet
Why Not! *'78*

Krystyna Janda
The Interrogation *'82*

Thomas Jane
Boogie Nights *'97*

Allison Janney
Big Night *'95*

David Janssen
S.O.S. Titanic *'79*

Ernst-Hugo Jaregard
Stubby *'74*

Jim Jarmusch
Sling Blade *'96*

Belinda Jarrett
Muriel's Wedding *'94*

Elzbieta Jasinska
Trois Couleurs: Rouge *'94*

Castalia Jason
Little Shots of Happiness '97

Star Jasper
True Love '89

Ricky Jay
Boogie Nights '97
House of Games '87

Michael Jayston
The Homecoming '73

Marianne Jean-Baptiste
Secrets and Lies '95

Jacqueline Jeanne
Dites-Lui Que Je L'Aime '77

Allan Jeayes
The Hidden Room '49
Saraband for Dead Lovers '48
They Drive by Night '38
The Scarlet Pimpernel '34

Soulfood Jed
Fly by Night '93

The Jefferson Airplane
Gimme Shelter '70

Barbara Jefford
Where Angels Fear to Tread '91

Peter Jeffrey
The Odessa File '74
If... '69

Lionel Jeffries
A Chorus of Disapproval '89

Roger Jendly
Jonah Who Will Be 25 in the Year 2000 '76

Allen Jenkins
Dead End '37

Jason Jenkins
Matewan '87

Ken Jenkins
Matewan '87

Megs Jenkins
The Innocents '61
Tiger Bay '59
John and Julie '55
Saraband for Dead Lovers '48

Richard Jenkins
Flirting with Disaster '95

Sam Jenkins
Twenty Bucks '93

Michael Jenn
Dance with a Stranger '85
Another Country '84

Lucinda Jenney
American Heart '92
Wired '89

Alex Jennings
The Wings of the Dove '97

David Jensen
The Underneath '95

Eulalie Jensen
Charley's Aunt '25

Kandeyce Jensen
Star Maps '97

Sasha Jensen
Dazed and Confused '93

Ebony Jerido
Just Another Girl on the I.R.T. '93

Clytie Jessop
The Innocents '61

Michael Jeter
Just Like in the Movies '90

Jimmy Jewel
The Krays '90

Ronny Jhutti
Wild West '93

Zheng Jian
Ju Dou '90

Wang Jianfa
The Story of Qui Ju '91

Penn Jillette
Hackers '95
Tough Guys Don't Dance '87

Elaine Jin
Love unto Waste '86

Ebony Jo-Ann
Fly by Night '93

Marlene Jobert
The Wonderful Crook '75

Cameron Johann
Last Exit to Brooklyn '90

Zita Johann
Struggle '31

Peter Johansen
The Brothers McMullen '94

Scarlett Johansson
Manny & Lo '96

Zizi Johari
The Killing of a Chinese Bookie '76

Elton John
Tommy '75

Georg John
M '31

Gottfried John
Mother Kusters Goes to Heaven '76

Mervyn Johns
The Intimate Stranger '56
1984 '56
Dead of Night '45
Pink String and Sealing Wax '45

Stratford Johns
Lair of the White Worm '88
Dance with a Stranger '85
Who Done It? '56

Tracy C. Johns
She's Gotta Have It '86

A. J. Johnson
House Party '90

Anne-Marie Johnson
Hollywood Shuffle '87

Ariyan Johnson
Just Another Girl on the I.R.T. '93

Brook Johnson
The Sweet Hereafter '96

Camilla Johnson
Sparrows '26

Carmencita Johnson
These Three '36

Celia Johnson
The Prime of Miss Jean Brodie '69
This Happy Breed '47
Brief Encounter '46

Craigus R. Johnson
Hollywood Shuffle '87

Don Johnson
A Boy and His Dog '75

Howard Johnson
Eddie and the Cruisers '83

Katie Johnson
John and Julie '55
The Ladykillers '55

Linda Johnson
Impact '49

Noel Johnson
Frenzy '72

Reggie Johnson
Platoon '86

Ron Johnson
Zebrahead '92

Sandy Johnson
Halloween '78

Scott Johnson
Bodies, Rest & Motion '93

Seeseell Ann Johnson
Sparrows '26

Tor Johnson
Plan 9 from Outer Space '56
Bride of the Monster '55

Vance Johnson
Red Rock West '93

Angelina Jolie
Hackers '95

Jonah
Jonah Who Will Be 25 in the Year 2000 '76

Angela Jones
Pariah '98

Barry Jones
Madeleine '50
Uneasy Terms '48

Claude Earl Jones
Miracle Mile '89

Damon Jones
Pariah '98

Duane Jones
Night of the Living Dead '68

Emrys Jones
Beware of Pity '46

Freddie Jones
Wild at Heart '90

Gemma Jones
Wilde '97

Gillian Jones
Echoes of Paradise '86

Hannah Jones
Blackmail '29

Henry Jones
The Grifters '90

James Earl Jones
The Ambulance '90
Grim Prairie Tales '89
Matewan '87

Jeffrey Jones
Enid Is Sleeping '90

Jennifer Jones
Beat the Devil '53

L. Q. Jones
Lightning Jack '94

Laurie Jones
In the Spirit '90

Marcia Mae Jones
These Three '36

Marie Jones
In the Name of the Father '93

Mickey Jones
Sling Blade '96

Nicholas Jones
Black Beauty '94

O-lan Jones
Shelf Life '94
Miracle Mile '89

Peter Jones
Hot Millions '68
John and Julie '55

Russell Jones
Squeeze '97

Sam Jones
American Strays '96

Tommy Lee Jones
House of Cards '92

Bobby Jordan
Dead End '37

Lewis Jordan
She's Gotta Have It *'86*

Richard Jordan
One Night Stand *'76*

Allen Joseph
Eraserhead *'78*

Paterson Joseph
In the Name of the Father *'93*

Erland Josephson
The Unbearable Lightness of Being *'88*
Face to Face *'76*
Scenes from a Marriage *'73*

Jennifer Jostyn
The Brothers McMullen *'94*

Milla Jovovich
Dazed and Confused *'93*
Chaplin *'92*

Mark Joy
Pecker *'98*

Robert Joy
A Modern Affair *'94*
Longtime Companion *'90*

Ella Joyce
Set It Off *'96*

Yootha Joyce
Having a Wild Weekend *'65*

Mario Joyner
Hangin' with the Homeboys *'91*

Michelle Joyner
Traces of Red *'92*

Ashley Judd
Normal Life *'96*
Smoke *'95*
Ruby in Paradise *'93*

Arline Judge
Girls in Chains *'43*

Raul Julia
Frankenstein Unbound *'90*
Kiss of the Spider Woman *'85*

Lenny Juliano
Not of This Earth *'88*

Jorge Juliao
Pixote *'81*

Ge Zhi Jun
The Story of Qui Ju *'91*

Ye Jun
The Story of Qui Ju *'91*

Tito Junco
Aventurera *'49*

John Junkin
A Handful of Dust *'88*
A Hard Day's Night *'64*

Katy Jurado
Reasons of State *'78*

John Justin
Lisztomania *'75*

Dalit Kahan
Song of the Siren *'94*

Khalil Kain
Love Jones *'96*

Toni Kalem
American Strays *'96*

Pascale Kalensky
The Unbearable Lightness of Being *'88*

A. Kaliaguine
The Orphans *'77*

Daria Kalinina
Welcome to the Dollhouse *'95*

Jacob Kalish
East and West *'24*

Sylva Kamenicka
Day for My Love *'77*

Byron Kane
Gog *'54*

Carol Kane
American Strays *'96*
Trees Lounge *'96*
Sticky Fingers *'88*
Valentino *'77*
Hester Street *'75*

Ivan Kane
Bound *'96*

Sandra Kane
Teenage Gang Debs *'66*

Takeshi Kaneshiro
Chungking Express *'95*

Paul Kantner
Gimme Shelter *'70*

Tracey Kapisky
American Heart *'92*

Ravi Kapoor
Wild West *'93*

Shashi Kapoor
The Deceivers *'88*
Sammy & Rosie Get Laid *'87*
Heat and Dust *'82*

Robin Karfo
Eddie and the Cruisers *'83*

Miriam Karlin
Hand in Hand *'60*
Room at the Top *'59*

Janice Karman
Switchblade Sisters *'75*

Tcheky Karyo
To Have and to Hold *'96*
La Femme Nikita *'91*
Sorceress *'88*

Harold Kasket
Moulin Rouge *'52*

Katherine Kath
Moulin Rouge *'52*

Nicky Katt
johns *'96*
SubUrbia *'96*

Maurice Kaufman
Fright *'71*

John Kavanagh
Widow's Peak *'94*
Bellman and True *'88*

Charles Kavanaugh
Public Access *'93*

Dorrie Kavanaugh
Hester Street *'75*

Oscar Kawagley
Salmonberries *'91*

Bernard Kay
In Possession *'84*
Interlude *'67*

Caren Kaye
My Tutor *'82*

Lila Kaye
Nuns on the Run *'90*

Norman Kaye
Warm Nights on a Slow-Moving Train *'87*

Fred Kaz
...And God Spoke *'94*

Costa Kazakos
Iphigenia *'77*

Stacy Keach
Road Games *'81*
The Killer inside Me *'76*
Luther *'74*

Marie Kean
The Dead *'87*
The Lonely Passion of Judith Hearne *'87*

Staci Keanan
Lisa *'90*

Bryan Keane
Art for Teachers of Children *'95*

Gillian Kearney
Shirley Valentine *'89*

Peter Keating
The Last of the High Kings *'96*

Michael Keaton
Jackie Brown *'97*
Much Ado about Nothing *'93*

Steven Keats
Hester Street *'75*

Lee Sau Kee
Eat a Bowl of Tea *'89*

Jeremy Keefe
The Boys of St. Vincent *'93*

Geoffrey Keen
Genevieve *'53*
The Fallen Idol *'49*

Monica Keena
Ripe *'97*

Tom (George Duryea) Keene
Plan 9 from Outer Space *'56*
Our Daily Bread *'34*

Catherine Keener
The Real Blonde *'97*
Box of Moonlight *'96*
Walking and Talking *'96*
Living in Oblivion *'94*

Matt Keeslar
Waiting for Guffman *'96*

Jack Kehler
Lost Highway *'96*

Harvey Keitel
Cop Land *'97*
FairyTale: A True Story *'97*
Smoke *'95*
Pulp Fiction *'94*
The Piano *'93*
Bad Lieutenant *'92*
Reservoir Dogs *'92*

Stella Keitel
Bad Lieutenant *'92*

Cecil Kellaway
I Married a Witch *'42*

Andrew Kelley
For a Lost Soldier *'93*

Barry Kelley
Too Late for Tears *'49*

Sheila Kelley
Passion Fish *'92*

Walter Kelley
Marty *'55*

Mike Kellin
Girlfriends *'78*
The Incident *'67*

Pamela Kellino
I Met a Murderer *'39*

Claire Kelly
Georgy Girl *'66*

David Patrick Kelly
Flirting with Disaster *'95*

Grace Kelly
The Children of Theatre Street *'77*

Judy Kelly
Dead of Night *'45*
The Private Life of Henry VIII *'33*

Moira Kelly
The Tie That Binds *'95*
Little Odessa *'94*
Chaplin *'92*

Patsy Kelly
Naked Kiss *'64*

Paula Kelly
Lost in the Stars *'74*

Moultrie Kelsall
The Battle of the Sexes '60
Abandon Ship '57

Gary Kemp
The Krays '90

Jeremy Kemp
Angels and Insects '95
Four Weddings and a Funeral '94

Martin Kemp
The Krays '90

Paul Kemp
M '31

Will Kempe
Metropolitan '90

Gerhard Kempinski
Beware of Pity '46
Thursday's Child '43

Rachel Kempson
Georgy Girl '66

Josef Kemr
Seclusion near a Forest '76

Felicity Kendal
Valentino '77

Jennifer Kendal
Heat and Dust '82

Henry Kendall
Rich and Strange '32

Kay Kendall
Genevieve '53

Aaron Leon Kenin
Morgan's Cake '88

Eliot Kenin
Morgan's Cake '88

Arthur Kennedy
Crashout '55
Champion '49
Too Late for Tears '49

Gordon Kennedy
Just Like a Woman '92

Graham Kennedy
Don's Party '76

Jamie Kennedy
Bongwater '98

Lyn Kennedy
Teenage Gang Debs '66

William Kennedy
High Stakes '89

Patsy Kensit
Grace of My Heart '96
Angels and Insects '95
Twenty-One '91
A Chorus of Disapproval '89
Absolute Beginners '86

Anno Kont
Widow's Peak '94

Diana Kent
Heavenly Creatures '94

Jace Kent
Little Odessa '94

Jean Kent
The Woman in Question '50

Keneth Kent
Night Train to Munich '40

Alexia Keogh
An Angel at My Table '89

Garrett Keogh
Widow's Peak '94

Jimmy Keogh
The Matchmaker '97

Deborah Kerr
The Innocents '61
Separate Tables '58
Black Narcissus '47

Corinne Kersten
Murmur of the Heart '71

Brian Kerwin
The Myth of Fingerprints '97

Mohamad Ali Keshavarz
Through the Olive Trees '94

Sara Kestelman
Lisztomania '75

Alice Key
Actors and Sin '52

Evelyn Keyes
The Prowler '51

Sajid Khan
Heat and Dust '82

Arsinee Khanjian
The Sweet Hereafter '96
Exotica '94

Eleonara Khilberg
Combination Platter '93

Michael Khumrov
Little Odessa '94

Margot Kidder
My Teacher Ate My Homework '98

Nicole Kidman
To Die For '95
Dead Calm '89

Udo Kier
The End of Violence '97
Breaking the Waves '95
My Own Private Idaho '91

Percy Kilbride
Guest in the House '44

Terence Kilburn
Lolita '62

Kevin Kildow
The Giving '91

David Kiley
Chameleon Street '89

Richard Kiley
The Little Prince '74

Val Kilmer
The Island of Dr. Moreau '96
Kill Me Again '89

Sandelle Kincaid
Vegas in Space '94

Andrea King
The Linguini Incident '92

Charmion King
Anne of Green Gables '85

Dave King
The Long Good Friday '80

Hazel King
Daughters of the Country '86

Loretta King
Bride of the Monster '55

Ben Kingsley
Photographing Fairies '97
Death and the Maiden '94
Maurice '87

Danitza Kingsley
Jack's Back '87

Susan Kingsley
Old Enough '84

Alex Kingston
Carrington '95

Maeve Kinkead
City of Hope '91

Melinda Kinnaman
My Life As a Dog '85

Roy Kinnear
Help! '65

Bruno Kirby
The Basketball Diaries '94
Golden Gate '93

George Kirby
Trouble in Mind '86

Michael Kirby
Swoon '91

Joe Kirk
Impact '49

Jess Kirkland
D.O.A. '49

Sally Kirkland
Cold Feet '89
High Stakes '89
Anna '87

Gene Kirkwood
The Crossing Guard '94

Mia Kirshner
Exotica '94
Love and Human Remains '93

Michael Kitchen
Enchanted April '92

Barry Kivel
Bound '96

Rudolf Klein-Rogge
Metropolis '26

Towje Kleiner
The Odessa File '74

Makka Kleist
Daughters of the Country '86

Rose Marie Klespitz
Stardust '74

Brandon Kleyla
Gods and Monsters '98

Kevin Kline
The Ice Storm '97
Chaplin '92

Joseph Knafelmacher
Kids '95

Bud Knapp
Never Take Candy from a Stranger '60

Tom Kneebone
The Luck of Ginger Coffey '64

Rob Knepper
Gas Food Lodging '92

Esmond Knight
Peeping Tom '60
Black Narcissus '47

Gladys Knight
Twenty Bucks '93

Wayne Knight
To Die For '95

Andrew Knott
Black Beauty '94

Kathryn Knotts
The Method '87

Mickey Knox
Cemetery Man '95
Frankenstein Unbound '90

Bogumil Kobiela
Ashes and Diamonds '58

Y. Kochurov
Professor Mamlock '38

Oja Kodar
Orson Welles: The One Man Band '95

Max Kohlhase
Joyless Street '25

Kristina Kohoutova
Alice '88

Clarence Kolb
Impact '49

Tetsu Komai
Bulldog Drummond '29

Maja Komorowska
The Balance '75

Gabor Koncz
The Hungarians '78

Tsang Kong
One Night Stand *'76*

Anna Konstam
They Drive by Night *'38*

Nada Konvalinkova
Dinner for Adele *'78*

Milos Kopecky
Dinner for Adele *'78*

Fritz Kortner
Pandora's Box *'28*
The Hands of Orlac *'25*

David Kossoff
1984 *'56*
Who Done It? *'56*

Elias Koteas
Crash *'95*
Exotica *'94*
Chain of Desire *'93*

Yaphet Kotto
Nothing but a Man *'64*

Maya Koumani
Fire Maidens from Outer Space *'56*

Karl Kozak
To Hell with Love *'98*

Linda Kozlowski
Pass the Ammo *'88*

Jeroen Krabbe
For a Lost Soldier *'93*
Kafka *'91*
Scandal *'89*
A World Apart *'88*

Werner Krauss
Joyless Street *'25*

Svetlana Krioutchkova
Burnt by the Sun *'94*

Sylvia Kristel
Emmanuelle *'74*

Marta Kristen
Body Count *'97*

Jason Kristofer
The Crossing Guard *'94*

Kris Kristofferson
Lone Star *'95*
Trouble in Mind *'86*
Message to Love: The Isle of Wight Festival, the Movie *'70*

Tracy Kristofferson
Trouble in Mind *'86*

Michael Kroecher
Every Man for Himself & God against All *'75*

Berry Kroeger
Gun Crazy *'49*

Derk-Jan Kroon
For a Lost Soldier *'93*

Christiane Krueger
Anne of Green Gables *'85*

Alma Kruger
These Three *'36*

Sonia Kruger-Tayler
Strictly Ballroom *'92*

David Krumholtz
The Ice Storm *'97*

Olek Krupa
Mac *'93*

Line Kruse
Emma's Shadow *'88*

Eva Krzyzewska
Ashes and Diamonds *'58*

Youki Kudoh
Picture Bride *'94*

Lisa Kudrow
The Opposite of Sex *'98*

Valentina Kuindzi
Aelita: Queen of Mars *'24*

Sophie Kullman
Where Angels Fear to Tread *'91*

Magda Kun
Dead of Night *'45*

Robert Kunsa
To Have and to Hold *'96*

Sakari Kuosmanen
Night on Earth *'91*

Swoosie Kurtz
Citizen Ruth *'96*
A Shock to the System *'90*

Tamiyo Kusakari
Shall We Dance? *'96*

Reiko Kusamura
Shall We Dance? *'96*

Finn Kvalen
The Feldmann Case *'87*

Kola Kwarian
The Killing *'56*

Susan Kyd
Dance with a Stranger *'85*

Sam Kydd
Eye of the Needle *'81*

David Kyle
Halloween *'78*

L. L. Cool J.
Halloween: H20 *'98*

Peg La Centra
Crime of Passion *'57*

Junior Labeija
Paris Is Burning *'91*

Pepper Labeija
Paris Is Burning *'91*

Matthew Laborteaux
A Woman under the Influence *'74*

Patrick Laborteaux
Heathers *'89*

Dominique Labourier
Jonah Who Will Be 25 in the Year 2000 *'76*
The Wonderful Crook *'75*

Philippe Labro
Cat and Mouse *'78*

Neil LaBute
Independent's Day *'97*

Bruce Lacey
Help! *'65*

Catherine Lacey
The Private Life of Sherlock Holmes *'70*
Pink String and Sealing Wax *'45*
The Lady Vanishes *'38*

Stan Lachow
The Luckiest Man in the World *'89*

Katya Ladan
32 Short Films about Glenn Gould *'93*

Taherek Ladania
Through the Olive Trees *'94*

Cheryl Ladd
Permanent Midnight *'98*
Lisa *'90*

Diane Ladd
Citizen Ruth *'96*
Rambling Rose *'91*
Wild at Heart *'90*

Margaret Ladd
The Whales of August *'87*

Walter Laderigast
Every Man for Himself & God against All *'75*

Dominique Laffin
Dites-Lui Que Je L'Aime *'77*

Bernadette LaFont
Waiting for the Moon *'87*
Violette *'78*

Valerie Lagrange
Cat and Mouse *'78*

Christine Lahti
Stacking *'87*

Connie Laird
Guest in the House *'44*

Jenny Laird
Village of the Damned *'60*
Black Narcissus *'47*
Beware of Pity *'46*

Ricki Lake
Serial Mom *'94*
Inside Monkey Zetterland *'93*
Last Exit to Brooklyn *'90*

Veronica Lake
I Married a Witch *'42*

James Lally
Critical Care *'97*

Michael Lally
The Secret of Roan Inish *'94*

David Lam
Project A: Part 2 *'87*

Jean LaMarre
Fresh *'94*

Anne Lambert
Picnic at Hanging Rock *'75*

Jack Lambert
The Ghost Goes West *'36*

Jack Lambert
Kiss Me Deadly *'55*

Lloyd Lamble
The Belles of St. Trinian's *'53*

Duncan Lament
The Woman in Question *'50*

Cynthia Lamontagne
Flirting with Disaster *'95*

Mark Lamos
Longtime Companion *'90*

Chus Lampreave
Matador *'86*

Ann Lancaster
The Railway Children *'70*
Hot Millions *'68*

Burt Lancaster
Legacy of the Hollywood Blacklist *'87*
Separate Tables *'58*

Stuart Lancaster
Faster, Pussycat! Kill! Kill! *'65*

Elsa Lanchester
The Ghost Goes West *'36*
The Private Life of Henry VIII *'33*

Mary Landa
Impact *'49*

Inga Landgre
Paradise Place *'77*

Inge Landgut
M *'31*

Bill Landis
Vortex *'81*

Carole Landis
Turnabout *'40*

Avice Landon
Leather Boys *'63*

Laurene Landon
The Ambulance *'90*

Pavel Landovsky
The Unbearable Lightness of Being *'88*

Ruth Landshoff
Nosferatu *'22*

Charles Lane
Acting on Impulse *'93*

Charles Lane
Bury Me Dead *'47*

Diane Lane
Chaplin *'92*

k. d. lang
Salmonberries *'91*

Perry Lang
Eight Men Out *'88*

Robert Lang
Interlude *'67*
Having a Wild Weekend *'65*

Stephen Lang
Last Exit to Brooklyn *'90*

Veronica Lang
Don's Party *'76*

Libby Langdon
Federal Hill *'94*

Hope Lange
Tune in Tomorrow *'90*
Blue Velvet *'86*

Jean Lange
Eraserhead *'78*

Jessica Lange
Cousin Bette *'97*

Frank Langella
Lolita *'97*

Heather Langenkamp
Wes Craven's New Nightmare *'94*

Jean Langer
Hard Eight *'96*

Margaret Langrick
American Boyfriends *'89*

Jean Langston
The Belles of St. Trinian's *'53*

David Langton
The Whistle Blower *'87*
Abandon Ship *'57*

George Lannes
Moulin Rouge *'52*

Victor Lanoux
In a Wild Moment *'78*
Servant and Mistress *'77*
Cousin, Cousine *'76*

Angela Lansbury
The World of Henry Orient *'64*
The Manchurian Candidate *'62*

David Lansbury
Gas Food Lodging *'92*

Luis Lantigua
Fresh *'94*

Anthony LaPaglia
Brilliant Lies *'96*
Trees Lounge *'96*

Daniel Lapaine
1999 *'98*
Muriel's Wedding *'94*

Yair Lapid
Song of the Siren *'94*

Victor Laplace
Letters from the Park *'88*

Jean Lapointe
The Orders *'75*

Jerome Lapperrousaz
Lumiere *'76*

Ring Lardner Jr.
Hollywood on Trial *'76*

Vincent Laresca
Ripe *'97*

Leon Larive
Children of Paradise *'45*

Chris Larkin
Angels and Insects *'95*

Diana Larkin
Color of a Brisk and Leaping Day *'95*

Mary Larkin
Galileo *'73*

Michele Laroque
Ma Vie en Rose *'97*

John Larroquette
Tune in Tomorrow *'90*

Michael Laskin
Passion Fish *'92*

Louise Lasser
Happiness *'98*
Sudden Manhattan *'96*
Frankenhooker *'90*

Tania Latarjet
The Vanishing *'88*

Zoltan Latonovits
The Unfinished Sentence in 141 Minutes *'75*

Ney Latorraca
The Fable of the Beautiful Pigeon Fancier *'88*

Matt Lattanzi
My Tutor *'82*

Carina Lau
Center Stage *'91*
Project A: Part 2 *'87*

Jeff Lau
Combination Platter *'93*

John Laughlin
Motorama *'91*

Charles Laughton
Sidewalks of London *'38*
The Private Life of Henry VIII *'33*

S. John Launer
Crime of Passion *'57*

Matthew Laurance
Eddie and the Cruisers 2: Eddie Lives! *'89*
Eddie and the Cruisers *'83*

Odette Laure
Daddy Nostalgia *'90*

James Laurenson
A House in the Hills *'93*

Christine Laurent
Cat and Mouse *'78*

Hugh Laurie
Cousin Bette *'97*
Spice World: The Movie *'97*
Strapless *'90*

John Laurie
Madeleine *'50*
Clouds over Europe *'39*
Nine Days a Queen *'36*
The 39 Steps *'35*

Piper Laurie
The Crossing Guard *'94*
Boss' Son *'78*

Sandie Lavelle
Ladybird, Ladybird *'93*

Gabriele Lavia
The Devil Is a Woman *'75*

Jude Law
I Love You, I Love You Not *'97*
Wilde *'97*

Phyllida Law
Much Ado about Nothing *'93*

Christopher Lawford
Mr. North *'88*

Josie Lawrence
Enchanted April *'92*

Marc Lawrence
The Big Easy *'87*

Martin Lawrence
House Party *'90*

Rick Lawrence
Campfire Tales *'98*

Linda Lawson
Night Tide *'63*

Wilfred Lawson
Room at the Top *'59*
Thursday's Child *'43*
Pygmalion *'38*

Frank Lawton
A Night to Remember *'58*

Abe Lax
American Matchmaker *'40*

Freida Lay
Vegas in Space *'94*

Renee Le Calm
When the Cat's Away *'96*

Brent Le Page
Halloween *'78*

Bernadette Le Sache
The Vanishing *'88*

Nigel le Vaillant
Christabel *'89*

Rosemary Leach
A Room with a View *'86*
That'll Be the Day *'73*

Cloris Leachman
S.O.S. Titanic *'79*
Kiss Me Deadly *'55*

Marianna Lead
Little Odessa *'94*

Denis Leary
The Matchmaker *'97*
The Real Blonde *'97*
Suicide Kings *'97*

Jean-Pierre Leaud
The 400 Blows *'59*

Madeleine LeBeau
8½ *'63*

Samuel Lebihan
Trois Couleurs: Rouge *'94*

Bryan Leder
Metropolitan *'90*

Erwin Leder
Das Boot *'81*

Francis Lederer
Pandora's Box *'28*

Virginie Ledoyen
La Ceremonie *'95*

Anna Lee
Non-Stop New York *'37*

Belinda Lee
Who Done It? *'56*
The Runaway Bus *'54*
The Belles of St. Trinian's *'53*

Bernard Lee
10 Rillington Place *'70*
Whistle down the Wind *'61*
Beat the Devil *'53*
The Fallen Idol *'49*
The Third Man *'49*

Bill Lee
She's Gotta Have It *'86*

Christopher Lee
A Feast at Midnight *'95*
The Private Life of Sherlock Holmes *'70*
Moulin Rouge *'52*

Dixie Lee
Legacy *'75*

Franchesca Lee
Children of the Damned *'63*

Jason Lee
Chasing Amy *'97*
Mallrats *'95*

Joanna Lee
Plan 9 from Outer Space *'56*

Joie Lee
She's Gotta Have It *'86*

Robbie Lee
Switchblade Sisters *'75*

Ruta Lee
Funny Bones *'94*

Sheryl Lee
Homage *'95*
Backbeat *'94*
Wild at Heart *'90*

Sophie Lee
Muriel's Wedding *'94*

Spike Lee
She's Gotta Have It *'86*

Virginia Lee
D.O.A. *'49*

Waise Lee
Center Stage *'91*

Adam LeFevre
Return of the Secaucus 7 *'80*

Christian Leffler
Killer Flick *'98*

Denise Legeay
I Have Killed *'24*

Alison Leggatt
Never Take Candy from a Stranger *'60*
This Happy Breed *'47*

Michel Legrand
The World of Jacques Demy *'95*

James LeGros
The Myth of Fingerprints *'97*
Destiny Turns on the Radio *'95*
Safe *'95*
Living in Oblivion *'94*
Guncrazy *'92*
Blood & Concrete: A Love Story *'90*
Drugstore Cowboy *'89*

John Leguizamo
Hangin' with the Homeboys *'91*

Janet Leigh
Halloween: H20 *'98*
The Manchurian Candidate *'62*

Jennifer Jason Leigh
Bastard out of Carolina *'96*
Georgia *'95*
Kansas City *'95*
Mrs. Parker and the Vicious Circle *'94*
Short Cuts *'93*
Last Exit to Brooklyn *'90*
Miami Blues *'90*

Vivien Leigh
Sidewalks of London *'38*

Barbara Leigh-Hunt
Paper Mask *'91*
Frenzy *'72*

Margaret Leighton
Galileo *'73*

Donovan Leitch
I Shot Andy Warhol *'96*
Gas Food Lodging *'92*

Chloe Leland
Wish You Were Here *'87*

Rachel Lemieux
Mommy *'95*

Tutte Lemkow
Moulin Rouge *'52*

Jack Lemmon
Short Cuts *'93*

Genevieve Lemon
The Piano *'93*

Jarrett Lennon
Short Cuts *'93*

John Lennon
The Rolling Stones Rock and Roll Circus *'68*
Help! *'65*
A Hard Day's Night *'64*

Loles Leon
Tie Me Up! Tie Me Down! *'90*

Robert Sean Leonard
I Love You, I Love You Not *'97*
Much Ado about Nothing *'93*

Marco Leonardi
Like Water for Chocolate *'93*
Cinema Paradiso *'88*

Tea Leoni
Flirting with Disaster *'95*

Philippe Leotard
Death of a Schoolboy *'91*
Cat and Mouse *'78*
First Communion *'77*
The Wonderful Crook *'75*

Paul Leperson
Phantom of Liberty *'74*

Ken Lerner
Mother's Boys *'94*

Michael Lerner
Eight Men Out *'88*

Angela Leslie
Chameleon Street *'89*

Albee Lesotho
A World Apart *'88*

Len Lesser
Shack Out on 101 *'55*

Richard Lester
The Making of "A Hard Day's Night" *'94*

Jared Leto
The Last of the High Kings *'96*

Dan Lett
Paris, France *'94*

Tony Leung Chiu-Wai
Happy Together *'96*
Chungking Express *'95*
Center Stage *'91*
Love unto Waste *'86*

Ted Levine
Georgia *'95*

Ashlee Levitch
Star Kid *'97*

Joseph Gordon Levitt
Halloween: H20 *'98*

Stan Levitt
Carnival of Souls *'62*

Adam Levy
The Governess *'98*

Eugene Levy
Waiting for Guffman *'96*

Jose Lewgoy
Kiss of the Spider Woman *'85*

Fiona Lewis
Lisztomania *'75*

Harry Lewis
Gun Crazy *'49*

Huey Lewis
Short Cuts *'93*

Jerry Lewis
Funny Bones *'94*

Jonathan Lewis
The Boys of St. Vincent *'93*

Juliette Lewis
The Basketball Diaries *'94*
Kalifornia *'93*

Richard Lewis
Hugo Pool *'97*
Leaving Las Vegas *'95*

Edward Lexy
Sidewalks of London *'38*

Leo Leyden
The Luck of Ginger Coffey *'64*

Gong Li
The Story of Qui Ju *'91*
Ju Dou *'90*

Mitchell Lichtenstein
The Wedding Banquet *'93*

Jim Lichtscheidl
With or Without You *'98*

Anki Liden
My Life As a Dog *'85*

Michael Liebman
2 by 4 *'98*

Albert Lieven
Beware of Pity *'46*
Night Train to Munich *'40*

Miguel Ligero
Apartment Zero *'88*

Cody Lightning
Smoke Signals *'98*

Marilyn Lightstone
Anne of Green Gables *'85*

Denis Liliegren
Caged *'97*

Matthew Lillard
Hackers *'95*
Serial Mom *'94*

Beatrice Lillie
On Approval *'44*

Bridget Lin
Chungking Express *'95*

Aida Linares
U-Turn *'97*

Abbey Lincoln
Nothing but a Man *'64*

Dagny Lind
Paradise Place *'77*

Jane Lind
Salmonberries *'91*

Traci Lind
The End of Violence *'97*

Sven Lindberg
Face to Face *'76*

Cec Linder
Lolita *'62*

Viveca Lindfors
The Linguini Incident *'92*
Girlfriends *'78*

Delroy Lindo
Mountains of the Moon *'90*

Olga Lindo
The Hidden Room *'49*

Robert Lindsay
That'll Be the Day *'73*

Rosaleen Linehan
The Matchmaker *'97*

Ruan Ling-Yu
Love and Duty *'31*

Theo Lingen
M *'31*

Richard Linklater
The Underneath *'95*
Slacker *'91*

Joe Linnane
The Woman in Question *'50*

Edilson Lino
Pixote *'81*

Richard Linton
The Cater Street Hangman *'98*

Therese Liotard
One Sings, the Other Doesn't *'77*

Ray Liotta
Cop Land *'97*

Lu Liping
The Blue Kite *'93*

Arthur Lipson
Struggle *'31*

Joe Lisi
Traces of Red *'92*

Michel Lisowski
Trois Couleurs: Blanc *'94*

Leon Lissek
The Unbearable Lightness of Being *'88*

Moira Lister
Abandon Ship *'57*
John and Julie *'55*
Uneasy Terms *'48*

Tommy (Tiny) Lister
Body Count *'97*
Jackie Brown *'97*

John Litel
Pitfall *'48*

John Lithgow
A Good Man in Africa *'94*

Mickey Little
Gun Crazy *'49*

Lucien Littlefield
Charley's Aunt *'25*

Gary Littlejohn
Badlands *'74*

Roger Livesey
The Entertainer *'60*
The Intimate Stranger *'56*

Sam Livesey
The Private Life of Henry VIII *'33*

Ron Livingston
Campfire Tales *'98*

Tony Llewellyn-Jones
Cosi *'95*

Christopher Lloyd
The Real Blonde *'97*
Twenty Bucks *'93*
Eight Men Out *'88*

Danny Lloyd
The Shining *'80*

Emily Lloyd
Wish You Were Here *'87*

Jeremy Lloyd
Murder on the Orient Express *'74*

John Bedford Lloyd
Tough Guys Don't Dance *'87*

Norman Lloyd
He Ran All the Way *'51*

Enrico Lo Verso
Lamerica *'95*

Tony LoBianco
City of Hope *'91*

Amy Locane
Bongwater *'98*
Carried Away *'95*

David Lochary
Female Trouble *'74*

Katherine Locke
Try and Get Me *'50*

Sondra Locke
Second Coming of Suzanne *'80*

June Lockhart
Bury Me Dead *'47*

Evan Lockwood
Rambling Rose *'91*

Gary Lockwood
Number One *'76*

Margaret Lockwood
The Slipper and the Rose *'76*
Night Train to Munich *'40*
The Lady Vanishes *'38*

Barbara Loden
Wanda *'70*

John Loder
Non-Stop New York *'37*
Sabotage *'36*
The Private Life of Henry VIII *'33*

David Lodge
The Railway Children *'70*
The Intimate Stranger *'56*

Roger Lodge
Not of This Earth *'88*

Judy Loe
In Possession *'84*

Fiona Loewi
Love and Death on Long Island *'97*

Phyllis Logan
Secrets and Lies *'95*

Robert Loggia
Lost Highway *'96*
Coldblooded *'94*

Marie Lohr
Abandon Ship *'57*
Pygmalion *'38*

Gina Lollobrigida
Beat the Devil *'53*

Herbert Lom
Return from the Ashes *'65*
The Frightened City *'61*
The Ladykillers *'55*

Herbert Lomas
The Ghost Goes West *'36*

John R. Lombardi
Poison *'91*

Jason London
Dazed and Confused *'93*

Jeremy London
Mallrats *'95*

Julie London
The Red House *'47*

John Lone
Echoes of Paradise *'86*

Nia Long
Love Jones *'96*

John Longden
Clouds over Europe *'39*
Young and Innocent *'37*
Blackmail *'29*

Victoria Longley
Celia: Child of Terror *'90*

Anne Lonnberg
The Unbearable Lightness of Being *'88*

Michael (Michel) Lonsdale
The Remains of the Day *'93*
Phantom of Liberty *'74*
Galileo *'73*
Murmur of the Heart *'71*

Nancy Loomis
Halloween *'78*

Rod Loomis
Jack's Back *'87*

Theodore Loos
M *'31*
Metropolis *'26*

Iguandili Lopez
Hombres Armados *'97*

Ivonne Lopez
Letters from the Park *'88*

Jennifer Lopez
U-Turn *'97*
My Family *'94*

Traci Lords
Serial Mom *'94*
Not of This Earth *'88*

Sophia Loren
A Special Day *'77*

James Lorinz
Frankenhooker *'90*
Last Exit to Brooklyn *'90*

Jean-Pierre Lorit
Trois Couleurs: Rouge *'94*

Marion Lorne
The Graduate *'67*

Peter Lorre
Beat the Devil *'53*
The Man Who Knew Too Much *'34*
M *'31*

Heidi Lotito
Star Kid *'97*

Sahara Lotti
Lover Girl *'97*

Samantha Louca
High Stakes *'89*

Lance Loud
Inside Monkey Zetterland *'93*

Jean Louis
A Virgin Named Mary *'75*

Helene Louiselle
The Orders *'75*

Helen Lounck
Nothing but a Man *'64*

Bessie Love
Isadora *'68*

Courtney Love
Kurt and Courtney *'98*
Basquiat *'96*

Montagu Love
Bulldog Drummond *'29*

Patti Love
The Long Good Friday *'80*

Frank Lovejoy
Shack Out on 101 *'55*
Try and Get Me *'50*
Home of the Brave *'49*

Lyle Lovett
The Opposite of Sex *'98*
Bastard out of Carolina *'96*
Short Cuts *'93*
The Player *'92*

Jon Lovitz
Happiness *'98*

Arthur Lowe
If... *'69*
Kind Hearts and Coronets *'49*

Chad Lowe
Trading Favors *'97*

Holger Lowenadler
Paradise Place *'77*
Lacombe, Lucien *'74*

Elina Lowensohn
Basquiat *'96*
Nadja *'95*

Klaus Lowitsch
The Odessa File *'74*

Kenneth Lu
Combination Platter *'93*

William Lucas
The Very Edge *'63*

Joseph Lucien
The City of Lost Children *'95*

Charles Ludlam
The Big Easy *'87*

Patrick Ludlow
Evergreen *'34*

Laurette Luez
D.O.A. *'49*

Bela Lugosi
Plan 9 from Outer Space *'56*
Bride of the Monster *'55*
Glen or Glenda? *'53*

Peter Luhr
The Marquise of O *'76*

Paul Lukas
The Lady Vanishes *'38*

Jorge Luke
Salvador *'86*

Folco Lulli
Variety Lights *'51*

Carl Lumbly
To Sleep with Anger *'90*

Joanna Lumley
Shirley Valentine *'89*

Lydia Lunch
Vortex *'81*

Sihung Lung
Eat Drink Man Woman *'94*
The Wedding Banquet *'93*

Romilly Lunge
Sidewalks of London *'38*

Cui Luowen
The Story of Qui Ju *'91*

Ida Lupino
Private Hell 36 *'54*

Robert LuPone
Palookaville *'95*
High Stakes *'89*

Federico Luppi
Hombres Armados *'97*

Peter Lupus
Acting on Impulse *'93*

Dorothy Lyman
Ruby in Paradise *'93*

Alfred Lynch
The Krays *'90*

Heather Lynch
Wildflower *'91*

Jennifer Lynch
Eraserhead *'78*

John (Carroll) Lynch
Fargo *'96*
The Secret of Roan Inish *'94*
In the Name of the Father *'93*

Kelly Lynch
Forbidden Choices *'94*
Drugstore Cowboy *'89*

Pauline Lynch
Trainspotting *'95*

Richard Lynch
High Stakes *'89*

Susan Lynch
The Secret of Roan Inish *'94*

Carol Lynley
In Possession *'84*

Melanie Lynskey
Heavenly Creatures *'94*

Sue Lyon
Lolita *'62*

Wendy Lyon
Anne of Green Gables *'85*

James Lyons
I Shot Andy Warhol *'96*
Poison *'91*

Stanislav Lyubshin
To See Paris and Die *'93*

Tzi Ma
Golden Gate *'93*

Sybil Maas
Cousin, Cousine *'76*

Eric Mabius
I Shot Andy Warhol *'96*
Welcome to the Dollhouse *'95*

Ellie MacCarthy
Sirens *'94*

Bruce MacDonald
Return of the Secaucus 7 *'80*

Edmund MacDonald
Detour *'46*
The Lady Confesses *'45*

Jennifer MacDonald
Campfire Tales *'98*
Clean, Shaven *'93*

Kelly Macdonald
Cousin Bette *'97*
Trainspotting *'95*

Andie MacDowell
The End of Violence *'97*
Four Weddings and a Funeral *'94*
Short Cuts *'93*
sex, lies and videotape *'89*

Moyna MacGill
Gaslight *'40*

Niall MacGinnis
Never Take Candy from a Stranger *'60*

Jack MacGowran
Start the Revolution without Me *'70*

Eileen Maciejewska
Christabel *'89*

Helen Mack
Struggle *'31*

Barry Mackay
Evergreen *'34*

John MacKay
Trust *'91*

Stephen MacKenna
Eye of the Needle *'81*

Alex Mackenzie
The Battle of the Sexes *'60*

Kenneth Mackintosh
Three Sisters *'70*

Steven Mackintosh
Different for Girls *'96*
London Kills Me *'91*

Kyle MacLachlan
Blue Velvet *'86*

Samantha MacLachlan
Set It Off *'96*

Barton MacLane
You Only Live Once *'37*

Deborah MacLaren
Naked *'93*

Mary MacLeod
If... *'69*

Aline MacMahon
Guest in the House *'44*

Will MacMillan
Salvador *'86*

Peter MacNeill
Crash *'95*

Norman MacOwen
The Battle of the Sexes *'60*

Elle Macpherson
Jane Eyre *'96*
Sirens *'94*

Duncan MacRae
The Little Kidnappers *'53*
The Woman in Question *'50*

William H. Macy
Boogie Nights *'97*
Fargo *'96*
Oleanna *'94*
Twenty Bucks *'93*

Marianne Maddalena
Wes Craven's New Nightmare *'94*

Victor Maddern
Abandon Ship *'57*

James Madio
The Basketball Diaries *'94*

Michael Madsen
A House in the Hills *'93*
Reservoir Dogs *'92*
Kill Me Again *'89*

Virginia Madsen
Mr. North *'88*

Christian Maelen
I Think I Do *'97*

Patrick Magee
Luther *'74*
Galileo *'73*
The Very Edge *'63*

Anna Magnani
Passionate Thief *'60*
Bellissima *'51*
The Miracle *'48*

Ann Magnuson
Hugo Pool *'97*
Heavy Petting *'89*
Vortex *'81*

Oliver Maguire
Butley *'74*

Tobey Maguire
The Ice Storm *'97*

Bill Maher
Cannibal Women in the Avocado Jungle of Death *'89*

Alix Mahieux
L'Amour en Herbe *'77*

John Mahoney
She's the One *'96*
Betrayed *'88*
Eight Men Out *'88*

Nuno Leal Maia
Kiss of the Spider Woman *'85*

Caludette Maille
Like Water for Chocolate *'93*

Marjorie Main
Turnabout *'40*
Dead End *'37*

Valerie Mairesse
One Sings, the Other Doesn't *'77*

Mike Maker
Sore Losers *'97*

Mako
The Wash *'88*

Karl Malden
Hot Millions *'68*

Ruth Maleczech
The Ballad of Little Jo *'93*
In the Soup *'92*
Anna *'87*

Arthur Malet
A Little Princess *'95*
Halloween *'78*

Laurent Malet
Roads to the South *'78*

Annet Malherbe
Abel *'87*

Dimitry Malikov
To See Paris and Die *'93*

Eddie Malin
A Hard Day's Night *'64*

Judith Malina
Household Saints *'93*

John Malkovich
Queens Logic *'91*

Miles Malleson
Peeping Tom *'60*
Kind Hearts and Coronets *'49*
Saraband for Dead Lovers *'48*
Dead of Night *'45*
Nine Days a Queen *'36*

Odile Mallet
The City of Lost Children *'95*

Matt Malloy
In the Company of Men *'96*

Jan Malmsjo
Scenes from a Marriage '73

Bonz Malone
Slam '98

Dorothy Malone
Private Hell 36 '54

Jena Malone
Bastard out of Carolina '96

Mark Malone Jr.
Straight out of Brooklyn '91

George Malpas
The Missing Reel '90

H. F. Maltby
Pygmalion '38
Young and Innocent '37

Leonard Maltin
Forgotten Silver '96

Albert Maltz
Hollywood on Trial '76

Elly Malyon
I Married a Witch '42

Irina Malysheva
100 Days after Childhood '75

Alex Man
Rouge '87

Nick Mancuso
Ticket to Heaven '81

Rena Mandel
Vampyr '31

Miles Mander
The Private Life of Henry VIII '33

Nino Manfredi
Down & Dirty '76

Camryn Manheim
Happiness '98

Dave Manley
Struggle '31

Dudley Manlove
Plan 9 from Outer Space '56

Claude Mann
French Provincial '75

Gabriel Mann
High Art '98

Leslie Mann
She's the One '96

Peter Mannering
Time Lock '57

Lucie Mannheim
The 39 Steps '35

Predrag Manojlovic
Tito and Me '92

Laszlo Mansaros
The Unfinished Sentence in 141 Minutes '75

Joe Mantegna
Queens Logic '91
House of Games '87

Joe Mantell
Marty '55

Michael Mantell
City of Hope '91

Leslie Manville
Secrets and Lies '95
High Season '88
Dance with a Stranger '85

Mary Mara
Bound '96

Jean Marais
The World of Jacques Demy '95
White Nights '57
Beauty and the Beast '46

Andre Maranne
Return from the Ashes '65

Fredric March
The Iceman Cometh '73
Tomorrow the World '44
I Married a Witch '42

Colette Marchand
Moulin Rouge '52

Guy Marchand
Coup de Torchon '81
Cousin, Cousine '76

Paul Marco
Plan 9 from Outer Space '56
Bride of the Monster '55

Saverio Marconi
Padre Padrone '77

James Marcus
Oliver Twist '22

Stephen Marcus
My Beautiful Laundrette '85

Elio Marcuzzo
Ossessione '42

George Margo
Who Done It? '56

Mark Margolis
Pi '98

Miriam Margolyes
Different for Girls '96
Little Dorrit, Film 1: Nobody's Fault '88
Little Dorrit, Film 2: Little Dorrit's Story '88

Constance Marie
My Family '94

Jean-Pierre Marielle
Coup de Torchon '81
In a Wild Moment '78

Jacques Marin
Forbidden Games '52

Ed Marinaro
Queens Logic '91

P. J. Marino
Little Shots of Happiness '97

Jane Marken
Children of Paradise '45

Melinda Markey
Crashout '55

Olivera Markovic
Tito and Me '92

Alfred Marks
Valentino '77
The Frightened City '61

Scott Marlowe
A Cold Wind in August '61

Percy Marmont
Young and Innocent '37
Rich and Strange '32

Richard Marner
The African Queen '51

Peter Marquardt
El Mariachi '93

Ron Marquette
Public Access '93

Gene Marrin
Teenage Gang Debs '66

Moore Marriott
Don't Take It to Heart '44

Kenneth Mars
Citizen Ruth '96

Marjorie Mars
Brief Encounter '46

Betty Marsden
Leather Boys '63

James Marsden
Campfire Tales '98

Garry Marsh
Who Done It? '56
Dead of Night '45
Pink String and Sealing Wax '45

Jean Marsh
Frenzy '72

Mae Marsh
Impact '49

Bryan Marshall
The Long Good Friday '80

Gary DeWitt Marshall
New Jersey Drive '95

Herbert Marshall
Gog '54

Ruth Marshall
Love and Human Remains '93

Stephen Marshall
The Whole Wide World '96

Tully Marshall
Queen Kelly '29

Zena Marshall
So Long at the Fair '50

Lisa Repo Martell
American Boyfriends '89

Cynthia Martells
A Modern Affair '94

Rica Martens
Living in Oblivion '94

Christopher Martin
House Party '90

Edie Martin
The Ladykillers '55
Genevieve '53

Gregory Mars Martin
Kalifornia '93

Helen Martin
Hollywood Shuffle '87

Jared Martin
Second Coming of Suzanne '80

John Martin
The Underneath '95

Michael Martin
In the Company of Men '96

Millicent Martin
Alfie '66

Nan Martin
Number One '76

Strother Martin
Kiss Me Deadly '55

Vivian Martin
The Belles of St. Trinian's '53

W. T. Martin
High Stakes '89

Margo Martindale
Critical Care '97
Dead Man Walking '95

A. Martinez
Powwow Highway '89

Mario Ivan Martinez
Like Water for Chocolate '93

Nacho Martinez
Law of Desire '86
Matador '86

Reinol Martinez
El Mariachi '93

Pete Marvel
Caged '97

Lee Marvin
The Iceman Cometh '73
Shack Out on 101 '55

Vincent Marzello
The Missing Reel '90

Marino Mase
The Belly of an Architect '91
A Virgin Named Mary '75

Mac Mashorian
Easy Rider *'69*

Joe Masiell
Jacques Brel Is Alive and Well and Living in Paris *'75*

Giulietta Masina
Variety Lights *'51*

Ace Mask
Not of This Earth *'88*

Virginia Maskell
Interlude *'67*

Elliot Mason
On Approval *'44*
The Ghost Goes West *'36*

James Mason
Voyage of the Damned *'76*
Georgy Girl *'66*
Lolita *'62*
I Met a Murderer *'39*

Jana Mason
The Wild Party *'56*

Laurence Mason
Hackers *'95*

Lea Massari
Allonsanfan *'73*
Murmur of the Heart *'71*

Michael Massee
Lost Highway *'96*

Anna Massey
Angels and Insects *'95*
Impromptu *'90*
Another Country *'84*
Frenzy *'72*
Peeping Tom *'60*

Daniel Massey
In the Name of the Father *'93*
Scandal *'89*
Dance with a Stranger *'85*
The Entertainer *'60*

Edith Massey
Female Trouble *'74*

Raymond Massey
The Scarlet Pimpernel *'34*

Christopher K. Masterson
Campfire Tales *'98*

Danny Masterson
Star Kid *'97*

Mary Stuart Masterson
Mr. North *'88*

Chiara Mastroianni
Three Lives and Only One Death *'96*

Federica Mastroianni
Creepers *'85*

Marcello Mastroianni
Three Lives and Only One Death *'96*
101 Nights *'95*
A Special Day *'77*
Allonsanfan *'73*
8½ *'63*
White Nights *'57*

Richard Masur
And the Band Played On *'93*

Clelia Matania
A Virgin Named Mary *'75*

Heather Matarazzo
Hurricane Streets *'96*
Welcome to the Dollhouse *'95*

Mahdu Mathen
Children of the Damned *'63*

Aubrey Mather
Sabotage *'36*

Joshawa Mathers
The Return of Tommy Tricker *'94*

Marion Mathie
Lolita *'62*

Ginette Mathieu
Blue Country *'77*

Samantha Mathis
The Thing Called Love *'93*

Marlee Matlin
It's My Party *'95*
The Linguini Incident *'92*

Dakin Matthews
Permanent Record *'88*

Jessie Matthews
Evergreen *'34*

Liesl Matthews
A Little Princess *'95*

Walter Matthews
Naked Kiss *'64*

Robin Mattson
Island of the Lost *'68*

Carmen Maura
Women on the Verge of a Nervous Breakdown *'88*
Law of Desire *'86*
Matador *'86*
Dark Habits *'84*

Mollie Maureen
The Private Life of Sherlock Holmes *'70*
Twisted Nerve *'68*

Peggy Maurer
I Bury the Living *'58*

Claire Maurier
The 400 Blows *'59*

Dawn Maxey
Normal Life *'96*

Max Maxudian
I Have Killed *'24*

John Maxwell
The Prowler *'51*

Larry Maxwell
Public Access *'93*
Poison *'91*

Lois Maxwell
Lolita *'62*

Marilyn Maxwell
Champion *'49*

Norman (Max) Maxwell
Wildflower *'91*

Roberta Maxwell
Dead Man Walking *'95*

Elaine May
In the Spirit *'90*

Jodhi May
Sister My Sister *'94*
A World Apart *'88*

Martin May
Das Boot *'81*

Melinda May
Hot Millions *'68*

Rik Mayall
Eye of the Needle *'81*

Jerry Mayer
Vanya on 42nd Street *'94*

Kathrine Mayfield
The Unbelievable Truth *'90*

Bill Maynard
Confessions of a Window Cleaner *'74*

Ferdinand "Ferdy" Mayne
Abandon Ship *'57*

Melanie Mayron
Sticky Fingers *'88*
Girlfriends *'78*

Debi Mazar
Trees Lounge *'96*
Red Ribbon Blues *'95*
Inside Monkey Zetterland *'93*
In the Soup *'92*

Janet Maze
The Cater Street Hangman *'98*

Paul Mazursky
Scenes from the Class Struggle in Beverly Hills *'89*

Joseph Mazzello
Star Kid *'97*

M.C. Lyte
Fly by Night *'93*

Des McAleer
Butterfly Kiss *'94*

Ray McAnally
My Left Foot *'89*

Simon McBurney
Kafka *'91*

Ruth McCabe
My Left Foot *'89*

Michael McCafferty
To Hell with Love *'98*

Lon McCallister
The Red House *'47*

David McCallum
Hear My Song *'91*
A Night to Remember *'58*

John McCallum
The Woman in Question *'50*

Tom McCamus
The Sweet Hereafter *'96*

Donal McCann
The Dead *'87*

Sean McCann
Affliction *'97*

Andrew McCarthy
Mrs. Parker and the Vicious Circle *'94*
Waiting for the Moon *'87*

Eoin McCarthy
The Cater Street Hangman *'98*

Kevin McCarthy
My Tutor *'82*

Nobu McCarthy
The Wash *'88*

Sheila McCarthy
My Teacher Ate My Homework *'98*

Paul McCartney
Help! *'65*
A Hard Day's Night *'64*

Norma McCarty
Plan 9 from Outer Space *'56*

Charles McCaughan
Heat and Dust *'82*

Libby McClintock
The Luck of Ginger Coffey *'64*

Doug McClure
The Land That Time Forgot *'75*

Greg McClure
Bury Me Dead *'47*

Marc McClure
Grim Prairie Tales *'89*

Edie McClurg
Ted *'98*
Eating Raoul *'82*

Matthew McConaughey
Lone Star *'95*
Dazed and Confused *'93*

Patty McCormack
Mommy *'95*

Timothy McCormack
Gal Young 'Un *'79*

Emer McCourt
London Kills Me '91

Malachy McCourt
Q (The Winged Serpent) '82

George McCowan
She's the One '96

Alec McCowen
Frenzy '72
A Night to Remember '58

Sid McCoy
Medium Cool '69

Tony McCoy
Bride of the Monster '55

Joel McCrea
Dead End '37
These Three '36

Colin McCredie
Shallow Grave '94

Alex McCrindle
Eye of the Needle '81

Andrew McCulloch
The Land That Time Forgot '75

Kyle McCulloch
Careful '92

Bill McCutcheon
Tune in Tomorrow '90

George McDaniel
Legacy '75

Dylan McDermott
Destiny Turns on the Radio '95
Twister '89

Seamus McDonagh
2 by 4 '98

Marie McDonald
Guest in the House '44

Robin McDonald
The Hours and Times '92

Caitlin Grace McDonnell
Art for Teachers of Children '95

Mary McDonnell
Passion Fish '92
Matewan '87

Frances McDormand
Fargo '96
Lone Star '95
Palookaville '95
Short Cuts '93
Blood Simple '85

Betty McDowall
Time Lock '57

Roddy McDowall
It's My Party '95

Malcolm McDowell
Hugo Pool '97
Chain of Desire '93
Voyage of the Damned '76
If... '69

Nelson McDowell
Oliver Twist '22

Brian McElroy
Bad Lieutenant '92

John McEnery
Black Beauty '94
The Krays '90
The Land That Time Forgot '75
Galileo '73

Peter McEnery
Entertaining Mr. Sloane '70
Victim '61

Bobby Joe McFadden
Red Rock West '93

Monica McFarland
Back Street Jane '89

Olive McFarland
The Frightened City '61

Mark McGann
Let Him Have It '91

Paul McGann
FairyTale: A True Story '97
Paper Mask '91
Dealers '89
Withnail and I '87

Parnell McGarry
Bedazzled '68

Darren McGavin
Blood & Concrete: A Love Story '90

Patrick McGaw
The Basketball Diaries '94
Forbidden Choices '94

Gwen McGee
New Jersey Drive '95

Paula McGee
Chameleon Street '89

Vonetta McGee
To Sleep with Anger '90

Bruce McGill
Waiting for the Moon '87

Kelly McGillis
Grand Isle '91
The House on Carroll Street '88

John C. McGinley
Set It Off '96
Mother's Boys '94
Platoon '86

Sean McGinley
Michael Collins '96

Boris McGiver
Little Odessa '94

John McGiver
The Manchurian Candidate '62

Mike McGlone
She's the One '96
The Brothers McMullen '94

Frank McGlynn
These Three '36

Terrence McGoff
2 by 4 '98

Elizabeth McGovern
The Wings of the Dove '97
A Shock to the System '90
Tune in Tomorrow '90

Rose McGowan
The Doom Generation '95

Tom McGowan
Mrs. Parker and the Vicious Circle '94

Leueen McGrath
Pygmalion '38

Matt McGrath
1999 '98

Charles McGraw
The Killer inside Me '76
A Boy and His Dog '75

Ewan McGregor
Trainspotting '95
Shallow Grave '94

Kim McGuire
Acting on Impulse '93

Stephen McHattie
Sticky Fingers '88

Tim McInnery
FairyTale: A True Story '97

Burr McIntosh
Way Down East '20

Elizabeth P. McKay
The Brothers McMullen '94

Scott McKay
Guest in the House '44

Donna McKechnie
The Little Prince '74

Gina McKee
Naked '93

Julie McKee
To Hell with Love '98

Don McKellar
Exotica '94

Ian McKellen
Gods and Monsters '98
And the Band Played On '93
The Ballad of Little Jo '93
Scandal '89

Alex McKenna
Campfire Tales '98

Breffini McKenna
The Crying Game '92

T. P. McKenna
Perfect Friday '70

Virginia McKenna
The Smallest Show on Earth '57

Hannah McKenzie
Forgotten Silver '96

Julia McKenzie
Shirley Valentine '89

Nancy McKeon
Teresa's Tattoo '94

Leo McKern
Help! '65

Kevin McKidd
Trainspotting '95

Mark McKinney
Spice World: The Movie '97

Mona McKinnon
Plan 9 from Outer Space '56

Kellie A. McKuen
The Giving '91

Ivor McLaren
Evergreen '34

Gibb McLaughlin
The Scarlet Pimpernel '34
The Private Life of Henry VIII '33

Mary Frances McLean
Sparrows '26

Gordon McLeod
Clouds over Europe '39

Allyn Ann McLerie
France, Incorporated '74

John McLiam
The Iceman Cometh '73

Ed McMahon
The Incident '67

Sue McManus
Teenage Gang Debs '66

John McMartin
A Shock to the System '90

Kenneth McMillan
True Confessions '81
Girlfriends '78

Roddy McMillan
The Battle of the Sexes '60

T. Wendy McMillan
Go Fish '94

Skipper McNally
Crime of Passion '57

Pat McNamara
The Daytrippers '96

William McNamara
Wildflower '91

Alan McNaughton
Victim '61

Gus McNaughton
Clouds over Europe '39
Sidewalks of London '38
The 39 Steps '35

Julia McNeal
The Refrigerator '91

The Unbelievable Truth '90

Ian McNeice
The Englishman Who Went up a Hill But Came down a Mountain '95
Funny Bones '94
The Lonely Passion of Judith Hearne '87

Kris McQuade
Strictly Ballroom '92

Frank McRae
Lightning Jack '94

Gerard McSorley
Michael Collins '96
An Awfully Big Adventure '94
Widow's Peak '94
In the Name of the Father '93

Janet McTeer
Carrington '95
Hawks '89

Stanley Meadows
Performance '70

Colm Meaney
The Last of the High Kings '96
The Englishman Who Went up a Hill But Came down a Mountain '95

Anne Meara
The Daytrippers '96

Meat Loaf
Spice World: The Movie '97
Motorama '91

Paul Medford
Black Joy '77

Patricia Medina
The Killing of Sister George '69
Don't Take It to Heart '44

Frank Medrano
Suicide Kings '97

Dana Medricka
Day for My Love '77

Michael Medwin
Genevieve '53

Donald Meek
Turnabout '40

Ralph Meeker
Kiss Me Deadly '55

Edith Meeks
Poison '91

Conrad Meertin Jr.
New Jersey Drive '95

Hannes Meesember
The Odessa File '74

Armand Meffre
Blue Country '77

Armin Meier
Mother Kusters Goes to Heaven '76

Kurt Meisel
The Odessa File '74

Mariangela Melato
Dear Michael '76
Swept Away... '75

Michele Melega
Death of a Schoolboy '91

Migdalia Melendez
Go Fish '94

Jack Melford
The Ladykillers '55

Jill Melford
Abandon Ship '57

Andree Melly
The Belles of St. Trinian's '53

Tomas Melly
I Like It Like That '94

Christopher Meloni
Bound '96

Sid Melton
Girls in Chains '43

Jean-Pierre Melville
Breathless '59

Neil Melville
Brilliant Lies '96

Pauline Melville
Mona Lisa '86

Murray Melvin
Let Him Have It '91
The Krays '90
Lisztomania '75
Start the Revolution without Me '70
Alfie '66

Ben Mendelsohn
Cosi '95
Sirens '94

Antonio Mendoza
Easy Rider '69

Asha Menina
House of Cards '92

Adolphe Menjou
Turnabout '40

Nina Menschikova
100 Days after Childhood '75

Oleg Menshikov
Burnt by the Sun '94

Irfan Mensur
The Dog Who Loved Trains '78

Yehudi Menuhin
32 Short Films about Glenn Gould '93

Vivien Merchant
The Maids '75

The Homecoming '73
Frenzy '72
Alfie '66

Chantal Mercier
Small Change '76

Denis Mercier
Le Sexe des Étoiles '93

Marianne-Coquelicot Mercier
Le Sexe des Étoiles '93

Melina Mercouri
A Dream of Passion '78

Paul Mercurio
Red Ribbon Blues '95
Strictly Ballroom '92

Burgess Meredith
True Confessions '81

Christel Merian
Salmonberries '91

Macha Meril
Robert et Robert '78

Epatha Merkinson
She's Gotta Have It '86

Valentine Merlet
La Ceremonie '95

Joanna Merlin
Mystic Pizza '88

Mary Merrall
The Belles of St. Trinian's '53
The Obsessed '51
Dead of Night '45
Pink String and Sealing Wax '45

Dina Merrill
Open Season '95
Suture '93
The Player '92

Gary Merrill
The Incident '67

Clive Merrison
Photographing Fairies '97
The English Patient '96
An Awfully Big Adventure '94
Heavenly Creatures '94

George Merritt
Clouds over Europe '39
Young and Innocent '37

William Merrow
The Good Soldier '81

William Mervyn
The Railway Children '70
The Battle of the Sexes '60

Galina Messenzeva
The Children of Theatre Street '77

Francesco Messina
In the Soup '92

Eric Messiter
Kind Hearts and Coronets '49

Jeannine Mestre
Roads to the South '78

Laurie Metcalf
U-Turn '97
Leaving Las Vegas '95

Mark Metcalf
Mr. North '88

Lili Metodieva
Last Summer '74

Nancy Mette
Matewan '87

Jim Metzler
Delusion '91
One False Move '91
River's Edge '87

Jason Mewes
Chasing Amy '97
Mallrats '95
Clerks '94

Bruce Meyers
The Governess '98

Gerard Meylan
Nenette and Boni '96

Pascal Meynier
L'Amour en Herbe '77

Michelle Meyrink
Permanent Record '88

S. Mezhinski
Professor Mamlock '38

Myriam Meziere
Jonah Who Will Be 25 in the Year 2000 '76

Robert Miano
Smoke Signals '98

Cora Miao
Eat a Bowl of Tea '89

Jordan Christopher Michael
Motorama '91

Ralph Michael
Children of the Damned '63
A Night to Remember '58
Abandon Ship '57
Dead of Night '45

Beverly Michaels
Crashout '55
Wicked Woman '54

Panos Michalopoulas
Iphigenia '77

Jeff Michalski
Star Maps '97

Marcella Michelangeli
Padre Padrone '77
Dear Michael '76

Keith Michell
The Deceivers '88

Tracy Middendorf
Wes Craven's New Nightmare *'94*

Gabrielle Middleton
Two for the Road *'67*

Guy Middleton
The Belles of St. Trinian's *'53*

Josephine Middleton
The Woman in Question *'50*

Noelle Middleton
John and Julie *'55*

Kenneth Midwood
The Good Soldier *'81*

Julia Migenes-Johnson
The Krays *'90*

Judy Mihei
Chan Is Missing *'82*

Nadia Mikhalkov
Burnt by the Sun *'94*

Nikita Mikhalkov
Burnt by the Sun *'94*

Andre Mikhelson
The Intimate Stranger *'56*

Alyssa Milano
Body Count *'97*
Hugo Pool *'97*
Old Enough *'84*

Adolph Milar
Bulldog Drummond *'29*

Bernard Miles
The Smallest Show on Earth *'57*
Great Expectations *'46*

Elaine Miles
Smoke Signals *'98*

Sarah Miles
White Mischief *'88*
Bride to Be *'75*
Blow-Up *'66*

Penelope Milford
Normal Life *'96*
Heathers *'89*

Piro Milkani
Lamerica *'95*

Peter Millard
32 Short Films about Glenn Gould *'93*

Betty Miller
High Stakes *'89*

Dick Miller
Motorama *'91*
After Hours *'85*

Jacob Miller
Rockers *'79*

Jason Miller
Mommy *'95*

John Miller
Young and Innocent *'37*

Jonny Lee Miller
Afterglow *'97*
Hackers *'95*
Trainspotting *'95*

Joshua Miller
River's Edge *'87*

Kristine Miller
Too Late for Tears *'49*

Larry Miller
Waiting for Guffman *'96*

Martin Miller
Children of the Damned *'63*
Peeping Tom *'60*

Mary Louise Miller
Sparrows *'26*

Penelope Ann Miller
Chaplin *'92*

Rebecca Miller
Mrs. Parker and the Vicious Circle *'94*

Sarah Jane Miller
Mommy *'95*

Danny Mills
Female Trouble *'74*

Donna Mills
The Incident *'67*

Hayley Mills
Twisted Nerve *'68*
Whistle down the Wind *'61*
Tiger Bay *'59*

John Mills
Tiger Bay *'59*
This Happy Breed *'47*
Great Expectations *'46*
Nine Days a Queen *'36*

Sandra Milo
8½ *'63*

Billy Milton
Hot Millions *'68*

Ernest Milton
The Scarlet Pimpernel *'34*

Esther Minciotti
Marty *'55*

Charlotte Mineau
Sparrows *'26*

Sal Mineo
Who Killed Teddy Bear? *'65*

Lau Siu Ming
Eat a Bowl of Tea *'89*

Kelly Jo Minter
Miracle Mile *'89*
Popcorn *'89*

Miou-Miou
Roads to the South *'78*
Dites-Lui Que Je L'Aime *'77*
Jonah Who Will Be 25 in the Year 2000 *'76*
Victory March *'76*

Brigitte Mira
Mother Kusters Goes to Heaven *'76*
Every Man for Himself & God against All *'75*

Helen Mirren
Critical Care *'97*
The Madness of King George *'94*
The Comfort of Strangers *'91*
Where Angels Fear to Tread *'91*
The Long Good Friday *'80*
S.O.S. Titanic *'79*

Karen Mistal
Cannibal Women in the Avocado Jungle of Death *'89*

Charlotte Mitchell
Village of the Damned *'60*

Colin Mitchell
Combination Platter *'93*

Darryl (Chill) Mitchell
Fly by Night *'93*

Doug Mitchell
Teenage Gang Debs *'66*

Eddy Mitchell
Coup de Torchon *'81*

Joni Mitchell
Message to Love: The Isle of Wight Festival, the Movie *'70*

Leslie Mitchell
Genevieve *'53*

Mary Mitchell
Spider Baby *'64*

Radha Mitchell
High Art *'98*

Warren Mitchell
Help! *'65*

Yvonne Mitchell
Tiger Bay *'59*

Ilan Mitchell-Smith
The Chocolate War *'88*

Bentley Mitchum
Ruby in Paradise *'93*

Robert Mitchum
Dead Man *'95*
Mr. North *'88*
The Night of the Hunter *'55*

Labina Mitevska
Before the Rain *'94*

Mitsuko
A-Ge-Man: Tales of a Golden Geisha *'91*

Nobuko Miyamoto
A-Ge-Man: Tales of a Golden Geisha *'91*

Shaul Mizrahi
Zohar: Mediterranean Blues *'93*
Ricochets *'87*

Matthew Modine
The Real Blonde *'97*
And the Band Played On *'93*
Equinox *'93*
Short Cuts *'93*

Gaston Modot
Children of Paradise *'45*
The Rules of the Game *'39*

Monica Moench
Clay Pigeons *'98*

Donald Moffat
The Unbearable Lightness of Being *'88*

D. W. Moffett
Lisa *'90*

Jay Mohr
Suicide Kings *'97*

Gunnar Moller
The Odessa File *'74*

Gretchen Mol
The Funeral *'96*

Alfred Molina
Boogie Nights *'97*
Dead Man *'95*
Enchanted April *'92*

Angela Molina
Black Litter *'77*

Miguel Molina
Law of Desire *'86*

Darbnia Molloy
Frankie Starlight *'95*

Phyllis Monkman
Blackmail *'29*

Darren Monks
The Last of the High Kings *'96*

Sydney Monkton
The Obsessed *'51*

Lili Monori
Nine Months *'77*

Bruno Monsaingeon
32 Short Films about Glenn Gould *'93*

Lee Montague
Moulin Rouge *'52*

Yves Montand
Roads to the South *'78*
The Crucible *'57*

Haoui Montaug
Vortex *'81*

Germaine Montero
Robert et Robert *'78*

Reggie Montgomery
Hangin' with the Homeboys *'91*

Marikeva Monti
Apartment Zero *'88*

Andre Montmorency
Once upon a Time in the East *'74*

Keith Moon
Tommy *'75*
Stardust *'74*
That'll Be the Day *'73*
Message to Love: The Isle of Wight Festival, the Movie *'70*

Paul Mooney
Dance with a Stranger *'85*

Alvy Moore
A Boy and His Dog *'75*

Andre Moore
New Jersey Drive *'95*

Deborah Maria Moore
Chaplin *'92*

Diane Moore
Who Killed Teddy Bear? *'65*

Dudley Moore
Bedazzled *'68*

Duke Moore
Plan 9 from Outer Space *'56*

Evelyn Moore
Bedazzled *'68*

Ian Moore
Sling Blade *'96*

Ida Moore
Money Madness *'47*

Julianne Moore
The Big Lebowski *'97*
Boogie Nights *'97*
The Myth of Fingerprints *'97*
Safe *'95*
Vanya on 42nd Street *'94*
Short Cuts *'93*

Kaycee Moore
Ninth Street *'98*
Daughters of the Dust *'91*

Mary Tyler Moore
Flirting with Disaster *'95*

Matt Moore
I Bury the Living *'58*

Melba Moore
Lost in the Stars *'74*

Michael Moore
Roger & Me *'89*

Roger Moore
Spice World: The Movie *'97*

Stephen Moore
Under Suspicion *'92*

Terry Moore
Shack Out on 101 *'55*

Agnes Moorehead
Tomorrow the World *'44*

Esai Morales
My Family *'94*

Pauline Moran
The Good Soldier *'81*

Richard Morant
Scandal *'89*

Kenneth More
The Slipper and the Rose *'76*
A Night to Remember *'58*
Genevieve *'53*

Jeanne Moreau
I Love You, I Love You Not *'97*
The World of Jacques Demy *'95*
La Femme Nikita *'91*
Hu-Man *'76*
Lumiere *'76*
French Provincial *'75*
Dangerous Liaisons *'60*
The 400 Blows *'59*

Mantan Moreland
Spider Baby *'64*

Andre Morell
10 Rillington Place *'70*
Madeleine *'50*
So Long at the Fair *'50*

Rita Moreno
Carmen Miranda: Bananas Is My Business *'95*
I Like It Like That *'94*
Boss' Son *'78*

Sergio Moreno
The Hours and Times *'92*

Linda Moretti
The Postman *'94*

Michele Moretti
French Provincial *'75*

George Morfogen
Twenty Bucks *'93*

Debbi Morgan
Eve's Bayou *'97*

Garfield Morgan
The Odessa File *'74*

Michele Morgan
Cat and Mouse *'78*
The Fallen Idol *'49*

Priscilla Morgan
Separate Tables *'58*

Shelley Taylor Morgan
My Tutor *'82*

Stephanie Morgenstern
The Sweet Hereafter *'96*

Naoki Mori
Spice World: The Movie *'97*

Cathy Moriarty
Cop Land *'97*
Hugo Pool *'97*

Michael Moriarty
Q (The Winged Serpent) *'82*

P. H. Moriarty
The Long Good Friday *'80*

Tara Morice
Sorrento Beach *'95*
Strictly Ballroom *'92*

Philippe Morier-Genoud
Trois Couleurs: Blanc *'94*

Johnny Morina
The Boys of St. Vincent *'93*

Miki Morita
Turnabout *'40*

Louisa Moritz
True Confessions *'81*

Karen Morley
Our Daily Bread *'34*

Robert Morley
Little Dorrit, Film 1: Nobody's Fault *'88*
Little Dorrit, Film 2: Little Dorrit's Story *'88*
Hot Millions *'68*
The Battle of the Sexes *'60*
Beat the Devil *'53*
The African Queen *'51*

David Morne
Madeleine *'50*

Anita Morris
Absolute Beginners *'86*

Aubrey Morris
Lisztomania *'75*

Beth Morris
That'll Be the Day *'73*

Garrett Morris
Motorama *'91*

Jeff Morris
The Crossing Guard *'94*

Johnny Morris
Forgotten Silver *'96*

Lana Morris
The Woman in Question *'50*

Libby Morris
Two for the Road *'67*

Phil Morris
Clay Pigeons *'98*

Sarah Ann Morris
Gods and Monsters *'98*

Jim Morrison
Message to Love: The Isle of Wight Festival, the Movie *'70*

Temuera Morrison
The Island of Dr. Moreau *'96*

Bruce Morrow
Dirty Dancing *'87*

David Morse
The Crossing Guard *'94*

Helen Morse
Caddie *'76*
Picnic at Hanging Rock *'75*

Robin Morse
Marty *'55*

Mary Morter
The Little Girl Who Lives down the Lane *'76*

Emily Mortimer
The Last of the High Kings *'96*

Trisha Mortimer
Perfect Friday *'70*

Antony Morton
Performance *'70*

Clive Morton
Lucky Jim *'58*
Kind Hearts and Coronets *'49*

Danny Morton
Money Madness *'47*

Joe Morton
Lone Star *'95*
City of Hope *'91*
Trouble in Mind *'86*

Gastone Moschin
The Conformist *'71*

William R. Moses
Fun *'94*
Mystic Pizza *'88*

D'Alan Moss
Street Music *'81*

Mireille Mosse
The City of Lost Children *'95*

Donny Most
Acting on Impulse *'93*

Josh Mostel
The Basketball Diaries *'94*
City of Hope *'91*
Heavy Petting *'89*
Matewan *'87*

Zero Mostel
Hollywood on Trial *'76*
Rhinoceros *'74*

Greg Mottola
Independent's Day *'97*

John Moulder-Brown
Deep End *'70*

Gilberto Moura
Pixote *'81*

Benjamin Mouton
The Whole Wide World *'96*

Wood Moy
Chan Is Missing *'82*

Pat Moya
In the Soup *'92*

Zofia Mrozowska
The Balance *'75*

Cookie Mueller
Female Trouble *'74*

Julia Mueller
The Unbelievable Truth *'90*

Maureen Mueller
Enid Is Sleeping *'90*

Armin Mueller-Stahl
Shine *'95*
The House of the Spirits *'93*
Kafka *'91*
Night on Earth *'91*

Marianne Muellerleile
The Trouble with Dick *'88*

Anita Mui
Rouge *'87*

Gavin Muir
Night Tide *'63*

Jack Mulcahy
The Brothers McMullen *'94*

Declan Mulholland
The Land That Time Forgot *'75*

Chris Mulkey
Gas Food Lodging *'92*
Jack's Back *'87*

Arthur Mullard
Morgan! *'66*

Barbara Mullen
The Very Edge *'63*

Patty Mullen
Frankenhooker *'90*

Peter Muller
25 Fireman's Street *'73*

Marius Muller-Westernhagen
The Second Awakening of Christa Klages *'78*

Rod Mullinar
Dead Calm *'89*
Echoes of Paradise *'86*

Dermot Mulroney
Bastard out of Carolina *'96*
Box of Moonlight *'96*
Kansas City *'95*
Living in Oblivion *'94*
The Thing Called Love *'93*
Silent Tongue *'92*
Longtime Companion *'90*

Kieran Mulroney
The Spitfire Grill *'95*

Robert Munic
Death of a Schoolboy *'91*

Marjorie Munks
On Approval *'44*

Molly Munks
On Approval *'44*

Pep Munne
Barcelona *'94*

Rocio Munoz
High Heels *'91*

Nan Munro
Morgan! *'66*

Ona Munson
The Red House *'47*

Christine Murillo
Why Not! *'78*

Christopher Murney
Last Exit to Brooklyn *'90*

Peter Murnik
Golden Gate *'93*

Annette Murphy
Star Maps *'97*

Brittany Murphy
Bongwater *'98*
Freeway *'95*

Donald Murphy
Shack Out on 101 *'55*

Kim Murphy
Campfire Tales *'98*

Martin Murphy
Dance with a Stranger *'85*

Mary Murphy
The Intimate Stranger *'56*

Michael Murphy
Kansas City *'95*
Salvador *'86*

Jan Murray
Who Killed Teddy Bear? *'65*

Stephen Murray
The Stranger's Hand *'54*
Pygmalion *'38*

Kate Murtagh
Switchblade Sisters *'75*

James Murtaugh
The Rosary Murders *'87*

Nata Murvanidze
Lullaby *'94*

Tony Musante
The Incident *'67*

Hans Musaus
Every Man for Himself & God against All *'75*

Pip Mushin
Strictly Ballroom *'92*

Alexander Musky
Joyless Street *'25*

Linda Mvusi
A World Apart *'88*

Bruce Myers
The Unbearable Lightness of Being *'88*

Dwight Errington Myers
New Jersey Drive *'95*

Byron Myrick
Ninth Street *'98*

Don Nagel
Bride of the Monster *'55*

Bill Nagy
Never Take Candy from a Stranger *'60*

Ajay Naidu
SubUrbia *'96*

Joanne Nail
Switchblade Sisters *'75*

Laurence Naismith
Village of the Damned *'60*
A Night to Remember *'58*

Jack Nance
Lost Highway *'96*
Motorama *'91*
Blue Velvet *'86*
Eraserhead *'78*

Agnes Nano
Cinema Paradiso *'88*

Charles Napier
The Grifters *'90*
Miami Blues *'90*

Russell Napier
Twisted Nerve *'68*
The Mark *'61*

Darling Narita
Bang *'95*

Arthur J. Nascarelli
Cop Land *'97*

Graham Nash
Gimme Shelter *'70*

Lori Naslund
Vegas in Space *'94*

Adam Nathan
Parting Glances *'86*

Zoe Nathenson
Mona Lisa *'86*

Francesca "Kitten" Natividad
My Tutor *'82*

Joey Naudic
Teenage Gang Debs *'66*

Anthony Naylor
Stardust *'74*

Tom Neal
Detour *'46*

Brent Neale
Careful *'92*

Laurel Near
Eraserhead *'78*

Philip Needs
Hand in Hand *'60*

Liam Neeson
Michael Collins *'96*
Under Suspicion *'92*

Pola Negri
The Yellow Ticket *'18*

Sam Neill
Forgotten Silver *'96*
Sirens *'94*
The Piano *'93*
Dead Calm *'89*
The Good Wife *'86*

Phyllis Neilson-Terry
Look Back in Anger *'58*

Marina Nejelova
With You and Without You *'74*

Kate Nelligan
Eye of the Needle *'81*

Barry Nelson
The Shining *'80*

Margaret Nelson
Picnic at Hanging Rock *'75*

Merritt Nelson
Trust *'91*

Novella Nelson
Manny & Lo *'96*

Sean Nelson
Fresh *'94*

Franco Nero
Victory March *'76*

Cathleen Nesbitt
Separate Tables *'58*
So Long at the Fair *'50*
Pygmalion *'38*

Derren Nesbitt
Victim *'61*

Loni Nest
Joyless Street *'25*

Lois Nettleton
The Man in the Glass Booth *'75*

Trish Nettleton
Anne of Green Gables *'85*

John Neville
My Teacher Ate My Homework *'98*

Sarah Neville
Careful *'92*

Derek Newark
Bellman and True *'88*

George Newbern
It Takes Two *'88*

Bob Newhart
Hot Millions *'68*

Chase Newhart
Switchblade Sisters *'75*

Michael Newland
Bang *'95*

David Newsom
Wes Craven's New Nightmare *'94*

Mary Newton
Tomorrow the World *'44*

Robert Newton
The Hidden Room *'49*
This Happy Breed *'47*

Gaslight *'40*

Olivia Newton-John
It's My Party *'95*

Marie Ney
Uneasy Terms *'48*

Lawrence Ng
Center Stage *'91*

Bonnie Ngai
Life Is Cheap...But Toilet Paper Is Expensive *'90*

Dustin Nguyen
Hundred Per Cent *'98*

Tien Ni
One Night Stand *'76*

Paul Nicholas
Lisztomania *'75*
Tommy *'75*
Stardust *'74*

Anthony Nicholls
If... *'69*
Victim *'61*

Patti Nicholls
Rita, Sue & Bob Too *'87*

Phoebe Nicholls
FairyTale: A True Story *'97*
Persuasion *'95*
Maurice *'87*

Barbara Nichols
The Wild Party *'56*

Dandy Nichols
Confessions of a Window Cleaner *'74*
Georgy Girl *'66*
Leather Boys *'63*
The Fallen Idol *'49*

Taylor Nichols
Barcelona *'94*
Metropolitan *'90*

Jack Nicholson
The Crossing Guard *'94*
The Shining *'80*
Tommy *'75*
Easy Rider *'69*

Daria Nicolodi
Creepers *'85*

Asta Nielson
Joyless Street *'25*

Craig Nigh
Trading Favors *'97*

Bill Nighy
FairyTale: A True Story *'97*

E. Nikitina
Professor Mamlock *'38*

Jan Niklas
The House of the Spirits *'93*

Valery Nikolaev
U-Turn *'97*

Jose Nilson dos Santos
Pixote *'81*

Rob Nilsson
Heat and Sunlight *'87*

Leonard Nimoy
The Balcony *'63*

Willi Ninja
Paris Is Burning *'91*

David Niven
Separate Tables *'58*

Marni Nixon
I Think I Do *'97*

Tony Noakes
Breakaway *'95*

Paul Nocholls
The Return of Tommy Tricker *'94*

Daniele Noel
Bedazzled *'68*

Hubert Noel
The Little Girl Who Lives down the Lane *'76*

Tsachi Noi
The Garden *'77*

Philippe Noiret
The Postman *'94*
Cinema Paradiso *'88*
Coup de Torchon *'81*

Jeanette Nolan
True Confessions *'81*

Lloyd Nolan
Abandon Ship *'57*

Robin Nolan
Teenage Gang Debs *'66*

Claude Nollier
Moulin Rouge *'52*

Jacques Nolot
Nenette and Boni *'96*

Nick Nolte
Affliction *'97*
Afterglow *'97*
U-Turn *'97*

Christine Noonan
If... *'69*

John Ford Noonan
Flirting with Disaster *'95*

Tom Noonan
What Happened Was... *'94*

Kathleen Noone
Citizen Ruth *'96*

Peter Noone
The Making of "A Hard Day's Night" *'94*

Marjorie Norman
Rockers *'79*

Susan Norman
Safe *'95*
Poison *'91*

Zack Norman
Tracks *'76*

John Normington
Stardust *'74*

Jeremy Northam
Carrington *'95*

Ralph Nossek
Citizen X *'95*

Silvana Nova
Vegas in Space *'94*

Donald Novis
Bulldog Drummond *'29*

Jerzy Nowak
Trois Couleurs: Blanc *'94*

Jan Nowicki
Nine Months *'77*

Danny Nucci
Homage *'95*

Bill Nunn
The Last Seduction *'94*
Def by Temptation *'90*

Rudolf Nureyev
Valentino *'77*

Mike Nussbaum
House of Games *'87*

Pascal Nzonzi
Night on Earth *'91*

Barbara O
Daughters of the Dust *'91*

Cicely Oates
The Man Who Knew Too Much *'34*

John Oates
Heavy Petting *'89*

Warren Oates
Badlands *'74*

Charles Oberly
Flirting with Disaster *'95*

Merle Oberon
These Three *'36*
The Scarlet Pimpernel *'34*
The Private Life of Henry VIII *'33*

Jack Oblivian
Sore Losers *'97*

Chris O'Brien
Private Hell 36 *'54*

Colleen O'Brien
Combination Platter *'93*

Edmond O'Brien
1984 *'56*
D.O.A. *'49*

Gary O'Brien
Strapless *'90*

Kieran O'Brien
Bellman and True *'88*

Richard O'Brien
Spice World: The Movie *'97*

Tom O'Brien
The Big Easy *'87*

Richard O'Callaghan
Butley *'74*
Galileo *'73*

Ronan O'Casey
1984 *'56*

Jacki Ochs
Heavy Petting *'89*

U. A. Ochsen
Das Boot *'81*

Deirdre O'Connell
Pastime *'91*

Eddie O'Connell
Absolute Beginners *'86*

Hugh O'Conner
The Boy from Mercury *'96*

Derrick O'Connor
Dealers *'89*

Jeannette O'Connor
Body Count *'97*

Kevin J. O'Connor
Gods and Monsters *'98*
Equinox *'93*
Special Effects *'85*

Simon O'Connor
Heavenly Creatures *'94*

Hugh O'Conor
My Left Foot *'89*

Denis O'Dea
The Fallen Idol *'49*

Judith O'Dea
Night of the Living Dead *'68*

Fritz Odemar
M *'31*

George T. Odom
Straight out of Brooklyn *'91*

Cathy O'Donnell
The Amazing Mr. X *'48*
Bury Me Dead *'47*

"Spec" O'Donnell
Sparrows *'26*

Rynagh O'Grady
Widow's Peak *'94*

Michael O'Hagan
Gods and Monsters *'98*

Brian O'Halloran
Mallrats *'95*
Clerks *'94*

Claudia Ohana
The Fable of the Beautiful Pigeon Fancier *'88*

Brad O'Hara
Longtime Companion *'90*

Catherine O'Hara
The Last of the High Kings *'96*
Waiting for Guffman *'96*
After Hours *'85*

David O'Hara
The Matchmaker *'97*

Dan O'Herlihy
The Dead *'87*
Actors and Sin *'52*

Carol Ohmart
Spider Baby *'64*
The Wild Party *'56*

Jodi Lynn O'Keefe
Halloween: H20 *'98*

Michael O'Keefe
Nina Takes a Lover *'94*

Miles O'Keeffe
Acting on Impulse *'93*

Bill Oland
Special Effects *'85*

Daniel Olbrychski
The Unbearable Lightness of Being *'88*

William Oldham
Thousand Pieces of Gold *'91*
Matewan *'87*

Gary Oldman
Basquiat *'96*
Criminal Law *'89*

Ken Olin
Queens Logic *'91*

Lena Olin
The Unbearable Lightness of Being *'88*

Ingrid Oliu
Stand and Deliver *'88*

Anthony Oliver
The Runaway Bus *'54*

Kareem Oliver
Killer Flick *'98*

Tristan Oliver
Another Country *'84*

Laurence Olivier
Three Sisters *'70*
The Entertainer *'60*
Clouds over Europe *'39*

Edward James Olmos
Caught *'96*
My Family *'94*
Stand and Deliver *'88*
Alambrista! *'77*

Richard Olsen
Wildflower *'91*

Anny Ondra
Blackmail *'29*

Anne O'Neal
Gun Crazy *'49*

Ryan O'Neal
Tough Guys Don't Dance *'87*

Tatum O'Neal
Basquiat *'96*

Chris O'Neill
2 by 4 *'98*
Backbeat *'94*

Maggie O'Neill
Under Suspicion *'92*

Maire O'Neill
Sidewalks of London *'38*

Yoko Ono
The Rolling Stones Rock and Roll Circus *'68*

Lupe Ontiveros
My Family *'94*

Evelyne Opela
False Weights *'74*

Shai K. Ophir
The Garden *'77*
Daughters, Daughters *'74*

Jerry Orbach
Delusion *'91*
Last Exit to Brooklyn *'90*
Dirty Dancing *'87*

Julian Orchard
The Slipper and the Rose *'76*
Perfect Friday *'70*

Kathleen O'Regan
Thursday's Child *'43*

Vera Orlova
Aelita: Queen of Mars *'24*

Roscoe Orman
New Jersey Drive *'95*

Brefni O'Rorke
Don't Take It to Heart *'44*

Lujza Orosz
The Unfinished Sentence in 141 Minutes *'75*

Leland Orser
Red Ribbon Blues *'95*

Marina Orsini
Eddie and the Cruisers 2: Eddie Lives! *'89*

Bud Osborne
Bride of the Monster *'55*

Homes Osborne
Affliction *'97*

Henry Oscar
The Man Who Knew Too Much *'34*

Per Oscarsson
Metamorphosis *'75*

John O'Shea
Forgotten Silver *'96*

Kevin O'Shea
Black Joy *'77*

Milo O'Shea
The Matchmaker *'97*

K. T. Oslin
The Thing Called Love *'93*

Jacek Ostaszewski
Trois Couleurs: Bleu *'93*

Robert Osterloh
I Bury the Living *'58*
Wicked Woman *'54*
The Prowler *'51*
Gun Crazy *'49*

Bibi Osterwald
The World of Henry Orient *'64*

Beth Ostrosky
Flirting with Disaster *'95*

Michael O'Sullivan
Careful *'92*

Richard O'Sullivan
The Stranger's Hand *'54*

Hideji Otaki
A-Ge-Man: Tales of a Golden Geisha *'91*

Peter O'Toole
FairyTale: A True Story *'97*

Barry Otto
Cosi *'95*
Strictly Ballroom *'92*

James Ottoway
That'll Be the Day *'73*

Andre Oumansky
Burnt by the Sun *'94*

Sverre Anker Ousdal
The Feldmann Case *'87*

Peter Outerbridge
Paris, France *'94*

Park Overall
House of Cards *'92*

Alun Owen
The Making of "A Hard Day's Night" *'94*

Bill Owen
In Celebration *'75*
Georgy Girl *'66*

Clive Owen
Century *'94*

Megan Owen
Clean, Shaven *'93*

Seena Owen
Queen Kelly *'29*

Timothy Owen
Terminal Bliss *'91*

Marjorie Owens
Crime of Passion *'57*

Catherine Oxenberg
Lair of the White Worm *'88*

Daphne Oxenford
That'll Be the Day *'73*

Tommy Pace
Vegas in Space *'94*

Charles Lloyd Pack
If... *'69*
Bedazzled *'68*
Victim *'61*

Roger Lloyd Pack
Fright *'71*

Stephanie Pack
The Hours and Times *'92*

Hugh Paddick
The Killing of Sister George *'69*

Anna Padgett
Pariah *'98*

Genevieve Page
The Private Life of Sherlock Holmes *'70*

Geraldine Page
The Trip to Bountiful *'85*

Grant Page
Road Games *'81*

James E. Page
Charley's Aunt *'25*

Leonie Page
Strictly Ballroom *'92*

Mary Page
Wildflower *'91*

Nicola Pagett
An Awfully Big Adventure *'94*

Maggie Paige
The Killing of Sister George *'69*

Nestor Paiva
The Wild Party *'56*

Aleksa Palladino
Manny & Lo *'96*

Anita Pallenberg
Performance *'70*

Eugene Pallette
The Ghost Goes West *'36*

Andrea Palma
Aventurera *'49*

Geoffrey Palmer
Mrs. Brown *'97*
Christabel *'89*

Lilli Palmer
Beware of Pity *'46*

Chazz Palminteri
The Usual Suspects *'95*
Bullets over Broadway *'94*

Gwyneth Paltrow
Shakespeare in Love *'98*
Hard Eight *'96*
Mrs. Parker and the Vicious Circle *'94*

Miguel Paneque
Letters from the Park *'88*

Franklin Pangborn
Turnabout *'40*

Joe Pantoliano
Bound *'96*
Eddie and the Cruisers *'83*

Tatiana Papamoskou
Iphigenia *'77*

Joe Paparone
Mac *'93*

Irene Papas
High Season *'88*
Iphigenia *'77*

Ignazio Pappalardo
Johnny Stecchino *'92*

Anna Paquin
Jane Eyre *'96*
The Piano *'93*

John Paragon
Eating Raoul *'82*

Norrie Paramor
The Frightened City *'61*

Michael Pare
Eddie and the Cruisers 2: Eddie Lives! *'89*
Eddie and the Cruisers *'83*

Marisa Paredes
Life Is Beautiful *'98*
Three Lives and Only One Death *'96*
High Heels *'91*
Dark Habits *'84*

Mila Parely
Beauty and the Beast *'46*
The Rules of the Game *'39*

Manda Parent
Once upon a Time in the East *'74*

Judy Parfitt
Wilde *'97*
Maurice *'87*
Galileo *'73*

Anne Parillaud
Frankie Starlight *'95*
La Femme Nikita *'91*

Jerry Paris
Marty *'55*

Virginia Paris
Stand and Deliver *'88*

Kris Park
I Love You, I Love You Not *'97*

Steve Park
Fargo *'96*

MacDonald Parke
Never Take Candy from a Stranger *'60*

Cecil Parker
The Ladykillers *'55*
The Lady Vanishes *'38*

F. William Parker
Hard Eight *'96*

Jean Parker
The Ghost Goes West *'36*

Kim Parker
Fire Maidens from Outer Space *'56*

Leonard Parker
Nothing but a Man *'64*

Mary-Louise Parker
Reckless *'95*
Bullets over Broadway *'94*
Longtime Companion *'90*

Michael Parker
My Own Private Idaho *'91*

Nicole Parker
Boogie Nights *'97*
The End of Violence *'97*

Robin Parkinson
Twisted Nerve *'68*

Ted Parks
Red Rock West *'93*

Rick Lee Parmentier
Stardust *'74*

Emory Parnell
I Married a Witch *'42*

Bobby Parr
The Land That Time Forgot *'75*

David Parr
Street Music *'81*

Leslie Parrish
The Manchurian Candidate *'62*

Ken Parry
Lisztomania *'75*

Loretta Parry
Hand in Hand *'60*

Kate Parselle
To Hell with Love *'98*

Milton Parsons
Bury Me Dead *'47*

Percy Parsons
Blackmail *'29*

Christine Pascal
Le Grand Chemin *'87*
The Best Way *'76*

Richard Pasco
Mrs. Brown *'97*
Room at the Top *'59*

Christina Pascual
Dark Habits *'84*

Adrian Pasdar
Just Like a Woman *'92*
Grand Isle *'91*

Jean Passanante
Return of the Secaucus 7 *'80*

Daniel Passer
Ted *'98*

Earl Pastko
The Sweet Hereafter *'96*

Vinny Pastore
Walking and Talking *'96*
True Love *'89*

Wally Patch
Night Train to Munich *'40*
Pygmalion *'38*
The Private Life of Henry VIII *'33*

Bill Paterson
Spice World: The Movie *'97*
Chaplin *'92*
The Witches *'90*

Ratna Pathak
Heat and Dust *'82*

Mandy Patinkin
Hombres Armados *'97*
Impromptu *'90*
The House on Carroll Street *'88*

Charles Paton
Blackmail *'29*

Jason Patric
After Dark, My Sweet *'90*
Frankenstein Unbound *'90*

Nigel Patrick
Uneasy Terms *'48*

Robert Patrick
Cop Land *'97*

Elizabeth Patterson
I Married a Witch *'42*

Frank Patterson
The Dead *'87*

Jay Patterson
Street Smart *'87*

Kenneth Patterson
Private Hell 36 *'54*

Lee Patterson
Time Lock *'57*

Oliver Patterson
The Giving *'91*

Robert Patterson
Nuns on the Run *'90*

Will Patton
The Spitfire Grill *'95*
In the Soup *'92*
A Shock to the System *'90*
After Hours *'85*

Parveen Paul
Heat and Dust *'82*

Richard Paul
Pass the Ammo *'88*

Scott Paulin
From Hollywood to Deadwood *'89*
Grim Prairie Tales *'89*

Adam Pawlikowski
Ashes and Diamonds *'58*

Bill Paxton
One False Move *'91*
Pass the Ammo *'88*

Collin Wilcox Paxton
Wildflower *'91*

Bruce Payne
For Queen and Country *'88*
Wonderland *'88*

Eric Payne
She's Gotta Have It *'86*

Dennis Payton
Having a Wild Weekend *'65*

Cezary Pazura
Trois Couleurs: Blanc *'94*

Mary Peach
Room at the Top *'59*

Guy Pearce
The Adventures of Priscilla, Queen of the Desert *'94*

Jacqueline Pearce
White Mischief *'88*

Mary Vivian Pearce
Pecker *'98*
Female Trouble *'74*

Patrick Pearson
Closing Numbers *'93*

Richard Pearson
The Woman in Question *'50*

Sierra Pecheur
Kalifornia *'93*

Bob Peck
FairyTale: A True Story *'97*

Brian Peck
Twisted Nerve *'68*

David Peck
Gal Young 'Un *'79*

Tom Pedi
The Iceman Cometh *'73*

Salmaan Peer
Twisted Nerve *'68*

Amanda Peet
1999 *'98*
She's the One *'96*

Yakira Peguero
Kids *'95*

Ting Pei
One Night Stand *'76*

Lanah Pellay
Eat the Rich *'87*

Jean-Pierre Pellegrin
One Sings, the Other Doesn't *'77*

Mark Pellegrino
Blood & Concrete: A Love Story *'90*

Tobie Pelletier
Le Sexe des Étoiles *'93*

Matti Pellonpaa
Night on Earth *'91*

Ron Pember
The Land That Time Forgot *'75*

Charles Pemberton
Black Joy *'77*

Tony Pemberton
Poison *'91*

Elizabeth Pena
Lone Star *'95*
The Waterdance *'91*

Freddie Pendavis
Paris Is Burning *'91*

Austin Pendleton
The Ballad of the Sad Cafe *'91*

Susan Penhaligon
The Land That Time Forgot *'75*

Christopher Penn
The Funeral *'96*
Short Cuts *'93*
Reservoir Dogs *'92*

Sean Penn
Hugo Pool *'97*
U-Turn *'97*
Dead Man Walking *'95*

Nicholas Pennell
Isadora *'68*

John Penrose
Kind Hearts and Coronets *'49*

Alan Pentony
Frankie Starlight *'95*

Barbara Pepper
Girls in Chains *'43*
Our Daily Bread *'34*

Marilia Pera
Pixote *'81*

Esme Percy
Dead of Night *'45*
Pygmalion *'38*

Michel Perelon
Cat and Mouse *'78*

Tony Perenski
The Underneath *'95*

Jose Perez
Miami Blues *'90*

Rosie Perez
Night on Earth *'91*

Anthony Perkins
Murder on the Orient Express *'74*

Clare Perkins
Ladybird, Ladybird *'93*

Elizabeth Perkins
Enid Is Sleeping *'90*

Dr. Arpad Perlaky
Adoption *'75*

Rebecca Perle
Not of This Earth *'88*

Max Perlich
Georgia *'95*
Drugstore Cowboy *'89*

Rhea Perlman
Enid Is Sleeping *'90*

Ron Perlman
The Island of Dr. Moreau *'96*
The City of Lost Children *'95*

Stephen Perlman
Pi *'98*

Dara Perlmutter
My Teacher Ate My Homework *'98*

Florence Pernel
Trois Couleurs: Bleu *'93*

Jean-Francois Perrier
La Ceremonie *'95*

Mireille Perrier
Shades of Doubt *'93*

Jacques Perrin
Cinema Paradiso *'88*

Harold Perrineau Jr.
Smoke *'95*

Leslie Perrins
Nine Days a Queen *'36*

Barbara Perry
Naked Kiss *'64*

Luke Perry
American Strays *'96*
Normal Life *'96*
Terminal Bliss *'91*

Lisa Jane Persky
The Big Easy *'87*

Nehemiah Persoff
Voyage of the Damned *'76*
The Wild Party *'56*

Sean Pertwee
London Kills Me *'91*

Ladislav Pesek
Dinner for Adele *'78*

Bernadette Peters
Impromptu *'90*

Brock Peters
Lost in the Stars *'74*
The Incident *'67*

Clarke Peters
Mona Lisa *'86*

Mattie Peters
Helen's Babies *'25*

Ralph Peters
I Married a Witch *'42*

Cassandra Peterson
Acting on Impulse *'93*

Edward Petherbridge
An Awfully Big Adventure *'94*

Anton Petje
Fear *'75*

Hay Petrie
Great Expectations *'46*
On Approval *'44*
Clouds over Europe *'39*
The Ghost Goes West *'36*
The Private Life of Henry VIII *'33*

Christopher Pettiet
Carried Away *'95*

Brian Pettifer
If... *'69*

Frank Pettingell
Gaslight *'40*

Chuck Pfeiffer
Basquiat *'96*

Robert Phalen
Halloween *'78*

Kate Phelps
The Shining *'80*

John Philbin
Shy People *'87*

Gerard Philipe
Dangerous Liaisons *'60*

Angie Phillips
Manny & Lo *'96*

Frank Phillips
The Runaway Bus *'54*

John Phillips
Village of the Damned *'60*

Leslie Phillips
Scandal *'89*
The Smallest Show on Earth *'57*

Lou Diamond Phillips
Teresa's Tattoo *'94*
Stand and Deliver *'88*

Michelle Phillips
Valentino *'77*

Robert Phillips
The Killing of a Chinese Bookie *'76*

William Phipps
The Wild Party *'56*

V. Phipps-Willson
Eraserhead *'78*

Joaquin Rafael (Leaf) Phoenix
Clay Pigeons *'98*
U-Turn *'97*
To Die For *'95*

River Phoenix
The Thing Called Love *'93*
Silent Tongue *'92*
My Own Private Idaho *'91*

Beatrice Picard
Once upon a Time in the East *'74*

Maureen Picard
Little Shots of Happiness *'97*

Robert Picardo
Motorama *'91*
Jack's Back *'87*

Michel Piccoli
101 Nights *'95*
The World of Jacques Demy *'95*
Martha and I *'91*
Phantom of Liberty *'74*

Andrew Piccone
She's Vintage *'98*

Sarah Pickering
Little Dorrit, Film 1: Nobody's Fault *'88*
Little Dorrit, Film 2: Little Dorrit's Story *'88*

Mary Pickford
Sparrows *'26*

Ronald Pickup
Three Sisters *'70*

Molly Picon
East and West *'24*

Jim Piddock
Traces of Red *'92*

Jacques Pieller
Three Lives and Only One Death *'96*

Claude Pieplu
Dites-Lui Que Je L'Aime *'77*
The Best Way *'76*
Phantom of Liberty *'74*

Justin Pierce
Kids *'95*

Wendell Pierce
Hackers *'95*

Sarah Pierse
Heavenly Creatures *'94*

Angela Pietropinto
Welcome to the Dollhouse *'95*

Alexandra Pigg
Strapless *'90*
A Chorus of Disapproval *'89*

Tim Pigott-Smith
The Remains of the Day *'93*

Nova Pilbeam
Young and Innocent *'37*
Nine Days a Queen *'36*
The Man Who Knew Too Much *'34*

Lorraine Pilkington
The Last of the High Kings *'96*

Reuben Pillsbury
Death of a Schoolboy *'91*

Bronson Pinchot
It's My Party *'95*
After Hours *'85*

Renato Pinciroli
A Virgin Named Mary *'75*

Larry Pine
Dead Man Walking *'95*
Vanya on 42nd Street *'94*
Anna *'87*

Robert Pine
Body Count *'97*

Vincent Pinel
First Communion *'77*

Jada Pinkett Smith
Set It Off *'96*
Menace II Society *'93*

Dominique Pinon
The City of Lost Children *'95*

Roni Pinovich
Ricochets *'87*

Allan Piper
Starving Artists *'97*

Frederick Piper
The Frightened City *'61*
Pink String and Sealing Wax *'45*
Sabotage *'36*

James Pirrie
Non-Stop New York *'37*

Joe Piscopo
Open Season *'95*

Marie-France Pisier
Cousin, Cousine *'76*
French Provincial *'75*

Anne Pitoniak
House of Cards *'92*
The Ballad of the Sad Cafe *'91*
The Wizard of Loneliness *'88*
Old Enough *'84*

Brad Pitt
Kalifornia *'93*

Marek Piwowski
The Balance *'75*

Mary Kay Place
Pecker *'98*
Citizen Ruth *'96*
Manny & Lo *'96*
Smooth Talk *'85*

Michele Placido
Lamerica *'95*
Victory March *'76*

Tony Plana
Salvador *'86*

Roger Planchon
Roads to the South *'78*

Scott Plank
Pastime *'91*

Karl Platen
M *'31*

Oliver Platt
Funny Bones *'94*

Angela Pleasence
The Favor, the Watch, and the Very Big Fish *'92*

Donald Pleasence
Creepers *'85*
Halloween *'78*
The Battle of the Sexes *'60*
Look Back in Anger *'58*
1984 *'56*

Martha Plimpton
Pecker *'98*
I Shot Andy Warhol *'96*
Forbidden Choices *'94*
Mrs. Parker and the Vicious Circle *'94*
Inside Monkey Zetterland *'93*
Shy People *'87*

Jack Plotnick
Gods and Monsters *'98*

Hilda Plowright
Separate Tables *'58*

Joan Plowright
Jane Eyre *'96*
Sorrento Beach *'95*
Widow's Peak *'94*
Enchanted April *'92*
Three Sisters *'70*
The Entertainer *'60*

Eve Plumb
...And God Spoke *'94*

Amanda Plummer
Freeway *'95*
Butterfly Kiss *'94*
Pulp Fiction *'94*

Glenn Plummer
Menace II Society *'93*
Pastime *'91*

Denis Podalydes
Pas Tres Catholique *'93*

Eric Pohlmann
The Belles of St. Trinian's *'53*
Moulin Rouge *'52*

Pavel Pol
Aelita: Queen of Mars *'24*

Priscilla Pointer
Carried Away *'95*
Blue Velvet *'86*

Talitha Pol
Return from the Ashes *'65*

Lina Polito
Everything Ready, Nothing Works *'74*

Sydney Pollack
Independent's Day *'97*
The Player *'92*

Kevin Pollak
The Usual Suspects *'95*

Michael J. Pollard
Motorama *'91*
Enid Is Sleeping *'90*

Sarah Polley
The Sweet Hereafter *'96*
Exotica *'94*

Ellen Pollock
Non-Stop New York *'37*

Teri Polo
Golden Gate *'93*
The House of the Spirits *'93*

John Polson
Sirens *'94*

Eusebio Poncela
Law of Desire *'86*

Marcel Poncin
So Long at the Fair *'50*

Rachel Pond
Morgan's Cake *'88*

Maria Luisa Ponte
Black Litter *'77*

Erich Ponto
The Third Man *'49*

David Pontremoli
Servant and Mistress *'77*

Iggy Pop
Dead Man *'95*

Paulina Porizkova
Anna *'87*

Anthony Portillo
Night on Earth *'91*

Paulo Porto
The Marriage *'76*

Mary Portser
Passion Fish *'92*

Jason Posey
Pariah *'98*

Parker Posey
The House of Yes *'97*
Basquiat *'96*
The Daytrippers *'96*
SubUrbia *'96*
Waiting for Guffman *'96*
Party Girl *'94*
Dazed and Confused *'93*

Pete Postlethwaite
The Usual Suspects *'95*
In the Name of the Father *'93*

Charlie Potter
The Witches *'90*

Annie Potts
Pass the Ammo *'88*

Georges Poujouly
Forbidden Games *'52*

Melvil Poupaud
Three Lives and Only One Death *'96*

Addison Powell
The Rosary Murders *'87*

Clive Powell
Children of the Damned *'63*

Dick Powell
Pitfall *'48*

Nosher Powell
Eat the Rich *'87*

Robert Powell
Tommy *'75*

Hartley Power
Dead of Night *'45*
Evergreen *'34*

Taryn Power
Tracks *'76*

Tyrone Power
Abandon Ship *'57*

Tyrone Power Jr.
Shag: The Movie *'89*

William Powers
The Balance *'75*

Stanley Prager
Gun Crazy *'49*

Mike Pratt
Repulsion *'65*

Otto Preminger
Hollywood on Trial *'76*

Paula Prentiss
The World of Henry Orient *'64*

Harve Presnell
Fargo *'96*
The Whole Wide World *'96*

Lawrence Pressman
The Man in the Glass Booth *'75*

Jason Presson
The Lady in White *'88*

Billy Preston
Wired *'89*

Kelly Preston
Citizen Ruth *'96*

Michael B. Preston
Matewan *'87*

Dana Preu
Gal Young 'Un *'79*

Francoise Prevost
L'Amour en Herbe *'77*

Dmitry Preyers
Little Odessa *'94*

Brendan Price
In Possession *'84*

Dennis Price
Victim *'61*
Kind Hearts and Coronets *'49*

Lindsay Price
Hundred Per Cent *'98*

Lonny Price
Dirty Dancing *'87*

Vincent Price
The Whales of August *'87*

Martin Priest
Zebrahead '92
Nothing but a Man '64

Jason Priestley
Love and Death on Long Island '97
Coldblooded '94

Adriana Prieto
The Marriage '76

Alec Primrose
Teenage Gang Debs '66

Barry Primus
Cannibal Women in the Avocado Jungle of Death '89
Heartland '81

Akili Prince
Went to Coney Island on a Mission from God...Be Back by Five '98

Freddie Prinze Jr.
The House of Yes '97

Juergen Prochnow
The English Patient '96
Das Boot '81

Tim Progosh
My Teacher Ate My Homework '98

Elena Proklova
The Only One '76

Robert Prosky
Dead Man Walking '95

Paul Provenza
Ted '98

Guy Provost
The Orders '75

Juliet Prowse
Who Killed Teddy Bear? '65

Jonathan Pryce
Carrington '95
Voyage of the Damned '76

Richard Pryor
Lost Highway '96

Matthew Puckett
Spanking the Monkey '94

Robert Pugh
Priest '94

Bill Pullman
The End of Violence '97
Lost Highway '96
The Last Seduction '94
Cold Feet '89

Bernard Punsley
Dead End '37

Reginald Purdell
Clouds over Europe '39

Louise Purnell
Three Sisters '70

Olivier Py
When the Cat's Away '96

Denver Pyle
Too Late for Tears '49

Zhu Qanging
The Story of Qui Ju '91

Liu Pei Qu
The Story of Qui Ju '91

Al Quagliata
Poison '91

Dennis Quaid
The Big Easy '87

Randy Quaid
Curse of the Starving Class '94

John Qualen
Our Daily Bread '34

Helmut Qualtinger
False Weights '74

Pu Quanxin
The Blue Kite '93

Robert Quarry
Crime of Passion '57

Anna Quayle
A Hard Day's Night '64

Anthony Quayle
Saraband for Dead Lovers '48

Queen Latifah
Set It Off '96

John Quentin
Isadora '68

Ginger Quest
Vegas in Space '94

Hugues Quester
Trois Couleurs: Bleu '93

Gerry Quigley
32 Short Films about Glenn Gould '93

Denis Quilley
Murder on the Orient Express '74

Veronica Quilligan
Lisztomania '75

Aidan Quinn
Michael Collins '96

Anthony Quinn
The Wild Party '56

Elizabeth Quinn
Love and Death on Long Island '97

Francesco Quinn
Platoon '86

Glenn Quinn
Campfire Tales '98

Martha Quinn
Motorama '91

Francesco Rabal
Tie Me Up! Tie Me Down! '90
The Devil Is a Woman '75

Pamela Rabe
Cosi '95
Sirens '94

Catherine Rabett
Frankenstein Unbound '90

Francine Racette
Lumiere '76

Rosemary Radcliffe
Anne of Green Gables '85

Ronald Radd
Galileo '73

Basil Radford
Dead of Night '45
Night Train to Munich '40
The Lady Vanishes '38
Young and Innocent '37

John Rae
Morgan! '66
The Little Kidnappers '53

Alex Rafalowicz
Shine '95

Frances Rafferty
Money Madness '47

Howard Ragsdale
Badlands '74

William Ragsdale
Smooth Talk '85

Theodore (Ted) Raimi
Evil Dead '83

Jack Raine
The Killing of Sister George '69

Patricia Raine
Madeleine '50

Ella Raines
Impact '49

Sheryl Lee Ralph
To Sleep with Anger '90

Esther Ralston
Oliver Twist '22

Cecil Ramage
Kind Hearts and Coronets '49

Nandi Luna Ramirez
Hombres Armados '97

Charlotte Rampling
The Wings of the Dove '97
Georgy Girl '66

Steven Randazzo
Mac '93
In the Soup '92

Elsie Randolph
Rich and Strange '32

John Randolph
The Wizard of Loneliness '88

Michael Rapaport
Cop Land '97
The Basketball Diaries '94
Zebrahead '92

Sara Rapisarda
Everything Ready, Nothing Works '74

Anthony Rapp
Dazed and Confused '93

Stephen Rappaport
...And God Spoke '94

David Rasche
Twenty Bucks '93

Richard Rasof
The Man in the Glass Booth '75

Fritz Rasp
Metropolis '26

John Ratzenberger
The Good Soldier '81

Thyrza Ravesteijn
Antonia's Line '95

Adrian Rawlins
Breaking the Waves '95
Mountains of the Moon '90

Robin Ray
A Hard Day's Night '64

Bill Raymond
City of Hope '91

Candy Raymond
Don's Party '76

Cyril Raymond
Brief Encounter '46

Gary Raymond
Look Back in Anger '58

Robin Raymond
Girls in Chains '43

Minnie Rayner
Gaslight '40

Michael Raynor
Federal Hill '94

Stephen Rea
The Last of the High Kings '96
Michael Collins '96
Citizen X '95
The Crying Game '92

Ronald Reagan
Hollywood on Trial '76

Craig Reay
Red Rock West '93

Mark Rector
In the Company of Men '96

Keith Reddin
Lolita '97

Quinn Redeker
Spider Baby '64

Ian Redford
Just Like a Woman '92

Rockets Redglare
In the Soup *'92*
After Hours *'85*

Corin Redgrave
Persuasion *'95*
Four Weddings and a Funeral *'94*
In the Name of the Father *'93*

Lynn Redgrave
Gods and Monsters *'98*
Shine *'95*
Georgy Girl *'66*

Michael Redgrave
The Innocents *'61*
1984 *'56*
Dead of Night *'45*
The Lady Vanishes *'38*

Vanessa Redgrave
Wilde *'97*
Little Odessa *'94*
Mother's Boys *'94*
The House of the Spirits *'93*
The Ballad of the Sad Cafe *'91*
Murder on the Orient Express *'74*
Isadora *'68*
Blow-Up *'66*
Morgan! *'66*

Amanda Redman
For Queen and Country *'88*

Liam Redmond
The Luck of Ginger Coffey *'64*

Rob Reece
The Method *'87*

Alan Reed
Actors and Sin *'52*

George Reed
Helen's Babies *'25*

James Reed
Eight Men Out *'88*

Oliver Reed
Funny Bones *'94*
Castaway *'87*
Lisztomania *'75*
Tommy *'75*

Donough Rees
Crush *'93*

Roger Rees
Sudden Manhattan *'96*

Christopher Reeve
The Remains of the Day *'93*
Street Smart *'87*

Keanu Reeves
Much Ado about Nothing *'93*
My Own Private Idaho *'91*
Tune in Tomorrow *'90*
Permanent Record *'88*
River's Edge *'87*

Kynaston Reeves
Hot Millions *'68*

Saskia Reeves
Different for Girls *'96*
Butterfly Kiss *'94*

Steve Reevis
Fargo *'96*

Benoit Regent
Trois Couleurs: Bleu *'93*

Serge Reggiani
Cat and Mouse *'78*

Paul Regina
It's My Party *'95*

Regine
Robert et Robert *'78*

Hans-Michael Rehberg
Death of a Schoolboy *'91*

Hans Leo Reich
Metropolis *'26*

Alice Reichen
Dear Victor *'75*

Beryl Reid
Entertaining Mr. Sloane *'70*
The Killing of Sister George *'69*
The Belles of St. Trinian's *'53*

Christopher Reid
House Party *'90*

Kate Reid
A Delicate Balance *'73*

Sheila Reid
Three Sisters *'70*

Tara Reid
The Big Lebowski *'97*

Andrew Reilly
Lisztomania *'75*

John C. Reilly
Boogie Nights *'97*
Hard Eight *'96*
Georgia *'95*

Luke Reilly
Zebrahead *'92*

Rob Reiner
Bullets over Broadway *'94*

Ray Reinhardt
The Tie That Binds *'95*

Judge Reinhold
Enid Is Sleeping *'90*

Joseph D. Reitman
Clay Pigeons *'98*

Sylvia Reize
The Second Awakening of Christa Klages *'78*

Devi Rekha
Kama Sutra: A Tale of Love *'96*

James Remar
Drugstore Cowboy *'89*

Lee Remick
A Delicate Balance *'73*

Bert Remsen
Hugo Pool *'97*

Albert Remy
The 400 Blows *'59*
Children of Paradise *'45*

Simone Renant
Dangerous Liaisons *'60*

Gilles Renaud
Once upon a Time in the East *'74*

Georges Renavent
Turnabout *'40*

Scott Renderer
Poison *'91*

Michael Rennie
Uneasy Terms *'48*

Jean Reno
La Femme Nikita *'91*

Jean Renoir
The Rules of the Game *'39*

Pierre Renoir
Children of Paradise *'45*

Gastone Renzelli
Bellissima *'51*

Maggie Renzi
Passion Fish *'92*
City of Hope *'91*
Eight Men Out *'88*
Matewan *'87*
Return of the Secaucus 7 *'80*

Clive Revill
Let Him Have It *'91*
The Little Prince *'74*
Galileo *'73*
The Private Life of Sherlock Holmes *'70*

Roberta Rex
Children of the Damned *'63*

Fernando Rey
Seven Beauties *'76*

Burt Reynolds
Boogie Nights *'97*
Citizen Ruth *'96*

Nancy Reynolds
Crime of Passion *'57*

Paul Reynolds
Let Him Have It *'91*

Robert Reynolds
The Cater Street Hangman *'98*

Hossein Rezai
Through the Olive Trees *'94*

Ving Rhames
Pulp Fiction *'94*

Julian Rhind-Tutt
The Madness of King George *'94*

Cynthia Rhodes
Dirty Dancing *'87*

Geoffrey Rhue
Squeeze *'97*

Miranda Stuart Rhyne
Angela *'94*

Paul Rhys
Nina Takes a Lover *'94*
Chaplin *'92*

Jonathan Rhys Myers
The Governess *'98*
Michael Collins *'96*

Giovanni Ribisi
SubUrbia *'96*

Marissa Ribisi
Dazed and Confused *'93*

Christina Ricci
The Opposite of Sex *'98*
Pecker *'98*
The Ice Storm *'97*
Bastard out of Carolina *'96*
The Last of the High Kings *'96*

Bill Rice
Vortex *'81*

Mandy Rice-Davies
Absolute Beginners *'86*

Matty Rich
Straight out of Brooklyn *'91*

Addison Richards
Our Daily Bread *'34*

Beah Richards
Drugstore Cowboy *'89*

Keith Richards
Gimme Shelter *'70*

Kyle Richards
Halloween *'78*

Joely Richardson
Loch Ness *'95*
Sister My Sister *'94*

Katie Ryder Richardson
The Cater Street Hangman *'98*

Kevin M. Richardson
Bound *'96*

Miranda Richardson
The Apostle *'97*
Kansas City *'95*
Century *'94*
The Crying Game *'92*
Enchanted April *'92*
Dance with a Stranger *'85*

Natasha Richardson
Widow's Peak *'94*
The Favor, the Watch, and the Very Big Fish *'92*
The Comfort of Strangers *'91*

Patricia Richardson
Ulee's Gold *'97*

Ralph Richardson
The Fallen Idol '49
Clouds over Europe '39

Clive Riche
Cemetery Man '95

Ralph Richer
Das Boot '81

William Richert
My Own Private Idaho '91

Charles Richman
Struggle '31

Fiona Richmond
Eat the Rich '87

Tony Rickards
Castaway '87

Alan Rickman
Michael Collins '96
An Awfully Big Adventure '94
Closet Land '90

Robert Ridgely
Boogie Nights '97
Hard Eight '96
Who Am I This Time? '82

Judith Ridley
Night of the Living Dead '68

Peter Riegert
Coldblooded '94
A Shock to the System '90

Richard Riehle
Trading Favors '97
Lightning Jack '94

Edward Rigby
Don't Take It to Heart '44
Young and Innocent '37

Terence Rigby
The Homecoming '73

Diana Rigg
A Good Man in Africa '94

Mariana Rigillo
The Postman '94

Roger Rignack
True Love '89

Brad Rijn
Special Effects '85

Jack Rikess
The Method '87

Eleanor Riley
Turnabout '40

Michael Riley
...And God Spoke '94

Walter Rilla
The Scarlet Pimpernel '34

Shane Rimmer
Dreamchild '85

Vince Rimmer
Careful '92

Todd Rippon
Castaway '87

Sara Risher
Wes Craven's New Nightmare '94

Jacques Rispal
Dear Victor '75

Michael Rispoli
Household Saints '93

Lazar Ristovski
Tito and Me '92

Cyril Ritchard
Blackmail '29

Blake Ritson
Alambrista! '77

John Ritter
Sling Blade '96

Thelma Ritter
The Incident '67

Emmanuelle Riva
Shades of Doubt '93

Julien Riviere
Ma Vie en Rose '97

Colin Rix
Eye of the Needle '81

Margaret Roach
Turnabout '40

Linus Roache
The Wings of the Dove '97
Priest '94

Jason Robards Jr.
A Boy and His Dog '75
Isadora '68
A Thousand Clowns '65

Sam Robards
Mrs. Parker and the Vicious Circle '94
The Ballad of Little Jo '93

David Robb
The Deceivers '88

Tim Robbins
Short Cuts '93
The Player '92
Five Corners '88

Alice Roberts
Pandora's Box '28

Allene Roberts
The Red House '47

Arthur Roberts
Not of This Earth '88

Christian Roberts
Twisted Nerve '68

Danyel Roberts
She's Vintage '98

Davis Roberts
To Sleep with Anger '90

Doris Roberts
Hester Street '75

Emma Roberts
Persuasion '95

Eric Roberts
American Strays '96
It's My Party '95
The Ambulance '90
Nobody's Fool '86

J. H. Roberts
Uneasy Terms '48
Young and Innocent '37
Nine Days a Queen '36

Joe Roberts
Shakespeare in Love '98

Judith Anna Roberts
Eraserhead '78

Julia Roberts
Michael Collins '96
Mystic Pizza '88

Leonard Roberts
Love Jones '96

Nancy Roberts
Black Narcissus '47

Pascale Roberts
Le Grand Chemin '87

Rachel Roberts
Picnic at Hanging Rock '75
Murder on the Orient Express '74

Rick Roberts
Love and Human Remains '93

Steve Roberts
Gog '54

Tony Roberts
Popcorn '89

Tracey Roberts
Actors and Sin '52

Robbie Robertson
The Crossing Guard '94

Liliane Robin
Breathless '59

Michel Robin
The Wonderful Crook '75

Betty Robinson
Naked Kiss '64

Charles Robinson
Set It Off '96

Dewey Robinson
The Lady Confesses '45

Eartha D. Robinson
Daughters of the Dust '91

Edward G. Robinson
Actors and Sin '52
The Red House '47

Jay Robinson
The Wild Party '56

John Robinson
Uneasy Terms '48

Karen Robinson
My Teacher Ate My Homework '98

Madeleine Robinson
Camille Claudel '89

Flora Robson
Saraband for Dead Lovers '48
Black Narcissus '47

Wayne Robson
Affliction '97

Alex Rocco
Wired '89
The Lady in White '88

Billy Roch
Strapless '90

Sebastien Roche
Household Saints '93

Julien Rochefort
La Ceremonie '95

Niva Rochelle
Sweet Sweetback's Baadasssss Song '71

Crissy Rock
Ladybird, Ladybird '93

Sam Rockwell
Box of Moonlight '96
Last Exit to Brooklyn '90

Shmuel Rodensku
The Odessa File '74

Anton Rodgers
Impromptu '90

Gaby Rodgers
Kiss Me Deadly '55

Reginald Rodgers
I Shot Andy Warhol '96

Celia Rodriguez
I Am Cuba '64

Paul Rodriguez
Rhythm Thief '94

Daniel Roebuck
River's Edge '87

Alva Rogers
Daughters of the Dust '91

Anthony Rogers
Tommy Tricker & the Stamp Traveller '87

Mimi Rogers
Trees Lounge '96
Street Smart '87

Paul Rogers
The Homecoming '73
The Mark '61

Eduardo Lopez Rojas
My Family '94

Jaime Rojo
The Refrigerator '91

Ruben Rojo
Aventurera '49

Guy Rolfe
Saraband for Dead Lovers *'48*

Esther Rolle
House of Cards *'92*

Rolling Stones
The Rolling Stones Rock and Roll Circus *'68*

Henry Rollins
Lost Highway *'96*

Yvonne Romain
The Frightened City *'61*

Rick Roman
Actors and Sin *'52*

Ruth Roman
Champion *'49*

Anna Romantowska
The Interrogation *'82*

Cesar Romero
Carmen Miranda: Bananas Is My Business *'95*
Hot Millions *'68*

Carla Rominelli
Steppenwolf *'74*

Eric Romley
Little Shots of Happiness *'97*

Michael Rooker
Bastard out of Carolina *'96*
Mallrats *'95*
Eight Men Out *'88*

Amanda Root
Jane Eyre *'96*
Persuasion *'95*

David Roper
The Cater Street Hangman *'98*

Francoise Rosay
Saraband for Dead Lovers *'48*

Gabrielle Rose
The Sweet Hereafter *'96*

George Rose
A Night to Remember *'58*

Guy Rose
If... *'69*

Claude-Emile Rosen
First Communion *'77*

Alan Rosenberg
Miracle Mile *'89*

Annie Ross
Short Cuts *'93*

David Ross
Little Odessa *'94*

Gene Ross
Lost Highway *'96*

Katharine Ross
Voyage of the Damned *'76*
The Graduate *'67*

Lee Ross
Secrets and Lies *'95*

Michael Ross
D.O.A. *'49*

Monty Ross
She's Gotta Have It *'86*

Willie Ross
Rita, Sue & Bob Too *'87*

Adrian Ross-Magenty
Another Country *'84*

Isabella Rossellini
The Funeral *'96*
Big Night *'95*
Wild at Heart *'90*
Tough Guys Don't Dance *'87*
Blue Velvet *'86*

Leo Rossi
River's Edge *'87*

Michele Rossignol
Once upon a Time in the East *'74*

Norman Rossington
Let Him Have It *'91*
The Krays *'90*
A Hard Day's Night *'64*

Leonard Rossiter
Luther *'74*

Dzsoko Roszics
Nine Months *'77*

Carlo Rota
32 Short Films about Glenn Gould *'93*

Tim Roth
Little Odessa *'94*
Pulp Fiction *'94*
Bodies, Rest & Motion *'93*
Reservoir Dogs *'92*
A World Apart *'88*

Jean Rougerie
Servant and Mistress *'77*

Raymond Rouleau
The Crucible *'57*

Richard Roundtree
Q (The Winged Serpent) *'82*

Simon Rouse
Butley *'74*

Jean-Louis Roux
Salut Victor! *'89*

Michel Roux
Pas Tres Catholique *'93*

Michael J. Rowe
Hard Eight *'96*

Gena Rowlands
Night on Earth *'91*
A Woman under the Influence *'74*

Dylan Roy
With or Without You *'98*

Lise Roy
The Boys of St. Vincent *'93*

Cornell (Kofi) Royal
Daughters of the Dust *'91*

Patricia Royce
To Cross the Rubicon *'91*

Selena Royle
He Ran All the Way *'51*

Gregory Rozakis
Five Corners *'88*

Maria Rubia
The Marriage *'76*

Jennifer Rubin
Delusion *'91*
Permanent Record *'88*

Saul Rubinek
Open Season *'95*
And the Band Played On *'93*
Ticket to Heaven *'81*

Zelda Rubinstein
Acting on Impulse *'93*

Alan Ruck
Just Like in the Movies *'90*

John Ruddock
The Fallen Idol *'49*

Claude-Oliver Rudolph
Das Boot *'81*

Verena Rudolph
Strongman Ferdinand *'76*

Kristin Rudrud
Fargo *'96*

Gene Ruffini
Little Odessa *'94*

Rufus
Jonah Who Will Be 25 in the Year 2000 *'76*

Waldemar Ruhl
The Good Soldier *'81*

Jose Carlos Ruiz
Salvador *'86*

Kicki Rundgren
My Life As a Dog *'85*

RuPaul
Red Ribbon Blues *'95*

Helena Rupport
His Picture in the Papers *'16*

Deborah Rush
Reckless *'95*

Geoffrey Rush
Shakespeare in Love *'98*
Shine *'95*

Claire Rushbrook
Spice World: The Movie *'97*
Secrets and Lies *'95*

Jared Rushton
The Lady in White *'88*

Sheila Ruskin
The Cater Street Hangman *'98*

Shimen Ruskin
Gun Crazy *'49*

Robert Rusler
Shag: The Movie *'89*

William Russ
Traces of Red *'92*
Pastime *'91*

Dick Russell
River of Grass *'94*

Kimberly Russell
Hangin' with the Homeboys *'91*

Robert Russell
Bedazzled *'68*

Theresa Russell
Kafka *'91*

Victoria Russell
Tommy *'75*

James Russo
American Strays *'96*
My Own Private Idaho *'91*
Vortex *'81*

Leon Russom
The Big Lebowski *'97*

Margaret Rutherford
The Smallest Show on Earth *'57*
The Runaway Bus *'54*
Blithe Spirit *'45*

Allison Rutledge-Parisi
Metropolitan *'90*

Sif Ruud
Paradise Place *'77*
Face to Face *'76*

Bridget Ryan
Palookaville *'95*

Eileen Ryan
The Crossing Guard *'94*

Fran Ryan
Suture *'93*

John P. Ryan
Bound *'96*

Kathleen Ryan
Try and Get Me *'50*

Madge Ryan
Frenzy *'72*

Marisa Ryan
With or Without You *'98*

Michael Ryan
The Crossing Guard *'94*

Robert Ryan
The Iceman Cometh *'73*

Tim Ryan
Detour *'46*

Derek Rydell
Popcorn *'89*

Winona Ryder
The House of the Spirits '93
Night on Earth '91
Heathers '89

Patrick Ryecart
Twenty-One '91

Mark Rylance
Angels and Insects '95

Rex Ryon
Jack's Back '87

Bruno S
Every Man for Himself & God against All '75

Sabu
Black Narcissus '47

Nicholas Sadler
Acting on Impulse '93

Isabelle Sadoyan
Trois Couleurs: Bleu '93

Marianne Saegebrecht
Martha and I '91

Aniko Safar
The Unfinished Sentence in 141 Minutes '75

William Sage
High Art '98

Eric Saiet
Body Count '97

Susan Saiger
Eating Raoul '82

Raymond St. Jacques
Lost in the Stars '74

Susan St. James
S.O.S. Titanic '79

Michelle St. John
Smoke Signals '98

Octavia St. Laurant
Paris Is Burning '91

Helen St. Rayer
I Married a Witch '42

Louis Sainteve
Forbidden Games '52

Gene Saks
A Thousand Clowns '65

Chic Sale
You Only Live Once '37

Pamela Salem
Gods and Monsters '98

Mary Jo Salerno
A Modern Affair '94

Soupy Sales
...And God Spoke '94

John Salew
Kind Hearts and Coronets '49
Beware of Pity '46

Emmanuel Salinger
101 Nights '95

Tomi Salmela
Night on Earth '91

Jeffrey D. Sams
Fly by Night '93

Samantha Sams
Caged '97

Laura San Giacomo
Suicide Kings '97
Nina Takes a Lover '94
Under Suspicion '92
sex, lies and videotape '89

Barry Sand
Eddie and the Cruisers '83

Paul Sand
Second Coming of Suzanne '80

Dominique Sanda
The World of Jacques Demy '95
Steppenwolf '74
The Conformist '71

Walter Sande
The Red House '47

Otto Sander
Wings of Desire '88
The Marquise of O '76

Ann D. Sanders
Straight out of Brooklyn '91

George Sanders
Village of the Damned '60

Henry Sanders
Boss' Son '78

Jay O. Sanders
The Matchmaker '97
Just Like in the Movies '90

Richard Sanders
Forbidden Choices '94

Martyn Sanderson
An Angel at My Table '89

Debra Sandlund
Tough Guys Don't Dance '87

Christopher Sandord
Deep End '70

Stefania Sandrelli
The Sleazy Uncle '89
The Conformist '71

Julian Sands
Leaving Las Vegas '95
Grand Isle '91
Impromptu '90
A Room with a View '86

Ellen Sandweiss
Evil Dead '83

Yip Sang
Center Stage '91

Barbara Sanon
Straight out of Brooklyn '91

Renoly Santiago
Hackers '95

Phyllis Sanz
The Refrigerator '91

Eric Sapp
Little Shots of Happiness '97

Richard Sarafian
Bound '96
The Crossing Guard '94

Susan Sarandon
Dead Man Walking '95
Who Am I This Time? '82

Martine Sarcey
In a Wild Moment '78

Dick Sargent
Acting on Impulse '93

Lewis Sargent
Oliver Twist '22

Daniel Sarky
Emmanuelle '74

Gailard Sartain
Open Season '95
The Spitfire Grill '95
Equinox '93
The Grifters '90
Trouble in Mind '86

Tura Satana
Faster, Pussycat! Kill! Kill! '65

Gary Sauer
The Unbelievable Truth '90

Jennifer Saunders
Spice World: The Movie '97

Didier Sauvegrain
Roads to the South '78

Ann Savage
Detour '46

John Savage
American Strays '96
The Crossing Guard '94
Salvador '86

John Savident
Impromptu '90
Mountains of the Moon '90
Butley '74

Joe Savino
The Crying Game '92

Camille Saviola
Last Exit to Brooklyn '90

Joseph Sawyer
The Killing '56

David Saxon
A Hard Day's Night '64

John Saxon
Wes Craven's New Nightmare '94

John Sayles
City of Hope '91
Eight Men Out '88
Return of the Secaucus 7 '80

Greta Scacchi
The Player '92
White Mischief '88
Heat and Dust '82

Hubert Scales
Sweet Sweetback's Baadasssss Song '71

Prunella Scales
An Awfully Big Adventure '94
A Chorus of Disapproval '89
The Lonely Passion of Judith Hearne '87
Room at the Top '59

Renato Scarpa
The Postman '94

Diana Scarwid
Bastard out of Carolina '96

Johnathon Schaech
The Doom Generation '95

Joshua Schaefer
johns '96

Rebecca Schaeffer
Scenes from the Class Struggle in Beverly Hills '89

William Schallert
Gog '54

Sabrina Scharf
Easy Rider '69

Roy Scheider
The Myth of Fingerprints '97

Maria Schell
Voyage of the Damned '76
The Odessa File '74
The Mark '61
White Nights '57

Maximilian Schell
Little Odessa '94
The Man in the Glass Booth '75
The Odessa File '74
Return from the Ashes '65

Jean Schertler
Pecker '98

Vincent Schiavelli
Cold Feet '89

Peter Schildt
Metamorphosis '75

Fred Schiller
Who Done It? '56

Heinz Schimmelpfennig
Strongman Ferdinand '76

Daniel Schlachet
Swoon '91

Jean Schlegel
Trois Couleurs: Rouge '94

Morgan Schmidt-Feng
Morgan's Cake *'88*

Hellena Schmied
Barcelona *'94*

Sybille Schmitz
Vampyr *'31*

Stefan Schnabel
Anna *'87*

Helen Schneider
Eddie and the Cruisers *'83*

Maria Schneider
Jane Eyre *'96*

Peter Schneider
The Second Awakening of Christa Klages *'78*

G. H. Schnell
Nosferatu *'22*

Lutz Schnell
Das Boot *'81*

Barbara Schock
From Hollywood to Deadwood *'89*

Michael Schoeffling
Longtime Companion *'90*

Jill Schoelen
Popcorn *'89*

Frank Schorpion
Random Encounter *'98*

Bitty Schram
Caught *'96*

Max Schreck
Nosferatu *'22*

Liev Schreiber
The Daytrippers *'96*
Walking and Talking *'96*
Party Girl *'94*

Ernst Schroder
The Odessa File *'74*

Greta Schroder
Nosferatu *'22*

Eric Schrody
Bang *'95*

Steven Schub
Caught *'96*

Heinz Schubert
Strongman Ferdinand *'76*

Maurice Schutz
Vampyr *'31*

Rusty Schwimmer
A Little Princess *'95*

Annabella Sciorra
Cop Land *'97*
The Funeral *'96*
The Addiction *'95*
True Love *'89*

Paul Scofield
A Delicate Balance *'73*

Alan Randolph Scott
Night on Earth *'91*

Campbell Scott
The Daytrippers *'96*
Big Night *'95*
Mrs. Parker and the Vicious Circle *'94*
Longtime Companion *'90*

Eileen Scott
Teenage Gang Debs *'66*

Evelyn Scott
Wicked Woman *'54*

Lizabeth Scott
Too Late for Tears *'49*
Pitfall *'48*

William Lee Scott
The Opposite of Sex *'98*

Kristin Scott Thomas
The English Patient *'96*
Angels and Insects *'95*
Four Weddings and a Funeral *'94*
A Handful of Dust *'88*

Bobbie Scroggins
The Woman in Question *'50*

Sean Scully
Phobia *'88*

Jenny Seagrove
A Chorus of Disapproval *'89*

Heather Sears
Room at the Top *'59*

John Sebastian
Message to Love: The Isle of Wight Festival, the Movie *'70*

Jean Seberg
Breathless *'59*

Kyle Secor
Delusion *'91*

Jon Seda
I Like It Like That *'94*

Kyra Sedgwick
Critical Care *'97*

Robert Sedgwick
Tune in Tomorrow *'90*

Alison Seebohm
A Hard Day's Night *'64*

George Segal
Flirting with Disaster *'95*
It's My Party *'95*

Nena Segal
The Refrigerator *'91*

Mil Seghers
Antonia's Line *'95*

Frederick Sehreicker
The Third Man *'49*

Edda Seipel
The Marquise of O *'76*

John Seitz
Five Corners *'88*

Jirinaova Sejbalova
Day for My Love *'77*

Marian Seldes
Affliction *'97*

Doug Self
Men in Love *'90*

Elizabeth Sellars
Madeleine *'50*

Tom Selleck
Open Season *'95*

Peter Sellers
The World of Henry Orient *'64*
Lolita *'62*
The Battle of the Sexes *'60*
The Smallest Show on Earth *'57*
John and Julie *'55*
The Ladykillers *'55*

Charles Sellon
Bulldog Drummond *'29*

Mortan Selten
The Ghost Goes West *'36*

Martin Semmelrogge
Das Boot *'81*

Willy Semmelrogge
Every Man for Himself & God against All *'75*

Rade Serbedzija
Before the Rain *'94*

Ivan Sergei
The Opposite of Sex *'98*

Assumpta Serna
Chain of Desire *'93*
Matador *'86*

Julieta Serrano
Tie Me Up! Tie Me Down! *'90*
Women on the Verge of a Nervous Breakdown *'88*
Matador *'86*
Dark Habits *'84*

Nestor Serrano
Hangin' with the Homeboys *'91*

Josephine Serre
Jane Eyre *'96*

Jacques Serres
Blue Country *'77*

John Serret
Return from the Ashes *'65*

John Sessions
Cousin Bette *'97*

Roshan Seth
London Kills Me *'91*
Little Dorrit, Film 1: Nobody's Fault *'88*
Little Dorrit, Film 2: Little Dorrit's Story *'88*
My Beautiful Laundrette *'85*

Chloe Sevigny
Trees Lounge *'96*
Kids *'95*

Ninon Sevilla
Aventurera *'49*

Rufus Sewell
Carrington *'95*
Twenty-One *'91*

Brendan Sexton III
Pecker *'98*
Hurricane Streets *'96*
Welcome to the Dollhouse *'95*

Athene Seyler
Non-Stop New York *'37*

Delphine Seyrig
Dear Michael *'76*

Glenn Shadix
The Applegates *'89*
Heathers *'89*

Serge Shakurov
100 Days after Childhood *'75*

Tony Shalhoub
Big Night *'95*

Amelia Shankley
Dreamchild *'85*

Ethel Shannon
Charley's Aunt *'25*

Harry Shannon
The Red House *'47*

Johnny Shannon
That'll Be the Day *'73*

Marlene Shapiro
Back Street Jane *'89*

Rick Shapiro
True Love *'89*

Abdul Hassan Sharif
Zebrahead *'92*

Ray Sharkey
Zebrahead *'92*
Scenes from the Class Struggle in Beverly Hills *'89*
Wired *'89*

Anastasia Sharp
Go Fish *'94*

Lesley Sharp
Priest *'94*
Naked *'93*
Rita, Sue & Bob Too *'87*

James Sharpe
Bang *'95*

N. Shaternikova
Professor Mamlock *'38*

Billy Joe Shaver
The Apostle *'97*

Helen Shaver
Open Season *'95*

Zebrahead '92

Anabel Shaw
Gun Crazy '49

Denis Shaw
Who Done It? '56

Fiona Shaw
Jane Eyre '96
Persuasion '95
London Kills Me '91
Mountains of the Moon '90
My Left Foot '89

Glen Byam Shaw
Look Back in Anger '58

Robert Shaw
The Luck of Ginger Coffey '64

Sandie Shaw
Eat the Rich '87
Absolute Beginners '86

Sebastian Shaw
High Season '88

Susan Shaw
Fire Maidens from Outer Space '56
The Woman in Question '50

Wallace Shawn
Critical Care '97
Mrs. Parker and the Vicious Circle '94
Vanya on 42nd Street '94
Scenes from the Class Struggle in Beverly Hills '89

Lin Shaye
Trading Favors '97

Robert Shaye
Wes Craven's New Nightmare '94

Chris Shearer
The Whole Wide World '96

Harry Shearer
Blood & Concrete: A Love Story '90

Jack Shearer
Golden Gate '93

Moira Shearer
Peeping Tom '60

Ally Sheedy
High Art '98

Gladys Sheehan
Hear My Song '91

Charlie Sheen
Eight Men Out '88
Platoon '86

Martin Sheen
Ninth Street '98
The Little Girl Who Lives down the Lane '76
Badlands '74
The Incident '67

Michael Sheen
Wilde '97

Barbara Shelley
Village of the Damned '60

Rachel Shelley
Photographing Fairies '97

Adrienne Shelly
Sudden Manhattan '96
Teresa's Tattoo '94
Trust '91
The Unbelievable Truth '90

Jean Shelton
The Method '87

Joy Shelton
Uneasy Terms '48

Lindsay Shelton
Forgotten Silver '96

Lei Lao Sheng
The Story of Qui Ju '91

Samuel Sheng
She's Vintage '98

Ben Shenkman
Pi '98

Chaz Lamas Shepard
Set It Off '96

Jewel Shepard
My Tutor '82

Jack Shepherd
Twenty-One '91

Suzanne Shepherd
Lolita '97
Palookaville '95

Mark Sheppard
In the Name of the Father '93

Anthony Sher
Shakespeare in Love '98
Mrs. Brown '97

Dinah Sheridan
The Railway Children '70
Genevieve '53

Jamey Sheridan
The Ice Storm '97

Richard Sheridan
The Secret of Roan Inish '94

Geraldine Sherman
Interlude '67

Lowell Sherman
Way Down East '20

Anthony Sherwood
Eddie and the Cruisers 2: Eddie Lives! '89

Siu Sheung
Center Stage '91

Vladek Sheybal
Return from the Ashes '65

Brooke Shields
Freeway '95

Steve Shill
The Missing Reel '90

Joseph Shiloah
Daughters, Daughters '74

Shogo Shimada
A-Ge-Man: Tales of a Golden Geisha '91

Sab Shimono
Suture '93
The Wash '88

Ronald Shiner
Thursday's Child '43
They Drive by Night '38

Zarifeh Shivah
Through the Olive Trees '94

Samia Shoaib
Pi '98
SubUrbia '96

Craig Shoemaker
Acting on Impulse '93

Dan Shor
Red Rock West '93

Florence Short
Way Down East '20

Winifred Shotter
John and Julie '55

John Shrapnel
How to Get Ahead in Advertising '89

Elisabeth Shue
Cousin Bette '97
Leaving Las Vegas '95
The Underneath '95
Twenty Bucks '93

Mort Shuman
The Little Girl Who Lives down the Lane '76
Jacques Brel Is Alive and Well and Living in Paris '75

Amanda Shun
The Last of the High Kings '96

Dorothy Shupenes
Wanda '70

Peter Shupenes
Wanda '70

William Sickingen
Medium Cool '69

Harold Siddons
Genevieve '53

Ann Sidney
Performance '70

Sylvia Sidney
Dead End '37
You Only Live Once '37
Sabotage '36

George Siegmann
Oliver Twist '22

Casey Siemaszko
Teresa's Tattoo '94

Nina Siemaszko
Suicide Kings '97
Twenty Bucks '93

Clovis Siemon
Blessing '94

Simone Signoret
Room at the Top '59
The Crucible '57

Maurice Sigrist
I Have Killed '24

Herbert Siguenza
Star Maps '97

Tusse Silberg
Citizen X '95

Karen Sillas
What Happened Was... '94

Henry Silva
The End of Violence '97
The Manchurian Candidate '62

Trinidad Silva
Alambrista! '77

Joe Silver
Rhinoceros '74

Veronique Silver
Dites-Lui Que Je L'Aime '77

Evan Silverberg
Happiness '98

Jonathan Silverman
Teresa's Tattoo '94

Alastair Sim
The Belles of St. Trinian's '53

Jean Simmons
So Long at the Fair '50
Black Narcissus '47
Great Expectations '46

Margi Simmons
With or Without You '98

Joey Simmrin
Star Kid '97

Francois Simon
Lumiere '76

Hugh Simon
Christabel '89

Luc Simon
Lancelot of the Lake '74

David Simonds
The Refrigerator '91

Brian Simpson
Star Kid '97

Peggy Simpson
The 39 Steps '35

Joan Sims
The Belles of St. Trinian's '53

Frank Sinatra
The Manchurian Candidate *'62*

Leon Singer
My Family *'94*

Lori Singer
Equinox *'93*
Short Cuts *'93*
Trouble in Mind *'86*

Cheryl Singleton
She's Gotta Have It *'86*

Joseph Siravo
Walking and Talking *'96*

Jeremy Sisto
Bongwater *'98*
Suicide Kings *'97*

Errol Sitahal
A Little Princess *'95*

Jimmie F. Skaggs
Thousand Pieces of Gold *'91*

Lilia Skala
House of Games *'87*
Heartland *'81*

Stellan Skarsgard
Good Will Hunting *'97*
Breaking the Waves *'95*
The Unbearable Lightness of Being *'88*

Hal Skelly
Struggle *'31*

Alison Skilbeck
The Missing Reel *'90*

Anita Skinner
Girlfriends *'78*

Claire Skinner
Naked *'93*

Keith Skinner
The Slipper and the Rose *'76*

Irene Skobline
Coup de Torchon *'81*

Ione Skye
Went to Coney Island on a Mission from God...Be Back by Five *'98*
Gas Food Lodging *'92*
Guncrazy *'92*
River's Edge *'87*

Pavel Slaby
The Unbearable Lightness of Being *'88*

Barbara Slater
The Lady Confesses *'45*

Brandon Slater
Pariah *'98*

Christian Slater
Heathers *'89*

Helen Slater
A House in the Hills *'93*
Sticky Fingers *'88*

Carrie Slaza
I Love You, I Love You Not *'97*

Cynthia Sley
Rhythm Thief *'94*

Grace Slick
Gimme Shelter *'70*

Stephane Slima
Mina Tannenbaum *'93*

Phillips Smalley
Charley's Aunt *'25*

Jimmy Smallhorne
2 by 4 *'98*

Amy Smart
Campfire Tales *'98*

Rebecca Smart
Celia: Child of Terror *'90*

Feark Smink
For a Lost Soldier *'93*

Marten Smit
For a Lost Soldier *'93*

Alexis Smith
The Little Girl Who Lives down the Lane *'76*

Allison Smith
Wildflower *'91*

Barry Smith
Caged *'97*

Britta Smith
In the Name of the Father *'93*

Brooke Smith
Kansas City *'95*
Vanya on 42nd Street *'94*

Buck Smith
Poison *'91*

Cedric Smith
Anne of Green Gables *'85*

Charles Martin Smith
And the Band Played On *'93*

Cyril Smith
John and Julie *'55*
Sidewalks of London *'38*

Ebbe Roe Smith
The Big Easy *'87*

Gregory Smith
My Teacher Ate My Homework *'98*

Howard Smith
I Bury the Living *'58*

J. Smith
Gal Young 'Un *'79*

Janet Smith
The Rosary Murders *'87*

Joe Smith
Starving Artists *'97*

Kent Smith
The Balcony *'63*

Kevin Smith
Chasing Amy *'97*
Independent's Day *'97*
Mallrats *'95*

Kurtwood Smith
Citizen Ruth *'96*
To Die For *'95*

Lewis Smith
Diary of a Hitman *'91*

Liz Smith
Apartment Zero *'88*

Lois Smith
Dead Man Walking *'95*

Madeleine Smith
Galileo *'73*

Maggie Smith
The Lonely Passion of Judith Hearne *'87*
A Room with a View *'86*
The Prime of Miss Jean Brodie *'69*
Hot Millions *'68*

Mike Smith
Having a Wild Weekend *'65*

Muriel Smith
Moulin Rouge *'52*

Russell Smith
The Giving *'91*

Thaddeus Smith
Road Games *'81*

Jimmy Smits
My Family *'94*

Ladislav Smoljak
Seclusion near a Forest *'76*

Jake Smollett
Eve's Bayou *'97*

Jurnee Smollett
Eve's Bayou *'97*

Meredith Snaider
Habit *'97*

William Snape
The Full Monty *'96*

Wesley Snipes
The Waterdance *'91*

Carrie Snodgress
The Ballad of Little Jo *'93*

Michele (Michael) Soavi
Creepers *'85*

Steven Soderbergh
Independent's Day *'97*

Sonja Sohn
Slam *'98*

Rudy Solari
Boss' Son *'78*

Helena Solberg
Carmen Miranda: Bananas Is My Business *'95*

Laly Soldevilla
Spirit of the Beehive *'73*

Vicente Soler
Bride to Be *'75*

P. J. Soles
Halloween *'78*

Paul Soles
Ticket to Heaven *'81*

Yulia Solntseva
Aelita: Queen of Mars *'24*

Jimmy Somerville
Orlando *'92*

Josef Sommer
The Rosary Murders *'87*

Gale Sondergaard
Hollywood on Trial *'76*

Agnes Soral
In a Wild Moment *'78*

Alberto Sordi
An Average Little Man *'77*

Alexandra Sorina
The Hands of Orlac *'25*

Mira Sorvino
Barcelona *'94*

Roberto Sosa
Hombres Armados *'97*
Cabeza de Vaca *'90*

Ann Sothern
The Whales of August *'87*

Zinedine Soualem
When the Cat's Away *'96*

J. D. Souther
To Cross the Rubicon *'91*

Mathe Souverbie
Why Not! *'78*

Roger Souza
The Vanishing *'88*

Kurt Sowinetz
False Weights *'74*

Arthur Space
The Red House *'47*

Sissy Spacek
Affliction *'97*
Badlands *'74*

Kevin Spacey
The Usual Suspects *'95*
Swimming with Sharks *'94*

James Spader
Critical Care *'97*
Crash *'95*
sex, lies and videotape *'89*
Jack's Back *'87*

Merrie Spaeth
The World of Henry Orient *'64*

Douglas Spain
Star Maps '97

Timothy Spall
Secrets and Lies '95

Vincent Spano
The Tie That Binds '95
City of Hope '91

Bogdan Spasov
Last Summer '74

Bernard Spear
Bedazzled '68

Phil Spector
Easy Rider '69

Hugo Speer
The Full Monty '96

Tori Spelling
The House of Yes '97

Peter Spellos
Bound '96

Sebastian Spence
The Boys of St. Vincent '93

Timmy Spence
Vegas in Space '94

Charles Spencer
Another Country '84

John Spencer
Cop Land '97

Jeremy Spenser
Kind Hearts and Coronets '49

Shirley Speril
Glen or Glenda? '53

David Spielberg
Red Ribbon Blues '95

Mickey Spillane
Mommy '95

Frank Spinella
Teenage Gang Debs '66

Victor Spinetti
The Making of "A Hard Day's Night" '94
The Krays '90
Voyage of the Damned '76
The Little Prince '74
Start the Revolution without Me '70
Help! '65
A Hard Day's Night '64

Tony Spiridakis
Queens Logic '91

Lisa Spoonhauer
Clerks '94

Gregory Sporleder
Clay Pigeons '98

Elizabeth Spriggs
Impromptu '90

Dina Spybey
SubUrbia '96

Bill Stacey
Road Games '81

Jerry Stahl
Permanent Midnight '98

Ernest Stahl-Nachbaur
M '31

Philip Stainton
Who Done It? '56

Marion Stalens
Trois Couleurs: Rouge '94

Sylvester Stallone
Cop Land '97

Terence Stamp
The Adventures of Priscilla, Queen of the Desert '94
Hu-Man '76

Joan Standing
Oliver Twist '22

John Standing
Chaplin '92

Natalie Stanford
Swoon '91

Goran Stangertz
Paradise Place '77

Jill Stanley
Tommy Tricker & the Stamp Traveller '87

M. Louise Stanley
Morgan's Cake '88

Don Stannard
Pink String and Sealing Wax '45

Vivian Stanshall
Black Joy '77

Harry Dean Stanton
Wild at Heart '90
Twister '89
Mr. North '88

Barbara Stanwyck
Crime of Passion '57

Don Stark
Switchblade Sisters '75

Graham Stark
Alfie '66

Emerald Starr
Men in Love '90

Fredro Starr
The Addiction '95

Ringo Starr
Lisztomania '75
That'll Be the Day '73
Help! '65
A Hard Day's Night '64

Dina Stat
The Fable of the Beautiful Pigeon Fancier '88

Imelda Staunton
Shakespeare in Love '98
Citizen X '95

Much Ado about Nothing '93

Alison Steadman
Shirley Valentine '89

Rick Stear
Went to Coney Island on a Mission from God...Be Back by Five '98

Barbara Steele
8½ '63

Karen Steele
Marty '55

Jan Steen
Antonia's Line '95

Mary Steenburgen
My Family '94
The Whales of August '87

Rod Steiger
The Ballad of the Sad Cafe '91
The Mark '61

Andrea Stein
Shelf Life '94

Franz Stein
M '31

June Stein
High Stakes '89

Saul Stein
New Jersey Drive '95

Wolfgang Steinberg
Salmonberries '91

Michael Steinhardt
High Stakes '89

Vladimir Steklov
To See Paris and Die '93

Karel Stepanek
The Fallen Idol '49

Aram Stephane
French Provincial '75

Martin Stephens
The Innocents '61
Village of the Damned '60

Nancy Stephens
Halloween: H20 '98
Halloween '78

Robert Stephens
Century '94
Chaplin '92
High Season '88
Wonderland '88
Luther '74
The Private Life of Sherlock Holmes '70
The Prime of Miss Jean Brodie '69
Morgan! '66

Toby Stephens
Cousin Bette '97
Photographing Fairies '97

Maureen Stephenson
The Wild Party '56

Jan Sterling
The Incident '67
1984 '56

Tisha Sterling
The Whales of August '87
The Killer inside Me '76

Agnes Stevenin
Hu-Man '76

Jean-Francois Stevenin
Small Change '76

Brinke Stevens
Mommy '95
Acting on Impulse '93

Fisher Stevens
Hackers '95
Nina Takes a Lover '94

Michael Stevens
The Return of Tommy Tricker '94

Scott Thompson Stevens
Acting on Impulse '93

Cynthia Stevenson
Happiness '98
The Player '92

Alexandra Stewart
Black Moon '75

Charlotte Stewart
Eraserhead '78

Jack Stewart
The Little Kidnappers '53

Kate McGregor Stewart
Safe '95

Paul Stewart
The Wild Party '56
Kiss Me Deadly '55
Champion '49

Peggy Stewart
Girls in Chains '43

Roy Stewart
Sparrows '26

Ben Stiller
Permanent Midnight '98
Flirting with Disaster '95

Stephen Stills
Gimme Shelter '70

Sting
Julia and Julia '87

Michael Stipe
Color of a Brisk and Leaping Day '95

Nigel Stock
Victim '61

Carl Stockdale
Oliver Twist '22

Dean Stockwell
The Player '92
Blue Velvet '86
Tracks '76

John Stockwell
Eddie and the Cruisers *'83*

Jean Stoddard
You Only Live Once *'37*

Malcolm Stoddard
Luther *'74*

Mink Stole
Pecker *'98*
Serial Mom *'94*
Female Trouble *'74*

Shirley Stoler
Frankenhooker *'90*
Miami Blues *'90*
Sticky Fingers *'88*
Seven Beauties *'76*

Eric Stoltz
Grace of My Heart *'96*
Pulp Fiction *'94*
Bodies, Rest & Motion *'93*
The Waterdance *'91*

Lena Stolze
The Nasty Girl *'90*

Elly Stone
Jacques Brel Is Alive and Well and Living in Paris *'75*

John Stone
The Frightened City *'61*

Julia Stone
Sirens *'94*

Marianne Stone
In Possession *'84*
Having a Wild Weekend *'65*
Lolita *'62*

Philip Stone
The Shining *'80*

Sharon Stone
Diary of a Hitman *'91*

Adam Storke
Mystic Pizza *'88*

Olaf Storm
Metropolis *'26*

Peter Stormare
The Big Lebowski *'97*
Fargo *'96*

Sandra Storme
Clouds over Europe *'39*

Ken Stott
Shallow Grave *'94*

Jerry Stovin
Lolita *'62*

Madeleine Stowe
Short Cuts *'93*
Closet Land *'90*

Jason Stracey
Ladybird, Ladybird *'93*

Susan Stranks
Madeleine *'50*

Fritz Strassny
The Hands of Orlac *'25*

David Strathairn
Passion Fish *'92*
City of Hope *'91*
Eight Men Out *'88*
Matewan *'87*
Return of the Secaucus 7 *'80*

John Stratton
Abandon Ship *'57*

Meryl Streep
The House of the Spirits *'93*

Russell Streiner
Night of the Living Dead *'68*

Stephen Strimpell
Hester Street *'75*

Jenny Stringfellow
Gal Young 'Un *'79*

Elaine Stritch
Who Killed Teddy Bear? *'65*

Oliver Stritzel
Das Boot *'81*

Shiloh Strong
House of Cards *'92*

Don Stroud
The Killer inside Me *'76*

John Stuart
Village of the Damned *'60*
John and Julie *'55*

Imogen Stubbs
A Summer Story *'88*

Jerzy Stuhr
Trois Couleurs: Blanc *'94*

Neil Stuke
Century *'94*

Michael Stumm
Swoon *'91*

Tara Subkoff
Lover Girl *'97*
All Over Me *'96*

Michel Such
Dites-Lui Que Je L'Aime *'77*

David Suchet
A World Apart *'88*

Yoko Sugi
Picture Bride *'94*

Ania Suli
Fun *'94*

Francis L. Sullivan
Great Expectations *'46*
Non-Stop New York *'37*

Hugh Sullivan
In Possession *'84*

Michelle Sullivan
Poison *'91*

Sarah Sullivan
Red Rock West *'93*

Frank Summerscales
Children of the Damned *'63*

Scott Sunderland
Pygmalion *'38*

Bjorn Sundquist
The Feldmann Case *'87*

Donald Sutherland
Citizen X *'95*
The Rosary Murders *'87*
Eye of the Needle *'81*
Start the Revolution without Me *'70*
Interlude *'67*

James Sutherland
The Little Kidnappers *'53*

Kiefer Sutherland
Freeway *'95*

Dudley Sutton
Orlando *'92*
Leather Boys *'63*

Frank Sutton
Marty *'55*

Janet Suzman
Nuns on the Run *'90*
Voyage of the Damned *'76*

Zdenek Sverak
Seclusion near a Forest *'76*

B. Svetlov
Professor Mamlock *'38*

Dominique Swain
Lolita *'97*

Robert Swann
If... *'69*

Gloria Swanson
Queen Kelly *'29*

Kristy Swanson
Lover Girl *'97*

Maureen Swanson
Moulin Rouge *'52*

Peter Swanwick
The African Queen *'51*

Don Swayze
Shy People *'87*

Patrick Swayze
Dirty Dancing *'87*

Swedish National Soccer Team
Stubby *'74*

Birdie Sweeney
The Crying Game *'92*

D. B. Sweeney
Eight Men Out *'88*

Vonte Sweet
American Strays *'96*
Menace II Society *'93*

Clive Swift
Frenzy *'72*
Having a Wild Weekend *'65*

Nora Swinburne
Interlude *'67*

Tilda Swinton
Orlando *'92*

Deborah Swisher
The Method *'87*

Meera Syal
Sammy & Rosie Get Laid *'87*

Derek Sydney
Hand in Hand *'60*

Kary Sylway
Face to Face *'76*

Sylvia Syms
A Chorus of Disapproval *'89*
Shirley Valentine *'89*
Victim *'61*

Laszlo Szabo
The Unbearable Lightness of Being *'88*
The Red Poster *'76*
Adoption *'75*

Sandor Szabo
The Hungarians *'78*

Presco Tabios
Chan Is Missing *'82*

Kristopher Tabori
Girlfriends *'78*

Ljuba Tadic
Fear *'75*

Sydney Tafler
Alfie *'66*
Fire Maidens from Outer Space *'56*
Uneasy Terms *'48*

Cary-Hiroyuki Tagawa
Picture Bride *'94*

Hiromasa Taguchi
Shall We Dance? *'96*

Taj Mahal
The Rolling Stones Rock and Roll Circus *'68*

Akira Takayama
Picture Bride *'94*

Naoto Takenaka
Shall We Dance? *'96*

Odette Talazac
The Rules of the Game *'39*

Gloria Talbot
Crashout *'55*

Lyle Talbot
Plan 9 from Outer Space *'56*
Glen or Glenda? *'53*

Michael Talbot
Acting on Impulse *'93*

William Talman
Crashout *'55*

Russ Tamblyn
Gun Crazy '49

Jeffrey Tambor
A House in the Hills '93
Pastime '91
Lisa '90

Zoe Tamerlis
Special Effects '85

Mary Tamm
The Odessa File '74

Jessica Tandy
The House on Carroll Street '88
Butley '74

Mark Tandy
Maurice '87

Gordon Tanner
Time Lock '57

Quentin Tarantino
Destiny Turns on the Radio '95
Pulp Fiction '94
Reservoir Dogs '92

Lilyan Tashman
Bulldog Drummond '29

Rolf Tasna
The Devil Is a Woman '75

Larenz Tate
Love Jones '96
Menace II Society '93

Aino Taube-Henrikson
Face to Face '76

Bernd Tauber
Das Boot '81

Bertrand Tavernier
The World of Jacques Demy '95

Nils Tavernier
Mina Tannenbaum '93

Tuvio Tavi
The Garden '77

Christine Taylor
Campfire Tales '98

Dolly Taylor
The Killing of Sister George '69

Frank Hoyt Taylor
Matewan '87

Henry Taylor
You Only Live Once '37

Holland Taylor
To Die For '95

Lili Taylor
Pecker '98
I Shot Andy Warhol '96
The Addiction '95
Girls Town '95
Mrs. Parker and the Vicious Circle '94
Household Saints '93
Short Cuts '93
Mystic Pizza '88

Meshach Taylor
House of Games '87

Mick Taylor
Gimme Shelter '70

Noah Taylor
Shine '95

Rod Taylor
Open Season '95
Separate Tables '58

Valerie Taylor
Repulsion '65

Ivan Tchenko
Isadora '68

A. Tcherstvov
The Orphans '77

Godfrey Tearle
The 39 Steps '35

Verree Teasdale
Turnabout '40

James Telfer
Apartment Zero '88

Isabel Telleria
Spirit of the Beehive '73

Jean Temple
His Picture in the Papers '16

Johanna Ter Steege
The Vanishing '88

Studs Terkel
Eight Men Out '88

Solveig Ternstrom
Paradise Place '77

John Canada Terrell
Def by Temptation '90
She's Gotta Have It '86

Yolande Terrell
They Drive by Night '38

Terry-Thomas
Lucky Jim '58

Desmond Tester
Non-Stop New York '37
Nine Days a Queen '36
Sabotage '36

Katharina Thalbach
The Second Awakening of Christa Klages '78

Torin Thatcher
Great Expectations '46
Young and Innocent '37
Sabotage '36

John Thaw
Chaplin '92
Business As Usual '88

Phyllis Thaxter
The World of Henry Orient '64

Jerome Their
Wanda '70

Marian Their
Wanda '70

Diana Theodore
My Teacher Ate My Homework '98

Justin Theroux
Body Count '97

Ernest Thesiger
The Battle of the Sexes '60
Who Done It? '56
Beware of Pity '46
Don't Take It to Heart '44
They Drive by Night '38

David Thewlis
The Big Lebowski '97
The Island of Dr. Moreau '96
Black Beauty '94
Naked '93

Alan Thicke
Open Season '95

Kevin Thigpen
Just Another Girl on the I.R.T. '93

Ben Thomas
Sorrento Beach '95

Dudley Thomas
My Beautiful Laundrette '85

Harry Thomas
Glen or Glenda? '53

Henry Thomas
Suicide Kings '97
Curse of the Starving Class '94

Hugh Thomas
If... '69

Jeffrey Thomas
Forgotten Silver '96

Koran C. Thomas
New Jersey Drive '95

Leonard Thomas
Bad Lieutenant '92

Marlo Thomas
The Real Blonde '97
In the Spirit '90

Robin Thomas
Star Maps '97

Trevor Thomas
Black Joy '77

Wynfold Vaughn Thomas
John and Julie '55

Florence Thomassin
Mina Tannenbaum '93

Greg Thomey
The Boys of St. Vincent '93

Anna Thompson
I Shot Andy Warhol '96

Derek Thompson
The Long Good Friday '80

Elizabeth Thompson
Metropolitan '90

Emma Thompson
Carrington '95
In the Name of the Father '93
Much Ado about Nothing '93
The Remains of the Day '93
Impromptu '90

Jack Thompson
Caddie '76

Lea Thompson
The Wizard of Loneliness '88

Marshall Thompson
Crashout '55

Patsy Ann Thompson
Tomorrow the World '44

Shelley Thompson
Just Like a Woman '92

Sophie Thompson
Persuasion '95
Four Weddings and a Funeral '94
Twenty-One '91

Teri Thompson
Breakaway '95

William C. Thompson
Glen or Glenda? '53

Pat Thomsen
Strictly Ballroom '92

Sally Thomsett
The Railway Children '70

Anna Thomson
Angela '94

R. H. Thomson
Ticket to Heaven '81

Frankie Thorn
Bad Lieutenant '92

Sybil Thorndike
Hand in Hand '60
Nine Days a Queen '36

Billy Bob Thornton
The Apostle '97
U-Turn '97
Sling Blade '96
Dead Man '95
One False Move '91

David Thornton
High Art '98

Peggy Thorpe-Bates
Georgy Girl '66

Ingrid Thulin
Return from the Ashes '65

Dechen Thurman
I Think I Do '97

Uma Thurman
Pulp Fiction '94

Sophie Thursfield
Sister My Sister *'94*

Brigid Tierney
Affliction *'97*

Lawrence Tierney
Reservoir Dogs *'92*
City of Hope *'91*
Tough Guys Don't Dance *'87*

Maura Tierney
Fly by Night *'93*

Kevin Tighe
City of Hope *'91*
Eight Men Out *'88*
Matewan *'87*

Ramon Tikaram
Kama Sutra: A Tale of Love *'96*

Viatcheslav Tikhonov
Burnt by the Sun *'94*

Grant Tilly
Brilliant Lies *'96*

Jennifer Tilly
American Strays *'96*
Bound *'96*
Bullets over Broadway *'94*

M. Timofeyev
Professor Mamlock *'38*

Alec Timoushin
The Children of Theatre Street *'77*

Tiny Tim
Message to Love: The Isle of Wight Festival, the Movie *'70*

Tippi
Vegas in Space *'94*

Ann Tirard
Perfect Friday *'70*

Daniel Tisman
...And God Spoke *'94*

Stephen Tobolowsky
Nobody's Fool *'86*

Ann Todd
Madeleine *'50*

Michael Todd
Caged *'97*

Richard Todd
The Very Edge *'63*

Sonia Todd
Shine *'95*

Zen Todd
Killer Flick *'98*

Niall Toibin
Frankie Starlight *'95*

Boris Tokarev
100 Days after Childhood *'75*

Marilyn Tokuda
My Tutor *'82*

Yu Tokui
Shall We Dance? *'96*

Kathleen Tolan
The Rosary Murders *'87*

Michael Toland
Eddie and the Cruisers *'83*

Joe Tolbe
Men in Love *'90*

Concetta Tomei
Twenty Bucks *'93*

Marisa Tomei
Equinox *'93*
Chaplin *'92*

Frances Tomelty
Bellman and True *'88*

Joseph Tomelty
A Night to Remember *'58*
John and Julie *'55*

Tamlyn Tomita
Hundred Per Cent *'98*
Picture Bride *'94*

Lily Tomlin
Flirting with Disaster *'95*
And the Band Played On *'93*
Short Cuts *'93*

David Tomlinson
So Long at the Fair *'50*

Ricky Tomlinson
Butterfly Kiss *'94*

Jacqueline Tong
How to Get Ahead in Advertising *'89*

Chaim Topol
Galileo *'73*

Peta Toppano
Echoes of Paradise *'86*

Kimberly Topper
2 by 4 *'98*

Silva Torf
Joyless Street *'25*

Rip Torn
Cold Feet *'89*
Heartland *'81*

Regina Torne
Like Water for Chocolate *'93*

Pip Torrens
A Handful of Dust *'88*

Ana Torrent
Spirit of the Beehive *'73*

Toto
Passionate Thief *'60*

Merle Tottenham
This Happy Breed *'47*

Tamara Toumanova
The Private Life of Sherlock Holmes *'70*

Sheila Tousey
Medicine River *'94*
Silent Tongue *'92*

Lorraine Toussaint
Mother's Boys *'94*

Roland Toutain
The Rules of the Game *'39*

George Tovey
Frenzy *'72*

Constance Towers
Naked Kiss *'64*

Tom Towles
Normal Life *'96*

Toke Townley
The Runaway Bus *'54*

Omar Townsend
Party Girl *'94*

Robert Townsend
Hollywood Shuffle *'87*

Pete Townshend
Tommy *'75*
Message to Love: The Isle of Wight Festival, the Movie *'70*

Sheila Ivy Traister
Back Street Jane *'89*

Daniel J. Travanti
Who Killed Teddy Bear? *'65*

Bill Travers
The Smallest Show on Earth *'57*

Linden Travers
Beware of Pity *'46*
The Lady Vanishes *'38*

Susan Travers
Peeping Tom *'60*

Nancy Travis
Destiny Turns on the Radio *'95*
Chaplin *'92*

John Travolta
Pulp Fiction *'94*

Susan Traylor
Bastard out of Carolina *'96*
To Die For *'95*

Emerson Treacy
The Prowler *'51*

Edouard Trebaol
Oliver Twist *'22*

David Tree
Clouds over Europe *'39*
Pygmalion *'38*

Lady Tree
The Private Life of Henry VIII *'33*

Viola Tree
Pygmalion *'38*

Yann Tregouet
Trois Couleurs: Bleu *'93*

Jerzy Trela
Trois Couleurs: Blanc *'94*

Christine Tremarco
Priest *'94*

Adam Trese
Palookaville *'95*
The Underneath *'95*

N. Tretyakova
Aelita: Queen of Mars *'24*

Hilda Trevelyan
The 39 Steps *'35*

Frederick Treves
Paper Mask *'91*

Austin Trevor
Abandon Ship *'57*
So Long at the Fair *'50*
Night Train to Munich *'40*
Sabotage *'36*

Claire Trevor
Dead End *'37*

Leopoldo Trieste
Cinema Paradiso *'88*
A Virgin Named Mary *'75*
The Profiteer *'74*

Paul Trinka
Faster, Pussycat! Kill! Kill! *'65*

Jean-Louis Trintignant
Trois Couleurs: Rouge *'94*
The Conformist *'71*
Dangerous Liaisons *'60*

Jan Triska
Seclusion near a Forest *'76*

Massimo Troisi
The Postman *'94*

Karen Trott
Return of the Secaucus 7 *'80*

Cecil Trouncer
Pygmalion *'38*

Tom Troupe
My Own Private Idaho *'91*

Sinolicka Trpkova
Death of a Schoolboy *'91*

John Trudell
Smoke Signals *'98*

Jim True
Affliction *'97*
Normal Life *'96*

Rachel True
With or Without You *'98*

Francois Truffaut
The 400 Blows *'59*

David Trughton
Dance with a Stranger *'85*

Raoul Trujillo
Medicine River *'94*
Paris, France *'94*

Ralph Truman
Beware of Pity '46

Dalton Trumbo
Hollywood on Trial '76

Brad Trumbull
Crime of Passion '57

Christos Tsangas
Iphigenia '77

Paris Tselios
High Season '88

Nikolai Tseretelli
Aelita: Queen of Mars '24

Irene Tsu
Island of the Lost '68

Masahiko Tsugawa
A-Ge-Man: Tales of a Golden Geisha '91

Maria Tucci
To Die For '95

Stanley Tucci
The Daytrippers '96
Big Night '95
A Modern Affair '94
In the Soup '92

Chris Tucker
Jackie Brown '97

Richard Tucker
Helen's Babies '25

Patrick Tull
Parting Glances '86

Marco Tulli
Beat the Devil '53

D'iana Tunnell
Sore Losers '97

Robert Turano
Federal Hill '94

Joe Turkel
The Shining '80
The Killing '56

Jack Turlton
The Cater Street Hangman '98

John Turnbull
Nine Days a Queen '36
The 39 Steps '35
The Private Life of Henry VIII '33

Guinevere Turner
Go Fish '94

Ike Turner
Gimme Shelter '70

Janine Turner
The Ambulance '90

Jim Turner
Shelf Life '94

John Turner
The Slipper and the Rose '76

Kathleen Turner
The Real Blonde '97
Serial Mom '94
House of Cards '92
Julia and Julia '87

Marcus Turner
She's Gotta Have It '86

Mimi Turner
Chicken Hawk '94

Ray Turner
Turnabout '40

Tina Turner
Tommy '75
Gimme Shelter '70

Tyrin Turner
Menace II Society '93

Vickery Turner
The Good Soldier '81

Bahni Turpin
Daughters of the Dust '91

Aida Turturro
True Love '89

John Turturro
The Big Lebowski '97
Box of Moonlight '96
Grace of My Heart '96
Search and Destroy '94
Mac '93
Five Corners '88

Nicholas Turturro
Federal Hill '94
Mac '93

Rita Tushingham
The Boy from Mercury '96
An Awfully Big Adventure '94
Leather Boys '63

Shannon Tweed
Cannibal Women in the Avocado Jungle of Death '89

Geri Tyler
Teenage Gang Debs '66

Harry Tyler
I Married a Witch '42

Liv Tyler
U-Turn '97
Heavy '94

Susan Tyrrell
Motorama '91
The Killer inside Me '76

Cathy Tyson
Priest '94
Business As Usual '88
Mona Lisa '86

Alanna Ubach
Trading Favors '97
johns '96

Tracey Ullman
Bullets over Broadway '94
Household Saints '93

Liv Ullmann
Face to Face '76
Scenes from a Marriage '73

Edward Underdown
Beat the Devil '53

Blair Underwood
Set It Off '96

Jay Underwood
Afterglow '97

Avril Ungar
Room at the Top '59

Deborah Kara Unger
Crash '95

Mary Ure
The Luck of Ginger Coffey '64
Look Back in Anger '58

Nina Usatova
To See Paris and Die '93

Peter Ustinov
Hot Millions '68

Badi Uzzaman
My Beautiful Laundrette '85

Kari Vaananen
Night on Earth '91

Grigor Vachkov
Last Summer '74

Annette Vadim
Dangerous Liaisons '60

David Vadim
Little Odessa '94

Charlotte Valandrey
Orlando '92

Manuela Valasco
Law of Desire '86

Birgitta Valberg
Paradise Place '77

Vladimir Valenta
The Unbearable Lightness of Being '88

Jeanne Valeri
Dangerous Liaisons '60

Anne Valery
Kind Hearts and Coronets '49

Rosa Valetti
M '31

Frederick Valk
Saraband for Dead Lovers '48
Dead of Night '45
Night Train to Munich '40

Alida Valli
Dear Victor '75
The Stranger's Hand '54
The Third Man '49

Romolo Valli
An Average Little Man '77

Vampira
Plan 9 from Outer Space '56

Willeke Van Ammelrooy
Antonia's Line '95

Tomas Van Bromssen
My Life As a Dog '85

James Van Der Beek
I Love You, I Love You Not '97

Diana Van Der Vlis
The Incident '67

Kyle Van Horne
Killer Flick '98

Henry van Lyck
Every Man for Himself & God against All '75

Veerle Van Overloop
Antonia's Line '95

Frederik Van Pallandt
Hu-Man '76

Nina Van Pallandt
Cutter's Way '81

Mario Van Peebles
Sweet Sweetback's Baadasssss Song '71

Megan Van Peebles
Sweet Sweetback's Baadasssss Song '71

Melvin Van Peebles
Sweet Sweetback's Baadasssss Song '71

Alex Van Warmerdam
Abel '87

Alexander Van Wyk
Julia and Julia '87

Philip Van Zandt
Gog '54

Violet Vanbrugh
Pygmalion '38

Danitra Vance
Sticky Fingers '88

Marta Vancurova
Day for My Love '77

Renata Vanni
The Lady in White '88

Joanne Vannicola
Love and Human Remains '93

Evelyn Varden
The Night of the Hunter '55

Ingerid Vardung
The Feldmann Case '87

Antonio Vargas
Strictly Ballroom '92

Jacob Vargas
My Family '94
Gas Food Lodging '92

Beatrice Varley
Room at the Top *'59*
Young and Innocent *'37*

Indira Varma
Kama Sutra: A Tale of Love *'96*

Michael Vartan
The Myth of Fingerprints *'97*

Tatyana Vasilyeva
Coffee with Lemon *'94*
To See Paris and Die *'93*

Peter Vaughan
The Remains of the Day *'93*
Mountains of the Moon *'90*
Valentino *'77*

Vince Vaughn
Clay Pigeons *'98*

Ron Vawter
Swoon *'91*
sex, lies and videotape *'89*

Yul Vazquez
Fresh *'94*
Fly by Night *'93*

Isidra Vega
Hurricane Streets *'96*

Vladimir Vega
Ladybird, Ladybird *'93*

Conrad Veidt
The Hands of Orlac *'25*

Michael Veitch
Brilliant Lies *'96*

Lauren Velez
I Think I Do *'97*
I Like It Like That *'94*

Martha Velez
Star Maps *'97*

Mauricio Venegas
Ladybird, Ladybird *'93*

Amy Veness
Madeleine *'50*
This Happy Breed *'47*

John Ventimiglia
The Funeral *'96*
Girls Town *'95*
Angela *'94*

Elena Verdugo
Boss' Son *'78*

Bernard Verley
Pas Tres Catholique *'93*
Phantom of Liberty *'74*

Guy Verney
This Happy Breed *'47*

Jerry Verno
The Belles of St. Trinian's *'53*
Sidewalks of London *'38*
Non-Stop New York *'37*
Young and Innocent *'37*
The 39 Steps *'35*

Glenn Vernon
I Bury the Living *'58*

John Vernon
A Special Day *'77*

Richard Vernon
A Hard Day's Night *'64*
Village of the Damned *'60*

Valerie Vernon
Gog *'54*

Todd Verow
Little Shots of Happiness *'97*

Veruschka
Blow-Up *'66*

Arie Verveen
Caught *'96*

Charlotte Very
Trois Couleurs: Bleu *'93*

Edy Vessel
Passionate Thief *'60*

Ondrej Vetchy
Martha and I *'91*

Maria Vico
Bride to Be *'75*

Charles Victor
The Woman in Question *'50*

Erico Vidal
The Marriage *'76*

Henri Vidal
Sois Belle et Tais-Toi *'58*

Lisa Vidal
I Like It Like That *'94*

Steven Vidler
The Good Wife *'86*

Susan Vidler
Naked *'93*

Vince Vieluf
Clay Pigeons *'98*

Gyongyver Vigh
Adoption *'75*

Florence Vignon
Trois Couleurs: Bleu *'93*

Tom Villard
Popcorn *'89*
The Trouble with Dick *'88*

Libby Villari
The Whole Wide World *'96*

Gerardo Villarreal
Cabeza de Vaca *'90*

Jacques Villeret
The Favor, the Watch, and the Very Big Fish *'92*
Robert et Robert *'78*

James Villiers
Let Him Have It *'91*
Mountains of the Moon *'90*
Repulsion *'65*

Pruitt Taylor Vince
The End of Violence *'97*
Heavy *'94*
Shy People *'87*

Alex Vincent
Just Like in the Movies *'90*

Frank Vincent
Cop Land *'97*
She's the One *'96*
Federal Hill *'94*

Helene Vincent
Ma Vie en Rose *'97*
Trois Couleurs: Bleu *'93*

Al Vincente
Star Maps *'97*

Alan Vint
Badlands *'74*

Enzo Vitale
Seven Beauties *'76*

Juan Vitale
Apartment Zero *'88*

Joe Viterelli
American Strays *'96*
Bullets over Broadway *'94*
The Crossing Guard *'94*

Michel Vitold
France, Incorporated *'74*

Judith Vittet
The City of Lost Children *'95*

Monica Vitti
Phantom of Liberty *'74*

Sandra Voe
Breaking the Waves *'95*

Emmett Vogan
The Lady Confesses *'45*

Nikolas Vogel
Dangerous Liaisons *'60*

Tony Vogel
Isadora *'68*

Karl Michael Vogler
Deep End *'70*

Jon Voight
U-Turn *'97*
The Odessa File *'74*

Dimitrie Vojnov
Tito and Me *'92*

Andre Volbert
I Have Killed *'24*

Franco Volpi
Johnny Stecchino *'92*

Phillipe Volter
Trois Couleurs: Bleu *'93*

Sasha von Scherler
Party Girl *'94*

Gustav von Seyffertitz
Sparrows *'26*

Max von Sydow
Citizen X *'95*
Voyage of the Damned *'76*
Steppenwolf *'74*

Gustav von Wagenheim
Nosferatu *'22*

Hertha von Walther
M *'31*

Danielle von Zerneck
Living in Oblivion *'94*

Lena Voronzova
The Children of Theatre Street *'77*

George Voskovec
The Iceman Cometh *'73*

Frank Vosper
The Man Who Knew Too Much *'34*

Andreas Voutsinas
A Dream of Passion *'78*

Milena Vukotic
Phantom of Liberty *'74*

Vladimir Vyssozki
The Only One *'76*

Steven Waddington
Carrington *'95*

Michael Wade
The Boys of St. Vincent *'93*

Julian Wadham
The English Patient *'96*
The Madness of King George *'94*

Anthony Wager
Great Expectations *'46*

Natasha Gregson Wagner
Lost Highway *'96*

Elsie Wagstaff
Whistle down the Wind *'61*

Mark Wahlberg
Boogie Nights *'97*
The Basketball Diaries *'94*

Eric Tsiang Chi Wai
Eat a Bowl of Tea *'89*

Rupert Wainwright
Another Country *'84*

Tom Waits
Short Cuts *'93*
Queens Logic *'91*
Cold Feet *'89*

Hugh Wakefield
Blithe Spirit *'45*
The Man Who Knew Too Much *'34*

Rick Wakeman
Lisztomania *'75*

Aesha Waks
Went to Coney Island on a Mission from God...Be Back by Five *'98*

Anton Walbrook
Gaslight '40

Hynden Walch
Sudden Manhattan '96

Gregory Walcott
Plan 9 from Outer Space '56

Christopher Walken
Suicide Kings '97
Basquiat '96
The Funeral '96
The Addiction '95
Pulp Fiction '94
Search and Destroy '94
The Comfort of Strangers '91
Who Am I This Time? '82

Amanda Walker
Heat and Dust '82

Arnetia Walker
Scenes from the Class Struggle in Beverly Hills '89

Corban Walker
Frankie Starlight '95

Helen Walker
Impact '49

Jimmie Walker
Open Season '95

Kathryn Walker
Girlfriends '78

Kerry Walker
Cosi '95
The Piano '93

Kim Walker
Heathers '89

Mark Walker
Random Encounter '98

Nicholas Walker
Body Count '97

Polly Walker
Enchanted April '92

Robert Walker Jr.
Easy Rider '69

Stephen Walker
Alambrista! '77

Sydney Walker
Who Are the DeBolts and Where Did They Get 19 Kids? '78

Tippy Walker
The World of Henry Orient '64

Willie Boy Walker
Morgan's Cake '88

Anita Wall
Scenes from a Marriage '73

Max Wall
Little Dorrit, Film 1: Nobody's Fault '88
Little Dorrit, Film 2: Little Dorrit's Story '88

Jack Wallace
Boogie Nights '97

Leroy Wallace
Rockers '79

Dee Wallace Stone
Popcorn '89

Eli Wallach
Girlfriends '78

David Waller
Perfect Friday '70

Gunn Wallgren
Metamorphosis '75

Sandy Walper
The Whole Wide World '96

J. T. Walsh
Sling Blade '96
The Last Seduction '94
Red Rock West '93
The Grifters '90
Wired '89
House of Games '87

Kathleen Walsh
Killer Flick '98

Kay Walsh
This Happy Breed '47

M. Emmet Walsh
Equinox '93
Blood Simple '85

Percy Walsh
Thursday's Child '43

Susan Walsh
Female Trouble '74

Ray Walston
Popcorn '89

Harriet Walter
The Governess '98

Mr. Walter
Glen or Glenda? '53

Tracey Walter
Destiny Turns on the Radio '95
Delusion '91

Hal Walters
Sabotage '36

Hugh Walters
Having a Wild Weekend '65

Julie Walters
Just Like a Woman '92
Sister My Sister '94

Melora Walters
Boogie Nights '97
American Strays '96
Hard Eight '96
Twenty Bucks '93

Thorley Walters
Twisted Nerve '68
Who Done It? '56

Lisa Waltz
Red Ribbon Blues '95

Irene Wan
Love unto Waste '86

Madame Sul Te Wan
Queen Kelly '29

Sam Wanamaker
Voyage of the Damned '76
The Battle of the Sexes '60

Zoe Wanamaker
Wilde '97

Faye Wang
Chungking Express '95

Garrett Wang
Hundred Per Cent '98

Peter Wang
Chan Is Missing '82

Yu-Wen Wang
Eat Drink Man Woman '94

Grzegorz Warchol
Trois Couleurs: Blanc '94

Christy Ward
Sling Blade '96

Colin Ward
Mother's Boys '94

Dave Oren Ward
Pariah '98

Fred Ward
Equinox '93
Short Cuts '93
Two Small Bodies '93
The Player '92
Miami Blues '90

Mary B. Ward
Smoke '95
Hangin' with the Homeboys '91

Rachel Ward
After Dark, My Sweet '90
How to Get Ahead in Advertising '89
The Good Wife '86

Ronald Ward
Sidewalks of London '38

Sophie Ward
Little Dorrit, Film 1: Nobody's Fault '88
Little Dorrit, Film 2: Little Dorrit's Story '88
A Summer Story '88

Wally Ward
The Chocolate War '88

Harlan Warde
Money Madness '47

Jack Warden
Bullets over Broadway '94

S. J. Warmington
Sabotage '36

Gordon Warnecke
London Kills Me '91
My Beautiful Laundrette '85

David Warner
Mr. North '88
S.O.S. Titanic '79
Perfect Friday '70
Morgan! '66

Jack Warner
The Ladykillers '55

Jeremiah Warner
The Wizard of Loneliness '88

Maggie Warner
High Stakes '89

Richard Warner
Village of the Damned '60

Steven Warner
The Little Prince '74

Betty Warren
So Long at the Fair '50

C. Denier Warren
Lolita '62

Gary Warren
The Railway Children '70

Jennifer Leigh Warren
Grace of My Heart '96
The Crossing Guard '94

Katherine Warren
The Prowler '51

Ruth Warrick
Guest in the House '44

Kenneth Warrington
Beware of Pity '46

Dan Warry-Smith
My Teacher Ate My Homework '98

Richard Warwick
If... '69

Robert Warwick
I Married a Witch '42

Mona Washbourne
If... '69

Beverly Washburn
Spider Baby '64

Denzel Washington
Much Ado about Nothing '93
For Queen and Country '88

Don Washington
Ninth Street '98

Isaiah Washington
Love Jones '96

Jerard Washington
Just Another Girl on the I.R.T. '93

Andre Wasley
Forbidden Games '52

Dick Wassel
Pitfall '48

Eriko Watanabe
Shall We Dance? *'96*

Dennis Waterman
Fright *'71*

Wayne Waterman
Salmonberries *'91*

Russell Waters
The Hidden Room *'49*

Sam Waterston
Serial Mom *'94*

Gwen Watford
The Very Edge *'63*
Never Take Candy from a Stranger *'60*

Tuc Watkins
I Think I Do *'97*

Deborah Watling
That'll Be the Day *'73*

Jack Watling
A Night to Remember *'58*

Alberta Watson
The Sweet Hereafter *'96*
Hackers *'95*
Spanking the Monkey *'94*

Emily Watson
Breaking the Waves *'95*

Jack Watson
Peeping Tom *'60*

Minor Watson
Dead End *'37*

Wylie Watson
Don't Take It to Heart *'44*
The 39 Steps *'35*

Richard Wattis
The Belles of St. Trinian's *'53*

Charlie Watts
Gimme Shelter *'70*

Jeanne Watts
Three Sisters *'70*

Queenie Watts
Alfie *'66*

Al Waxman
Critical Care *'97*

Damon Wayans
Hollywood Shuffle *'87*

Keenen Ivory Wayans
Hollywood Shuffle *'87*

Tishan Waymire
She's Vintage *'98*

Keith Wayne
Night of the Living Dead *'68*

Ken Wayne
One Night Stand *'76*

Naunton Wayne
The Hidden Room *'49*
Dead of Night *'45*
Night Train to Munich *'40*
The Lady Vanishes *'38*

Jacki Weaver
Cosi *'95*
Caddie *'76*
Picnic at Hanging Rock *'75*

Sigourney Weaver
The Ice Storm *'97*
Death and the Maiden *'94*

Hugo Weaving
The Adventures of Priscilla, Queen of the Desert *'94*

Alan Webb
Entertaining Mr. Sloane *'70*
Interlude *'67*

Chloe Webb
The Belly of an Architect *'91*
Queens Logic *'91*

Rita Webb
Frenzy *'72*

Timothy Webber
The Boys of St. Vincent *'93*

Dewey Weber
Ulee's Gold *'97*
Chain of Desire *'93*

Steven Weber
Leaving Las Vegas *'95*

Rupert Webster
If... *'69*

Ann Wedgeworth
The Whole Wide World *'96*
Love and a .45 *'94*

Jimmie Ray Weeks
Dead Man *'95*

Dan Weene
Pariah *'98*

Li Wei
Ju Dou *'90*

Robert Weil
Rhinoceros *'74*

Harvey Weinstein
Forgotten Silver *'96*

George Weiss
Glen or Glenda? *'53*

Elizabeth Welch
Dead of Night *'45*

Raquel Welch
Bedazzled *'68*

Tahnee Welch
I Shot Andy Warhol *'96*

Renee Weldon
The Last of the High Kings *'96*

Gwen Welles
Sticky Fingers *'88*
Nobody's Fool *'86*

Orson Welles
Orson Welles: The One Man Band *'95*
Voyage of the Damned *'76*
Start the Revolution without Me *'70*
The Third Man *'49*

Margaret Wells
Pitfall *'48*

Sheilah Wells
Island of the Lost *'68*

John Welsh
Lucky Jim *'58*

Margaret Welsh
American Heart *'92*
Smooth Talk *'85*

George Wendt
Spice World: The Movie *'97*

John Wengraf
Gog *'54*

David Wenham
Cosi *'95*

Klaus Wennemann
Das Boot *'81*

Zhang Wenyao
The Blue Kite *'93*

Jenny Werner
The Third Man *'49*

Oskar Werner
Voyage of the Damned *'76*
Interlude *'67*

Otto Wernicke
M *'31*

Francois Wertheimer
One Sings, the Other Doesn't *'77*

Devon West
She's Vintage *'98*

Julian West
Vampyr *'31*

Lockwood West
Bedazzled *'68*
Leather Boys *'63*

Samuel West
Carrington *'95*
A Feast at Midnight *'95*
Persuasion *'95*

Timothy West
Twisted Nerve *'68*

John Westbrook
Room at the Top *'59*

David Westhead
Mrs. Brown *'97*

Cecil Weston
Money Madness *'47*

Celia Weston
Dead Man Walking *'95*
Flirting with Disaster *'95*

Jack Weston
Dirty Dancing *'87*

Patricia Wettig
Bongwater *'98*

Frank Whaley
Went to Coney Island on a Mission from God...Be Back by Five *'98*
Homage *'95*
Pulp Fiction *'94*
Swimming with Sharks *'94*

Joanne Whalley
A Good Man in Africa *'94*
Mother's Boys *'94*
Kill Me Again *'89*
Scandal *'89*
Dance with a Stranger *'85*

Kevin Whately
The English Patient *'96*

Thomas Wheatley
Where Angels Fear to Tread *'91*

Rich Wheeler
Bodies, Rest & Motion *'93*

Alison Whelan
My Left Foot *'89*

Forest Whitaker
Smoke *'95*
The Crying Game *'92*
Diary of a Hitman *'91*
Platoon *'86*

Millie White
Poison *'91*

Sheila White
Confessions of a Window Cleaner *'74*

Steven C. White
Open Season *'95*

Wynn White
Hard Eight *'96*

Andrew Whitehead
Tommy Tricker & the Stamp Traveller *'87*

Billie Whitelaw
Jane Eyre *'96*
The Krays *'90*
Maurice *'87*
Frenzy *'72*
Start the Revolution without Me *'70*
Twisted Nerve *'68*

Jon Whiteley
The Little Kidnappers *'53*

Lynn Whitfield
Eve's Bayou *'97*

Peter Whitford
Strictly Ballroom *'92*
Warm Nights on a Slow-Moving Train *'87*

Gordon Whiting
The Railway Children *'70*

Stuart Whitman
The Mark *'61*
Crime of Passion *'57*

Leanne Whitney
Little Shots of Happiness *'97*

May Whitty
The Lady Vanishes *'38*

William Whymper
The Missing Reel *'90*

Jeffrey Wickham
Another Country *'84*

Saskia Wickham
Angels and Insects *'95*

Ellen Widmann
M *'31*

Richard Widmark
Murder on the Orient Express *'74*

Kai Wiesinger
Backbeat *'94*

Rudy Wiesler
Tomorrow the World *'44*

Dianne Wiest
Bullets over Broadway *'94*

Wiley Wiggins
Dazed and Confused *'93*

Peter Wight
Naked *'93*

Robert Wightman
Living in Oblivion *'94*

Carlton Wilborn
Grief *'94*

James Wilby
A Handful of Dust *'88*
A Summer Story *'88*
Maurice *'87*
Dreamchild *'85*

Marty Wilde
Stardust *'74*

Gene Wilder
The Little Prince *'74*
Rhinoceros *'74*
Start the Revolution without Me *'70*

Webb Wilder
The Thing Called Love *'93*

John Wildman
American Boyfriends *'89*

Judie Wildman
The Little Girl Who Lives down the Lane *'76*

Valerie Wildman
Salvador *'86*

Catherine Wilkin
Brilliant Lies *'96*

Tom Wilkinson
The Governess *'98*
Shakespeare in Love *'98*
Wilde *'97*
The Full Monty *'96*
Priest *'94*
Paper Mask *'91*

Fred Willard
Permanent Midnight *'98*
Waiting for Guffman *'96*

Adam Williams
Crashout *'55*

Barbara Williams
City of Hope *'91*

Branden Williams
Halloween: H20 *'98*

Burt Williams
Public Access *'93*

Clarence Williams III
Tough Guys Don't Dance *'87*

Cynda Williams
The Tie That Binds *'95*
One False Move *'91*

Edy Williams
Naked Kiss *'64*

Elexa Williams
Pariah *'98*

Emlyn Williams
They Drive by Night *'38*

Gareth Williams
Palookaville *'95*
Blessing *'94*

Guinn "Big Boy" Williams
You Only Live Once *'37*

Harcourt Williams
The Obsessed *'51*

Heathcote Williams
Orlando *'92*

Kimberly Williams
Coldblooded *'94*

Leigh Williams
Squeeze *'97*

Lori Williams
Faster, Pussycat! Kill! Kill! *'65*

Michelle Williams
Halloween: H20 *'98*

Natalie Williams
To Hell with Love *'98*

Polly Williams
The Slipper and the Rose *'76*

Robin Williams
Good Will Hunting *'97*

Ryan Williams
Menace II Society *'93*

Samm-Art Williams
Blood Simple *'85*

Saul Williams
Slam *'98*

Scot Williams
Backbeat *'94*

Treat Williams
Smooth Talk *'85*

Mykelti Williamson
Miracle Mile *'89*

Noble Willingham
Pastime *'91*

Bruce Willis
Pulp Fiction *'94*

Shauntisa Willis
Passion Fish *'92*

Noel Willman
The Odessa File *'74*
Abandon Ship *'57*

Kevin Willmott
Ninth Street *'98*

Drusilla Wills
Non-Stop New York *'37*

Channing Wilroy
Female Trouble *'74*

Brian Wilson
I Just Wasn't Made for These Times *'94*

Bridgette Wilson
The Real Blonde *'97*

Carnie Wilson
I Just Wasn't Made for These Times *'94*

David Wilson
Eddie and the Cruisers *'83*

David Lee Wilson
Pariah *'98*

Elizabeth Wilson
The Graduate *'67*

K. J. Wilson
An Angel at My Table *'89*

Lambert Wilson
The Belly of an Architect *'91*

Luke Wilson
Bongwater *'98*

Owen C. Wilson
Permanent Midnight *'98*

Peter M. Wilson
She's Vintage *'98*

Richard Wilson
How to Get Ahead in Advertising *'89*

Scott Wilson
Clay Pigeons *'98*
Dead Man Walking *'95*

Stuart Wilson
Death and the Maiden *'94*

Wendy Wilson
I Just Wasn't Made for These Times *'94*

Penelope Wilton
Carrington *'95*

Barry Winch
Tommy *'75*

Michael Wincott
Basquiat *'96*
Dead Man *'95*

Marc Wincourt
Murmur of the Heart *'71*

Marie Windsor
The Killing *'56*

Debra Winger
Betrayed *'88*

Lucyna Winnicka
25 Fireman's Street *'73*

Mare Winningham
Georgia *'95*
Miracle Mile *'89*
Shy People *'87*
Nobody's Fool *'86*

George Winship
Teenage Gang Debs *'66*

Kate Winslet
Heavenly Creatures *'94*

Hattie Winston
Jackie Brown *'97*

Ray Winstone
Ladybird, Ladybird *'93*

Vincent Winter
Time Lock *'57*
The Little Kidnappers *'53*

Kristoffer Ryan Winters
With or Without You *'98*

Shelley Winters
Heavy *'94*
An Average Little Man *'77*
Alfie *'66*
The Balcony *'63*
Lolita *'62*
The Night of the Hunter *'55*
He Ran All the Way *'51*

Siegfried Wischnewski
Strongman Ferdinand *'76*

Googie Withers
Shine *'95*
Dead of Night *'45*
Pink String and Sealing Wax *'45*
On Approval *'44*
The Lady Vanishes *'38*

Jimmy Witherspoon
Georgia *'95*

Reese Witherspoon
Freeway *'95*
Wildflower *'91*

Glenn Withrow
Pass the Ammo *'88*

Alicia Witt
Bongwater *'98*
Citizen Ruth *'96*
Fun *'94*
Bodies, Rest & Motion *'93*

Karen Witter
Popcorn *'89*

Bess Wohl
Starving Artists *'97*

Rita Wolf
My Beautiful Laundrette *'85*

Michael J. Wolfe
True Love *'89*

Donald Wolfit
The Mark *'61*
Room at the Top *'59*

Carol Wolveridge
1984 *'56*

John Womack Jr.
Badlands *'74*

Anna May Wong
Impact *'49*

Russell Wong
Eat a Bowl of Tea *'89*

Victor Wong
Life Is Cheap...But Toilet Paper Is Expensive *'90*
Eat a Bowl of Tea *'89*

Arthur Wontner
Genevieve *'53*

George Woo
Chan Is Missing *'82*

David Wood
If... *'69*

Edward D. Wood Jr.
Plan 9 from Outer Space *'56*
Glen or Glenda? *'53*

Elijah Wood
The Ice Storm *'97*

Evelyn Wood
Glen or Glenda? *'53*

John Wood
Jane Eyre *'96*
Citizen X *'95*
The Madness of King George *'94*
Orlando *'92*

Tom Wood
Ulee's Gold *'97*

Victor Wood
Time Lock *'57*

Alfre Woodard
Passion Fish *'92*

Bokeem Woodbine
Freeway *'95*

George Woodbridge
The Fallen Idol *'49*

Eric Woodburn
The Innocents *'61*

Heather Woodbury
Habit *'97*

James Woods
Curse of the Starving Class *'94*
Chaplin *'92*
Salvador *'86*

John Woodvine
Persuasion *'95*

Morgan Woodward
The Killing of a Chinese Bookie *'76*

Sarah Woodward
The Cater Street Hangman *'98*

Tim Woodward
Closing Numbers *'93*
Galileo *'73*

Emily Woof
Photographing Fairies *'97*

Norman Wooland
Madeleine *'50*

Susan Wooldridge
Just Like a Woman *'92*
Twenty-One *'91*
How to Get Ahead in Advertising *'89*
Butley *'74*

Henry Woolf
Galileo *'73*

Mary Woronov
Grief *'94*
Acting on Impulse *'93*
Motorama *'91*
Scenes from the Class Struggle in Beverly Hills *'89*
Eating Raoul *'82*

Nicholas Worth
Blood & Concrete: A Love Story *'90*

Helmut Woudenberg
White Nights *'57*

Fay Wray
Crime of Passion *'57*

John Wray
You Only Live Once *'37*

Amy Wright
Girlfriends *'78*

Jeffrey Wright
Critical Care *'97*
Basquiat *'96*

Jenny Wright
A Shock to the System *'90*
Twister *'89*
The Chocolate War *'88*

Marie Wright
Gaslight *'40*

N'Bushe Wright
Fresh *'94*
Zebrahead *'92*

Nicola Wright
Christabel *'89*

Steven Wright
1999 *'98*

Wendell Wright
Jack's Back *'87*

Robin Wright Penn
The Crossing Guard *'94*

Chien-Lien Wu
Eat Drink Man Woman *'94*

Robert Wuhl
Open Season *'95*

Kari Wuhrer
The Crossing Guard *'94*

Jane Wyatt
Pitfall *'48*

Noah Wyle
The Myth of Fingerprints *'97*

Frank Wylie
Three Sisters *'70*

Bill Wyman
Gimme Shelter *'70*

Patrick Wymark
Repulsion *'65*

Geraint Wyn Davies
Daughters of the Country *'86*

Robert Wyndham
Dead of Night *'45*

Joel Wyner
Random Encounter *'98*

Peter Wyngarde
The Innocents *'61*

Keenan Wynn
The Killer inside Me *'76*
Shack Out on 101 *'55*

Charlotte Wynters
Struggle *'31*

Diana Wynyard
Gaslight *'40*

Amanda Wyss
Powwow Highway *'89*

Miss X
Vegas in Space *'94*

Xaleese
Hard Eight *'96*

Yang Liu Xia
The Story of Qui Ju *'91*

Anji Xtravaganza
Paris Is Burning *'91*

Venus Xtravaganza
Paris Is Burning *'91*

Mickey Yablans
Halloween *'78*

Jeff Yagher
Shag: The Movie *'89*

Koji Yakusho
Shall We Dance? *'96*

Emily Yamasaki
Chan Is Missing *'82*

Jin Yan
Love and Duty *'31*

Kuei-Mei Yang
Eat Drink Man Woman *'94*

Chen Yanyan
Love and Duty *'31*

The Yardbirds
Blow-Up *'66*

Margaret Yarde
Thursday's Child *'43*

Ellen Yeung
Chan Is Missing *'82*

Li Yi
Love and Duty *'31*

Zhang Yi
Ju Dou *'90*

Dwight Yoakam
Sling Blade *'96*
Red Rock West *'93*

Malik Yoba
Cop Land *'97*

Lee Yoke-Moon
Children of the Damned *'63*

Kathleen York
Cold Feet *'89*

Michael York
Murder on the Orient Express *'74*

Sarah York
Evil Dead *'83*

Susannah York
A Summer Story *'88*
The Maids *'75*
The Killing of Sister George *'69*

Aden Young
Cousin Bette *'97*
Cosi *'95*

Bruce A. Young
Normal Life *'96*

Burt Young
Last Exit to Brooklyn *'90*

Joan Young
The Fallen Idol *'49*

Karen Young
Criminal Law *'89*

Nedrick Young
Gun Crazy *'49*

Polly Ann Young
Turnabout *'40*

Jim Youngs
Nobody's Fool *'86*

Tom Yourk
Teenage Gang Debs *'66*

Jimmy Yuill
Much Ado about Nothing *'93*
Paper Mask *'91*

Harris Yulin
Loch Ness *'95*

Chow Yun-Fat
Love unto Waste *'86*

Grace Zabriskie
Bastard out of Carolina *'96*
Chain of Desire *'93*
My Own Private Idaho *'91*
The Waterdance *'91*
Wild at Heart *'90*
Drugstore Cowboy *'89*
The Big Easy *'87*

Ann Zacarias
France, Incorporated *'74*

Steve Zahn
SubUrbia *'96*

Konstantin Zaklinsky
The Children of Theatre Street *'77*

Roxana Zal
River's Edge *'87*

Zbigniew Zamachowski
Trois Couleurs: Blanc *'94*

Billy Zane
Orlando *'92*
Blood & Concrete: A Love Story *'90*
Dead Calm *'89*

William Zappa
Crush *'93*

Waclaw Zastrzezynski
Ashes and Diamonds *'58*

Yuri Zavadski
Aelita: Queen of Mars *'24*

Rosel Zech
Salmonberries *'91*

Vesko Zehirev
Last Summer *'74*

Renee Zellweger
The Whole Wide World *'96*
Love and a .45 *'94*

Mai Zetterling
The Witches *'90*
Abandon Ship *'57*

Monica Zetterlund
Stubby *'74*

Otto Zhakov
Professor Mamlock *'38*

Lin Zi
The Story of Qui Ju *'91*

Vanessa Zima
Ulee's Gold *'97*

Joey Zimmerman
Mother's Boys *'94*

Dan Ziskie
Zebrahead *'92*

Bata Zivojinovic
The Dog Who Loved Trains *'78*
False Weights *'74*

Valery Zolothuhin
The Only One *'76*

Louis Zorich
City of Hope *'91*

Olga Zuiderhoek
Abel *'87*

Jose Zuniga
Hurricane Streets *'96*

Anne Zupa
Pariah *'98*

Milena Zupancic
Fear *'75*

Elsa Zylberstein
Mina Tannenbaum *'93*

Director Index

The "Director Index" provides a complete listing of directors cited within the reviews. The directors' names are listed alphabetically by last name, and the films they directed that are reviewed in this book are listed chronologically, from most recent to the oldest film. Take a peek back at the "Cast Index" to see if your favorite director also had a walk-on in his/her own or his/her best friend's film.

Ivan Abramson
East and West *'24*

Rodney Ackland
Thursday's Child *'43*

Peter Adair
Word Is Out: Stories of Some of Our Lives *'77*

Catlin Adams
Sticky Fingers *'88*

Lisa Addario
Lover Girl *'97*

Percy Adlon
Salmonberries *'91*

Jordan Alan
Terminal Bliss *'91*

Rafael Morena Alba
Bride to Be *'75*

Robert Aldrich
The Killing of Sister George *'69*
Kiss Me Deadly *'55*

Rand Alexander
Caged *'97*

Marc Allegret
Sois Belle et Tais-Toi *'58*

Woody Allen
Bullets over Broadway *'94*

Michael Almereyda
Nadja *'95*
Twister *'89*

Pedro Almodovar
Kika *'94*
High Heels *'91*
Tie Me Up! Tie Me Down! *'90*
Women on the Verge of a Nervous Breakdown *'88*
Law of Desire *'86*
Matador *'86*
Dark Habits *'84*

Robert Altman
Kansas City *'95*
Short Cuts *'93*
The Player *'92*
Secret Honor *'85*

Gianni Amelio
Lamerica *'95*

Jon Amiel
Tune in Tomorrow *'90*

Allison Anders
Grace of My Heart *'96*
Gas Food Lodging *'92*

Lindsay Anderson
The Whales of August *'87*
In Celebration *'75*
If... *'69*

Michael Anderson Sr.
1984 *'56*

Paul Thomas Anderson
Boogie Nights *'97*
Hard Eight *'96*

Wendell Jon Andersson
With or Without You *'98*

Roger Andrieux
L'Amour en Herbe *'77*

Michelangelo Antonioni
Blow-Up *'66*

Michael Apted
35 Up *'91*
Stardust *'74*

Manuel Gutierrez Aragon
Black Litter *'77*

Gregg Araki
The Doom Generation *'95*

Alfonso Arau
Like Water for Chocolate *'93*

Denys Arcand
Love and Human Remains *'93*

Emile Ardolino
Dirty Dancing *'87*

Dario Argento
Creepers *'85*

George Armitage
Miami Blues *'90*

Gillian Armstrong
Not Fourteen Again *'96*

Robin B. Armstrong
Pastime *'91*

Darren Aronofsky
Pi *'98*

Miguel Arteta
Star Maps *'97*

Karen Arthur
Legacy *'75*

Ash
Bang *'95*

Anthony Asquith
The Woman in Question *'50*
Pygmalion *'38*

Richard Attenborough
Chaplin *'92*

David Attwood
Wild West *'93*

Bille August
The House of the Spirits *'93*

Beth B
Two Small Bodies *'93*
Vortex *'81*

Scott B
Vortex *'81*

Hector Babenco
Kiss of the Spider Woman *'85*
Pixote *'81*

Theodore Bafaloukos
Rockers *'79*

Norma Bailey
Daughters of the Country *'86*

Paule Baillargeon
Le Sexe des Étoiles *'93*

Roy Ward Baker
A Night to Remember *'58*

Albert Band
I Bury the Living *'58*

Jack Baran
Destiny Turns on the Radio *'95*

Bruno Barreto
Carried Away *'95*
The Story of Fausta *'88*

Lezli-Ann Barrett
Business As Usual *'88*

Zelda Barron
Shag: The Movie *'89*

Michael Barry
Second Coming of Suzanne *'80*

Paul Bartel
Shelf Life *'94*
Scenes from the Class Struggle in Beverly Hills *'89*
Eating Raoul *'82*

David Beaird
It Takes Two *'88*
Pass the Ammo *'88*

William Beaudine
Sparrows *'26*

Martin Bell
American Heart *'92*
Streetwise *'84*

Marco Bellocchio
Victory March *'76*

Roberto Benigni
Life Is Beautiful *'98*
Johnny Stecchino *'92*

Obie Benz
Heavy Petting *'89*

Bruce Beresford
A Good Man in Africa *'94*
Don's Party *'76*

Ingmar Bergman
Face to Face *'76*
Scenes from a Marriage *'73*

Alain Berliner
Ma Vie en Rose *'97*

Joe Berlinger
Paradise Lost: The Child Murders at Robin Hood Hills *'95*
Brother's Keeper *'92*

Claude Berri
In a Wild Moment *'78*

John Berry
He Ran All the Way *'51*

Bernardo Bertolucci
The Conformist *'71*

Dan Bessie
Hard Traveling *'85*

Luc Besson
La Femme Nikita *'91*

Radha Bharadwaj
Closet Land *'90*

Tony Bill
Five Corners *'88*

Kevin Billington
The Good Soldier *'81*
Interlude *'67*

Mira Reym Binford
Diamonds in the Snow *'94*

Antonia Bird
Priest *'94*

Whitney Blake
Reno's Kids: 87 Days Plus 11 *'87*

Bertrand Blier
Too Beautiful for You *'88*

Yurek Bogayevicz
Anna *'87*

Peter Bogdanovich
The Thing Called Love *'93*

James Bond III
Def by Temptation *'90*

John Boorman
Having a Wild Weekend *'65*

Arthur Borman
...And God Spoke *'94*

Costa Botes
Forgotten Silver *'96*

John Boulting
Lucky Jim *'58*

Roy Boulting
Twisted Nerve *'68*
Lucky Jim *'58*

Jenny Bowen
The Wizard of Loneliness *'88*
Street Music *'81*

George Bowers
My Tutor *'82*

Don Boyd
Twenty-One *'91*

Danny Boyle
Trainspotting *'95*
Shallow Grave *'94*

John Brahm
Guest in the House *'44*

Kenneth Branagh
Much Ado about Nothing *'93*

Andre Brassard
Once upon a Time in the East *'74*

Michel Brault
The Orders *'75*

Robert Bresson
Lancelot of the Lake *'74*

Matthew Bright
Freeway *'95*

Clive Brook
On Approval *'44*

Nick Broomfield
Kurt and Courtney *'98*

Ricou Browning
Island of the Lost *'68*

Kevin Brownlow
Cinema Europe *'96*

Franco Brusati
The Sleazy Uncle *'89*

Colin Bucksey
Dealers *'89*

Richard Bugajski
The Interrogation *'82*

Luis Bunuel
Phantom of Liberty *'74*

Charles Burnett
To Sleep with Anger *'90*

Edward Burns
She's the One *'96*
The Brothers McMullen *'94*

Steve Buscemi
Trees Lounge *'96*

Michael Cacoyannis
Iphigenia *'77*

Barry Caillier
To Cross the Rubicon *'91*

Simon Callow
The Ballad of the Sad Cafe *'91*

Ken Cameron
The Good Wife *'86*

Donald Cammell
Performance *'70*

Martin Campbell
Criminal Law *'89*

Jane Campion
The Piano *'93*
An Angel at My Table *'89*

Dyan Cannon
Number One *'76*

Marcel Carne
Children of Paradise *'45*

Marc Caro
The City of Lost Children *'95*

John Carpenter
Halloween *'78*

John Cassavetes
The Killing of a Chinese Bookie *'76*
A Woman under the Influence *'74*

Frank Cassenti
The Red Poster *'76*

Joseph Cates
Who Killed Teddy Bear? *'65*

Michael Caton-Jones
Scandal *'89*

Peter Cattaneo
The Full Monty *'96*

Alberto Cavalcanti
Dead of Night *'45*

Claude Chabrol
La Ceremonie *'95*
Violette *'78*

Judy Chaikin
Legacy of the Hollywood Blacklist *'87*

Jackie Chan
Project A: Part 2 *'87*

Tony Chan
Combination Platter *'93*

Peter Chelsom
Funny Bones *'94*
Hear My Song *'91*

Lisa Cholodenko
High Art *'98*

Joyce Chopra
Smooth Talk *'85*

Christo Christov
Last Summer *'74*

Gerard Ciccoritti
Paris, France *'94*

Rene Clair
I Married a Witch *'42*
The Ghost Goes West *'36*

Larry Clark
Kids *'95*

Alan Clarke
Rita, Sue & Bob Too *'87*

Jack Clayton
The Lonely Passion of Judith Hearne *'87*
The Innocents *'61*
Room at the Top *'59*

Rene Clement
Forbidden Games *'52*

David Coburn
To Hell with Love *'98*

Jean Cocteau
Beauty and the Beast *'46*

Fred Coe
A Thousand Clowns *'65*

Wayne Coe
Grim Prairie Tales *'89*

Joel Coen
The Big Lebowski *'97*
Fargo *'96*
Blood Simple *'85*

Eli Cohen
Ricochets *'87*

Larry Cohen
The Ambulance *'90*
Special Effects *'85*
Q (The Winged Serpent) *'82*

Max Allan Collins
Mommy *'95*

Peter Collinson
Fright *'71*

Carl Colpaert
Delusion *'91*

Bill Condon
Gods and Monsters *'98*

Kevin Connor
The Land That Time Forgot *'75*

Martha Coolidge
Rambling Rose *'91*

Matt Cooper
Campfire Tales *'98*

Roger Corman
Frankenstein Unbound *'90*

Alain Corneau
France, Incorporated *'74*

Henry Cornelius
Genevieve *'53*

Michael Corrente
Federal Hill *'94*

Constantin Costa-Gavras
Betrayed *'88*

Manny Coto
Star Kid *'97*

Michael Covert
American Strays *'96*

Ronnie Cramer
Back Street Jane *'89*

Wes Craven
Wes Craven's New Nightmare *'94*

Charles Crichton
The Battle of the Sexes *'60*
Dead of Night *'45*

Donald Crombie
Caddie *'76*

David Cronenberg
Crash *'95*

Alfonso Cuaron
A Little Princess *'95*

Julie Cypher
Teresa's Tattoo *'94*

John Dahl
The Last Seduction *'94*
Red Rock West *'93*
Kill Me Again *'89*

Damiano Damiani
The Devil Is a Woman *'75*

Anthony Darnborough
So Long at the Fair *'50*

Julie Dash
Daughters of the Dust *'91*

Sean Dash
Breakaway *'95*

Jules Dassin
A Dream of Passion *'78*

Delmer Daves
The Red House *'47*

Martin Davidson
Eddie and the Cruisers *'83*

Nick Davis
1999 *'98*

Robin Davis
Dear Victor *'75*

Tamra Davis
Guncrazy *'92*

Andre de Toth
Pitfall *'48*

Emile DeAntonio
Point of Order *'64*

Basil Dearden
Victim *'61*
The Smallest Show on Earth *'57*
Who Done It? *'56*
Saraband for Dead Lovers *'48*
Dead of Night *'45*

Edward Dein
Shack Out on 101 *'55*

Steve DeJarnatt
Miracle Mile *'89*

Peter Del Monte
Julia and Julia *'87*

Jeffrey Dell
Don't Take It to Heart *'44*

Eames Demetrios
The Giving *'91*

Jonathan Demme
Who Am I This Time? *'82*

Claire Denis
Nenette and Boni *'96*

Maya Deren
Meshes of the Afternoon *'43*

Robert Derteno
Girl Gang *'54*

Joseph Destein
The Method *'87*

Tom DiCillo
The Real Blonde *'97*
Box of Moonlight *'96*
Living in Oblivion *'94*

Thorold Dickinson
Gaslight *'40*

Mick Diener
Which Way, Por Favor? *'98*

John Dingwall
Phobia *'88*

Edward Dmytryk
The Hidden Room *'49*

David Dobkin
Clay Pigeons *'98*

Stanley Donen
The Little Prince *'74*
Bedazzled *'68*
Two for the Road *'67*

Arthur Dong
Licensed to Kill *'97*

Martin Donovan
Apartment Zero *'88*

Robert Dornhelm
Cold Feet *'89*
The Children of Theatre Street *'77*

Robert Downey
Hugo Pool *'97*

Tony Drazan
Zebrahead *'92*

Carl Theodor Dreyer
Vampyr *'31*

Martin Duffy
The Boy from Mercury *'96*

Martine Dugowson
Mina Tannenbaum *'93*

John Duigan
Sirens *'94*

Robert Duvall
The Apostle *'97*

Ivo Dvorak
Metamorphosis *'75*

Nicolas Echevarria
Cabeza de Vaca *'90*

Uli Edel
Last Exit to Brooklyn *'90*

Christine Edzard
Little Dorrit, Film 1: Nobody's Fault *'88*
Little Dorrit, Film 2: Little Dorrit's Story *'88*

Jan Egleson
A Shock to the System *'90*

Atom Egoyan
The Sweet Hereafter *'96*
Exotica *'94*

Gary Ellenberg
Ted *'98*

Stephan Elliott
The Adventures of Priscilla, Queen of the Desert *'94*

Bob Ellis
Warm Nights on a Slow-Moving Train *'87*

Maurice Elvey
The Obsessed *'51*
Beware of Pity *'46*

John Emerson
His Picture in the Papers *'16*

Cy Endfield
Try and Get Me *'50*

Victor Erice
Spirit of the Beehive *'73*

Bente Erichson
The Feldmann Case *'87*

Chris Eyre
Smoke Signals *'98*

Zoltan Fabri
The Hungarians *'78*
The Unfinished Sentence in 141 Minutes *'75*

William Fairchild
John and Julie *'55*

Rainer Werner Fassbinder
Mother Kusters Goes to Heaven *'76*

Federico Fellini
8½ *'63*
Variety Lights *'51*

Leslie Fenton
Tomorrow the World *'44*

Rene Feret
First Communion *'77*

Abel Ferrara
The Funeral *'96*
The Addiction *'95*
Bad Lieutenant *'92*

Larry Fessenden
Habit *'97*

Annie Flenburgh
The Windsors: A Royal Family *'94*

Mike Figgis
Leaving Las Vegas *'95*

Cinda Firestone
Attica *'74*

Terence Fisher
So Long at the Fair *'50*

Richard Fleischer
10 Rillington Place *'70*

Theodore J. Flicker
The Troublemaker *'64*

John Florea
Island of the Lost *'68*

James Foley
After Dark, My Sweet *'90*

Bryan Forbes
The Slipper and the Rose *'76*
Whistle down the Wind *'61*

Phillip R. Ford
Vegas in Space *'94*

Lewis R. Foster
Crashout *'55*

Eytan Fox
Song of the Siren *'94*

Cyril Frankel
The Very Edge *'63*
Never Take Candy from a Stranger *'60*

John Frankenheimer
The Island of Dr. Moreau *'96*
The Iceman Cometh *'73*

The Manchurian Candidate '62

Carl Franklin
One False Move '91

Richard Franklin
Brilliant Lies '96
Sorrento Beach '95
Road Games '81

Stephen Frears
The Grifters '90
Sammy & Rosie Get Laid '87
My Beautiful Laundrette '85

Morgan J. Freeman
Hurricane Streets '96

Bart Freundlich
The Myth of Fingerprints '97

Samuel Fuller
Naked Kiss '64

Sidney J. Furie
Leather Boys '63

Bruno Gantillon
Servant and Mistress '77

Lee Garmes
Actors and Sin '52

Jozsef Gemes
Princess and the Goblin '92

Chris Gerolmo
Citizen X '95

Nicolas Gessner
The Little Girl Who Lives down the Lane '76

Yervant Gianikian
From the Pole to the Equator '87

Brian Gilbert
Wilde '97

Lewis Gilbert
Shirley Valentine '89
Alfie '66

David Gill
Cinema Europe '96

Frank D. Gilroy
The Luckiest Man in the World '89

Francois Girard
32 Short Films about Glenn Gould '93

Richard Glatzer
Grief '94

Jean-Luc Godard
Breathless '59

Jill Godmilow
Waiting for the Moon '87

Sandra Goldbacher
The Governess '98

Daniel Goldberg
A Kiss to This Land '94

Sidney Goldin
East and West '24

Steve Gomer
Fly by Night '93

Nick Gomez
New Jersey Drive '95

Keith Gordon
The Chocolate War '88

Claude Goretta
The Wonderful Crook '75

Leonid Gorovets
Coffee with Lemon '94

Marleen Gorris
Antonia's Line '95

Alberto Gout
Aventurera '49

F. Gary Gray
Set It Off '96

James Gray
Little Odessa '94

Guy Green
Luther '74
The Mark '61

Peter Greenaway
The Belly of an Architect '91

Maggie Greenwald
The Ballad of Little Jo '93

D. W. Griffith
Struggle '31
Way Down East '20

Ulu Grosbard
Georgia '95
True Confessions '81

Nikolai Gubenko
The Orphans '77

Ruy Guerra
The Fable of the Beautiful Pigeon Fancier '88

Christopher Guest
Waiting for Guffman '96

Val Guest
In Possession '84
Confessions of a Window Cleaner '74
The Runaway Bus '54

Tomas Gutierrez Alea
Letters from the Park '88

Philip Haas
Angels and Insects '95

Piers Haggard
A Summer Story '88

Fred Haines
Steppenwolf '74

Billy Hale
S.O.S. Titanic '79

Peter Hall
The Homecoming '73
Perfect Friday '70

Mark Halliday
Just Like in the Movies '90

Lasse Hallstrom
My Life As a Dog '85

Robert Hamer
Kind Hearts and Coronets '49
Dead of Night '45
Pink String and Sealing Wax '45

Christopher Hampton
Carrington '95

Justin Hardy
A Feast at Midnight '95

David Hare
Strapless '90

Curtis Harrington
Night Tide '63

Leslie Harris
Just Another Girl on the I.R.T. '93

Wendell B. Harris Jr.
Chameleon Street '89

Matthew Harrison
Rhythm Thief '94

Mary Harron
I Shot Andy Warhol '96

Hal Hartley
Trust '91
The Unbelievable Truth '90

Harold (Herk) Harvey
Carnival of Souls '62

Byron Haskin
Too Late for Tears '49

Masami Hata
Little Nemo: Adventures in Slumberland '92

Masanori Hata
The Adventures of Milo & Otis '89

Kayo Hatta
Picture Bride '94

Todd Haynes
Safe '95
Poison '91

Ben Hecht
Actors and Sin '52

Chris Hegedus
The War Room '93

Josef Heifetz
The Only One '76

Sarah Hellings
The Cater Street Hangman '98

David Helpern
Hollywood on Trial '76

John Henderson
Loch Ness '95

Frank Henenlotter
Frankenhooker '90

Denis Heroux
Jacques Brel Is Alive and Well and Living in Paris '75

Mark Herrier
Popcorn '89

Rowdy Herrington
Jack's Back '87

Juraj Herz
Day for My Love '77

Werner Herzog
Every Man for Himself & God against All '75

Douglas Hickox
Entertaining Mr. Sloane '70

Scott Hicks
Shine '95

George Roy Hill
The World of Henry Orient '64

Jack Hill
Switchblade Sisters '75
Spider Baby '64

John Hillcoat
To Have and to Hold '96

Arthur Hiller
The Man in the Glass Booth '75

Alfred Hitchcock
Frenzy '72
The Lady Vanishes '38
Young and Innocent '37
Sabotage '36
The 39 Steps '35
The Man Who Knew Too Much '34
Rich and Strange '32
Blackmail '29

P. J. Hogan
Muriel's Wedding '94

Nicole Holofcener
Walking and Talking '96

Billy Hopkins
I Love You, I Love You Not '97

Dennis Hopper
Easy Rider '69

Harry Horner
The Wild Party '56

Leslie Howard
Pygmalion '38

George Huang
Swimming with Sharks '94

Jean-Loup Hubert
Le Grand Chemin '87

Reginald Hudlin
House Party '90

Marc Huestis
Men in Love *'90*

Albert Hughes
Menace II Society *'93*

Allen Hughes
Menace II Society *'93*

Tim Hunter
River's Edge *'87*

William T. Hurtz
Little Nemo: Adventures in Slumberland *'92*

Anjelica Huston
Bastard out of Carolina *'96*

Danny Huston
Mr. North *'88*

John Huston
The Dead *'87*
Beat the Devil *'53*
Moulin Rouge *'52*
The African Queen *'51*

Nicholas Hytner
The Madness of King George *'94*

Dan Ireland
The Whole Wide World *'96*

John Irvin
Widow's Peak *'94*

Sam Irvin
Acting on Impulse *'93*

Aline Issermann
Shades of Doubt *'93*

Juzo Itami
A-Ge-Man: Tales of a Golden Geisha *'91*

Anatoli Ivanov
The Last Days of the Last Tsar *'92*

James Ivory
The Remains of the Day *'93*
Maurice *'87*
A Room with a View *'86*
Heat and Dust *'82*

Arnaldo Jabor
The Marriage *'76*

Douglas Jackson
Random Encounter *'98*

Peter Jackson
Forgotten Silver *'96*
Heavenly Creatures *'94*

Alan Jacobs
Nina Takes a Lover *'94*

Nicholas A. E. Jacobs
The Refrigerator *'91*

Just Jaeckin
Emmanuelle *'74*

Henry Jaglom
Tracks *'76*

Steve James
Hoop Dreams *'94*

Nan Janelidze
Lullaby *'94*

Victor Janson
The Yellow Ticket *'18*

Jim Jarmusch
Dead Man *'95*
Night on Earth *'91*

Lionel Jeffries
The Railway Children *'70*

Jean-Pierre Jeunet
The City of Lost Children *'95*

Neal Jimenez
The Waterdance *'91*

Mark Joffe
The Matchmaker *'97*
Cosi *'95*

Sande N. Johnson
Teenage Gang Debs *'66*

Aaron Kim Johnston
Daughters of the Country *'86*

F. Richard Jones
Bulldog Drummond *'29*

L. Q. Jones
A Boy and His Dog *'75*

Neil Jordan
Michael Collins *'96*
The Crying Game *'92*
Mona Lisa *'86*

Mikhail Kalatozov
I Am Cuba *'64*

Tom Kalin
Swoon *'91*

Scott Kalvert
The Basketball Diaries *'94*

Marek Kanievska
Another Country *'84*

Wong Kar-Wai
Happy Together *'96*
Chungking Express *'95*

Philip Kaufman
The Unbearable Lightness of Being *'88*

David Keating
The Last of the High Kings *'96*

Diane Keaton
Wildflower *'91*

Douglas Keeve
Unzipped *'94*

Roy Kellino
I Met a Murderer *'39*

Nancy Kelly
Thousand Pieces of Gold *'91*

Burt Kennedy
The Killer inside Me *'76*

Roeland Kerbosch
For a Lost Soldier *'93*

Lodge Kerrigan
Clean, Shaven *'93*

Irvin Kershner
The Luck of Ginger Coffey *'64*

Abbas Kiarostami
Through the Olive Trees *'94*

Mark Kidel
Boy Next Door *'93*

Krzysztof Kieslowski
Trois Couleurs: Blanc *'94*
Trois Couleurs: Rouge *'94*
Trois Couleurs: Bleu *'93*

Cedric Klapisch
When the Cat's Away *'96*

Randal Kleiser
It's My Party *'95*

Matjaz Klopcic
Fear *'75*

Alexander Kluge
Strongman Ferdinand *'76*

John Knoop
Cafe Nica: Portraits from Nicaragua *'87*

Amos Kollek
High Stakes *'89*

Andrei Konchalovsky
Shy People *'87*

Alexander Korda
The Private Life of Henry VIII *'33*

John Korty
Who Are the DeBolts and Where Did They Get 19 Kids? *'78*

Eric Koyanagi
Hundred Per Cent *'98*

Karl Kozak
To Hell with Love *'98*

Soeren Kragh-Jacobsen
Emma's Shadow *'88*

Randolph Kret
Pariah *'98*

Bill Krohn
It's All True *'93*

Lisa Krueger
Manny & Lo *'96*

Stanley Kubrick
The Shining *'80*
Lolita *'62*
The Killing *'56*

Martin Kunert
Campfire Tales *'98*

Hanif Kureishi
London Kills Me *'91*

Stanley Kwan
Center Stage *'91*
Rouge *'87*
Love unto Waste *'86*

Richard Kwietniowski
Love and Death on Long Island *'97*

Neil LaBute
In the Company of Men *'96*

Frank LaLoggia
The Lady in White *'88*

Mary Lambert
Grand Isle *'91*

Fritz Lang
You Only Live Once *'37*
M *'31*
Metropolis *'26*

Simon Langton
The Whistle Blower *'87*

James Lapine
Impromptu *'90*

Jerome Lapperrousaz
Hu-Man *'76*

Alberto Lattuada
Variety Lights *'51*

Charles Laughton
The Night of the Hunter *'55*

Frank Launder
The Belles of St. Trinian's *'53*

J. F. Lawton
Cannibal Women in the Avocado Jungle of Death *'89*

Philip Leacock
Hand in Hand *'60*
The Little Kidnappers *'53*

Anton Leader
Children of the Damned *'63*

David Lean
Madeleine *'50*
This Happy Breed *'47*
Brief Encounter *'46*
Great Expectations *'46*
Blithe Spirit *'45*

Ang Lee
The Ice Storm *'97*
Eat Drink Man Woman *'94*
The Wedding Banquet *'93*

Spike Lee
She's Gotta Have It *'86*

Michael Lehmann
The Applegates *'89*
Heathers *'89*

Mike Leigh
Secrets and Lies *'95*
Naked *'93*

David Leland
Wish You Were Here *'87*

Claude Lelouch
Cat and Mouse *'78*
Robert et Robert *'78*

If I Had It to Do Over Again '76

Kasi Lemmons
Eve's Bayou '97

John Lemont
The Frightened City '61

Murray Lerner
Message to Love: The Isle of Wight Festival, the Movie '70

Michael Lessac
House of Cards '92

Richard Lester
Help! '65
A Hard Day's Night '64

Marc Levin
Slam '98

Jefery Levy
Inside Monkey Zetterland '93

Ben Lewin
The Favor, the Watch, and the Very Big Fish '92

Joseph H. Lewis
Gun Crazy '49

Victoria Lewis
Mystery of the Last Tsar '97

Gunnel Lindblom
Paradise Place '77

Michael Lindsay-Hogg
Frankie Starlight '95
The Rolling Stones Rock and Roll Circus '68

Richard Linklater
SubUrbia '96
Dazed and Confused '93
Slacker '91

Roger Lion
I Have Killed '24

Oldrich Lipsky
Dinner for Adele '78

Miguel Littin
Reasons of State '78

Jennie Livingston
Paris Is Burning '91

Frank Lloyd
Oliver Twist '22

Ken Loach
Ladybird, Ladybird '93

Sondra Locke
Trading Favors '97

Barbara Loden
Wanda '70

Richard Loncraine
Bellman and True '88

Roy London
Diary of a Hitman '91

Temistocles Lopez
Chain of Desire '93

Jean-Claude Lord
Eddie and the Cruisers 2: Eddie Lives! '89

Joseph Losey
Roads to the South '78
Galileo '73
The Intimate Stranger '56
The Prowler '51

Arthur Lubin
Impact '49

Angela Ricci Lucchi
From the Pole to the Equator '87

Baz Luhrmann
Strictly Ballroom '92

Sidney Lumet
Critical Care '97
Murder on the Orient Express '74

David Lynch
Lost Highway '96
Wild at Heart '90
Blue Velvet '86
Eraserhead '78

Adrian Lyne
Lolita '97

Jonathan Lynn
Nuns on the Run '90

Alexander MacKendrick
The Ladykillers '55

John MacKenzie
The Long Good Friday '80

Alison Maclean
Crush '93

Alan Madden
Mushrooms '95

John Madden
Shakespeare in Love '98
Mrs. Brown '97
Golden Gate '93

Guy Maddin
Careful '92

Norman Mailer
Tough Guys Don't Dance '87

Terrence Malick
Badlands '74

Louis Malle
Vanya on 42nd Street '94
Black Moon '75
Lacombe, Lucien '74
Murmur of the Heart '71

David Mamet
Oleanna '94
House of Games '87

Milcho Manchevski
Before the Rain '94

James Mangold
Cop Land '97
Heavy '94

Daniel Mann
Lost in the Stars '74

Delbert Mann
Separate Tables '58
Marty '55

Stuart Margolin
Medicine River '94

Goran Markovic
Tito and Me '92

Ross Kagen Marks
Homage '95

Richard Marquand
Eye of the Needle '81

James Marsh
Walk on the Wild Side '93

Tonie Marshall
Pas Tres Catholique '93

Darnell Martin
I Like It Like That '94

Peter Masterson
The Trip to Bountiful '85

Rudolph Mate
D.O.A. '49

Daisy von Scherler Mayer
Party Girl '94

Al Maysles
Gimme Shelter '70

David Maysles
Gimme Shelter '70

Derek Mazur
Daughters of the Country '86

Des McAnuff
Cousin Bette '97

Jim McBride
The Big Easy '87

John Michael McCarthy
Sore Losers '97

Michael McClary
Curse of the Starving Class '94

Scott McGehee
Suture '93

Jim McKay
Girls Town '95

John McNaughton
Normal Life '96

Nancy Meckler
Sister My Sister '94

Peter Medak
Let Him Have It '91
The Krays '90

Myron Meise
It's All True '93

Ramon Menendez
Stand and Deliver '88

Chris Menges
A World Apart '88

Jiri Menzel
Seclusion near a Forest '76

Marta Meszaros
Nine Months '77
Adoption '75

Nicholas Meyer
The Deceivers '88

Russ Meyer
Faster, Pussycat! Kill! Kill! '65

Nikita Mikhalkov
Burnt by the Sun '94

Christopher Miles
The Maids '75

Gavin Millar
Dreamchild '85

Claude Miller
Dites-Lui Que Je L'Aime '77
The Best Way '76

Rebecca Miller
Angela '94

Robert Ellis Miller
Hawks '89

Steve Miner
Halloween: H20 '98

Anthony Minghella
The English Patient '96

Adolph Minkin
Professor Mamlock '38

Roger Mitchell
Persuasion '95

Moshe Mizrahi
Daughters, Daughters '74

Christopher Monger
The Englishman Who Went up a Hill But Came down a Mountain '95
Just Like a Woman '92

Mario Monicelli
An Average Little Man '77
Dear Michael '76
Passionate Thief '60

Jennifer Montgomery
Art for Teachers of Children '95

Michael Moore
Roger & Me '89

Simon Moore
Under Suspicion '92

Philippe Mora
Swastika '73

Christopher Morahan
Paper Mask *'91*

Jeanne Moreau
Lumiere *'76*

Errol Morris
A Brief History of Time *'92*
The Thin Blue Line *'88*

Greg Mottola
The Daytrippers *'96*

Ray Muller
The Wonderful, Horrible Life of Leni Riefenstahl *'93*

Christopher Munch
Color of a Brisk and Leaping Day *'95*
The Hours and Times *'92*

F. W. Murnau
Nosferatu *'22*

Susan Muska
The Brandon Teena Story *'98*

Mira Nair
Kama Sutra: A Tale of Love *'96*

Rodion Nakhapetov
With You and Without You *'74*

Silvio Narizzano
Georgy Girl *'66*

Sergio Nasca
A Virgin Named Mary *'75*
The Profiteer *'74*

Gregory Nava
My Family *'94*

Ronald Neame
The Odessa File *'74*
The Prime of Miss Jean Brodie *'69*

Mike Newell
An Awfully Big Adventure *'94*
Four Weddings and a Funeral *'94*
Enchanted April *'92*
Dance with a Stranger *'85*

Sam Newfield
Money Madness *'47*
The Lady Confesses *'45*

Mike Nichols
The Graduate *'67*

Rob Nilsson
Heat and Sunlight *'87*

Tom Noonan
What Happened Was... *'94*

Victor Nord
The Garden *'77*

Phillip Noyce
Dead Calm *'89*
Echoes of Paradise *'86*

Victor Nunez
Ulee's Gold *'97*
Ruby in Paradise *'93*
Gal Young 'Un *'79*

Bruno Nuytten
Camille Claudel *'89*

Vern Oakley
A Modern Affair *'94*

Peter O'Fallon
Suicide Kings *'97*

Susanne Ofteringer
Nico Icon *'95*

Mo Ogrodnik
Ripe *'97*

Tom O'Horgan
Rhinoceros *'74*

Greta Olafsdottir
The Brandon Teena Story *'98*

Laurence Olivier
Three Sisters *'70*

Kathy O'Neill
The Windsors: A Royal Family *'94*

Gerd Oswald
Crime of Passion *'57*

G. W. Pabst
Pandora's Box *'28*
Joyless Street *'25*

Goran Paskalyevic
The Dog Who Loved Trains *'78*

Ivan Passer
Cutter's Way *'81*

Robert Patton-Spruill
Squeeze *'97*

Peter Patzak
Death of a Schoolboy *'91*

Alexander Payne
Citizen Ruth *'96*

Richard Pearce
Heartland *'81*

Larry Peerce
Wired *'89*
The Incident *'67*

Sean Penn
The Crossing Guard *'94*

D. A. Pennebaker
The War Room *'93*

Clare Peploe
High Season *'88*

Wolfgang Petersen
Das Boot *'81*

Scott Peterson
Out of the Loop *'97*

Donald Petrie
Mystic Pizza *'88*

Maurice Phillips
Enid Is Sleeping *'90*

Rex Pickett
From Hollywood to Deadwood *'89*

Harold Pinter
Butley *'74*

Allan Piper
Starving Artists *'97*

Sarah Pirozek
Free Tibet *'98*

Anne Claire Poirier
Salut Victor! *'89*

Roman Polanski
Death and the Maiden *'94*
Repulsion *'65*

Stephen Poliakoff
Century *'94*

Sally Potter
Orlando *'92*

Michael Powell
Peeping Tom *'60*
Black Narcissus *'47*

Emeric Pressburger
Black Narcissus *'47*

Alexander Proshkin
To See Paris and Die *'93*

Yakov Protazanov
Aelita: Queen of Mars *'24*

Evelyn Purcell
Nobody's Fool *'86*

Michael Radford
The Postman *'94*
White Mischief *'88*

Bob Rafelson
Mountains of the Moon *'90*

Kevin Rafferty
Feed *'92*

Sam Raimi
Evil Dead *'83*

Herbert Rappaport
Professor Mamlock *'38*

Mark Rappaport
The Silver Screen: Color Me Lavender *'97*
From the Journals of Jean Seberg *'95*
Rock Hudson's Home Movies *'92*

Steve Rash
Queens Logic *'91*

Christopher Rawlence
The Missing Reel *'90*

Tim Rebman
Ninth Street *'98*

Carol Reed
The Fallen Idol *'49*
The Third Man *'49*
Night Train to Munich *'40*

Kelly Reichardt
River of Grass *'94*

Jeff Reiner
Blood & Concrete: A Love Story *'90*

Karel Reisz
Isadora *'68*
Morgan! *'66*

Norman Rene
Reckless *'95*
Longtime Companion *'90*

Jean Renoir
The Rules of the Game *'39*

Matty Rich
Straight out of Brooklyn *'91*

Peter Richardson
Eat the Rich *'87*

Tony Richardson
A Delicate Balance *'73*
The Entertainer *'60*
Look Back in Anger *'58*

James Ridgeway
Feed *'92*

Marlon Riggs
Color Adjustment *'91*

Eran Riklis
Zohar: Mediterranean Blues *'93*

H. Anne Riley
Street Music *'81*

Wolf Rilla
Village of the Damned *'60*

Pierre Rissient
One Night Stand *'76*

Hal Roach
Turnabout *'40*

Tim Robbins
Dead Man Walking *'95*

Bruce Robinson
How to Get Ahead in Advertising *'89*
Withnail and I *'87*

Mark Robson
Champion *'49*
Home of the Brave *'49*

Alexandre Rockwell
In the Soup *'92*

Robert Rodriguez
El Mariachi *'93*

Nicolas Roeg
The Witches *'90*
Castaway *'87*
Performance *'70*

Michael Roemer
Nothing but a Man *'64*

Eric Rohmer
The Marquise of O *'76*

George A. Romero
Night of the Living Dead *'68*

Joanelle Romero
Powwow Highway *'89*

Don Roos
The Opposite of Sex *'98*

Martin Rosen
Stacking *'87*

Stuart Rosenberg
Voyage of the Damned *'76*

Keva Rosenfeld
Twenty Bucks *'93*

Roberto Rossellini
The Miracle *'48*

Bobby Roth
Boss' Son *'78*

Cy Roth
Fire Maidens from Outer Space *'56*

Raymond Rouleau
The Crucible *'57*

Russel Rouse
Wicked Woman *'54*

Michael Rubbo
The Return of Tommy Tricker *'94*
Tommy Tricker & the Stamp Traveller *'87*

Alan Rudolph
Afterglow *'97*
Mrs. Parker and the Vicious Circle *'94*
Equinox *'93*
Trouble in Mind *'86*

Raul Ruiz
Three Lives and Only One Death *'96*

David O. Russell
Flirting with Disaster *'95*
Spanking the Monkey *'94*

Ken Russell
Lair of the White Worm *'88*
Valentino *'77*
Lisztomania *'75*
Tommy *'75*

Richard Sale
Abandon Ship *'57*

David Salle
Search and Destroy *'94*

Robert Sarkies
Forgotten Silver *'96*

Philip Saville
Wonderland *'88*

Victor Saville
Evergreen *'34*

Nancy Savoca
Household Saints *'93*
True Love *'89*

John Sayles
Hombres Armados *'97*
Lone Star *'95*
The Secret of Roan Inish *'94*
Passion Fish *'92*
City of Hope *'91*
Eight Men Out *'88*
Matewan *'87*
Return of the Secaucus 7 *'80*

Jerry Schatzberg
Street Smart *'87*

Richard Schenkman
Went to Coney Island on a Mission from God...Be Back by Five *'98*

Suzanne Schiffman
Sorceress *'88*

Rick Schmidt
Morgan's Cake *'88*

Julian Schnabel
Basquiat *'96*

Paul Schrader
Affliction *'97*
The Comfort of Strangers *'91*

Ettore Scola
A Special Day *'77*
Down & Dirty *'76*

Martin Scorsese
After Hours *'85*

Campbell Scott
Big Night *'95*

Sandra Seacat
In the Spirit *'90*

Richard Sears
Bongwater *'98*

William A. Seiter
Helen's Babies *'25*

David Semel
Campfire Tales *'98*

Dominic Sena
Kalifornia *'93*

Coline Serreau
Why Not! *'78*

Vernon Sewell
Uneasy Terms *'48*

Adrienne Shelly
Sudden Manhattan *'96*

Richard Shepard
The Linguini Incident *'92*

Sam Shepard
Silent Tongue *'92*

Adrian Shergold
Christabel *'89*

Jim Sheridan
In the Name of the Father *'93*
My Left Foot *'89*

Gary Sherman
Lisa *'90*

Bill Sherwood
Parting Glances *'86*

Barry Shils
Motorama *'91*

Mamoru Shinzaki
Barefoot Gen *'83*

Alex Sichel
All Over Me *'96*

Adi Sideman
Chicken Hawk *'94*

Scott Sidney
Charley's Aunt *'25*

David Siegel
Suture *'93*

Donald Siegel
Private Hell 36 *'54*

Vassili Silovic
Orson Welles: The One Man Band *'95*

Joan Micklin Silver
Hester Street *'75*

Marisa Silver
Permanent Record *'88*
Old Enough *'84*

Scott Silver
johns *'96*

Anthony Simmons
Black Joy *'77*

Yves Simoneau
Mother's Boys *'94*

Alexander Singer
A Cold Wind in August *'61*

Bryan Singer
The Usual Suspects *'95*
Public Access *'93*

Bruce Sinofsky
Paradise Lost: The Child Murders at Robin Hood Hills *'95*
Brother's Keeper *'92*

Jerzy Skolimowski
Deep End *'70*

Brian Sloan
I Think I Do *'97*

George Sluizer
The Vanishing *'88*

Jimmy Smallhorne
2 by 4 *'98*

John N. Smith
The Boys of St. Vincent *'93*

Kevin Smith
Chasing Amy *'97*
Mallrats *'95*
Clerks *'94*

Michele (Michael) Soavi
Cemetery Man *'95*

Steven Soderbergh
The Underneath *'95*
Kafka *'91*
sex, lies and videotape *'89*

Iain Softley
The Wings of the Dove *'97*
Hackers *'95*
Backbeat *'94*

Helena Solberg
Carmen Miranda: Bananas Is My Business *'95*

Mario Soldati
The Stranger's Hand *'54*

Todd Solondz
Happiness *'98*
Welcome to the Dollhouse *'95*

Sergei Solovjov
100 Days after Childhood *'75*

Richard Spence
Different for Girls *'96*

Bob Spiers
Spice World: The Movie *'97*

Roger Spottiswoode
And the Band Played On *'93*

Michael Steinberg
Bodies, Rest & Motion *'93*
The Waterdance *'91*

Martin Stellman
For Queen and Country *'88*

Robert Stevenson
Non-Stop New York *'37*
Nine Days a Queen *'36*

Peter Stewart
Money Madness *'47*

Whit Stillman
Barcelona *'94*
Metropolitan *'90*

Oliver Stone
U-Turn *'97*
Platoon *'86*
Salvador *'86*

Joseph Strick
The Balcony *'63*

Wesley Strick
The Tie That Binds *'95*

Herbert L. Strock
Gog *'54*

Charles Sturridge
FairyTale: A True Story *'97*
Where Angels Fear to Tread *'91*
A Handful of Dust *'88*

Kevin Sullivan
Anne of Green Gables *'85*

Masayuki Suo
Shall We Dance? *'96*

Jan Svankmajer
Alice *'88*

Joe Syracuse
Lover Girl *'97*

Istvan Szabo
25 Fireman's Street *'73*

Jean-Charles Tacchella
Blue Country *'77*
Cousin, Cousine *'76*

Daniel Talbot
Point of Order *'64*

C. M. Talkington
Love and a .45 *'94*

Alain Tanner
Jonah Who Will Be 25 in the Year 2000 *'76*

Quentin Tarantino
Jackie Brown *'97*
Pulp Fiction *'94*
Reservoir Dogs *'92*

Bertrand Tavernier
Daddy Nostalgia *'90*
Coup de Torchon *'81*

Paolo Taviani
Padre Padrone *'77*
Allonsanfan *'73*

Vittorio Taviani
Padre Padrone *'77*
Allonsanfan *'73*

Alan Taylor
Palookaville *'95*

Andre Techine
French Provincial *'75*

Julien Temple
Absolute Beginners *'86*

Antony Thomas
Thy Kingdom Come, Thy Will Be Done *'87*

Gerald Thomas
Time Lock *'57*

Ralph L. Thomas
Ticket to Heaven *'81*

Caroline Thompson
Black Beauty *'94*

J. Lee Thompson
Return from the Ashes *'65*
Tiger Bay *'59*

Billy Bob Thornton
Sling Blade *'96*

Eric Till
Hot Millions *'68*

Peter Timm
Meier *'87*

Giuseppe Tornatore
Cinema Paradiso *'88*

Bram Towbin
Just Like in the Movies *'90*

Robert Townsend
Hollywood Shuffle *'87*

Rose Troche
Go Fish *'94*

Francois Truffaut
The Man Who Loved Women *'77*
Small Change *'76*
The 400 Blows *'59*

Stanley Tucci
Big Night *'95*

Ann Turner
Celia: Child of Terror *'90*

John Turturro
Mac *'93*

Edgar G. Ulmer
Detour *'46*
Girls in Chains *'43*
American Matchmaker *'40*

Michael Toshiyuki Uno
The Wash *'88*

Roger Vadim
Dangerous Liaisons *'60*

Melvin Van Peebles
Sweet Sweetback's Baadasssss Song *'71*

Gus Van Sant
Good Will Hunting *'97*
To Die For *'95*
My Own Private Idaho *'91*
Drugstore Cowboy *'89*

Alex Van Warmerdam
Abel *'87*

Agnes Varda
101 Nights *'95*
The World of Jacques Demy *'95*
One Sings, the Other Doesn't *'77*

Joseph B. Vasquez
Hangin' with the Homeboys *'91*

David Veloz
Permanent Midnight *'98*

Michael Verhoeven
The Nasty Girl *'90*

Todd Verow
Little Shots of Happiness *'97*

Dziga Vertov
The Man with the Movie Camera *'23*

King Vidor
Our Daily Bread *'34*

Luchino Visconti
White Nights *'57*
Bellissima *'51*
Ossessione *'42*

Erich von Stroheim
Queen Kelly *'29*

Lars von Trier
Breaking the Waves *'95*

Margarethe von Trotta
The Second Awakening of Christa Klages *'78*

Bernard Vorhaus
The Amazing Mr. X *'48*
Bury Me Dead *'47*

Kurt Voss
Body Count *'97*

Andy Wachowski
Bound *'96*

Larry Wachowski
Bound *'96*

Jonathan Wacks
Powwow Highway *'89*

Andrzej Wajda
Ashes and Diamonds *'58*

John Walker
Hidden Children *'94*

Gary Walkow
The Trouble with Dick *'88*

Fred Walton
The Rosary Murders *'87*

Bu Wancang
Love and Duty *'31*

Wayne Wang
Smoke *'95*
Life Is Cheap...But Toilet Paper Is Expensive *'90*
Eat a Bowl of Tea *'89*
Chan Is Missing *'82*

Jennifer Warren
Forbidden Choices *'94*

Don Was
I Just Wasn't Made for These Times *'94*

John Waters
Pecker *'98*
Serial Mom *'94*
Female Trouble *'74*

Mark Waters
The House of Yes *'97*

Bruce Weber
Let's Get Lost *'88*

Mark Weidman
Killer Flick *'98*

Claudia Weill
Girlfriends *'78*

Peter Weir
Picnic at Hanging Rock *'75*

Jiri Weiss
Martha and I *'91*

Orson Welles
It's All True *'93*

Wim Wenders
The End of Violence *'97*
Wings of Desire *'88*

Lina Wertmuller
Seven Beauties *'76*
Swept Away... *'75*
Everything Ready, Nothing Works *'74*

Haskell Wexler
Medium Cool *'69*

Claude Whatham
That'll Be the Day *'73*

Tim Whelan
Clouds over Europe *'39*
Sidewalks of London *'38*

Stephen White
The Windsors: A Royal Family *'94*

Stephen Whittaker
Closing Numbers *'93*

Harriet Wichins
Silent Witness *'94*

Bernhard Wicki
False Weights *'74*

Bo Widerberg
Stubby *'74*

Ken Wiederhorn
A House in the Hills *'93*

Robert Wiene
The Hands of Orlac *'25*

Billy Wilder
The Private Life of Sherlock Holmes *'70*

Stephen Williams
My Teacher Ate My Homework *'98*

Nick Willing
Photographing Fairies *'97*

Kevin Willmott
Ninth Street *'98*

Peter M. Wilson
She's Vintage *'98*

Richard Wilson
It's All True *'93*

Sandy Wilson
American Boyfriends *'89*

Simon Wincer
Lightning Jack *'94*

Charles Winkler
Red Ribbon Blues *'95*

Michael Winner
A Chorus of Disapproval *'89*

Michael Winterbottom
Butterfly Kiss *'94*

Theodore Witcher
Love Jones *'96*

Andy Wolk
Traces of Red *'92*

M. Wallace Wolodarsky
Coldblooded *'94*

Edward D. Wood Jr.
Plan 9 from Outer Space *'56*
Bride of the Monster *'55*
Glen or Glenda? *'53*

Arthur Woods
They Drive by Night *'38*

Mary Woronov
Eating Raoul *'82*

Robert Wuhl
Open Season *'95*

William Wyler
Dead End *'37*
These Three *'36*

Jim Wynorski
Not of This Earth *'88*

Boaz Yakin
Fresh *'94*

Peter Yates
The House on Carroll Street *'88*

Zhang Yimou
The Story of Qui Ju *'91*
Ju Dou *'90*

Bud Yorkin
Start the Revolution without Me *'70*

Hiroaki Yoshida
Twilight of the Cockroaches *'90*

Harold Young
The Scarlet Pimpernel *'34*

Robert M. Young
Caught *'96*
Alambrista! *'77*

Krzysztof Zanussi
The Balance *'75*

Franco Zeffirelli
Jane Eyre *'96*

Paul Zehrer
Blessing *'94*

Marina Zenovich
Independent's Day *'97*

Tian Zhuangzhuang
The Blue Kite *'93*

Rafal Zielinksi
Fun *'94*

Lee David Zlotoff
The Spitfire Grill *'95*

Charlotte Zwerlin
Gimme Shelter *'70*

Terry Zwigoff
Crumb *'94*

Category Index

So look up "Comedy" or "Drama" if you must. But you could be more specific and look up "Black Comedy" or "Tearjerkers." And the truly inspired among you will look up "Disorganized Crime," or "Edibles," or "Dates from Hell," or one of the many creative and slightly off-the-wall categories we categorize by. The "Category Index" includes subject terms ranging from straight genre descriptions (Westerns, Documentaries) to more unique categories (Flashback, Gender Bending). These terms can help you identify unifying themes (Late Bloomin' Love, Mad Scientists), settings (Nifty '50s, France), events (World War II, the Great Depression), occupations (Shrinks, Struggling Musicians), or foreign films by country of origin (French, German). Category terms are listed alphabetically. Have fun.

Action Adventure
See also: Adventure Drama; Romantic Adventures; Swashbucklers
Blood & Concrete: A Love Story
Body Count
Breakaway
Bulldog Drummond
Diary of a Hitman
El Mariachi
Faster, Pussycat! Kill! Kill!
Island of the Lost
Mona Lisa
Project A: Part 2
Salvador
Set It Off
Switchblade Sisters
Try and Get Me

Adolescence
See: Coming of Age; Summer Camp; Teen Angst

Adoption & Orphans
See also: Hard Knock Life; Only the Lonely
Adoption
Anne of Green Gables
Flirting with Disaster
Great Expectations
Jane Eyre
Oliver Twist
Pixote
Queen Kelly
Secrets and Lies
Sidewalks of London
Sois Belle et Tais-Toi
Sparrows
Streetwise
The Tie That Binds

Adventure Drama
See also: Action Adventure; Drama
Abandon Ship
The Adventures of Milo & Otis
The Deceivers
Hackers
Mountains of the Moon
Platoon

Africa (Locale)
The African Queen
A Good Man in Africa
White Mischief
A World Apart

African America
See also: New Black Cinema
Black Joy
Daughters of the Dust
Eve's Bayou
Fly by Night
Fresh
Hangin' with the Homeboys
Hollywood Shuffle
Home of the Brave
Hoop Dreams
House Party
Just Another Girl on the I.R.T.
Kansas City
Lone Star
Love Jones
Menace II Society
New Jersey Drive
Nothing but a Man
One False Move
Paris Is Burning
Pastime
Pulp Fiction
Secrets and Lies
Set It Off
She's Gotta Have It
Slam
Straight out of Brooklyn
Sweet Sweetback's Baadasssss Song
To Sleep with Anger
Zebrahead

AIDS
And the Band Played On
Closing Numbers
It's My Party
Longtime Companion
Men in Love
Parting Glances
Red Ribbon Blues

Alcoholism
See: On the Rocks

Alien Beings
Not of This Earth
Plan 9 from Outer Space
Vegas in Space
Village of the Damned

American Film Theatre (AFT) Productions
Butley
A Delicate Balance
The Homecoming
The Iceman Cometh
Jacques Brel Is Alive and Well and Living in Paris
Lost in the Stars
Luther
The Maids
The Man in the Glass Booth
Rhinoceros
Three Sisters

American Indians
See: Native America

American South
The Apostle
The Ballad of the Sad Cafe
Bastard out of Carolina
The Big Easy
Eve's Bayou
Nothing but a Man
One False Move
Passion Fish
Rambling Rose
Ripe
River of Grass
Shag: The Movie
Shy People
Sling Blade
The Trip to Bountiful
Tune in Tomorrow
Wildflower

Animals
See: Cats; Dogs; Horses

Animation
Barefoot Gen
Little Nemo: Adventures in Slumberland
Princess and the Goblin
Twilight of the Cockroaches

Anime
See also: Animation
Barefoot Gen
Twilight of the Cockroaches

Anthology
See also: Horror Anthologies
Actors and Sin
Night on Earth
Pulp Fiction

Short Cuts
Slacker

Anti-Heroes
See also: Rebel with a Cause
Easy Rider
Palookaville
Set It Off
U-Turn

Anti-War War Movies
See also: Satire & Parody
Forbidden Games
Hombres Armados
Platoon

Art & Artists
Backbeat
Basquiat
The Belly of an Architect
Camille Claudel
Carrington
Crumb
I Shot Andy Warhol
Morgan!
Moulin Rouge
Sirens

Asia (Locale)
See also: China; Japan
Eat Drink Man Woman
Emmanuelle

Asian America
Chan Is Missing
Color of a Brisk and Leaping Day
Combination Platter
Eat a Bowl of Tea
Golden Gate
The Wedding Banquet

Assassinations
See also: Hit Men; Spies & Espionage
Ashes and Diamonds
La Femme Nikita
The Man Who Knew Too Much
The Manchurian Candidate
Michael Collins

At the Movies
The movie within a movie or movies about watching the movies. See also: Behind the Scenes
Apartment Zero
Boogie Nights
Cinema Paradiso
Love and Death on Long Island
Popcorn
The Real Blonde
Wes Craven's New Nightmare

Australia (Locale)
See: Down Under

Australian (Production)
The Adventures of Priscilla, Queen of the Desert
Brilliant Lies
Caddie
Celia: Child of Terror
Cosi
Dead Calm
Don's Party
Echoes of Paradise
A Feast at Midnight
The Good Wife
Muriel's Wedding
Mushrooms
Phobia
The Piano
Picnic at Hanging Rock
Road Games
Shine
Sirens
Sorrento Beach
Strictly Ballroom
To Have and to Hold
Warm Nights on a Slow-Moving Train

Austrian (Production)
East and West
The Hands of Orlac

Automobiles
See: Motor Vehicle Dept.

Bad Dads
See also: Monster Moms; Parenthood
Affliction
Bastard out of Carolina
The Myth of Fingerprints
The Shining
Star Maps
U-Turn

Baseball
Eight Men Out
Pastime

Basketball
The Basketball Diaries
Hoop Dreams

BBC TV Productions
Christabel
Mrs. Brown
Persuasion
Priest

Behind Bars
See: Men in Prison; Women in Prison

Behind the Scenes
A peek behind the show business curtain. See also: At the Movies; Film History
Actors and Sin
...And God Spoke
Bullets over Broadway
Chaplin
A Chorus of Disapproval
Cosi
The End of Violence
Gods and Monsters
Grief
Help!
Hollywood Shuffle
In the Soup
Killer Flick
The Killing of Sister George
Living in Oblivion
Open Season
Pastime
The Player
Search and Destroy
Secret Honor
Spice World: The Movie
Swimming with Sharks
Through the Olive Trees
Waiting for Guffman
Wes Craven's New Nightmare

Belgian (Production)
Ma Vie en Rose
One Sings, the Other Doesn't

Biography
See: This Is Your Life

Bisexuality
See also: Gays; Lesbians
Closing Numbers
The Crying Game
Pas Tres Catholique
Why Not!

Black Comedy
See also: Comedy; Comedy Drama; Satire & Parody
After Hours
Alice
American Strays
The Applegates
Beat the Devil
Careful
Clerks
Coldblooded
Coup de Torchon
Critical Care
Don's Party
The Doom Generation
Eat the Rich
Eating Raoul
Enid Is Sleeping
Entertaining Mr. Sloane
Fargo
Female Trouble
Funny Bones
Happiness
Hawks
Heathers
High Heels
The House of Yes
How to Get Ahead in Advertising
In the Company of Men
The Killing of Sister George
Kind Hearts and Coronets
The Ladykillers
Matador
Miracle Mile
Muriel's Wedding
Mushrooms
The Opposite of Sex
Pulp Fiction
Reckless
Serial Mom
Seven Beauties
Shallow Grave
Spanking the Monkey
Sticky Fingers
The Story of Fausta
Sudden Manhattan
Suicide Kings
Swimming with Sharks
Tie Me Up! Tie Me Down!
To Die For
Trainspotting
Trois Couleurs: Blanc
The Unbelievable Truth
Withnail and I
Women on the Verge of a Nervous Breakdown

Boating
See: Sail Away

Bowling
The Big Lebowski

Boxing
Champion
Pulp Fiction

Brazilian (Production)
Kiss of the Spider Woman
Pixote
The Story of Fausta

Bringing Up Baby
See also: Parenthood; Pregnant Pauses
Celia: Child of Terror
Helen's Babies
The Miracle
The Very Edge

British (Production)
Abandon Ship
Absolute Beginners
The African Queen
Alfie
Angels and Insects
Another Country
Apartment Zero
An Awfully Big Adventure
Backbeat
The Ballad of the Sad Cafe
The Battle of the Sexes
Bedazzled
Before the Rain
The Belles of St. Trinian's
Bellman and True
The Belly of an Architect
Black Joy
Black Narcissus
Blackmail
Blithe Spirit
Blow-Up
Boy Next Door
Brief Encounter
Butley
Butterfly Kiss
Carrington
Castaway
The Cater Street Hangman
Century
Chaplin
Children of the Damned
A Chorus of Disapproval
Christabel
Closing Numbers
Confessions of a Window Cleaner
Dance with a Stranger
The Dead
Dead of Night
Dealers
The Deceivers
Deep End
A Delicate Balance
The Devil Is a Woman

Different for Girls
Don't Take It to Heart
Dreamchild
Eat the Rich
Enchanted April
The Englishman Who Went up a HIll But Came down a Mountain
The Entertainer
Entertaining Mr. Sloane
Evergreen
The Fallen Idol
The Favor, the Watch, and the Very Big Fish
Fire Maidens from Outer Space
For Queen and Country
Four Weddings and a Funeral
Frenzy
Fright
The Frightened City
From the Pole to the Equator
The Full Monty
Galileo
Gaslight
Genevieve
Georgy Girl
The Ghost Goes West
The Good Soldier
Great Expectations
Hand in Hand
A Handful of Dust
A Hard Day's Night
Having a Wild Weekend
Hawks
Hear My Song
Heat and Dust
Help!
The Hidden Room
High Season
The Homecoming
Hot Millions
How to Get Ahead in Advertising
I Love You, I Love You Not
If...
In Celebration
In Possession
In the Name of the Father
The Innocents
Interlude
The Intimate Stranger
Isadora
Island of the Lost
John and Julie
Just Like a Woman
Kind Hearts and Coronets
The Krays
Kurt and Courtney
The Lady Vanishes
Ladybird, Ladybird
The Ladykillers
Lair of the White Worm
The Land That Time Forgot
The Last of the High Kings
Leather Boys
Let Him Have It
Lisztomania
Little Dorrit, Film 1: Nobody's Fault
Little Dorrit, Film 2: Little Dorrit's Story
The Little Kidnappers
The Little Prince
Loch Ness
Lolita
London Kills Me
The Lonely Passion of Judith Hearne
The Long Good Friday
Look Back in Anger
Love and Death on Long Island
Lucky Jim
Ma Vie en Rose
The Madness of King George
The Maids
The Man Who Knew Too Much
The Mark
The Marriage
Maurice
Mrs. Brown
Mona Lisa
Morgan!
Much Ado about Nothing
Murder on the Orient Express
My Beautiful Laundrette
Naked
Never Take Candy from a Stranger
Night Train to Munich
Nine Days a Queen
1984
The Obsessed
The Odessa File
On Approval
101 Nights
Orlando
Paper Mask
Perfect Friday
Performance
Persuasion
Photographing Fairies
Pink String and Sealing Wax
Priest
The Prime of Miss Jean Brodie
The Private Life of Henry VIII
The Private Life of Sherlock Holmes
Pygmalion
The Railway Children
The Remains of the Day
Repulsion
Return from the Ashes
Rhinoceros
Rich and Strange
Rita, Sue & Bob Too
The Rolling Stones Rock and Roll Circus
Room at the Top
A Room with a View
The Runaway Bus
Sammy & Rosie Get Laid
Saraband for Dead Lovers
Scandal
The Scarlet Pimpernel
Secrets and Lies
Shallow Grave
Shirley Valentine
Sidewalks of London
Sirens
Sister My Sister
The Slipper and the Rose
The Smallest Show on Earth
So Long at the Fair
S.O.S. Titanic
Special Effects
Spice World: The Movie
Stardust
Start the Revolution Without Me
The Stranger's Hand
Strapless
A Summer Story
Swastika
10 Rillington Place
35 Up
The 39 Steps
This Happy Breed
Three Sisters
Thursday's Child
Tiger Bay
Time Lock
Trainspotting
Twenty-One
Twisted Nerve
Two for the Road
Under Suspicion
Uneasy Terms
Valentino
The Very Edge
Victim
Village of the Damned
Voyage of the Damned
Walk on the Wild Side
Where Angels Fear to Tread
The Whistle Blower
Whistle down the Wind
Who Done It?
Widow's Peak
Wild West
Wilde
The Windsors: A Royal Family
The Wings of the Dove
Wish You Were Here
Withnail and I
The Woman in Question
Wonderland
A World Apart
Young and Innocent

Buddies
The Adventures of Milo & Otis
Backbeat
The Basketball Diaries
A Boy and His Dog
Chasing Amy
Clerks
Easy Rider
Federal Hill
The Full Monty
Good Will Hunting
Hangin' with the Homeboys
Hard Eight
Heavenly Creatures
Hurricane Streets
Mallrats
Mina Tannenbaum
My Beautiful Laundrette
Mystic Pizza
One Sings, the Other Doesn't
Palookaville
Platoon
Return of the Secaucus 7
Robert et Robert
Shag: The Movie
Sling Blade
SubUrbia
Terminal Bliss
Trainspotting
Trees Lounge
Walking and Talking
Withnail and I

Bulgarian (Production)
Last Summer

Buses
The Adventures of Priscilla, Queen of the Desert
The Runaway Bus
Spice World: The Movie
The Sweet Hereafter
The Trip to Bountiful

Cabbies
Night on Earth
She's the One

Campus Capers
See: School Daze

Canada (Locale)
American Boyfriends
Anne of Green Gables
The Boys of St. Vincent
Clean, Shaven
Eddie and the Cruisers 2: Eddie Lives!
Love and Human Remains
The Sweet Hereafter
Time Lock

Canadian (Production)
American Boyfriends
Anne of Green Gables
The Boys of St. Vincent
Butley
Crash
Daughters of the Country
A Delicate Balance
Eddie and the Cruisers 2: Eddie Lives!
Exotica
Galileo
Hidden Children
The Homecoming
In Celebration
Le Sexe des Etoiles
The Little Girl Who Lives down the Lane
Love and Death on Long Island
Love and Human Remains
The Luck of Ginger Coffey
The Maids
Medicine River
My Teacher Ate My Homework
Once upon a Time in the East
The Orders
Paris, France
Random Encounter

The Return of Tommy Tricker
Rhinoceros
Salmonberries
Silent Witness
The Sweet Hereafter
32 Short Films about Glenn Gould
Ticket to Heaven
Tommy Tricker & the Stamp Traveller

Cannibalism

See also: Edibles

A Boy and His Dog
Cannibal Women in the Avocado Jungle of Death
Eat the Rich
Eating Raoul
Night of the Living Dead

Carnivals, Circuses & Amusement Parks

Carnival of Souls
The Third Man
Shag: The Movie
Variety Lights
The Woman in Question

Cats

The Adventures of Milo & Otis
When the Cat's Away

Central America (Locale)

Cafe Nica: Portraits from Nicaragua
Hombres Armados
Salvador
Which Way, Por Favor?

Child Abuse

Bastard out of Carolina
The Boys of St. Vincent
Never Take Candy from a Stranger
Ripe
Shades of Doubt
2 by 4
Wildflower

Childhood Visions

See also: Murderous Children

American Heart
Angela
Bastard out of Carolina
Black Beauty
Cinema Paradiso
Emma's Shadow
Eve's Bayou
FairyTale: A True Story
The Fallen Idol
For a Lost Soldier
Forbidden Games
Fresh
The Lady in White
Le Grand Chemin
A Little Princess
Ma Vie en Rose
My Life As a Dog
My Teacher Ate My Homework
The Orphans
Pixote
The Railway Children
Sling Blade
Small Change
Spirit of the Beehive
Star Kid
Tito and Me
Welcome to the Dollhouse
Whistle down the Wind
The Wizard of Loneliness
A World Apart

China (Locale)

The Blue Kite
Ju Dou
The Story of Qui Ju

Chinese (Production)

The Blue Kite
Ju Dou
Love and Duty
Project A: Part 2
The Story of Qui Ju

Christmas

See: Holidays

CIA

See: Spies & Espionage

Circuses

See: Carnivals, Circuses & Amusement Parks

Cities

See: Urban Drama

Civil Rights

Home of the Brave
The Orders

Classic Horror

See also: Horror; Horror Anthologies; Horror Comedy

Bride of the Monster
Carnival of Souls
Frankenstein Unbound
Lair of the White Worm
Nosferatu
Pandora's Box
Vampyr

Cold War

See: Red Scare

Comedy

See also: Black Comedy; Comedy Drama; Horror Comedy; Musicals; Romantic Comedy; Satire & Parody; Screwball Comedy; Slapstick Comedy

Alfie
...And God Spoke
The Belles of St. Trinian's
Bullets over Broadway
Cold Feet
Confessions of a Window Cleaner
Cosi
Daughters, Daughters
Dazed and Confused
Dinner for Adele
Flirting with Disaster
The Full Monty
Having a Wild Weekend
Helen's Babies
His Picture in the Papers
Hot Millions
House Party
Hugo Pool
Hundred Per Cent
I Think I Do
In a Wild Moment
In the Spirit
Johnny Stecchino
Jonah Who Will Be 25 in the Year 2000
Kika
Killer Flick
Law of Desire
Life Is Beautiful
Life Is Cheap...But Toilet Paper Is Expensive
Lightning Jack
Living in Oblivion
Love and Death on Long Island
The Luckiest Man in the World
Lucky Jim
Mallrats
Meier
Motorama
Old Enough
Party Girl
Pas Tres Catholique
Passionate Thief
Pecker
Perfect Friday
Pygmalion
Red Ribbon Blues
Rita, Sue & Bob Too
The Runaway Bus
Shall We Dance?
She's Vintage
Sirens
The Sleazy Uncle
Small Change
Starving Artists
Sudden Manhattan
Teresa's Tattoo
Three Lives and Only One Death
To Hell with Love
The Troublemaker
Walking and Talking
Welcome to the Dollhouse
When the Cat's Away
Who Done It?
Wild West

Comedy Drama

See also: Black Comedy; Comedy

American Boyfriends
Antonia's Line
Barcelona
The Best Way
Big Night
Bongwater
Boogie Nights
Box of Moonlight
Carried Away
A Chorus of Disapproval
Chungking Express
Combination Platter
Cousin, Cousine
The Daytrippers
Destiny Turns on the Radio
Different for Girls
Down & Dirty
Drugstore Cowboy
Eat a Bowl of Tea
Eat Drink Man Woman
Everything Ready, Nothing Works
Five Corners
Georgy Girl
Girlfriends
A Good Man in Africa
The Graduate
Grief
Hangin' with the Homeboys
Household Saints
In the Soup
Inside Monkey Zetterland
Like Water for Chocolate
Loch Ness
Love and Human Remains
Lover Girl
Ma Vie en Rose
Metropolitan
Mr. North
Murmur of the Heart
My Beautiful Laundrette
My Life As a Dog
Mystic Pizza
The Nasty Girl
Night on Earth
1999
Powwow Highway
The Prime of Miss Jean Brodie
Return of the Secaucus 7
Rhinoceros
Robert et Robert
The Rules of the Game
Shag: The Movie
Shirley Valentine
A Shock to the System
Short Cuts
Smoke Signals
Star Maps
Street Music
Swept Away...
A Thousand Clowns
Thursday's Child
Tito and Me
To Sleep with Anger
True Love
Trust
Twenty Bucks
Twenty-One
Twister
Two for the Road
Went to Coney Island on a Mission from God...Be Back by Five
Why Not!
Widow's Peak
Wired
Wish You Were Here
The World of Henry Orient

Coming of Age

See also: Teen Angst

All Over Me
American Boyfriends
Anne of Green Gables
An Awfully Big Adventure
The Blue Kite
Blue Velvet
Boss' Son
Dirty Dancing
Eat Drink Man Woman

For a Lost Soldier
The 400 Blows
Gas Food Lodging
The Graduate
Hangin' with the Homeboys
Heathers
Hurricane Streets
I Love You, I Love You Not
Le Grand Chemin
Le Sexe des Etoiles
Lover Girl
Martha and I
Metropolitan
Murmur of the Heart
My Life As a Dog
My Tutor
Mystic Pizza
Old Enough
Palookaville
Platoon
Rambling Rose
A Room with a View
Smooth Talk
Spanking the Monkey
Stacking
Twenty-One
Walking and Talking
Went to Coney Island on a Mission from God...Be Back by Five

Computers
Hackers
Pi

Concentration/ Internment Camps
See also: Nazis & Other Paramilitary Slugs
I Love You, I Love You Not
Life Is Beautiful

Concert Films
See also: Rock Stars on Film
Free Tibet
Gimme Shelter

Contemporary Noir
See also: Film Noir
After Dark, My Sweet
After Hours
The Big Easy
Blood Simple
Blue Velvet
Bodies, Rest & Motion
Cutter's Way
Dance with a Stranger
The Grifters
Guncrazy
Hard Eight
Kill Me Again
The Last Seduction
The Manchurian Candidate
One False Move
Performance
Pulp Fiction
Red Rock West
Reservoir Dogs
River of Grass
sex, lies and videotape
Trouble in Mind
True Confessions
U-Turn
The Usual Suspects
Wild at Heart

Cooking
See: Edibles

Cops
See also: Detectives
Affliction
Bad Lieutenant
Bang
The Big Easy
Blackmail
Chungking Express
Cop Land
Coup de Torchon
Fargo
Jackie Brown
Lone Star
Miami Blues
New Jersey Drive
The Prowler
Traces of Red
Two Small Bodies
The Usual Suspects

Corporate Shenanigans
The Battle of the Sexes
Dealers
Hackers
How to Get Ahead in Advertising
In the Company of Men
Open Season
The Player
Roger & Me
A Shock to the System
Swimming with Sharks
Vortex

Courtroom Drama
See: Order in the Court

Creepy Houses
In Possession
The Innocents
The Shining

Crime & Criminals
See also: Crime Sprees; Disorganized Crime; Organized Crime; Serial Killers
Betrayed
The Big Easy
Breathless
Clean, Shaven
Cold Feet
Criminal Law
Dead Man
Dead Man Walking
Down & Dirty
Fargo
Federal Hill
Female Trouble
Frenzy
The Frightened City
The Funeral
The Grifters
Hot Millions
A House in the Hills
Hurricane Streets
The Incident
The Intimate Stranger
Jackie Brown
Kansas City
The Ladykillers
Let Him Have It
Little Odessa
Lone Star
Mona Lisa
New Jersey Drive
Nuns on the Run
Ossessione
Perfect Friday
Pink String and Sealing Wax
Pixote
Red Rock West
River's Edge
Sois Belle et Tais-Toi
Suicide Kings
Sweet Sweetback's Baadasssss Song
10 Rillington Place
They Drive by Night
Tiger Bay
To Die For
Too Late for Tears
Tough Guys Don't Dance
The Troublemaker
Twisted Nerve
Two Small Bodies
U-Turn
The Underneath
The Usual Suspects
Violette
Wanda
The Wild Party

Crime Drama
See also: Drama
Cop Land
The Intimate Stranger
Jackie Brown
Normal Life
Return from the Ashes

Crime Sprees
See also: Lovers on the Lam
Butterfly Kiss
Love and a .45
Normal Life
Set It Off
The Tie That Binds

Crop Dusters
Down on the farm.
Blessing
Curse of the Starving Class
Our Daily Bread
Stacking

Cuban (Production)
I Am Cuba
Letters from the Park
Reasons of State

Cult Films
Apartment Zero
Badlands
Bedazzled
Blood Simple
Blow-Up
Blue Velvet
A Boy and His Dog
Breathless
Bride of the Monster
Cannibal Women in the Avocado Jungle of Death
Careful
Carnival of Souls
Crash
Detour
Easy Rider
Eating Raoul
Eraserhead
Evil Dead
Faster, Pussycat! Kill! Kill!
Female Trouble
Frankenstein Unbound
Glen or Glenda?
A Hard Day's Night
Kiss Me Deadly
Naked Kiss
The Night of the Hunter
Night of the Living Dead
Peeping Tom
Performance
Plan 9 from Outer Space
Spider Baby
Start the Revolution without Me
Twister
Vortex

Cults
See also: Occult
The Deceivers
Safe
Ticket to Heaven
Withnail and I

Czech (Production)
Alice
Day for My Love
Dinner for Adele
Seclusion near a Forest

Dance Fever
Boogie Nights
The Children of Theatre Street
Dirty Dancing
Faster, Pussycat! Kill! Kill!
Isadora
Paris Is Burning
Shag: The Movie
Shall We Dance?
Strictly Ballroom

Danish (Production)
Breaking the Waves
Emma's Shadow
The Last of the High Kings

Dates from Hell
See also: Singles
After Hours
Miracle Mile
Walking and Talking
What Happened Was...

Death & the Afterlife
See also: Funerals; Ghosts, Ghouls, & Goblins; Occult; Suicide
Blithe Spirit
Carnival of Souls
Cemetery Man
D.O.A.
The English Patient
The Entertainer
Hawks
I Bury the Living
I Married a Witch
It's My Party
The Lady in White
Night of the Living Dead

Death Row
See also: Men in Prison; Women in Prison
Dead Man Walking
Let Him Have It
Lost Highway
The Thin Blue Line
Under Suspicion

Dedicated Teachers
See also: School Daze
Carried Away
The Prime of Miss Jean Brodie
Reno's Kids: 87 Days Plus 11
Stand and Deliver

Deserts
The Adventures of Priscilla, Queen of the Desert
American Strays
The English Patient
Faster, Pussycat! Kill! Kill!

Detectives
See also: Cops
Blackmail
Bulldog Drummond
Cat and Mouse
From Hollywood to Deadwood
Kill Me Again
Kiss Me Deadly
Murder on the Orient Express
Pas Tres Catholique
Private Hell 36
The Private Life of Sherlock Holmes
Under Suspicion
Uneasy Terms
Vortex
Who Done It?

Dinosaurs
The Land That Time Forgot

Disorganized Crime
See also: Crime & Criminals; Organized Crime
Fargo
Palookaville
Reservoir Dogs
Suicide Kings

Divorce
See also: Marriage; Singles
The Only One
Saraband for Dead Lovers
Scenes from a Marriage

Doctors & Nurses
See also: AIDS; Sanity Check; Shrinks
And the Band Played On
Century
Critical Care
The English Patient
Guest in the House
Hombres Armados
The Madness of King George
Mr. North
Paper Mask
The Unbearable Lightness of Being

Docudrama
See also: Documentary
And the Band Played On
Glen or Glenda?
Kids
S.O.S. Titanic
The Thin Blue Line
32 Short Films about Glenn Gould

Documentary
See also: Docudrama
The Brandon Teena Story
A Brief History of Time
Brother's Keeper
Carmen Miranda: Bananas Is My Business
Chicken Hawk
The Children of Theatre Street
Cinema Europe
Crumb
Diamonds in the Snow
Feed
Free Tibet
Heavy Petting
Hidden Children
Hollywood on Trial
Hoop Dreams
Independent's Day
It's All True
A Kiss to This Land
Kurt and Courtney
Legacy of the Hollywood Blacklist
Let's Get Lost
Licensed to Kill
The Making of "A Hard Day's Night"
The Man with the Movie Camera
The Missing Reel
Mystery of the Last Tsar
Nico Icon
Not Fourteen Again
Orson Welles: The One Man Band
Out of the Loop
Paradise Lost: The Child Murders at Robin Hood Hills
Paris Is Burning
Point of Order
Reno's Kids: 87 Days Plus 11
Roger & Me
Silent Witness
The Silver Screen: Color Me Lavender
Streetwise
Swastika
The Thin Blue Line
35 Up
Thomas Jefferson: A View from the Mountain
Thy Kingdom Come, Thy Will Be Done
Unzipped
Walk on the Wild Side
The War Room
Who Are the DeBolts and Where Did They Get 19 Kids?
The Windsors: A Royal Family
The Wonderful, Horrible Life of Leni Riefenstahl
Word Is Out: Stories of Some of Our Lives
The World of Jacques Demy

Dogs
The Adventures of Milo & Otis
A Boy and His Dog

Down Under (Locale)
Australian and New Zealand settings.
The Adventures of Priscilla, Queen of the Desert
Caddie
The Good Wife
Heavenly Creatures
Muriel's Wedding
Shine
Sirens
Sorrento Beach
Strictly Ballroom

Drama
See also: Adventure Drama; Comedy Drama; Historical Drama; Musicals; Romantic Drama; Tearjerkers; Tragedy
Actors and Sin
Adoption
Affliction
Alambrista!
All Over Me
Allonsanfan
American Heart
And the Band Played On
An Angel at My Table
Angela
Anna
Anne of Green Gables
Another Country
The Apostle
Art for Teachers of Children
Ashes and Diamonds
An Awfully Big Adventure
Backbeat
Bad Lieutenant
Badlands
The Balance
The Balcony
Bang
The Basketball Diaries
Basquiat
Bastard out of Carolina
Bellissima
Bellman and True
The Belly of an Architect
Betrayed
Black Beauty
Black Narcissus
Blessing
The Blue Kite
Bodies, Rest & Motion
Boss' Son
The Boys of St. Vincent
Breaking the Waves
Brilliant Lies
The Brothers McMullen
Burnt by the Sun
Business As Usual
Butley
Butterfly Kiss
Caught
Celia: Child of Terror
Center Stage
Century
Chameleon Street
Champion
Chaplin
The Chocolate War
Christabel
Cinema Paradiso
Citizen X
City of Hope
Clean, Shaven
Closet Land
Closing Numbers
A Cold Wind in August
Color of a Brisk and Leaping Day
The Conformist
Cousin Bette
Crash
Crashout
Crime of Passion
The Crossing Guard
The Crucible
Crush
The Crying Game
Curse of the Starving Class
Daddy Nostalgia
Dance with a Stranger
Dangerous Liaisons
Das Boot
Daughters of the Dust
The Dead
Dead End
Dead Man Walking
Dealers
Death and the Maiden
Deep End
A Delicate Balance
Detour
The Devil Is a Woman
Dirty Dancing
A Dream of Passion
Dreamchild
Easy Rider
Echoes of Paradise
Eddie and the Cruisers
Eddie and the Cruisers 2: Eddie Lives!
8½
Eight Men Out
Emmanuelle
Emma's Shadow
The End of Violence
The Entertainer
Equinox
Every Man for Himself & God against All
Eve's Bayou
Exotica
Face to Face
The Fallen Idol
A Feast at Midnight
Federal Hill
For a Lost Soldier
For Queen and Country
Forbidden Choices
Forbidden Games

The 400 Blows
Frankie Starlight
French Provincial
Fresh
From the Journals of Jean Seberg
Fun
The Funeral
Galileo
Gas Food Lodging
Georgia
Girls in Chains
Girls Town
Glen or Glenda?
The Good Wife
Good Will Hunting
Great Expectations
The Grifters
Hand in Hand
A Handful of Dust
Happy Together
Hard Traveling
He Ran All the Way
Heartland
Heat and Sunlight
Heavenly Creatures
Heavy
Hester Street
Homage
Hombres Armados
Home of the Brave
The Homecoming
The Hours and Times
House of Cards
The House of the Spirits
Hurricane Streets
I Am Cuba
I Like It Like That
I Love You, I Love You Not
I Met a Murderer
The Ice Storm
The Iceman Cometh
If...
If I Had It to Do Over Again
In Celebration
In the Name of the Father
The Interrogation
Iphigenia
Isadora
johns
Ju Dou
Just Another Girl on the I.R.T.
Kalifornia
Kansas City
Kids
Kill Me Again
The Killing
The Killing of a Chinese Bookie
Kiss of the Spider Woman
The Krays
La Femme Nikita
Lacombe, Lucien
Ladybird, Ladybird
Lamerica
Lancelot of the Lake
Last Exit to Brooklyn
Le Grand Chemin
Le Sexe des Etoiles
Leather Boys
Leaving Las Vegas
Let Him Have It
Lisztomania
Little Dorrit, Film 1: Nobody's Fault
Little Dorrit, Film 2: Little Dorrit's Story
Little Odessa
Little Shots of Happiness
Lolita
London Kills Me
The Lonely Passion of Judith Hearne
The Long Good Friday
Longtime Companion
Look Back in Anger
Lost Highway
Love and a .45
Love unto Waste
The Luck of Ginger Coffey
Lumiere
Mac
The Madness of King George
The Maids
The Man in the Glass Booth
Manny & Lo
Matewan
Maurice
Medium Cool
Men in Love
Menace II Society
Metamorphosis
Michael Collins
Mina Tannenbaum
The Miracle
Mrs. Brown
Mrs. Parker and the Vicious Circle
Mother Kusters Goes to Heaven
Moulin Rouge
My Family
My Left Foot
My Own Private Idaho
The Myth of Fingerprints
Nadja
Naked Kiss
Nenette and Boni
Never Take Candy from a Stranger
Nine Months
1984
Ninth Street
Nothing but a Man
Oleanna
Oliver Twist
Once upon a Time in the East
One False Move
100 Days after Childhood
One Sings, the Other Doesn't
Orlando
The Orphans
Ossessione
Our Daily Bread
Padre Padrone
Paper Mask
Pariah
Paris, France
Parting Glances
Passion Fish
Pastime
Permanent Record
Phobia
Photographing Fairies
Pi
Picture Bride
Pink String and Sealing Wax
Pitfall
Pixote
The Player
Poison
The Postman
Priest
Private Hell 36
Public Access
Queen Kelly
The Railway Children
Rambling Rose
The Remains of the Day
Reservoir Dogs
Rhythm Thief
Ricochets
Ripe
River of Grass
River's Edge
Ruby in Paradise
Safe
Salmonberries
Scandal
The Scarlet Pimpernel
Scenes from a Marriage
Second Coming of Suzanne
Secret Honor
The Secret of Roan Inish
Secrets and Lies
Separate Tables
sex, lies and videotape
Shack Out on 101
Shades of Doubt
Shine
Shy People
Sidewalks of London
Sister My Sister
Slacker
Sling Blade
Smoke
Smooth Talk
Sorceress
Sorrento Beach
Special Effects
Spirit of the Beehive
The Spitfire Grill
Stacking
Stand and Deliver
Stardust
Steppenwolf
The Story of Qui Ju
Straight out of Brooklyn
The Stranger's Hand
Street Smart
SubUrbia
The Sweet Hereafter
Sweet Sweetback's Baadasssss Song
Swoon
Ted
Terminal Bliss
That'll Be the Day
These Three
They Drive by Night
32 Short Films about Glenn Gould
This Happy Breed
Three Sisters
Ticket to Heaven
Time Lock
Tomorrow the World
Too Late for Tears
Tracks
Trees Lounge
The Trip to Bountiful
Trois Couleurs: Bleu
Trois Couleurs: Rouge
True Confessions
25 Fireman's Street
2 by 4
Two Small Bodies
Ulee's Gold
Valentino
Vanya on 42nd Street
Variety Lights
Victim
Vortex
Voyage of the Damned
Waiting for the Moon
Wanda
The Wash
The Waterdance
The Whales of August
What Happened Was...
Where Angels Fear to Tread
Which Way, Por Favor?
Whistle down the Wind
The Whole Wide World
Wicked Woman
Wilde
Wildflower
The Wizard of Loneliness
A Woman under the Influence
A World Apart
You Only Live Once
Zohar: Mediterranean Blues

Drugs
See: Pill Poppin'

Dutch (Production)
Abel
Antonia's Line
For a Lost Soldier
Orlando
The Vanishing

Eating
See: Cannibalism; Edibles

Edibles
See also: Cannibalism
Big Night
Combination Platter
Eat a Bowl of Tea
Eat Drink Man Woman
Eat the Rich
Like Water for Chocolate
The Spitfire Grill

Ethics & Morals
Cutter's Way
The Ice Storm
Platoon
Private Hell 36
Twenty-One

Etiquette
Phantom of Liberty
Pygmalion
True Love

Family Ties
See also: Moms; Parenthood
American Heart
Angela
Angels and Insects
Antonia's Line
Barcelona
Bastard out of Carolina
Bellissima
Big Night
Blessing
The Blue Kite
Boss' Son
Brilliant Lies
Brother's Keeper
The Brothers McMullen
Burnt by the Sun
Caught
Clean, Shaven
Cousin Bette
Cousin, Cousine
The Crossing Guard
Crumb
Crush
Curse of the Starving Class
Daddy Nostalgia
Daughters of the Dust
The Daytrippers
Down & Dirty
East and West
Eat a Bowl of Tea
Eat Drink Man Woman
Enid Is Sleeping
The Entertainer
Entertaining Mr. Sloane
Equinox
Eve's Bayou
Face to Face
Flirting with Disaster
Forbidden Choices
Frankie Starlight
The Funeral
Funny Bones
Gas Food Lodging
Georgia
Golden Gate
Halloween: H20
Heavy
High Heels
Homage
House of Cards
The House of the Spirits
The House of Yes
Household Saints
Hugo Pool
Hurricane Streets
I Love You, I Love You Not
I Met a Murderer
The Ice Storm
In Celebration
In the Name of the Father
Inside Monkey Zetterland
Iphigenia
It's My Party
Kind Hearts and Coronets
The Krays
La Ceremonie
The Last of the High Kings
Law of Desire
Le Sexe des Etoiles
Life Is Beautiful
Like Water for Chocolate
Little Dorrit, Film 1: Nobody's Fault
Little Dorrit, Film 2: Little Dorrit's Story
Little Odessa
A Little Princess
Lone Star
Lover Girl
Ma Vie en Rose
Mac
The Madness of King George
Manny & Lo
Martha and I
Mother's Boys
Murmur of the Heart
My Family
The Myth of Fingerprints
Nadja
Nenette and Boni
The Night of the Hunter
The Opposite of Sex
Padre Padrone
Pecker
Peeping Tom
Persuasion
Pitfall
The Railway Children
The Secret of Roan Inish
Secrets and Lies
Seven Beauties
Shades of Doubt
She's the One
Shine
Shy People
Silent Tongue
Sister My Sister
The Sleazy Uncle
Smoke Signals
Sorrento Beach
Spanking the Monkey
Spider Baby
Star Maps
Strapless
Struggle
Suture
The Sweet Hereafter
This Happy Breed
A Thousand Clowns
Thursday's Child
Ticket to Heaven
The Tie That Binds
Tito and Me
To Sleep with Anger
The Trip to Bountiful
Trois Couleurs: Blanc
Trois Couleurs: Bleu
True Confessions
True Love
Twister
2 by 4
Two Small Bodies
Ulee's Gold
Uneasy Terms
Violette
The Wedding Banquet
Welcome to the Dollhouse
The Whales of August
Wild at Heart
Wild West
Wildflower
The Wings of the Dove
The Wizard of Loneliness
A Woman under the Influence
Women on the Verge of a Nervous Breakdown
A World Apart

Fantasy
See also: Animation; Musicals
Alice
Blithe Spirit
The City of Lost Children
Dreamchild
Eraserhead
I Married a Witch
Julia and Julia
Little Nemo: Adventures in Slumberland
Night Tide
Princess and the Goblin
Reckless
The Return of Tommy Tricker
The Secret of Roan Inish
Tommy Tricker & the Stamp Traveller
Trouble in Mind
Wings of Desire
The Witches

Farming
See: Crop Dusters

Female Bonding
See also: Women
Antonia's Line
Girls Town
Lover Girl
Manny & Lo
Passion Fish
Set It Off
Walking and Talking

Femme Fatale
Carried Away
Crime of Passion
Crush
Detour
Faster, Pussycat! Kill! Kill!
Frankenhooker
Impact
Lair of the White Worm
The Last Seduction
Night Tide
The Opposite of Sex
Scandal
Too Late for Tears
Trading Favors
U-Turn
Under Suspicion

The Fifties
See: Nifty '50s

Film History
Cinema Europe
Cinema Paradiso
8½
Forgotten Silver
Heavy Petting
Hollywood on Trial
Legacy of the Hollywood Blacklist
The Missing Reel
Orson Welles: The One Man Band
Way Down East
The Wonderful, Horrible Life of Leni Riefenstahl

Film Noir
See also: Contemporary Noir
Delusion
Detour
D.O.A.
Gun Crazy
The Killing
Kiss Me Deadly
Naked Kiss
Pitfall
The Prowler
The Red House
The Third Man
Too Late for Tears
The Underneath
Vortex

Film Stars
See also: Price of Fame
Carmen Miranda: Bananas Is My Business
Chaplin
From the Journals of Jean Seberg
Rock Hudson's Home Movies
Thursday's Child
Valentino

Filmmaking
See also: At the Movies; Behind the Scenes
...And God Spoke
Independent's Day
It's All True
Killer Flick
Living in Oblivion
The Making of "A Hard Day's Night"
Orson Welles: The One Man Band
The Player
The Silver Screen: Color Me Lavender
Special Effects
Swimming with Sharks
Wes Craven's New Nightmare
The Wonderful, Horrible Life of Leni Riefenstahl

Flashback
Antonia's Line
Carried Away
Eve's Bayou
Exotica
Frankie Starlight
Nina Takes a Lover
Reservoir Dogs
Smoke Signals
The Underneath
The Usual Suspects
Valentino

Flower Children
Easy Rider
Gimme Shelter
Grace of My Heart

Food
See: Edibles

Foreign
See: Australian; Austrian; Belgian; Belgian; Brazilian; British; Bulgarian; Canadian; Chinese; Cuban; Czech; Danish; Dutch; French; German; Greek; Hong Kong; Hungarian; Indian; Iranian; Irish; Israeli; Italian; Jamaican; Japanese; Macedonian; Mexican; New Zealand; Norwegian; Polish; Russian; Spanish; Swedish; Swiss; Taiwanese; Yugoslavian

Frame-Ups
The Lady Confesses
The Obsessed

France (Locale)
Breathless
Children of Paradise
The Favor, the Watch, and the Very Big Fish
La Ceremonie
Mina Tannenbaum
Moulin Rouge
Night on Earth
The Rules of the Game
The Scarlet Pimpernel
Sister My Sister

French (Production)
Beauty and the Beast
Before the Rain
The Best Way
Black Moon
Blue Country
Breaking the Waves
Breathless
Burnt by the Sun
Camille Claudel
Carrington
Cat and Mouse
Children of Paradise
The City of Lost Children
The Conformist
Coup de Torchon
Cousin, Cousine
The Crucible
Daddy Nostalgia
Dangerous Liaisons
Dear Victor
Dites-Lui Que Je L'Aime
Emmanuelle
The End of Violence
The Favor, the Watch, and the Very Big Fish
First Communion
Forbidden Games
The 400 Blows
France, Incorporated
French Provincial
Fresh
Hu-Man
I Have Killed
I Love You, I Love You Not
If I Had It to Do Over Again
In a Wild Moment
Jacques Brel Is Alive and Well and Living in Paris
La Ceremonie
La Femme Nikita
Lacombe, Lucien
L'Amour en Herbe
Lancelot of the Lake
Le Grand Chemin
The Little Girl Who Lives down the Lane
Lumiere
Ma Vie en Rose
The Man Who Loved Women
The Marquise of O
Mina Tannenbaum
Murmur of the Heart
Nenette and Boni
101 Nights
One Night Stand
One Sings, the Other Doesn't
Orlando
Orson Welles: The One Man Band
Pas Tres Catholique
Phantom of Liberty
Reasons of State
The Red Poster
Roads to the South
Robert et Robert
Servant and Mistress
Shades of Doubt
Small Change
Sois Belle et Tais-Toi
Sorceress
Three Lives and Only One Death
Too Beautiful for You
Trois Couleurs: Blanc
Trois Couleurs: Bleu
Trois Couleurs: Rouge
The Vanishing
Victory March
Violette
When the Cat's Away
White Nights
Why Not!
The Wonderful Crook
The World of Jacques Demy

Friendship
See: Buddies

Front Page
See also: Shutterbugs
Fun
Mrs. Parker and the Vicious Circle
Nina Takes a Lover
The Odessa File
Salvador
Shy People
Spice World: The Movie
Street Smart
A World Apart

Funerals
See also: Death & the Afterlife
Four Weddings and a Funeral
Heathers
The Wings of the Dove

Gambling
Eight Men Out
Hard Eight
House of Games
Household Saints
The Underneath

Gangs
See also: Crime & Criminals; Organized Crime
Gimme Shelter
Menace II Society
Pariah
Performance
Slam
Sticky Fingers
Teenage Gang Debs
Too Late for Tears
Wonderland

Gays
See also: Bisexuality; Gender Bending; Lesbians
And the Band Played On
Another Country
The Best Way
Carrington
Closing Numbers
The Conformist
The Crying Game
Entertaining Mr. Sloane
For a Lost Soldier
Four Weddings and a Funeral
Go Fish
Grief
Happy Together
The Hours and Times
I Think I Do
It's My Party
Kiss of the Spider Woman
Longtime Companion
Love and Death on Long Island
Love and Human Remains
Maurice
Men in Love
My Beautiful Laundrette
My Own Private Idaho
The Opposite of Sex
Paris Is Burning
Parting Glances
Priest
Rock Hudson's Home Movies
Swoon
Victim
The Wedding Banquet
Wilde
Withnail and I
Wonderland

Gender Bending
See also: Gays; Lesbians; Role Reversal
The Adventures of Priscilla, Queen of the Desert
The Brandon Teena Story
The Crying Game
Different for Girls
Glen or Glenda?
I Like It Like That
I Shot Andy Warhol
Just Like a Woman
Law of Desire
Le Sexe des Etoiles
Ma Vie en Rose
Nuns on the Run
Orlando
Paris Is Burning
Vegas in Space

Generation X
Bodies, Rest & Motion
Chasing Amy
Clerks
Mallrats
Party Girl
Slacker
SubUrbia

German (Production)
The Conformist
Das Boot
Deep End
Every Man for Himself & God against All
False Weights
I Love You, I Love You Not
Joyless Street
La Ceremonie
M
The Marquise of O
Martha and I
Meier
Metropolis
Mother Kusters Goes to Heaven
The Nasty Girl
Nico Icon
Nosferatu
The Odessa File
Orson Welles: The One Man Band
Pandora's Box
Salmonberries
The Second Awakening of Christa Klages
Strongman Ferdinand
Two Small Bodies
Vampyr
Victory March
Wings of Desire
The Wonderful, Horrible Life of Leni Riefenstahl
The Yellow Ticket

Germany (Locale)
Backbeat
Nico Icon
The Odessa File
Salmonberries
Wings of Desire

Ghosts, Ghouls, & Goblins
See also: Death & the Afterlife; Occult
Don't Take It to Heart
The Ghost Goes West
In Possession
The Innocents
Rouge
Silent Tongue

Governesses
See: Nannies & Governesses

Grand Hotel
Dirty Dancing
Separate Tables
The Shining

Great Britain (Locale)
See also: Ireland; London; Scotland

Angels and Insects
An Awfully Big Adventure
Carrington
The Englishman Who Went up a Hill But Came down a Mountain
FairyTale: A True Story
For Queen and Country
Four Weddings and a Funeral
Funny Bones
The Innocents
The Krays
The Long Good Friday
The Madness of King George
Mrs. Brown
Naked
Nine Days a Queen
Persuasion
Pink String and Sealing Wax
Scandal
35 Up
The Whistle Blower
White Mischief
The Windsors: A Royal Family

Great Depression
See also: Hard Knock Life; Homeless
The Ballad of the Sad Cafe
The Funeral
Hard Traveling
Our Daily Bread
Rambling Rose
The Whole Wide World
Wildflower
You Only Live Once

Greek (Production)
A Dream of Passion
Iphigenia

Growing Older
See also: Death & the Afterlife; Late Bloomin' Love
Anna
Daddy Nostalgia
Lamerica
Lightning Jack
Pastime
The Private Life of Henry VIII
Queens Logic
Salut Victor!
Shirley Valentine
A Shock to the System
Street Music
Two for the Road
The Whales of August

Hard Knock Life
See also: Great Depression; Homeless
Blessing
Forbidden Choices
The Full Monty
Lamerica
Set It Off
The Story of Fausta

Hard Knuckle Sandwich
See: Boxing

Heists
See also: Scams, Stings & Cons
Bellman and True
Body Count
Bound
Destiny Turns on the Radio
Gun Crazy
The Killing
Lightning Jack
Motorama
Normal Life
Palookaville
Passionate Thief
Reservoir Dogs
Set It Off
The Underneath
The Usual Suspects

Hell High School
See: School Daze

Hispanic America
I Like It Like That
Lone Star
My Family

Historical Drama
Cabeza de Vaca
Children of Paradise
Death of a Schoolboy
FairyTale: A True Story
I Shot Andy Warhol
Kama Sutra: A Tale of Love
Luther
The Marquise of O
Mrs. Brown
Nine Days a Queen
The Orders
The Private Life of Henry VIII
Saraband for Dead Lovers
The Scarlet Pimpernel
White Mischief

Hit Men
See also: Assassinations
Breakaway
Diary of a Hitman
El Mariachi
The Funeral
La Femme Nikita
Little Odessa
Pulp Fiction
Red Rock West
U-Turn

Holidays
Century
Halloween
The House of Yes
The Ice Storm
The Myth of Fingerprints
The Night of the Hunter
1999
The Railway Children
Reckless
Tommy Tricker & the Stamp Traveller

The Holocaust
See also: Germany; Judaism; Nazis & Other Paramilitary Slugs; World War II
Christabel
Diamonds in the Snow
Hidden Children
I Love You, I Love You Not
Life Is Beautiful

Homeless
See also: Great Depression; Hard Knock Life; Yuppie Nightmares
Caught
Oliver Twist
Streetwise

Homosexuality
See: Bisexuality; Gays; Lesbians

Hong Kong (Production)
Center Stage
Chungking Express
Happy Together
Love unto Waste
One Night Stand
Rouge

Horror
See also: Classic Horror; Creepy Houses; Horror Anthologies; Horror Comedy; Monsters
The Addiction
The Ambulance
Campfire Tales
Cemetery Man
Creepers
Dead of Night
Def by Temptation
Evil Dead
Grim Prairie Tales
Habit
Halloween
Halloween: H20
The Hands of Orlac
In Possession
The Innocents
The Island of Dr. Moreau
Mommy
My Teacher Ate My Homework
Night of the Living Dead
Popcorn
Teenage Gang Debs
Wes Craven's New Nightmare

Horror Anthologies
Campfire Tales
Dead of Night
Grim Prairie Tales

Horror Comedy
Frankenhooker
Q (The Winged Serpent)
The Refrigerator
Spider Baby
The Witches

Horse Racing
See: Gambling; Horses

Horses
Black Beauty
Cold Feet

Hostage!
See also: Kidnapped!; Missing Persons
Body Count
Death and the Maiden

Hungarian (Production)
Adoption
The Hungarians
Nine Months
25 Fireman's Street
The Unfinished Sentence in 141 Minutes

Identity
See also: Mistaken Identity; Role Reversal
Ma Vie en Rose
Orlando
Return of the Secaucus 7
Ruby in Paradise
Secrets and Lies
The Woman in Question

Immigration
Combination Platter
Hester Street
A Kiss to This Land

Incest
See also: Family Ties
Angels and Insects
The Grifters
The House of Yes
Spanking the Monkey
The Sweet Hereafter
U-Turn

India (Locale)
Black Narcissus
The Deceivers
Heat and Dust
Kama Sutra: A Tale of Love

Indian (Production)
The Deceivers
Kama Sutra: A Tale of Love

Interracial Affairs
Pariah
The Wedding Banquet
Zebrahead

Iranian (Production)
Through the Olive Trees

Ireland (Locale)
See also: Great Britain
The Crying Game
The Dead
Frankie Starlight
Hear My Song
In the Name of the Father
The Last of the High Kings
The Lonely Passion of Judith Hearne
The Matchmaker
Michael Collins
My Left Foot
The Secret of Roan Inish
Widow's Peak

Irish (Production)
The Boy from Mercury
The Crying Game
Frankie Starlight
In the Name of the Father
The Last of the High Kings
My Left Foot

Island Fare
Echoes of Paradise
The Island of Dr. Moreau
Island of the Lost
The Postman
Swept Away...

Israeli (Production)
Coffee with Lemon
Daughters, Daughters
The Garden
Ricochets
Song of the Siren
Zohar: Mediterranean Blues

Italian (Production)
Allonsanfan
An Average Little Man
Bellissima
The Belly of an Architect
Blow-Up
Cemetery Man
Cinema Paradiso
The Conformist
Creepers
Dangerous Liaisons
Dear Michael
The Devil Is a Woman
Down & Dirty
8½
Everything Ready, Nothing Works
From the Pole to the Equator
Johnny Stecchino
Julia and Julia
Lamerica
Life Is Beautiful
The Miracle
Ossessione
Padre Padrone
Passionate Thief
The Postman
The Profiteer
Seven Beauties
The Sleazy Uncle
A Special Day
The Stranger's Hand
Swept Away...
Variety Lights
Victory March
A Virgin Named Mary
White Nights

Italy (Locale)
Cemetery Man
Cinema Paradiso
The Conformist
Enchanted April
Life Is Beautiful
Ossessione
The Postman
A Special Day
Spice World: The Movie
Where Angels Fear to Tread
The Wings of the Dove

Jamaican (Production)
Rockers

Japan (Locale)
See also: Asia
Shall We Dance?

Japanese (Production)
A-Ge-Man: Tales of a Golden Geisha
The Adventures of Milo & Otis
Barefoot Gen
Picture Bride
Shall We Dance?
Twilight of the Cockroaches

Journalism
See: Front Page

Judaism
See also: The Holocaust
American Matchmaker
Coffee with Lemon
East and West
Hester Street
Hidden Children
I Love You, I Love You Not
A Kiss to This Land
Martha and I
Voyage of the Damned

Justice Prevails...?
See also: Order in the Court
In the Name of the Father
Let Him Have It
The Story of Qui Ju
Wilde

Kidnapped!
See also: Hostage!; Missing Persons
The Big Lebowski
The City of Lost Children
The Crying Game
The End of Violence
Fargo
Kansas City
Lullaby
Manny & Lo
Suicide Kings
Teresa's Tattoo
Tie Me Up! Tie Me Down!
Try and Get Me

Killer Bugs and Slugs
The Applegates
Creepers
Lair of the White Worm

Killer Dreams
Dead of Night
Wes Craven's New Nightmare

Kindness of Strangers
The Matchmaker
Mr. North

Kings
See: Royalty

Korean War
The Manchurian Candidate

Late Bloomin' Love
See also: Growing Older
The African Queen
Brief Encounter
Gal Young 'Un
The Lonely Passion of Judith Hearne
Shirley Valentine

Law & Lawyers
See also: Order in the Court
Brother's Keeper
Criminal Law
Critical Care
Death and the Maiden
In the Name of the Father
The Island of Dr. Moreau
The Sweet Hereafter
Swoon
Trois Couleurs: Rouge
Victim

Lesbians
See also: Bisexuality; Gays; Gender Bending
All Over Me
Bound
Butterfly Kiss
Chasing Amy
High Art
The Killing of Sister George
Law of Desire
Nadja
Set It Off
These Three

Loneliness
See: Only the Lonely

Lovers on the Lam
Badlands
Gun Crazy
Guncrazy
Kalifornia
Love and a .45
Wild at Heart

Macedonian (Production)
Before the Rain

Mad Scientists
Bride of the Monster
The City of Lost Children
Frankenhooker
Frankenstein Unbound
The Island of Dr. Moreau

Made for Television
See: TV Movies

Mafia
See: Organized Crime

Marriage
See also: Divorce; Otherwise Engaged; War Between the Sexes; Wedding Bells; Wedding Hell
Afterglow
American Matchmaker
Breaking the Waves
Caught
Crash
Dangerous Liaisons
The Dead
Eat a Bowl of Tea
Eating Raoul
Emmanuelle
The Entertainer
Eve's Bayou
Gaslight
The Good Wife
Grace of My Heart
Grand Isle
A Handful of Dust
I Like It Like That
In Celebration
It Takes Two
Ju Dou
Lost Highway
Martha and I
Marty
Muriel's Wedding
Nina Takes a Lover
Normal Life
On Approval
The Only One
Paris, France
The Piano
Picture Bride
The Prowler
Red Rock West
Rich and Strange
Scenes from a Marriage
She's the One
Silent Tongue
Too Beautiful for You
True Love
Two for the Road
Walking and Talking
The Wash
Way Down East
Where Angels Fear to Tread
Why Not!
Wilde
A Woman under the Influence

The Meaning of Life
The Apostle
Badlands
My Own Private Idaho
The Remains of the Day
Wings of Desire

Men in Prison
See also: Women in Prison
Crashout
In the Name of the Father
Kiss of the Spider Woman
Lost Highway
Slam
Ulee's Gold

Merchant Ivory
The Ballad of the Sad Cafe
Maurice
The Remains of the Day
A Room with a View

Mexican (Production)
Aventurera
Cabeza de Vaca
El Mariachi
A Kiss to This Land
Like Water for Chocolate
Reasons of State

Mexico (Locale)
Which Way, Por Favor?

Middle East (Locale)
Ricochets
Through the Olive Trees

The Military
Das Boot
Platoon

Missing Persons
See also: Hostage!; Kidnapped!

From Hollywood to Deadwood
The Lady Vanishes
Picnic at Hanging Rock
The Vanishing

Mistaken Identity
See also: Gender Bending; Role Reversal
The Ballad of Little Jo
The Big Lebowski
Chameleon Street
Charley's Aunt
El Mariachi
Evergreen
A House in the Hills
Johnny Stecchino
Lisa
Lost Highway
The Obsessed
Paper Mask
The Player
Red Rock West
Suture
10 Rillington Place
The Thin Blue Line
The 39 Steps
Withnail and I

Moms
See also: Bad Dads; Monster Moms; Parenthood
Bastard out of Carolina
Manny & Lo
Spanking the Monkey

Monster Moms
See also: Bad Dads; Moms; Parenthood
Bellissima
The Grifters
Mommy
Serial Mom
Spanking the Monkey

Monsters
See also: Ghosts, Ghouls, & Goblins; Killer Bugs and Slugs; Mad Scientists; Vampires; Zombies
Bride of the Monster
Evil Dead
Fire Maidens from Outer Space
Frankenstein Unbound
Loch Ness
Q (The Winged Serpent

Motor Vehicle Dept.
Crash
Motorama
Night on Earth
Roger & Me

Murderous Children
See also: Childhood Visions
Children of the Damned
The Little Girl Who Lives down the Lane
Village of the Damned

Musicals
Absolute Beginners
Evergreen
Help!
The Little Prince
The Slipper and the Rose
Spice World: The Movie
Tommy

Musician Biopics
Nico Icon
Shine
Zohar: Mediterranean Blues

Mystery & Suspense
See also: Psycho-Thriller
Acting on Impulse
After Dark, My Sweet
The Amazing Mr. X
Betrayed
The Big Easy
Blackmail
Blood Simple
Blue Velvet
Bulldog Drummond
Bury Me Dead
Cat and Mouse
The Cater Street Hangman
Chain of Desire
Clouds over Europe
Criminal Law
Cutter's Way
Delusion
Dites-Lui Que Je L'Aime
D.O.A.
Eye of the Needle
Frenzy
Fright
From Hollywood to Deadwood
Gaslight
Guest in the House
Help!
The Hidden Room
High Stakes
A House in the Hills
The House on Carroll Street
I Bury the Living
Impact
In the Spirit
Jack's Back
Julia and Julia
Kafka
La Ceremonie
The Lady Confesses
The Lady in White
The Lady Vanishes
Lisa
The Little Girl Who Lives down the Lane
Madeleine
The Man Who Knew Too Much
The Manchurian Candidate
Miami Blues
Money Madness
Mother's Boys
Murder on the Orient Express
The Night of the Hunter
Night Train to Munich
Non-Stop New York
The Obsessed
The Odessa File
Picnic at Hanging Rock
The Private Life of Sherlock Holmes
The Prowler
Random Encounter
The Red House
Red Rock West
Repulsion
Rich and Strange
Road Games
The Rosary Murders
Sabotage
So Long at the Fair
Sois Belle et Tais-Toi
10 Rillington Place
The Third Man
The 39 Steps
Tiger Bay
To Have and to Hold
Tough Guys Don't Dance
Traces of Red
Twisted Nerve
Under Suspicion
Uneasy Terms
The Usual Suspects
The Vanishing
The Very Edge
Violette
Warm Nights on a Slow-Moving Train
The Whistle Blower
White Mischief
The Woman in Question
Wonderland
Young and Innocent

Nannies & Governesses
See also: Bringing Up Baby; Parenthood
Cousin Bette
The Governess
The Innocents

Native America
Daughters of the Country
Dead Man
Powwow Highway
Silent Tongue
Smoke Signals

Nazis & Other Paramilitary Slugs
See also: Germany; The Holocaust; Judaism; World War II
Closet Land
The Conformist
Eye of the Needle
The House on Carroll Street
Life Is Beautiful
The Man in the Glass Booth
Martha and I
The Nasty Girl
Night Train to Munich
The Odessa File
Pariah
The Red Poster
Swastika
Tomorrow the World

New Black Cinema
See also: African America
Hangin' with the Homeboys
Hollywood Shuffle
Just Another Girl on the I.R.T.
Menace II Society
Set It Off
She's Gotta Have It
Straight out of Brooklyn
To Sleep with Anger

New Year's Eve
See: Holidays

New Zealand (Locale)
See: Down Under

New Zealand (Production)
An Angel at My Table
Crush
Forgotten Silver
Heavenly Creatures

Newspapers
See: Front Page

Nifty '50s
Absolute Beginners
Badlands
Big Night
Celia: Child of Terror
Dance with a Stranger
Dirty Dancing
Last Exit to Brooklyn
Mac
Shag: The Movie
Stacking
That'll Be the Day

Nightclubs & Bars
Backbeat
The Killing of a Chinese Bookie
Party Girl
Pecker
Trees Lounge
Wonderland

Norwegian (Production)
The Feldmann Case

Nuns & Priests
See also: Religion
Black Narcissus
The Boys of St. Vincent
Dead Man Walking
Nuns on the Run
Priest
The Rosary Murders
Sorceress
True Confessions

Obsessive Love
Brief Encounter
Chungking Express
The English Patient
Homage
Kama Sutra: A Tale of Love
Love and Death on Long Island
Wilde

Occult
See also: Witchcraft
The Amazing Mr. X
Evil Dead

Oceans
See: Shipwrecked

Oldest Profession
See also: Women in Prison
The Balcony
Frankenhooker

High Stakes
Jack's Back
johns
Leaving Las Vegas
Miami Blues
Mona Lisa
My Own Private Idaho
Naked Kiss
Pandora's Box
Queen Kelly
Star Maps
Street Smart
Sweet Sweetback's Baadasssss Song
Thousand Pieces of Gold
Warm Nights on a Slow-Moving Train

On the Rocks
See also: Pill Poppin'
Affliction
The Big Lebowski
The Crossing Guard
The Entertainer
Georgia
Leaving Las Vegas
Little Shots of Happiness
The Luck of Ginger Coffey
Mrs. Parker and the Vicious Circle
Sling Blade
Struggle
Trees Lounge

Only the Lonely
The Ballad of Little Jo
A Chorus of Disapproval
Eat Drink Man Woman
Every Man for Himself & God against All
Eye of the Needle
Heavy
The Lonely Passion of Judith Hearne
Marty
Pi
The Prime of Miss Jean Brodie
Rhythm Thief
Robert et Robert
Separate Tables
What Happened Was...
When the Cat's Away

Order in the Court
See also: Justice Prevails...?; Law & Lawyers
Hard Traveling
In the Name of the Father
Madeleine
The Man in the Glass Booth
Swoon
Wilde

Organized Crime
See also: Crime & Criminals; Disorganized Crime; Gangs
Bound
Breakaway
Bullets over Broadway
Coldblooded
The Frightened City
The Funeral
High Stakes
Johnny Stecchino
Kansas City
Kill Me Again
The Killing of a Chinese Bookie
The Krays
Last Exit to Brooklyn
Little Odessa
The Long Good Friday
Lost Highway
Pulp Fiction
To Die For

Otherwise Engaged
See also: Romantic Triangles; Wedding Bells; Wedding Hell
Four Weddings and a Funeral
The Graduate
The House of Yes
Shag: The Movie
Shakespeare in Love

Painting
See: Art & Artists

Parenthood
See also: Bad Dads; Bringing Up Baby; Moms; Monster Moms
American Heart
Daddy Nostalgia
Eat Drink Man Woman
Flirting with Disaster
Gas Food Lodging
Ladybird, Ladybird
Padre Padrone
The Red House
Secrets and Lies
Ulee's Gold

Philanthropy
See: Kindness of Strangers

Photography
See: Shutterbugs

Physical Problems
The Big Lebowski
Breaking the Waves
A Brief History of Time
Cop Land
Frankie Starlight
Hugo Pool
In the Company of Men
Lightning Jack
My Left Foot
Passion Fish
The Waterdance
The Whales of August
Who Are the DeBolts and Where Did They Get 19 Kids?

Pill Poppin'
See also: On the Rocks
Bad Lieutenant
The Basketball Diaries
Basquiat
The Big Lebowski
Blood & Concrete: A Love Story
Bongwater
Boogie Nights
Chungking Express
Dazed and Confused
The Doom Generation
Down & Dirty
Drugstore Cowboy
Easy Rider
Federal Hill
France, Incorporated
Fresh
Georgia
High Art
Hugo Pool
Kids
Let's Get Lost
London Kills Me
Mrs. Parker and the Vicious Circle
Nico Icon
One False Move
Performance
Pulp Fiction
River's Edge
Suicide Kings
The Sweet Hereafter
The Third Man
Trainspotting
Twenty-One
Ulee's Gold
The Usual Suspects
Wired
Withnail and I
Women on the Verge of a Nervous Breakdown

Poetry
The Postman
Slam

Poisons
D.O.A.
Safe

Polish (Production)
Ashes and Diamonds
The Balance
The Interrogation
Trois Couleurs: Blanc
Trois Couleurs: Rouge

Politics
See also: Presidency
And the Band Played On
The Blue Kite
Burnt by the Sun
Death and the Maiden
Don's Party
Feed
A Good Man in Africa
Hollywood on Trial
Hombres Armados
The House of the Spirits
I Am Cuba
In the Name of the Father
Kansas City
Lamerica
The Matchmaker
Medium Cool
Michael Collins
Point of Order
Tito and Me
The War Room

Postwar
An Awfully Big Adventure
Cinema Paradiso
Eat a Bowl of Tea
The Man in the Glass Booth
The Odessa File
Photographing Fairies
The Third Man
Wish You Were Here

Pregnant Pauses
See also: Bringing Up Baby
Eraserhead
Fargo
Just Another Girl on the I.R.T.
Manny & Lo
A Modern Affair
Nenette and Boni
Spice World: The Movie

Presidency
See also: Politics
Feed
Secret Honor
Thomas Jefferson: A View from the Mountain
The War Room

Price of Fame
See also: Rags to Riches
Champion
Eddie and the Cruisers
Eddie and the Cruisers 2: Eddie Lives!
A Hard Day's Night
Pecker
The Thing Called Love
Wired

Princes/Princesses
See: Royalty

Prison
See: Men in Prison; Women in Prison

Prostitutes
See: Oldest Profession

Protests
See also: Rebel with a Cause
In the Name of the Father
Matewan

Psychiatry
See: Shrinks

Psycho-Thriller
See also: Mystery & Suspense
Apartment Zero
Blow-Up
Bound
The Comfort of Strangers
Dead Calm
Freeway
House of Games
The Incident
Julia and Julia
The Killer inside Me
The Last Seduction
M
The Mark
Peeping Tom
Performance
Repulsion
Shallow Grave
The Shining
Suture

The Tie That Binds
To Have and to Hold
The Vanishing
Who Killed Teddy Bear?

Psychotics/ Sociopaths
Apartment Zero
Badlands
Homage
Kalifornia
The Killer inside Me
The Little Girl Who Lives down the Lane
Mother's Boys
Repulsion
Reservoir Dogs
The Shining
To Die For
U-Turn

Queens
See: Royalty

Race against Time
D.O.A.
Miracle Mile
Time Lock

Rags to Riches
See also: Price of Fame; Wrong Side of the Tracks
Boogie Nights
Pygmalion
Trois Couleurs: Blanc

Rape
See also: Sexual Abuse
Bad Lieutenant
Bastard out of Carolina
Dead Man Walking
Death and the Maiden
Girls Town
Guncrazy
Kika
Pariah

Rebel with a Cause
See also: Rebel without a Cause
The Applegates
Basquiat
In the Name of the Father
Luther
The Scarlet Pimpernel

Rebel without a Cause
See also: Rebel with a Cause
Badlands
A Boy and His Dog
Breathless
Easy Rider
Guncrazy
If...
sex, lies and videotape

Red Scare
See also: Russia/USSR
Golden Gate
The Interrogation
Mother Kusters Goes to Heaven
Tito and Me

Religion
See also: Judaism; Nuns & Priests
The Addiction
...And God Spoke
Angela
The Apostle
Before the Rain
Breaking the Waves
Citizen Ruth
The Crucible
Dead Man Walking
Def by Temptation
The Favor, the Watch, and the Very Big Fish
Hand in Hand
Household Saints
Luther
The Miracle
Pass the Ammo
Pi
Priest
A Virgin Named Mary
Whistle down the Wind

Repressed Men
See also: Men
Box of Moonlight
Love and Death on Long Island
Maurice
The Remains of the Day
Sirens

Revenge
Aventurera
The Ballad of the Sad Cafe
Bang
Chan Is Missing
Cousin Bette
Creepers
The Crossing Guard
Death and the Maiden
The Funeral
Halloween
The Hidden Room
A House in the Hills
I Married a Witch
I Met a Murderer
The Lady in White
Reservoir Dogs
Trois Couleurs: Blanc

Road Trip
See also: Motor Vehicle Dept.
The Adventures of Milo & Otis
The Adventures of Priscilla, Queen of the Desert
Box of Moonlight
Butterfly Kiss
Delusion
Detour
The Doom Generation
Easy Rider
Flirting with Disaster
It Takes Two
Kalifornia
Lamerica
Lolita
Love and a .45
My Own Private Idaho
Night on Earth
The Opposite of Sex
Powwow Highway
Reckless
Road Games
The Runaway Bus
Smoke Signals
Trading Favors
Two for the Road
Wild at Heart

Roaring '20s
Bullets over Broadway
Eight Men Out
Mrs. Parker and the Vicious Circle

Rock Stars on Film
See also: Concert Films
Absolute Beginners
Backbeat
Blow-Up
Boy Next Door
The Crossing Guard
A Hard Day's Night
Having a Wild Weekend
Help!
Lisztomania
Performance
Spice World: The Movie
That'll Be the Day
Tommy

Role Reversal
See also: Gender Bending; Identity
A Dream of Passion
La Femme Nikita
The Lady Vanishes
Performance
The Scarlet Pimpernel
Turnabout

Romance
See: Late Bloomin' Love; Lovers on the Lam; Otherwise Engaged; Romantic Adventures; Romantic Comedy; Romantic Drama; Romantic Triangles; Torrid Love Scenes

Romantic Adventures
The African Queen
Destiny Turns on the Radio
Gun Crazy
Guncrazy

Romantic Comedy
American Matchmaker
Blue Country
Charley's Aunt
Chasing Amy
Don't Take It to Heart
East and West
The Englishman Who Went up a Hill But Came down a Mountain
Four Weddings and a Funeral
Go Fish
Hear My Song
I Married a Witch
Impromptu
It Takes Two
Just Like a Woman
The Last of the High Kings
The Linguini Incident
Love Jones
The Man Who Loved Women
The Matchmaker
A Modern Affair
Morgan!
Much Ado about Nothing
My Tutor
Nina Takes a Lover
Nobody's Fool
On Approval
Queens Logic
Roads to the South
Shakespeare in Love
She's Gotta Have It
She's the One
Song of the Siren
Strictly Ballroom
The Thing Called Love
To Cross the Rubicon
Too Beautiful for You
Tune in Tomorrow
The Wedding Banquet
Who Am I This Time?

Romantic Drama
The African Queen
Afterglow
Angels and Insects
The Ballad of the Sad Cafe
Beauty and the Beast
Before the Rain
Beware of Pity
Breathless
Brief Encounter
Caddie
Camille Claudel
Carrington
Castaway
Enchanted April
The English Patient
Gal Young 'Un
Golden Gate
The Governess
Grand Isle
Heat and Dust
High Art
It's My Party
Jane Eyre
L'Amour en Herbe
Letters from the Park
Martha and I
Marty
Persuasion
The Piano
Room at the Top
A Room with a View
Rouge
A Special Day
Strapless
A Summer Story
Through the Olive Trees
Trouble in Mind
The Unbearable Lightness of Being
White Nights
Wild at Heart
Wings of Desire
The Wings of the Dove
With or without You

Romantic Triangles
See also: Otherwise Engaged

Carried Away
Carrington
Caught
The Doom Generation
The English Patient
High Art
Homage
The Opposite of Sex
A Room with a View
She's Gotta Have It
U-Turn
The Unbearable Lightness of Being
The Underneath
The Wedding Banquet
The Wings of the Dove

Royalty
See also: Historical Drama
Kama Sutra: A Tale of Love
Kind Hearts and Coronets
Lancelot of the Lake
The Madness of King George
Mrs. Brown
Nine Days a Queen
Orlando
The Private Life of Henry VIII
Queen Kelly
Shakespeare in Love
Start the Revolution without Me
The Windsors: A Royal Family

Russia/USSR (Locale)
See also: Red Scare
Burnt by the Sun
Citizen X

Russian (Production)
Aelita: Queen of Mars
Burnt by the Sun
The Children of Theatre Street
I Am Cuba
The Man with the Movie Camera
100 Days after Childhood
The Only One
Orlando
The Orphans
Professor Mamlock
To See Paris and Die
With You and without You

Sail Away
See also: Shipwrecked
Abandon Ship
The African Queen
Beat the Devil
Das Boot
Dead Calm
Loch Ness
A Night to Remember
Voyage of the Damned

Sanity Check
See also: Doctors & Nurses; Shrinks
Affliction
An Angel at My Table
Camille Claudel
Dead of Night
Easy Rider
Fright
Heat and Sunlight
Heavenly Creatures
The House of Yes
How to Get Ahead in Advertising
The Last Seduction
Morgan!
Mother Kusters Goes to Heaven
Pecker
Peeping Tom
Performance
Poison
The Shining
Sling Blade
Star Maps
Tracks
Twister
A Woman under the Influence

Satire & Parody
See also: Black Comedy; Comedy
Abel
...And God Spoke
Citizen Ruth
Dark Habits
Down & Dirty
Forgotten Silver
Genevieve
High Season
Love and a .45
Open Season
Pass the Ammo
Phantom of Liberty
The Player
Sammy & Rosie Get Laid
Scenes from the Class Struggle in Beverly Hills
Search and Destroy
Serial Mom
A Shock to the System
Swimming with Sharks
The Troublemaker
A Virgin Named Mary
Waiting for Guffman
White Mischief

Scams, Stings & Cons
See also: Heists
The Amazing Mr. X
The Big Lebowski
Chameleon Street
Destiny Turns on the Radio
Fargo
The Grifters
House of Games
In the Soup
Jackie Brown
The Killing
Kind Hearts and Coronets
Lamerica
Ossessione
Pass the Ammo
Suicide Kings

School Daze
The Belles of St. Trinian's
Black Narcissus
The Chocolate War
Creepers
Dazed and Confused
Girls in Chains
Girls Town
Good Will Hunting
Halloween: H20
Heathers
Heavenly Creatures
If...
A Little Princess
Lucky Jim
My Teacher Ate My Homework
Oleanna
The Prime of Miss Jean Brodie
Stand and Deliver
Star Kid
Zebrahead

Sci Fi
See also: Fantasy
Aelita: Queen of Mars
A Boy and His Dog
Children of the Damned
Fire Maidens from Outer Space
France, Incorporated
Gog
Hu-Man
Island of the Lost
The Land That Time Forgot
Metropolis
1984
Not of This Earth
Plan 9 from Outer Space
Sore Losers
Star Kid
The Trouble with Dick
Vegas in Space
Village of the Damned

Scotland (Locale)
See also: Great Britain
Breaking the Waves
The Governess
Loch Ness
Madeleine
The Prime of Miss Jean Brodie
Trainspotting

Screwball Comedy
See also: Comedy; Romantic Comedy; Slapstick Comedy
Bedazzled
Don't Take It to Heart
The Favor, the Watch, and the Very Big Fish
A Hard Day's Night
The Smallest Show on Earth
Start the Revolution without Me
Turnabout

Serial Killers
See also: Crime & Criminals; Crime Sprees
American Strays
Butterfly Kiss
Citizen X
Freeway
Kalifornia
Love and Human Remains
M
The Rosary Murders
Serial Mom
10 Rillington Place
The Seventies
See: Swingin' '70s

Sex & Sexuality
Acting on Impulse
Afterglow
Alfie
Angels and Insects
Art for Teachers of Children
Bad Lieutenant
Blue Velvet
A Boy and His Dog
Breaking the Waves
Business As Usual
Carried Away
Chain of Desire
Chasing Amy
Chicken Hawk
The Comfort of Strangers
Crash
Crush
Dites-Lui Que Je L'Aime
Don's Party
Eating Raoul
Echoes of Paradise
Emmanuelle
Exotica
Female Trouble
Frankenstein Unbound
Frenzy
Georgy Girl
Glen or Glenda?
The Graduate
Habit
Heavy Petting
Isadora
Kama Sutra: A Tale of Love
Kids
Kika
The Last of the High Kings
Like Water for Chocolate
Lolita
Love and Human Remains
Love unto Waste
Lover Girl
The Man Who Loved Women
Nenette and Boni
Paris, France
Peeping Tom
Performance
Rambling Rose
Repulsion
Ripe
Rita, Sue & Bob Too
Salmonberries
Salut Victor!
Sammy & Rosie Get Laid
Scenes from the Class Struggle in Beverly Hills
sex, lies and videotape
She's Gotta Have It
Sirens
Tie Me Up! Tie Me Down!
Twenty-One
2 by 4
The Unbearable Lightness of Being
Under Suspicion
Wild at Heart
Wish You Were Here

Women on the Verge of a Nervous Breakdown

Sexual Abuse
See also: Rape
The Boys of St. Vincent
Priest

Sexual Harrassment
Brilliant Lies
Oleanna

Ships
See: Sail Away; Shipwrecked

Shipwrecked
Cabeza de Vaca
Eye of the Needle
Island of the Lost
Rich and Strange
Swept Away...

Showbiz Comedies
Bullets over Broadway
Funny Bones
Hear My Song
Hollywood Shuffle
The Real Blonde
Tune in Tomorrow
Waiting for Guffman

Showbiz Dramas
Actors and Sin
Anna
Boogie Nights
From the Journals of Jean Seberg
Grace of My Heart
The Player
Second Coming of Suzanne
Sidewalks of London
Wired

Shrinks
See also: Doctors & Nurses
Face to Face
Good Will Hunting
House of Games
The Myth of Fingerprints

Shutterbugs
See also: Front Page
Art for Teachers of Children
Backbeat
Blow-Up
The Favor, the Watch, and the Very Big Fish
The Governess
Heat and Sunlight
High Art
High Season
Pecker
Peeping Tom
Photographing Fairies
Spice World: The Movie
The Unbearable Lightness of Being

Silent Films
Aelita: Queen of Mars
Charley's Aunt
East and West
The Hands of Orlac
His Picture in the Papers
Joyless Street
The Man with the Movie Camera
Metropolis
Nosferatu
Oliver Twist
Pandora's Box
Queen Kelly
Sparrows
Vampyr
Way Down East

Singles
See also: Dates from Hell
Metropolitan
Mystic Pizza
The Thing Called Love
When the Cat's Away

The '60s
See: Flower Children

Slapstick Comedy
See also: Comedy; Screwball Comedy
The Battle of the Sexes
Nuns on the Run

South America (Locale)
See also: Central America
Apartment Zero
Death and the Maiden
Happy Together
The House of the Spirits
It's All True
The Story of Fausta

Spain (Locale)
Barcelona

Spanish (Production)
Black Litter
Bride to Be
Cabeza de Vaca
Dark Habits
The Fable of the Beautiful Pigeon Fancier
High Heels
Kika
Law of Desire
Matador
Spirit of the Beehive
Tie Me Up! Tie Me Down!
Women on the Verge of a Nervous Breakdown

Spies & Espionage
See also: Terrorism
The English Patient
Eye of the Needle
The House on Carroll Street
Night Train to Munich
The Odessa File
Sabotage
Shack Out on 101
The Third Man
The 39 Steps
The Whistle Blower

Sports
See: Baseball; Basketball; Boxing; Bowling

Strained Suburbia
See also: Yuppie Nightmares
Blue Velvet
The Graduate
Hugo Pool
Serial Mom
Short Cuts

Strippers
Exotica
The Full Monty
Pecker

Struggling Musicians
Backbeat
Eddie and the Cruisers
Eddie and the Cruisers 2: Eddie Lives!
Stardust
SubUrbia

Suicide
See also: Death & the Afterlife
American Strays
Bedazzled
Crumb
Golden Gate
Heathers
Leaving Las Vegas
Mother Kusters Goes to Heaven
Peeping Tom
Permanent Record

Summer Camp
The Best Way
Evil Dead
Grim Prairie Tales
100 Days after Childhood

Survival
Abandon Ship
Das Boot
Dead Calm
Delusion
The Interrogation
Island of the Lost
The Land That Time Forgot
Last Exit to Brooklyn
Little Dorrit, Film 1: Nobody's Fault
Little Dorrit, Film 2: Little Dorrit's Story
Sweet Sweetback's Baadasssss Song

Suspense
See Mystery & Suspense

Swashbucklers
See also: Action Adventure
Project A: Part 2
The Scarlet Pimpernel

Swedish (Production)
Face to Face
Metamorphosis
My Life As a Dog
Paradise Place
Scenes from a Marriage
Stubby

Swingin' '70s
Boogie Nights
Dazed and Confused
The Ice Storm
The Last of the High Kings

Swiss (Production)
A Dream of Passion
Jonah Who Will Be 25 in the Year 2000
Orson Welles: The One Man Band
Steppenwolf
Trois Couleurs: Blanc
Trois Couleurs: Rouge
The Wonderful Crook

Taiwanese (Production)
Eat Drink Man Woman
The Wedding Banquet

Tearjerkers
A Little Princess
Sparrows
Struggle
Thursday's Child
Way Down East

Teen Angst
See also: Coming of Age
All Over Me
Art for Teachers of Children
The Basketball Diaries
Carried Away
Dazed and Confused
Dead End
The Doom Generation
Freeway
Fun
Gas Food Lodging
Girls Town
Hackers
Halloween
Heathers
Heavenly Creatures
Hoop Dreams
Hurricane Streets
If...
Just Another Girl on the I.R.T.
Kids
L'Amour en Herbe
The Last of the High Kings
Lisa
Lover Girl
Manny & Lo
Metropolitan
My Own Private Idaho
Mystic Pizza
Nenette and Boni
New Jersey Drive
Paradise Lost: The Child Murders at Robin Hood Hills
Pecker
The Prime of Miss Jean Brodie
Rambling Rose
Ripe
River's Edge
Shag: The Movie
Shine
Squeeze
Stand and Deliver
Sticky Fingers
Straight out of Brooklyn
Terminal Bliss
To Die For
Trading Favors
Trust
Wish You Were Here
Zebrahead

Terrorism
See also: Crime & Criminals; Spies & Espionage
The Applegates
Barcelona
The Crying Game
In the Name of the Father
Women on the Verge of a Nervous Breakdown

Thanksgiving
See: Holidays

This Is Your Life
See also: Musician Biopics
An Angel at My Table
Backbeat
Basquiat
Boy Next Door
Cabeza de Vaca
Caddie
Camille Claudel
Carmen Miranda: Bananas Is My Business
Carrington
Center Stage
Chaplin
Crumb
Dance with a Stranger
Dreamchild
From the Journals of Jean Seberg
Gods and Monsters
The Hours and Times
I Shot Andy Warhol
Isadora
Kurt and Courtney
Let's Get Lost
Lisztomania
Michael Collins
Mrs. Parker and the Vicious Circle
Moulin Rouge
My Left Foot
Nico Icon
Padre Padrone
Saraband for Dead Lovers
Secret Honor
Shine
Ted
32 Short Films about Glenn Gould
Thomas Jefferson: A View from the Mountain
Valentino
Waiting for the Moon
Wilde
Wired
The Wonderful, Horrible Life of Leni Riefenstahl

Thrillers
See: Mystery & Suspense; Psycho-Thriller

Titanic
A Night to Remember
S.O.S. Titanic

Torrid Love Scenes
See also: Sex & Sexuality
The Big Easy
Blue Velvet
Law of Desire
Men in Love
Swept Away...
The Unbearable Lightness of Being
Wild at Heart

Tragedy
See also: Drama; Tearjerkers
Deep End
Forbidden Choices
From the Journals of Jean Seberg
House of Cards
Law of Desire
Martha and I
Silent Tongue
The Sweet Hereafter
Trois Couleurs: Bleu
Where Angels Fear to Tread

Trains
Color of a Brisk and Leaping Day
The Lady Vanishes
Murder on the Orient Express
Night Train to Munich
Tracks
Warm Nights on a Slow-Moving Train

Transvestites & Transsexuals
See: Gender Bending

Trapped with a Killer!
See also: Psychotics/Sociopaths
Dead Calm
Eye of the Needle
Kalifornia
The Shining
The Tie That Binds

Troma Films
Def by Temptation
Vegas in Space

True Crime
See also: Crime & Criminals; This Is Your Life; True Stories
Citizen X
Normal Life
Paradise Lost: The Child Murders at Robin Hood Hills
Sister My Sister
Swoon

True Stories
See also: This Is Your Life; True Crime
And the Band Played On
Art for Teachers of Children
Backbeat
Badlands
The Ballad of Little Jo
The Basketball Diaries
The Boys of St. Vincent
Cabeza de Vaca
Castaway
Chameleon Street
Christabel
Citizen X
Dance with a Stranger
Drugstore Cowboy
Eight Men Out
Every Man for Himself & God against All
Heartland
Heavenly Creatures
I Shot Andy Warhol
In the Name of the Father
It's My Party
The Krays
Ladybird, Ladybird
Let Him Have It
Madeleine
Matewan
Michael Collins
Mountains of the Moon
My Left Foot
The Nasty Girl
A Night to Remember
Normal Life
River's Edge
Scandal
Shine
Stand and Deliver
Street Smart
10 Rillington Place
The Thin Blue Line
Thousand Pieces of Gold
True Confessions
Violette
Voyage of the Damned
White Mischief
The Whole Wide World
A World Apart

TV Movies
Acting on Impulse
And the Band Played On
An Angel at My Table
Anne of Green Gables
Bastard out of Carolina
The Boys of St. Vincent
Christabel
Citizen X
Eat a Bowl of Tea
Face to Face
Grand Isle
Letters from the Park
Longtime Companion
Persuasion
Priest
Smooth Talk
S.O.S. Titanic
Under Suspicion
Waiting for the Moon
Wildflower

Twins
See also: Family Ties
Equinox
The Krays
Ripe
Start the Revolution without Me

Up All Night
See also: Vampires
After Hours
Dazed and Confused
Little Nemo: Adventures in Slumberland

Urban Drama
American Heart
Bad Lieutenant
Fly by Night
Fresh
Just Another Girl on the I.R.T.
Menace II Society
Naked
New Jersey Drive
Slam
Squeeze
Straight out of Brooklyn
Zebrahead

Vacations
Dirty Dancing
Enchanted April
The Last of the High Kings
The Man Who Knew Too Much

Vampires
The Addiction
Habit
Nadja
Nosferatu
Not of This Earth
Vampyr

Vietnam War
See also: Postwar
Platoon
Return of the Secaucus 7

Voodoo
See also: Occult
Eve's Bayou
Household Saints

Waitresses
Hard Eight
Heavy
Mystic Pizza
The Spitfire Grill

War between the Sexes
See also: Divorce; Marriage; Singles
The African Queen
The Ballad of the Sad Cafe
Beware of Pity
Cannibal Women in the Avocado Jungle of Death
Castaway
Dangerous Liaisons
Much Ado about Nothing
Song of the Siren
The Story of Fausta
True Love
Women on the Verge of a Nervous Breakdown

War, General
See also: Anti-War War Movies; Korean War; Postwar; Terrorism; Vietnam War; World War I; World War II
Before the Rain
Hombres Armados
Ricochets

Wedding Bells
See also: Marriage; Otherwise Engaged; Wedding Hell
Four Weddings and a Funeral
Ma Vie en Rose
Muriel's Wedding

Wedding Hell
See also: Marriage; Otherwise Engaged; Wedding Bells
Bride of the Monster
The Graduate
I Think I Do
True Love
The Wedding Banquet

Westerns
See also: Western Comedy
The Ballad of Little Jo
Cold Feet
Dead Man
Grim Prairie Tales
Heartland
Lightning Jack
Lone Star
Silent Tongue
Thousand Pieces of Gold

Witchcraft
See also: Occult
The Crucible
I Married a Witch
Sorceress
The Witches

Women
See also: Femme Fatale; Moms; Women in Prison
Anna
Antonia's Line
The Ballad of Little Jo
Bang
Business As Usual
Carmen Miranda: Bananas Is My Business
Citizen Ruth
Daughters of the Dust
Enchanted April
Enid Is Sleeping
From the Journals of Jean Seberg
Gas Food Lodging
Girlfriends
Grace of My Heart
Heat and Dust
Household Saints
I Like It Like That
Just Another Girl on the I.R.T.
Ladybird, Ladybird
Legacy
Lumiere
Mina Tannenbaum
One Sings, the Other Doesn't
Passion Fish
Ruby in Paradise
Salmonberries
Set It Off
Sorceress
The Spitfire Grill
The Story of Qui Ju
Twenty-One
Widow's Peak
Women on the Verge of a Nervous Breakdown
The Wonderful, Horrible Life of Leni Riefenstahl

Women in Prison
See also: Men in Prison
Fun
Girls in Chains

World War I
The African Queen
Death of a Schoolboy
FairyTale: A True Story
The Land That Time Forgot
Photographing Fairies

World War II
See also: The Holocaust; Postwar
Ashes and Diamonds
Brief Encounter
Christabel
Das Boot
Diamonds in the Snow
The English Patient
Eye of the Needle
For a Lost Soldier
Forbidden Games
Home of the Brave
Life Is Beautiful
The Nasty Girl
Seven Beauties
25 Fireman's Street
Voyage of the Damned
The Wizard of Loneliness

Writers
See also: This Is Your Life
The Basketball Diaries
Kafka
Love and Death on Long Island
Mrs. Parker and the Vicious Circle
Shakespeare in Love
Slam
Street Smart
The Third Man
The Whole Wide World
Wilde

Wrong Side of the Tracks
See also: Rags to Riches
Dirty Dancing
Federal Hill
Last Exit to Brooklyn
Pygmalion
Room at the Top
Set It Off
sex, lies and videotape

Yugoslavian (Production)
The Dog Who Loved Trains
Fear
Tito and Me

Yuppie Nightmares
See also: Strained Suburbia
City of Hope
Dead Calm
In the Company of Men
In the Spirit
Mother's Boys
sex, lies and videotape
A Shock to the System
The Tie That Binds

Zombies
See also: Death & the Afterlife; Ghosts, Ghouls, & Goblins
Carnival of Souls
Cemetery Man
Night of the Living Dead
Plan 9 from Outer Space